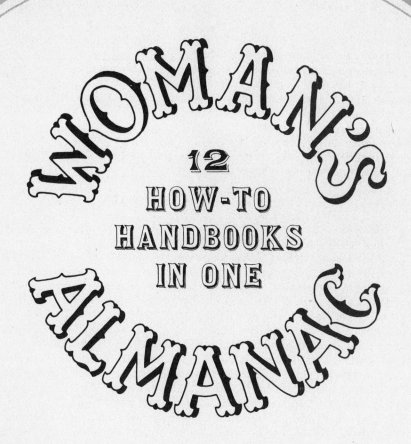

WOMAN'S ALMANAC

12 HOW-TO HANDBOOKS IN ONE

Compiled and edited by

Kathryn Paulsen and Ryan A. Kuhn

Designed by

Holly Alderman McLellan

An Armitage Press / Information House Book

J.B. Lippincott Company

Philadelphia and New York

To our mothers, our sisters and our daughters

Permissions: Jody Sheff
Production: Stephen V. Lines, George Harrar
Editorial Assistants: Ellen McManus, Jody Sheff, Barbara Dziorney
Design and Production Assistants: Florence P. Rawls, Linda Alexsa, Anne Fiske, Deborah Zimmerly McLellan, Mary B. Adams, Pamela Hertzel, Elizabeth D. Hengen, Linda D. Harrar, Ruth Hayes
Photographer: Paul C. Cabot III
Picture Research: Pamela Hertzel, Jody Sheff
Contributing Editors: Marcia L. Storch, M.D. (Health), Roslyn L. Kramer (Finance), Holly Alderman McLellan (Woman's Directory)

Acknowledgments: First to Peg Cameron, Pat Pennington, Gary Yanker, and Fletcher A. McLellan, who inspired us to make this the best book we could.

And to Caroline I. Ackerman, Bissell Alderman, Mrs. and Mr. Edward L. Bernays, Victoria Blaine, Jean Blashfield, Alison Bond, Donna Bridgeman, Century Typography Ltd., Diana Chace, Shelley Clayman, Mary Connors, Harvard *Crimson,* George C. Cutler, John B. Davidson, Martha Davidson, Melinda Davis, Michelle Demers, Carole Deseram, Dover Pictorial Archives Series, Nancy Doyne, Dick Eales, Allan Edmands, Dodie Gerson Edmands, Susan Edmiston, Phyllis Ewen, Kathryn Exon, Paul A. Freund, John Getsinger, Mitzi Haggard, Jeremiah Harrison, Marianne Kehrli, Herta Loeser, Mary A. Lord, Stephen D. McLellan, T.J. Lyons, Naomi Mermelstein, Mary-Elizabeth Murdock, Robert S. Neuman, Nancy Northrup, Nancy Palmer, William L. Pardee, John Patterson, Daniel H. Paulsen, Victoria Pellegrino, the editors of *Population Reports,* Eileen Price, Elaine Romanelli, Marya Rosenthal, Katherine Ball Ross, Schlesinger Library (Radcliffe College), Roberta Shea, Bob Sheffield, Gonnie Siegel, Dian Smith, Dr. Phillip Stubblefield, Sheila Tobias, N. Morrison Torrey, Adrian Tronson, Wendy Watriss, Heidi C. Whitman, Joanne Woodard, and Barbara Yacono for their invaluable service, assistance, and encouragement.

Included in *Woman's Almanac* is a very small amount of male-oriented reprinted material. The editors believe that its value to the readers will outweigh feminist objections.

U.S. Library of Congress Cataloging in Publication Data

Main entry under title:

Illustrated woman's almanac.

1. Women's encyclopedias and dictionaries.
2. Women—Societies and clubs—Directories.
I. Paulsen, Kathryn.   II. Kuhn, Ryan A.
III. Title: Woman's almanac.
HQ1115.I37   301.41'2   76-2055
ISBN-0-397-01113-X
ISBN-0-397-01138-5 (pbk.)

Contents

Introduction 11

"ANNALS OF WOMANKIND"
A Footnote Chronology of the Political, Social, Religious and Legendary
Evolution of Women Throughout the World from the Earliest Period to the Present

DeLysle Ferree Cass and Ryan A. Kuhn   Pages 14-568

The Health Adviser

The Psychological Adviser

The Sex Adviser

Motherhood

Education

Working

Your Own Business

The Money Manager

The Legal Adviser

Politics and the Community

Handywoman

Simple Pleasures

Woman's Directory

Classified listings of more than 1500 local and national women's 577
services, resources and special interest organizations

Stephen V. Lines and the Woman's Almanac Correspondents

Introduction

These days all sorts of people have bold plans for women—plans for us to embark on brand new careers, rear better families, have more free time, enjoy more exciting sex lives, become financially independent and politically powerful. But no matter how these grand dreams inspire us, what they often lack is the means to make them reality—solid, practical information, the kind of information we need to actually ask for a raise, start a daycare center, establish a credit identity.

Woman's Almanac grew out of a desire to bring together in one place just such essential information in the basic areas of women's lives. To create it, we combed hundreds upon hundreds of sources, looking for the best in how-to literature for women—from nineteenth-century periodicals to modern how-to manuals. We selected the most helpful parts of some very good books, valuable articles from the back pages of out-of-print magazines, information from little-known pamphlets, and a few classics from women's writings about women. When what we needed either didn't appear in print or required updating, we found an expert in the field to write it or update it, or advise us in writing it ourselves.

There are hundreds of books around that tell you how to do one thing or deal with one sort of problem. The *Almanac* tells you not only how to rewire a lamp, but how to start a business at home, how to cope with anxiety, how to make babyfood, how to play poker, how to run for office—and much, much more. In addition, the "Woman's Directory," a yellow-pages section at the back of the book, lists a wealth of organizations and facilities for women. We think that the *Almanac* has something substantial to offer every woman in every corner of the country, whatever her age, occupation, or political persuasion.

We should like to thank all those who helped make the *Almanac* possible and especially the many women's organizations that permitted us to reprint from their publications and guided us to sources we might otherwise have overlooked. We hope you, too, will share with us for any future editions of the *Almanac* any information you or your organization might have that you feel should reach a wider audience of women. Write to *Woman's Almanac,* 211 East 51st Street, New York, New York 10022.

The Health Adviser

Menstrual Problems

Hilary Maddux

Dysmenorrhea is the medical term for any of those unpleasant things that women experience at the time of, or shortly before, their monthly periods. Doctors recognize two distinct types of dysmenorrhea, spasmodic and congestive, the latter variety really being a form of premenstrual syndrome.

Spasmodic dysmenorrhea, as the name suggests, is marked by spasms of dull and/or acute lower abdominal pain, usually experienced by the woman on the first day of menses and sometimes, to some degree, on Days 2 through 4. Spasmodic dysmenorrhea is localized period pain, usually involving only the lower abdomen and the genital area. But at times it may radiate out to include the entire pelvic area, the inside of the thighs, and the lower back. It is most often diagnosed in the younger woman, between the ages of fifteen to the mid- to late twenties. It is also possible that a woman will experience this kind of period pain for her full reproductive life, although there is now some evidence that the symptoms of spasmodic dysmenorrhea disappear after a woman has had a child. As with so many other questions surrounding menstruation, it's not completely understood why this should make such a difference, but it's thought to be related to the extension, stretching, and final relaxation of the uterine muscles that take place during pregnancy and childbirth.

Abdominal cramping is believed to result from changes that occur inside the uterus in preparation for the implantation of a fertilized egg during each cycle. If such fertilization does not take place, the entire uterine lining must change again.

The uterus is made up of layers of muscle tissue. The evolution and eventual dissolution of the uterine lining mark the overall menstrual cycle, and the musculature of the uterus enables this process to be carried out. Cramping must therefore be viewed as one of the unfortunate side effects of this evolutionary process. That is not to say, however, that a normal side effect need not be treated.

In most cases, the expulsion of the menstrual discharge will relieve the pain of spasmodic dysmenorrhea after a day or two. Even so, it is a common experience for a woman to feel very much out of sorts until the pain is relieved one way or another. Many women experience such acute cramping in the lower abdomen that they are put out of commission for a day or two each month.

Congestive dysmenorrhea is very different from spasmodic period pain. The congestive variety is marked by one or more symptoms occurring together or at different times just *before* the onset of menstruation. The symptoms include dull aching in the lower abdomen; bloatedness and swelling of the tissues in the abdomen, breasts, genitals or extremities (a condition known as *edema*); headache and back ache; nausea, constipation and/or diarrhea; pains in the joints; and more general feelings of depression, fatigue, tension and irritability, just to mention a few. The symptoms of this variety of menstrual pain are often those that alert a woman to the coming of her period days or even a week in advance of actual flow. For example, a woman may feel bloated or lethargic as much as a week before she begins menstruating, but the symptoms are generally the most severe on the day before her flow begins and may disappear altogether on the first day of her menses or on the day the discharge is greatest (usually the first or second day).

Women can suffer from congestive dysmenorrhea up until the menopause, although it may come and go and its severity may vary

Adapted from *Menstruation* by Hilary C. Maddux. Copyright © 1975 by Hilary C. Maddux. Available from Tobey Publishing, Box 428, New Canaan, Connecticut 06840.

Personal Products Company, Advertisement, 1951

Girls never look their best on "those days"

widely from month to month and year to year. Unlike spasmodic dysmenorrhea, the congestive variety does not usually abate with pregnancy and may even worsen.

Few thoroughgoing studies have been made of either type of dysmenorrhea, but some general patterns seem to exist. It is believed there is a hereditary factor involved. Women who suffer from one form of menstrual pain often report having mothers, aunts, sisters and other blood relatives who suffered from the same variety. In such cases, it may be difficult to isolate whether hereditary factors are involved or whether this relationship results from behavior learned in the home. A daughter brought up by a mother who suffered from spasmodic dysmenorrhea is very likely to have learned how to respond to menstruation by her mother's example. The daughter may be suffering from real symptoms of a real problem, but one not entirely analogous to her mother's. More and better information on menstruation might help both in dealing with their respective problems.

Premenstrual syndrome is used to describe a range of symptoms a woman may exhibit during the *premenstruum* (the period of time immediately before menstruation). It is the generic name for congestive dysmenorrhea and as such, refers to a broader range and a less specific type of period pain, although pain may be the wrong word to use here. What makes premenstrual syndrome different is that the term usually describes the more behavioristic changes that a woman experiences premenstrually with *each* period. Emotionally, women suffering from premenstrual syndrome show signs of depression, irritability, lethargy and fatigue, tension, changes in sleep patterns, anger, anxiety or a host of other related behavior disorders. The physical symptoms—gastro-intestinal upsets, cardiovascular problems, nausea, skin problems, eye problems, respiratory difficulties (asthma and allergies), urinary tract problems and many others—may be absent altogether. The symptoms of the syndrome, whatever they consist of and however they manifest themselves, are *not* in a woman's head. Anyone who has spent any time around a woman with one or more of these problems knows just how they can affect her and those close to her. Nor can a woman's edginess or depressive behavior, premenstrually, simply be written off to "unhealthy attitudes about sex" or to strictly "female" emotional instability, as some writers would have us believe.

Prehistoric. Ancient religions have an array of special deities for childbirth, all of these gods feminine, of course: in Greece, Eilithyia, Lucino, and Ossipaga; in China, Chang Hsien; in Egypt, Meskhenet and Maut; in Ireland, Ana, Rigu, and Mor; in India,

In dealing with the physical pain of spasmodic dysmenorrhea, abdominal cramps and lower back pain, many women choose the age-old remedy of heat applied to the affected areas. This remedy does have medical validity in that heat applied to muscles in spasm tends to ease the discomfort and accompanying pain by relaxing the muscles. A heating pad or hot water bottle is most often used for this purpose. Some women prefer to rub their backs or stomachs with deep-heating oils and creams. There are many such products on the market that can be bought without a prescription. Just plain massaging the affected area or having someone else massage it for you can also be helpful. Massaging creates heat and also stimulates blood circulation. One particularly beneficial technique is to gently massage the lower back and lower abdomen with your fingertips. This does not provide heat, but it does create a numb sensation that can give considerable relief from cramps and other muscle aches and spasms.

Some women swear by a hot bath when menstrual cramps become overpowering, but be sure not to soak in water that is too hot. Hot drinks, such as mint or herbal teas, hot clear broths or other light soups can be very soothing. If a woman relaxes best with a little alcohol in her system, she might like hot teas with rum or whiskey in them. Women who suffer from any of the symptoms of water retention—weight gain, edema, or feelings of bloatedness and general fatigue—should probably *not* drink large amounts of fluid. It would only heighten the symptoms.

Women who have learned to expect cramping in the natural course of their cycles—and one learns it quickly—often carry nonprescription or prescription drugs with them in the event they are suddenly doubled over by pain. Aspirin is probably the most common medication taken for cramps, but many women can't take aspirin. Women suffering from ulcers, gastritis, or other stomach disorders can buy aspirin-like products on the market without the aggravating compound. Some of these products are Tylenol, Nebs, and APAP.

There's a whole series of nonprescription drugs marketed especially for menstrual pain and/or premenstrual syndrome. Together with mild pain-killing compounds, they often contain varying amounts of diuretic agents, substances to increase the volume of urine excreted from the body, thus relieving the sensations of bloatedness and actual swelling symptomatic of congestive dysmenorrhea. These drugs can be bought in any drugstore, but tell your doctor you are taking the medication even though a prescription is not required for its purchase. Women must experiment to determine which of the many brands is the best for them. But experimentation does not mean taking one on top of the other, or trying more than one at a time. Some brand names are Midol, Pamprin, Trendar, Femicin and Humphreys #II. They usually consist of caffeine, an ammonia chloride compound acting as a diuretic, quinine, and sometimes a belladonna derivative used as an antispasmodic.

Lydia Pinkham Herbal Tonic (now available only in tablet form in most states) is an age-old remedy many women still think is *the* answer. Even though its effectiveness has been questioned, it is still bought over the counter by many women and used with good results. If it works for you, no need to give it up. If you think it will work for you, give it a try. Another nonprescription tonic that is available in many drugstores is Cardui. Cardui is a vegetable bitter-tonic and stomachic, which has, as its label reads, "antispasmodic properties valuable in relieving functional dysmenorrhea."

Any prescription drugs that may be deemed necessary for a woman suffering from menstrual pain must of course be secured through a doctor. GPs and gynecologists often avoid prescribing more powerful

Myths and Misconceptions about Menstruation
Judith Ramsey

1. Women must restrict their activities during their menstrual period. They should not exercise, have sexual relations or take tub baths.

There is no medical reason for any of these restrictions. Most doctors say that women should do whatever feels appropriate for them.

2. If a woman misses a menstrual period, poisonous materials will build up in her body.

Not so. If a woman misses a period it will not make her sick nor lead to the accumulation of "dirty" waste products in her body. A missed period for reasons other than a pregnancy can be caused by many factors: emotional upsets, travel, changes in a home or work environment. It is only of concern when it is a symptom of an underlying health problem.

3. It is "safe" for a woman to have intercourse during her period because

it means she has ovulated.

Women do *not* always ovulate 12-14 days before their period begin. In rare instances, ovulation can occur before, during or immediately after a period. Only endocrine tests can tell for certain. For this reason gynecologists recommend using some form of protection during a period if a woman wishes to have sexual relations. For example, use of a diaphragm during a menstrual period is not only perfectly safe, it has the additional advantage of temporarily halting the passage of blood from the vagina.

4. A menstrual period that lasts less than three days or more than five is abnormal.

Not necessarily. Three to five days is the average time span for a period. But it is also normal to bleed for only one day—or seven. Sometimes menstruation may be preceded or followed by a day or two of slight bleeding (known as spotting). As long as this spotting comes within the period, it is not abnormal. Some women may occasionally spot slightly in mid-cycle. This light bleeding is usually associated with ovulation, and in a healthy woman probably isn't of any consequence. Bleeding at any other time, should be brought to the attention of a physician immediately.

5. A heavy flow is abnormal.

Menstrual flow may be light, moderate or heavy. The amount of flow varies from woman to woman. Most women tend to overestimate the amount of blood they actually lose. In an average menstrual period, about one to three ounces of blood is lost. If a woman feels that her blood loss is excessive she should keep track of how many tampons or pads she saturates in a given day and discuss the matter with her physician.

Avaloktitsevara; in Babylon, Nintud, and so forth. But this is just a small portion of the feminine gods, not to speak of those controlling the forest, darkness, the rainbow, dawn, and feminine virginity.

drugs than those already mentioned unless many other methods of treatment have been tried and have failed. When the situation does warrant it, a doctor might prescribe an *analgesic* (pain-killer) such as Darvon or one of the many codeine-derivative drugs. Women should be warned of the possible side effects of any prescription drug and should be careful about driving or drinking while taking certain medications. In treating the various forms and symptoms of dysmenorrhea, many doctors have put together their own medications with contents and quantities they can adjust according to the specific needs of the woman and the symptoms she exhibits. If a doctor does recommend a prescription drug for your particular problem, ask questions about it. Find out what it is for, what it contains, and whether the drug has any side effects. Ask your druggist to put the name of the drug on the label, the expiration date of the drug's effectiveness, and to spell out the instructions for its use carefully, in words you can understand. This is good advice with *any* medication, and it is your right and responsibility to have such information.

Research into medications that can make life easier for women during menses continues, but is proving difficult since many of the causes of menstrual distress are not yet fully known or understood.

Where drug research fails, some unusual studies have succeeded. One current theory is that some symptoms of dysmenorrhea seem related to increases in the amount of blood in the genital area, resulting in tension, dullness, and cramping sensations. And a method that seems to relieve such pressure and discomfort is *orgasm,* induced either through sexual intercourse or by auto-erotic (masturbatory) means. Some women have discovered this for themselves, but now, for the first time, it is being put together with scientific data and research. Masters and Johnson have made clinical studies showing that a woman's orgasm is a powerful means of relieving tension throughout the body. It follows that orgasm might be a viable method of treating menstrual and premenstrual tension and distress, and more studies will undoubtedly be made along these lines.

In dealing with the emotional symptoms of dysmenorrhea and premenstrual syndrome, there are few cure-alls and fewer home remedies available. Generally speaking, women must learn to anticipate and adjust to the moods brought on by menstruation. If a woman is aware she often feels irritable, angry, or depressed before or during her period, it is wise for her to deal with these feelings as they come, rather than allow them to build into a pitch of rage, hysteria or violence.

Amenorrhea (absence of menstruation): Primary amenorrhea, defined as the failure of menstruation to occur after a woman has reached and passed the age when it should have occurred, can be caused by many factors. Primary amenorrhea can result from the absence, malformation or underdevelopment of the female reproductive organs. In such cases, careful medical diagnosis and treatment are necessary. One example of primary amenorrhea is that caused by the blocking of the vaginal opening by an over-imperforated hymen. This condition can usually be corrected with minor surgery.

Primary amenorrhea is not a disease in and of itself, but rather a symptom. In the majority of cases, the condition results from hormonal imbalances. With proper hormone therapy (always prescribed by a doctor), the woman's system can be brought back into balance and menstruation will begin.

Secondary amenorrhea is defined as the absence of menstruation after three months have elapsed since the last period. Usually this is a normal condition and may only indicate that a woman is pregnant or is breastfeeding her child. Secondary amenorrhea is also normal in women shortly after the menarche or during the months or years leading to the menopause. Climate, changes in living conditions, and emotional traumas, such as fear of things to come, anticipation of a big event, or a shocking event in a woman's life, can cause secondary amenorrhea. The situation can usually be normalized with no detrimental effect. However, there are instances in which secondary amenorrhea is due to different pathological conditions. A woman who suffers from primary or secondary amenorrhea should consult her doctor. One of the most common causes of both forms of amenorrhea is general poor health. Any woman who carries out a regular program of preventive health care will have far fewer difficulties with menstruation, and is likely to notice a marked improvement in her general health and sense of well-being.

Menorrhagia (excessive menstruation): It is often difficult for women to determine how much menstrual flow is too much. In general, any woman who cannot keep up with her menstrual flow by using 6 to 8 napkins or tampons a day and/or notices large clots in her menstrual discharge should call her doctor. There may be many reasons for such excessive flow, including the presence of infection, inflammation, benign or malignant tumors, glandular imbalances, organic malfunctioning or emotional factors. In order to rule out the possibility of the presence of any of these abnormalities, it may be necessary for the doctor to perform a D & C. Again, this is done as a diagnostic and curative measure and is often the best method available to a doctor for an accurate diagnosis of the woman's condition. Hormone therapy might be prescribed to prevent the symptoms from recurring in subsequent cycles.

Irregular periods: Irregular periods are most often experienced by women in the early and final months of reproductive life. Irregular periods experienced in the months in between are often due to slight and innocuous disruptions in nature's timetable because of numerous environmental, physical, and emotional factors. Most women put up with these irregularities in the natural course of things. However, any woman who experiences an abnormal loss of blood at *any* time during her cycle, or is concerned about other irregularities, should consult a doctor immediately. Many diseases and disorders can cause irregular periods, the most serious being, of course, cancer.

Once disease has been ruled out, a woman might be put on a program of hormone therapy to normalize this condition.

Pain at Ovulation (Mittelschmerz): Experiencing pain with ovulation is not an uncommon problem but it can vary widely in severity, from a mild twinge of pain at the exact moment of expulsion of the egg from the ovary, to acute pain suffered over a longer period of time. Diagnosis in the latter case is sometimes difficult because the symptoms of mittelschmerz can often mimic the symptoms of appendicitis. If the patient suffering such symptoms has kept a menstrual chart, differentiating one from the other is made easier. Given accurate dates of a patient's menstrual cycles, a doctor can then estimate when ovulation should occur in any given cycle. By combining this information with other medical facts of the case, the doctor can usually make an accurate diagnosis.

If the diagnosis is mittelschmerz, the only effective way of treating it is to block ovulation. This therapy technique, as previously described, can be administered for acute and recurring pain with ovulation. But the technique is a rather radical procedure for the symptoms involved. Doctors will usually advise a woman to ride out the pain as best she can, after, of course, determining there is nothing else wrong with her.

Prehistoric. One of the earliest known forms of popular government is the matriarchies of the small-statured, long-headed race of the Van Lake region in Asia Minor. They are cave dwellers ruled by a "Wise Woman who wields magical and autocratic powers." Bands of these people, each led by its individual matriarch, march westward to Europe, reaching as far as Spain. They are the aborigines of England, Ireland, and Scotland.

The Gynecological Examination

Donna Cherniak and Allan Feingold

After puberty, a woman should have an annual gynecological examination to make sure that the pelvic organs are healthy. Some conditions such as gonorrhea and cervical cancer often do not produce symptoms and may only be discovered during such an examination. Most general practitioners are qualified to do this procedure; therefore, if a woman has a GP who knows her medical history there is no reason for her to see a specialist.

Most women have mixed feelings about the gynecological examination. During this procedure it is necessary to allow the doctor greater intimacy with our bodies than we are used to giving to anyone but our lovers. Few of us really understand the "internal" or how it is performed. We may catch a glimpse of the instruments being used but, for most of us, their function is unknown. We are vulnerable because we lack this knowledge. We are vulnerable because we are physically exposed. We are vulnerable because we are so dependent on the doctor for our health.

How do doctors respond to our vulnerability? A few take advantage of it and exploit us sexually; but most doctors simply ignore our feelings. Most medical students start with some sensitivity but medical school grinds this sensitivity out before they graduate. In gynecological training, the medical student hears his clinical teachers contemptuously refer to women of all ages as "girls" who "urinate once a day, defecate once a week, menstruate once a month, parturate (give birth) once a year and copulate at any conceivable moment." Most medical students, eager to become doctors, succumb to the constant anti-woman attitude that is so typical of North American medical schools.

When doctors are not supportive of women, the quality of medical care goes down. Fearing a lecture on morality, many women give inadequate or misleading sexual histories. Women are so tense during the internal examination that it is difficult for the doctor to interpret what he is feeling. Some doctors try to get the woman to relax by asking superficial questions about her children, her school-work, her job - about anything except what is being done and why. Doctors must learn to understand that even if a woman is relatively relaxed, her entire attention is directed at what his hands are doing to her body. It is the doctor's responsibility to act patiently and explain everything he is doing in terms which the woman can understand.

We must learn about our bodies and the medical procedures necessary for the maintenance of our health. With this knowledge, we will be in a better position to be active participants in decisions about our own health.

History: On the first visit to a doctor, a woman's general medical history should be taken, including past illnesses or operations, allergic reactions to drugs, present illnesses and medication, and general state of health. The woman should give the following information about her gynecological history: At what age did she begin menstruating? Are her cycles regular? What is the duration and amount of menstrual flow? Does she have cramps before, during or after her period? Does she use external pads or internal tampons? What method of birth control has she used and with what success? Has she had any gynecological problems and how have they been treated? If a woman has been pregnant, she should also give an obstetrical history including: number of pregnancies, miscarriages or induced abortions; type of delivery (vaginal or caesarean); premature or full term delivery; weight of newborn; complications before, during or after delivery; whether or not she breastfed; and plans for future pregnancies.

Such thorough questioning is not necessary at each visit. Women attending clinics where the doctor is rarely the same at each visit should ask if their charts have been read prior to examination.

If the woman has come to the doctor because of uncomfortable symptoms or suspected disease, the history of this immediate problem should be taken in detail. When did she first notice the problem? Is it causing her pain or discomfort? Is it always noticeable or does it come and go? Is it worse or better during any particular activity such as urinating or making love? Has she done anything to make it better (medication, douching) and has this worked? These symptoms should direct the doctor's approach to the physical examination. For example, if the woman used a douche just before seeing the doctor, the nature of a discharge may be temporarily changed. If the woman says she has been very sore, the doctor should be especially gentle and sympathetic when examining her.

Physical examination: The woman is left alone to undress, and is given a robe or sheet to wear. A nurse records the woman's height, weight and blood pressure. If the woman has had burning or

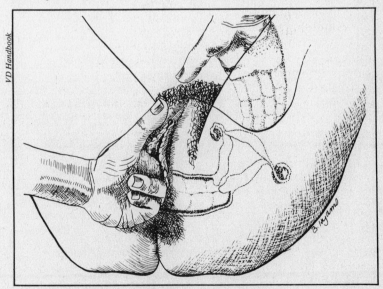

Pelvic examination ("internal"): an internal-external view. The doctor puts two fingers in the vagina and presses down on the lower abdomen with the other hand. The pelvic organs can be felt between the two hands.

Prehistoric. Ancient man entertains deeply ingrained fears of menstruation, a regularly recurring phenomenon to which he himself is never subject. Hence the restrictions since time immemorial, the universal custom of primitive societies being to seclude women at menstruation to neutralize their dangerous influences. Two major precautions observed by nearly all such societies are that the women may not touch the ground nor see the

pain on urination, she will be asked to give a "mid-stream" sample of urine. To do this, the woman first washes her external genitals with a soap-filled pad. She sits on the toilet and only after she has begun to urinate does she hold a bottle under the stream to collect the sample. The bottle should be removed before the woman finishes urinating. The urine is sent to the laboratory where it is tested for bacteria. The mid-stream procedure ensures that any bacteria found in the urine come from the bladder and not from the urethra or external genitals.

While the woman sits on the examining table the doctor examines her head, neck, breasts, lungs, heart and abdomen. With the woman lying on her back, a further check is made of the breasts, abdomen and groin. The doctor looks for swellings, unusual growths or other signs of disease. Women should be instructed how to examine their own breasts, and encouraged to do so once each menstrual cycle.

For examination of the vulva and pelvic organs, the woman lies on her back with her legs apart in stirrup-like supports. The doctor examines the vulva for inflammation, sores, color changes or growths.

To inspect the vagina and cervix, the vaginal walls are held apart by a speculum. The speculum is a metal or plastic instrument with rounded blades which should be warmed and lubricated before being inserted into the vagina. When the blades are opened gently, the vaginal walls are separated.

The Pap test for cervical cancer is done with the speculum in place. With a flat stick, cells are gently scraped from the surface of the cervix especially from around the cervical canal. These cells are placed on a glass slide and sent to a laboratory where the cells are examined for changes typical of cancerous cells. This procedure may be uncomfortable, but not painful.

Sexually active women should have a test for gonorrhea at least once a year, whether or not they have symptoms. This is also done with the speculum in place. A cotton-tipped swab is inserted about ½ inch into the cervical canal. If the woman is relaxed, this procedure may be uncomfortable but should not be painful. A sample of cervical secretions is sent to a lab for the growth and identification of bacteria.

If the woman complains of itchiness or vaginal discharge the doctor should take a sample of vaginal secretions to examine under a microscope immediately.

The doctor removes the speculum by closing the blades and withdrawing it gently. The doctor then performs an "internal" or pelvic examination in order to feel the size, shape, texture and mobility of the pelvic organs. Two fingers of a surgically gloved hand are inserted deep into the vagina. With the other hand on the lower abdomen, the doctor moves the uterus from side to side and feels for unusual growths. Unless there is swelling or abnormal growth, the ovaries and fallopian tubes cannot be felt.[1] If the woman is healthy and relaxed, the internal may be uncomfortable but should not be painful.

If an abnormality is detected during a pelvic examination the doctor may perform a similar examination of the rectum. The doctor can reach higher into the pelvis by this route and in some conditions such as inflammation of the fallopian tubes, rectal examination is less painful than vaginal examination. Rectal examination is important in older women for the early detection of rectal cancer.

Gynecological hygiene: The genital organs require no special care. Washing the vulva with soap and warm water during a bath or shower is enough. There is no reason why a woman should not bathe or shower during her period. Douching (flushing out the vagina with a warm solution) is unnecessary and usually does more harm than good. Douching often upsets the balance of micro-organisms in the vagina by changing their environment.

Vaginal sprays and deodorants are useless products forced on women through high powered advertising campaigns. In healthy women the vulva has a characteristic smell which many sexual partners find exciting. A woman should seek medical attention if her genitals smell bad rather than disguising this symptom with deodorants and perfumes. The vaginal sprays often dry up normal vaginal secretions causing irritation and discomfort.

When a woman wipes herself after moving her bowels, she should wipe from front to back to avoid bringing bacteria from the anus to the urethra and vagina.

For similar reasons, internal tampons are preferable to external pads during the period. The pad provides a direct link from the anus to the vagina and urethra. The blood on the pad is an environment in which bacteria thrive.

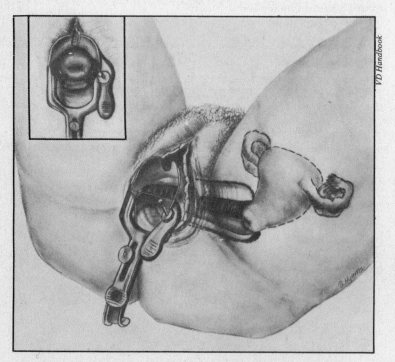

VD Handbook

Use of the speculum: an internal-external view of the speculum in place in the vagina. The blades of the speculum are opened holding the vaginal walls apart. Inset: the cervix as the doctor sees it with the speculum in place.

---

[1] It is very difficult to feel a normal ovary, even in a slender woman, but easy to feel an enlarged ovary. —Ed.

---

sun. The general effect, then, to keep them suspended between heaven and earth. Whether enveloped in a hammock or slung up to the roof, as in South America, or raised above the ground in a dark and narrow cage, as in Polynesia, she may be considered out of the way.

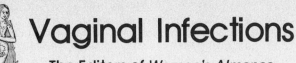

Vaginal Infections

The Editors of *Woman's Almanac*

Sometime during their lives half of all American women will experience these unmistakable symptoms: a maddening vaginal itching and burning, aggravated by scratching and upon urination; a malodorous discharge, called leukorrhea; and a generalized inflammation of the vulvo-vaginal membranes. Any disease causing these symptoms is called vaginitis. It can be "specific" (that is, caused by one or a number of identifiable microscopic organisms) or "nonspecific" (simply meaning that there is no immediately identifiable physical or biological reason for the irritation).

Many cases of "nonspecific" vaginitis have later been proved to be, in fact, infections by organisms normally associated with other sites in the body, like the throat or the intestines. For instance, sometimes strep or staph organisms are detected on the vaginal membranes. But generally speaking, nonspecific vaginitis is readily cured with simple treatments, mild antiseptic douches, or medicated creams.

The specific forms of vaginitis are more severe and demand more attention to treat them successfully. Fortunately, about 95 percent of all women with vaginitis can be cured, and many experts claim that cure rates would be higher yet if doctors took greater care in their diagnoses. Just examining the genitals or discussing your complaints will not tell a physician what *kind* of vaginitis you may have and therefore what course of treatment would be most effective. For that, she or he must take the time to carry out certain standard clinical tests, with smears of vaginal secretions and a microscope to identify the organism(s) responsible.

Specific vaginitis is most often the work of one of two organisms: *Trichomonas vaginalis* (a single-cell animal) and *Candida albicans* (a yeast fungus). Lesser but still sizable numbers of women—and some say up to one third of those already suffering from trichomoniasis—are infected with the *Hemophilus vaginalis,* a flulike bacillus causing milder symptoms than the other two. It is possible for a woman to play host to all three of these organisms simultaneously or in any combination.

Trichomonas vaginalis (trich, TV, trichomoniasis).

As the most common cause of vaginitis, the trichomonad has been found in nearly 25 percent of all women undergoing a routine gynecological exam, according to several studies. The infection is even more common among pregnant women, whose altered vaginal chemistry favors trichomonad growth. Though many women harbor the organism with no signs of infection, the trich has never been considered a "normal" inhabitant of the human body.

Its chief symptom is a vaginal discharge that may be thin and milky but more often is thick and either a frothy greenish or yellowish white. The discharge, itself a powerful irritant, may be so plentiful that it chafes the inner thighs and rectal area, and its odor is the most unpleasant of any vaginal infection. The vaginal membrane may be covered with many small, round, red bumps; the entire region may be sore or may itch or burn; and very often intercourse is painful.

It is now thought that the great majority of trich infections are transmitted from one partner to the other only during genital-to-genital contact. Its home is in the vagina or within the urinary tract of males.

There have been cases of trich blamed on exchanged washcloths, damp bathing suits, the swimming pool, and that old bugaboo, the toilet seat, but these are considered very rare. Since up to 80 percent of infected women's male partners also carry the trich in their urinary tract, most doctors believe this to be the primary source of original or continuing infection. Incidentally, only a few men occasionally exhibit symptoms of infection, usually a burning sensation after urination or ejaculation.

Currently the most effective medication for trich is medronidazole (Flagyl). A regimen of this drug will cure fully 95 percent of those afflicted, provided the other partner is treated at the same time. Symptoms will typically begin to subside within two or three days of taking the pills (usually 250-milligram doses three times a day for ten days), but the therapy must be continued to the end, or you will risk a resurgence of the disease.

Recently a controversy has arisen over the safety of Flagyl, however. Certain experiments on bacteria suggest a possible cancer risk attached to using the drug. The FDA has not yet reacted to this finding, and until it does, the most prudent course of treatment might be to try one of the less effective treatments first, such as a vaginal cream—which would have no effect on trichomonads cached away in the urinary tract—then use metronidazole only if the cream fails to eradicate the symptoms.

Candida vaginalis (vaginal thrush, moniliasis, condidiasis, yeast infection).

Candida albicans is a fungus normally found in the vaginas of about four in ten women. The organism has been detected as well in urine, semen, saliva, the folds of skin creases, and fecal matter, among other sites. If a woman does not harbor the yeast, she may be infected easily and at any time by any one of these sources, but only under certain conditions will the fungus reproduce rapidly enough to provoke the symptoms of vaginitis.

In general, whenever the sugar content of the vaginal cells is higher than normal, the fungus may multiply to take advantage of this rich food supply. Hormones, such as estrogen, associated with pregnancy and with the Pill cause more cellular glycogen or sugar to be stored in the vaginal walls (low-estrogen Pills would, of course, have a lesser effect). As a result, as many as 25 percent of all pregnant women experience the symptoms of moniliasis, and many of them recover spontaneously after delivery, when estrogen production drops back to normal.

For similar reasons, the diabetic—with her higher levels of accumulated unmetabolized sugar in the body—is especially susceptible. It is even possible to court an attack of yeast infection by eating a lot of candy.

Sometimes wide-spectrum antibiotics like tetracycline, prescribed by a doctor for something like a strep throat, encourage the explosive growth of candida by wiping out its microscopic competition while leaving the fungus untouched.

Finally, moniliasis can gain a foothold whenever the body's natural resistance to disease is reduced through fatigue, emotional turbulence, poor eating habits, and so forth.

In the right combination of conditions, the fungus multiplies at geometric rates. Some women may help the transmission of the fungus along by spreading it from their own anus to the vagina with menstrual pads or by wiping themselves from the rectum to the vagina after a bowel movement. There is some evidence that candida, like trich, can transfer from a man's foreskin or urinary tract to his partner's vagina.

While the extreme itching of an acute moniliasis infection can drive a woman to desperation, another woman may be unaware that she has an infection until a doctor tells her. Often the amount of discharge is small, though both amount and texture vary among women. Most commonly, the leukorrhea is watery, with thick, white curdlike chunks mixed in, and smells somewhat like cheese or baking bread. Sometimes the woman may complain of a dry vulva or vagina and the lips and barrel of the the vagina may become covered with whitish patches.

The best treatment for candida vaginitis is probably miconazole (Monistat) cream, which is inserted into the vagina with an applicator once each evening for two weeks. The cream may also be applied to the vulva to soothe any external irritation. Mystatin (Mycostatin) suppositories are the second choice. Candida can be very stubborn to dislodge. Those on the Pill may find it advisable to discontinue that contraceptive until all traces of the disease can be removed. Often pregnant women must simply resign themselves to it until term.

In particularly entrenched cases the doctor may suggest painting the affected area with a deep purple dye, Gentian Violet, but this treatment is quite messy. Another technique, eating yogurt, can help suppress the number of intestinal candida fungi and may, in turn, prevent reinfection of the vagina *via* the anus, but yogurt or Mycostatin oral medication cannot act directly on the yeast causing the vaginitis symptoms.

Hemophilus vaginalis.

It has only been a short while since the hemophilus bacillus has been isolated and identified as an independent agent of vaginitis. The organism must now be considered a possible cause of some forms of vaginitis that have resisted other methods of treatment or that used to be labeled "nonspecific."

Hemophilus is the mildest vaginitis. Often its only symptom is a slight vaginal discharge, grayish white and somewhat unpleasant smelling.

It is thought that most hemophilus infections are passed along through sexual intercourse. For instance, we know that women with untreated male partners have a high rate of reinfection.

An oral antibiotic administered over the course of a week or so will usually neutralize the organism. An effective local cream or suppository treatment is also available.

What can you do to help prevent a vaginitis infection or reinfection? If you think a male partner may be carrying one of these diseases, have him visit a doctor or at least wear a condom during intercourse. Contraceptive foams, jellies, and creams can also provide some protection. If you have been plagued with recurrent infections, use tampons instead of sanitary napkins during your periods. They cut down on bacterial and fungal traffic between the anus and vagina.

But if despite your preventative measures you contract vaginitis, be sure not to douche the day before your examination, since douching may make accurate diagnosis impossible. Take the full regime of whatever medication your doctor prescribes, rather than stopping as soon as symptoms disappear. This will give the medication the best chance to knock out the infection completely.

Self-help

An Interview with Marcia L. Storch, M.D.

For several years women have been meeting in what are known as self-help groups to discuss women's health problems and sexuality. One of the activities for which these groups are best known is the self-administration of vaginal examinations by using a speculum and a mirror. Many a woman has had the experience of seeing her own cervix for the first time in a self-help group—an experience often described as awesome. Below, Dr. Storch discusses the activities of these groups.

Q: What in your opinion is the main value of self-help groups?

A: I think that self-help is marvelous in the following areas:

Most important—education, including anatomy of the genital area and, to some extent, physiology. You should know what's inside your vagina.

It can also help women understand how to use contraception correctly, for example, by seeing where the diaphragm should be placed to cover the opening of the cervix.

Besides what you see in a self-help group, it provides a good opportunity to talk with other women, not just about medical things but about sexuality. Self-help groups can be a form of consciousness-raising. For some women it might be easier to talk about sex in a self-help group than in a consciousness-raising group.

Q: Do some of the home remedies discovered by self-help groups really work?

A: The only remedy that self-help groups have actually discovered so far is putting yogurt into the vagina to treat vaginitis. [See pages 19-20.] The yogurt works by increasing the lactobacillus population, which is the normal bacterial inhabitant of the vagina.

However, some of the other remedies the self-help movement is credited with discovering have been known to the medical profession for some time, for example, that vinegar douches can increase the acidity of the vagina, which discourages infection; that drinking cranberry juice, which similarly creates an acid environment in the urethra, can help prevent chronic cystitis; that high fluid intake—flushing out the bladder—can also help prevent cystitis.

Q: What should a self-help group do to prevent passing around vaginal infections by using the same speculum?

A: Ideally, every woman in a self-help group should have her own speculum. However, think of a speculum as a plate or a toothbrush. Ordinarily, it doesn't have to be sterilized between uses, just adequately cleaned. Inexpensive plastic speculums should be well scrubbed and soaked in a detergent solution for at least an hour before being reused. Stainless-steel speculums, which are less porous, just need scrubbing.

Q: Do you think that regular self-examination of the vagina can be useful in telling you when you're getting an infection or are pregnant?

A: A woman who examines her vagina regularly will become familiar with its appearance, but that doesn't mean that she can rely on changes she sees to tell whether or not she's pregnant or has an infection. A woman who thinks she has an infection shouldn't rely on self-diagnosis and treatment. Nor, obviously should a woman who thinks she's pregnant; she should have a pregnancy test.

---

founders of Rome, are born of a virgin coupling with the god Mars. There are literally thousands of such examples, perhaps the most prominent being the birth of Christ by the Virgin Mary.

Herpes Genitalis

Carol V. Horos

A type of virus closely related to that responsible for causing the common cold sore or fever blister is presently the second most prevalent venereal disease in the U.S. It surpasses syphilis in frequency and rivals gonorrhea as the number one venereal disease. Herpes genitalis is a frightening, bizarre infection. It produces painful, blister-like sores on the genital organs which cause misery to those who are unfortunate enough to be infected. Unlike other venereal diseases, which are completely cured by proper medication, the herpes virus can remain in the human body indefinitely. Seventy per cent of the people with herpes type 2, once infected, remain infected. The virus lies dormant within the body for varying lengths of time, only to strike again and again.

But herpes is more than just cold sores on the genitals. It has been linked to producing cervical cancer in women and can kill newborn babies. At present, herpes genitalis is an epidemic, with an estimated 250,000 persons developing the disease in 1974. No one knows why herpes has suddenly reached epidemic proportions. No one can predict how long it will last or how many infant deaths or cases of cervical cancer will result before herpes type 2 can be controlled. Clinics are now seeing more cases of herpes genitalis than either syphilis or gonorrhea. What was once a little understood medical oddity has become a major venereal disaster.

"Herpes" is derived from the Greek word "to creep" and describes a sore made up of tiny bumps or blisters. The medical term for the infection is *Herpes simplex* and it is caused by a virus called herpes virus hominis (HVH). Herpes simplex is divided into two different categories or types; herpes type 1 and type 2. Picture an imaginary line cutting across the waist. Herpes type 1 strikes in the areas above the waist and generally limits itself to the face, but it can also be spread to the genitals. It is primarily responsible for causing the unsightly cold sores or fever blisters. Anyone who has ever had a fever blister knows that it may appear at what seems are irregular intervals, causing a minimal amount of physical discomfort but somewhat more mental anguish by producing an unwanted blemish on your face. The fever blister eventually bursts and heals in a week or two. It may or may not return.

Type 1 can also affect the eyes. In some instances, the infection scars the cornea (lens of the eye), leading to partial or complete blindness. In relatively few cases, the infection of the cornea progresses to the brain passages and causes encephalitis. If you should have a fever blister on your face, *never* wipe your eyes with the fluid from the sore.

Herpes type 2 or herpes genitalis hits the areas below the waist and most often affects the genital organs, buttocks and thighs. Tiny, painful blisters appear singly or in clusters. After a few days, the blisters break, leaving open, red sores which ultimately form scab tissue and then heal completely.

Transmission

Herpes type 2 is primarily spread by direct sexual contact, through vaginal, oral-genital or anal intercourse with an infected partner. The virus can also enter the body through even the slightest cut or break in the skin.

A person with herpes is highly contagious when she or he has a moist blister or open sore on the body. The fluid that oozes from the blister is loaded with the herpes virus particles. An infection can be spread easily by transferring the liquid to a susceptible skin surface. The line of demarcation separating the two types of herpes (above or below

From *Vaginal Health* by Carol V. Horos. Available from Tobey Publishing, Box 428, New Canaan, Connecticut 06840.

the waist) is not a rigid rule. Although herpes type 1 occurs predominately above the waist, it can be spread to the genital areas as well. This transfer of type 1 infection to the genitals often happens during oral-genital intercourse, when the genitals touch a moist fever blister or cold sore on a person's mouth. The reverse is also true. If an infected penis or vulva (type 2) comes into direct contact with a person's mouth or face, the result is a type 2 infection on the facial area. Inadequate personal hygiene is another route of infection. Wiping your eyes or face after touching your own or someone else's infected genitals can transfer a type 2 infection to your face.

You may wonder if there is any difference between herpes types 1 and 2 other than their location on the body. There is a big difference between the two, but it is not visibly noticeable. The virus responsible for type 2 is a variety or strain biologically different from the type 1 virus. The only way a doctor can verify the strain is to take a specimen of the blister and culture it on a special charcoal medium. The specimen is then sent to a laboratory where technicians differentiate the two strains.

The Course of Herpes Type 2 Infection

When the virus enters the body, it moves to some area other than the point of infection. There it remains dormant for an undetermined period of time. Some physicians believe the herpes virus stays within the sheaths or nerve coverings in a latent, inoperative state. After the incubation period (the amount of time between exposure and first symptoms), one or several small blisters appear on the genital organs. They may be bunched together in groups or colonies, or scattered over the surface of the skin.

In women, the blisters are generally hidden within the vagina or on the cervix. This situation makes herpes type 2 especially serious, since an internal infection usually produces no symptoms to warn a woman of her infection. The blisters also appear externally on the vaginal lips, perineum (area between the vagina and rectum), clitoris, anus, buttocks or thighs. Men generally find the blisters on the glans or shaft of the penis. Homosexual men find them near the anus as well.

The infected area becomes red and tender. Tiny raised bumps or blisters begin to form on the skin. They are filled with fluid and are painful to the touch. One to three days after the formation of the blisters, the blister ruptures, leaving a soft, terribly painful open sore called an erosion. The moist erosion is covered by a yellow-grey pus and the sore is highly contagious to yourself and to others. During this stage you can spread the infection to other areas of your body. The rupture of blisters on the vaginal lips may spread the fluid over the surface of the vulva, buttocks and thighs. Just one minute break in the skin is necessary for the virus to gain a foothold in another area.

About one week later, scabs begin to form over the open sores, which gradually heal themselves. The crusted scab resembles the chancre of syphilis and is often mistaken for it. The first attack of herpes type 2 may last a month to six weeks before the symptoms of the virus disappear. In addition to the painful sores, some people have fever, headaches, itching, swelling of the lymph nodes and general malaise or weakness. These symptoms, similar to flu, gradually diminish as the infection progresses.

Recurring Infections

For many people, the first bout with herpes type 2 is only the beginning of many more painful episodes which can disrupt the normal

---

Prehistoric. Classical Greek and Latin mythology is one long chronicle of coition between the gods, demigods, and mortal women. Heracles is the son of Alcmene by Zeus; Apollo cohabits with the mortal Creusa whose human husband never before nor

routine of daily life. A person's lack of a natural resistance to viral infections is thought to play a major role in recurrent herpes. The infection may reappear every week or two and continue so for years, bringing the miserable flu-like feeling with it. Subsequent attacks are shorter in duration, lasting about a week to ten days.

Certain factors are known to trigger recurring herpes infection. Doctors have found a direct correlation between body temperature and the onset of herpes. Whenever the body temperature is raised, however slightly; it can set off another infection. A return of the virus' activity is almost certain, since any kind of physical exertion raises body temperature. Exposure to sunlight causing a mild sunburn, emotional stress, tension, colds, fever, the strain of sexual intercourse and sports may trigger the virus. Anything that raises the internal temperature may bring back the symptoms. Some women experience a monthly battle with herpes. The herpes appear about a week before each menstrual period because of the elevation of the body temperature after ovulation.

If you are a victim of recurrent herpes, you can take some precautions to stave off another infection. When you are outside for any length of time, wear a sunscreen to avoid sunburn. Taking aspirin in times of stress or exertion can help keep the temperature down. Applying cool, wet compresses to susceptible areas also affords some relief.

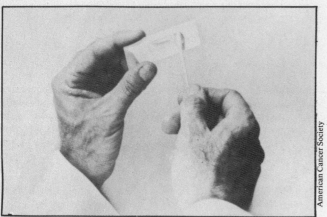

In a pap test, a sample of vaginal secretions is smeared on a glass slide and, after a series of preparations, is studied under the microscope for early evidence of cancer.

Cervical Cancer

The exact relationship between herpes type 2 and cervical cancer is not fully understood, but studies indicate that a woman with a herpes infection on the cervix is eight times more susceptible to developing cervical cancer than an uninfected woman. It is also estimated that six per cent of women with cervical herpes develop cancer within five years of the time of infection. This second most common form of cancer (breast cancer is number one) has been found to strike most frequently in women who began to have sexual intercourse at an early age and who have had multiple partners. It occurs infrequently in women who do not engage in sexual intercourse.

The problem with a herpes type 2 infection of the cervix is that it does not produce symptoms. The cervix is relatively free of nerve endings, so you won't feel any pain. Even if the infection is a recurrent one, you won't know it is there. The only way to insure against cervical cancer is to have regular internal examinations. Go at least once a year; every six months if you have an active and varied sex life.

Herpes and Pregnancy

An active herpes infection of the cervix or vagina in a woman late in pregnancy poses a tremendous threat to the life of the newborn.

Transmission of the disease occurs as the infant passes through the birth canal during delivery. The infant mortality rate from this disease is high. One out of every four babies dies at birth and one third of all children who survive are seriously damaged.

If a pregnant woman has active sores on her genitals near the time of delivery (about the 38th week), a Caesarean section (delivery from an incision on the abdomen) is performed to prevent the child from becoming infected. But even birth by Caesarean section is not a 100 per cent guarantee of delivering a healthy baby.

Treatment

Like most viruses, herpes simplex (type 1 and type 2) cannot be killed by antibiotics. Surface skin creams, such as sulfa cream or nonprescription products such as Campho-Phenique, offer some relief from the burning and itching symptoms, but the infection will continue to run its course. Sometimes the doctor prescribes Pontocaine, a surface anaesthetic, or a combination of aspirin and codeine to alleviate the pain.

Breakthroughs have occurred in the treatment of herpes simplex, but the results are, as yet, inconclusive. The dye-light therapy is a recent, though highly controversial, method of treatment. Some physicians believe the therapy may trigger cancer in normal cells. In this procedure, the blisters are painted with proflavine dye, a common, inexpensive yellow dye mixed in a 0.1% aqueous solution. After the blisters are painted, the area is exposed to an ordinary 15–watt fluorescent desk lamp for about 15 minutes. The area is exposed to the light again six to eight hours later. The treatment has been found to be 50 per cent effective in reducing the number of recurrent infections, but long-term experiments in animals have shown that the dye-light technique may be responsible for producing cancer in normal, healthy cells. Until further studies conclude that the dye-light therapy does not trigger cancerous cells in humans, its use in the treatment of herpes simplex should be questioned.

Perhaps the best hope for curing herpes simplex is the development of a safe and effective vaccine. Vaccines are preparations composed of disease-causing organisms (which have been killed) that produce an immunity to infectious diseases. Researchers have discovered several vaccines for herpes. The most promising is a German preparation called *Lupidon G,* which specifically works against type 2 herpes. Although the results of the vaccine have been quoted as high as 95 per cent effective, it too has been found to cause cancer in experimental animals. For this reason, the Food and Drug Administration has banned import of Lupidon G to the U.S.

Preventing Herpes

For the present, medical science can safely offer a person with herpes little more than solace and painkillers. But you can take simple precautions against developing this debilitating infection

1. Never kiss or have oral-genital intercourse with a person who has a cold sore or fever blister on the mouth. The reverse is also true. Refrain from kissing or having oral-genital intercourse if you have a cold sore or fever blister. Once the cycle runs its course and the sore disappears, you may resume sexual relations.
2. Look at your partner's genitals *before* intercourse. If you notice any unusual sore or swelling, don't have intercourse.
3. If you have herpes, be careful not to spread the fluid from the blisters to other areas of your body, particularly the eyes.
4. If you have new or multiple sex partners, your best protection is to have them wear condoms. Don't rely on the man to carry a condom with him; have your own supply.
5. To insure against cervical cancer, have a routine internal examination at least once a year.

afterward can impregnate her. The problem gets so out of hand that, much later, medieval Catholic popes solemnly issue bulls condemning intercourse between incubi (invisible male demons) and women.

Your Medical Data Bank
Marcia L. Storch, M.D.

It's a good idea to establish health facts about yourself at whatever age you are, and to have them updated periodically. This information about what's normal for you will make diagnosis easier should you later develop any medical problems.

EKG: If you're over 25, you should have an electro-cardiogram (EKG). Between the ages of 25 and 40 you should have an EKG done at least every five years, and after that, every year.

Chest X-ray: Chest x-rays, which have very little radiation, can help detect lung cancer and tuberculosis. If you are under 40, you should have a chest x-ray every five years. If you are over 40, or work in the health professions or live in a poor area, you should have one yearly.

Blood Work: Everyone should have a complete blood count and a test for syphilis every year. Until age 40, tests for levels of blood sugar and cholesterol and for liver-kidney function should be done every five years; after that they should be done yearly.

Blood Pressure: Blood pressure should be taken yearly, or whenever you go to the doctor, at whatever age you are, and possibly more often if you are taking oral contraceptives or are over 40. Often a doctor won't volunteer to tell you your blood pressure if it's normal. Feel free to ask.

Mammogram: At age 35, if she hasn't had one before, every woman should have a mammogram (breast x-ray) done. If you are in a high-risk group for breast cancer, you should have one done at whatever age you are. Then when you approach the age at which members of your family were discovered to have breast cancer, which is the age at which your risk becomes greatest, you should get professional advice about having more frequent periodic mammograms (and manual breast examinations as well; for further information see page 13). Make sure you're getting a low-dose mammogram, a maximum of two rads per breast. If your doctor or clinic won't tell you how much radiation you're being exposed to, have the x-ray done elsewhere.

Proctoscopic Exam: After age 40 you should have yearly proctoscopic exams of the rectum.

After age 40, you should see an internist at least once a year to have a complete physical examination done, including the above procedures.

Rubella Vaccination: Any woman who expects to be pregnant should be tested for immunity to measles and, if necessary, vaccinated before pregnancy. You should never be vaccinated during pregnancy. Before vaccination you should take a pregnancy test, and for three months after vaccination you should use an effective means of contraception.

Bladder Infections
Healthright, Inc.

Another infection which many women suffer from is cystitis, which is the medical term for a bladder infection. Urine is stored in the bladder and normally does not contain bacteria, so the infection does not start there. However the openings of the rectum, vagina and bladder (the urethra) are close together and the whole area is warm and moist so it's easy for germs to spread from the rectum or vagina to urethra and bladder. Bladder infections can occur in children and celibate women, but like vaginal infections they occur more often among women who make love with men. (In the days when women were virgins at marriage, cystitis was often called 'honeymoon disease').

Symptoms: There is pain and a burning feeling when you pass urine. You may want to pee frequently, yet when you do there is very little urine in your bladder. In a bad case there may be blood in the urine.

Cause: Several different germs can infect the bladder including those that are normally present in the rectum. If a woman is diabetic and there is sugar in her urine, bacteria will grow more easily. If you don't respond to the first drug a doctor prescribes, he/she may do a 'urine culture' test. A sample of urine is treated so that any bacteria present will grow, and the type of bacteria can be identified and tested to see which drugs it responds to.

Treatment: Gantrisin is a sulfa drug and is widely used. In some cases the bacteria may be resistant to Gantrisin and an antibiotic like Tetracycline is used. This medication should bring almost immediate relief of the symptoms. However, the infection is not immediately cured, so the medication should be continued for about two weeks. Some women have side effects when they take Gantrisin including headaches. In such cases Tetracycline is used.

Prevention: If you have a history of bladder or kidney infections, drink a lot of fluids because this dilutes the urine and flushes the kidneys. Pee regularly because the pressure of a full bladder can help inflame the tissues, and also peeing can wash out bacteria in the bladder and urethra. It is very important to be completely cured of bladder infections. Many people think that chronic bladder infections may result in serious kidney diseases after many years.

Crabs

These are lice that infest (live in) the pubic hair but may be found on any other hair. They suck the blood from the infested area. Lice are easily passed on sexually but may also be acquired from bedmates, sharing bedlinen and towels. They have been occurred recently in commune situations. Treatment is (a) thorough cleansing with Kwell in cream, lotion, or shampoo form and (b) using freshly washed underwear and bedding.

Infections of the Vagina © Health Organizing Collective. These and other pamphlets are available from Healthright, Inc., Suite 1319, 175 Fifth Ave., New York, NY 10010.

ca. **3350 B.C.** Egyptian women are acknowledged as the superior sex. Men inherit property and position through the rights of their wives and mothers. In the First Dynasty it is doubtful whether a king could reign unless he happened to be the husband of the queen, whose title comes to her through the female line.

Cervicitis and Endometriosis

Carol V. Horos

CERVICITIS

The cervix resembles a small, hollow cylinder about two inches long and one inch wide. It is the lower portion of the uterus which protrudes into the top part of the vaginal canal. The tissues of the cervix may be affected by inflammations, infections and cancer. Cervicitis is an inflammation of the cervix and is quite common.

Causes

Any number of bacteria which ordinarily live in the genital tract or which are introduced into the cervix from the outside can cause cervicitis. Viruses, protozoa (one-celled animals), fungi or any other type of organism may trigger the inflammation. Cervicitis frequently occurs in women who are infected with gonorrhea. Also, birth control pills are thought to produce a mild, chronic cervical inflammation. Childbirth is cited as another cause of cervicitis since tiny lacerations on the cervix resulting from delivery can become infected.

Symptoms

1. Often the only symptom is a persistent vaginal discharge. The discharge is generally white or yellowish.
2. Spotting or bleeding between menstrual periods or after intercourse may occur.
3. There can be pain during intercourse.
4. Urination may cause a burning sensation.
5. Sometimes a woman suffers from lower back pain and a slight fever.

Diagnosis

The cervix is examined with a speculum inserted into the vagina. The doctor usually sees a swollen, reddened cervix and a great deal of discharge coming from the cervical canal. A culture taken of the discharge determines what type of bacteria is causing the infection.

Treatment

Penicillin is the most preferred drug, followed by sulfa drugs and broad spectrum antibiotics. If the inflammation does not respond to antibiotic treatment, the doctor may cauterize the cervix. Cauterization is the burning of the tissue in order to seal the skin of the inflamed area and can be done either in the doctor's office or in a hospital with anesthesia. A speculum exposes the cervix and the vaginal and cervical canals are cleared of all discharge. The area is then cauterized by an electric cautery tip, a silver nitrate solution or by freezing. When done properly, this procedure is not painful since the cervical tissues are comparatively insensitive to heat.

After the cautery is performed, a woman notices an increase in her vaginal discharge, which may be muddy-looking and sometimes streaked with blood. The color is due to the shedding of the burned cells of the cervix. The discharge usually lasts four to six weeks and complete healing takes place in seven to eight weeks. A woman should not have intercourse for about two weeks after cauterization.

Cervical Erosion

These are large or small sores found on the surface of the cervical opening. There may be an increase in the vaginal discharge and, less commonly, bleeding. Depending on the size of the erosion, the doctor may leave them alone since they are not harmful. In some instances, the erosion should be cauterized.

Prevention of Cervicitis

Seek out early treatment for vaginal infections before they spread to the cervix and go for a routine gynecological examination at least once a year. Vaginal hygiene is also extremely important since outside bacteria (from the feces) can produce cervical inflammation.

ENDOMETRIOSIS

The endometrium is the membrane that lines the inner surface of the uterus. During the menstrual cycle, the endometrium thickens and grows to provide nourishment for the fertilized egg. If the egg is not fertilized, the endometrium shrinks and its lining crumbles into the cervical canal, forming the menstrual flow.

Sometimes the cells of the endometrium grow in places other than the uterine lining. This is called endometriosis. Common sites of tissue growth are: on the ovaries, Fallopian tubes, rectum, bladder, vagina, vulva, cervix and lymph glands. Endometriosis ordinarily occurs during the reproductive years between the ages of 25 and 45, and most often affects women who have not had children. Since the tissues may grow on the internal reproductive organs, infertility is a common consequence of endometriosis.

Symptoms

Symptoms vary, depending on the location of the tissue growth. There may be pain before, during and after the menstrual period and, in some instances, pain is felt during sexual intercourse. Sometimes a woman may have pain in the abdomen and lower back.

Diagnosis

Endometriosis is difficult to detect in its early stages because its symptoms are variable and can be attributed incorrectly to other problems. The doctor performs a pelvic examination to feel for any abnormal growths on the internal organs.

Treatment

In some cases, hormones similar to those contained in birth control pills are given to cure the condition. But, if the tissue growth is extensive, surgery may be required to remove the cyst.

ca. **3000 B.C.** Poetry written by ancient Egyptians indicates that women take the active part in courting rituals, choosing and wooing their men. Also, certain other written materials make reference to women leaving the home each day to earn a living while their husbands domestically remain behind.

Syphilis and Gonorrhea
Planned Parenthood League of Massachusetts

The term venereal disease is applied to various infections which are transmitted from an infected person to a partner during intimate contact. The two main venereal diseases, *syphilis* and *gonorrhea*, usually are passed via the genitalia during intercourse. In rare instances, syphilis may be spread by kissing or touching the infected area, or by a blood transfusion. However, since the organisms causing the infection need a warm, moist environment to survive, it is important to dispel the myth that venereal diseases can be contracted from toilet seats, wash basins, drinking cups, fountains, etc. In the 1950's VD was considered to be almost under control. Since 1960, however, VD, particularly gonorrhea, has grown to epidemic rates. VD is particularly common among the young. According to statistics, about one in every twenty-five persons in the 20-24 age group will contract gonorrhea, as will one in every fifty teenagers. However, available statistics are definitely lower than the actual figures, since all too often VD remains undetected and untreated. Only about one-third of diagnosed cases are reported to public health authorities. VD is fairly easy to detect in the male but all too often goes undetected in infected females. The problem lies in recognizing the symptoms of VD. It is possible to have more than one venereal disease at one time; also, all of the symptoms may not be present in a particular individual.

Of the two common venereal diseases, syphilis is the more dangerous. Untreated mothers can transmit the disease through the bloodstream to an unborn child. Untreated syphilis can result in damage to any of the vital organs, lesions of the skin, and inflammation of the bones, joints, eyes, and especially the brain and cardiovascular system. These are the effects of late syphilis. It is important that the disease be diagnosed and treated in its early stages before permanent body damage can be done.

The first symptom of syphilis, a sore or chancre, appears anywhere from 9 days to three months after initial exposure. The sore is caused by a concentration of white corpuscles packed so tightly in the infected area that the surrounding tissue is destroyed. The sore may resemble a cold sore and is painless. It appears at the site of the infection, usually in the genital, oral, or anal areas. In women a genital chancre is often internal and, therefore, unnoticeable. The sore will disappear within three to four weeks with or without treatment.

However, without treatment, syphilis persists and enters a second stage. It is during these first two stages that the disease is most contagious.

The symptoms of the second stage vary widely and are often mistaken for other illnesses. Hence, syphilis is known as "The Great Imitator." The most common of these symptoms is a rash which may cover the whole body or only a small area. The rash is often present on the soles of the feet and palms of the hands. This differs from rashes caused by other diseases. Other symptoms of the secondary stage include headaches, sore throat, swollen glands, especially in the genital area, and pain in the bones or joints. If syphilis is not treated, these symptoms can appear and disappear for a period of four years.

After this time, the disease enters a latent stage in which no symptoms are visible, but the disease is still present in the body. When the symptoms do reappear, they are quite serious. The danger of infecting others during this stage is greatly decreased. At any stage the disease can be arrested with treatment but the damage done cannot be undone. Untreated syphilis can be fatal at this stage.

Syphilis is fairly easily detected by a blood test. For this reason, most states require proof of a negative blood test before issuing a marriage license. These blood tests have also become part of the routine physical exam done in the Armed Forces, during pregnancy, and for admission to a hospital. If a person has one or more of the symptoms listed above, a blood test is necessary.

Adapted from *Everybody's Guide to Every Body.* Reprinted with permission of Planned Parenthood League of Massachusetts.

Gonorrhea (GC) or "the clap" is essentially a disease of the linings of the genito-urinary organs. It can cause sterility and a form of arthritis. An infected mother can transmit the organism during delivery to the eyes of her baby, thus causing blindness. Adults in rare cases have also been blinded by accidentally rubbing their eyes with their hands after contact with the vaginal or urethral discharge, and in this way, accidentally infecting the eyes.

The symptoms of gonorrhea differ in the sexes. Eighty percent of infected women have no symptoms with an early infection. A few women may have some pain when urinating or a slight vaginal discharge. The disease is generally discovered in a woman only when the obvious symptoms show up in her male partner. It is, therefore, essential that a man with a positive gonorrhea test inform his sexual contact(s) immediately. If the disease is untreated, it can infect the bladder causing cystitis; the rectum—proctitis; or the fallopian tubes—salpingitis which can result in sterility.

A man generally has much more acute symptoms, including burning or painful urination and a discharge from the urethra. He may also suffer from cystitis, epididymitis, and genito-urinary tract complications.

It is possible to contract gonorrhea in the throat or anus. Anyone who has anal or oral-genital sex should be sure to tell this to the physician.

Current methods of diagnosis for gonorrhea differ with the sexes. In the male, there is usually a sufficient number of organisms present to swab the discharge, make a slide and examine it immediately. In the female, however, the organisms are not as numerous. During a pelvic examination a swab of the cervical and urethral discharge can be taken and cultured. About two days are required for the bacteria to grow and the diagnosis confirmed. Treatment for both sexes must be prompt to avoid permanent damage to the infected area.

If a test is positive, one is usually asked about sexual contacts. Any names given are treated in confidence. Any names not given should be informed immediately by the infected man or woman. Since the symptoms of VD are so varied and elusive, this may be the only way that partners of an infected person will ever find out they have the disease. Having had VD does not produce any natural immunity, and one can be reinfected by any contagious contact. Remember that it is not just last night's partner who may be infected. If one is being treated for early syphilis, all contacts within the last three months should be notified. For gonorrhea, all contacts within one month of diagnosis should have a test done. Any temporary embarrassment is insignificant compared to the risk to the health, and possibly the life, of another person.

Successful treatment consists of one or a series of injections of penicillin or other antibiotic. To be sure not to transmit the infection it is recommended that sexual intercourse be avoided for at least four days after the final injection. Even if a condom is used, one cannot be sure that the infection will not be transmitted.

A simple inexpensive blood test to detect gonorrhea has recently become available. It produces a result in only two minutes and can be performed in a medical office or clinic. The advantage of the test is its simplicity and that it will detect gonorrhea in an asymptomatic female (due to pain and discharge most men know they have an infection). It has a sensitivity of 80%, 10% better than the culture method. A positive blood test will mean that the woman has gonorrhea now, or has had it in the past (there is a 5% false positive rate).

This is the first blood test for gonorrhea and as time goes on will no doubt be made more sensitive.

In most cities there are clinics and hospitals where one can obtain tests for and treatment of VD. Care at these clinics is usually free, although some may ask you to pay what you can afford. For the name of the clinic nearest you, call the Department of Public Health.

---

ca. **2460 B.C.** Babylon opens its perpetual marriage mart, where huge throngs of young girls are kept on regular display by parents seeking husbands for them.

Methods of Abortion

Donna Cherniak and Allan Feingold

There are several different medical methods of abortion. The choice of which method to use is determined mainly by the length of the pregnancy that is to be interrupted.

Suction abortion

Suction abortion, also called vacuum curettage, is a simple technique for sucking the fetus out of the uterus through a narrow tube which is inserted into the cavity of the uterus through the cervix. Suction abortion can be performed quickly and easily, with little blood loss and a very low risk of complications. It can be performed in an outpatient clinic since the full facilities of a hospital operating room are not needed. Originally developed in China in 1958, suction abortion has since replaced the older method of dilatation and curettage for abortions performed up to the 12th week of pregnancy, and has become the most widely used method of abortion.

Very little special preparation is needed for suction abortion. The woman must have her blood type determined. To prevent vomiting, the woman should not eat for three hours before the operation. The woman should bathe the day of the operation. Shaving the pubic hair is not necessary.

Before beginning the abortion the doctor should perform an internal gynecological examination to determine the size and position of the uterus. As the fetus grows, the uterus becomes progressively larger and softer. An experienced doctor can determine the age of the pregnancy by determining the size of the uterus. Once the woman has been pregnant for more than 12 weeks, the fetus becomes too large and the uterus becomes too soft for suction abortion to be performed safely. In most cases, suction abortion should not be performed after the 12th week of pregnancy.[1]

Having performed the internal examination, the doctor inserts a speculum into the woman's vagina. The speculum is an instrument that holds the vaginal walls apart so that the doctor can see the cervix (opening of the uterus).

If the operation is performed gently, a local anesthetic ("freezing") is enough to prevent pain. The technique of local anesthetic commonly used for abortion is called the paracervical block which "blocks" pain coming from the cervical canal and uterus. To establish the "block" the doctor injects a small amount of an anesthetic drug into the back walls of the vagina, next to the cervix. The injections themselves are not painful since the deep end of the vagina has few nerve endings. Some doctors also give their patient a small amount of nitrous oxide gas ("laughing gas") which has harmless, temporary and pleasant effects. In almost all cases of suction abortion performed early in pregnancy, local anesthetic is sufficient and general anesthetic should not be used. In contrast to local anesthetic which is quite harmless, general anesthetic can have side effects which are considerably more dangerous than the abortion itself.

Once the local anesthetic drug is injected, the cervical canal is dilated (widened) so that surgical instruments can be passed through the cervical canal and into the uterus. To dilate the cervical canal the doctor inserts a series of increasingly larger polished metal rods into the canal. The first rod is about the width of a soda straw and the last rod is about the width of a finger. The canal becomes a little wider as each rod is inserted and removed. The muscles around the cervical canal stretch more easily in women who have had children. Although the local anesthetic prevents severe pain, some women, especially those who have never given birth, experience menstrual-like cramps during dilatation of the cervical canal.

Once the cervical canal is dilated, the doctor inserts a suction curette into the uterus until it touches the fetus. The suction curette is a rigid, hollow, plastic tube 8 mm (about 1/3 of an inch) wide, which is connected by transparent plastic tubing to a vacuum bottle. (There is also a narrower, flexible suction curette which can be used for very early abortions, up to the 9th week of pregnancy). With the suction curette within the cavity of the uterus, the vacuum pressure is turned on for 20 to 40 seconds. This breaks up the fetus and pulls it into the vacuum bottle. Once the uterus is emptied, the doctor inserts a small spoon-like instrument called a curette, and gently scrapes the inner lining of the uterus to make sure that none of the fetus or placenta ("afterbirth") is left behind. This scraping is the same as in a dilatation and curettage operation (D and C).

The whole suction abortion takes 5 to 10 minutes. The woman should rest for 15 to 30 minutes after the operation. The woman should get up slowly from the operating table, to prevent fainting. Recuperation after suction abortion is rapid. Although most women have menstrual-like cramps after the operation, these cramps are usually not severe and can be controlled with pain killers such as aspirin with codeine. The woman should take it easy for a day or two after the abortion.

After an abortion a woman will have menstrual-like bleeding for a day to a week. The woman may use either pads or tampons to absorb the flow. Some doctors forbid the use of tampons immediately after abortion, claiming that they can cause infection in the immediate post-abortion period; however, there is no evidence to show that tampons can cause infection.

Ovulation (release of an egg from an ovary) usually occurs 10 to 35 days after abortion. The first menstrual period usually begins 3 to 6 weeks after abortion. The woman should consider herself fertile immediately after the operation and she should start using a birth control method if she plans to have sexual intercourse. If the woman wants to start using the birth control pill, she can take the first pill of a package within 5 days of the abortion; if more than 5 days go by after the operation, the woman must wait until her first normal period before starting the Pill.[2] If the woman wants to use an IUD, she must wait for at least 8 weeks before having the device inserted since IUD insertion too soon after abortion can cause infection and other complications.[3]

From *Birth Control Handbook*, a publication about contraception, sterilization, and abortion, published and copyright (1974) by Montreal Health Press, Inc., a nonprofit group. Individual copies available for 35 cents pp.; bulk orders $82 per thousand, from The Health Press, Box 1000, Station G, Montreal, Canada, H2W2N1.

ca. **2430 B.C.** Lady Ch'ang-O, Chinese "Ravisher of Hearts," weds Hou-I, prince of Ch'ung and the most celebrated archer in the service of Emperors K'u and Yao. According to legend, she steals the drug of immortality away from her husband and flees with it to the moon, only to be turned into a toad.

After suction abortion, a woman can have sexual intercourse as soon as she likes.[4] A woman must not douche after an abortion. The cervix remains slightly dilated for several days and a douche can force water and air into the uterine cavity; this can cause complications. The woman can take a tub bath, or shower which does not force fluid into the vagina or uterus.

Some doctors give antibiotics such as penicillin to all women who have an abortion in an attempt to prevent post-abortion infections; such routine use of antibiotics is neither effective nor wise. Antibiotics work best when used to cure an existing infection; however, antibiotics are not good at preventing infections. When suction abortion is properly performed, infection is an uncommon complication.

Abortion for women who have Rh negative blood

Blood is not exactly the same in every human being. Human blood can be classified into different types, according to the exact chemical make-up of the surface of the red blood cells. Two important classification systems for human blood are the ABO and the Rh systems. According to the ABO system, a person's blood is type A, B, AB or O; according to the Rh system, a person's blood is either Rh positive or Rh negative. Most people are Rh positive: 13% to 17% of white people and about 5% of black people are Rh negative. Blood type, like other body characteristics such as eye or hair colour, is inherited in a complicated way from a person's mother and father.

An Rh positive woman can have either an Rh positive or an Rh negative fetus, and an Rh negative woman can have an Rh positive or negative fetus. During every pregnancy and delivery, a few of the red blood cells from the fetus enter the mother's blood circulation. If both mother and fetus have the same Rh blood type, there is no problem; also, the entry of blood from an Rh negative fetus into an Rh positive woman does not cause any problem; however, the entry of blood from an Rh positive fetus into an Rh negative mother causes the woman's blood to develop "antibodies" against Rh positive blood. These antibodies, circulating in the woman's blood, are chemicals which can attack and destroy Rh positive blood. Such antibodies do not develop before the end of the first Rh positive pregnancy and therefore, the first Rh positive baby that an Rh negative woman has is not affected by the antibodies; but the second and every other Rh positive baby that the Rh negative woman has may be attacked and even killed by the antibodies in the mother's blood.

A special blood product called **Rh immune globulin** can be injected into an Rh negative woman after pregnancy to prevent her from developing antibodies against Rh positive blood. All Rh negative women should receive this drug after every pregnancy in which the baby is Rh positive. Since the blood type of an aborted fetus cannot be determined easily, **all Rh negative women who have an abortion should receive Rh immune globulin.**

In the United States, Rh immune globulin is manufactured and sold by Ortho Pharmaceuticals Inc. and other private drug companies under Ortho's license. Ortho charges about $40.00 for one injection's worth of the drug. Many clinics and private doctors charge women undergoing abortion as much as $75.00 for the

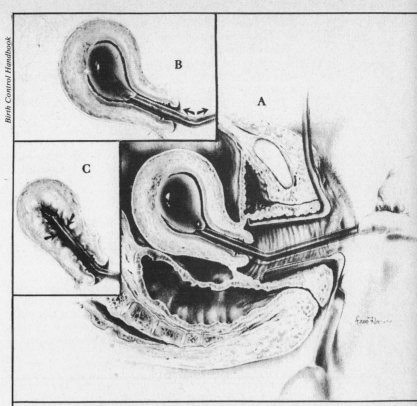

Vacuum curettage: A. vacurette inserted through cervical canal; B. Suction turned on, material flows through tubing; C. empty uterus "tugs" on vacurette.

same drug. In Canada, Rh immune globulin is manufactured by a nationalized drug company for about $3.00 per injection and is provided to patients for free by the Canadian Red Cross.

Complications of suction abortion

Suction abortion is one of the safest of all surgical operations. It is considerably safer than normal childbirth; however, suction abortion occasionally does cause complications.

Post-abortion pain: Most women experience some discomfort and menstrual-like cramping after abortion. Normally, such cramps are not severe and disappear within several hours. If the pain is severe it should be reported to the doctor who performed the operation.

Infection: In about 15 cases out of every 1000 abortions, an infection of the uterus and fallopian tubes develops soon after the operation. The symptoms of such an infection are fever, lower abdominal pain and possibly nausea and vomiting. If a woman develops such symptoms after having an abortion, she should see a doctor immediately. Post-abortion infections are usually cured easily with antibiotics.

Perforation of the uterus: In about 1 to 2 cases in 1000 abortions, the doctor accidentally pushes one of the surgical instruments right through the wall of the uterus. This can injure the abdominal organs such as the intestines or tear blood vessels, causing internal bleeding. In about half of the cases of perforation, an abdominal operation is necessary to repair the damage and stop the bleeding.

Incomplete abortion: In about 3 to 4 cases out of 1000, the operation is not complete and small parts of the fetus or placenta ("afterbirth") are left behind.

ca. **2375 B.C.** Se-ling-Shi, queen of the usurping Chinese Emperor Huang-te, is said to be the first to notice the silk thread produced by worms, to unravel their cocoons, and to weave their filaments into a web of fine fabric.

This causes continuous bleeding and cramping. In such cases the suction operation is repeated.

Heavy bleeding: In about 2 to 10 cases out of 1000 abortions, the woman bleeds heavily from her uterus after the operation. In some cases blood transfusions are necessary.

Death: In extremely rare cases, one of the above complications causes death after suction abortion. In New York City between July 1970 and July 1972 there were 4 deaths out of 261,700 suction abortions, that is, a death rate of 1.5 per 100,000 abortions. In contrast, childbirth causes the death of the mother in about 23 cases out of 100,000 pregnancies.

Dilatation and curettage (D and C)

Before the development of suction abortion, dilatation and curettage was the standard method of abortion in early pregnancy. The D and C is still used for the diagnosis and treatment of diseases of the inner lining of the uterus.

To perform a D and C the doctor first dilates the cervical canal and then inserts a curette into the cavity of the uterus. The curette is a long surgical instrument with a spoon-like tip. Using the curette, the doctor scrapes loose the fetus and placenta and removes the fragments with forceps.

The D and C abortion is more difficult to perform, takes longer, is more painful and is considerably more dangerous than suction abortion. The D and C should no longer be used for early abortion.

Saline abortion

After the 12th or 13th week of pregnancy, the fetus is too large to be removed safely by suction abortion.[5] The safest way to perform a late abortion is to stimulate the uterus to push the fetus out, that is, to stimulate a miscarriage. If a fetus dies, the uterus contracts and forces it out. It is possible to stimulate a miscarriage by killing the fetus within the uterus. In the saline method of abortion, the fetus is killed by an injection of a concentrated salt solution.

A local anesthetic ("freezing") is injected into a small area of skin on the lower abdomen several inches below the navel. A long needle is inserted through the abdominal and uterine walls, into the cavity of the uterus. The fetus is surrounded by a protective sac called the amniotic sac which is full of fluid. When the needle is in the right place in the uterine cavity, the amniotic fluid can be withdrawn through the needle. About 50 ml (about 2 fluid ounces) of amniotic fluid is withdrawn and about 200 ml of concentrated salt solution (saline) is injected into the amniotic sac. This procedure must be performed slowly and carefully. A misdirected injection of the salt solution into the woman's bloodstream instead of into the amniotic sac of the fetus can seriously harm the woman. If the salt solution is accidentally injected into the woman's bloodstream, it immediately causes symptoms of tingling, numbness, headache, pain and faintness. If such symptoms develop, the injection is stopped immediately, thus preventing serious harm to the woman.

The salt solution kills the fetus and stops production of pregnancy-supporting hormones. Contractions of the uterus usually begin 6 to 48 hours after the injection. The cervical canal gradually dilates open. Eventually the amniotic sac breaks open, releasing the salty fluid out through the vagina. The uterine contractions become harder and occur closer together until the fetus is pushed out of the uterus and through the vagina. In most cases the woman is given injections or pills of pain-killing drugs to reduce the pain of the uterine contractions. In some hospitals the woman is taken to an operating room when the fetus is coming out of the vagina; however, in most hospitals the woman miscarries in her bed and the dead fetus is taken away as soon as it is out of the woman's vagina. In 25% to 50% of cases the placenta ("afterbirth") does not come out of the uterus by itself and has to be removed by a gentle tug on the umbilical cord of the dead fetus. In about 10% of cases a vacuum curettage or a D and C has to be performed to remove parts of the placenta which are stuck within the uterus.

Throughout the saline abortion procedure the woman must remain in the hospital. Some hospitals have discharged women after they have received the salt injection, with instructions to return to hospital when uterine contractions begin. This is extremely dangerous for during the time between the injection and the beginning of uterine contractions, complications can develop which require immediate in-hospital attention. Women who are having saline abortion should refuse to leave the hospital before the entire operation is completed.

Menstrual Extraction
An Interview with Marcia L. Storch, M.D.

Menstrual extraction is the term applied to the removal of the contents of the uterus by a process that can be used either for very early abortions or for removal of the menstrual period. It is performed with a device called a flexible cannula, which is small enough so that the cervix need not be dilated to admit it; hence, no anesthetic is required.

Q: Do you know whether many members of the self-help groups are doing menstrual extraction on each other?
A: There were never very many groups doing extraction, and I doubt whether more than a very few, if any, are still doing it.

Q: What do you think of the practice of using extraction for removal of the menstrual period, either occasionally or regularly?
A: Considering that all you gain is not having a period, it's unduly dangerous. There is a risk of introducing infection into the uterus.

Q: What about the use of menstrual extraction for abortion?
A: Menstrual extraction for abortion must be done very soon after a missed period, and many women have it done before they know whether they're actually pregnant. I'd recommend waiting for a positive pregnancy test for the following reasons:

First, obviously a number of women who have extraction without knowing they're pregnant turn out not to have been pregnant. These women are undergoing an unnecessary procedure that has some risk attached that there's no need for them to run.

When menstrual extraction is done on a pregnant woman within a week of what would have been the first day of the first missed period, there's a greater likelihood that the pregnancy site will be missed, since the fetus is still so small, at best the size of a pea. Then the woman just has to have an abortion later anyhow.

The best of the new pregnancy tests are 98-percent accurate as early as ten days after what should have been the first day of the missed period. At this time extraction can still be done, if the woman prefers this to vacuum aspiration.

---

ca. **2300 B.C.** Inscription on a Sumerian baked-clay tablet: "A woman is a pit, a trap for unwary men. . . a sharp sword of iron that is liable to cut the neck of man."

After saline abortion the woman will have menstrual-like bleeding and cramps for several days. Care after saline abortion is similar to that after suction abortion, although greater caution is the rule. Douching is forbidden and it is best not to have sexual intercourse until the menstrual-like bleeding has stopped. Symptoms such as severe menstrual cramps or lower abdominal pain, fever, heavy bleeding, nausea or vomiting should be reported immediately to the doctor who performed the abortion.

Because of possible complications related to the use of the concentrated salt solution, women who have severe high blood pressure or severe heart or kidney disease, must not have a saline abortion.

Complications of saline abortion

The risks of saline abortion are about as high as the risks of normal childbirth. The safety of the saline abortion is greatly affected by the skill of the doctor and by the conditions of the hospital. Saline abortion is a significant surgical procedure and must be carried out with great caution.

Complications after saline abortion include infection, incomplete abortion with some of the placenta remaining within the uterus, heavy blood loss from the uterus, injuries to the uterus which sometimes occur during miscarriage, and whole-body complications such as blood clotting problems. In most cases, such complications are detected and cured easily while the woman is still in hospital. Antibiotic drugs and blood transfusions are sometimes required.

In rare cases, complications after saline abortion kill the woman. In New York City between July 1970 and July 1972 there were 10 deaths out of 53,300 saline abortions, that is, a death rate of about 19 per 100,000 saline abortions. In comparison, normal pregnancy and delivery is the cause of death in about 23 cases out of 100,000 pregnancies.

For the woman's safety, abortions should be performed before the 12th week of pregnancy so that suction abortion can be used and saline abortion avoided.[6] The similarity of the salt-induced miscarriage to normal childbirth makes the saline abortion an unpleasant experience both for the pregnant woman and the medical personnel taking care of her. The medical profession has the responsibility to make early abortion easily available to any woman who wants the operation so that the saline abortion becomes a rarely needed procedure.

Hysterotomy

Hysterotomy is similar to a cesarean section delivery and involves major surgery with a hospital stay of about one week. An incision is made in the abdominal wall just above the pubic bone and a second incision is made in the uterine wall. The fetus and placenta are removed and both incisions are sewed closed. Hysterotomy is sometimes necessary when an injection of salt solution fails to start a miscarriage; otherwise, hysterotomy must not be used.

Prostaglandins

Prostaglandins are a group of naturally occurring chemicals which contribute to the normal functioning and contractions of "smooth muscle" organs such as the uterus and intestines. Prostaglandins have been discovered in all parts of the human body and the full range of their effects remains a mystery.

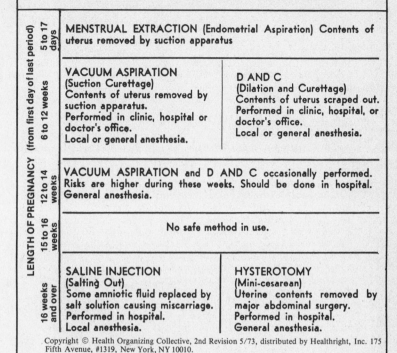

Two kinds of prostaglandins, E2 and F2-alpha, are being used experimentally to stimulate miscarriage. The prostaglandin can be given to the pregnant woman by mouth, by injection into the bloodstream or by injection into the cavity of the uterus. The prostaglandin causes miscarriage in most cases; however, unpleasant side effects of nausea, vomiting and diarrhea often occur. Side effects are more common with the high dosages necessary when the drug is given by mouth or by injection into the blood. More favourable results with fewer side effects have been obtained with the direct application of prostaglandins into the uterus. When perfected, prostaglandins may replace the saline method for abortions past the 12th week of pregnancy.

---

1. There is recent and persuasive evidence that in skilled hands suction abortion at 13 to 14 weeks is safer than waiting for a saline or similar method of abortion at 16 weeks. These "late suctions" are usually performed in hospitals.

2. Many doctors recommend that, in case the Pill is not acting effectively during the first cycle after abortion, you protect yourself against pregnancy by using an additional method of contraception.

3. Most doctors believe that IUD insertion directly after an abortion is good medical practice. However, some studies show a slightly higher rate of expulsion for IUDs inserted at this time, and a 30 percent higher rate for IUDs inserted directly after childbirth. Perhaps the safest though less convenient course, then, is to wait to have your IUD inserted until your next regular period.

4. If you do resume intercourse immediately it is a good idea to have your partner wear a condom because after an abortion the uterus is more susceptible to infection. Many experts maintain that you should not engage in intercourse for as long as two weeks after an abortion.

5. See note 1.

6. See note 1. —Ed.

---

ca. **2200 B.C.** Ancient Sumerian code: "If the wife hates her husband and denies him, they shall throw her into the river. If the husband divorces his wife, he shall pay her fifty shekels of silver."

Aftermath of Abortion

Elizabeth B. Connell, M.D.

In spite of the development of new and better contraceptive techniques and services, a study presented at the 21st International Planned Parenthood Association Conference last October in Brighton, England, showed, abortion is still the commonest method of birth control. On a world-wide basis, nearly one pregnancy in three is deliberately terminated and more than half the money spent on all forms of birth control goes for abortion.

It has been estimated that this year, barring the enactment of certain pending restrictive and discriminatory legislation, more than 1.5 million abortions will be carried out in the United States alone. If this estimate is accurate, abortion will become the most frequently performed of all surgical procedures. For this reason it seems appropriate to look at certain of the medical aspects of abortion, about which we have by now learned a great deal. In this article I will deal primarily with the effects of simple abortion procedures carried out early in pregnancy, but many of the generalizations made here apply also to the somewhat more complicated abortions performed later.

The first and most obvious physical changes that a woman should expect following an abortion are uterine cramps and vaginal bleeding, which are direct results of the abortion procedure itself. For a day or two after surgery most women have mild to moderate cramping, which responds well to the administration of aspirin. Bleeding may range from spotting to a flow comparable to that of a normal menstrual period.

The amount of postoperative bleeding depends on a number of things—the woman's own spontaneous bleeding pattern, the number of previous pregnancies she has had and, most important, the length of the pregnancy before it was aborted. Abortions carried out in the first few weeks of pregnancy tend to cause very little bleeding, in contrast to those performed later. In general, bleeding should not last for more than a week, although spotting sometimes continues for an additional two to three weeks. For a number of women the bleeding stops, then starts a few days later, lasts several days and then stops once again. If this is not accompanied by fever or any other abnormal signs, it usually is not cause for concern.

Bleeding must be considered excessive when several pads are thoroughly soaked in two to three hours, and the woman should contact her doctor, for it may be suggestive of certain complications. The commonest cause of ex-

cessive bleeding is failure of the uterine muscles to clamp down properly. In most instances the uterus will contract spontaneously; sometimes, however, medication may be necessary. Much less commonly a piece of tissue not removed from the uterus during the abortion may cause continued bleeding; this, of course, will have to be removed.

Following an abortion, patients are advised by most physicians to take their temperature twice a day for one week, the first thing in the morning and after dinner in the evening. Any fever that goes over 101 degrees and remains elevated should prompt a woman to seek medical advice.

When the pregnancy has proceeded for a number of weeks prior to abortion, breast soreness is frequently noticed and lactation occasionally may occur. The discomfort is usually mild and can be handled by aspirin or similar medications. The same general rules for care of the breasts after a full-term pregnancy apply here: A tightly fitting brassiere should be worn until the swelling, the soreness and the milk have disappeared.

Women often ask their doctors when they will be "back to normal." When abortion is done very early there frequently is no alteration in a woman's general feeling of strength and well-being. She may be able to return to work on the same day and resume in all respects the general level of her activity prior to the procedure. When the abortion is done somewhat later, however, the woman may feel a bit tired and must return more gradually to full activity.

Another question patients often ask is when sexual relations may be safely resumed. It is usually recommended following an early abortion that at least one week be allowed to pass. If sexual relations are carried out before that

time, most physicians feel, it is safer if the man uses a condom in order to decrease the risk of infection. For later abortions the length of time is usually longer, and is determined by the type of procedure performed.

Some women also ask when they may begin to douche again. Many doctors feel that douching is not necessary unless there is a specific medical problem. For women accustomed to douching, however, it is generally advised that they wait until approximately six weeks after the abortion procedure and after their follow-up examination.

Questions are frequently asked as to when sports activities may be resumed. Mild forms of exercise can be reinstituted almost immediately. The more vigorous sports, such as skiing and horseback riding, usually are better postponed until the bleeding has stopped and the woman feels completely recovered.

Old wives' tales in the past discouraged women from returning to normal activity after a pregnancy, and to an amazing degree many of them still persist. These same taboos, without any basis in fact, are now being applied to abortions. Some women believe, for example, that it is very dangerous to wash their hair after a term pregnancy or after an abortion. According to another belief it is hazardous to use tampons after an early abortion. This also is not true.

A third area of fear relates to driving a car; some women have become convinced that they should not drive after having a baby or a minor surgical procedure. Any woman who feels well enough to be up and around and carrying on her normal activities is able to drive her car safely. Finally, many women have great anxiety relating to taking baths. We now know that bath water does not enter the vagina, and bathing can be allowed immediately after an abortion. In addition to the hygienic aspects, which are important, a warm bath is relaxing and may be therapeutic for women who are having mild cramping.

Doctors are increasingly offering birth-control measures to patients immediately following abortion. IUDs frequently are inserted directly after the abortion procedure. Although this may produce a slight, temporary increase in uterine cramping and bleeding, it has proved over-all to be a highly effective method of preventing another unwanted pregnancy. Or the use of oral contraceptives may be instituted at the time of the abortion; they are being prescribed more and more.

Approximately six weeks after having an abortion a woman should have a fol-

ca. **2100 B.C.** It is customary for both rich and poor Babylonian women to give out their babies to be suckled by the temple harlots.

low-up examination, for several reasons. First, it is important to be sure that the uterus has returned completely to normal. Second, many women have questions that have arisen during this time, and these should be discussed. Third, if contraceptive methods were begun at the time of the abortion, they should be checked; if they were not, a birth-control technique may well be selected and started.

In general, both women and their physicians are unhappy with the continued need for abortion services. The prevention of an unwanted pregnancy is infinitely to be preferred over its termination. Even under the best of circumstances the procedure itself always carries a risk, albeit exceedingly small when it is done early. For example, in rare instances perforation of the uterus may occur. Similarly, infection may develop afterward and, if severe, prevent future childbearing. Rh sensitization may occur if proper blood tests and treatment are not carried out at the time of the abortion.

All these and most other complications become increasingly commoner as pregnancy advances. Women must be made to realize that the earlier an abortion is carried out, the safer it is.

In addition to these immediate problems, as more data are collected from areas such as Eastern Europe, where abortion has been widely practiced for many years, certain other potential delayed complications are beginning to come to light. There is early evidence to suggest that abortion, or perhaps repeated abortion, may predispose a woman to an increased incidence of spontaneous abortion and/or premature delivery in subsequent pregnancies. For all these reasons abortion, vital as it is at the present time, must not be considered just another means of contraception.

While abortion' is necessarily a somewhat negative experience, it is very important to realize that with sympathetic care and good counseling, abortion also can have certain positive effects. It can be highly beneficial ultimately if it provides a woman an opportunity to assess with professional help her own particular role and status in life, the way she views herself and the people around her. If properly handled, an abortion not only can terminate an unwanted pregnancy but also can be the impetus toward greater growth and development, and toward self-knowledge and self-education.

With the increased use of new and better contraceptive methods, it is believed that abortion gradually will become less necessary in the years ahead. However, whether because of fear, ignorance or medieval medical, ethical or legal restrictions regarding contraception, abortion will undoubtedly continue to be an essential part of the medical scene for some time to come.

Legal Facts on Abortion

Association for the Study of Abortion

ON JANUARY 22, 1973, the U. S. Supreme Court declared the abortion laws of two states to be unconstitutional invasions of the right of privacy. Its holdings resulted in all the rest of this country's abortion laws being unconstitutional too.

Because of this decision, a whole new set of rules about abortion came into being and some old questions received new answers.

Do I have the right to have an abortion?

Yes. The decision now rests with you and your doctor. Only after viability—the point at which the fetus may be able to live outside the uterus—may the state prohibit some abortions. But until then the woman's right to privacy and the protection of her health are the only factors to be considered.

Can I be forced to have an abortion?

No. The whole point of the Supreme Court's decision is to make it unlawful for the state to force you—or any other woman— to have an unwanted child, because that would violate your constitutional rights. It is clear that these rights would be just as seriously invaded if you could be forced to have an abortion. (As a matter of fact, in one case the parents of a minor tried to force her to have an abortion and a state court said that not even parents could do that.)

Do parents have to consent to a minor's abortion?

Parents may not force a minor to have an abortion against her will; probably they can't force her to have the baby either.

The Supreme Court did not decide this question but there is a growing body of law which recognizes that minors do have fundamental constitutional rights—among them the right to make some important decisions which affect their private lives.

Adapted from *The Supreme Court Decision on Abortion: New Legal Facts* by the Association for the Study of Abortion.

ca. **2013 B.C.** Sebek-Neferu-Ra, who reigns alone in Egypt as queen, is one of the greatest builders of her era. Among her constructions is one of the Seven Wonders of the Ancient World, the Labyrinth.

Does a husband have to consent to his wife's abortion?

This is another area of consent the Supreme Court did not consider. Some states require the husband's consent; most do not and there is considerable legal support for the argument that requiring the husband's consent violates the constitutional rights of the wife.

Does my doctor have the right to do an abortion?

Yes. During the first three months of pregnancy a doctor has a right to do an abortion if his patient requests one and if he thinks it should be done. During the second three months the state may, if it wants to, tell him where the abortion may be done and set forth other conditions to safeguard the health of the woman but it cannot prohibit abortions. In the final three months of pregnancy, the state may, if it chooses, forbid abortions but must make exceptions where the doctor thinks abortion is necessary to protect the woman's life or health.

Can my doctor be forced to do an abortion?

No. Again, the whole effect of the Supreme Court decision is to emphasize freedom of choice. So the Court was very careful to say that doctors do not have to do abortions if they have some moral or religious objection. In that case, of course, the doctor should refer the patient to another doctor who does not have such an objection.

How can state law regulate abortion during the first three months of pregnancy?

The only regulation the state may make about abortion in the first three months is that it must be done by a licensed physician.

The state can have nothing to say about the decision to have an abortion. It cannot disapprove of a woman's reasons for requesting an abortion or the doctor's reasons for doing one.

How can state law regulate abortion during the second three months of pregnancy?

Again, the decision as to whether or not to have an abortion rests with the woman and her doctor. The state cannot interfere.

But, because the operation is more difficult during this time period, the state may, if it chooses, tell the doctor where the abortion must be done—in a hospital or a specially equipped clinic, for example—and set forth other conditions directed to protecting the health of the woman.

How can state law regulate abortion in the final three months of pregnancy?

Abortions are almost always done during the first five or six months of pregnancy since after this time the fetus may live. For this reason, the Court held that abortions may be prohibited during the last three months of pregnancy unless they are necessary to protect the woman's life or health.

Does the state have to regulate abortion?

No. The Supreme Court decision makes it clear that the states can regulate abortions in the ways described above but they are not required to do even that much. And, in the absence of new state legislation, the Court's decision is the law of the land.

To the extent that state abortion laws are more restrictive than the decision handed down by the Court they are unconstitutional. No further action by the states is required to nullify their old laws. The Court's decision did that automatically. And, in varying degrees, all of the 50 state abortion laws were unconstitutionally restrictive.

Furthermore, the states do not have to pass new laws that bring their statutes into agreement with the Court's decision. If they want to they may pass laws that are less restrictive than the Court's decision but they do not have to have an abortion law at all. Nor may any governmental agency (such as a board of health) or agent (such as an attorney general) issue regulations that are more restrictive than the Court's decision.

---

ca. **1897 B.C.** According to Hebrew legend, when Abraham the Patriarch is one hundred years old and his wife Sarah is ninety, she astounds both him and herself by conceiving and bearing a son, Isaac.

How to Examine Your Breasts

American Cancer Society

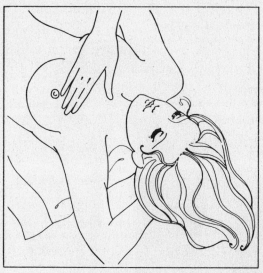

If you didn't, you should. If you don't know how, we'll tell you.

Once a month, while you're taking a shower, and your skin is still wet and slippery, begin:

Keep your fingers flat, and touch every part of each breast. Feel gently for a lump or thickening. After the shower, continue with a more thorough check.

Don't be afraid.

1. Lie down. Put one hand behind your head. With the other hand, fingers flattened, gently feel your breast. Press ever so lightly. Now examine the other breast.

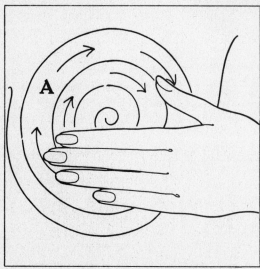

2. This shows you how to check each breast. Begin at the A and follow the arrows, feeling gently for a lump or thickening. Remember to feel all parts of each breast.

3. Now repeat the same procedure sitting up, with the hand still behind your head (right hand if you're checking the right breast, left hand up in checking the left breast).

It's what you don't know that can hurt you.

Most women discover breast changes by themselves. If there is a change, the earlier you find it, the better. But some women don't discover it early enough.

You can avoid that mistake by examining your breasts once a month after your menstrual period. Be sure to continue these check-ups after your change of life.

See your doctor as soon as you discover a lump or thickening. In most cases, it turns out to be a perfectly harmless condition. But only the doctor can tell you that for sure.

 For another method of breast examination, use downward strokes beginning by moving the hand down from the armpit, and cover the chest from one side to the other. —Ed.

ca. **854 B.C.** Ban-Gamulat, the Assyrian king Shalmaneser's beautiful concubine, falls ill but the harem keeper dares not admit any male visitor, not even a badly needed doctor without the absent king's permission. Finally he writes: "She is constantly ill. Let the Great King send orders so that some physician may be allowed to go and attend her."

Signs and Symptoms of Breast Cancer

George Crile, M.D.

The most important thing to remember is that after the age of 20 any lump in the breast may be a cancer.

1. A lump. A single, painless lump in the breast is by far the commonest sign of breast cancer. Usually it is the woman herself who first recognizes its presence. In women under 30 years of age, a lump is most apt to be a fluid-filled cyst. But after the menopause, unless the woman is taking estrogens continuously in small doses, which prevents the division of cells, the odds are strong that the lump is a cancer. Normal cells don't divide after menopause, but cancer cells are partly autonomous and divide independently of estrogen control. Estrogens benefit some patients with cancer by inhibiting the lactogenic hormone of the pituitary gland.

2. A pucker. Cancer does not always form a round, firm lump. More often it invades the breast tissue in such a way that it forms an area of thickening. Often the little strands of tissue that lead from the breast to the skin become involved in the tumor in such a way that the skin is pulled down by them so that it forms a dimple. This is almost always a sign of cancer. The dimple can best be seen by looking in a mirror and raising the arms above the head. Sometimes it is revealed when the hands are placed on the hips and the chest muscles are tightened to put pressure on the hips.

3. Inversion of the nipple. Inversion of one nipple is very apt to signify the presence of a cancer, provided, of course, that the nipple was not always inverted. It is difficult to feel a tumor that is located beneath the nipple so that often it is the retraction of the nipple rather than a lump that is first noticed. The retraction can be seen more clearly when the arms are raised as described above.

4. Shrinking of one breast. Some cancers invade the breast tissue and pucker it up, a sign of breast cancer that gave cancer its name: "the crab." Thus if a breast

seems to be puckering up and getting smaller and firmer, one should suspect cancer.

5. Swelling or enlargement of the breast. Some types of cancer produce large tumors but these are relatively rare. Swelling of the entire breast also is occasionally a sign of cancer. The breast is heavy and swollen, and if one looks closely, one can see that the skin too is swollen, making the pores more easily visible and giving the "orange skin" appearance that is characteristic of skin in which fluid is retained. Usually this sign is accompanied by extensive involvement of the lymph nodes which blocks the flow of lymph and causes the tissues to swell.

6. A lump under the arm. Occasionally even when no lump or other abnormality can be detected in the breast, an enlarged and hard lump in the armpit may be the first sign of cancer. When this is the case, there is a tiny tumor in the breast, so small that it cannot be felt, but nevertheless it has already spread to the nodes and requires prompt treatment.

7. A sense of discomfort. A persistent sense of discomfort or a tingling sensation in one area of one breast in a patient

who has passed the menopause and is taking no estrogens, can be the first sign of cancer, but this is rare. Most cancers do not at first cause pain or discomfort.

8. Bloody discharge from the nipple. Bloody discharge from the nipple is nearly always a sign of benign papilloma, a small wartlike tumor about the size of a glass pinhead, that is present in one of the ducts. Occasionally, however, bleeding may be a sign of cancer.

9. Irritation of the nipple. A persistent eczemalike irritation of the skin of the nipple and central breast may be the first sign of Paget's disease, a rare form of breast cancer that affects the central ducts and overlying skin.

Signs and symptoms that are not caused by breast cancer

1. Pain and tenderness of the breasts, continuous or with the menstrual periods, are not symptoms of breast cancer. Neither is having pain or tenderness in both breasts when a woman is taking estrogen. Enlargement, engorgement and tenderness of the breast are normal reactions to estrogen. The same reactions occur, of course, in response to the increased estrogen levels that occur in early pregnancy.

2. Discharge from both nipples is not a sign of breast cancer. The discharge may be clear, milky, yellow, gray or green, but if it is present on both sides and not bloody there is little to worry about. A Pap test can be made of the secretion, but it almost never shows abnormal cells. Surgical treatment is not indicated. The discharge is the result of some imbalance in the function of the ovaries and other endocrine glands and usually disappears after the menopause unless the woman takes estrogen.

3. Repeated abscesses and chronic drainage of pus from infections near the nipple are not due to cancer and do not cause it. These infections often occur in women with inverted nipples and are the results of abnormal development of the lining of the milk ducts. They usually persist until corrected by a minor operation.

ca. **800 B.C.** At six-month intervals all the damsels of Lacedaemonia, Greece, excepting slaves, are shut up in a large dark room to which a lesser number of young bachelors are admitted. Whatever youth a girl catches in the brief time before the doors are thrown open is required to marry her without demanding a dowry.

RATING YOUR RISK

American Cancer Society

Age Group			Your Risk
20-34 (10)	35-49 (40)	50+ (90)	

Race Group			
Oriental (10)	Black (20)	Caucasian (30)	

Family History			
None (10)	Mother, sister, aunt or grandmother with breast cancer (50)	Mother **and** sister (100)	

Your History		
No breast cancer (10)	Previous breast cancer (100)	

Maternity			
First baby before 25 (10)	First baby 25 or after (15)	No childbirth (20)	

Your Total

The risk test shown at left involves three steps. First, answer each question by filling in the percentage number in parentheses under the description that best fits you. Check your total on the risk scale to see where you fall. Then, follow the instructions which tell what your score means to you. This test is meant to compute your risk of getting breast cancer. Any changes in your breast should receive prompt, expert medical attention no matter where your risk score falls on the scale.

WHAT YOUR SCORE MEANS TO YOU

Women 225 and higher on the scale should practice monthly breast self-examination (BSE) and have physical examination of the breast every six months, with annual breast x-ray (mammography).

Women between 100 and 220 on the scale should practice BSE and have physical examination of the breast as part of an annual check-up. Periodic breast x-ray should be included as the doctor may advise.

Women below 100 on the scale should practice BSE and have physical examination of the breast as part of an annual checkup.

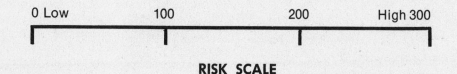

0 Low   100   200   High 300

RISK SCALE

Excerpted with permission of the American Cancer Society, Illinois Division.

ca. **750 B.C.** Lupercalia, the most durable of all Roman public festivals, is established in honor of the legendary she-wolf that suckled the infant twins Romulus and Remus, founders of Rome. As part of the ritual, naked priests run around Palatine Hill with leather thongs, striking at the bared buttocks of the assembled women to insure their fertility.

Frequently Asked Questions
about Breast Cancer

George Crile, M.D.

What are lymphatics?

Lymphatics are small vessels that drain the fluid from the tissues and return it to the blood, usually by way of the lymph nodes. This circulation of lymph can also carry cancer cells to lymph nodes or into the bloodstream.

What are lymph nodes?

The nodules or "kernels" in the neck that swell and get sore when you have a sore throat are lymph nodes. Lymph nodes are present throughout the body, notably in the groins and armpits. They contain a type of white blood cell called lymphocytes that are the body's chief defense against some types of infection and also against cancer.

What do axilla and axillary mean?

The axilla is the armpit and axillary is that which is situated in or grows from the axilla. An axillary node is a lymph node in the axilla.

What does malignant mean?

Malignant means cancerous. It implies that the tumor grows progressively, invades tissues around it, and often spreads through the bloodstream to other parts of the body.

What is metastasis?

Metastasis is the process by which cells from a cancer enter the bloodstream or the lymphatics and spread to other parts of the body, causing another cancer.

What is a cure?

Cure means that the cancer has been permanently eliminated. In some types of cancer, a patient can be considered to be cured if she remains well for five years. Cancers of the breast, however, are unpredictable and occasionally may reappear even after 30 years following treatment. In this type of cancer, it is better to measure the success of treatment in terms of survival, meaning whether or not the patient is still living after five years, ten years, and so on, and to specify the length of time.

How common is cancer of the breast?

Cancer of the breast is by far the commonest malignant tumor in women. Approximately one American woman in 17 is destined to have cancer of the breast.

Who is apt to be affected by breast cancer?

Breast cancer rarely occurs before the age of 30, almost never in women under the age of 20, and occurs only one-one hundredth as often in men as in women.

How dangerous is cancer of the breast?

Cancer of the breast is the commonest single cause of death in women between 37 and 55 years of age. In old age, although the incidence of breast cancer continues to rise, heart disease catches up with it as the commonest killer.

What is a biopsy?

Biopsy involves removing a specimen for the pathologist to examine or putting a fine needle into the lump to see if it is just a fluid-filled cyst. If the needle draws fluid, the lump goes away and the patient is cured. If no fluid is obtained, an attempt is made to draw a little tissue juice and some cells into the needle and to make a "Pap smear." If cancer cells are found on the smear, the tumor is malignant.

A positive Pap smear from the breast fluid means cancer, but a negative one means only that no cancer cells were seen in that specimen. Then the only way to tell whether cancer is present is to remove a specimen for the pathologist to examine. This minor operation

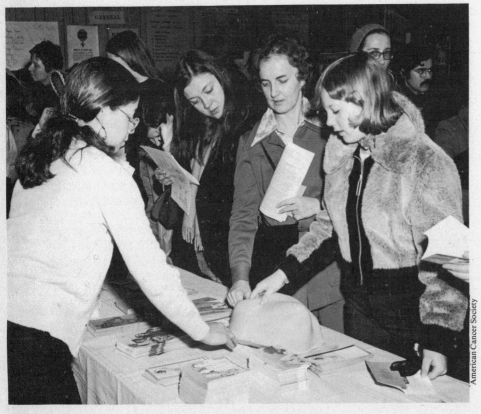

Betsi Bosom, the American Cancer Society's plastic model, is used to demonstrate the technique of self-examination during a public education program

American Cancer Society

Reprinted with permission of Macmillan Publishing Co., Inc. from *What Women Should Know about the Breast Cancer Controversy* by George Crile, Jr. Copyright © 1973 George Crile, Jr. Originally appeared in *Ms.* Magazine.

ca. **714 B.C.** The Roman king Numa institutes the religious Order of the Vestal Virgins, dedicated to perpetual chastity, limited to six in number, and declared temple guardians of the sacred objects upon which the stability of Rome is thought to depend.

need not involve an overnight hospital stay.

Many surgeons do not aspirate cysts or do needle biopsies. The reason for this is not clear, since aspirating the fluid from a cyst almost always cures it permanently. Cancer lumps rarely contain fluid, so if a lump can be reduced by aspiration, it is most likely not cancerous.

Since cysts tend to be multiple, some women are subjected to many needless operations for removal of cysts that could have been just as successfully treated in the office.

Putting a needle into a cancer does not increase its tendency to metastasize. Studies from the Walter Reed Army Hospital in Washington and elsewhere show that there is no harm done by taking a biopsy of a breast cancer and waiting a few days before completing the operation if it proves necessary. In fact, if the biopsy removes the tumor completely (that is, excisional biopsy), there may be a slight advantage in waiting a few days before removing the breast, because during this period the cancer cells are drained out of the area and their growth arrested by the lymphatics so that there is less chance of local recurrence.

Breast cysts do not turn into cancers. The only reason for treating them is to be sure that the lump is caused by a cyst and not by a cancer. This procedure can be done more easily in an office with a needle than in an operating room.

The interpretation of the biopsy specimen is done by the pathologist. A number of samples of the tissue are taken, sliced thin, and stained and mounted on glass slides. This process takes about 24 hours unless the surgeon asks for a "frozen-section." This must be processed specially, and is much more costly than the regular sections. It does not stain as well as the regular sections, and usually only one or two samples of the tissue are cut and examined. The advantage of a frozen-section is that it only takes 10 or 15 minutes to prepare. On the basis of this evidence, the pathologist must make a decision as to whether or not cancer is present. And, on the basis of this decision, the surgeon decides what operation to do.

Even when a patient is past the menopause and has a lump that is almost certainly a cancer, one would not remove the breast without a definite diagnosis proved by biopsy.

The Dispute over Surgery
for Breast Cancer

The Editors of *Good Housekeeping Magazine*

Of all diseases, women fear breast cancer the most. Not only is it the leading cause of cancer deaths in women, but the usual treament for it involves surgical removal of the entire affected breast, with or without related tissue.

Consequently, the recent publicity concerning a procedure, called *partial mastectomy*, that avoids removing the entire breast (and makes surgical reconstruction possible then or at a later time) has aroused intense interest. It has also whipped up a storm of controversy over the long-range effectiveness of the procedure in saving lives.

Women confused by the debate should know one thing from the outset: The overwhelming majority of experts in the field of breast cancer—including the American Cancer Society, the National Cancer Institute in Washington, D.C., and Memorial Sloan-Kettering Cancer Center in New York City—do not accept the claims made for partial mastectomy. They say that, for the present, there are not enough data to prove its effectiveness. Their opposition is heightened by their fear that widespread misinterpretation of the limited claims made for partial mastectomy by its principal exponent, Dr. George Crile, Jr., emeritus consultant in surgery at the Cleveland Clinic in Cleveland, Ohio, may lead many women afflicted by breast cancer to endanger their lives by insisting on this procedure in preference to more radical surgery.

Just What Is Involved in a partial mastectomy and why has it become so controversial? As Dr. Crile performs it, the tumor along with the overlying skin and a wide segment of normal breast tissue and the underlying *fascia* (membrane that covers the muscle) are removed. Later the breast can be surgically reconstructed, leaving it smaller than it was originally but with the same contour.

It must be stressed that Dr. Crile does *not* advocate a partial mastectomy for every woman who has breast cancer. He does say he will perform a partial mastectomy for any woman who wants it, in certain circumstances—*if* the cancer is small in relation to the size of the woman's breast, apparently localized to one area of the breast, and not located near the nipple.

"My feeling is that many women avoid treatment of breast cancer until dangerously late because they are terrified of radical mastectomy," Dr. Crile says. "When women know that radical mastectomy need not always be done, that radiation is often not necessary or even desirable, that in many cases the breast itself can be preserved—in short, when women lose their fear of the treatment of breast cancer—they will be motivated to seek treatment at once."

To Support His Theory That Partial Mastectomy can be successful in selected cases, Dr. Crile compared 53 patients treated by partial mastectomy with 53 patients treated by total (simple) mastectomy, carefully matching them for size of tumor and whether or not there were signs of cancer in

712 B.C. King Numa also decrees an annual New Year's Day—Matronalia—in honor of Juno, goddess of marriage and wives. Since the festival celebrates the sanctity of the matrimonial tie, only matrons and maidens of stainless character may participate.

Breast Cancer
THE HEALTH ADVISER 37

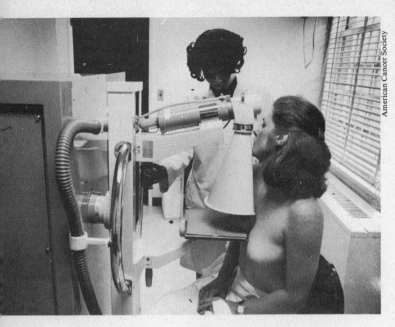

Demonstrating a mammography: the patient's breasts are placed, alternately, on a metal plate and the X-ray taken from different angles, from the side and from above.

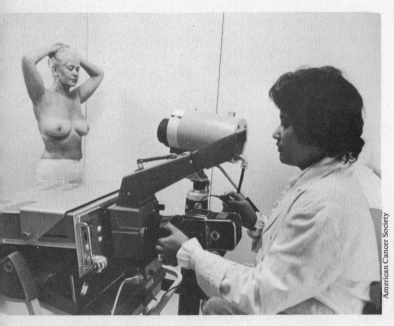

This woman is having a thermogram of her breasts— a process which indicates "hot spots" or changes in temperature of breast tissue. Three positions of the breasts are X-rayed: facing front, left breast and right breast, all with the patient's hands on her head.

the lymph nodes in the armpit. Dr. Crile found that after five years, 77 percent of the patients treated by partial mastectomy were living, compared with 71 percent of those treated by total mastectomy. (The ten-year survival rate for those women who had partial mastectomies was only 34.4 percent. But Dr. Crile says this figure is based on fewer cases—32 patients—and that ten years ago partial mastectomy was often used in treating advanced cases of cancer. In Dr. Crile's opinion the low ten-year survival rate therefore reflects the selection of poor risk patients for partial mastectomy.)

In opposition to Dr. Crile, most experts in the cancer field support some form of surgery that totally removes the breast (see box). Their major arguments are that any surgery that does less than remove the entire breast may leave cancer within the patient and decrease her chances of survival, and that only radical surgery can reveal whether the cancer has spread to another part of the body.

The American Cancer Society (ACS) Says, "Limited surgical procedures that remove less than the entire breast have not been scientifically proven to be as effective as mastectomy." What is more, the ACS is concerned that some benefits of early diagnosis may be canceled out by inadequate and unproven methods of treatment, and that the current controversy may divert attention from the importance of early diagnosis—through breast self-examination, periodic physical examination of the breasts by physicians and other proven detection methods.

Dr. Arthur I. Holleb, ACS senior vice-president for medical affairs and research, fears that many women will misinterpret what Dr. Crile says by believing that any case of breast cancer can be treated by partial mastectomy. "At least 70 percent of Dr. Crile's patients have the breast removed," points out Dr. Holleb. "Only a very small, carefully selected group of his patients have had partial mastectomies."

The National Cancer Institute (NCI) says it is not known now which surgical procedure (see box) provides the best treatment. But Dr. Paul P. Carbone, chairman of the treatment committee of the NCI breast cancer task force, believes that current evidence indicates that women who demand surgical treatment less drastic than radical or modified mastectomy must accept the risk that they may have as little as a 30 percent chance of surviving five years following surgery.

This is because by the time breast cancer is detected it may have traveled to some other part of the body and be lodged in the brain, bone marrow, liver or lung. Currently, this risk cannot be known for sure unless the lymph nodes in the armpit are removed in the course of surgery. Cancer-positive nodes are indicators of trouble—evidence that the disease may have filtered through the nodes and traveled in the bloodstream to other parts of the body. The prompt detection of this development permits the use of chemotherapy to treat the cancer right after surgery rather than after recurrence presents a visible tumor.

Experts At New York City's Memorial Sloan-Kettering Cancer Center also are primarily concerned that a less-than-adequate operation may leave cancer within the patient. One of several variations of radical surgery is the best treatment for breast cancer, says Dr. Jerome A. Urban,

ca. **660 B.C.** Semonides, Greek poet, writes his famous poem "The Pedigree of Women," tracing their descent from different animals according to their characteristics. He "derives" the dirty women from a hog, the cunning from a fox, the stubborn from an ass, the ugliest from an ape, and the good from a bee.

attending surgeon of breast service at Memorial Sloan-Kettering. Which radical operation he performs depends upon the size of the tumor and the extent to which he believes the cancer has spread. Dr. Urban cites a 60 percent ten-year survival rate for *all* his patients who had radical surgery, and a 98 percent five-year survival rate for those whose tumors were minimal.

Dr. Guy F. Robbins, acting chief of the breast service at Memorial Sloan-Kettering, completely rejects the data used by Dr. Crile to support partial mastectomy. "Even Dr. Crile agrees that it would be better to quote a ten-year survival rate, but for now he is relying on a five-year survival rate except for 13 cases that he states had a 34 percent ten-year survival as compared to 321 cases he operated on in 1960 that have a 60 percent ten-year survival after surgery involving breast removal," says Dr. Robbins.

Dr. Bernard Fisher, professor of surgery at the University of Pittsburgh, says that until acceptable data are developed that indicate just what form of surgery is best for treating cancer, the controversy cannot be resolved.

Current surgical treatment of breast cancer includes:

RADICAL SURGERY

• **Radical Mastectomy.** This involves removal of the entire breast, underlying chest muscles and lymph nodes in the *axilla* (armpit). In extreme cases the internal mammary lymph nodes also may be removed.
• **Modified Radical Mastectomy.** The entire breast and the lymph nodes in the axilla are removed. Chest muscles are left intact.
• **Simple Mastectomy** (recently renamed *Total Mastectomy*). In this operation the breast is removed completely, but the underlying chest muscles and axillary lymph nodes are not.

CONSERVATIVE SURGERY

• **Partial Mastectomy.** The cancer and at least an inch of surrounding breast tissue are removed as well as the overlying skin and underlying *fascia* (connective tissue that covers the muscle).
• **Lumpectomy or Local Excision.** Only the tumor itself, with or without a small amount of surrounding breast tissue or overlying skin, is removed.

The development of such data is still a long way off, although the groundwork for a possible future study comparing the effectiveness of partial versus radical mastectomy is now being laid by a National Surgical Adjuvant Breast Project. Headed by Dr. Fisher, this project is comparing the effectiveness of radical mastectomy, total (simple) mastectomy, and total mastectomy plus radiation therapy. At least 1,000 patients (the total eventually will reach 1,500) from across the country are in the study, and data comparing the survival and recurrence rates among the patients should begin to be available shortly.

Only after this current study determines whether total mastectomy is equivalent to radical mastectomy in effectively treating cancer will it be feasible to compare the effectiveness of total versus partial mastectomy in selected cases, says Dr. Nathaniel I. Berlin, chairman of the NCI breast cancer task force which, along with an NCI grant, are funding Dr. Fisher's project.

In spite of their fears that many women will be misled by current publicity about partial mastectomy, some cancer experts do think that a certain amount of good will evolve from it. Dr. Holleb of the ACS, and Dr. Robbins of Memorial Sloan-Kettering, for example, say that the publicity is creating more public awareness of the problems of breast cancer and the necessity of detecting it early, and that surgeons are becoming more willing to discuss the disease openly with their patients and the public.

One Thing All Experts Agree On is that early diagnosis of the disease is vital. And a primary method of early diagnosis is breast self-examination. If a woman does not know how to give herself a monthly breast self-examination, she should ask her doctor or contact a local division of the American Cancer Society. If she does find a lump on her breast, she should see her doctor at once. Chances are she will have nothing to worry about—contrary to the widespread belief that most breast lumps are cancerous, biopsies reveal that from 65 to 80 percent of such lumps are relatively harmless. But if the lump in her breast does prove to be malignant, immediate treatment may well save her life.

There are also X-ray and heat-detection tests that can detect the disease. *Mammography* is an X-ray procedure than can detect lumps so small that they could not be discovered either by the woman or her physician during a fingertip examination of the breast. *Thermography* measures heat emanating from the breasts. Tissues that reproduce faster than those around them—as do malignant tumors—give off more heat. By measuring heat radiation from the various areas of the breast, thermography can detect a malignant tumor.

The American Cancer Society and the National Cancer Institute are jointly sponsoring a project utilizing these advanced methods in order to determine if the new techniques can be brought to vast numbers of women in their home communities at a reasonable cost. Twenty seven detection centers have been set up throughout the country to annually screen 10,000 women over a five-year period. Dr. Berlin of the NCI says a combination of these advanced methods is the most effective means for early detection of the disease. If a woman and her physician do not know the location of the detection center nearest her, she should write the NCI in Washington, D.C.

ca. **609 B.C.** Amytis marries Nebuchadnezzar, later King of Babylon. Because she wearies of the flat Babylonian plains and pines for the airy verdure of her native hills, the king constructs for her the Hanging Gardens of Babylon, one of the Seven Wonders of the Ancient World.

The Greening of the Womb   Deborah Larned

A year and a half ago Mrs. J., a 47-year-old Queens' school-teacher, ran out of birth control pills, and, because her regular gynecologist had retired, she made an appointment with another highly recommended Ob/Gyn in her neighborhood. She was feeling fine, just needed a new pill prescription, pap smear and pelvic. As things turned out, she got all that and more.

"After my examination," Mrs. J. recalls, "the doctor told me to come into his office. I sat down, and in the most

Gynecological examination.

nonchalant manner he told me that I had 'a uterine fibroid the size of a lemon' and needed a hysterectomy as soon as possible. He, of course, was going to do the operation."

The doctor neglected to tell Mrs. J. that fibroids are almost always benign and are so common (1 in every 5 women of childbearing age) that some doctors would go so far as to say that it's normal to get them. "The only thing I heard was the word 'tumor,'" says Mrs. J., "and when I asked, 'Are these things always cancerous?' all the doctor said was, 'Sometimes when we go in we find them to be cancerous.' I was so upset I could hardly talk. My husband was furious about the casual way I had been treated. When he suggested to the doctor that we get another opinion, the doctor just said, 'That's up to you.'"

Mrs. J. never had the hysterectomy. Two subsequent consultations proved that she had only a "tiny" fibroid, which was nothing to worry about. Like most fibroids, it would probably shrink as she approached menopause.

Looking back on it now, Mrs. J. feels lucky. "I'm 47 and very healthy. I feel and look younger than I am. I was happy with the pill and had no interest in sterilization. The last thing I needed was an unnecessary operation." But she worries about the women who might not be so lucky. And she should.

American women are experiencing the effects of a mysterious and highly contagious epidemic. But it's not the disease that's gotten out of hand; it's the treatment. We're having a hysterectomy outbreak and though doctors have been aware of it—even promoting it—for several years, most women still believe that hysterectomies are performed rarely (after all, it is major surgery), and then only to alter the course of some critical disease like uterine cancer.

Hysterectomy, the surgical removal of the uterus, is in fact the fourth most commonly performed operation in the U.S. today—after tonsillectomy, hernia repair and removal of the gall bladder. And though this procedure is still used as a cure for uterine cancer, over the last 30 years hysterectomy has come to be regarded by many gynecologists as a "simple" solution for everything from

ca. **576 B.C.** All single women in Rome, maidens as well as widows, are subjected to a special tax, imposed to supply the *equites*, or knights, with barley money for their horses. The idea is that since the *equites*, as shock calvary, protect otherwise helpless females from assault, these women should help defray the expense.

backaches to contraception. Once considered a surgical last resort, hysterectomy is now put forth as "the only logical approach to female sterilization." American women are being sold an attractive, albeit expensive, all-purpose surgical package—no more periods, cramps, babies or bother—and if they do not readily accept the medical recommendation, they are often bamboozled into sterilization on highly questionable grounds.

While hysterectomy as a means of sterilization is a relatively new phenomenon, the controversy over hysterectomies is an old one.

For nearly a century doctors have been arguing over which "female conditions" warrant the removal of the uterus. In the mid-1800s hysterectomies were performed for such symptoms as general "troublesomeness," "eating like a ploughman," "erotic tendencies" and even "simple cussedness."

By the early part of the 20th century science had replaced superstition, and only so-called medical problems were considered adequate reasons for performing a hysterectomy. To name just a few—uterine cancer, inexplicable menstrual bleeding, small nonmalignant tumors (fibroids), dysmenorrhea (what most women just call "cramps") and vaginal laxness (a condition in which the vaginal walls lose their firmness, often as a result of childbearing).

Even then, many doctors weren't convinced, claiming that for most of these symptoms, rest, relaxation, hormones or scraping of the uterus (D+C) were all treatments that should be tried before major surgery. When a cancerous condition existed, or when a woman had a severely disabling pelvic disease that did not respond to less drastic treatments, no one quibbled over the necessity of a hysterectomy. But would a conscientious surgeon remove a woman's uterus because of simple backache? They've been doing it for years and, needless to say, not everyone is happy about it.

Out of the estimated 2 million unnecessary operations performed in the U.S. each year (a "conservative figure," according to Dr. Sidney Wolfe of Ralph Nader's Health Research Group), hysterectomies are one of the biggest offenders. Several medical studies—one as early as 1946—have shown that at least one-third of all the hysterectomies in the U.S. have been performed on women with *normal* uteri. In many cases women who underwent hysterectomies had not presented any symptoms prior to surgery.

So for years, gynecologists have been recommending major surgery for women who don't need it—and that's bad enough. Lately, however, doctors have simply abandoned the question of which medical symptoms warrant surgery and have wholeheartedly endorsed this operation for the sole purpose of sterilization—which is a clever and disarming move since such labels as "necessary" and "unnecessary" no longer apply. Doctors are off the hook. They've even changed the name. Now a woman may elect to have a "hysterilization." If she has an additional pelvic problem or two, all the better.

In hospitals throughout the country sterilization by hysterectomy, once unthinkable, has now become routine. At the Los Angeles County-University of Southern California Medical Center, for example, the total number of hysterectomies performed for any reason increased 293 percent between July 1968 and the end of 1970. If only elective hysterectomy for the purpose of sterilization is counted, the increase was an astounding 742 percent.

"Up until the last few years," says Dr. Lester T. Hibbard, author of the L.A. County-USC Medical Center study, "no hysterectomies were performed at this institution unless functional or organic pathology was documented. . . . In 1970, sterilization by hysterectomy had become a commonplace and widely accepted operation . . . both for women with normal pelvic function and women with relatively minor abnormalities which otherwise

would not justify a major operative procedure."

Although the general public is largely unaware of the sudden upsurge in hysterilizations, physicians have been quietly arguing about it in professional journals for the last five years. Finally in 1971, Hibbard's report and other indications of the soaring hysterectomy rate—California Blue Cross announced a 79 percent increase in hysterectomies for the last half of 1970—forced a showdown between the pro and anti factions.

At its 1971 annual meeting held in San Francisco, the American College of Obstetrics and Gynecology sponsored what is now fondly remembered as the "Great Debate" on the merits of hysterilization. Following the exchange, physicians were asked to register their approval or disapproval of this procedure by their applause. The acclaim for hysterilization lasted a full 25 seconds; the applause for the "no" position, only 10 seconds. What's more, according to *Audio Digest*'s decibel meter, the intensity of the advocates' applause was double that of the opposition.

Though this victory may well have been pulled off by a rowdy band of partisans, there's no denying that hysterilization generates extraordinary enthusiasm among many gynecologists. It seems to have a lot going for it.

Contrary to popular belief, a hysterectomy does not bring on menopause, hasten the aging process, or physi-

Female physicians performing ancient Arabic uterus treatment.

Bettmann Archive

ca. **570 B.C.** Sappho establishes her famous school of lyric poetry on the island of Lesbos, the only students admitted being the loveliest and brightest young women available. No fewer than six Greek comedies satirize Sappho's "Lesbian Love," but her fame as a poet grows to rival even Homer's. Plato is to call her, after Homer, "the Tenth Muse."

Hysterectomy
THE HEALTH ADVISER 41

ologically interfere with sexual enjoyment. The ovaries continue to produce eggs and hormones each month, but because the uterus has been removed, menstruation and any accompanying discomforts are eliminated. As Dr. Joseph H. Pratt Jr. of the Mayo Clinic rather over-enthusiastically pointed out at the Great Debate, "No more monthly curse, no napkins, no Tampax, no accidents, no embarrassment, no poring over a calender to see when a trip is feasible."

Other hysterilization promoters point to the fact that hysterectomy is 100 percent effective in preventing pregnancy, whereas tubal ligation (a less complicated procedure involving tying of the Fallopian tubes) has a failure rate of from 2.2 percent to 1 percent. The removal of the uterus also eliminates further pelvic disorders, an important consideration since recent studies have shown that many women who undergo tubal ligation develop an unusually high percentage of pelvic problems in later life. (Whether these disturbances are a direct result of the ligation, however, is unclear. Some experts suggest that women who are no longer able to conceive are simply unwilling to tolerate even minimal discomforts.)

It all adds up to an attractive proposition, and yet for most women the nuisance of menstruation, the chance of contraceptive failure, or the remote possibility of future pelvic problems do not provide enough of an incentive to undergo major surgery. By far the most persuasive medical argument—for many women the real clincher—is that hysterectomy will prevent uterine cancer. As one woman who underwent a hysterectomy recently said, "I went into the hospital to get my tubes tied. When the doctor suggested that I have a hysterectomy instead, the whole idea was horrifying to me. But when he told me that I wouldn't have to worry about cancer of the uterus, I decided that maybe that was the best thing to do after all."

Dr. Ralph C. Wright, a Connecticut gynecologist and perhaps the most outspoken advocate of routine hysterectomy, views the possibility of cancer as fundamental. "When the patient has completed her family," Wright contends, "total hysterectomy should also be performed as a prophylactic procedure. Under these circumstances, the uterus becomes a useless, bleeding, symptom-producing, potentially cancer-bearing organ and therefore should be removed. . . . To sterilize a woman and allow her to keep a useless and potentially lethal organ is incompatible with modern gynecological concepts.

Hysterectomy is the only logical approach to surgical sterilization of women."

Even ignoring Wright's apparent view that it is now the gynecologist's prerogative to decide which organs a woman may be "allowed" to retain, it is the "lethal organ" argument that has provoked the most heated debate. This view, says hysterilization detractors, not only appeals to an unreasonable fear of cancer but is patently misleading.

According to Washington, D.C.'s Health Research Group, which recently concluded a study of surgical sterilization practices in federally funded clinics, what hysterilization advocates fail to tell their patients is that the death rate for hysterectomy itself (1,000 out of every 1 million women annually) is, in fact, *higher* than the death rate for uterine/cervical cancer. The American Cancer Society estimates that of the approximately 44,000 cases of uterine or cervical cancer reported each year, 12,000 are fatal (or 100 out of every 1 million women each year). In addition, the Cancer Society claims, a majority of these deaths could be prevented if regular gynecological exams and Pap smears were available to all women.

Hysterectomy will, of course, prevent cancer; if you don't have a uterus you can't get uterine cancer. However, many cancer experts regard this procedure as a risky exercise in "surgical overkill." Dr. Sidney Arje, a gynecologist and vice-president of professional education for the American Cancer Society, points out that there are cheaper and, in the long run, safer ways of preventing death from uterine cancer. A simple Pap smear is 95 percent effective in detecting the earliest signs of cervical cancer, and though the same test is only 60 percent accurate in diagnosing cancer of the uterus, symptoms such as excessive irregular bleeding followed by a diagnostic D+C provide an early enough warning signal for successful treatment. "If the only reason for performing a hysterectomy is sterilization," says Dr. Arje, "you are probably exposing a woman to a danger equal to or greater than the risks of uterine cancer."

Planned Parenthood Federation, along with many others, takes issue with what they call "hacking 'preventatively' at future possibly offending flesh." For most women, the chances of *not* getting cancer far exceed the chances of getting it. "Preventative lobotomies," says Planned Parenthood in an effort to point out the absurdity of the argument, "for young people at statistically high risk of developing violent psychoses or ophthalmectomy

for those populations found most likely to get cancer of the eye at some future time have not been suggested by physicians writing in psychiatric or ophthalmologic specialty journals." They might also have pointed out that though cancer of the prostate frequently occurs in men over 50, male urologists are not suggesting routine prophylactic prostectomy.

Medicine is a complicated business and no single explanation can account for the high rate of hysterectomy or for the growing acceptance of hysterilization.

Many gynecologists blame their patients for insisting upon the operation. And yet the evidence does not bear this out. At the L.A. County Hospital, one-third of all the patients who received hysterectomies had originally requested tubal ligations. In another hospital in Florida, where hysterilizations outnumber tubal ligations 2 to 1, tubal ligations are "discouraged by general staff agreement."

Women are not clamoring to have their uteri taken out, but they are demanding more reliable birth control methods. Hysterectomy is sold as a fail safe and if physicians are unable to "persuade" a woman to undergo hysterectomy, more devious methods can be used.

Dr. Bernard Rosenfeld, a California physician who is currently studying sterilization practices in the U.S., describes one doctor's tactic that is especially employed among Third World women.

"I remember treating a young black woman with several children who was having trouble with her IUD. She was

ca. **560 B.C.** Chi Nu has two lovers, one living to the right, the other to the left of her residence. Her father, exasperated by her delay in marrying, commands her to show her preference by tucking up that sleeve which corresponds to the man of her choice. She tucks up both sleeves, explaining that she wants to eat with her rich lover and cohabit with the handsome one.

interested in trying another type of device and was referred to the family planning clinic of the hospital to have her present IUD removed. About two weeks later I accidentally ran into her at the hospital. She looked upset and I asked her why. She said, 'They just told me I needed a hysterectomy.' I knew from having examined her that she did not *need* a hysterectomy, so I went and looked up her file. On her medical chart the doctor had recorded, 'Patient *requests* hysterectomy.' "

Black women have long been aware of this kind of medical practice. In the old days it was called a "Mississippi appendectomy." You'd go into the hospital to have a baby and come out minus your uterus. Now doctors are more subtle, but the results are the same. When the doctor decides you've had too many children, he tells you that you "need" a hysterectomy and then writes down that you "asked" for it.

So the question remains: why are doctors "electing" hysterectomy for their female patients?

To begin with, 97 percent of all gynecologists in the U.S. are men, and to some extent their attitudes toward their female patients inevitably reflect the current view of women held by society as a whole. A woman medical student, for example, remembers this winner from her Ob/Gyn lecturer: "The only significant difference between a cow and a woman is that a cow has more spigots."

One of the more obvious reasons for unnecessary hysterectomy is that medical students need operating experience. Dr. James Ryan describes an exchange which took place while he was a medical student at Boston University Medical School.

"When the student asked the resident why this woman was having a hysterectomy instead of a tubal ligation, he was told, '. . . We like to do a hysterectomy, it's more of a challenge . . . you know, a well-trained chimpanzee can do a tubal ligation . . . and it's good experience for the junior resident . . . good training.' "

But over-zealous residents account for only a fraction of unnecessary hysterectomies. It's out there in the world of private practice where it's happening and the reasons, many experts say, can be summed up in one word: greed.

Dr. Norman F. Miller, author of the earliest study of unnecessary hysterectomies, first hinted at it in 1946. Referring to the fact that 30.8 percent of all the hysterectomy patients he studied

showed no uterine pathology following their operations, he could not help but conclude that a substantial number of women had undergone "acute remunerative or hip-pocket hysterectomies." The now famous "hip-pocket" theory of hysterectomy—an operation performed primarily to fatten a doctor's wallet—still holds true today. There's a joke going around the medical schools—Professor: what are the symptoms for a hysterectomy? Student: A Blue Shield card and $200. But only the doctors are amused.

For a "relatively easy" operation, hysterectomies aren't cheap. Prices run from $1,500 to $2,000 (five to seven times more expensive than a tubal ligation), not to mention the additional loss of a patient's income due to a four to six week recovery period. Like most of us, doctors have to make ends meet. And with a host of borderline justifications to choose among—from the population explosion to the patient's need for dependable contraception—hysterectomies are a tempting solution to inflation.

"It seems inevitable," says Dr. Charles E. Lewis, professor of preventative medicine at UCLA, "that in any occupation where considerable income is available on the basis of events called operations, a small percentage of people can well identify this as a marvelous, income-producing device. . . . Medicine is one of the few fields . . . where, if your wife wants a new coat, all you have to do is a couple more hysterectomies and she can buy it." Or, he might have added, if the doctor wants a Ferrari.

Other critics take a slightly less cynical view. "Human beings," says John R. Knowles, former director of Massachusetts General Hospital, "rationalize what they do without any conscious effort to be dishonest or greedy. Doctors are human. A significant number of them—20 to 30 percent—are de facto fleecing the public while 'knowing they are doing good.' "

Conscious or unconscious, most experts agree that what makes the hysterectomy business so lucrative and what may influence the high rate of needless surgery is the hospital-oriented, fee-for-service system of payment that dominates U.S. medical care. Comparative studies of fee-for-service medical practices (financed largely by insurance plans such as Blue Cross/Blue Shield and Medicaid) and prepaid medical plans (such as California's Kaiser Permanente or Health Insurance Plan of Greater New York) suggest that the incentive of fee-for-service

medicine not only fosters more hospital admissions in general but as much as 50 percent more hysterectomies than prepaid plans that employ salaried physicians. Add to this a surplus of surgeons in many U.S. cities and you have a situation ripe with surgical possibilities.

"There are twice as many surgeons in proportion to population in the United States as in England and Wales," says Stanford anesthesiologist John P. Bunker, "and they perform twice as many operations." Consistent with these overall figures, U.S. gynecologists perform proportionately twice as many hysterectomies as their British counterparts.

Are American women sicker than British women? Some flatly say no, claiming that the U.S. is just experiencing a medical version of Parkinson's Law: the more surgeons you have, the more surgery is performed simply because the surgeons are there and need to make a living. Bunker's own study, "Surgical Manpower" (and here, as it applies to gynecologists, the choice of the word *man*power seems particularly appropriate) attributes discrepancies in the rate of surgery not to differences in U.S. and British health needs but to differences in the organization of health care.

One of the crucial factors—important to the hysterectomy controversy—can be found in the consultant system.

"The British surgeon is a true consultant," Bunker notes. "He sees patients only as they are referred to him by a general practitioner or internist, and he is hospital based. The American surgeon by contrast . . . may be the primary physician/general practitioner referring the patient to himself for surgery and thus creating his own demand."

What women tend to forget (and it's not surprising since in the majority of cases a woman isn't sick when she sees her Ob/Gyn) is that gynecologists are trained surgeons. Perhaps more than any other single group of medical consumers, women rely upon gynecological specialists, not as consultants but as their primary physicians. More than likely, if gynecologists had no vested interest in recommending surgery, fewer unnecessary hysterectomies would be performed.

But at present, with the childbirth business drying up, we have a lot of supertrained gynecologists running around with nothing to do. From the point of view of a physician who may benefit from "self-referral," hysterectomy may be the ideal form of birth control. For a woman to see a gynecologist under these circumstances,

ca. **451 B.C.** Roman law makes it an offense, punishable by death, to administer an aphrodisiac to a person of either sex and to engage in sorcery, particularly "as practiced by women."

Hysterectomy
THE HEALTH ADVISER 43

says Dr. Ed Stim, medical director of a New York women's clinic, "It's like sending a fly into a spider's web."

The case for hysterectomy has not been made. Despite the claims of gynecologists that surgical advances have made hysterectomy a "relatively easy" procedure—it may now be done through an incision in the vaginal wall as well as through the abdomen—it remains a major operation and, thus, all the complications of anesthesia, bleeding, infection, pneumonia and blood clots may occur. Moreover, there is always the possibility of serious local complications, such as injury to the intestine, vagina, bladder or the tube that connects the bladder to the kidney. Although the death rate for hysterectomy is commonly accepted to be equal to or only slightly higher than tubal ligation (.18 percent), the total complication rate for simple vaginal hysterectomy is 10 to 20 times higher than the complication rate for tubal ligation.

Beyond the cancer argument in favor of hysterectomy—in most cases a scare tactic—is the more fundamental question of how "useless" the uterus really is. Many American physicians would agree with hysterilization advocate Dr. Ralph Wright: the uterus functions primarily as an "incubator" and when conception is either no longer possible or no longer desirable, it loses its function. And yet such unsolicited remarks as "You're 42 and don't need your uterus anyway," or "When you're finished with your family come in for your birthday hysterectomy," are regarded as cavalier and presumptuous by many women.

But even granting that at some point in a woman's life her uterus becomes something akin to excess baggage, the medical profession largely ignores the emotional impact that a hysterectomy may have on a woman's life.

Psychiatrists agree that a hysterectomy is often a blow to a woman's identity, yet doctors continue to discount the evidence—chalking it all up to female neurosis or sentimentality. "Gynecologists persist in believing," says Sylvia Oliver, a psychotherapist in Seattle, "that most women feel relieved by no longer having to suffer the nuisance of menstruation, and that with adequate counseling a 'well-adjusted' woman will be able to realistically cope with her hysterectomy. On both counts gynecologists are often wrong."

Dr. Peter Barglow, a psychiatrist on staff at the Michael Reese Hospital in Chicago, finds "that hysterectomy is clearly and immediately visualized as an irreversible, drastic procedure, which removes an organ with high value in the ego's image of the body, as well as with considerable conscious value in the woman's sense of identity and femininity. Surely, the loss of an organ whose presence was reaffirmed monthly cannot easily be denied." By contrast, Barglow and his associates suggest, "tubal ligation . . . involves a less drastic change to the body image . . . ."

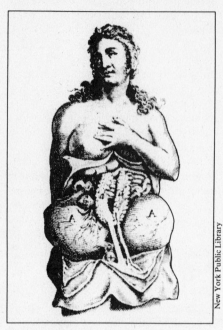

New York Public Library

Of course, depression following a hysterectomy is not a universal reaction. With strong support from friends and family and with a clear understanding of the possible physiological and psychological effects of the operation, most women can handle the loss of their uterus. Many women who have had hysterectomies for severe medical problems *and* who do not plan to have any more children have an easier time of adjustment. "The uterus," says one woman who recently underwent a hysterectomy for chronic pelvic infection, "is not a sacred organ. After what I went through, worrying about my femininity is the furthest thing from my mind. I'm just so relieved to feel like a *person* again."

The story is a little different, however, for women who have been rushed into elective hysterectomy with little preparation. A 36-year-old mother of three says her operation was first suggested by her gynecologist. "My doctor somehow convinced me that a hysterectomy would solve the contraception problem and that I wouldn't have to be bothered with my heavy periods. I am embarrassed now at how reluctant I was to ask questions. I still find it hard to believe that I went along with it. Afterwards I became depressed. Even though I didn't want to have any more children, I realized that I wanted to have the option.

"I finally went and saw a counselor. In one sense, the whole thing was good because I could no longer think of myself as only a 'mother.' I had a chance to figure out who else I was. But I still feel upset and angry. All my life I was valued, sometimes overvalued, as a mother. Then I had my uterus removed and everyone, especially my doctor, expected me to go along like nothing happened. It seems like you just can't win."

The best way to "win" is for a woman to learn as much as possible about the reasons for her hysterectomy and the alternative forms of treatment. If there are medical indications for surgery, a second opinion is advisable.

If a woman is considering hysterectomy as a means of sterilization, or, as is often the case, it looks like her physician is electing it for her, she should ask her doctor to explain not only the risks of the procedure but also the alternative forms of contraception, including tubal ligation.

"It is the prerogative of the patient," states a recent precedent-setting California Supreme Court decision, "*not* the physician, to determine for himself the direction in which he believes his interests lie." A physician may not remain silent about risks or alternatives to proposed surgery, the court states, "simply because divulgence might prompt the patient to forgo the therapy that the physician feels the patient really needs. This attitude assumes instability or perversity for even the normal patient."

So, at least in California and now more recently in the District of Columbia, informed consent is a patient's right (not her privilege), and she may sue a doctor not only for physical damages but for failure to state the alternatives to proposed treatment. And it's about time.

With a hard sell, half-truths and a leave-it-to-me-dear, thousands of women have been buffaloed into major surgery, and hysterectomy has become one of the fastest growing and most questionable elective medical procedures in the U.S. The gynecological profession, led by such devotees as Dr. Wright, has a real head-start and women have a lot of catching up to do. But with the California Supreme Court ruling in one hand and even a copy of *In Celebration of My Uterus* in the other, at least women can give the doctors a run for their money.

---

ca. **450 B.C.** Nico, an exceptionally beautiful harlot, is nicknamed "The Goat" (known for its lechery and appetite) after having attracted a visiting merchant and "so nearly devouring him" erotically that he says weakly after leaving her house, "Let no one tell me hereafter that a woman's mouth is not her most debilitating part."

Menopause

The Boston Women's Health Book Collective, Inc.

MENOPAUSE is defined as the period of cessation of menstruation, occurring naturally between the ages of forty-five and fifty. Menopause involves the gradual decline of the working of our ovaries. Our ovaries can begin to produce less estrogen starting even in our late twenties. But most of us do not actually begin to notice *signs* of menopause until our late thirties or early forties. In other words, menopause is a long process which ends with the complete cessation of menstruation and of our ability to conceive and bear children. Our bodies have to adjust to these changes in ovarian and hormonal function. The length of time and the quality of this adjustment will vary from woman to woman. Removal of both ovaries (as in a total hysterectomy) before the age of natural menopause will bring on menopause symptoms.

A few older friends sat down and told some of us recently what their experiences of menopause had been like:

* * *

I have found life after 55 and the menopause very similar to life before 55 and the menopause.

* * *

Just beautiful not to have to worry about the damn periods. And no more birth control!

* * *

I was tired in the afternoons for a couple of years and worried that I was going into a decline, but being luckily a vigorous person, I kept going with my work. Then one day I realized it must have been the menopause.

* * *

I don't really think of telling my kids I'm in the menopause because that would be overplaying its importance.

* * *

When I was about age fifty-six I began to menstruate less often and felt mildly nervous at times. The woman gynecologist to whom I had been going yearly for Pap smears probed at some length into any possible dangers and then recommended a daily amount of Premarin, and when this brought back the periods, suggested halving the daily pill. This was six years ago and I have had no menopausal symptoms since.

* * *

Although we know that not every woman has the easy time with menopause that these particular women did, it was a relief for us to hear such positive things about menopause, because so much that we have heard and absorbed about "the change of life" has been negative and scary. The popular image of the typical menopausal woman is negative—she is exhausted, haggard, irritable, bitchy, unsexy, impossible to live with, driving her husband to seek other women's company, irrationally depressed, unwillingly suffering a "change" that marks the end of her active (re)productive life. Our idea of menopause has been shaped by ads like the one in a current medical magazine that pictures a harassed middle-aged man standing by a drab and tired-looking woman. The drug advertised is "For the menopausal symptoms that bother him most." Menopause is presented as an affliction to us that makes us an affliction to our friends and families.

Because almost all of us at some point during menopause will go to a doctor about physical symptoms, it will be really important to us to insist on good medical care and advice. Many women up until now have been adversely affected by their doctors' own ignorance and carelessness. One woman told us that she went from doctor to doctor asking why she was so tired all the time—not one of them suggested she was going through menopause. Another woman, feeling tired, went to her doctor and complained that she couldn't do as much as she was accustomed to doing. Her doctor said, "Well, after all, you *are* getting old." Used to bowing to his authority, she accepted his verdict and resigned herself to her loss of energy. Pitifully little research has been done into symptoms and cures for symptoms of a physical experience more universally shared by women even than childbirth.

WHAT ARE THE SYMPTOMS?

The symptoms that occur because of the new balance of hormones are chiefly the result of your body's reaction to a drop in estrogen after it has been used to lots of it. Some symptoms usually associated with menopause may occur very early.

The most commonly reported symptom is the hot flush, or the hot flash, with sweating. This is called a vasomotor disturbance, and although the hormonal process causing it is not totally understood, hot flushes are often relieved by estrogen therapy. A typical hot flush is usually a sudden wave of heat from the waist up; you may get red and perspire a lot; then when the flush goes away, you feel very cold and chilled and sometimes shiver. It lasts from a few seconds to a half hour and may occur several or many times a day. When hot flushes occur at night, they can cause insomnia, and sometimes perspiration may be heavy enough to require a change of bedclothes.

* * *

Suddenly, without warning my temperature seemed to skyrocket about a hundred degrees. It wasn't the sensa-

ca. **411 B.C.** Aristophanes, master author of comic plays, writes *Lysistrata*, a popular, bawdy satire ridiculing the current agitation among women for cessation of war. In another comedy, *Ekklesiazusai* (392 B.C.), Aristophanes satirizes the late fifth century "feminist" movement of which the tragedian Euripides was an ardent champion.

tion of standing in front of an open oven, as some have described it, but the breathless feeling of having stayed too long in a hot shower or a steam bath. I was hot, I was wet, and I was breathless. Charging across the room I slammed up the window and began to gulp down the cool, comforting fresh air.

The book said "hot flashes" were named by woman. Right on. They had to be, the name is so accurate. How to describe them—like a wash of wet heat; unexpected, unwanted and uncontrollable.

* * *

Lack of estrogen allows the usually acidic vaginal secretions to become less acidic, thus increasing the likelihood of vaginal infection. Some women have a heavy discharge as a result. Without as much estrogen, the skin and mucous membranes atrophy somewhat, particularly those of the genitourinary tissues. The vagina starts to become narrow, shorter, and less elastic, and the surface of the vagina is easily eroded and may bleed and become ulcerated. This condition can make intercourse painful and may be responsible for so-called emotional problems such as "frigidity" or irritability during and after menopause. Lack of skin and muscle tone often leads to fre-

quency of urination, pain on voiding, and incontinence. After menopause there is often a loss of fat and shrinkage of tissues; breasts usually shrink and droop.

Estrogen, besides being necessary for your general skin tone, is apparently needed for bone tone. Osteoporosis (porous and brittle bones) is related to the long-term metabolic effects of declining estrogen, and estrogen therapy has been shown to arrest mineral loss from osteoporotic bones. Low backache in menopausal women may be the beginning of osteoporosis; as postmenopause advances, women often lose height and develop "dowager's hump" as their spines compress.

The lower estrogen level of postmenopause is now thought also to be related to an increase in coronary heart disease (atherosclerosis) and cancers in postmenopausal women. Some doctors feel that after their estrogen level drops, women become as vulnerable as men to heart disease and more vulnerable to cancer.

A whole range of other physical complaints—common ones are insomnia, headache, fast-beating heart and palpitations, vertigo, vague abdominal pains, constipation or diarrhea, nausea and vomiting, gas, tiredness, loss of appetite or weight gain, and back or other muscle aches

---

ca. **400 B.C.** The practice of stitching together the vulva and mutilating the clitoris of women (partly as a rite analogous to male circumcision and partly because it is believed to make women more passionate) is common custom in Arabia, Egypt, southern Syria, and a large portion of Africa.

—are not always so clearly related to the lower estrogen level. We feel that these very common symptoms, so often dismissed by doctors as psychosomatic, deserve thorough medical research to find causes and cures. If every male doctor went through menopause, no doubt this research would already be well on its way.

Emotional symptoms of menopause include irritability, nervousness, depression, frigidity, lack of memory, difficulty in concentrating, and temporary distortions in close personal relationships. These emotional symptoms can be caused or aggravated by a feeling of ill health due to some of the physical symptoms of menopause. We feel that they can often be minimized when a woman feels generally happy about herself and involved in what she is doing.

WHAT YOU CAN DO ABOUT IT

Since so many of the physical discomforts of menopause are caused by insufficient estrogen, estrogen-replacement hormone therapy is a solution that many women can turn to, being careful to consult a knowledgeable doctor about its possible side effects and dangers. Before talking about hormone therapy, however, we want to emphasize that there are other important ways of dealing with and preventing some of menopause's discomforts. Good diet, exercise, enough rest, where these are possible, can give our bodies enough physical vigor and good health to minimize menopause's physical effects, just as work that is meaningful to us either in or outside our home can help tremendously to minimize the emotional effects often associated with menopause.

If you are having uncomfortable physical symptoms you might want to discuss estrogen therapy with your doctor. Estrogen may relieve low-estrogen symptoms like hot flushes, sweating, cold hands and feet, osteoporosis, and discharges from the vagina. Sometimes relieving low-estrogen symptoms brings general relief from irritability or depression. Estrogen is commonly given in the natural form, Premarin, or in synthetic forms, Stilbestrol, Progynon, and Meprane. Stilbestrol, however, has been mentioned as a carcinogen (cancer-causing agent) in some research. A natural form is usually well tolerated; side effects from the synthetics include nausea, allergies and pain in the breasts, but they are more powerful and cheaper and you and your doctor may feel they're worth trying. The Maturation Index test is done to determine how much estrogen you should take; it simply involves examining a sample of your vaginal secretions or cells. Estrogen is not generally prescribed for women with severe kidney or liver disease, some heart problems, or a history of breast or uterine cancer. *(It is important to take estrogen or any prescription drug only under the guidance of a doctor.)*

According to recent studies women who take estrogen for treatment of menopause symptoms run a substantially increased risk of developing uterine cancer, a risk that increases the longer the estrogen is taken. It may therefore be advisable for a doctor to prescribe such medication or a woman to accept it only for severe symptoms. A woman taking estrogen should be examined every six months.—Ed.

The majority of those receiving estrogen at menopause are being given it in cycles: they take a pill daily for three weeks, then stop for a week. This is very similar to many birth-control pill regimes, and similar to the timing of the estrogen a woman's own body produced.

* * *

Here I am, one of the lucky females, taking Premarin since August, a little yellow pill every day for three weeks, then none for a week. I guess this is the answer for me. The gynecologist did not routinely prescribe it until I complained about the depression, the spilling over with tears at very slight provocation, and then I realized that intercourse was really painful. This must have justified his decision, along with the Maturation Index from the Pap smear, to prescribe the hormone.

* * *

Bleeding is a common effect of estrogen, especially on the week you don't take it. For this reason some regimes include progesterone, which brings the total hormone situation closer to the premenopause state in that it promotes a predictable endometrial bleeding—an induced period in effect. You have a menstrual-type flow and feel very much as though you had a regular period but the flow is not as heavy nor for as many days. This "medical curettage" avoids protracted bleeding, which can occur when estrogen only is taken. Relief of menopause symptoms, however, can usually be obtained with estrogen doses small enough so that no bleeding occurs. Mid-cycle bleeding on an estrogen-induced cycle should be checked immediately by a doctor. In fact, any bleeding at all that occurs in a postmenopausal woman, whether or not she is taking estrogen, should be carefully investigated by a doctor; it may be a first sign of endometrial or cervical cancer. In about one-third of the cases reaching surgery the bleeding proves to be of malignant origin.

Possible side effects from too much estrogen are gastrointestinal disturbances, fluid retention and weight gain, breast and pelvic pains due to swollen tissues, headache, high blood pressure, vaginal discharge, and skin pigmentation. As with birth-control pills—most of which also contain estrogen—sensitivities vary enormously. It looks as though you're damned if you do, damned if you don't take estrogen—the trick is to find the right amount, if any, for you, to get regular check-ups twice a year if you are taking estrogen, and to find a doctor who is aware of both the positive uses and the potential risks of estrogen, who will be very careful about what s/he prescribes.

What can you do about weight gain? Eat less, especially refined carbohydrates, and exercise more. Estrogen relief of some of your other physical symptoms may improve your general feeling of health enough so that this will be easier for you. If the extra weight bothers you, it is probably worth losing; thinner people live longer, according to insurance statistics—and they've got money on it. Excessive weight can also make activity difficult. A good diet and sensible exercise have done a lot to help many women feel better through menopause.

ca. **325 B.C.** Chung-Li Ch'un—at forty appallingly ugly, unmarried, and therefore a disgrace to her family—secures an audience with Hsuan Wang, prince of the Feudal State of Ch'i. Despite the ridicule of the courtiers, she so impresses his Highness with her wit that he marries her forthwith.

Varicose Veins

The word, "varicose," means "swollen." Thus, varicose veins, which doctors may call "varicosities," are swollen, enlarged veins. They are found most frequently on the inner side and back of the calf and on the inner side of the thigh. Bluish in color, they are visible through the skin when close to its surface—and look something like a map's drawing of a river and the streams that flow into it.

The superficial veins, those lying just under the skin, are most commonly affected. The deep veins, which run inside the muscles of the leg and thigh, are seldom seriously afflicted with varicosities because they are surrounded and supported by the muscles.

WHAT CAUSES VARICOSE VEINS?

Veins contain valves which permit the blood to flow only in the direction of the heart. One of the main causes of varicose veins seems to be valves that leak, allowing blood to flow backward into the vessel rather than continuing on its way to the heart.

This increases blood pressure in the section of the vein below the faulty valve. Veins are low-pressure vessels. Their walls are thinner and have less muscle in them than do the walls of arteries. When continually subjected to abnormally high pressures, the veins become stretched and swollen. The result is the condition which we know as "varicose veins."

Inherited weakness in the structure of the veins greatly increases the individual's susceptibility to varicose veins. Other contributing factors are diseases, such as phlebitis—an inflammation of the veins, which weakens or damages the walls and valves of the veins.

Abdominal pressure, from the stomach muscles—such as that caused by heavy lifting, coughing, and straining—may also contribute to the development of varicose veins.

Obesity and increasing age are other factors in causing varicose veins. Obesity's useless, fat weight may play a role in overworking the veins. With increasing age there is a loss of tone of the skin and tissues which surround the veins and help to support them.

WHO HAS VARICOSE VEINS?

Varicose veins are widespread throughout the population and affect almost all ages. However, they are most common in people over forty, affecting one out of every two women and one out of every four men in this age group.

Occupation may be a factor in acquiring varicose veins. Persons in occupations that require a great deal of standing, such as elevator operators, beauticians, dentists, and salespeople, seem more prone to varicose veins than people with sit-down jobs. To illustrate this point: it has been found that pressure in the leg veins is increased 5 times when a person stands erect from lying down.

From *Varicose Veins*, 1966, Department of Health, Education and Welfare.

But people in jobs requiring sitting in one place for long periods of time also have a problem. These people should walk around or elevate their feet from time to time to prevent excessive pooling of blood in the veins of the lower leg.

WOMEN IN PARTICULAR

Pregnant women frequently develop varicose veins, sometimes rather early in pregnancy, but more often during later months. The main factors contributing to their development are:

- increased abdominal pressure resulting from the enlarging uterus
- increased bloodflow to and from the lower abdominal and pelvic areas

Both factors act indirectly to hinder return flow from the leg veins, thus increasing blood pressure in these blood vessels.

Unless severe, varicose veins of pregnancy frequently improve substantially without treatment, after delivery.

One of the main kinds of varicose veins, the smaller "spidery type," appears most frequently among women, particularly among women of middle age and those past the menopause.

Among women, a contributing cause of varicose veins is the use of tight garters, girdles, and other clothing which tends to obstruct the veins' bloodflow and thus to increase pressure on the veins. By eliminating or reducing the use of these constricting items from the wardrobe, women can themselves do much to prevent varicose veins or to reduce their severity.

Girdles are made primarily for the standing woman and tend to press down and tightly constrict the big veins of the leg when she sits down. Those with varicose veins, or with a tendency toward

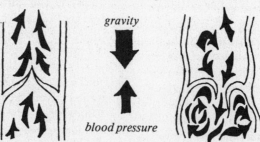

gravity

blood pressure

them, should not wear girdles, especially if they are going to sit for a long time, as on a long trip by plane, automobile, or train.

SYMPTOMS

Most victims of varicose veins have a combination of many symptoms. Among these symptoms are changes in the appearance of the leg; increased tendency to fatigue of the leg muscles; a sensation of fullness and congestion; soreness in the region of the veins after standing for a long period of time; muscular cramps, particularly at night; and itching and burning sensations in the region of varicose veins.

DIAGNOSING VARICOSE VEINS

In medical terms, there are several kinds of varicose veins. Some can be helped by surgery, some by injection therapy, and some by other simpler measures. An examination is necessary for the doctor to determine the best treatment.

All who have, or suspect they may have, varicose veins should have a complete physical examination. This is important because the presence or absence of other possible diseases is significant for the physician in considering diagnosis and treatment.

Although the doctor, by inspecting and manipulating areas of the leg, can usually establish their presence, various other tests have been developed to aid in diagnosing varicose veins. One of these procedures is called venography. In this test, a radiopaque substance is injected into the veins. Then the blood flow and the working of the valves in the vessels are checked by means of X-rays.

TREATMENT

Conservative Therapy. In mild cases of varicose veins it may be possible to relieve much of the discomfort and to prevent the veins from becoming worse by wearing support hosiery. This hosiery helps to provide additional support to offset excessive blood pressure within the veins. Support hosiery, available in stockings for women and socks for men, should be carefully fitted on the basis of precise leg measurements. With the improved stretch yarns now available, it is possible to make this hosiery attractive and at the same time functional in giving needed support to the legs.

The person with mild varicose veins should also get adequate periods of rest with his feet and legs elevated. He should try to avoid prolonged periods of standing. But, if this is unavoidable because of occupation or other factors, elastic bandages may provide better support than can usually be obtained with support hosiery.

"Bicycling" exercises while lying on the back, swimming, and walking are recommended forms of exercise for persons with mild varicose veins.

Injection. Varicose veins can be injected with a sclerosing (hardening) solution to block off the part of the vein that is swollen. The blood normally car-

"Transparent Woman"

ried by that vessel is re-routed through other veins. For a time after injection, the injected vein may be swollen and tender, but this subsides within a few hours or days. Thereafter, the injected section usually withers and gradually disappears over a period of weeks to months. This process may be hastened by removing some of the coagulated blood from the blocked section through a small incision.

Injection is probably best reserved for the treatment of the small varicose veins lying very near the surface of the skin.

Injection treatment has some drawbacks, however. Permanent results cannot be guaranteed, numerous injections may be necessary, and elastic pressure bandages have to be worn for the duration of treatment.

Surgery. Surgery for tying off or removing the vein is quicker and the results are more likely to be permanent. If the patient is otherwise in good health, the surgical risk is slight. However, surgery does require a hospital stay and is relatively expensive.

To the question of how well a victim can get along without the veins that are being injected, tied off, or removed, the answer is: far better than he can get along with them. Varicose veins are inefficient in carrying out their function of returning blood "uphill" to the heart. In fact, in a severely affected vein, blood flow may be in the opposite direction. Thus, blocking or removing that vein actually improves the overall performance of the system of veins.

The physician is the only one who can determine the best course of treatment. After the examination, he will take into account such factors as the patient's general state of health, weight, reaction to drugs, and high or low blood pressure. Then he can suggest the best specific therapy indicated for the individual case. The fact that one has varicose veins does not always have to mean discomfort. Even the worst case is usually responsive to treatment.

---

ca. **169 B.C.** The Roman senate decrees "the most unjust law ever passed," according to Saint Augustine. It states that no woman may inherit the estate of her husband if he was worth over a certain trifling amount.

Hypertension

Ellen Switzer

Jane Andrews is one of those women who feels so marvelous all the time that some of her friends (especially the ones with problems) tend to get annoyed. She's 35 years old, happily married to a successful architect, has three children who never seem to get into trouble, and a good part-time job as a copywriter for a magazine. She sees her gynecologist once a year for a checkup, and knows enough to get a "Pap" smear and have her breasts examined for early cancer detection. Since Jane hasn't had even a serious sore throat in the past five years, she sees no other physician—a fact of which the gynecologist is not aware. One day, just before having her teeth cleaned at the dentist's office, the dentist's nurse produced a blood-pressure cuff and sphygmomanometer and attached it to her arm. After getting a reading, she looked puzzled. "What does my blood pressure have to do with my *teeth?*" Jane asked. "We've been asked by our state dental association to take our patients' blood pressures as part of a pilot project," the nurse explained. At any rate, after Jane got out of the dentist's chair, her pressure was taken again, this time by the dentist. He looked a little grim. "When was the last time anybody took your blood pressure?" he inquired. Jane couldn't even remember, but she thought during her last pregnancy—about eight years ago. "Mrs. Andrews, I think you have a problem," the dentist said. "Your blood pressure is much too high. I suggest you make an appointment to see your family physician promptly. Your hypertension should be controlled."

The fact is that millions of American women have undiagnosed hypertension, which, if left untreated, eventually may kill or cripple them. Physicians are exceedingly worried about this situation. The World Health Organization (WHO) in 1972 declared high blood pressure (or hypertension, the accurate medical term for this condition) "a widespread epidemic." According to WHO, it affects one in every ten adult persons in the world, with only a small fraction knowing that they suffer from it and even fewer receiving correct treatment. The situation is even worse in the United States where about 22 million persons (20 percent of all adults) are afflicted with hypertension. Over 13 million are women; over 8 million, men. For some unknown reason, hypertension occurs more frequently in females, but is more deadly to males. Blacks have a greater tendency towards the disease than whites.

The reason so many people with this potentially deadly condition don't know they have it is that, in the early stages, it produces no symptoms. As a matter of fact, most hypertensive people feel just fine. Many people don't see a physician unless they feel sick, and the person with early hypertension doesn't feel sick. Women who have been thoroughly indoctrinated about prenatal care and early cancer detection through "Pap" smears and breast palpation often use their gynecologist as their family doctor. Many of those specialists don't take blood pressures except when their patient is pregnant or on birth control pills. They just assume that she is also seeing another physician. So, particularly in women, high blood pressure can go undetected for decades (usually, the decades between the time she has her last child and her early fifties, when she may ask her physician for endocrine-replacement therapy for menopausal symptoms).

What exactly is hypertension? The medical term is itself confusing. Although emotional tension and anxiety may increase blood pressure temporarily (as a matter of fact, some people's blood pressure goes up simply because they are anxious about having it taken, making it necessary to do several readings), most physicians feel that the disease probably is not primarily psychosomatic. "We know the ulcer type or the colitis type. We even have clues to the heart-attack type. But we've not been able to identify a unique hypertensive personality," says Dr. Campbell Moses of the American Heart Association.

When a physician measures blood pressure, he is measuring the force of the blood against the artery walls. Since artery walls are elastic and muscular, they stretch and contract with the heart beat, which pumps blood through them. Each time the heart relaxes between beats, blood

Deborah Taylor

ca. **77 B.C.** Amaesia Sentia, a respected member of the Roman patrician class, argues her own case in court before the praetor, the first recorded instance of a woman personally prosecuting her rights. She is so vigorous in pressing her attack that she comes to be called "Androgyne," a fusion of Greek words meaning "having both male and female characteristics."

pressure goes down; when it beats, pressure goes up. The lower pressure is called "diastolic pressure." Physicians tend to be concerned more about diastolic pressure, with a measurement of around 80 considered normal and everything over 90 abnormal.

On the other hand, naturally *low* blood pressure, which formerly was considered a problem by some physicians, is now generally regarded as an asset.

In a hypertensive patient, the smallest arteries of the body, known as the arterioles, clamp down, requiring more pumping to distribute blood through the system. This means that the heart has to work harder to pump blood through the body since it is acting against the resisting pressure.

The heart is a muscle and the extra effort tends to enlarge it, just as a ballet dancer's leg muscles tend to enlarge through intensive use. An enlarged heart is often a symptom of the degree of hypertension that has persisted for a number of years; however, *it is not a cause of the condition.*

When it comes to causes, little is known. A very few patients have some kind of specific disease (such as malfunctioning kidneys or a tumor of the adrenal glands) which may be cured by surgery. But the vast majority of patients have "essential hypertension," another very confusing term since, in this instance, "essential" does not mean "necessary" but "of unknown cause."

Among the suspected causes are genetic factors (men and women with family histories of high blood pressure seem to have a greater susceptibility to hypertension); lifelong food habits (a black physician, Dr. Elijah Saunders of the University of Maryland, suspects that the large amount of sodium in "soul food" may have some impact on the high incidence of hypertension in young black patients); constant emotional turmoil (one secretary reported that her blood pressure dropped almost immediately after her obnoxious boss was fired); or, most likely, a combination of all these factors, plus some others that researchers have not yet discovered.

Moderate hypertension is eminently treatable. The patient may be asked to lose some weight and to make sure to keep his or her weight normal. Smoking is absolutely *out,* since it puts a strain on even a healthy heart and arteries. On the other hand, a modest amount of alcohol is probably *in,* since it releases nervous tension. However, some medications given for hypertension don't mix well with liquor, so it's a good idea to ask the doctor whether a pre-dinner drink is still in order. Usually, the body gives out warning signals (such as nausea or fatigue) if the alcohol and the medicine are having an undesirable effect on each other. Physicians usually will prescribe a diet that is low in sodium. Sodium is present in many foods, including milk and cheese, but its most common form is table salt. The patient probably will be advised to put a minimum amount of salt in his food and to leave the salt shaker off the dinner table. Such high-salt foods as pickles (one large pickle contains about as much salt as a whole year's worth of lightly salted scrambled eggs), sauerkraut, frankfurters, bologna, and any kind of pickled meats, including ham, are also taboo. Salt has a tendency to retain fluid in the body and that extra water, pressing on the arterioles, can inhibit an already difficult blood-pumping process even further, thus raising the pressure.

If hypertension is very mild (some physicians tend to call this "a borderline condition"), diet alone may be prescribed to control it. If that doesn't work, the physician will probably prescribe a diuretic, which stimulates the kidneys and thus helps the body get rid of water and sodium. However, right along with eliminating these hazards, a necessary chemical, potassium, may also be eliminated in excess amounts. A potassium deficiency can cause a patient to be tired and out of sorts, and potassium supplements may then be prescribed.

Next on the list of weapons against hypertension are drugs that depress the activities of the sympathetic nervous system. The best known of these is reserpine, a drug originally used in India as a specific agent for lowering blood pressure. Subsequently, its properties as a tranquilizer were also noticed, and it is now sometimes given to calm down high-strung people, even if they don't have hypertension. However, it has an unfortunate side effect on some patients: serious depression.

When reserpine is used, it usually is appropriate to alert the patient and/or his family to report any symptoms of depression, which may include anxiety, waking up very early in the morning, or a sudden lack of appetite. An early warning signal may be, strange as it may seem, a stuffy nose. Since depression may persist even a few weeks after the drug has been discontinued, it's important to report any and all signs, including nasal stuffiness not associated with a cold. Some other medication which doesn't produce dangerous side effects may be substituted.

A third variety of drug, used most frequently in serious cases of hypertension, blocks the transmission of nerve impulses. These medications have to be carefully adjusted, usually starting with a very low dose and increasing it until hypertension is controlled. The side effects may be a slight feeling of dizziness as one gets out of bed in the morning or takes a hot shower. Some men particularly hate these drugs, since they make it impossible for them to ejaculate during sexual intercourse. Again, both the type of drug and the dosage can be adjusted, so that the side effects will disappear with the control of hypertension.

In recent years, several universities in Russia and in the United States have experimented with a form of autosuggestion (called bio-feedback) in which the patient attempts to lower his or her blood pressure. Up to a point, this works. The only trouble with the system is that for the blood pressure to go down the patient must put himself into a form of trance. One physician stated at a recent conference on ⟶

ca. **100 B.C.** Among the pagan Germanic tribes the husband is absolute ruler of his household, though the marriage is one of affection and constancy. Women are thought to possess a sacred and prophetic element, many of them being consulted as oracles in matters of importance. These *Velledas,* or prophets, play a prominent part in German myth and history.

hypertension sponsored by the American Heart Association: "Blood pressure goes down also if the patient is asleep. It's dubious that a system which requires some form of perpetual half-sleep would be very useful as an effective form of therapy."

As Dr. Moses indicated earlier, statistics show that women tend to suffer from hypertension much more frequently than men, but they tolerate it better. This means that women with elevated blood pressures probably can live longer without disastrous medical results. However, women are not *immune* to the damage produced by high blood pressure and there are certain times in every woman's life when she *must* make sure that her blood pressure is checked regularly:

1. When she is taking birth control pills

Oral contraceptives can cause hypertension in a few women. Any woman who is receiving a supply of pills that will last a year should insist that her blood pressure be taken within three months after starting to take the pills. Actually, oral contraceptives may provide a useful clue in bringing to light certain women who run an inherited risk of developing high blood pressure, according to research reported last year by Dr. James W. Woods, Jr. of the University of North Carolina. Dr. Woods suggested that these women, whose blood pressures rose slightly above normal only after starting on the pill, might fall into a category designated as "pre-hypertensive." In any case, a woman whose blood pressure rises when she takes birth control pills should use some other form of contraception.

2. Pregnancy

Some women experience a drastic rise in blood pressure during pregnancy. In its most extreme form, this condition is called "eclampsia" and can seriously harm the mother and the unborn child. One of the reasons physicians have asked women to restrict their weight gain during pregnancy, and sometimes to go on a low-salt diet, is to avoid such a medical emergency. Recent research in England and Sweden has indicated that the drastic restriction on weight gain that has been imposed on pregnant women by their physicians may also have been bad for the

baby, by keeping its birth weight too low. However, a generally sensible diet is still advisable in all cases of pregnancy (who wants to be faced with losing 40 pounds after the birth of a baby anyhow?) and a more drastic diet may be advised if the blood-pressure level goes up.

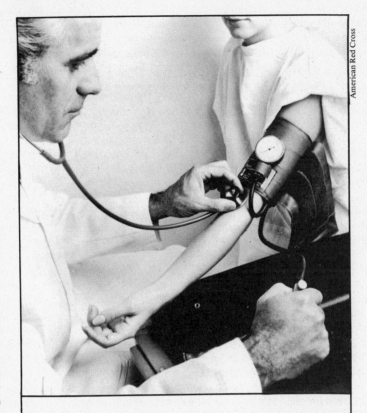

Hypertension is measured with a blood pressure cuff and a sphygmomanometer.

American Red Cross

3. Menopause

Nobody really knows why menopausal women tend to become hypertensive more frequently than their younger sisters. Some researchers believe that the physical and emotional stresses and strains of the menopausal years may be the cause; others, that the changes in hormone production may encourage the development of hypertension. This is one of the reasons why some physicians advise estrogen-replacement therapy . . . although there is no definite proof that this will make a substantial difference.

Whatever the cause of hypertension, it's one of our most treatable diseases. The most complete

study of the effects of early treatment on mildly and moderately hypertensive patients was reported in 1971 by Dr. Edward Freis, senior medical investigator of the Veterans Administration Hospital in Washington, D.C. He put more than 800 male patients with mild hypertension into a double-blind study. Some were assigned at random to an active drug program, some others to placebos (pills containing no active ingredients). Among the 800 mildly hypertensive men who were tested in a three-year study, 56 of those on placebos developed cardiovascular complications versus only 22 of those in the treated group.

Another group of 143 patients with moderately high blood pressures were assigned to a similar experiment. Of the 143 patients, *27* of those receiving placebos developed major cardiovascular complications during the study period. Among the patients receiving treatment (a diuretic plus reserpine), only *one* suffered from

complications. The experiment was ended and all patients in this group put on the active drugs after twenty months, because it was so evident that the men who were getting the placebos in place of active drug treatment were in real physical jeopardy.

The researchers felt that this study proved that for men, at least, *early* treatment can make the difference between a patient's leading a normal, healthy life or suffering serious illness.

No similar study has been reported for women, "partly because we don't have as handy a female patient population as those males who are in a veterans' hospital," Dr. Moses says. The Heart Association is most eager to see such a study done and several major corporations who employ large numbers of women (insurance companies, for instance) are attempting a study similar to the one conducted by Dr. Freis and the Veterans Administration patients.

All in all, hypertension can be a silent medical menace, even a killer, if left undetected and untreated. In the vast majority of cases, this is exactly what happens. Therefore, every woman, even one who feels perfectly healthy and fit, should have regular blood-pressure checkups at least once a year. If her primary physician is a gynecologist who does not take a routine reading, she should ask for one. The doctor won't think she's a hypochondriac, just an intelligent patient.

Whatever type of medical care she receives, she should insist on a blood-pressure reading regularly, and make sure her husband gets one, too. If hypertension runs in one or both families, even teen-age youngsters should be checked with a fair amount of regularity; it might also be a good idea to "forget" to buy salted peanuts, potato chips, pickles, and other high-sodium foods on supermarket shopping trips.

If a test turns up hypertension, it's important not to panic. Remember, you or your hypertensive family member are one of 20 percent of all Americans who have the disease—and they are not dropping dead like flies on all sides of you. Indeed, those who are getting the right kind of treatment (and sticking with it) will live longer and more comfortably than those who never knew they had a problem. If there's one outstanding truth about hypertension, it is that what you don't know will most definitely hurt you.

ca. **66 B.C.** Roman legions, in pursuing Mithridates, king of Pontus, across Asia Minor to the Black Sea, run into a horde of hostile barbarians at the wild, unexplored Caucasus region. After fighting them off in a vicious day-long battle, the Romans wander around the littered corpses and discover that these warriors are all women. The "Amazons" living here are said to make war their constant occupation and to tolerate men only once

How to Live with Arthritis

William A. Nolen, M.D.

Arthritis is a mysterious disease. It exists everywhere, troubles millions of people, has been the subject of endless investigations. Yet we still don't know the cause of it—let alone the cure.

Actually, arthritis—from "arthron" (joint) and "itis" (inflammation of)—is not one disease but many. *Still's disease* is a special form of arthritis that strikes children; *infectious arthritis* can be caused by any bacteria, including those that cause tuberculosis and gonorrhea; people in their 60s or 70s, and younger people who may have injured joints (athletes in particular), may develop *osteoarthritis,* a degeneration of the joint without inflammation. But the arthritis that is by far the most common in women, especially those between 35 and 50—the painful, crippling kind we know so little about —is *rheumatoid arthritis.* When I refer to arthritis in this article, unless I specify otherwise, I'm talking about the rheumatoid kind.

Rheumatoid arthritis is three times as common in women as in men. No one knows why. Sometimes it comes on abruptly, with chills, high fever and pain and swelling in several joints; more often it begins insidiously, with moderate stiffness and pain in one or two joints and only a slight fever, if any. In the insidious cases, the victim often doesn't realize at first that she has arthritis. She may attribute her sore knee or finger to a strain or sprain. Only when the symptoms persist for several weeks, or spread to other joints, is she likely to consult a doctor. He will make the diagnosis on the basis of her medical history, a physical examination, an X ray and blood tests.

Once the disease is diagnosed, patients may remember that they "hadn't really felt well" for a week or two before the symptoms appeared. They may recall that they were easily tired, or had lost weight,

or had a tingling in their hands or feet. These are the so-called "prodomal" (forerunning) symptoms of arthritis. And often patients will associate the onset of their first obvious symptoms with an episode of acute physical or emotional stress. It's difficult to prove statistically, but it seems to be true that severe emotional upheavals can precipitate the onset of arthritis.

Just as there are variations in the way this disease begins, so are there variations in the course it follows. Sometimes it may strike one joint, persist for a few weeks or months and then disappear for years. More often, unfortunately, it will strike one joint, move to another, disappear for a few weeks or months and then return, either to the same joints or to others. Each time a little more lasting damage is done to the affected joint; over the course of several years it may become progressively more deformed and disabled. But only rarely does joint damage lead to bed or wheelchair confinement, and then only after 15 or 20 years of repeated attacks.

The elbows, ankles, fingers, hips and knees are the joints most commonly involved. In the ankles and knees, the swelling isn't always obvious, but in the hands it's usually easy to see. For some reason, only the first two joints of the fingers, rarely the last, are affected.

Along with the joint symptoms, patients often suffer from anemia, weight loss and fatigue. They may also develop "rheumatoid nodules" —rubbery lumps about the size of a marble or walnut—beneath the skin near the ankle or knee. After repeated attacks, the skin over deformed joints may become red, smooth and shiny. This again is particularly obvious in the hands.

Since we don't know the cause of arthritis, treatment is not curative, but good, sound management of the disease can delay and sometimes prevent the crippling that ensues

when it is ignored. It's possible to live out a perfectly normal life-span with minimal inconvenience and discomfort if you learn how to live with and manage your disease.

The first step in assuring yourself of sound treatment is to find a doctor you like. This is very important, since the two of you may have to see a lot of each other over the years.

Also, you'd better make certain your doctor is interested in arthritis —not all doctors are. It's not a "glamorous" disease, and there are few real "triumphs" for the doctor who treats it.

Once you've found your doctor, the two of you may at one time or another, in collaboration, use one or all of the various means of treatment. Since arthritis comes and goes for no apparent reason, there will be times when you won't need any treatment at all. On the other hand, if you have a severe, acute flare-up, with high fever and pain in several joints, you may need hospitalization. Not only must treatment be individualized but it has to be reassessed constantly even in the same individual.

Currently, treatment of arthritis may include any or all of these:

Rest. This is essential, particularly in the early stages. When arthritis strikes a weight-bearing joint, such as the knee or ankle, the patient may require bed rest until the inflammation subsides. But even when the disease is in remission, patients should be careful to avoid getting overtired.

Relief of pain. There is still no drug superior to aspirin. Some patients need only two aspirin every four hours; others may require three or four. Some doctors prescribe very large doses—as much as the patient can tolerate without developing signs of aspirin toxicity (ringing in the ears is one such sign). Sometimes narcotics are necessary but very rarely.

Treatment of the joints. Heat and exercise are the key. Heat—warm, wet towels or a heating pad—may be applied locally; if several joints are involved, generalized heat to the body—for example, in a hot bath or a steam room—may be helpful.

From *McCalls* Magazine, November 1973. Reprinted by permission of the author's agent, Lurton Blassingame. Copyright © 1973 McCall Publishing Company.

each year for a two-month interval—just long enough to become impregnated by them. They chose their short-lived mates from among neighboring Gelea and Leges peoples under a temporary truce. Alexander the Great is also thought to have encountered them in his campaigns.

Twenty minutes of generalized heat at any one time are about all a patient should have; more than that tends to be exhausting.

Exercise is important for the preservation of muscle tone and to prevent stiffness of the joints. Even acutely inflamed joints should be put through a range of motion exercises every day. Your doctor can show you what exercises to do and which to avoid; excessive exercise is unwise.

Orthopedic support. At some time your doctor may call on an orthopedist for help. The orthopedist may construct plaster splints to help relieve the pain in acutely inflamed joints; he may also advise surgery to prevent crippling deformities or to correct them when they occur. In the last few years there has been a growing tendency to operate on joints *before* they develop advanced arthritic deformities.

General health care. Arthritis is a generalized disease. It's important to remember this and to avoid the mistake of treating the joints and ignoring the rest of the body.

Now and then you'll hear of a special diet that is good for arthritis. This is nonsense. Research of all sorts has been done on the subject, and the conclusion is that there is no "magic" diet. But patients with arthritis tend to be underweight and undernourished, so it is important that they eat a well-balanced diet with plenty of protein and calories. Vitamin supplements are sometimes prescribed, but they aren't necessary if the patient eats wisely.

Arthritis patients—for a reason we do not know—are often anemic. Usu-

Arthritic hands

ally the anemia isn't severe, and generally it doesn't respond to the usual medications—iron and vitamin B_{12}—though occasionally these are helpful. If the blood level drops to a point that leaves the patient exhausted, then an occasional transfusion may be necessary, but this situation is rare.

Any obvious infection anywhere in the body should be treated.

But beware of the doctor who suggests an appendectomy or a hysterectomy on the off chance that these organs may be precipitating attacks of arthritis. Medical experience has shown that this shotgun approach to organs that are "potentially infected" doesn't work.

Some arthritis victims get relief when they move to a warm, dry climate; Arizona and New Mexico are favorite refuges. But not all patients are benefited, and before considering a radical change of locale the wise pa-

tient will try a temporary move—say, for three or four months—just to see.

"Special" therapy. Most arthritis can be successfully managed with one or all of the fairly simple methods of treatment I've described here. But if the disease is particularly severe, other measures are available. They include injection of gold salts and the use of cortisone. I mention these only in passing because anyone who is going to be treated with either of these potent drugs deserves a lengthy, thorough discussion of the potential benefits and risks; this must be a matter between the individual patient and her doctor.

Let me end with a warning. Arthritis is a cyclical disease with frequent ups and downs, and cyclical diseases are prime targets for quacks. Almost anything you give an arthritis patient—whether it's a sugar pill, a kooky diet or a massage with an electric vibrator—is likely to be followed by an improvement in her condition. The patient attributes the improvement to the bizarre treatment (when actually it's just another fluctuation in the normal course of the disease), and the quack takes credit. Word gets around and soon the quack has a thriving practice. Don't be one of those patients who forgoes sound medical therapy to chase a nonexistent magic cure. You'll only hurt yourself.

Fortunately, research into the causes of arthritis continues to be vigorous. Perhaps soon there will be a breakthrough—and a cure. Until then, a great deal can be done to help the arthritis victim live a long and comfortable life.

The Natural Way to Prevent an Aching Back
The Editors of *Harper's Bazaar*

"Stress, exhaustion, tension all manifest themselves in our most vulnerable spot. And in our sedentary society one of our most vulnerable spots is the back, especially the lower back," says Dr. Willibald Nagler, Physiatrist in Chief at the New York Hospital.

When we look at the figures, bad backs seem a national epidemic. It's the second largest cause of work days lost in the United States. Over eight million people suffer from impairments of the back or spine. Women are especially affected by lower back pain after childbirth and after the onset of menopause.

Yet, it is one of the most avoidable problems. Excluding backaches that are the result

of disease or spinal misalignments that only your doctor should deal with, there are an infinite number of things you can do in your daily life to avoid this latest plague. Clinical studies have shown that 80 per cent of back pain is a result of under-exercised muscles.

HOW AND WHERE TO SLEEP according to the American Academy of Orthopedic Surgeons' Symposium on the Spine and Dr. Nagler:
(1) Sleep on a very firm mattress. Sometimes a ¾-inch wooden bed board helps when placed between the box spring and mattress, but not when the mattress is so far gone that it begins to sag.
(2) Sleep alone or in a king-sized bed.
(3) Sleep on your side with your knees drawn up, with pillow under your head and pillow be-

tween your legs. If you feel most comfortable sleeping face down, put a pillow under your abdomen. If you must sleep on your back, put a rolled up blanket or pillow under your knees.
(4) When you get out of bed, move first to the side of the bed, draw up your knees, then swing your legs over the side, and support yourself with your arms when getting into the sitting position.
WHAT KINDS OF SHOES TO AVOID:
For women, sling-back shoes or very high heels that pitch the body forward can be very dangerous.
ROUTINE CARE DURING THE DAY:
(1) If you are very tall, think about getting furniture scaled to your size.
(2) Never sit with your legs straight out on an ottoman. Always bend the knees.

(3) When you're driving, adjust the car seat so that you sit up straight, and have your knees and hips bent.
(4) If you're short and will be riding in a car for long periods use a low foot rest to bring your knees up.
(5) Sit with the buttocks tucked under.
(6) Avoid deep sofas.
(7) Avoid standing for long periods. If you must, for instance when ironing, place one foot on a low footstool.
(8) Walk with your abdomen drawn in.
LIFTING AND REACHING:
(1) When reaching down toward floor, bend from the hips, knees and ankles. Keep back straight.
(2) When lifting objects (or children), bend properly, and bring and keep objects as close as possible to your midline while you rise.

ca. **60 B.C.** Liu Hsaing, prolific Chinese author and imperial minister of state, writes his popular *Biographies of Famous Women,* the first work of its kind in Chinese.

EXERCISES:

These are a series of exercises that can be done without supervision devised for us by Dr. Nagler. He advises you not to begin them if you are in constant pain, or have sudden, acute pain. You should see a doctor first and get his advice. But if you don't yet suffer from backache, begin these immediately. They could save you hours of untold agony in the future.

(1) Lie on stomach, pillow under abdomen. Squeeze buttock muscles together and hold 5 seconds before relaxing.

(2) Lie on back, knees bent. Squeeze buttock muscles and flatten lower back into the floor (the "pelvic tilt"). Hold 5 seconds, then relax. Do not hold your breath, but try to be relaxed and breathe normally as you hold the "tilt" position.

(3) Lie on back, knees bent. Bring one knee up towards chest as far as possible, then lift head up and try to touch forehead to knee. Repeat and touch other knee.

(4) Lie on back with knees bent and feet anchored. Raise head and shoulders off floor and curl up your trunk as far as possible with arms reaching forward until you come close to sitting position. *Slowly* uncurl back down. (As you gain strength, do sit-ups with arms crossed on chest; when you are even more advanced, put hands behind neck, but always curl up and down again.

(5) Sit-ups with knees bent—as you sit up, rotate body nearly 90 degrees as you curl upwards, so that elbow reaches towards opposite knee. (This one is particularly good for waistline.)

(6) This one is more advanced—do it after you have strengthened your muscles. It's great for abdominal muscles. Sit on floor, arms extended forward, knees bent and feet off the floor. (You should look like an oarsman ready to row.) Bring elbows back (bending them) as you straighten legs without touching feet to floor. (When you are even stronger, rotate legs in circles or do scissors-kick while legs are extended.) Repeat 5 times and work up to 15 to 20 times.

Some of the headaches which are alarm signals for prompt and thorough medical checkup are:

Sudden, severe headache "out of the blue."
Headache associated with fever.
Headache associated with convulsions.
Headache accompanied by confusion or lessening of consciousness.
Headache following a blow on the head.
Headache associated with local pain in the eye, ear, or elsewhere.
Headache beginning in the older person, previously free of headache.
Recurring headache in children.
Headache at any age which interferes with normal living.
Daily or frequent headache.

How do doctors classify headache?

Headache may be classified as acute or chronic. The acute headache occurs suddenly and occasionally, and is an unpleasant part of many illnesses.

Chronic headaches recur more or less frequently, and doctors classify them in various ways, such as:

1. Migraine and other headaches due to blood vessel (vascular) changes

Headaches associated with blood vessel (vascular) changes include the painful *migraine* or "sick" headache and its variations, such as *cluster headache* which is also called *histamine headache*.

Research proved that a temporary narrowing (vasoconstriction) of the blood vessels in the head marks the early painless stage of migraine. Perhaps 8 to 10 percent of migraine patients experience a warning of the impending headache, such as jagged streaks of light or other "fireworks" of vision, numbness, tingling, and perhaps nausea. Some feel weak, tired, or over-excited.

This warning "aura" allows the individual to lie down in a dark, quiet room, or to take immediately the medicine his doctor has prescribed. These means may ward off the threatening head pain.

The second and painful stage begins in minutes or hours with a severe, throbbing, one-sided or two-sided headache, and distended, throbbing arteries sensitized by certain chemical substances. Distension of arteries by the sun or a hot bath

Adapted from *Headache: Hope Through Research*, 1973, Department of Health, Education and Welfare.

ca. **60 B.C.** Gaia Afrania, renowned as the most contentious woman in Rome, is constantly involved in lawsuits and invariably pleads her cases before the judge. Her nearly continuous appearances before the courts may have been responsible for the edict passed thereafter forbidding any woman from arguing in her own defense.

Jane's Headache

does not cause pain unless sensitization of the arteries also occurs. Medicine to contract dilated arteries may end a migraine attack.

A third stage may follow—the steady headache—which is either part of the original migraine attack, or a complicating muscle-contraction (tension) headache resulting from muscles held stiffly in the neck.

2. The muscle-contraction (tension) headache

Undoubtedly the commonest of chronic headaches is the muscle-contraction headache which comes from stiffly set muscles in the neck. A popular name is "tension headache."

The trigger which sets the person to holding these muscles stiffly is some kind of conflict or stress. It could be an emotional conflict when a person or event is hated or viewed with anxiety.

Or, the trigger could be physical—a cold draft from an air conditioner, eye-muscle fatigue, straining to hear because of partial deafness, or pain anywhere in the body. Muscle-contraction headache can complicate other types of headache.

Muscle-contraction headache comes without warning symptoms or signs. It usually affects both sides of the head, or the back of the head and neck, or the forehead, face, or jaw muscles, or a band around the head. The pain is steady or pressing or "tight" rather than throbbing.

Muscle-contraction headache may occur occasionally or frequently. Such a headache at times disappears quickly, at other times lasts for days or weeks. The pain can be mild, or more severe than some "dangerous" headaches.

3. Headaches associated with various structural changes

A small but important group of recurring headaches are associated with a variety of structural changes. These include headaches due to high blood pressure, virus infection, tumors, brain abscesses, defects and malformations of blood vessels, and certain diseases of the neck and spine, and headache related to the menstrual cycle.

In women with migraine, the attacks may appear just before, during, or after the menses. The exact role that hormones play in menstrual migraine is still to be determined. Research indicates that retention of fluid is not the direct and invariable cause of menstrual headache. Recent evidence suggests that falling levels of estradiol (estrogen) may play a role in menstrual migraine but the role is not completely understood.

Headache in persons with *high blood pressure* takes many forms, and can accompany sudden rises of blood pressure. A distinct type of hypertensive headache occurs in the morning upon awakening and eases as the day goes on.

Certain headaches involving structural changes may resemble migraine, adding to the doctor's problem of diagnosis.

4. Some truths about headache

Persons who have headache of unknown cause or after prolonged use of the eyes should have a complete eye examination. Properly fitted glasses, if necessary, and good reading light promote comfort. If discomfort continues after new glasses are fitted, a physician should be consulted promptly.

Headache and constipation are separate results of tension, fatigue, or disrupted routine. There is no scientific evidence that constipation causes headache. Worry about constipation, like other worries, can cause headache.

Chronic sinus trouble is an uncommon headache cause; but acute sinus inflammation often is accompanied by headache.

A severe headache can be a dangerous headache; often it is not.

A mild headache, similarly, could be serious or not serious.

A steady headache is no more and no less likely to be serious than an occasional one.

Excessive use of sedatives, even sedatives for treatment of headache, can be dangerous and might cause a headache. Don't take larger amounts of painkillers than your doctor orders. Don't take sedatives more often or over a longer period than your doctor orders. If you are doubtful of a sedative's effect on you, stop it until you can ask your doctor's advice.

Careless home use of household and garden chemicals can cause a headache. Read the directions carefully and follow the warnings against skin contact and inhaling of household and garden chemicals.

Treatment of headache is not a do-it-yourself project.

Understanding these truths helps patients to avoid wasting time and money going from doctor to doctor. Allowing one doctor the time necessary to solve the sometimes complicated headache problem is usually the best practice.

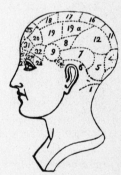

Phrenologist's view

---

ca. **18 B.C.** A series of laws bring marriage under the province of the Roman government, exclude women from public athletic exhibitions, and limit their expenditures on lavish homes, servants, banquets, jewels, and dress.

Women and Smoking

Jane E. Brody and Richard Engquist

New York Public Library

*Woman smoking
(from an old print)*

New York Public Library

"La Charmante Tabagie"

To give up smoking is not easy—except for a few lucky individuals who are able to "take it or leave it alone." Smoking is a habit, and like all habits it must be unlearned, or, to put it another way, replaced with a different habit: nonsmoking.

A continuing decline has been shown in the per capita consumption of cigarettes per day by Americans 18 years and older: 11.73 cigarettes per day in 1967; 11.44 in 1968; 10.94 in 1969; 10.93 in 1970; and 10.86 in 1971.

These impressive statistics should give heart to current smokers who fear they may not be able to quit. Dr. Donald T. Fredrickson, who is Project Director for the Inter-society Commission for Heart Disease Resources in New York City, has helped thousands of people to give up smoking through withdrawal clinics. He says, however, that most smokers don't really need clinics, provided they make a firm decision to break the smoking habit. According to Dr. Fredrickson, it is the decision that is all-important, and it must be a firm decision, reinforced frequently. A California housewife who stopped smoking several years ago, and is glad she did, nevertheless admits that not a single day goes by that she does not want a cigarette. In effect, every day she makes her decision to be a nonsmoker.

But some people really need the support of one other person at least—one who would say, "Let's quit together." As one woman reported, "The first week was rough, but the fact that there were two of us made all the difference."

For most habitual smokers who decide to "quit cold" and do so, there are a few days of acute craving for cigarettes. But within two or three weeks, the desire to smoke has become "occasional." Many researchers—though not all—believe that withdrawal discomfort is mostly psychological rather than physical, for smoking is not an addiction in the sense that the body's biochemistry has been altered by exposure to and subsequent dependence on a drug.

Once learned, the smoking habit can be very strong because smokers tend to use tobacco like a drug—to modulate their feelings. That is, smoking is used as a tranquilizer in times of stress, or to enhance pleasurable situations such as coffee breaks, after meals, and the cocktail hour. Removing the pleasure-enhancing smoke, or the smoke that acts as a safety valve under stressful situations, poses psychological difficulties for the person who is trying to give up smoking. In effect he must concentrate on learning to be a nonsmoker, and this will help to make up for the sense of loss resulting from his giving up the smoking habit.

On the positive side, many people find that they experience no psychological withdrawal pangs, or that the relief of having decided to quit more than makes up for the initial discomfort.

But not all withdrawal discomfort is psychological, for a variety of physical symptoms have been reported by those in the process of breaking the smoking habit. A temporary increase in coughing, for example, may be an indication of the healing process at work, for as soon as smoking is stopped, the body begins to replace damaged tissues. Other physical symptoms, such as shortness of breath, headaches, dizziness, fatigue, and even heart palpitation, probably result from the body's adjustment to a sudden increase in nervous tension. Almost always they subside rapidly, within a few days.

Adapted and reprinted with permission from *Women and Smoking* by Jane E. Brody and Richard Engquist, Public Affairs Pamphlet No. 475. Copyright © 1972 the Public Affairs Committee, Inc.

ca. **9 B.C.** A *Velleda*, or prophetess, of the pagan German tribes confronts the invading Roman commander Drusus on the banks of the Elbe River with a warning that his life is about to end. He scornfully laughs her off, then, weeks later, falls off his horse and dies soon after.

Happily, the discomfort of withdrawal is soon replaced in most cases by a sense of well-being and other distinct benefits, both psychological and physical.

Another side benefit that many ex-smokers have noted is a marked increase in sexual appetite and the ability to perform sexually. Dr. Alton Ochsner reported on several striking examples of this phenomenon in an article in *Human Sexuality*. Dr. Ochsner states that "it has been the observation of many individuals dealing with patients who have discontinued smoking that there is a prompt return in libido, particularly in men and to a lesser degree in women."

And he quotes L. Johnston, who wrote in the British medical journal *Lancet* some years ago, "The symptoms of tobacco smoking become apparent to the sufferer only after the disease has been arrested, and he has given up smoking. An accession of high spirits, energy, appetite, and sexual potency, with recession of coughing, makes the chief symptoms of tobacco smoking plain."

The fear of gaining weight inhibits many people—especially women—from making the effort to stop smoking. Actually, weight gain may not be a serious problem; in fact, many people tend to *lose* weight when they give up tobacco. But there is no question that for some eating becomes a substitute for smoking, and for them the risk of gaining weight is a real one. The health hazard of some increase in weight, of course, is almost nothing compared to the hazard of continued smoking. Actuarial statistics have shown that a person would have to gain 100 pounds before he equaled the health risk of two packs of cigarettes a day.

Aside from the fact that some ex-smokers begin to nibble when they would otherwise reach for a cigarette, there is some evidence that weight gain following withdrawal from smoking is caused by the body's using less oxygen, and therefore metabolizing food at a slower rate. Five Philadelphia doctors who stopped smoking for a month in a test partly supported by the National Institutes of Health found that they gained an average of six and a half pounds. But one of the doctors, who greatly increased his physical activity, gained nothing.

An increase in exercise is virtually a must. Daily physical exercise, increased on weekends, burns calories as well as improving circulation and muscle tone and adding to a sense of well-being.

Part of the problem of increased food intake after withdrawal from tobacco is that food tastes better, and some people respond by going on an eating binge. Weight control is easier if you step on the scale every day and carefully watch your diet, rather than allowing yourself to plunge into an orgy of eating and discovering a month later that you have put on 15 pounds. Removing excess weight is far more difficult than avoiding it in the first place.

For reasons not well understood, women have more difficulty than men in giving up cigarettes. Male ex-smokers outnumber females two to one. Many women quit, but before you know it they are back to smoking again. The weight problem may have something to do with the high relapse rate, but clearly that is not the whole story. Dr. Steinfeld suggests that the housewife who is alone for part or most of the day may turn to the cigarette for companionship. On the other hand, the working woman may use a cigarette in an effort to achieve a sense of equality with her male colleagues. And it is possible that some working wives and mothers seek in cigarette smoking relief from some of the heavy tensions of their several roles.

It also seems that women get a bigger "kick" out of cigarettes than do men, apparently because they are more susceptible to the effects of nicotine.

American Cancer Society

Smoking robot: simulating the smoking manner of humans, this automatic device puffs on cigarettes and collects smoke residue, trapping tars which—when painted on the backs of mice—produce cancer.

American Cancer Society

Two thousand cigarettes (shown heaped on the table) produce the amount of tobacco tar shown in the flask.

---

4 B.C. Mary, bride-to-be of the carpenter Joseph, grows heavy with child. She dispels his suspicions, convincing him of her Immaculate Conception, and the two of them, in turn, convince the high priest.

The most eminent fathers of the Church are skeptical of Mary's claim for the three centuries after Christ's death and, at any rate, do not consider the matter important. Her

The Mind of the Rapist
James Selkin, Ph.D.

The most personal felony follows
a predictable course, from isolating
the victim to testing her docility
to scaring her silent afterward.
Best advice:
resist loudly, firmly—and early.

RAPE IS A SCARE WORD. It arouses in
women almost as much fear as the word
murder, and in a sense it kills both rapist
and victim. The offender dies emotionally because he no longer can express or
feel tenderness or love, and the victim suffers severe emotional damage.

Women have nightmares about being
sexually assaulted, and they anguish over
what to do. They can either resist, hoping
to fend off the rapist; or they can obey his
commands, hoping he will depart without
maiming or killing them. My clinical experience in treating rapists and their victims, and my study of sexual offenders
and their prey, suggests that a woman's
best strategy is to resist, to refuse to allow
her attacker to intimidate her.

Intimidation is the rapist's stock in
trade, a necessary precondition to rape.
Those who say there is no such thing as

rape and sneer that you can't put a pencil
through a moving doughnut, do not understand this. Rapists threaten to kill their
victims, and often brandish weapons to
punctuate their point. The victim has to
cope with this threat. By the time the sexual assault takes place, she often has been
terrorized into cooperating with her assailant or is immobilized with fear.

Emotionally Healthy Resisters. Many
women thwart a rapist by screaming, flee-
ing, or physically resisting. These women
do not differ in age or socioeconomic
status from those who don't resist, but
they do score differently on personality
tests. At the Violence Research Unit at
Denver General Hospital we tested 20
rape victims and 16 women who had successfully resisted attacks, and found the
resisters scored higher on measures of
dominance, sociability, social presence
and communality. Their scores indicated
they felt more socially competent than
the rape victims, and they could express
themselves better, both verbally and physically. The resisters were more self-accept-
ing and had a greater sense of well-being.

These data suggest that women who resist rapists are more socially flexible than
women who don't. They also are more
likely to understand another person's
point of view, including the rapist's. We
also have found that they are less anxious,
less depressed and show fewer symptoms
of psychological stress after the ordeal. So,
women who escape rape seem to have
stronger personalities and, not surprisingly, fare better psychologically after the
attempt than rape victims.

Because men are fairly consistent in
how they go about rape, I have been able
to analyze their strategies and behavior to
show how and why women can successfully resist.

My description, however, is limited to
rape cases in which a woman was approached by a man she had never seen before. More than half of all reported cases
are of this type. Other rapes involve persons who know one another, for example,
neighbors, separated husbands and wives,
fathers and daughters, prostitutes and dissatisfied clients. There are also gang rapes.
These encounters follow different patterns. It is the stranger-to-stranger rape
that women fear most, and it is this type
that follows an identifiable pattern.

Choosing His Victim. First, a potential rapist looks for a woman who is vulnerable to
attack. Rapists differ in defining who is
vulnerable. Some look for victims who are
handicapped or who can't react appropriately or swiftly to the threat of rape. Such
a man might prey upon retarded girls, old
women, sleeping women, or women who
are intoxicated. Between mid-1970 and
mid-1972, almost one fourth of the victims of sexual assault in Denver were under the influence of drugs or alcohol at
the time of the offense.

Still other assailants look for environments that are easily entered and relatively safe. They make certain that the
victim is alone, and that they will not be
interrupted. They often commit their
crimes in the run-down section of town,
where residences are rickety, and where
many women live alone. More than three
fourths of the Denver victims were single
women.

Older homes, converted into apartments, are the easiest residences for a rapist to get into; basement or first-floor
apartments are especially tempting. Two
thirds of Denver's sex offenses that took
place in buildings during a two-year period occurred in the basement or on the
ground floor. Large apartments with door-
men or security guards are the most difficult residences for a rapist to enter.

Rapists often select their victims long
before they actually approach them, and
they may be very consistent in how they
do it. One rapist in Denver always identified single women living alone in a sec-
ond-story apartment with an accessible
window. He used a ladder to reach his victims and to flee the scene.

Rapists may have a sixth sense for identifying women who live alone, or be particularly good at finding streets, empty
laundromats or theater restrooms that are
isolated, but draw unsuspecting victims.

Friendly Women Court Danger. While
housing that is easy to enter and the isolation of the victim are two obvious factors
that make women particularly vulnerable
to rape, women who are characteristically
friendly and who like to help others also
are courting danger. One fourth of the
women in Denver who were attacked by
strangers from 1970 to 1972 were responding to the offender's request for help.
Teachers, nurses and other women who

miraculous conception is bitterly debated during the fourth century A.D., but the
question peaks in the twelfth century when nearly all leading Christian theologians
consider the idea an "absurdity" and the entire Dominican order voices its disbelief. The
Franciscans are true believers, however, and finally, in 1854, the pope declares it to be
fact.

have learned to serve others, be charitable, and give of themselves are especially vulnerable to sexual exploitation.

A woman's first act of resistance should be to refuse to help or be helped by strange men. It is unwise to stop on the street to give a man a light or explain street directions. Women should refuse to let a stranger in their houses to make an emergency phone call or for any other reason. These may be ploys, and there are hundreds of clinical case histories and police offense reports in which a gullible or trusting woman has fallen for such chicanery.

One man in Denver would pull up next to a woman driver parked at a stop light, tell her that her tire was flat, and if she reacted with anxiety or concern, he would gallantly offer to assist her. He would then direct her to follow him to an isolated street off the boulevard. When she stopped her car, he would approach her with a tire iron, threaten her life, and then rape her.

Another rapist would walk into an apartment house and ring several doorbells asking for "Sally." When he found a woman who was helpful, attractive and presumably alone, he would explain how hot and tired he was and ask for a drink of water. Then he asked to use the bathroom so he could look around and make sure the victim was alone. Finally he would ask for a second drink of water and then approach the victim as she stood at the kitchen sink. With a knife at her throat and cut off from help, the victim usually capitulated.

Rapists Test, Then Threaten. These examples illustrate the second and third stages of the rape process, testing and threatening the victim. After finding a vulnerable target, the rapist proceeds, in essence, to ask his victim, "Can you be intimidated?" If she can, he then threatens her life. For instance, a rapist may approach a victim on the streets and ask her for a light. If she provides it, he may ask her an intimate question. If she reacts submissively or fearfully, he knows he has intimidated her and that she likely will submit to his demands.

The testing phase is crucial for the rapist. If he guesses wrong about whether a woman can be intimidated, he will lose the opportunity to rape her. And if he is incorrect about the victim's situation, he may be caught, convicted and sentenced to the penitentiary. So by verbal questions, threats or intimidations such as "Don't scream!" "Don't shout!" "Take your clothes off!" the rapist tests his victim's responses.

Rapists frequently test women on the street or in semipublic places. They make suggestive or insinuating remarks, caress or grab the victim, or gauge her reactions by first robbing her. They can thus easily identify a terrified victim who is ripe for rape.

The safest stance for a woman alone, either on the street or in her home, is to be aloof and unfriendly. This is her first line of resistance to rape.

But when a rapist attacks a woman without warning, climbs into her bedroom while she is asleep or pulls her into a dark alley, she must decide whether to use more direct methods of resistance or to submit. My view is that a clear refusal to cooperate, no matter what form it takes, is by far the best way of repelling a would-be rapist.

The Denver Anticrime Council studied all reported cases of sexual offenses in Denver between 1970 and 1972. These crimes included child molestation, rape attempts, rapes and exhibitionism. In 304 of the 915 cases, women successfully resisted a potential rapist. They resisted in a variety of ways: 24 percent ran away, 18 percent resisted physically, and another 15 percent screamed for help.

Most Rapists Aren't Murderers. It is vital to ask, however, how many women who resist rape are injured seriously or killed. Less than nine percent of the Denver victims sustained anything more serious than a cut or bruise. From 1970 to 1972 there were 140 murders in Denver and only one was a rape murder; in the first 10 months of 1974 there were about 60 homicides and not one was a rape murder. Police officers in Los Angeles report that probably less than one percent of all murders in that city also involve sexual assault. A San Diego police detective could recall only one murder last year in which the victim was sexually assaulted. And in a 1965 study of 1,206 sexual offenses in New Jersey, only nine percent of the attacks involved force by the offenders.

It is important that a woman resist at the very beginning of the attack, when the assailant first makes his intentions known. At this point he has not committed a serious crime, and it's easier for him to look for a more cooperative victim than to struggle to overcome one who has already shattered his hopes for a smooth sex-fantasy trip. Immediate resistance in a residence is most effective because the offender hasn't had a chance to explore the premises to make sure no one else is present.

Officer John Petrosky of the Los Angeles

Police Department stresses the point: "Scream bloody murder," he says. "It will alarm the rapist and hopefully the surrounding community." In cases where the attacker is not armed, officer Petrosky believes the woman should resist physically. "Keep cool, lash out at him with your fingernails, and give him a quick jab in the eyes," says Petrosky, who adds that if a man is armed, each woman has to decide how far she is going to stick her neck out. If he has a gun at her head, it is probably wiser to submit, but if he is coming across the room with a knife in his hand, she has a chance to flee.

An Invitation to Murder. It is necessary to stress the fact that playing along with an assailant to calm his anxiety, and then counterattacking with a kick in the genitals may be an invitation to murder. If a victim first responds passively, the intruder can check the premises to make sure the victim is alone, and that he is in a relatively safe place. Once so assured, he has little compunction about acting out his sexual fantasies on the victim. If she should suddenly resist him or try to hurt him, nothing but his inadequate ego is available to stop him from maiming or murdering her.

I found that in the few reports where victims of sexual assaults were murdered, the act was committed in an environment where the murderer felt very safe and comfortable. The Richard Speck case is a good example of this situation. Seven of his eight victims allowed him to tie and gag them without making a sound. They offered no resistance as he took them one by one into another room and slashed their throats. This heinous crime probably could have been averted if even a few of those girls had screamed, scratched him, or tried to get help.

As we move into the third or threat stage of rape, we find the rapist telling his victim what he wants from her, and what he will do to her if she refuses to cooperate. Most important, he tells her what reward she will receive if she submits. Typically he says he will kill her if she does not cooperate, and he will not hurt her if she does. If the victim is terrified, immobilized or hysterical, the rapist may reassure her. He'll repeatedly promise her that nothing will happen to her if she does as he tells her. He may express concern for her health or future relationships with her husband or boy friend.

Above all, the rapist needs ordered and controlled behavior from his victim. As one rapist explained in John MacDonald's book, *Rape: Offenders and Their Victims:*

ca. **A.D. 7.** Julia the Younger, granddaughter of the Emperor Augustus of Rome, conducts a sensational and much gossiped about intrigue with Silanus, the poet Ovid lending them his villa as a place of rendezvous. When their illicit goings-on are discovered

"I'd try to wake her with caution, want to control her to keep her from becoming too scared . . . I would try to make sure the victim was covered with blankets so I could control her movements when she woke up . . . I'd start talking to her right away as soon as she woke up. 'Be still, be still, don't move, do just exactly what you're told and you won't get hurt. I've got a gun.' These phrases I might repeat several times and interchange, depending on how much resistance I felt from the woman."

Rapist's Fantasies During Sex. The next stage in rape is the sexual transaction itself. Vaginal intercourse occurred in less than half of the rape victims who came to the Denver Hospital Emergency Room; anal or oral intercourse are common. In this fourth stage we can see the rapist's fantasy life in full bloom. Here he imprints his unique personality on the crime. Some assailants will create a false identity and describe a nonexistent person to the victim. Others will reveal their split personalities by telling the victim, "It isn't really me doing this," or "I can't help it."

In my clinical work with rapists, I have found that they fall into two groups. Most are victims of what analysts call ego splits. They are married, young, employed, and living a life that one would not describe as typical of a person who is mentally ill. But their family life is disturbed. They can't relate successfully to their wives or parents; as youngsters they had problems with an older sister or aunt who they say "messed on them."

After the crime these men will deny their behavior. Typically they'll say, "I don't remember. It wasn't me," or "I felt like I was watching a movie." If they don't harm their victims, these rapists often get a suspended sentence or are sent to reformatories where they can get work releases and return to the community in a matter of months. The courts generally give them a second chance on the condition they receive psychotherapy. But if they murder or cut up a victim, they usually receive long prison sentences.

I call the other type of rapist a predator. Often, he's a man who goes into a place to rob it. In the course of the crime he enters a bedroom where he finds a lone woman sleeping. On the spur of the moment he decides to rape her. These men are out to exploit or manipulate others, and sometimes they do it through rape. But most rapists fall into the first category, and it is these men I treat in therapy.

Inadequate Lovers. The rapist who requires his victim to pretend to respond sexually has often failed to please his wife or lover. On a deeper level he may be trying to maintain his shaky defenses about his own sexual inadequacy.

The rapist who boasts about fantasized exploits as a Green Beret is also describing his feelings of weakness and inadequacy. One man in MacDonald's book tells about his own power fantasies, and his need for intimacy with his victim: "I had a complete fantasy life that involved my being stronger than all men, irresistible to all women, a doer of great things . . . I had fantasies about the woman I was raping,

how she felt physically, where she had been in life, some resentment that she'd done things in life without me. I had a longing to do things in general with people. Sometimes I'd verbalize these fantasies if the woman was quite submissive, otherwise I'd just take the trip within myself."

Most rapists have narcissistic and self-centered relationships with women. They have only the tiniest awareness of their partner's social needs or of the social situation itself.

A rapist also writes his diagnostic signature in the sign-off or termination stage of rape. A rapist who assumes the victim will report the crime, terminates the rape by trying to confuse the woman. He'll say, "Don't move until you count to 100," and then he'll go into another room, and slam the door. A minute later he will reenter the room, find the victim has moved, and berate her for failing to follow his directions. Again he will tell her to count, and then he will leave. Other offenders are guilty or apologetic when they leave. They plead for the victim not to call police. Still others threaten future harm if she calls for help.

Keys to Diagnosis. The themes of omnipotence, guilt, fear of retribution, or anger which occur early in the rape process continue in the final leave-taking. These themes affect the rapist's method of operation; they are keys to diagnosing his sickness; and they are educational tools we can use to help potential victims understand what happens in stranger-to-stranger rapes. One hopes that this understanding will help them develop a strategy to avoid it.

The ultimate tragedy in rape is the dehumanization of both victim and assailant. One rapist, lying in jail awaiting sentencing, expressed his own revulsion to his acts: "I wish no harm on anyone. If I cannot overcome my sickness I would not want to live anymore. Suicide is always with me, but I still have hope that I can become a useful member of society. If I cannot overcome this evil in me, if I am to be controlled by this, if somebody else does not kill me, I will kill myself instead of bringing pain on another human being. My death would be sorrow for a few. My evil acts would be sorrow for many."

Unfortunately most rapists can neither admit nor express the fact they are a menace to society. Even convicted rapists who are serving long prison terms deny their culpability. They tenaciously insist women encourage and enjoy sexual assault. These men will tell you they are the greatest lovers in the world.

Bibliotheque Nationale, Paris

Fantasy: woman being carried to libidinous satyr, by L.D. after Primacaccio, 1547

by the emperor, he disgraces and exiles Ovid from Rome and rusticates Julia and her paramour to the seclusion of separate country estates. There Julia will remain isolated until her death, in A.D. 28.

Don't Take It Lying Down

Carole Wade Offir

For years, authorities have warned women that to resist rape is to court death. Yet to submit is to court humiliation.

Many a smirking lawyer has defended his rapist client by arguing that you can't thread a moving needle, implying that if the woman did not resist, she probably "wanted it." Juries will often fail to convict if the victim cannot prove she put up a strenuous fight against her assailant. It's a cruel version of the old double bind.

Now women are beginning to break out of that bind. Most of the credit must go to the women's movement, which encourages women to be self-reliant, to think about the unthinkable and prepare themselves mentally and physically for it. Rape crisis and prevention centers staffed by women, are springing up all over the country. New books, like *Against Rape* by Andrea Medea and Kathleen Thompson, are full of information on how to fight back. Some police departments are giving women pointers about self-defense.

There are certain basic precautions a woman can take. She should be sure the doors and windows of her home lock securely and that there are lights at entrances. If she lives alone or with other women, she should not put her first name on the mailbox or in the telephone book but should use an initial instead, e.g., "C. Smith." If a woman who is alone answers a knock at the door and is not expecting anyone, she might first call out "I'll get it, Jack." The best policy is not to open the door to any strangers.

The cautious woman will also refuse rides from men; as an alternative for female hitchhikers, many women's groups now encourage their members to "Give a Sister a Ride." A woman should not walk alone at night, and should check the back seat of her car before entering it. She should avoid dark streets and parking lots, and stay out of high-crime areas of town if she can. In effect, and unfair as it is, women have to live under a curfew. Until men stop preying on women, the simple freedom to take a stroll after sunset will carry risks.

When a woman is confronted by a rapist, or thinks she is going to be, she should run away if at all possible, preferably toward a populated area. She can also yell; some authorities suggest shouting "Fire!" because that often gets a better response from bystanders than "Help!" or "Rape!" In any case, she should forget about being ladylike, and bellow with everything she's got.

Women who think their voice may fail them can now purchase devices that will make noise. A number of stores carry small whistles that can be worn on a watch band or charm bracelet. One whistle consists of two parts that you separate and throw away to start the device screeching.

There is some disagreement about whether you should try to calm a rapist by talking to him. There are cases where women have talked an assailant out of rape. In other instances, the rapist has been provoked to more violent behavior. But if a woman decides to talk, she should not show fear or submissiveness.

Some women carry arms—guns, knives, or Mace sprays. But carrying a concealed weapon is a crime in most states. In addition, women usually are not versed in the use of a weapon, and the rapist may turn it on his victim. There are many items, though, that women can use effectively against an attacker. A spray of underarm deodorant, perfume or hairspray, or a squirt of concentrated lemon juice from a plastic lemon can temporarily blind a man and give a woman time to flee. These items should be kept accessible, not at the bottom of a handbag. An umbrella, strategically placed, will also do a lot of harm. If you have a lighted cigarette, you can smash it out on his face or in his eyes. All these devices, though, should be used *only* if the attacker is unarmed, and only to gain enough time to flee.

More and more rape counselors are advising women to resist physically, as long as only one man is involved and he is unarmed. Some advocate training in one of the martial arts, like karate, aikido or judo. Courses are available at special schools, universities, local Ys, women's centers, rape crisis centers and other locations.

But Detective Linda Simmons of the San Diego Police Department points out that martial skills take years to master. She believes that for most women, automatic responses like clawing with the fingernails, biting, pulling the man's hair, jabbing him in the neck or solar plexis with an elbow, and giving him a fast, short kick in the crotch are more useful. This kind of fighting does not require any thought or planning, and most women have known how to do it since childhood. A man's ears, eyes, nose, mouth and Adam's apple are especially vulnerable to attack. A woman should not try to fend off an attacker simply by raising her arms, since he can grab them and force her to the ground. If you kick, you must be careful not to lose your balance. It is often better to use one's heels and aim for the knees, shin or instep.

Each woman must use her own judgment and common sense about fighting back. Rape is traumatic, especially when accompanied by the threat of violence, but it is not a fate worse than death. If you do choose to use either a weapon or your body to resist, you must act quickly, without hesitation and with all your strength. A half-hearted struggle is worse than none at all; you must be prepared to hurt your attacker, and to get hit yourself. Once the attacker is distracted, the woman should run as fast as she can. Like Lot's wife, she must not look back.

Most women will never have to defend themselves against a rapist, but a startling number will. There were 51,000 reported rapes in the U.S. in 1973. And, according to educated estimates, the total number would be two to 10 times larger if unreported incidents were included.

In order to get a better picture of what these statistics mean to a woman living in an urban area, PT used crime and census statistics from the city of Los Angeles to compute the probability of confronting a rapist. According to the Los Angeles Police Department, there were 2,205 reported rapes and attempted rapes in 1972. At the last census (1970), there were 1,256,020 women 16 years of age or older residing in Los Angeles. If we make the conservative assumption that there were at least as many unreported as reported cases, then in 1972 the chances of a woman meeting up with a rapist was about 3.5 in 1,000. Since the number of unreported instances is probably larger than we have assumed, this estimate is undoubtedly low. And it does not tell the whole story. If one assumes that most women are not approached more than once, and that the current rate is going to continue, then the chances of a Los Angeles woman meeting a rapist at some time during a 30-year period is about one in 10.

These are the odds a modern woman must live with. She should not take them lying down.

For a more detailed discussion of how the courts deal with rape, see Rape and the Law *on page 438—440.*

---

ca. **A.D. 9.** Anula, lusty and ambitious queen of the usurper King Choranaga of Ceylon, tiring of her mate after fourteen years of wedlock, poisons him and encourages her son (by the deceased King Mahachuli, whom she had deposed beforehand) to at last assume his inherited rights as king. Dominating the youth, Anula will spend the next three years as chief of his wives; then, wearying of him, she will poison him too.

If You Should Be Raped

Andra Medea and Kathleen Thompson

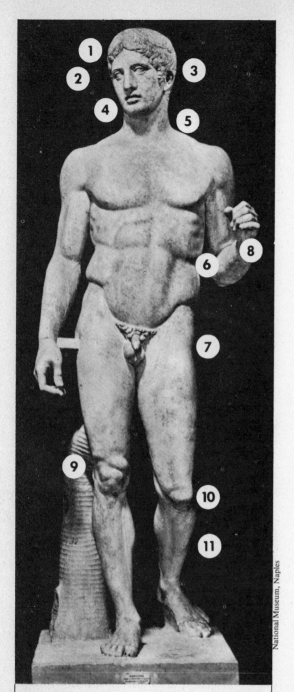

National Museum, Naples

1. **If he leans forward, grab his hair and double him over**
2. **Claw at eyes; use spray**
3. **Blow to ear or temple**
4. **Slam heel of hand up under chin or nose**
5. **Poke to hollow of throat**
6. **Jab to solar plexus**
7. **Snap knee into groin (do not try a kick unless it is very fast)**
8. **Wrench little finger; try to break it**
9. **Kick to kneecap**
10. **If grabbed from rear, bring heel down over kneecap**
11. **Keep kicks aimed low**

During the rape

Stay calm.

Talk sanely, quietly, to remind him you are a human being.

If he asks you a question that you can't answer without exciting him, say something else such as calmly, factually stating, "You're hurting my arms."

Memorize the details of his face and clothing, and describe him to yourself.

Think about something concrete and routine, such as what you should do later.

Don't show any pain or weakness if you can avoid it, for it will only make him more violent.

Whether to report to the police

Can you give a clear description?

Did you know him well?

Did you do anything which could be interpreted as provocative?

How were you dressed?

Do you have bruises?

Did he use a weapon?

Did he commit any other crimes, such as theft?

Do you have the kind of background that will support an investigation?

If reported to the police

Don't take a bath.

If possible, call a friend first, then the police. If the police arrive first, wait until your friend gets there.

Don't take any flak from anybody.

Insist on going to the hospital.

Give as clear and comprehensive a description of your attacker as possible.

At the hospital

Ask for antibiotics for VD.

Consider your medical background before you accept the "morning after" pill.

Have your friend check all medication given you.

If you don't want to report it

Don't take a bath.

Find a friend.

Get yourself to a doctor—you may later decide to report the rape.

Get treatment for VD.

If you must go to a hospital, remember that you don't necessarily have to talk to the police.

ca. **A.D. 10.** Conchobar, pagan ruler of Ireland, announces that henceforth he himself will deflower all virgins in his skingdom as a duty to his subjects. This is to spare his countrymen the risks attending defloration: visitations by demons.

The Heimlich Maneuver to Stop Choking
The Editors of *Emergency Medicine*

If the victim is standing or sitting:

Stand behind him and wrap your arms around his waist. If he is sitting, do this from behind his chair.

Placing your fist thumb side against the victim's abdomen slightly above the navel and below the rib cage, grasp the fist with your other hand.

Press your fist into the victim's abdomen with a quick upward thrust.

Repeat several times if necessary.

The person whose trachea is obstructed by a bolus of food can't breathe, can't speak, turns cyanotic, and collapses. He has only four minutes to live—unless you save him.

If the victim is lying on his back:

Facing him, kneel astride his hips.

With one of your hands on top of the other, place the heel of your bottom hand on the victim's abdomen, slightly above the navel and below the rib cage.

Press with the heel of your hand into the victim's abdomen with a quick upward thrust.

Repeat several times if necessary.

If the victim is lying face down:

Turn him over and proceed as above.

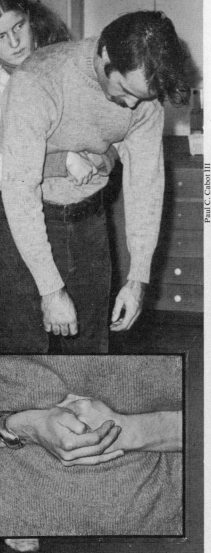

Paul C. Cabot III

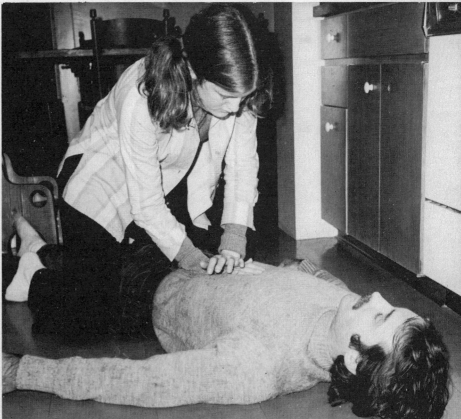

Adapted from *Emergency Medicine*, February 1975. Copyright © 1975 Emergency Medicine. Reprinted with permission. The Heimlich Maneuver was developed by Henry J. Heimlich, M.D., Director of the Jewish Hospital, Cincinnati, OH. For educational materials, brochures, posters, etc., send a stamped, self-addressed envelope to Edumed, Inc., Box 52, Cincinnati, OH 45201.

A.D. 16. Anula, aging queen of Ceylon, has reigned alone for the past four years after having poisoned six paramours. Unexpectedly, her rule is threatened by an armed revolt of her disgusted subjects. The young brother of her second murdered mate emerges from a Buddhist monastery, raises an army, slays Anula, and makes himself king, promising a just reign.

First Aid

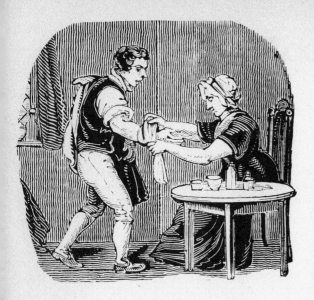

Bleeding. Place sterile pad directly on wound and apply pressure by hand or by bandaging firmly.

Elevate an arm or leg if bleeding does not stop, provided you think no bones are broken.

Use a tourniquet only if a limb is badly crushed, blood is gushing from a wound, or if bleeding is not stopped by a pressure bandage. Place the tourniquet on upper arm or leg between injury and heart. Leave the tourniquet in place until the bleeder has been tied off; if bleeder cannot be tied off, leave the tourniquet in place until physiological amputation is complete. Keep the treatment area as warm as possible.

Control of Bleeding. Serious bleeding must be controlled at once. In only a few minutes, life can ebb away; and without the ability to replace the blood, the life is lost.

Direct pressure compresses will stop most bleeding. Use of a tourniquet under such circumstances may sacrifice a limb or, if improperly applied, may increase the bleeding. Application of strong pressure may be required until the seriously bleeding vessel can be tied off with thread or a fine string. If reasonably sure that the bleeder is in a given bit of tissue, the entire area can be tied off, thus stopping the bleeder. This may be done by using a large needle to pass into the tissue and around the area of severe bleeding and tying the entire mass securely.

Cessation of Breathing. The best form of artificial respiration is the mouth-to-mouth type. It is the only technique which guarantees enough air exchange to revive the unconscious person, and allows the "operator" to insure that the airway is open. If there is an obstruction, air cannot enter the lungs regardless of the method of artificial respiration used.

There are three main causes for obstruction:

1. Liquid, false teeth, or other foreign matter in the mouth or throat.

2. Relaxation of the jaw. The tongue is attached to the jaw so that it falls backward and blocks the throat (called "swallowing the tongue").

3. Position of the neck. When the neck is bent forward so that the chin is near the chest, the throat becomes "kinked" and blocks the passage of air.

Adapted from *Search and Rescue Survival*, 1969, U. S. Air Force.

Pressure Points for Control of Bleeding

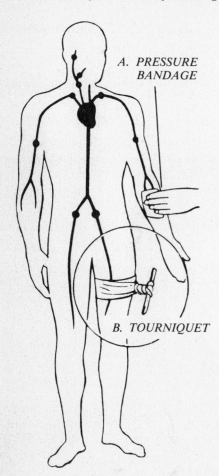

A. PRESSURE BANDAGE

B. TOURNIQUET

BLEEDING BELOW THE KNEE AND ELBOW

A. Place pressure dressing/bandage directly over injury.

B. Place tourniquet just above wound UNLESS bleeding is just below knee or elbow; in which case place tourniquet just above the joint.

BLEEDING IN SCALP ABOVE THE EAR
Light pressure in front of middle ear.

BLEEDING ON OUTSIDE OR INSIDE OF HEAD
Moderate pressure on neck about 3" above collarbone—push artery against spine.

BLEEDING IN THE CHEEK
Very light pressure in notch on under edge of jaw 2/3 back from tip of chin.

BLEEDING IN THE LOWER ARM
Strong pressure on inside of arm halfway between shoulder and elbow.

BLEEDING IN THE ARM
Firm pressure behind the middle of collarbone—push artery against first rib.

BLEEDING ABOVE THE KNEE
Strong pressure in groin with heel of hand—push artery against pelvic bone.

A.D. 19. Occia, one of the sacred vestal virgins of Rome, dies after faithfully discharging the strict duties of her priesthood for fifty-seven years.

To correct any of the above conditions, place the patient on his back looking upwards and hold the lower jaw forward.

Procedure

1. Turn the victim on his back.

2. Clean the mouth, nose, and throat. If the mouth, nose, and throat appear clean, start exhaled-air artificial respiration immediately. If foreign matter such as vomitus or mucus is visible in the mouth, nose, and throat, wipe it away quickly with a cloth or by passing the index and middle fingers through the throat in a sweeping motion.

3. Place the victim's head in the "sword-swallowing" position. The head must be placed as far back as possible so that the front of the neck is stretched.

4. Hold the lower jaw up. Approach the victim's head, preferably from his left side. Insert the thumb of your left hand between the victim's teeth at the midline. Pull the lower jaw forcefully outward so that the lower teeth are further forward than the upper teeth. Hold the jaw in this position as long as the victim is unconscious. A piece of cloth may be wrapped around your thumb to prevent injury by the victim's teeth.

5. Close the nose. Close the victim's nose by compressing it between the thumb and forefinger of the right hand.

6. Blow air into the victim's open mouth with your open mouth with airtight contact. Blow rapidly and forcefully until the chest rises.

7. Let air out of victim's lungs. After chest rises, quickly separate lip contact with the victim, and allow the victim to exhale by himself.

If the chest did not rise when you blew in, improve the support of the victim's air passageway, and blow more forcefully. Repeat the inflations of the lungs 12 to 20 times per minute. You'll need to breathe slightly deeper and faster than usual to get enough air for yourself, but don't worry about this point. Continue rhythmically without interruption until the victim starts breathing or is obviously dead. A smooth rhythm is desirable, but split-second timing is not essential.

If the victim appears to be breathing to some degree, keep his air passageway open until he awakens by maintaining the support of his lower jaw. If his tongue or fingernails are blue rather than pink, he is not breathing adequately and requires assistance.

Although the victim may appear to be breathing because of movement of his chest and abdomen, air may not be moving into his lungs due to complete obstruction of the air passageway from improper positioning of the head and jaw. For this reason, it is most important to determine whether or not there is any movement of air in and out of the mouth and nose by listening closely.

Heart Stoppage. If the heart has stopped, external cardiac massage (manual heart compression) must be given simultaneously with mouth-to-mouth resuscitation.

Manual Heart Compression

1. A few puffs of air should immediately be given by mouth-to-mouth resuscitation as above. (It should be continued by another person; but if there is no one else, you can interrupt massage every 15 to 30 seconds to fill the lungs with air two or three times and then return to the massage.)

2. Place yourself on your patient's right with your left hand on the lower third of his sternum (breastbone) so that the heel of that hand will deliver the pressure. Rest your right hand on the left, fingers pointing to his chin. Your position should be such that your body weight can be used in applying pressure.

3. Apply pressure vertically, downward, approximately once per second so that the patient's sternum moves one and a half to two inches toward his spine.

4. At the end of each stroke, lift your hands so that his chest will expand fully by recoil.

5. After heart action has resumed, manual heart compression should be continued until the pulse is strong.

Shock. A person in shock may have pale, cold skin; they may sweat, breathe rapidly, and have a weak pulse; they may be confused or unconscious.

Lay the patient down flat, with feet raised.

Keep him warm, but not overheated. If he is conscious and not injured internally, give him warm drinks; *do not give alcohol.*

Give oxygen if it is available.

Eye Injury. Clean wound and eye by irrigating with clean water.

To remove a foreign body from the eye, first irrigate with clean water. If not successful, then wind sterile cotton on a match stick to make an applicator. Moisten with clean water and attempt to dislodge the foreign body by several gentle swipes over the affected area. If this is unsuccessful, make no further attempt to remove it.

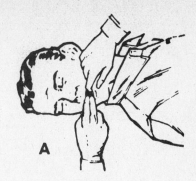
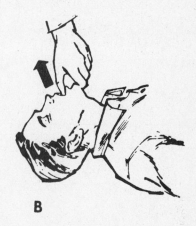

A

B

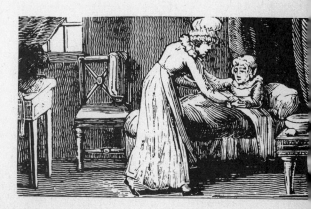

C

Mouth-to-Mouth Resuscitation

ca. **A.D. 20.** Chao-Yun, a waiting woman in the family of Wang Shen, saves her master and other Chinese officials by going in disguise to the mountain encampment of the rebellious Mantzu aborigines. There she so charms the savages with her marvelous flute playing that they are won back to allegiance.

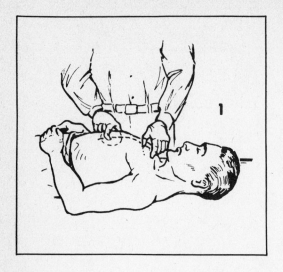

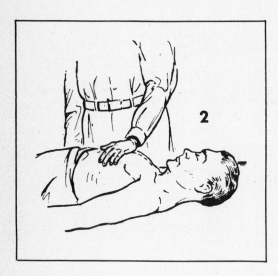

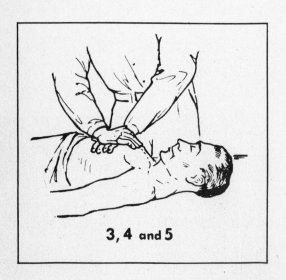

3, 4 and 5

Sprains. Bandage and keep sprained part at rest. Application of local cold may prevent swelling. When swelling has decreased (in 6 to 8 hours) application of local heat will ease pain. Elevate the injured extremity.

If it is necessary to use the sprained limb, immobilize the injured area as much as possible with a splint or heavy wrapping. If no broken bones are involved, a sprained limb can be used.

To Prevent Infection. Cut away clothing necessary to get at a wound. Don't touch a wound with fingers or dirty objects. Don't suck wounds, except snake bites, and then only if there are no cuts or sores in your mouth.

Apply sterile dressing with firm pressure to wound. Tie firmly but not too tightly.

Keep wounded part at rest.

Iodine may be used to sterilize skin areas surrounding a wound but should not be poured directly into an open wound. Let iodine dry in air before applying bandage.

Burns. Burns cause severe pain, often result in shock and infection, and offer an avenue for the loss of body fluid and salts. The initial treatment is directed toward the relief of pain and prevention of infection.

Maintenance of body fluids and salts is essential to the recovery from burns. Administer fluids by mouth. Drink quantities of water following the burn damage.

Don't touch a burned part with fingers. Apply thick gauze pack; bandage firmly. Don't change bandage.

Frostbite. Frostbite is the freezing of some part of the body. As a rule, the first sensation of frostbite is numbness rather than pain. You can see the effects of frostbite, a grayish or yellow-white spot on the skin, before you can feel it.

Get the frostbite casualty into a heated shelter if possible.

When only the surface skin is frozen (frost nip or superficial frostbite), it becomes "spongy" to the touch. It can be rewarmed by body heat. If deeper tissues are involved (deep frozen), the thawing process must take place quickly. Ideally, thawing is accomplished in warm water. Because refreezing of a thawed part means certain loss of tissue, it is better, in some cases, to continue with a frozen part as it is rather than to thaw it when there is a chance of refreezing. Thawing must, however, be accomplished as soon as possible.

Warm the frozen part rapidly. Frozen parts should be thawed in water until soft, even though the treatment is painful. This treatment is most effective when the water is between 105° and 110°F (comfortably warm to a normally protected part such as an elbow). If warm water is not available, wrap the frozen part in blankets or clothing and apply improvised heat packs. Thawed extremities should be immobilized.

Use body heat to aid in thawing. Hold a bare, warm palm against frostbitten ears or parts of the face. Grasp a frostbitten wrist with a warm, bare hand. Hold frostbitten hands against the chest, under the armpits, or between the legs at the groin. Hold a frostbitten foot against a companion's stomach or between his thighs.

When frostbite is accompanied by breaks in the skin, apply sterile dressing. Do not use strong antiseptics such as tincture of iodine.

Never forcibly remove frozen shoes and mittens. Place in lukewarm water until soft and then remove gently.

Never rub frostbite. You may tear frozen tissues and cause further tissue damage. Never apply snow or ice; that just increases the cold injury. Never soak frozen limbs in kerosene or oil.

Do not try to thaw a frozen part by exercising. Exercise of frozen parts will increase tissue damage and is likely to break the skin. Do not stand or walk on frozen feet. You will only cause tissue damage.

Severe Chilling. If you are totally immersed in cold water for even a few minutes, your body temperature will drop. Long exposures to severe dry cold on land can also lower your body temperature. The only remedy for this severe chilling is warming the entire body. Warm by any means available. The preferred treatment is warming in a hot bath. Severe chilling may be accompanied by shock.

Snowblindness. Symptoms of snowblindness are redness, burning, watering, or sandy feeling eyes, the halo one sees when looking at lights, headaches, and poor vision. Remember that snowblindness may not appear until 4-6 hours after exposure. For this reason, it is often not suspected because the symptoms do not appear until well after sunset.

Treat snowblindness by protecting the eyes from light and relieving the pain. Protect the eyes by staying in a dark shelter or by wearing a lightproof bandage.

ca. **A.D. 20.** Chao-Yin, the accomplished and beautiful mistress of the famous Chinese poet, Su Tung-p'om, accompanies her lover on his banishment to Hui-chow in Kwangtung, and there dies with these words on her lips:

"Like a dream, like a vision, like a bubble, like a shadow, like dew, like lightning." A tablet to her memory stands on the shores of the Western Lake.

Relieve the pain by putting cold compresses on the eyes, if there is no danger of freezing, and by taking aspirin. Use no eye drops or ointment. Most cases recover within 18 hours without medical treatment. The first attack of snow-blindness makes the victim susceptible to future attacks.

Carbon Monoxide Poisoning. Carbon monoxide poisoning can be caused by a fire burning in an unventilated shelter. Usually there are no symptoms; unconsciousness and death may occur without previous warning. Sometimes, however, there may be pressure at the temples, headache, pounding pulse, drowsiness, and nausea. Treat by getting into fresh air at once; keep warm and at rest. If necessary, apply artificial respiration. Give oxygen if available.

Heat Cramps. The first warning of heat collapse usually is cramps in leg or belly muscles. Keep the patient resting; give him salt dissolved in water.

Heat Exhaustion. Patient is first flushed, then pale, sweats heavily, has moist, cool skin, and may become delirious or unconscious.

Treat the patient by placing him in the shade, flat on his back. Give him salt dissolved in water.

Heat Stroke. Heat stroke may come on suddenly. The face is red, skin hot and dry. All sweating stops. There is severe headache; pulse is fast and strong. Unconsciousness may result.

Treat the patient by cooling him off. Loosen his clothing; lay him down flat, but off the ground, in the shade. Cool by saturating his clothes with water and by fanning. Do not give stimulants.

Snakebite. If you are bitten, immediately apply a constriction band (tourniquet) only tight enough to shut off venous, i.e., return, flow of the blood between the snakebite and the heart. Then make a single cut parallel to the long axis of the limb about one-quarter inch deep through each fang mark and immediately apply suction over the bite by mouth if there are no open sores in the mouth, and spit out poison immediately. In the moist tropics, instead of making the cuts, use deep massage with the teeth combined with strong oral suction.

Immobilize and splint the injured member. Apply cool compresses to reduce pain, and remain quiet as much as possible. *Don't give alcohol!*

APOPLEXY

Apoplexy, cerebral hemorrhage, or stroke is spontaneous rupture of a blood vessel within the skull, causing a hemorrhage into the brain tissues. It usually occurs in elderly persons.

Besides spontaneous rupture of a blood vessel within the brain, blows to the head may cause cerebral hemorrhage. In all head injuries, symptoms of cerebral hemorrhage should be looked for, and if present, the treatment for apoplexy should be administered.

The patient becomes unconscious gradually or suddenly. Unconsciousness may be preceded by a sense of pressure and pain within the head. When the hemorrhage occurs, blood from the ruptured blood vessel accumulates in the part of the brain near the rupture; as the accumulation increases, there is pressure on the substance matter of the brain, usually leading to paralysis of the part of the body controlled by the section of the brain where the pressure is exerted.

Symptoms

The patient usually is unconscious. The face is flushed and warm but sometimes may appear ashen gray. The pulse at first is slow and strong but later becomes rapid and weak. Respiration is slow and snoring in type, the lips and cheeks puffing out at each expiration. The pupils of the eyes are unequal in size, and often one eyelid droops. Frequently the mouth is drawn to one side, and if the patient tries to talk, he mumbles out of one side of the mouth. Usually only one side of the body is paralyzed.

Treatment

Have the patient lying down with the head well raised by a pillow or good-size pad under the shoulders and head.

Allow plenty of fresh air but keep the patient warm with covers.

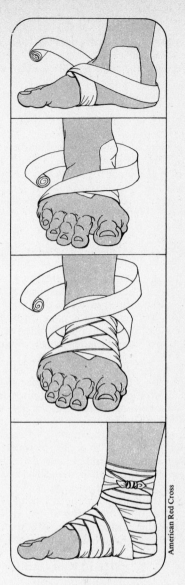

Figure-eight bandage for the ankle

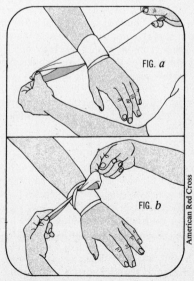

Circular turn, or wrist wrap

Apply cold applications or an ice bag to the head.

Give no stimulants.

Keep the patient absolutely quiet, and do not move him unless necessary.

Obtain medical care as soon as possible.

DIABETIC COMA

Diabetic coma is a state of unconsciousness which results when the body's chemistry is altered due to inability to metabolize carbohydrates. The patient is thrown into a state medically known as "acidosis". If this becomes sufficiently severe, the patient gradually becomes confused, disoriented, and stuporous; and he eventually lapses into diabetic coma.

Symptoms

The face is flushed, the lips are cherry-red in color, the skin is very dry, the temperature is lowered although the patient may look as though he has a fever. Breathing may come in gasps. Characteristically, there is the sickly-sweet odor of acetone (it smells like nail-polish remover) on the breath. Do not confuse it with alcohol. This condition is preceded by excessive thirst, excessive urination, excessive appetite followed by loss of appetite, and increasing weakness leading into drowsiness.

Treatment

A doctor should be called immediately. The immediate need is for the administration of sufficient insulin to correct the acidosis. If a doctor cannot be reached, treat the case as one of shock and administer fluids in large amounts by mouth. If the patient is unconscious, and medical aid cannot be obtained in a short time, a salt solution (1 teaspoon to a glass of water) or bicarbonate of soda in the same concentration should be given, by rectum, in amounts up to two quarts or more. Do not give sugar, carbohydrates, fats, or alcoholic beverages.

Make sure the patient does not "swallow his tongue," and if vomiting occurs, turn the head to one side. He should be placed in a semi-reclining position rather than in a true shock position since a complicating heart condition may also be present.

EPILEPTIC SEIZURES

A epileptic seizure is probably the most common cause of convulsions which are likely to require the services of the first aid man. Quite often, the patient realizes that something is going to happen. He then loses consciousness, falls, and goes into the familiar convulsion. There are severe spasms of the muscle of the jaw. The patient may vomit, or the muscle spasms may force the stomach contents from his mouth. He may also urinate. The face is livid and the veins of the neck are swollen. Breathing is loud and labored with a peculiar hissing sound.

The attack lasts only a few minutes, but sometimes one attack follows another. Usually, however, the patient passes into a deep sleep and awakens with little or no knowledge of what has happened.

Treatment

Keep calm. Do not restrain the person in his convulsions but protect him against injury. Prevent him from biting his tongue in the convulsive spasms of the jaw by placing a protective pad such as a folded handkerchief between the jaws on one side of the mouth. Do not obstruct his breathing. Prevent vomited matter from being sucked back into the lungs. When the jerking is over, loosen the clothing about the neck and allow him to lie flat with the head turned to one side. When the patient recovers, he should rest. If he arises immediately, he may suffer another attack. Give him a drink of water or tea. Protect him from onlookers, and see that he is taken home or to a hospital.

EMERGENCY MEDICAL IDENTIFICATION

All persons with existing medical problems, or who are subject to spontaneous or recurring attacks that should be known in an emergency, should wear some type of identification which will alert rescue personnel, doctors, nurses, and hospital staff members to such conditions. This would include:

1. Persons with known allergies to certain drugs and medications such as penicillin or other antibiotics, horse serum, morphine derivatives, novocain or other anesthetics, barbital, or aspirin.

2. Persons using certain medications, such as antabuse, cortisone, anticoagulants, digitalis, dilantin, insulin, mercupurin, etc.

3. Persons subject to certain physical conditions, such as hemophilia, multiple sclerosis, myasthenia gravis, glaucoma, amnesia, diabetes, and epilepsy.

4. Persons with surgically created conditions, such as a laryngectomy, uretero-intestinal anatomosis, a removed lung or kidney, or an implanted pacemaker.

5. Persons who work as divers, or under elevated pressures; those who wear contact lenses; and deaf-mute persons.

Some of the organizations from whom information may be obtained relative to emergency medical identification are as follows: American Medical Association, American College of Surgeons, American College of Allergists, American Association of Nursing Homes, and Medic Alert Foundation International.

EMERGENCY MEDICAL IDENTIFICATION

prepared by the
AMERICAN
MEDICAL ASSOCIATION
535 N. Dearborn St.
Chicago, Illinois 60610

ATTENTION
In an emergency where I am unconscious or unable to communicate, please read the other side to know the special care I must have.

PERSONAL IDENTIFICATION

Name_____
Address_____
_____
_____
Religion_____

NOTIFY IN EMERGENCY (A)

Name_____
Address_____
_____
Phone_____

Name_____
Address_____
_____
Phone_____

My Doctor is_____
_____
Address_____
_____
Phone_____

MEDICAL INFORMATION
(with date of notation)

Present Medical Problems_____

Medicines Taken Regularly_____

Dangerous Allergies_____

Other Important Information_____

Last Immunization Date
Tetanus Toxoid_____ Polio: Salk_____
Diphtheria_____ Sabin_____
Smallpox_____ Typhoid_____
Others_____

REMEMBER: This is the minimum medical and personal information needed by those who help you in an emergency. It is not designed to be a complete medical record. Check its accuracy with your doctor.

A.D. 30. Saint Veronica, living in Jerusalem on the route taken by Christ and his condemned companions to crucifixion, is—as legend has it—in the crowd gathered to watch the sorry procession. Seeing Jesus stagger past, bearing his cross and covered with blood, sweat and dust, she impulsively runs to him with her kerchief to wipe his face.

Pretty Poisons

The Editors of *Consumer Contact*

Plants—in gardens, fields, forests and homes—are often pretty but sometimes poisonous.

While meaningful figures on plant poisonings are hard to get (the government doesn't count every kid's sore tummy) the possible danger to health can't be ignored.

Poisonous plants may harm a person in four ways. They may cause:

(1) stomach and intestinal irritation
(2) poisoning of the system
(3) mouth and throat lining irritation
(4) skin irritation

The seriousness of plant poisoning will usually depend upon the amount swallowed. For some plants, even a small amount can be dangerous.

Points to remember about poisonous plants:
- **Learn about those in your area that could cause harm;**
- **Don't eat wild plants, including mushrooms, unless you are sure of their identity and safety;**
- **Don't brew home-made medicines from plants;**
- **Teach children how to recognize the most common poisonous plants, such as poison ivy. Tell them not to eat unknown plants, or to suck plant nectar, and not to play with plants. Keep plant seeds and bulbs well away from small children.**

 The list of common toxic plants below indicates the hazards that may be present. The numbers represent the effects we have listed above.

HOUSE PLANTS
Caladium (3 & 1)
Castor Bean (1 & 2)
Dieffenbachia (3 & 1)
Elephants Ear (3 & 1)
Lantana (2)
Mistletoe (1 & 2)
Poinsettia (4)
Philodendron (3 & 1)

FIELD PLANTS
Buttercup (1)
Death Camas (2)
False Hellebore (2)
Poison Hemlock (2)
Pokeweed (Inkberry) (1 & 2)
Snow-on-the-Mountain (4)
Thornapple (Jimsonweed) (2)
Poison Ivy (4)

VEGETABLE GARDEN
Potato (new shoots) (2)
Rhubarb (leaf blade) (2)

FLOWER GARDEN PLANTS
Autumn Crocus (Meadow Saffron) (2)
Christmas Rose (1 & 4)
Foxglove (leaves & seeds) (2)
Golden Chain (2)
Daffodil (1)
Hyacinth (1)
Iris (Blue Flag) (1)
Larkspur (Delphinium) (2)
Lilly-of-the-Valley (2)
Monkshood (2)
Morning Glory (2)
Narcissus (1)
Snowdrop (1)
Sweet Pea (in large amounts) (2)

ORNAMENTAL PLANTS
Daphne (1)
Mountain Laurel (2)
Rhododendron (2)
Wisteria (1)
Yew (1)

TREES AND SHRUBS
Black Locust (1 & 2)
Box (1 & 2)
Cherry (twigs, leaves and bark) (2)
Elderberry (Black Elder) (2)
Horsechestnut (1 & 2)
Privet (1)

MARSH PLANTS
Cowslip (Marsh Marigold) (1)
Skunk Cabbage (3 & 1)
Water Hemlock (cowbane) (2)

FOREST PLANTS
Baneberry (1 & 2)
Bloodroot (1 & 2)
Fly Agaric Mushroom (2)
Deadly Amanita (2)
Jack-in-the-pulpit (3 & 1)
Moonseed (2)
Mayapple (1)
Poison Ivy (4)
Poison Oak (4)

A number of other poisonous plants also are grown indoors.

Adapted from *Consumer Contact*, 1973, Consumer and Corporate Affairs, Government of Canada.

Jesus momentarily takes the "napkin" with one hand and presses it to his face, then returns it to the compassionate woman. It is miraculously marked with the exact imprint of his features. The kerchief eventually becomes one of the holiest relics of the Church, and is claimed to be capable of working miracles.

Dangerous Drug Combinations

Ruth Winter

A successful working wife and mother attended an after-theater party where she had a number of cocktails before going home. Hoping for a restful night's sleep after a busy, exciting day, she swallowed several sleeping pills. It was the last thing she ever did.

An aging business executive, depressed by the combination of waning sexual powers and young lions biting at his corporate heels, swallowed a prescribed antidepressant capsule, and sat down to a gourmet lunch hoping to forget his troubles. He sipped wine, nibbled Camembert cheese and keeled over, paralyzed on one side of his body.

A young housewife, fighting the pressures of caring for small children, a busy husband and an isolated sub-

The Scream, by Eduard Munch

Oslo National Gallery

urban household, awoke one morning with a bad cold. She took a tranquilizer for her nerves, aspirin and an antihistamine for her cold, an appetite suppressant to help her lose weight and a birth control pill. On the way back from driving her husband to the railroad station, she wrapped her car around a tree.

These three people all made an increasingly common but exceedingly dangerous mistake. They swallowed chemicals that are individually beneficial but lethal in combination.

Americans are the biggest pill-poppers in the world. We swallow thirty-seven billion doses of tablets, powders and elixirs each year. More than a billion drug prescriptions were filled during 1970—a rate of five for every man, woman and child—double the number of just ten years ago.

In addition to taking prescribed medications, many people swallow over-the-counter preparations, inhale and ingest chemical pollutants, drink alcoholic beverages and eat rich food —all of which can cause complicated chemical interactions and unexpected physical effects.

Dr. Raymond Randall, a Mayo Clinic endocrinologist, maintains the big problem today is "that many people take vitamin pills, tranquilizers and birth control pills by habit—just like cleaning their teeth. They don't think of these pills as medication and often neglect to tell the examining doctor about them."

Which examining doctor? That is another complication. Formerly, the same family doctor cared for all a patient's ills and prescribed all his medications. Now, Americans hop from doctor to doctor, taking each symptom to a different specialist who prescribes a new medication.

Dr. Walter Alvarez, a retired Mayo Clinic physician, tells about a woman who came to see him complaining that she couldn't stay awake. She had even slept in the taxi on the way to his office. He discovered that she had

been to see six different specialists, including a neurologist and a dermatologist, and that each had observed her nervousness and prescribed a tranquilizer. She'd taken them all— simultaneously. "I'm surprised she could stay awake long enough to swallow them," said Dr. Alvarez.

Failure to discontinue one medication when starting another for the same illness is a common cause of adverse reactions to drugs. Even more complicated is the interaction of dissimilar drugs prescribed for different purposes. The majority of drugs are metabolized by liver enzymes that detoxify and break them down into usable form. In healthy adults, the activity of drug-metabolizing enzymes remains fairly constant, but disease or poor nutrition modify this capacity. Drug tolerance is also affected by genetic factors, age, weight and sex. In newborns, for instance, the liver enzymes are absent or minimally active, making babies especially sensitive to drugs.

Complicating the interaction problem still further is the fact that as many as two hundred drugs—phenobarbital being the most common— speed up metabolism by increasing the synthesis of enzymes. Phenobarbital taken along with another drug, therefore, can make the second less effective. In one tragic example, a sixty-year-old man hospitalized with a heart attack was given phenobarbital to calm him down and induce sleep. He was also given an anticoagulant to prevent his blood from clotting and producing another heart attack. His blood's clotting time was carefully measured as the dosage of anticoagulant was built up to effective levels. Doses larger than usual were made necessary by the phenobarbital's enzyme-stimulating properties. When the man was discharged from the hospital, he was given a prescription and instructed to continue taking anticoagulants. Since he was home in his own bed, he didn't think he needed

ca. **A.D. 35.** Cheng Tse and Cheng Erh, two sisters, lead an uprising in Tonking to free the region from Chinese imperialism. Their undisciplined army is shortly overwhelmed, and the sisters are put to death.

70 Incompatible Drugs
THE HEALTH ADVISER

This is only a sampling of some of the most common drug interactions.   *No action should be taken without checking with your own doctor.*

TRANQUILIZERS	combined with	interaction
Diazepam derivatives (Librium, Valium, Serax, etc.) and meprobamate (Miltown)	alcohol	increases effects of both
	barbiturate	increases effects of both
	MAO-inhibiting antidepressants (Nardil, Parnate, Marplan, Eutonyl)	oversedation
	phenothiazine tranquilizers (Thorazine, Compazine, etc.)	increases effects of both
	tricyclic antidepressants (Elavil, Aventyl, Tofranil, Pertofrane)	increases effects of both
Phenothiazines (Thorazine, Mellaril, Compazine, etc.)	alcohol	oversedation
	antihistamine	increases effects of both
	antihypertensive drugs	increases blood-pressure-lowering action
	barbiturate	increases sedation
	MAO-inhibiting antidepressants (Nardil, Parnate, Marplan, Eutonyl)	makes antidepressant less effective
	Demerol	increases sedation
	diazepam derivatives (Librium, Valium, etc.)	increases action of both
	thiazide diuretics (Diuril, HydroDiuril)	causes shock
	tricyclic antidepressants (Elavil, Aventyl, Tofranil, Pertofrane)	increases action of both

ANALGESICS	combined with	interaction
Aspirin	anticoagulant	increases the blood-thinning effect and could cause bleeding
	para amonosalicylic acid (PAS)	makes PAS toxic
Meperidine (Demerol)	MAO-inhibitor antidepressants (Nardil, Parnate, Marplan, Eutonyl)	increases action of Demerol
	phenothiazine tranquilizers (Thorazine, Compazine, etc.)	increases sedation
Phenylbutazone	anticoagulant	increases the blood-thinning effect and could cause bleeding
	oral antidiabetic drugs (Orinase, Diabenese)	may make the blood sugar too low

ANTIHISTAMINES	combined with	interaction
Diphenhydramine (Benadryl), chlorpheniramine (Chlor-Trimeton), dimenhydrinate (Dramamine), promethazine (Phenergan) and others	alcohol	increases sedation
	barbiturate	nullifies both
	hydrocortisone	lessens effect of hydrocortisone
	phenothiazine tranquilizers (Thorazine, Compazine, etc.)	increases effects of both
	reserpine	depresses central nervous system
	anticholinergics (slows intestinal movement)	makes the anticholinergic more potent

ANTIDEPRESSANTS	combined with	interaction
MAO-inhibitors (Marplan, Nardil, Parnate, Eutonyl)	alcohol	increases depression of central nervous system
	amphetamine	increases effect of amphetamine
	barbiturate	makes barbiturate more potent
	Demerol	makes Demerol more potent
	diazepam tranquilizers (Librium, Valium, etc.)	increases effect of tranquilizer markedly
	thiazide diuretics (Diuril, HydroDiuril)	lowers blood pressure and increases action of MAO-inhibitor
	tricyclic antidepressants (Elavil, Aventyl, Tofranil, Pertofrane)	increases effects of both
Tricyclic antidepressants (Elavil, Tofranil, Aventyl, Pertofrane, etc.)	diazepam derivatives (Librium, Valium, etc.)	increases effects of both
	phenothiazine tranquilizers (Thorazine, Compazine, etc.)	increases effects of both
	reserpine	lessens effect of reserpine

ANTIBIOTICS	combined with	interaction
Tetracycline	penicillin, antacid or milk	makes tetracycline less effective
Penicillin G	chloramphenicol (Chloromycetin), antacid or tetracycline	makes penicillin less effective
Griseofulvin (Fulvicin, Grisactin, Grifulvin)	anticoagulant	may make the anticoagulant less effective
	phenobarbital	makes griseofulvin less effective
Sulfonamide	antacid	makes sulfa less effective
	anticoagulant	makes the anticoagulant more potent
	antidiabetics (Dymelor, Orinase, Diabenese)	makes antidiabetics too powerful
Furazolidone (Furoxone)	alcohol	lessens bacterial action of drug and could skyrocket blood pressure
	amphetamine	increases effect of amphetamine
	barbiturate	increases action of the barbiturate
	MAO-inhibitor antidepressants (Nardil, Parnate, Marplan, Eutonyl)	increases effects of both
	phenothiazine tranquilizers (Thorazine, Compazine, etc.)	increases effects of tranquilizers
	tricyclic antidepressants (Elavil, Aventyl, Tofranil, Pertofrane)	increases effects of antidepressant

DRUGS THAT MAY INTERACT WITH ALCOHOL

Antibacterials—inhibits germ-killing action of antibacterials.

Antidiabetic agents (including insulin)—may lower blood sugar to dangerous levels. Insulin also increases the effects of alcohol.

Antihistamines—depresses central nervous system.

Antihypertensives—increases the blood-pressure-lowering effect of drugs.

Antidepressants—increases the effect of alcohol and depresses the central nervous system.

Tranquilizers—affects coordination and depresses the central nervous system.

Sedatives and hypnotics—causes oversedation and depression of the central nervous system.

FOOD INTERACTIONS

Milk and dairy products combined with antibacterials (such as tetracycline) make the antibacterial less effective.

Aged cheese, broad beans, chocolate, bananas, passion fruit, pineapples, tomatoes and *lemon* combined with MAO-inhibiting antidepressants cause blood pressure to increase to dangerous levels.

Soybean preparations, Brussels sprouts, cabbage, cauliflower, kale, turnips, peaches, carrots and *pears* may enlarge thyroid glands in susceptible people and make thyroid tests inaccurate.

DRUGS THAT MAY CAUSE SKIN ERUPTIONS WHEN PATIENT IS EXPOSED TO THE SUN

Antibacterial sulfas.
Antidiabetic drugs like Orinase and Diabenese.
Thiazide diuretics such as Diuril and HydroDiuril.
Tranquilizers, including Librium and Compazine, among others.
Antihistamines, particularly Benadryl.
Anti-itching preparations.
Antibiotics, including Aureomycin and Terramycin.
Antifungal agents.
Birth control pills.

ca. **A.D. 37.** Caligula, Emperor of Rome, institutes the *vectigal,* or tax paid by all persons subsisting by prostitution—a custom which is continued profitably by all succeeding Roman emperors down to Theodosius. A contemporary writer describes the

Incompatible Drugs
THE HEALTH ADVISER

phenobarbital any longer, but without its inhibiting effect, the dose of anticoagulant was too high and he suffered a severe hemorrhage.

On the other hand, drugs like allopurinol (Zyloprim), prescribed for gout, and nortriptyline (Aventyl), prescribed for depression, inhibit enzyme production and make other drugs more toxic. Dr. Elliot S. Vesell, chairman of the Department of Pharmacology, Hershey Medical Center, Hershey, Pennsylvania, believes that physicians whose patients are taking these drugs should monitor the drug levels in their blood, and adjust dosages to prevent the extremes of toxic accumulation or undertreatment.

When phenobarbital, nortriptyline or any other drug that acts on the central nervous system is taken with alcohol, the results may be dire (as in the case of the working wife mentioned earlier). Yet vast numbers of Americans drink alcoholic beverages, and some two hundred twenty million prescriptions for various tranquilizers, amphetamines, barbiturates (sleeping pills) and related psychopharmaceuticals are written every year.

The type of alcohol, the speed at which it's consumed and the amount of food eaten with it all affect the body's reaction to other drugs. The higher the concentration of alcohol in the beverage, the faster it is absorbed. Thus, vodka and gin are absorbed most rapidly and table wines and beers most slowly. Presence of food in the stomach may reduce the peak amount of alcohol in the blood by as much as 50 percent.

Alcohol is also absorbed more readily if the emptying of the stomach is hastened by fear, anger, stress or nausea. And the less a person weighs, the more concentrated the alcohol in his blood will be. Doctors have found that drinkers of hard liquor suffer more severe alcohol-drug comas than those who drink only beer and wine. They attribute this to the fact that hard liquor not only causes higher blood-alcohol levels, but also irritates the stomach, which, in turn, promotes more rapid absorption of the drug.

Alcohol increases the action of many antihistamines, tranquilizers and drugs like reserpine (for lowering blood pressure) and scopolamine (contained in many over-the-counter sleeping and nerve preparations), making such combinations extremely dangerous. Severe damage to the nervous system and even death has resulted when diabetics combined alcohol and insulin. Alcohol has also been reported to nullify the benefits of certain antibiotics and anticoagulants.

Staying away from dangerous alcohol-drug combinations is not as easy as it may seem. Many people fail to realize that a large number of over-the-counter preparations—such as liquid cough medicine, antihistamines and tonics—all contain appreciable amounts of alcohol. Physicians prescribing drugs with the potential for interaction with alcohol may not know that their patients are also taking over-the-counter products containing alcohol.

Alcohol and drugs are not the only culprits. Some foods also contain chemicals that may interact with drugs. The antidepressant that the aging business executive swallowed was an inhibitor of monomine oxidase (MAO), an enzyme that

helps to control blood pressure. Both the aged cheese he ate and the wine he drank contained pressor amines, which raise blood pressure. Without the controlling effect of MAO, these amines skyrocketed his blood pressure and caused a stroke. Significant amounts of pressor amines are also present in certain yeast extracts, some broad beans, bananas, herring, passion fruit, pineapples, tomatoes, licorice and lemons. The effect they have when combined with MAO-inhibiting drugs depends upon how much is eaten and how much amine is released in the digestive process.

Anyone taking female hormones (estrogen and progesterone), male hormones androgens) or corticosteroids should consult with his doctor before taking any other drugs—including such common ones as antihistamines and barbiturates. Some drugs decrease the effect of the hormones, while others are, themselves, nullified by hormones.

People with stomach trouble often destroy the effectiveness of certain stomach-soothing drugs by taking antacids. Colloidal antacids such as aluminum hydroxide gel (Gelusil, Maalox, Wingel, Estomul and others) can cause malabsorption of the phenothiazine tranquilizers (Thorazine, Compazine, Sparine, Stelazine, etc.). Such people also invite disaster by taking more than one drug that slows intestinal activity.

Few drugs have but a single specific action. Most have several effects on the body. According to Dr. Edward S. Brady of the University of Southern California School of Pharmacy, the prime problem of drug interaction is "the assignment of a single function to drugs by the person who uses them."

A number of drugs have secondary intestine-slowing action. These include antihistamines, tricyclic antidepressants (Elavil, Tofranil, Aventyl, Pertofrane, etc.) and meperidine-like analgesics (Demerol, Mepergan). Nitrates—preservatives in food and pollutants of water from fertilizers—also slow down the intestines. Severe constipation, dryness of the mouth and even fatal paralysis of the intestines have been reported when more than one intestine-quieting drug has been taken.

That generally innocent drug, aspirin, which Americans gulp at the rate of twenty to thirty tons a day, also affects the gastro-intestinal tract and interacts with other drugs, according to studies by Dr. Gerhard Levy of the State University of New York at Buffalo. Aspirin may also inhibit the elimination of additional drugs from the body. And although aspirin is effectively used by many arthritics, when it is taken along with such anti-arthritic drugs as phenylbutazone (Butazolidin) or indomethacin (Indocin), the patient's susceptibility to ulcers may be increased—all three drugs irritate the lining of the stomach.

Aspirin also can cause a 50 percent decrease in salt excretion for three to four hours. This effect, reported by pharmacist Mickey McDougal in an article in *The Journal of the American Pharmaceutical Association,* suggests that people on low-salt diets, diuretic therapy or digitalis (heart stimulant) should take aspirin only under medical supervision. Those on anticoagulants should also be careful, for aspirin augments the anti-blood-clotting ability of these drugs—a situation that can

lead to hemorrhages.

Sun and certain drugs make unpleasant, if not exactly dangerous, combinations. Commonly prescribed antihistamines, antibiotics and tranquilizers, for instance, sometimes cause skin reactions when patients taking them are exposed to direct sunlight for any length of time. Birth control pills also seem to increase the incidence of dark skin blotches (similar to the so-called mask of pregnancy) in susceptible women.

Not all drug combinations are bad. Doctors have been highly successful in prolonging the lives of leukemia and other cancer victims with combinations of drugs that individually could not do the job. Resistant kidney disease is also responding to drug combinations in cases where single drugs were ineffective.

Although relatively few drug interactions are known to have practical applications in human drug therapy, Dr. Jean Weston of the National Pharmaceutical Council says, "More are becoming apparent all the time. It should be noted as well that drug interactions may eventually be used with benefit to the patient if the knowledge available is used effectively."

In the meantime, the unwise combinations are so vast that many researchers feel only computers will be able to keep track of them. Dr. John Voigt, Director of Pharmaceutical Extension Service at Rutgers University, warns against taking any drug unless you are really sick. "Drugs are foreign to the body and basically affect the liver and kidneys," he says. Dr. Voigt also believes that it's one of the coming responsibilities of the local pharmacist to keep a patient's drug record and to alert doctors and patients to possible adverse drug interactions.

Leo Dubrow, past president of the New Jersey Pharmaceutical Association, believes record keeping is a good reason for families to patronize one pharmacy. He told of a woman given a diuretic by her internist because of her heart disease. Her eye doctor prescribed another diuretic because she had pressure in her eye due to glaucoma. Her pharmacist knew from her record that she was already taking a diuretic and might become seriously ill by taking another. He alerted her eye doctor and treatment was altered accordingly without alarming the patient.

Unfortunately, not all drug store customers are that lucky. Anyone who takes any medication for any reason would do well to heed the following advice of Dr. Edward Brady:

1. Tell your doctor about all medications you're taking, even infrequently used over-the-counter drugs.

2. If you change doctors, do not take any of the former physician's prescriptions without checking with the new doctor.

3. Avoid self-treatment with nonprescription drugs while taking prescription drugs.

4. Do not take old prescription drugs. Self-diagnosis and self-treatment with possibly decomposed drugs are always dangerous.

5. Do not trade medicines with friends or relatives with similar symptoms. Their drug needs may be entirely different.

To these, Dr. Voigt adds a sixth: "Do not take any drugs if you are going to a cocktail party."

imperial agents hunting for prostitutes in baths, taverns, and bawdy houses, forcing them to purchase, by tax payment, the right to pursue their calling. The women's complaints, according to this source, are frequent and loud.

Cut the Cost of Prescription Drugs

The Editors of *Consumer Reports*

According to the Consumer Price Index of the Bureau of Labor Statistics, the price of prescription drugs in the U.S. has been rising at a much slower pace than other consumer goods. It has risen only about 4 per cent in the past year and 4½ per cent in the past five years. But those figures are deceptive. The CPI measures a relatively fixed "market basket" of drug products. It was not designed to reflect the impact of expensive new drugs that replace cheaper ones.

Until a rational drug marketplace is developed in the U.S., consumers must fend for themselves when buying prescription drugs. To help you cut prescription costs now, CU offers the following advice:

■ **Ask your doctor to prescribe a drug by its generic name.** As we noted earlier, generic drugs tend to be substantially less expensive than brand-name drugs. Although a pharmacist may not actually sell you the least expensive form of the drug, the CEP study uncovered this interesting fact: Pharmacists often charge less for a generic prescription than for a brand-name prescription *even when the same product from the same manufacturer is used to fill both.*

■ **Ask your doctor to specify the manufacturer who sells the cheapest equivalent product.** That will assure you the lowest-cost therapy, provided the druggist passes on the savings. Unfortunately, price information is not readily available to doctors. But they can try to obtain it by consulting pharmacists, pharmaceutical company representatives, and by obtaining catalogs from generic drug companies. Under the HEW reimbursement plan, price information would be published at least once a year for all physicians and pharmacists and made available to the general public.

■ **If you are going to continue a specific drug for a long period, ask your doctor to prescribe it in a large quantity.** Large-quantity prescriptions are generally more economical and will save repeated trips to the pharmacy. But be sure to check the expiration date of the product with the druggist. If the date will fall before you are scheduled to use up the drug, you should buy a smaller quantity. To preserve the life of a drug as long as possible, ask the pharmacist about the best method of storage.

■ **Shop around.** Numerous surveys, including CU's ("What's the Price of an Rx Drug," CONSUMER REPORTS, May 1970), have documented a wide difference in drug prices from store to store in the same city. But many states restrict retail advertising of prescription-drug prices. So you may have to shop for price. If you prefer to shop by telephone, you may be able to find out drug price information without leaving your home. Organizations that are interested in consumer issues may wish to conduct price surveys of commonly prescribed drugs at local pharmacies.

If it's not an emergency situation, ask a number of pharmacists the cost of a prescription before you have it filled. If it's a generic prescription without a manufacturer specified, ask for the least expensive version of the drug.

If you live in California, Michigan, Minnesota, New Hampshire, New York, Texas, Vermont, Washington, or the city of Boston, your drug shopping will be made somewhat easier by posters listing the prices of the top-selling prescription drugs (though you may have trouble ferreting out the posters in some stores). Price-posting is mandatory in Boston and those eight states; in some other states it is permitted but not required. If your prescription is for a drug not listed on the poster, you'll have to ask for its price.

Wherever you live, inquire about discounts sometimes given routinely to the elderly and to other special categories of patients—but first find out the standard consumer price.

While this report has emphasized drug prices, you should also consider what pharmaceutical services you want—credit, home delivery, personal attention, 24-hour availability in case of emergency, records of your purchases, for example. Such services may be available only at pharmacies that price prescriptions on the high side to cover the extra expense. Only you can decide if such services are worth higher prices.

A.D. 41. Saint Paul states, in recommending celibacy over marriage, "It is good for a man not to touch a woman." He continues, "The unmarried women cares for the things of the Lord, that she may be holy in both body and spirit, but she that is married cares for the things of the world and how she may please her husband."

The No-nonsense Approach to

Any skin, regardless of the problems it may have, requires *cleansing, oil-balance control,* and *toning.*

The overview of skin-care products that follows is a guide through the labyrinth of modern beauty products in the light of 20th-century biology and medicine.

CLEANSING

Cleansing removes the outer layer of dead cells, stale oil, perspiration, and soot from the skin's surface. If this layer is not removed, the skin looks dull and flaky. The oil glands can block up and form whiteheads and

pimples, even in normally dry skin.

Of the huge array of products offered for cleansing, each has different properties and should be applied to different types of skin.

SOAP: Used as early as 200 A.D., soap is the oldest and still the most common kind of cleanser. Basic toilet soap consists of a mixture of fat, alkali salt, and water. Frequently, coconut oil or palm kernel oil is added for lathering. Soap removes the dry, dead cells that coat the skin's surface, and dissolves stale oil and dirt. Special ingredients are often added to give soaps unique properties.

Whatever soap you choose, work it into a lather in your hands and spread it on your already moist face. People with normal or oily skin may use a washcloth. Rub the soap thoroughly over the face and rinse off just as thoroughly. The rubbing motion helps to loosen the dead cells and dissolve the grease.

Superfatted soap, containing extra amounts of oil and fat, is good for people with normal or slightly dry skin. The increased fat and oil content interferes with the soap's ability to remove oil and, as a result, some oil remains and dry skin is in less danger of becoming dehydrated.

Castile soap contains olive oil as its main fat. It is no less drying or richer than basic toilet soap.

Transparent soap, made with glycerin and alcohol—both of which draw water from the skin—is best for people with normal skin.

Deodorant soap contains antibacterial chemicals that kill the bacteria present on the skin's surface. Under normal circumstances these bacteria feed on the perspiration from the apocrine glands, changing it from an odorless liquid to its characteristic pungent state. Since there are no apocrine glands on the face, these

Peter Costello

Adapted from *The Medically Based No-Nonsense Beauty Book* by Deborah Chase. Copyright © 1974 Deborah Chase. Reprinted by permission of Alfred A. Knopf, Inc. as seen in *Ms.* Magazine.

ca. **A.D. 105.** Soranus of Ephesus, renowned Greek physician, writes one of the earliest treatises on obstetrics, care of the new mother, and infant feeding.

Cleaning Your Face

Deborah Chase

soaps serve no special purpose for that part of the body.

French milled soap has been specially processed to reduce alkalinity. A low alkalinity makes the soap less drying to the skin.

Floating soap floats because it contains extra water and has air trapped in it. It has no special properties for the skin.

Detergent soap is synthetic or "soapless" soap. Although the word "detergent" conjures up an image of harsh chemicals, just the reverse is often true. The cosmetic chemist can adjust the properties of a detergent soap to make it less alkaline, less dehydrating, and less irritating than plain soap to sensitive skin.

Soap with fruit, vegetable, or herb extracts is very popular today. These additives rarely enhance the cleansing properties of a soap. Their only value is the appeal of fresh fruit, vegetables, or herbs to the senses. Whatever vitamins or enzymes these ingredients may possess in the raw state are usually destroyed in the manufacturing process.

Cocoa butter soap uses cocoa to provide the basic fat ingredient in the soap. This fat, while not giving any special property to the soap, has sometimes been associated with skin allergies.

CREAM AND LOTION CLEANSERS: *Cold cream*, the simplest and most commonly used cleansing cream, is made up of mineral oil, wax, and borax. When cold cream is rubbed on the skin, it dissolves the oils on the surface and loosens the superficial dead cells. When the cream is taken off with tissues, the oil and cells are removed, but an oil film that contains some dirt may remain.

Cleansing cream is made of wax, mineral oil, alcohol, water, and some kind of soap or detergent. Cleansing cream is rubbed on the face and the excess is taken off with tissues. After this treatment the skin may feel sticky and unclean because thick cream, when rubbed on the skin, cannot create enough friction to remove the dead cells, which clump together and remain on the skin's surface. In addition, the soap in cleansing cream remains in a film that coats the skin, damaging it and drying it out.

A skin freshener with alcohol or another strong solvent may remove the remains of the cream, but these products also strip the skin of its natural oils.

Cleansing lotion is made of the same ingredients as cleansing cream, but contains more water. Otherwise like solid cleansing cream, it has the same drawbacks.

Liquefying cleansing cream has the same ingredients as solid cleansing cream, but it is formulated to melt at body temperature.

Washable cream and *lotion* are made of ingredients similar to those described above, but have been formulated to make them water-soluble. After application to the face, the cream or lotion dissolves stale oils and loosens dead cells, and is then washed off with water. This rinsing removes any trace of soap along with the dirt. Washable creams do a thorough but gentle job of cleansing and are the best type of cleanser for normal and dry skins. They do not have enough degreasing power for oily skin.

Milky cleanser is made of soap, water, alcohol, and mineral oil, and contains more soap and less oil than washable creams or lotions. Milky cleansers are wiped on and rinsed off with water. Since they are primarily soaps, they are good for normal and slightly oily skin, but are too harsh for dry skin.

Scrubbing cleanser is soap with tiny, hard grains that rub off the surface of the skin. It should be used daily on oily skin, weekly on normal skin, and monthly on dry skin.

OIL-BALANCE CONTROL

Every type of skin, with the exception of oily and acned skin, needs lubrication. Oils and creams shield against loss of water, which every skin needs to be healthy, and supplement the skin's own natural oil shield. Many products are available for this purpose and are intended for both day and night use.

DAY CREAM is designed to be worn under makeup, and should be nongreasy. It is meant to prepare the skin for a foundation. Because the cream seems to disappear into the skin, it is often called a *vanishing cream*. (Actually the cream stays on the surface of the skin, spreading out in an imperceptible film on the very top layer.) Day creams are made of wax, water, oil, and soap, or soaplike chemicals—to make the cream less greasy so that it does not dissolve makeup. The soap in these products makes them bad for dry skin.

Daytime lotion, frequently called *moisturizer,* is healthier for the skin. It contains more water and much less soap than daytime cream. These lotions may have the additional ingredients of estrogen or synthesized Natural Moisturizing Factors (NMF), which help the skin maintain a better water balance. They are excellent products for dry skin. However, they should be used judiciously on normal skin and avoided for oily skin.

All-purpose hand, body, and face lotion is made with four basic ingredients: water, wax, oil, and glycerin. Although somewhat oilier than the under-makeup moisturizer, these lotions will not discolor makeup. They usually do not contain NMFs or other chemicals that encourage the skin to hold water.

An important question to ask yourself in buying such a cosmetic is what oil it contains. There are three categories of oils, all of which are meant

---

ca. **A.D. 137.** Baine, daughter of the Celtic king of Britain, "whose skin was like the first blush of dawn," weds Tuathal, king of Meath, or Ireland.

to coat the skin and delay the evaporation of water. None have any special power to delay aging or prevent lines and wrinkles:

• Animal fat, like codfish oil, lanolin (which is derived from sheep), mink oil, and turtle oil.

• Vegetable oil, such as corn, safflower, olive, wheat germ, and all the nut oils.

• Mineral oil, such as regular mineral oil, or petroleum derivatives.

Of all the oils, *animal fat*—particularly lanolin—most closely resembles the natural human oil (sebum). Not only do animal fats maintain the skin's water level, but they do not interfere with the skin's normal activities—such as breathing, perspiring, and eliminating the natural waste products of the skin's rapidly growing cells. The most expensive animal fats, mink and turtle oil, do the same job as cheaper ones. Mink oil is extracted from the scraps of minks discarded by furriers. Turtle oil has no special vitamins or antiaging properties.

Vegetable oil protects the skin well enough, but it is not as good as animal oil. Polyunsaturated oil (vegetable oil), while probably good for your diet, has no unique or magic powers on your skin. There is little difference in moisturizing ability among the various vegetable oils. Apricot kernel oil, even though it is scarcer and harder to extract, is no better than corn oil.

Mineral oil is very bland and mild and is used as a base for many cosmetics. It is not as good as either animal or vegetable oil for very dry skin, since it has a tendency to dissolve the skin's own natural oil, and can thereby increase dehydration.

NIGHT CREAM: More nonsense has been written about night cream than any other beauty product. A night cream merely helps the skin to retain a better supply of water. It does not rejuvenate the skin, prevent lines or wrinkles, reach deep down into the pores, or wake up sleepy complexions. A night cream, by shielding the skin against water evaporation, allows it to build up a supply of water, and this, in turn, makes the skin feel soft and smooth. Some night creams, containing estrogens and other water-holding substances, do a better job of retaining water in the skin. Night creams are good for dry skin, not necessarily helpful for normal skin, and not needed for oily skin.

A night cream consists of wax, oils, water, and emulsifiers (for instance, soap or borax). It is usually much thicker and oilier than a day cream since it is not worn under makeup. Although a night cream provides a somewhat heavier shield against water loss, a daytime moisturizer can double very satisfactorily as a night cream, thus sparing you the expense of two products.

Many additives in night creams are promoted as having special beautifying properties, but most are useless. Some of the more common additives are:

Amino acids. These are the building blocks of protein, which is a basic ingredient in virtually every part of the body. However, the skin can never absorb or utilize foreign proteins or amino acids that are coated on its surface.

Collagen. This is the structure in the dermis that gives the skin its strength and flexibility. The strength of the collagen fiber lies in its ordered structure; it is not a substance that can be absorbed into the skin. The chopped-up extract that is now incorporated into creams is cosmetically worthless.

Eggs. The lecithin (a fat compound) that occurs naturally in eggs is used as an emulsifier; that is to say, it keeps the cosmetic in cream form and does not let the water separate from the solid components of the cream. The surface of the skin cannot absorb the protein, minerals, or vitamins found in eggs.

Honey. The presence of honey in a cream can cause nasal congestion and skin rashes in those people who are allergic to flowers, grasses, and other natural allergenic materials.

Vitamins. Only vitamins A and D can be absorbed by the skin, and thereby have an effect on its health. (They help regulate the growth of skin cells.) All other vitamins, including the much-heralded vitamin E, cannot pass through the topmost layer of the skin's protective coating; therefore they cannot in any way influence the skin's condition.

TONING

Toning makes the skin look firm, lively, poreless, and smooth; all types of skin require toning. The three basic cosmetic tools for toning are lotions, masks, and saunas.

A TONING LOTION is applied after the skin is washed and dried, before moisturizer and makeup. These lotions can temporarily shrink facial pores, make the skin look firmer, and reinforce a healthy coloring. Different toning lotions have different properties, but they are not consistently labeled; different names can be applied to the same kind of substance and different formulas can bear the same name. The three basic types of toning lotions are *skin fresheners, astringents,* and *clarifying lotions.*

A *skin freshener* is an alcohol compound with various additives, such as herb extracts and camphor or menthol. Also called *freshening lotion* or *skin tonic,* a freshener cools and refreshes the skin, but it can be irritating to normal and dry skin, since it is used primarily for oily-skin problems. A freshener can also be used to remove the sticky residue of nonwashable cleansing cream.

An *astringent,* also called a *pore lotion,* contains water, less alcohol than skin fresheners, and most importantly aluminum or zinc salts. The salts, by causing a slight puffiness or swelling of the skin around the pores, makes them seem smaller. (Once a pore is stretched it can never be closed, even temporarily.) An astringent is a much more effective pore

ca. **A.D. 141.** The crown of the queen of Ireland is stolen from her during the great conclave of kings at her husband's court.

closer than a skin freshener, and, in general, is much less irritating to all types of skins.

Here are some points to remember when you choose an astringent.

• Concentrate on products with "astringent" in the name. By definition, these lotions are supposed to contain astringent substances (aluminum or zinc salts)—but beware, there is no *legal* definition of astringent, so that there is no guarantee that you are really getting an astringent.

• Beware of astringents that cause sharp, stinging sensations. These products probably contain only camphor or menthol (without any aluminum or zinc salts). Called *rubefactants,* they often have a smell of peppermint. In its place, a rubefactant is a good cosmetic aid; it jolts the circulation in the skin and gives the face a nice rosy glow. But to hide pores you want an astringent.

• Do not buy any astringent that is meant to remove makeup. To do this, the product must contain chemicals that dissolve grease, and it will not have sufficient pore-hiding properties.

Finally, you can make your own astringent by adding alum (a type of aluminum salt) to the skin freshener or toner that works best for you. Alum is used in the canning of fruits and vegetables and is available on the spice rack at about 15 cents an ounce. One half teaspoon of alum added to eight ounces of freshener will make an excellent astringent. If your freshener is really an astringent, the extra alum will not make it too strong.

A *clarifying lotion,* also known as an *exfoliating lotion,* contains water, alcohol, glycerin, and a chemical that dissolves the keratin that makes up most of the skin's top layer of dry, dead cells. The skin looks brighter and cleaner after using a clarifying lotion. These lotions include salicylic acid, resorcinol, and benzoyl peroxide, which presently must by law be listed on the label. Papain, an enzyme extracted from papayas, and brome-

lin, an enzyme extracted from pineapples, can also dissolve keratin, but neither has to be listed on the label. Both are very powerful agents and have been associated with allergies and chemical burns.

A clarifying lotion may also be formulated to be extremely alkaline or have a high alcohol content. Either formula can remove the topmost keratin layer, but both may damage healthy skin, in addition to removing the dry, dead skin cells.

3 times 10 are 30.
My face is very dirty.

Clarifying lotions can be used once a week for oily skin and about once a month for normal skin. Despite their somewhat scary concept, they can make the skin look brighter, smoother, and clearer. Clarifying lotions are frequently the special secret technique that cosmeticians use in their expensive facials.

MASKS come in two basic forms— *clay* and *gel.*

A *clay mask* absorbs excess oil and dirt from the skin. It picks up the cellular debris and gives the skin a smooth, even texture. As the mask dries, the tightening action stimulates circulation and makes the skin glow.

The clay itself contains mild bleaching agents that cause a gentle lightening of the skin. Clay also soothes the skin, reducing any in-

flammation and soreness.

Finally, a clay mask acts as a complete barrier against evaporation, allowing the skin to store up a large supply of water for as long as it remains on the skin.

A *gel mask* is made of a clear, thick gel that is usually bought in a tube. It is spread on the face and allowed to dry. After drying, it is either pulled off in one piece or washed off with water. A gel mask is especially good for restoring water or rehydrating normal, normal to dry, and dry skin. It does not soak up oil, but its solid, stretched film encourages the skin to store up water. As it dries and hardens, it gives a gentle boost to the circulation. When the mask is pulled off the face, the loose, flaky skin on the surface comes off with it.

Most of the value of a mask is based on the clay or gel base that forms the mask itself. Although certain ingredients are useful, like mint or vitamin A, many commercial masks have other exotic ingredients that do not perform any function.

SAUNAS: These are marvelous for every type of skin. The warm, moist heat loosens the skin's top dried layer so that it can be removed, melts clogged-up oil in the pores, stimulates circulation, and provides water for the skin.

Electric facial saunas—whatever the price—do very much the same thing; they bathe the face in gentle steam. Some are used with herbs or other additives in the water, which do not really improve their value.

Just as efficient is the sauna that can be made at home. Boil some water in a large pot, carry the pot to a steady table, sit down in front of it, and drape a towel over your head and shoulders to envelop you and the pot in a towel tent. Be sure to keep your face at least a foot away from the steaming pot; this is much hotter than a commercial sauna, so be careful not to burn yourself. Examine your skin after five or ten minutes. Lines seem to disappear and the skin feels very soft.

ca. **A.D. 150.** Ma Ku, famous for her witchcraft, magically reclaims from the sea a large area of the Kiangsu coast and causes mulberry orchards to grow over it in profusion.

Recommended Weights for Women and Calorie Expenditure Guide

Louise Page and Nancy Raper

Height (without shoes)	Weight (without clothing)		
	Low	Average	High
5 feet	100	109	118
5 feet 1 inch	104	112	121
5 feet 2 inches	107	115	125
5 feet 3 inches	110	118	128
5 feet 4 inches	113	122	132
5 feet 5 inches	116	125	135
5 feet 6 inches	120	129	139
5 feet 7 inches	123	132	142
5 feet 8 inches	126	136	146
5 feet 9 inches	130	140	151
5 feet 10 inches	133	144	156
5 feet 11 inches	137	148	161
6 feet	141	152	166

Type of activity: *Calories per hour*

Sedentary activities, such as: Reading; writing; eating; watching television or movies; listening to the radio; sewing; playing cards; and typing, officework, and other activities done while sitting that require little or no arm movement. — 80 to 100.

Light activities, such as: Preparing and cooking food; doing dishes; dusting; handwashing small articles of clothing; ironing; walking slowly; personal care; officework and other activities done while standing that require some arm movement; and rapid typing and other activities done while sitting that are more strenuous. — 110 to 160.

Moderate activities, such as: Making beds, mopping and scrubbing; sweeping; light polishing and waxing; laundering by machine; light gardening and carpentry work; walking moderately fast; other activities done while standing that require moderate arm movement; and activities done while sitting that require more vigorous arm movement. — 170 to 240.

Vigorous activities, such as: Heavy scrubbing and waxing; handwashing large articles of clothing; hanging out clothes; stripping beds; walking fast; bowling; golfing; and gardening. — 250 to 350.

Strenuous activities, such as: Swimming; playing tennis; running; bicycling; dancing; skiing; and playing football. — 350 or more.

Adapted from *Food and Your Weight*, 1973, Department of Agriculture.

ca. **A.D. 205.** Women are, for the first time, admitted to official life at the Chinese court. Several of them actually rise to high positions in the state, but few appear after the eighth century A.D.

The Great Diet Ripoff

The Editors of *Consumer Guide*

Here, as reviewed by *Consumer Guide* Magazine, are a few of the dangerous or dubious diet fads you're likely to hear about. Before going on one of these, or any other reducing diet, consider its claims carefully and make sure your physician approves it.

Staplepuncture

Acupuncture is the ancient Oriental art of inserting needles into specific parts of the body to kill pain or to cure disease. In 1974 a new use for acupuncture—losing weight—was introduced in California and has since spread to other regions. Although treatments are usually given by physicians, in some states anyone can perform acupuncture.

Acupuncture for weight loss is concentrated in an area of the external ear known as the concha. The theory is that the vagus nerve, which runs from the brain, down neck and chest, to the stomach, has a branch that extends into the area of the ear. When the sharp point of a needle finds the branch of this nerve, it sends signals through the nerve that inhibit the contractions of the stomach.

Acupuncturist and anesthesiologist Anastacio T. Saavedra, of Chicago, explains that the ear treatment itself does not cause a person to lose weight. Rather it helps a person stave off appetite. Dr. Saavedra inserts a stainless steel surgical staple in a patient's ear and instructs the patient to jiggle the staple with a clean finger every time he or she feels the urge to nibble, and

Adaption from *Consumer Guide® Rating the Diets*. Copyright © Publications International, Ltd. Reprinted with permission. Copies available from Consumer Guide Magazine, 3323 West Main St., Skokie, IL 60076.

before sitting down to a meal. If a staple in one ear does not work, he suggests a staple in the opposite ear.

The American Medical Association, however, considers all acupuncture experimental. Robert H. Moser, M.D., editor of the AMA's journal, says, "This is pure hokum," and points out that most ear acupuncturists give their patients low-calorie diets along with the staples. The going price is about fifty dollars.

Consumer Guide Magazine points out that the only real hazard of the procedure is infection from an unclean staple. But more important, the treatment smacks more of gimmickry than of soundness. Controlling weight is a lifelong effort; staples are, at best, of only temporary benefit.

The "Mayo Clinic" Diet

Yes, there is a real Mayo diet, an exchange diet of moderate protein and high fats and carbohydrates detailed in the Clinic's official diet manual. But it's probably eclipsed by the fake Mayo diets, which have been passed around for years on much-folded mimeographed or machine-copied sheets of paper. They are also known by such names as the Egg Diet, the Grapefruit Diet, and the Tomato Juice Diet. The most common of these is based on the fraudulent premise that grapefruit has certain enzymes that somehow subtract calories by acting as a catalyst to increase the fat-burning process.

The danger in a diet that carries a respected name, such as Mayo, is that too

A.D. 218. Julia Soemis, whose son has just become Emperor Elagabalus of Rome, is scandalously chosen as a counselor, taking her place as the first female in the senate. She soon installs herself at the head of a female parliament that regulates matters connected with morals, dress, etiquette and the equipage of Roman matrons.

Diet Fads
THE HEALTH ADVISER   **79**

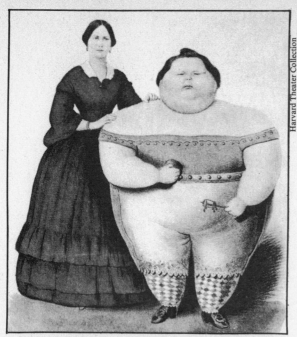

VANTILE MACK, THE INFANT LAMBERT, OR
GIANT BABY!!
7 Years old, Weights 257 pounds!
*Measures 61 inches around the chest,
36 inches around the leg!!*

many dieters will accept its claims un-critically and follow its directions, absurd though they may be. According to some of the most popular Mayo diets, for example, you should always eat until stuffed full, even if this includes one or two dozen slices of bacon and as many eggs, cooked in as much butter as you wish.

Dr. Atkins' High-Fat Diet

High-fat diets are not new or revolutionary; they've been around for more than a century. Dr. Atkins' "revolution"—one of the latest—follows in the footsteps of many.

Atkins' diet (described in his book *Dr. Atkins' Diet Revolution,* coauthored by Ruth West) calls for an initial week of zero-carbo-hydrate menus that include an abundance of fats. At the end of the week, says Atkins, "most men will have lost seven or eight pounds, most women five or six pounds."

After this weight loss occurs, you may go on to "Level Two" of the diet, which allows you to add food with carbohydrates—about five grams more each day of the week. You yourself will discover when you must level off, for you will be testing your urine daily with Ketostix for the presence of fat, called ketones, which indicates that your body is burning fat (or is in the state of ketosis). As soon as your urine-stick stops turning purple,

it means that your are not releasing ketones anymore, or that your body is no longer burning fat. At this point you must stop adding carbohydrates to your diet.

Cutting down on carbohydrates, the authors claim, triggers secretion of the fat-mobilizing hormone, or FMH, to keep the body's metabolic fires fueled with fat. You convert your body "from being a carbo-hydrate-burning engine into being a fat-burning engine."

The main weakness of the Atkins diet is the absence of scientific reasons for its high-fat content. It remains unclear in logic and undemonstrated in experiments just how eating lots of fat will stimulate the body to release fat it has stored away weeks or months before. More likely, your body will continue to store the extra fats you eat and do not burn.

Consumer Guide Magazine feels that the danger of high-fat diets to the heart and art-eries is reason enough to stay away from them. The unhealthy state of ketosis is another reason. Pregnant women, especially, should avoid all ketogenic diets, which can lead to brain damage in the unborn child. So should anyone likely to have kidney prob-lems or gout, which can be aggravated by ketosis. Among other conditions resulting from ketosis can be disturbances in the rhythm of the heartbeat, diarrhea, fatigue, low blood pressure, nausea, and depression.

Zen Macrobiotic

In spite of its name, the Zen Macrobiotic diet has little to do with Zen Buddhism. But, more important, the diet is dangerous—so dangerous in fact, that there have been reports of young people starving themselves to death on it.

Defenders of the macrobiotic diet deny that it is harmful. They claim that the diet will cure or prevent every disease, including epilepsy and cancer. (Such claims, of course, have not been proved.)

According to zen philosophy everything in the world is composed of two parts, Yin (identified with woman, inactivity, passivity, silence, happy-go-lucky, mental, heaven) and Yang (identified with man, activity, sound, businesslike, physical, earth). Each quality is constantly changing in its proportion to the other, and either, carried to its extreme, turns into the other. Thus everything changes; everything is striving for balance. So far, so good.

She is thought to be as depraved as her degenerate son and boasts of herself as the inventor of several novel perversions, parading about "indiscreetly and making her position as a moral regulator a travesty."

But the way adherents of the macrobiotic diet apply zen philosophy is to say that the balance in food should be in a five-to-one ratio of yin to yang. Sugar and most fruits are frowned on as too "yin"; meats and eggs are heavily yang. The perfect food is brown rice, and on the most perfect macrobiotic diet only brown rice and tea are permitted. To prepare the body to live only on brown rice, the macrobiotic program prescribes moving through six stages of diets, each more severe than the last.

Dr. Frederick J. Stare, M.D., chairman of the Department of Nutrition at Harvard University, explains the danger of the macrobiotic diet accordingly: "taking away certain elements in the usual variety of foods without adequately replacing them can be extremely dangerous. . . . At almost any stage of the diet it is possible to become anemic from lack of iron. The diet is also deficient in most vitamins. . . I think it is the most dangerous fad diet around."

Dr. Neil Solomon, Chief Health Officer of Maryland and assistant professor at The John Hopkins University School of Medicine, put it more succinctly: "The macrobiotic ('long life') diet is injurious and even fatal and is really a microbiotic ('short life') diet."

Lecithin Vinegar, Kelp, B_6

The hottest diet fad of 1974-75 was that of Mary Ann Crenshaw, which first appeared in *Family Circle* magazine and then in her book *Super Beauty*. A number of pharmaceutical companies, who saw gold in Crenshaw's formula, jumped on the kelp boat as well and have sold to dieters millions of dollars' worth of pills containing her "Four Friends."

Lecithin "is full of Vitamin E, the sexy shaperupper," wrote Ms. Crenshaw. "Pronounce it less-i-thin and call it a miracle." *Consumer Guide* Magazine, consulting medical and nutritional textbooks, agrees that it must be a miracle—if it works. Lecithin helps fats in foods to be absorbed in the intestines because it acts as an emulsifier to suspend droplets of fat in watery tissue fluids.

Ms. Crenshaw also advises drinking a teaspoonful of cider vinegar in a glass of water after every meal. Her "scientific reasoning": "After all, oil and vinegar don't really mix. Maybe vinegar and my fat wouldn't either, and vinegar might just win out."

Such use of cider vinegar hark back to Dr. D.C. Jarvis and his folk-medicine craze of the late 1950's. Another practice Ms. Crenshaw

John Getsinger

borrowed from Ol' Doc Jarvis was eating the seaweed known as kelp. Her reasoning: kelp contains iodine; the thyroid gland, which regulates the rate of metabolism, needs iodine—ergo, eat lots of iodine and you raise the rate of metabolism enough to burn off excess fat.

Fortunately, the body does not work by such distorted logic. If you eat seafood or use any iodized salt in your food, you are getting enough iodine. Indeed, if you jam too much iodine into your body, you might depress the effects of thyroid on your metabolism and actually slow it down.

B_6, also known as pyridoxine, is Crenshaw's last miracle. What this vitamin has to do with losing fat is a mystery. Its known use in the body is in the metabolism of amino acids, not fat.

All in all, the Crenshaw diet is merely a a low-calorie diet with some "natural food" supplements sprinkled on. *Consumer Guide's* evaluation: Super Baloney.

---

ca. **A.D. 280.** Fu Hsuan writes a famous poem, "Woman," which deplores the low social position of even highborn Chinese women. The first line reads: "How sad it is to be a woman! Nothing on earth is held so cheap."

Aerobic Exercises
for Fitness and Heart Health

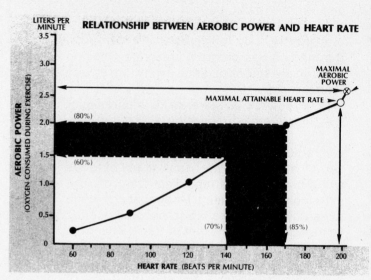

Fig. 1

Pinch Test

- Pinch up a fold of skin and fat at the back of your upper arm over the triceps muscle area.
- Do not include the triceps muscle itself.
- Remove your fingers maintaining the "measurement."
- Measure the space between your fingers with a ruler.
- If you have more than an inch of combined skin and fat between your fingers then you are fat—maybe not over-weight—but fat.

Exercise training will normalize the relationship between lean body mass and fat. When a reducing diet plus exercise programming work together, you lose not only weight, but flabby fat.

GUIDELINES FOR EXERCISING

The Target Zone

There is an amount (intensity or vigorousness) of exercise which is enough to condition the muscles and cardiovascular system leading to physical fitness, but is not overly strenuous. That is, there is a target zone in which there is enough activity to achieve fitness, but not too much to exceed safe limits. The name of the game is finding your target zone.

Each individual's target zone is between 60 and 80 per cent of his own *maximal aerobic power*. Below 60 per cent of his capacity he achieves little fitness benefit (unless he has been bedridden for a prolonged period). Above 80 per cent there is little added benefit from a great deal of extra exercise. The concept of maximal aerobic power (sometimes called maximal aerobic capacity or maximal oxygen intake) is merely the technical description of the fact that there is a point for each of us where, despite our best efforts, the heart and circulation cannot deliver any more oxygen to the tissues and we cannot exercise much longer or harder without approaching exhaustion.

At this point, the lungs are making oxygen available to the bloodstream, but that oxygen cannot be transported by the blood to the muscles fast enough to create energy for exercise. The muscles can't work aerobically any more. Almost simultaneously with reaching this limitation of oxygen supply, the heart becomes unable to beat any faster.

In normal active individuals, the points where maximal aerobic power and *maximal attainable heart rate* are reached are very close. In fact, the target zone of 60 to 80 per cent of maximal aerobic power is at approximately the same level as 70 to 85 per cent of maximal attainable heart rate (Fig.1). If you have had a "road test" or exercise stress test, your doctor will be able to tell you your maximal aerobic power and maximal attainable heart rate. If you have been sedentary these may be below the levels for normal active individuals. Nevertheless, your particular target zone will then also be 60 to 80 per cent of your *individually measured* maximal aerobic power or 70 to 85 per cent of your measured maximal attainable heart rate.

Adapted from "Beyond Diet . . . Exercise Your Way to Fitness and Heart Health," by Lenore R. Zohman, M.D. Copyright © 1974 CPC International, Inc. Reprinted with permission.

These values may be different for you and a friend who may be the same age, since in addition to age they depend primarily on your natural hereditary endowment, as well as your original state of physical fitness and your health. Because we are able to count our own heart rates, but cannot easily determine our own aerobic power, the heart rate target zone gives us a means of regulating our own exercise performance. If you cannot have your actual maximal heart rate measured, you could assume you are "average" and look up your maximal and target zone heart rates on the chart which follows.

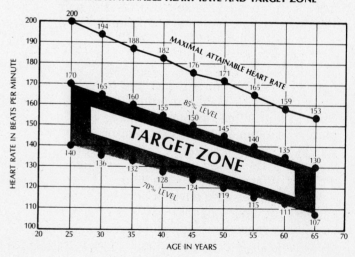

Fig. 2

This figure shows that as we grow older, the highest heart rate which can be reached during all-out effort falls. These numerical values are "average" values for age. Note that one-third of the population may differ from these values. It is quite possible that a normal 50-year-old man may have a maximum heart rate of 195 or that a 30-year-old man might have a maximum of only 168. The same limitations apply to the 70 per cent and 85 per cent of maximum lines.

---

ca. **A.D. 286.** Hua-Ts'un, daughter of the minister of state, is famous as a student and practitioner of witchcraft. One day, according to legend, she swallows some purifying drugs and, in broad daylight, ascends directly to heaven.

Example: A 20-year-old man has a maximal heart rate of 200. His target zone would then be 140 (70 per cent) to 170 (85 per cent) beats per minute heart rate. However, a 65-year-old man with a maximal attainable heart rate of 150 beats per minute, would have a target zone of 107 (70 per cent) to 130 (85 per cent) beats per minute.

Age and Heart Rate

From the above examples it is obvious that there is a relationship between age and the highest heart rate which can be reached at all-out effort. The older one gets, the lower become both the maximal aerobic power and the maximal attainable heart rate (see Fig. 2). This fact is important because a senior citizen may be expending the same degree of effort in exercising as a younger person but his heart rate may be considerably less. He is not lazy! He is at the same percentage of his maximum capacity as the younger man. Women can reach the same maximal heart rates as men of a comparable age. This value is roughly 220 minus age (in years).

How To Use The Target Zone

The crucial part of a workout is the duration one stays at the target zone, the 70 to 85 per cent of maximal heart rate zone. (Fig. 3).

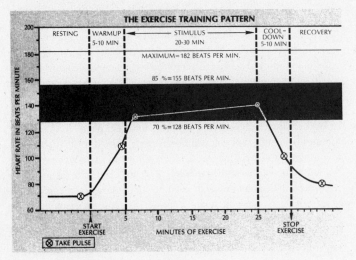

THE EXERCISE TRAINING PATTERN

Fig. 3

Usually 20 to 30 minutes in the target zone will provide a significant conditioning effect on the cardiovascular system. The 70 per cent of maximum level should be sufficient to promote cardiovascular fitness. Although it is not *necessary* to do so, the 85 per cent level provides an upper limit which may be sustained if a more intense workout is desired. The period at target (called the stimulus period) should be preceded by a warmup of 5 to 10 minutes so that the heart and circulation are not suddenly taxed. This warmup is also beneficial to joints and muscles and helps to prevent injuries and soreness.

After the stimulus period, there should be a 5 to 10 minute cooldown in which the intensity or strenuousness of the effort is lessened before exercise is stopped. Abruptly stopping exercise when one has been vigorously working out may trap all the blood in the muscles which have suddenly stopped moving. Not enough blood circulates back to the brain or heart or intestine, and related symptoms result, i.e., dizziness or faintness may occur when there is too little blood to the brain, extra heart beats when there is too little blood getting back to the heart muscle itself or nausea if the intestine is getting too little.

How To Count Your Pulse

To determine whether you are in the target zone, learn to count your pulse. Since the pulse count is almost always the same as the number of heart beats per minute (the heart rate), placing your hand over the heart is a simple method. However, since clothing may prevent your clearly feeling the beat, it is usually easier to obtain an accurate count over either one of the large arteries at the side of the neck—the carotid arteries. With the thumb on the chin, the fingers can easily palpate (feel) the opposite carotid artery in front of the strip of muscle running vertically in the neck, called the sternocleidomastoid muscle (Fig. 4).

However, any location where a full pulse can be felt is satisfactory, such as at the wrist on the thumb side, inside the bend of the elbow towards the body side or even in the groin. The count will be the same (Fig. 5).

Fig. 4

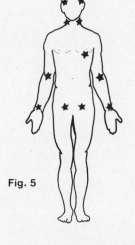

Fig. 5

When To Count The Pulse

It is important to count the pulse *immediately* upon stopping exercise because the rate changes very quickly once exercise is slowed or stopped. Find the beat within a second and count for 10 seconds. Then multiply by six to obtain the count for a minute. Do not count for the whole minute or even for 15 seconds because the fall-off is too fast.

By trial and error, develop an exercise pattern that seems easy for 5 to 10 minutes and count your pulse immediately after this warmup. It should be less than 50 per cent of your age-related maximal attainable heart rate. Then exercise more vigorously to get to the target zone. Count again after 3 to 5 minutes at this level to check whether you are doing enough to be on target. If your heart rate is below 70 per cent of your maximum, exercise more strenuously. Conversely, if it is above 85 per cent of your maximum, exercise less vigorously either by exercising slower or less forcefully.

For example, jog instead of run, or walk briskly instead of trying to jog, or pedal your stationary bicycle slower or against less resistance. Repeat counting at five minute intervals until you have determined just how much exercise is necessary to put you in the target zone.

Cooldown after you have been at target for 20 to 30 minutes. Ease up gradually over a 5 to 10 minute period before stopping. Do not come to a screeching halt; even horse trainers walk the horse after the race!

Once you have thoroughly checked out your own responses to exercise, you will begin to recognize certain normal sensations you get when you are in the target zone such as an awareness of a certain amount of rapid heart action or breathlessness. You will recognize how much effort it takes to get you there and will no longer need to continue to count your heart rate during each exercise session. You will be able to perceive intuitively with reasonable accuracy just how high your heart rate is and whether you are in the target zone.

ca. **A.D. 365.** Isidora the Simple, virgin nun, dies this year in the desert. In order to better please God by "mortifying" herself, she publicly "acted like a complete fool for Christ's sake," enduring the predictable insults and derision as her secretly cherished reward.

Type and Frequency of Exercise

Not all types of exercise are equally useful for becoming physically fit. The way in which the cardiovascular system is challenged by the exercise is all important. Only those exercises which significantly augment the continuous flow of blood through the heart and large skeletal muscles will help cardiovascular fitness. For example, both weight lifting and isometrics cause the muscle being strengthened to shorten (contract or tense up). This pressure squeezes the blood vessels letting less blood pass instead of more. By contrast, jogging, requiring continuous movement of the legs (and arms to some extent) results in rhythmic tensing and relaxing of muscles. This aids the flow of blood and promotes cardiovascular fitness. The table on page 85 lists the exercises that improve cardiovascular fitness if done correctly as well as those which do not.

Of course, exercises which do not improve cardiovascular fitness have other benefits. They may increase muscle strength or athletic skill—but they do not improve stamina or endurance or "wind." Those which improve cardiovascular fitness are rhythmic, repetitive and involve motion, and are called "isotonic" or *dynamic*.

Certain other exercises may enhance blood flow but still do not improve cardiovascular fitness because they cannot be kept up for a sufficiently long period of time. Thus, the second requisite for the right kind of exercise is that it must be capable of being *sustained*. It must be "aerobic." Aerobic exercise is the type which steadily supplies enough oxygen to the exercising muscles for as long as the exercise is continued. Any rhythmic, repetitive, dynamic activity which can be continued for two or more minutes, without huffing and puffing afterwards, is probably aerobic. If enough oxygen was not being provided to the muscles, the exercise could not be continued, or if it was continued through sheer willpower, the body would immediately have to pay back the extra oxygen it borrowed from its own tissues by continuation of hard breathing after the exercise was stopped.

For example, sprinting is not aerobic. The sprinter can't keep going at that pace. By contrast, the jogger, bicycle rider or swimmer seems to cover long distances effortlessly because he has attained a balance between the oxygen he needs and the oxygen he is getting through his lungs and cardiovascular system.

Dynamic, aerobic exercise must be carried out three times weekly with no more than two days elapsing between workouts or gains will begin to be lost. Exercising Monday, Wednesday and Friday, or Tuesday, Thursday and Sunday are frequent exercise plans for YMCA's and YMHA's respectively.

Making Progress

After two to three weeks of regular exercise according to the principles described, you will begin to improve your physical fitness level, and after four to six weeks there should be some measurable improvement. You will begin to be able to carry out the exercise more easily;

it will take more exercise for you to reach your target zone and your resting heart rate may be less (Fig. 6). Your body has become more efficient. You may begin to sleep better, be less tired at the end of the day, and will often find that you miss the invigorating feeling you get from a workout if you skip your exercise for even one scheduled day.

As you begin to improve your physical fitness level and become "trained," you must increase the vigor of the exercise you do or you will make no further progress. If you have been walking briskly to achieve the 70 per cent level of heart rate, and you no longer reach 70 per cent, begin to jog for part of the walking time and check yourself out again as described in the section on "When to Count Your Pulse." When jogging becomes too light for you, try running. Increase the resistance against which you pedal your home bike, the number of laps you cover in the pool, or the number of skips per minute with your jump rope, but be sure to keep your heart rate in the target zone for 20 minutes. Every four to six weeks, re-evaluate yourself and upgrade your program. Use the heart rate profile sheet at the end of the booklet to record your progress.

Any activity which gets your heart rate into the target zone for 20 minutes is suitable, but you will not become trained for that activity if you switch to others too frequently. Your leg muscles will become trained after six weeks of stationary bicycling, and your heart rate response will become slower as evidence of cardiovascular improvement. But if you then work out on a rowing machine, for example, you will again show less of a training response on heart rate since your arm muscles have not had six weeks of this kind of exercise. The best type of program is one which uses both your arms and legs and achieves the training effect on the cardiovascular system by conditioning the muscles of both.

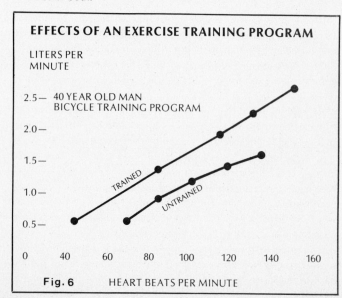

EFFECTS OF AN EXERCISE TRAINING PROGRAM

LITERS PER MINUTE

40 YEAR OLD MAN
BICYCLE TRAINING PROGRAM

TRAINED

UNTRAINED

Fig. 6   HEART BEATS PER MINUTE

---

ca. **A.D. 380.** It is determined by the ecclesiastical Council of Saragossa in Spain that hereafter no woman may devote herself to the religious life until she has attained the age of forty, by which time it is hoped that her sexuality will have cooled.

RELATIVE MERITS OF VARIOUS EXERCISES IN INDUCING CARDIOVASCULAR FITNESS

Note: Energy range will vary depending on skill of exerciser, pattern of rest pauses, environmental temperature, etc. Caloric values depend on body size (more for larger person). Table provides reasonable "relative strenuousness values" however.

Energy Range	Activity	Comment
1.5–2.0 Mets* or 2.0–2.5 Cals/min. or 120–150 Cals/hr.	Light housework such as polishing furniture or washing small clothes	Too low in energy level and too intermittent to promote endurance.
	Strolling 1.0 mile/hr.	Not sufficiently strenuous to promote endurance unless capacity is very low.
2.0–3.0 Mets or 2.5–4.0 Cals/min. or 150–240 Cals/hr.	Level walking at 2.0 miles/hr.	See "strolling".
	Golf, using power cart	Promotes skill and minimal strength in arm muscles but not sufficiently taxing to promote endurance. Also too intermittent.
3.0–4.0 Mets or 4–5 Cals/min. or 240–300 Cals/hr.	Cleaning windows, mopping floors, or vacuuming	Adequate conditioning exercise if carried out continuously for 20–30 minutes.
	Bowling	Too intermittent and not sufficiently taxing to promote endurance.
	Walking at 3.0 miles/hr.	Adequate dynamic exercise if low capacity.
	Cycling at 6 miles/hr.	As above.
	Golf–pulling cart	Useful for conditioning if reach target rate. May include isometrics depending on cart weight.
4.0–5.0 Mets or 5–6 Cals/min. or 300–360 Cals/hr.	Scrubbing floors	Adequate endurance exercise if carried out in at least 2 minute stints.
	Walking 3.5 miles/hr.	Usually good dynamic aerobic exercise.
	Cycling 8 miles/hr.	As above.
	Table tennis, badminton and volleyball	Vigorous continuous play can have endurance benefits but intermittent, easy play only promotes skill.
	Golf—carrying clubs	Promotes endurance if reach and maintain target heart rate, otherwise merely aids strength and skill.
	Tennis—doubles	Not very beneficial unless there is continuous play maintaining target rate—which is unlikely. Will aid skill.
	Many calisthenics and ballet exercises	Will promote endurance if continuous, rhythmic and repetitive. Those requiring isometric effort such as push-ups and sit-ups are probably not beneficial for cardiovascular fitness.
5.0–6.0 Met or 6–7 Cals/min. or 360–420 Cals/hr.	Walking 4 miles/hr.	Dynamic, aerobic and of benefit.
	Cycling 10 miles/hr.	As above.
	Ice or roller skating	As above if done continuously.
6.0–7.0 Mets or 7–8 Cals/min. or 420–480 Cals/hr.	Walking 5 miles/hr.	Dynamic, aerobic and beneficial.
	Cycling 11 miles/hr.	Same.
	Singles tennis	Can provide benefit if played 30 minutes or more by skilled player with an attempt to keep moving.
	Water skiing	Total isometrics; very risky for cardiacs, pre-cardiacs (high risk) or deconditioned normals.
7.0–8.0 Mets or 8–10 Cals/min. or 480–600 Cals/hr.	Jogging 5 miles/hr.	Dynamic, aerobic, endurance building exercise.
	Cycling 12 miles/hr.	As above.
	Downhill skiing	Usually ski runs are too short to significantly promote endurance. Lift may be isometric. Benefits skill predominantly. Combined stress of altitude, cold and exercise may be too great for some cardiacs.
	Paddleball	Not sufficiently continuous but promotes skill. Competition and hot playing areas may be dangerous to cardiacs.
8.0–9.0 Mets or 10–11 Cals/min. or 600–660 Cals/hr.	Running 5.5 miles/hr.	Excellent conditioner.
	Cycling 13 miles/hr.	As above.
	Squash or handball (practice session or warmup)	Usually too intermittent to provide endurance building effect. Promotes skill.
Above 10 Mets or 11 Cals/min. or 660 Cals/hr.	Running 6 miles/hr.=10 Mets 7 miles/hr.=11.5 8 miles/hr.=13.5	Excellent conditioner.
	Competitive handball or squash	Competitive environment in a hot room is dangerous to anyone not in excellent physical condition. Same as singles tennis.

*Met= multiple of the resting energy requirement; e.g. 2 Mets require twice the resting energy cost, 3 Mets triple, etc.

ca. **A.D. 400.** The Byzantine emperors pursue a curious Cinderella-like custom in the selection of their wives. Imperial envoys summon the most beautiful and ambitious young women to a gigantic beauty contest in Constantinople, where the emperor inspects, interviews, and chooses his empress, who may come from any background no matter how humble.

The table distinguishes between these immediate and delayed symptoms. The first three symptoms described are cause for consulting a physician before carrying out the next exercise session. If you cannot consult a physician, discontinue your exercise program. Symptoms 4 and 5 have suggested remedies which may be tried prior to consulting a physician. The other symptoms listed may usually be remedied without medical advice by the measures described. However, if the suggested measures fail to work, of course medical evaluation is indicated.

Warnings and What to do About Them

STOP — SEE A PHYSICIAN BEFORE RESUMING

SYMPTOM	CAUSE	REMEDY
1 Abnormal heart action; e.g. —pulse becoming irregular —fluttering, jumping or palpitations in chest or throat —sudden burst of rapid heartbeats —sudden very slow pulse when a moment before it had been on target. (Immediate or delayed)	Extrasystoles (extra heart beats), dropped heartbeats, or disorders of cardiac rhythm. This may or may not be dangerous and should be checked out by physician.	Consult physician before resuming exercise program. He may provide medication to temporarily eliminate the problem and allow you to safely resume your exercise program, or you may have a completely harmless kind of cardiac rhythm disorder.
2 Pain or pressure in the center of the chest or the arm or throat precipitated by exercise or following exercise. (Immediate or delayed)	Possible heart pain.	Consult physician before resuming exercise program.
3 Dizziness, lightheadedness, sudden incoordination, confusion, cold sweat, glassy stare, pallor, blueness or fainting. (Immediate)	Insufficient blood to the brain.	Do not try to cool down. Stop exercise and lie down with feet elevated, or put head down between legs until symptoms pass. Later consult physician before next exercise session.

REMEDIES WHICH MAY BE SELF-ADMINISTERED

SYMPTOM	CAUSE	REMEDY
4 Persistent rapid heart action near the target level even 5-10 minutes after the exercise was stopped. (Immediate)	Exercise is probably too vigorous.	Keep heart rate at lower end of target zone or below. Increase the vigor of exercise more slowly. If these measures do not control the excessively high recovery heart rate, consult physician.
5 Flare up of arthritic condition or gout which usually occurs in hips, knees, ankles, or big toe (weight bearing joints). (Immediate or delayed)	Trauma to joints which are particularly vulnerable.	If you are familiar with how to quiet these flare-ups of your old joint condition, use your usual remedies. Rest up and do not resume your exercise program until the condition subsides. Then resume the exercise at a lower level with protective footwear on softer surfaces, or select other exercises which will put less strain on the impaired joints; e.g. swimming will be better for people with arthritis of the hips since it can be done mostly with the arms. If this is new arthritis, or if there is no response to usual remedies, see physician.

CAN BE REMEDIED WITHOUT MEDICAL CONSULTATION

SYMPTOM	CAUSE	REMEDY
6 Nausea or vomiting after exercise. (Immediate)	Not enough oxygen to the intestine. You are either exercising too vigorously or cooling down too quickly.	Exercise less vigorously and be sure to take a more gradual and longer cool-down.
7 Extreme breathlessness lasting more than 10 minutes after stopping exercise. (Immediate)	Exercise is too taxing to your cardiovascular system or lungs.	Stay at the lower end of your target range. If symptoms persist, do even less than target level. Be sure that while you are exercising you are not too breathless to talk to a companion.
8 Prolonged fatigue even 24 hours later. (Delayed)	Exercise is too vigorous.	Stay at lower end of target range or below. Increase level more gradually.
9 Shin splints (pain on the front or sides of lower leg). (Delayed)	Inflammation of the fascia connecting the leg bones, or muscle tears where muscles of the lower leg connect to the bones.	Use shoes with thicker soles. Work out on turf which is easier on your legs.
10 Insomnia which was not present prior to the exercise program. (Delayed)	Exercise is too vigorous.	Stay at lower end of target range or below. Increase intensity of exercise gradually.
11 Pain in the calf muscles which occurs on heavy exercise but not at rest. (Immediate)	May be due to muscle cramps due to lack of use of these muscles, or exercising on hard surfaces. May also be due to poor circulation to the legs (called claudication).	Use shoes with thicker soles, cool down adequately. Muscle cramps should clear up after a few sessions. If "muscle cramps" do not subside, circulation is probably faulty. Try another type of exercise; e.g. bicycling instead of jogging in order to use different muscles.
12 Side stitch (sticking under the ribs while exercising). (Immediate)	Diaphragm spasm. The diaphragm is the large muscle which separates the chest from the abdomen.	Lean forward while sitting, attempting to push the abdominal organs up against the diaphragm.
13 Charley horse or muscle-bound feeling. (Immediate or delayed)	Muscles are deconditioned and unaccustomed to exercise.	Take hot bath and usual headache remedy. Next exercise should be less strenuous.

ca. **A.D. 485.** According to some historians, P'an Fei, favored concubine of China's Ch'i Dynasty, introduces at this time the practice of foot binding for upper-class women. Extremely painful and debilitating, the foot deformation excites rapture among Chinese men through countless later centuries. The crippled women's gait is compared to the "delicate weaving of a willow."

The
Psychological
Adviser

What We Know and Don't Know about Sex Differences

Eleanor Emmons Maccoby and Carol Nagy Jacklin

The physical differences between men and women are obvious and universal. The psychological differences are not. Yet people hold strong beliefs about sex differences, even when those beliefs fail to find any scientific support.

Some popular views of sex differences are captured in a scene from the Rodgers and Hammerstein musical, *Carousel*. A young man discovers he is to be a father. He rhapsodizes about the kind of son he expects to have. The boy will be tall and tough as a tree, and no one will dare to boss him around. It will be all right for his mother to teach him manners, but she mustn't make a sissy out of him. The boy will be good at wrestling, and able to herd cattle, run a riverboat, drive spikes.

Then the prospective father realizes with a start, that the child might be a girl. The music moves to a gentle theme. She will have ribbons in her hair. She will be sweet and petite, just like her mother, and suitors will flock around her. There's a slightly discordant note, introduced for comic relief from sentimentality, when the expectant father brags that she'll be half again as bright as girls are meant to be. But then he returns to the main theme: his daughter will need to be protected.

The lyrics in this scene reflect some common cultural stereotypes. There are also some less well-known stereotypes in the social science literature on sex differences. We believe there is a great deal of myth in both the popular and scientific views about male-female differences. There is also some substance.

In order to find out which generalizations are justified and which are not, we spent three years compiling, reviewing and interpreting a very large body of research—over 2,000 books and articles—on the sex differences in motivation, social behavior, and intellectual ability. We examined negative as well as positive evidence. At the end of our exhaustive and exhausting search, we were able to determine which beliefs about sex differences are supported by evidence, which beliefs have no support, and which are still inadequately tested.

MYTH ONE:
Girls are more "social" than boys.

There is no evidence that girls are more likely than boys to be concerned with people, as opposed to impersonal objects or abstract ideas. The two sexes are equally interested in social stimuli (e.g. human faces and voices), and are equally proficient at learning by imitating models. They are equally responsive to social rewards, such as praise from others, and neither sex consistently learns better for this form of reward than for other forms.

In childhood, girls are no more dependent than boys on their caretakers, and boys are no more willing than girls to remain alone. Girls do not spend more time with playmates; the opposite is true, at least at certain ages. The two sexes appear to be equally adept at understanding the emotional reactions and needs of others, although measures of this ability have been narrow.

Any differences that do exist in the sociability of the two sexes are more of kind than of degree. Boys are highly oriented toward a peer group and congregate in larger groups; girls associate in pairs or small groups of children their own age, and may be somewhat more oriented toward adults, although the evidence on this is weak.

Adapted and reprinted from *The Psychology of Sex Differences* by Eleanor Emmons Maccoby and Carol Nagy Jacklin, with the permission of the publishers, Stanford University Press. Copyright © 1974 the Board of Trustees of the Leland Stanford Junior University.

MYTH TWO:
Girls are more suggestible than boys.

Boys are as likely as girls to imitate other people spontaneously. The two sexes are equally susceptible to persuasive communications, and in face-to-face situations where there is social pressure to conform to a group judgment about an ambiguous situation, there are usually no sex differences in susceptibility. When there are, girls are somewhat more likely to adapt their own judgments to those of the group, although some studies find the reverse. Boys, on the other hand, appear to be more likely to accept peer group values when these conflict with their own.

MYTH THREE:
Girls have lower self-esteem than boys.

Boys and girls are very similar in overall self-satisfaction and self-confidence throughout childhood and adolescence. (The information on childhood is meager, but what there is indicates no sex difference.) The sexes do differ in the areas in which they report greatest self-confidence. Girls rate themselves higher in the area of social competence, while boys more often see themselves as strong, powerful, dominant, potent.

Through most of the school years, boys and girls are equally likely to believe they can influence their own fate, as opposed to falling victim to chance. During the college years (not earlier or later), men have a greater sense of control over their destiny, and are more optimistic in predicting their own performance on a variety of school-related tasks. However, this does not imply a generally lower level of self-esteem among women of this age.

MYTH FOUR:
Girls lack motivation to achieve.

In the pioneering studies of achievement motivation, girls were more likely to report imagery about achievement when asked to make up stories to describe ambiguous pictures, as long as the instructions did not stress either competition or social comparison. Boys need to be challenged by appeals to their ego or competitive feelings, for their achievement imagery to reach the level of girls'. Although boys' achievement motivation does appear to be more responsive to competitive arousal, that does not imply that they have a higher level of achievement motivation in general. In fact, when researchers observe behavior that denotes a motive to achieve, they find no sex differences or find girls to be superior.

A contrary—and more recent—view on the origin of foot binding is that the tradition sprung from the imagination of a Chinese emperor, possibly in an effort to stress the restrictions and subjugation visited upon all properly raised noble women. Submissive women were thought especially attractive.

MYTH FIVE:
Girls are better at rote learning and simple repetitive tasks. Boys are better at high-level tasks that require them to inhibit previously learned responses.

Neither sex is more susceptible to simple conditioning, in which stimuli become connected with responses in what is assumed to be a rather automatic process. Neither sex excels in rote-learning tasks, such as learning to associate one word with another. Boys and girls are equally proficient at tasks that call on them to inhibit various responses, e.g., discrimination of certain items from others, a task requiring the subject to avoid attending or responding to irrelevant cues.

Boys are somewhat more impulsive during the preschool years, but after that the sexes do not differ in ability to wait for a delayed reward or inhibit early, incorrect responses, or on other measures of impulsivity.

MYTH SIX:
Boys are more "analytic" than girls.

The sexes do not differ on tests of cognitive style that measure one's ability to analyze, i.e., the ability to respond to a particular aspect of a situation without

being influenced by the context, or restructure the elements of a problem in order to achieve a solution. Boys and girls are equally likely to respond to contextual aspects of a situation that are irrelevant to the task at hand. Boys are superior only on problems that require visual discrimination or manipulation of objects set in a larger context; this superiority seems to be accounted for by spatial ability, which we discuss below, and does not imply a general analytic superiority.

MYTH SEVEN:
Girls are more affected by heredity, boys by environment.

Male identical twins are intellectually more alike than female identical twins, but the two sexes resemble their parents to the same degree. Boys are more vulnerable to damage by a variety of harmful agents in the environment both before and after birth, but this does not mean that they are more affected by environmental influences in general.

The two sexes learn with equal facility in a wide variety of situations. If learning is the primary means by which the environment affects us, then the two sexes are equivalent in this regard.

MYTH EIGHT:
Girls are "auditory," boys "visual."

Male and female infants do not seem to respond differently to sounds. At most ages,

boys and girls are equally adept at discriminating speech sounds. There is no sex difference in memory for sounds previously heard.

No study shows a sex difference among newborns in time spent looking at visual stimuli. During the first year of life, neither sex emerges clearly as more responsive to what they see. From infancy to adulthood, the sexes exhibit a similar degree of interest in visual stimuli. They also seem to be alike in ability to discriminate among objects, identify shapes, estimate distances, and perform on a variety of other tests of visual perception.

Our examination of the social science literature also revealed some sex differences that are fairly well-established:

DIFFERENCE ONE:
Males are more aggressive than females.

A sex difference in aggression has been observed in all cultures in which aggressive behavior has been observed. Boys are more aggressive physically and verbally. They engage in mock-fighting and aggressive fantasies as well as direct forms of aggression more frequently than girls. The sex difference manifests itself as soon as social play begins, at age two or two and a half. From an early age, the primary victims of male aggression are other males, not females.

Although both sexes become less aggressive with age, boys and men remain more aggressive through the college years. Little information is available for older adults.

DIFFERENCE TWO:
Girls have greater verbal ability than boys.

Girls' verbal abilities probably mature somewhat more rapidly in early life, although a number of recent studies find no sex differences. During the period from preschool to early adolescence, the sexes are very similar in their verbal abilities. But at about age 11, they begin to diverge: female superiority increases through high school, and possibly beyond. Girls score higher on tasks that involve understanding and producing language, and on "high-level" verbal tasks (analogies, comprehension of difficult written material, creative writing) as well as "lower level" measures (such as fluency and spelling).

New York Public Library

ca. **A.D. 501.** Queen Chand Bibi of Bijapur, Hindustan, famous for her beauty and ability as a warrior, is so enamored of the dashing figure she cuts on the battlefield that she deliberately picks fights with neighboring rajahs. Now, however, she allows her vanity to get the better of her sense of precaution, is lured into enemy territory, and is at last fatally ambushed.

DIFFERENCE THREE:
Boys excel in visual-spatial ability.

Visual-spatial ability involves the visual perception of figures or objects in space and how they are related to each other. The visual-spatial test has the subject inspect a three-dimensional pile of blocks, and estimate the number of surfaces visible from a perspective different than his own. Another has him look at a figure, then select one from a set of four that matches the original if rotated in a plane. Male superiority on visual-spatial tasks is not found in childhood, but appears fairly consistently in adolescence and adulthood, and increases through the high school years. The sex differences are approximately equal on analytic tasks (those that require separation of an element from its background) and nonanalytic ones.

DIFFERENCE FOUR:
Boys excel in mathematical ability.

The two sexes are similar in their early acquisition of quantitative concepts and their mastery of arithmetic in grade school. Beginning at about age 12 or 13, however, boys' mathematical skills increase faster than girls'. The greater rate of improvement does not seem to be entirely due to the fact that boys take more math courses, although the question has not been extensively studied.

The magnitude of the sex difference varies depending on the study, and is probably not as great as the difference in spatial ability. Both visual-spatial and verbal processes are sometimes involved in solving math problems; some problems can be solved in either way, while others cannot, a fact that may help to explain why the size of the sex difference varies from one study to another.

On some questions, we found ambiguous findings or too little evidence on which to base conclusions. These questions are still open to further research.

QUESTION ONE:
Are there differences in tactile sensitivity?

Most studies of tactile sensitivity in infancy or ability to perceive by touch at later ages do not show sex differences.

When differences are found, girls are more sensitive, but since this finding is rare, we cannot be confident that it is meaningful. Most studies in which the results are analyzed by sex deal with newborns; more work is needed with other ages.

QUESTION TWO:
Are there differences in fear, timidity and anxiety?

Studies that involve direct observation of fearful behavior usually do not find sex differences. But teacher ratings and self-reports usually reveal girls as more timid or more anxious. The problem with self-reports is that we do not know whether the results reflect real differences, or only differences in people's willingness to report anxiety.

Since the very willingness to assert that one is afraid may lead to fearful behavior, the problem may turn out to be unimportant. But it would be desirable to have measures other than self-reports, which now contribute most of the data from early school age on.

QUESTION THREE:
Is one sex more active than the other?

Sex differences in activity level do not appear in infancy. They begin to show up when children reach the age of social play.

Some studies find that during the pre-school years, boys tend to be more active, but many studies do not find a sex difference. This discrepancy may be partially traceable to the kind of situation in which measurements are made. Boys appear to be especially stimulated to bursts of high activity when other boys are present. But the exact way in which the situation controls activity level remains to be established.

Activity level is also affected by motivational states—fear, anger, curiosity—and therefore is of limited usefulness in identifying stable individual or group differences. We need more detailed observations of the vigor and quality of children's play.

QUESTION FOUR:
Is one sex more competitive than the other?

Some studies find boys to be more competitive than girls, but many find the sexes to be similar in this regard. Almost all the research on competition has involved situations in which competition is maladaptive. For example, two people might be asked to play the prisoner's dilemma game, in which they have to choose between competitive strategies that are attractive to the individual in the short run, and cooperative strategies that maximize both players' gains in the long run. In such situations, the sexes are equally cooperative.

In settings where competitiveness produces greater individual rewards, males might be more competitive than females, but this is a guess based on common-sense considerations, such as the male interest in competitive sports, and not on research in controlled settings. The age of the subject and the identity of the opponent no doubt make a difference too; there is evidence that young women hesitate to compete against their boyfriends.

QUESTION FIVE:
Is one sex more dominant than the other?

Dominance appears to be more of an issue in boys' groups than in girls' groups. Boys make more attempts to dominate

---

ca. **A.D. 502.** Ethne the Terrible, "Daughter of the Druids" and warrior queen of the Irish king of Munster, is slain fighting alongside her husband in battle.

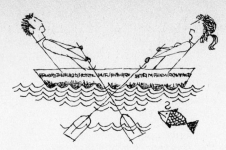

each other than do girls. They also more often attempt to dominate adults.

But the dominance relations between the sexes are complex. In childhood, the segregation of play groups by sex means that neither sex frequently tries to dominate the other; there is little opportunity. When experimental situations bring the two sexes together, it is not clear whether one sex is more successful in influencing the behavior of the other. In mixed adult groups or pairs, formal leadership tends to go to the males in the early stages of an interaction, but the longer the relationship lasts, the more equal influence becomes.

QUESTION SIX:
Is one sex more compliant than the other?

During childhood, girls tend to be more obedient to the commands and directions of adults. But this compliance does not carry over into relationships with peers. Boys are especially concerned with maintaining their status in their peer group, and therefore are probably more vulnerable than girls to pressures and challenges from that group, although this has not been well-established. It is not clear that in adult interactions, one sex is consistently more willing to comply with the wishes of the other.

QUESTION SEVEN:
Are nurturance and "maternal" behavior more typical of one sex?

There is very little information about the tendencies of boys and girls to be nurturant or helpful toward younger children or animals. Cross-cultural work does indicate that girls between six and 10 are more often seen behaving nurturantly. In our own society, the rare studies that report nurturant behavior involve observation of free play among nursery-school children. These studies do not find sex differences, but the setting usually does not include children who are much younger than the subjects being observed. It may be that the presence of younger children would elicit sex differences in nurturant behavior.

Very little information exists on how adult men respond to infants and children, so we can't say whether adult females are more disposed to behave maternally than adult males are to behave paternally. But if there is a sex difference, it does not generalize to a greater female tendency to behave altruistically. Studies of people's willingness to help others in distress have sometimes found men to be more helpful, sometimes women, depending on the identity of the person needing help and the kind of help that is required. Overall, the sexes seem similar in degree of altruism.

QUESTION EIGHT:
Are females more passive than males?

The answer is complex, but for the most part negative. The two sexes are highly alike in their willingness to explore a novel environment, when they both have freedom to do so. Both sexes are highly responsive to social situations of all kinds, and although some individuals tend to withdraw from social interaction and simply watch from the sidelines, they are as likely to be male as female.

We said earlier that girls are more likely to comply with adult demands, but compliance can take an active form; running errands and performing services for others are active processes. Young boys seem more prone than girls to put out energy in bursts of strenuous physical activity, but the girls are not sitting idly by while the boys act; they are simply playing more quietly. Their play is fully as organized and planned, possibly more so. When girls play, they actively impose their own design upon their surroundings as much as boys do.

Is it true that boys and men are more aggressive, but this does not mean that females are the passive victims of aggression —they do not yield or withdraw in the face of aggression any more frequently than males do, at least during the phases of childhood that have been observed. We have already noted the curious fact that while males are more dominant, females are not especially submissive, at least not to boys and girls their own age. In sum, the term "passive" does not accurately describe the most common female personality attributes.

We must conclude from our survey of all the data that many popular beliefs about the psychological characteristics of the two sexes have little or no basis in fact. Yet people continue to believe, for example, that girls are more "social" than boys, or are more suggestible than boys, ignoring the fact that careful observation and measurement show no sex differences.

The explanation may be that people's attention is selective. It is well-documented that whenever a member of a group behaves the way an observer expects him to, the observer notes the fact, and his prior belief is confirmed and strengthened. But when a member of the group behaves in a way that is not consistent with the observer's expectations, the behavior is likely to go unnoticed, so the observer's prior belief remains intact.

This probably happens continually when those with entrenched ideas about sex differences observe male and female behavior. As a result, myths live on that would otherwise rightfully die out under the impact of negative evidence.

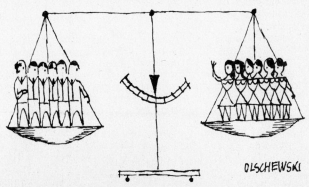

OLSCHEWSKI

ca. **A.D. 587.** Radegunde, the daughter of the king of Thuringia, founds Germany's first charitable institutions for aiding and nursing the sick and maimed.

How to Select Your Shrink

Rosemary Blackmun

A number of years ago, when I was considerably younger and not too smart, I had a friend who was in long-term, in-for-a-penny, in-for-a-pound psychoanalysis, and I asked him how he could bear to reveal himself so completely to someone who was almost a stranger. "There comes a time," he said, "when it hurts so much you want to." Which is still a pretty good gauge for anyone debating the question of therapy. Many people, of course, need to be "led" to therapy, a subtle process better performed by your family doctor or perhaps a trusted clergyman than by your best friend or your hairdresser no matter how close you are. This article is an attempt to show, after talking with experts in practice, some of the present varieties of therapy from which you can choose what seems congenial or pertinent.

Short-term psychotherapy

In recent years for several reasons, not the least of them economy, there has been a marked swing away from long-term therapy to something quicker and more immediate. Dr. Arnold A. Hutschnecker, who wrote *The Drive for Power,* feels there is no rigid standard by which one can judge whether short-term therapy is in order. It depends on the problems as they are assessed by the therapist and the patient, as well as the patient's expectations. "You're dealing," he explained, "with people who have lost their zest for life, their vigor, élan, joie de vivre; they find decisions hard to make; they start things and can't finish them. The problem may relate to any area—marriage, job, child-parent or parent-child relationships. These people are confused and don't know how to go on." Consideration must be given to the relative acuteness of the problem and the patient's ability to handle problems; it is often possible to estimate just how "together" a person is in his first session.

"When someone is confused," explained Dr. Hutschnecker, "the question of therapy is a matter of getting him out of a hole, to understand what triggered the confusion or depression. Then there is the question of how far you want to go." If the problem is merely a matter of fears, of anxieties, or mild depression, short-term therapy may well offer a solution—anything from a few sessions to roughly six months should take care of relieving symptoms. "It's like getting over an accident," he explained, "you learn to understand why this happened to you or by what compulsion you have made it happen. The important thing is to make the patient aware and to get him to pick himself up and shake it off. The therapist must mobilize what's in the person, his drive, his talents, his interests. He tries to create harmony and point out possible pitfalls in the patient's behavior patterns. . . . The object of short-term therapy is to understand the 'obstacle' and why you can't overcome it. The sum of the symptoms is the indicator of trouble. When you have a bright and functioning young person, for example, he probably has enough perception and courage to take hold quickly, and short-term therapy is probably the answer to his dilemma."

Short-term therapy is advisable when there is an acute conflict. Very often such patients are temporarily paralyzed by life, and short-term therapy may break the pattern if the patient has the determination to bring all his own initiative and creativity to bear on the problem rather than spending those energies in idleness or violence. "What really matters," said Dr. Hutschnecker, "is to have the capacity to love and the ability to give."

When is short-term therapy not enough? The answer (which may be painfully arrived at) is when the basic personality structure is in a tumult of confusion, when self-esteem is at a very low level, when there is no sense of worth and only a thin veneer of efficiency. A person in that state must first learn to walk, to feel the strength in his legs, to put life in proper perspective and learn how to balance things. That requires the long-term therapy that develops a strong ego; the subject should eventually be able to say to himself, "I do these things because I *want* to do them."

Psychoanalysis - the classic variety

If you have doubts, let me say that this is indeed the type of therapy in which a couch is used. The patient must go to his analyst four or five times a week for a period of three to six years. While he lies on the couch, the treatment situation is so organized that important facts and feelings emerge freely from his mind. There will be few directions, almost no questions and no judgments. The purpose is to get the patient to know what's going on in his mind: his thoughts, dreams, reactions. The analyst ultimately shows the connection between these thoughts, images and feelings and is able to demonstrate misconceptions and misconstructions in terms of past traumas and responses. Any neurosis is essentially a misinterpretation of the present caused by a misconception of the past. The analyst's values and personality are not permitted to intrude upon the patients' integrity.

My authority for this is an eminent New York psychoanalyst whom I shall call Dr. Brown. Dr. Brown finds that long-term analysis is indicated in a surprisingly small percentage of the people who come to see him—"not every neurotic should be hauled off to the couch." The patient must feel that his life is so disrupted that he wants to effect a radical change. He must have a deep sense of this, a moral commitment to change; he must also expend a great quantity of energy and must have an innate capacity to handle analysis; memories must be brought back and abreacted, put in their proper perspective. The premise is that everything depends on the understanding of the unconscious conflict which has been persistent from childhood on. Most people are unaware of their childhood wishes or fears or guilt, but they are aware of the effects of conflict. Neurotic symptoms include phobia, obsession, depression, severe inhibitions, compulsive habits such as checking the lock on the door not once but three times, fear of taking examinations or meeting their equivalent in later life. There may be physical symptoms: transient paralysis of the hand, disturbances in vision, skin eruptions, over-abundant blushing, and *globus hystericus*—the lump in the throat.

If you merely take symptoms away, a neurosis may be replaced by other symptoms or an abnormal character trait. Other things that bring people to couch-therapy may be certain unfortunate repetitive patterns in life, sexual disabilities and inhibitions, or such abnormalities as those of a man who can only love a debased woman. Certain symptoms are very intrusive; they interfere with life and may in fact govern a life-style or overwhelm the character. Habit formation is a way of getting away from anxiety produced by conflict.

There is always a direct relation between the personality structure and the symptom; for instance, phobic patients tend to be frightened people. The point is that it is necessary to explore the symptoms and find others as well as patterns of life that have escaped the subject. Since symptoms, character traits. inhibitions, etc. are interchangeable, it is necessary to examine and analyze all aspects of personality. Certain aspects of the problems are untouched by other forms of therapy.

Who benefits most from psychoanalysis? Dr. Brown believes, as most analysts do, that it is preferable to treat young adults—people from the mid-twenties to early forties. Ado-

ca. **A.D. 660.** Saint Odile, the blind daughter of Berswinde and warrior lord Adalric, is born. She awes her region, shortly thereafter, with her gift of "second sight," correctly foretelling the downfall of the Carolingian empire, the siege of Paris, and its near miraculous deliverance from attacking Norsemen.

lescence is too fluid; too much is changing too fast. . . . In recent years lack of self-esteem has taken center stage in the problems people present when turning to analysis. Twenty years ago it was anxiety. With lack of self-esteem goes the whole range of guilt feelings, feelings of worthlessness, expecting too much of oneself, often stemming from early humiliations and frustrations. Part of this is undoubtedly cultural and appears in large urban centers, whereas in more primitive areas doctors encounter old-fashioned hysterics. Paradoxically, the patient who evidences less suffering initially may require a longer period of treatment than one in acute distress.

Psychoanalytic treatment, as a rule, is available to most middle-class people but beyond the reach of many, although there are some low cost clinics. It will never be generally applicable to all who need it because society cannot (or will not) afford to train the number of psychoanalysts required. Compared to other healing practitioners, the psychoanalyst can treat only a handful of patients.

Therapy the group way

Mildred Newman and Bernard Berkowitz, the husband and wife authors (with Jean Owen) of the best selling book, *How To Be Your Own Best Friend,* are both practicing psychologist-psychoanalysts. Their combined use of individual and group analysis, they explained, "is grounded in traditional psychoanalytic theory implemented by insights and techniques adopted from more recent developments in ego-psychology."

Jointly, they lead each of their five groups which are composed of analysands who are in treatment with one or the other of them. A new patient usually spends a minimum of six to twelve months in individual sessions before entering a group. As in more classic analysis, the aim is to elucidate the influences of the past on the present.

In group the emphasis is on the present, and the interaction is often exciting, sometimes turbulent. One girl told a man in her group that she loved him. Thereupon another girl "relived her childhood pain of feeling left out of the love between her parents." It became clear that the second young woman was carrying through life a chronic sense of deprivation and exclusion which caused her much needless pain. "Paradoxically," said Newman and Berkowitz, "she would have to give up this sense of deprivation and whatever strange satisfaction it gave her in order to partake fully of what life has to offer." Most interesting of all was the fact that the whole group could see the psychodynamics of the situation fully displayed.

A group usually consists of six to nine members, and it requires a sharp pair of eyes, or in this case a quartet of eyes,

Freud's study, with the first couch of psychoanalysis.

New York Public Library

to follow the action. Neither Newman nor Berkowitz is a passive analyst, but the better the interaction of the group, the less they need to intervene. Each group develops its own lifestyle, its own way of dealing with such inflammable subjects as loving, stress, anger and the whole range of human emotions—as Zorba put it, "the full catastrophe." Newman and Berkowitz feel there is often too much intellectualization in therapy, and their groups focus on feelings, predominantly on subjective reactions to oneself and to others in the group. In a well-working group the emphasis is on what's happening that very moment.

Some people get more by speaking, others by listening. There was one completely silent man who stayed in his group for two years and then rose and made a formal speech to the others thanking them for enabling him to untangle his problems and embark on a new life.

How does the therapist put a group together? Both Ms. Newman and Dr. Berkowitz agree that some diversity is necessary and that intuition and judgment must go into striking just the right balance. Then the therapists must know when to put pressure on and when to take it off. They not only listen to what is said, but must also pay attention to facial expressions, breathing, and body posture. "It is, in fact," they said, "hard work to conduct a group." But both of these experienced therapists feel strongly that the richest and most therapeutic result a patient can have comes of the combination of individual and group analysis.

Interaction between patients is limited to the one-and-a-half-hour group sessions. Only first names are used. There is no smoking, no touching; patients are forbidden to meet socially outside the group. "For the person who joins in group therapy for the first time," said Newman and Berkowitz, "the experience is one of looking *out* of himself and seeing others." As one patient said, "It was the group that helped me to respect other people's feelings."

How much time goes into all this? It may take six months to a year before you are ready for group (although many other group therapists recommend a shorter period of one-to-one sessions). After that you may stay for several years in individual and group therapy.

Family Therapy

In the present era of concern and discussion about the nuclear family, many psychotherapists have developed special techniques for dealing with family problems. Dr. Paul Franklin, a practicing analyst, is one of them. "Family therapy," explained Dr. Franklin, "is a healing procedure which deals with the emotional pain underlying the problems of one person or a family." It attempts to deal with the presenting difficulty within the framework of that microcosm of society we call the family.

Dr. Franklin believes that no person is "sick by himself"—everyone with whom he has close emotional contact is involved; this includes, of course, other members of his living unit. Dr. Franklin believes emotional sickness is often an expression of imbalance within the family system. By observing the family it is possible to predict which member of the unit will show signs of disturbance, which person will be afflicted and what form the affliction will take.

Who seeks family therapy? Some patients are referred to a therapist; others come with such complaints as "our marriage is about to break," or "the family is falling apart" or "our son is a dropout and we feel intuitively we've contributed to his problems but we don't know why." At other times a person calls for individual therapy. In any case it is advisable to see the whole family diagnostically before the therapeutic goals are formulated. Seeing a person alone presents a monochromatic aspect of the problem. Seeing the living, interacting unit shows additional facets of his pain and disturbance and, most importantly, his strength.

The usual procedure is to see the whole family together for a consultation. At the end of one or two sessions, tentative diagnosis as well as therapeutic treatment is determined. Further sessions may involve the ——————————➤

ca. **A.D. 690.** The Empress Wu How of China changes her dynastic title to Chou and now calls herself "God Almighty."

whole family unit or a fragment of it—say, all the siblings, parent and child, father and child, mother and child, or both parents and one child, possibly a grandmother or a trusted housekeeper. These matters are interchangeable; there are no set rules and procedure is decided according to the needs of the patient or patients.

Individual therapy is not opposed—in fact, it may be essential concurrently or during certain segments of family treatment. It is essential that the same therapist see either individual sub-groups or the total family. Any emotional fragmentation is to be avoided. Sometimes, however, one member of a family should, for various reasons, be referred to another therapist with whom the original therapist can talk freely and is in constant communication.

During the therapy sessions the therapist has several roles to perform. He tries to identify the underlying conflicts and deal with them in an attempt at resolution. They are often unknown to the subjects or at best there is a dim awareness.

One of Dr. Franklin's most revealing case histories concerns a ten-year-old boy, a troublemaker who was aggressive, defiant, and claimed to have a B.B. gun he planned to use on one of his teachers. Consultation revealed that his parents' marriage had floundered from the beginning, and that his grandparents had suggested their having the child as a means of bringing them closer together. The husband was passive, detached, worked excessively long hours, then went bowling and came home at three o'clock in the morning. His wife was bitter, depressed, and biting. Her rage was frequently turned on her son. The conflict was thus identified as existing between the parents. Dr. Franklin, by placing the problem where it really existed, encouraged the parents to face it and resolve their differences so they could stop scapegoating the child. This was crucial because it freed the boy from a tremendous burden and permitted him to resume his normal growth pattern.

Dr. Franklin believes that aside from placing the problem, the therapist must activate the dormant positive elements in the relationships between the various members of the group. Sometimes hostility and togetherness exist at the same time, and those involved have only ineffectual means of coping with their emotions. It is the therapist's task to look for the positive links, which can't always be seen in individual therapy.

In contrast with other therapies in which the therapist's personality remains fairly anonymous, the family therapist becomes a *temporary* living member of the family unit—but only for the duration of therapy. At times he may be free to express his personal feelings about members of the family, having checked them first against rationality and appropriateness.

This encourages openness on the part of the others. He does not spell out his reactions to everything by any means; it is a technique to be used *occasionally* when intervention is indicated. By thus entering the family milieu as a real person the therapist serves as an unconscious model of feeling and reaction.

When is family therapy contra-indicated? It is of little value when there is danger of an uncontrolled outbreak of violence or little evidence of a viable relationship between people.

Crisis intervention

Dr. Arthur Meyerson, Director of the psychiatric acute care and emergency service at New York's Mt. Sinai Medical Center and an Assistant Professor at the Mt. Sinai School of Medicine, has several strings to his bow. Besides his role at the hospital which has a great deal to do with crisis intervention, he also maintains a small practice as a full-term analyst. His reasons for choosing the long way home for certain people are much the same as Dr. Brown's—he defines those patients as people whose personalities are getting in their way and who are willing to make a long commitment of time and money.

He feels strongly that the form of therapy people fall into now is largely a matter of chance. Two things are needed to correct this: complete honesty on the part of the referring doctor, who should be aware of the varieties of therapy available and some sound, disciplined research into the effectiveness of each type with long follow-up records.

Crisis intervention—new in the last decade or so—is a method of helping people in a moment of intense crisis resulting from death, divorce, or a psychosocial clash such as you find in ghetto areas. It puts together a team of doctors, social workers, paramedics and others to apply a battery of techniques working with an entire family or surrounding circumstances; it is a maximum arsenal of psychiatric-social help for a limited time. Even if one member of a group is resistant the team proceeds. Six months later, it has been found, people who have had the benefit of crisis intervention are better off than if they had been hospitalized. And, in spite of the array of talent, it is cheaper than hospitalization.

Medicine is moving rapidly to make crisis intervention a matter of clinical reality although training people is something of an obstacle. In crisis, professionals focus directly on one issue and both Mt. Sinai and Roosevelt Hospital have units in action now. Mt. Sinai also maintains a walk-in clinic with psychiatric facilities for everything but analysis. In three years they have progressed from having one psychiatrist on call to having two or three residents during the day and two on call at

night. These experts screen patients and evaluate their needs—should they be in-patients or out-patients, etc.

Another sort of crisis intervention

Dr. Milton C. Hollar, a black psychiatrist, has an analytical practice but works more on a level where he "can touch many people," which is the key to dealing with the small, grinding daily crises many of us experience. For instance, he has spent a great deal of time with seven sets of foster parents counseling them about how to deal with the thirty or forty children in their care.

Also, as director of the Lincoln Avenue branch of the New Rochelle Guidance Center, he has seen it grow from a basement operation (complete with odorous sewer pipes) to a brand new community center where the staff has worked things out so that a person in distress can be seen by a therapist within 2.5 days of applying—which is something of a record. They now have a day care center, group therapy, and a day camp for children with behavioral problems to give them both a summer camp experience and some therapy. These are children who are not acceptable elsewhere because they have been expelled from school, even from the specialized programs that exist for them. Concurrently with the day camp, they receive the benefit of a five hour school program every day. The aim is to get them back to school or, if necessary, arrange for them to have residential treatment.

Again in his behind-the-scenes role, Dr. Hollar is a consultant to a cooperative college that has many exciting, relatively experimental programs. Most of his time is spent in consultation and as a resource person to whom the staff can turn for advice rather than directly with the students. He guides the supervisory people in their evaluation of the need for therapy and what form it should take.

Dr. Hollar is one of the few psychiatrists with whom I talked who works with adolescents—both at the New Rochelle Center and in private groups. At the Center he lets his colleagues know how he sets up a peer group and how to keep it in balance. He finds group therapy excellent for young people, and more successful on the whole if they are drawn from diverse areas and don't have to face each other every day—"it's just easier to let it hang out that way." In such groups it is extremely helpful if one member has already coped with a problem another is hung up on. One of his most interesting findings is that a great number of high school seniors really don't feel ready for college; they don't rule it out but they want to do something else for a time first. He insists that they maintain a regular job schedule, either paid or volunteer.

ca. **A.D. 735.** Among the Norse and Danish vikings marriage is a contract of sale, barter, or personal gift between a woman's parents and her future husband. Fidelity is not expected of the husband, though the unfaithful wife may be put to death if caught. Wives are also frequently exchanged or sometimes shared in common between sworn warrior comrades.

"Intense Feeling" therapy

Just four years ago, Dr. Sidney Rose, in New York, read, at the insistence of a patient, Arthur Janov's book, *The Primal Scream.* He tried this new approach and found it very effective. Without any help or training from Janov, he has converted his entire practice to what he calls Intense Feeling therapy. For someone who had been Director of Group Analysis at the Karen Horney Clinic and on the faculty of the American Institute for Psychoanalysis for twenty years, this was, to say the least, an enormous change.

According to Dr. Rose, people who have tried other forms of therapy find that a few months of Intense Feeling has changed them more than years of other therapies.

What happens is this: You start out individually with a three-week crash program during which you spend two to three hours a day, six days a week with the therapist. During this time you must live in isolation in a hotel. The purpose is to take you away from everyday living—"you can't repair a road without stopping the traffic." You are forbidden to drink, smoke, look at TV, take tranquilizers, sleep excessively or do anything else that normally relieves your tensions. You can't read, but you can write about yourself. You learn to suspend your critical faculties and regress, to forget you're an adult and become a child, letting all the old bad feelings well up. The worse you feel the better. "Welcome the pain," advises Dr. Rose. "The pain and bad feelings will lead you back to childhood memories of the original causes. It even leads some people back to traumatic birth experiences.

Dr. Rose does not, however, believe that birth is necessarily traumatic, because the infant is programmed for it in advance. But there is no end to the hurts and traumas to which a growing child may be subjected. All involve a feeling that the world is hostile, unpredictable, confusing and unable to meet the child's need to be held, nourished and cherished. All hurts are recorded in the body-memory system

and exert their influence in later life. The neurotic who has had bad yesterdays expects bad tomorrows. "All the world's a stage," maintains Dr. Rose, "and every neurotic has stage fright."

Having learned to let the bad feelings surface during the crash program, the patient then enters a group. There is no interaction in these groups except at the end of the session when patients discuss the day's therapy experience. During the actual session patients lie on mats on the floor. While each one is in a state of regression he pays no heed to the others. If he talks, he talks to himself, and the language is child talk in the present tense or even the crying and screaming of a baby. While in the regressed state he *permits* the expression of feelings which he dared not feel at the moment they first occurred, and the small piece of his adult self he carries with him injects new elements into his old "memory-circuit." Changes occur physically: "A schlemiel looks like a schlemiel," comments Dr. Rose. Afterwards he doesn't.

Why is this therapy different? Dr. Rose feels it "goes to the core of neurosis and allows the most primitive feelings to surface. Time is not wasted trying to deal with all the complicated endless verbal tricks the neurotic uses to deceive himself and others. As soon as he gives up control and allows the sick, hurt child's feeling to surface, he is at one with himself and able to talk back to his parents as people outside him. The purpose is to free the patient from hangups from the past so he can become a whole person realistically at peace with the past and living fully in the present."

Who should have Intense Feeling therapy? "The person who wants it very badly," said Dr. Rose. The optimum age range is from about twenty-six to forty.

Hypnosis as a facilitator

"Hypnosis, in itself, is not a therapy," explained Dr. Herbert Spiegel, Associate Clinical Professor of Psychiatry at Columbia's College of Physicians and Surgeons, "but it can be used as a facilitator in conjunction with psychotherapy, even long-term psychotherapy. It is a matter of applying a strategy in appropriate circumstances." For example, at a point in treatment where there is an already well-defined problem, an analyst may decide that it would be helpful to have the patient go straight to hypnosis for the removal of certain symptoms. If the patient shows self-destructive habits such as smoking, then he may be exposed to hypnosis to conquer it. The triumphant feeling that results from successful hypnosis may, by what is known as "the ripple effect," help the patient to lose other self-destructing tendencies. Hypnosis is also useful in re-

moving the fear of flying, fear of dogs, and other phobias, plus insomnia, anxiety, weight control, and depression, and again the ripple effect may facilitate psychotherapy.

The truly professional hypnotists (psychiatrists or trained psychologists) can also do a certain amount of detective work for the analyst. Highly hypnotizable people get a great assist in recalling relevant data during the trance state. This is known as hypermnesia—the direct opposite of amnesia.

In other cases, people in analysis suffer from a sense of despair. Hypnosis may help to discover the cogent reasons for this and catapult the patient into the reconstructive part of analysis. All such hypnosis is done concurrently with modified analysis; it is a diagnostic tool to clarify what the patient wants to change.

In recent avant-garde experiments conducted by Dr. Spiegel and his associates at Columbia it has been discovered that by measuring the hypnotizability of individuals, it is possible to predict what forms of therapy would be most suitable for them. If you are low on hypnotizability— one of the critical people who always must know "why"—long-term introspective analysis is probably for you. If you are capable of hypnosis, you are probably more trusting and may do quite well with some counselling, and at times brief exploratory medication. Some people do very well with such direct encounters as religious conversion, Zen, or AA, depending on the problems.

One question Dr. Spiegel feels is often unanswered in the whole field of psychiatry is "Who has the capacity to change?" . . . . Some people just can't, and at this point we don't know how they can have been so damaged during the growing up process that they are unable to. Among this group are those unconsciously committed to predeterminism—they are the people who feel "I am a victim of circumstances." These feelings are the enemy of therapy; patients may go through the motions, but it's just a facade. Only professionals know how to zero in on those capable of changing, and let the others go.

At present, Dr. Spiegel feels, more people are being treated by incompetent lay healers than professionals. Some patients are not really disturbed to begin with and others are chronic patients for whom therapy is at best a diversion. Interestingly enough no harm is actually done to those who are not sick or are very sick; it is the middle range of people who are capable of change who are handicapped by impulsive selection of a therapist or possibly bad advice. However, patients who keep going back out of choice to the non-pros deserve what they get, and inept therapy *can* be mischievous or harmful.

A.D. 775. Lu Shih, a young woman of China's T'ang Dynasty, becomes famous for staying to protect her aged mother-in-law from robbers when all other members of the family have fled. "Ah" says the old woman afterward, quoting from Confucius's *Analects,* " 'tis in cold weather that we become aware of the endurance of the fir and pine.' "

Choosing a Shrink
THE PSYCHOLOGICAL ADVISER   **95**

Self-analysis Eleanor Yachnes, M.D.

Psychoanalysis, like the woman's movement, can help people to take a new look at relationships and behaviors that they have taken for granted. The aims of both are to help the individual to change, to take power for her life in her own hands; to feel equal and to be equal; to be able to choose her direction; to assent, consent, refuse; to express herself; to develop as fully and freely as possible. Both are devoted to reexamining and reevaluating what exists in the personality and, through action, to making it into something more satisfying.

Karen Horney was one of the earliest psychoanalysts, probably the earliest, to write that women have the same character elements as men, and that our culture pressures women toward a one-sided development and men toward a different one-sided development. She saw in her analytic work with patients that individual differences spanned both sexes, though she also acknowledged the few differing responses to biological differences that are impossible to compare. Her book, *Self Analysis,* is the major resource of this article.

Most people who wish help with psychological problems consult a psychoanalyst or therapist whom they see over an extended period of time, often several times a week. Obviously, however, most constructive changes are accomplished without direct professional input, since only a small percentage of people can get to see a shrink. Many people can and do shrink their own ballooned images. And even with a professional, you do the work yourself; it is not done for you.

My recommendation would be to do analysis with professional guidance if you have the choice, because
  1) you would have the expertise of a trained observer who can see elements and connections to which you may be blind;
  2) you would get into fewer blind alleys and spend less time circling around in them; it would be quicker;
  3) in the inevitable times of confusion and consternation, you would have the encouragement of an interested ally.

However, professional analysis may be unavailable to you at the moment, and self-analysis may be your only alternative. Your Introspections may have so far been haphazard, though fairly rewarding, and you are wondering whether you should undertake self-analysis in a more disciplined way.

Of What Use Is a More Searching Self-analysis?

• Most gratifyingly, you might get to feel more in charge of yourself instead of feeling you are floating along.
• You might create both more solidity and more flexibility within yourself.
• You might realign your personality in a basic way so as to be able to develop and use your paralyzed assets and count on continued growth.
• You might get to dissolve your hidden self-defeating patterns.
• You might become able to express your warmth, realistic anger, compassion, hopes, and fantasies spontaneously and appropriately.
• You might respond to opportunities and resist unjust, denigrating, or exploitative treatment, rather than failing to respond.
• You might unleash creativity of several kinds.
• You might give up needing to be superwoman, and appreciate your real (whole) self more.
• You might allow yourself to have, and even implement, dreams, wishes, pleasures, enjoyment.
• You might give up stereotyped values and develop your own value system.
• You might learn to respect your limitations and cease denigrating yourself and others for having them.
• You might become able to do something about the limitations that arise from inertia, not from biology.
• You might lose the notion that you have one static identity and acquire the awareness of your changing identities.
• You might realign yourself in the situations in which and with people with whom you automically feel uneasy, inferior, self-effacing; or automatically privileged, superior, arrogant; or fearful.
• You might redefine your place in the world as a person of the feminine gender.
• You might be able to increase your ability to be understanding and helpful without making a martyr of yourself.

For many women who are experiencing a rebirth of awareness of themselves as more capable, strong, intelligent, enduring, creative, and equal than they had dreamed (or had been misled to believe), self-analysis can lead to a much richer experience with men. This can become yet richer as men, too, give up misled, worn-out, decayed attitudes, which hobble them as well as women.

Unfortunately, many people avoid even occasional self-analysis in depth, because they mistakenly fear they will find out they are "really" bad or weak or powerless or despicable. Some popular literature and manners of speaking feed these misconceptions. When you read about "the masochistic personality," for example, it is very possible to conclude that this is a bed-rock (and specifically woman's) personality. If you apply this idea to yourself, you conclude, inaccurately, that you must resign yourself to being completely a "masochist." The formulation "the masochistic personality" refers only to those parts of you that are self-effacing, and totally ignores your impulses to assume responsibility for yourself for the joy of it.

Interestingly, your fear of finding out that you are "really terrible" may be a very good sign that being "terrible" (vindictive, mean, selfish, hypocritical) is not at all acceptable to you. The more good work you put in on yourself, the more likely you are to find out that your "real self" is, as Karen Horney said, "the possible self, in contrast to the 'idealized' self, which is impossible of attainment." The real self is "the original force toward individual growth and fulfillment, with which we may again achieve full identification, when freed of the crippling shackles of neurosis." She also defines an "actual self" as "everything a person is at a given time: body and soul, healthy and neurotic." The goal of self-analysis is to get to know the actual self and move toward the real self.

What Must You Bring to Self-analysis?

• A searching, introspective attitude about yourself and your external world; an open-mindedness and willingness to entertain other points of view from those you've held so far.
• The determination to make consistent effort to change.
• Resilience.
• An honesty that is ruthless to self-deceit and false modesty.
• The conviction that it is possible to change, that each human nature is changing, as is your own, right now.
• An awareness of some of the laws of psychology, accepting that they apply to *you,* not only to others.
• A recognition that it is not just *one* of your troublesome traits that is causing all the difficulty. Complexly interacting groups of safety maneuvers are creating general patterns, which have far-reaching effects within you.
• Acceptance of the working of unconscious motive forces beneath the surface expression of your feelings and behavior. "Something" of which you may be only dimly aware "makes" you do and feel things that surprise you, or that you don't want to do or feel. Good news! Some of these unconscious forces may be basically healthy, though unacceptable, impulses still striving to be expressed; but some may be the unacceptable consequences of those repressions. Only being open to them will sort them out.
• The realization that you must change by

A.D. 825. Sung Jo-Chao, celebrated author and scholar of the T'ang Dynasty, dies after devoting her life to study, writing the *Analects for Women* and other works, and gaining the title of "The Female Scholar," an unusual distinction for her sex then or at any other period in Chinese history.

Varujan Boghosian, Cordier & Ekstrom, NYC

These needs are "basic" in the sense that ill health will result from their being unsatisfied, much as absence of vitamins or certain amino acids may not cause death rapidly but will create deficiency diseases that hamper function, and in time create marked disability and death.

All of these needs and many more are needs of *every* person. It is not possible to choose one or two and do without some of them. They all apply.

"Symptoms" are a result of thwarting the satisfaction of these and many other needs. Some well-known symptoms that are disturbing and difficult to deal with are:
psychosomatic pains, headache, ulcer pains, stomachache
some high blood pressure
some palpitations
trembling
blushing
extravagant sweating at times
some asthmatic conditions
hives
colitis

Another well-known group includes:
anxiety
compulsive self-denigration
submissiveness
chronic depression
procrastination
suspiciousness
expectation of being exploited (beyond realistic cautions)
need for conquests of the opposite sex
compulsive work
expectation of disapproval
certainty that one will make the wrong choice

Some attitudes or behavior that are less often thought of as symptoms are:
intermittent clumsiness
blurting regretted remarks
"laziness"
avoidance of areas of living
compulsive high spirits no matter what
righteousness, the need to be right
inhibition about educating self
inhibition about assuming management
following the same routines, year in and year out
"successfully" masking feelings constantly
constant sarcasm
constant cynicism
constant denigration of everything
blandness, lack of enjoyment

Have hope! These are not inborn and unchanging. Symptoms are an attempt to make life streamlined, more predictable, and comfortable and they do succeed in part. For example, if you make yourself a "klutz," you can succeed in avoiding competition and the hope for anything good, thereby preventing any possible disappointment.

Our own special combinations of symptoms and ways of dealing with problems get

your own efforts, and not expect to be changed by magic, nor by merely intellectual grasp of psychological principles, nor by token efforts, nor by finding out one important thing about yourself. Nor can you expect to be changed by a professional analyst. This is impossible anyway, no matter what undue influence you may feel others can exercise upon you.

Some Principles of Psychology That Are Necessary and Useful

Below is a positive conceptualization of some of the "laws of psychology."
• Change is constant.
• The *fundamental* inner drives are toward survival and growth, and not toward death and exploitation of others (death "instinct" and aggressive "instinct"). The distorted drives (cruelty, overbearing behavior, even self-defeating behavior) are not instinctive but are for safety at any expense.
• Every human being, woman and man, has similar basic needs and impulses and the

same basic channels through which to express them. (It may be that there are some needs that differ in men and women, but we can't yet be certain.)

Some of the basic needs are for:
sustenance and security
acceptance
affection
approval
satisfaction of curiosity
expression of love, anger, intelligence, creativeness
sociability
solitude
meaning
greater responsibility
consideration and respect
feeling useful
self-protection, coping (ability to fight, to run)
variety in experience (active/passive, piquant/bland, light/dark, brilliant/subdued, sound/quiet, companionship/solitude, initiate/acquiesce)

ca. **A.D. 880.** The Byzantine priest Herembert, horrified, reports to the Emperor Basil that a vision has revealed the head of the Greek Orthodox Church to be a woman. The patriarch is thereupon accused and, "after having been despoiled of all her garments

together with our competencies and spontaneities to make up our character structures (or personalities). We repress parts of our needs. The neurotic parts of us may become mostly compliant, or mostly aggressive, or mostly detached from either compliancy or aggressiveness.

Still, the compliant person hasn't killed all assertiveness; it is submerged, or, more often, half drowned. The aggressive person, who needs people around most of the time in order to have someone to lead, has repressed but not lost the need to be alone at times, to enjoy herself without having to be admired. Often it is difficult to detect this. The aggressive woman may say, "I hate to be alone. I don't enjoy doing things by myself." She *needs* the admiration. The compliant woman may feel the same way but for the opposite reason. She can't enjoy things alone, because she feels unentitled to enjoy them unless she is arranging them for someone else's benefit.

In early self-analysis you will explore the pluses and minuses of your most frequently used patterns. In late self-analysis you will recognize the presence of the *other* patterns underneath. You will start to express these submerged needs, clumsily at first. As this happens, it will release the tension and other symptoms caused by the effort exerted in keeping them down.

How You Go About It

The method in self-analysis is the same as in formal analysis: you use free association to help to get to unconscious motivation and feelings.

To help yourself get into consistent work, you might want to free up some convenient time each day and arrange that there will be no interruptions, as you might when taking a course in something you enjoy. (It might be necessary to do this outside your home if your home offers little privacy. Or it might be good to set aside time early in the morning or very late at night.) You might want to keep a special notebook to jot down sequences of associations or feelings or thoughts or questions or fantasies or dreams, many of which tend to be forgotten. In any event, consistent, continuous work yields much more than does hit-and-run work.

But don't be slavish about it, because there is really no need to do it by pre-arrangement as with formal analysis. Outside important things may come up, or you may be really blocked or really tired. On the other hand, you may suddenly get a burst of interest or a series of insights at an off hour. Take advantage of this if you can. Spontaneity and responsiveness are to be cherished, in addition to reasonable consistency. In this respect, self-analysis may have some advantage over formal analysis—you can choose times when you feel like working, times that are most likely to be productive.

A good place to start is with whatever is on your mind. It is there because it bothers you or interests you. If it is a particular feeling, let it wash over you. Later, perhaps, you might ask yourself a lot of questions about it, but at first get the feel of it. Let associations and memories of having this feeling come back. Remember situations in which it occurred, and people with whom it is connected. Give attention to the bodily feeling of this emotion. Let whatever comes register. Later you can reject irrelevancies, after you determine that they really are irrelevant. At first you won't know.

But soon you will ask questions. Perhaps: Why such a strong feeling with such seemingly trivial precipitating occurrences? For example, you burst into tears when a stranger extends a kindness. You may be led into asking yourself about other exaggerated emotional responses. You should also review your appropriate responses and register them as strengths. Don't take them for granted. You may pursue what there is in yourself and in the situation that permits you a more fulfilling participation. What fantasies have you of alternate solutions? You will no doubt think back to related experiences in your earlier years and in childhood. This can lead to valuable connections, but it is also vital to connect with the present-day importance of whatever it is you are exploring.

This is true of dreams as well. Whatever conclusion you come to eventually about what is going on in your dreams, it is most useful to connect it with what "causes" or precipitates these particular dreams at this time. Dreams reflect your ongoing fears and wishes, often in disguised or possibly opposite form, and also the attempts to solve these conflicts, trying out various possibilities for size, so to speak.

You should work with dreams in a manner similar to the way you work with feelings—that is, first, by allowing as free a play of association as possible to the various aspects of your dreams. Do not get lost in a never-ending maze of dream associations and possible interpretations, but, keeping within reasonable limits, give attention to the drift of the story, the manifest content, and the general emotional feeling in the dream. What role or roles did you play in the story, were you in it at all, were there any others in it, what sort of problem or conflict was present? Is the situation resolved by chance, by you or by others, or is it not resolved? Keep in mind that the whole thing is *your* dream, that you wrote all the parts, designed the scenery, whether rickety or rich, and that you are empathizing with and interpreting all of the roles in your story. Are you active or otherwise, does everything fail, does everything end up in the air, do you feel threatened or safe, and are you in strange- or familiar-feeling surroundings? All of these and, of course, many other questions may give bits of answers as to how you regard yourself and your capabilities in your world. After some time, try to relate the prevalent feelings in your dreams to those in your waking life in the situations that the dream may symbolize.

It is very important to remember that there is no universal dream symbol. W element means is unique to each p The meaning of a particular obje sequence of events in a dream depend your particular life history and associatic It may mean different things to you different times in your life, and even in th same dream. It may mean the reverse o. what it is generally thought to mean or of what it has meant to you in the past.

A banquet table could convey an underlying hunger, which might possibly be for enough food. But it might instead be hunger, for status or for acceptance or for affection and a sense of belonging or for sensual pleasures or for something more expensive that you can "afford"—literally, such as a house, or figuratively, such as being your own boss. It might represent a yearning for power over others through conferring or withholding your invitation, or a desire to take revenge, or a disgust at waste, or jealousy, or a desire to express generosity, or loneliness overcome by people getting together, or four of the above or none of the above.

You might conclude that your giving is via feeding, perhaps literally, perhaps feeding someone else's or your own neurosis; or the opposite, that you are wanting to feed your own healthy impulses. Thus you should not arrive superficially at the interpretation, but you must connect your dream to your past and current strivings. At first get in touch with all the feelings you are having. Then let your associations and memories float freely around the element you are exploring. This is quite different from going mechanically and intellectually down a checklist of "is it this, is it that?" Later, when you are more sure of the meanings and directions you are headed for, your intelligence and critical judgment should be brought in to establish priorities, to eliminate self-defeating methods, to choose real versus unrealistic possibilities.

For example, the "angry people" you fear in a dream might represent your inability to deal in reality with angry people, fear of your own anger, fear of doing without your own anger, or feelings of impotence.

Wishes, fantasies, daydreams are normal and valuable practices for the real thing; they are escape valves and clues to other parts of your personality, which are extremely useful to look into in the same manner as dreams. They are not unimportant, time-wasting fluff, but give clues to our hopes and to the ways in which we expect them to be fulfilled, even though these ways may be at variance with our conscious positions.

For example, the standard (I hope outdated) vision of the young girl being swooped out of her boring existence by a gorgeous, strong but kind knight on a (rarely black) horse, into a life of happily-ever-after housekeeping in the castle is still fairly prevalent in present-day dress. Perhaps a young woman today dreams that a shipping magnate with an island in Greece, or a

until she was naked...," is discovered to be, in fact, a woman. She is promptly driven from the Church in disgrace to a nunnery. Herembert's "vision" was, it seems to some, more the product of a spy's report than a holy inspiration.

super-talented businessman, or even the male spiritual leader of a commune will find her vital to his well-being and will insist on taking her into his life. In such a fantasy she acquires a safe niche without asking for it, without working for it, but dependent on his enduring affection for her beauty, innate goodness, and sexual attractiveness, all of which she is unsure of. Nowadays (thank goodness) in fantasies her intelligence, too, must be brought out by his encouragement.

Look for patterns and clues to your personal meaning in fantasies and day-dreams. As with dreams in sleep, you may find it useful to ask about your daydreams some questions such as these: Do I have repeated daydreams? what roles do I play? are they active or passive? what aspects of myself do they emphasize or minimize? what feelings do I experience? in response to what? how does the story end? do I let daydreams substitute for activity? They probably represent attempts to both solve your conflicts and get them solved from the outside.

In examining your repeated behavior patterns you may ask, Do I feel free to do what I like? what might happen if I did? do I always act the same with certain people? are my actions misinterpreted by others?

Self-analysis is not something you have to do in isolation, feeling you are alone with your trials and errors. You can take a companion into your confidence. When your insights lead you to change your behavior in ways that might disconcert people close to you, try to let them know that you're trying to change. Just remember that they have made no contract to respond exactly as you wish, but will respond to the changes they see in you in their individual ways. Try to be open to their responses.

Don't assume that the way you think people feel is the way they actually do feel. Check out your interpretations and assumptions when you can. You might be pleasantly surprised. One middle-aged woman, for example, believed her children would feel rejected and angry if she did not baby-sit with the grandchildren whenever they asked. With some self-exploration, she reached the point that she could say, on occasion, that she had other plans. She was surprised that the children did not respond as though she was an ungiving, unloving (unsacrificing) mother. She discovered, with mixed feelings, that they had other sources of sitters—partly with relief, because she could now feel freer about her own time; partly with panic, as she feared this might lead to her being less important to them and that they would not want to see her as much if she did not serve some utilitarian function. So she examined herself further and became more aware of her ancient and current self-denigrating attitudes, and also that her children held her in affection.

An old dog can indeed learn new ways. This will not make the dog into a lion, but will indeed utilize more of her "dogness." Or his.

What Then?

You have become increasingly honest, you have discovered assets you didn't dream you had and self-defeating behavior you had glossed over and impulses you are not sure what to do with. You really must test your insights in daily living. Try another formulation, another assertion. Keep in mind that the new way may be less straightforward than you think, though it may be an improvement over your old way. Bring your courage to bear, and risk and risk again, even if your expectations are not met the first time, even if your move goes without notice. You are not "entitled" to success at the first try, just because you did try. That's right, there's no justice. Just finding the way.

Come to some decisions, a critique of what you have been aiming for, of what you have done and are now wanting. If you don't apply your intelligence and decisiveness, you'll be floating without direction. Call off the injunction against choosing and using your forces.

Difficulties in Self-analysis

At this point we will consider what are called "resistances." Horney later preferred to call them "blockages," which implies a concept that is not so oppositional and suggests a forward thrust that meets up with a block.

"Analysis is an explicit attack on the neurotic structure," she says. "The sources of resistance are the sum total of a person's interest in maintaining the status quo. . . . This interest is not—and emphatically not—identical with a wish to remain ill. . . . What the person wants to maintain is not the 'neurosis,' but those aspects of it which have proved to be of immense subjective value . . . and which . . . hold the promise of future security and gratification. The basic factors that no one wants to modify one iota are . . . those that concern . . . secret claims on life."

Therefore, resistances of great power and variety can be expected, expressed in the most convincing disguises and with elegant rationalizations, since the very roots of safety are being threatened—the old ways with which we are so familiar.

Often they are difficult to see, and many resistances are indeed not visible at all, though their presence may be inferred from the illusions and contradictions about ourselves that come to our attention. They are responsible for much of the work in formal analysis, and must be looked for very energetically in self-analysis.

Below are listed a few of the disguises under which resistance to change may operate, both in your life and in analysis. Such feelings are not, however, "all in the imagination." They are felt keenly and there is more than an element of actuality in them. Healthy people feel them, too, but in neurosis they may be magnified to near paralyzing dimensions.

chronic confusion
prolonged discouragement

constant fatigue (if no physical cause)
frequent boredom
general helplessness
oversensitivity
undersensitivity
righteousness
self-glorification
disparagement of intellect
disparagement of emotionality
compulsive disparaging
compulsive anything
automatic distrust
"forgetting," in or out of analysis
hopelessness
getting lost in details (circumstantiality)
being tangential
blind spots
self-castigation
taking partial insights as complete
self-denigration
believing self "medicore," i.e., a "failure"
feeling stupid
depression following real losses that is beyond the expected
depression without obvious cause
depression for seeming trivia
anxiety not oriented to reality
general resentment (chip on shoulder)

Following is an example of the workings—and working out—of a blockage:

An intelligent, undereducated, gifted woman of twenty-seven with an obvious core of vitality had moved into her own apartment for the first time a year before the events to be described. Formerly, she had lived with her family by whom she had allowed herself to be exploited, and for years had worked in a managerial capacity in a dull job, having few acquaintances and no friends. She felt very isolated, inferior, and actually shoddy. Her chief and reliable comfort had been food, and she was overweight.

After she had been in group and individual analysis for several years, she took a leave from both job and analysis and went to another city for awhile, which freed her from the influence of family and colleagues, and from the ruts she had been in. During this period she arrived at some lasting insights, made a few decisions, and slowly began acting on them. Of course she ran up against blockages on the way (par for the course), but was able to understand some of them.

She had almost given up hoping for respect and affection from her family, but was still expecting a miracle to reward her past services to them. Her overall role had been to be the alter housekeeper and parent, filling in for both parents, who were depressed. Her yearning for affection was hidden under a masklike expression and robotlike helplessness.

While she was away, she examined these relationships at leisure. She decided she would no longer collude with her father against her mother and that she would no longer neurotically fulfill the neurotic needs of the family, but would try to nourish her own needs. "I won't be their slave. I will not let them lean on me." So far, so good.

But this resolution led into a painful blockage and she had to face the question What now?, or, in other words, how to become more self-dependent. Nourish her needs? What needs? She didn't dare to acknowledge needs. She became anxious, couldn't sleep, raged at her family, the whole world, and herself. This effectively blocked her from becoming aware of how she struggled against trusting her own feelings, which she had usually felt as dangerous and which indeed had been consistently ridiculed in childhood. She felt the pull of the old familiar helplessness-compliance-anger combination that had sustained her so far. "I need them (family), but I also need myself, and I can't have one at the price of killing other. What I don't understand is how a healthy livable compromise gets worked out. I'm not sure it can be done. . . . I'm so damned worried about what other people think, about other people laughing at me ALL THE TIME. . . . I think one of the worst fears I have about getting close to people is that they will eventually use that closeness against me where I am most vulnerable."

A few days later she was able to say, "But my dream has to do with being able to enjoy myself even though important, domineering people in my family are standing there disapproving. . . . Screw you, I'm going to do what I want in spite of you."

She was stuck at this point for some time. She was torn between going back to the old life and chancing the new one. A conflict that had to be blocked, of which she was unaware, was between her feelings that she must be assertive and that her assertiveness necessitated hurting or killing someone, as the previously quoted phrases "killing the other" and "screw you" suggest. While she did recognize a loose connection between her self-hate and her frequently enormous hatred of others, she was completely blocked from realizing that these hostilities were paralyzing her.

After awhile she did accept some of her own part in alienating people, and she extended herself and made at least one interesting relationship. "Honesty is liquid and has a high tide and low tide, and during hot spells there can be an honesty drought. Just as I hate being labeled honest [because she is aware of her deceptions], I hate, hate, hate having anything anything about me called phony, even if it is phony. What phony test do I put people through? My fat? My fat is *not* phony, it's real, very real. It's a real expression of how I feel, of what I think about life, how I've reacted to my life. It's not hidden away like an ulcer, which I can smile over and pretend is not there. Is there something wrong with letting people know loud and clear from the start just what trouble they're liable to get into if they get mixed up with me? How I look does put a lot of people off! But that's too damn bad."

What follows is the beginning of working through the resistance against taking full responsibility for her whole self, rather than passively waiting for people to do archaeo-logical digs for the buried treasure within her.

"But I'm reminded of something. Maybe I shouldn't test people just with my fat. Some people once 'accused' me of deliberately showing only my dark side to people and hoarding away the good. They said it was unfair to people because they could never respond to the better parts of me, which then strengthened my bad opinions about others, and around the vicious cycle went again. I thought they were all nuts then; I didn't know what the hell they were talking about. Well, maybe I didn't want to know."

What Helps Are There from Inner Resources?

When you become aware that you are up against a blockage, everything else you are analyzing should be dropped in favor of analyzing the resistance. It shows you are near something very important to you. The method is, again, as in tackling a dream or a feeling, to associate as freely as you can to the resistant feeling and to review the recent work you have been doing in self-analysis, possibly consulting notes if you have any.

Try to recall where you started braking. If this opens up the new area, you are off on a brand new trip. If it stays bogged down, as often happens for awhile, give yourself a breather for a few days or longer if necessary. Do things that you know you enjoy, and give it a chance. Often the insights will surface when you are not expecting them at all. Then encourage your introspection.

What Helps Are There from Outside?

You may be fortunate to have a friend with whom you can share and perhaps discuss some aspects of what is going on. Do not ever expect a friend to be your "alter analyst," however.

Many women's consciousness-raising groups are very valuable in throwing light from a new angle onto old difficulties, giving necessary support and encouraging growth. Often what you thought was only your problem turns out to be a general one, and you can thus get insights more quickly with others. Or it may occur to you that the problem is a societal problem and that you need not take the whole thing on your own shoulders—only your own part of it. This has relieved the personal burden for many women and members of other minority groups.

Participating in active or activist groups that are trying to make changes in any area in which you have an interest will have a freeing and strengthening effect on you. This is definitely not to suggest that the goals of analysis can be accomplished through activism and without analysis itself, but only that exposure to all aspects of your interests can only give you more to work with and on. This is a superb way to get to use aspects of yourself that have been dying on the vine. You don't have to set the organization on its heels the first time you go! Sit back and observe.

Getting involved with groups for creative work in art, dance, writing, sport, or whatever forms of expression you may be familiar with or want to work in are a good course of action, especially when you need a breather. But don't make the unfortunate mistake of signing up for a course in order to solve all of your hangups and make life beautiful. It just doesn't happen that way. Do it for enjoyment. Don't take a punishment course ("I *should* take short-hand"), but branch out.

If you cannot get past important blockages, you may want to have one or a few consultations with your analyst, if you have one. If your analyst and you have the arrangement to exchange letters or tapes, you might make use of this. Sometimes an analyst will agree to receive your communications and respond briefly, rather than at length.

You may want to start formal therapy after you have gone part of the way yourself, either with a "private" analyst or at a low-cost psychoanalytic clinic, foundation, or school. At some of these places, group analysis may be available. Sources of therapy can be located through the Department of Mental Hygiene, the local medical association, through various social agencies and professional associations, and also through women's self-help referral services. Many good contacts have been made by the recommendation of a friend. In any case, you should inquire in detail about the training and orientation of the therapist you consult. This is information to which you are entitled, and it will be good assertive practice to make the inquiry of the therapist.

In conclusion, Horney felt that with will, honesty, a determination to achieve the fullest that you can, there is a good chance that you can overcome these resistances, both in your daily life and in your analysis, and begin to develop your "real self"—the self that uses your total assets, a self that you can honestly like, and a self that never stops growing.

Resources and Self-analysis
Some of the Many Good Books Available

Horney, Karen, M.D. *Self Analysis.*
———. *The Neurotic Personality of Our Time.*
———. *Feminine Psychology.*
———. *Our Inner Conflicts.*
———. *Neurosis and Human Growth.*
   all W. W. Norton Library, all in paperback.
Bardwick, Judith M. *Readings on the Psychology of Women.* New York: Harper and Row (in paperback).
Strouse, Jean, ed. *Women and Analysis.* New York: Grossman Publishers.
Nin, Anais. *Diaries.* New York: Harcourt Brace Jovanovich, Inc. (in paperback).
Sexton, Anne. *To Bedlam and Party Way Back.*
———. *All My Pretty Ones.*
———. *Transformations.*
———. *The Awful Rowing Toward God.*
———. *Live and Die.*
———. *The Book of Folly.*
   all Houghton Mifflin, all in paperback.

There are many other good books now on the shelves in the "women's section" of most book shops.

ca. **A.D. 915.** Bertha, Countess of Swabia, Germany, is celebrated as a model housewife and is pictured on various official seals as seated on her throne, industriously spinning. Memories of "the good old times when Bertha span" will continue to be passed down through the centuries.

Creative Dreaming

Patricia Garfield, Ph.D.

Your dream life can provide you with many marvelous gifts: creative products, delightful adventures, increased skill in coping with waking life, and a personal laboratory to develop any project of your choice. The party is held several times each night. You are the guest of honor. All you need to do is attend, enjoy, pick up your presents, and return to waking life. Of course, you need to be aware. Otherwise, unconscious and tipsy, you'll forget who was there, what they said, what you did, and lose your gifts before you reach home. *You can develop almost total recall for your nightly dream parties and become able to record and use your gifts in waking life.*

Skill in remembering your dreams begins with your attitude. Value your dreams. Don't reject any one of them. The dream you dismiss as ridiculous or trivial, like an orphan child, may be the very one with great potential to blossom beautifully when it's more developed. Accept each dream you remember. Treat it with respect. Write it down. Give it permanent form. You will be amazed to find, after you keep a dream diary for a few months, that seemingly unimportant symbols appear again and again. They change in shape and size but are clearly recognizable when written down. They literally grow. You can trace their development over time. Each dream you have is a child of your own. *Attend patiently to all your dreams and they will provide you with remarkable insights about yourself.*

High dream recallers can increase color, vividness, and detail of their dreams. By employing creative dream techniques outlined in this book, high dream recallers can reduce anxiety and learn to become more self-confident in waking life. *If you are already a high dream recaller, you can get even more learning from your dreams and at the same time increase skills and confidence.*

Recalling your dreams and then recording them in a permanent form will give you an invaluable document from which you can both contribute to knowledge in general and learn, in depth, more and more about yourself. You can not only learn *about* yourself, but also *from* yourself.

When you have collected a set of your own dreams, you are in a better position to examine them and learn from them than when you have only isolated dreams. Jung observed that when you examine a series of dreams, you can find certain themes recurring. An important personal point will be underlined by repetition; glaring omissions become apparent; later dreams comment on or interpret preceding ones.

You can learn amazing things about yourself as you attend to the unusual images in your dreams. Dreams often contain strange creatures or objects: a long furry white animal-bird with hundreds of legs that dances and glides over the snow (the marvelous snowbird); a creature as round as a ball, covered in feathers, with dark eyes, sitting on a stone wall (the puffball); a tiny green woman with a water lily on her

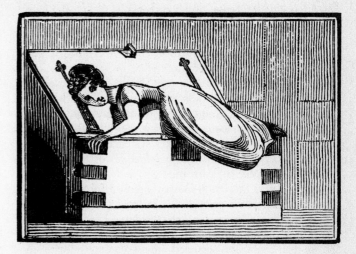

bottom who dives and swims in a pond (the water-lily lady); an object the size and color of half an orange, covered with candylike shreds, that turns into a jewelry box . . . .

Each idiosyncratic dream image offers us a chance to learn more about ourselves. When similar images recur over a series of dreams, they are shouting to their dream originator for attention. According to Ernest Rossi, a contemporary American dream theorist, any dream image that is unique, odd, strange, or intensely idiosyncratic in a dream is an emerging part of the dreamer from which new patterns of awareness may develop. Unique dream images are the "growing edge" of your personality. If you reflect on an unusual dream image, Rossi says, it can lead you to a new awareness; if you integrate your new awareness with your present self, you will be forming a new identity; as you form a new identity, you will be able to behave in new ways in waking life that will lead to new sensations and emotions, and eventually to new and different dream images. And so the cycle of growth continues.

The process of integrating new awareness from images is called psychosynthesis. The emphasis is upon making dream images part of your conscious awareness, rather than simply breaking down the parts of a dream to analyze them (as in psychoanalysis).

The way that you relate to your unique dream images will determine your future psychological development. Dreamers must take an active role within their dreams to integrate the newly emerging elements. As you actively cope with your dream images you will affect your waking behavior. Dreams in which you are overwhelmed by your dream images, chased, abused, ignored, or frustrated can leave you with a "dream hangover," clouding your waking activities. Dreams in which you successfully confront danger, have fascinating experiences, and discover creative products can leave you feeling covered with "dream dust," confident, happy, and full of zest for waking life.

Dreams are what you make of them. If you believe them to be meaningful, you will have and remember meaningful dreams; if you believe them to be creative, you will have and

ca. **A.D. 920.** Theodora, wife of the Count of Tusculum and a powerful woman in her own right, practically dominates the papacy. Her daughter Theodora the Younger, equally important in Roman politics, later marries Duke John, and their children become Popes John XIII and Crescentius I.

remember creative dreams. Dream states respond to waking attitudes. Perhaps, like the existentialist's view that the meaning of life is the meaning we give it, the meaning of dreams is the meaning we impose on them.

Thus, the first step in creative dreaming is to regard dreams as important and meaningful aspects of life. If you do not already have this attitude, you may wish to adopt it temporarily, as an experiment. You can proceed with the other steps, in any case, but you will be more likely to get good results if you value your dreams.

Assuming that you value your dreams, and you accept that you can consciously influence them, and you have accumulated much that is interesting to dream about, you can hasten creative dreaming by immersing yourself in the specific subject you wish to dream of. Every system employs this step. Ancient dreamers concentrated on thoughts of the god they expected to appear in a dream to heal them; past creative dreamers such as Stevenson exerted intense efforts to invent a story for a few days prior to his induced dream; American Indian youths on their vision quests endured hungry days and nights thinking about and waiting for their spirit guide's arrival; the Senoi are occupied almost constantly with the subjects of their dreams; don Juan urged Carlos to concentrate on his desired dream imagery; lucid dreamers such as Mary Arnold-Forster focused intensely on the flying dreams she wished to produce; and Yogi dreamers meditate upon the events of their dreams to come. Skills in meditation may increase dream control. *Whatever subject you wish to dream about, immerse yourself fully in it. Concentrate on it. Many creative dreamers stay deep in their subject up until a few minutes before sleep.*

As you concentrate on the subject you wish to dream about, *form a clear-cut intention to dream of that subject.* All systems employ this step, directly or indirectly. *Decide specifically what you want to dream about; intend to dream about it. Pick the topic of your dreams.*

After a clear-cut dream topic is decided upon, many dreamers put their intention into a concise phrase, such as, "Tonight I fly in my dreams. Tonight I fly. Tonight I fly." Only a few systems of dream control employ this step, so it may be helpful rather than essential. Those who advocate it repeat their phrase at intervals throughout the day and, while the body is deeply relaxed, repeat it again just prior to sleep. *You may wish to put your dream intention into a phrase, relax, repeat it, and visualize its fulfillment.*

All this *prior* preparation discussed so far will help you to remember what to do *during* your dreams. The more you think about what you want to do in your dreams while awake, the easier the same thoughts will come to you in your dreams. Think about the fact that dreams are not waking life and the things in them cannot hurt you, until you can remember this in the midst of a dream. Think about the cues that you might have used to become aware that you were dreaming until you can recognize them during a dream. For this is the crucial transition: *Remember while dreaming what you previously intended to do in your dream.* Once you have remembered your intentions during a dream, it is fairly easy to execute them.

One important principle to remember during your dream state is to find friendly dream images. All systems achieve a more cooperative dream state in some way: Ancient dreamers and American Indian dreamers induced helpful spiritual figures; the creative Stevenson had his "Brownies"; Senoi dreamers transform dream enemies into dream friends, or call on dream friends and they appear; don Juan achieves the dream images he desires; lucid dreamers can make friendly figures appear (or any other type); and Yogi dreamers are urged to be fond of, and merge with, their dream figures.

Build friendly figures into your dreams. Value the ones that appear spontaneously; respond to them in friendly ways during your dreams. Call on dream friends when you need them, induce them, make them part of you.

The most important thing to remember during your dream is *fearlessness of dream images.* As you gain control over various aspects of your dream life, you become aware that there is no need for fear because you can determine what will happen in your dreams. You can totally eliminate nightmares. You can both master and befriend your dreams. Fearlessness of dreams is easier if you are aware that you are dreaming.

Lucid dreaming, a feeling of consciousness during dreams, is one of the most exciting experiences a person can have. You can develop the skill of lucid dreaming from a brief flash of awareness to a prolonged dream adventure. As you learn to recognize prelucid moments you can test your dream experience and go into lucid dreaming. Frightening dream experiences, incongruities, or a strange dreamlike quality can alert your critical thought processes to the point that you realize you are in a dream state. You can learn to easily alter unpleasant dream experiences as they occur without having to escape them by awakening. To hold on to lucidity, you need to maintain a delicate balance between not becoming too emotional and not forgetting that you are dreaming. You may be able to maintain, as the Yogis do, consciousness throughout the transitions from waking to sleeping to dreaming to waking again.

Only two of the systems require high consciousness during the dream state: lucid dreamers and Yogi dreamers. You need *some* degree of dream consciousness to recognize that you are supposed to confront danger rather than run (in a dream) or to recall that you intended to look at your hands (in a dream). Lucidity is unimportant in the other systems and hence may limit their usefulness. You can shape your dreams without high consciousness, but the more aware you become of your dream state while you are in it, the more you will be able to actively relate to it and use it to your benefit. *Become conscious of your dream state.*

You may be able to develop lucid dreaming by increasing your number of flying dreams. My records confirm that both lucid dreams and flying dreams occur more often after several hours of rest and frequently occur in the same night. I made a special analysis of the appearance of color in my dreams and found that color, too, appears more frequently in my dreams after several hours of rest. Perhaps there is an underlying common chemical base for these findings. Or perhaps the cortex is more aroused at this time since, according to my records, various types of dream control often occur during the same night. In any case, consciousness in dreams is achieved more easily after several hours of sleep. Even before full consciousness occurs, you may become aware of directing

ca. **A.D. 941.** Olga, widow of the foully murdered Prince Igor, succeeds to his Slavic throne and leads her forces into pitched battle with his killers, burying many alive, torturing others, and finally, it is said, burning down their chief town by tying lit matches to the tails of homing birds.

SUMMARY OF SUGGESTIONS FOR KEEPING YOUR DREAM DIARY

1. You can develop almost total recall for your dreams. Accept and value each dream, no matter how foolish or fragmentary it may seem at the time. A complete record of your dreams can provide remarkable insights.

2. Before retiring, plan to remember whatever dreams come to you. Place a pad and pen within easy reach of your sleeping spot.

3. The best time to begin developing skill in dream recall is during an unpressured time in the morning when you awaken naturally (it will be from a REM period). If you have trouble recalling your dreams, plan a time when you can spontaneously awaken and be unhurried.

4. When you awaken from a dream, lie still and allow the dream images to flow back into your mind. If no images come, let yourself run through the important people in your life; visualizing them may trigger association to your recent dream.

5. When dream recall is complete in one bodily position, move gently into other sleeping positions to see whether you have additional dream recall in these positions. Always move gently into any recording position.

6. Record your dreams whenever they come to you, immediately, later in the day, or several days later.

7. Dream recall is richest and most detailed immediately following a REM period. You can learn to self-awaken from your REM periods throughout the night and make accurate records without disturbing your sleep. Record your dreams regularly in the morning with closed eyes in the method described and you may find yourself waking spontaneously from earlier REM periods. Recording dreams after spontaneous awakening from a REM will give most complete and accurate dream recall.

8. If you prefer, or if self-awakening does not develop, you may wish to use an artificial awakening method such as having a friend stay with you while you sleep and wake you at approximate ninety-minute intervals, when you are likely to be experiencing REM. Or, your friend can watch directly for rapid eye movements. You can also use an alarm clock. Remember that REMs toward morning are longer and you have a better chance of catching dreams then.

9. Regardless of the method used to collect your dreams, by writing or by tape, make the first record with your eyes closed. Opening your eyes will disrupt dream recall.

10. As you value your dreams, accept them, record them regularly, and work on building dream friends, you will develop a more cooperative dream state.

11. Make your records in the order that you recall your dreams. Exception: Make note of unique verbal expressions first (poems, names, unusual phrases), regardless of the order, before they are forgotten. Note unusual happenings while making your record (falling asleep, interruptions). You may wish to note hypnogogic experiences. Try to identify elusive elements such as simultaneous layers of dreams.

12. Sharing your dream with a friend will help you to remember it, but you need written records as well to get the most benefit from your dream diary. Put your dreams into permanent written form (even if originally taped) and into chronological order.

13. Selecting titles for your dream stories from their unique aspects helps you recall your dreams and also identifies elements deserving special attention.

14. You may wish to try a "translation" of your dreams in the method described. You can learn much about yourself from this practice.

15. Regardless of your current level of dream recall, researchers find that you can increase the amount of your dream recall and enhance the quality of it. As you give dreams an important role in your life, and time to attend to them, they will come more easily, more often, and be of more value to you. Keeping a dream record can lead to greater self-understanding and help you increase your confidence and skills.

ca. **A.D. 950.** Anglo-Saxon law stipulates that if a man seduces the wife of another, he must pay a fine to the husband and procure for him another woman for like use. Adultery fines are graduated according to the social rank of the seduced woman: the seducer of a nobleman's wife pays forty times the amount exacted for seducing the wife of a churl.

Creative Dreaming
THE PSYCHOLOGICAL ADVISER **103**

permanent form. Work with your dreams—question dream images; give particular attention to recurring dreams and idiosyncratic dream images. All systems use the valuable information they obtain from the dream state. Treasure your creative dream products. Produce them in waking life. Use them. Share them. Discuss your dreams with friends, as well as record them. Since this means listening to your friends' dreams, too, you may want to form a creative dreaming group.

Developing creative dreaming takes time. It takes practice to develop the necessary attitudes and behaviors before and after dreaming, so that awareness of previous intentions comes back to you *during* dreaming. One researcher found that children needed an average of *five weeks* before a self-suggested dream appeared. Some children were able to produce the desired dream in two weeks, several of them took less than four weeks, while one took as long as six months. It seems there are great individual differences in creative dreaming skills.

The fact that it is possible to become conscious during dreams and to control many events within them raises a question: Is there such a thing as "unconscious"? Perhaps dreams are simply part of the continuum of life. Perhaps there is no unconscious. *Perhaps there are only levels of awareness. Relate to your dreams creatively and you will become more aware at every level.*

Your dreams can become your own personal laboratory. All of the systems use dreams to make life better: Ancient dreamers got cured or received advice; past creative dreamers had products, such as a violin concerto or inspiration for a book; American Indian dreamers received permission for a life's career and assurance of support and help; Senoi dreamers receive daily creative products to share with their tribe; don Juan and some lucid dreamers feel able to obtain useful paranormal information; Yogi dreamers believe they attain salvation from the endless cycle of death and rebirth. Confronting and conquering danger in dreams has helped people to develop self-confidence in waking life and to develop independence. Successful problem solving in dreams carries over into waking life. By relating to your dreams in creative ways you can help integrate your personality. Here, then, is the beauty of creative dreaming: *You can use creative dreaming for your own purposes.*

Whatever you wish to do in your dreams you can do, especially as you develop dream consciousness. You can experiment. You can practice whatever skills you wish while dreaming and they will carry over to your waking state. You can overcome your fears. You can pick whatever matters to you, plan ahead, or decide during the dream what *you* want. It is an open system. You decide. *Use your dreams to help you. Decide what is important to you and dream on it.*

aspects of the dream while it occurs, a phenomenon I call "dream composing."

As you become conscious in your dreams, you can have limitless positive dream adventures, as well as turn off negative dream happenings. Delightful things can happen to you without dream consciousness—you can see a beautiful painting, get a brilliant idea for reorganizing the office, experience waves of passion, observe strange animals and people, or fly to a different land. However, when you become conscious in your dreams, your range of choice is multiplied a thousandfold. You can do all that can be done in other systems—and go beyond them. You are conscious. Your choice is unlimited. Would you feel all the joy of flying? Would you make love to orgasm with a particular person? Would you converse with a dead friend? Would you learn from a great sage? Would you travel to another place? Would you obtain answers to a question? Would you use the full creative resources of your mind? You can do any of this during your dreams because all the material exists within you. *Become conscious in your dreams and you can do all this—and more.*

Your behavior *after* your dreams is important, too. Visualize your dream, record it in the present tense, put it into a

---

A.D. 1000. About this time women become predominate in Japanese literature, retaining that edge into the twentieth century. Women write Japan's first fiction, verse, and history—according to some chroniclers, while their men are caught up in incessant feudal squabbles and wars.

Hypochondria:

Your Emotions Can Make You Sick

Howard R. and Martha E. Lewis

The hypochondriac is a person who suffers an obsessive preoccupation with his supposed ill health. He is "impossible and ludicrous company," says psychiatrist Morris D. Riemer, because he gives the impression of relishing his misery. He is wrapped up in his bodily afflictions and will talk endlessly about them.

At the same time, he bemoans his fate and punctuates his self-pitying with expressions of hopelessness. Yet he gives the impression that there is some source of satisfaction for him in being sick. He generally is overdemanding of his doctors, and also unappreciative of their help. Often he seems to take pride in foiling their best efforts. If a physician is persistent in trying to help him, the hypochondriac is likely to become angry. A doctor's psychological explanation will usually only make the sufferer more anxious.

The hypochondriac's symptoms rarely fit any pattern known to medicine. They come and go unaccountably, often mysteriously shifting from one part of the body to another. The degree of discomfort reported is usually excessive for the complaint.

Hypochondriacs generally follow a series of steps, almost a waltz, as they wend their way through the world of medical care. Their unwitting partner is the doctor, and the dance steps go like this: (1) The patient's demands for treatment are met by (2) the physician's determination to examine and reinvestigate, trying one medication after another, to avoid at all costs missing an organic cause. After each trial medication (3) the patient experiences some relief, followed by worsening—the net result being "no change." (4) The patient and the physician become frustrated with each other, and the angry doctor labels the patient a "crackpot" or "untreatable." Then (1) the cycle starts again elsewhere, in another doctor's office.

And yet, as annoying as they are to others, men and women who suffer from hypochondria merit sympathy. Psychiatrist David J. Vail of the University of Minnesota School of Medicine feels that the main difficulty doctors have with the

hypochondriac is that he does not behave according to accepted patterns.

Moreover, the hypochondriac's pains are totally real to him. They preempt most of his time. Often they disable him. And he is wholly sincere in his despair of ever finding relief.

A Yiddish proverb says, "If things are too good, it's bad." This might well be the slogan of hypochondria, for it often accounts for the hypochondriac's reluctance to surrender his physical symptoms. Even more than sufferers with other psychosomatic conditions, he unconsciously believes that, as long as he suffers, he is protected from a more dreaded punishment. Thus, in his mind, it would be dangerous to get well.

The hypochondriac's expectation of punishment is generally the result of unconscious feelings of guilt. Since guilt is painful, it is generally repressed from conscious awareness. It does not, however, cease to exist, but continues to motivate a need for expiation, perhaps in the form of the hypochondriac's symptoms or, as he desperately fears, something worse.

The unconscious mind follows certain primitive lines of reasoning, and these serve to intensify the hypochondriac's guilt feelings. For example, the infantile mind cannot distinguish between a thought and a deed. To the unconscious, a person is as liable for thinking a thing as doing it. In psychiatrist Charles William Wahl's experience, most hypochondriacs have felt powerful hatred toward their parents and siblings. Wishing a parent dead, for example, can make a person unconsciously convinced that he too must die. Guilt, the unconscious believes, can be relieved only by suffering. The hypochondriac therefore finds his symptoms welcome. As the Yiddish proverb suggests, if he felt better, he'd be worse off.

A hypochondriac's symptoms can also be a way for him to assert his identity, a sign of his uncertainty over his inner worth. Lacking self-esteem, he thrusts himself—in the form of his bodily complaints—onto all who will listen. Capturing someone's attention in part is a means of assuring himself that he exists, that he is "somebody."

Most psychosomatic disorders achieve for the sufferer an unconscious primary gain, usually relief from anxiety or guilt.

Almost always there are also unconscious secondary gains—additional advantages that help perpetuate the disorder.

As an example of secondary gain, physical symptoms may be used as a cover-up for psychiatric difficulties. To many people it is still humiliating to have emotional problems but quite acceptable to have a physical illness.

By contrast, the patient knows, the psychiatric "case" is often an object of dread and aversion to others. Treatment means being "put away"—a far cry from the comfortable bed in a medical hospital where he can be solaced by visitors, surrounded by gifts of candy and flowers, and deluged with get-well cards.

Secondary gains are nowhere more evident than in hypochondria. A hypochondriac, often concerned about being unloved and uncherished, can nurse himself in his illness to compensate for the love he feels he lacks. His illness allows him to be dependent, he can use it to command attention. He can employ it to punish others, as if to say, "Look what you've done to me," and, "You're worsening my condition."

Dr. Jackson A. Smith of the Illinois State Psychiatric Institute tells of a headache that is the basis of a marriage.

Wilma is 38 and outweighs her smallish husband by 60 pounds. George worries about Wilma. Not long ago he urged her to visit Dr. Smith to see if there was any "new" treatment for her chronic headache.

Wilma produced for the physician a packet of X-rays, lab reports, and consultation notes. While she gave her history, George nodded agreement to each symptom, occasionally emphasizing a pain or ache he felt his wife had insufficiently detailed.

Smith asked George to retire to the waiting room and sought to get more of Wilma's history. She had a headache even as a child, she said. Studying only made her headache worse. She couldn't keep up, so she dropped out in her junior year of high school "because I was sick so much."

Wilma married a man who was "most inconsiderate" of her condition. "He was oversexed," Wilma whispered. The marriage soon ended in divorce.

Then George came along. He is sympathetic and sincerely appreciates her condition. He accepts all her

---

A.D. 1001. Lady Murasaki Shikibu, accomplished Japanese novelist born in 978, writes the massive *Genji Monogatari*, fifty-four books and 4,234 pages long, while in a Buddhist monastery. To acquire writing paper for her project, she uses sheets from the holy temple sutras. Her sacrilege is discovered, and she is required to copy over all the sutras she has destroyed.

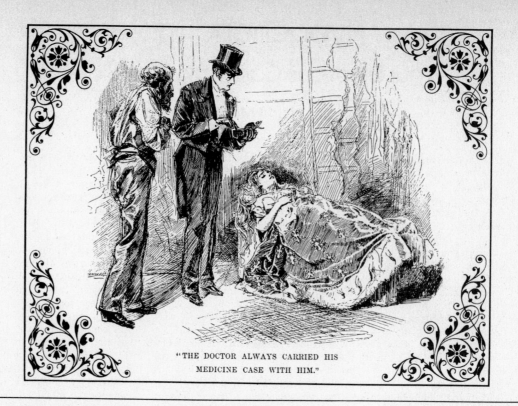

"THE DOCTOR ALWAYS CARRIED HIS
MEDICINE CASE WITH HIM."

complaints and makes no demands on her, sexual or otherwise.

George works hard at a service station he owns. He always goes home for lunch to see how Wilma is feeling and to fix her a bite to eat. In the evenings they watch television together. On long weekends they visit Wilma's mother. Wilma has never made many friends because "folks don't understand sick people."

"To be cured wouldn't offer an awful lot to Wilma," concludes Dr. Smith. She has long since ceased to think of herself as a well person. Her headache is more than a symptom. It's a way of life.

It gives her a reason to avoid the unpleasant. What she can't or doesn't want to do is always the result of her headache rather than her inabilities. Her complaint explains all her short-comings and is an ever-available topic of conversation.

Without the headache, observes Smith, there is no Wilma. If she were well, she would have to meet the ordinary routines of the day and night without fanfare or special consideration. She would need to forego the attention and sympathy her headache provides.

Superficially, it appears that George is losing out because of Wilma's condition. "Actually," Smith points out, "he gets everything from life that Wilma does, and besides, he doesn't have a headache.

First, all his friends agree he is an admirable character, a "nice little guy." They wonder how he "puts up with her." Next, Wilma's symptoms provide him with the quiet, undisturbed existence he

wants. Being a bachelor was difficult for him because his friends were always trying to get him married. Refusing invitations and saying no to people was unpleasant for him; he hated to hurt anyone's feelings. The marriage solved this problem. He obviously can't go any place because of Wilma's condition.

George had never been comfortable around women unless he was doing something for them. Wilma never deprives him of something to do for her. He has never felt right about sex, and with Wilma he is appreciated for letting her alone. He is intuitive enough never to let his joy over this arrangement shine through.

If by some magic Wilma were cured and became an independent, vigorous, sexually energetic female—"then," cautions Dr. Smith, "it might well be George who had the headache!"

Many changing ills

Barbara walked into a room at the psychiatric clinic of the University of Pittsburgh. For years she had circulated from doctor to doctor, asking for remedies to cure her many changing ills but was unable to obtain relief for long. As her chart grew thick, her doctors' patience wore thin. To avoid seeing her any more than he had to, a physician would tell her to return after six weeks, three months, or longer. Invariably Barbara would suffer a worsening of symptoms that forced her to come in sooner.

Now Barbara and seven other hypochondriacal women were placed in

experimental group therapy under the guidance of Dr. William D. Ogston, a psychiatrist, and Mary A. Mally, a professor of social work. The women were not considered good candidates for psychotherapy—hypochondriacs generally resist it—but they were offered the weekly group in an effort to afford them some help. Their medical records labeled them "pathetic," "helpless," "troubled," "inadequate."

The women ranged in age from 27 to 56. Their marital pictures were generally dim: two were single, and five of the remaining six were divorced or separated. None was self-supporting; all got either public assistance or money from relatives.

All had problems related to food. Two were grossly obese. Two others choked when they ate. Four were undernourished. In addition, all had complaints concerning their reproductive organs, such as cramps and vaginal discharge. Four of the women had undergone a hysterectomy.

Every one of the women was the least successful member of her family in terms of education, money, social achievement, and marriage. Barbara told the group: "I was hated by my mother, even though I was devoted to her." With one exception, the other women said the same.

Barbara would try to buy warmth and care from her mother by pleasing her with gifts and good deeds. She expected tenfold in return and ended up feeling angry over being used and misunder-

ca. **1011.** Freydis, called "The Valkyrie," or warrior-maiden, is the sole woman in a band of thirty who sail from Greenland to Vinland (the southern coast of New England).

stood. The other women followed this pattern.

Each also painted a vague picture of her father. Barbara (and three of the others) described hers as a remote, shadowy figure who was a source of apprehension and fear. The others were so emphatic about the intense love and devotion they felt toward their fathers that Dr. Ogston and Professor Mally believed that much of this description was fantasy.

In marriage Barbara had expected to be taken care of rather than to behave as an adult, responsible wife.

Now divorced, she recalled her marriage as turbulent and sexually unsatisfying. Sylvia and Margaret, the two who hadn't married, had had erratic courtships. They finally exhausted the patience of their suitors and remained with their mothers.

In establishing the group, Mally and Ogston hoped to answer: What made these individuals "untreatable"? How effective would group therapy be for them?

Almost immediately the women turned the group to serving their hypochondria. Discussion generally revolved around the subject of symptoms and medications. The women competed for the position of being the "sickest" in hopes of winning the sole interest of the leaders. When a member got into a troubling situation, she and the others expected Mally and Ogston to get her out of it, meanwhile resisting the insights the leaders tried to bring them to.

The group soon became the focus of the women's lives. Whenever a member tried to engage in an outside activity, such as getting a job or joining an organization, the others discouraged her. "Perhaps you're not well enough," she'd be told. If she persisted and failed, she would return to the group satisfied that she was ill. The other members welcomed her back with open arms.

Body language

It became clear to Ogston and Mally that from patients there is a lifelong cry to be taken care of. This is mixed with anger that there has never been enough love, protection, affection. Their symptoms arise evidently as a body language expressing their need to be cared for. They are appealing more for pity than for help.

The group met for about three years, and a seeming paradox emerged. On one hand, the women got little insight into themselves or their hypochondria. Their competitive, demanding, manipulative behavior within the group did not improve much.

On the other hand, there was some relief of their symptoms, and demands for medication became fewer.

What had happened? Why did treatment that by traditional standards failed have in large part a successful result? Mally and Ogston suggest that while such patients are searching for something, it is not really medical care per se. It is to be *taken care of*.

Hypochondriacs are best thought of as chronically handicapped people who require management rather than treatment. Psychiatrist Charles Wahl offers the following advice for laymen who must deal with the hypochondriac:
- **Listen.** A positive willingness to listen, rather than mere toleration, is what the hypochondriac wants and needs. He seeks a dependable relationship of trust and confidence. As soon as he is assured of this, his need for unreasonable amounts of attention is ordinarily diminished.
- **Take his symptoms seriously.** Don't tell him his pains are imaginary. Rather explain how tension can produce the symptoms that frighten him.
- **Focus on feelings.** Encourage him to talk openly about his deep feelings of fear and need. Help him to express other problem areas. Perhaps you can help him see that by concentrating on his health he may be avoiding other areas of difficulty.
- **Accentuate the positive.** Don't suggest alternative fearful possibilities concerning his symptoms. This can terrify him.

Don't urge new tests, either. Hypochondriacs are prone to develop hysterical complications following such procedures. Nor should you advise new medicines. The hypochondriac tends to overdose himself with drugs and become dependent on them.

There is also such a thing as a "reverse hypochondriac." The case of Lisa illustrates this.

"I guess I'm suffering from the tired housewife syndrome," Lisa said. She had four small children and a hectic household. This, agreed her doctor, could account for her fatigue and nondescript low-back pain. Bored, harassed homemakers frequently suffer this set of symptoms. The "tired housewife syndrome," as Lisa knew, is nearly always psychogenic (originating in the mind).

A less cautious doctor might have simply counseled Lisa to spend more time on herself and sent her off with a prescription for a mild tranquilizer. Fortunately Lisa's physician gave her a physical examination. He found a substantial tumor in her left breast.

Lisa evidently knew about the tumor all the time. But she denied it, put it out of her conscious mind. Even when she went to a tumor clinic on her doctor's recommendation, she talked not about the implications of cancer but about the difficulties of raising small children and keeping up with a busy household.

Lisa was manifesting "reverse hypochondria." Whereas the typical hypochondriac uses physical complaints to express an emotional disorder, Lisa was employing psychological symptoms to mask a physical condition.

Denial of illness is often part and parcel of a disease of the brain or central nervous system. If shown clear evidence that he is ill, the victim may very well become inattentive or he may change the subject or invent explanations.

"Fed Up"

Reverse hypochondria in part results from the public's increasing sophistication about psychiatric ills. People who've learned that mental illness is nothing to be ashamed of may find a psychiatric condition more palatable than a potentially life-threatening physical one. When their doctor asks, "How do you feel?" they are freer to give emotional answers like "Depressed," or "Fed up" than to honestly confront ominous physical ones such as "Short of breath," or "In pain."

One investigator, psychiatrist Robert Seidenberg of the Upstate Medical Center at Syracuse, N.Y., has found that many patients "psychologize" their symptoms with the unconscious conviction that a neurotic illness is easier to cure than an organic one.

In the face of bodily symptoms, they readily accept and use the concepts of psychosomatic medicine. If their doctor disagrees, they are likely to dismiss him as being psychologically unsophisticated. And when they are confronted with real evidence that they have an organic illness, many of them feel insulted.

Adolescents characteristically minimize their physical problems. "During the teens the herd instinct is at its peak," notes Dr. Harris C. Faigel. "No adolescent wants to be different from his friends." Since the teens are generally a healthy time of life, illness makes a youngster feel different. Not wanting to be an exception, he may deny his illness.

Among adults, denial of an organic illness often stems from an underlying fear of weakness and helplessness. The patient is likely to admit to physical symptoms but use psychological theory to explain them.

Reverse hypochondria is potentially far more perilous to the patient than hypochondria. The typical hypochondriac would do well to be less mindful of his symptoms. The reverse hypochondriac may ignore an organic condition until it is fatal.

---

ca. **1018.** Jaroslav the Great, Grand Prince of Novgorod, Russia, lays down his Code of Laws: "The life of a female may be considered worth half that of any man in case she be murdered illegally and blood-payment be demanded by her relatives."

Drugs Commonly Prescribed to Change Your Mind

Carl D. Chambers and Dodi Schultz

These are the psychotropic—mood-altering or mind-affecting—drugs with which respectable, middle-class Americans are increasingly "turning. on." Usually, they are obtained by prescription; often, they are not. You will undoubtedly recognize many of their names. We use the word "abuse" to mean use in excess of prescribed dosage, frequency, and/or duration of time.

Type of Drug	What They Do—And Can Do	Some Common Brand Names
Relaxants ("minor" tranquilizers)	*Reduce anxiety. Even in small doses, react with and boost effects of alcohol. Abuse can cause addiction.*	*Atarax, Equanil, Librium, Meprotabs, Miltown, Valium, Vistaril—also combined with analgesics and other substances in such medications as Deprol, Equagesic, Milpath.*
"Major" tranquilizers	*Modify psychotic symptoms; reduce fear and hostility. Dangerous in combination with alcohol or sedatives. Potentially addictive, but rarely abused due to unpleasant side effects.*	*Compazine, Frenquel, Mellaril, Serpasil, Sparine, Stelazine, Thorazine—also in combination drugs (see antidepressants below).*
Antidepressants ("mood elevators")	*Alleviate serious depression. Interact dangerously with alcohol, amphetamines, sedatives, a number of other substances. Side effects, including blurred vision and dizziness.*	*Aventyl, Elavil, Marplan, Sinequan, Tofranil—also combined with major tranquilizers in drugs such as Estrafon, Triavil.*
Amphetamines ("pep pills")	*Stimulate central nervous system, create feelings of confidence, prevent fatigue. High doses can cause toxic psychosis. Abuse can produce psychic dependence, possible addiction.*	*Benzedrine, Dexedrine (also see diet pills below).*
Diet pills	*Reduce appetite, create sense of well-being. Abuse poses all the risks of the individual ingredients.*	*Three major types: 1) amphetamines with barbiturates—Desbutal, Dexamyl, Nobese; 2) amphetamines with tranquilizers—Appetrol, Eskatrol; 3) other chemicals with amphetamine-like effects—Preludin, PreSate, Tenuate, Wilpo.*
Barbiturates	*Central nervous system depressants that sedate (calm) or, in larger doses, induce sleep. Can cause psychic dependence. Abuse causes addiction.*	*Amytal, Butisol, Luminal, Mebaral, Nembutal, Sandoptal, Seconal, Sombulex, Tuinal, Veronal—also in combination with antispasm drugs in such medications as Bentyl, Donnatal.*
Other powerful sedatives	*Similar to barbiturates in purpose and in trouble-making potential.*	*Chloral hydrate (Noctec, Somnos), Doriden, Noludar, Placidyl, Valmid.*
Controlled narcotics (opiates)	*Powerful analgesics that relieve pain, produce euphoria. Abuse causes addiction—which can sometimes occur with prescribed dosages as well.*	*Natural substances (opium, morphine, codeine, paregoric) plus semisynthetics and synthetics: Demerol, Dilaudid, Dolophine (methadone), Leritine, Levo-Dromoran, Numorphon, Percodan.*
Noncontrolled narcotics (not legally classed as narcotic drugs)	*Similar to controlled narcotics, except that normal (prescribed) dosages are not potentially addictive.*	*Butazolidin, Darvon, Indocin, Robaxin, Tandearil, Talwin.*

ca. **1024.** Countess Ida Von Toggenburg dies. Years before, a raven had flown away with her ring, left carelessly on the battlement of her castle, and a huntsman, Count Paul, found and wore it. Ida's husband, seeing the ring on the count's hand, concluded that his wife was unfaithful and hurled her through a window in the castle tower.

Change Can Make Us Ill

Thomas H. Holmes, M.D. and T. Stephenson Holmes, M.D.

New York Public Library

The average person has about two acute illnesses per year, according to Public Health Service statistics. These ailments require going to the doctor about four times and keep the person feeling under the weather for a total of about a week.

Most of these health changes represent more inconvenience than serious threat. However, during any given year, 10 per cent of the population will spend some time in the hospital (not including maternity cases).

The problem might be a serious illness, such as tuberculosis, a heart attack or high blood pressure. But the word "illness" is really too limited, so the term "health change" is usually used in this article.

We rarely think of a car accident or a suicide attempt as an illness. Surgical operations are not illnesses. But all of them involve a certain disruption of the state of health and functioning.

Psychiatric disorders such as depression and schizophrenia involve more than emotional imbalance. Depressed people, for example, almost always experience marked decreases in appetite and sex drive, along with weight loss, insomnia, fatigue and constipation.

The sophisticated instruments and laboratory tests we use to diagnose these ailments still do not tell us what accounts for individual susceptibility to illness. When the London or Asian flu comes around, not everybody gets it. Of those who do, some need to be hospitalized and may even die, while others have little more than a stomachache. Not every

heavy drinker becomes an alcoholic; not every alcoholic gets cirrhosis of the liver; not every cirrhotic even gets diagnosed.

We say that we get sick when our resistance is down. But resistance is hard to define. Is it related to fitness? Probably, but it is not unusual to read of an athlete or a coach, in the best of shape, dying suddenly of a heart attack. Conversely, many frail and sedentary people live to ripe old ages.

Is resistance related to mental attitude? Probably, but the most devout clergymen are heir to the same ailments as the rest of us. And we all probably have a hypochondriacal relative who has been expecting to die for 40 years.

Is resistance related to exposure to illness-producing agents? Probably, but most people who work for years in sanatoriums don't get tuberculosis.

Whatever the contributing factors, when our resistance goes down our risk goes up. One approach to the problem of what determines the behavior we call sick is to find a measure of risk, or susceptibility, to health change.

Given the rapidly accelerating pace of life today, with one national crisis after another, with unpredictable job market and social and political instability, one thing that touches us all is change. More and more of us are moving from small towns to urban areas; we move frequently; we eat on the run; we grab a nap when we can; we change jobs; we change spouses. Even those of us who stay put most of our lives have to contend with change. Our children are bussed to school; they grow up and leave home; our parish church is torn down to make way for a supermarket; property taxes go up; our old friends get sick and die; we make new ones.

The routine of our lives is constantly being revised. We have to filter incoming stimuli, assign them priorities and try to fit them into our own way of life. If we refuse or are unable to deal with this input, our

circuits may become overloaded with a massive life crisis and our systems are at great risk for a breakdown in function.

Alvin Toffler has popularized this phenomenon under the general heading of *Future Shock,* which he defines as "the distress, both physical and psychological, that arises from an overload of the human organism's physical adaptive systems and its decision-making processes." This idea has been around for many years. Adolf Meyer, professor of psychiatry at Johns Hopkins, recognized this idea around the turn of the century and began keeping "life charts" on his patients. They were abbreviated biographies that showed time and again that people tended to get sick around the time when clusters of major events took place in their lives. The concept was expanded in the 1940's and 1950's by the late Harold G. Wolff, professor of neurology and psychiatry at Cornell University Medical College, who studied intensively the life settings and emotional states surrounding many specific illnesses and symptoms.

In 1949, Dr. Thomas H. Holmes (a coauthor of this article), after working with Doctor Wolff at Cornell, began to apply Doctor Meyer's life chart idea systematically to the case histories of more than 5,000 patients. A number of life-change items were found to occur over and over and tended to cluster in the brief time period just prior to the onset of major illnesses. The items are listed in the chart shown here. They constitute various interactions of people with their environment, and make up essentially all the changes in life situations that we have to deal with, or reflect the fact that salient changes have occurred.

Some of the changes in life situation and life style are socially desirable and some are undesirable. We are all aware of the drain on energy and resources associated with such "stressful" events as divorce, troubles with the boss and death of a spouse.

Miraculously, she survived the great fall unhurt and escaped to live out the remainder of her life in seclusion and Christian sanctity. Eventually she will be canonized, and her holiness regionally celebrated throughout Germany and Switzerland.

In swaddling clothes behold the bud,
  Of sweet and gentle womanhood.
Next she foreshews with mimic plays,
  The business of her future days.
Now glorious as a full blown flower,
  The heart of manhood feels her power.
A husband now her arms entwine,
  She clings around him like the vine.

Now bearing fruit she rears her boys,
  And tastes a mother's pains and joys.
Like sparkling fountain gushing forth,
  She proves a blessing to the earth.
A busy housewife full of cares,
  The daily food her hand prepares.
As age creeps on she seeks for grace,
  Always to church and in her place.

Now second childhood loosens all her tongue,
  She talks of love and prattles with the young.
A useless cumberer on the earth,
  From house to house they send her forth.
Chained to her chair by weight of years,
  She listless waits till death appears.

But not all life changes are stressful in the usual negative sense. What could be more gratifying to a singer than finally to hit the big time? Concert tours, recording dates, parties, money and meeting famous people may represent all his dreams come true. But the way he lives his life will be radically changed. Think of the many changes brought about by the happiest marriage. Even a long-awaited vacation requires certain changes, if only for a relatively short time— eating in restaurants instead of at home, sleeping in a sleeping bag instead of a bed, snorkeling or playing tennis for the first time. Whether "positive" or "negative" to our way of thinking, all such events require us to cope, adapt or change to some degree.

The numbers in the right-hand column of the chart represent the amount, duration and severity of change required to cope with each item, averaged from the responses of hundreds of people. Marriage was arbitrarily assigned the magnitude of 50 points, and the subjects then rated the other items by number as to how much more or how much less change each requires in comparison with marriage. For instance, the scale implies that losing a spouse by death (100) requires, in the long run, twice as much readjustment as getting married (50), four times as much as a change in living conditions (25), and nearly 10 times as much as minor violations of the law (11).

The more changes you undergo in a given period of time, the more

points you accumulate. The higher the score, the more likely you are to have a health change. All the kinds of health changes previously discussed—serious illnesses, injuries, surgical operations, psychiatric disorders, even pregnancy— have been found to follow high life-change scores. And the higher your score, the more serious the health change will likely be.

If you scored below 150 points, you are on pretty safe ground— about a one in three chance of serious health change in the next two years. Remember, you already have a 10 per cent chance of winding up in the hospital some time during the year. If you scored between 150 and 300 points, your chances rise to about 50-50. The odds on Russian roulette are better than

1047. King Edward the Confessor imposes the following laws on Anglo-Saxon England: Of Adultery: He that shall defile the wife of another shall forfeit his Were (a fine) unto the lord. Of those that use violence (rape) against women: If so a man shall ravish a woman by force, he shall be punished by loss of limb. That a pregnant woman shall not

that. If you scored over 300 points, be sure your health insurance is paid up—your chances are almost 90 per cent.

It all sounds pretty grim. But there may be ways in which you can soften the blow. Change is not entirely random. You have a large amount of personal control over whether and when to marry, go to college, move or have a family. You may have little or no control over whether to get divorced, change jobs, take out a loan or retire. But you may have a pretty good idea of when these events might take place.

So the future is not a complete blank. You can predict it to a certain degree. And to this degree, you can order your life by managing the change that is a vital part of living. You can weigh the benefits of change against its costs, pace the timing of inevitable changes and regulate the occurrence of voluntary changes to try to keep your yearly life-change score out of the danger zone.

If you are considering your third job change in two years, you might stay put for a while and consider a more long-lasting alternative. Or if divorce is imminent, you might avoid the temptation to plan to re-marry right away and give yourself time to sort out the implications of all the changes that divorce brings with it. If you are approaching 65, a gradual rather than sudden transition from full-time work and responsibility could help reduce the feeling of uselessness that often accompanies retirement.

Life change is not something that you should avoid. After all, there are worse things in life than illness. Changing, adapting and evolving help all of us to live our lives to our fullest capacity and enjoyment. But too much change in too short a period of time takes its toll on the adaptive capabilities of the human body, lowers resistance and increases the risk of major changes in health.

If you can learn to regulate the major changes that inevitably affect you, you may yet be able to defuse their consequences.

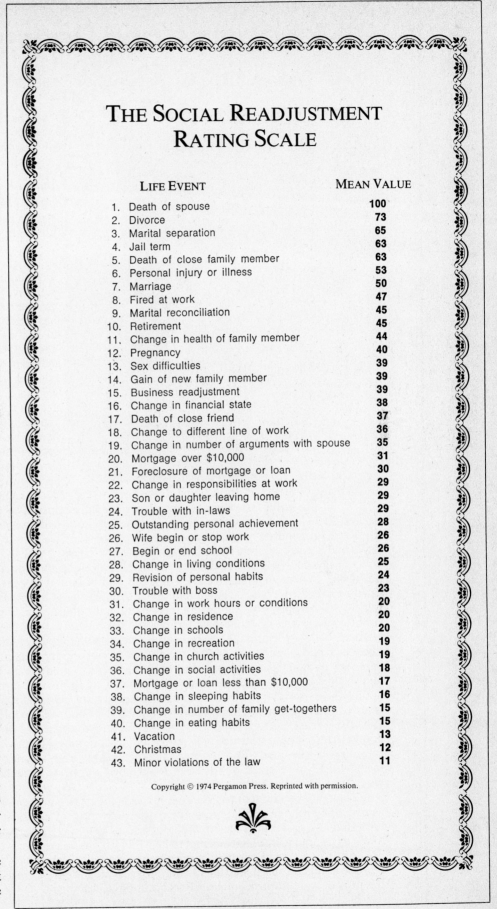

THE SOCIAL READJUSTMENT RATING SCALE

LIFE EVENT	MEAN VALUE
1. Death of spouse	100
2. Divorce	73
3. Marital separation	65
4. Jail term	63
5. Death of close family member	63
6. Personal injury or illness	53
7. Marriage	50
8. Fired at work	47
9. Marital reconciliation	45
10. Retirement	45
11. Change in health of family member	44
12. Pregnancy	40
13. Sex difficulties	39
14. Gain of new family member	39
15. Business readjustment	39
16. Change in financial state	38
17. Death of close friend	37
18. Change to different line of work	36
19. Change in number of arguments with spouse	35
20. Mortgage over $10,000	31
21. Foreclosure of mortgage or loan	30
22. Change in responsibilities at work	29
23. Son or daughter leaving home	29
24. Trouble with in-laws	29
25. Outstanding personal achievement	28
26. Wife begin or stop work	26
27. Begin or end school	26
28. Change in living conditions	25
29. Revision of personal habits	24
30. Trouble with boss	23
31. Change in work hours or conditions	20
32. Change in residence	20
33. Change in schools	20
34. Change in recreation	19
35. Change in church activities	19
36. Change in social activities	18
37. Mortgage or loan less than $10,000	17
38. Change in sleeping habits	16
39. Change in number of family get-togethers	15
40. Change in eating habits	15
41. Vacation	13
42. Christmas	12
43. Minor violations of the law	11

undergo death: If so a woman shall be adjudged to die or to suffer mutilation of her limbs (as punishment for some crime), and shall prove pregnant, execution of the sentence shall be deferred until she has been delivered of that in her womb. If a father finds his daughter in the act of adultery in his own house, he is at liberty to slay the adulterer. In a

Menopause and Depression

The Boston Women's Health Book Collective, Inc.

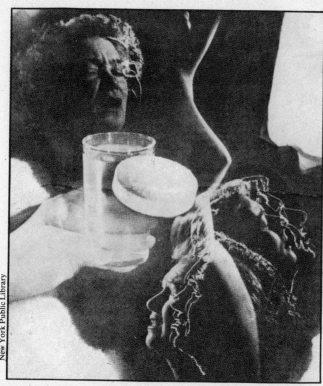

New York Public Library

About one in ten women experiences severe depression during menopause. Though physical changes do play a part in these depressions, Pauline Bart feels that we often become depressed simply because we are middle-aged. We have no clear or important role to play in our society. Very little if anything is expected of us. We have no status. But at the same time, our life span has lengthened, we have twenty or thirty good years ahead of us. If we have had children, we end our childbearing years sooner than we did in the past, and we are left with a lot of time on our hands and space in our lives. For there are no clear societal norms which give us a useful place in our children's lives. Often we are in their way after they leave home. If we have overprotected them or expected them to live out and fulfill our own lives for us, we are both angered by their leave-taking and saddened by our loss. Often, not understanding that we feel anger, unable to direct it toward our children or unable to express it in any way, we turn it inward onto ourselves and become severely and heavily depressed.

We are faced with other real losses. Some of us feel deeply saddened by the end of our ability to bear children. We are losing our youth. And if in general we feel unfulfilled personally, we may be bitter about not having achieved happiness yet.

If we are already working during menopause and middle age, we are less likely to suffer certain forms of depression, though heavy work can take its physical toll on us.

There are many legitimate reasons for our depression. We have to recognize that its causes are not so much personal as social; that is, our society does not recognize us as necessary or valuable members. More research needs to be done on both the physical and social causes of our depression. And we must try to provide discussion and work groups for ourselves and others to understand better our own feelings and capabilities, to share them, and to move out of depression into new and worthwhile lives.

It makes sense for each of us to try to prevent emotional problems at menopause by doing what we can to keep not only our bodies but our minds healthy. Our psychological state, how we cope with stress and maintain our security, is going to affect how we feel physically all the rest of our lives. Remember, the stress of menopause can often magnify already existing mental problems.

We must make sure that society does not make our later lives miserable by denying us rewarding roles in addition to motherhood. For many of us, dilettante interests are not enough to prevent the feeling of worthlessness that many older women experience. Many of us need to be employed and to be paid fairly by society for work that it values. We must at no time in our lives allow parents, guidance counselors, husbands or anyone else to talk us out of starting or continuing to pursue our interests and careers. It is our present and future mental health that is at stake, not theirs!

like manner, if the son finds his mother in the act of adultery, during the life of his father, he is at liberty to slay the adulterer.'' It is not recorded how many instances of such killing transpired during Edward's reign.

Depression...
How to Recognize and Cure It
Alice Lake

"We used to do a lot of things together as a family—going on picnics, tossing a ball around, playing miniature golf—but suddenly we couldn't get John to move. Instead of cracking jokes like his usual cheerful self, he just moped around. He'd always been very neat, but it got so even taking a bath seemed to be too much of an effort."

Three months of increasing misery passed before Marjorie Jenkins (not her real name) realized that her husband, John, was not merely ornery but sick—and that the illness had a name: *depression.* She'd thought depression was just a temporary bout with the blues, but this was far more disabling. As John struggled to pull out of it alone, he seemed to mire himself deeper—and to pull his wife and children down with him.

An estimated one in every twenty-five Americans is now suffering from depressive illness, and one in seven suffers some of its crippling symptoms. Public health officials consider it a major problem because it is on the rise and causes acute anguish—perhaps more pain than any other disease—for its victims and their families. What's more, the causes of depression are not clearly understood, and that makes it difficult to prevent.

On the brighter side, drugs developed in the last decade have proved effective in some 70 percent of cases. Patients who once languished in hospitals for months or even years are now treated in out-patient clinics or by their family doctors—with substantial recovery expected in a month or so. "The outlook for acute depression is now excellent," says Dr. Gerald Klerman, psychiatry professor at Harvard Medical School.

When a person is immobilized by depression, the whole family is in trouble. One woman, an enthusiastic cook who even baked her own bread, found it was all she could do to pour the breakfast coffee. Her husband took over the cooking, and the children did the laundry. But the emotional drain is often worse than the physical. "I wanted to shake my husband and yell, 'Get up and do something! Pull yourself out of it,'" a wife said. A husband recalls, "We seemed lost in a maze together. She kept predicting doom and calamity until it sounded like a cracked record. I tried to be sympathetic, but couldn't bear the interminable nonsense."

The spouse of a depressed person may be furious, but the children—particularly when their mother is sick—are hurt, confused and vulnerable to emotional damage. A study of forty depressed women treated at the Connecticut Mental Health Center (newly published as *The Depressed Woman* by Dr. Myrna Weissman and Dr. Eugene Paykel) found the mothers to be less affectionate than other mothers and highly irritable with their children. One woman left her youngsters alone because she couldn't bear their noise. Another force-fed her overweight three-year-old as a distorted way of denying she was a bad mother.

Depressive illness affects the entire body, "The patient is in a total disequilibrium," Dr. Klerman says. "Everything is sluggish. The hormonal system is out of balance, muscles in spasm, sex drive lost, appetite vanished, sleep disordered." Other bodily symptoms include constipation, dry mouth and, in women, menstrual irregularity. Yet the real diagnosis—the precursor to effective treatment—is often missed by members of the family and even by doctors. In one group of depressed persons, half were never treated for their illness although they swallowed hundreds of pills for headache, backache, stomach pain and other physical complaints that masked their depression.

Looking back, Marjorie and John Jenkins wonder how they could have failed to seek medical help for three miserable months—until it was almost too late. But at the same time it looked to them like a sordid marital problem. After ten years of marriage, John had had an affair with another woman. All he had wanted was to break it off, confess to his wife and be forgiven, but the episode touched off a cycle of guilt, self-hatred and deep despair that almost consumed him.

Getting up his nerve to tell Marjorie, John found he ——————→

New York Public Library

1050. The wife of Domenica Silvio, doge of Venice, rejects the rude table manners of Europe. "Being too dainty to touch her meats and other foods with her fingers," she uses a small golden fork "instead of eating like other people" with their hands. Her actions are thus considered "luxurious beyond belief."

could no longer concentrate on his job. For him this was the first significant symptom. "It got so I couldn't even add three numbers together," he recalls. After he made the confession, he felt even worse. He had trouble falling asleep, then thrashed all night and awoke before dawn. (Early-morning awakening is a prominent symptom of developing depression. So is shallow, restless sleep from which one awakes unrefreshed.) John began to lose weight. "Even the smell of food nauseated me." (Although most depressed persons lose their appetites, a few become gluttonous. Women are more likely to go on eating sprees while men get drunk in an attempt to ward off depression.)

John lost interest in sex and feared that he was impotent. This was misinterpreted by Marjorie who suspected he was seeing the other woman again. (The loss of sex drive, a significant symptom of depression, can play havoc with a marriage. Depressed women are likely to find sexual intercourse repugnant, even physically painful. When a doctor advised one husband to be more sympathetic to his depressed wife, the man exploded: "How about some sympathy for me? I haven't had any sex in four damn months!")

John felt exhausted. "Even brushing my teeth was a tremendous chore," he recalls. His lethargy was hard on the children —a girl of five and a boy of seven. They couldn't understand why their father would no longer play with them. "Daddy doesn't feel like it," he explained. "Maybe tomorrow." But when the next day came, the answer was still *no*. Bewildered, the children told their mother that Daddy never kept promises.

The worst burden for Marjorie was John's utter dependence on her. "He couldn't make the simplest decision," she says. "I even had to tell him what to wear. He'd send the children out of the room so we could talk when we'd just finished thirty minutes of pointless conversation. I watched their chins quiver, but there was nothing I could do. Then our son's grades started going down. He felt his father didn't care."

"When you're depressed," John explains, "you think only of yourself. You lose respect for yourself, so you can't love or respect someone else." When friends came to the house, John sat in a corner, silent and brooding. Sometimes he played grudgingly with his children, then blamed himself for not really wanting to do it. "You're a bad father," he told himself. "You're never going to be any better. Marjorie and the kids would be lucky if you were gone."

Feeling utterly hopeless, John began to talk

of suicide. His plans were serious, but he was crying out for help. "I felt I just couldn't handle it by myself anymore," he says. Marjorie was frightened. She kept an eye on him while he shaved, hid all the pills, checked constantly on his whereabouts and finally telephoned the family doctor. After a brief stay in a hospital in suburban New Jersey where they live, John was referred to a new depression clinic at the Hospital of the University of Pennsylvania. John Jenkins need not have flirted with death; both he and Marjorie know that now. If they'd

John Getsinger

recognized the symptoms earlier, they could have spared themselves and their children months of anguish. But how does one recognize depression and find appropriate treatment before the illness becomes life-threatening? Here is what the experts recommend:

Be alert to symptoms. According to Dr. Heinz Lehmann, professor of psychiatry at McGill University in Montreal, there are three key questions: (1) Are you less productive than a month or two ago? (2) Are you less interested in work, hobbies, friends, those you love? (3) Are you getting less enjoyment from life—a good dinner, a beautiful sunset, sexual intercourse? Affirmative answers are all that's needed to diagnose depression.

Other psychiatrists consider a person's behavior—the inability to function at a normal

level, disturbed sleep, loss of appetite—along with negative thoughts about himself, his relations with others and the future. The duration and intensity of symptoms—such as numbing grief that continues beyond a normal mourning period—are also significant. Hypochondriacal complaints—vague aches and pains all over the body—often mask depression.

See a doctor. If you're convinced that a loved one is suffering from depression, you must persuade him to consult a doctor—a task that is often quite difficult. "When my husband, who loves parties, started refusing to see our friends, and spent every evening slumped in front of the television set," one wife explained, "I insisted he call a doctor. But he flared, 'There's nothing wrong with me; leave me alone!' I finally delivered an ultimatum: Go to the doctor within a week, or I'm going to leave—and I don't know when I'll come back."

This may sound cruel, but Dr. Dean Schuyler, coordinator of the Depression Section at the National Institute of Mental Health, calls it "scary but motivating. So long as this wife tolerated her husband's depression, she was helping to maintain it. Once she said 'I refuse to live this way any longer,' she gave him the push he needed. If he had been suicidal, she should have taken him to the doctor's office herself."

Start with your family doctor. Some people hesitate to seek help because they don't know where to go, while others have visions of being locked up in a mental hospital or forced into shock treatment. Yet most cases of depression are treated by general practitioners and internists. If the doctors are knowledgeable about the use of antidepressant medication and can spare the time to listen, they're likely to do a good job. And there are definite advantages to having a doctor who knows the entire family and can comfortably advise other members on how to help.

Another resource is one of some 300 community mental health centers across the country. The therapists are usually psychiatric social workers and fees are geared to family income. Even if your family doctor recommends a psychiatrist, you needn't be concerned that you're in for years on the psychiatrist's couch. Several months of weekly or biweekly visits focused on everyday problems is typical. Some patients recover on medication alone.

Seek hospitalization, if necessary. About one in thirty persons with depression needs to be hospitalized—if he is suicidal and requires constant watching, if he is too ill for intermittent outpatient care, and usually if he requires shock treatment (electroconvulsive therapy or ECT). Although ECT has been overused and abused, all the experts I spoke to said it was highly ⟶

ca. **1050.** Throughout England and the rest of Europe the Law of Primogeniture begins to prevail in the disposition of all landed estates. Upon death of the landholder the title and property go to the eldest son, making younger sons largely his pensioners. Only should no male heirs be available would the eldest daughter receive the estate.

effective in selected cases—particularly when a patient fails to respond to antidepressant medication. It is still not known why producing a brief convulsive seizure by applying an electric current to the scalp knocks out a depression, nor what other effects it may have within the brain. But new techniques now minimize the transient loss of memory—once a serious side effect.

Don't forget the pills. Antidepressant medication is slow-acting; it must be taken for about two weeks before any improvement occurs. This lag is unlikely to confirm the patient's negativism—"the pills don't do any good"—and a family member may have to monitor the pill-taking at first. Frequently a depressed person thinks of himself as not really ill, just morally weak. He balks at taking pills because they appear to confirm his loss of self-control.

Be supportive, but firm. Anyone who unconsciously agrees that depression shows a defect in willpower is likely to do more harm than good. Urging the patient to "snap out of it" or implying that he is malingering merely reinforces his guilt. If he were capable of snapping out of the depression, he wouldn't be sick. An excess of sympathy is equally unhelpful. A depressed person is wholly wrapped up in himself and his misery. You make it worse by wallowing with him.

Living with someone who is depressed is physically and emotionally draining; he is irritable, irritating and often utterly irrational. One wife, for example, told her husband, "I was talking to Janet on the phone today, and she hung up on me. She said she had a doctor's appointment, but I know it's because she doesn't like me. I guess I have no friends." The temptation is to get sucked into an argument about this ridiculous statement, which winds up with an angry "You're just talking nonsense."

Instead of criticizing such distortions you should make the sick person question his own premise, says Dr. Aaron Beck, professor of psychiatry at the University of Pennsylvania Hospital and author of *Depression: Causes and Treatment.* When one young woman deserted by her husband wailed, "Life isn't worth living without him," Dr. Beck countered, "Really? Tell me how you managed before you met him."

A depressed person can be hurtful to those closest to him if they don't realize he's temporarily in a black mood. "I don't love you," one man told his wife. "I guess I never did." The wife admitted later that she "wanted to cry, but I reminded myself it was just a part of his negativism. Instead of protesting, I nodded and changed the subject."

Your own response to a depressed person's behavior can lead him toward recovery . . . or to a plateau of despair. Expect but don't demand some attempts to cope. Ignore failure, but praise success—and start small. Dr. Beck believes that when a task, however simple, is successfully accomplished, the depressed mood lifts and the patient is spurred on to try something harder. He often plans a schedule of daily activities and counts on the family to see that it's carried through. "You'll have to urge the patient along," Dr. Beck says. "Don't lay on the compliments about small accomplishments too thick. Try to be objective, but use your approval to motivate him further."

Watch out for suicide. The family of a depressed person must be ever alert to the possibility of suicide. While it's rare, records show that about 25,000 Americans kill themselves each year, and the true figure is probably three or four times higher. (What's recorded as an automobile accident, for instance, may well be suicide.) Suicide frequently follows depressive illness and is often preceded by suicide threats. While only about 10 percent of those who attempt suicide eventually succeed, it's important to listen for cues—particularly those indicating an utter hopelessness about the future, like John Jenkins's remark, "I'm thoroughly rotten. You'd be better off without me."

Relatives of depressed persons should not regard suicide as a taboo topic for conversation. "Bring it up yourself," advises Dr. Klerman. "You won't be putting new ideas in his mind. Someone considering suicide is usually conflicted, wavering. He wants you to help him fight for life." Nevertheless this is not a battle to be left to amateurs—however loving. A suicidal person should be under professional care, probably in a hospital. "But while you're waiting," Dr. Klerman says, "you must act as his private-duty nurse. Hide the pills, the razor, even the kitchen knives. And don't let him drive a car alone."

If you're at your wit's end about how to help a depressed person you love, new psychological techniques based on the common sense theory that the sadness will lift if the person can start to think and act differently may be helpful. John and Marjorie Jenkins worked with Dr. John Rush, a young psychiatrist associated with Dr. Beck, on several such projects. John's first task was to record each day's activities in a spiral notebook and to grade them with an *M* (Have I mastered the chore?) and a *P* (Has it given me pleasure?). As he wallpapered his daughter's bedroom with a gay flower pattern one Saturday, John stopped occasionally to scribble in the notebook. Marjorie poked her head in the room, surveyed his progress and wrote in her own notebook. The following week both husband and wife, notebooks in hand, discussed the experience with Dr. Bush.

"Saturday, 9 A.M. to 3 P.M., wallpapered daughter's room," John's notebook read. He did not add an *M* or a *P* because "I did a lousy job," he explained. "I couldn't get the flowers to line up straight." ("A depressed person perceives only those segments of experience that prove he has failed," Dr. Rush commented later.) But Marjorie's version was quite different. John had worked steadily for six hours—a startling improvement over the previous week when he couldn't muster the energy to rake the lawn. The job was difficult, he had never done it before and no one else noticed the slightest misalignment of the pattern. In fact, John's daughter hugged him with delight—and he even smiled briefly. ("Marjorie's contribution was to correct his distortion of reality and to confront him with it," Dr. Rush explained. "It also helped her understand the extent of his negativism and to be more supportive and less irritated.")

John kept up the notebook assignment for a month, adding only an occasional *M* or *P* at first. "I sort of enjoyed some things, but not really," he said. "I felt like I couldn't do anything, but when I looked back, I saw I *was* capable of some ⎯⎯⎯⎯⟶

New York Public Library

ca. **1057.** Lady Godiva, wife of the harsh and powerful Earl of Mercia, stands by helplessly as he imposes crushing taxes upon the Town of Coventry. Sympathetic to the plight of the people, Lady Godiva legendarily does penance for the earl's actions by riding through town "veiling the modesty she cherished solely with her long, unbound hair." In

Women are treated for depression two or three times as often as men. Feminists claim that this is because women suffer from chronically diminished self-esteem. Many researchers agree to the point that it's the social condition of women rather than their physical makeup that's responsible. Some psychiatrists suggest that a woman's changing status, her uncertainty about her role and a dichotomy between rising expectations and dull reality may all be factors in depression coin. For a woman prone to depression, getting a job outside the home may have a protective effect, according to Dr. Myrna Weissman, assistant professor of psychiatry at Yale Medical School.

Some researchers don't believe women *are* more depression-prone, however. "The figures are based on visits to clinics," Dr. Beck says, "and clinics are mostly open in the daytime when men are at work." Moreover, alcoholism in men and overt depression in women may be two sides to the same coin. "Depression is more likely to be masked and thus missed in men," suggests Dr. Beck. "Perhaps that's why the suicide rate is three times higher for men than for women."

Despite heartening advances in treatment, many questions about depression are still unanswered. While the new drugs treat symptoms effectively, they do not root out the vulnerability to stress that may precipitate a second depression. Current studies suggest that about two thirds of those treated for depression never suffer another attack; the others eventually experience some of the symptoms again. Maintenance doses of the antidepressant pills are proving effective in preventing a relapse during the first year after an acute episode, but it's still not known if continuing them longer will be useful.

The need is for more preventive techniques—like those John Jenkins is learning—to help people control feelings of guilt and self-hatred before they're overwhelmed by them. We also need an increased understanding of the dynamics of marriage to help husbands and wives strengthen their mates' egos rather than destroy them. The stress of an unhappy marriage appears to be common in precipitating depression, and treatment involving both spouses seems effective in guarding against recurrence. As one woman put it, "The medication made me feel better, and the psychotherapy helped me make my marriage better."

According to Dr. Klerman, depression does have a positive aspect. "It's a signal to stop and look at your life and make changes. A man may be in the wrong work. A woman may need to get out of the house. Husband and wife may have to learn to love each other again."

This is precisely what John and Marjorie Jenkins now feel they've accomplished. Last year their marriage appeared to be on the rocks; now they're both confident that it's stronger than ever. "It's like the old days," Marjorie says happily. "We can enjoy having a drink together and talking about anything. I used to go off alone to teach Sunday school; now we all go to church together and really enjoy it."

"I'm feeling great," John adds. "I look back and think yes, I was sick and yes, I made mistakes. That was yesterday. Now it's paid off for all of us. I count myself a very fortunate man."

things." In the same notebook, John jotted down his thoughts—good and bad. "I think the turning point came when I went on a business trip," he recalls. "In the motel room I started to feel low, and I wrote 'I'm a rotten husband and I ought to give Marjorie a divorce. I'm not good enough for my family.' Then I looked at it; did I write that? It's a bunch of bull. When you write things down, they look so foolish."

John brooded interminably over his feelings of guilt and failure. "Bad thoughts just took over my whole life," he said. To convince him that this was not accurate, Dr. Rush asked John to click on a stopwatch whenever a negative thought occurred, and to click it off when his mind turned elsewhere. He later noted on a sheet of graph paper the blocks of time the negative thoughts covered. He carried the stopwatch wherever he went. "I was watching a football game on television," John recalls, "when whammo, I had a bad thought—'I may never be capable of being a good person again.' I clicked on the stopwatch. Then I thought about getting a beer, so I clicked it off. You're convinced these thoughts are constantly on your mind, but the graph paper shows it isn't so. It helped me to step back and see what was really going on. I started acquiring tricks for controlling the thoughts and realized that I didn't need to be passive, that I *could* run my life again."

At the University of Oregon, Dr. Peter Lewinsohn is exploring new ways to help those who are depressed to get more fun out of life. When they're ill, he observes, these people unwittingly decrease their range of pleasant activities. For example, a woman who enjoys having weekly lunches with friends can't muster the energy to call them.

Instead of merely telling a patient to do something, Dr. Lewinsohn tries to mobilize him into activities enjoyed in the past. Lewinsohn asks his patients to choose from a checklist of 160 items—he calls it

a "Pleasant Events Schedule"—activities they consider pleasant, and then to do them more often. Those chosen by a twenty-year-old co-ed, for example, included going to a restaurant, driving a car, making snacks, visiting friends. "Activity schedules are not a panacea for depression," Dr. Lewinsohn admits. "Yet the more a person engages in pleasant activities, the better he feels."

While doctors are developing pragmatic techniques to treat depression, they still haven't solved the basic problem of what causes it. This much is known: depression often runs in families and may have a genetic base; it's usually preceded by a series of stressful events in a person's life; and this stress is not merely emotional but is accompanied by biochemical changes in the brain—probably in those areas that control sleep, appetite, sex drive, motor activity. (Antidepressant medication apparently reverses the biochemical changes.) Some people appear to overreact to stress, which results in more profound biochemical reactions and more severe depressions. Their heightened sensitivity may come from a genetic weakness, a vulnerability rooted in early childhood experiences or both. Adults who lost a parent in early childhood seem to be more prone to depression, perhaps because a new loss—real or fancied—triggers a flood of memories about the childhood episode.

The stress that triggers a depression can follow good news (a job promotion) or bad (a request for divorce), but it seems to depend on how the victim perceives it. A blow to self-esteem appears to be central. One husband went reeling into despair on learning he was sterile; his self-esteem was bound up in his sexual identity. A mother tumbled into depression each summer when her college son arrived home for vacation; she was shattered by his adolescent scorn for her life-style.

order to spare her feelings, the townsfolk stay indoors and close the shutters. All, that is, except "Peeping Tom" who steals a look and is instantly struck blind. The earl, impressed by his lady's self-sacrifice, calls off the oppressive taxes, and the couple become the town's greatest benefactors.

Overcoming Anxiety through Systematic Desensitization

C. Eugene Walker

Many of the anxieties that people experience are due to what psychologists call **conditioned reactions.** Simply stated, what psychologists mean by this is that things that frequently occur together in our experience become linked or associated with each other so that we respond to them in the same, or a highly similar, way when they happen again. Thus, if we are made anxious or afraid in the presence of certain factors (psychologists refer to them as stimuli), these same factors or stimuli will make us anxious later when they occur, even if the situation in reality no longer poses an actual threat. For example, a person may have had a number of experiences as a child in which a person in authority, such as a school principal, policeman, or guard, frightened him and perhaps punished him in some way. His reaction as an adult to a person in authority may produce considerably more anxiety in him than the situation really calls for. This is because of his previous conditioning of strong anxiety to this type of person. A person, so conditioned, might be driving along a highway and see a police car pull up behind him. He may feel considerable anxiety at the approach of the car. If the policeman stops him, the driver may have many symptoms of anxiety such as a pounding heart, rapid respiration, muscular tenseness, stuttering, and stammering speech. Of course, this is an overreaction to the situation. He was breaking no law and the officer may only want to tell him that his tail light is broken or warn him of a road hazard ahead. At worst, he may have broken a minor traffic law which would cost a few dollars fine. However, for many, the situation evokes anxiety near panic. Such effects often result from conditioned reactions.

Now, if many of our anxieties are conditioned reactions, what can we do about them? Are we the victims of our traumatic past, or can we overcome such anxieties? Fortunately, we can overcome them. In fact, they are amazingly easy to overcome if we work at them in the right way. For decades psychologists have studied conditioned reactions in research laboratories all over the world. A clinical procedure for eliminating such anxieties was developed by Dr. Joseph Wolpe, a psychiatrist, which makes use of the basic principles learned from research. It is called systematic desensitization. If done properly, it works almost every time.

Let's use the example of authority persons to see how to use systematic desensitization on your own. Suppose this is your problem. The first step would be to sit down with some index cards and on each card write a different situation or experience that causes you anxiety in this area. After you have a stack of cards, place them in order, with the one that causes least anxiety on top and the one that causes most anxiety on the bottom. Your list might look something like this (least anxiety causing at top, most at bottom; *see box, right).*

Next, you have to learn to relax completely. Believe it or not, you can actually train yourself to do this rather easily. First sit in a comfortable chair or lie on a couch or bed. Then say something like

1. Walking past and greeting one of the bosses at work who is only a little older than myself.
2. Walking past and greeting one of the bosses at work who is considerably older than myself—one with gray hair and a gruff but somewhat fatherly demeanor.
3. Encountering one of the bosses who is only a little older than myself in the coffee-break room, where we will have to talk and have coffee together.
4. Encountering one of the bosses who is considerably older than myself—with gray hair and a gruff but somewhat fatherly demeanor—in the coffee-break room, where we will have to talk and have coffee together.
5. Having one of the bosses who is only a little older than myself watch me, without seeming pleased or displeased, while I work.
6. Having one of the bosses who is considerably older than myself—watch me while I work—without seeming to pleased or displeased.
7. Having one of the bosses who is only a little older than myself watch me while I work and seeming to be displeased with what I am doing.
8. Having one of the bosses who is considerably older than myself watch me while I work and seem to be displeased with what I'm doing.
9. Having one of the bosses who is only a little older than myself watch me while I work and make a slightly critical comment to me after watching for a while.
10. Having one of the bosses who is considerably older than myself watch me while I work and make a slightly critical comment to me after watching for a while.
11. Having one of the bosses who is only a little older than myself watch me while I work and make a very critical comment after watching for awhile.
12. Having one of the bosses who is considerably older than myself watch me while I work and make a very critical comment after watching for a while.
13. Attending a conference in the office of one of the bosses who is only a little older than myself to discuss something about my work that should be improved.
14. Attending a conference in the office of one of the bosses who is considerably older than myself to discuss something about my work that should be improved.
15. Attending a conference with several bosses both young and old to discuss something about my work that should be improved.

the following to yourself, "I am going to relax completely. First, I will relax my forehead and scalp. I will let all the muscles of my ⟶

1059. Pope Nicholas II decrees that hereafter no churchman may be married, that only those who profess perpetual celibacy may be ordained as priests, and that no married priest may celebrate or even assist at Mass.

forehead and scalp relax and become completely at rest. All of the wrinkles will smooth out of my forehead and that part of my body will relax completely. Now, I will relax the muscles of my face. I will just let them relax and go limp. There will be no tension in my jaw. Next, I will relax my neck muscles. Just let them become tranquil and allow all of the pressure to leave them. My neck muscles are relaxing completely. Now, I will relax the muscles of my shoulders. That relaxation will spread down my arms to the elbows, down the forearm to my wrists, hands, and fingers. My arms will just dangle from the frame of my body. I will now relax the muscles of my chest. I will let them relax. I will take a deep breath and relax, letting all of the tightness and tenseness leave. My breathing will now be normal and relaxed, and I will relax the muscles of my stomach. Now I will relax all of the muscles up and down both sides of the spine; now the waist, buttocks, and thighs down to my knees. Now the relaxation will spread to the calves of my legs, my ankles, feet, and toes. I will just lie here and continue to let all of my muscles go completely limp. I will become completely relaxed from the top of my head to the tip of my toes."

If you try this one or two times, you will be amazed at just how relaxed you can become. If you have trouble doing this at first, you might try purposely tensing the muscles of various parts of your body a few times and then letting them relax completely immediately following the forced tension. This will teach you to discriminate clearly between the tense and relaxed state, and train you in producing relaxation at will.

After you are completely relaxed, you are ready to begin the systematic desensitization. Take the top card from the pile and look at it. Then close your eyes and visualize the situation described on it as vividly as you can in your imagination. Imagine it occurring and imagine that you are really there. As you do that, you may experience some anxiety. If so, *stop* the imaginary scene *at once* and go back to relaxing. Relax all of the muscles again. Generally, taking just a deep breath or two and letting all of the muscles rest will do the job. However, if you need to, go through the whole relaxation sequence in your mind again, muscle by muscle.

When you are again completely relaxed, wait a few seconds. Then look at the card and imagine the scene once more. If you feel anxiety, make your mind turn blank, stop imagining the scene and go back to relaxing. Do this over and over until you can imagine the scene without feeling anxiety. It may take only a couple of times, or it may take 15—20 times, but repeat it until you can imagine the scene without feeling anxiety. When you have accomplished this, go on to the second scene. Continue in this manner until you have gone through all the cards.

It is best to work on the scenes like this for about a half an hour at a time. You may want to do it every day or every other day or only a couple of times a week, depending on your schedule and how quickly you want to conquer the anxiety. Usually, from one session to the next, it is a good idea to start by going over the last item or two from the previous session that you were able to imagine without anxiety.

A variation of the above procedure, which some people use, is tape recording a vivid description of the scene in advance. They then relax and listen to the tape. If they feel anxious, they shut the tape off and relax. When calm, they back the tape up and begin again.

When you have completed the above process, you will find that situations which used to cause stabbing pains of anxiety at their mere thought can now be calmly thought about without disturbance. You have been desensitized. To make the treatment complete, you should now calmly go over in your mind what is the right thing to do in the situation that has caused you anxiety. Then make plans to actually do the right thing the next time the situation occurs. You will be amazed to find that your previous anxiety kept you so uptight that you avoided thinking or planning in this area; it

prevented you from thinking clearly when you were in the situation. This will all be different now. It is a good idea, as you desensitize yourself to the scenes on the cards, to plan how to handle such situations and then seek out several occasions when you can practice doing better. Some people go through the relaxation procedure just before confronting the real situation. Others just take a deep breath and get as relaxed and composed as they can.

If you have trouble going through the procedure alone, you might want to enlist the help of a friend. Often you can arrange to help each other by trading roles and desensitizing one another. If you do this, have the friend instruct you step by step to relax all of the muscles and then vividly describe the scene to you while you stay relaxed. You will need to tell the friend enough details about the scene so that he can weave an imaginary story, one you can really put yourself into and experience. If you feel anxiety, at any time, signal the friend by raising the index finger of your right hand. He should, at that instant, tell you to turn off your imagination, make your mind go blank, and return to relaxing. When you are relaxed, he can begin again.

Another way of handling conditioned anxiety that works just as well as the preceding method in most cases, and better in some, is called *in vivo* desensitization. The term *in vivo* simply means in this case, "in real life."

As an example of real life desensitization, suppose you have a lot of anxiety in social situations. After thinking about it you might develop a hierarchy that looks like this (least anxiety-causing at top, most at bottom):

1. Making small talk with a stranger, for example, at a bus stop.
2. Having a fairly extended conversation with a stranger, for example, in the doctor's waiting room.
3. Meeting a new person for the first time and talking only briefly with him, for example, being introduced to him by a mutual friend on the street as you happen to run into each other.
4. Meeting a new person at a party and having to make conversation with him for a few minutes.
5. Meeting several new people at a party and making small talk.
6. Meeting a new person who joins you and some mutual friends for dinner.
7. Meeting several new people who join you and some mutual friends for dinner.
8. Being the only new person who must meet several people for the first time and have dinner with them, for example, being placed at a table of strangers at a dinner party.

The way to attack the above problem would be to take the first item and look for naturally occurring occasions or even arrange for occasions to occur in which you can experience the event. You should prepare for the occasion in a way that is logical and appropriate. Being prepared is half the battle. In the above example, you might make it a point to read the newspaper in order to glean some topics to talk about. You might go over in your mind various pleasantries that seem to contribute to a congenial encounter. You might have an appropriate joke or anecdote in the back of your mind. You might search the other person's interests, once you meet, for one you share. A compliment on how he looks or on something he said will seldom lead you astray and will often make him a friend for life. The point is, plan in advance how you will handle the occasion. Then when you are in the situation, work out what you have planned.

Just before you enter the situation, go through the relaxation procedure or, at least, take a few deep breaths, shrug your shoulders, and get completely relaxed. Then go in and do the best you can.

After it is over, think about and analyze how things went. Learn from each experience how to perform better next time. Then do it

1125. Mabel, countess of Belesne, is described by the historian Odericus Vitalis as "politic, shrewd, fluent and extremely cruel." She rides about the countryside with a band of armed troops beating and robbing monks and she manages to reduce all her neighbors to poverty. One of them, however, gains access to her bedroom and there murders her, causing "much joy."

again. Eventually, the anxiety will be gone and you will have developed a repertoire of skills in handling such situations. At that point, you will no longer need the elaborate plans. It will just come "naturally."

Be sure to start with the least anxiety-provoking situation. Go on to the next highest and the next only after the ones below it have been conquered. Success depends on a careful, systematic attack.

Some people have used an approach that is in between the imagination approach and the real-life approach discussed above. It is called behavioral rehearsal. In this, you rehearse things with a friend that you would like to do without anxiety. For example, in a job interview, have a friend play the part of the interviewer. He can play the part of different kinds of interviewers (stern, hostile, friendly, etc.), and you can practice being calm and responding to the questions. At the end, you can discuss how you might have better handled the situation. Then, try it again. Do it over and over until you act without anxiety. The different types of interviews and different types of interviewers can be arranged in hierarchies and worked on using this method.

The hardest part of using these procedures is developing the hierarchies. Often just what it is that makes us anxious seems vague, hard to define or to separate out from other factors. The basic strategy is to keep the scenes as simple and straightforward as possible. The best way to start is simply to write down on cards as many situations that involve anxiety as possible without worrying about categories or hierarchies. After you have done that, sort them out into logical categories involving one dimension or a couple of dimensions that seem to go together well. Each of these piles will become a hierarchy of its own. Read over all the items in a given pile and fill in the gaps by writing new cards that obviously would fit in with the ones already written. Extend the range upward and downward by making up more or less extreme situations. Eventually, you will develop a hierarchy with 10 to 25 items. If you have too many more than that, break it into two or more hierarchies.

Many times people also wonder if they are including the "right" things in their hierarchies. The best way to handle this is to make them as specific and as close to real life as you can. If they are specific, real-life situations that make you anxious, they are right for the hierarchy.

When you start the desensitization procedure, if you have trouble staying relaxed and getting past the first item on the hierarchy, you have started out with one that is too threatening. Write some less anxiety-provoking items and extend your list downward. If you reach a point at which you have conquered the last item but the next one on the list seems not to be getting any better, say after 15 or 20 trials, you probably have made too big a jump. Write some additional items that would logically fit in between the two and work on them.

Sometimes we have anxiety about an event that doesn't seem to have a logical hierarchy to go with it. Often this is a very unique event, sometimes one that will happen only once in our lives. For example, your upcoming wedding might be causing anxiety. The way to use the systematic desensitization procedure for such events is to imagine the whole event, step by step, from beginning to end while staying relaxed. At the first sign of anxiety, stop, make your mind turn blank, then go back to the beginning and start over. Keep this up until you can imagine the whole thing without anxiety. You will find yourself much more relaxed when the event actually occurs than if you had not done this.

One further tip. Imagination, behavioral rehearsal, and *in vivo* desensitization all work on essentially the same principle. We generally use the imagination and rehearsal procedures for situations that don't occur often enough in real life to make the *in vivo* system practical or when the situation is so anxiety provoking that we are too terrified to try it in real life.

Simple Meditation Techniques

Lawrence LeShan

Do not expect to do a meditation "well" (focusing on it and nothing else) for a long period of time. The first major effect of meditation, strengthening the personality structure, comes from working consistently on it, not on doing it "well." The important thing about a meditation is how hard and consistently you work on it, not how well you do it. This point *cannot* be overstated. It is a crucial truth, but most people simply do not believe it. Only after a long period of practice can you expect to be really just doing a meditation and not anything else. Saint Bernard of Clairvaux (who had certainly worked long and hard on his meditations) was once asked how much, when he was meditating, he was really "into it," really just doing it. He replied with a sigh that still echoes down the centuries, "Oh how rare the hour and how brief its duration!"

A story about Saint Theresa of Avila illustrates the same point. One of her novices remarked that it must be wonderful to be like Theresa and not be bothered by distractions in her prayers and meditations. Saint Theresa replied, "What do you think I am, a saint?"

1143. Portugal revamps its laws this year. Several highlights: "If a married woman commit adultery and her husband complain to a judge—and the judge be the King— the adulterer and adultress shall be condemned to the flames; but if the husband retain his wife, neither offending party shall be punished." If, however, a woman of the aristocracy

It is only after you have worked a long time and reaped the benefit of the first part of the path in its personality strengthening, increased ability to relate to and cope with the world, ability to accept and express your own feelings, etc., that the second effect—helping you to attain a new way of being in the world, a new metaphysical system—emerges. The road is long and often frustrating, but the game is worth the candle. Let us fare on.

Start by finding a comfortable position in a quiet time and place. If the place feels good to you also (has "good vibes"), that is nice too; it is not essential, but helpful.

The Meditation of Contemplation

This meditation—called in Eastern schools "One-pointing"—is used by a wide variety of mystical schools. Essentially it is learning to look at something actively, dynamically, alertly, but without words. You pick an object to work with (generally speaking, it is best for most people to start with a natural object, a bit of seashell, a pebble, a twig) and look at it with the same structure as if you were feeling it, as if you were using your sense of touch to stroke a piece of velvet.

Let me try to make this clearer. Take a part of your sleeve or the cloth covering your thigh. Stroke it with your hand, "feel" it. Do this for half a minute or a minute. Then look at it for the same amount of time. Really *look* at it, learn it by eye. For most people there is a real difference between the two perceptions. With the visual sense, you tend to use words to describe the sensation, to translate the experience into language. With the tactile sense, you tend to accept the experience on a nonverbal level.

Contemplation is a structured meditation of the outer way. You take the object, hold it at a comfortable eye range for you, feeling free to move it closer or farther away as you please, and just *look* at it.

It is very hard. Give yourself permission to make constant slips from the directions. You will make them anyway and will be much more comfortable—and get along better with this exercise—if you give yourself permission in advance. Treat yourself as if you were a much-loved child that an adult was trying to keep walking on a narrow sidewalk. The child is full of energy and keeps running off to the fields on each side to pick flowers, feel the grass, climb a tree. Each time you are aware of the child leaving the path, you say in effect, "Oh, that's how children are. Okay, honey, back to the sidewalk," and bring yourself gently but firmly and alertly back to just looking. Again and again you will suddenly notice that you are thinking about something else or translating your perception into words or something of the sort. Each time, you should say the equivalent of "oh, that's where I am now; back to work," and come back to looking.

In training her students in this technique, Saint Theresa of Avila wrote, "I do not require of you to form great and serious considerations in your thinking. I require of you only to look." A Byzantine mystic, Nicophorus the Solitary, put it, "Attention is the appeal of the soul to itself." The Baal Shem Tov wrote, "God's miracles belong to those who can concentrate on one thing and limit themselves." And a statement attributed to the Buddha runs in part, "In what is seen should be only the seen."

Patanjali, an Eastern sage, called this technique "fixed attention" and described it as "binding the mind staff to a place." We must, however, bind ourselves gently and with humor and compassion at our own lack of discipline.

This lack of trained discipline of our own will becomes immediately apparent as we do this exercise. In the words of one student of it, we find ourselves "itching, twitching and bitching." We find ourselves constantly needing to change our physical position, or getting sleepy, or using words to describe our perception, or suddenly solving problems we have been concerned with for weeks, or unable to concentrate, or anything else we can dream up to avoid the discipline. Or we notice that for a moment we were "just looking" and begin to think about how well we are doing at the meditation and, thereby, of course, stray right off the track. (This has been called The Law of the Good Moment, otherwise known as "Here I am, wasn't I!")

One way we frequently avoid discipline is by the production of what the Zen people call "Makyo." Makyo are illusions that we project on reality as an aid to escaping from the directions. Your seashell or pebble may develop a pretty corona of colored light or apparently begin to accordion in size, growing larger and smaller. You may feel yourself grow lighter or heavier or feel as if currents of rather pleasant energy are running through you. Every sort of sensation from smells to touches to sounds to lights is possible. The Suringama Sutra (a mystical training document of ancient India) lists fifty types of Makyo and then goes on to explain that these are only the most typical types. The best way to respond to these is to say to yourself, in effect, "Oh, that's what I'm perceiving now. How interesting. I wonder what I will make up next to avoid the discipline. Now, back to just looking." Yasutani Roshi, an experienced Zen teacher, said of these, "Makyo do not occur when you are dawdling, neither do they appear when your practice has ripened. . . . They indicate the intensity of your concentration." He goes on to warn you to be careful not to get too interested or involved with them as they prevent progress if you do.

The task is to look actively and alertly. You must keep trying to bring more and more of yourself to just doing this one thing—looking. You are aiming at being totally involved, from your head to your toes, in this intense, nonverbal activity, to be as totally involved as is a dog pointing at a rabbit. In the words of the

is raped, all her assaulter's property is given over to her. Should she not be a member of the nobility, on the other hand, and if she be single the rapist must marry her regardless of his own social rank.

120 Meditation
THE PSYCHOLOGICAL ADVISER

feel good about it, a small, fairly plain piece of personal jewelry.

Staying with the same object tends to make the exercise go better. Work for ten-minute periods for the first two weeks on a daily basis. If your schedule makes this impossible, work at least five times a week. After two or three weeks, increase the time to fifteen minutes and a month later to twenty minutes. After a month of this you will know where you stand with this meditation and may want to increase it to one-half hour, or you may feel twenty minutes are right for you. Or that you wish to leave it out of your meditational program.

Expect it to be different each time. The fact that it goes "well" one period makes no prediction for the next. There will be "good" sessions and frustrating, discouraging ones. About all you can predict as you go on is a tendency to go to more and more extremes and that when they are good they are very good and when not good, intensely frustrating. This is a tough but excellent meditation and, in the words of Richard Rolle, the beautiful thirteenth-century British mystic, "Contemplative sweetness not without full great labour is gotten."

Bhagavad-Gita, "to hold the senses and imagination in check and to keep the mind concentrated upon its object."

Hold the object you have chosen at a comfortable visual distance for you and be flexible about this distance. Do not stare at one point on the object. Dynamically explore it without words. Treat it as a fascinating new continent you are exploring nonverbally. If you stare or strain your eyes during the exercise you will simply increase the illusions (eye fatigue plus Makyo) and slow yourself down. Contemplation is "binding the mind staff to a place." It is not binding the retina to a place.

Stay, if at all possible, with the same object for several weeks (at least) at a time. A nature object is often best, but do not choose a flower. A flower as a contemplation object is, for many people, too easy and we tend to slip into dazed, trancelike states with it. There are also some objects that, because of their symbolic, unconscious and archetypal meanings, are quite difficult and should not be used until you are thoroughly experienced with this exercise. (This means a minimum of several months of daily work.) These difficult objects include a cross, a fire, a mandala. Save these until much later or your work will probably be greatly slowed.

In my own training seminars I have the participants use a paper match. (Christmas Humphreys uses brass doorknobs.) These are generally fine when working with the aid of the discipline of an intensive group. However, if working alone, they are frequently just too dull and dispiriting; nature objects are better or, if you

The Meditation of Breath Counting

There are a very wide variety of meditations utilizing your own breathing. The particular one described here is, with a minor modification, used particularly in Zen training.

In this structured meditation of the outer way, the object again is to be doing just one thing as completely and fully as possible. In this case the one thing is counting the exhalations of your breath, your breathing out. You strive to be aware of just your counting and to be as fully aware of it as possible. All your attention is gently and firmly and repeatedly brought to bear on this activity. The goal is to have your whole being involved in the counting. Saint Anthony the Great described something of the goal you are working toward when he wrote, "The prayer of the monk is not perfect until he no longer realizes himself or the fact that he is praying."

In this exercise one is paying as full and complete attention as possible to the counting itself. Thoughts, feelings, impressions, sensory perceptions, to the degree that they are conscious, are a wandering away from the instructions. In the words of Bhagavad-Gita, "The tortoise can draw in his legs/The seer can draw in his senses." It is this "drawing of the senses" you are working toward in this discipline.

It is probably best for most Westerners to count up to four and repeat. In Zen, the usual practice is to count up to ten. However, after working with a fairly large number of Westerners on this exercise, it seems to me that this makes the work unnecessarily difficult.

ca. **1150.** Early medieval Russia practices marriage as a commercial transaction. The bride is purchased by her suitor when he pays a negotiated "bride-price" to her father. Haggling over this price is a regular fixture of nuptial preparations.

Meditation
THE PSYCHOLOGICAL ADVISER **121**

Typically, when you get to seven, eight and nine in your counting you begin to worry if you will remember to change over at "ten" and so get thrown off stride.

Another variation is to count sequentially as high as you go during each session. The problem here is that it is very difficult to avoid self-competition, the sort of inner statement that goes, "Yesterday I counted up to 947. Will I go higher today?" All in all, a count of four seems like the best available compromise.

When you find yourself thinking about your counting (or about anything else), you are wandering away from the instructions and you should bring yourself gently back. If you find yourself modifying your breathing, this also is a straying from the exercise.

One permissible variation on the exercise as given here is to include an "and" between the counts to "fill up" the space between exhalations. This makes it easier for some people. Thus you would count "one" for the first exhalation, "and" for the next inhalation, "two" for the second exhalation, "and" for the next inhalation, and so forth. After trying it for a few sessions with just the "one, two, three, four" try it for a session with the "and" included and then make your own decision. As in all meditations, it is essential before you start a session to decide exactly what it is to consist of and then stick to it.

Be comfortable and set a timer or put a clock face where it is in your line of vision. For most people this exercise goes better with the eyes closed since there is less distraction. Experiment and see whether it is better for you with your eyes opened or closed. If closed you will have to "peek" once in a while to see how your time is going. Start with fifteen minutes at a time on a daily, or else a five times a week basis if necessary. After a few weeks, increase to twenty minutes, and after another month to twenty-five or thirty minutes. After working this last schedule for a month or two, you should be able to determine your own future course with this meditation.

The Meditation of the Bubble

This is a structured meditation of the inner way. In meditations of this sort, you observe your own consciousness in a special way (through the structured design of the meditation) while interfering with it as little as possible. You meditate on the stream of your own consciousness.

Picture yourself sitting quietly and comfortably on the bottom of a clear lake. You know how slowly large bubbles rise through the water. Each thought, feeling, perception, etc., is pictured as a bubble rising into the space you can observe, passing through and out of this space. It takes five to seven or eight seconds to complete this process. When you have a thought or feeling, you simply observe it for this time period until it passes out of your visual space. Then you wait for the

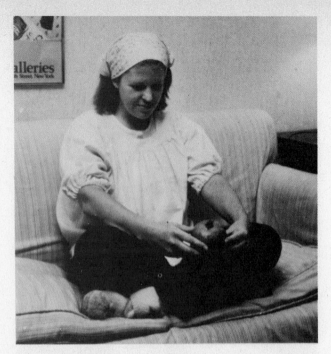

next one and observe it for the same amount of time, and so on. You do not explore, follow up or associate to a bubble, just observe it with the background of "oh, that's what I'm thinking (or feeling or sensing) now. How interesting." Then, as it passes out of visual space (as the imaginary bubble rises), you calmly wait for the next bubble.

Do not be thrown off the meditation if the same "bubble" rises several times. If you just go on, this will pass. And do not be disturbed if you cannot see the connection between the bubbles or the source of your thoughts. If you simply stay with the discipline long enough, most confusing connections will clear up. If your mind seems to go "blank," why, feeling "blank" makes a fine bubble!

The purpose of the concept of bubbles rising through the water is to help you to do two things. The first is to keep the timing. You learn to simply contemplate each thought or perception for (approximately) a definite time and then to let it go. Secondly, the structure helps you look at each one individually and not constantly feel you must find connections between them. Since these are crucial reasons for this structure, those who find the idea of sitting at the bottom of a lake unsympathetic or disturbing can picture themselves on a warm, windless day on the prairie watching large, separate puffs of smoke rise from a campfire as if it were an Indian signal fire.

Another variation of this is the Tibetan "thoughts are logs" discipline. In this you picture yourself sitting on the bank of a broad, gentle river. From time to time logs come floating down the river; you follow the same procedure, using the logs concept instead of the bubble concept. This approach is preferable for some people while others find it extremely difficult and confusing. The structure and purpose of the two ways of

1170. Jaufre Rudel, Prince of Blaye, France, and a noted troubadour, hears of the Countess of Tripoli's great beauty and falls desperately in love with her from afar. He actually gets sick in his longing for her, so he decides to at least meet her in person before he dies. Arriving by boat in Palestine, Rudel is too weak to disembark, but the countess has heard about this man and, moved by such an extreme display of love (and probably

bubbles and logs are the same. For most people the bubble concept seems to go better.

Start with ten minutes a day for two weeks. If you are having especial difficulties, on the fourth to seventh day experiment for a session with either the "puffs of smoke" or the "thoughts are logs" conceptualization. Try both of them if you wish, one session for each. After that choose one of the conceptualizations and stay with it. After the two weeks of ten minutes each, go to twenty minutes a day (one-half hour if this is clearly a "right" meditation for you at this period in your development) for three weeks to a month. At the end of that time you should know how to include this meditation in your own program.

The Mantra Meditation

The Mantra is one of the most widely used forms of meditation. We find it in every major mystical training school, with the possible exception of Hasidism. It consists of a word or phrase or sentence chanted over and over and over again. The basic goal is to be doing one thing at a time, in this case chanting and being aware of your chanting and only of your chanting. Whether one chants the Eastern "Hare Krishna," or "Aum," the Christian "Deus in adjutorium meum intende" ("Oh God, come to my aid"), the Sufi "Allah hu" or any other sounds, the basic goal remains the same.

It is necessary to say here that two other reasons are given for the value of mantras by various mystical training schools. Although I personally do not agree that these reasons are valid, the contrary opinion is held by many men who are very serious students of the subject and whose viewpoints must be treated with respect.

The first set of reasons concerns the *content* of the mantra. Many meditators believe that a specific content has real value in helping you comprehend and *know* its validity. Thus the chant "All is One," if repeated enough, will, from this viewpoint, bring you closer to the knowledge that this is true. Similarly, chants such as "God is One" or "God is good" are believed to have beneficial effects because of their content.

The second set of reasons given for the positive value of mantras is believed by some to be in the "vibrational" qualities of certain sounds and the effect of these vibrations on specific parts of the body or personality. Thus certain sounds are supposed to vibrate chiefly in certain organs of the body and to thereby stimulate these organs into greater effectiveness and/or to bring them into a better relationship with other organs and personality areas. This type of explanation is found chiefly in the Yoga and Sufi schools. Although I must confess that I cannot understand exactly what they are talking about, these claims are made by men of such seriousness and experience that they cannot be

taken lightly.

However, anybody who gives (or sells) you a mantra designed just for you on the basis of ten minutes' conversation is pulling your leg. The mantra will probably work but certainly not because it is designed for you, but because you use it as a mantra.

A short phrase is chosen. I prefer meaningless phrases since I believe that the meaning of the content makes it harder to stay with the structure, but if you feel fairly strongly that a phrase with positive content would be more sympathetic, use one of these. I have known people to usefully work with mantras such as "Love one another," "Peace," "Peace to all," etc. The classic Eastern and Christian phrases just mentioned have also been useful to many. One man I know of used Thoreau's phrase "I have heard no bad news" effectively, although this is a bit long. "Kyrie eleison" ("Christ is risen") and "Alleluia" have also been used. Saint Gregory of Sinai recommends, "I am the way, the truth and the light." One mystical training school believes all mantras should be seven syllables in length, but I do not understand their reasoning.

One of the nonsense phrases I have used with groups is "La-de" ("Lah-dee"). This mantra was designed by means of LeShan's Telephone Book Method, which is probably as effective as any other. Open a telephone book at random and put a finger down blindly. Take the first syllable of the name you hit. Repeat

by curiosity as well), she goes aboard.

Inside, "she took his hand and spoke graciously and cheeringly to him." Troubadour Rudel barely falters out his thanks before, "overcome in a rush of emotion, he expired before her eyes."

Meditation
THE PSYCHOLOGICAL ADVISER 123

the procedure. Link the two syllables and you have a mantra.

Find a comfortable position but do not slouch in such a way as to constrict your chest and throat. Start chanting the phrase. Do this aloud if possible, but if not, do it without making actual sounds. It's best to do it audibly but not too loudly or you will strain your voice, or even hyperventilate (breathe more rapidly and deeply than your oxygen needs require) and so alter the chemical environment of your brain. This can make you dizzy and produces other symptoms sometimes. It is generally a pretty silly thing to do.

Keep trying to chant and nothing else. Keep bringing yourself back to the task and trying to involve yourself more and more in it. Find one rhythm that seems sympathetic to yourself and the phrase. Stay with that rhythm. Stay with it through all the silliness you will dream up, seeing new meanings in the phrase, punning on it, finding its meaning break down into nonsense (if it isn't nonsense already), and God knows what else. Your task is to follow the discipline and to keep working at doing nothing else but chanting and being aware of your chanting. If a mantra is right for you at this stage of your development, after five to eight sessions you will find increasing periods of time (five seconds or up to twenty) when you are only aware of your chanting.

Start with fifteen minutes at a time. Then, after two weeks, increase this to twenty minutes (or a half hour if you feel really good about this discipline) and keep this up for another two to three weeks. Then decide if, and if so, how, you wish to integrate this form of meditation into your own meditational program.

A Sufi Movement Meditation

This meditation requires a group of from five to fifteen people. It is a meditation of movement and chanting and is described here in order to introduce and give the flavor of this type of meditation work.

In movement meditations, as in the other forms I have described, the primary goal is to learn to do, at will, one thing at a time. In addition, movement meditations are the best overall route for some people and are an exceedingly valuable variation and change of pace in a meditational program for many others. I strongly recommend that somewhere in your own program you try this meditation.

The change to the route of physical movement also releases the whole organism you are and makes it more coherent and integrated by including the body instead of leaving it out. There is, to my knowledge, no serious mystical training school that does not include some movement work, and this, in itself, should tell us something.

In this meditation you and your companions form a circle with hands clasped. Leave some distance between each of you, but not so much that you are stretching your arms. Place your feet comfortably apart so that you are solidly set on the earth. Slowly lean backward, raise your face to the sky and your hands upward, and when looking as straight up as is comfortable say in a ringing voice, "Ya Hai." Bring the body and head forward and the arms down and back until you are facing as directly downward as is comfortable. Say in the same voice "Ya Huk." Now move upward to the "Ya Hai" position and repeat. Move together until you find a group speed and rhythm that feel right. Many groups do this at between ten and fourteen pairs per minute, but find your group's own best pace. The "Ya Hai" is a ringing, upward, triumphant call. The "Ya Huk" has the same qualities, but its abrupt ending produces a different feeling. Once you have found the pace, keep at it. Your goal is total involvement of your awareness in the movement and chant. When going well the group should be opening and closing like a flower.

You must be aware of the physical condition of each person in this. If anyone feels he is pushing himself where he should not be, he steps back, brings together the hands of the persons on each side of him and leaves the circle intact as he withdraws. Everyone must feel free to do this or it is a mistake to do the exercise.

Practice it for ten to fifteen minutes about ten times until you really begin to feel the group getting into it and that no one is uncomfortable or strained by the exercise. If it goes well, begin to increase it to a half hour. The goal is to be able to go past the fatigue point to where you are moving and chanting so completely and so unaware of anything else that fatigue drops away and the only awareness of the self and the universe is the total harmony and action of movement and sound. If this exercise is right for you, you will find this way of being and notice afterward that you were so completely integrated and doing only one thing so completely that you were hardly tired at all once you had gone past the first fatigue, gotten your "second wind." Once you have reached this place a few times you will be able to decide whether and (if so) how to include this exercise in your meditational program.

None of these meditations are "easy" or "gentle" ones. They hold the possibility of shaking you up more than you expect. They must be done with persistence and courage, courage to face the unexpected in you and to look at it and attempt to let yourself comprehend it. Freud once wrote, "The essence of analysis is surprise." This is not only true of analysis, but, in some ways, of all growth. Heraclitus said, "If we do not expect the unexpected, we will never find it." I would add only "expect and try to welcome" to this statement.

Assertiveness Training   Patricia Jakubowski-Spector

Many women find that their anxiety about producing interpersonal conflicts often prevents them from taking stances and expressing their true feelings, beliefs, and opinions. In other words, their anxiety prevents them from being assertive. Women feel internal pressures for growth at the same time that they feel unprepared to meet their raised aspirations. Thus, there is an increased awareness and concern about personal limitations and a great desire to overcome these limitations. A major limitation for many women is not being able to be as assertive as they would like. This has led to a growing demand for assertive skill training.

Before describing the assertive training procedure, it is important to distinguish among assertive, non-assertive, and aggessive behavior.

Assertive Behavior

Assertive behavior is that type of interpersonal behavior in which a person stands up for her legitimate rights in such a way that the rights of others are not violated. Assertive behavior is an honest, direct and appropriate expression of one's feelings, beliefs and opinions. It communicates respect (not deference) for the other person, although not necessarily for that person's behavior. There are various levels of quality in assertive responses. For example, when a woman's verbal message clearly conveys an assertion of her rights, but her body posture, voice level, facial expression and breathing tempo all convey undue anxiety and may even contradict her verbal message, her assertive response is of a lower quality than if both her verbal and non-verbal behaviors were consonant.

Non-Assertive Behavior

Non-assertive behavior is that type of interpersonal behavior which enables the

Adapted from *The Counseling Psychologist*, Vol. 14, No. 1. Copyright © 1973 Patricia Jakubowski-Spector. Reprinted with permission.

person's rights to be violated by another. This can occur in two ways: First, she fails to assert herself when another person deliberately attempts to infringe upon her rights. For example, when a friend, who rarely returns favors, asks her to babysit, *knowing* that she's made other social plans for the evening, her failure to tell the friend her plans enables the other to take advantage of her. Second, the other person does not want to encroach upon her rights, but her failure to express her needs, feelings, etc. results in an inadvertent violation. For example, when a neighbor drops in for coffee *not knowing* that she is terribly busy, her failure to assert her needs results in her sacrificing or violating her own rights.

A non-assertive person inhibits her honest, spontaneous reactions and typically feels hurt, anxious, and sometimes angry as a result of her behavior. She frequently sends double messages. Verbally she says, "Sure, I'll be glad to babysit," while nonverbally her tight mouth, weak voice, and averted eyes indirectly communicate the opposite message.

Most non-assertive behaviors are situation specific; that is, they characteristically occur only in certain situations. Alberti and Emmons (1970) have called this "situational non-assertiveness." Although most people have some situational non-assertiveness, some people are generally unable to assert themselves under most or nearly all situations. A "generally non-assertive" person is not able to do anything that would disturb anyone. Deep feelings of inadequacy, extreme inhibition and lack of appropriate emotional responsiveness require more extensive and complex therapy than the assertive training procedure which is discussed in this article.

In some cases non-assertive behavior can be construed as a subtle type of manipulation in which the individual abdicates her rights in order to influence certain kinds of behavior from the other person. Figure 1 illustrates how this takes place. Since these bargains or exchanges are seldom explicitly stated, the other person

usually fails to fulfill the terms of the unspoken bargain and generally takes the self-sacrifice for granted. The woman then feels bitter and cheated. It would be better if she were more assertive and directly asked to have her needs met.

Aggressive Behavior

Aggressive behavior is that type of interpersonal behavior in which a person stands up for her own rights in such a way that the rights of others are violated. The purpose of the aggressive behavior is to humiliate, dominate, or put the other person down rather than to simply express one's honest emotions or thoughts. It is an attack on the person rather than on the other person's behavior. Aggressive behavior is quite frequently a hostile over-reaction or outburst which results from past pent-up anger. Letting someone else know your angry feelings at the time they occur can be assertive behavior. Making that person responsible for your feeling angry, or degrading the other person because you feel angry is aggressive behavior. Figure 2 compares non-assertive, assertive, and aggressive behavior. Because assertion and aggression are frequently confused, a series of brief examples may help to further distinguish the two. In each of the following examples, the first response given is aggressive and the second is assertive:

*** Complaining about the unsatisfactory nature of love-making:

   . . . Bill, you're really inadequate as a lover. If this is how our sex life is going to be, we might as well forget it right now. I could get more satisfaction doing it myself.

   . . . Bill, I'd like to talk about how we could act differently in sex so that I could get greater satisfaction. For one thing I think you really need to slow down a lot so that I could start tuning into my own sensations.

* * *Refusing a roommate's request to borrow clothes:

   . . . Absolutely not! I've had enough of your leeching clothes off of me.

Figure 1	The Unspoken Bargain	
I Won't Assert Myself When You:		*In Exchange For Your:*
Boyfriend	constantly talk about your past girlfriends, only socialize with your friends, ridicule my opinions.	dating only me, changing these objectionable behaviors without my having to ask you to.
Husband	make me the scapegoat for your business frustrations, give me the "silent" treatment, are abrupt in sex.	staying married to me and maintaining our home.
Employer	constantly ask me to work on my lunch hour for no extra pay, unfairly criticize me.	giving me a raise without my having to ask for it, never firing me.

1188. The great debate at Constance's court—she is an English countess of French Thoulouse—is "Whether or not real love may exist between married persons." She renders the following decision: "We declare and affirm that Love cannot exercise its powers on married persons, for it has been proved conclusively that, without being

A Comparison of Non-Assertive, Assertive, and Aggressive Behavior

	Non-Assertive Behavior	Assertive Behavior	Aggressive Behavior
Characteristics of the behavior:	Emotionally dishonest, indirect, self-denying inhibited	(Appropriately) emotionally honest, direct, self-enhancing, expressive	(Inappropriately) emotionally honest, direct, self-enhancing at expense of another, expressive
Your feelings when you engage in this behavior:	Hurt, anxious at the time & possibly angry later	Confident, self-respecting at the time & later	Righteous, superior, depreciatory at the time & possibly guilty later
The other person's feelings about herself when you engage in this behavior:	Guilty or superior	Valued, respected	Hurt, humiliated
The other person's feelings about you when you engage in this behavior:	Irritated, pity, disgusted	Generally respect	Angry, vengeful

Modified from Robert E. Alberti & Michael L. Emmons, *Your Perfect Right: A Guide to Assertive Behavior,* San Luis Obispo, California: Impact, 1970.

. . . I'm sorry, but the last time you borrowed my sweater you were careless with it and really got it dirty. I don't want to loan you any more of my clothes.

* * * Refusing to type term papers for a boyfriend:

. . . Where in the hell did you get off asking me to type your papers? What do you think I am—some sort of slave?

. . . I think that it's about time I told you how I feel when you constantly ask me to type your papers. I'm getting irritated, and I feel like I'm being taken for granted when you assume that I'll type for you. I hate typing and I think that you're asking too much when you expect me to do that for you. Please don't ask me to type any more.

* * * Reprimanding one's children:

. . . You kids are so sloppy. . . sometimes I hate you. You've got to be the worst kids in the whole city! If I had known motherhood was going to be like this, I would never have had any kids at all!

. . . Listen, I feel as though I'm being taken advantage of when you are this sloppy in cleaning up after yourselves. I can't enjoy myself with you in the evening when I have to spend all that extra time cleaning up after your mess. This is a problem that must be solved. What are your ideas?

As therapists become sensitized to deficits in assertive skills, they will frequently find that upon closer examination many psychological problems will also involve assertive problems. The following examples will illustrate how the presenting problems were ultimately treated with assertive training:

* * * *Presenting Problem:* Mild depression soon after the wedding in the absence of other marital problems. This may particularly occur among women who have had some fulfillment in their careers before marriage, who have established their own identities, and who do not want to "live vicariously" through their husbands.

Assertive Problem: Fears of becoming too dominated or "totally submerged" by her husband's personality are exacerbated by not knowing how or being afraid to stand up for her legitimate rights. A frequent underlying issue concerns how the women can be assertive *and* be a good wife.

* * * *Presenting Problem:* Consistent inability or great difficulty in "achieving" orgasm in intercourse with a boyfriend.

Assertive Problem: Attempts to use Masters and Johnson's (1970) sexual shaping therapy are thwarted when the women cannot be assertive to tell the man what she finds sexually stimulating, irritating, etc., to refuse sex when she's not sufficiently stimulated, or to ask for tenderness after sex. Common underlying assertive issues concern the woman's right to refuse sex and her fear of hurting the man if she tells him that she is not being sexually satisfied.

* * * *Presenting Problem:* Various somatic complaints—headaches, stomach-aches, backaches—which have a psychogenic origin.

Assertive Problem: When the situations that arouse the tension and anxiety are ones in which the woman fails to stand up for her rights and where she inhibits her spontaneous reactions, swallowing her hurt, irritation, or humiliation, the woman can benefit from assertive training.

* * * *Presenting Problem:* Impulsively quits attractive jobs and bitterly complains about how she was "treated" by her employer and fellow employees: "The other workers didn't do their job, and I had to do all their work as well as my own. The boss unjustly criticized me for mistakes the others made. I kept having to do extra work and run errands for my boss during my lunch hour, etc."

Assertive Problem: Quite commonly in this type of employment problem the woman is failing to assert reasonable small complaints as they occur. Instead she continues pretending that she is not irritated until her anger finally overwhelms her, and she suddenly quits her job.

Assertive Training Procedure

This article will describe a semi-structured assertive training approach which has three goals: 1) to educate the woman to her interpersonal rights; 2) to overcome whatever blocks exist to acting assertively; and 3) to develop and refine assertive behaviors through active practice methods. Many techniques may be used to achieve these goals; however, only a few will be de-scribed here. Although this assertive training program will be described as occurring in a series of successive steps, in actual practice these steps may occur in virtually any order.

Developing a Belief System

A major goal of assertive training is building a personal belief system which will help the client to support and justify her acting assertively. This is important so that the client: 1) can continue to believe in her right to act assertively even when she is unjustly criticized for her assertive behavior; 2) can counteract her own irrational guilt that later occurs as a result of having asserted herself; 3) can be proud of her assertion even if no one else is pleased with this behavior; and 4) can be more likely to assert herself.

An important part of this belief system concerns the client's acceptance of certain basic interpersonal rights. While most of these interpersonal rights are very simple and naturally assertive people act on these rights without even considering them as such, this is not the case with non-assertive people, many of whom do not really believe that they have a right to their feelings, beliefs, or opinions. These interpersonal rights are usually identified in the context of discussing several specific situations in which the clients failed to assert themselves.

The following example illustrates how several group members helped one woman to identify and accept her right to refuse an acquaintance's request to borrow her records.

Case Example:

Susan: Why didn't you tell her that you didn't want to loan that record?

Anne: I was afraid that she'd think I was petty.

Leader: What about your right to say "No"?

Anne: I don't know . . . I guess deep down I believe I *shouldn't feel* that I don't want to loan my records.

Leader: So what's wrong with your feeling that way?

Anne: Well. . . it's wrong to be selfish. I shouldn't be so possessive about my things.

Ericka: That's sure different than the way

constrained by motives of obligation or necessity, married persons, on the contrary, are compelled as a *duty* to submit to one another. ...Let this decision which we have arrived at with great deliberation and after taking counsel with the ladies of the Court, be held henceforth as a confirmed and indisputable truth."

I see it!

Anne: What do you mean? (curiously)

Ericka: If you've got bad feelings about loaning records, then you really shouldn't loan them. I mean like . . .I don't mind loaning some of my things. It's not any big moral issue. . . I'm not doing it to be a better person. It's just that I don't really mind loaning things like my hair dryer and stuff. But—wow—when it comes down to clothes, I do mind. I believe my feelings matter. *They should matter,* if not to other people, at least to myself. I have a right to have my feelings respected. And you've got a right to your feelings, and I don't see anything wrong with that! The other person may not like your feelings, but that doesn't take away from the legitimacy of your feelings.

Leader: Anne, are you still worried about what the other person will think of you?

Anne: Well . . . if I've got a right to my hang-ups—my little idiosyncracies—I guess that the other person will just have to respect that. If they don't like it, well, I'm sorry. I guess that's just too bad.

In helping the client to build a belief system which will effectively support her assertive behavior, it is important that in addition to believing that she has certain rights which she is entitled to exercise that she also hold two other convictions.

The first conviction is that *she will be happier if she appropriately exercises her rights.* When a person is learning how to become assertive, she is not merely changing a simple behavior; she's also changing how she interacts with others and consequently how she feels about herself and to some extent even what she values. Most importantly she has to learn to accept her own thoughts and feelings even when they are different than one "should" supposedly feel. This self-acceptance almost invariably results in a raised self-concept and increased personal happiness. There is, however, one important exception. If the woman's relationship with another person is *dependent* upon her continuing to act non-assertively, then her becoming assertive may very well end the relationship unless the other person can also reciprocally change. When the relationship is with an intimate male and the woman wants to maintain the relationship, it is advisable that the therapist also see the male in an attempt to prepare him for the experience and to help him change. Sometimes the end result of such intervention is a more satisfying and healthy relationship.

The second conviction is that *non-assertion is hurtful in the long run.* It hurts relationships since it prevents the person from sharing her genuine thoughts and feelings, and this essentially limits the closeness and intimacy that can only grow out of risking authentic encounters with others. Furthermore, non-assertion can inadvertently reinforce hurtful behavior on the part of others. For example, when a wife aquiesces to her domineering and critical husband, her non-assertive behavior may serve to strengthen his destructive behavior. In addition, the wife's modeling of self-effacing behavior may bring about ambivalent feelings within the daughter concerning her own femininity, viewing it as a source of weakness rather than strength.

When the client has the needed assertive skills in her repertoire but is inhibited from acting upon them because she lacks an appreciation of her rights, a discussion about rights and the resulting insight alone are frequently sufficient to prompt assertive behavior. However, usually the client also has certain anxieties about assertion which must be overcome before assertion can comfortably occur. These anxieties also need to be reduced if the client does not have the requisite assertive skills in her repertoire.

Behavior Rehearsal

Those clients who do not have the needed assertive skills in their repertoire must acquire these skills in *addition* to their developing a supportive belief system and reducing their anxieties about assertion. Behavior rehearsal is the most common technique used to teach these skills. This procedure involves a special kind of role-playing experience in which the client practices or rehearses those specific assertive responses which are to become part of her behavioral repertoire.

Behavior rehearsal can be quite useful in reducing a client's anxiety about assertion in two ways: 1) when the client perceives her increased skill in handling successively difficult role-play experiences, her confidence increases, and 2) when the client learns through the course of the role-play that nothing catastrophic happens when she enacts the assertive response, her irrational anxiety decreases.

The following steps are most commonly used in arranging the non-systematic role-play experiences for the client:

Step 1: *A Rationale for the Client:* The client is given a brief explanation of how behavior rehearsal may help her to acquire assertive skills. The client's hesitations and embarrassment about role playing are discussed.

Step 2: *Devising the First Role Play:* The therapist and client discuss situations the client has had difficulty in responding to assertively. They decide to role-play either a signifi-cant encounter that has occurred recently or one that is to occur in the near future. This situation is discussed until the therapist understands the other party's behavior well enough to role-play that person. If the therapist cannot play the other party, she may ask the client to demonstrate that person's behavior to her through role-play.

Step 3: *The First Role-Play:* The client plays herself while the therapist plays the other party. The client is instructed to role-play as though the scene were happening right then and to act as she usually does in that situation. The therapist is careful to play the role in such a way that the client is not overwhelmed with feelings of failure or anxiety. Succeeding role-plays portray increasingly difficult encounters.

Post Discussion: The therapist elicits the client's reactions to her performance including her thoughts regarding possible alternative responses. The therapist reinforces the client for any small approximations of more effective behavior. If additional feedback is needed and no video equipment is available, the therapist imitates the client's performance so that the client can then observe her own behavior.

Step 4a: *Role-Play Reversal:* The therapist and client reverse roles. The therapist demonstrates more effective assertive behavior.

Post Discussion: The therapist elicits and selectively reinforces the client's reactions to the role-play experience. The client is encouraged to evaluate the demonstrated behaviors and to determine which of these she could incorporate.

Step 4b: *An Exception to the Reversal:* If, during the first role-play discussion, the client clearly indicates that she is now ready to change her performance and says something to the effect of, "If I had to do it over again now, I'd do it a lot different," the therapist re-enacts the first role-play and skips the role reversal as it is now unnecessary. This procedure is then identical to the Step 5 role-play.

Step 5: *The Third Role-Play:* The first role-play situation is replayed. The client practices the more effective assertive responses which were previously demonstrated and discussed.

Post Discussion: The therapist asks for the client's reactions to her performance. As always the therapist warmly reinforces the client and provides positive feedback before supplying a limited amount of negative feedback which is always followed with concrete suggestions for im-

---

1189. The fickle and flirtatious Countess Louve de Penaultier attracts the attentions of young Piere Vidal, a wandering troubadour whom she comes to know when he arrives in her neighborhood wounded. Once in the castle, Piere attempts to impress her by making a play on her baptismal name, Loba de Peugnautier (she-wolf): He sneaks away, clothes himself in a wolfskin, and approaches the castle in the twilight, strumming and singing

Step 6: From this point on, the role-plays are increasingly difficult.

Step 7: *Transfer:* As soon as the client can comfortably and effectively role-play a particular situation, the therapist and client discuss how the client can try out her newly acquired behavior.

Case Example: In this example a 21 year-old woman is learning how to assert her right to govern her own life. The therapist is concentrating on the content of the client's verbal message to her mother and is gradually shaping more assertive verbal responses through successive role-play experiences. If this client were seriously deficient in her non-verbal messages—extremely quiet voice, speech disfluency, no eye contact, inappropriate smiling, immobile body expression, or standing an inappropriate distance from the other person—these behaviors would also become the focus of behavior rehearsal.

The dialogue in the following example is condensed so that the sequence of role-plays in step 3 through 6 can be more clearly illustrated. The symbols "Ther/Mom" and "Ther/Clt" refer to the therapist playing the role of the mother and the therapist playing the role of the client, respectively. A likely future encounter between the mother and daughter is being role-played as the dialogue starts.

Step 3: *The First Role-Play*

Ther/Mom: Honey, I just wanted to remind you that you have a dentist appointment tomorrow, and don't forget to tell him about that chipped tooth, and remember that there's free parking in the back of the building.

Client: Ma, I know that. Listen I can take care of myself.

Ther/Mom: Of course you can, dear. I know that. I just wanted to remind you because I knew you'd feel so bad if you forgot.

Discussion:

Therapist: What were your reactions to your performance?

Client: Not too good. It's what I always do, and it doesn't seem to make much of an impact on my mother.

Step 4a: *Role-Play Reversal*

Therapist: O.K., let's reverse roles. I'll play you. When I do, notice both what I say and what effect it has on you as the mother.

Ther/Clt: Ma, I think it's time that I told you how I feel. I know that you love me, but to tell you the truth when you tell me what to do—like you just did—I feel as though I'm 2-years old and that's awful! I would like you to stop treating me that way.

Discussion:

Client: You sounded sure of yourself. I felt like you were telling me something that was very important to you. But if I were really my mother I'd also feel kind of defensive.

Therapist: How was my response different than your typical one?

Client: I guess that I usually don't give all that much feedback to my mother. Mostly I say, "Aw, Ma" and assume that she'll get the message.

How'd you ever come up with that reply?

Therapist: I took stock of my thoughts and feeling and simply reflected back what I felt when she acted that way and specifically how I wanted her behavior to change. I kept calm by remembering that I had a right to tell her how I felt and a right to at least ask her to change. I also reminded myself not to try to put her down. Now, before we do another role-play, you mentioned that your mother would get defensive. What did you mean by that?

Client: That she wouldn't like that. She might get hurt or angry.

Therapist: Yes, she might not like that. After all, you're telling her that she's not perfect and that you'd like her to change a little. Is that so unreasonable?

Client: I hadn't thought of it that way.

Therapist: If she gets a little defensive, that's O.K. She has a right to. But remember that you're not saying that she's a bad mother. You're just asking to take responsibility for your own life and not to be 2 years old. O.K.? Let's try it again.

Step 5: *The Third Role-Play*

Client: Mom, did you know that when you tell me how to go to the dentist like that, I feel just like I am 2 years old again? I know that you don't mean to do that but that's how I feel. I would like you to stop reminding me how to take care of myself.

Ther/Mom: But, honey, I was *just* trying to help you.

Client: But it's just that which I object to. In the future, please stop reminding me.

Discussion:

Therapist: Great. . .I liked the way you modified my statement and really made it your own. That was certainly assertive! You stood up for yourself but you didn't put her down. How'd you feel?

Client: It was easier than I thought it would be.

Therapist: O.K., this time I'm going to make it a little harder.

Step 6: *Increasingly Difficult Role-Playing*

Ther/Mom: My goodness! A mother can't say two words without her daughter jumping down her throat. O.K., tell me just what I should do. . .never say anything?

Client: See, I can't carry on a conversation with you without it ending in a fight!

Ther/Mom: So who's arguing now? All I asked you is what I should do!

Discussion:

Therapist: O.K., do you see what's happened here? Your mom got defensive and you got sucked into fighting. You forgot your assertive message. When you assert yourself, you have to remember what your goals are. Here your goal is to get your mother to stop reminding you. Let's try that again. Would you like me to demonstrate how to do that?

Client: No. I think I can do it.

Step 6: Client: Mom, I don't mean to jump down your throat. I just would be happier if you would simply not remind me to do things.

Ther/Mom: But you have often forgotten to do things in the past. You just haven't remembered.

Client: Yes, I have forgotten in the past. But now I want to take total responsibility for remembering my own appointments and other things. If I forget, then I'll take the consequences. Deal?

Future role-plays would expose the client to a variety of potential maternal reactions ranging from complete indifference to hostility. The client needs to learn assertive responses which are appropriate for *each* of these situations. In addition role-plays which prepare the client for other people's negative reactions to her assertive behavior are needed. For example, when people, who have confused assertion with masculinity, wrongly reprimand the client for her so-called "unfeminine," assertive behavior, the client will need to know how to defend herself.

A Final Comment

In the course of training, clients usually do a fair amount of "assertion for the sake of assertion." By the end of training, hopefully they have a natural assertiveness which they can choose to exercise if they wish. When people know that they have the necessary skills to assert themselves, they frequently feel less of a need to do so. When they decide not to assert themselves it's because they *choose to* and not because they're afraid to.

love songs. Castle hunstmen, thinking the apparition to be a real wolf, set their dogs on him and pursue Piere across the darkening countryside. Only an alert dog master saves him from the frenzied pack, and they carry him back to the castle once again badly wounded. There the countess makes "secret amends with her person for the pain her wooer has suffered."

How to Talk to Practically Anybody About Anything

Barbara Walters

Undoubtedly inner confidence is the key to making genuine contact with another person. Nervous people are too involved with their own alarm bells and flashing signals. In any new encounter, you have valid reason to be concerned, if only because your self-esteem sags so badly when you know you haven't made a good impression. If an additional strain such as meeting your husband's boss or your boy friend's mother is added, you can be in real trouble.

To offset some of the panic, assess the situation ahead of time. What is the worst thing that can happen? Try to envision what it is and consider how it can be handled. Perhaps you dread being thought of as stupid and uninformed; if that's the case, plan ahead of time what subjects you can discuss comfortably and try to bring them up—and vow that if the topic gets out of your field you'll be candid and say, "I'm interested in what you're talking about, but I'm ashamed to say that I don't know much about it." Don't bluff: there is no surer road to ruin.

If the worst that you can imagine is the fear of arriving at a party where you don't recognize a soul and you're left orphaned by the door, analyze that possibility. It won't last long, though it may seem forever, and you can

stall away a few minutes by being busy selecting hors d'oeuvres or checking in your purse for a handkerchief. Find a telephone and make a call, hoping the situation will have improved when you're finished. You can also take a deep breath and join the least formidable cluster of guests, introducing yourself with as agreeable and relaxed an expression as you can muster. Most people know how tough it is to break into a party and will be kind.

Nervousness causes some people to become helplessly garrulous. They listen in horror to their own voices going on and on, trying to rescue one silly wrong-taste remark with another that turns out to be worse. If this happens to you, try to steady yourself by taking deep slow breaths. Deep breaths are very helpful at shallow parties. It also helps to be just plain candid. I liked the heroine in a recent novel who said, "Forgive me for talking so much. I always do that when I don't have anything to say."

Some people have an opposite reaction when nervous. They retreat into themselves, pulling down all the shades. The meek mouse approach won't give offense to anyone, but it lessens the likelihood that you'll enjoy yourself. Get your courage up and participate: it's like exercising a muscle, the more you do it, the better it works.

ca. **A.D. 1200.** In the Early Middle Ages, women are viewed as the "Devil's Gateway" to temptation and sin. Marbode, Bishop of Rennes, writes: "Of the numberless snares that the crafty enemy spreads before us... the worst, and the one which scarcely anyone can avoid, is woman—sad stem, evil root, vicious fount, which in all the world propagates

Woman in the Middle

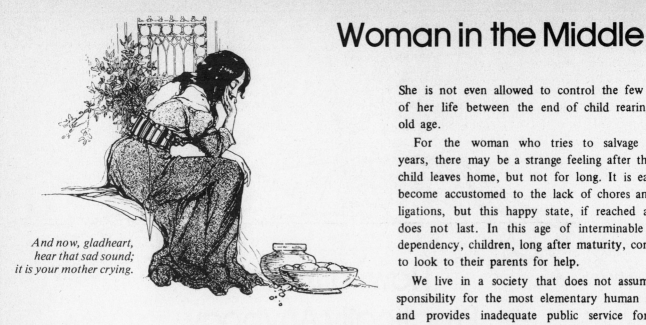

*And now, gladheart,
hear that sad sound;
it is your mother crying.*

The woman in the middle is between forty and fifty-five years of age and at the point in her life when her aging parents are becoming increasingly dependent and her children, past eighteen, should be increasingly independent, but are not. Her parents may become helpless, ill, and although her children may be in college or living away from home, they come back for holidays, also become ill, get into trouble and mother is needed. The woman in the middle is caught between two generations. She has about ten or maybe fifteen good years left and if she does not use them for herself, she will never have another opportunity.

Contrary to popular opinion, many women look forward to this period in life when, free at last, they can be concerned with only themselves. Some women plan to go back to school, take a job, study music, travel, or just enjoy some well-earned leisure. There may be those who break down from lack of household chores, absence of children, or the feeling of not being wanted, but that is only because these women have had no alternative way to live beyond child care and housework. If a woman has skills, job opportunity, lives in a world that does not discriminate against women, particularly older women, and is not programmed to believe in her own uselessness, loss of dependent children will never be a problem. The woman in the middle is depressed not because she is going through her menopause or her children have left home, but because wherever she turns, she is prevented from fulfilling herself as a human being.

She is not even allowed to control the few years of her life between the end of child rearing and old age.

For the woman who tries to salvage those years, there may be a strange feeling after the last child leaves home, but not for long. It is easy to become accustomed to the lack of chores and obligations, but this happy state, if reached at all, does not last. In this age of interminable child dependency, children, long after maturity, continue to look to their parents for help.

We live in a society that does not assume responsibility for the most elementary human needs and provides inadequate public service for the poor, sick, aged, and young. The old, sick, and poor individual is at the mercy of a community with so little concern for human life that it allows old people to die alone every day from neglect and starvation. Similarly, young people with few legal rights are subject to abuse, exploitation, and forced destructive relationships with parents and guardians. Children and the aged have no protection beyond the family. Because society has failed to make provision, it is, as always, the wife, mother, or daughter who must cope with and find solutions for the needs of the family members. She may do a good job, a bad job, or overwhelmed, may even walk away from the job, but no matter which way it goes, the responsibility for the care of the dependent person belongs to the woman.

My training as a female to fill this role started at an early age. I was the baby daughter, cute, and, I'm told, always had a lot of feeling for other people. At age four, when I saw my mother scrubbing the kitchen floor, I said, "Mommy, why do you work so hard for everyone?" My mother remembered the words well and told them to me very often. She was grateful to have a daughter who could really feel for her. She often commented that a boy is wonderful but a girl really cares.

At age eight I was awakened in the middle of the night by my father's angry shouts and my mother slamming down the window so the neighbors wouldn't hear. Soon I became aware that my parents' quarrels were part of our normal family life. When I asked my mother why she and father hated each other so much, she told me not to be silly, they really loved each other, but, since I was her only daughter and showed interest, and, since

many scandals. Oh woman! Sweet evil, honey and poison alike. Who persuaded our first parent to taste the forbidden thing? A woman! Who tamed the strong by robbing him of his hair? A woman! Who cut off the head of a just man with a sword? A woman!" Such loathing of the female sex marks countless pages of the early Church fathers' writings.

Florence Rush

she had to have someone to talk to, and since I was a big girl (age ten), she thought it was time I knew what kind of a man my father really was.

When my father learned that my mother confided in me, he demanded equal time and they both complained to me about each other. I was later surprised to learn that my brother, ten years my senior, was totally unaware and unaffected by my parents' actively hateful relationship. They never involved him because he was, after all, a man.

Later, after I married and my children were finally grown and in the process of leaving home, my father had two massive heart attacks. I was drawn into a nightmare of nurses, doctors, and hospitals, while my mother, crying and helpless, also needed attention. I asked my brother to help and he gladly agreed but since he had no preparation for this kind of work, the instruction and supervision required more effort than the job itself, so I did everything. I was soberly informed by family and friends that I had this neurotic attachment to my father which would not allow me to have anyone else care for him. My father got better and enjoyed one good year when we learned he had terminal cancer. Doctors agreed that he had nine months to live but he survived for two years, and I was needed more than ever. I became very efficient at dealing with hospital personnel, became an expert at sick benefits and insurance, and even learned how to read X-rays.

Anyway, my father died and left all his money to my brother. I didn't get a penny but fortunately my mother had enough money to manage. At my father's funeral, my mother's widowed state was much discussed but was not of great concern because she had a daughter to care for her. Later, I saw her regularly. I took her shopping, for doctor's appointments, kept her finances in order and responded, in addition, to frequent emergencies — she fell, was cheated by Macy's, or a neighbor insulted her. After a year, it struck me that half my life was spent with my mother. I figured out that my mother, now eighty, in good health and with a family history of longevity, would probably live till ninety and, if I owed her for the rest of her life, I would not finish paying my dues until I was fifty-five.

During this period, I noticed that my husband was never plagued by similar problems. His mother lived with and was supported by an unmarried sister. When, at my suggestion, my husband sent a check to help with the burden of support, his mother returned the money. She would take help from her daughter but not from her son. I once asked a young woman who was active in the women's liberation movement and wise in the ways of sexism, why men responded so differently from women to human needs and suffering, and she told me to examine how differently the sexes are raised by their parents. I compared the attitudes of my parents to myself and my brother, and then my husband's parents' attitudes to him and his sister. Males are trained to do different jobs, have different responsibilities, and are programmed to feel different feelings than females.

At the other end of the spectrum, I had to cope with my grown children and these problems were no less disturbing or complicated. For eighteen years I had raised my children practically alone because this is regarded as woman's work and my husband

DEDICATED TO THE PIONEER WOMEN OF KANSAS

Sophia Smith Collection, Smith College

ca. **1200.** A number of Christian churches forbid women to enter beyond the "Galilee" porch or chapel annex. A portion of the nave is sometimes marked off to define the boundary.

had little to do with the job. I nursed them when they were ill, ran to school when called, helped with homework, made costumes for Halloween, prepared birthday parties, supervised their sex education, worried about stammering, thumbsucking and other neurotic symptoms, in addition to doing the usual cooking and cleaning.

Before I married, I had been trained and worked as a social worker, so when Bob, my oldest son, went off to college, and Anne, my daughter, was in high school, and Bill, my youngest son, was in junior high, I decided to go back to work. I found an agency that would employ me after my long years of absence. Although initially nervous, I soon found the change of scene, the challenge of the job, and the weekly pay check the most rewarding experience in eighteen years. Even though extremely busy, I managed children, husband, home, and job. Six weeks after Bob left for school, he returned in a succession of holidays, usually with guests, that made my head spin and kept me hopping. I never realized that Thanksgiving, Christmas, and intersession were so close. I looked forward eagerly to the free time between intersession and Easter when, soon after intersession, Bob called from school to tell us that he had seriously injured his knee. His father fetched him home and this represented the total sum of his parental obligation.

Bob had to be put in traction for about six weeks. Hospitalization was impossible because of the length of time involved, so there was no question but that I would take care of him at home. I carried trays, turned TV channels, entertained visitors, got books from the library, and, because he was a young, healthy man who became bored and irritable from being confined, I also received a large amount of abuse. My supervisor kept wanting to know when I'd come back to work and finally I suggested she find someone to take my place. After seven weeks, Bob went back to school and I was without a job.

It took me six months to find other employment. After a year and a half on my second job, the agency offered to send me back to school, at their expense, to get my master's degree. It would mean giving up income for a year but I would receive, in return, after a year, a supervisory position and a substantial increase in salary. While completing my school application, Bill's school counselor informed me that my youngest child was failing miserably in junior high. He had never been a good student and since third grade I ran regularly to school conferences, supervised his studies and forced him to do hated homework. Nothing helped. The counselor offered no solution to the present problem, thought the difficulty might stem from the home, put it to me to figure something out, and of course I did.

I found a very expensive private school fully staffed with hand-picked educators and psychiatric experts dedicated to help the underachiever. I gave up my school plans in order to earn the money necessary to pay for Bill's private school. Almost every penny I earned went for tuition, psychiatric treatment, carfare, lunches, etc. The school, steeped in psychiatric principles, maintained that students who could not function academically usu-

ally suffered from disturbed parental relationships. Since Bill's father had little to do with raising his son, it was naturally I who was the controlling and domineering parent unable to let her son grow up. With years of experience and authority in all matters pertaining to education, and in order to obtain each student's confidence, the school established the rule that parents were not permitted to communicate with any staff member. Since the mother was usually the greatest threat to the child, the school director emphasized for my benefit that I would not be given any information regarding my son's progress. I was not permitted a phone conversation with a teacher and I was warned against trying to wheedle information from my son. I was advised to trust the school and relax control. No one seemed to notice that since I had previously given so much time and energy to Bill and his school problems, what they suggested was like a welcomed vacation. I gladly obeyed.

One year later, I received a phone call from the school psychiatrist who did not bother to disguise his annoyance and impatience with me. He questioned my lack of interest in my son, wondered why I never contacted the school or asked for a progress report. Before I could protest, I was informed that my son was not only failing everything, but was also using hard drugs. When I broke down in tears and confusion, I was told I had good reason to cry because my son was seriously emotionally ill and needed to be hospitalized.

Later, when I confronted Bill, he swore he did not use drugs, was having the same problems in private school as in public school, and never spoke of this before because he was advised to consult only with staff and never to discuss anything with his parents. I didn't believe him. I dragged him to doctors, put him through physical and psychological tests until one kind psychologist held me down long enough to convince me that Bill was not on drugs, was not sick, and there was no reason to have him hospitalized. When the panic passed, I gained my senses and took Bill out of school. Very soon after, he got himself a job in a hospital working on a brain research program, ran a computer, experimented with cats, loved his work, and is now getting along just fine.

When my daughter Anne graduated from college, she embarked on a career to conquer the world, and I was her assistant. She went on a diet, lost fifteen pounds, went shopping, got great clothes, got her hair done at Sassoon, got an exciting job, and, thus armed, moved out of my home to the world, life, and adventure.

To her horror and mine, she discovered that there were millions out there like herself. Her work, which consisted of an enormous amount of detailed and boring writing, was credited to her boss, and with all her clothes and fantastic figure, no one cared if she lived or died. Married women would not associate with a single girl and a single woman would not be seen with another single woman who was looking for friends. Men, generally in great demand, did not find it necessary to be even passingly polite, and their style was one of utter contempt, particularly toward a woman eager for a relationship. Anne, far away from the

security and community of friends at college, had no one but me and this forced dependency resulted in hostility and fear. Unable to cope with the outside rejection and isolation, Anne moved back home, let her frustration out on me, and we fought constantly.

Finally she left her job and experimented with different life styles. She moved to a farm and came home; she went to the coast and came home; she found a commune and came home and nearly exhausted me with her activity and anxiety. Anne's father never got too involved because he did not wish to interfere in problems between mother and daughter. Finally, Anne became aware of her desperate behavior, stopped, found a better and more independent way to live, and we were again good friends.

It is hard, if not impossible, to estimate the cost to a human being in terms of time, energy, pain, and guilt as a result of the above relationships. The woman in the middle is the target of all negative emotions stemming from each family member's failure and frustration, and the damage can never be measured. When things go wrong, and they always do, she bears the burden, the responsibility, and the blame.

If she is to save herself, the woman in the middle must learn to reject the myths regarding her family ties and responsibilities. She must no longer accept as natural her designated role as servant to all. She must question and challenge the privilege that excludes men from responsibilities and involvement with other human beings. She must reject the passivity of husbands, fathers, and brothers who sit by while wives, daughters, and sisters struggle alone with the devastating hardships involved in caring for the dependent. She must reject the lies and advices of the patronizing professionals and experts who, because of their own incompetence and inadequacy, have mystified reality and have shifted the blame for their failure to find social, economic, psychological, and educational remedies onto the mother, wife, and woman.

I am told that the women's liberation movement is for young women, but older women are looking to be liberated from their particular oppression, as well as the oppression common to all women. The only reason I am writing this paper instead of sitting with my poor old mother or sweating over a large family dinner for children and relatives is because my right to my own life has been supported by my sisters in the movement. Being fifty is not so bad if you are not torn by guilt, brutal obligation, and socially induced feelings of low self-esteem. Sooner or later, the woman in the middle is you and me, and together we must find a way not to be crushed.

ca. **1230.** Juliana, a nun at Liege, in Flanders, legendarily has a vision in which she sees the full moon missing a chunk of its orb and is simultaneously told by "a voice from heaven" that this signifies the need for an additional Church festival. She convinces the bishop of Liege to start the feast in 1246, and in 1264 Pope Urban IV declares it the holy day of Corpus Christi.

| "Woman" | "Peace" One woman under a roof | "To Quarrel" Two women together | "Intrigue and Slander" Three women together | "Home" A pig under a roof | "Marriage" A woman and a pig under one roof | "A Wife" A woman and a broom | "Son" | "Good" Woman and male child |

Starting a Consciousness-raising Group
Women's Equity Action League

☐ What is a "support" group?

Most support or "consciousness-raising" groups have six to twelve women usually meeting once a week to discuss their lives and experiences. They come to get support from others, to get perspective on their lives, to find a serious hearing for experiences usually treated as trivial, and for other reasons as diverse as the participants.

There is no one kind of group. What emerges depends on the people who come. There are no books, no leaders, no special expertise. The philosophy is that each woman is an expert on herself and has a lot to offer the others—if only she will.

☐ There is one rule: don't criticize another woman.

You can go just about anywhere in the world for criticism and advice; this is the place to go to listen and be listened to—carefully—no matter how different you are. The only reason for judging another woman is if you think she is judging you or someone else in the group. Then you can challenge her for putting you down, or at least talk about it.

☐ What do you talk about?

At first it may be useful to go around the room and have each woman say why she came, or comment on some topic chosen for the day (there is a list of possible topics at the end of this article). Often a member will want to discuss a particular idea or personal situation, and this is the best way to begin.

No matter where you start talking, if the conversation is good you will end up somewhere else. It's impossible to conclude a topic in one session, so it's easier not to try; just plan to return to the subject frequently over the months.

☐ There are no leaders

Though this sounds chaotic, it usually works extremely well. Women are good observers of social situations and practiced at encouraging reticent participants. A group with no formal leader is not free of the greater influence of its more outgoing members, but over time members usually begin to assert themselves more evenly—a bonus of this type of organization.

☐ Types of groups

If you want a close, confiding group, avoid joining one with many neighbors, friends or colleagues. It is extremely

Adapted from *Support/Consciousness-Raising Groups* by Women's Equity Action League, National Press Building, Washington, D.C. 20045. Reprinted with permission.

difficult to be open with people whom you will see tomorrow in another setting. Conversely, diversity in age and background usually contributes to the conversation once you get over the initial bewilderment. There is nothing wrong with more homogeneous groupings of age, neighborhood, etc.; just expect such a group to be less personal and decide if you want that.

☐ How to start a group

Put a notice in a local newsletter or on a bulletin board. Most women's organizations keep a list of women who are interested in forming a small group and if you give them your name, they will call you when one is starting. Meetings are usually in the members' homes, since this is simplest to arrange.

After an initial period, if there is a stable core of members, you may want to close the group to outsiders. This limits the number of members, making it easier to speak freely (talking is easier in a smaller group) and helps create a background of information and trust. But this is not always done and each group must decide on membership, visitors, frequency of meetings, privacy outside meetings, etc. for itself.

Tip: Keep food and drink to a minimum. Coffee, tea, or juice is fine. You may also want to rotate meeting places so hostessing does not always fall on one member.

☐ How long does a meeting last?

Each meeting lasts two or three hours. You may want to establish a time limit so that you'll begin more promptly and end before exhaustion sets in.

☐ How long do groups last?

Groups continue meeting as long as the members want, usually from six months to a year and a half. Groups of women in more stable situations tend to last longer than groups of younger women, women who move frequently, or women who are experiencing a lot of upheaval in their lives.

One suggestion is to arrange a date at which the group will look at itself and decide whether to change direction (take up a project, for example), disband, re-form, or continue as it has for another period of time. This sort of appraisal offers flexibility both to the group and its members; it provides a useful focus for new ideas and an escape hatch for tensions. The date set can be six months, a semester, a school year. Between six and nine months from the first meeting is a good length of time.

1250. Sheger-Ud-Durr, onetime harem slave in the Turkish sultan's quarters, has risen to the position of favorite wife. When the sultan dies as Christian crusaders led by Louis IX of France are advancing after the capture of Damietta, Egypt, she breaks Moslem tradition, assumes the regency, and reorganizes her panicking army. The invaders are defeated and the French survivors become her prisoners, later to be ransomed off.

Consciousness-raising group

POSSIBLE TOPICS OF CONVERSATION
Peggy King and June Myers

GROWING UP

1. Was your education affected by your sex?
2. Did your parents influence your ideas about male and female roles by word or deed? Did you have brothers and were they treated differently?
3. How did your religion affect your life as a woman? If you didn't have any, was that a help or hindrance?
4. Is your mother an oppressed woman?
5. Is your father a sexist?
6. How can we raise our daughters and sons to be liberated?
7. What were our mothers like?
8. What were our fathers like?
9. How do you feel about aging? Menopause?

WORK AND MONEY

1. Is there sexism where you work? (This includes work at home.)
2. Who controls money in your family? What advantages does that person have?
3. What jobs or tasks make you feel like a servant? What tasks make your man feel like one?
4. How can we liberate ourselves from housework?
5. Do you feel that politics is a man's field? Do you think they've done a good job? How are women's interests expressed in politics? By whom?

LOVE AND SEX

1. What is love?
2. What do we consider sexually attractive?
3. Do men get sexually aroused faster?
4. Should men be more experienced sexually?
5. Do you enjoy sex?
6. Do you recognize yourself when you read sex manuals?
7. What do you think of prostitution? Rape?
8. How do you feel about your body?
9. What do you think of abortion?
10. Do you touch other people easily? Do people with higher status usually initiate touching?

WOMEN AND WOMEN

1. What keeps women separate from other women?
2. Were you taught to compete with other women for men?
3. How do you feel about other women?
4. What is your attitude toward lesbians?

WOMEN AND MEN

1. How do you feel about men?
2. Can a woman be a friend to a man? Has it ever happened to you?
3. Do you admire dominance in a male? Enjoy it?
4. How can we get men to accept ideas of liberated women?
5. How do women threaten men? How do men deeply hurt women?
6. Are there innate psychological differences between the sexes?

LIVING ARRANGEMENTS

1. Would you—or do you—like to live alone?
2. Were you programmed to be married?
3. What are possible alternative living arrangements?
4. What would you consider a good marriage?

LANGUAGE AND IMAGE

1. What is masculine? Feminine?
2. Is aggression a male trait? Are nagging, gossip, manipulation aggressive? What's the difference between aggression and self-expression?
3. Did you ever admire Miss America?
4. Who are your heroines? (Can't count wives of famous men.)
5. Do you like being called a lady?
6. What's your image of divorce? How do you feel about it?
7. Is it important to you to use language which has fewer sex-specific terms? (e.g., "chairperson", "humanity" rather than "mankind", "they" rather than "he", etc.)

FREEDOM OF MOVEMENT

1. If you were in a dangerous situation would you rather defend yourself or have a man defend you? Could you defend yourself?
2. What are your thoughts on violence and death?
3. Are you flattered by street whistles?
4. What kind of put-downs can men use on women and *vice versa*? What kind of body language can men use to control women and *vice versa*?

GENERAL

1. What are you guilty about?
2. What are you angry about?
3. What are your ambitions?
4. What are your fears?
5. Would you feel easy making public speeches?
6. Who are the most sexist people you have met and how do you feel about them?
7. What are some of the ways you are treated as a woman that you don't like? That you do like?
8. Would you—or do you—prefer to have children of one sex or the other? Why?
9. Would you—or do you—bring up sons and daughters differently? In what ways?
10. What are your own enemies that prevent you from being liberated?

Adapted from *Support/Consciousness-Raising Groups* by Women's Equity Action League, National Press Building, Washington, D.C. 20045. Reprinted with permission.

1274. Margarethe, duchess of Henneberg, meets a woman carrying twins in her arms—so the legend goes— and rebukes her plea for assistance, calling the mother a harlot, saying that it is impossible to bear two children simultaneously by one man. Calling on God, the abused woman prays that He will cause the duchess to have as many children as there are days of the year. Sure enough, "At her next confinement the

The
Sex Adviser

Anatomy and Reproduction

Planned Parenthood League of Massachusetts

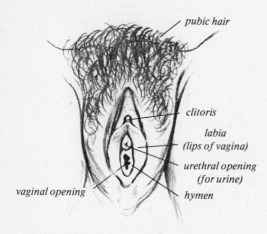

The female's internal sex organs

pubic hair

clitoris

labia
(lips of vagina)

urethral opening
(for urine)

vaginal opening

hymen

Russ Hoover

Different types of hymen

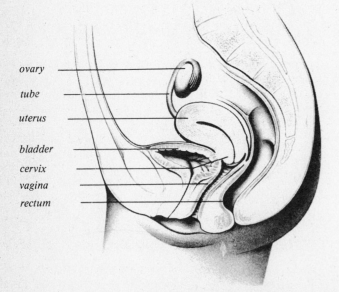

ovary

tube

uterus

bladder

cervix

vagina

rectum

Detailed view of female genital area

FEMALES

External Sex Organs

The vulva, or external female sex organ includes the mons veneris, the labia majora, the labia minora, the clitoris, and the hymen. The mons veneris is the mound of fat covered by pubic hair. The two rounded hair-covered folds of skin lying on either side of the vulva are the labia majora, and the two thin folds of skin lying between the labia majora and the vaginal opening are the labia minora. The urinary meatus lies between the clitoris and the vaginal opening and is the orifice through which urine is passed. The clitoris is a small, hooded, erectile structure located just above the urinary meatus in the upper triangle of the vulva. It corresponds to the penis in the male, has a glans which is highly packed with nerve endings, like the glans penis, and is the center of sexual excitement in the female. However, unlike the penis, it plays no direct role in reproduction and contributes solely to sexual pleasure. The hymen (maidenhead) is a membrane which partially covers the external opening of the vagina in many, but not all, virgin females. In rare cases, the hymen is particularly tough and may have to be cut or stretched by a doctor. The presence of a hymen may cause women pain and bleeding at the first intercourse. However, some women with hymens experience no pain, some women have no hymen, and often the hymen has been previously stretched by using tampons, by petting, or by masturbation.

Internal Reproductive Organs

The woman's internal reproductive organs consist of the ovaries, the fallopian tubes, the uterus, and the vagina.

The ovaries lie on either side of the uterus and are homologous (correspond) to the testes in the male. They produce ova and the hormones estrogen and progesterone. Each ovary is about the size and shape of an almond and contains many tiny cavities where ova are stored. Known as Graffian follicles, some 200,000-400,000 of these ova-containing cavities are present at birth. However, since the average woman is fertile for about 35 years and ovulates 13 times a year, only 400-500 of these thousands of ova are ever released.

The fallopian tubes begin close to the ovaries with finger-like projections (fimbria) which pick up the released egg and carry it to the uterus by means of rhythmic tubal contractions and waving hair-like cilia. Approximately four inches long and the width of a telephone cord, the fallopian tubes are attached high to either side of the uterus.

The uterus is a muscular organ, about the size and shape of a small pear, sitting above the bladder. The uterus narrows at its lower end to form the neck-like cervix, a muscle which extends into the vagina. The vaginal canal extends from the cervix outside to the vulva. By inserting a finger into her vagina, a woman can feel her cervix; it feels firm like the end of a nose if she has not had a baby, softer, like a chin if she has.

The walls of the vagina are normally in contact with each other but are stretched open by a penis during intercourse and by a baby at birth. The vagina cleanses itself constantly by secreting a small amount of mucoid-like substance which some women notice as a light vaginal discharge. This discharge is normal—douching is unnecessary except under explicit medical supervision, generally for a specific problem.

Adapted from *Everybody's Guide to Every Body*. Reprinted with permission of Planned Parenthood League of Massachusetts.

Duchess gave birth to 365 children, all living and each about the size of a little chick, half of them boys, half girls, all of them baptized in two huge basins by the Bishop of Utrecht. He christened all the boys John and all the girls Elizabeth but they all, as well as the Duchess, died that day."
An inscription still to be seen in an abbey near The Hague, Holland: "Margarethe,

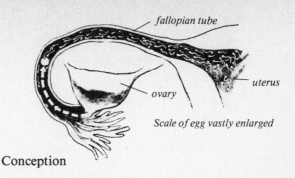

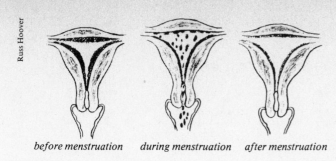
before menstruation during menstruation after menstruation

fallopian tube

uterus

ovary

Scale of egg vastly enlarged

The Menstrual Cycle

The average menstrual cycle lasts approximately twenty-eight days, including a three to seven day period of menstrual bleeding. The first day of a period is considered day one of the cycle. The bleeding represents the sloughing off of the uterine lining caused by a decrease in the body's levels of estrogen and progesterone, hormones which are produced in the ovaries. As the period nears its end these hormone levels rise and the uterus begins to rebuild its lining. These hormones prepare the uterus and other organs for the possible fertilization and implantation of the ovum, which is released approximately fourteen days before the end of each menstrual cycle. When fertilization does not occur, the level of hormones drops and the sloughing off (menstrual flow) begins again.

Conception

Fertilization occurs when a sperm from the male unites with the woman's ovum. This normally takes place in the fallopian tube. After ejaculation the sperm move through the cervix, up the cervical canal, into the uterus and up into the fallopian tubes.

The fertilized egg starts to move along the tube and takes around four days to reach the uterus and implant therein. This process is called nidation.

Throughout the pregnancy the walls of the uterus expand to accommodate the growing baby. The pregnancy, if normal, ends with the involuntary contractions of the uterus delivering the baby through the cervix which widens to allow its passage. The gestation period, from conception to delivery, is approximately thirty-eight weeks.

MALES

The penis is the male organ for intercourse and urination. It is composed almost entirely of erectile tissue which fills with blood and becomes stiff when a man is sexually aroused. The most sensitive part of the penis is the glans, or head, which is covered by a loose flap of skin called the foreskin. Shortly after birth, the foreskin may be removed in a minor operation called circumcision, a procedure which is very common.

The two skin pouches which hang below the penis make up the scrotum. Contained in these pouches are the testicles or testes, two small oval glands in which sperm and the male hormone, testosterone, are produced. Sperm are actually created in tiny tubes coiled within the testes called seminiferous tubules. They then progress to the epididymis, another network of tubes lying behind the testes. Here they spend a few hours undergoing final maturation.

Since a temperature lower than the normal body temperature favors sperm production, the scrotal muscles regulate the testes' temperature by

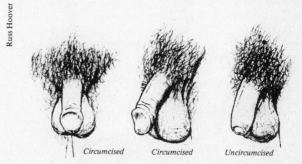
Circumcised　　Circumcised　　Uncircumcised

Detailed view of male genital area

pulling them up close to the body in cold weather and allowing them to hang lower when they are warm. The scrotum is covered with sweat glands which also regulate temperature.

The sperm are transported from the epididymis by the action of tiny, hair-like cilia in two tubes, the vas deferens. These tubes extend upward into the abdominal cavity, passing several glands whose secretions contribute to sperm transport. Each vas passes around the urinary bladder and then enlarges to form the ampulla, which stores sperm. The ampullae lead into two sacs called the seminal vesicles which lie behind the bladder.

Immediately below the bladder is the prostate gland. As the sperm pass through from the seminal vesicles, the prostate adds a thin fluid which forms the greater part of semen, the transporting fluid for the sperm which is released at ejaculation. At this point the two vasa come together to form the ejaculatory ducts which then lead directly into the urethra, the tube in the penis through which semen is ejaculated and through which urine is passed.

During sexual excitement the urethra is lubricated and its acidity neutralized with an alkaline fluid secreted from the cowper's gland, thus facilitating the passage of sperm. At the same time, a muscular constriction closes off the tube from the bladder, so that urination is impossible during coitus.

After ejaculation, the sperm are motile—they can propel themselves without ciliary action. If sexual intercourse has occurred, the sperm—some 200 million per ejaculation—have begun a journey through the female reproductive system, traveling at the speed of one inch every eight seconds.

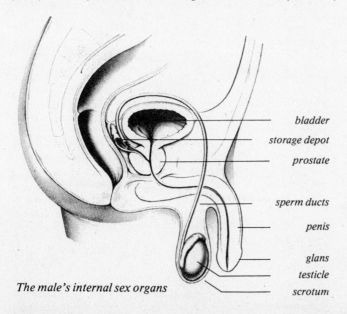

bladder

storage depot

prostate

sperm ducts

penis

glans

testicle

scrotum

The male's internal sex organs

...sister of William, King of Germany was delivered at nine o'clock of the Friday morning before Easter, in the year of 1276, of 365 babies in the presence of several lords and gentlemen. All (children) died soon after, as did the Mother, and all were buried in the sepulchre here.''

The Pill
Planned Parenthood League of Massachusetts

The Pill is the most effective and the most controversial contraceptive in general use. While the controversy has prevented complacency and spurred exhaustive research, it has also led to much confusion, doubt, and fear. What follows is a brief look at the most up-to-date information.

There are two kinds of oral contraceptives: the combination pill and the sequential pill. Both types contain synthetic versions of the female hormones progesterone and estrogen. The difference between the two is the way in which the hormones are combined. The combination pills contain estrogen and progesterone in each tablet. The sequential pills contain only estrogen for the first 14-16 days of the cycle and then a combination of estrogen and progesterone for the remainder.

Sequential pills have more disadvantages than combination pills. Most of the side effects and serious complications that result from taking the Pill have been linked to estrogen. It is known that certain kinds of synthetic progesterone counter some of the effects of estrogen. With sequential pills which involve taking solid estrogen for 14-16 days, the anti-estrogenic effect of progesterone is absent for most of the cycle. In addition, sequential pills are not quite as effective as combination pills. For these reasons sequential pills are not highly recommended for most women.

When the Pill was first produced, it contained as much as 10 mg. synthetic estrogen and 25 mg. synthetic progesterone. Most pills now contain smaller doses, .05 mg. estrogen and 1 mg. progestin, although some may contain up to 1 mg. estrogen. Brands which are commonly used are: OrthoNovum, Ovral, Ovulen, Norinyl, Demulen, and Norlestrin. Although the action of all pills is the same, they are composed of slightly different versions of the synthetic hormones. If a woman experiences side effects while taking one brand of pills, switching to another brand (only with a physician's consent) may reduce or eliminate the problem.

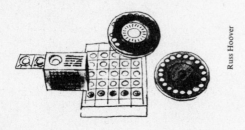

Russ Hoover

How the Pill Works

The Pill mimics the hormone levels found during pregnancy in a woman's body. The body assumes a "pseudo-pregnancy" as a result of the estrogen and progesterone being administered and no ova are released. The combination pills have two back-up effects as well: the progesterone in the pill causes the cervical mucus, which normally becomes thin at the time of ovulation, to remain thick and impenetrable. Progesterone also disrupts the growth of the lining of the uterus so that it is not receptive to a fertilized egg.

Obtaining a Prescription

The Pill is issued only by prescription after a routine gynecological examination. It is not recommended for everyone and proper medical screening is important in determining who can take the Pill. It will probably not be prescribed for women who have had thromboembolism, thrombophlebitis, pulmonary embolism, a stroke, retinal thrombosis, heart disease or heart defect, severe endocrine disorder, or some forms of cancer. Women who have had migraine headaches, diabetes, varicose veins, high blood pressure, epilepsy, or psychiatric disorders can probably take the Pill

Adapted from *Everybody's Guide to Every Body.* Reprinted with permission of Planned Parenthood League of Massachusetts.

if they are closely supervised. These are not hard and fast rules, but only general indications. Only a medically qualified person who knows the individual's medical history can make the final decision.

A prescription is issued for either six months or a year and an appointment for a return visit is made at the end of this time for a new prescription and a check-up. The Food and Drug Administration (FDA) has set no limit on how many years the Pill may be taken.

How To Take the Pill

Complete and explicit instructions accompany every brand of pill. It is recommended that intercourse be avoided or another contraceptive method used for the first 14 days for the first pill cycle, since it is possible that ovulation could occur before the Pill has its full effect. The first pill is taken on day five of the cycle, counting the first day of menstruation as day one. One pill is taken each day at approximately the same time for 20 or 21 days (depending upon the brand). The pills are stopped when the package is empty, and menstruation should begin within two or three days. The next cycle of pills is begun one week after the last pill of the previous cycle. If they were started on a Thursday, they would be finished Wednesday and started again one week later on the following Thursday. Thursday would always be the starting day.

Some combination pills now come in a 28-day series. The last seven pills, which are a different color, contain no contraceptive. A woman taking these pills takes one every day, even while she has her period, and begins the next cycle the day after taking the last pill.

Sometimes menstruation does not occur. This is not an indication of pregnancy if the pills have been taken correctly, and the next cycle should be started seven days after the last one ended. If two periods are missed, a doctor should be consulted.

If one combination pill is forgotten, it should be taken as soon as it is remembered. The next pill should be taken at the regular time and the pills continued for the rest of the cycle. If a sequential pill or two combination pills are forgotten the missed pill or pills should be taken and continued for the rest of the cycle but another method of contraception should also be used for the rest of the cycle.

When use of the pills is stopped, the next period may be delayed a week or two, or missed altogether. As soon as the pills are stopped, one is potentially fertile again and another reliable method of birth control should be used.

Side Effects

Side effects from the Pill can generally be broken down into two categories: nuisance effects and serious complications. The majority of women experience few, if any, side effects. Most nuisance effects should disappear by the third or fourth cycle, especially if the woman is on a low-dose pill. Such effects are:

Nausea: Women who experience nausea usually adjust to the Pill and tolerate it better as they continue to take it. Taking the pill with supper or before going to bed (instead of on an empty stomach in the morning) sometimes helps. The newer, low-dose pills are less likely to cause nausea.

Weight changes: This varies with the individual, some gain, some lose, some remain the same. Some degree of weight gain may be caused by water retention due to the estrogen in the pill. A change of brands or a corrective diet may help.

Breakthrough bleeding or spotting: Occasionally this occurs but it should disappear after the second cycle. If not, a doctor should be consulted.

Anxiety or depression: A small percentage of women develop anxiety or a depression and lethargy that persist beyond the third or fourth month

---

1288. The first recorded leap year: Margaret of Norway, Queen of Scotland, enacts a law that gives women permission to propose marriage to eligible men. Men may be penalized if they refuse the offer or treat their female suitors scornfully.

on the Pill. The reasons for this are unknown. Many of these women stop taking the Pill. Many women, on the other hand, feel elated while on the Pill because the fear of pregnancy is absent.

Sore breasts: Some women experience either sore breasts or breast enlargement. Breast tenderness should disappear in a couple of months. If the breasts enlarge slightly they may remain enlarged while on the Pill but will return to normal when it is discontinued.

Vaginal discharge: Vaginal mucus becomes slightly more sticky with the use of the Pill but this is seldom even noticed. The vagina becomes more susceptible to yeast (Monilia) infections, which are sometimes difficult to treat without discontinuing the Pill.

Complexion: Although some women's complexions greatly improve, a few may develop blotches or changes in pigmentation called cholasma. Changing the brand of pill does not help.

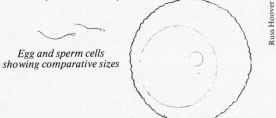

Egg and sperm cells showing comparative sizes

Russ Hoover

Advantages

The combination pill, if taken according to instructions, is virtually 100% effective. The pills cost about $2.25-3.00 per packet—a relatively small price for such high effectiveness. The Pill regulates the menstrual cycle and in most cases produces comfortable periods with reduced bleeding and cramps. The Pill is therapeutic treatment for women with some menstrual disorders, and is also used to treat premenopausal problems.

Disadvantages

The Pill was developed in 1955-56 and its long-term use is still being studied. It must be taken daily, regardless of how infrequently the woman may have intercourse. Some patients report side effects, which usually disappear when the Pill is discontinued. However, more serious complications do sometimes occur.

THE MINI PILL

The Federal Drug Administration has recently approved a new type of oral contraceptive, the "mini-pill." The new drug contains progesterone only and is taken daily without a break.

Experience to date indicates that the effectiveness of progesterone-only pills is lower than that of sequential or combination pills. The pregnancy rate with the combined pill is generally less than one pregnancy per 100 women users, while with the progesterone-only products approximately 3 pregnancies might occur per 100 women users.

On the mini-pill menstrual bleeding does not follow a regular pattern. The lapse between one period and another can vary considerably, the length of periods vary and a pattern may never develop.

Studies have not yet been done to determine if progesterone-only contraceptives have the same association with thromboembolic disorders (stroke, deep vein thrombosis, pulmonary embolism) as do other oral contraceptives. However, it must be emphasized that this newest oral contraceptive, although a pure synthetic progesterone, has its own "built-in" estrogenic component. It has been estimated that up to 8% of the degradation products of the synthetic progesterone become biologically active estrogens.

The mini-pill is thought to prevent conception by changing the cervical mucus, making it thick and impenetrable to sperm and by altering the development of the endometrium (the lining of the womb), therefore making it unreceptive to a fertilized egg.

The progestin in a mini-pill may also alter an enzyme used by sperm to break down and penetrate the ovum wall, and it may interfere with the normal coating on that wall itself.

Prop Art

HAVE YOU HAD YOUR PILL TODAY

COMPLICATIONS

The risk of developing *blood clots* (venous thrombosis) in the veins, usually of the legs, although about 5½ times greater in pill users than in nonusers, does not frequently occur. The incidence of this condition decreases when lower doses of estrogen are used in the pill. Women who have had a previous attack of venous thrombosis will be discouraged from taking birth control pills.

Women who are *breastfeeding* may be discouraged from using the Pill since some of the hormones will be secreted in the breast milk and thus be taken in by the baby. The Pill may also decrease the amount of breast milk produced.

The Royal College of General Practitioners reporting on Oral Contraceptives and Health have recently concluded that estrogen and progesterone used in the Pill *do not cause cancer.*

The risk of *heart attack* (coronary thrombosis) to Pill users in the forty to forty-four year-old groups appears to be 5.7 times greater than that of nonusers, says the Food and Drug Administration. Between the ages of thirty and thirty-nine, the risk was estimated at almost three times that of nonusers. (The FDA has no plans to ban the Pill, since the death rate from pregnancies for women in these age groups is higher than the mortality figures for women heart attack victims.)

1292. To prevent virtuous women from being confused with the numerous prostitutes abroad in the streets of Paris, King Philip of France declares that all harlots must wear an identifying scarlet shoulder knot as a badge of their profession.

The IUD

The Editors of *Woman's Almanac*

An IUD, or intrauterine device, is an object inserted into the uterus to prevent pregnancy. Though precursors of the modern IUD have been known and used for millennia, only since the early sixties have relatively safe and effective devices been developed and come into popular use. No one is exactly sure how the IUD works. At present it is thought that any object planted in the uterus somehow interferes with the implantation of the fertilized egg on the uterine wall while at the same time stimulating white blood cells there to attack sperm. Through these and possibly even more elaborate interactions (none of which has been related to cancer), the IUD makes the womb inhospitable.

Modern IUDs have come in hundreds of shapes, sizes, and materials, from handmade coils of nylon filaments (used in Egypt) to recently developed "drug delivery systems" that release timed portions of the hormone progesterone something like the Pill. But most IUDs are now made of plastic that is firm yet flexible enough to allow them to be twisted to fit inside the thin, hollow tube through which they are inserted into the uterus. The IUD springs back into shape after emerging from the delivery tube and fits snugly against the uterine walls.

Because of recent technological advances or medical studies, we now know to avoid some IUDs. The Dalkon Shield has been taken off the market altogether because it caused a serious infection in the wombs of a number of women who became pregnant while wearing the Shield. The stainless-steel Majzlin Spring—also off the market—had a tendency to bury itself in the uterine wall, necessitating surgical removal. The family of "closed ring" IUDs could become entangled in internal organs should they perforate the uterine wall and escape into the abdomen. The Margulies Coil was bulky and therefore unduly difficult to insert and to wear.

If you are still wearing one of these once popular devices, ask your gynecologist to replace it with a newer model.

Modern IUDs

Three IUDs are in common use today: the Lippes Loop, the Saf-t-Coil, and the Copper 7. The Lippes Loop is probably the best choice for the woman who has had children, though its relatively large size can make it very uncomfortable for the nulliparous woman, the woman who has never given birth. The Saf-t-Coil is delivered to the uterus in a smaller inserter, but it is perhaps more often expelled than the Lippes Loop.

The newest of the three is the Copper 7 (or the Cu 7), a plastic, "7"-shaped rod with its lower half wound in fine copper wire that slowly releases minute quantities of the metal (which has an antifertility effect) into the uterine fluids. Although the Copper 7 has not been in use long enough for firm conclusions to be reached about its effectiveness, studies so far indicate that it may be somewhat more effective than the Lippes Loop or the Saf-t-Coil.

The "bioactive" Copper 7 (and the Copper T, not yet released) seems to cause less increase in menstrual bleeding than the larger devices. Because of its smaller size and ease of insertion, it is at present the first choice for nulliparous women. (Studies show that even a slight reduction in the standard diameter of the IUD inserter can reduce by 50 percent the incidence of bleeding and pain on insertion.)

Inserter size and design is especially important to nulliparous women, since their cervical canals are narrower and less elastic than those of mothers. The Copper 7 offers the smallest inserter now available.

The Copper 7 does have a drawback, however. It must be removed and replaced every two years or so when the copper becomes exhausted. Fortunately, removal and replacement of the IUD is a great deal less taxing than the original insertion. New models of the Copper 7, not yet generally distributed, with copper bands or sleeves rather than wire, may have a four- or five-year lifespan. But because the current Copper 7 must be periodically replaced, women who have had children usually use the Lippes Loop or the Saf-t-Coil, which have no dissolving parts and need not be replaced unless problems develop.

IUD Insertion and Its Timing

If you decide to try the IUD, the first step is a complete gynecological examination. Be sure to mention to the doctor if you have ever had a venereal disease. If your ovaries, cervix, uterus, and Fallopian tubes all seem healthy and you have had a child, the doctor may be willing to insert the IUD immediately. Most, however, prefer to wait until your next period, when the cervical canal is naturally somewhat dilated, especially if you have never had children. This way the doctor can also be sure you are not already pregnant.

It has been proved that the more experience a doctor has had in IUD insertion, the less painful and complicated the procedure is. Try to find a gynecologist who is very familiar with the type of IUD you will probably use.

Although there is some evidence that a woman is more likely to expel an IUD inserted immediately after abortion, most doctors feel that, as long as the patient is aware of the risk, insertion at that time is good medical practice, since the cervix is stretched and relaxed then. However, because there is even a higher rate of expulsion of IUDs inserted after delivery, most doctors recommend that a woman wait till at least her first postpartum menstrual period before insertion.

To begin the procedure the doctor places a speculum in your vagina to hold the walls apart, then, using a pair of forceps, gently grasps and pulls the cervix down, straightening the cervical canal and aligning the cervix with the uterus. The cervix and vaginal walls are swabbed with an antiseptic solution to discourage the transportation of bacteria into the womb along with the inserter. Next, the doctor slips a "sound," or long, very narrow tube, through the cervix in order to determine the shape and depth of the uterine cavity, and calculate how deeply to insert the IUD. Finally the IUD itself is introduced, pushed through the tube into the uterus. The whole thing takes only a few minutes, but it may be painful. Before the Copper 7, it was especially so for nulliparous women; but now most of them experience only mild pain.

Some women get cramps after a Copper 7 insertion; after a Lippes Loop insertion, most experience the familiar low abdominal pain and backache usually associated with periods. A simple analgesia like Darvon or aspirin usually relieves this discomfort.

IUD insertion can also trigger a "cervical shock" reaction

---

ca. **1300.** Canon law of the early Christian Church declares that women, even relatives, are not to live in the same houses as priests. Women may not approach the church altar, nor fill any public office of the faith. In certain cases, the testimony of women is not legally admissible.

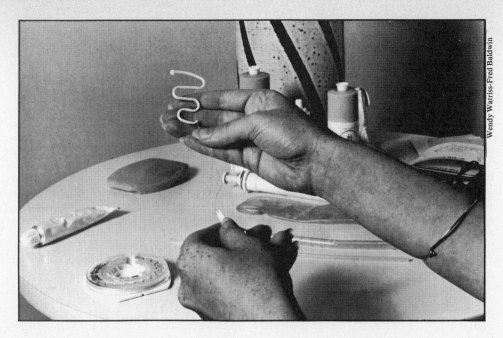

The Lippes Loop

in the woman, depressing her blood pressure and causing fainting. And among some women the pain of insertion and cramps is severe and simply intolerable. For these reasons, you should remain in the doctor's office for about half an hour after insertion for rest and observation.

The most common, but still rare (about .04 percent), complication of IUD insertion is perforation of the uterus. (It is thought that this happens most often during the insertion process itself, not afterward.) Sometimes a perforation causes pain, other times not. If you cannot feel the tail of the inserted IUD (a thread attached to the IUD, which descends through the cervix and into the upper vagina) with your fingers, and you do not think it has been expelled (you have examined your menstrual pads or tampons for it at each period), then there is a chance that the device may have penetrated into or through the uterine wall. Should you be unable to locate your IUD after a careful search, call your doctor for a closer examination.

Living with the IUD

The advantages of the IUD are convenience, relative reliability, cheapness, and long-term effectiveness. Many women also prefer the straightforward mechanical action of the IUD on a specific portion of the body to the widespread and sometimes insidious chemical changes caused throughout the body by the Pill.

The main disadvantage of the IUD is not its failure rate of 2 to 4 percent (a pregnancy rate higher than the Pill but still much less than that of any other single form of contraception, except perhaps the diaphragm used scrupulously), nor its expulsion rate of 3 to 15 percent, but rather the high rate of medical removal—from 5 to 20 percent, depending on the group studied—made necessary by menstrual bleeding, pain, or infection. Of all women fitted for an IUD, about 25 percent will be forced to abandon the device within a year of insertion.

IUDs substantially increase the amount of menstrual flow and lengthen the menstrual periods of most women, especially of those whose periods were scanty before IUD insertion. Studies have shown that the Copper 7 causes the least additional blood loss, with the Saf-t-Coil coming next.

infection, most often pelvic inflammatory diseases (PID), a generalized infection of the internal reproductive organs, is second only to bleeding and pain as a cause of IUD removal. Symptoms of PID are a fever, tenderness in the lower abdomen, low back pain, sometimes a vaginal discharge, menstrual-like cramps, and a diffuse feeling of ill-health. PID is dangerous if left untreated, though antibiotics usually bring it under control rapidly. The IUD itself does not introduce PID to the body; but it can worsen a preexisting condition, especially if the woman has an incompletely cured case of gonorrhea. From 2 to 4 percent of women wearing an IUD will contract PID. The infection typically flares up soon after insertion, and it is necessary to remove the device for proper treatment.

About half the women who become pregnant despite the IUD miscarry. Sometimes the IUD causes such miscarriages to be complicated with infection.

Also, since the device acts only on the walls of the uterus, it is less effective in preventing the ectopic pregnancy, a pregnancy in which the fertilized egg implants on the ovaries or inside a Fallopian tube instead of developing in the womb. Approximately 5 percent of women who become pregnant on the IUD have ectopic pregnancies. Such pregnancies must be terminated surgically.

The Federal Drug Administration has found that IUDs are "a safe and reliable means of contraception and they compare favorably with . . . oral contraceptives. The mortality rate from the IUD is between 1 and 10 deaths per million women years, while with oral contraceptives it is 22 to 45 per million women years."

Research now going on will likely develop even better versions of the IUD in the near future. However, the newest device to reach the market, Progestasert, doesn't seem to offer significant advantages over other IUDs, except perhaps to those women who are unable to tolerate any other type. Progestasert is a T-shaped device that continuously releases into the uterus a very small quantity of progesterone, smaller even than that in the mini-Pill. Its failure rate and its rate of medical removal are about the same as those of other IUDs in current use. It has the drawback of needing yearly replacement.

ca. **1348.** German towns punish women who use abusive language and "quarrel so as to come to blows" by requiring them to carry two 50-pound stones—each usually carved to represent a woman's head with protruding tongue—the length of the village. One is burdened with the stones while the other prods her with a needle on a pole. Then they switch positions.

The Diaphragm, Spermicides, Condom,

Planned Parenthood League

THE DIAPHRAGM

The diaphragm is a round, bowl-like rubber cup with a spring rim. It holds a sperm-killing cream or jelly over the cervical area, providing a chemical barrier to sperm moving toward the cervix. Because women's internal organs vary in size, diaphragms range from 50-105 millimeters (2-4 inches) in diameter and each woman must be fitted individually. A pelvic exam is necessary. The inside of the vagina at the cervix is measured and the correct diaphragm size assessed. The woman is instructed to familiarize herself with the proper position and then practice insertion and removal. A diaphragm should be refitted after a pregnancy or after a weight gain or loss of more than ten pounds, or if the original fitting was before frequent intercourse. If properly fitted and inserted, it should not interfere with intercourse.

Using a Diaphragm

The contraceptive cream or jelly should be spread generously (about a teaspoon) on the inside of the bowl of the diaphragm and around the rim. The rim is squeezed together and the diaphragm inserted into the vagina. The further part of the rim is guided past the cervix and the front part is pressed up behind the bony arch above the front vaginal wall. The diaphragm can be inserted with a plastic or metal "introducer." An applicator full of contraceptive cream or jelly can be inserted after the diaphragm is in place for additional protection. The cervix should be felt through the diaphragm — it feels like the end of a nose. It may be easiest to lie down for insertion, but the diaphragm may be inserted from a standing or squatting position.

Adapted from *Everybody's Guide to Every Body*. Reprinted with permission of Planned Parenthood League of Massachusetts.

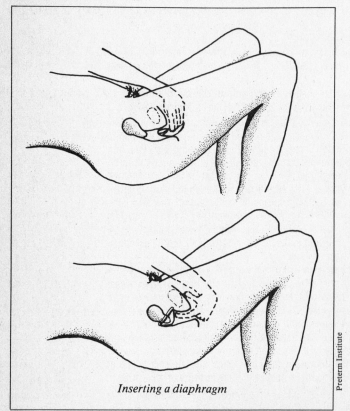

Inserting a diaphragm

Preterm Institute

The diaphragm must be used with cream or jelly during *every* intercourse. It can be inserted as much as two hours prior to intercourse, but not more than two, as the cream or jelly loses its effectiveness. *The importance of using a spermicide with the diaphragm cannot be overemphasized.* In their studies on human sexual response, Masters and Johnson found that the vaginal canal expands during sexual excitement so the diaphragm may become displaced from the cervix. If this happens the spermicide must take over the job of contraception.

The diaphragm must not be removed for 6-8 hours following the last intercourse, as it takes this long for all the sperm to be killed. To have intercourse again before the eight hours is up, more cream or jelly must be applied without removing the diaphragm. This is done by means of a syringe-like applicator that applies the cream or jelly to the outside of the diaphragm. A douche should be done no sooner than eight hours after the last intercourse, but it is not at all necessary to douche. A diaphragm can be left in place for 24 hours or more with no discomfort or ill effect.

The diaphragm is removed by placing the forefinger behind the front portion of the rim and pulling it down and out. It should then be washed in warm, soapy water, dried, dusted with cornstarch, and replaced in its container in a cool place. A well cared-for diaphragm can last for two or more years, although you should check often for holes or tearing, by holding it up to the light.

Advantages

The diaphragm is a highly effective method of birth control that has no side effects. It is also inexpensive: a diaphragm lasts a long time and each application of spermicide costs only $.10-.15.

Disadvantages

Proper use of a diaphragm requires strong motivation on the part of both partners and very conscientious use. Precise understanding and practice are absolutely necessary for success. Some people argue that insertion of the diaphragm interrupts love-making but the insertion can be used as a prelude to intercourse.

Effectiveness

The diaphragm is 95-98% effective if used with sufficient cream or jelly and used at every intercourse. Recent studies have shown that out of every 100 women who rely upon a diaphragm for a year, 12 will get pregnant. Obviously, in many of these cases, the diaphragm did not fail, but the person did by not using enough cream, by not leaving the device in long enough, or by not using it at all.

NOTE: Some of the contraceptive jellies and creams, such as Lorophyn and Koromex, contain phenylmercuric acetate — an organic mercuric compound. Although this substance does not cross the cell wall and would not normally constitute a health hazard, the presence of lacerations within the vagina or cervix increase the chances of absorption. Because of the *potential* hazard and the availability of other contraceptive jellies and creams *without* organic mercury, we would recommend the use of contraceptive preparations without organic mercury. A new brand of Koromex (Koromex II) contains no mercury.

Adapted from *Contraceptive Technology*. Reprinted with permission of Emory University Family Planning Program.

ca. **1350.** The Order of the Garter is legendarily named this year after an incident in which King Edward III retrieved the dropped garter of a lady and then — rebuking snickering bystanders — proclaimed in French "Shame to him who thinks ill of it," the order's motto.

Rhythm and Combined Methods

of Massachusetts

VAGINAL SPERMICIDES

Inserting spermicidal agents into the vagina is a contraceptive technique that has been used for many years. Today, there are several spermicides available in the form of foams, creams, jellies, tablets, and suppositories. Tablets and suppositories are not very effective and should not be used by anyone who is seriously trying to avoid pregnancy.

All vaginal preparations intended for birth control are made of chemicals which kill sperm. The foams work in two ways: the spermicidal agent kills the sperm, and the foaming agent provides a barrier over the cervix. Creams and jellies very often fail to spread over the cervix and are therefore not as effective.

Using Vaginal Spermicides

The foam comes in an aerosol can with a syringe-like applicator. After the can is shaken well, the applicator is filled by putting it over the opening of the can. The woman lies on her back and inserts the applicator into the vagina like a tampon, then pushes on the plunger of the applicator to release the foam. The procedure is the same for creams and jellies, except they come in tubes. For more complete protection it is best to use two applications with each intercourse.

The spermicide can be inserted up to half an hour before intercourse. It is probably not wise to stand up or walk around as this may displace the foam from the cervix. A fresh application is required for each subsequent intercourse or if more than half an hour elapses. If the woman wants to douche, she should wait for six to eight hours after the last intercourse. However, douching is not necessary. The applicator should be washed and dried after each use.

Obtaining Vaginal Spermicides

Vaginal spermicides may be bought at most drug stores without a prescription. Foams (including applicator) usually cost about $3.50. The applicator need only be purchased once and can be used repeatedly. The foam alone costs about three dollars. A can of foam contains about twenty single applications. It is important to examine the applicator each time to be sure it's full, because when the can is nearly empty, mostly air may be coming out of it. Creams and jellies are less expensive (about $2.50 including the applicator) and contain about twenty-five single applications in each tube.

Advantages

Vaginal spermicides are easy to obtain and to use properly and are available without prescription or fitting. They are convenient to use if pills are forgotten or if an IUD is expelled, and generally have no side effects. However, some women or men may be allergic to some of the products. If irritation occurs, stop using the product and try another brand. They are relatively cheap, 10-15 cents per application. They are mildly lubricating and do not stain clothing or sheets. If pregnancy should occur, the spermicide does no harm to the baby. Vaginal spermicides do not cause cancer or any other diseases.

Disadvantages

Vaginal spermicides are an intercourse-related method, and may therefore cause interruptions. They can be inserted ahead of time or as a part of foreplay. Many women complain of leakage or dripping during or after intercourse. Some couples find the smell and taste of the spermicidal preparations distasteful.

Contraceptive foam

Russ Hoover

Applicator for contraceptive jelly

CONDOMS

Rolled

In package

Unrolled

Contraceptive jelly

Contraceptives

Effectiveness

Foam is the most effective spermicide and is reported to have an effectiveness of 94-96%, although this may be an overly high estimate. The jellies and creams are less effective—90-95% depending upon the product used. The suppositories are the least effective of vaginal spermicides.

THE CONDOM (Prophylactic, Safe, Rubber)

The condom is a thin skin or latex sheath which comes packaged and ready to be unrolled onto the erect penis. The open end has a small rubber band inside it which forms an elastic rim to keep the condom from slipping off the penis. The semen is held in the condom at the time of ejaculation and cannot escape into the vagina.

Using a Condom

It should be put on the penis shortly after attaining erection — not just prior to ejaculation, as the first few drops of discharge can contain enough sperm to cause pregnancy. The condom should cover the entire penis and some empty space without a lot of air in it (so the condom won't explode) should be left at the end to receive ejaculated semen. Some condoms come with a reservoir tip at the end for this purpose.

Following ejaculation, there is always some loss of erection. As long as the rim remains tight against the penis, intercourse can continue. If the rim does not fit snugly, some semen can leak from the open end of the condom, or it may slip completely off the penis into the vagina. When withdrawing, the open end of the condom should be held tightly against the base of the penis. If the condom slips off into the vagina, it should be removed immediately with the rim held tightly closed. The semen-filled condom is then thrown away. Some brands can be washed, dried, and powdered and used a second time; but no condom should be used more than three times. If the condom is to be used more than once, it should be checked carefully for holes or tearing.

Condoms should never be used with vaseline or petroleum jelly as they tend to rot the rubber. If a lubricant is needed, pre-lubricated condoms can be bought. If preferred, contraceptive gel, K-Y jelly, or a similar product can be applied to the outside of the sheath after it has been rolled onto the penis. Contraceptive foam or jelly provide a lubricant as well as offering the advantage of double contraceptive protection. Condoms should be left in their protective containers, not kept in a wallet or pocket, since moisture and heat deteriorate the rubber.

---

ca. **1350.** As morals loosen up, suspicious husbands and fathers institute the custom of paid chaperonage for their wives and daughters. By 1400 the tradition is passed to Spain, where it flourishes even into the late twentieth century. England follows suit in 1700, with Germany taking up the practice in 1800. In the United States, the idea remains in use until about 1900.

Obtaining a Condom

A prescription is not needed. They may be purchased at most drugstores. Because quality control is checked by the U.S. Food and Drug Administration, reliable brands bought at drugstores are generally acceptable.

Advantages

Condoms are easy to obtain and use. There are no side effects and they provide some protection against venereal disease. Some men find that condoms enable them to prolong intercourse by delaying orgasm.

Disadvantages

Some men claim that the condom cuts down on sensation and therefore decreases the pleasure of sex. The skin condom is better than the latex type if this is a problem. Some women find the rubber irritates the inner walls of the vagina. Use of a pre-lubricated condom, a lubricating jelly, or a contraceptive cream or jelly might alleviate this problem.

Failure Rates of Contraceptives

The Editors of *Contraceptive Technology*

(PREGNANCIES PER 100 WOMAN YEARS)

	Theoretical Failure Rate	Actual Use Failure Rate
Abortion	0+	0+ *
Abstinence	0	?
Hysterectomy	0.0001	0.0001
Tubal Ligation	0.04	0.04
Vasectomy	Less than 0.15	0.15
Oral Contraceptives (combined)	Less than 1.0	2-5**
I.M. Long Acting Progestin	Less than 1.0	5-10
Condom + Spermicidal Agent	1.0	5
Low-Dose Oral Progestin	1-4	5-10
IUD	1-5	6
Condom	3	15-20
Diaphragm	3	20-25
Spermicidal Foam	3	30
Coitus Interruptus	15	20-25
Rhythm (calendar)	15	35
Lactation for 12 months	15	40***
Chance (sexually active)	80	80

* Among women actually depending upon abortion as a means of fertility control, effectiveness is less than 100% as in some instances women change their minds.

** Oral contraceptive failure rates may be far higher than this, if one considers women who become pregnant after discontinuing oral contraceptives, but prior to initiating another method. ORAL CONTRACEPTIVE DISCONTINUATION RATES OF AS HIGH AS 50-60% in the first year of use are not uncommon in family planning programs.

*** Most women supplement breast feedings, significantly decreasing the contraceptive effectiveness of lactation. In Rwanda 50% of non-lactating women were found to conceive by just over 4 months postpartum, while among lactating women 50% had conceived at just over 18 months postpartum (Bonte, M. and van Balen, H., *J. Biosoc. Sci* 1: 97, 1969).

Adapted from *Contraceptive Technology*. Reprinted with permission of Emory University Family Planning Program.

Effectiveness

The condom is about 95% effective if used properly.

COMBINING METHODS

It is advisable to use a combination of methods to obtain better contraceptive protection. For instance, the use of the foam and a condom is almost 100% effective and is easy to obtain and use.

RHYTHM (Safe Period, Calendar Method, Temperature Method)

The rhythm method is not as effective as other methods, and should not be used by anyone who is seriously trying to avoid a pregnancy. It is, however, the only method approved by the Catholic Church. It depends upon abstaining from sexual intercourse on those days every month when a woman is most likely to conceive. This may sound easy enough but menstrual cycles are unpredictable.

Using the Rhythm Method

To calculate accurately the fertile period, several factors must be considered: time of ovulation, life span of the egg, and the life span of the sperm. We know that ovulation occurs about fourteen days before the beginning of the next menstrual cycle and that an egg can be fertilized within only twelve, possibly twenty-four hours after ovulation. It is now believed that sperm may stay alive in a woman's body for at least 72 hours, and as long as seven days.

This means that sperm deposited in the body as long as four days before ovulation may patiently await the arrival of the egg. Therefore, to use the rhythm method effectively, you must abstain for four days before the earliest chance of ovulation and 48 hours after the latest possible chance.

The Temperature Technique

The temperature technique is based on the fact that body temperature often, but not always, drops slightly about 24 hours before ovulation and rises about ½ degree on the day after ovulation. This is due to the thermogenic effect of progesterone. As the rise and fall are slight and could probably not be determined with a regular thermometer, a special one known as a basal thermometer is easier to use. Since body temperature varies with daily activity it is taken immediately upon waking up in the morning even before getting out of bed. This procedure will give you the basal body temperature which must be recorded daily on a special chart. The fertile period (time when one cannot have intercourse) is then calculated from the beginning of the cycle until the third day after a rise in basal temperature. A combination of the calendar and the temperature methods can be used to shorten the unsafe periods.

Advantages

It is the only approved method of the Catholic Church.

Disadvantages

Even when used conscientiously with medical advice and help, this method is not very reliable. It should not be used by young girls who have not yet established regular cycles or by women approaching menopause. A recent abortion, breast feeding, childbirth, emotional problems, illness, miscarriage, travel, etc. can upset the menstrual cycle enough to make the rhythm method an impossibility. For women with irregular periods, the unsafe period may stretch out to include most of every cycle.

ca. **1385.** The highly cultured Anne of Bohemia, bride of King Richard II, popularizes the sidesaddle among the noble classes. This particularly modest form of horseback riding is to persist in England up to the beginning of the twentieth century.

One Answer: Sterilization

Association for Voluntary Sterilization

What is sterilization?

It is a permanent method of birth control for men or women who want no children or who have all of the children desired.

How is this done?

The operation is accomplished by closing a pair of small tubes so that egg and sperm cannot meet and result in pregnancy. Sterilization does not involve the removal of the reproductive glands (ovaries in the female, testicles in the male) and is not castration.

Sterilization for a woman, salpingectomy or "tubal ligation", can be achieved by a variety of surgical procedures.

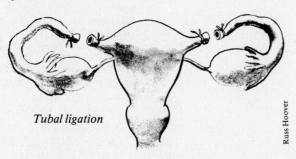

Tubal ligation

Russ Hoover

- Laparotomy: This is the classic approach through an incision in the abdominal wall in order to cut and close the fallopian tubes. This procedure may be done at the time of delivery or other surgery, including cesarean section, making a separate hospital stay unnecessary.

- Laparoscopy: This is a technique which permits a trained physician to view the abdominal cavity by means of a laparoscope, a tube containing a telescope and light. A harmless gas is used to distend the abdomen to prevent internal injuries. Through one or two small incisions below the navel, the physician inserts the laparoscope and an instrument into the cavity to seal off the fallopian tubes. After the instruments are removed and the gas is released,

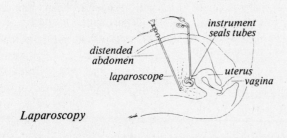

instrument seals tubes
distended abdomen
laparoscope
uterus
vagina

Laparoscopy

Association for Voluntary Sterilization, Inc., 708 Third Ave., New York, NY 10017.

the incision may be covered with a band-aid and therefore the operation has become known as "band-aid" surgery.

- Colpotomy: This is a vaginal approach leaving no external scars. Through an incision in the vagina the physician is able to reach and close the fallopian tubes.

- Culdoscopy: Also a vaginal approach, this technique, like laparoscopy, employs the use of a lighted instrument, a culdoscope, by which a trained physician is able to view the fallopian tubes and seal them.

Laparotomy is considered major surgery under general anesthesia and usually requires several days hospitalization. For the other techniques, local or general anesthesia may be used and hospitalization ranging from a few hours to several days may be required. Not all techniques are suitable for all women, and the physician will determine which technique is advisable in consultation with the patient.

If desired, sterilization can be performed in conjunction with abortion making a separate hospitalization unnecessary.

Sterilization for a man, vasectomy, is minor surgery and is usually performed in the physician's office or clinic under local anesthesia. The physician makes one or two incisions in the scrotum through which each sperm-carrying tube, the vas deferens, can be lifted out, cut and closed, thus blocking the passage of sperm.

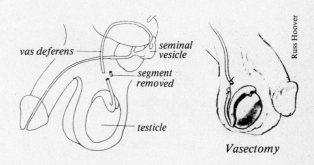

vas deferens
seminal vesicle
segment removed
testicle

Russ Hoover

Vasectomy

For some time after the operation residual sperm are found in the semen, other contraception must be used until tests show sperm are no longer present in the ejaculate. After the operation the testicles continue to produce sperm which then disintegrate and are absorbed by the body.

1400. Statues of the popes are displayed in the cathedral of Siena, and among them is included Pope Joan. According to the most widely circulated story, Joan was born in A.D. 838, the illegitimate daughter of an English priest. Under her father's tutelage she grew into a beautiful and brilliant young woman. By her twelfth birthday her learning

Is sterilization effective?

There is no guarantee that a surgical procedure of any kind will be 100% effective, or that after a sterilization the tubes will not grow back together. The risk of this is extremely small, however, and sterilization is the most reliable form of birth control available today.

Are there physical changes?

Other than the inability to reproduce, there are no known physical changes. A woman's menstrual periods and age of menopause are unaffected. A man continues to have an erection and ejaculate but his semen contains no sperm.

Are there emotional changes?

Voluntary sterilization obtained after thorough consideration, with full understanding of the nature of the operation, and without coercion, usually results in relief and peace of mind for both partners. Many patients report increased enjoyment of sex when the fear of pregnancy has been removed.

Is it safe?

All surgery carries some risk. Complications are rare. The possible discomfort, complications, and risks associated with the sterilization method to be used should be freely discussed with the doctor prior to surgery. For female sterilization, the risk is probably the same as that of removing an appendix or having a baby. The risk associated with vasectomy is even less.

Is it permanent?

The operation is ordinarily performed as a permanent measure and should not be considered unless the individual is sure no children will be wanted in the future. Continuing research is improving the techniques for surgical restoration of fertility (reversal), but a successful reversal cannot be assured in any individual case.

Vasectomy operation

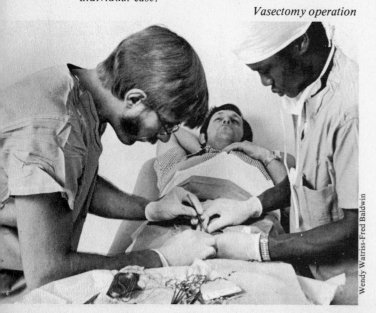

Wendy Watriss-Fred Baldwin

Is it legal?

Yes. In all 50 states, sterilization is legal without restriction as to the reason it is performed.

Is spousal consent required by law?

Only three states require it: Georgia, Virginia, and New Mexico. Throughout the country, however, many doctors and hospitals are reluctant to perform a sterilization for the married without spousal consent.

Is it expensive?

Charges vary according to such factors as type of surgery or hospital arrangements. If other medical costs are usually paid by Medicaid, welfare or private health insurance, all or part of the costs for sterilization may be covered. Uncovered medical expenses for sterilization are tax deductible.

When is sterilization indicated?

It is indicated:
- if no pregnancies are wanted in the future
- if pregnancy is likely to endanger a woman's health
- if physical, mental or emotional factors prevent fulfilling the responsibilities of parenthood
- if there is possibility of transmitting an hereditary defect.

It is not indicated:
- if there is uncertainty about the desire to terminate fertility
- if the wish is to delay assuming the responsibilities of parenthood
- if the hope is to reverse the operation in case of remarriage, death of children, or other change of circumstances.

Which partner should be sterilized?

Whoever is most positive in the desire for permanent birth control.

Can any doctor perform sterilization?

It is advisable to choose a physician experienced in performing the operation. The personal or family physician may perform the procedure or may be able to make referral to a colleague. The local family planning agency, health department, hospital, or county medical society may also be able to suggest an experienced doctor in this field.

Is voluntary sterilization a widely used method?

According to the 1970 National Fertility Study, sterilization has become a very popular method of preventing conception and nearly three million Americans had already chosen sterilization for contraceptive reasons. AVS estimates that the number has increased by about one million each year since 1970.

---

outdistanced the most distinguished men in southwest Germany.

But at fourteen she discovered romance and, at the stern urgings of her priest-teachers, prepared to enter a nunnery. However, she instead disguised herself as a boy and studied at a Benedictine abbey. There a young monk accidentally discovered her

Future Techniques
Planned Parenthood League of Massachusetts

Unfortunately, no perfect method of contraception yet exists. The ideal birth control method would have a long list of desirable qualities. It would be 100% effective, inexpensive, and convenient. It would have no effect upon the body except to render it temporarily infertile. It would have no connection with the act of sexual intercourse since mistakes are most likely to occur at this time. There *would be no possible room for error* such as forgetting a pill, and it would not reduce the opportunities for intercourse, as the rhythm method now does. Unfortunately, we are still a long way from this ideal method.

Progestin-only Preparations

As estrogen seems to be responsible for most of the serious complications from the Pill, some very promising experiments are using progestin alone.

For several years researchers have been administering progestin injections to women once a month, once every three months, or once every six months. The "progestin-only" shot causes very irregular bleeding and missed periods, and may result in future infertility. A combined estrogen and progestin shot promises to be more effective with less sporadic bleeding.

Another progestin preparation involves inserting under the skin a silastic pellet, which is a small capsule filled with the hormone. The capsules are made of a synthetic rubber that diffuses the progestin at a very constant rate. Thus a low level of progestin is secreted into the body daily. Because the rate of release is continuous, there are no high peaks of medication. This may eliminate the side effects present in the mini-pill. The life of the pellet is controlled by its size. Presumably pellets could be designed to last five, ten, or even twenty years. To implant the pellet, a small area of skin is anesthetized and the pellet is injected under the skin by a large needle. Should a woman desire to become pregnant, the capsule can be removed.

The silastic ring is a synthetic rubber impregnated with progestin which is placed in the vaginal canal like a diaphragm. It does not interfere with intercourse and releases the hormone in the same way that the pellets do. The device is inserted the first day of menstruation and left in place for 21 days. Then it is removed to allow for normal menstrual flow. A new one is used for each cycle except when a pregnancy is desired.

MORNING AFTER MEDICATION

If, after having intercourse without effective contraception, a woman fears she may become pregnant, she may wish to consider taking the "morning after medication."

Diethylstilbesterol (DES) or the "morning after pill" has

Adapted from *Everybody's Guide to Every Body*. Reprinted with permission of Planned Parenthood League of Massachusetts.

Wendy Watriss—Fred Baldwin

Waiting room of a birth control clinic

been used for some gynecological disorders for more than thirty years. Recently it has been linked with vaginal and cerivcal cancer in the daughters of some women who had taken the drug during pregnancy to prevent threatened miscarriage.

American farmers used DES as a growth hormone in cattle feed until August 1972 when reports that it had caused cancer in laboratory animals led the government to proscribe this use of the drug. On February 21, 1973, the FDA approved prescription of DES as a morning after contraceptive in emergency situations, but with the caveat that "this usage is to be considered as an emergency treatment only and should not be considered as a method for birth control with continuous and frequently repeated therapy." The FDA suggested that rape and incest qualified as emergency situations but left the decision to prescribe DES to the individual physician.

The morning after pill is a high dose of estrogen, usually stilbesterol. It is thought to prevent pregnancy after unprotected intercourse by altering the lining of the uterus, making it hostile to implantation of the fertilized egg. It should be taken as soon as possible after intercourse, although it is considered effective if taken within 72 hours. A prescription is required for the medication, which is generally taken in pill form for five consecutive days. It tends to cause nausea, vomiting and dizziness and is usually given in conjunction with anti-nausea medication (either orally or in rectal suppositories) and it also tends to disrupt the menstrual cycle, causing an early or late period.

true sex, they fell in love, and, dreading detection, they left the abbey to wander over Europe. Later the lovers settled in Athens, Europe's center of learning, and Joan at the age of twenty took on the whole of human knowledge and studies offered by the famous Greek schools. But her lover suddenly died and, finding it increasingly difficult to

Birth Control:
The Middle Class Offensive
Barbara Ehrenreich and Deirdre English

Public health was always respectable, but the birth control movement started out in the disreputable company of anarchists, socialists, and extreme feminists. Emma Goldman was jailed for speaking on birth control, and the young Margaret Sanger pushed it in her socialist/feminist journal *The Woman Rebel*. At first, other middle-class reformers saw birth control as a wicked scheme to "take the penalty out of vice," and "degrade the wife to the level of the prostitute."

But as the movement matured under Sanger's single-handed leadership and attracted the support of thousands of upper-middle- and upper-class women, it began to make a frank appeal to upper-middle-class self-interest. By the late 1910s Sanger was blaming all the problems of the world—war, poverty, prostitution, famine, feeblemindedness—on overpopulation, and she put the blame for overpopulation squarely on women:

> While unknowingly laying the foundations of tyrannies and providing the human tinder for racial conflagrations woman was also unknowingly creating slums, filling asylums with the insane, and institutions with other defectives. She was replenishing the ranks of prostitutes, furnishing grist for the criminal courts and inmates for prisons. Had she planned deliberately to achieve this tragic total of human waste and misery, she could hardly have done it more effectively.

And in case that did not make clear *which* women Sanger blamed, she wrote, in 1918, that "all our problems are the result of overbreeding among the working class."

Birth control offered the possibility of qualitative as well as quantitative control of the population. "More children from the fit, less from the unfit—that is the chief issue of birth control," Sanger declared in 1919. Just who was fit and who was unfit—and how you would impose birth control on one group and keep it away from the other—was not altogether clear. Ms. Sanger usually limited her definition of the "unfit" to the feebleminded (as judged by the newly invented IQ test), but some of her associates in the American Birth Control League were explicitly racist.

Guy Irving Burch, an officer of Sanger's National Committee on Federal Legislation for Birth Control, explained his interest in birth control thus:

> My family on both sides were early colonial and pioneer stock and I have long worked with the American Coalition of Patriotic Societies to prevent the American people from being replaced by alien or Negro stock, whether it be by immigration or by overly high birth rates among others in this country.

Another birth control advocate urged that "to offset the so-called 'yellow peril,'" the United States should, "spread birth control knowledge abroad so as to decrease the quantity of people whose unchecked reproduction threatens international peace."

A few farsighted physicians joined in the campaign to make contraception acceptable to the middle class by

Adapted from *Complaints and Disorders: The Sexual Politics of Sickness* by Barbara Ehrenreich and Deirdre English. Copyright © 1974 Barbara Ehrenreich and Deirdre English. Published by The Feminist Press, Box 334, Old Westbury, New York 11568. Reprinted with permission.

Above, Margaret Sanger leaving Brooklyn Court of Appeals; below, Margaret Sanger under arrest for advocating birth control.

Sophia Smith Collection, Smith College

Sophia Smith Collection, Smith College

maintain her disguise among the bearded men of Greece, she decided to go to Rome, where it is the custom to shave. Now she attempted to dull her loss by immersing herself in scholarship and teaching. She gained appointment as a notary at the papal court, and then worked her way up to become a cardinal. Still no one suspected her sex.

Top left, the street where birth control was born; left, volunteers selling the Birth Control Review; top right, Margaret Sanger at rest; right, Margaret Sanger at the opening of a Planned Parenthood Clinic in Tucson, Arizona, in 1965.

pointing out its possibilities for population control. In his 1912 presidential address to the AMA, Dr. Abraham Jacobi endorsed birth control, citing the high fertility of immigrants and the rising cost of welfare. Dr. Robert Dickinson, a gynecologist and one of Sanger's most steadfast medical allies, urged his fellow doctors in 1916 to "take hold of this matter [birth control] and not let it go to the radicals." With the help of men like Dr. Dickinson, Ms. Sanger was able to begin the first birth control services—appropriately enough, in the slums of New York City.

Contraception did not become legal until a 1938 court ruling allowed physicians to import, mail, and prescribe birth control devices. This was a great step forward for women, and the credit goes largely to Margaret Sanger's courage and determination.

We want to be clear about our position on this issue. We think birth control should be available on demand for all women, of all classes and ethnic groups. We do not subscribe to the view that birth control is liberating for some women, but "genocidal" for others. What we are criticizing is the line that the birth control movement advanced in order to make its gains. The fact that the birth control movement took a racist and classist line makes even the final victory a dubious one.

But here we must ask ourselves: Could the birth control movement have succeeded any other way, given the context of American society at the time? If the birth control movement had advanced purely feminist arguments for contraception, would it have had the power or influence to succeed? We might ask a similar question about the public health movement: Would there have been any public health reforms if these had not been in the direct self-interest of wealthy and powerful people? These questions are, of course, unanswerable, but they do point to the fundamental ambiguity of reform in an otherwise oppressive society.

In A.D. 855, so the story goes, Joan was selected as the next pope, after the death of Leo IV. She was ordained according to the rituals and she ruled for over two years with tact and skill, even appointing Ludwig Holy Roman Emperor of the West. She was known as Pope John VIII, the Angelic.

However, in A.D. 856, Joan grew restless and took herself a lover, her first since

The Physiology of Erotica

Julia R. Heiman

FOLKLORE AND FRATERNITIES have had great fun over the years speculating about what arouses women sexually. No one seems to know for sure, but everyone does agree that women aren't turned on by erotica. "They like romantic flights of emotional fantasy," runs the popular view. "So give 'em passion, not pornography."

The problem with finding out what women like is that some of them don't know and others don't think they should know. Some researchers believe—and women agree—that many females learn early in childhood to suppress or reinterpret signs of sexual excitement. And the matter is further complicated because women tend to define arousal—and orgasm—in different ways, from gentle tingling to bells clanging. Men, of course, don't have quite the same problem. They have a handy feedback system that announces that they are aroused, as any suffering male adolescent can tell you.

But women today are more willing to admit their sexual fantasies and respond to erotica than they ever were, as the popularity of Erica Jong's *Fear of Flying* and other explicit books about female sexuality suggests. When the smoke clears after the last battle of the sexes, I suspect we will find that men and women aren't as different as we thought—not in needs, not in desires, not in sexual response. Jong's fantasy of the "zipless fuck" is, after all, what males have yearned for and joked about for years: a sexual encounter with literally no strings attached—neither physical ones, such as zippers and girdles, nor emotional ones, such as feelings of guilt and anxiety.

My research finds, indeed, that women like erotica as much as men do, that they are as turned on by sexual descriptions, that their fantasies are as vivid and self-arousing. In my experiment, males and females responded to erotic stories in order to resolve some of the arguments about what turns women on, in comparison to men. Because sex is a matter of mind and body, I also explored the way fantasy may aid self-arousal, and compared subjective reports of sexual excitement with objective physiological measures. The experiment also tested the cultural assumption that women are slower to become aroused

than men. It is possible that they are merely slower to *admit arousal*.

I began with a group of 42 male and 77 female college students. They completed a questionnaire to assess their sexual experience and attitudes, with particular attention to how liberated they were about sex and sex roles.

Sexually Sophisticated Students. This group of students was pretty experienced, as one might expect of volunteers for such an experiment. A minority of both sexes, only 22 percent, had never had intercourse, and both males and females were having sex with roughly the same frequency. The women, however, reported fewer partners than the men, were slightly older at the age of first intercourse, fantasized less during masturbation, and for

that matter masturbated less often. The great majority of women, 84 percent, claimed to have reached orgasm, a major change from their Kinsey age-mates a generation ago, when only 53 percent reported orgasm. These young women either know what they're doing, know what they should be saying, or define orgasm differently from women in the 1930s and '40s.

Having determined that I had a sample of experienced subjects who knew what sexual arousal was all about, I launched the second phase, the psychophysiological study of sexual response.

Physiological measures of male response are easy: erection—yes, sort of, no. For more precise measurement—how much yes, what degree of sort of—we used a mercury-filled strain gauge that meas-

Pottery vessel in the form of reclining ithyphallic man (from Colima, Mexico, after A.D. 300).

Paul C. Cabot III

Athens. She guarded his identity so well that his name has never been mentioned by chroniclers. Their relationship would remain unreported had she not become unexpectedly pregnant. (Medieval accounts describe her anguish over this circumstance in detail, depicting her thrashing alone in her bed at night.) Although close to term, she was required to lead a solemn procession through the streets of Rome on the holy Day of

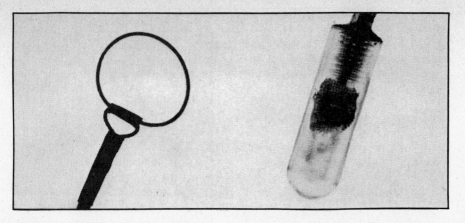

Left, the penile strain gauge consists of wire attached to a flexible band that fits around the base of the penis; right, the photoplethysmograph, an acrylic cylinder containing a photocell and light source, is placed just inside the vagina.

ures blood volume and pressure pulse in the penis. The gauge, which is a flexible circlet the thickness of a rubber band, fits unobtrusively around the base of the penis. Numerous researchers have used this strain gauge to study male response to pornography and to other erotic stimuli.

Physiological measures of *female* response aren't so easy, and until recently researchers had to rely on asking women what they felt. Last year George Sintchak and James Geer of SUNY Stony Brook developed a way to measure blood volume and pressure pulse in the vagina. (Genital vasocongestion, as Masters and Johnson have shown, is a principal physiological response during the initial stages of sexual arousal for both sexes.) Sintchak and Geer came up with a simple device with a cumbersome name, the photoplethysmograph, an acrylic cylinder that is only 1¾" by ½", which contains a photocell and light source. The photocell registers diffused light as vaginal pressure pulse and blood volume change. (It is placed just inside the entrance of the vagina, and is not used if the woman is menstruating.) The photoplethysmograph can detect relatively low levels of arousal, and validation studies indicate that the device does reliably measure sexual response—as opposed, say, to anxiety, boredom, or apprehension.

Every subject put on the genital instrument in privacy, remained fully clothed throughout the test, and recorded subjective reactions during the study in the absence of the experimenter. A male experimenter worked with the men and a female experimenter with the women to explain the gadget and the procedure, but he or she did not lurk about to add to the students' possible nervousness. We left each subject alone with his or her dreams and devices.

Erotic Vs. Romantic. We assigned each student to one of four groups. The first group heard four different *erotic* tapes, each six to eight minutes long. (I had a fairly entertaining time rummaging through pornography and popular novels to find my excerpts, which a panel of judges independently verified for erotic value.) Then I modified the tapes for the other groups. Group two heard four *romantic* tapes—the expurgated version of the same scenes, now without explicit sex. Instead, the couple in each tape expressed tenderness and affection for each other, verbally but not physically. Group three heard *romantic-erotic* tapes, in which the couples both expressed affection and had sex. Group four got to listen to tapes of couples sharing conversation, dinner, or wine, but not each other. The control tapes had no erotic or romantic elements.

The erotic tapes described sex between a man and a woman, occasionally preceded by masturbation. There were no elements of homosexuality, sadomasochism, incest, bestiality, or other fashions dear to pornographers.

But the four erotic and erotic-romantic tapes did vary on what I call an action dimension. Most pornography is directed at males, so in most plots men initiate the sex and description concentrates on the woman's genitals and reactions. I wondered how modern students would react to an erotic story that emphasized the man's body, or in which the female was the sexual aggressor.

So I modified the tapes according to whether the man or the woman initiated the sexual encounter and also according to whether the erotic description concentrated on the female's genitals, body, and pleasure, or the male's. Tape one was male-initiated, male-centered; two was female-initiated, male-centered; three was female-initiated, female-centered; and four was male-initiated and female-centered.

At the start of the session, each student sat and relaxed for five minutes to give us baseline physiological measures. We then asked the students to try to conjure up a sexually arousing fantasy for two minutes, and to rate briefly the vividness of their fantasy—and its effectiveness in turning them on. Finally we started the tapes. After each one, the student rated its erotic value and described whether and how it was arousing. The process of reporting was enough to get the student's genital response back to baseline before the next tape. If it didn't, we asked him or her to count backwards in multiples; that squelched most everyone's arousal.

Again at the end of the session, each student fantasized for two minutes. With this procedure, we could determine whether the erotic stimuli helped or inhibited sexual fantasy and arousal. About 10 days later, we ran the whole procedure over again.

We found, first of all, that explicit sex, not romance, is what turns people on—women as well as men. The great majority of both sexes responded physiologically and subjectively to the erotic and erotic-romantic tapes, and not to the romantic or control contents. Women, in fact, rated the erotic tapes as more arousing than men did. Our assumption that women would react only to the romantic tapes, or at least that they would prefer eroticism that was tempered with romance to straight-out sex, was simply wrong.

The Power of Sexual Thinking. A small proportion of men and even fewer women reacted sexually to the unprovocative control tapes. I have always suspected that men can interpret the most unsexy situations as erotic, and there they were, turned on by a bland narrative of a student couple discussing the relative benefits of an anthropology major over premed. Perhaps anticipation of what they *thought* they were going to hear and a lot of cognitive acrobatics turned them on. In any case, by the second session a week later, everyone's expectations were clari-

Rogations. One chronicler described what followed:
 "Mounted on her horse, she went to the Church of Saint Peter, clothed in her pontifical garments, preceded by the Cross and accompanied by. . .bishops, cardinals, priests, deacons, nobles, magistrates, and a huge crowd of citizens. After presiding over ceremonies there, she again set forth at head of that pompous procession for the Church

Physiology of Erotica
THE SEX ADVISER **151**

*Warrior standing
in erotic stimulation
(from Colima, Mexico)*

**Vaginal pressure pulse during
erotic and non-erotic tapes**

**Penile pressure pulse during
erotic and non-erotic tapes**

fied. Students listening to control and romantic tapes were not sexually aroused, while those who heard the erotic and erotic-romantic tapes still were.

One erotic tape of the four was especially sexy to women: the female-initiated, female-centered story. Their physiological response to that tape was significantly greater than to the others, and the same tended to be true for males. The second-favorite tape, again for both sexes, was the male-initiated, female-centered one. The description of the woman's body and her sexual response is apparently an important ingredient in the erotic script for men and women alike. It makes sense; pornography and advertising spend much money and effort to make the female an erotic object—and that message is effective with women as well as men.

I was fascinated that both sexes preferred the female as initiator. Perhaps this

group was unusually liberated—especially the women—although from their questionnaires I don't think they were terribly unlike most college students. Perhaps they were responding to the beach scene in which the sexual activities took place. Or perhaps this particular fantasy gives women a sense of sexual control that they do not have usually, while it allows men a chance to lie back and enjoy it, without having to worry about performance.

Men and women alike were able to turn themselves on through fantasy, significantly increasing their blood volume and pressure pulse. (And in less than two minutes, at that.) The erotic tapes did not increase their ability to fantasize, as I had expected; people began and ended the experiment with about the same degree of fantasy skill. Arousal through fantasy, especially for women, was relatively independent of exposure to erotic stimuli. In a

few cases, people who listened to the erotic tapes were *less* able to arouse themselves during the posttape fantasy than students who listened to nonerotic tapes. Of course, this was not a clinical group with sexual problems, so they were not motivated to improve. On the contrary, by the end of the session most were tired, as one student said, "of being turned on."

I had predicted that women would find it more difficult than men to detect when they were, by all objective measures, sexually aroused. The answer is: yes and no.

Knowing When You Throb or Tickle. We asked all the students to describe their reactions after each tape: did he or she feel "any physical arousal" (because many women describe arousal in general, not genital, terms); any "throbbing, tickling, or other genital sensations"; and any erection (males) or lubrication (females). I

of Saint John; but, before arriving at the public square between the Church of Saint Clement and the Colosseum, the pangs of childbirth siezed her with such violence that... she fell from her horse to the street, where she writhed and rolled about, uttering fearful groans. "Well-meaning clerics immediately removed her stiff and weighty robes, and no sooner did they discover her womanhood than she gave birth on the spot. In the

could then cross-tabulate the yes-no answer to each of these questions with each student's measured genital arousal, categorized from very low to very high.

The measures of physiological arousal and self-report correlated highly for both sexes, indicating that the majority of these students could label their arousal accurately. But women did make more mistakes than men.

For example, I looked at the women's responses to the first tape they heard, regardless of content. Of those who showed the *largest* physiological change in vaginal blood volume, 42 percent said they felt *no* physical response, 54 percent reported no vaginal sensations at all, and 63 percent said they felt no signs of lubrication. As you might imagine, the men were terrific at recognizing when they were turned on. Exactly zero percent were able to ignore an erection—the male approximation of genital blood-volume change.

The women's self-appraisal didn't improve much over time and subsequent tapes; large percentages remained unaware of their extreme changes in vaginal blood volume. However, women did better in identifying changes in vaginal pressure pulse, a less generalized measure of vasodilatation. Those women who showed a very strong sexual reaction to the tapes as measured by pressure pulse

were more likely to report subjectively that they were turned on.

The discrepancy may be a problem of measurement. Blood volume increases more slowly than pressure pulse and takes longer to return to baseline; thus women may adapt to blood-volume changes more easily. For these reasons, pressure pulse does seem to be a more accurate indicator of immediate fluctuations in arousal.

But I also think that the discrepancy between body arousal and verbal report comes partly from women's learned reactions to sexual excitement. When I looked more carefully at the discrepant cases, I found that most of the women who made such mistakes were those responding to the *nonerotic* tapes.

The women who were excited by the erotic tapes would, logically, find it difficult to deny their arousal—especially in a situation in which it is obviously legitimate for them to be aroused, and especially for young women who are fairly liberated about admitting such things. But as soon as the women did not have external erotic cues to make their arousal legitimate, they had trouble recognizing physiological excitement. The women who were turned on during the control and romantic tapes, for reasons that only they and their fantasies know, did not have a social validation for their physical

response. So their minds denied or ignored their bodies.

Beyond Pedophilia. Most sex researchers have concentrated on the exotic rather than the erotic: until Masters and Johnson published, we knew more about mackintosh fetishes and masochism than about normal human sexiness. More people have studied trans-, homo-, bi-, and nonsexuals than the ordinary hetero variety, and the field hums with other curious forms, such as pedophilia (sexual attraction for children) and kleptolagnia (sexual arousal through stealing). Before we can know more about why some people *do* become sexually deviant, we might do well to ask why most people *don't*.

By knowing how normal women—workers and housewives as well as students—respond to fantasy and erotica, for example, we can begin to understand why some women are nonorgasmic. Their problem may result from not being turned on at all, from not recognizing and labeling the signs of arousal, or from not being able to let themselves go from high arousal to orgasm.

Further, knowledge of the sexual responses of normal women challenges myths, misconceptions and stereotypes. Women who turn on the way men do to erotica often think they are deviant. They aren't.

Odalisque, by Eugene Delacroix

confusion, the priests packed in around her to prevent others from witnessing the scene or giving assistance. According to one account, Pope Joan "could not support the humiliation of having been seen by all the people in so terrible a position and... she expired." A more popular story is that the enraged priests turned her over to the mob, who tore her apart and threw her remains into the Tiber River while priests dispatched

The Liberated

Orgasm

Barbara Seaman

Years ago Margaret Mead suggested that, "the human female's capacity for orgasm is to be viewed. . .as a potentiality that may or may not be developed by a given culture."

We don't need to be anthropologists to realize that our Western culture has not only failed to develop that potentiality, but it has stifled and repressed it.

As a result, we women have been afraid to think for ourselves about our own sexual tastes and pleasures. We have tried to model our own preferences after the prevailing views of normality. We have been shy about telling our lovers what we want. We have feared it would be unwomanly to do other than let the male take the lead, however ineptly.

The modern sex manuals are filled with misinformation—for instance, the standard advice to men that they should flail away at the sensitive clitoris. But even when their suggestions are applicable to some women in some moods, they are rarely applicable to all women in all moods, and they foster a certain

technical rigidity that is antithetical to really good sex.

Female sexuality is so easily bruised and buried in the myths and medical models of the prevailing culture that the self-awarensss needed for liberation will be difficult to achieve unless women explore their own true sexual feelings and needs.

We know that all orgams are similar on a motor level, and that all orgasms are different on a sensory level.

We know also that there is no ideal or norm, except in our own imaginations. The truth is that the liberated orgasm is an orgasm *you* like, under any circumstances *you* find comfortable. (The only qualification is that liberated persons don't exploit each other—that's just for masters and slaves.)

In the spring of 1971, my research assistant Carol Milano and I completed an informal but we think rather enlightening sex survey of 103 women. They were career women or students: models of the new woman who enjoys more than average sexual awareness and freedom.

In our survey all but six regularly achieved some sort of orgasm with

relative ease. This is substantially higher than the figure for women in general in our society, especially when you consider that perhaps one-third of the women in our survey were under 25. (From the Kinsey report and more recent investigations, we know that while the majority of women do achieve orgasms sooner or later, for many it is later. It often takes years or even decades for adult women to achieve sexual satisfaction.)

There was a group in our survey who could not comment on the clitoral *versus* the vaginal orgasm at all and said that to them the whole debate seemed meaningless. These women simply did not experience their orgasms in one place more than the other. But with this group left out, there were the two extremes of women who stated a preference for, or more frequent experience of, one type or the other. That is to say, regardless of the actual physiology of the event, they *felt* most of their orgasms in either the vagina or the clitoris.

Women are so varied in their sexuality that even those who seem alike are different. Let us contrast two, whom I shall call Marie and Antoinette.

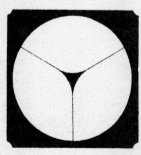

---

the infant.

Yet another account maintains that both her and her child's remains were interred on the very spot where she fell. The incident supposedly so shook the Church of Rome that a decree was passed prohibiting future papal processions on that accursed street. (To this day the procession formed on the Day of Rogations makes a long circuit around it.)

Both women are sexually informed and active, and both have given considerable thought to their sexual needs. To achieve orgasms, both require direct clitoral stimulation.

They are not militant clitorists, for neither doubts that some women obtain orgasms via vaginal stimulation, but it doesn't work for them. Marie says, "I know that lots of girls do *not* need as much direct stimulation as I do—but I think this is because they have larger and better placed clitorises." Antoinette says, "I don't think anyone really knows what percentage of women have orgasms during intercourse. It would seem to depend on individual anatomy and placement of the clitoris."

Although clitorises are highly variable in size as well as placement, Masters and Johnson say that in eleven years of research they found no evidence to support the belief that differences in clitoral anatomy can influence sexual response. This, however, must be viewed as a highly tentative finding since they were unable to observe any clitorises during orgasms. Masters and Johnson think that in certain women the thrusting penis does not exercise the traction on the labia and clitoral hood that it does for others. So perhaps idiosyncrasies of the vagina, rather than the clitoris, better explain the anatomical need for direct stimulation. Direct clitoral stimulation can be obtained in sexual intercourse, provided the woman is on top or the couple is side by side, and the pubic bones of the man and woman are touching.

What, in the experience of Marie and Antoinette, is the most common lovemaking error that men make?

Marie: "Not enough direct manipulation of the clitoris."

Antoinette: "Many men don't realize that the clitoris is the source of orgasms."

Two peas in a pod. Of all the women in my survey, there were no two who were more similar. . .and yet Marie loves sexual intercourse, while Antoinette finds it dull.

Marie: "Intercourse to me is very exciting! I get depressed if sexual contact doesn't include penetration, and a man doesn't come inside me."

Antoinette: "How a man performs intercourse is unimportant to me; I've never achieved and never expect to achieve orgasm during coitus."

Marie isn't the only woman who swears that for a first-rate orgasm she requires a penis or other object within the vagina. Nor is Antoinette the only one who is indifferent. No doubt there are many psychological as well as anatomical variations that might influence a woman's perceived degree of vaginal sensitivity.

Analysts are undoubtedly telling us the truth when they report that they have "converted" thousands of women to vaginally experienced orgasms. The point is merely that, for some women at least, the strong desire to notice vaginal sensations makes these more noticeable. If Masters and Johnson are correct, all orgasms are essentially the same and quite sensibly involve all the pertinent parts God gave us.

But if all orgasms are the same, why do women not recognize the fact? Are we hopelessly stupid or recalcitrant?

Or are we complex human organisms whose responses are as varied and individual as we are ourselves? Some women noted a difference in their response to vaginal stimulation after childbirth. Several other women noted that they first experienced "vaginal" orgasm—that is, orgasm without direct clitoral stimulation—during intercourse with men who could either sustain vaginal thrusting for an exceptionally long period of time (compared to other lovers) or who had organs that seemed exceptionally large and "filling." One woman also noted a difference in male "sex rhythms"(". . .with some of my lovers I need my clitoris fondled to reach orgasm, and with others I don't. I find that every man has his own individual sex rhythm and way of thrusting. This is something a man cannot control, no matter how much he may wish to. Some men make short, rapid, jerky thrusts, and other men make longer, deeper thrusts, which I like better. With a man who takes the longer thrusts, I can have orgasms without clitoral manipulation and with a man who takes jerky thrusts I can't. This is oversimplifying of course, because every one of my fourteen lovers had his own unique sex rhythm, and I more or less enjoyed orgasm all, even though some required that the man use his finger in supplementation. I believe that I could recognize most of my lovers blindfolded, just on the basis of their own unique sex rhythms. This, to me, is one of the most fascinating differences in men."

Several of the women who need direct clitoral stimulation gave what appeared to be very sound anatomical explanations of their preference. Here is one example: "Before the birth of my son, who weighed over nine pounds and had an inordinately large head, I used to reach orgasm without needing to have my clitoris massaged. I don't believe that my vagina was repaired properly after childbirth. I think it must have gotten stretched out of shape because my same husband, with the same penis (and to whom I feel closer than ever),

Joan's story passed into literature and common belief in the late thirteenth century, providing grist for such writers as Petrarch and Boccaccio. In 1415, the Council of Constance, comprised of many of the most brilliant theologians in Europe, regarded the existence of Pope Joan as fact. Joan's life was proved a myth, however, in the sixteenth

cannot bring me to orgasm so easily by his thrusting alone. I enjoy sex more than ever. My desire, if anything, has increased. But something is different about me, and if my understanding of Masters and Johnson is correct, I believe that the difference is that my vagina was slightly damaged, so that my husband's thrusting no longer provides as much traction on my clitoris."

So, allowing for the probability that there are anatomical differences that may have a strong bearing, what were the other differences between "vaginal" and "clitoral" women?

From the evidence gathered in our survey, there were more women in the vaginal group whose early experience with men had been favorable and who had not had to struggle to learn to enjoy sex. These women, perhaps because they were more "trusting" or perhaps, more simply, because their earliest lovers were better controlled and had stimulated them vaginally for long enough periods to bring them to orgasm by that route, had somehow learned to experience "feeling" in their vaginas and to let themselves come to orgasms through vaginal stimulation alone.

The "clitoral" types generally had been exposed to more selfish or fumbling lovers, particularly in their early experiences. Some, of course, had themselves insisted on the practice of merely "petting to climax" in order to preserve a token virginity during their premarital years.

Outside or in, clitoral or vaginal, we are in no way as standardized as Hugh Hefner's airbrushed and siliconed playmates. For example, while fourteen women in our survey complained that their lovers did not engage in enough physical foreplay, and eight others complained that their lovers did not engage in enough verbal foreplay,

pillow talk, or conversation, two respondents took the opposite position. They like to get down to the main business of sex more swiftly than their lovers. One observed: "I find foreplay detrimental. When I really get into rubbing up against him, the feelings become sensuous, non sensual. Sex is more direct—from the inside out." So that is how one woman feels, and she is sexually active and well realized. The second woman asks wryly: "I have very little interest in foreplay. Is that an inhibition or a total lack of it?"

Or consider the question of the handsome stranger, an alleged apparition in the dreams of younger females. Most of the women in my survey dislike sex with strangers. Over and over they emphasized the importance (to them) of warmth, intimacy, trust, tenderness. For example, "I appreciate kindliness in a man—and one who appreciates and loves women (i.e., me). Too many people use sex as an outlet—it should be a mutual experience of lovingness. . . ."

Yet, undeniably, for some women intimacy breeds boredom or contempt. One girl admitted, "I can only be uninhibited in sex with men I do not know very well."

Some women even deem it best to withdraw entirely from men. A prominent feminist confided: "I think it's wonderful that women have discovered masturbation, because it will enable us to keep apart from men as long as necessary. When you have work to do, you can't allow yourself to be diverted by sexual relationships. Masturbation is what male revolutionaries have always used to relieve themselves. Some of the women I know are so pathetic. They run around looking for a man, any man at all."

A 55-year-old woman admits: "I was born too early and too late. Unlike my

mother, I realized that I too had sexual desires, but unlike my daughter, I considered it unthinkable to vocalize them. In the early years of my marriage I suffered unbearable frustration because I couldn't bring myself to tell my husband what he was doing wrong. By the time I worked up the courage he had lost most of his interest in sex. I've learned how to satisfy myself with an electric massager, but it's lonely. Some women are very sexy, and it's cruel to all concerned that delicacy prevents them from expressing it."

But what precisely is the female orgasm (which may or may not be developed by a given culture) and where does it take place? A woman knows when she's had one (if she doubts it, she hasn't), but since her orgasm is not punctuated by the sure sign of ejaculation, men have felt free to develop lunatic theories about it, and women have not learned to trust their own bodies.

A woman's external sex organs consist of labia majora, or outer lips; labia minora, or inner lips; and the highly eroticized clitoris, the only organ known to man or woman whose sole purpose is to receive and transmit sexual pleasure. The hood of the clitoris is attached to the labia minora, which are directly affected by penile thrusting. Thus, intercourse causes the labia to exert traction on the clitoral hood, producing rhythmic friction between it and the clitoris itself.

Masters and Johnson have proved—or believe they have proved; their work has not yet been replicated—that virtually all feminine orgasms, however vaginal some of them may seem, do include indirect clitoral stimulation, the labia minora being the agent of mediation. Some Freudian analysts have long maintained that vaginal orgasms are entirely distinct from clitoral orgasms and are, indeed, the hallmark of a sexually mature woman. If clitoral stimulation, whether direct or transmitted through the labia, occurs in all orgasm, then distinguishing them is invalid. So is the complicated mystique attached to the distinction. Vaginal women have been said to be mature, feminine, loving and happy, while

century, though Protestant clerics continued to use her in their anti-papal polemics long afterward. Even though most consider the tale a myth today, nonetheless it was thought of as fact for over two hundred years, perhaps in recognition of the powerful women who exercised great influence over the early medieval papacy.

clitoral women have had all the opposite traits attributed to them.

However, if I read Masters and Johnson correctly, they are saying that clitoral stimulation may occur in orgasm, but orgasm does not chiefly occur in the clitoris.

To the contrary, orgasm, which is a total body response, is always marked by vaginal contractions. No specific physiologic response in the clitoris has yet been recorded.

Let us review the physiology of the female sex cycle:

STAGE ONE: Excitement. Within ten to thirty seconds after erotic stimulation starts, the vaginal lining is moistened with a lubricating fluid. Nipples erect, and the breasts begin to swell, increasing in size by one-fifth to one-quarter in women who have not nursed a baby. (Breasts that have been suckled do not enlarge as much.) Other changes start to occur in the clitoris, labia, and vagina as vasocongestion (the engorgement of vessels and organs with blood) and muscular tension start to build. Late in the excitement phase, some women may start to develop a measles-like rash, or sex flush, across their bodies. (Seventy-five percent of the women evaluated by Masters and Johnson showed this response on some occasions.)

STAGE TWO: Plateau. The tissue surrounding the outer third of the vagina engorges and swells, creating an "orgasmic platform." The deeper portion of the vagina balloons out to form a cavity. The uterus enlarges. The swelling of the outer third of the vagina reduces its diameter, allowing it to grip the penis better. The clitoris retracts, and it becomes harder to locate.

Just prior to the orgasmic phase, the labia minora undergo a marked color change called the sex skin reaction. In the woman who has not had children, the labia minora turn pink or bright red. In the mother, they turn bright red or deep wine (presumably because she has a greater number of varicosities). This coloration remains throughout orgasm, but disappears ten to fifteen seconds afterward. When a woman develops sex skin, she is almost certain to go on to orgasm. Women who are aroused to plateau levels but not

brought to orgasm experience a prolonged and sometimes uncomfortable ebbing away of vasocongestion and muscular tension.

STAGE THREE: Orgasm. The typical orgasm lasts only ten or fifteen seconds, if that long. Changes occur throughout the body. Muscles of the abdomen, buttocks, neck, arms, and legs may contract; pulse and breathing are more rapid; and blood pressure climbs. The woman experiences a series of rhythmic muscular contractions in the outer third of the vagina and the tissues surrounding it and in the uterus. These contractions, each taking about four-fifths of a second, serve to discharge the accumulated vasocongestion and tension that have been brought on by sexual stimulation. A mild orgasm usually involves three to five contractions; an intense one, as many as fifteen.

From time to time a woman may experience what some Samoan Islanders call the "knockout" orgasm, and what Masters and Johnson term the "status orgasmus." Masters and Johnson suspect, but are not certain, that the woman is probably having rapidly connected multiple orgasms, over a time period of sixty seconds or so.

In prolonged intercourse a woman may have three, four, or five separate orgasms, and in a few primitive cultures, where men have good control of themselves, multiple female orgasms are apparently the norm. Some masturbating women can have up to fifty successive orgasms according to clinical observation.

Multiple orgasms are most apt to occur when intercourse is prolonged. Thus, while the much vaunted "mutual orgasm" has some very nice features, it also has some drawbacks from the women's point of view. Or to put it

another way, there is no need for a woman to hold back deliberately, for if the male can maintain effective thrusting for a long enough period, the woman will have several preliminary orgasms and, quite possibly, another when he reaches his.

Women who don't have multiple orgasms may fear that they are missing something, but women who do have them often report that these are not their most pleasurable experiences. "If I've had a great orgasm, I can't bear to go on," one such woman explained.

This mysterious thing called orgasmic intensity is measured, principally, in the number of contractions. Masters and Johnson maintain that females have the most intense orgasms when they are free to please themselves only—"without the distraction of a partner." But they do qualify it. "A woman might tell me that she had a delightful experience with the machine," Dr. Masters commented at the New York Academy of Medicine in 1968, "but the next night with her husband might have been even better, in her opinion, although we registered fewer orgasmic contractions."

STAGE FOUR: Resolution. Blood vessels emptied and muscular tensions relieved, the various parts and organs return to their normal condition, some rapidly and some slowly. One woman in three develops a film of perspiration across her body.

According to Masters and Johnson, the clitoris contributes crucially to the buildup of sexual tensions, but orgasm itself is more correctly described as centering in the vagina. Tensions established, it is vaginal contractions that bring relief by emptying engorged organs and vessels. Masters and Johnson call these vaginal contractions "the visible manifestations of female orgasmic experience."

1401. Lady Barbe de Cilley of the French court, married to a particularly ugly though noble husband, astonishes her friends by taking as a lover a man even more "foul." "I do so," she informs jesting courtiers, "the better to accustom me to my husband's ugliness."

Yet, even for those lucky women who can fantasy to orgasm, the clitoris serves as receptor and transformer of sexual stimuli, while vaginal contractions punctuate the orgasm itself.

However, it is important to note that some women who do not possess a clitoris seem to be capable of orgasm. Dr. Michael Daly, a Philadelphia gynecologist, reports that he has studied in depth two patients in whom the total clitoris was removed because of cancer. Both continued to have orgasms, and both said that their sexual responsiveness after surgery was as great as it was before.

There also are established cases of women in whom an artificial vagina had to be created, because they were born without one. These women also are capable of reaching orgasm.

Apparently, it is lucky for us that most of our sex tissue is internal and can be stimulated by an almost infinite variety of methods.

It is clearly false to say "vaginal orgasm is a myth." But does the vagina contribute to sexual arousal? Or (as some sex researchers, most notably Kinsey, and some women have thought) does it have no feeling?

Yes, it does. Vaginal sensations are believed to be proprioceptive, which means that they are sensations resulting from a stimulus within our own bodies, not imposed from outside.

Close your eyes; extend an arm and bend it. If you can describe the position of your arm, if you know whether it is bent or straight, you are receiving and using proprioceptive information. Ordinarily, we do not pay much conscious attention to our proprioceptive intelligence, but without it we would not even be able to walk.

The vagina is most apt to develop proprioceptive abilities during states of sexual arousal and distention. In unaroused states, as, for example, when a gynecologist inserts a speculum, it may be quite unresponsive.

Obviously, there is a crucial distinction between motor experience (what's happening) and sensory experience (what we're aware of). Masters and Johnson do not always draw this distinction as sharply as many psychologists (and women) might wish.

Some orgasms seem to be experienced vaginally or deep in the vagina, while others seem to be in the clitoris. Some orgasms occur while direct clitoral stimulation is taking place, while others occur only with vaginal stimulation. The experts who have been discussing us have never even defined the terms "vaginal" and "clitoral" orgasm, and women could hardly be sure whether a clitoral orgasm meant an orgasm that was induced by clitoral stimulation, an orgasm that seemed to be experienced in the clitoris, or both.

The same woman may, at different times, experience orgasms in different locations or from different types of stimulation. Women know this, but as a rule men appear to have difficulty comprehending it. In 1968, Drs. Jules

Glenn and Eugene Kaplan accused psychoanalysts of assuming, incorrectly, that clitorally stimulated orgasms are necessarily experienced clitorally. They described a patient who, following a fleeting touch to the clitoris, experienced intense orgasms localized deep within the vagina which did not involve any conscious clitoral sensations at all. Glenn and Kaplan classify such orgasms as "clitorally stimulated, but vaginally experienced."

They go on to say that their patients have reported a great variation in the location of the experienced orgasm. Occasionally, sites other than the vagina and clitoris (the abdomen, the anus) seem to be the focus of feeling. The area in which the orgasm is experienced need not be the area of stimulation, and there is great variation in the area or areas stimulated, as well as the area or areas where orgasm is felt. The terms "vaginal orgasm" and "clitoral orgasm," according to Glenn and Kaplan have been "widely used but ill-defined."

The charge of technical rigidity is frequently leveled against not only writers of certain types of sex manuals, but also sex researchers, such as Kinsey, and Masters and Johnson.

There is a great deal that can be said against Masters and Johnson, and some of it has been said very well and very publicly. Among the many eloquent critics, Yale psychologist Kenneth Keniston has observed that Masters and Johnson are, although unintentionally, "helping to perpetuate rather than to remedy some of the more prevalent ills of our time—the confusion of human sexuality with the physiology of sexual excitement, naivete with regard to the psychological meaning of the sexual act, and an inability to confront the ethical implications of sex." He also points out how little has been told of actual laboratory procedures and adds, "Masters and Johnson repeatedly reduce human sexuality to physical responses."

Dr. Natalie Shainess considers the Masters and Johnson view one in which "sex seems little more than a stimulus-response reflex cycle, devoid of intra-psychic or interpersonal meaning. . . . What is the attitude toward sex in a researcher who says, 'Masturbating women concentrate on their own sexual

The National Trust

Cerne Giant

1430. Jeanne d'Arc (Joan of Arc) and her French comrades retake Compiegne from the English, but she herself is captured later. At English instigation, the University of Paris demands that Joan be tried for sorcery. She is found guilty, burned at the stake, and her "accursed" ashes thrown into the River Seine.

demand without the distraction of a coital partner'? Distraction! Is that the meaning of a partner in sex? This points to a dehumanizing view even if it is necessary to consider the effect on an individual of giving command sexual performances in the presence of others."

But with all this, the fact remains that Masters and Johnson have recorded some sexual response cycles in women, and have done it in a way that helps clarify many issues for us. If we use their findings in a self-destructive way, it is we who are choosing to do so. It is probably too much to ask that they be humanitarians and love advisers, as well as intrepid researchers.

Some of the anatomical details Masters and Johnson unearthed are interesting and useful to know, certainly for gynecologists and perhaps for women. And yet the interest we express in their work is, above all, a testament to the abysmal limits put on us by our own timidity.

Certain marriage counselors have long maintained that a loving wife is content merely to satisfy her husband, for instance, and that it need be of no consequence if she fails to achieve satisfaction. We have Masters and Johnson to thank for convincing them that sexual frustration can even give a woman cramps and headache. But how sad it is that we had to wait for sex researchers to demonstrate it. Didn't we know it all the time?

If there is going to be a breakthrough in human sexuality—and I thank that such a breakthrough may be in the wind—it is going to occur because women will start taking charge of their own sex lives. It is going to occur because women will stop believing that sex is for men and that men (their fathers, their doctors, their lovers and husbands, their popes and kings and scientists) are the authorities. We need only study a little anthropology or history to understand that sexuality is incredibly plastic and easily repressed.

Women must discover and express their own sexuality, without shame or inhibition. And instead of following sex manuals or trusting the lockerroom sexpertise of their fellows, men must learn to seek and receive signals from the women they love.

Getting in Shape for Love

Lonnie Barbach

An important physical characteristic of the vagina is the large muscle that surrounds the opening; it also covers the whole pelvic floor (from the pubic bone to the tail bone). This is called the pubococcygeal muscle, or "PC muscle," and it is one of the muscles that contracts during orgasm. If you put your finger into the entrance to your vagina and/or the entrance to your anus or both during an orgasm, you usually can feel this muscle contract. This muscle may be lacking in tone in some women, especially after childbirth. Like any other muscle, the PC muscle needs exercise to keep it in its best condition. A series of exercises popularly referred to as "Kegels" were developed by Dr. Arnold Kegel for women with the common problem of urinary incontinence. These women would expel urine when they sneezed or coughed and these exercises were designed to tighten the PC muscle, and help them contain the urine. Many gynecologists recommend these exercises routinely to women after they have had a baby. "Kegeling" is also taught in many natural childbirth classes.

Some of the women who followed Dr. Kegel's advice reported that after about six weeks of practicing the exercises they experienced increased pleasure during sexual intercourse. The women I have worked with have also found that exercising this muscle increases sensitivity in the vaginal area. In addition, strengthening the PC muscle helps reduce spontaneous urination with orgasm, an occurrence which is not unusual among women. I highly recommend that you practice the following Kegel exercises.

To locate your pubococcygeal muscle, urinate with your legs apart; the muscle you squeeze to stop the flow of urine is the PC muscle. Practice stopping the flow of urine a few times in order to become familiar with the

1485. Pope Innocent VIII issues a bull affirming the existence of witches on earth. It is the duty of each decent citizen to hunt them, expose them, and, finally, to execute them.

muscle. Then, lie down and put your finger in the opening of your vagina and contract the PC muscle. See if you can feel the contraction around your finger.

After practicing the following exercises for about six weeks, see if you notice any difference in the strength of your PC muscle when you put your finger in your vagina and squeeze.

The first Kegel exercise consists of squeezing the PC muscle for three seconds, then relaxing the muscle for three seconds, and squeezing it again. At first, do ten three-second squeezes at three different times during the day. It may be difficult at first to keep contracting for a full three seconds. If that is the case, contract for one or two seconds and build up the time as the muscle gets stronger. The advantage to these exercises is that you can do them anywhere and at any time and no one can tell you're doing them. Practice when you stop the car for a red light or in the morning when you wake up. Or do them when you answer the telephone at home or at work, or when you are lying down to rest. The muscles surrounding your anus may also move during the exercise, but if you find that you are moving your thigh muscles, your stomach or buttocks, you are probably squeezing the wrong muscle.

The second exercise is like the first except that the objective is to squeeze the muscle, release it, squeeze again and release as quickly as possible. This is nicknamed the "flutter" exercise. Again, squeeze and release ten times at three different times during the day. When you first start doing this exercise, it may feel like a tongue twister; you may not be able to tell if you are contracting or releasing and for a while it may keep getting muddled all together. However, after working at it slowly, you will gradually be able to do the flutter more rapidly.

The third exercise consists of imagining that there is a tampon at the opening to the vagina and that you are sucking it up into your vagina.

The fourth exercise consists of bearing down as during a bowel movement, but with the emphasis more on the vagina than the anal area. This exercise is more apparent to an observer. Both the sucking in and the bearing down should be held for three seconds, as with the first exercise.

All four exercises should be practiced ten times each at three different times during the day. As you progress with these Kegel exercises, slowly increase the number in each series until you are able to do twenty of each exercise in succession. You can do them as frequently during the day as you can find time, but consider three times daily a minimum.

If you notice some discomfort or tightness in the pelvic area at the beginning, reduce the number of daily contractions, but do not abandon the exercises. Like any muscle that is being exercised for the first time, it may get a little stiff at first. It is quite important to keep this muscle, like others in your body, in tone. The exercises can become as much of a habit as brushing your teeth and, like brushing your teeth, they should be continued for the rest of your life.

Why Masturbation

Lonnie Barbach

Masturbation is one of the best ways to learn about your sexual responses. Once you learn about how you respond —through stimulating yourself while free of outside distractions—you will be in a better position to shift your own body movement during love-making to achieve more pleasure or to teach your partner how to stimulate you in the manner that is most likely to lead you to sexual pleasure and eventually to orgasm.

Of all sexual practices, masturbation is probably the most difficult to talk about. It is an intimate and very personal experience which we have been taught is dirty, sinful, shameful, even physically debilitating. The guilt, fear, anxiety, and repulsion that surrounds masturbation is astounding, especially when one realizes not only how pervasive it is among human beings, but how beneficial, pleasurable, and relaxing an experience it can be. Most importantly, from the standpoint of the pre-orgasmic woman, it is the surest, most effective way to achieve orgasmic release. Many women don't consider the orgasms they have with masturbation as being "real." They believe that "true orgasms" occur only during intercourse.

But all orgasms are real no matter how they are produced, although the total subjective experience may differ depending on the situation and mode of stimulation.

Sixty-two per cent of the women Kinsey interviewed masturbated, and only 4 to 6 per cent of these women masturbated without reaching orgasm. The ones who did experience orgasm were able to do so in 95 per cent of their masturbatory experiences. Hence, almost all women who masturbate enjoy orgasm through self-stimulation almost every time that they undertake to do so.

Over all, Kinsey found that "the type of premarital activity in which the female had acquired her experience did not appear to have been as important as the fact that she had or had not experienced orgasm." Women who had experienced orgasm premaritally, through any means, were able to respond orgasmically with marital sex three times as often as women who had no orgasmic experience prior to marriage. Masters and Johnson found that the orgasms produced by masturbation occurred more dependably, more rapidly, and were of greater intensity than those achieved through stimulation by a partner. These are just a few of the statistics that support the value of masturbation as an excellent way to go about discovering and learning about your own sexuality, and to achieve orgasm.

The reason self-stimulation works so well to produce orgasm is that you are the only one involved. There is

1488. "Mother Shipton" is born of a woman who claims the child to have been conceived in rape by the devil. A hunchback at birth and "affrightingly ugly of face," she nonetheless is to acquire an international reputation for "extraordinary understanding." Of her famous twenty prophecies of world significance, all but two will come true before 1645, exactly as forecast. Her predictions are concrete and unambiguous, but the most

no one else to distract you or for you to worry about pleasing. You can focus totally on yourself, take as much time as you need, and you don't need a partner who is willing to co-operate. You are the one in control, which has benefits. First of all, once you are free from being observed you can focus all your attention on the different kinds of touches, pressures, and positions. The instant feedback of self-stimulation allows you to change things to meet your needs.

If you are uncertain as to whether you have ever experienced orgasm or are certain that you haven't, masturbation can be the key to orgasmic discovery.

Once you have learned to overcome your inhibitions and abandon yourself to the physical sensations of orgasm with masturbation you may become more capable of responding in a similar way with your partner—if you want to. The successful experience of having orgasms with masturbation helps to build up positive expectations of having more orgasms by yourself and eventually with a partner. If you choose to continue to hold back the orgasm you can do so, but at least you'll have the choice.

Contrary to popular belief, women do not get "hooked" on masturbation, thereby becoming incapable of having orgasms in any other way.

Even if you achieve orgasm frequently there are many good reasons to masturbate. For example, masturbation is always available including times when your partner isn't—either because you are physically separated or be-

cause your lover is not in the mood at the same time that you are. Your ability to produce your own orgasm can reduce pressure on your partner to perform. Also, there may be times when you don't feel like interacting, times when you would prefer to be totally self-engrossed, forget the need to respond to him, and enjoy masturbation just for the relaxing satisfaction it provides you. Your mate can also benefit from your self-sufficiency. If you are self-sufficient, both people in the relationship gain more freedom to express their own needs in their own style rather than having to adapt their sexual tempo to that of a partner. And in no way need participation in masturbation be viewed as a reflection on the adequacy of the couple's sexual relationship. Masturbation can enlarge your sex life, not restrict it. Furthermore, masturbation can afford you a sense of control and self-confidence while helping you to like and enjoy your body better.

Still, a reasonable proportion of women don't masturbate for a variety of reasons. During the 1800s many books were written by physicians describing the horrors of masturbation.

Masturbation was alleged to cause warts on one's hands, hair on the palms of hands, blindness, acne, sterility, and deformed babies. It was deemed responsible for all sorts of psychological problems. The source of this belief is an interesting one. It appears that doctors observed institutionalized mental patients and found that they masturbated. Of course, it should be noted that because these people were institutionalized, no sexual outlet was available other than masturbation. Bizarre as it may sound, these were the observations that led to the conclusion that masturbation was the cause of the lunacy.

Other common reasons that prevent women from masturbating include moral proscription, not being aware that women could do it, or not knowing how to do it. Margaret Mead says, "The female child's genitals are less exposed, subject to less maternal manipulation and less self-manipulation." Therefore, it is likely that female children may fail to discover that their sex organs are sensitive to pleasurable stimulation.

Other obstacles to masturbating stem from the partner and the social situation. Many women feel a sense of self-devaluation if they masturbate, because they assume that a woman resorts to masturbation only if she can't get anything better.

Many men feel threatened by the idea that women masturbate, especially with a vibrator. A man may feel that if his partner can be sexually fulfilled on her own, she will have no need for him. He often does not recognize the previously mentioned advantages that masturbation affords him. What is inferred is that masturbation will lower a woman's desire for sexual contact with a partner. In reality, a study by Greenberg showed no statistically significant relation between the frequency of masturbation and the frequency of intercourse among the women polled. Most women who masturbate have enough sexual energy to allow for masturbation as well

amazing are the following, all of which—excepting the last line—are realized as late as four hundred years after her death (the exact date of which she also foretold):

"Carriages without horses shall go,
And accidents fill the world with woe.

as sexual activity with a partner.

A considerable number of women avoid masturbation because they consider it morally wrong. Several religious denominations have condemned masturbation, sometimes in the context of a broader condemnation of any sexual activity that is not aimed at reproduction, or because it reflects carnal as opposed to spiritual pursuits. These moral grounds have been a prime factor in preventing numerous women from beginning to masturbate. However, once a woman has discovered masturbation as a sexual release, evidence indicates that she will only rarely discontinue the practice because of religious condemnation. Instead, she is likely to continue masturbating while experiencing significant feelings of guilt.

Harmful effects of masturbation come from the worry or concern women have about the abnormality of the activity rather than from the activity itself. According to Kinsey ". . . some millions of the females in the United States, and larger number of males, have had their self-assurance, their social efficiency, and sometimes their sexual adjustments in marriage needlessly damaged—not by their masturbation, but by the conflict between practice and moral codes. There is no other type of sexual activity which has worried so many women."

It could hardly be expected that after reading these passages, you will automatically and magically lose all of the negative feelings you may have about masturbation. The first time that you contemplate it you probably won't feel very comfortable with the idea that self-stimulation is a good thing for you. But the act itself, and the positive learning about your sexual self that can be derived may, in time, make you more comfortable with the idea.

Despite the substantial negative conditioning surrounding the act of masturbation, Hunt and Kinsey both obtained figures that showed that 6o to 65 per cent of the women interviewed had masturbated at some time during their lives. Heterosexual petting is the form of sexual activity the largest number of females report participating in before marriage; coitus is the sexual activity most frequently performed after marriage; and masturbation is the second most common activity that women engage in both before and after marriage.

Females can stimulate themselves sexually in many ways. Most commonly, female masturbation consists of manipulating the clitoris, the inner lips, or the whole genital area. Or, by simply creating pressure by exerting muscular tension of the thighs and buttocks. Other methods include running water directly on the clitoris; use of a vibrator, douches, rubbing of the genitals against pillows, clothing, or other objects.

Masturbation can be the first step in becoming orgasmic. Not only is it a pleasurable and natural activity, but also it provides effective tools for change which will be used later.

The Pleasing Touch

Lonnie Barbach

If you follow the steps in this section carefully and closely, chances are excellent that you will be able to become orgasmic within several weeks of practice.

You will need to practice the exercises. An hour a day, *every day*, should be set aside for two to five weeks if you want to re-establish the sexual connections that have been disconnected for all these years.

Once you have made the decision to find an hour each day, think about how you can feel in a more sensual mood. Your mood is important, so pick a time when you are at ease and your energy level is fairly high. Take a long shower or bath; bring some fresh flowers into the room, light some candles, or burn some incense if you like. Or do whatever will create a sensual scene for you. Pretend a lover is returning from a long trip and arrange the room in the kind of romantic setting you know you both would enjoy. Lie down and enjoy the time; one of your favorite lovers can be you.

In our culture achieving sexual ease and comfort does not come naturally, any more than learning to walk would if you had spent your early years contained in a small box. In order to have orgasmic sexual experiences you may have to learn about sexual stimulation from the beginning, in the comfortable setting you've designed for yourself. Don't rush things. You have lots of time. All you need is practice and determination. You have to begin feeling that you have the right to an orgasm, for yourself, rather than to keep your partner from feeling inadequate as a lover; you deserve the pleasure that a satisfying sexual relationship can bring.

For now, concentrate on learning to have an orgasm on your own through self-stimulation. Later you can concentrate on transferring the orgasm to the partner relationship.

Examine your body thoroughly, visually and through touch, for that first hour. During your hour the next day, examine your genitals with a mirror and explore each area to see if you notice any difference in sensitivity or sensations in the various parts of the genital area. Don't forget the Kegel exercises.

The exercise for the third night is to begin the actual masturbation. You may need to use some oil—massage oil, baby oil, coconut oil, or even vegetable oil will do. Do not use Vaseline; it is not water soluble and can cause problems if it gets in the vagina or urethra. Scented massage oils can add to your sensual experience, but be careful that the oil contains no alcohol, since alcohol can irritate the mucous membranes of the genitals.

Use oil, saliva, or the natural lubrication of the vagina to keep the genital tissues moist so that no irritation de-

Around the world thoughts shall fly
In the twinkling of an eye.
The world upside down shall be,
And gold be found at the root of a tree
Through hills man shall ride

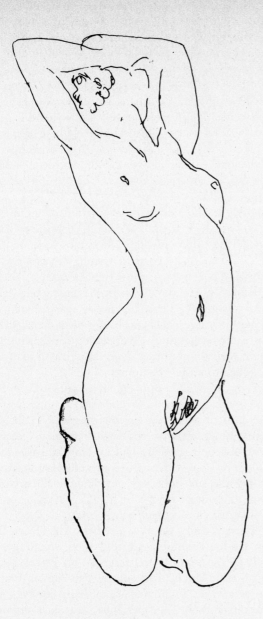

Kneeling Nude, Arms Overhead
by Henri Matisse, 1918

velops. Explore by stimulating the area with various types of strokes and pressures. What do very light feathery touches feel like? How about harder rubbing? Try massaging the clitoral area with your fingertips by making gentle but firm circular motions. Some women like to stimulate the glans of the clitoris directly while others find this area too sensitive for direct stimulation and prefer to massage the areas directly surrounding the clitoris above, below, or to the sides. Find out what feels best for you. Many women rub one finger back and forth over the clitoris with varying speeds and intensity. Or the clitoris could be massaged between the forefinger and middle finger, massaging also the whole area by stroking up and down the clitoral shaft. Many women enjoy having their fingers or something else in their vagina while the clitoris is being stroked.

If you notice some irritation of the area, you may be rubbing the skin surface rather than the structures below. A deeper type of rubbing generally produces less irrita-

tion to the genitals; rub as though you were massaging a tense muscle and wanted to reach the structures below the skin. It may take a day or two for the genital area to get used to the stimulation.

Remember, you're on a fact-finding mission now. You're learning. Feel whatever there is to feel. Don't hold back in anticipation; don't measure your sensations. Instead, just tune in to any feelings that you do experience and enjoy them.

In our groups we found that women tend to get stymied at various stages in the process of self-stimulation. The most consistent initial difficulty is finding the time to practice. Women try masturbating once or twice for a short period of time and, feeling discouraged and guilty, conclude that there never will be any hope for them, that there must be an easier way—and they give up. Many women require an hour every day for two to five weeks, so if you don't feel anything during the first few days, stick with it. You have lots of time ahead of you.

And no horse be at his side.
Under water man shall walk,
Shall ride, shall sleep, shall talk.
In the air men shall be seen,
In white, in black, in green.

If you're still finding masturbation and the thought of it disagreeable and offensive, don't try to fight the feelings. Exaggerate them! While you are stimulating yourself, let yourself feel disgusted. Make disagreeable sounds and exaggerate the motions that offend you. Stay with the foolish or uncomfortable feelings. Exaggerating them for a couple of hours should help to neutralize your negative feelings about the exercise.

Another difficulty that may arise for many women is that they say they feel *nothing*, even after a number of days of consistent practice. If you are one of these women, let's compare with your expectations the feelings you label as "nothing." Are you really feeling nothing? Compare the feeling in your clitoris to that in your elbow. Any difference? A good strategy is to concentrate on what *is* happening rather than on what is not happening. At the beginning you are looking for information about yourself—*not* instant orgasm. Even negative information—discovering the things that don't turn you on—is important.

Involve other parts of your body in addition to your genitals in the sexual stimulation. Massage your inner thighs, breasts or nipples, or other erotically sensitive areas with one hand as you stimulate the genital area with the other. Stimulate any sensitive area in the manner that feels best to you. You, and you alone, know what is most exciting and pleasurable to you.

Don't forget the mental aphrodisiacs. Erotic writings, pictures or films, and fantasy can help take your mind off the cares of the day and focus it on the sensual feelings. Edna had her first orgasm after returning from seeing her first pornographic movie. Many women enjoy the "most patient lover" fantasy. Pretend that you are making love and your lover is infinitely patient. Your lover is willing to do anything and everything for you. A second enjoyable fantasy might be to imagine yourself as the world's most sensuous woman who is teaching an inexperienced lover the art of pleasing a woman.

Using muscular tension by rhythmically contracting the muscles in the pelvic and thigh region, or doing the Kegels while stimulating the clitoral area manually can

enhance your pleasure. A glass of wine or a martini might relax you for your hour so that you are better able to concentrate on the good feelings. If you find that your mind wanders while you are masturbating, take some time off to think about various nonerotic things. We all need some time to daydream, so acknowledge that need.

Let yourself go. Experiment. Darlene found it a turn-on to do the exercises while partially clothed. She said she felt like a dancer in a burlesque show and the thought really enhanced her sexual mood. Also, remember that music may either enhance arousal, or it can interfere with it.

You might find that without the aid of group support to make you stick with it, it's likely that you will find all sorts of ways to procrastinate. Here are some of the common problems I have heard from the women in the groups, and also ways to solve them. Perhaps by recognizing them you can devise ways to get beyond the early natural resistance. If you've never masturbated before, your natural urges have probably been blocked by factors in your background. Overcoming these factors means sticking with the exercises even though you may find the task difficult at the beginning.

Evelyn complained that her hand got tired, so we suggested more movement of the fingers and less of the whole arm or vice versa depending upon the muscles which were being affected. If this problem persists, cut the exercise time down to half an hour and add five minutes to your time with each succeeding day until you are spending the full hour. It's very common for women to require an hour or even two hours of stimulation before that first orgasm occurs.

Margaret would do the exercises for fifteen seconds while reading pornography and then would get so involved in the reading that she would forget about the manual stimulation. Remember that discontinuing the physical stimulation in females usually lowers the level of sexual arousal. To experience your first orgasm it is important to keep your level of physical arousal high.

If this process is going to work, you have to really want the orgasm. If you don't think it worth the effort or if you don't expect results, you will probably be the victim of a self-fulfilling prophecy. Because you don't really try, it will fail.

If you've been practicing the exercises for an hour a day for about ten days to two weeks and still aren't getting aroused (I don't mean not having orgasms, I mean not having any sexual feelings at all), there are some nonmanual techniques that may be just what you need to awaken your sexual feelings. I don't recommend using these techniques at the outset because I've found that it is better for women to touch themselves directly, to become comfortable with the genital area and get used to their bodies and their sexual feelings. In the long run, directly confronting the negative and guilty feelings that arise can make us much more relaxed and at ease with sex.

Iron in the water shall float,
As easily as a wooden boat.
Gold shall be found and shown
In a land that's now not known.
Fire and water shall wonders do;

A good compromise would be to use a vibrator or the running water technique as an addition to manual masturbation. It might make good sense to begin with manual stimulation and then after about ten to fifteen minutes employ another technique. Or, use one method one day and another the next day.

Many children discover the running water or bathtub technique. It consists of lying in the tub and maneuvering your body so that the genitals are directly under the faucet (this may not be physically possible given the shape of your body and the design of your tub); or attach a small hose to the faucet. Direct the stream of warm water onto the clitoral area. The sensation produced is akin to that of a thousand tiny fingers rapidly moving over the genitals. The pressure of the water on this sexually sensitive area can produce an orgasm. I say "can" because, as with other types of stimulation, it is possible to fight the orgasm and prohibit it from happening, despite the effectiveness of the physical stimulation. I shall discuss this process in greater detail later. The best thing to do is to get used to the sensations gradually. Stay under the water for a while and then move away when you begin feeling some sensations that are unfamiliar to you. Then move under again as you gradually become more comfortable with these new feelings.

Another popular alternate technique is to use one of the many types of vibrator/massagers available at most drug and department stores. They can also be ordered by mail. An electric one is generally preferable. The inexpensive battery operated massagers are fine for some women, but many complain that they are noisier than the electric ones. Heating elements do not seem to be important, but a massager equipped with a variety of attachments can afford the versatility required for individual preferences. The small ball-shaped attachment appears to be a favorite among many women. Again, choice here is totally individual. Some women prefer a gentle vibrator while others like a heavier, more intense machine. If the sensation is too strong, use a towel or some clothing between your body and the vibrator to soften the intensity.

Some women are hesitant to use a vibrator for fear that they will get "hooked" on it and not be able to have orgasms any other way. First of all, if you haven't been experiencing orgasm any other way, using a vibrator surely can do no harm, especially since there is an excellent chance that you'll become orgasmic this way. Secondly, there is no evidence that women who have orgasms with vibrators are unable to have orgasms with other kinds of stimulation. However, stimulation produced by using water or a vibrator is significantly different from other forms of stimulation, so women who may be orgasmic easily with a vibrator may have to spend more time when other types of stimulation are used. A vibrator sometimes stimulates the urethra, which may result in unintentional urination, but this should cause no alarm. If this should happen to you, practice the Kegel

exercises. Urinate before using the vibrator and put a towel on the bed if it makes you feel more secure. But really, why should we be so concerned over expelling a few drops of urine? A vibrator may be equivalent to using training wheels to learn to ride a bicycle. You get the feeling of what the experience is like and then, if you want to, you can practice without the machine. However, there is no reason to stop using a vibrator, either alone or with a partner, if you enjoy it. Many women have very successfully integrated the vibrator into their sexual relationship with a partner before, during, after, or instead of intercourse. Some men enjoy the sensation of the vibrator on their body and genitals too.

If the masturbation is working and you are beginning to feel new and different sexual feelings, you may find this as upsetting as not feeling any sensations at all. Angela found that the more she became interested in sex and enjoyed it, the more guilty she felt. As we feel more, it seems that the old sexual taboos come back to haunt us. We think we have gotten over the guilt and fears, and then they show up again to plague us once more: Maybe we really will lose consciousness or become a nymphomaniac.

As you masturbate, let the fears come. Try to make them bigger; then smaller. Have fun changing the size and intensity of the fears. Play with them and let them wash over you like waves. Getting to know them well can keep them from seeming so overwhelming, so scary, and can keep them from interfering with your sexual progress.

Some women experience intense feelings when they first begin the masturbation assignments and then suddenly feel nothing during successive efforts. If this happens to you, don't worry—if you could feel the sensations once, you can feel them again. More than likely, the intensity of the initial sensations frightened you and caused you to hold back. Discontinue the masturbation for a few days and then very slowly begin again.

Become familiar with your new sexual feelings. You don't have to discover the whole range of feelings in one day or even one week. Move on slowly and push a little bit further ahead each time.

Getting close to orgasm often feels like a sneeze that doesn't quite happen. Frequently, reaching these high levels of excitement without release can be as irritating and frustrating as that lost sneeze. The women with whom I work call these levels of excitation "plateaus." All the excitement and sexual tension is there, but they just can't find a way to move beyond to orgasm. After a number of sessions that stop at this plateau, women can become quite demoralized and discouraged.

The responsibility for overcoming this last barrier to reaching orgasm is primarily yours. Try to push beyond this point by stimulating yourself a few seconds beyond the time when you would ordinarily stop. With each succeeding session, continue the stimulation until you reach a level of slightly higher intensity before stopping. Sometimes the feelings will build and at other times they

England shall at last admit a foe.
The world to an end will come
In eighteen hundred and eighty-one.
As fantastic as these utterances seem in her day, Mother Shipton accurately describes
the advent of automobiles, airplanes, electronic communications, submarines and scuba

Masturbation
THE SEX ADVISER 165

will diminish. Just at the point you may think that you've lost them forever, they may suddenly return.

If you are stuck at the high plateau level but have not succeeded in going over it to experience the release of orgasm, you're probably expending as much energy fighting the orgasm as you are trying to make it happen. Relax, but don't stop the stimulation. There is one kind of muscular tension that fights the orgasm and another kind that enhances it. If you feel your whole body becoming a tightened spring, try to relax, but continue to stimulate the genital area. Breathe deeply; imagine the air being breathed in and out of your vagina, rather than your mouth. This helps to ease the anxiety. Change positions to eliminate some of the excess tension. If breathing deeply and regularly doesn't work, maybe you need to hold your breath. Lydia found that holding her breath helped her get over the plateau stage while Sally experienced just the opposite. Experiment with several different breathing patterns to see what works for you; for example some women prefer panting in short rhythmic gasps. If you are becoming extremely frustrated, get up and take a thirty-second walk; look out the window. One of the women in the group would get up and brush her teeth when she felt stuck. Stopping won't cause you to lose the feelings completely. They'll return when you start to stimulate yourself again.

Building up sexual tension, letting it ebb and then increasing it again, can produce a level of arousal that some women experience as frightening. Some women fear that the release won't be great enough for the tension that has been built up. Or, that the release will be too great. How can you be sure that you won't explode or disintegrate if all that tension is released? Intellectually, you may know that you won't, but the intensity of the feelings could make you hold back.

Some women find that it helps if they role-play. When they reach a plateau, they move their body around as if they were having an orgasm. Exaggerate the pretend orgasm. Act as if it were very intense. Make lots of sounds and exaggerate the body movements. Sarah did this and to her surprise a real orgasm followed soon after the simulated one.

Don't give up, but if you feel discouraged and frustrated don't pretend that those feelings don't exist either. Rather, attempt to get in deeper touch with them. Allow your whole body to feel discouraged. Consider the possibility that you may never allow yourself to take that final leap, because only you can do it for yourself. Janice was very discouraged and I told her to get in touch with the fact that she might never have an orgasm. I told her to go home and really think about that possibility. This really made her angry. She said, "Why should I get in touch with never having an orgasm? I've been in touch with that for thirty years. I'm not going to think about that. I'm going to have it if it kills me!" And she did—the very next day.

Don't forget about experimenting with the expression of other feelings too if you have a tendency to keep everything, including sexual feelings, safely locked inside. Holding emotions inside requires a tremendous amount of energy, energy that could be better used in being creative, productive, feeling intimate and sexual. Experiment for a week or two. Allow your feelings to "hang out" for that length of time by expressing the feelings as soon as you feel them. If you tend to cover things over with a smile it may be especially important to practice expressing feelings. Ellen had a fight with her husband. It was the first time she had expressed her angry feelings in a long time. She did the exercises that night and had her first orgasm. She said it measured 10 on the Richter scale.

In general, however, first orgasms are not very intense. They take a long time to achieve and may be barely noticeable. Sometimes women are disappointed after all the work and effort. The lack of intensity in the beginning frequently results from the amount of energy invested in fighting the orgasm. As you experience more orgasms and become less afraid and anxious, the orgasms can become more intense.

After experiencing the first orgasm, many women become afraid that they won't be able to have another one. Frequently, they repeat the exercises immediately to see if it can happen again.

It takes a while before you can be comfortable and assured that orgasm will occur. Most of the time it will. Occasionally it won't so don't worry, it's not lost. You may have to relax a bit more, or be more in the mood.

Sometimes the orgasm doesn't come simply because you're trying to force it to happen. It seems that when the pressure is turned on, the orgasm is turned off. Laurie found it helped to be able just to enjoy the feelings without having to reach an orgasm. Inevitably, when she could relax and just feel good with no goal in mind, the orgasm would occur. Sexual sensations ebb and flow. You may feel turned on, and then lose the feeling. There is no need to struggle for the lost sensation as another one will develop soon if you relax.

First, learn to be comfortable about having orgasms on your own. Then, you can try to integrate them into your love-making with your partner—if you want to.

Once you are experiencing orgasms with masturbation you may find at first that sex with your partner can be disappointing. This is not uncommon. Polly became comfortable with masturbation, and enjoyed the orgasms which resulted, but she felt frustrated by love-making with her partner because she could not attain the same release. Soon, however, when the novelty of the masturbation wore off, Polly renewed her interest in partner sex again.

Whether or not you are orgasmic with your partner, there is no reason to stop masturbating. Instead of looking at self-stimulation from an antiquated perspective—as a substitute for the "real thing"—why not view it as one of many alternative forms of sexual expression—provided by nature for a party of one.

gear, steel ships; the discovery of gold in California, Alaska, and Australia; steam power; and three invasions of England. This particular prophecy is repeatedly published and ridiculed each succeeding century until suddenly it begins to come true. Then, with 1881 hard by, entire English towns and cities empty and flee to the hills, their populations numbly prepared to watch Judgment Day and to receive their fate.

Coital Positions

Derek Llewellyn-Jones, M.D.

Embraces carved in stone: above, the ancient temple at Orissa, India; below, The Kiss by Brancusi.

Sexual intercourse can take place in a variety of positions. These have been described in the literature of all cultures, and ancient Indian literature is particularly informative, as shown by Vatsyayana's *Kama-Sutra*, written in 200 B.C., and in the sculptures on the temples of Khajuraho. Basically, the positions can be reduced to about half a dozen, all of which are 'normal'.

Face to face, the man on top: The man lies on top of the woman, either putting his weight upon her, or supporting most of his weight on his elbows or hands. She spreads her legs apart, and may for variety flex her knees, sometimes placing them around her partner's waist. She may place a pillow beneath her buttocks to lift her pelvis. There are many variations of this basic position. The women may keep her legs stretched out, her partner's legs inside hers, or she may bring her legs together, so that her partner's knees are outside. She may flex her thighs more so that her legs are clasped round his shoulders.

This position is the most usual, and has the advantage that it makes penile entry into the vagina easy; the bodies of the two partners are in close proximity so that they can kiss and caress each other during coitus; it permits the male to set the pace and slow or hasten coitus to reach an orgasm at a desired speed; and it is probably the best position for pregnancy to occur, as after ejaculation the seminal fluid bathes the cervix. The disadvantages of the position are that it restricts the woman's movements and thrusts; male orgasm is often reached too quickly; penetration may be painfully deep, and the male is unable to caress the woman's clitoris during coitus, which she may desire.

Face to face, woman on top: The man lies on his back, the woman squats over him and guides his penis into her vagina. Once this has occurred, she may lie upon him, her weight resting on his body; she may support her weight on her arms; or she may sit upright across his thighs. The man may lie flat, raise himself on his arms, or clasp his legs around the woman's waist.

This position is an advantage if the man is very heavy, his wife light in weight. In it the women has the greatest freedom of movement, and the male can caress her clitoris and vulval area during coitus.

The disadvantages are that some women cannot control the depth of penile penetration too easily, and it may be too deep and so painful. During coitus the man's penis may slip out of the vagina, which is uncomfortable for both and spoils smooth coital sequence.

Man's face to woman's back, rear entry: There are several variations of this position. The man may lie behind the

Adapted from *Everywoman and Her Body* by Derek Llewellyn-Jones (Taplinger Publishing Company 1971). Copyright © 1971 Derek Llewellyn-Jones. Reprinted by permission.

1492. Queen Isabella and King Ferdinand of Spain—ignoring scholars' predictions of failure—become convinced that Columbus's plans to reach the Indies by sailing west may, in fact, work. The monarchs give him three ships, and he sets forth on August 3. On October 12 he sights land—not the Indies, however, but America.

Paul C. Cabot III

Philadelphia Museum of Art

Pages from Orissan postures manual

Red figure cup, Triptolemos painter

woman, his hands around her to caress her breasts or clitoris. She lies in front of him, her legs bent at the hips, her body slightly curved away from his. The man's penis is inserted into the woman's vagina from the rear, and once inside she presses her thighs together and pushes backwards so that her buttocks make a firm contact against his lower abdomen and scrotum. Alternatively, she may lie on her stomach with her pelvis raised and her legs apart. The man lies on top of her, entering her vagina from the rear. Or she may kneel on hands and knees, her head and breast touching the bed, the man kneeling behind her. In another variation, the man sits on the edge of a chair, or the bed, and the woman, with her back to him, sits upon his penis and as it slips into her vagina, eases herself onto his lap.

The advantages of these positions are that the contact of the woman's buttocks on the man's abdomen, legs and scrotum may stimulate them both; he can readily caress her breasts or her clitoris during coitus; and the couple can rest on their sides during coitus. In late pregnancy, this position is the most suitable one.

Face to face, side by side: This position is, in fact, not exactly side by side, for penile entry would be almost impossible if it were. Usually the couple's legs are interlocked, and the man may lie largely on his back, the woman resting on his chest, or, alternatively, the woman may lie largely on her back, one thigh beneath him.

Sitting positions: The man sits on a chair, or the edge of the bed, and the woman sits astride his lap, his penis within her vagina, his arms around her body, and hers around his. Alternatively, the man can squat behind the woman's thighs, as she lies on her back facing him, with her legs on his hips. He can then make thrusting motions, or pull the woman's pelvis back and forth. Another alternative is for the woman to squat between the man's thighs, supporting her weight on her outstretched arms, whilst he lies on

ca. **1500.** Any woman in the kingdom of Ceylon allowing herself to be religiously "contaminated" through intermarriage between herself and a member of a lower caste runs a high risk: She automatically forfeits all her property and rights to inheritance and is liable to even more severe measures by her family, who may kill her.

his back with his legs apart. Once his penis is inside her vagina, she moves her pelvis in a circular fashion.

Standing positions: By bending his legs, the man can introduce his penis either facing the woman, or from the rear. She may put her hands around his neck and clasp his hips between her thighs. The couple may move around during coitus, or coitus may take place in surroundings different from normal, such as during a shower.

The advantages of the sitting and standing positions are that they may be more exciting because they are unusual and not used routinely.

Extravaginal coitus

The man may obtain stimulation by rubbing his penis between the woman's thighs, or between her breasts. The sole advantage of these positions, apart from variety, is that the chance of conception occurring is remote, although ejaculation outside the vulva may lead to conception.

One notorious extravaginal position is quite normal and often followed by a deep emotional release. This is the simultaneous caressing of the woman's clitoris and vulva by the man's tongue, whilst she puts his penis in her mouth and caresses it with her tongue until they both have a simultaneous orgasm.

For sexual intercourse to be truly satisfying, the penile entry into the vagina, or caressing with the tongue, should only come at the end of a sequence of foreplay activities which draw the bonds between the partners closer, surrounding them with feelings of warmth to each other, and joy in their mutual embraces. Sexual intercourse is not just a silent monotonous thrust of an urgent penis into an indifferent vagina. It is a complex, varied group of activities leading to the maximum sexual joy for both participants.

Red figure cup, Briseis painter

1503. Mona Lisa, an obscure merchant's wife, becomes a portrait model for Leonardo da Vinci, who works over the painting for four years. It has since presided over many tragedies of the French royal family, one in particular, the breakup of King Louis XVI and his wife Queen Marie Antoinette, aggravated, some say, by his profound admiration of the face and her distaste for "that smirking monster." The picture has figured in

Improving Your Sex Life
Albert Ellis

1. Be more communicative and expressive about your sex desires and feelings. Some male partners will resent this. Perhaps, this is the best way to discover those individuals who cannot or will not attempt to satisfy their partners sexually as well as emotionally. When you have, perhaps by the process of active experimentation and elimination, found a partner who is more than willing to learn what pleases and displeases you, confess, as fully as you can, your enthusiasms and your limitations. Let him know how you feel!

2. Be assertive. *Go* after what you want, in action as well as words. In looking for a suitable partner, don't merely wait to be chosen—actively **choose!. . .Women in our culture, in spite of women's lib, still shy away from actively selecting and pursuing a male of their choice because they foolishly construe being rejected as horrible, terrible, and demeaning.**

In rational-emotive psychology, I and my associates teach that rejection is merely rejection. It is frustrating, annoying, and inconvenient; but that's *all* it is. It has nothing to do with one's value as a human; it presents no evidence that the rejected person will be continually rejected in the future. Quite the contrary! The more you risk failure, at almost anything, the more you will normally succeed. For, statistically, you will increase your chances; and you will also get the practice and the experience that will enhance your skills and make you more likely to make the right move the next time.

As with dating and love, so with sex. If you want your mate to please you with certain coital and noncoital methods, tell him what you want. And instruct him nonverbally. Take his finger, for example, and put it on your clitoral region and show him how to massage this area to your satisfaction. Put your breast into his mouth and let him kiss and suck it. Without asking, give him the best kind of soul kiss that you know how to give, and see if you can get him to enjoy it.

3. Consider your own likes and preferences, and your individual differences from other humans. Don't think that because *many* or *most* women enjoy *x* or abhor *y* sex activity, you must, to be "normal" and "healthy" enjoy or abhor the same modes. . . .

Try to discover, experimentally, what *you* really want; and do your damnedest to get it. You don't *have* to equal or surpass any other women in your sex-love proclivities. You may. . .enjoy intercourse without. . .orgasm. You may enjoy orgasm without requiring much precoital play. You may enjoy "foreplay" as an end in itself. You may even find little enjoyment, throughout your life, in sexual activities and still experience a highly emotional, full love life. The important thing is: what do *you* want in this area of your life? Seek; experiment; find!

4. Both ultraconventionality and rampant unconventionality may be unrewarding and unhealthy for you as an individual. . . You. . .might be well advised to be sexually independent, as well as to look for other than purely sexual values and to try to make your sex and your love lives somewhat coterminous. You certainly can have sex partners that you hardly care for, and have love partners that don't send you in bed. But although sex and love don't *necessarily* have to go together, it is frequently *preferable* when they do.

5. Don't let yourself get compulsively hung up on any one form of sex. In the old days, almost all single and married partners were fixated on intercourse, and insisted that unless they ended up, at least, with this form of sexual performance, their acts were "abnormal," "perverse," "unnatural," or "unhealthy." During the last quarter of a century this kind of monolithic, and essentially puritanic, attitude toward sex, has largely disappeared. Almost all the present authorities in the field quite agree that noncoital sex acts are not deviant—unless they are performed in some rigid, compulsive, phobic manner. . . .

6. In more ways than one, use your head. Kinsey and his associates

Adapted from Albert Ellis, epilogue to *Sex and the Intelligent Woman* by Manfred F. DeMartino, pp. 279—284. Copyright © 1974 Springer Publishing Co., 200 Park Avenue South, New York, New York. Reprinted with permission.

implied that females are "naturally" inferior to men in their ability to fantasize sexually. Maybe they were right; but the evidence in this study of intelligent women, as well as that recently amassed by Nancy Friday and other investigators, tends to belie their conclusion. . . Bright women have considerable ability to fantasize sexually, and probably often surpass men in this respect.

Not—let me again warn—that you *must* develop your capacity to dream up sexually arousing images. Not at all. Women, like most men, fairly easily perform at least two different kinds of mental focusing when they masturbate or engage in interpersonal sex. They are quite capable of fantasizing, that is, imagining romantic or sexualized "stories" in their heads, and seeing themselves engaging in various kinds of acts with humans, animals, or objects. Like men, they can range far and wide in these sex-love fantasies; women can deliberately get themselves from a state of passivity to one of extremely high arousal and can help themselves achieve orgasmic reactions.

Secondly, even more frequently perhaps than men, women are able to focus intently on sexual and and sensual sensations, and thereby enhance their own reactions. Physical focusing is a natural part of the human repertoire; very few individuals are totally incapable of doing it. In the progressive relaxation technique of Dr. Edmund Jacobsen, for example, people are taught (or teach themselves) to focus intently on the various muscles of their bodies and to relax these muscles, so that finally they achieve a state of almost complete muscular repose, and sometimes fall asleep.

Sensual-sexual focusing is somewhat the opposite of this relaxation process, and achieves exciting rather than quiescent results. It may even be a required part of heightened stimulation. . . .

When a woman (or a man) does not utilize concrete fantasies to stimulate herself and help bring on orgasm, she frequently seems to focus, quite cerebrally, on her own sensations. She concentrates on her genital feelings, or on lip, breast, or other sexualized feelings. She literally heightens her passions by partially blocking out other thoughts and sensory input and by temporarily obsessing herself, as it were, with her own sensual-sexual responses. If she does not do this, she may have trouble getting fully aroused and going "over the top."

So, if you do not already do this "naturally," teach yourself to focus. Pay close attention to your general and specific sexual sensations. During masturbation and partnership sex play, see that your genital area—especially your clitoral region—is adequately stimulated; and, at the same time, get into your vulva with your head. Focus; think; center yourself on your physical reactions. Force yourself, if necessary, to concentrate on your erogenous zones. Keep yourself focused there, until you are aroused and verging on orgasm. You may slip back and forth, if you wish, from pictoral fantasy to sensate focusing; or you may concentrate mainly on one of these two different kinds of sexualized ideation. As ever, experiment. It is likely that you will, thereby, enhance your reactivity.

7. Knowledge is power. If you and your partner can communicate openly with each other, both of you will learn about each other's particular sexual pleasures and consequently will be able to achieve maximum satisfaction. There are other sources of sex knowledge from which both of you can learn, including: magazines, books, films, recordings, and other types of written and spoken communications.

So-called pornography often comes up in this respect. Women, according to the Kinsey researchers, are usually not as aroused or as enthusiastic about "pornographic" presentations as are men;. . . however, many women thrive, as it were, on "obscene" writings and illustrations and find that their sex lives, including those with their husbands, at least temporarily are enhanced by this kind of reading and viewing.

Highly sexualized presentations, moreover, are often educational. When asked what the important factors in promoting the sexual revolu-

countless suicides, crimes, and general breaches of the peace among those who view it. Today, countless love letters are laid at its feet in the museum, while numberless women have attempted to shred it. Some who gaze steadily at the painting claim her expression changes from one of placidity to either lush sensuality or sneering ridicule. When it was

Museo del Prado, Madrid

Garden of Earthly Delights, by Heironymus Bosch

tion in the Western world during the last decade are, I point out that one of these factors is the wide dissemination of hard-core "pornography." Ever since Grove Press won the legal fight to publish the works of Henry Miller, the Marquis de Sade, and many other classic writers of "obscene" material, millions of modern women have been reading "pornographic" books, where previously this type of reading was almost exclusively the privilege of males. Although many of these women are not aroused by such writings, and some are even repelled, they have incidentally learned about many sex practices—such as oral-genital and anal-genital relations—that they were aware of only vaguely. They have consequently been much more prone to try these practices in their own bedrooms and have often added considerably to their sexual repertoires.

If you are a full-blooded female, seek a wide range of sexual information. Beware, however, of some of the fictional presentations, such as *Fanny Hill* and *The Story of O,* that are truly just that—man-made imaginings of the way women presumably react. Even these fictional portrayals may give you ideas with which you may experiment. You may also purchase, on any paperback newsstand today, nonfictional manuals

that, along with some exaggerated "sensuosity" allegations, will give you some excellent suggestions to choose among.

8. Be aware of and work to overcome your general emotional inhibitions which may impair your sex-love functioning. Like men, women in our culture are often terrified about being generally disapproved of and unloved; and they have, in innumerable instances, enormous fears of sexual failure. They frequently tend to have unrealistic notions of how they *should, ought,* and *must* succeed in their sex-love relationships; these irrational ideas sabotage much of their potential or actual involvement.

If you are blocked significantly in your sex or love life, your real problem may well be general rather than specific. Your self-downing tendencies about *anything* may easily sabotage and spoil your sex-love affairs. Once you learn to fully accept yourself, with whatever your failings happen to be, you are much more likely to have a good love life. Through self-analysis (guided by adequate reading) or by more direct professional help (with a competent, reputable therapist), you may well be able to help yourself.

stolen in 1912, the Parisian police received thousands of letters, half being jubilant celebrations of the loss, half sorrowfully deploring the theft. One read, "I have taken her, that monster of the Renaissance! Her diabolical smile shall no longer mock an honest Frenchman."

No-nonsense Therapy for Six Sexual Malfunctions

Helen Singer Kaplan

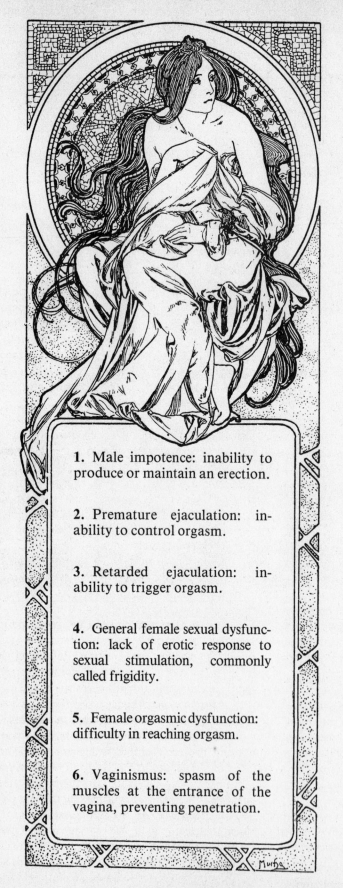

1. Male impotence: inability to produce or maintain an erection.

2. Premature ejaculation: inability to control orgasm.

3. Retarded ejaculation: inability to trigger orgasm.

4. General female sexual dysfunction: lack of erotic response to sexual stimulation, commonly called frigidity.

5. Female orgasmic dysfunction: difficulty in reaching orgasm.

6. Vaginismus: spasm of the muscles at the entrance of the vagina, preventing penetration.

SINCE WILLIAM H. MASTERS AND VIRGINIA E. JOHNSON published their research on the physiology of sexual intercourse, and talk about sex has become respectable, a growing number of men and women know they are being cheated. They are seeking help at new sex therapy clinics throughout the nation.

In our clinic at Cornell University Medical School, we see couples who have one or more of the six basic sexual problems.

As sex therapists we deal first and foremost with immediate sexual problems, so that women and men can enjoy sex to its fullest. However, we also attack the conflicts and defenses that are obstacles to sexual functioning. We are, of course, concerned with *why* a man persists in wilting his erection by obsessively monitoring his own behavior, or why he is so worried about performing sexually, or what experiences and fantasies make a woman so insecure that she cannot ask her lover to stimulate her clitoris. But we are primarily interested in teaching individuals to abandon themselves completely to the erotic experience of sexual intercourse.

To do this, we teach patients sexual exercises to remove the immediate anxieties and defenses that create and maintain their anti-erotic environment. We employ psychotherapy when deep anxieties or underlying pathologies impede our progress. I present a detailed discussion of our philosophy and treatment in *The New Sex Therapy,* published by Brunner/Mazel.

Friction and Fantasy. We begin treatment of all sexual dysfunctions with a psychiatric examination of both partners, a detailed history and assessment of their sexual functioning, and an evaluation of the marital relationship. We give the couple a clear picture of what to expect during treatment, and we make a therapeutic contact with them that clearly establishes their responsibility for treatment.

Adapted and reprinted from *Psychology Today* Magazine, October 1974. Copyright © 1974 Ziff-Davis Publishing Company. All rights reserved.

1505. Margaret, countess of Richmond and mother of England's King Henry VII, founds Christ's College, and later, Saint John's College, at the University of Cambridge.

Sex is composed of friction and fantasy; deficiencies in either can produce problems. A pleasurable sexual response depends both on receiving the proper sexual stimulation and responding freely to it. Most couples with sexual problems practice poor, insensitive and ineffectual sexual techniques.

Some inadequate lovemaking results merely from a couple's misinformation or ignorance about sex. Frequently, for instance, neither spouse knows where the clitoris is or recognizes its potential for eliciting erotic pleasure. They have intercourse as soon as the husband has an erection, and he ejaculates without considering whether his partner is ready. Such couples genuinely wonder why the wife does not reach orgasm. Both partners contribute to this sexual ineffectiveness. She will not ask for the kind of stimulation she wants because she is unaware of her own needs; he doesn't know that he's not a very effective lover. So, in silence, they continue their unsatisfactory sexual habits.

In other couples, feelings of guilt or anxiety about erotic needs prevent one or both partners from enjoying sex. They may actively discourage their partners from stimulating them effectively. Careful questioning often reveals that such persons respond to sexual excitement by immediately stopping the activity which produces it. The man who is excited by an actively seductive woman may literally forbid his wife to be aggressive. The woman who is responsive only to slow tender caresses may push her husband away when he tries to kiss her breasts or to caress her buttocks. Patients who avoid effective sexual expression tend to focus on genital stimulation and on orgasm, and are apt to neglect the sensual potential of the rest of their bodies and of nonorgasmic eroticism.

Some persons have as much difficulty giving pleasure as others do in receiving it. These individuals don't provide their partners with enough sexual stimulation because they lack either the knowledge and sensitivity to know what to do, or they are anxious about doing it. Others are consciously or unconsciously hostile towards their mates and don't really want to please them.

Sexual Defenses. Therapists have overlooked immediate sources of anxiety until the advent of the new sex therapy. Traditional approaches to sexual dysfunction looked for subtle and profound anxiety sources, such as oedipal conflicts and marital power struggles. We find there are

also more obvious reasons for sexual anxiety, such as fear of sexual failure, fear that the partner expects too much, or fear that the partner will reject sexual advances. These fears create various sexual defenses and introduce conscious control into lovemaking, which in turn prevents persons from abandoning themselves to the experience.

We have found that the three male dysfunctions, impotence, retarded ejaculation, and premature ejaculation all seem to be associated with some form of sexual conflict, but there are different symptoms for each dysfunction, and each of them responds to different therapeutic strategies and tactics.

1

Premature ejaculation is one of the most common and easily relieved male complaints. Men with this malady are unable to control voluntarily their ejaculatory reflex. Once they become sexually aroused, they reach orgasm very quickly. Some ejaculate after several minutes of foreplay, others just prior to or immediately upon entering their partner's vagina, and others after only a few pelvic thrusts. The essential problem, however, is not how quickly the man ejaculates, but his inability to control the reflex. In contrast to a premature ejaculator, an effective lover continues to engage in sex play while he is in a highly aroused state. He is able to forestall climax until his partner, who is slower to respond, can reach orgasm. At the least, prematurity restricts the couple's sexuality; at worse, it destroys it.

Most men who suffer this distress are unhappy about their condition, and often employ a variety of common-sense techniques to relieve the difficulty. They shift their attention to nonsexual thoughts during intercourse, tense their anal muscles, bite their lips or dig their fingernails into their palms. In this manner they can delay the onset of intense erotic arousal, but once aroused, they still can't control ejaculation. They feel sexually inadequate, and guilty that they have not satisfied their partners.

The term "primary prematurity" refers to a man who has never been able to control orgasm. If he is otherwise healthy, there is little reason to suspect his difficulty arises from a physical cause. On the other hand, a physician should conduct

thorough urological and neurological exams on the secondary ejaculator, a man who has developed the problem after a history of good control. Diseases of the posterior urethra or pathology along the nerve pathways serving the orgasmic reflex mechanisms may cause secondary prematurity. Sex therapy should begin only after a physician rules out any physical basis for the condition.

Small Comfort. Different therapeutic schools emphasize various psychological explanations for premature ejaculation. Psychoanalysts say it is the result of a neurosis, marriage counselors believe it comes from hostilities between the partners, common-sense theorists blame it on excessive sensitivity to erotic sensation. Masters and Johnson contend that stressful conditions during a young man's initial sex experiences bring on premature ejaculation, while Wardell Pomeroy, co-author of the Kinsey reports, says that anxiety is the culprit. All these speculations may be theoretically interesting, but they are of little comfort to the patient.

In 1956, James Semans, a urologist, demonstrated a simple manipulative technique to help cure premature ejaculation. Semans realized that the distinguishing feature of premature ejaculation was the rapidity of the orgasmic reflex. Consequently, his treatment goal was to prolong the reflex. To do this, he directed the patient's wife to stimulate her husband's erect penis until he felt he was just about to have orgasm, and signaled her to stop. When he could recapture control, the patient would tell her to resume stimulation until he again felt the sensations that signaled ejaculation. Again she would stop. Over a period of several weeks the couple practiced this stop-start method until the patient could tolerate stimulation without ordering a halt. At this point, his prematurity was permanently cured.

Semans reported on eight men who were premature ejaculators, and in every case the symptom disappeared. Other clinicians have used his method with the same success. I believe the technique works because it focuses a man's attention on the sensations preceding orgasm. Apparently he has previously failed to acquire control because he has not received, or let himself receive, the sensory feedback necessary to bring the reflex under control.

In our treatment program at Cornell we teach the patient to clearly identify his intensely erotic preorgasmic sensations and, initially, to avoid being distracted by his

ca. **1530.** Germany invents the pedal-driven spinning wheel, greatly speeding the manufacture of clothing by women in their homes. Thus the term "spinster" comes to be the legal designation of an unmarried woman.

wife's needs. We advise the couple that, provided they adhere to the prescribed therapeutic exercises, we can cure the symptom in most cases.

We use a variation of the Semans "stop-start" method in our treatment. The couple carries out their exercise assignments in their home. After three or four of these noncoital sessions, the patient usually feels he has attained some improvement in orgasmic control. We then suggest that the couple attempt intercourse using the same stop-start method. They first have coitus with the woman in the superior position, then while both lie on their sides, and finally with the man on top. Since this is usually the most stimulating position for the male, he has conquered his problem when he can maintain control in this position.

Husband First. This procedure can be quite unexciting and frustrating for the wife. Therefore, we suggest that the couple work out an agreement previous to treatment where the husband stimulates his wife to orgasm before or after the stop-start treatment. If the wife is unable to have an orgasm, we tell her that our first goal is to cure her husband's prematurity, then we can shift treatment to her.

If either partner resists any part of the treatment procedures, we root out the cause and intervene with appropriate psychotherapy. This might involve marriage counseling, psychoanalysis, or anxiety-reduction techniques. During therapy we continue to reinforce the couple's progress by reminding them that in a relatively short time, most, if not all, premature ejaculators respond to treatment.

Whereas the man suffering from prematurity cannot control orgasm, the retarded ejaculator cannot trigger it. Men with a mild form of this disorder can ejaculate by employing fantasy or distracting themselves from their sexual worries, or by additional stimulation. A few others have never experienced orgasm. At one time clinicians thought retarded ejaculation was a relatively rare phenomenon. Now it appears it may be highly prevalent, at least in its mild forms. At Cornell, we are seeing an increasing number of patients with this difficulty.

The Old-Time Religion. In its mildest form, a man's ejaculatory inhibition is confined to specific anxiety-provoking situations, such as when he is with a new partner, or when he feels guilty about the sexual encounter. The patient who seeks help, however, usually is more severely restricted in his sexuality. The man who suffers from primary ejaculatory retardation has had the difficulty since his first attempt at sexual intercourse, has never achieved orgasm during coitus, but may be able to achieve it by masturbation, manipulation or oral stimulation. Secondary retarded ejaculators enjoyed a period of good sexual functioning before the onset of retarded ejaculation; commonly, a specific trauma brought on their difficulty. Like the premature ejaculator, the retarded ejaculator often anticipates failure and frustration, which can eventually impair his ability to sustain an erection.

Few physical illnesses play a role in retarded ejaculation. Clinical evidence suggests that a strict religious upbringing, sexual conflict from an unresolved oedipal complex, strongly suppressed anger, ambivalence toward one's partner, fear of abandonment, or a specific sexual calamity are causes of retarded ejaculation.

Our treatment goal is to overcome the mechanism that inhibits ejaculation and resolve the underlying problems that impede sexual functioning. We use a series of progressive sexual exercises to relieve the patient of his anxieties and fears about the sexual act. We start with the couple performing the sexual practices that can elicit any existing ejaculatory capacity. As the patient is successful in one situation, he moves on to a more threatening or difficult one. Concurrently, the psychotherapy sessions at the clinic foster the patient's insight into any of his irrational fears, traumatic memories or destructive interactions with his partner that inhibit ejaculation.

Masters and Johnson cured 14 out of 17 retarded ejaculators using a similar method. Our preliminary results are similar to theirs. One of our successful cases was Mr. J., who had been in psychoanalysis for some time when he came to our clinic.

No Ejaculation. We traced Mr. J.'s difficulty to the traumatic termination of a sexual relationship. He had left his wife and four children for another woman, who subsequently left him. He became deeply depressed and sought psychoanalytic treatment. Although his depression subsided during analysis, he continued to have ejaculatory problems.

The patient had remarried, and his new wife agreed to cooperate in our sex ther-

apy program. Before entering treatment, they had worked out a way to have frequent and enjoyable sex, except for the limits imposed by his inability to ejaculate during intercourse. They would engage in imaginative sex play and have intercourse until she reached orgasm. Then she would stimulate him manually or orally until he achieved orgasm.

Treatment in this case was brief and effective. First we instructed the couple to participate in sex play without intercourse or orgasm. Then she stimulated him to orgasm with his penis near the mouth of her vagina. Finally, we told the wife to stimulate her husband almost to orgasm, at which point he was to enter the vagina with strong pelvic thrusting. In order to ejaculate during coitus, Mr. J. initially needed to fantasize that his wife was stimulating him orally, but gradually he could ejaculate without distracting himself from lovemaking with fantasy.

At the same time that Mr. and Mrs. J. practiced the sexual desensitization exercises at home, we conducted psychotherapy with them at the clinic. Their relationship had many immature elements in it. He was infantile, jealous and demanding, and haunted by the fear that his wife would leave him. At times, she acted like a stubborn, irresponsible and provocative child. In the therapeutic sessions we discussed the quality of their relationship from this perspective. Two years after we terminated therapy, we were pleased to learn that the patient had retained his ejaculatory competence, felt well, and seemed more assertive and less anxious.

A man who suffers from impotence is often almost unbearably anxious, frustrated and humiliated by his inability to produce or maintain an erection. Although he may become aroused in a sexual encounter and want to make love, he can't. He feels his masculinity is on the line. Clinicians and researchers estimate that half the male population has experienced at least transient impotence. Men seek help only when the problem becomes chronic.

Primary impotence is the rarest and most severe form of the disorder; men who suffer from it have never been potent with a woman, although they may be able to attain good erections in other situa-

---

1536. Queen Anne Boleyn, second wife of England's Henry VIII, has been ordered beheaded by the king. Her last words, upon being asked to bare her throat on the block, are: "The executioner is, I believe, very expert, and my neck is very slender."

tions. Secondary impotence is less severe, but still debilitating. These patients functioned well for some time prior to their erectile difficulties. The prognosis for treating impotence depends on how long the patient has suffered from it and how severe it is. Here again, the prospective candidate should have a thorough physical checkup before he goes into therapy. Stress, fatigue, undiagnosed diabetes, hepatitis, narcotics use, low androgen levels and other physical factors may cause impotence.

Depression and Discord. Although some traditional therapists believe impotence is always a sign of a deep underlying pathology, we believe there are often more obvious and immediate causes. Fear of sexual failure, pressures created by an excessively demanding wife, and guilt or conflict may prevent a man from producing or maintaining an erection. Therefore, we feel our brief, symptom-focused form of treatment is preferable to lengthy, reconstructive insight therapy that essentially ignores the immediate antecedents of impotence. Masters and Johnson report they cured 70 percent of their secondary impotent patients using treatment very similar to ours.

Because depression or marital discord can accompany or cause impotence, we must often relieve these symptoms before we can treat the man's impotence. Therefore, we always combine sexual tasks at home with therapeutic sessions in the clinic. The following case history demonstrates the variability and flexibility of this combined approach.

A 26-year-old Jewish law student applied for treatment. Although he and his 29-year-old West-Indian wife reported they had enjoyed a good sexual relationship during the year and a half they lived together, he began to have erectile difficulty after they were married, and she admitted that even while they lived together, intercourse was often hurried and more infrequent than she wished. Most recently, the patient had been unable to achieve an erection under any circumstances, and had lost all interest in sex. In the course of our initial evaluation and interview, the patient admitted that he had experienced potency problems with girls of his own ethnic background before he met his wife. But he emphasized that he had functioned well with her at first.

The wife had no sexual problems. She had orgasm during coitus, but only if intercourse lasted for 10 minutes or more. She could climax through clitoral stimulation, but was reluctant to allow him to engage in this activity.

Although there were many elements in the patient's psychiatric and family history that could indicate underlying psychological reasons for his impotence, we did not raise those issues in therapy. They had no immediate relevance to our belief that the cause of the patient's impotence was his wife's demands for frequent intercourse of long duration, and his progressive fear of failure.

We saw the couple in our office once a week. We also instructed them to gently caress each other during sexual play at home, but not to engage in coitus. We encouraged the wife to accept clitoral stimulation to orgasm if her sexual tension became excessive. These exercises produced intense excitement in both partners. He experienced a spontaneous erection, and, "against our advice," their passion led them to try coitus. The wife did not reach orgasm, but the patient felt sufficiently encouraged by his success to attempt intercourse again the following night. This time, he lost his erection when he became afraid he would be unable to sustain it long enough to bring his wife to orgasm.

Erotic Abandon. We talked about their experience in the next therapeutic session. When the wife understood the destructive effect of her sexual demands, she admitted for the first time that her husband was not very skilled at clitoral stimulation. Moreover, she said she felt this form of stimulation was "homosexual." We corrected her misconception and encouraged the couple to communicate more freely with each other about their sexual responses.

This couple developed a good sexual partnership, free of the pressures and demands which had caused his impotence. Without making her husband feel deficient the wife achieved postcoital orgasm by clitoral stimulation when she did not climax during intercourse. He learned to abandon himself to his erotic sensations. We terminated treatment after four therapeutic sessions, conducted over a three-week period, and the couple reported no difficulty in sexual functioning a year later.

This case was relatively simple. Others are more difficult. Impotence can be tenacious, and we often have to employ extensive psychotherapy to relieve the anxieties produced by deep-seated pathology or by marital discord.

In contrast to male dysfunctions, the female sexual dysfunctions are not as clearly understood. For example, the term "frigidity" is confusing on two counts. Be-

cause it has traditionally referred to all forms of female sexual inhibition, covering both total lack of erotic feeling and the inability to have orgasm, it fails to convey the fact that these are two separate components of the female sexual response. It also implies that women who suffer from inhibitions are cold and hostile to men, which is both inaccurate and pejorative.

Confusion also centers on the relationship between female orgasm and coitus. Some clinicians believe that if a woman cannot achieve orgasm during coitus, she suffers from sexual dysfunction. Others do not attach any particular importance to how a woman reaches a climax. Our clinical experience supports the second viewpoint. A woman who is otherwise orgasmic, but who does not reach orgasm during coitus, is neither frigid nor sick. This pattern seems to be a normal variant of female sexuality for some women. Our impression is that eight to 10 percent of the female population has never experienced orgasm, and of the 90 percent who have, only about half do so regularly during intercourse.

Women are slower than men to become aroused, and their arousal signs are much less obvious than the male's erect penis. Because men cannot easily discern whether or not a woman is ready for intercourse, and because women are culturally conditioned to put their husbands needs first, couples often proceed to coitus before the woman is sufficiently aroused to reach orgasm during intercourse.

Gentle Sensitivity. A woman's reluctance to express her needs, however, is not always based on cultural paranoia. Women may run a real risk of displeasing their husbands if they become sexually assertive. Such behavior repels some men, who regard women who assume active roles in sex as aggressive, castrating females. Other men feel threatened when their wives express sexual needs. They think their partners are challenging their sexual adequacy. Too often men fail to realize that they can become good lovers if they simply supply their partners with gentle, sensitive stimulation instead of perpetual erection.

The inability of some women to become aroused even though they receive adequate stimulation probably indicates some underlying sexual conflict. A restrictive upbringing; a hostile marital relationship; severe psychopathology; conflicts about the female role in lovemaking; fear of men, of losing control, of rejection and abandonment can cause female sexual dysfunctions.

4

General sexual dysfunction, usually referred to as frigidity, is the most severe of the female inhibitions. Women plagued with it derive little, if any, erotic pleasure from sexual stimulation. They are essentially devoid of sexual feelings. Many nonresponsive women consider sex an ordeal. Those who suffer from primary frigidity have never experienced erotic pleasure, and those who have secondary general sexual dysfunctions responded at one time to sexual stimulation, but no longer do so. Typically, these patients were aroused by petting before marriage, but lost the ability to respond when intercourse became the exclusive objective of all sexual encounters.

To help these nonresponsive women, we create a relaxed, sensuous ambience to permit the natural unfolding of sexual responses during lovemaking. To help foster such an environment, we encourage the couple to communicate openly about their sexual feelings and wishes, and we prescribe systematic sensuous and erotic experiences for the couple to perform at home.

Masters and Johnson developed a technique called sensate focus which is an ingenious and invaluable tool in treating general female sexual dysfunction. This exercise consists of having the couple forego sexual intercourse and orgasm while the wife caresses her husband's body, after which he stimulates her in like manner. By telling the wife to act first, we help counteract her guilt about receiving something for herself, and her fear that her husband will reject her. When we free women from the pressure to produce orgasm, they often experience erotic and sensuous sensations for the first time.

When the patient reports that she feels sensuous and erotic during the sensate focus exercises, we expand the caressing to include light, teasing genital play. After the husband caresses his wife's body he gently touches her nipples, clitoral area, and vaginal entrance. The woman guides his actions verbally and nonverbally. If, during these sessions, he becomes too sexually aroused, we tell the patient to bring him to orgasm manually or orally after she has had a chance to experience nonpressured, reassuring genital play.

Premonitory Sensations. Genital stimulation typically produces a definite increase in the patient's sexual responsiveness. When she reaches a high level of erotic feeling during these exercises, the couple moves on to intercourse. On top of her husband, she initiates coitus with slow and exploratory thrusts at first, while she focuses her attention on the physical sensations emanating from her vagina. If her partner's urge to ejaculate becomes too intense during her thrusting, we tell the couple to separate. The husband manually stimulates his wife until his premonitory orgasmic sensations disappear and they can resume intercourse. They repeat this cycle several times until she feels like driving for orgasm. If she does not want to try to reach climax, the couple proceeds with coitus until the husband reaches orgasm.

Frequently these sexual experiences evoke highly emotional responses and resistances in the patient. We use these feelings to help identify the specific obstacles which impede her eroticism. We deal with these obstacles on both an experiential level and in psychotherapy.

There is a good chance that women who suffer from general sexual dysfunction will improve. To a great extent the outcome of treatment seems to depend on the quality of the patient's relationship with her husband. If he does not reject her and she has no deep-seated psychopathology, the great majority of these women learn to enjoy sex and to reach orgasm.

5

Problems in reaching orgasm are probably the most prevalent sexual complaint of women. A woman suffers from primary orgasmic dysfunction if she has never experienced an orgasm, and from secondary orgasmic dysfunction if the disorder developed after a period of being able to reach orgasm. An inorgasmic woman has an absolute problem if she can't achieve orgasm under any circumstances, and a situational one if she can reach a climax only under specific circumstances. Women who suffer solely from orgasmic problems frequently have strong sex drives. They fall in love, enjoy sex play, lubricate copiously, and love the sensation of phallic penetration. They simply get stuck at or near the plateau phase of the sexual response.

Women who can achieve orgasm only by masturbation when they are alone, or those who must use vibrators for half an hour to reach orgasm obviously have a problem. But when a clinician sees a woman who can climax during masturbation, or when her husband stimulates her either manually or orally, but she cannot reach orgasm during coitus, he often faces a dilemma. It is difficult for a therapist to decide whether she is suffering from a pathological inhibition or whether she merely exhibits a normal variation of female sexuality. If the clinician cannot uncover any sexual anxieties, conflicts or fears during his initial interview with the couple, he should probably reassure them that she functions within the normal sexual range, and encourage them to work out lovemaking patterns that satisfy them both. However, if they still want to achieve coital orgasm, we will accept them, and try to increase her sexual responsiveness. Some of these women learn to climax during coitus, and others do not.

At Home, Alone. The first goal of therapy with a woman who has never experienced orgasm is to eliminate as many inhibiting factors as possible from the sexual environment so she can have her first climax. Because it is the rising tide of clitoral sensations which triggers the female climax, and because women are least threatened when they are alone, we first instruct the inorgasmic woman to masturbate at home alone in an environment free from possible interruption. If several attempts at

1540. Vesalius, the first genuine anatomist in Europe, performs his first systematic dissection upon the body of a woman, which he has stolen at night from an Italian cemetery.

this fail to produce orgasm, we tell her to use an electric vibrator to stimulate her clitoris. Some sexologists feel the vibrator is the only significant advance in sexual technique since the days of Pompeii. Because the patient may become "hooked" on this device, however, we transfer her to manual stimulation as soon as she has had a few orgasms using the vibrator.

When she can stimulate herself to orgasm regularly, we bring her husband into the treatment program. First we instruct them to make love in the usual way, telling her not to make any special effort to achieve orgasm during coitus. After he has ejaculated, and there is no pressure on her to perform quickly, he uses the vibrator or stimulates her manually to orgasm. We tell her to be utterly "selfish," and to focus on her own sensations. After a few of these sessions some women climax during intercourse without the manual stimulation.

One of our patients was a 28-year-old social worker who had never experienced orgasm. Her husband was a 34-year-old physician. They were very much in love, and were frequent and passionate lovers. During the early years of their marriage, Mrs. E. had simulated orgasm because she was afraid her husband would feel hurt and guilty if he knew she could not climax. A year before they sought treatment, she admitted to Dr. E. that she could not reach orgasm, and since then he had tried to bring her to orgasm by clitoral stimulation.

Mrs. E. arrived for the initial interview alone. She explained she had been reluctant to ask her husband to come because of his busy schedule. This was typical of her overprotectiveness of him. We explained that he would have to participate in treatment, and scheduled the first therapy session for two weeks later. In the meantime we instructed her to try to reach orgasm with an electric vibrator.

Missed Signal. At our next meeting, Mrs. E. told us she had easily achieved orgasm with a vibrator in solitude. But she was afraid to ask her husband to use the vibrator to stimulate her clitoris. She thought it would repel him and make him feel inadequate. He reassured her that this was not true, and said he was eager to try to bring her to orgasm.

We also learned that Mrs. E. never abandoned herself completely to her sexual feelings, because, like many other women, she was overly concerned with satisfying and pleasing her husband. This meant that the couple's lovemaking was never governed by her needs. This was not Dr. E's fault. Often he aroused her to a high level of sexual tension, but at this point she would think, "That's enough, he must be getting tired." And she would signal him to begin coitus. Not surprisingly, he misinterpreted her signal to mean that she was ready to commence coitus because she too was ready to have an orgasm.

It became clear that the patient's orgasmic inhibition was not associated with severe psychopathology or marital difficulties. It was her great need to please her husband, motivated by her own insecurity.

We treated this couple by enhancing the communication between them, prescribing sexual experiences to sensitize Mrs. E. to her own feelings, and by helping her develop a sense of responsibility for obtaining her husband's adequate stimulation to bring her to orgasm. Both the therapist and her husband reassured her that her sexually assertive behavior would not diminish her husband's sexual enjoyment or jeopardize their relationship.

We encouraged Mrs. E. to develop sexual autonomy during lovemaking, and to assume responsibility for obtaining pleasure, first during foreplay and then during coitus. We instructed her to ask her husband to stimulate her, and tell him where to kiss and caress her. If he ejaculated during intercourse, she was to ask him to stimulate her to orgasm. We also helped her stop monitoring her own progress toward orgasm, which distracted her from her sexual sensations.

Dr. E.'s acceptance of Mrs. E.'s growing sexual maturity and activity helped her progress. After 12 sessions, she easily reached orgasm via clitoral stimulation and was beginning to experience coital orgasm. Both enjoyed sex tremendously, and after therapy Mrs. E. became more assertive and happier in general.

More common than the woman who has never had an orgasm is the patient who is orgastic in low tension situations, but cannot reach a climax under circumstances that make her even slightly anxious. She may be able to climax during solitary masturbation, but not when she is with a partner. We treat these patients by uncovering and resolving the specific conflicts which inhibit the patient.

Bridge Maneuvers. With a woman who cannot have orgasm during intercourse, our goals are to identify and remove any psychic blocks or marital problems that inhibit her during coitus, to have her perform erotic tasks to heighten her sexual arousal, enhance her awareness of and pleasure in her vaginal sensations and to maximize clitoral stimulation. We find that techniques that combine coitus with clitoral stimulation are very helpful. These are called "bridge" maneuvers.

A great majority of women, including those who suffer from absolute primary orgasmic inhibition, are able to achieve orgasm after a relatively brief period of therapy. Indeed, orgasmic inhibition is virtually 100 percent curable if the sole criterion for cure is the ability to reach orgasm. But, as mentioned before, some women never reach orgasm during intercourse, which suggests that the phenomenon is a normal variant of female sexual response.

6

The third, and relatively rare, female sexual dysfunction is vaginismus. Anatomically, a vaginismic woman is normal, but whenever a man tries to penetrate her vagina, the vaginal muscles literally snap the entrance shut so that intercourse is impossible. Physicians often must conduct vaginal examinations on these women under anesthesia. This disorder is due to an involuntary spasm of the muscles surrounding the vaginal entrance. These patients are usually afraid of vaginal penetration, and intercourse. They often suffer from general sexual dysfunction or orgasmic inhibition. However, many women who seek treatment for vaginismus are sexually responsive and highly orgastic.

Vaginismus results from a woman's association of pain or fear with vaginal penetration. The precipitating event may be physical pain or psychological stress. A rigid hymen, inflammatory pelvic diseases and tumors, childbirth pathologies, and hemorrhoids may cause it. Strict religious upbringing, a husband's impotence, or the psychological effects of rape also may bring on vaginismus, or it may result from ignorance and misinformation about sex, or guilt caused by deep sexual conflicts.

Tolerating Motion. Our basic strategy for treating vaginismus is simple, provided all physical pain-producing conditions have been corrected. Our first goal is to uncover the basis for the patient's phobic avoidance of vaginal entry. Then, with progres-

1545. Lady Anne Berkeley becomes the first female judge in English history. She is empowered by Henry VIII to decide the guilt and punishment of some rioters who set fire to her Gloucestershire estate hayricks.

sive sexual exercises, we try to decondition the involuntary spasm of the muscles that guard the entrance to the vagina.

First we have both the patient and her husband examine her genitals in the privacy of their well-lit bedroom. We tell them to find and examine the exact location of the vaginal opening. In the first sexual assignment, we tell the woman to gently insert her own or her husband's finger into her vagina. When her usual discomfort disappears we tell her to move her finger back and forth inside her vagina until she can tolerate the motion without discomfort. We always allow the woman to control the situation to reduce her fears and apprehensions. Next, the husband or wife inserts two fingers in the vagina, and then rotates them gently, stretching the walls of the vagina. When she can tolerate this, the couple proceeds to intercourse. First they lie still with the man's penis inserted in his wife, then the husband begins gentle thrusting at his wife's signal and withdraws if she wishes him to. Finally the couple thrusts to orgasm. Concurrently we conduct therapy sessions with the couple to work on the patient's phobia about vaginal penetration.

We have achieved excellent and permanent results with women who suffer from vaginismus. Masters and Johnson report they achieved a 100 percent cure rate. We find that the length of treatment is more variable than that for the other sexual dysfunctions because of the tenacity of the phobia. But we have been able to resolve the phobic avoidance in 10 psychotherapy sessions. Within three to 14 weeks, we can go on to cure the vaginal spasm with four to eight home exercise sessions.

Sex therapy promises, and experience suggests it delivers, rapid and permanent relief of distressing sexual problems for many. But we have not scientifically substantiated its merits in a controlled study.

There can be no doubt, however, in light of the clinical evidence and the compelling conceptual considerations which underlie this approach, that the new methods merit further trial and development. We need to know which kinds of problems we can best treat with sex therapy, and under what conditions. We must learn precisely what components of these complex methods are actually responsible for the observed changes. At the present stage in its development, however, sex therapy appears to have great value. Indeed, it may close the door on sexual boredom and agony in America.

Who Is the Lesbian?

Del Martin and Phyllis Lyon

So little is known about the Lesbian that even Lesbians themselves are caught up in the myths and stereotypes so prevalent in our society.

When we first started living together as a couple we knew practically nothing about female homosexuality. We only knew that we loved each other and wanted to be together. Somehow that tagged us as Lesbians and bound us to some mysterious underground "gay" society of which we were only barely aware. That was back in the days when the term "gay" was an in-group password, a means of double talk in a hostile "straight" (heterosexual) society. It was a word you could use to let someone else know you were homosexual without the fear that anyone overhearing it would understand—unless, of course, they were in the know.

Del had read a few books—that's all there were in the earlier days. She had been to a number of gay bars, which was always a twitchy experience, since police raids were commonplace then. She had met a few Lesbians and had one previous affair.

Phyllis had been vaguely aware of homosexuality, but, like so many other women, never heard or thought of it in terms of the female, only in terms of the male. That the reason she and her roommate had been thrown out of their college dorm was undoubtedly due to implied homosexuality never occurred to her until years later. The dean of women and the housemother had charged that Phyllis and Jane were "too close," that they engaged in double talk at the dinner table, that they did not mix socially with the other girls in the dormitory, and that they had missed "lock out" a couple of times.

Although she liked men, dated them and even once went so far as to become engaged, Phyllis still had reservations about taking that final step down the aisle. She sought a career in journalism and enjoyed her independence. She had always maintained a number of close friendships with women and recalls feeling very resentful when one of them would call up and cancel a prior engagement to go to the movies with her, just because some man had asked for a date.

That's about where we were. Hardly the ideal background from which to launch a Lesbian "marriage," which is the way we thought of our relationship. The only model we knew, a pattern that also seemed to hold true for those few Lesbians we had met, was that of mom-and-dad or heterosexual marriage. So Del assumed the role of "butch" (she was working at the time) and Phyllis, being completely brainwashed in society's role of woman anyway, decided she must be the "femme." Like her mother before her, she got up every morning to make breakfast—at least for the first week.

The closest friends we had at the time were a newly married heterosexual couple. They, too, assumed that Lesbians would adopt

butch-femme roles. Sam happily encouraged Del to be a male chauvinist, slapping her on the back and plying her with cigars, all the while telling her she had to keep Phyllis in her place and coaching her on maintaining the upper hand. Meanwhile Sue and Phyllis plotted the traditionally sneaky ways women devise to gain and maintain the upper hand. If this sounds like an arm-wrestling match, it was. Like so many heterosexual couples, we played the roles in public, and with Sue and Sam, and then we went home and fought about them. The only thing that saved our relationship was Phyllis's stubborn resolve that it would last at least a year. The fact we had known each other for more than three years and had established a basic friendship was the other thing we had going for us.

In the course of our nineteen years together we have learned that many Lesbians in our age group (late forties) went through the same kind of role playing. While a few become trapped in this butch-femme pattern, most come in time, as we did, to the realization that they are both women and that's why they are together.

Most of you can probably recall a distant cousin or a maiden aunt about whom the family whispered vaguely. But few of you wish to admit that the Lesbian in your life was really much closer to home. For we are also your daughters, your sisters, even sometimes your mothers. The Lesbian comes from all walks of society, every economic class, every educational level, every racial and ethnic group, every religious background. She is in every type of work, of every political persuasion, and in every part of the world.

For her own protection, learned through painful experience, the Lesbian generally maintains a dual life—one that is visible and one that is kept secret. Understandably, this can lead to emotional conflicts, and time and energy wasted on weaving a web of lies. It can lead to a loss of self and potential in the process of facesaving conformity.

Understandably, too, since the Lesbian in our society is generally hidden, her existence has generated a great deal of conjecture and intrigue, out of which a whole body of folklore has been perpetrated on the public as fact.

Once aware of the Lesbian's existence, most people tend to view her solely as a sexual being. She is seen as a sad caricature of a male, trying to dress and act in the manner she deems "masculine," and generally aping some of men's worst characteristics. Or she is conceived of as a hard, sophisticated female who indiscriminately seduces innocent girls or women into the mysteries of some "perversion" they know little or nothing about. On the other hand, she is seen as an unfortunate, pitiable spinster, who, unable to catch a man, has settled for a less desirable substitute in another woman as her lover—whom, of course, she will immediately abandon when and if she meets "him." Some men fantasize the Lesbian as a voluptuous, sensuous mistress who is unscrupulous in her sexual

ca. **1550.** The branks, or "Scold's Bridle," becomes popular in Scotland and England as a device for punishing loose-tongued or shrewish women. It is a hooped headpiece of iron hinged to clamp over the face and to insert a metal flange into the mouth. Wearing this apparatus, an offending women is marched through the streets to general ridicule.

tastes, insatiable in her sexual appetite and therefore indiscriminate in her choice of sexual partner.

These stereotypes are based upon the false assumption that the Lesbian is first and foremost **sexual** in all her thoughts, desires and actions. What people fail to realize is that being a Lesbian is not merely indulging in physical acts or lovemaking. For the woman involved it is a way of life, encompassing the structure of her whole personality, one facet of which is, of course, her sexuality. For her it is the expression of a way of feeling, of loving, of responding to other people.

Furthermore, Lesbians are no more preoccupied with sex than are other people. We don't spend all our time in bed—and neither does anyone else we know. We, too, go to work, clean house, do the shopping, watch television, go to the movies, work on hobbies, have guests in for dinner, visit friends, and do all the other ordinary humdrum things which make up life in America today.

Also contrary to popular belief, most Lesbians seek relationships with those in their own age bracket. They do not put a premium on youth, as do many male homosexuals, but prefer partners with whom they have something in common besides sex. They look for companionship, community of interests, and all those other ingredients necessary to make any relationship work over a period of time.

Yet one of the myths that seems to hang on in our society is that Lesbians molest little girls and seduce young women. In actuality, childhood homosexual experiences are usually episodes of experimentation between little girls of the same age. Del recalls engaging in such experimentation at the age of nine with a girl who may have been a year younger and who, incidentally, was the initiator. But the incident bore no particular significance for Del at the time, since most of the youngsters, male and female, were in the habit of "playing doctor" and examining each other's bodies and genitals. Instances of an adult woman molesting a small child are so rare that we have not run into even a single case.

A 1959 survey by the Daughters of Bilitis indicated a very high ratio of Lesbians in the teaching profession. In writing up the research, however, these women were lumped in with the "professional" classification which comprised 38 percent of the sampling. This particular point of information we purposely withheld at the time lest a witch hunt be initiated in the California school system. Discovery or even the mere accusation of a teacher's homosexual orientation was cause for immediate dismissal or request for one's resignation, along with revocation of one's teaching credential, until 1969.

Despite the large number of Lesbians who are teachers, there is no data available, other than in fiction, that they have seduced or become sexually intimate with their female students. Yet the myth persists. It has always mystified us that the public remains so fearful of Lesbian teachers when criminal statistics clearly indicate that young girls who are seduced or raped are invariably victimized by men.

Women have always been carefully warned to shun the Lesbian; after all, the sanctity of home and family must be protected. Men, on the other hand, become increasingly fascinated by the unattainable, independent woman who is not an adjunct or appendage to a man, who does not seek nor require his approval for her existence, who even dares to compete with him not only in the job market but for "his" women as well.

But this woman-to-woman relationship, because it is contrary to the accepted and expected man-woman relationship and because there is so little known about it, is regarded as something weird, mysterious— and downright "queer." By community standards anything that is different must also be wrong. Consequently some people's first reaction, on learning that someone is a Lesbian, is that there must be something wrong with her physically. She must be some kind of biological freak whose genitals are somehow malformed; or perhaps she is the unfortunate victim of some type of hormone imbalance.

Phyllis was left with her mouth hanging open in astonishment when, on a guest appearance on his television show a few years ago, she was asked by the late Louis Lomax, "What are the physiological differences between Lesbians and other women?" Susan, who more recently, as part of her "liberation," felt the need to tell her mother about her Lesbian life, was equally appalled when her mother grasped her hand and asked very solemnly, "But why don't you have an operation, dear?"

Because there is no such operation. Neither our bodies nor the way they function is different from those of other females. Like other women we come in all sizes and shapes. Some of us are tall and lanky; some of us are short and fat. We are young and old, beautiful and homely, blonde and brunette, short-haired and long-haired, fair-skinned and dark-skinned—whatever the combination or variation. And no matter how you may look at it, we are and must be recognized and dealt with as women. In order to understand the Lesbian, it is therefore necessary that you think of her as a living, feeling, thinking human being: a woman. The Lesbian looks, dresses, acts, and **is** like any other woman.

Wherever you find two women living together you cannot assume, however, that they are Lesbians, since many heterosexual women share apartments out of economic necessity or for companionship. Nor can you be sure that two women, because they date men, are heterosexual. It may only be a cover to protect their Lesbian relationship from gossip and innuendo. Karen recalls the time when a coworker who was driving her home after an overtime stint at the office declared emphatically, "I can spot a 'queer' every time!" The fact that she was talking to one had completely escaped her.

Another fallacy is the assumption that "it takes one to know one": that there is some telltale sign, Morse Code signal or knowing glance exchanged between Lesbians at a mixed gathering. In all likelihood any Lesbian present at such a gathering would be very much on guard lest she give herself away—even to one of her own kind, whom she still regards as a threat in such social situations.

Appearance can also be misleading in trying to detect a woman's sexual orientation. Nancy, on return from a camping trip at Yosemite National Park, told us she had finally figured out the way you can tell the Lesbians from the straight women. The "stomping butch" types wearing men's jeans and boots usually had a husband and a number of kids trailing along behind them; the Lesbians, however wore capris or women's slacks so as to appear more "feminine" and not so obvious.

Lesbians in our society are perceived by men as sexually permissive in choice of partner and sexual act. Many a Lesbian, too, has been surprised to realize that the heterosexual couple whom she has befriended, whom she believed to be sympathetic and understanding, was actually conspiring to lure her into their conjugal bed.

And so it has gone through the years. The descriptive phrases, commonplace in the literature about the Lesbian, have always been ambivalent and tend to create an aura of sexual mysticism: "the exciting, alluring and tantalizing promise of a woman's closeness"; "a strange, tempting, forbidden love"; "perverse, yet compelling attraction"; "sordid and ugly revelation of the unleashed passions of evil and of love"; "the quirk of nature that lures young women into the lonely, isolated and tragic twilight world." Although such language makes for dramatic effect in fiction and attention-getting headlines for newspaper sensation-seekers, it has little to do with the realities of Lesbian life, and has led to the existing state of confusion among the general public as well as among Lesbians themselves.

Little scientific research has been done on the Lesbian, and what has been done is based primarily upon childhood background and sexual practices. Until recently most subjects were drawn from captive samples of women in prison or in psychotherapy. And it has always bothered us that the emphasis of research has been devoted almost exclusively to causation rather than to those facets of the Lesbian life itself which could help to explode some of the myths and foster better understanding.

We have also maintained a strong objection to measuring the Lesbian in terms of happiness or unhappiness. A Lesbian who is struggling with her identity or who may be trying to repress her sexuality will, of course, be unhappy during that period of her life. The woman who has come to terms with her identity and has crossed the bridge of self acceptance may have gained self confidence but not yet a lover, and so feels lonely and unhappy for a time. The Lesbian who has hurdled the identity crisis and established a meaningful and satisfying relationship with another woman may still feel somewhat unhappy on occasion because of society's strictures. Happiness is not stationary: it is fluid; it fluctuates. As Lesbians we have experienced great joy and happiness and love. We have also known despair, conflict and unhappiness. This is the human condition. The same may be said for heterosexuals, for whose miseries Lesbians have often expressed compassion and empathy. Unfortunately the concern is not reciprocal. The fact that the Lesbian is not generally thought of in terms of her humanity, her close relationship to family, her deep involvement with society, her sameness rather than her difference, is responsible for the negative self image she often adopts or must struggle to overcome.

1550. Venetian nobleman and merchants, suspicious of their wives during extended business trips, devise an improved chastity belt. This model, unlike the crude Crusaders' soldered-on piece, is equipped with intricate locks.

Sex and Menopause

The Boston Women's Health Book Collective, Inc.

Many of us have feared that menopause would bring an end to our sex lives. But Masters and Johnson tell us, "There is no time limit drawn by the advancing years to female sexuality." And an older friend says, "I was curious to see if my sexual life would be the same after menopause and am delighted to find that it is." Many women report that they enjoy sex even more after menopause because they no longer have to worry about getting pregnant.

There *can* be problems with sex for us as we grow older:

Our sex organs gradually atrophy (deteriorate) with the lowering of estrogen, and vaginal lubrication can become scarce, so intercourse can become painful in menopause or post menopause. A lubricant like saliva or K-Y Jelly may help, and estrogen therapy might correct it.

Other non–sexually related symptoms of menopause—tiredness, emotional irritability, nervousness, hot flashes, headaches, and so on—can do a lot to lessen our sexual drive and pleasure. Once we are past these symptoms, through time or hormone therapy, our sexual life can be as good as ever.

Sometimes in going through menopause we may feel that we have "lost our womanhood." It is true that we can no longer offer our partner the chance to produce a child, but the odds are good that our partner wouldn't want one anyway.

Many of us as we get older get fewer chances for heterosexual sex. Middle-aged men often go through a change of life in which they are impotent for anywhere from two months to a couple of years. Divorce, death, and a cultural norm which pushes men to seek younger sex partners, leave many middle-aged women without partners, and in the past it seems that many of them resigned themselves to a life without sex. But an increasing number of women are breaking the silly convention that women should pair up only with men older than they are. We are enjoying male company without insisting on marriage, so that the male-female numbers ratio is not so important. And there are many good kinds of sexual expression that don't involve men.

Here is one woman's experience with sex in middle age:

* * *

Sex was great—probably—until I had a hysterectomy for fibroid tumors five years ago. After the surgery I was sore and rather dead for a long time. Foreplay was less good because there was a broken link—no visceral response when he played with my breasts, and this had been very nice to feel before.

Sex became less joyful. Coincidentally, my husband became ill and was prescribed a tranquilizer which overdosed him to near impotence. My frustration was total, and for the first time in my life, at forty, I masturbated to orgasm. Out loud, in wonder, I said, "So that's what it is!"

I spent about three and a half years trying to reconcile the two very different experiences, very different pleasures, of intense masturbatory orgasm and intense shared love-making with little increments of sensation which make me rest and relax before returning for more sharing. By now I just figure I have two great goods for my pleasure. My husband doesn't thrive on thinking about the vibrator, and I don't have as good an orgasm with it if he's there, so it's a private pleasure. I recommend it to everyone (not person-to-person or door-to-door, but here, anonymously).

* * *

The writer Simone de Beauvoir talks about sex and older people. She points out that for some the joy of sex lies in their own physical beauty, and as this fades from youthful prime, they derive less and less joy from sex. They may even be unwilling to participate at all. However, she says, those for whom sex is a joyous, friendly act will frequently continue to enjoy it into the seventies and later.

1553. Margaret of Austria describes her intimate relations with Laodamia Fortenguerre, an attractive Italian woman, as "a pure and holy love that passeth human understanding."

Motherhood

Adoption Advice

Joan McNamara

You've made up your mind. You have looked at this question of adoption from all sides and you have decided that, yes, I want to adopt a son or a daughter. And that decision raises new questions. Such as, how do you start? And where do you turn?

The first step is to decide if you want to adopt through an adoption agency or if you want to try to arrange a nonagency, or independent, adoption. Basically, there are three types of adoption agencies: public agencies, which usually are run by county or city departments of welfare or social services; private agencies, which place a broad range of homeless children; and sectarian agencies, which specialize in adoptions for children and parents of specific religions such as Jewish, Catholic, or Lutheran, although some may place across religious lines.

Independent adoptions usually are arranged through lawyers or doctors. These are the "gray market" or, in some cases, the "black market" adoptions you have heard about. Before you opt for the independent route, make sure you understand how adoption agencies work today. You may find that certain assumptions you may have about the rigidity and requirements of agencies no longer hold true.

More than 75 percent of all adoptions in the United States are agency adoptions. One reason is the increased flexibility of adoption agencies in recent years. Another is the greater assurance of legal safeguards with an agency adoption. Adoption agencies in most states are licensed and regulated by state governmental bodies such as a department of public welfare or a department of social services. These departments set legal standards that adoption agencies must follow to keep their licenses. For example, to avoid the possibility that an adopted child could be taken away from you by a biological parent, there are steps such agencies must take to ensure that a child has been legally released for adoption. In addition to legal protections, agencies also provide a screen of anonymity between the bio parents and adoptive parents, whereas in some private adoptions you might come into contact with a bio parent. Agencies also are able to provide preadoption guidance for parents *and* children, as well as postadoption guidance for adopted children and their parents.

In a few states there is no specific adoption licensing. However, all states do have certain standards that are followed, and there are efforts under way in some of the states to institute legal guidelines for agency adoptions (as well as for independent adoptions).

The policies and practices of adoption agencies across the country vary widely, so it is impossible to generalize about comparisons between public agencies and private ones. One type of agency is not necessarily "better" than another, contrary to an old wives tale that private agencies placed a "better class" of baby (whatever that meant) than public ones. A private agency adoption usually will cost more than a public agency placement, but about all adoption agencies today have one thing in common: a severe shortage of infants and a re-

Adapted from *Adoption Advisor*. Copyright © 1975 Information House. Reprinted with permission.

sulting sharp decline in placements. For example, at the Los Angeles County Department of Adoption, the largest public agency in the United States, placements in 1973 dropped to about 1,100 children, from an annual rate of about 2,500 in the late 1960s. The private Spence-Chapin Adoption Service in New York City placed 110 youngsters in 1973, down from a high of 475 in 1967.

So the first thing you want to do is to find an agency that will accept your application to adopt a child and will put you on a waiting list for a homestudy. What is a homestudy? It used to be an intense investigation by an agency into the intimate details of your private life and finances, with a social worker literally and figuratively peeking under your carpets. Or at least that was the way many adoption applicants felt after going through a homestudy. But today most agencies use homestudies, which usually include personal visits to your home by a social worker, as a way to help parents reach their own decisions about adoption rather than acting out the old stereotype of a homestudy as an opportunity for a minor inquisition. The homestudy is the final step before the search for a child to be placed in your home.

Locating a Child

Ideally, after you have been approved for an adoption, your caseworker soon will find a child she feels would be right for you.

The caseworker then will invite you to the agency to see a picture of the child or to meet the child. She also will give you some information on the child's background. If you are adopting an older child, the caseworker may arrange for you and the youngster to size each other up in the less official atmosphere of a park, museum, or zoo, rather than at the agency office. It is possible that you may feel the child is not right for your family; expressing doubts or even rejecting a placement does not jeopardize your chances of getting a child. If, however, you decide this is the child for you, your new son or daughter will be placed in your home.

But what if the weeks roll by and that phone call doesn't come and your agency tells you it may be many months before a child is found for you? Or what if you have not even been able to get on a waiting list because the agencies in your area say the type of children you are interested in are not available in large enough numbers?

If you are seeking a healthy infant or toddler, there is little you can do to speed the process because there simply are not enough children to meet the demand. Otherwise, there are two possible courses of action you can take: One, you can sit and wait for a year or two until a child is put in your arms or you finally are placed on a waiting list. Two, you can shorten the wait by becoming better informed about the children who actually are available for adoption, both in your area and elsewhere, and, if necessary, by trying to locate among these children a child who would fit into your life.

1556. "Bloody" Queen Mary of England, a Roman Catholic, continues her religious purges by burning alive many high officials of the Protestant church.

This can be helpful to your agency if you have been approved for adoption. If you haven't gotten that far, locating a child first may enable you to convince an agency to do a homestudy on you. Again, be sure that the problem isn't that you are limiting yourself by being inflexible about the type of child you will accept. The more flexible you are, the easier it will be for either you or your agency to locate a child for your family.

Whether or not you have been approved by an agency, probably the most reliable sources you can tap for information on available children are the adoption exchanges established by private organizations, parent and citizen groups, or state and city agencies. These exchanges list children who are waiting to be adopted, and some also list prospective parents who wish to adopt. Some groups generally list children for whom local agencies have had difficulty finding homes.

All the exchanges have the same purpose—to help children find homes that may not be readily available in the community or state where the child presently is located. And, second, to help prospective parents who cannot locate adoptable children in their own areas. Ed and Sharon Barco, for example, had been waiting for a baby for eight months after their homestudy was completed, and there seemed little likelihood that a child would be available from their agency in the near future even though the Barcos were willing to accept a hard-to-place child. Finally, the couple urged their caseworker to register them with the various exchanges. This was not done automatically in their state.

About another eight months later, through one of the exchanges, the Barcos located in a nearby city a sixteen-month-old boy with a heart defect. They were shown a picture of a slightly undersized baby with very large brown eyes. The child had been released for adoption less than two months before because his biological mother could not cope with the special needs of a child with a serious heart condition.

By consulting with their family doctor and a heart specialist he recommended, Ed and Sharon learned that the baby's heart condition was operable and that the baby would have a better than average chance for recovery and eventual normal activity. Their insurance would cover part of the surgical costs, and their agency assured them the state would pick up the remaining expenses as part of its medical subsidy plan for adoptive children. So the Barcos took into their home a son—Edward Harold Barco—whom they might never have found if they had not taken the initiative to expand their adoption search beyond their own community.

If you have been approved by an agency for adoption, and if the wait has been longer than three or four months with little prospect for a placement soon, make sure the agency has listed you with local, state, and national adoption exchanges. Your adoption worker should do this; if she has not, talk to her about it. Almost every state now has a central listing of children available for adoption, updated monthly according to current information from each licensed adoption agency in the state. Since 1970 California has used a computer to match adoptive children and families. There have been proposals in Congress to establish a computerized National Adoption Information Exchange to centralize such matching on a national scale through the Department of Health, Education and Welfare.

Whether or not you have completed a homestudy, you can directly contact groups that run exchanges for information on what children are available. Some groups, such as the Adop-

Erika Stone

tion Resource Exchange of North America (ARENA), regularly publish newsletters, sent to parent groups and agencies, containing descriptions of representative children listed with that exchange. Others, such as the Illinois Multiple Listing Service of the Child Care Association of Illinois, distribute in book form information on children available for adoption in specific geographic areas. Photographs and brief descriptions of waiting children are included in such books, which are periodically updated. You can obtain information about these newsletters and listings by writing directly to the groups that operate the exchanges.

The exchanges work on the same principle as multiple listing in real estate. The theory is that you can reach more prospective parents and benefit more children if you centralize and share information that can lead to these children finding homes.

While such exchanges generally list "hard-to-place" children, what is difficult for one agency in one community may be routine for another agency elsewhere. A Mexican-American child may be hard to place in California but not in Iowa. A black child from Georgia may be placed more readily in Minnesota. Children may be considered difficult to place because of age, racial background, medical or emotional problems, or because several brothers or sisters must be placed together.

Adoption applicants and adoption agencies from any state can contact these exchanges about any child listed; they will be put in touch with the local agency that has custody of the child. The groups that operate the exchanges, with some exceptions, do not place children themselves. Adoption agencies generally view the exchanges as valuable aids that help their own adoption workers to help prospective adoptive parents. If you do not have an agency, you will have to get one to do a homestudy and to decide, along with the agency that has custody of the child in whom you are interested, if the placement would be a potentially good one. Some agencies are reluctant to study a family that insists on a specific child in advance because it commits the agency to approving or disapproving the applicants on the basis of a single child who the agency

---

1555. Madame de Maldemeure, having given birth to one child the first year, twins the second, triplets the third, quadruplets the fourth, quintuplets the fifth, and finally, sextuplets the sixth, dies. She leaves her husband with twenty-one children in six years.

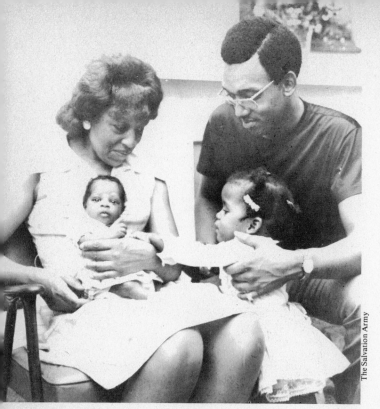

The Salvation Army

as the Barcos found, you may have to do some prodding and searching. Finding a child depends upon your worker being informed and aggressive in the hunt for sources of children. If you can help, you will be shortening your wait for a child.

Independent adoptions are private adoptions generally arranged by lawyers, obstetricians, clergymen, or other intermediaries without the services of a licensed adoption agency.

The Gray Market

Perhaps the best way to understand how a gray market adoption works is to see how a real one was completed. When Bill and Laura Fried decided to adopt, they were referred by their family doctor to a lawyer who arranged adoptions independently. The lawyer, in turn, worked with another lawyer in Florida who had contacts with unwed mothers there.

This is the so-called "gray market" adoption. It is legal in all states except Connecticut and Delaware, assuming certain requirements are met under varying state laws.

When the Frieds had their first appointment with the lawyer recommended to them, they briefly discussed their feelings about adoption and their inability to have a biological child. The lawyer was convinced that they both were sincere and mature in their approach to adoption, but he warned them that it could be as long as five years before a healthy white infant could be placed with them for adoption. This was discouraging, but the Frieds decided to work with the lawyer. They placed half of the estimated fees for the services and medical care for the baby and biological mother, about $1,500, in escrow.

Almost two years later the Frieds received a telephone call from the lawyer. He knew of a child, now in a Florida hospital, who was born with a club foot. The couple who had been promised this child for adoption could not accept the handicap. Would the Frieds be interested?

Laura initially said no. But after she talked it over with Bill later in the evening, they decided to call the lawyer back and ask to see the child. The next morning the lawyer showed them biographies of the child's parents, with family names removed, and the Frieds made arrangements to fly to Florida to see the child at the hospital.

Meanwhile, the biological mother in Florida had agreed to a change in parents for her child. She signed a new surrender form stipulating that she was placing her child for adoption with the Frieds. Legally speaking, placement of the child was made by the bio mother, not the lawyers, and it had to be approved by the courts before final adoption.

When the Frieds arrived at the hospital, they arranged to have the child examined by a staff orthopedist, who explained to them the type of surgery needed to correct the condition. Bill had checked with his insurance company before leaving home, and he knew his medical plan would cover such procedures.

Bill and Laura decided they wanted to adopt the baby boy. They signed the necessary papers and brought their new son home the next day. A few weeks later their lawyer filed an adoption petition in their home state, and the Frieds subsequently were visited by a court representative. The court official sat and chatted casually in their living room as she examined various documents relating to the adoption. Laura had housecleaned frantically for days in preparation for the

may or may not decide is suitable for that family. Other agencies may be more willing to consider you for a homestudy if you can show that there are children available for adoption that they can place with you. And having a specific child in mind may be the one consideration that will get you in the door at these agencies.

Addresses of the major adoption exchanges are listed in the directory of this book.

Television and radio shows or newspaper articles about adoption can be potential sources for locating a child. Such shows and articles tend to concentrate on the "hard-to-place" children available. But by showing specific children in need of homes, and by showing what a "hard-to-place" child is really like (not so different from other kids, after all), these shows and articles give prospective adoptive parents a chance to consider adoption in the light of real live kids, not just statistics and stereotypes.

Television programs such as "The Ben Hunter Show" in Los Angeles and "Midday Live" in New York have regularly shown children waiting to be adopted. There are adoption newspaper columns in some cities, such as Ruth Carleton's "A Child Is Waiting" in the Detroit *News*. Such columns usually include pictures of the children described. Since there is no central listing of the programs and columns dealing with adoption, the only way to discover if they exist in your area is to contact local stations and newspapers. If they don't have such programs or columns, you may plant an idea.

What these exchanges, programs, and columns show is that, despite the shortage of adoptable babies, there is no shortage of kids waiting for homes. If you are running into "Sorry, no children" responses from local agencies, you may be able to shortcut the process by checking these outside adoption sources to determine if the children who do need homes also would fit into your family.

If you have been approved by an agency, in many cases your caseworker will locate a child for you within a few months after your homestudy is completed, without your ever becoming involved in the locating process. If there is a delay,

1560. Catherine de' Medici, acting regent of France for her son Charles IX, who is a minor, organizes her "Flying Squadron" of court maids-of-honor and uses their seductions of noblemen to reveal her enemies. She is the most powerful figure in France.

visit, but the court study appeared to be a formality in this case.

The Frieds' lawyer filed an adoption petition asking the court to approve the adoption. The legal proceedings took place about six months later, and the Frieds were issued a new birth certificate for their son, Roy, with their own names typed in the space marked "Parents."

The Frieds' adoption was fairly typical of most private adoptions in the gray market. They contacted a reputable professional, in this case a lawyer, who located a baby and helped arrange the legal details of the surrender and adoption. In the Frieds' case, their lawyer and the court both made an informal type of homestudy. In other cases the adoptive family may undergo an actual homestudy by a caseworker from a government adoption agency in the state where the child is located. And they may go to court in that state. As with agency adoptions, complete legal records are kept with gray market placements.

The main advantage of a gray market adoption until recently was that it was a way to get infants without the years of waiting increasingly being required by agencies. But now that advantage is gone. The wait for infants in private adoptions is as long as for agency adoptions. Some people may prefer private adoptions for other reasons—they want to avoid agency red tape. They don't want an agency prying into their lives. Perhaps they cannot get accepted or approved by an agency. Or maybe they still feel a private contact can find them a baby faster than an agency will. You may feel that a private adoption could offer some advantages. But be sure to weigh these against the potential pitfalls. Pitfalls such as:

• Lack of adequate legal safeguards. For one, there is the problem of the biological mother's legal release of her child for adoption and the possibility that she could withdraw her consent before the child is placed. You probably will have a lawyer to protect your interests. But the laws governing adoptions outside licensed agencies are vague and contradictory in many states. Whether or not you will be protected if you run into legal complications, such as the mother deciding she wants the child back, may depend on the laws in your state and the skill of your lawyer. Private adoptions usually involve little, if any, counseling for the unwed mother involved, and it is possible that a court could find she was unduly pressured to release her child for adoption if she should decide to challenge your adoption later.

The rights of the unwed father also have been recently established by the courts. He must sign a release form or at least be notified that his biological child is being released for adoption. Of course, the legal procedures of adoption agencies are not foolproof either, but agencies are more closely regulated than gray market intermediaries.

• No guarantee of anonymity—either for you or for the biological parents of your adopted child. In cases where the adopted parents are known by the bio mother, the adoptive couple may frequently worry about the possibility that the bio mother will return at some future time and demand to see "her"—"my"—child. In reality, this rarely happens; if it does, there is usually no legal basis for the demand to be honored. But the thought can be disturbing.

• Medical and cost uncertainties. If the child you have contracted to adopt dies, is born with serious birth defects, is mentally retarded, or has some other major physical problem, you still may be responsible for all medical and hospital costs even though you may end up without a child. You usually are not obligated to take personal responsibility for a handicapped child. Even if the baby is born healthy, delivery complications and other medical problems could double or triple the estimated hospital bills that you contracted to pay for the mother and child.

The major concern about gray market adoptions in the United States today, however, is that you could lapse unknowingly into the black market. How do you know? The sure way is to follow the dollar signs. In a gray market adoption, you pay the legitimate expenses to arrange the adoption—medical fees for the bio mother and child, legal fees for the placement, plus the cost of your own lawyer. On average this ranged between $1,600 and $3,400 total in 1974. Once the price rises over $5,000—and surely over $10,000—there's a good chance you may be moving into the black market.

The Black Market

At first glance, black market adoptions appear not unlike gray market ones. You contact an intermediary, sometimes a lawyer, and he arranges to place a baby with you if you agree to pay certain costs. The key difference is that such operators are not finding homes for babies in return for reasonable fees, they are selling babies at a profit, which makes it a modern type of slave trade. Indeed, in mid-1974 the Los Angeles County Grand Jury indicted five persons on charges of operating an interstate, black market baby-selling racket in California. Prosecutors alleged the group signed contracts with pregnant women and sold their babies out of state for $10,000 to $15,000 per child.

In such operations, middlemen approach unwed mothers, women visiting abortion clinics, doctors, lawyers, and social workers to offer them large amounts of money if they can provide healthy, white babies for adoption. In an article on rising black market adoptions in the *Christian Science Monitor* in the fall of 1974, reporter Curtis J. Sitomer wrote that some pregnant and unwed college girls said they had been offered cash sums up to $25,000 for their babies. Another source reported that prostitutes are being recruited to produce children "for sale" at black market prices, according to the *Monitor* article.

Moral objections aside, there are practical problems with black market adoptions. To start with, selling babies for profit violates the law in many states. So such sellers are likely to avoid certain legal niceties in arranging placements. They may obtain the release for adoption of the child without the proper consent of the biological parents as mandated by law; they may coerce the mother into releasing the child; and they may forge or alter birth records, adoption records, and placement documents. Any one of these acts can invalidate the release or the final adoption. If so, your custody of the adopted child is threatened.

Another problem, as with some gray market adoptions, is a possible lack of anonymity. With a black market adoption, this can have threatening overtones. It leaves you open to extortion or harassment by unscrupulous individuals who may claim, falsely or not, that the biological parents want your baby back unless you pay protection money. If the adoption is on shaky legal ground, you may feel that you have no choice but to pay.

Stay away from people who offer you a child for the "right" amount of money, people who have babies for sale. Not only are they morally and legally suspect, but they may not even be

---

1563. Madame Godard de Blois, a minor French noblewoman, is hanged for having accepted the advances—each Sunday after church—of "never less than a dozen" young male members of the congregation. She asked "only the text of the sermon as a password to her compliance." What made her crime even worse was her habit of practicing it "sometimes in the Consistory itself."

able to come up with a healthy child for you. Again, the best way to tell when you are crossing into the black market is by the dollar amount involved. Such operators have a way of escalating fees beyond the first estimate, for "unexpected" complications that supposedly arise.

How to Protect Yourself

It is possible for independent adoptions to be made safely and with legal safeguards in most states, at least in the case of gray market adoptions. But to protect your welfare and that of your prospective child, you should be cautious about private placements. Parents who have adopted children through independent contacts make the following recommendations for others who wish to follow the same route without falling into the dangers of the black market:

• Deal only with reputable intermediaries.

The people you trust to locate your child should have impeccable professional and personal references from parents who have worked with them, from adoptive parents groups, and from those within their own field of expertise—other lawyers, doctors, and so forth. Honest intermediaries can be found through the grapevine of adoptive parents. Also check your doctor, lawyer, friends, and relatives. Ask them to make inquiries in their own professional and social circles. Clergymen often know of independent sources for adoption, as do many private social workers and psychologists.

• Hire your own lawyer to represent you.

This is an extra cost, but it will be worth it to have someone you know or someone specifically looking out for your interests to research all the legal aspects of private adoption in your state. This lawyer can protect you from fraudulent practices and legal loopholes. Since many independent placements take place outside the adoptive parents' state of residence, your lawyer also should look into the private adoption laws of the child's state of residence. (Many independent placements take place in Florida, Texas, Arizona, and California.) *Again, note that this is a lawyer in addition to any who may be involved with arranging the adoption for you.*

• If you contract to pay expenses, make sure you get a specific breakdown of the expenses—hospital bills of the biological mother, delivery fees, legal fees, travel costs, and so on. Make certain the fees to the intermediary are limited to reasonable fees for the type of service rendered and are not for procurement of a child. The average fee for private adoptions in mid-1974 of $1,600 to $3,400 included medical and delivery costs for mother and child (averaging between $700 and $1,400) and legal fees averaging around $500 to $1,000 for each lawyer involved. Costs could rise higher if there are medical or legal complications. And with inflation, prices go up quickly. Your own lawyer and doctor can advise you if the estimated costs seem out of line.

• Once a child is located for you, get as much information as possible on that child.

Get specific details from the intermediary or the public agency assigned to do a formal or informal homestudy on you about the circumstances of surrender for adoption and any medical problems of the biological parents. Before you sign any documents or take legal possession of the child, have the child's physical condition evaluated by your own doctor, if possible, or by a doctor you choose or have recommended to you from the pediatric staff in the hospital where the baby is located.

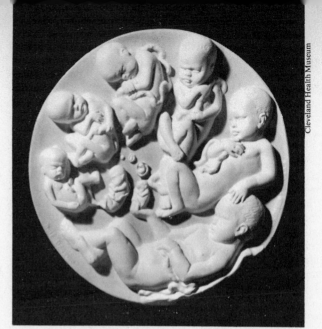

Ten fetal and embryonic stages

Confirming the Pregnancy
Planned Parenthood League of Massachusetts

A late menstrual period is not a sure sign of pregnancy since menstrual irregularity can have a variety of physiological or psychological origins. Other bodily changes in early pregnancy provide clues. The breasts enlarge, become sensitive, and the area around the nipple may darken. Some women also experience nausea, a sudden weight gain, and fatigue but it is not until the fourth or fifth month that the pregnancy begins to "show." The best way to confirm a pregnancy is through a pregnancy test.

Urine Pregnancy Test

A urine test is most accurate two weeks after a missed period or at least 41 days from the beginning of the last menstrual period. The urine of a pregnant woman contains HCG (human chorionic gonadotropin), a hormone secreted by the developing placenta. After about the sixteenth week of pregnancy the level of HCG decreases again and the urine test is no longer reliable.

Urine pregnancy tests provide an indication of pregnancy or non-pregnancy but not a medical diagnosis. They are about 95-98% accurate. A woman with a negative test is always advised to have the test repeated about a week later if no period occurs or if the period is abnormally light. Occasional false positives can result from the presence of certain drugs in the system and some medical conditions, or in menopausal or post-menopausal women. False negatives usually result from insufficient hormone and/or insufficient concentration of urine.

The following procedure insures the greatest possible accuracy:

1. Drink no liquids after 9:00 or 10:00 the night before the test.
2. Urinate before going to bed and discard.
3. The next morning, before eating or drinking anything, collect the first urine of the day in a clean, dry container.
4. Cover and refrigerate until taken to the lab.

"Gestest" (Progesterone Test)

The "Gestest" involves the administration of progesterone either orally (10-20 mgs. per day for 5 days) or by injection (single dose). If the missed period is due to failure of or delay in ovulation, the progesterone will simply bring the onset of flow, usually within the next two-to-four days, possibly longer. The progesterone acts to produce endometrial maturation which is then followed by withdrawal bleeding as the progesterone effect subsides. If the missed period is due to pregnancy, no flow will occur.

Adapted from *Everybody's Guide to Every Body*. Reprinted with permission of Planned Parenthood League of Massachusetts.

1570. Ivan the Terrible of Russia keeps all the most beautiful women of his domain in captivity at Alexandrovskoe for more than a year. After using them as he sees fit, he finally selects one from the two thousand as his wife.

Will My Baby Be Normal?

Alan J. Anderson, Jr.

Each day, roughly 700 sets of parents throughout the United States are cruelly reminded that medicine has not yet conquered genetic disease. About one in 14 babies is born with a genetic disorder; the afflicted range from the diabetic who may become a tennis champion to the hopeless cripple who may live only a few days. Genetic mistakes, according to the National Foundation-March of Dimes, afflict some 2.9 million Americans with mental retardation, 4 million with diabetes, 1 million with congenital bone, muscle or joint disease, 500,000 with complete or partial blindness, 750,000 with impaired hearing and some 6 million others with imperfect organ systems.

While these mistakes cannot be corrected, the curse of genetic disease is slowly being lifted. A new kind of specialist called the genetic counselor can now detect more than 60 disorders in unaffected "carriers" and, equally important, within the developing fetus itself. As recently as 10 years ago, doctors faced the complexity of human deformity armed with little more than 19th-century peas-and-flowers genetics. Today, genetic counselors, who are usually M.D.'s with extensive training in genetics, can call upon a growing arsenal of sophisticated tools to probe within the cell and even among the invisible genes themselves. Perhaps more important, they can now offer parents considerably more than guesswork when asked the heavy question: "Will my baby be normal?"

Even the most optimistic counselors are quick to admit that genetic diseases will never be eliminated; natural mutations constantly replenish the stock of defective genes. But they are quickly learning to identify high risk women most likely to need help: Those over the age of 35; those with deformed children or a family history of genetic trouble; those with diabetes, hyperthyroidism or some 125 other metabolic diseases; those plagued by miscarriages or stillborn infants; and those of a few susceptible ethnic groups. Greeks and Italians of Mediterranean origin, for example, should be tested for thalassemia (a rare type of anemia), Eastern European Jews for Tay-Sachs disease and blacks for sickle-cell trait. Close relatives are counseled against having children. First cousins, for example, have one-eighth of their genes in common. Thus a man carrying the gene for cystic fibrosis has one chance in 400 of marrying another carrier if she is unrelated—but one in eight if she is a first cousin.

Parents who fall in a high-risk category will find a session with a genetic counselor an intensive experience. In one Manhattan clinic, typical of big-city facilities, a counselor first talks with parents by phone, explaining the procedure and requesting complete family medical records. Next, the parents come in for a morning or afternoon session. They

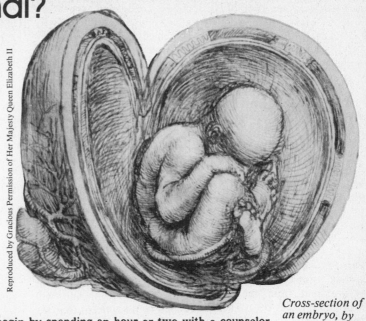

Reproduced by Gracious Permission of Her Majesty Queen Elizabeth II

Cross-section of an embryo, by Leonardo da Vinci

begin by spending an hour or two with a counselor who draws a detailed "pedigree," a schematized medical geneology essential for tracing inheritance patterns. If the parents are accompanied by a child with an ailment suspected to be genetic, the child is given a thorough physical exam. (A counselor's medical training is important at this point, since it enables him to screen out nongenetic disorders.)

The family then is asked to wait while the counselor enters a closed-door session with a group of specialists. This group discusses the case, deciding whether enough is known for a diagnosis or if further tests are needed. If the parents have lost a child to cystic fibrosis, for example, the counselors can quickly tell them that they are both unaffected carriers of the gene and that each succeeding child will have one chance in four of inheriting the disease. If biochemical or chromosomal tests must be done, the counselor explains why and makes another appointment. Such tests may take from three to six weeks and are designed to indicate whether crucial genes are functioning normally.

A gene is simply a portion of a ladderlike molecule of DNA—a substance present in the nucleus of every cell. The structures of various genes will set the patterns of cell growth and so determine such inherited traits as hair, skin and eye color, body structure and the like. In addition, gene structures determine how normal chemical reactions will occur within the cell, and how body functions that depend on those reactions will take place. Although no one has ever seen a gene, the proper functioning of tens of thousands of them is essential to producing and maintaining a normal human body.

To test this functioning, researchers grow large numbers of similar cells from samples of blood or skin, in much the same way "cultures" of bacteria are grown from small colonies. This has made it feasible to discover cell irregularities that could not be determined from the examination of a single cell. For example, the culture of cells can be as-

1573. The Huguenot women of the city of La Rochelle, France, fight side by side with their men in defending the walls from an attack by the Catholic army under Francois, Duc d'Alencon. It is said their courage was such that, during a lull in the battle, the besieging Catholic gentlemen doff their hats and bow, while the common soldiers cheer them lustily.

sayed biochemically for signs of trouble such as the ineffectiveness or lack of an essential enzyme. This could well indicate a genetic error, since if any of the dozens of genes thought to order the production of an enzyme are not formed properly, that enzyme could be disorganized and useless. The enzyme galactase, for example, is essential to digestion of milk sugar; if the enzyme is defective, a child who drinks milk will develop a disorder known as galactosemia, causing cataracts, cirrhosis of the liver, mental retardation and even death within the first month. If galactosemia is detected in prenatal testing for genetic problems, milk can be withheld from the newborn infant's diet before damage can begin.

By cell culturing, a scientist can also produce good samples for chromosome analysis. The chromosomes (really long chains of genes) are visible only when they divide, an event that occurs as the cell and its nucleus are reproduced. Scientists have learned how to use chemical processes to "freeze" them in the act of dividing so that they may be scanned for missing sections or irregularities. A counselor may, for example, be asked to determine what is wrong with an adolescent girl with infantile sex organs, drooping eyelids, a webbed neck, and short stature. Seeing these symptoms, an experienced counselor will immediately suspect Turner's syndrome and order a chromosome scan. If each of the girl's cells lacks one female sex chromosome (the x chromosome), the counselor must confirm his suspicions to the parents: The girl will never be able to bear children. At the same time, knowing why usually comes as a relief to all concerned.

These new tests can also be used to detect genetic mistakes early in a pregnant woman who has reason to expect trouble (one who belongs to a high-risk group, or who has been exposed during pregnancy to X-rays, German

measles or some drugs). Doctors have developed a relatively painless procedure called amniocentesis, usually performed after the 13th week of pregnancy, in which a small amount of fluid is drawn from the amniotic sac in a hollow needle passed through the abdomen. Because the baby moves actively and even breathes in this fluid, it carries fetal cells. Like the blood or skin samples, these cells can be cultured and then scanned for chromosome irregularities, or broken down for biochemical tests.

Requests for amniocentesis come most frequently from doctors of older women concerned about having a child with Down's syndrome, or Mongolism. The counselor will explain to the woman that the chances of bearing a Mongoloid child increase rapidly toward middle age: Before age 30, they are about one in 3,000; from age 30 to 34, they rise to one in 600; from 35 to 39, one in 280; from 40 to 44, one in 100, and after 45, one in 50. Because a woman's lifetime supply of egg cells is formed even before she is born, the odds of "over-ripeness" or environmental damage increase as she grows older. Thanks to amniocentesis and cell-culturing, it is now easy to pick out the telltale irregularity of Down's syndrome—an extra chromosome No. 21.

Then comes the hard part. The counselor will probably tell the parents that if mental retardation is severe, the child may have to spend life in an institution. He will also point out that advances in heart surgery and antibiotic use have extended the lifespan of many Mongoloids far past the old limit of childhood. Then it is up to the parents whether to have the child and hope that its symptoms will be mild, or to end the pregnancy by abortion and try again. The choice is a cruel one, but most parents would prefer the option to a *fait accompli* in the delivery room.

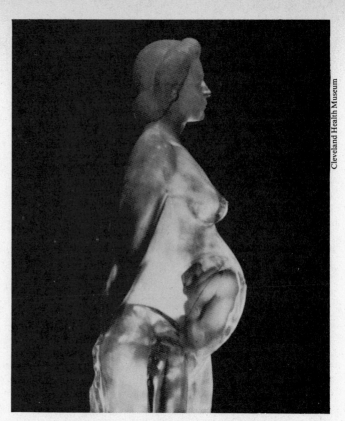

Transparent plastic model of a pregnant woman

Both Turner's and Down's syndromes belong to the class of defects caused by chromosome mistakes. Such a mistake occurs when any one of the 46 chromosomes present in every normal cell is missing, duplicated or broken. These errors occur either in the egg or sperm before conception, or in the embryo after, and are passed on to many or all of the subsequent cell divisions. Each chromosome may be composed of hundreds of genes, so such a mistake will disrupt a vast number of genetic instructions. Of these mistakes, those affecting the two sex chromosomes, x and y, are thought to be the mildest; individuals with Turner's syndrome do, at least, survive. When a defect involves a mistake on one of the 44 autosomes (nonsex chromosomes), the damage is far more severe. As many as 65 symptoms have been described in Mongoloids, and all this disruption is caused by merely an extra copy of one of the smallest autosomes. Children lacking any autosome, even the smallest, are never born alive.

Chromosome mistakes are so gross that they are usually visible under a microscope. Most of the 2,000 or so known genetic defects, however, are caused by only one or a few invisible genes. Since the popularization of Mendel's laws of genetic behavior after the turn of the century, geneticists have been tracing and classifying these heritable errors. The three best-known are dominant, recessive and sex-linked. The names are strictly behavioral; presumably, a dominant gene would look just like a recessive gene if they were visible.

Mendel discovered that all genes are inherited in pairs— one from the male parent and one from the female. If a defect is caused by a dominant gene, that gene will "mask" the efforts of its normal partner, producing the defect. In the case of some chronic glaucomas, Huntington's chorea, achondroplastic dwarfism, polydactyly (too many fingers or toes) and nearly 1,000 other ailments, the defective gene is dominant to its normal matching gene. If a person with one of these traits

1575. Among the many versions of the Transylvanian "Vampire Countess" tale, the following is commonly repeated: Elizabeth Bathory becomes convinced this year that bathing her aging body in the fresh blood of virgins will rejuvenate her. With the aid of her dwarf, Ficsko, and an old crone nurse, she murders more than fifty of her castle

has children, each of them stands a chance of one in two of picking up the bad gene. (Just as a coin may come up heads three or four times in a row, however, such odds do not guarantee that a healthy child will follow an abnormal child; gamblers and geneticists agree that "chance has no memory.")

A recessive disorder is one caused by genes whose possible effects are usually masked by dominant normal genes. For a child to inherit any of about 800 recessive diseases, such as cystic fibrosis, galactosemia, sickle-cell disease, or Tay-Sachs disease, he must receive the defective gene from each parent, and the defective genes must be paired together. Thus, even if both parents carry the defective recessive gene, the child has only a one-in-four chance of being afflicted, a two-in-four chance of being a healthy carrier, and a one-in-four chance of being neither a carrier nor a sufferer.

Another 150 or so diseases are also recessive, but sex-linked as well. That is, the gene appears only on the x, or female, sex chromosome. (The y, or male, sex chromosome carries no known genetic information except male reproductive orders.) Because females have two x chromosomes, the normal dominant usually masks the recessive that causes such traits as color blindness, muscular dystrophy, hemophilia, and agammaglobulinemia (lack of normal defense against disease). Males, on the other hand, have only one x chromosome to go with their y. If that x is defective, there is no other x to mask it. Queen Victoria was perhaps history's best-known carrier of a sex-linked disease, hemophilia; unaffected herself, she passed it on to several royal sons and grandsons. When such a female carrier marries, each son has one chance in two of inheriting the trait; each daughter has a one-in-two chance of being a carrier. Affected men who bear children will produce only carrier daughters; sons, who inherit his y

chromosome, cannot get his x-linked trait.

Less understood, and less predictable, are malformations caused by combinations of genes, such as hydrocephaly, clubfoot, cleft lip and/or palate, and spina bifida. Something like 20 seperate genes are thought to cause anencephaly, or incomplete brain and skull formation. The mother may have 15 of these genes, the father 10; neither would be affected, but in combination they may produce an affected offspring. In the population as a whole, about one in 1,000 newborns is anencephalic. If parents have one child with such a disease, most genetic counselors predict that the odds of having another are about one in 20; if two children, about one in 10. Fortunately, these usually fatal spinal and cranial distortions can be detected in utero by a sonarlike ultrasound profiler (now used routinely with amniocentesis) or by protein tests on amniotic fluid.

The effectiveness of these new tests in averting years of suffering is illustrated in the case of Rachel R., whose sister had lost two infants to Tay-Sachs disease. When Rachel married, she and her husband John feared the same fate for their children: Both were descendents of Ashkenazic Jews, one in 30 of whom carry this recessive gene. Tay-Sachs babies seem normal at birth, and are often exceptionally beautiful. But at the age of six months, development begins to slow because of an error in body chemistry. Nerve cells rupture and die, responses slow gradually, and the brain deteriorates.

Before Rachel became pregnant, she and John were both tested by a genetic counselor and told the bad news that both of them, although healthy themselves, were carriers of the Tay-Sachs gene. Each child of theirs would stand a 1-in-4 chance of inheriting the fatal disorder. But after their counselor told them that Tay-Sachs can now be picked up by amniocente-

sis, they decided to try for a child. Rachel was tested during her 14th week of pregnancy and, to her delight, the results were negative. Their baby would be born free of the disease, and she could look forward to the rest of pregnancy with peace of mind. On the other hand, the child would have to be tested again after birth: It would have a 2-in-3 chance of being an unaffected carrier, and would want to know with certainty before having children.

The big challenge to genetics, of course, is not simply to identify early the genetic mistakes that cause Tay-Sachs babies, but to correct them. Already a few halting steps have been taken in this direction. One young boy with agammaglobulinemia, the sex-linked inability to stave off disease and infection, was rescued by injection of about a billion bone-marrow cells from his sister. Even more ambitious are plans to implant slow-dissolving microcapsules of enzymes to supplement a faulty metabolic system, or even to inject bits of genetic material to replace or correct faulty genes.

Such genetic wizardry is not yet part of the counselor's repertoire. In fact, some counselors complain that popularization of amniocentesis has led to impossible requests by women who want a "beautiful baby" or a "perfect child." Counselors also spend much of their time dealing with false alarms. Dr. Laurence Karp of the University of Washington reports a case of a pregnant woman whose doctor thought amniocentesis should be performed as a "last resort," because her brother was mentally retarded. The brother's problem could not be assigned to a known genetic syndrome, however, and Dr. Karp had to explain that amniocentesis would not help. Another physician requested Karp's group to "check the chromosomes" of a patient known to be a Tay-Sachs carrier. The counselors

explained that a chromosome check would be useless; to detect Tay-Sachs disease, cells of the fetus must be grown in a test tube and then analyzed biochemically, and the process would take several weeks. The woman declined the tests, saying that by then she would be feeling the baby move and could not consider abortion.

Although most patients are still referred by their private physicians, many now seek genetic advice on their own. "People are becoming more sophisticated," says a counselor at Albert Einstein College of Medicine. "More than a third of our patients are calling us direct." Most counselors work at large medical centers where they combine clinical sessions with community screening programs. An in-clinic counseling session typically costs $25, a Tay-Sachs test $10 per couple, a chromosome analysis $75, and amniocentesis, including culture and analysis, $100 to $150. The procedures are usually covered by medical insurance; for those without coverage who cannot pay, there is usually no charge. "The last thing we want," says Lynn Godmilow of Mount Sinai Medical Center, "is for people to stay away because they think they can't pay."

The training of the counselors themselves has barely begun. As recently as 10 years ago, only a handful of medical schools offered courses in genetics; now most do. Thus, of the few hundred counselors in the entire country, most have entered the field within the last few years. If every patient in a high-risk category were to seek help, their ranks would be overwhelmed. Yet to these hardy pioneers, every new patient may bring the cause of another genetic disease, and with the cause the hope of a new cure. "Hardly a week goes by when we don't discover something new," says a busy counselor between sessions. "If anyone has any questions about genetics, they should call us."

maids over time. Later her husband dies, leaving her alone to indulge her appetite till her 641st victim escapes alive to tell all. Convicted of her crimes, Elizabeth is confined to her own dungeon, where she eventually goes raving mad and dies. Claims circulate that the spectre of the Vampire Countess still haunts the ruins of the castle.

Common Complaints of Pregnancy

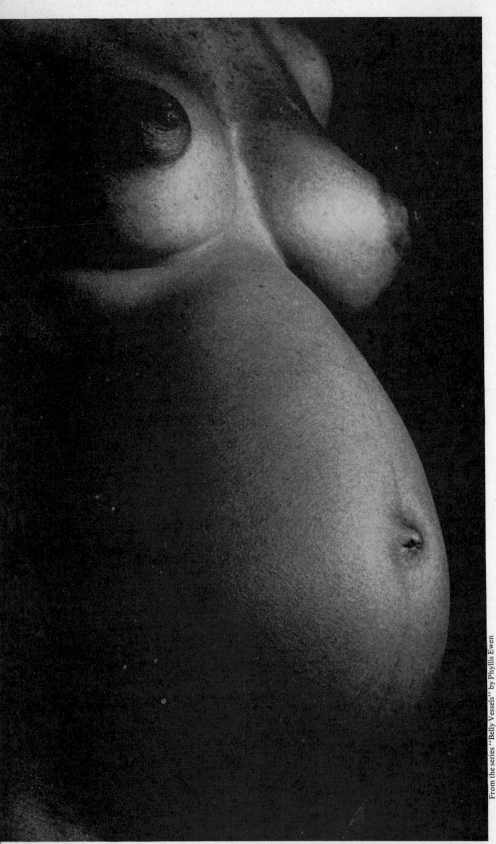

From the series "Belly Vessels" by Phyllis Ewen

Fatigue. As your pregnancy progresses, you will feel less tired. The only thing for you to do is to get plenty of sleep at night and rest occasionally during the day.

Frequent Urination. About the third month of pregnancy you will find that this will not be as much of a problem. In the last month of your pregnancy, the desire to empty your bladder frequently will reoccur. At this time, it is due to the baby pressing against your bladder as it is getting ready to be born.

There is nothing much you can do to prevent frequent urination. If however you have a burning sensation when you urinate, tell your doctor.

Morning Sickness. Early morning nausea is usually due to body changes that take place early in pregnancy and generally ends about the third month. A few of you may have it throughout the day. If vomiting continues and you can not keep fluids down you should report this to your doctor.

Morning sickness can often be relieved by eating a dry piece of toast or a cracker about a half-hour before getting out of bed in the morning. When you get up, move slowly.

Greasy, fried foods and any food that you know disagrees with you should not be eaten at this time. Unsweetened popcorn has helped some women. Eating 5 small meals a day often works better than 3 large meals, and small amounts of gingerale or coke are often helpful.

Heartburn. Heartburn is a burning sensation caused by indigestion.

Do NOT take baking soda or sodium bicarbonate to relieve your heartburn. Try some of the same hints as with morning sickness.

Tell your doctor about heartburn because there are some medicines which he can prescribe for you if you are uncomfortable. Don't take medicines

From *Prenatal Care*, 1973, Department of Health, Education and Welfare.

1575. Mary Herbert, countess of Pembroke, "had a pritty, sharpe-ovall face" but she was also "very salacious, & shee had a contrivance that in the spring of the yeare (deletion) ...the stallions (another deletion) were to be brought before such a part of the house, where she had a *vidette* (small window) to look on them while (deletion)."

advertised on television, radio or in magazines.

Constipation. There are several things you can do to relieve constipation. Drink lots of water—6 to 8 glasses a day. Eat fruits and vegetables, preferably raw ones as they add roughage to your diet. Exercise every day as this keeps your body toned up. Make a habit of going to the bathroom every day at the same time. If you continue to be troubled after trying these, tell your doctor about it. Do not take enemas or harsh laxatives on your own.

Backache. As your pregnancy progresses, your posture changes because your womb is growing and your pelvic bone joints relax. This causes your back to ache. Low heeled supporting shoes may be helpful.

Good posture is important in preventing backache. Remember that if there is someone around who can lift things for you, have someone do it.

There are several exercises which should help you.

The squatting position helps to avoid back strain and to strengthen muscles you will use in labor. This position is a good one to take to reach low drawers or for lifting a child or object from the floor:

Lower your body slowly into a squatting position by using the wall as a support. Keep your feet parallel and heels on the floor.

Hold onto a heavy piece of furniture. Squat down on your heels and allow your knees to spread apart. Keep your heels flat on the floor and your toes straight ahead.

Pick up your child or object from the floor by squatting. Hold your child or object close to your body. Rise slowly, using your leg muscles.

The following exercise, called the "Pelvic Rock" increases the flexibility of your lower back, and strengthens your abdominal muscles. It not only relieves backache, but will help improve your posture and appearance. Practice it every day and try walking and standing with your pelvis tilted forward. This provides your baby with a cradle of bone in which to lie instead of your abdominal wall.

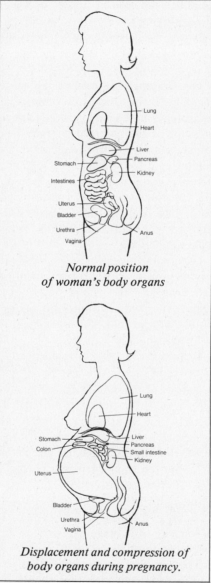

Russ Hoover

Lung
Heart
Liver
Pancreas
Stomach
Kidney
Intestines
Uterus
Bladder
Urethra
Anus
Vagina

*Normal position
of woman's body organs*

Lung
Heart
Liver
Stomach
Pancreas
Colon
Small intestine
Kidney
Uterus
Bladder
Urethra
Anus
Vagina

*Displacement and compression of
body organs during pregnancy.*

When you practice the pelvic rock standing up you can use a chair. Stand about 2 feet away from the back of the chair and bend slightly forward from your hips. Place your hands on the chair back and keep your elbows straight. Rotate your hips backward and sag with your abdominal muscles. You have a real "sway back" this way.

Flex your knees slightly and then slowly rotate your hips forward. Tuck your buttocks under as if someone were pushing you from behind.

Practice the pelvic rock lying on your back, knees bent and feet flat on the floor. Tighten your lower abdominal muscles and muscles of the buttocks. This causes the tailbone to be elevated and the small of your back pressed into the floor. Then—relax your abdominal and buttock muscles. As you do this, arch your back as high as you can. Repeat tightening your abdominal and buttock muscles being sure that the small of your back presses tightly into the floor.

There are other exercises which you can be shown at prenatal classes.

Shortness of Breath. Difficult breathing or shortness of breath is due to the baby taking up so much space in your abdomen. This will go away as soon as the baby is born.

Moving slowly conserves your breath. Lying flat may be difficult and you may feel more comfortable in using more than one pillow. Lying on your side may also help.

Varicose Veins. Varicose veins are an enlargement of your veins. They usually occur in your lower legs, but may extend up into the pelvic area or exist as hemorrhoids. Your enlarged uterus presses on your abdominal veins and interferes with the return of blood from your legs. Frequently, these varicose veins get smaller and disappear during the first few weeks after you have your baby.

It is wiser to try to avoid problems than cure them. You can help avoid varicose veins by not wearing round garters or tight clothing. If at all possible, do not stand in one place for a long period of time. If you have a job that requires you to stand, walk about at break time to circulate the blood. If you can, sit down and put your feet up occasionally. Do not sit with your legs

ca. **1585.** Paralleling Greek and Oriental practices of this time, Russian women are required to live in a separate portion of the house. It is a Russian proverb that "Russian wives are unhappy and say their husbands do not love them unless they are beaten regularly." Laws governing domestic relations are similarly enlightened.

crossed or with the pressure of a chair under your knees. Sitting down jobs such as being a secretary or assembly line worker often aggravate varicose veins.

The position shown in the picture, where you can lie on a bed, couch, or floor and raise your feet and legs up in the air, resting your heels against the wall, is a good position to take if you have varicose veins or swelling in your legs. Take this position for 2 to 5 minutes several times a day if possible.

You may be asked to wear elastic bandages or elastic stockings during the day. "Support" hose will help you some, but they are not as effective as elastic hose. If you are told to wear elastic stockings, put them on before you get up in the morning, before your veins get filled with blood. Take your hose off at night before you go to bed and wash them in mild soap. If you are using elastic bandages, they should be put on before getting out of bed in the morning and taken off at night. Apply the bandages spirally with a firm, even pressure. Begin at the foot and move up the leg until you are above the varicose veins. Your doctor or nurse will help show you how to apply elastic bandages.

If you have varicose veins around your vaginal area, try to take frequent rest periods by lying down with a pillow under your buttocks. This position elevates your hips and gives you some relief.

Hemorrhoids. Again, prevention is important. Try not to become constipated so that you need not strain when you have a bowel movement. Straining may cause hemorrhoids to protrude through your rectum. If this should happen, tell your doctor. The doctor or nurse will show you how to push them back into the rectum.

The position in the illustration, of lying down on your side with your hips on a pillow will help relieve your hemorroids.

An ice bag or a compress of clean gauze or fabric soaked in cold witch hazel or a solution of Epsom salts will give you relief.

If your hemorrhoids bleed, let your doctor know.

Leg Cramps. Leg cramps are more common during the later months of your pregnancy and are generally due to pressure of the enlarged uterus. You can get some relief from leg cramps by holding on to a back of a chair, standing about 6 inches away from it. Slide the foot as far back as you can and keep the heel on the floor. This stretches the calf muscle and helps relieve the cramp.

If you are lying down and someone is around to help, extend the cramped leg and have another person push down against your knee and push up against the sole of your foot so that your foot is at a right angle to your leg.

If cramps continue, tell your doctor.

Vaginal Discharge. During pregnancy, there is an increase in vaginal secretions. It is usually nothing to be concerned about. However, if you notice that the discharge has one of the following you should tell your doctor.
☐ yellow or greenish color
☐ bad odor
☐ heavy and frothy flow
☐ burning or itching
☐ bloody flow
There is always a possibility that you may have an infection that should be treated.

Skin Changes. You may notice pink or reddish streaks on your abdomen and breasts. This is due to stretching of your skin. These streaks grow lighter in color or a silvery-white after pregnancy. There is not too much you can do about stretch marks. Do not gain an extra amount of weight. Skin changes do not occur in all women. This is probably because some skin is more elastic.

Some women notice blotches on their face. Do not become upset as they go away right after you have your baby.

Abdominal Discomfort. This is frequent during the last 2 to 3 months of pregnancy. Your pelvic joints are more moveable and getting your body ready for the baby to be delivered. There are other possible reasons for this discomfort such as being constipated, having an infection or even appendicitis. So let your doctor know if you are uncomfortable.

Complications of Pregnancy

Although I mentioned that childbearing is normal, the line between health and sickness can be difficult to draw because there are so many changes going on in your body. Early and continuous care during your pregnancy will help prevent illness. Most complications will give you some warning and immediate care by your doctor will help you prevent serious illness to both you and your baby. Some of the first warnings of a complication may show up in a change in your blood pressure, urine or weight. This is why these are usually checked each time you go to the doctor.

What Should I Look For Between Checkups? You may be the first one to notice symptoms which are at times referred to as the "danger signals." They are:
☐ Bleeding, no matter how slight, from any place—vaginal, rectal, breast, nipple, or coughing blood
☐ Swelling or puffiness of your face or hands and a sudden excessive weight gain
☐ Severe, continuous headache
☐ Dimness, blurring of vision, or flashes of light or spots before your eyes
☐ Sharp or continuous pain in your abdomen
☐ Severe or continuous vomiting

1585. Johann, archbishop of Treves, Germany, sentences so many to be burnt at the stake as witches that only two women remain alive in his two districts.

192 Complaints of Pregnancy
MOTHERHOOD

☐ Chills and/or fever
☐ Sudden escape of fluid from the vagina

If you should have any of the above symptoms, notify your doctor right away. Do not wait for your next checkup. If anything is wrong, treatment should be started immediately.

Miscarriage. A miscarriage, or, medically speaking, abortion, means that the baby is born before it has developed enough to live outside your body. The majority of miscarriages occur during the first three months of pregnancy. A miscarriage may follow a fall, infection or health problems. About one in every ten pregnancies ends this way. If you notice any bleeding from your vagina, go to bed immediately even though bleeding does not always mean that you are having a miscarriage. Call your doctor and save the pads you wear to catch the blood, clots and tissue. The doctor will want to inspect these.

Miscarriages are not usually dangerous to you and most women have little difficulty becoming pregnant again and have a normal baby.

Severe Vomiting. Morning sickness is a common complaint. However, if you keep vomiting and cannot keep anything down, you should report this to your doctor. You need to be nourished and so does your baby. If you keep vomiting neither of you are getting the foods and liquids you need.

Anemia or Low Hemoglobin or Low Blood Count. The actual amount of your blood increases when you are pregnant. Hemoglobin is a substance in your blood that carries oxygen to all your tissues and to your baby. You may be anemic because you are not eating enough foods high in iron. When you are pregnant you need more iron than usual. Foods high in iron are lean meats, liver and eggs. Often your doctor will prescribe iron pills to give you the added iron you need.

You may be anemic due to other blood disease such as Sickle Cell. This disease is most common among black people. You are checked to see if you

have this disease when your laboratory work is done on your first or an early visit to the doctor. If you should have this kind of blood disease you will be told about it by your doctor and you will be given whatever special care that may be necessary.

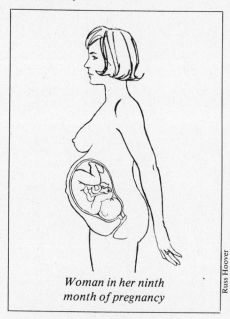

Woman in her ninth month of pregnancy

Russ Hoover

Bladder and Kidney Infections. You are more likely to get a urinary infection now because of changes in this part of your body. You may have symptoms such as abdominal pain, chills, fever, frequent or burning on urination and possible blood in your urine. If you have such problems, contact your doctor as there are certain medicines he can prescribe for you to help clear this infection. One important thing you can do is to drink as much water as you possibly can if you should have a urinary infection.

Toxemia. This is a complication which may be very serious. At the time of this writing, medical scientists do not know why this complication may occur in some women. The important thing is that it can be treated. You should notify your doctor immediately if you have a sudden weight gain, or swelling of your feet and hands, severe headaches, dizziness, blurred vision, or spots before your eyes.

Changes in your urine and an increase in your blood pressure may be signs of toxemia.

As long as problems are found early,

taken care of immediately, and you follow the instructions that are given you, the chances are that toxemia can be controlled at home. This is a serious enough complication that some women must be hospitalized to be cared for properly because it can be dangerous both for you and your baby.

Rh Factor. At your visit when your blood is taken for laboratory examination, it is checked to see if you have a substance called Rh in your blood. If you have this substance you are Rh positive; if you do not your blood is Rh negative. If both you and the father of the baby are Rh negative there is no problem. However, if you are Rh negative and the father of the baby is Rh positive, the baby's blood may be Rh positive. If that is so, your body may manufacture an antibody which affects your baby's Rh positive blood cells. Antibodies are normally useful because they protect you against many common diseases, but at this time they can make the baby anemic.

Fortunately, this is not a big problem with your first pregnancy even if you are Rh negative. Only about 15% of white women are Rh negative. This is much less common in black women.

If you should be a woman who is Rh negative, your doctor will do certain tests to find out just how much affect it is having on your blood and your baby's blood. It may be necessary to deliver the baby before it is full term.

There is a medicine that you may be given after each pregnancy to protect each baby of your future pregnancies from this problem. It is effective for the greater majority of women. Your doctor will tell you more about this if you should need the medicine.

German Measles or Rubella. You may know this disease as "three day measles." If you should get this disease just prior to, or early in your pregnancy, your baby may be harmed. If you learn that you have been in contact with anyone who has German measles, tell your doctor as he may want to do some tests on you and will also want to be extra careful in examining your baby when it is born.

Birth Methods

Marcia L. Storch, M.D., Helen Swallow, and Jean Marzollo

METHOD	ADVANTAGES	DISADVANTAGES
1. Prepared Childbirth. Also called natural, psychoprophylactic, and (mistakenly, many feel) "painless" childbirth. The mother is educated about the process of birth and is coached by a partner, usually the father, who shares her education and is present during labor and delivery. Medication is not used unless necessary, and when used, usually given in lower quantities. The most well-known method of prepared childbirth is the Lamaze method, which teaches special breathing, concentration, and relaxation. Other methods are: the Bradley method, which encourages the mother to accept, rather than control, her body and feelings; and the Jacobson method, which stresses relaxation.	Less medication required and less likelihood of forceps being used. Feelings of great joy and triumph afterwards. Pushing is cooperative and effective. The recuperative process after birth is shortened and more pleasant. The mother and father can fully experience the birth event. Education valuable in allaying fears during pregnancy.	If pain is experienced, the couple sometimes feels they did something wrong. Such feelings of failure are found most often in women who do not fully understand the event, but what first mother does? If a woman expects only joy and beauty, she may find the work, pain, and sweat unattractive and unacceptable.
2. Analgesia (medication given during labor to relieve pain), e.g., Demerol. Given to the mother by injection but not before labor is well established and not when delivery is imminent. The analgesia is usually given along with a potentiator, such as Vistiril.	Diminishes perception of labor pains. May help cervix to relax, thereby decreasing pain and accelerating labor.	Women respond individually: some get high; some have nausea. May cause temporary depression of the newborn's respiration.
3. Regional Anesthesia for Labor Only. Paracervical block. An injection of a numbing substance alongside the cervix provides pain relief during latter half of labor without drowsiness or paralysis.	Easy to do. Short-acting. The mother can still feel the urge to push and respond vigorously to it.	Does not provide pain relief for the delivery. May cause temporary slowing of baby's heartrate.
4. Regional Anesthesia for Labor and Delivery. Various kinds: epidural (also called peridural), and caudal. Pain relief is provided without drowsiness but sometimes with paralysis by injection of a numbing substance beside the spinal nerves.	Relief of pain after administered, though doctors often wait until labor is well established to give the medication.	The mother cannot feel the urge to push so must be told when to do so. Medication can temporarily slow down baby's heartbeat.
5. Regional Anesthesia for Delivery and Episiotomy. Various kinds: spinal, saddle block (also called low spinal), pudendal block, and local anesthesia. The spinal and saddle block provide pain relief with paralysis below the waist by the injection of a numbing substance into the spinal canal. For a pudendal block an injection through the side walls of the vagina numbs the lower vagina and the perineum. For local anesthesia, an injection in the perineum numbs that area.	Saddle block provides relief for painful forceps delivery. Spinal (and peridural) provides safe anesthesia for Caesarean section. Pudendal and local provide easy, safe relief for normal delivery and episiotomy.	In the case of spinal and saddle block, paralysis may be undesired, and the injection into the spinal canal can be complicated by infection or injury, though this is rare. Headache following delivery is not uncommon.
6. General Anesthesia. Medication renders mother unconscious. Use primarily for Caesarian section and difficult forceps deliveries.	Can be done quickly. Provides good relaxation of uterus and complete pain relief.	Can be a respiratory depressant on the baby. Mother misses out on birth experience.
7. Other Medications. Tranquilizers may be given during labor to relax the mother and decrease dosage of analgesia. Barbiturates may be given to a mother in false labor to help her sleep.	As stated.	None, if usage is not abused.
8. Other Methods. Twilight sleep (includes use of Scopolamine or Scope) is an amnesiac and hallucinogen given in combination with other drugs early in labor. Trilene, N_2O (Nitrous Oxide), and Penthrane are inhalation analgesias for delivery administered by a mask. Hypnotism and acupuncture are not described in this chart.	Twilight sleep makes the mother forget her delivery—a debatable advantage. Inhalation analgesias: may be self-controlled; are minimally dangerous.	Twilight sleep, unpopular today, can be dangerous for the mother and baby. Inhalation analgesia can make the mother feel dopey or silly. Excessive use may depress infant.

From *9 Months 1 Day 1 Year: A Guide to Pregnancy, Birth, and Babycare,* written by Parents, compiled by Jean Marzollo. Copyright © Jean Marzollo. Reprinted by permission of Harper & Row, Publishers, Inc.

1589. At Quedlinburg, Germany, 133 witches are burnt in one day "for having danced sacrilegiously at a witches' congress on Blocksberg mountain and for having emptied the cellars of fourteen of the wealthiest people in the vicinity of their wine for unholy use on that occasion."

Hospital and Home Births

Sometimes it makes sense to select a hospital before a doctor, especially if what you want is one of the more innovative hospitals that offers a family-oriented maternity plan geared to provide humane, personalized care for the new baby and the new baby's family. Characteristically such plans invite full participation of the father during labor, delivery, and after the baby is born; they offer rooming-in (an arrangement whereby the baby rooms with the mother for most or all of the day); they encourage breastfeeding; they allow sibling visitation. Some hospitals may have some of these features but not others. Lamaze-trained physicians are not necessarily affiliated with family-oriented hospitals. It makes sense to call the hospital directly to inquire about their policies.

Another reason to select a hospital before a doctor is if you have heard from reliable sources that a particular hospital is better than others in your area. Some women feel that the best medical care is provided by university teaching hospitals.

If you like your doctor but not his or her hospital and if you are having a normal pregnancy without complications and if you are so inclined, you might consider the possibility of giving birth at home with your doctor there to help. In some areas a portable operating unit is driven to a home in which a delivery is occurring. Parents pay for the security of having emergency facilities on hand, whether or not they need to be used.

If you want or have to give birth at a particular hospital even if it doesn't have the features you'd like, resist, when feasible, pressures that go against your own nature. For example, if you want to breast-feed but know your hospital doesn't especially encourage it, bring along a book on breast feeding and proceed with the author's help. Ignore nurses who discourage you. Your determination may help them be more openminded to the next nursing mother.

Doctors

Some obstetricians work alone; others work in groups. The advantage of the former is that you see the same person at each visit and are apt to develop a closer relationship with the doctor.

A group practice, on the other hand, assures that you will know the doctor who delivers your baby. Since the doctors work as a team, rotating check-ups, you see each one several times. It doesn't matter if one goes on vacation; the others automatically substitute for him.

An obstetrician who works alone makes arrangements ahead of time for you to see a colleague if your due date comes during his or her vacation.

Prenatal clinics at good hospitals offer excellent maternity care if you don't mind the waiting before each check-up. One mother suggests that if you use a clinic you get there first thing in the morning before the number of patients builds up. Teaching hospitals can usually be depended on to have good clinics, and in most hospitals clinic patients have the same benefits as private patients: the same kind of labor and delivery rooms, the same staff and staff training. If the staff is trained for Lamaze, clinic patients will be encouraged to use the method. One disadvantage of clinics is that you never know who will deliver your baby. This can be offset by low costs and the fact that many clinics employ nurse-midwives who give a kind of personalized care that hurried doctors seldom provide.

Midwives

Nurse-midwifery is a growing profession in this country. According to the American College of Nurse-midwives, "the nurse-midwife is a Registered Nurse who by virtue of added knowledge and skill gained through an organized program of study and clinical experience recognized by the American College of Nurse-midwives has extended the limits of her practice into the area of management of care of mothers and babies throughout the maternity cycle so long as progress meets criteria accepted as normal."

Nurse-midwives provide prenatal care, care at the time of birth, and unlike obstetricians, they continue to care for the mother *and* newborn baby. Many women report that midwives are more sympathetic, compassionate, and respectful than the average male obstetrician.

Nurse-midwives function within the framework of medically-directed health centers. Their license to practice is determined by the legal jurisdiction in which they are employed.

For more information, write the American College of Nurse-midwives, Suite 500, 1000 Vermont Ave., N.W., Washington, D.C. 20005.

Not all midwives are nurse-midwives. Many others operate outside of medical institutions, as they've been doing for millennia (midwifery being one of the oldest professions). In recent years a renaissance of lay midwifery has developed in California with many families enjoying home birth under a midwife's care.

1595. Chand Bibi, Sultana of Bijapur in India, defends her city from the Mogul invasion, despite the advice of her city commander, Nasir Kahn, who is ready to surrender. Covering her face with the required veil, she personally leads the fray, successfully lifting the siege.

Birth of Baby

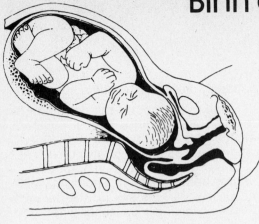

1. Just before birth, baby rests head downward. Delivery has started, but not necessarily labor pains.

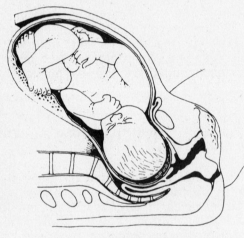

2. Labor has begun. Cervix is dilating; baby's head is pressing downward through the opening.

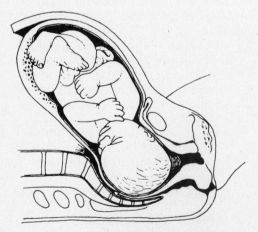

3. Cervix has dilated and head rests on pelvic floor. Membrane around the fetus has not yet ruptured.

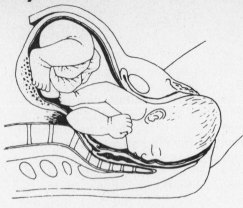

4. The mother's "tail bone" or coccyx is bent back. Baby's body is streamlined to make the exit easier.

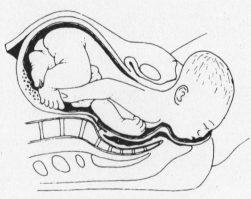

5. The head emerges and turns upward, accentuating the lengthening of the baby's head.

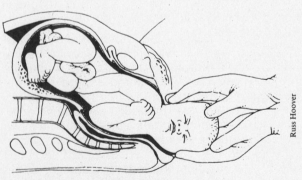

6. While shoulders emerge, doctor's hands support head. Baby's cry indicates it has started to breathe.

Russ Hoover

ca. **1600.** In England, the ducking stool becomes a uniform fixture of justice reserved for shrewish or scolding wives. On the Continent, the stool is replaced by a large hamper or cage suspended from a gallows. The imprisoned woman is plunged at sunset into the nearest pond—basket and all—however many times stipulated by her court sentence.

The Leboyer Way:
Birth Without Violence

Ellen Goodman

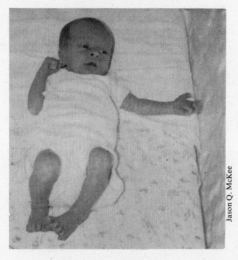

Jason Q. McKee

He is a gentle man, this Dr. Leboyer from France. A peaceful man.

And when you look at pictures of newborn babies with him, he insists that you use your eyes. And when you hear the sounds of a newborn, he insists that you use your ears.

"Do you believe that birth is an enjoyable experience for the baby?" he asks.

"When babies are born they start shouting and screaming. Why don't they just breathe? Could it be that being born is as painful for the baby as it used to be for the mother?"

With these questions and the gentle insistence that we respond to a newborn as the most sensitive of humans, Frederic Leboyer, a French obstetrician, has begun something of a revolution in the way children are born.

The wiry, gray-haired doctor had delivered thousands of babies the traditional way, hearing the shrieking through his mind as the sound of good healthy lungs, and seeing the thrashing of agitated limbs as those of an active newborn.

Then, in the process of psychoanalysis, as he tells it, with a primal scream therapist who led him back and back through a series of pivotal traumas in his own life, he re-experienced birth, and rediscovered it as a horrible wrench from a quiet, darkened environment into a cold, glaring, loud and painful one. An environment in which the infant is neither deaf nor blind, but blinded and deafened, he believes by the harsh hospital room.

Gradually, to the horror of the French medical establishment, he began smoothing the transition from womb to world through a method that assumes not only the existence but the importance of the emotional life of a newborn. He calls it simply, "Birth Without Violence."

To an audience at the Harvard Medical School that included only one obstetrician, he talked about the simple non-technical ways he has turned the focus of birth toward the baby.

The newborn is massaged and gently laid on the mother's stomach in a darkened, quiet room, and the umbilical cord severed only as it stops beating. Then the baby is bathed, rocked and caressed with water as it resimulates its own birth.

He showed a beautiful film of the infant slowly opening its eyes, looking around and beginning to explore with its fingers and feet. The same infant, at less than 24 hours old, was playing and smiling.

There seemed to be nothing radical about this nurturing attention. Yet, Dr. Leboyer has become something of a cause celebre in his own country, accused of risking the health of a newborn for radical psychological ideas.

This is partly because he sees birth as an enormously important part of our emotional life. It sets up the primary expectation in a child of how life will be.

"Our aggression as adults," he says, "is a response to early suffering. And birth is the earliest pain. Have you asked yourself why the experience of being left alone is so painful to us as adults? After all, being alone can be painful or pleasant. But we remember it as painful because the first separation is painful," he says opening his arms as if to say, "how simple."

"When I was a medical student we took it for granted that a newborn was essentially a digestive tract. That it couldn't see or hear and had no emotions. But we know that a young baby needs one kind of food that we know very little about: love. We've been giving them medicine because it seems more practical than love."

Leboyer is convinced that a "Birth Without Violence" —also the name of his poetic book (Knopf $7.95)—will make a difference in the lives of children delivered by this method. An independent psychologist is researching 104 of the babies who are now as old as eight, and while the study isn't complete, she has discovered one fact that neither of them can account for: All 104 children are ambidextrous.

Leboyer is willing to admit that he may be overemphasizing the importance of birth. But even if it made no difference, even if it were simply a more humane borning, he asks "Why not try?"

If a child is crying, he reminds us, all of our instincts tell us it is in pain. If a newborn shrieks, we say it is healthy.

He says to look and listen: "For years we said that women had to give birth in pain and now we say, 'No, no that's not right.' Now we have to say the same to the baby."

Much of the American establishment has heard Leboyer's argument and is not amused. Many obstetricians claim that there is no evidence that a traditional birth produces emotional scarring or that Leboyer's method makes happier babies. More important perhaps, they fear that in the Leboyer method insufficient attention is paid to the establishment of proper infant breathing after birth, not necessarily an automatic mechanism. Many of them remain unconvinced that a baby's first cry is one of terror instead of the breath of life. The debate will doubtless continue for years. —Ed.

1600. Anna Roemer of Hamelin, Germany, gives birth to seven children—two boys and five girls—simultaneously on January ninth. The tablet inscription is still to be seen at her home.

The Pros and Cons of Induced Labor

Jane E. Brody

In most women, labor begins spontaneously within two weeks before or after the due date. Sometimes, however, the doctor considers inducing labor—that is, starting it artificially—usually by breaking the amniotic sac, or bag of waters, that surrounds the baby or by injecting a drug called oxytocin (Pitocin) or by a combination of the two methods. Oxytocin also can be used to "stimulate" a labor that is progressing too slowly.

Sometimes labor must be induced because a complication has arisen that threatens the baby's survival.

The induction of labor for nonmedical reasons—so-called "elective" induction, or induction of convenience—is highly controversial. Some doctors say that labor should never be induced solely for the convenience of the physician or the mother. Dr. Ralph Gause, former head of obstetrics at Roosevelt Hospital, in New York City, and former director of research at the National Foundation–March of Dimes, maintains that "elective inductions should never be performed unless the woman is living in a lighthouse in the middle of the ocean." But others point to decided advantages of a "programed" labor and delivery.

These advantages, according to Dr. Edward Bishop, of the University of North Carolina, include being sure that the woman will reach the hospital in time; allowing the mother to prepare her household and to find someone to watch other children at home; and scheduling the labor and delivery for a time when hospital personnel and facilities are optimally available and when the physician is free of other duties.

However, Dr. Bishop says, he is an "absolute tyrant" about when and on whom elective induction should be performed. He emphasizes that the woman must understand the procedure and be willing to undergo it. The doctor must know with certainty that the baby is fully mature. This pregnancy and previous pregnancies must be "uncomplicated" by any condition that might impair the mother's health or endanger the baby. The baby must be lying head down in the uterus and in a position indicating he or she is ready to be born. The cervix must be thinned out and soft, prepared for dilatation.

Once labor has been induced, there is another "absolute" requirement, according to Dr. Harry Fields, a gynecologist at the University of Pennsylvania, who has written a book on the induction of labor: "The doctor should be on the hospital floor at all times (to deal with any complications that may arise) and a nurse should be listening to the fetal

Adapted and reprinted from *Redbook* Magazine, September 1975. Copyright © 1975 The Redbook Publishing Company.

heart and monitoring the mother's contractions continuously. Someone must be beside the patient every second; it this is not possible, the induction should not be done."

In light of these conditions why, then, is elective induction of labor so controversial? A main reason is that many inductions are done under less than ideal conditions. Dr. Merton C. Hatch, professor emeritus of obstetrics and gynecology at Upstate Medical Center in Syracuse, New York, points out: "Outside the major medical centers, doctors don't have the setup and personnel adequate to monitor the fetal heart constantly, and the doctor doing relatively few deliveries a year doesn't have the expertise to select the cases properly."

New York Public Library

One of the snafus that may result from elective induction is prematurity. Dr. Gause estimates that perhaps 10 per cent of cases of prematurity are due to elective induction of labor and elective cesarean section. Dr. Hatch explains: "There isn't anybody smart enough to know every time whether the baby is mature enough to live outside the uterus." There is, however, a test that can be performed on the fluid in the womb, which indicates whether the baby's lungs are mature enough to function well after birth.

Elective induction also has the potential for depriving the baby of needed oxygen. During the normal process of labor, each contraction temporarily reduces the exchange of blood between mother and baby, which also diminishes the amount of oxygen the baby is getting. Then the uterus relaxes and the baby's supply of blood and oxygen is restored. According to Dr. Roberto Caldeyro-Barcia, president-elect of the International Federation of Gynecologists and Obstetricians, when labor is enhanced by drugs the uterine contractions tend to be stronger, longer and with shorter relaxation periods between them. This decreases the ability of the baby to restore his supply of needed oxygen, and if he is deprived of oxygen

long enough, brain damage may result.

Dr. Karlis Adamsons, obstetrician turned neonatal physiologist at Mount Sinai School of Medicine, in New York City, postulates an even grimmer turn of events: "With one contraction following another, the fetus doesn't have a chance to recover—like being caught in the surf. The result can be sudden, unexpected fetal death."

Although several smaller studies revealed no adverse effects from inducing labor in normal pregnancies, in one study of 1,000 induced labors at New York City's Columbia-Presbyterian Medical Center the birth of a "disquieting number of depressed infants" (twice as many as in 1,000 spontaneous labors) was related to the rapidity of the induced labor. In the first minutes after birth a depressed baby is likely to have difficulty breathing, appear blue in color and be floppy from lack of muscle tone. The authors of the study pointed out, however, that the patients in the induced group were so "ripe" that they might have had rapid labor whether induced or not.

Induced labor also may have some disadvantages for the mother. When labor is induced, the woman who is hoping to go through labor and delivery without the use of painkilling drugs may have a harder time coping with the relatively sudden onset of strong contractions. In addition, according to the Columbia-Presbyterian study, tearing of the cervix and hemorrhaging after delivery were commoner with induced labor.

Does this mean that a woman should automatically say no when her doctor suggests elective induction? Not necessarily. But it does mean that if she agrees to induction, she should be sure that the hospital is equipped to monitor closely the progress of her labor and that the advantages of induction to her clearly outweigh the possible risks.

The expectant mother is likely to have less to say about whether her labor is stimulated with oxytocin. Statistics gathered by the National Institutes of Health indicate that in this country oxytocin is used in at least 1 in 5 births—a ratio many doctors would consider too high. Dr. Hatch, for example, believes that stimulation should not be done very often; perhaps it might be used on the woman who has had a lot of babies and has a "tired-out" uterus or if labor has been slowed by the excessive use of painkilling drugs.

Dr. Fields says that when done carefully, stimulation carries no increased risk; but as with induction, the doctor must be on the floor at all times and a nurse must be with the patient, monitoring the fetal heartbeat.

1602. It is decided by English law that remarriage after legal separation is now null and void. "The gate of exit from true matrimony is completely closed except by death."

Assisting at Emergency Childbirth

Judy Wilson, M.D.

Above, preparations for emergency childbirth; below, midwifery as illustrated in the Encyclopaedia Britannica's *first edition, 1771.*

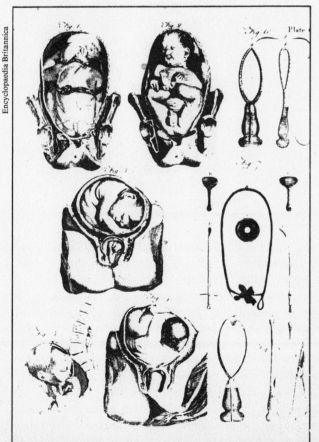

Encyclopaedia Britannica

Not too many generations ago the home was the only proper place for a child to be born, and any written instruction for that function would likely have been found in the Ladies Domestic Science Book somewhere between berry preserves and brine for curing bacon. Home child birth was, for lack of any other place, a necessity and as much a part of homestead life as haying in the early summer. Only after the population began its exodus to the city in quest of the unfulfilled promises of an industrial society did it become fashionable to have children in a hospital. Like their grandmothers did before them, many homestead ladies today are having their children at home. There are some excellent books on the subject of home child birth and if you are considering having your child at home you should study these carefully and have the assistance of a trained midwife or doctor at the time of your delivery.

If the mother should begin labor, though, and the bridge has just been washed out by a storm or the snow is up to the tops of the fence posts on the road, you may find yourselves delivering the baby at home whether or not you had planned it. Once labor begins, the baby will not be inclined to wait until a more convenient time. The information here is presented to help with an EMERGENCY BIRTH.

You will need to get together some items in preparation for the delivery.

1.   A covered soup pot for sterilization. Fill the pot with soapy water, boil the water for a few minutes, dump and rinse thoroughly, refill it with clean water and bring it to a boil again. This water will be used for sterilization.

2.   Lots of clean towels.

3.   A clean feed pan or something to receive the afterbirth.

4.   A pair of sharp scissors from the sewing kit.

5.   Warm clean blankets and clothes for the baby.

Birth of new young is a natural spring happening all around the homestead. As the only animals that have been alienated from the land and natural childbirth for a couple of generations, we need to relearn much of that folk knowledge lost to us during that time. The mother needs to understand that childbirth is a natural thing and that a part of her brain with which she may not even be familiar is equipped by heritage to tell her body the right things to do.

From *Mother Nature's Homestead First Aid.* Copyright © 1975 Judy Wilson, M.D. Reprinted with permission of Oliver Press.

1603. Queen Elizabeth, last of the Tudor dynasty and the greatest queen of England, dies at age sixty-nine, after a glorious reign of forty-five years. Vain to the last, she repeatedly asked for a mirror to inspect herself on her deathbed. When told she was dying, she gasped her last words: "All my possessions for but a moment of time!"

Probably the most important thing in helping a mother with childbirth is to give her reassurance and confidence in herself. She needs to be calm and her muscles relaxed in order for her natural instincts to direct the birth. If she is tense and frightened, it can only prolong the labor and make the delivery difficult and painful.

The beginning of labor is often noted by the discharge of a mass of blood-stained mucus. In other cases, the breaking of the bag of water which the baby is suspended in will soon be followed by labor contractions, although breaking of the water bag may precede labor contractions by several hours. Contractions will become rhythmical and the time between them will become shorter. The mother should be washed well and made comfortable on a clean bed, though if she wants to walk at this time, let her.

If the baby is going to have to be delivered at home, you should have stoked the fire well for boiling water, and have the delivery room ready by the time the contractions are within five minutes apart. Wash your hands (up to your arms) carefully, at least twice, and rinse in water as hot as you can stand.

By now, she should be in whatever position is most comfortable for her to give birth. Lying on her back is the standard hospital and textbook position, but there are many who feel this is the most difficult position for the mother. Lying on her side, on hands and knees, or squatting, or even standing, are some positions that are more and more frequently being used.

Toward the end of the first stage of labor, the contractions will become stronger and harder, as the opening to the uterus enlarges to let the baby's head enter the birth canal. The mother usually will enter a form of mild shock at this time. She will appear to remove herself from the reality of her experience between contractions.

After the uterus has enlarged, and the baby's head has slipped into the birth canal, the labor pains will ease. The mother will begin to feel a pressure on her rectum as though she were having a hard bowel movement. She may want to help the delivery by bearing down with the final contractions. The first sign of the baby will be the top of his head appearing in the enlarged opening of the vagina. Many times the birth will be completed on the next contraction after the head is born and you must be ready to catch him.

The labor will usually be slow at this time, and you may reassure the mother that the birth is nearly over. If not, you may press gently with your finger on the mother's skin between the anus and the vagina where you will feel the baby's chin. Lift up gently and guide his chin through the opening of the vagina.

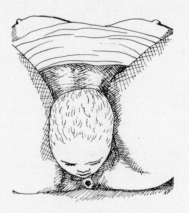

The mother will usually relax after the head has been born. Don't attempt to hurry the birth by pulling on the head of the baby. Permanent injury to the spine and the nerves may result. If the head appears and is still covered by the bag of water, it must be opened so the baby can breathe. Very carefully open it with your fingernails or a sterile knife or scissors. Wipe off the face of the baby with a clean cloth. The mother should be reassured that everything is cool and to bear down on the next contraction. This usually delivers a brand new, slimy blue baby into the world.

Sometimes the baby's shoulder will be caught on the pelvic bone and some assistance may be needed. If the baby has already started to cry, he may stay in that position as

Medieval chair and apparatus for delivery

1604. Excerpt from the will of Akbar the Great, Emperor of India: "Every man should have at least four wives—a Hindu to bear children, a Persian for conversation, an Afghan to keep house, and a Turk to beat up as an example to the other three."

long as he wishes. If he is not crying and breathing, which is usually the case, he must be delivered in the next two contractions as fast as possible, without hurting the mother.

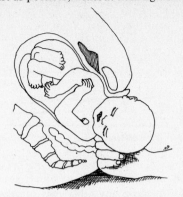

If the shoulders still are not out after two more contractions, locate with your finger the shoulder nearest the mother's backbone. Hook your finger under the arm and pull gently while rotating the shoulder towards the baby's face. This assistance is normally not required and should only be given when the above methods have not worked. Sometimes the cord is wrapped around the baby's head; wait until the delivery is finished and the baby is completely out before untangling it.

Hold the baby's face down or to the side so he can cough and sneeze the mucus from his mouth and nose. Don't attempt to wash or wipe out his mouth.

Be sure to hold the slippery little cuss firmly with both your thumb and fingers locked tightly around his ankles as well as a hand under the neck and head. By this time the baby will have started crying and breathing freely. Lay him face down on the mother's abdomen or between her legs, then pat him dry with clean towels, and cover him with warm blankets.

You can now go out on the cabin porch, give three strong rebel yells and have a stiff medicinal belt of whiskey on your way back through the kitchen.

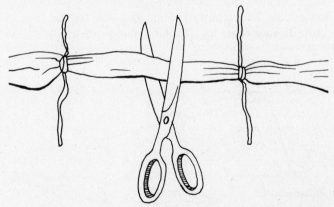

Let the baby cry for a few minutes until the cord has become thinner and changed from bluish color to very pale. About twelve inches from the baby's belly make two tight knots with sterilized cloth tape, about an inch or two apart. These must be tight enough to stop the flow of blood between the baby and the mother. When this is done, cut the cord with the scissors (after they have been sterilized by boiling for at least five minutes).

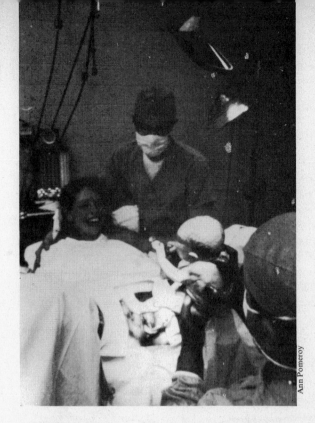

Ann Pomeroy

Massage the uterus which will be felt as a soft mass under the now very relaxed stomach muscles. Massage through the stomach by kneading it between your finger tips and base of your hand. As you knead, you will feel it become hard. This is what you want to happen.

With everything under control, you can fix mom a cup of coffee, congratulate her and collapse for a few minutes, to wonder again how it is that nature was designed to work so well.

When the mother feels like it, clean her off and change the sheets on the bed. Don't clean the baby by wiping, as he comes into the world with a special finish on his skin for protection. Pat him gently with a clean soft towel.

You can now place the baby at the mother's breast; when he starts to suckle, it begins the biological impulse which helps expel the after-birth. The after-birth should be caught in a pan and saved for a doctor or midwife to check that it has been expelled. Don't pull on the after-birth as it may cause hemorraging from the uterus. The after-birth is usually delivered within a few minutes but may sometimes take several hours. If the mother is not bleeding there is no hurry.

1604. Ahmed, Turkey's new sultan, is a noted athlete and pleasure seeker. He maintains over three thousand concubines in the palace harem, in addition to numerous legitimate wives. By the time he reaches thirty, thirteen years later, he is dead of "complete nervous exhaustion."

Exercises to Get Back Into Shape

Marion Slatin

Some physicians suggest that you start exercises to strengthen your muscles within a few days after you have had your baby. This is on an individual basis and depends upon your condition and how your doctor feels about exercises. Getting up out of bed and moving around is almost always all right and helps strengthen your muscles. Nothing strenuous should be done until after the red bleeding has stopped.

Lying on your abdomen may help your uterus return to normal position. The exercises shown are commonly done but check with your doctor to see if they are all right for you to do.

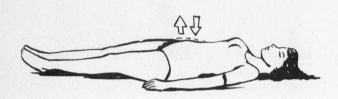

Lie flat—breathe in deeply from your abdomen and expel—repeat about 5 times.

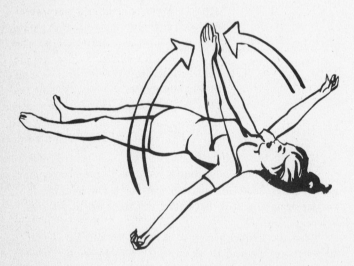

Lie flat with your arms at your side, then move your arms out to the side with your elbows stiff. Raise your arms over your head and bring your hands together. Repeat about 5 times.

From *Prenatal Care*, 1973, Department of Health, Education and Welfare.

Lie flat, then raise your head to touch your chin to your chest. Try not to move any other part of your body. Repeat several times.

The next exercises are more strenuous and should definitely not be done until the red bleeding stops. It is usually suggested that you do not do these during the first week postpartum.

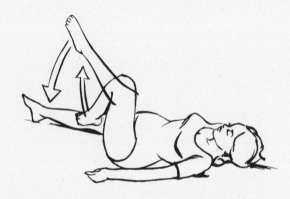

Raise one knee and draw your thigh down on your abdomen. Lower your foot to buttock. Straighten your leg and lower it. Then do your other leg. Do this about 5 times.

Spread your legs slightly and slide your feet toward you so that your knees bend almost at a right angle. Raise buttocks and rest your body on the soles of your feet and shoulders. Press your knees together and contract the abdominal muscles.

1604. In Naumburg, Germany, a woman is accused of transforming herself into a black cat for evil, nocturnal purposes, and of magically depriving a town burgher of one of his eyes. She is burned as a witch.

Do You Believe in Breast Feeding?

Marvin J. Gersh, M.D.

There has been a great deal of debate about the advantage and disadvantage of breast-feeding. The average mother is in need of some help in deciding whether she should or should not breast-feed.

All mothers should breast-feed their babies, except of course those mothers who shouldn't. The problem is primarily psychological. If a mother feels on a superficial level that she should, but on a deeper level that she shouldn't, then she shouldn't. If, on the other hand, she feels that she shouldn't when basically she knows that she should, then she should, providing that she knows on which level she is operating.

There are so many misconceptions about breast-feeding that I hardly know where to begin. It sounds logical to begin at the breast. It is generally agreed that the size of the breast is of no importance for feeding, but it is not generally well appreciated how important the shape of the breast is. Dr. Mavis Gunther, who spent several years observing mothers breast-feeding, was able to predict, simply by observing the

Adapted from the book *How to Raise Children at Home in Your Spare Time.* Copyright © 1966 Marvin J. Gersh. Reprinted with permission of Stein and Day/Publishers.

shape of the breast, whether the infant would be able to feed effectively or not. She teaches that the "nipple is like a cherry on a stalk." The "cherry" nipple should not be grasped between the gums, but rather should go to the back of the mouth. When the nipple goes into the back of the mouth, it touches

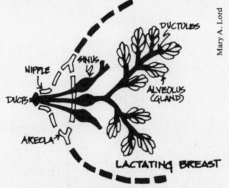

the tongue, the soft palate, and the tissues of the mouth. This seems to stimulate the infant to suck vigorously. When the nipple cannot be or is not so placed, the infant is apathetic and behaves as if he does not want the breast. It actually is not a question of wanting, or even a matter of taste; it is a complex reflex pattern independent of the good intentions of the mother.

The breast has three parts: the breast itself, the nipple and the areola. The areola is the red, dark area surrounding the nipple. Dr. Gunther found that the "protractility" of the areola was important. Protractility refers to the capacity of this tissue, when squeezed by the infant's jaws, to thrust the nipple forward. The nipple, thus thrust forward, causes the reflex pattern I have described to come into action, and successful feeding takes place. It all sounds so mechanical and unromantic, doesn't it?

Chance plays a role, too, in the success of breast-feeding. Dr. Gunther noted that there were infants who, when they started to feed, would struggle and seem to beat the breast with their fists. She noticed that this behavior was similar to that of babies who had had their oxygen supply cut off. That is precisely what happened to these babies. Either their upper lip or Mother's breast got pressed against the nose, making it difficult for the infant to breathe. If this happens two or three times without anyone realizing what is happening, the infant gets conditioned against the breast, and it may become

---

1608. Mistress Forrest and her maid, Anne Burras, are the first English women colonists of record in America. Anne Burras's marriage in Virginia the following year is also the first wedding.

practically impossible to get him to breast-feed.

Dr. Gunther noted, too, that brunettes seemed to be more successful at breast-feeding than fair-haired people. Blondes may have more fun, but not at breast-feeding.

So you see if you cannot breast-feed, there is no need to feel guilty or unmotherly or inadequate or whatever derogatory term you choose. It may be out of your control.

If all this is true, and modern woman is really not at fault, what did women in earlier times do? For one thing, they used wet nurses. Where this was not possible, all-glass bottles were used. What do primitive women do? They also use wet nurses if available. In some African communities, if the baby does not feed well from the breast, the mother puts her finger into the baby's mouth to make it swallow and then tips in the milk with the palm of her hand. It is a sure bet she does not sit in her hut analyzing herself.

Is Breast Best?

Breast milk is, of course, an excellent source of nutrition. It is not perfect, however, and must be supplemented by vitamins. It does not cause allergies as cow's milk might. It is also unlikely to be contaminated. Babies who are breast-fed seem to develop resistance to certain types of infection. Nevertheless, with the availability of a variety of formulas that can be used if allergy is to be

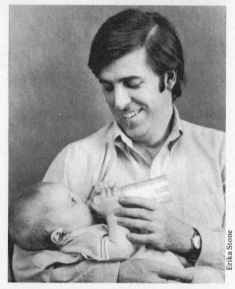

prevented or alleviated, with good sterilization and refrigeration so that infection in bottle-fed babies is rare, with a wide variety of antibiotics available should infection arise, I do not think a case can be made for breast-feeding on a *physical* basis.

People often argue that breast-feeding is better from a psychological point of view. There is no evidence that breast-fed infants are psychologically different or emotionally more stable than bottle-fed infants. As a matter of fact, Dr. Robert Fredeen of Kansas has had mothers cup-feed babies for many years. Recent psychological studies done retrospectively on this group show no evidence of emotional disturbance as a result.

1611. Artemisia, beautiful and "elegant" daughter of the famous Italian portrait painter Orazio de Gentileschi of Pisa, herself studies under Guido and becomes renowned as a painter of huge canvasses on historical subjects, the most famous of which is *Judith and Holofernes,* a powerful depiction of the physical horror of war.

Erika Stone

Erika Stone

Practical Hints on Breast Feeding

Most women find that a good nursing bra, one that provides good uplift and that opens easily for nursing, makes nursing easier and more comfortable. Many wear such a bra day and night during the months they are nursing.

Use the first few days, when there is little milk in the breast, to get your nipples used to your baby's nursing. Let him suck for only two minutes at each breast at each feeding the first day, three minutes the second day, and five minutes the third day. If your nipples get sore at any time later, you can limit nursing time to five minutes at each breast. Even a slow nursing infant gets at least four-fifths of the milk in his first five minutes at breast.

Find a position that is comfortable for you and your baby; a foot stool, a pillow and a chair with arms are often helpful.

Touch the baby's cheek with the nipple to start. He will turn his head to grasp the nipple. (If you try to push him to the nipple with a finger touching his other cheek or chin he will turn away from the nipple toward the finger.)

Allow him to grasp the entire darkly colored part of the

From *Infant Care*, 1973, Department of Health, Education and Welfare.

breast in his mouth. He gets the milk by squeezing it from the nipple, not by actually sucking. His grasp on your nipple may hurt for the first few seconds, but the pain should disappear once he is nursing in a good rhythm. When you want to remove his mouth from your breast, first break the suction by inserting your finger in the corner of his mouth. This will save sore nipples. If your entire breast becomes sore, you may be able to relieve the painfulness simply by lifting and supporting the breast with one hand during nursing.

A small amount of milk may come out of your nipples between feedings. A small nursing pad or piece of sanitary napkin inserted in the bra over the nipple will absorb this milk, keeping the bra clean and preventing irritation of the nipple.

Wash your nipples with mild soap and water at least once a day, and rinse off any messiness with clean water before or after most feedings.

If you notice a spot of tenderness or redness on your breast or nipple that persists for more than two feedings be sure to seek medical advice promptly.

1612. Anne Bradstreet, poet, is born. Of her work, thought to be the first verse written by an American woman, Adrienne Rich has said: "To have written these, the first good poems in America, while rearing eight children, lying frequently sick, keeping house at the edge of wilderness, was to have managed a poet's range and extension within

Infant Feeding Theories

Selma H. Fraiberg

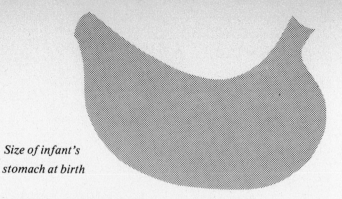

*Size of infant's
stomach at birth*

PERHAPS you remember our attempts in the '20's and '30's to discipline the infant stomach. The by-the-clock feeding schedules of this era were derived from a psychological theory that character formation begins from the day of birth, and orderly habits of feeding were expected to lay the foundations for a firm character. The four-hour-feeding schedule was based upon the observation that the average baby will waken for feedings *about* every four hours during the first months. The statistically average baby with a built-in Swiss Movement probably did not suffer much from this scientific caprice unless he frivolously changed over from Standard to Daylight Saving Time, or Eastern to Central, in which case he was in trouble, too. But the Independent, the Radical, whose stomach contracted under another time system or with no time system to speak of, fell into bad times during this era. The task of disciplining this unruly fellow, of getting the stomach to contract with the average, became a career for conscientious parents of that time. A good mother of the period closed her ears to the noise, set her teeth, and waited until the kitchen clock registered hunger. The consequence of "giving in" to such eccentric appetites in infants was set forth in stern addresses to parents in home magazines. This was known as coddling and was destined to lead to malformations of character.

The proponents of these theories were able to testify that in time most babies, regardless of personal idiosyncracies, were won over to Standard Time, i.e., the four-hour schedule. This might appear to be a tribute to the plasticity of human beings, but the facts are that most babies, without benefit of the clock or the caprices of psychology, arrive at something like a four-hour schedule after the first two or three months. This is a matter that has to do with the size of the baby at birth, the growth needs of a particular baby and a number of other factors, but all our contemporary evidence seems to show that it cannot be masterminded by an adult with a clock.

Our experiment in getting babies' stomachs to contract at orderly intervals produced some unforeseen consequences. A struggle over food was set up in the earliest months of infancy and very often the battle over food was waged over the family dinner table for years afterward. Eating problems were high on the list of complaints to pediatricians and child guidance clinics in the '20's and '30's. The thwarted instincts got their revenge.

Today's baby is fed when he shows signs of hunger, and if this seems trite to the contemporary reader, let me remind him that twenty years were devoted to the reform of infant stomachs before we emerged with this cliché. Today's baby, with his unreconstructed stomach, shows every sign of flourishing under this regime. His relationship with his mother is more harmonious than that of the clock baby because his mother satisfies his hunger. And since food and the obtaining of food creates no struggle between him and his mother, feeding problems have dropped way down on the list of complaints to pediatricians and guidance clinics.

"How do we know," says a cautious mother, "that today's

theory is a better theory? These theories begin to resemble women's fashions. How do we know that clock feeding won't come back next year along with a change in the hem line?"

Parents have a right to be skeptical when they survey the eccentric turns of child-rearing practices in the past twenty-five years. But what makes a good theory? A theory is not, after all, a fashion. A scientific theory derives from observation. It is a valid theory when it passes rigid tests in use. The theories of infant feeding we described in use in the '20's were poor theories because they were not derived from a large body of observation. They were poor theories, also, in that they made assumptions regarding the physical and mental equipment of an infant that could not have been verified through infant observation. All available information then, as well as now, shows that the infant in the early months has no mental processes that could enable him to postpone satisfaction of his hunger or suppress his appetite. The infant's hunger is imperative, the drive for satisfaction is urgent, biologically reinforced to insure survival. To withhold satisfaction of this hunger is to oppose the most necessary and impelling drives of the infant. With this information we could predict from an arm-chair—no need for large-scale experimentation—that withholding of satisfaction would produce reactions of extreme helplessness and distress in an infant and produce conflict between him and his mother.

We think today's theories of infant feeding are better theories because they take into strict account the nature of the infant and the kind of equipment he brings into the world. We think they are better theories because they have held up well in the test. The methods derived from our present-day theories promote a harmonious infant-mother relationship. They have substantially reduced the incidence of serious feeding disturbances in children.

Our present-day methods of infant feeding are not really new at all, of course. They are practically as old as the human race. All that is new is the empirical evidence that has been built up to give scientific support to the methods. Fashions in feeding infants? Unless we should choose to ignore an enormous body of scientific information on infant development—or unless a new breed of infants appears on the face of the earth, there is probably not much chance that these methods will be drastically revised.

But why do we go to so much trouble to discuss old and new theories of infant rearing? It's a roundabout way of arriving at a point which is really the point of this book. A method of child-rearing is not—or should not be—a whim, a fashion or a shibboleth. It should derive from an understanding of the developing child, of his physical and mental equipment at any given stage and, therefore, his readiness at any given stage to adapt, to learn, to regulate his behavior according to parental expectations.

confines as severe as any American poet has confronted." A book of her poems was first published, without her knowledge or permission, in England. Its title: *The Tenth Muse Lately Sprung Up in America. Or Several Poems,* compiled with great variety of Wit and Learning, full of delight. ... by a Gentlewoman. ...

Make Your Own Baby Foods

The Editors of *Consumer Reports*

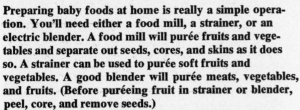

Preparing baby foods at home is really a simple operation. You'll need either a food mill, a strainer, or an electric blender. A food mill will purée fruits and vegetables and separate out seeds, cores, and skins as it does so. A strainer can be used to purée soft fruits and vegetables. A good blender will purée meats, vegetables, and fruits. (Before puréeing fruit in strainer or blender, peel, core, and remove seeds.)

Once your baby is old enough to eat strained solids, you can adapt foods prepared for family meals. Simply take out the baby's portion after the food is cooked but before you add seasonings and spices, then purée. Prepared this way, homemade baby foods should cost less overall than commercial foods. Use fresh foods only. Canned foods may contain added salt and other undesirable additives; frozen foods, though a bit better, often contain added salt.

Here are some basics for preparing baby foods:

Fruits. A baby's first fruit is usually bananas, which you need only mash with a fork. All other fruits should be cut up into small pieces, steamed until soft, and puréed.

Vegetables. Babies usually like carrots, zucchini, peas, and sweet potatoes. Cut vegetables into small pieces, cook, then purée. Avoid spinach and beets, since they may contain an excess of harmful nitrates. Cabbage, broccoli, and cauliflower may produce gas, and corn is difficult for an infant to digest.

Meats, poultry, fish. These can be baked, broiled, poached, stewed, or braised, but not fried. It's probably best to start with chicken, since it is easily digested.

Simply cook it, remove the skin and any bones, cut up, and purée. Fish is also easy to digest. When you prepare any fish, even fillet, go through it carefully for bones before puréeing. Cooked, cut-up lamb, veal, beef, and pork can be puréed in a blender.

Eggs. Some pediatricians feel that infants shouldn't eat egg whites. Others disagree. Consult your own doctor on the matter. But whether your baby eats both the white and the yolk or just the yolk alone, hard-boil the egg, then mash what you need with a fork to make a smooth paste. Custard is an egg-rich food. To make it, simply follow a standard recipe, omitting sugar, nutmeg, cloves, and similar spices.

Other foods. Cottage cheese is an easily digested food for babies. Purée it first and add a little puréed fruit, if you like. Soup is another good choice. When you fix a pot of soup for the family, take out a cup for the baby before you add spices; purée if necessary.

Prepare baby food with clean hands (to prevent any spread of harmful bacteria) and clean, freshly washed utensils. When the food is ready, cover and refrigerate the unused portions immediately; they'll keep for three days. Or better, cover a tray with foil, drop on spoonfuls of the prepared foods, then freeze and individually wrap the portions. They'll keep for one month in the freezer. Once you've started the baby on a portion, do not keep it for more than a day.

Almost any food can touch off an allergic reaction, so introduce strained solids one at a time. If the baby has an unfavorable reaction—diarrhea, a rash, spitting up—discontinue the food, then check with your doctor.

THE TWO LOWER CENTRAL INCISORS, 5TH TO 9TH MONTH.

THE FOUR UPPER INCISORS, 8TH TO 12TH MONTH.

TWO LATERAL INCISORS, 12TH TO 15TH MONTH.

FOUR ANTERIOR MOLARS, 15TH TO 18TH MONTH.

THE FOUR CANINES ARE NEXT, 18TH TO 24TH MONTH.

FOUR POSTERIOR MOLARS COMPLETE THE TEMPORARY SET, 24TH TO 30TH MONTH.

RECOMMENDATIONS

CU believes that homemade baby foods are better for babies than the commercial variety. And making your own baby food isn't that difficult. You can often feed the baby the same food you're preparing for the rest of the family, but minus the seasonings and spices, and puréed.

Of course, commercial baby foods are very convenient, and we won't say they shouldn't be used at all. We simply suggest that you give thought to preparing your own baby foods and using commercial food only when you can't make your own. Whichever you use, take care to avoid overfeeding, which many physicians believe may lead to overweight later in life.

If you do use commercial strained baby foods, here are a few suggestions:

■ Read the ingredients list carefully when buying. Avoid the foods that list water first. When possible, buy foods that

don't list added salt, starches, or sugar. For safety's sake, check the joint between the jar and the lid for debris, and make sure that the vacuum seal has not been broken. (The "safety button" at top center of the lid should be concave; if it has popped up, the seal is broken.)

■ Stress the meats. They are the most nutritious of all the commercial foods tested. They provide protein and some vitamins; there's added salt but no starches or sugar.

■ Try to avoid the dinners and high-meat dinners. Those we tested all contained added salt and starches. Some contained added sugar. All were less preferable than the tested commercial meats and vegetables. Combine equal amounts of a meat and a vegetable for a much more nutritious "dinner."

■ Avoid the desserts. The tested desserts were high in calories and low in nutrients. They almost always contained added starches, sugar, and even salt. A balanced diet does not require such commercial desserts.

1621. The price of "tobacco brides" goes up to 150 pounds. Virginia male colonists pay with the weed to cover the expenses of their future wives' transportation from England.

A Letter on the Postpartum Blues   Melodie Cooey

The editors wish to thank Geraldine Carro, contributing columnist of *Ladies' Home Journal*, who passed this letter on to us. It was written in response to a reader questionnaire on postpartum life, which she ran in "Mothering," her monthly news and information column for parents.

Dear Mrs. Carro:

This problem of "postpartum blues" seems to have been wrapped up and neatly packaged by physicians, psychologists, and even other women. Just blame it all on hormones, give her six weeks of patronizing, and your "normal" new mother will bounce back to her old self.

Not that easy, as I'm sure you realize.

I'll explain my situation briefly, then give you some thoughts on what the problems are.

My husband, Peter, and I were married for three years before we decided to have a child. We were both working at interesting, professional jobs, and our income had always been between $11,000 and $17,000. We tried for several months, so when I was finally pregnant, we were both quite happy. Our anticipations grew, we went to Lamaze classes, and in April 1974 we *both* delivered a beautiful baby girl (my choice) whom we named Claire. Claire turned one year old earlier this month. She's a delightful, smart, happy child, and we both love her very much.

However, this past year has been the worst of my life. My husband and I almost got divorced; what had been a close, trusting relationship went sour, and I became a person I didn't enjoy being and didn't know how to change.

If La Leche League has set up a hot line for emergency calls regarding breast feeding, I certainly believe there is a need for a hot line for calls from desperate mothers. Books are fine, but so many questions need answering *NOW!* My main problem was in taking the whole mothering role too seriously, in feeling (and being) left out of the "outside" world's activities, and in hiding these feelings from others. I bet many a first-time mother spends *most* of her waking hours asking herself questions like, Do I pick her up now or let her cry? Will I ruin her for life if I go back to work? What will she think if I leave her with a new baby-sitter? How can you (anyone) listen to Walter Cronkite when our daughter is grinning like that? Will I turn her into a sugar freak if I put honey into her cereal? HELP!!

As helpful as others are, no one can possibly be as concerned about that little being

as its *mother*. Perhaps that in itself is the problem. This gargantuan task of mothering is uninteresting to most people (how long can it carry you through a conversation in mixed company?), unrewarded economically and by those other means our society has of showing that someone is special (TV coverage, medals, awards, degrees, etc.), yet it is one of the toughest jobs I've ever taken on. (No executive has ever sweated more about a decision than a worried mother with her baby's temperature rising in the middle of the night.) I was a Peace Corps volunteer in rural Brazil, and many times my self-image and security were shaken by challenging situations, but those situations weren't half as complicated as adjusting to the new *threesome* of a family. Peter and I were unable to talk calmly about Claire, her needs, and ours. There was never enough time (I'm a day person, he a night person), and neither of us took the initiative to MAKE time. There were complicated little scenarios of "mommy trying to get daddy to spend more time with baby"—not a bad idea in itself, but daddy *knew* when he was being manipulated. And there was a developing sense that I didn't trust Peter with the baby because she cried more with him than she did with me. "Hormones," he said. "Bunk," I said. "You just don't know how to hold her right."

The romance evaporates, sex becomes a fantasy or only a chore, and you begin to wonder where that vital, vibrant person(s) has gone.

Now, from a vantage point of one year later, I have some observations. First, that former person (single or "young married," chic, moneyed, carefree) does indeed disappear, but no one really tells you that it's not forever. Perhaps both parents should just accept that and stop trying so damn hard to be anything else. Forget about sex if you don't feel like it, forget trying to "get out" alone together. (All you think about anyway is what the sitter is doing to the baby.) Plan, instead, neat things to do with the baby and with friends who have babies—potluck suppers, picnics in the park, afternoon get-togethers. Be social, but don't try to go back as before to an old office crowd or political party, where you would be the only one with kiddies on the brain.

I wish new parents would get counseling—or that a plethora of classes like Lamaze would spring up to cover the part after the baby comes. Fathers are brought into this wonderful event, and then, if they go back to work and the woman stays home, they are dropped somewhat

abruptly from intimate involvement in the baby's development.

Mainly, I think the problem is one for society as a whole to face. If children are important, if we can teach them and learn from them, then the job of "mothering" should require more thoughtful input from all sectors of society. Men must become more involved, and women must be more aware of what their needs are (perhaps that will be not to be a mother at all, or to have just one child).

I personally took some steps to retain my own marriage, my sanity, and my "other selves." I still worry extremely much about how I mother my daughter, I still have disagreements with my husband over what to do with her, but I've taken one major step—I've cut down on the actual time I have to worry and have forced my thoughts and energies into other areas. This might not work for all women, but it did for me. Actually, I am bored "just" being a mother. That is because I don't do many of the home things other women do (sewing, baking, gardening, writing, etc.). I often wish I were more creative on my own so that those things satisfied me. However, I'm sure many others who've worked in an office realize that part of working is social interaction, responsibility, and pay! So I think the only answer is to get out of the house. Every child-care book, from Spock to Salk to Brazelton, will counsel the mother not to leave her baby "unless she has to" until the child is two or three. What constitutes "having to"?—a normal, intelligent human being going crazy? Why not take some drastic steps like the father taking a leave of absence to care for the child—particularly if he objects to a baby-sitter? And what about day care? It's generally not available for infants, but we must work to change that situation.

As for me, I decided to go back to graduate school. Claire's care is now divided equally between her father, the day-care center (an excellent one), and me. I am much happier. Claire is adjusting well to the new scene, and her father (like so many really wonderful men) is just happy to see me happy. And I'm beginning to feel like the thirty-one-year-old *person* I am, rather than like an over-the-hill matron with concerns narrowed by the parameters of a household.

While not applicable to all, this solution may help some. I think just sharing the experience, which is certainly more than "postpartum blues" implies, will help many women (and men).

Sincerely, Melodie Cooey

1638. Margaret Brent, maintained by many to be America's first feminist, alights on the shores of Maryland and becomes the first woman to possess property in her own name. A relation to Lord Baltimore and secretary to Governor Calvert, she agitates constantly for a voice in the general-assembly proceedings. Upon the death of the governor, she is

A Bill of Rights for Parents

Daniel Rosenblatt, Ph.D.

Where does it all lead? When you are young, you are encouraged to be good, and if not, to be guilty or ashamed or anxious or depressed. It all seems hopeless, but at least there is the possibility of growing up, of being independent, autonomous, in charge of yourself. So you do it. Not without travail, you grow up. Then what happens? You get married, have a family, and find the cycle has begun all over again. Now you feel guilty, ashamed, anxious or depressed because you are not having perfect relationships with your spouse and child. You resent this because, having finally learned how not to be guilty toward your parents, you thought you were through with guilt. But you're not; instead you're just in a new trap.

Your child can't take care of himself. He is helpless and dependent on you. What you do to and for him will mark him for life. You are responsible for his coming into this world and you are responsible for what happens to him now and, implicitly, for the rest of his life. Because it is humanly impossible to meet all your child's desires, you can only feel guilty. And what about your partner? If he or she isn't happy, isn't that your fault too?

Somehow you've got to figure out a means of surviving the snares of guilt and torture. Instead of ruining yourself by trying slavishly to fulfill everyone else's desires, give yourself some rights as a parent.

1. The right to have some time for yourself and no one else. You need to be free to waste time, to stay in bed, watch television, gossip, or to play with the cat whom you really love because she can take care of herself (if only she could just manage to work the electric can opener). Forbid yourself to be useful twenty-four hours a day, salvaging extra minutes to make baby's juice in the blender.

2. The right to feel negative feelings toward the baby. Are you jealous because your husband comes home and plays immediately with his child, because he is more interested in that new tooth than your new dress? Well then, permit yourself to feel neglected. Are you depressed because your older sister is a "better mother," and your mother-in-law has undying enthusiasm? They both love to sew cute outfits for the baby; they just love the way a baby smells. Well, feel free not to compete with them or any other "better mother." Your baby is stuck with you, just as you are stuck with him. And just as one of the ways you can torture him is to make invidious comparisons with other babies (how smart they are, how cute, how sweet, how well they eat and sleep), so you can torture yourself with invidious comparisons with other mothers.

3. The right to be a baby yourself. Everyone at some point needs to get as well as to give. We are not inexhaustible wells of loving kindness, generous souls supplying all of the wants of another person. See what you can get for yourself from your baby, and if, because he is too small or too ignorant, he is not able to give you anything now, then let your partner give you what you need. Don't be afraid to ask for it because he is a partner. If he can't offer it right now, don't sulk but ask instead later on or from someone else. That's what friends and relatives are for. If they all fall through, why, then use your own imagination and see how you can give TLC to yourself.

4. The right not to be a slave. Get over the notion that your child is so fragile. Read the literature of primitive tribes or of the nineteenth century. Your baby has had to be strong to survive itself; he can take a lot. If you pamper him too much, then he will expect that from everyone else; if you neglect him, he will be wounded in another fashion. Try to develop a sensitivity to what his needs are, not just his desires. If you confuse the two, you become his slave. But if you satisfy his needs in a caring way, you will be rewarded by the development of his own strengths.

5. The right to know your own baby. Let him teach you what you need to know about him. Forget norms and averages. Maybe your baby hasn't read the books that say he'll sleep through the night at one month.

6. The right to know yourself as a parent. Stop trying to live up to the standards of "good mothers." Maybe you hate changing diapers or hate feeding him pablum or hate nursing him. Well, one thing babies are very good at doing is picking up your tensions, so if you are engaged in an interior monologue of guilt and resentment about his diapers or diet, try to accept that the kind of mother you are is one who doesn't really love taking care of infants. He can accept you, if you can accept yourself. And if you can't accept yourself, well, then you will probably find ways of teaching him not to accept you either.

7. The right to skip something. If you're too tired, forget the baby's bath. He will survive. If his clothes are dirty, he will forgive you if you don't change him. If his fingers are grubby and grimy, he'll probably bless you if you let him suck on them without scrubbing them.

8. The right to have lurid fantasies about your child. Don't feel guilty; they are, after all, just fantasies. If you fear he can read your mind, imagine what would happen if you could read his. Better not. Next time you feel lewd, vicious, violent or punitive, just sit back and enjoy your ability to put on a show for yourself.

From *9 Months 1 Day 1 Year: A Guide to Pregnancy, Birth, and Babycare,* written by Parents, compiled by Jean Marzollo. Copyright © 1975 Jean Marzollo. Reprinted by permission of Harper & Row, Publishers, Inc.

made his executrix and therefore becomes acting governor, presiding over the very colonial body she could never force to grant her the vote. They refuse her many requests on the grounds that "it would set a bad example to ye wives of ye colony."

COMMON COMMUNICABLE DISEASES

Disease	First Signs	Incubation period*	Prevention	How long	What you can do
Chickenpox	Mild fever followed in 36 hours by small raised pimples which become filled with clear fluid. Scabs form later. Successive crops of pox appear.	2-3 weeks, usually 13-17 days.	None. Immune after one attack.	6 days after appearance of rash.	Not a serious disease; trim finger-nails to prevent scratching: a paste of baking soda and water, or alcohol, may ease itching.
German measles (3-day measles)	Mild fever, sore throat or cold symptoms may precede tiny, rose-colored rash. Enlarged glands at back of neck and behind ears.	2-3 weeks, usually 18 days.	Vaccine may be given at 1 year of age as measles-rubella, rubella-mumps or measles, mumps, rubella combined vaccines; priority immunization should be given to children in kindergarten and elementary school; all children should receive vaccine.	Until rash fades. About 5 days.	Generally not a serious disease in childhood, complications rare; give general good care and rest.
Measles	Mounting fever; hard, dry cough; running nose and red eyes for 3 or 4 days before rash which starts at hair line and spreads down in blotches. Small red spots with white centers in mouth (Koplik's spots) appear before the rash.	1-2 weeks, usually 10 or 11 days.	All children should receive measles vaccine at 12 months of age. If an unvaccinated child is exposed to measles, gamma globulin given shortly after exposure may lighten or prevent the disease.	Usually 5 to 9 days, from 4 days before to 5 days after rash appears	May be mild or severe with complications of a serious nature; follow doctor's advice in caring for a child with measles, as it is a most treacherous disease.
Mumps	Fever, headache, vomiting, glands near ear and toward chin at jaw line ache and these develop painful swelling. Other parts of body may be affected also.	11-26 days, usually around 18 days.	Live mumps vaccine may be used at any age after 1 year. Combination measles-mumps-rubella, rubella-mumps may be used.	Until all swelling disappears.	Keep child in bed until fever subsides; indoors unless weather is warm.
Roseola	High fever which drops before rash or large pink blotches covering whole body appear. Child may not seem very ill despite the high fever (103°-105°) but he may convulse.	About 2 weeks	None. Usually affects children from 6 months to 3 years of age.	Until seems well.	No special measures except rest and quiet.
Strep throat (septic sore throat) and scarlet fever (scarletina).	Sometimes vomiting and fever before sudden and severe sore throat. If followed by fine rash on body and limbs, it is called scarlet fever.	1-7 days, usually 2-5.	Antibiotics may prevent or lighten an attack if doctor feels it wise.	7-10 days. When all abnormal discharge from nose, eyes, throat has ceased.	Frequently less severe than formerly, responds to antibiotics which should be continued for full course to prevent serious complications.
Whooping cough	At first seems like a cold with low fever and cough which changes at end of second week to spells of coughing accompanied by a noisy gasp for air which creates the "whoop."	5-21 days, usually around 10 days.	Give injections of vaccine to all children in infancy; if an unvaccinated child has been exposed, the doctor may want to give a protective serum promptly.	Usually no longer after 4th week.	Child needs careful supervision of doctor throughout this taxing illness.

*Incubation period is the usual amount of time which elapses between exposure to the disease and onset of the first symptoms. For example, if a child is exposed to chickenpox, he can safely play with other children until 12 or 13 days afterwards. The following week, he should be kept away from other children since he may be in the early stages of the disease and it will be contagious before you notice any symptoms.

1647. Achsah Young is the first witch to be executed in Massachusetts Bay Colony. Another killing follows in Boston next year.

Childhood Diseases and Disorders

Laura L. Dittmann, Ph.D.

The following brief descriptions of common diseases and disorders give background information needed by parents as they live with children—children and their spots, runny noses, and wheezes. Of course, such information does not replace the doctor's diagnosis of your child. And, while the list may look alarming, no child contracts them all.

The disorders are grouped so parents can look up any group of symptoms, not as they would be in a medical textbook.

Allergies

What are they? When a person is sensitive to a normally harmless substance, he has an allergy. If he receives more of the irritant than he can tolerate, he will show an allergic reaction. An allergy may look like a cold, an upset stomach, a skin disease or a number of other disorders.

There is such a variety of allergic reactions that a series of tests are usually necessary to determine their true nature. Allergies are not infections and cannot be "caught" or given to anyone else. While seldom fatal, they cause discomfort and inconvenience—mild to severe—and can lead the way to infections.

A child with an allergy should be under the care of a doctor who will, by means of tests, trial diets, and changes in the child's surroundings try to determine what the child is sensitive to.

What causes allergies? Any child may inherit a tendency to allergy, but his reaction to a substance may differ from the reaction of his parents, or he may be allergic to quite different substances. Any child may develop an allergy, however. Climate, season, degree of exposure, state of mind and other factors seem to contribute to the frequency and intensity of reaction. And the reaction itself may change or disappear as the child grows older. Frequently the doctor will study the child's whole life—the stresses and tensions he lives with—as well as specific irritants in order to get at the cause.

A person may be allergic to certain foods (such as eggs, chocolate, strawberries, milk, fish); to fine particles which are breathed (dust, pollen, feathers); to irritants which he touches (poison ivy, dog or cat hair, wool, glue, soap, detergent); to drugs which are taken by mouth or injections (sedatives, antibiotics, antitoxins); or to germs which are released in the body by an infection.

Sometimes it is relatively easy to find the cause and eliminate it from the child's life so that he gets complete relief. In other cases, the child is sensitive to so many things or to such widely present or obscure substances that the particular offenders cannot be eliminated.

From *Your Child from 1 to 6*, 1962, Department of Health, Education and Welfare.

Some common allergic reactions are:

Asthma, an irritation of the bronchial tubes, narrows the air passages and produces mucus so there is difficulty in breathing. The child wheezes and coughs in an alarming fashion. It may be worse when the child lies down, and he has to sleep propped up. Attacks frequently occur at night, and will vary considerably with the season of the year. Sometimes a cold precedes an asthmatic episode.

Hay fever resembles the common cold, with sneezing, itching and weeping eyes, and a stuffed-up head caused by swelling of the membranes of the nose. It is usually caused by pollens of weeds, grasses, and trees and therefore, unlike a cold, usually comes only at regular seasons of the year. It is rarely seen in children under 3 years of age.

Eczema is a red, thickened rough patch on the skin, frequently on the cheeks, folds of skin at the elbow and behind the knee. It will itch, and scratching causes oozing which forms crusts. While it is not contagious, the open sores may readily become infected.

Hives are itching, raised welts on the skin which resemble large mosquito bites. They usually appear and disappear suddenly. The child with hives can be made more comfortable by applying ice to the welts, or giving a warm soda bath (1 cup of baking soda for a small tub).

Child who is under-par

If a child tires quickly, is pale and listless, and lacks the bounce you expect, something is wrong although no sign of acute illness develops. Chronic ill health and lack of vitality have various causes. Until you know the source, you can't treat the condition effectively. Don't buy special foods and tonics. Get a physical checkup for the child. Then, if the doctor prescribes something special, you'll know you're treating your child's specific needs.

The child who lacks energy and seems run down may be suffering from:

A chronic infection which drains him of vitality.

Lack of sufficient rest. Slow down the pace of the child's day, plan for a midday rest, and arrange an earlier bedtime. It may do wonders for him, and you, too!

Anemia, lack of sufficient red coloring matter (hemoglobin) in the blood. Anemia may occur when a child loses a great deal of blood or has had a severe illness. Unless the loss is severe, he'll build new red blood cells in time, but the doctor may feel that a transfusion of whole blood is necessary to replenish the supply quickly. Or the doctor may prescribe iron as a medicine. Otherwise, good general care is all that is needed, with

special emphasis on foods rich in iron, such as meats (especially liver, kidney, and heart), egg yolk, green leafy vegetables, whole-grain and enriched bread and cereals, molasses, raisins and other dried fruits.

Anemia may also be caused by disease which destroys the blood, by faulty diet, or by an inherited condition. In each case, the cause will determine the treatment.

Poor nourishment. In some instances, a child is run down because the foods he eats fail to supply his body with energy and the building substances he needs. In rare instances, a child's body is unable to use the materials present. Your doctor will have to prescribe for such a condition.

Emotional problems. A child who lives in a tense, unhappy home is sure to suffer deeply. So much of his energy is bound up in worry and distress, he is apt to tire readily and care little about play. Even his posture will show dejection. Sometimes a child may be disturbed by problems and you have no idea why.

If you suspect that your child is trying to handle emotional problems which are beyond him—and you—don't hesitate to seek professional help. Your doctor, or a social worker in a family agency, may be the one to start with.

1647. In Russia now, as for centuries past, a national beauty contest is held when the czar or his heir needs a wife. This year, two hundred daughters of the lesser nobility are weeded down to six finalists, who are lined up and inspected by the Czar Alexis. He

You may wish to seek psychiatric aid through a child guidance clinic.

Colds and other respiratory infections

During the preschool years, children seem to get a discouraging number of coughs and colds and sore throats. There is an array of possibilities: croup, aching or running ears, flu, grippe, swollen glands and so on. Some are named for the part involved: laryngitis, tonsillitis, adenoiditis, bronchitis, pharyngitis. Many mothers feel as if they can name them all. It is some help to know that the child will be less susceptible as he grows older and will have less severe reaction to those which he does get.

You never know at the beginning what you're dealing with. What looks at first like a simple running nose may become in a day or two a common childhood disease with typical eruption, chickenpox for instance. It may be the first sign of a more serious infection. Or it may, despite a furious onset with high fever or a convulsion, settle down to be an ordinary cold. Many times children produce their own typical response to infection. One will get croup every time. Another never does, but screams with earache.

About all a parent can do is to decide that every cold and cough and sore throat deserves

the safest treatment. Check with the doctor, and keep in touch with him as symptoms change. He'll decide whether he needs to see

the child. Keep the child indoors, in bed if there's fever, and unroll all the tender-loving care routine you know so well.

In this way, you're going to avoid complications which can result when a slight infection opens the way for a more serious one.

Be wary of nose drops or cough medicines without a doctor's instructions. These will not cure the infection. Keep the child comfortable, with grease or cream under his nose to prevent soreness; keep the room warm but not overheated; add moisture to the air if you feel it will help; and keep the child away from others.

Diphtheria, a serious disease, can be avoided. A child who has received 3 injections in infancy, and booster shots on schedule has practically no chance of catching it. It begins with sore throat and fever; hoarseness and sharp cough may develop. The throat and tonsils may become whitish in appearance. If a child who has not been immunized is exposed to diphtheria, the doctor will give him antitoxin immediately in an effort to prevent the disease.

A sore throat caused by a streptococcus is called a **"strep throat"** or, if a rash is present, **scarlet fever.** Be sure to continue the medicine the doctor advises for the full period he prescribes even though the symptoms clear up quickly. To avoid later complications it

LESS COMMON INFECTIOUS DISEASES

Disease	First signs	Incubation period	Prevention	How long contagious	What you can do
Infectious hepatitis (catarrhal jaundice).	May be mild with few symptoms or accompanied by fever, headache, abdominal pain, nausea, diarrhea, general weariness. Later, yellow skin and white of eyes (jaundice), urine dark and bowel movements chalklike.	2-6 weeks, commonly 25 days.	Injection of gamma globulin gives temporary immunity if child is exposed.	May last 2 months or more.	May be mild or may require hospital care.
Infectious mononucleosis (glandular fever).	Sore throat, swollen glands of neck and elsewhere, sometimes a rash over whole body and jaundiced appearance, low persistent fever.	Probably 4-14 days or longer.	None.	Probably 2-4 weeks but mode of transmission is not clear.	Keep in bed while feverish, restrict activity thereafter.
Meningitis	May be preceded by a cold; headache, stiff neck, vomiting, high temperature with convulsions or drowsy stupor; fine rash with tiny hemorrhages in the skin.	2-10 days.	None.	Until recovery.	Immediate treatment is necessary. Take child to hospital if doctor unavailable. Continue treatment with antibiotics as long as doctor advises.
Polio (infantile paralysis or poliomyelitis).	Slight fever, general discomfort, headache, stiff neck, stiff back.	1-4 weeks, commonly 1-2 weeks.	Be sure to complete the series of the Sabin vaccine.	1 week from onset or as long as fever persists.	Hospital care is usually advised.
Rocky Mountain spotted fever.	Muscle pains, nosebleed occasionally, headache, rash on 3d or 4th day.	About a week after bite of infected tick.	Injections can be given to a child who lives in heavily infested area.	Spread only by infected ticks.	New drugs have improved treatment.
Smallpox	Sudden fever, chills, head and back ache. Rash which becomes raised and hard, later blisters and scabs.	6-18 days, commonly 12.	Routine smallpox vaccination is no longer recommended.	Until all scabs disappear.	Doctor's care necessary.

chooses tall, striking Eufemia Vsevolozhsky, and she faints in the excitement. But their union is never consummated: jealous courtiers accuse her of being an epileptic, and charge her father with fraud, banishing him to Siberia.

should be continued for the full course of treatment.

A sore throat that gets out-of-bounds may lead to infection elsewhere in the body. **Rheumatic fever** is one such complication, and a serious disease because it can affect the heart. School-age children are more apt to be affected, but it occasionally occurs in preschool children.

Rheumatic fever takes on different forms, and may be deceptively mild—simply a low recurrent fever—or acute with pain and swelling in the joints. It tends to recur again and again, so take seriously the first attack, however mild. Furthermore, the mildness of the symptoms bears no relation to the damage it can cause. The doctor can guide you in ways to ward off further attacks, and may prescribe regular preventive doses of medicine.

A doctor needs to check any child who complains of aching legs or mild joint pains, who is pale and tired, or who has slight fever for more than a few days without obvious cause.

Chorea, or **St. Vitus Dance**, may be a symptom of rheumatic fever. The child has jerky movements of face, arms, trunk, or legs which may vary each time. Don't confuse chorea with the restlessness of a child who's tired of sitting, or with nervous twitches such as eye blinks, head jerks, or other mannerisms which the child repeats. A child with chorea should be under a doctor's care. He needs sympathetic handling at home, too, for he's apt to cry easily and be frustrated by the jerkiness that appears when he wishes to dress or feed himself, pick up small objects, or use a pencil.

Infection following a sore throat may center in the kidney, causing **nephritis**. With nephritis, the urine is scanty, dark-colored or bloody. Tell your doctor at once of any change in the amount or color of a child's urine.

Pneumonia is a general name for infection of the lungs and can be caused by a virus, bacteria, or foreign object. Each type has a different treatment. As a rule there is fever, cough and difficult, rapid breathing. Modern drugs bring about prompt recovery in most cases when the treatment is started early. A child with pneumonia may not seem to be very sick, but the disease may last a long time and needs medical supervision throughout.

Tonsils and **adenoids** are small, spongy masses of tissue at the back of the throat which are similar in their function to other glands in the body, particularly those at the side of the neck, in the armpit and groin. Like these other glands, tonsils and adenoids combat germs; they become involved whenever the child has a cold or throat infection. After repeated respiratory troubles, they may remain so swollen they can interfere with breathing or swallowing. If the situation becomes urgent, the doctor may feel that obstructive tonsils or adenoids should be removed. Nowadays, the operation is never done routinely, in a general attempt to improve the child's health in some vague way. Don't urge your doctor to remove tonsils or adenoids; he'll do it if he's convinced it is necessary.

Immunization Schedule for Children

The American Academy of Pediatrics

2 mo	DTP [1]	TOPV [2]
4 mo	DTP	TOPV
6 mo	DTP	TOPV
1 yr	Measles [3]	Tuberculin Test [4]
	Rubella [3]	Mumps [3]
1½ yr	DTP	TOPV
4-6 yr	DTP	TOPV
14-16 yr	Td [5]	and thereafter every 10 years

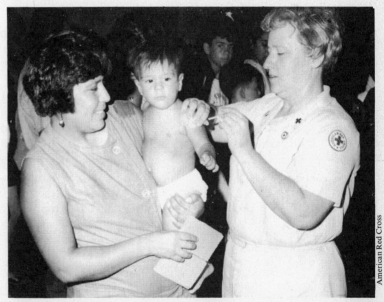

American Red Cross

[1] DTP—diphtheria and tetanus toxoids combined with pertussis vaccine.
[2] TOPV—trivalent oral poliovirus vaccine. This recommendation is suitable for breast-fed as well as bottle-fed infants.
[3] May be given at 1 year as measles-rubella or measles-mumps-rubella combined vaccines.
[4] Frequency of repeated tuberculin tests depends on risk of exposure of the child and on the prevalence of tuberculosis in the population group. The initial test should be at the time of, or preceding, the measles immunization.
[5] Td—combined tetanus and diphtheria toxoids (adult type) for those more than 6 years of age in contrast to diphtheria and tetanus (DT) which contains a larger amount of diphtheria antigen. *Tetanus toxoid at time of injury:* For clean, minor wounds, no booster dose is needed by a fully immunized child unless more than 10 years have elapsed since the last dose. For contaminated wounds, a booster dose should be given if more than 5 years have elapsed since the last dose.

Immunization Schedule recommended by the American Academy of Pediatrics. Reprinted by permission.

1652. Lady Eleanor Ratcliffe, countess of Sussex, whose husband dies this year, proves herself to be "a great and sad example of the power of lust and the slavery to it. She was as great a bewtie as any in England and had a good witt. After her lord's death, she sent for one who was formerly her footman; and she made him the groom of her chamber,

Your Child's Vision

James R. Gregg

Here are some signs of poor vision in infants:
1. *Baby is visually very unresponsive.*
2. *He holds things very close to see them.*
3. *He often bumps into large objects.*
4. *He cannot pick up small objects with accuracy.*
5. *He constantly favors one eye when looking at an object.*
6. *One or both eyes turn in or out for noticeable periods of time.*
7. *Baby squints or closes one eye frequently.*

Once the youngster can respond to instructions, it is possible to check his eyesight more accurately. Here are some ways to test visual responses of preschool children.

1. The child should be able to recognize the open side of a letter E which is ¾ inch high and twenty feet away with each eye separately. Hold the letter pointed in different directions; have him indicate the open side. (This is about 20/40 vision.)
2. Drop a small bead on the floor, using one nearly the same color as the rug. He should spot it immediately and pick it up accurately. Try it with each eye alone, and each hand with each eye.
3. The child should be able to follow with his eyes the point of a pencil moved side to side, up and down, when held three feet away. The eyes should track smoothly with no head movement. The test should be done with each eye alone and both together.

Such check tests are never substitutes for a complete vision examination. A child might appear to do all the above satisfactorily and still have visual difficulties. Nevertheless, parents doing these simple tests would find many of the youngsters with faulty vision who might otherwise go unnoticed. Any signs or symptoms call for attention.

The fundamental clues to vision difficulties in children are as simple as *ABC*. *A* stands for *appearance* of the child's eyes when they do not see properly. *B* stands for his *behavior* which is so often a warning sign. *C* stands for the *complaint* he sometimes makes when vision doesn't do the job properly.

appearance

Frequent styes, red and swollen eyelids, and inflamed eyes, although caused by infectious organisms, may have an underlying basis of eyestrain. Lids which droop, pupils of unequal size, or any inflammation of the eyes may require investigation by a physician trained in eye care.

Persistent redness and watering, particularly following intense use of the eyes, may be an indication of poor vision, or inadequate coordination of the two eyes. Crossed eyes, though present only part of the time, of course show something is wrong.

behavior

Restlessness and irritability may occur if pressure is put on to perform what for the child is a difficult visual task. Avoiding use of the eyes is an easy, and actually a clever, way out of difficulty. A variety of excuses for not studying, misbehavior to divert attention in order to avoid exposure of poor reading skills, can all come from faulty eyesight.

One of the most significant indicators is failure to learn at the expected achievement level. Poor school performance, if not readily accountable in any other way, may be an indication that the eyes need attention. Any child not keeping up with his grade level should have a visual analysis to be sure what role his eyesight is playing in his low achievement.

Play activity can also be a source of information about eyesight. Frequent tripping or stumbling, poor hand and eye coordination in playing ball or picking things up, temper tantrums, even unsociability can have a visual basis.

Some kinds of reading behavior may also indicate a visual problem, even though speed and comprehension are adequate. Holding the book too close to the face, frequent blinking, closing one eye, tilting the head, poor posture, rubbing the eyes, frequently losing the place are significant signs.

complaints

A child cannot be relied on to complain about his blurry vision. Eventually he will realize he doesn't see as clearly as those around him, but he may be well along in school before this happens because he finds nothing unusual about fuzzy vision. He thinks everyone sees his way; he has no standard of clear vision to judge by.

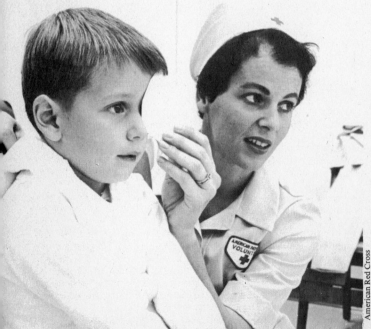

American Red Cross

Adapted and reprinted with permission from *Parent's Guide to Children's Vision* by James R. Gregg, O.D., Public Affairs Pamphlet No. 339. Copyright © 1972 the Public Affairs Committee, Inc.

though he then had the pox and she well knew it, and was a damnable sot to boot. He was not verry handsom, but his body was of an exqusit shape. About 1666 this deplorable Countess dyed of the pox that she got from him."

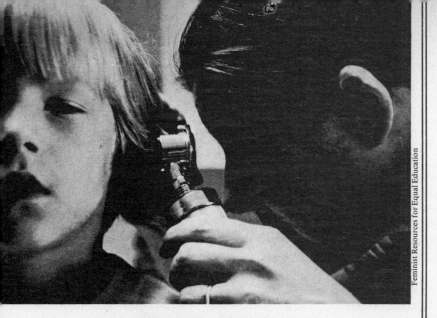

How to Detect
Hearing Problems
Samuel Moffat

danger signals

What do you look for to find out whether a child is hearing normally or not? Here are six danger signals that have been outlined by the Bell Association and Dr. William G. Hardy, director of the Hearing and Speech Center of Johns Hopkins Hospital in Baltimore:

1. A newborn does not act startled when someone claps sharply within three to six feet;
2. At three months the child does not turn his eyes toward the sound;
3. At eight months to one year the child does not turn toward a whispered voice, or the sound of a rattle or a spoon stirring in a cup, when the sound originates within three feet behind him;
4. At two years the child cannot identify some object when its name is spoken, cannot repeat a word with a single stimulus, cannot repeat a phrase, and does not use some short phrases while talking;
5. The child is not awakened or disturbed by loud sounds, does not respond when called, pays no attention to ordinary crib noises, uses gestures almost exclusively instead of verbalization to establish needs, or watches parents' faces intently;
6. The child has a history of upper respiratory infections and chronic middle ear trouble.

diagnosis

Once someone suspects that a child does not hear normally, a thorough evaluation should be made. This will probably begin with the child's pediatrician or the family doctor. But if you are not referred to a hearing specialist and some question persists, the evaluation should not stop there. Not all physicians are aware of developments in hearing and speech rehabilitation, and the child should be seen by a specialist if there is any doubt at all.

Dr. Robert J. Ruben, head of the Department of Otorhinolaryngology at Albert Einstein College of Medicine in New York City and long a student of problems of hearing-impaired children, gives this advice: "If there is any question in your mind about your child's hearing, make sure that he is taken to an otologist or a hearing and speech center. No child is too young for a hearing test."

Ideas for Forming a
Babysitting Pool
The Editors of *Good Housekeeping*

► If you have young children, one way to save money is to join a baby-sitting pool in which members give and receive sitting services free of charge. If there is no pool in your neighborhood, consider forming one using the following method, recommended by Rita Rabinowitz, director of Family Life Education of the Child Study Association of New York.

If you do not know any prospective members, there are several ways to find them. For example, run an advertisement in your local newspaper or get permission to place signs in local storefronts and on bulletin boards in community schools, churches and civic centers.

WHEN YOU HAVE A GROUP of 20 to 25 interested people— a larger group would be difficult to work with—set a time and place to meet to establish a system for operation and elect officers. You will need a chairperson to call meetings whenever necessary and to officiate at them, a corresponding secretary to notify members of meetings and of other news, and a recording secretary to keep the records of how many hours each member owes or should receive from the pool.

After the organizational meeting, each person should receive from the corresponding secretary a complete list of members, including each member's name, address, telephone number, most convenient times for sitting and the number of her children and their ages. Using this list, members then can make the sitting arrangements with one another. Both the giver and the recipient of the services should notify the recording secretary of the number of hours sat, by whom, for whom and when.

USE OF A POINT SYSTEM IS THE BEST and fairest way for the recording secretary to keep track of the services each member owes or should receive from the pool. For instance, one weekday hour might be assigned one point, one weekend hour two points. (Be sure to include half hours—at half the above point value—because they will add up over a period of time. But the number of children sat for usually does not affect the number of points.) The point system awards plus credits to the sitter and minus credits to the member using the service. Anyone with over 25 plus or minus points should be notified by the corresponding secretary to do more sitting or more going out.

Other responsible members of your family—your husband or older children—can fill in for you as a sitter. Although no money passes hands for the hours sat, your group may choose to have each member pay minimal dues to cover mailing costs and other incidentals. If you have any complaints about how the pool is functioning or about a particular member who has sat for you, contact the chairperson.

A baby-sitting pool can do more than save its members money and eliminate worries about not being able to find a sitter. Sometimes members arrange to have their children play together and share toys. A baby-sitting pool can also provide a means of exchanging children's clothing or the names of children's specialists, such as pediatricians or dentists, and other information, as well as an opportunity for parents to share mutual concerns and personal experiences about rearing children.

1655. Changing its attitude toward officially licensed houses of public prostitution, the city of Hamburg, Germany, enacts strict laws in reference to visiting suspected places. The "woman-houses" are pulled down by the city, and their inmates expelled.

Probably the greatest fear a pregnant woman has is that her child will be born with some deficiency or abnormality. There are over seven million mentally, physically, or emotionally impaired children in the United States, but there are relatively few parents prepared to deal with raising such a child. Understandably, the task is a difficult one. Many of the everyday problems of child raising are magnified, but the real burden of caring for a handicapped child lies not in the disability itself but in the response of other people toward the handicapped. Often looked upon as subhuman, handicapped persons have been excluded from our society and denied many of the rights and privileges other people take for granted.

The most important of these rights is the right to an education. Without educational resources parents in the past had few options to choose from when deciding how to care for a handicapped child. Institutionalization was usually advised, even though life in an institution can impair a child's intellectual, emotional, and even physical growth. The only alternative was for parents to provide total care themselves, often for the rest of the child's life.

Today the situation has changed for the better. Over the past two decades there has been a dramatic change in public policy toward the handicapped. Schools have begun providing programs for special children. Important progress has been made in the courts, as parents have started challenging the legality of schools' denying their children an education.

The first landmark case in establishing the educational rights of handicapped children was *Brown v. Board of Education*, in 1954 (better known as the case that mandated an end to racial segregation in the schools), in which the courts ruled that education is a basic right of all citizens. Since then, the courts have continued to uphold the rights of the handicapped. Their decisions have forced some schools to implement educational services for special children and have helped provide the impetus for mandatory education laws.

Thirty-seven states now have laws mandating education for all handicapped children. Most of the other states have laws providing services for children with certain types and degrees of disability. At the federal level there has also been an increase in legislation for the handicapped. The Vocational Rehabilitation Amendment of 1973, P193-112, section 504, now guarantees the civil rights of the handicapped and provides vocational rehabilitation for them, with priority given to those who are severely handicapped. Other federal legislation provides for funding for special-education services, elimination of architectural barriers to the physically handicapped, and vocational opportunities.

But as is often the case there is a sizable time lag between legislation and court rulings and their implementation. According to the Bureau of Education for the Handicapped, of the 7 million handicapped children in the United States fewer than 40 percent are receiving educational services. Even when services are available, the dispersal of information is so inadequate that many children who are eligible don't receive them. The most difficult and important task of parents of the handicapped today is to see that their children receive the care to which they are entitled.

If you suspect that your child has a mental or physical handicap, take action at the earliest possible moment. Early identification and treatment of problems can relieve parents of many burdens and often lessen the severity of the handicap. The first step in obtaining services for your child is notifying the proper agency that you have or may have a handicapped child. Who to get in touch with may vary in each state and local area. The intermediate-school district is a good place to start, since in many states the responsibility for identifying, diagnosing, and providing services for the handicapped lies with the schools. If they are unable to help you, go to the public health department in your county, which can refer you to the proper state agency offering free diagnostic services.

Inform the school or agency in a letter with duplicate copies that you may have a handicapped child and request an evaluation of

---

1656. Ann Austin and Mary Fisher are the first two Quakers to arrive in America; both Englishwomen are subjected to a rigid examination by Massachusetts's Puritan authorities and imprisoned for five weeks while it is determined whether they are witches.

Handicapped Child   Kristine Paulsen

at cutting through red tape, digging up information, exploiting available resources in a community, and providing understanding and support for their members. The value of these groups cannot be stressed enough; they are responsible for much of the progress in obtaining rights for the handicapped.

Many of these parent groups are national organizations, such as the Association for Children with Learning Disabilities, the Association for Education of the Visually Handicapped, and the Association for Emotionally Disturbed Children. (In the Woman's Directory at the end of the *Almanac* you will find addresses of the national offices of these and other organizations that may be helpful.)

The next step is having your child diagnosed. In most states the school or agency you have contacted will make the arrangements for an evaluation of your child. An evaluation and diagnosis can provide valuable information and recommendations, often identifying a physical cause for what had appeared to be a mental disability. But it can also pose a real threat to your child's welfare. A diagnosis is essentially a labeling process, and there is a strong stigma attached to many of the labels given handicapped persons. If your child receives one of these labels, she or he will be subject to discrimination and alienation.

The possible consequences of being mislabeled, as the result of diagnostic error, are very serious. Obviously, a mislabeled child would not receive the services appropriate to his or her needs; but, even more tragic, a child will often adopt the intellectual and behavioral characteristics associated with the label even if she or he is capable of doing better. Also, once a child is given a label, it may stay with him or her for life.

There is the greatest danger of your child's being falsely labeled in the categories "educable mentally impaired," "learning disabled," "socially maladjusted," or "emotionally impaired." Most of the children placed in these categories do not have severe problems and are usually not identified until after entering school. The validity of labeling these children and segregating them from

your child. If you do not receive a response, send a copy of your letter to the director of Special Education Services in your state. Your department of public health can guide you to this agency which is located in your state capitol.

You should also learn as much as possible about available diagnostic and placement services and how to obtain them. For this information do not rely solely on public agencies. Consult a variety of other sources, particularly outside the public school system, in order to obtain an objective, independent opinion.

Parent organizations, made up of people who have dealt with the same problems you are facing, are especially helpful for this. They can give you specific information and evaluations of the services and professional people in your area. Parent groups are good

---

1656. The first American jury composed of women is ordered by the General Provincial Court of Patuxent, Maryland. The case concerns a woman suspected of murdering a child. The verdict is not guilty.

"normal" children is questionable. Many people feel, too, that the selective process involved in labeling these children reflects the prejudices in our society, and the racial make-up of the various disability groups tends to support this idea. The racial makeup of children diagnosed as having physical or severe mental handicaps is in the same proportion as that of the overall population in the United States, while in the categories I mentioned above, minority groups are grossly over-represented.

What can you do to ensure that your child is not mislabeled? First, familiarize yourself with the diagnostic process. Find out who is evaluating your child, what tests are used, what kinds of information are being sought, what conclusions are being drawn and for what purposes they will be used. Keep accurate records of what you learn. Talk to all the persons who will evaluate your child, ask for copies of their reports, and make sure you understand fully any diagnosis that is made.

Parents now have the legal right to examine and challenge their children's school records.

Erika Stone

Use this right! Find out what has been said about your child and have any inaccurate or biased information stricken from the files. The more information you have, the better able you will be to evaluate the diagnosis and placement of your child.

There are several things to look for in a good evaluation. First, an evaluation should never consist of just an IQ test. An IQ test is a general and sometimes inaccurate assessment of a child's intellectual level and does not provide sufficient information for diagnosis and placement. This is especially important if your child is from a racial or ethnic minority background, because most standardized tests, particularly those stressing verbal skills, are culturally biased and are partly responsible for the overrepresentation of minority groups in certain disability areas.

If English is not the primary language spoken in your home, demand that your child be tested in the language she or he speaks most fluently. Request that some of the persons testing and evaluating your child be of the same racial or ethnic background as your child. An evaluation can be very subjective and whether or not the evaluators are familiar with your child's culture and language can make a big difference in their results.

A good evaluation includes clinical data, educational data, and input from parents or other people who have had dealings with the child. There are many sources for obtaining clinical data, and the more sources used the better chance of an accurate evaluation. Some possible diagnosticians are psychologists, psychiatrists, audiologists, physical and occupational therapists, nutritionists, dentists, pediatricians, social workers, and nurses. Educational data come from regular teachers, special-education teachers, reading specialists, counselors, and other education specialists. One valuable source of information often overlooked is input from parents. Parents know more about their children than anyone else does, so make sure your observations are included in the report.

A good evaluation begins with a screening for general problem areas and then moves toward a more complex assessment of specific disabilities and abilities. This assessment could include various kinds of standardized achievement tests in specific skill areas plus

1658. Following the death of his wife, Czar Alexei calls for the usual national beauty contest in quest of a more congenial second wife. From among seventy contestants, he chooses Natalie Narishkin, a noblewoman. She is to become the mother of several royal offspring, among them Peter the Great.

your child's performance. Ideally there should be both formal and informal assessments, given over an extended period of time by more than one person. *Never allow your child to be placed on the basis of one test given one time by one person.*

What else can you do to ensure a suitable placement for your child? Before your child is placed, find out exactly what the recommended program is like and what alternatives exist. Parent organizations should be able to provide you with much of this information. Visit the program—that's one of the best ways to evaluate it. Consider questions such as these: What is the atmosphere like? Is the teacher enthusiastic? What is the teacher-student relationship like? Are the students active and is the activity constructive? One of the biggest problems with many special-education services is that they do nothing more than babysit. Handicapped children have even greater educational needs than "normal" children, so make sure that the program provides a learning experience. Do goals and objectives seem designed for each child, applicable to each child's own particular needs? Is instruction individualized? Ask the teacher how she or he assesses the children's progress. A good program may appear chaotic, but there is usually a good deal of organized teaching and evaluation involved. Does the program provide for parent input and involvement? Talk to parents of children in the program to get some of this information.

Most important of all, is this program the least restrictive alternative and does it work at moving children toward normalization? Recently courts have ruled that placements of handicapped children must be the least restrictive alternative. This means that children are to be placed where they will receive an education appropriate to their needs in a setting closest to the mainstream of society and restricting as few of their liberties as possible.

Does the program being considered integrate or work at integrating handicapped children with those in regular classrooms? This is important because it may prevent much of the alienation and stigma that accompany many handicaps. An essential requirement of any program is that it provide frequent, automatic reevaluation to ensure proper placement.

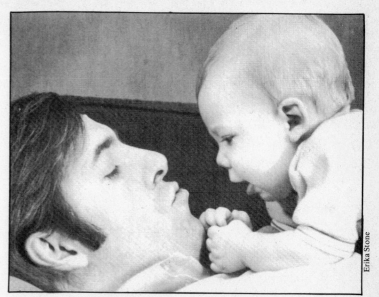

Handicapped children have greater educational needs than normal children.

What can you do if you disagree with the diagnosis and placement of your child? Request a reevaluation. Some schools or public agencies will be glad to cooperate. If you dislike any of the diagnosticians, you have the right to insist upon a qualified diagnostician of your own choice. Many states have well-defined procedures for appealing a diagnosis, placement, or lack of placement.

If you still don't receive any satisfaction, then take your child's case to court and sue the school or state. Write to the National Association for Retarded Children for their *How-to-Sue Package for Mental Health Civil Righters.* The address is N.A.R.C. Regional Office, 420 Lexington Ave., New York, N.Y. 10017. The Council for Exceptional Children also has information on the litigation process in the pamphlet *"Legal Change for the Handicapped through Litigation"* and publishes the bulletin *"A Continuing Summary of Pending and Completed Litigation Regarding the Education of Handicapped Children."* You can obtain both pamphlet and bulletin by writing to the State-Federal Information Clearinghouse for Exceptional Children, Suite 900, 1411 S. Jefferson Davis Highway, Arlington, Va. 22202.

As a parent of a handicapped child you must be willing to take any steps necessary to ensure that your child receives the rights and services to which she or he is entitled.

1665. Mrs. Coleman, the first female performer on the English stage, makes her appearance in London as Lanthe in Davenport's *Siege of Rhodes*. Other women actresses shortly dare to follow her lead at the Drury Lane Theatre.

Choosing a Day Care Home for Your Child

Carol Seefeldt, Ph.D., and Laura L. Dittmann, Ph.D.

The Department of Social Services in your community is often a good source of information for helping you to find a family day care home. A local planning council, religious organization, Head Start center, or neighborhood day care center or school may also be able to help you find a home suited to your needs.

John Getsinger

Some family day care homes are part of a "system" or group of homes operated by an agency, school or child development center. These homes are usually licensed or approved by the sponsoring group and supervised by them. If the home you are considering is affiliated with a system of homes, find out how much supervision is given the home and what the agency requirements and standards are. It may be that this home is well qualified to offer quality family day care for your child.

In some areas of the country, family day care homes must be licensed. A license will protect you and your child. If a license is required in your state, ask to see the licensing requirements. Do these requirements represent the kind of quality you are looking for? Check for yourself whether the home meets the requirements, since it is not always possible for state licensing agencies to make frequent inspections.

Visit several homes, trying to find some that are located close to your own home so that transportation will not be difficult and the children will stay in their own neighborhood, among people and things they know.

As you visit the home, ask yourself:
- Is there a space for the children to play inside?
- Is there a space for the children to play outside? Is it fenced? Away from traffic or other danger?
- Are the rooms well lighted, safe and in good repair?
- Is there adequate heating and ventilation?
- Where will the children rest? Does each child have his own cot? Is there enough space for all of the children to rest?

From *Day Care 9: Family Day Care*, 1975, Department of Health, Education and Welfare.

1665. Frances Stewart, later duchess of Richmond, is used as the model for the symbol of England—Britannia—which is stamped on the copper coins of the realm.

- Is there some space for them to keep their own things?
- Is the kitchen clean, and are all appliances working?
- Is the bathroom safe for children? Are there footstools for the children to reach the faucets and toilet? Are these in good working order?
- If there are stairs, are they guarded and do they have a handrail?
- Is there a place to keep a child who becomes ill?
- Are there books for the children to read, or the mother to read to the children?
- Is there someplace for the school age child to study?
- Is there a workable fire extinguisher available?
- Are emergency numbers posted near the telephone?
- Are the walls free of lead paint?

Before you make the final decision about placing your child in a family day care home be sure that you are at least satisfied that:
- you and your child have visited the home at least once while other children are there;
- you like the way the day care mother works with the other children in the home and how she will work with yours;
- your child will feel welcome in the home by the other children or anyone else living in the home;
- the day care mother has a good idea of what she will do with the children during the day, that she has routines which include rest, meals, snacks and play planned for at regular times;
- the house is safe and comfortable for children—that there are not too many "breakables" around or sharp edges and that there is good light;
- there are enough exits for the children if an emergency arises and that the children are able to practice what they should do in an emergency;
- there are no other people in the home, or likely to visit it, whom you would not like around your children.

If Your Choice is a Mistake

If, after several weeks, the way your child acts tells you that he is happy about going to the family day care home, then you will know you have chosen wisely. If your child is getting along fine in the home, he will:
- talk about the things he did during the day
- talk about the caregiver, what she does and says
- be eager and happy to go to the home in the morning, and just as happy to return to his own home in the evenings
- be active and cheerful
- continue in his same eating, sleeping patterns
- be eager to learn new things and go new places

It's natural for a child to cry when he's been left. He may be worried that his mother or father is not coming back, or he may be expressing his unhappiness over having to leave his own home. However, if your child:
- cries when you take him to the home
- becomes afraid to let you out of his sight
- starts sucking his thumb, wetting in the bed, or pulling at his hair, or in other ways tells you he is tense
- appears listless, refuses to eat, is afraid to sleep

then you may want to check to see if the home you have chosen is the best for you and the child. First talk to the caregiver to see if she or he knows what is troubling the child. Or you might contact the agency to see if there is someone with whom you can talk with and could help you. You and the caregiver should not be embarrassed if the home is not the right place for your child. The caregiver and you should understand that not every place, no matter how good the care is, can meet the needs of every child.

1691. The Magdalen hospital of Saint Nicholas de Barre is founded in Madrid, Spain, for women of the better classes who have been banished from the homes of their fathers and husbands for sexual misconduct.

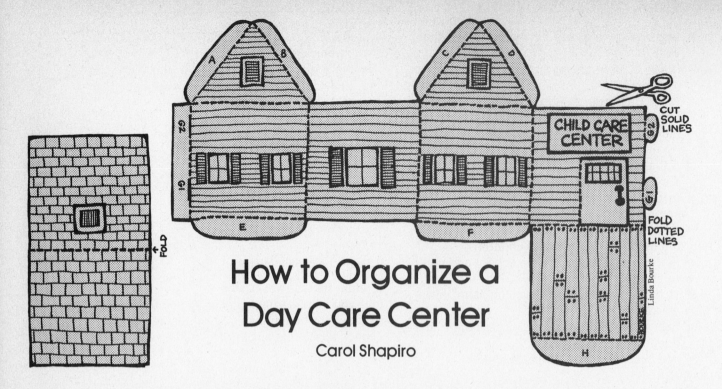

Linda Bourke

How to Organize a Day Care Center

Carol Shapiro

Starting a child care center involves putting a lot of pieces together. This should help you start thinking about those pieces, provide you with some ideas, and direct you to other sources of information and assistance.

In designing a child care center that both uses and services the community, you will have to thoroughly study not only the requirements of all aspects of running a center but also the size, population characteristics and available services of the community itself. It will take, initially, a lot of research and brainstorming to sort through the many options that you have. Once you have begun putting the design into effect, remember to keep an open mind towards recognizing any mistakes and finding new and better ways to proceed.

Getting a group together. The first thing you need do is to get together a group of people to plan and to make decisions about the kind of child care center you will have. If you do not already have a working group, first define your community. A community may be a geographical neighborhood, a factory or office, or a college or university campus. Next put notices on bulletin boards, in publications, or in places where people with children congregate (stores, schools, playgrounds, etc.). Call a meeting of interested people from which a working group can be established. Efforts should be made to insure that the group involves parents and represents the ethnic, cultural and racial makeup of the population it serves. The group should select the center's Board of Directors or appoint themselves a temporary Board and make provision for the selection of a permanent Board which truly represents the community.

Deciding what types of programs children and parents need. In deciding what programs your center will offer, it is most important to keep in mind the needs of the children and parents in the community. Generally, an initial meeting or

some kind of written or oral survey of the community to be served will help you determine the needs of the parents and children who will use the center. If school age children are being left untended after school or children are getting into trouble because there is nothing to do after school, consider after-school programming. If many parents work in other than 9-to-5 jobs, for example, night shifts in hospitals or factories, etc., think about flexible hours for your center or perhaps a 24-hour program. Whatever programming you decide to include in your center, be sure it is based on the needs of those who use the center—children and parents.

Deciding what programs to offer. Based on the needs of children and parents discussed above, the planning group should decide what kinds or combination of child care programs to offer.

- *Infant program* - includes care for children ages eight weeks to two or three years.

- *Preschool program* - includes children from two years to first grade.

- *After-school program* - includes children from first grade through eighteen years. Since it usually begins at 3:00 p.m., teachers can be hired on a part-time basis. (The hours should reflect the school schedule of the children the center serves.) Some day care centers where the schools are on split session have both a morning program and afternoon program. The program can integrate school-age and pre-school children. This can be a rewarding experience for both.

- *Programs for handicapped children* - some centers today are planning more organized programs for handicapped children. They have developed a variety of programs to help children with all kinds of handicaps and to find solutions to the problems that arise be-

1692. In the spring of this year, in Salem village, two hysterical adolescent girls accuse Martha Corey of bewitching them, the first in a string of over 150 arrests and numerous executions inspired by the girls. Dragged before a hearing, Martha stoutly insists that her accusers are "poor distracted creatures" whose addled talk must be disregarded.

tween handicapped and nonhandicapped children. (For more information, write to Children's Circle Day Care Center, 1332 Fulton, Bronx, New York, Ms. Edith Hicks, Director.)

- *Twenty-four hour program*—the children do not stay in the center twenty-four hours, but the center is open twenty-four hours in order to serve families where the parents work on night shifts.

- *Drop-in care*—occasional use of a child care center for any number of reasons such as shopping, medical appointments, emergencies, training programs or classes that do not meet daily. A drop-in program can be much more than babysitting. Most children come once or twice a week regularly. This means they can become involved with continuing education while they are there. The difference it makes in the home for parents to be able to get tasks done without worrying about their children helps the child's overall development. Such care is, however, very difficult to arrange and provide properly and must be thought through carefully in advance.

Curriculum. Planning your child care center's curriculum is part of deciding on your program. Your curriculum includes everything you do in your child care center in order to reach the goals you have set for your children and yourselves, including integration of parents and community with the center, making the classroom experience relevant, and the recruitment and training of the teaching staff. In the long run, your program is about people's lives—parents and children—and how people can lead satisfying and productive lives.

This obviously takes in much more than classroom activity. Children do not live or learn in a vacuum, separated from their parents, their community and society in general. So, first, don't protect them from the reality of the outside world, but think of ways to integrate that world in your program. Second, the curriculum and learning experiences at school must be supported and confirmed at home. What will happen when the child goes home? When she or he goes to public school? Will she or he drop out or graduate? If the program does not take these things into account, your program will have made no appreciable impact on the child's future or on the child's possibilities for development.

Parents and the Community. First, begin with parents. Try to involve all the parents in some aspect of planning, operating, and evaluating the program. What you all learn about child development will make you better parents. And when your children enter public school, what you have learned about education, about supervising teaching staff and about organizing yourselves will help you work to influence the public school curriculum so that your children continue to enjoy learning and continue to learn.

Find out what the parents' outside needs are. For example, how good are health services that are available in your community? A coalition of parents from a child care center can be more effective than a single parent in making hospi-

tals and clinics in the neighborhood more responsive to the needs of the community and in pressuring hospital and clinic personnel to treat patients promptly and with respect.

As you explore these other needs and begin to develop appropriate programs and activities to meet them, you will find that many of them relate directly to the classroom program, like health services. For example, a sick child who is not getting proper medical treatment will probably be a poor learner.

Poor nutrition also causes learning problems. In addition to giving the children good meals at the center, the center can act to help improve the amount and quality of food available in the home. For example, the center can start or join a food buying club.

Making the Classroom Experience Relevant. Your classroom program can expand a child's experience and knowledge. The first step in planning the program is to set goals for what you want the children to learn. Some examples of goals that centers set are:

- that the children enjoy school;
- that they develop free of stereotyped role images, thus opening up life's options for both girls and boys;
- that they develop a positive self-image and gain self-confidence; and,
- that they learn to cooperate with other children.

Your group will be able to think of many specific things you want for your children. Then you can look into ways of reaching these goals in the classroom. You can learn a lot about what you want and what you don't want by visiting other child care centers and by watching and asking questions. Once you have done work on developing these ideas, you will have a better idea of what kind of teaching staff you want.

Learning state and federal rules and regulations. One of the first things to do in organizing your center is to get hold of a copy of the various federal, state and local rules and regulations for day care centers. Licensing by state is mandatory except in North Carolina. In most states the licensing agency is the Department of Welfare. However, in Kansas, Maryland, Massachusetts, and New Mexico, the Department of Public Health handles licensing; in New Jersey it is handled by the Department of Education; and in Washington, D.C., by the Department of Human Resources.

Regulations differ from state to state but generally they deal with health and safety conditions in the physical surroundings and have little to do with educational standards. Please do not consider minimum standards, federal, state, or local, as a guide to a good developmental child care program. These standards usually are designed to assure custodial care only and should be regarded as such. For information about day care standards, contact: Child Welfare League of America, Inc., 67 Irving Place, New York, New York 10003.

All day care which will be supported in any degree by federal funds must meet the Federal Interagency Day Care Requirements. The requirements cover a range of areas

---

Nevertheless, by September she and seven others are hanged for witchcraft, the last set of killings in Salem. She goes to her death, resigned to her powerlessness against the mania but still protesting her innocence. Later in 1706, Ann Putnam—Martha's chief accuser—admits her horrid charade.

Finding Space for Your Center   Vicki Breitbart

The space you look for is somewhat determined by the kind of program you want and how large you think your group will be. Guidelines for day care usually advise 35 square feet of indoor space for each child in the center (100 square feet per child is recommended for outdoor space). But if you want enough space for children to group themselves in a variety of activities, both active and quiet, then you'll need more like 50 square feet of classroom space per child. This doesn't include the kitchen and special-function rooms. If you have a choice of sites, here are some things you might consider before making a final decision.

- Does the space provide separate areas for different groupings of children, for different activities, for different age groups? If not, can it be so partitioned?
- Does it have an adjacent or nearby outdoor playground?
- Does the indoor space have easy access to the outdoors?
- Is the place well lighted, well ventilated, pleasant? In other words, is it a place in which *you* would want to spend a lot of your time?
- Is it safe (no loose wires, no lead-base paint), or can it be made safe with little additional expense?
- Do you have to share the space with another group at night or on weekends? And if so, do you have to move all your equipment before others use the space?
- Does it have kitchen facilities and toilets?
- Is the landlord friendly, or at least comparatively friendly?
- What does it cost?
- With necessary renovations, what does it cost?

Renovation can mean anything from painting, where the paint and labor can be donated and cost you nothing, to rewiring and major plumbing, which are very expensive. If major renovations are necessary, you might be able to get the landlord to do it for a slight increase in the monthly rent, instead of having to pay it in a lump sum. The site of your center can determine:

- *The size of your group.* You may have already decided how many children will be in your

including:

- Comprehensive social, health and nutrition services;
- teacher/child ratios of 1:5 for three year olds, 1:7 for four and five year olds, and 1:10 for children over 6;
- parent participation on all levels;
- group sizes of no more than 15 for three year olds, 20 for four and five year olds, and 25 for children over 6;
- continuous in-service training for all staff; and
- no specific education or experience requirements are included for teaching staff and volunteers may be used.

These regulations have been in the process of revision for more than two years, but until formally changed, they should be strictly followed.

You can obtain copies for the Federal Interagency Day Care Requirements from your state welfare department or regional Health, Education and Welfare office or Office of Child Development, Department of Health, Education and Welfare, Washington, D.C.

Incorporating. The corporation is the principal form of organization for doing business in the United States. To an increasing extent, groups formed for non-business purposes such as charities, community groups, educational and social groups are also organizing in corporate form. Unlike business corporations, charitable corporations do not have stockholders but instead have members or a board of directors that perform decision-making functions.

Corporations are formed under the provisions of a particular state law. Most states have a number of different corporation laws covering groups with different purposes, each with its own procedures and requirements. It is necessary to consult a lawyer to become incorporated. Perhaps some community agency will volunteer its legal staff to help you. Or ask a lawyer in your community to help you. Your elected officials who are lawyers will often help you incorporate without charging a fee. Getting a lawyer is the most important first step in this entire process.

A good reason for incorporating is that it limits the liability of the members of the group. That means that the members who control the corporation are not legally responsible for the corporation's obligations (debts). This reduces a lot of the risks involved in a group venture. Incorporating guarantees your legal existence even if the director or key members leave. Incorporating also makes it easier to get a tax exempt status from the Internal Revenue Service.

1692. Rebecca Nurse speaks out against the witchcraft hysteria gripping Salem Village, "observing that there were persons spoken of (as guilty of witchcraft) that were as innocent as she was." She is hanged four months later as a witch.

group, but if you find a large community room with extra space, will you expand to include more children?

- *Who will use your center?* Who lives in the immediate area? If you are on a university or college campus, will the surrounding community be able to use the program?
- *Additional resources for your center.* A center located in a church may get donations from the congregation. If the center is on a campus, then there is the possibility of using food and medical facilities, as well as recruiting volunteers for the program. Arrangements can be made with teacher training schools, etc.
- *What the program will look like.* If there is an adjacent outdoor play area, children can flow in and out instead of having a special time for outdoor play. If there is an adequate kitchen, children can use it for supervised cooking activities. What about quiet places? What about building platforms or other semi-permanent structures?

How involved will you become with city, state, and federal regulations? A center in a hospital or in a community room in a public housing project is more likely to be monitored by the authorities.

If the group has money to rent space, then privately owned storefronts, community rooms, or even apartments and houses can be on your list. Space is also available in most churches and synagogues, but getting it for a day care center is a different problem. If a member of the group or relatives of a member are in any way connected with a religious institution in the community, it's a place to start. Many groups canvass the entire neighborhood to find the most convenient, most attractive, and in other ways most desirable space. And then they start a campaign to get it. It may be that the institution you choose is looking for a way to serve the community. But more likely you'll have to make at least one appointment to see a member of the board; make a second and third appointment; find a lawyer particularly adept at dealing with nonprofit institutions that are not at the moment serving the needs of the community (see below); get help from other community groups. Other possibilities for low-cost or free space include places where you work or study or such possibilities as: recreation buildings in parks; campaign headquarters and offices of sympathetic politicians or political groups; buildings and storefronts taken over by the city; buildings in good condition, but awaiting—although not in the too-near future—demolition.

The last way to get space is to TAKE IT. With enough community support, groups have occupied unused—or used—buildings and storefronts.

The Bank Street College of Education, Day Care Consultation Service has a complete chapter on incorporation in its *Manual on Organization, Financing, and Administration of Day Care Centers in New York City*. Although incorporation laws differ in each state, the manual can provide help for your lawyer—should she or he need it—on how to proceed, and problems that may arise.

Federal funds. *Title IV-A* can provide partial funding for child care centers. This is a section of the Social Security Amendments of 1967 that authorize the Federal Government to pay states three-quarters of the costs of a broad range of programs.

Day care programs funded under Title IV-A are administered by a state agency, usually the state Welfare Department. Approval and ultimate authority rests with the Federal Government (Community Services Administration, Social and Rehabilitation Services of the Department of Health, Education and Welfare).

While Title IV-A is the major source of funds, it has been changed from an open-ended program, to a limited one. The Revenue-Sharing Act of 1972 placed a national limit of $2.5 billion annually on Title IV-A day care funds. This amount was divided up among the states, roughly in proportion to population. As a result, more populous, industrialized states (such as New York and California) which had previously received large amounts of matching Title IV-A funds, were limited to approximately the same amount they had been spending, thus making expansion of federally-assisted day care impossible. On the other hand, some less populous states with less commitment to day care programs were allotted much more than they had been spending. It is important to remember that no state automatically gets its allotment of these funds; it must apply. So if your state does not have a large day care program in operation, some pressure to apply for these Title IV-A/Revenue-Sharing funds may help.

Who is Eligible. Title IV-A allows states, if they choose, to provide day care and other services to past and potential AFDC recipients, as well as to those presently receiving assistance. Each state submits a State Plan to the Department of Health, Education and Welfare which defines which services it intends to provide, how programs and services will be implemented. A past recipient is a parent who is likely to become a recipient again if the

---

1696. Letter sent by the Duchesse d'Orleans in Paris to her friend, the Duchesse of Hanover, in September: "If it is possible to recover one's virginity after having not slept with one's husband for nineteen years, assuredly my virginity is restored."

needed child welfare service (child care) is not available. Potential recipients include four categories:

- individuals who are medically needy;
- individuals who would qualify if the earning exemptions granted to recipients applied to them; and
- those who are likely to receive financial assistance within five years.

Talk to your lawyer about getting a tax exempt status. Aside from the tax benefits this will also enable you to be eligible for foundation grants and federal funding. It will also provide an incentive for voluntary contributions since they can be written off as tax deductions.

A site for your center. Before you even start to look for a site for your center, you should find out what the licensing requirements are. Ask for help from officials who take care of licensing and can translate rules and regulations into real life terms. Building inspectors, the Department of Sanitation, Fire and Safety Marshalls, and the Zoning Commission will probably all have to be involved.

Be sure *not* to sacrifice quality of staff and program for perfect quarters for your center. Check with state and local housing authorities or local realtors for available space. Keep in mind that churches may have Sunday School classrooms that are empty on weekdays. Check on schools and other community centers for available space.

Recruitment and training of staff. We feel the traditional concept that preschool teachers are only female is detrimental to child development. Many children using these services are from single parent families where the father is absent. The child care classroom could provide the only male identification for young girls and boys. Ideally each classroom should have a female and male teacher.

In addition to including both sexes, it is important for the staff to reflect a variety of racial and ethnic backgrounds, especially those represented in the community the center serves. At a time when a child's attitudes are being formed she or he will have more of a chance of growing up free of prejudices if she or he has a chance to develop relationships with children and adults of different racial and ethnic backgrounds.

When it is time for the Board of Directors to hire a director (director hires staff), you must begin to think of the work that needs to be done, the qualifications for that job and kind of person you want for the job. At this point, it is important to keep in mind the goals that have been set for your center and the kind of people you would like to have working with your children.

In-service training programs are necessary for the continued growth of staff, for keeping in touch with attitudes of staff. For example, if the elimination of sexism and racism are important components of your center, it is important to have on-going consciousness-raising sessions in those areas. The best curriculum tools and materials will fail if the teachers' negative attitudes show through. Also, in order to enhance your sessions, guests (or community people) that have a particular field of expertise can be invited in for specific presentations from time to time.

Funding. Getting money is an important part of starting a day care center. Good day care is expensive. The cost of adequate care even on a low budget is about $2500 per child per year. Some child care centers are run with money raised privately by parents themselves, using volunteer staff, donated spaced, charging parent fees, getting contributions, and finding what is available free. This is a very hard job and a lot of work. Within the next few years we hope legislation will be enacted for a national, comprehensive, developmental child care program which will make large scale funding available for a broad spectrum of the population. Until then, funding a center is a matter of collecting funds from a variety of public and private sources.

Check State Plans. The State Plan submitted by each state is the document which outlines how broad the range of services may be and how they are delivered. The State Plan also tells what advisory boards are to be established to administer or advise on the delivery of services.

The State Plan, however, is only half the picture. The other half is how much money each state has appropriated to actually operate programs which are referred to in the State Plan. Many states list a broad range of possible programs on the State Plan and then actually provide the local matching funds for only a few programs or none at all.

State welfare departments have exerted little initiative in maximizing spending for services. This is related in part to the lack of pressure on them from communities. State welfare departments may be resistant to putting up 25 percent of the cost or even of permitting it to be raised (they may not want to be bothered with the extra paperwork). Get hold of a copy of the State Plan; then map out a strategy to pressure the state into implementing the plan.

The Talmadge Amendment. The Talmadge Amendment to the Social Security Act, which went into effect July 1, 1972, provides for 90 percent of the cost of child care to welfare recipients that register for work training programs.

Special Feeding Program. The Special Food Service Program for Children is part of the National School Lunch

1696. Mademoiselle Ninon de L'Enclos, a celebrated French fascinator of men, caps her birthday by yielding to the advances of a twenty-nine-year-old abbot. Her lover asks her why she had denied him for so long until now: "Was it because I happen to be a churchman? Or perhaps you could not quite make up your mind?"

Act. Breakfast, lunch, or supper and snacks are offered to pre-school children from low-income areas where there are large numbers of working mothers. Any private or public non-profit child care center is eligible.

The Federal Government (Department of Agriculture) will pay up to 80 percent of the cost of preparing and serving meals. Only children who can afford the cost have to pay. Children from low-income families get free or reduced price meals.

Get an application booklet from: Herbert Rorex, Director, Child Nutrition Division, U.S. Department of Agriculture, Washington, D.C. 20250.

For more information or assistance contact: The Children's Foundation, 1026 17th Street, N.W., Washington, D.C. 20036.

Private funding. [1] *Local Resources.* Think of what your center will need and then try to tap local resources. Ask toy stores, furniture stores, etc., to donate equipment. (If you get a tax-exemption, their contributions will be tax deductible plus it can be good publicity for them.) Local colleges may be willing to do free consulting. Churches may be willing to donate space. Community action programs may have funds available. Ask community professionals and non-professionals to donate services. Retired professionals may be especially willing to donate time to the program. Everyone potentially has something to give; don't be afraid to ask!

[2] *Foundations.* Most cities and states have private foundations that may give money to educational programs. The public library should have a listing of these foundations in *The Foundation Directory.* Contact these foundations and talk to them about your plans to see if they would be interested.

[3] *Corporations.* Many corporations and banks now have community affairs divisions that give money to community projects. Contact the community relations director of each organization for specific information on how grants are made. If your center will serve the employees of a corporation, the company's support should be actively solicited. Likewise, colleges and universities should be approached for funds and space when the center will serve the campus community. (For articles on corporation and campus child care, see *Day Care - Who Cares?* in resource list.)

[4] *Fund Raising.* There are always the old standbys: bake sales, rummage sales, raffles, theatre benefits, etc. They take a lot of time and energy but they can be quite profitable. And, finally, you may want to try to find several wealthy individuals who will support your efforts because they believe in what you are doing.

Opening your center. Child care centers cannot be put together overnight. It usually takes from six to nine months from the time that you begin planning your center to the time you can open it. Once the center is open, it usually takes several more months before it is operating effectively and efficiently. If your center is to survive as a useful community resource, you will have to make a commitment of many months' time. Everyone involved should be told what to realistically expect so that parents needing services will not become frustrated and disappointed.

Evaluating the program. Centers, especially those that are aimed at serving community people, need to be continually evaluated to be sure they are meeting the needs that were originally identified and to be sure that parents, children, and staff are pleased with the progress being made. It may be that the needs identified early in the planning process will change. It is certain that in most areas, the job situation, the transportation system, the schools, and political considerations will make part of the planning outdated. For this reason, all of those involved with the centers—parents, children, and staff—must be looked at separately, and each segment of the community served by the center (or serving the center) must take a look at its own role. Constant re-evaluation should be built into your program.

Making necessary changes. Changes are as difficult to make in community-responsive institutions (and a child care center is an institution) as in any institution. All institutions tend to become defensive, to rely on what has been said or done or written, and to resist changes of any kind. Parents that had a strong role in putting together centers will want to continue their role, even if their particular ideas are no longer representative of the real needs. Children may cease to be the focus for services. Staff, like people everywhere, may become set in their ways. They may resist change because they feel that they have experienced enough and that no one else can tell them how to do the job better. Although it may be difficult, try to insist that the parents of children attending the center have final and conclusive power to make any changes necessary. This will include an insistence that the director replace even the most dedicated staff that may no longer be serving the needs of the children. This will also include, if necessary, the courage to close a center that no longer serves the needs of its children and parents, and to start over again.

"Hardly," she replies. "I was merely waiting for this particular date to arrive, wanting ability to boast that I am one of the few women ever to crown her eightieth birthday in this manner."

The Family and Its Purposes

John Holt

Erika Stone

Erika Stone

SOME FEAR THAT giving or offering children the right to greater independence will threaten or weaken or destroy "the institution of the family." But the family of which most people speak now—Mom, Pop, and the kids—is a modern invention. The family even as most people knew it in this country a hundred years ago has been almost entirely destroyed, mostly by the automobile and the restless and rootless society it has helped to create. That family was in turn very different from the European family of three hundred years before, when the whole notion of the home and the family as private had not yet been invented. In any case there is much evidence that the modern nuclear family is not only the source of many people's most severe problems but also is breaking down in many ways or changing into new forms.

Whatever is strong and healthy in families, whatever meets real human needs, enhances and enriches life, cannot and will not be threatened by what I propose here. Any institution that really works is immune to attack, however severe. Reality has its own strength. People with genuinely strong religious beliefs are not threatened by talk that God does not exist or is dead. Happily married couples who after many years get great strength and joy from each other's company simply smile and go on with their life when they hear that marriage is nothing but a device for the exploitation of women, or whatever it may be. Their experience tells them better.

At its very best, the family can be what many people say it is, an island of acceptance and love in the midst of a harsh world. But too often within the family people take out on each other all the pain and frustrations of their lives that they don't dare take out on anyone else. Instead of a ready-made source of friends, it is too often a ready-made source of victims and enemies, the place where not the kindest but the cruelest words are spoken.

This may disappoint us, but it should not surprise or horrify us. The family was not invented, nor has it evolved, to make children happy or to provide a secure emotional and psychological background to grow up in. Mankind evolved the family to meet a very basic need in small and precarious societies—to make sure that as many children as possible were born and, once born, physically taken care of until they could take care of themselves. "Be fruitful and multiply," commanded the Bible. A society or community that did not was sure to be wiped out, by drought, famine, plague, or war. The rulers of these societies solved their problem in a way that is the foundation of our moral codes today, though these codes now do not meet, but oppose, our most urgent survival needs. What they did was to harness the sexual drives of young men to the begetting and nurturing of young children. The rules boiled down to this. You can't have sex except to make a baby; you have to take care of the woman who will be the baby's mother; and when the baby is born you have to take care of it as well. This was a burden, heavy then

1697. Mary Astell, English author and reformer, publishes in London her *Serious Proposal to the Ladies wherein a Method is Offered for the Improvement of their Minds*. With this goal in mind, she elaborates a scheme for ladies' colleges, which is favorably entertained by Queen Anne but which is not implemented because of the interference of Bishop Burnet.

Paul C. Cabot III

as now, which most young men would have avoided if they could. But loopholes were tightly closed, the rules strictly forbade getting sexual release or pleasure in any other way. And society sweetened the deal a little bit. In return for the trouble of taking care of this woman and her child or children, society gave them to the man as his property. They had to work for him and do what he told them. Since human energy was both a scarce resource and a valuable form of capital, a man with a large family was generally felt to be rich and fortunate. The invention worked, and the people multiplied. How they did multiply! In short, the family was an institution in which some people were owned by others. Men owned women, and male and female children learned to own and be owned.

If the family became other things besides, as it often did, it was because people who live close together for a long time have to find some way to make this somewhat palatable and workable and because man is a social and affectionate creature who, with any luck, will become fond of many of the people he is closest to. But the family was not invented to give people someone to love. To the extent that came, it was extra. Basically the family was and is a tiny kingdom, an absolute monarchy. Roman law gave the father the right to life and death over his wife and children, as over his slaves. Fathers in some Arab countries have rights close to this even today. Within the past months a father in one Arab country, who had killed his fifteen-year-old daughter because she was too friendly with the boys—there was no charge that she was having sexual relations with them—and who had spent seven months in prison for doing this, was granted full pardon by the head of state, a very popular decision. Within the past few weeks I have read accounts in major newspapers and magazines of parents kidnapping their children, often well into their twenties, and keeping them prisoner, often for weeks, in order to free them from the "influence" of certain religious com-

munities. Nobody suggests that in such cases our otherwise rather severe laws against kidnapping should apply. Apparently kidnapping is okay if it is your own kid—no matter how old he is.

It is the family in this sense that is most heatedly defended. Most of those people who talk angrily about saving the family or bringing back the virtues of the family do not see it as an instrument of growth and freedom but of dominance and slavery, a miniature dictatorship (sometimes justified by "love") in which the child learns to live under and submit to absolute and unquestionable power. It is a training for slavery.

Others, more kindly, insist that only in the family can children grow up healthy. Elizabeth Janeway puts it thus:

> . . . Children do indeed need to be brought up, and brought up in intimate surroundings. They need love, stability, consistent and unequivocal care and lasting relationships with people who are profoundly enough interested in them to look after them with warmth, gaiety, and patience. *

This notion that a child cannot grow up healthy unless he is at every moment under the eye of some adult who has nothing to do but watch over him is very modern.

And Ms. Janeway, in other parts of her book, shows over and over again that most children never had the kind of care modern dogma says they must have. Thus on page 180:

> . . . Most women who work do so because they need the money. They work at unglamorous jobs, not at careers—and they always have.

This suggests something interesting about the context of our mythic statement that woman's place is in the home. We have seen that, as far as history goes, it is very much a middle-class myth . . . . The myth as we know it reflects a society that can afford to hold women off the labor market and keep them at home in a more or less Veblenesque situation. *

Another modern idea is that children get from the family their models of grown-up life, their ideas of what it is to be a man or a woman. Ms. Janeway quotes the sociologist Talcott Parsons as saying that "children learn about the world and the culture in which they live by growing up in the subdivision of that culture which we call the nuclear family. . . . Later he learns that the members of his family represent social relationships that are common to the rest of the world he lives in." Today, it is hard to find much truth in this. And what need had children of such "models" when the life of the adults went on all around them, in full view, when they lived their own lives in the middle of that adult life, when they joined the adults often in work, play, ceremony, festival, death, mourn-

1697. Hannah Dustin, American Colonial heroine, is captured and carried off by a band of marauding Indians while her family is dispersed. One night as her captors lie asleep, Hannah escapes from her bonds and frees those of a servant and a young white boy. Together they kill ten of the twelve Indians, at last returning to the settlement safely.

ing? And what kind of model of adult life does the modern child get, who sees his father come home in the evening, sit down, perhaps read the paper, and spend the rest of the evening and much of the weekend watching television, or who sees the mother doing household chores? Is this, then, all that men and women do? Not only is the modern nuclear family a very bad model of adult and social life, because so incomplete and distorted, but it is its isolation from the world that creates the need for models.

For many reasons children need a much larger network of people to relate to. The small family is so often unhelpful or destructive because it is so small. The relationships are too intense, too much is always at stake. Many parents find it hard to say no to their children even though they say it much too often, because it seems to threaten their ideal relationship with the child. They have to get angry before they can say no, and then they are doubly angry at the child for

Erika Stone

"making" them say no. The family is so dependent on these high-powered feelings, so shut in on itself, so non-involved with others or with the community, so devoid of purposes outside of itself, that it is fragile, easily threatened by a quarrel. Human relations cannot be only about human relations. If there is nothing in a family but feelings, if it is only an arena for feelings, if its life depends on everyone feeling good about or loving everyone else, if the members have no other way of being really useful to each other, then it is constantly threatened by anything that might upset the good feelings, and perfectly normal differences and quarrels take on too much importance.

A pat phrase of our time is "sibling rivalry." We take as healthy and right what is only "normal" in the

sense that it is all too common—that the children in a family should actively dislike each other and compete frantically and ruthlessly for the too scarce attention and "love" of their parents. Why should the competition be so frantic? Because the wanted and needed attention, concern, advice, companionship and protection are so scarce. Why so scarce? Because there is no one but the parents to give it.

Children need many more adult friends, people with whom they may have more easy relationships that they can easily move out of or away from whenever they need to or feel like it. Perhaps they found many of these in extended families, among various grandparents, aunts, uncles, cousins, in-laws, and so on. Perhaps they found them living in smaller communities, villages, or towns, or neighborhoods in larger cities. But these communities, in which people have a sense of place and mutual concern, are more rare all the time, disappearing from country as well as city. The extended family has been scattered by the automobile and the airplane. There is no way to bring it together so that children may live close to numbers of older people who will in some degree have an interest in them and care about them.

What we need is to re-create the extended family. Or rather, we need to allow, encourage, and help young people create extended families of their own. There is no reason why the adult friends of a child should be friends of his parents. Parents generally want friends like themselves. Children may like more variety so that they may get some things from one person and some things from another. During my sister's growing up one of her closest friends, and one very important to her, was an older woman that our parents hardly knew and might well not have liked. Many young people in their twenties and thirties are now trying to re-create the lost extended family or community in organizations of one kind or another. These are often good for them but may be less good for their children, if only because the people who live in these communes tend to be too much alike. And there is no reason why the network of people with whom we, or children, are most closely linked—what Vonnegut in *Cat's Cradle* called a *karass*—should all have to live close to us.

Robert Frost, in his poem "Death of the Hired Man," put it very well. The hired man, now too old and ill to work, is sitting exhausted in the kitchen of a younger farm couple. The husband, not quite knowing what to do about him or with him, wonders why he has come to their house, since he has other relatives nearby. For answer his wife says to him—it could not be said better—"Home is where, when you have to go there, they have to let you in."

Just so. Children need many such homes. Perhaps we all do. But I think many adults, much more than children, have a sense of having many homes, places where in time of bad need or trouble we could go and be sure of getting help, or at least shelter. But the making and finding of these homes is not, on the whole, something that society can do for people. Each person as he lives must find and make his own. This is what I want to allow and help children to do.

ca. **1699.** Mary De La Riviere Manley, prominent member of London society, scandalizes the public with her series of debauched books on the ruling class and politics. She is widely believed to be the "Sappho" of the famous Tatler letters.

Smart Child Rearing

Ryan A. Kuhn

As LITTLE KATHY ROUNDS the corner on nine months, suddenly the odds change in her favor; she's become a mobile engine of curiosity and destruction, randomly ranging throughout the house. So it's time to pop her into the playpen, equip it with lots of toys, switch on the nearby tube and return to your neglected homework/housework/personal life, right? Definitely not, cautions developmental psychologist Burton L. White, Ph.D., director of the ambitious Preschool Project at Harvard's Laboratory of Human Development. In fact, her explorations at this age — roughly from eight to eighteen months — play a critical role in her future achievements and abilities.

The following guidelines for effective child rearing practices were drawn up by Dr. White and his colleagues after they had closely observed the behavior both of particularly competent children and their skillful mothers, and conversely, of especially unsuccessful children and their mothers.

As standard operating procedure, young Kathy should be allowed to roam far and wide, or as much as possible. So that she can rummage to her curiosity's content, place valuable or potentially dangerous objects outside her reach. Set the Ming vase on the mantel and remove the Drano from under the kitchen sink. Do, however, leave harmless cooking utensils, yesterday's newspaper, the contents of the utility closet accessible. Such common household items are just as intriguing as expensive toys to children this age.

Child Rearing Checklist

1. Don't cage or confine your child over long periods or regularly.

2. Don't allow her to become so dependent that she constantly follows you around.

3. Don't allow tantrums to develop by ignoring her more conventional attempts to attract your attention.

4. Don't worry that she will stop loving you if you refuse her from time to time.

5. Don't try to win all spats with her, especially when she enters the negative period around the eighteenth month.

6. Don't try to prevent her from cluttering up the house; it's a typical sign of a healthy, curious baby.

7. Don't be over-protective.

8. Don't overpower her. Let her do what she wants whenever feasible.

9. Don't, if you can afford it, take a full-time job or otherwise absent yourself from her life during these important months.

10. Don't bore your child if you can help it.

11. Don't worry about how fast she memorizes the alphabet, numbers, etc. Don't even worry if she's slow to talk, as long as she seems to understand more language over time.

12. Don't force toilet training. By the time she's two or so it will be easy.

13. Don't spoil her; she may think the world's at her fingertips.

If these conditions are met—Kathy (or little Johnny) is permitted a large area of play, she stumbles into a good variety of engrossing objects, and you are nearby—she will inevitably attempt to attract your attention. When she does:

1. Respond to her overtures as quickly and as favorably as possible.

2. Make an effort to understand her purpose of the moment.

3. Set limits. Don't give in to unreasonable requests.

4. Supply generous amounts of encouragement, enthusiasm and assistance whenever appropriate.

5. Use words frequently, both those the child understands and those slightly beyond her present vocabulary. Also use words to convey ideas related to the matter at hand. If she knocks over the dish of Doggie Munchies, make a game of cleaning it up: "Now we put them back."

6. Interact with the child only as long as she shows interest, often less than ten seconds.

7. Encourage "pretend" activities.

1705. Anne Bonny and Mary Read are two of the most notorious female pirates of the high seas. Their ships, captained by the infamous Jack Rackham, prey upon international trade in the Caribbean. Both women have a price on their heads.

Problems of the Single Mother
Barbara Trecker

Love and marriage, they used to say, go together like a horse and carriage. Well, that may not be so true anymore, but marriage and children still seem to be a natural pair, at least in society's notion of what ought to be. If a woman has a husband, she'd better have children or a darned good excuse not to. If, on the other hand, she has children but no husband, the penalties are even greater.

Society doesn't really buy the idea of a woman raising her children alone, and it doesn't matter whether you're an unwed mother, widowed, or divorced, although the stigma attached to unwed motherhood is greatest. And, unless you've made a superhuman effort to rid yourself of the values you grew up with, you probably harbor, somewhere inside of you, the notion that children need a father and, with that notion, guilt because you're not providing one. If you're a single mother, you probably have financial problems; very likely you need to work to provide for your children. Yet, because you're a woman, you no doubt make less money than a male head of the family would.

The number of single mothers in this country has been increasing along with the divorce rate. Also increasing is the number of women who make a choice from the outset to raise their children alone.

One, a New York City clothing designer, said she had one advantage that most other single mothers don't have—money. Even so, she said, it is no easy task.

Jennifer was a successful dress designer, selling to sixty or seventy top stores throughout the country, when at the age of twenty-nine, she became pregnant. She was not married, and the father left her during her third month of pregnancy.

"I gave it a lot of thought," Jennifer said. "It would have been easy to have had an abortion. But when you really want a child and you're getting older . . . I just couldn't have an abortion. Every woman I know is taking care of that child alone. Some of them have accomplished Herculean things. The thing that makes it difficult is money. But I was making enough money at the time. And I felt I could spend time with the baby because I work at home. The baby cries and I'm right here.

"I thought a great deal about whether I could do it. I never thought about anything so much in my life. I spoke to social workers, doctors. But there's no professional advice you can give, because it depends on the person. In the fourth month I tried to find a woman's group. I was very scared. I thought again about having an abortion. I needed moral support. None of my closest friends had ever had children, and I needed to talk to someone. I finally found a group, mostly welfare mothers, and they were incredibly supportive."

If it weren't for the welfare mothers, Jennifer said, she might not have made it through the pregnancy. "There are all kinds of changes happening in your body; you don't have a husband; you're scared; you need someone to talk to. Someone to tell you that everything you're going through is normal."

Jennifer wanted to have a natural childbirth, so she took the course along with a girl friend. "It was very painful," she recalled, "to see all those couples." Her hospital at first refused to allow her girl friend to accompany her in the labor and delivery rooms and only gave in and granted permission after a running battle during the latter weeks of her pregnancy.

Other single women are hesitant to take natural childbirth classes because they, too, feel uncomfortable doing it alone. One dropped out halfway along because she couldn't stand to be alone while all the other women had their husbands with them.

One of Jennifer's biggest problems during her pregnancy was an unsympathetic obstetrician, who, as her pregnancy wore on, could not conceal his feelings about unmarried mothers. At one point, Jennifer said, she complained to him about some problems she was having and his response was, "That's what women have husbands for." After the delivery he asked her, "What do you think of your women's-lib baby?"

It definitely pays to shop around for a doctor you like, one whom you can confide in and who will make no value judgements about your marital status. Another woman, recently divorced, was fortunate enough to find a very supportive pediatrician. She told him she was worried about raising a child alone, and his reply was, "You're not crippled, are you? You'll manage."

Often the most traumatic moment for a single mother is checking into the hospital to have the baby, since hospitals often automatically assume that a husband is involved. If you've got a supportive doctor, he may pave the way for you at the hospital, so that you won't be faced with any embarrassing questions. One woman, who had left her husband during her pregnancy, received great help from her doctor, who made sure the hospital didn't make any last minute trouble. She showed up at the hospital with a male friend, to whom she was very close and whom she'd wanted to coach her in childbirth. Since the staff assumed he was the husband, he was allowed into the labor room.

Of course, most single mothers don't start out single. Instead, death, divorce, or separation suddenly leaves them as head of the family. A thirty-year-old Hispanic woman who works in a day-care center described her feelings when her husband was suddenly killed in an accident and she was left to care for her three young children alone: "I'm pretty stable, but after my husband died, I was a nervous wreck. Being the only one scares me. Knowing you're the only one. That there's no male image. But working, having a job, helped me."

Since most single mothers have to work for financial reasons, they carry a double load of guilt—guilt about there not being a father around and guilt about being away from home so much. But the woman who lost her husband in the accident said that after a while her guilt about working gave way to a good feeling of responsibility and independence. By working, she said, she had the money that meant extras for her children—such as a trip to the movies. And, she said, "I like to think of myself as a working mother. I think it's a good thing. I'm showing my children that even though I'm a woman, I can get up and go to work and have responsibilities, and I'm proud of it."

Lonely. Resourceful. Independent. Frightened. Single mothers are often all of these things at once. Or

1707. Henrietta Johnston takes up brush and chalk to become America's first pastellist and first woman painter. Her subjects are mostly the women of South Carolina.

their experience may take them on a continuum from loneliness and depression to true independence.

A woman whose husband left her with two small boys after ten years of marriage was at first desolate. She had been for those ten years nothing more than a wife and mother. Her friends were all married women who, like her, had never worked.

But, after a while, she dropped those friends and made new ones. Each time her sons asked where Daddy was, the pangs were somewhat less sharp. She began to take courses at night on how to manage her money and how to fix things around the house. She became outraged at the difficulties she encountered when applying for her own credit cards and bank loans. Where once she had been committed to being a full-time mother, she now began thinking of getting a job although her financial situation was secure. Where once she had scoffed at the women's rights movement, she became, in one year, a truly liberated woman, in both her thinking and her actions.

There is little doubt that the women's rights movement has done two things for single mothers —increased their number and made their plight easier, at least psychologically. Women, it seems, are no longer willing to stay in a bad marriage "for the sake of the children," as they once were. Increasingly, women who are dissatisfied with their marriages are leaving and taking their children with them. And many say that the women's rights movement has made them feel less guilty about what they are doing. Also, they say, it has affected the attitudes of the other people with whom they deal.

Erika Stone

Mary is a thirty-four-year-old single mother who lives with her two young boys in a fourth-floor walk-up apartment in New York's Greenwich Village. The family had gone to Ethiopia because her husband was transferred there. When their marriage of thirteen years broke up, she packed up herself and her two children and arrived in New York City with no job, no apartment, very little money, and just a few friends.

"First I got an apartment," she said. "Then I got the children into nursery school. And then I started job hunting." Her life now is radically different from what it was before. When she was married, her husband expected her to be a full-time wife and mother—her job consisted of getting the meals on the table. Now she is making her own furniture for the apartment, including the platform beds her children sleep on, and she teaches belly dancing three evenings a week, both for the money and because she likes it. The day-to-day business of her life is strung together on a thin thread of baby-sitters.

"Things get pretty complicated," she said. "There's a lot you have to hold in your mind at one time. But it hasn't really been all that difficult. If one thing doesn't work out, you try another."

When she compares her life now with her earlier married life, she is satisfied that she made the right move. "Marriage required more dependence than I really wanted," she said. "I have a freer life now. My life is simpler because I don't have as many commitments. The demands on my life now are much less. True, you have to plan more, and I spend more money on baby-sitters now than if there were someone else around. But I've been lucky. I've been helped by friends who've given me a kick in the ass when I needed it. When I've felt too dependent. You know, you *can* take care of yourself."

Single mothers react to their status in various ways. While most find it useful to share the burden with others—friends, the father, or even just a baby-sitter—a few seem to thrive on being independent. Sharon, a thirty-year-old divorced editor, said she went through a series of different arrangements in her search to get someone to help her with her young daughter: a women's commune, a reciprocal baby-sitting arrangement with a friend, housekeepers, and living with another divorced woman. "It was all a dream, trying to get someone else to help me take care of my child. I had to realize that this child is my responsibility. No one is going to help me take care of her." But she doesn't feel that that puts her in any worse a position than most married women with children, since, she said, it is the woman who bears the major responsibility for raising her children, whether she's married or not.

But although most single mothers need to be independent, they don't usually thrive on it. Jennifer, the dress designer, felt the need to seek out other women during her pregnancy. She now makes sure she always has a full-time baby-sitter to help her with her daughter. She goes out with men and doesn't rule out marriage. Although she doesn't regret for a moment the way she had her daughter, she said, "It must be really wonderful to have a baby with a man you love beside you."

Jennifer has also found it useful to integrate her work life and her home life. Like many single mothers, she doesn't want to box herself and her child into a world apart from everything else. She is committed to working, but she is also committed to making her child a part of her work life. For her that is easy to do, since her

1715. The first patent granted to an American by England is Number 401, issued to "Thos. Masters, Planter of Pennsylvania, for an Invention found out by Sibylla his wife, for cleaning & curing Indian corn growing in the severall colonies in America."

dress designing career involves a small factory employing a few women and her loft apartment is divided into personal and business areas. Her daughter often moves back and forth from the living part of their loft to the factory part. She knows the women who work there. She is used to other adults besides her mother. "I'm not the only one in her life," Jennifer said, "and to me that is very important." Her daughter goes with her on every business trip, whether it's to Florida or Europe. Some people don't approve, she said, but she doesn't care. "I tell them she's my kid and she's coming with me. You want me, she comes along."

Most single mothers agree that their problems lessen as their children grow older. As one mother said, "It's hard to realize that one day your child won't be three years old anymore, but it does happen." Single mothers usually feel a tremendous sense of freedom once their youngsters start school. Sending a child off to school for the day carries none of the guilt that might come with a baby-sitter or day-care arrangement.

On the other hand, when a child grows up and leaves home, say for college, the experience can be particularly painful for a single mother. One woman, divorced since her children were three and two, was desolate at the imminent prospect of both children going away to college. "I feel like I'm losing my best friends too, not just my children."

Isolation is one of the single mother's greatest enemies. If she works, as she usually does, she rushes home afterward to her children. Between her two jobs, there's little time to relax, let alone socialize. So many single mothers find it useful to combine their two worlds— home and job—to bring their children more into the outside world. They take them to their office occasionally, they take them on vacation, they let their children get to know their friends and build relationships with some of them.

One woman who has been separated since her third month of pregnancy solves her problem by taking her year-old daughter to work with her all the time. Mary works in a fashion-consulting firm in the heart of New York's garment district. There are six women in the office plus her child, who uses the conference room. The little girl has a Porta-crib, a walker, and all the other comforts a growing toddler requires. If she has disrupted the routine of the office, no one, including the boss (also a working mother), seems to mind. And for Mary it's a way of saving child-care costs and, more important, sharing the burden of raising her child. "At first I was worried about some of the women in the office, especially the older ones who aren't married and who've never had children. But it's been wonderful. They are the ones that are having the best time with the baby. The baby is a calming factor. After the pressures of work, she is like a little bit of reality."

Mary has been helped partly by discovering new reserves of strength within herself. "I found I can do things by myself that I never thought I was able to. I have more strength. You find that when you have to do it, you do it."

But, more than anything else, she said, she has been helped by her friends. Often a single mother finds that her friends change. But whether they are old or new, single mothers say they are invaluable. "My friends have been wonderful," Mary said. "They baby-sit, they run errands, they keep me company. I've become a totally new person now that I have seen how nice people are to me. I wouldn't change this experience for anything else in the world."

Paul C. Cabot III

Confessions of a Child Abuser

Judith Reed

What I can tell you is what you won't get from the other speakers—the guts of a person going through child abuse. Being there doesn't automatically make you an expert on child abuse but it tells what it's like . . .

"Child abusers are going through hell. We have a vision of how powerful our anger can be, a concept of where this anger will take us if we are pushed too far, and the constant dread that we will be pushed that far. For abuse is usually not a singular incident but part of a consistent pattern . . .

"We don't like being child abusers any more than society likes the problem of abuse. If a positive approach is offered abusers, they will usually respond . . .

"I'm convinced that parents are aware of their feelings and let others know. But we don't know how to listen. Too many of our parents have told society time and time again: 'Help me! I'm at my wit's end. Help me before I bring my kid there too!' How can we learn to listen and respond? Too many parents are afraid to go to agencies because they fear that their child will be taken away . . .

"Our defense mechanisms may make it difficult to read us but look to see what went into our lives to make us this way . . . It's true that we're socially alienated, most of us with good reason. Ninety percent of us were abused as children. I can remember not being loved when I was a child. But I just thought I was a rotten little kid and that's why I was being tossed from foster home to foster home. Since most of us grew up viewing others as part of negative, hurtful relationships, why should we form more relationships now?

From *Children Today*, 1975, Department of Health, Education and Welfare.

1716. Lady Mary Montague, daughter of the duke of Kingston and the toast of English society, returns from Turkey convinced of the therapeutic aspects of inoculation. Against great public outcry, she vaccinates her only son against smallpox and introduces western Europe, against its will, to one of medicine's finest accomplishments.

"The feeling parents most often talk about in P.A. is fear—fear of what they're doing, fear of what will happen if they don't get help and fear of what will happen if they do. And, of course, their fears are reality-based.

"Many of us in P.A. also have a constant dread that our behavior is indicative of insanity, that we are losing our minds. We think: 'I had no control over a lot of things in my life and now I have no control over even my mind!' Many times we also work in symptoms that we have read about—game-playing, attention-getting. Then comes fear that we really are that psychopathic . . .

"I've abused my child physically and emotionally. Now I can talk in retrospect. I live in bits and pieces of those feelings now, but not the hell!!"

The speaker is Jolly K., graduate of 35 foster homes, former abusive parent and founder of Parents Anonymous, Inc. of Los Angeles, California, a private organization of self-help groups that now has 1,500 members in 150 chapters in the United States and Canada.

Jolly founded her organization, first known as Mothers Anonymous, in 1970. It happened, as she tells it, in response to her bitter complaints to her therapist that there was no place for fearful abusers—and potential abusers—to turn for services. "Well, why don't you start one?" was his answer.

In 1974 Parents Anonymous received a grant from the Children's Bureau, OCD, to help establish additional chapters—by preparing and distributing materials on the organization and by providing technical assistance to communities wishing to form such groups, including the training of regional coordinators and local group leaders.

How is a P.A. chapter formed? Who are the parents who join such groups? Who leads them and what do they do in their meetings?

How do your members learn about Parents Anonymous?

Jolly K.: Surprisingly, over 80 percent of our members come by themselves after hearing about us on television or radio programs or through newspaper stories and other published materials. The remaining 20 percent are referred through agency contacts, the courts, mental health practitioners and friends, neighbors or relatives.

How does a new chapter get started and where may a chapter meet?

Jolly K.: New chapters are the direct result of someone's dedicated interest coupled with his or her willingness to work in developing the chapter. Chapters may be started by a parent with an abuse problem or a professional or a service agency wishing to help such parents. More specific information on starting a chapter is contained in our new *Chapter Development Manual*.

A chapter may meet in any non-threatening environment, such as a YMCA or YWCA, church, school or community center. We definitely must not meet in a city, county, state or Federal agency such as a Department of Public Welfare, Bureau of Adoptions or police department. Because feelings like "I have to have a clean house" and "Those kids better behave" can lead to potential pressure situations, we do not recommend that chapter meetings be held in private homes.

Are most of your members parents who have abused their children or are a good proportion mothers or fathers who fear they may? What percentage of members have had a child removed from their home?

Jolly K.: The majority of P.A. parents have already experienced the anguish of having an active problem, but we are beginning to see more and more parents become involved prior to actual abusive behavior. By the end of 1976 we expect to have more concrete information on this. We also will be gathering data on the percentage of parents who have children in placement.

Who, besides parents, are involved in the chapters?

Jolly K.: All chapters have a Sponsor and Chairperson. The sponsor should be a professional who has a profound respect for the self-help concept and understands group dynamics. Our sponsors include psychiatrists, psychologists, marriage and family counselors, social workers, ministers and others. If a sponsor is already employed by an agency that has an authoritative position in regard to parents with abuse problems, such as a protective service agency, he or she must work with P.A. autonomously, not as a representative of the agency.

The chairperson is always a parent. He or she may be the parent who helped start the group, or one of several who worked to form the chapter and who was later chosen informally to serve as chairperson by the other parents.

Many of our chapters also have various volunteers working with and for the chapter. Babysitters who care for the children during meeting times constitute the largest number of volunteers. We also have volunteers who help by providing transportation, hanging P.A. posters, circulating P.A. literature, making public contacts on our behalf and raising funds.

Can you tell us something about what happens at a meeting?

Jolly K.: Meetings begin and take shape in many different ways. Sometimes they start by someone saying, in response to the body language of a member, "Hey, what's happening?" Other times it begins by picking up on a problem a member was discussing at the last meeting or by asking for follow-up on a phone crisis call.

If I were at a meeting of a new group I might say, "Look, we're meeting here for a purpose—we're here to talk about what's churning inside us. Let's do something now to stop this behavior." We'd exchange telephone numbers and addresses and begin to form a lot of support contact.

I remember one meeting when a member, Lenny, was sitting on the couch, sharing with us how "down" she felt. Questioned many times as to the whys and wherefores, Lenny answered by saying, "I don't know," "I'm so confused" and "Stop badgering me." All the while she was quietly crying. She appeared so vulnerable, so young at that moment and most of all, so very needy.

I reached out, put my arms around her, practically putting her into my lap as if she were a lonely, lost child. At this, Lenny cried openly, much in the same way that a hurt, pained child cries. We as a group then knew, and verbally discussed the fact, that there are times when our need for nurturing exceeds our need to know the whys and wherefores. We also found out that when this overwhelming need is fulfilled—for Lenny it was within a half an hour's time—we can then turn our attention and response to the realities of our daily situations. Most of all, we learned that we can ask for inner fulfillment, that some others will respond with positive methods to help, and that we are not bad, unloveable people.

Another typical moment came at a meeting when Joel told other members: "I did it! Last week," she said, "I got so teed off at my son!" (He is five). "But instead of abusing him I squashed the milk carton I was holding until the milk went all over the place . . . I released my anger in a more positive way and it worked. Now I know I can do

1717. Maria Theresa, eldest daughter of Austria's Charles VI, is born. She will later be known to her subjects, after her ascension to the Austrian throne, as the "Mother of Her Country," abolishing torture and the worst elements of feudalism, organizing a system of education and more equitable taxation, putting the feared Inquisition on a shorter leash, and—in a word—endearing herself to her people.

other things besides being abusive when I'm uptight."

Sure, the members laughed, but most important, we learned. Joel had shown us that a potential abusive situation can be averted, that we can be non-abusive regardless of how uptight we are! Call these heavy times or light times in a meeting. More than anything else, we in P.A. call the meetings "our time." The times with Lenny and Joel were very real moments in Parents Anonymous.

How do members support one another between meetings and in emergencies?

Jolly K.: My last answer illustrated support but also a lot of caring. Suppose Joel had not squashed the milk carton. Alternate ways to release angry feelings include calling another member and releasing the feelings over the phone. Joel could also have asked another member to care for her boy until she "pulled it together," or she could have asked to have someone care for her (meaning stay with her) for a while.

Have you found that there are certain kinds of parents with whom P.A. cannot work successfully? Are you able to guide them to other help?

Jolly K.: We've not found "certain kinds" of parents that we're not able to work with. We have found that some people find our program to be less successful for them. Again, we're not the "cup of tea" that they find comforting. When we are made aware of this, yes, we usually are able to guide them to other helping resources.

We have also found that persons who are acutely mentally ill and who come to a P.A. meeting may find that the group can't offer them the comprehensive services they need. It may also be that the group feels it is not prepared to deal with the behavior that may arise from their illness. In such cases the group, with the assistance of the sponsor, is able to refer the person to a more appropriate source.

What is the rate of recidivism for those who attend meetings? Do you follow up former members?

Jolly K.: Recidivism has been very, very low. In the five years of the program's existence, we know of only two incidents which resulted in a child's hospitalization. That's not to say all is sweetness and roses and that our members have become instant Pollyannas. It is to say that life- or limb-threatening abuse has been vastly reduced.

No, we do not do a formal follow-up on former members.

Do you feel that members of P.A., who have voluntarily sought help, are typical of most abusive parents?

Jolly K.: Yes . . . emphatically, yes. We are seeing much the same, and then some, of the parents so often described in the available literature and research studies. We are seeing the very withdrawn, the very aggressive, the isolationist, the uptight, the psychotic . . . in short, we are seeing human beings displaying a lot of different "typical human traits."

How many members meet in an average group and how long do most parents remain members?

Jolly K.: Average group size is between six to 10 members, with most members staying in for one or more years.

What is the percentage of men to women in your groups?

Jolly K.: Too small a percentage. The average among the groups would probably be 25 to 30 percent men. Confirmed percentages are not currently available.

Do both parents in an abusive family usually attend meetings? And what have you found the role of the non-abusing (passive) parent to be?

Jolly K.: No. Again, this is not one of our most successfully realized objectives. Incidentally, we've found the passive parent to be not so darn passive as people think. We know that a whole lot of "behind the scenes setting of the stage" is going on and contributing to the activeness of the active abusing parent.

What action is taken if the group learns that a member has committed an abusive act or fears that he will?

Jolly K.: Group peer pressure, group commitment to work extra hard with the parent and, as an extreme last resort, if P.A. doesn't work and the parent doesn't stop, then with or without the parent's agreement other people will be asked to intervene and provide services that will guarantee the safety of the child or children and the parent.

The Child Abusive Pattern

In order for a child to be physically injured or neglected by his parents or guardian, several pieces of a complex puzzle must come together in a very special way. To date, we can identify at least three major criteria.

First, a parent (or parents) must have the potential to abuse. This potential is acquired over the years and is made up of at least five factors:

* *The way the parents themselves were reared, i.e., did they receive a negative "mothering imprint?"*

* *Have they become very isolated individuals who cannot trust or use others?*

* *Do they have a spouse who is so passive that he or she cannot give?*

* *Presence of a poor self-image.*

* *Do they have very unrealistic expectations for their child (or children)?*

Second, there must be a child. *As obvious as that might sound we point it out because this is not just any* child, *but a very special child—one who is seen differently by his parents; one who fails to respond*

in the expected manner; or possibly one who really is different (retarded, too smart, hyperactive, or has a birth defect). Most families in which there are several children can readily point out which child would have "gotten it" if the parents had the potential. Often a perfectly normal child is "seen" as bad, willful, stubborn, demanding, spoiled or slow.

Finally, there must be some form of crisis, or a series of crises, that sets the abusive act into motion. These can be minor or major crises—a washing machine breaking down, a job lost, a husband leaving, no heat, no food, a mother-in-law's visit and the like. It is most unlikely for the crisis to be the cause *for the abuse, as some would like to believe; rather, the crisis is the precipitating factor. The simplistic view that child abuse is caused by parents who "don't know their strength" while disciplining their child has been shown to be false.*

It is this combination of events that, when they occur in the right order and at the right time, lead to physical abuse.

1718. Mary Butterworth invents an ingenious counterfeiting technique, which makes no use of highly incriminating metal printing plates. Instead, she employs a disposable muslin cloth to take up the image of a bill and transfer it to a blank sheet of paper. Members of the family are put to work in the kitchen, each on a specialized assembly-line

Education

Before You Sign Up with a
Vocational School

The Editors of *Changing Times*

Don't assume that money you spend for schooling is sure to be money well spent. The education marketplace can be as full of consumer pitfalls as a car lot or a home-improvement deal. When unemployment is high, as now, shopping for vocational education is especially fraught with hazards, the chief one being the come-on that holds out the false promise of a job.

A number of organizations—from the U.S. Office of Education and the Federal Trade Commission to private accrediting agencies—are looking into ways to protect you when you shop for postsecondary vocational education. Some new laws and tougher enforcement of existing regulations may result. But no rules or regulations can make any vocational school a fail-safe investment, whether it's public, nonprofit or profit-making. The only sure way to select the right one will continue to be the slow and tedious, but tried and true approach outlined here.

First, narrow the field

While the proprietary, or commercial, school probably is the most widely known of your alternatives, there are many different kinds of vocational schools. Training in job skills is available in vocational high schools and adult education programs of public schools; vocational and extension divisions of community and four-year colleges; schools run by major companies or trade groups to train potential employees; apprenticeship programs run by unions, companies and local groups; on-the-job and classroom training programs for members of the armed forces. Job training in these will probably cost you less than at commercial schools, so check on them first. But just because a school is free or cheap doesn't mean it is the best deal for you.

Many considerations other than cost are involved. For one thing, your choice of job may limit your choice of schooling. Take a look at the Department of Labor's *Occupational Outlook Handbook* at your library. It will tell you, for instance, that major airlines train their flight attendants in airline-operated schools; that you can become a full-fledged appliance repairman strictly through on-the-job training, but vocational schooling can enable you to qualify sooner. On the other hand, if you eventually want a position requiring a bachelor's degree, pick a school where you can earn credits toward a four-year degree while taking courses for a beginning-level job.

A good commercial school could be well worth your investment—which might run to $1,000 or more—if it teaches the specific job skills you are after, is more in tune with the needs of employers than a non-profit school and offers concentrated course cycles that will allow you to enter the job market sooner.

Manpower Magazine

Here's how to select a school that will give you the most value for your money. Use this same general approach to evaluate nonprofit as well as commercial schools.

Start by making a list of all the schools in the area you're interested in that offer the kind of training you need. Check school directories in your library (a good one is the *New York Times Guide to Continuing Education in America*). Ask for suggestions from these sources: your high school teachers and guidance counselors; past employers; employers you'd like to work for; career counselors with the Veterans Administration and branches of the military service; state employment agencies; union or U.S. Labor Department officials familiar with apprenticeship training; relatives and friends, especially those in your chosen line of work.

Next, collect some information from the schools on your list. Reputable schools will be happy to give you publications that describe their courses, facilities and services. Schools need students to stay in business, of course, so a recruiter may take any sign of interest on your part as an invitation to sell you on his school. Warning: Do not commit yourself at this stage. If the recruiter has no printed compilation of the information you need or is not willing to give you material without obligation, cross his school off your list at once.

When you've narrowed the possibilities to just a few places, visit each one to talk about your plans. Get specifics about costs, financial aid and training requirements for the job you'd like. Look over the school facilities and meet some of its students and staff—teachers, guidance counselors, placement people,

task, with Mary reportedly running a very tight ship. Within a short time she becomes quite rich, attracting the attention of Rhode Island authorities and neighbors. When a charge is finally brought to bear and she is arraigned in court, prosecution is unable to produce evidence of the crime. Since no plates can be found, she is acquitted.

not just the recruiter or salesman. If you like, take along a more experienced friend or relative who can advise you.

Obtain copies of enrollment contracts as well as financial-aid and installment-payment forms required by the school so you can read them at your leisure. As with any contract, before signing, be sure you understand all the implications—for you and the school. If you're not absolutely clear about what the contract says, get help from a lawyer or other adviser you trust.

Now, check each school point by point

Here are the most important questions you'll need to get answered at each school you look into. Some items are less critical than others, but the best schools should pass muster on all these criteria.

☐ Is the school accredited by an agency officially "recognized" by the U.S. Office of Education? If so, then it has met at least minimum standards. To find out what these standards are, write to the accrediting agency. If you're in doubt about the school's standing, write to the U.S. Office of Education (see address in the box.)

☐ Is the school licensed, registered or approved by a state or local government agency?

☐ Will you qualify for government financial aid at the school? A member of the staff should explain the major aid programs to you and point out the financial liabilities as well as the benefits of each plan.

☐ Will the courses qualify you for the kind of job you want within a reasonable time? Will you later have to pass exams for licenses or undergo a period of apprenticeship? The *Occupational Outlook Handbook,* mentioned earlier, will give you information on this and on employment prospects.

☐ Does the school have a placement officer who will assist you without further charge in finding a job? To check on the effectiveness of the placement office, talk

---

---

to recent graduates (a good school will give you the names of some) and to potential employers.

☐ Does the enrollment contract clearly spell out everything included in the stated cost of your course? Will any necessities cost you extra?

☐ Does your payment contract protect you against default by the school? In many states if a contract is sold to a bank or other third party, you may be obligated to pay all of it even if the school backs out on its part of the deal unless there is specific language in the contract to protect your interest in such a case.

☐ Does the school have a printed refund policy? Good schools have a reasonable refund arrangement for students who drop out.

☐ What percentage of the students complete their courses? A high drop-out rate can mean either poor courses or faulty evaluation of students' aptitudes and qualifications, or both.

☐ How many graduates are successful at landing the jobs they trained for? A recent survey of over 2,000 public and private vocational school graduates in six occupational fields showed that only one of five graduates in accounting, computer programming and electronics technician programs got the jobs for which they had been trained. The study found no difference in this respect between nonprofit and commercial schools. Graduates of secretarial, dental assistant and cosmetology courses fared better, with four out of five finding the jobs they wanted. Again, the best way to gauge the success of a school's graduates is by talking to them and to employers if you can.

SOME WARNING SIGNALS

If a vocational school you're considering does the following, reject it:
● Says or implies it will "guarantee" you a job after completion of the course. Only employers give out jobs. A number of major U.S. firms own vocational schools, but graduation from them is no assurance you'll land a job with the parent company.
● Advertises for students under such headings as "Help Wanted," "Employment" or "Business Opportunities." Legitimate ads for students belong under the headings "Schools, " "Education" or "Training."
● Pressures you to sign a contract quickly.
● Makes extravagant claims about the success of graduates, your prospective earnings and the demand for workers. The New York City Consumer Affairs Department recently found that potential computer school students were being told that their opportunities would be virtually unlimited, when in truth the market for programmers without a college education had become extremely tight.

1718. While Sara Drew and her lover, John Hewet, are cavorting in a haystack, lightning strikes their shelter and electrocutes them both. Clergymen use the couple's fate as an object lesson in the wages of sin. Alexander Pope, among other writers of the day, defends them in romantic epitaphs.

Know the Facts

Choosing a private vocational school is a big decision. You probably want to know: "What is the cost?" "How hard is it?" "How long does it take?" These are good things to find out. *But don't be fooled about how much the training will help you get a good job.* Before you sign any vocational school contract, get the *straight facts*.

First, and most important, contact *prospective employers. These are the people who may be hiring you.* They know what they want in an employee. Their opinions and general impressions are valuable even if they don't have the exact answers to your questions.

1. Go to the yellow pages of the telephone book. Make a list of three companies in your field of interest who might be possible employers.
2. Visit, write or call the Personnel Offices to get answers to the Most Important Questions

Can you tell me:

1. **"Would you hire graduates of the school?"**
2. **"How many have you actually hired in the last year?"**
3. **"Were they hired because of school training?"**
4. **"Did training make any difference in starting salary?"**

Are there jobs available for the skills you want? Talk to:
  Companies that should be hiring
  Your state or local employment agency
  Labor unions and trade associations

Are there complaints or recommendations about the school/course? Talk to:
  Chamber of Commerce or Better Business Bureau
  Federal Trade Commission, contact office nearest you
  Present or former vocational school students. (Get names from military or high school counselors.)

For personal counseling and further information, visit:
  V.A. and military education counselors
  Present or former high school counselors
  Career counselors at local or state employment agencies
  The school itself. A personal inspection is worth many phone calls. Compare the school to its ads. Then compare it with other public and private schools offering similar courses.

From *Pocket Guide to Choosing a Vocational School,* 1973, Federal Trade Commission.

1721. Eighty young women, shipped out from a French house of corrections, arrive on the shores of Louisiana to become wives for the settlers.

Getting Credit for What You Know

Have you wondered how you really could?

What credit? We're talking about educational credit, the kind of credit that puts you in a position for a better job or for advancement, or gives you a second chance at college and higher education.

Did you know that more than two out of every five adult citizens have not graduated from high school?

Of the 111.1 million persons 25 years of age and over in March 1972, 46.5 million had not completed their formal high school education. Of these, 24.6 million were women.

Did you know that people without a high school education have more difficulty finding employment, and those who do frequently must settle for low-paying, uninteresting, dead end jobs?

Unemployment rates were much higher in March 1972 for women who were high school dropouts (10.7 percent) than for high school graduates (5.8 percent) or for college graduates (3.1 percent).

Did you know that average earnings increase with more schooling?

Median incomes of women 25 years of age and over who worked full time year round in 1971 were

- $3,946 for those with less than 8 years of schooling
- $5,808 for high school graduates
- $9,162 for college graduates

Did you know that there are new ways of building educational credit without "going to school"?

A high school diploma is a *must* for almost all desirable jobs today, and in many cases college-level credit is needed for advancement. You may be able to get the equivalent of a high school diploma, college credit, or even a degree, by taking examinations which evaluate learning no matter how it has been acquired — through

- on-the-job training
- correspondence or extension courses
- adult education programs
- educational TV
- independent study

Such alternatives to formal schooling can help you meet the compelling need for educational credentials.

From *Get Fair Credit for What You Know*, Women's Bureau, Department of Labor.

These new ways of getting educational credit have special meaning for women who want to return to school or to work, and who want to return at levels equal to what they have already learned through their life experiences.

Getting High School Credit

Q. It seems as if every job I want to apply for requires at least a high school diploma, but it's been years since I left school without graduating. Do you mean I can get a diploma without going back to a classroom?

A. Yes, by taking a high school equivalency examination. It is designed to test individual competence in certain subject areas. When you pass the General Educational Development (GED) tests, you will get a certificate accredited by your State department of education that is accepted on the same basis as a high school diploma. You may already have the knowledge to pass the examinations without even realizing it!

Q. What kinds of tests are the GED's?

A. There are five parts to the examinations: English, social studies, natural sciences, literature, and mathematics. The tests are designed to measure one's ability to think clearly about ideas and concepts rather than his or her knowledge of facts. Spanish versions of the GED have been available since 1971 and are administered in 29 States.

Q. Who is eligible to take the high school equivalency examination?

A. Any adult who wishes to apply. GED tests are given at approximately 2,000 official centers throughout the country.

Q. Is GED testing widely used?

A. Yes. During 1971 a total of almost 400,000 adults took the GED tests, representing a fourfold increase during the past 10 years.

The average age of those tested was 28 years; the average number of years of formal schooling these individuals had attained was equivalent to tenth grade.

Q. Who determines standards for passing the examinations?

A. Each State department of education establishes its minimum score for the issuance of a certificate.

Q. Is it necessary to prepare for the tests?

A. Many people will feel ready to take them with-

1722. The earliest recorded instance of a professional female prize fight appears this year when Elizabeth Wilkinson advertises in London papers that she will box Hannah Hayfield in a public bout. Police threaten to jail both women if they go through with it. They don't.

out further preparation. For some who do not, help in preparing for the examinations may be obtained from organizations and agencies conducting special programs for adults. These include Federal and State civil service commissions, public and private schools, businesses and industries, the Job Corps, and other government agencies.

● For information about programs in your area, contact your local Superintendent of Schools or Adult Education Supervisor, or write to the Adult Education Association of the United States of America, 1225 19th Street NW., Washington, D.C. 20036.

● The Federal Government has many training programs which provide basic literacy skills, remedial reading, and brushup courses. Contact your local State employment service about how to get into such a program.

Q. What if I cannot attend regular classes?

A. You may want to consider independent study or correspondence courses, as many adults prefer. About 1,200 high schools provide personally supervised correspondence study. The Federal Government sponsors correspondence courses for military personnel and courses in work-related subjects for other employees. In addition, colleges and universities, businesses and industries, labor unions, religious denominations, and private home-study schools offer a wide range of courses.

Q. If I decide on correspondence study with a private home-study school, how do I select a school?

A. You are more likely to be on safe ground when you choose an accredited correspondence school. Special care should also be exercised in the selection of courses to be sure they meet individual goals and will be completed.

The National Home Study Council has been designated by the U.S. Office of Education as the recognized accreditation agency for private home-study schools. While many nonaccredited schools may be reliable, only 188 of the more than 800 private correspondence schools presently in operation are accredited.

● For a directory of accredited schools, write to the National Home Study Council, 1601 18th Street NW., Washington, D.C. 20009.

To check on schools that are not accredited, contact your State department of education, local Chamber of Commerce, or the Veterans Administration.

Q. Is there any other way I can obtain assistance in getting my certificate?

A. Yes, TV High School was developed for this purpose by the Manpower Education Institute, a private organization sponsored jointly by labor and management. The course consists of 60 half-hour lessons covering the five subject areas tested. A home-study kit, with 10 paperback texts and a study guide containing lesson outlines, study aids, and bibliographies, is available for a nominal fee.

Programs based on this curriculum have been used in communities throughout the country. State-wide coverage with broad citizen support was undertaken in Arizona. TV High School has also been shown in Georgia, Michigan, Nebraska, Ohio, South Carolina, Washington, and the District of Columbia. In a number of cases, businesses and industries have set up viewing centers for their employees and given them time off from work to view the TV courses.

● For information, write to: Manpower Education Institute, 450 Lexington Avenue, New York, N.Y. 10017; or, Great Plains Instructional Television Library, University of Nebraska, Lincoln, Nebr. 68508; or, Dr. Catherine G. Nichols, College of Education, Arizona State University, Tempe, Ariz. 85281.

Local educational TV stations often provide public service programs of this type. Contact your Superintendent of Schools or your local stations about this.

Q. How can I get further information about taking the GED examinations and getting a diploma?

1725. At about this time, the French government is unable to convince Frenchwomen to settle in the Canadian wilderness. Finally, invoking a long disused law, the government forces Parisian prostitutes out of the city and ships them to Canada as prospective wives for the lonely colonists.

A. Ask your local board of education or community college about the program, or write to the Commission on Accreditation of Service Experience, American Council on Education, 1 Dupont Circle NW., Washington, D. C. 20036 for:

- State policies on the issuance of high school certificates based on the GED results
- a list of official GED centers
- information on the granting of high school credit for military educational experience

Getting College Credit

Q. Is there any way to receive credit for college-level achievement whether or not high school has been completed?

A. Yes, many colleges and universities grant such credit through special examinations. The tests provide a way to secure academic credit and give people a chance to show that they have the equivalent of some college education even though they never went to college. In other words, these examinations give credit for what a person knows no matter how he or she learned it.

Q. What kinds of examinations would enable me to get college credit or advanced placement without formal classroom preparation?

A. There are programs through which examinations may be taken.

- The College Proficiency Examination (CPE) was established in 1963 by the New York Board of Regents. The primary areas where credit may be obtained through CPE are health education, the nursing sciences, foreign languages, and professional education.

- The College-Level Examination Program (CLEP) was conceived in 1965 and introduced in the fall of 1967 by the College Entrance Examination Board. Thirty-three General and Subject Examinations are currently being used. You may take one or several tests, depending upon your goals, needs, and motivations. The General Examinations provide a way to show that you have acquired some general education, the equivalent of what is offered in required freshman and sophomore courses at many colleges. General Examinations are given in five basic areas: English composition, mathematics, natural sciences, social sciences, and humanities. The Subject Examinations are a more intensive measure of ability in special areas such as general

psychology, American government, and introductory economics.

Q. Who gives the credit for CPE and CLEP tests?

A. In both programs, the colleges and universities which are among the participating institutions decide the amount of credit to grant and specify the scores they require. More than 200 institutions in New York and other northeastern States grant credit toward completion of degree requirements through CPE. More than 1,300 colleges and universities throughout the country award credit through CLEP. Neither CPE nor CLEP grants college credits.

Q. What are some advantages of taking the tests?

A. The test scores are used as a means of developing appropriate procedures for the admission and placement of persons who wish to continue their education. In some States, certification boards and licensing agencies accept CLEP results in lieu of college training to meet requirements for such professions as library science, law, and accounting. Businesses and industrial organizations also make use of the programs in determining qualifications of individuals for higher positions, or in filling jobs with special requirements.

Q. How can I get help in preparing myself to take college-level examinations?

A. One means is through independent study. The National University Extension Association is a major national organization of those public and private institutions which offer such courses. For a list of accredited colleges and universities where home-study courses are offered, write for the booklet titled "Guide to Independent Study." (75 cents) For degree programs through independent study, write for "A Directory of U. S. College and University Degrees for Part-Time Students." ($1.95) Both are available from the National University Extension Association, Suite 360, 1 Dupont Circle NW., Washington, D. C. 20036.

Q. How can I arrange to take the examinations?

A. For information about participating institutions, registration, location of test centers, description of examinations, and other details of the program, write

- Dr. Donald J. Nolan, Director, College Proficiency Examination Program, State Education Department, Albany, N.Y. 12224.

- CLEP, College Entrance Examination Board, Box 1821, Princeton, N.J. 08540, or Box 1025, Berkeley, Calif. 94701.

1731. Nine corpses, seven of them female, are exhumed from their graves, and the villagers of Olmutz, Bohemia, drive stakes through their hearts. It is believed that the bodies were becoming vampires by night and were preying upon sleeping citizens of the opposite sex.

Returning to School

Whether you are just beginning to think about returning to school or are ready for actual re-entry, you are not alone. Many women—younger, older and your age—are part of the back-to-school trend among adults that has grown considerably during the past decade and promises even greater participation in the future.

You are not alone

Let's look at the statistics. There are more than 850,000 American men and women over 35 in college part-time and full-time; more than half of these, 53 percent, are women. In contrast, only 42 percent of college students under 35 are women.

Of more than 450,000 women over 35 enrolled in continuing education and college-degree programs, 70 percent are married. The majority of these students are in part-time programs.

The number of younger returning students continues to increase as well. More 25-to 35-year-old women than ever before are part of the returning student scene. This includes young mothers, married and single women, in part-time and full-time studies. Some are also employed. Some are homebound.

Returning students include job and career-oriented women who are learning that, if they are married, they are likely to work for 24 years after age 35 and, if single or divorced, they are apt to work 28 years after 35.

If you are ready to return to school, or just contemplating a possible re-entry, it will help if you realize that you will not be the only adult on the registration line or in the classroom.

What are your concerns?

Some of the fears returning women have faced center on money, age, ability to perform as a student and ability to function in multiple roles.

Worries about money

"How can I spend money on myself when I really do not have it? when I have some but have it earmarked elsewhere in the family budget? or when I am reluctant to accept a loan from family, friend or banker?"

The prospective returning student's concern about financing her education, from tuition to the necessary extras, may be justified. The supply of scholarships, fellowships, grants and loans falls far short of the growing demand. Financial assistance for part-time studies, the route preferred by most returning women, is particularly skimpy. There is some comfort, however, in the fact that, although the supply does not approach the demand, increasing attention is being given to the financial needs of returning students and new avenues are being explored for financial aid, some of which have already proved fruitful.

Whether or not you, personally, can benefit from available aid is something you have to find out for yourself. Review your resources and explore your community and find out what its institutions and organizations have to offer.

Look into the availability of funding through the government, from the specific school of your choice, from your bank or from your family.

From *The Returning Student*. Copyright © 1975 Catalyst, Inc. Adapted and reprinted with permission.

Family savings set aside for a rainy day may be spent wisely now for your education, as an investment in your future. Some returning students, hard-pressed for school fees, are choosing to use money that was put aside for their children's college education, spending it on their own because the youngsters will have a chance at scholarships not available to returnees.

You might take a part-time job to pay for part-time schooling, or you may boost your income by tapping saleable talents. One woman, for example, cashes in on her extra-curricular skills to pay school tuitions by exhibiting and selling art works she originally did strictly for pleasure.

Look to community colleges, which have been a valuable entry point for many returning students throughout the country, and a point at which funding is increasingly available. Or consider state colleges or local junior colleges as possible alternatives to private institutions.

Explore financial assistance possibilities through indirect aid, which is another way colleges and institutions are beginning to help women who are serious about their return to studies. Reduced tuition and fee schedules are one major method. One university's "family plan," for example, enables a woman or man to return to school at a financial discount if a member of the family is already enrolled full-time.

Some alumni organizations aid returning students. One university, whose scholarship program for adult women began as far back as 1966, recently began encouraging alumni to bequeath their estates for part-time scholarship monies. Several have already agreed.

Employers sometimes are the avenues to assistance. If you are already employed, find out whether or not there is a reimbursement plan that would help in financing your studies, whether they are job-related or not.

Try to keep up-to-date on new available funding. Additional attention to women as a significant segment of the higher education population has led to current explorations into funding. Potential sources include the government, colleges and universities, industry, alumni organizations and women's associations.

While you are wondering about the costs involved in your return to school, do not overlook the extras, such as costs of books, transportation, child care or whatever needs you anticipate in addition to tuition.

Although the increasing attention being given to the needs of returning students and to the development of financial assistance resources is encouraging, you should be aware of the basic facts of financial life which affect returning students. Federal funding has generally been geared to full-time students even though most adult women, particularly those with family responsibilities, prefer to return to studies part-time. Financial aid for full-time study sometimes is disallowed when a combined income in a household exceeds $15,000, which means a husband's income can deter a wife's education if financial assistance is a necessity.

Although there are shortcomings in many financial assistance programs in terms of the returning adult woman, there are some indications that the financial picture may brighten in the coming decade, particularly if the overall state of the economy improves. Indeed, more and more educators, administrators and counselors are realizing that financial aid can be a psychological as well as a practical boost for women reluctant to spend family funds on themselves for re-entry.

1736. A Mrs. Hicks and her nine-year-old daughter become the last women to be executed as witches in England.

Take time to find out which funds may be available in your area for you now, or later, as your educational commitment expands. You may be pleasantly surprised, or disappointed. But you certainly should inquire. There are many potential sources of financial assistance for returning students.

Federal Loan Programs. Loans have the dual advantage of allowing you to concentrate solely on your studies and enabling you to repay after your earning power has been increased. The Federal government sponsors the Guaranteed Student Loan Program, through which you may borrow money from a bank. You must be enrolled on at least a half-time basis. A listing of state agencies which administer this program is available from the U.S. Office of Education. The National Direct Student Loan Program, through the financial aid offices of colleges, offers long-term, low-interest Federal loans for both undergraduate and graduate study. Contact the Division of Student Financial Aid, Office of Education of the U.S. Department of Health, Education and Welfare, for current information on these programs.

Other loans. Be aware that loans from banks, insurance companies and commercial loan programs usually carry high rates of interest and stiff repayment terms.

Cooperative and Work-Study Programs. If you feel you can handle the time commitment, explore these possibilities for funds. In a cooperative program, the student alternates periods of full-time study with periods of full-time employment. A work-study program usually requires that you be a full-time student with part-time employment. Besides enabling you to earn money, these programs often offer the opportunity to gain experience in a chosen career field. For information, contact:

The Cooperative Education Association
Drexel University
Philadelphia, Pennsylvania 19104

Work-Study Branch
Division of Student Financial Aid
Bureau of Higher Education
U.S. Office of Education.
Washington, D. C. 20202

Aid of Field of Study. If you know which career field you wish to study, particularly on the graduate or professional level, a letter to its national association may elicit further sources of aid. Examples include the American Library Association, the Council on Social Work Education, the American Bar Association and the Society of Women Engineers. These are listed in the U.S. Department of Labor's *Occupational Outlook Handbook* and in various directories of associations which are available at most schools and in public libraries.

Worries about age

"How can I go back to school when, even as a 25-year-old, I feel 'over the hill' compared to traditional college beginners of 18? or when I've been out of school 10 or 15 years, or much longer?"

You are probably concerned about the differences you expect to find between yourself and the 18 to 21 year-old you may have as a classmate. But all the plusses are not on her side. She may be younger and even have the advantages of living in the school environment all day, of consecutive years as a full-time student, and of not running off to the other kinds of commitments you have after school hours. But you are bringing to your new role as a student an enrichment that comes from past experiences and present responsibilities.

You will be able to attend classes, read, talk and listen with a more keenly developed sense of purpose than a young student has or than you had as a younger student.

The give-and-take between you and the younger student should be a boon to you both. Women who have returned to school report that their classroom and extra-curricular exchanges with younger students, some of whom may be their own children's ages, are a bonus to their educational experience.

Worries about ability

"How will I be able to develop study habits? write term papers? study for exams?"

You will. Counselors at women's centers at universities and colleges across the country report that it takes just one or two courses to bring most returning women to the point at which doubts about their abilities begin to diminish and are replaced by excitement, enthusiasm and seriousness that enable them to move ahead into their studies.

The woman who came to class yesterday with timidity and reluctance learns quickly that she can and should speak up, pursue her interests and open her mind to the ideas and avenues that will help her advance in her aspirations.

Some women's abilities strengthen in special programs for returning women, such as self-development workshops; others come into their own in the traditional mainstream of student life, the classroom.

Enough returning students have succeeded in a variety of educational settings to demonstrate that, despite the fears of women contemplating re-entry, returning students do not have less physical stamina than younger students and they usually overcome difficulties in developing study habits and juggling demands upon their time. Returning students are succeeding in their educational endeavors, their strengths far offsetting their worries and their real or imagined weaknesses.

If you are uncertain about your educational plans, make your return to school a slow one, possibly beginning with just a course or two. It is wiser to take a single course and find you can handle more than to take several courses, find the load overwhelming and proclaim, "I knew I couldn't do it." A sampler course is apt to whet your appetite for more, help you determine your educational goals and result in a boost to your self-confidence.

Other worries

Do you have other concerns about returning to school? If you are the mother of young children, are you worrying about how you can go back to school when they are still at home?

Increasing attention has been given to the growing need for child care facilities for women involved in school and/or work. As in the matter of financial aid, the existing facilities do not meet or even approach the demand. The lack of adequate child care programs is particularly evident as the average returning student gets younger and some, married women and single parents, return to college before all of their children enter kindergarten.

In some communities, child care facilities are available at educational institutions that range from community colleges to universities. There are universities at which child care has become a fact of academic life for students, faculty and staff requiring it. Other communities offer no child care at all.

Not only do the availability and quality of child care facilities vary in each locale, but so does the structure. Some child care centers, for example, are affiliated with the schools at which they are located; others are sponsored by neighborhood organizations or private groups. Some are less formal, sometimes organized by a group of working/studying mothers and fathers.

Explore your community and the alternatives open to you so that you can plan for your children's supervision as you prepare for re-entry.

1737. Bettina Gozzi, daughter of an Italian shoemaker, is Casanova's first love. Being slightly older and more worldly-wise, she tantalizes him, then jilts him in favor of another shoemaker.

Are you also asking yourself if school is an essential step for you? If you are not certain that a degree will move you toward your career goal, find out first what the employment possibilities and outlook are with your present credentials. You may confirm that you must have the degree — undergraduate, graduate or doctoral — or realize that it is not essential for you after all.

If you recognize that you are not fully prepared for the career of your choice — or even a second, more realistic choice — take the time now to prepare for it by completing the educational requirements. If you feel, however, that you need or want a taste of work first, or a period of testing your interest in a specific career field, then start your job campaign even if it means working at a lower level as a first step.

Invest in planning before you plunge into long-term studies, regardless of whether you are a 25-year-old, or her mother or grandmother!

Where do you return?

There are more educational facilities than most people imagine as they contemplate returning to school. For many women, the choices are many. Much will depend, however, on where you are located and what your geographic boundaries are.

Accept the fact that researching what is available for you educationally is a task that you must begin to do for yourself.

Check out your community for:
- state colleges and universities
- private educational institutions
- two-year community colleges
- junior colleges
- technical institutes

Explore:
- noncredit programs
- undergraduate programs
- graduate studies

Consider:
- traditional formal courses
- less formal workshops and seminars
- traditional semester-long courses
- short-term courses: summer session, intersession, week-end
- day session
- evening session
- full-time study
- part-time study

Look into:
- skills courses
- self-development courses

Explore other possibilities that may help you to clarify your goals and improve your present abilities.

How fortunate you are to be returning at a time when you can choose from a smorgasbord of educational fare, from traditional academic courses in a vast array of enrichment and career fields — including many formerly reserved for men — to a broad range of in-depth workshops, seminars and conferences that deal with self-assessment, self-development, career-planning and goal-setting, all designed to help you decide what you will do with the rest of your life.

The spectrum of nontraditional study

There is yet another educational route open to the returning adult. Nontraditional study programs have not only increased in availability and diversity in recent years but they have also gained in student popularity and academic respect.

Alternatives to traditional study include such recent innovations as ''life-learning'' credit, independent study and television courses, some of which are offered in combination with each other or in conjunction with regular classes. They are designed not only for the returning woman, but also for working adults seeking further job-related education, for older adults who are retired or approaching retirement and for traditional students who seek additional college experiences different from those of the classroom.

Special degree programs and other forms of nontraditional study are not a mid-twentieth century phenomenon. The University of London has awarded degrees by examination to students since 1836 and several American universities have offered extension services to part-time students since the early 1900s. Today, however, the American Council on Education estimates that special external and evening degree programs are developing at the rate of eleven per week in the United States.

Nontraditional education requires independent study and emphasizes off-campus learning. Instead of living on or near an institution of higher learning and attending classes regularly, the student may engage in some combination of the following:

Independent study

Independent study is perhaps the oldest and best known nontraditional method of learning. Under the supervision of a faculty member, the student receives lectures through the mail, does her own reading and writing assignments, and submits a paper or examination by which the teacher can assess her learning. There is a minimum of on-campus contact and, as can be expected, this form of study relies heavily on the discipline, initiative and motivation of the student. It is particularly advantageous to a person who needs or prefers to work on her own at home. Independent study permits greater flexibility and tailoring of courses to the interests of the individual student and helps overcome geographic boundaries. A student in Kansas, for example, can enroll in a study program conducted from an institution in Vermont.

Originally reserved as ''honors'' courses, a certain number of independent study courses may be found in almost any institution. A growing number of degree programs, however, are almost exclusively independent in format. A few of these are described in the paragraphs that follow. For others, check with the schools in your area.

- University Without Walls, formed by the Union of Experimenting Colleges and Universities, emphasizes independent study with no fixed length of time for completing degree requirements. Admissions policy and evaluation procedures are set by each participating college and university, a list of which may be obtained from University Without Walls, 2700 Bancroft Way, Berkeley, California 94704.
- The Open University began in Britain in 1969 and has since been

1738. Elizabeth Timothy, whose husband dies this year, continues printing his *South Carolina Gazette,* the first newspaper in the colonies, and becomes the first American woman to publish a newspaper.

246   Returning to School
EDUCATION

adapted by four American universities: the University of Maryland, University of Houston (Texas), Rutgers State University (New Jersey), and Salem State College (Massachusetts). An additional sixty institutions offer one or more "Open University" courses. The teaching system includes correspondence study, courses on television and personal contact with tutors and counselors by mail, telephone or at learning centers. Sometimes called the "University of Second Chance," it is structured to meet the needs of busy people seeking education.

• The Regents External Degree program awards bachelor and associate degrees entirely by examination in such fields as business administration and nursing science. For information, contact The Regents External Degree Program, State Education Department, 99 Washington Street, Albany, New York 12210.

• Thomas A. Edison College in New Jersey has awarded more than 300 associate degrees and bachelor of science degrees in business administration. It received state approval for a bachelor of arts program in 1974. Counseling, self-education and work experience are emphasized. Students do not have to live in New Jersey and they have the option of attending other colleges for particular courses. Tuition ranges from $250 to $400 for a degree. For information, contact Thomas A. Edison College, Department of Higher Education, 225 East State Street, Trenton, New Jersey 08625. Another example of a comparable state-sponsored independent study program is New York's Empire State College. For information, contact Empire State College, Saratoga Springs, New York 12866. Several other states are planning similar schools.

• Other programs include the Adult Degree Program at Goddard College, Vermont, which enrolls students from all over the country and which consists of short resident planning periods followed by longer independent study periods. The College of Liberal Studies at the University of Oklahoma also includes resident periods, independent study periods and examinations for students from every state. The University of Pittsburgh's External Degree Program features independent study with three Saturday seminars during each course. Many other independent study programs can be found by checking with colleges and libraries.

Local and national institutions are expanding into educational sources. Summer credit programs in music at Aspen, and in the biological sciences at Rocky Mountain National Park, are available through the University of Colorado Extension Division. York County Community College in Maine offers a program that utilizes local libraries, museums and community centers.

It is even possible to get a taste of college study without committing yourself to an entire program. Transylvania University in Lexington, Kentucky, allows students over 25 to audit courses with the option for credit. A "Degree Provisional Student" at the University of Pittsburgh who completes from twelve to eighteen credits may then enroll in a degree program. Bay de Noc Community College in Delta County, Michigan, runs an "Introduction to College" program for prospective students.

The Women's Re-Entry Education Program (WREP) in Santa Clara Valley, California, serves women from low-income areas who have had limited schooling. Students are admitted regardless of educational background. It has expanded into four California colleges and emphasizes support services, counseling and tutoring. Information is available from Ms. Beatrice Cossey, Director, De Anza College, 21250 Stevens Creek Boulevard, Cupertino, California 95014. Similar efforts have been undertaken at schools such as Tufts University in Medford, Massachusetts, and Brooklyn College in New York. The organization, Washington Opportunities for Women (WOW) sponsors an on-the-job and academic training program for social service aides, which can lead to an associate of arts degree from Federal City College in Washington, D.C.

If you are thinking of pursuing a nontraditional educational program, carefully explore not only its offerings but its expected

Mount Holyoke College

accreditation and anticipated advantages for you. Be particularly wary of so-called "diploma mills" that award "degrees" for money. If you have any questions concerning a correspondence course, or any other nontraditional program, check with the Accrediting Commission of the National Home Study Council, the United States Office of Education, the National University Extension Association or your local Better Business Bureau.

Steps toward admission

Whether you are certain of what, where or when you want to study or are still exploring the idea, begin now to make a serious and systematic task of gathering information that will help you make choices and move ahead. Begin an orderly compilation of relevant information for present or future use, recording important data such as school fees, registration dates, prospective educational contacts and admission requirements.

ca. **1740.** Czarina Anna of Russia rules her country capriciously, delighting in rather extreme practical jokes. She forces two servants, both clowns, to marry; then she builds a house of ice, down to the kitchen utensils, dishes, chairs, and beds, leads a procession through the snowy streets with the bride and groom locked in a large cage atop an

Find out initially from local colleges, from the library, from friends and family, the names of all educational institutions in your area and the range of traditional or nontraditional study programs that are offered. Write to each for catalogs, admissions applications and any available materials for returning students.

Note that each educational institution has its own policies and procedures regarding such matters as the college calendar, semester plan, admission requirements, grading system, advanced standing requirements, pre-entrance examinations, admissions application deadlines, testing dates and locations, financial assistance plans and individual counseling.

Find out, at the outset, any information that is particularly significant for you. This can include whether the school is accredited, if you can attend part-time, how many credits are required in a full-time program, how few credits can be carried by a part-timer and whether you can begin graduate studies or must take prerequisite courses. Is there the possibility of financial aid? Are child care facilities available? What is the policy regarding credit transfer, not only from previous schools you may have attended, but from that college to others at which you may continue later?

The college bulletins or catalogs you use must be current. Do not leaf through an old one used a couple of years ago by a friend because, in some educational institutions, there have been recent changes in some policies and procedures.

When sending for information about college program possibilities, also send for whatever transcripts you may need from secondary schools or colleges you have attended.

Assemble references from your educational past, your employment past or present, and from your volunteer life as well. You may seek the recommendation of the professional head of a program in which you were involved as a volunteer, the chairperson of a local school board on which you served, instructors of noncredit or credit courses you took and former teachers who still remember you and are willing to put a good word in writing. Former or present employers may also be pleased to endorse your new educational aspirations in a recommendation by citing your strengths in previous and current undertakings.

Depending on what other basic information you need, check such sources as *The New York Times Guide to Continuing Education in America*, a nationwide directory of college-level institutions and study programs for mature students. If you want a list and description of thousands of career fields, including educational requirements and employment outlook for each, explore the U.S. Department of Labor's *Occupational Outlook Handbook*. For these reference books or others, consult a school or local library.

It may also be appropriate for you to assemble and keep up-to-date a life experience portfolio that reveals tangible evidence of your efforts and abilities in both paid and volunteer work. Even if the college to which you apply does not grant life experience credits, the dean or other representative who interviews you for admission may recognize your potential through the work you show. It may also come in handy later when you are involved in a job search.

If entrance examinations are required for the undergraduate or graduate program you plan to pursue, find out whether, where and when review courses are given—and when, where and how the examinations are administered. For the Graduate Record Examination information bulletin, write to GRE, Educational Testing Service, Box 955, Princeton, New Jersey 08540.

At this point, or earlier if you have unanswered questions about study programs, career fields or personal goals, contact a woman's center for information and/or counseling. You may come away from an exploratory interview with facts about entrance requirements for special educational programs, with a realistic appraisal of job opportunities in the field you have chosen, with the name of someone to contact in an educational field that interests you, or even with the dates for a self-assessment workshop that may give you the emotional boost you need at this point.

Once you have gathered together as much information as you can on your own—from schools, libraries, counseling centers or elsewhere—call the admissions office of the school or schools you are considering. Many colleges routinely schedule interviews with admissions officials for prospective adult students. Make the appointment and use that interview to find out more about what is offered that will suit your educational goals.

Throughout your planning and preparing for re-entry, and in the years ahead, there is a need for you "to hang loose," as one veteran counselor advises adult women as well as younger students. "This means leaving yourself open, at all times, to receive new information, some of which may confirm your plans and goals, but some of which may lead you to make adjustments in them or even to alter your initial direction."

Do not constrict yourself to what you feel is expected of you or what you expect of yourself because you are a woman—such as extensions of home and work roles you have accepted in the past. You may feel comfortable as mother, homemaker, teacher, secretary, nurse, social worker, librarian. But your interests may be broader. Listen when someone across a dinner table or in a career workshop talks about new opportunities for women in such nontraditional fields as insurance, accounting, banking or industrial management.

Once you've returned

After you have enrolled in a study program, an advisor or counselor may be assigned to you. You may find this person available for assistance at each step or you may have to seek that individual out as situations occur in which you would like some advice or guidance.

If you are fortunate enough to be re-entering at a school or in a setting which has a special center or group for returning students, take advantage of this excellent opportunity to share experiences and problems, even decision-making discussions, with mature returnees like you. If you do not have time for such an extra-curricular group, or the school or center does not have one, try to organize informal get-togethers with friends who are recent or prospective returning students.

If you, like most women who re-enter school, have plans for working eventually, either in a former career field or in a new one, try to envision the link between education and employment right from the start. Unfortunately, many career-minded returning students who carefully select major fields of study neglect looking ahead toward the jobs they hope to have. Keeping informed about your profession by regularly reading the professional journals and, if possible, talking with people in the field, are pre-employment essentials. Know what special tools and materials are being used in your field, whether there are new training programs and courses, how the economy affects the field and, of course, what the current employment outlook is and what the outlook is likely to be when you are ready to start working.

During the time you are in school you can look ahead in terms of future employment possibilities as well. It is important to seek advice but be your own counselor, too, not only reading the appropriate journals, but making contacts in your field, seeking out professors who may know when jobs are available or what future graduate studies will be necessary for you. Your contacts for the future also may include the college placement office, alumni organization, women's center, job recruitment seminars and workshops that bring professionals from the field to the school. Classmates and instructors, even co-workers and employers, also may offer advice, or advice leading to employment opportunities. Seek them out.

elephant, presides over an enormous banquet, and, to the hooting of the crowd, locks them into their frigid bedroom for the night. The following morning they are found frozen to death.

Reading for degree

Organizing for Effective Study

William F. Brown and Wayne H. Holtzman

If you are at all typical of the vast majority of students, you have at least one, if not more, of the following study faults. First, you don't get as much studying done as you should. Not that you don't try or even that you don't go through the motions of studying, but somehow or other you don't manage to accomplish as much as you should. Second, you waste time going from one thing to another. You try to study too many things the same day or evening or even within an hour. Hence, you are so disorganized that you do not stay with one thing long enough to get much done. Finally, you have difficulty settling down to work. You are

always getting ready to study, but for one reason or another, a lot of time goes by before you actually tackle your assignments.

All three difficulties are slightly different aspects of the same problem. When you study, you fail to use your time wisely and to concentrate effectively so that you really accomplish something. Fortunately, these study faults may be corrected. Setting up a schedule for studying is of value to good as well as poor students. A well-planned schedule permits more effective use of time. It keeps you from vacillating about what you are going to do next so that you aren't disorganized about your studying. It assigns time where time is needed, prevents your studying a subject more

William F. Brown and Wayne H. Holtzman, *A Guide to College Survival*, pp. 52-59. Copyright © 1972 William F. Brown and Wayne H. Holtzman. Adapted and reprinted by permission of Prentice-Hall, Inc., Englewood Cliffs, New Jersey.

ca. **1742.** Empress Elizabeth of Russia turns the affairs of state over to trusted advisors and embarks on a life of ''prodigious'' extravagance. Her wardrobe contains 1,000 dresses, many of which are never worn, several thousand pairs of shoes, and more French lingerie than ''any other living woman.'' It is a crime against the court to wear clothes styled in the same fashion as hers.

than is required, and generally insures that you are doing the right thing at the right time. With your time thus organized, there will be more time to devote to your most difficult subjects and also more time for activities other than study.

Time budgeting principles

Several general principles may prove helpful in distributing your study time. When preparing for a *participation course* where you will be called upon in class, reserve some time *just before* the class period to study your daily lesson. In this way you will be fresh and ready to do your best work in class. For a *lecture course,* keep the time *immediately following* the class period free to spend reviewing what was said in class, organizing and expanding your notes so they will be coherent later when you study the reading assignment accompanying the lecture. If, instead, you wait till that night or the next day, you will have difficulty remembering what the instructor had to say. Besides, if the instructor is at all stimulating, you'll be in the best frame of mind to study that topic immediately after the lecture. Break long periods of study with a short relaxation period. A good rule is to take a five- to ten-minute break after each hour of concentrated study. Studying a given subject in fairly short, daily periods is far superior to occasional long periods, especially if you need to remember the material later. For example, when you are trying to learn a lot of detailed material, it is much better to study a subject one hour each day for four days than to mass four hours of study into one day.

Most students who have spent the morning and early afternoon in class or in the library studying find the late afternoon best for recreation and relaxation. Then they are able to resume their studying with refreshing vigor for several hours after dinner. It is of great importance that you achieve the proper balance between sleeping, eating, studying, working, and recreation. All work and no play will indeed make life dull, but all play and no work will assure academic failure. Experiment until you find the proper balance for you, and then stick to it. *Building up habits of regularity is essential to scholastic success.* It requires much practice and self-discipline, but pays off pleasant dividends in terms of better grades now and better work habits for the future. Remember, the work habits that you develop now will surely influence your future success in executive and professional life.

How to prepare a time budget

Efficient time budgeting requires painstaking, systematic planning. The resulting time schedule must be both realistic and practical; that is, it must be sufficiently flexible to handle changing requirements and be adequately balanced between work and play. For best results, the following five-step sequence should be employed in preparing a daily activity schedule.

1. Record Fixed Time Commitments Write in all your regularly scheduled activities, such as classes, labs, church services, employment, band practice, etc.

2. Schedule Daily Living Activities Set aside ample (but not excessive) time for eating, sleeping, dressing, etc.

3. Schedule Review Time Reserve time for reviewing either before or after each class, as appropriate.

4. Schedule Recreation Time

5. Schedule Preparation Periods For each course, schedule sufficient time for preparing outside assignments. The amount of time to be scheduled for each course will depend upon the difficulty level of the material, your ability to master the material, the grade you wish to receive, and the efficiency of your study methods. Preparation periods should be scheduled at times when interference is at a minimum and should be long enough to permit the accomplishment of a significant amount of work. Incidentally, be sure to write the name of each course in all time periods when you plan to study it.

Ten hints for time planning

You will find, below, a set of ten specific suggestions for efficient time planning. Read these suggestions carefully. Then, make out a study schedule for yourself using the principles suggested. First prepare a preliminary daily activity schedule. Live with this tentative schedule for a few days and note whether or not your allotment of study time is really adequate to meet the needs of each of your courses. Also, ask your advisor or a friend to look over your schedule and suggest improvements. Then, prepare a revised schedule in accordance with these suggestions and any new ideas that you might have. Finally, post your final schedule in your room or insert it in the notebook that you carry with you.

Schedule Around Fixed Commitments

Plan Sufficient Study Time Most college classes are planned to require about two hours of outside work per week per credit hour. By multiplying your credit load by two you can get a good idea of the time you should provide for studying. Of course, if you are a slow reader, or have other study deficiencies, you may need to plan more time.

Set Realistic Study Requirements You should know from experience about how long it will take you to write a 500-word English composition, to work 30 algebra

1744. Abigail Smith Adams, consummate writer of letters and wife of the second U.S. president, is born. In a note to her statesman husband, Abigail warns Congress: "Remember the ladies, and be more generous and favourable to them than your ancestors. Do not put such unlimited power into the hands of husbands. Remember all

problems, to read a 35-page history textbook chapter, or to translate two pages of Spanish sentences. Be realistic in scheduling your preparation time. Don't underestimate!

Study at Regular Times and Places Establishing habits of regularity in studying is extremely important. Knowing what you are going to study, and when, saves a lot of time in making decisions, finding necessary study materials, etc. Avoid generalizations in your schedule such as "study." Commit yourself more definitely to "study history" or "study chemistry" at certain hours.

Study as Soon after Class as Possible Check over lecture notes while they are still fresh in your mind. Start assignments while your memory of the assignment is still accurate. Remember, one hour of study immediately after class is probably better than two hours of study a few days later.

Utilize Odd Hours for Studying Those scattered one or two hours of free periods between classes are easily wasted. Using them for reviewing materials already known from previous study will result in free time for recreational activities later one.

Set a Two Hour Limit After studying one subject for two hours, many people begin to tire and their ability to concentrate decreases rapidly. To keep up your efficiency, take a break and then switch to studying another subject.

Study Your Hardest Subject First Begin a long study session by starting with the subject that is the least stimulating or most difficult for you. Not only will your mind be fresh while you are doing your hardest work, but you can switch to something more interesting when you begin to feel fatigued.

Study on the Weekends Some time should always be set aside on the weekends since this is a particularly good time to work on special projects (especially those requiring use of library materials). It is also a good idea to schedule a special study session for Sunday evening in order to catch up on back reading or other delayed assignments.

Borrow Time—Don't Steal It Whenever unexpected demands arise that take up time you had planned for study, decide immediately where you can trade for "free" time to make up the missed study time and adjust your schedule for that week accordingly.

USING THE DAILY ACTIVITY SCHEDULE

Time planning is no magic formula. Its value depends upon study, thought and effort. The plan suggested here can be a valuable asset to anyone who has the self-discipline to carry it through. To make it work for you, however, you cannot give up and quit after a half-hearted initial effort. Make out your schedule and follow it until it becomes the natural thing to do. Don't expect a week's trial to establish the habit of efficient time management.

Successful college students agree that study is a lonely business. You must learn to isolate yourself from the rest of the world and study alone.

Paul C. Cabot III

Passing Exams

William F. Brown and Wayne H. Holtzman

Taking mid-term and final examinations is often the downfall of many otherwise capable students. Since course grades are assigned largely on the basis of these exams, students frequently become easily rattled and blow a big test by forgetting material that they could previously recall without much trouble. Why? For most, the basic cause is fear—they know that failure is a very real possibility and they feel that they are inadequately prepared for the exam, or they lack confidence in their test-taking skills. Thus the two keys to conquering such fears are to study the subject matter thoroughly and to develop efficient test-taking techniques.

Rules for preparing for tests

1. Don't Fall Behind Keep up with your reading assignments so that studying for an exam will only involve a thorough reviewing and tying together of familiar materials. Frantic last-minute cramming of new material usually undermines your confidence and results in faulty remembering.

2. Underline To avoid completely rereading textbook assignments later, prepare them for reviewing by underlining key words and phrases and writing summary notes in the page margins as you go along.

3. Clarify Ask your instructor or a competent classmate to clarify material that you do not understand.

men would be tyrants if they could. If particular care and attention is not paid to the ladies, we are determined to foment a rebellion, and will not hold ourselves bound by any laws in which we have no voice or representation."

concentrate on understanding general concepts, principles and theories. Study for tests of the problem-solving type by working examples of each type of problem that might appear on the exam.

10. Review Briefly   On the night before a big test, quietly rethink the materials through a comprehensive final review and then go to bed early so as to be mentally and physically alert when the time comes to take the exam. Remember, your mind and body will not be fully alert if you have spent most of the previous night drinking coffee and taking pills in a desperate effort to stay awake while you frantically scramble for last-minute facts.

General rules for taking tests

1. Be on Time   Arrive early instead of barely on time so as to be organized and ready instead of in a panic. Try to go into the test alert but calm. As you work, try to do your best without becoming tense and anxious. Concentrate on what you are required to do on the test instead of worrying about the unpleasant consequences of possible failure.

2. Don't Panic   Regard lapses of memory as perfectly normal, and do not let them throw you into a panic. If you block on answering one question, leave it for a while and return to it later.

3. Read the Directions   Make certain that you fully understand the directions for a test before attempting to solve any problems or answer any questions. Don't goof up and lower your grade because you did not listen or read carefully.

4. Plan Your Time   Plan how you will use your time during the exam. Look quickly over the entire test and then divide your available time according to the number and type of questions that you find. Pace yourself carefully; otherwise you will find yourself with insufficient time to try to answer all the questions.

5. Read Thoroughly   Read each test question carefully and completely before marking or writing your answer. Reread again if you are at all confused. If you still have no idea how to answer a given question, go on to the next one, returning later after you have finished the others.

6. Clarify Questions   Ask your instructor for help in interpreting a test question that is unclear or ambiguous to you. He will probably want to clear up the misunderstanding for everybody if the question really is misleading or confusing.

7. Do Your Own Work   Be very careful not to give any impression of cheating. Do your own work and do not give *any* help to others. Avoid all temptation. Not only should your work be your own but you simply cannot afford the risk of being caught.

8. Don't Rush   Do not be disturbed about other students finishing before you do. Take your time, don't panic, and you will do much better on the test.

9. Recheck   Don't try to be the first one to leave—you don't win a prize for being the first one finished. If you have any time left over, edit, check, and proofread your answers.

You cannot remember something unless you first understand it!

4. Review   Review the past material learned in each course at least once every two weeks during the semester. Reread class notes, outside reading notes, textbook underlining, etc.

5. Familiarize   In reviewing, spend most time on the material that is least familiar, but also review briefly the material that is most familiar.

6. Test Yourself   In reviewing, look for likely test questions and make certain that you can give the correct answer to each in your own words.

7. Study Previous Tests   Keep, correct, and review returned quizzes and exams. Find out what you did wrong so that you won't make the same mistakes again. Remember, previous tests are probably the best source of clues as to what kind of questions your instructor is likely to ask.

8. Ask Questions   When an exam is announced, ask your instructor what materials will be covered and what type of test it will be. Find out as much as possible about the scope and scoring of the test and the nature and form of the questions. Remember, forewarned is forearmed!

9. Study Properly   Orient your studying to the type of exam that has been announced. For an objective test, you will need to concentrate on memorizing factual details such as names and formulas; for an essay exam, you will want to

1745. Christine Zeller, having planned and overseen the construction of a fort in Lebanon, Pennsylvania, for the protection of the colonists, finds herself there alone when Indians attack. She dispatches three of them with an axe as they climb through a window; the rest flee.

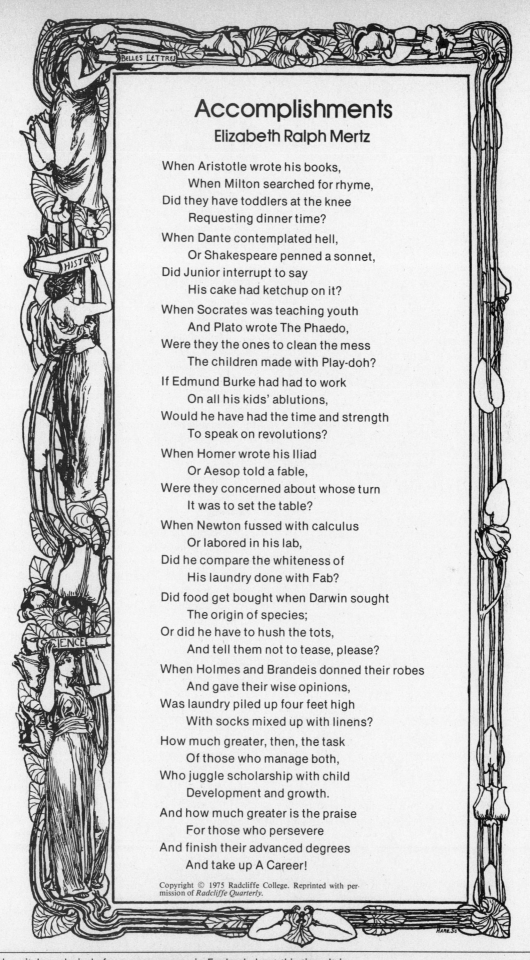

Accomplishments
Elizabeth Ralph Mertz

When Aristotle wrote his books,
     When Milton searched for rhyme,
Did they have toddlers at the knee
     Requesting dinner time?

When Dante contemplated hell,
     Or Shakespeare penned a sonnet,
Did Junior interrupt to say
     His cake had ketchup on it?

When Socrates was teaching youth
     And Plato wrote The Phaedo,
Were they the ones to clean the mess
     The children made with Play-doh?

If Edmund Burke had had to work
     On all his kids' ablutions,
Would he have had the time and strength
     To speak on revolutions?

When Homer wrote his Iliad
     Or Aesop told a fable,
Were they concerned about whose turn
     It was to set the table?

When Newton fussed with calculus
     Or labored in his lab,
Did he compare the whiteness of
     His laundry done with Fab?

Did food get bought when Darwin sought
     The origin of species;
Or did he have to hush the tots,
     And tell them not to tease, please?

When Holmes and Brandeis donned their robes
     And gave their wise opinions,
Was laundry piled up four feet high
     With socks mixed up with linens?

How much greater, then, the task
     Of those who manage both,
Who juggle scholarship with child
     Development and growth.

And how much greater is the praise
     For those who persevere
And finish their advanced degrees
     And take up A Career!

1745. The first hospitals exclusively for women appear in England about this time. It is soon found that the larger the hospital's bed capacity, the greater the mortality rate. A survey of 888,302 hospital deliveries shows a death frequency of 3.5 percent, while home deliveries produce only .0048 deaths per hundred. Overcrowding, lack of individual

Using the Library and Its Card Catalogue

Mona McCormick

THE GIANT STEP forward in any reference project is familiarity with the library and an understanding of the library card catalog.

CLASSIFICATION SYSTEM

Books are arranged within the library according to a classification system. They are classified or sorted into groups so that books on the same subject are located together.

There are two main classification systems used by libraries: the Dewey Decimal System (used in most libraries because it can be easily adapted to the needs of a small book collection) and the system of the Library of Congress (used in very large collections because it allows for greater subdivisions without making lengthy class numbers). These two systems are divided into the main groups illustrated.

Dewey Decimal Classification: First Summary		Library of Congress Classification	
		A	General works—polygraphy
000	General works	B	Philosophy—religion
		C	History—auxiliary sciences
100	Philosophy	D	History and topography (except America)
200	Religion	E-F	America
		G	Geography—anthropology
300	Social sciences	H	Social sciences
		J	Political science
		K	Law
400	Language	L	Education
		M	Music
500	Pure science	N	Fine arts
		P	Language and literature
600	Technology	Q	Science
		R	Medicine
		S	Agriculture—plant and animal industry
700	The arts	T	Technology
		U	Military science
800	Literature	V	Naval science
900	History	Z	Bibliography and library science

Within each of these large groups there are further divisions indicated by numbers or letters.

In the Dewey system, for example, the 900s are shown above as the identification for history. But within that, 940 is the number for European history and 973 begins American history. And within the 973s you will find still more divisions such as:

973 American History
973.1 American discovery & exploration
973.2 American Colonial Period
973.3 American Revolution
973.4 American Constitutional Period
973.5 Early 19th Century America
973.6 Middle 19th Century America
973.7 American Civil War

and so on into the 20th century. That's how it works. You don't need to remember it. Use the card catalog to get the number.

CALL NUMBER

The location of a book in the library is determined by the call number. The call number is a combination of the subject classification number and a letter or letter number indicating the author. The *Encyclopedia of the American Revolution* by Mark M. Boatner might have this call number: 973.3 / B

or in larger libraries a more precise author identification: 973.3 / B63 which will appear on the spine of the book and on the cards in the catalog which refer to that book. Books are arranged on the shelves according to number and then alphabetically by the author's name.

CARD CATALOG

Depending on the classification system, the size of the collection (and perhaps the whim of the person assigning the numbers), a book may be given different numbers in different libraries so always check the card catalog. Often fiction (though usually alphabetically by author) and biographies (though usually alphabetically by biographee) are treated differently from library to library.

The card catalog shows what books the library has and where you will find them.

There are three kinds of cards in the catalog: author cards, title cards, and subject cards, usually arranged in one alphabet. So you have three approaches to locating a book if you know the author, title or subject you want.

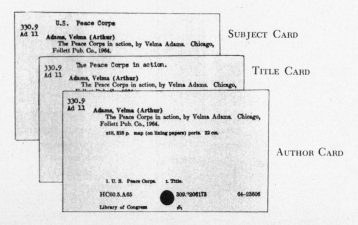

330.9 Ad 11 — U.S. Peace Corps — Adams, Velma (Arthur) — The Peace Corps in action, by Velma Adams. Chicago, Follett Pub. Co., 1964. — SUBJECT CARD

330.9 Ad 11 — The Peace Corps in action. — Adams, Velma (Arthur) — The Peace Corps in action, by Velma Adams. Chicago, — TITLE CARD

330.9 Ad 11 — Adams, Velma (Arthur) — The Peace Corps in action, by Velma Adams. Chicago, Follett Pub. Co., 1964. — xiii, 218 p. map (on lining papers) ports. 22 cm. — AUTHOR CARD

1. U. S. Peace Corps. 2. Title.
HC60.5.A65 — 309.²205173 — 64-23606
Library of Congress

attention, and the septic practice of doctors who come from autopsy tables directly to the patient's bedside to participate in the birth all contribute to the fatalities. It is to be many years before the medical profession is convinced that rigorous hand washing is necessary between work on corpses and attention to living women.

The most complete information is given on the author card, where you will find:

> the call number of the book
> the author's name
> title and subtitle
> the name of the publisher
> copyright date or date of publication

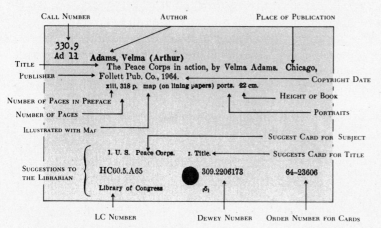

CALL NUMBER — AUTHOR — PLACE OF PUBLICATION

330.9
Ad 11

TITLE —
PUBLISHER —

Adams, Velma (Arthur)
The Peace Corps in action, by Velma Adams. Chicago,
Follett Pub. Co., 1964. — COPYRIGHT DATE
xiii, 318 p. map (on lining papers) ports. 22 cm. — HEIGHT OF BOOK

NUMBER OF PAGES IN PREFACE
NUMBER OF PAGES
ILLUSTRATED WITH MAP

PORTRAITS

SUGGEST CARD FOR SUBJECT

1. U. S. Peace Corps.   i. Title. — SUGGESTS CARD FOR TITLE

SUGGESTIONS TO
THE LIBRARIAN

HC60.5.A65   309.2206173   64–23606

Library of Congress   [5]

LC NUMBER — DEWEY NUMBER — ORDER NUMBER FOR CARDS

When person, place, subject and title are the same the arrangement (usually) is as follows:

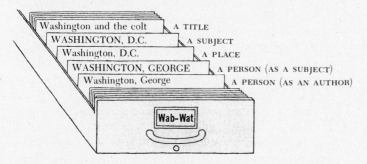

Washington and the colt — A TITLE
WASHINGTON, D.C. — A SUBJECT
Washington, D.C. — A PLACE
WASHINGTON, GEORGE — A PERSON (AS A SUBJECT)
Washington, George — A PERSON (AS AN AUTHOR)

Wab-Wat

The card catalog also has "see" and "see also" references. A sample of a "see" reference—a direction from a heading not used to the heading used:

PEACE CORPS
see
U.S. Peace Corps

A sample of a "see also" reference—a direction to related material:

GHOSTS
see also
Demonology
Spiritualism
Superstition

ALPHABETIZATION

Knowing the alphabet does not mean you're home free. Alphabetization for indexes and filing cards has two major systems. One is a word by word system (as used in the Encyclopedia Americana) and the other is a letter by letter system (as used in the Encyclopedia Britannica) where each entry, no matter how many words, is treated as though it spelled one word.

Word by Word	*Letter by Letter*
West Point	Western Union
West York, Pa.	Westminster Abbey
Western Union	West Point
Westminster Abbey	Westward Ho!
Westward Ho!	West York, Pa.
Wheat	Wheat
Wheat germ	Wheatear (bird)
Wheatear (bird)	Wheat germ

Filing of names, especially foreign names, is complicated but three common stumbling blocks are:

> The St., in for example St. Valentine's Day, is usually filed as though spelled out: Saint Valentine's Day.

> Names beginning with Mc are sometimes filed ahead of all the M's, sometimes filed as though spelled Mac, and sometimes filed as Mc in a letter by letter style.

> Prefixes such as Lord, Mrs., Viscount are usually ignored in filing: Long, *Mrs.* Adam
> Long, *Baron* Paul

If you can't find something you expect to find in a certain source or in the card catalog, check the instructions, try an alphabet variation, or ask for assistance.

Only the most common arrangements and catalog cards are discussed here. There are many variations on basic classification systems (as mentioned in the classifying and filing of biographies) and there are other kinds of catalog cards—those, for example, with an institution as an author or a card for a special series of books. Each library has its own unique character. Take the time to know your library and if you can't find something or do not understand a card reference, ask the librarian.

Remember that modern libraries have much "non-book" material available. Pamphlets and clippings are kept in what are known as "vertical files." Record albums and films may be borrowed from some libraries. Many libraries have special programs for book discussions and some libraries offer books in braille and "talking books" (books on records or tapes) for the blind. Libraries today are not just storage places for books. They are a vital source not only of information but also of entertainment.

1745. Samuel Johnson, curmudgeon and autocrat of the English language, makes the statement "Nature has given women so much power that the law has very wisely given them little."

Women and Fellowships

NO MATTER WHAT FIELD OF STUDY you may take up, there is a fellowship—probably a series of them—specifically designed to broaden your base of experience. Fellowships may count very heavily in an evaluation of your educational background, besides providing financial support for studies or research.

While women now compete for degrees alongside men, they still have difficulty in attracting the "extras," such as fellowships. Part of the problem is that women are unaware of the range of opportunities. Often professors and friends do not tell women about fellowships, assuming that since most of the winners are male, a woman wouldn't stand a chance. In addition, the rituals and procedures required of a fellowship applicant are extremely complex. Any inside information a woman can discover about this process will be highly useful. Following are a few tips from the inside.

A word of caution: Do not underestimate how much time is necessary to fill out applications, write project descriptions, develop narrative biographies, rationalize your proposed expenditures in a budget, and agonize over recommendations. Those who have persisted through all this, however, say there are unexpected benefits in learning how to present oneself professionally, and that in many ways this involved evaluation is the first step in forming a perspective on career goals. It also helps in successfully competing for grants offered by foundations and government agencies.

We at WEAL have found an important difference in the way men and women applicants approach their task. Men do not seem to take the inevitable rejections personally. Women do. Men tend to see their fellowship applications as a professional chore, or as just another game. One man described the selection process as a great lottery in which the outcome depends on such uncontrollable factors as the year's competition and the makeup of the selection panel. Women need to pick up some of that sense of gamesmanship.

All fellowship applications will demand at least several of these items:

1) *Application Forms.* Carefully review what is being requested of you. If you don't understand what information is expected on a given question, call and ask.

2) *Recommendations.* One of the most important parts of your application. Those who recommend you must speak about you and your work with authority, so pick them carefully. Try to select people who are familiar with the fellowship program and who have written such recommendations before.

Warning: "Big names" do carry weight with selection

Judith Nies, Director Project on Fellowships, Women's Equity Action League. Reprinted with permission.

panels. However, they are likely to be asked by a number of others for recommendations to the very program you have in mind. Needless to say, if your big name has little interest in you, you run the risk of an indifferent recommendation. If you must approach people who do not know you or your work well, send them extra documentary material—a narrative biography, reprints of articles, etc.

3) *Project Description.* Emphasize how the proposed project will build on your previous experience, how it will allow you to maintain continuity in your work, to extend past efforts into the future. Focus on your unique capabilities to accomplish this particular project—such concrete advantages as language skills, experience with creative children, knowledge of Irish immigrants, and so forth. Relate the significance of your work to other work in the field. Be specific in what you plan to do within the time covered by the fellowship. (They don't expect miracles.) Have an experienced person, preferably a former recipient of the fellowship, give your project a preliminary critique.

4) *Narrative Biography.* This is supposed to be an integrated portrait of past experience. As such it should show a pattern of success, consciousness of goals, and your progressive development as a personality and as a professional. The following hints on how to write a narrative biography are derived from Richard Irish's book *Go Hire Yourself an Employer* (Doubleday, 1973).

Compose a list of personal achievements and job accomplishments no matter how silly they appear. Inventory all your education: special training courses, conferences, seminars, discussion groups. List all your employment: part- or full-time, volunteer, vocational. Then set it all down as if you were writing your own obituary in the year 2000, in 600 words or less.

5) *Budget.* Grants or fellowships that do not award a specific sum of money may require you to submit a budget. Selection boards have an aversion to handing out subsistence stipends. They would rather finance a scholar's visit to Turkish Hittite sites than pay the rent.

Get down to nuts and bolts. If the budget covers travel abroad, call a travel agent for quotes on fares. Research authoritative *per diem* costs for subsistence at home or abroad. (The federal government issues standard tables revised annually.) Know the average grant your program gives.

Some general suggestions: Investigate the workings of the program and the mechanics of its selection process. Examine the biographies of recent recipients for clues as to what type of background is emphasized and what level of achievement is expected. Talk things over with one of the program's fellows and, especially if you are scheduled for an interview, discuss what questions are asked and what qualities are favored.

1747. Jane Wardley co-founds the Shakers with her husband, James. The sect is so called for their transports into religious ecstasy, wild dancing and violent trembling. Jane is regarded by her followers as the "spirit of Saint John the Baptist operating in the female line." A tenet of their belief is that God is a dual person—male and female.

Women's Equity Action League

Is There a Fellowship For You?

Thousands of fellowships are awarded each year, in all fields and for many puposes, so many, in fact, that a Chicago company sells a computer service that will—for a $250 fee—match your accomplishments with the appropriate program. However, there are less expensive ways to research fellowships. Visit your library. Countless sources are listed in its many reference books.

Often applicants approach the fellowship hunt with the attitude, "I'll take whatever's available." We think this is the wrong approach. Fellowships are designed to provide a specific experience. The successful applicant is one who demonstrates she understands what that experience is.

For example, you have a B.A. and would like to do graduate work in a foreign country, learning another language and spending time living abroad. A prime choice might be the Fulbright-Hays Graduate Study Program, devised to promote "mutual understanding between peoples of the U.S. and other countries through the exchange of persons, knowledge and skills." The Institute of International Education at 809 United Nations Plaza, New York, New York 10017, administers its grants for graduate study almost anywhere for almost anything, including the creative arts. At this level women do fairly well.

Year	Total Recipients	Number of Women
1968	723	290
1969	273	104
1970	286	103
1971	300	113

Say you have a Ph.D., want to study or research abroad, and need a travel grant and a cost-of-living allowance. You might try the Senior Fulbright-Hays Advanced Research Grants, administered by the Committee on the International Exchange of Persons at 2101 Constitution Avenue N.W., Washington, D.C. 20418. The grants enable scholars and specialists to conduct postdoctoral research in other countries or to lecture in foreign universities. Here, women do not do well.

Year	Total Recipients	Number of Women
1968	152	7
1969	56	3
1970	72	1
1971	112	6
1972	90	7

When WEAL suggested that this poor showing might be a result of the absence of women from the selection panels, the State Department responded by asking us to come up with a list of women qualified to sit on the panels. (The critical party is commonly asked to supply the cure.)

Now suppose you are a graduate student working toward a Ph.D. in political science, or a journalist with several years' work on a magazine, or a lawyer who has taught one year at a law school, or a federal employee with at least a G.S.—13 rating. You want direct exposure on Capitol Hill, working for a senator or congressperson and learning how policy directives are translated into law. You might consider Congressional Fellows's offer of a year's work on the Hill. Administered by the American Political Science Association at 1527 New Hampshire Avenue, Washington, D.C. 20036, both federal employees and outside political scientists, journalists, and lawyers work six months in Congress and six months in the Senate. Women won very few of these grants until 1972, when WEAL began querying members of Congress about their underrepresentation in the program.

Year	Total Recipients	Number of Women
1968-69	40	1
1969-70	42	4
1970-71	34	4
1971-72	44	8
1972-73	41	8
1973-74	46	9

Finally, let's say your mathematical research is of potential value to NASA's space program. They offer a series of postdoctoral and resident fellowships for experimental and theoretical research projects in the physical, mathematical, life, space, or engineering sciences that relate to their goals. For a number of reasons, one of them having to do with the way NASA deals with women in professional positions (Ruth Bates Harris, a civil-rights coordinator there, resigned in protest at this treatment), women rarely rate the fellowships.

Year	Total Recipients	Number of Women
1968	111	3
1969	143	2
1970	117	3
1971	133	5

For more information about NASA's program write the Office of Scientific Personnel, National Research Council, 2101 Constitution Avenue N.W., Washington, D.C. 20418.

To make a rather broad generalization, women tend to fare badly in physical-science and business-management fellowships. Though women hold 12 percent of the Ph.D.'s in economics, 6 percent in physics, and 6 percent in business management, they are nearly invisible on the rolls of these fellowships. (For more information on fellowship and scholarship sources, turn to the "Directory" at the end of this book.)

1760. The adage "No woman takes one lover" (implying that she takes either none or many, on the same theory that few men are ever able to content themselves with a single drink) is invented by a French court wit and attains widespread cynical belief.

Top to botton, left to right: Jim Reinig, *Harvard Crimson*, Steven Geovanis, Paul Donahue, Ed Forman

1770. The English Parliament declares that "all women. . .that shall impose upon, seduce and betray into marriage any of His Majesty's subjects by scents, paints, cosmetic washes, artificial teeth, false hair, Spanish wool, iron hoops, high-heeled shoes and bolstered hips shall incure the penalty of the law in force against witchcraft. . .and the marriage shall stand void."

HEW's Rules on
Women and Education

The Editors of the *Washington Post*

With all the hullabaloo over the impact on college sports of the new federal sex bias rules, it is easy to overlook the real importance of those rules which is that they should open the country's educational institutions to women in a way they have never been open before. That will mean, in the long run, more female doctors and other professionals, more female scholars and college teachers, more females in technical jobs, and, to some extent, more female athletes. The rules mean, simply, that the nation is taking another significant step toward a time when intellect and talent and competence in general will be recognized as such in all endeavors—whether academic or athletic—regardless of the sex of the person concerned.

In that sense, the fight over what these rules will do to sports and athletic programs is a side issue. The real impact of them will be on things that matter much more in life—things like admission to vocational and professional schools and public colleges, access to courses and scholarship funds, and employment practices. In these areas, as well as in athletics, educational institutions at all levels have consistently discriminated against women down through the years. The new rules, if they are properly enforced by HEW, will do much to eliminate that discrimination.

There is also a matter of basic fairness involved in the athletic programs and if it takes a complete change in the nature of intercollegiate sports to produce that fairness, so be it. There is something fundamentally wrong with a college or university or, for that matter, a lower level school, that relegates its female athletes to second-rate facilities or second-rate equipment or second-rate travel arrangements solely because they are female. There is nothing in the Constitution or in the nature of the world that says only males can be athletes or that male athletes are entitled, if they are good enough, to free education, free food and free medical care.

Indeed, we suspect that there are a good many university presidents who, way down deep inside, are cheering that part of the HEW rules having to do directly with sports. The emphasis on all too many campuses has reached the point where it appears the purpose of the university is not to educate young people but to produce winning football or basketball teams. The presidents know this—and despair at what it is doing to their institutions—but many of them have felt unable to tackle the problem because of the power their athletic departments have with alumni. These new rules may provide the impetus they need to begin to bring the right perspective back to the campuses. If so, HEW's efforts will serve not only to give to women what is rightfully theirs but to restore some balance between what is meaningful in higher education and what is fun and games.

Paul C. Cabot III

1772. Martha Wayles, through inheritance from her father, brings her new husband, Thomas Jefferson, 40,000 acres of land and 135 black slaves.

What You Can Do about
Sexism in the Schools
Women's Equity Action League

Is there evidence of sex discrimination in your children's schools? If so, what is to be done about it?

First, get the facts. One woman, making a few afternoon phone calls, can determine how many women principals run schools in her district and how many of them head schools above the elementary level. Two or three women visiting local secondary schools can quickly find out what vocational courses are offered, how many of them are for boys only, and whether girls are limited to cooking, sewing, and home-health-care classes. A day or two spent talking to guidance counselors should give you a good idea of how they shape the career plans of girls and boys.

One of the best sources for advice on making such studies is *Sexism in*

Adapted from *WEAL K-12 Education Kit* by Women's Equity Action League, National Press Building, Washington, D.C. 20045. Reprinted with permission.

Schools, A Handbook for Action, published by Nina Rothchild, a member of a Minnesota school board, which gives many practical suggestions within the limitations of small groups or single individuals. (Her address is: 14 Hickory St., Mahtomedi, Minnesota 55115.)

Second, publicize your results. Do a quiet study, then issue a loud press release. Publicity encourages change. Occasionally a well-placed story in local papers will itself provoke the changes you want. For example, Minnesota WEAL studied discrimination in school-administration hiring practices one winter, published the results that spring, got a fine story in a city paper, and by June one more female principal had been hired. She was quickly followed by a new woman assistant principal and yet another woman principal, swelling the ranks of women

in administration by 300 percent over the count of one for the previous September.

Talk to the people who make policy. If yours is the typical American school

board, it's 80 percent male, takes its responsibilities seriously, and really wants to do the right thing. However, in many cases (as in the controversy over textbooks, mentioned in detail below), board members may never have even heard of sex-stereotyping before, such as the preponderance of male high school principals. Other conditions may seem so "natural" to them that they have never considered an alternative. Certainly in both these instances they are not unlike most Americans. It's up to us to do a little consciousness-raising.

Point out where discrimination lies, what needs to be done about it, and what other school boards are doing about it. For example, the New Jersey State Board of Education set up a Women's Equal Rights program to insure equal employment opportunities, in-service training for career counselors,

---

1773. Marie Slocum, the former nun and celebrated French midwife, achieves public recognition for her work in the previously ignored field of infant and maternal mortality, especially among the poor and middle classes.

the distribution of sex-discrimination literature to local school districts, and statewide conferences on stereotyping in textbooks, courses, and extracurricular activities.

Friendly discussions with school superintendents can also produce changes. Here again, it is helpful to point out what is happening in other school districts. Recently, the Cedar Rapids, Iowa, Superintendent announced several steps: A one-hour "Awareness-Packet" was designed and presented to elementary teachers; and two in-service courses were started in the fall, one on stereotyping in curriculum materials, the other called "Everything You Always Wanted to Know About Sex Roles." (For further information, contact Mary Carson, Family Life Coordinator, Cedar Rapids Schools, Cedar Rapids, Iowa.)

Work with teachers and principals. Catch them where they congregate. Get permission to put up a display rack at local teachers' meetings. Supply them with studies of curriculum materials like *Dick and Jane as Victims*[1] or the piece on history texts by Janice Trecker.[2] More important are samples of materials teachers can use to supplement their curriculums. Also include nonsexist counseling information, such as the pamphlets put out by the Women's Bureau, and biographies of women achievers.

Even better than the display rack is a workshop—one morning, evening, or day long:

for Teachers. Focus on curriculum materials supplementing those distributed by the school system, on the teachers' ability to create their own materials, and on class-discussion techniques.

for Counselors. Examine what affirmative action counselors can take to guide girls into non-traditional careers, professional or otherwise (invite a woman doctor, lawyer or carpenter to speak at your workshop); review any nonsexist counselor's material available; discuss biases in vocational tests.

for Parents, Teachers and Students. Arrange a career night about the changing roles of women in which you may speak and the ways that girls can enter new fields.

A last word about workshops: Consider holding a session for your organization's members and other local

[1] Published by Women on Words and Images, Box 2163, Princeton, N.J.

[2] *Women in U.S. History High School Textbooks* by Janice Trecker; published in *Social Education,* March, 1971. Available from National Council for Social Studies, 1201 16th St, NW, Washington, DC 20016.

Mamma and Miss Ann

MAMMA. Go and buy a Toy, Ann.
ANN. I can buy a gun.
MAMMA. A gun is not fit for you, Ann.
ANN. Why is not a gun fit for me?
MAMMA. A gun is only fit for a boy.
ANN. May I buy a top?
MAMMA. No, but you may buy a mop.

circa 1810

What to do About Sexism in School Textbooks
Women's Equity Action League

Long range action. Publishers publish the offending textbooks, so write them directly with your complaints. Make your views known to teachers, curriculum planners, librarians, principals, school boards, and purchasing agents. Try to convince them too to pressure the publisher. The only trouble with this approach, however, is that it can take a half million dollars and five years to deliver a textbook series from writer to child, and people don't move fast when that much capital and time are wrapped up in a product. But this shouldn't discourage you. After all, what publisher would consider a new series if customers never complained about the old one?

Immediate action. Meanwhile we must work to supplement regular classroom materials now. Bibliographies of nonsexist books are easily available; better yet, buy some books yourself and show them to the teachers.

Ask teachers in the lower grades to "edit" as they read aloud, occasionally substituting *policewoman* for *policeman,* and so forth. Suggest that they discuss with the class some of the sex bias found in the books. One teacher read *What Will I Be, From A to Z* and, with her class, went over the list of twenty jobs described, deciding which ones could be performed by women. They concluded that all could, with the possible exception of the quarterback. Later, the teacher met a class mother who said that her son had been delighted to learn that girls could become judges.

ca. **1774.** Elspeth, daughter of an innkeeper in Banff, Scotland, begins to preach the faith of the Buchanites. She claims that the Scriptures reveal that the time is close at hand when there will be "no more marrying and the thistles of the roadside will bloom as luscious fruits." An advocate of all property and women being held in common among

Sexism in Schools
EDUCATION **261**

Girls and their Careers

Women's Equity Action League

Dr. Phyllis Boring, now WEAL Education Committee head, tells of an interview she had with a guidance counselor after she had completed a series of tests while in tenth grade. The counselor told her that she had performed excellently in tests measuring engineering aptitude, then went on, "But I know you don't want to be an engineer."

Fifteen years old and a child of her culture, Boring nodded her head and never gave engineering another thought—until recently. Today she is aware that 40 percent of all those demonstrating engineering aptitude are women, but only 1 percent of all American engineers are women. And she understands why: The girls have been steered away from the field.

Another study shows that while nine-year-old boys and girls show little difference in science writing ability, by the time they reach thirteen a gap develops that widens through young adulthood. Our society encourages boys to take an interest in math and physics, while girls get the message that to become involved in this field is somehow "unfeminine." A New York student has testified that her physics teacher told the girls in class to put down their hands when he asked for volunteer lab assistants; he was only interested in working with the boys.

Dr. Boring tells of another high school physics teacher who noticed that while only 25 percent of his classes were girls, they took home 50 percent of the A's. When he inquired why so few of them went on in science, he was told that the guidance counselors encourage only the very best to pursue it. That may explain why there are only 280 women with Ph.D.'s in physics living in this country.

Another WEAL member, Dr. Gloria Leon, has written a critique of the Strong Vocational Interest Test, widely used to guide students undecided about their careers. Until recently, the men's test required its subjects to indicate their choice among high school principal, dentist, or hotel-manager occupations. The women's test requested its takers to choose among high school teacher, dental assistant, and hotel-nursery manager. While males wavered between "travel to outer space" and "the bottom of the ocean," women were offered the life of either a rancher's or a corporation president's wife. The men's and women's versions of this test have since been combined into a new form, but the scoring remains sex-biased. Some counselors, when criticized for using the Strong, have responded, "Don't take that away from us. The other tests are worse."

women not affiliated with the educational system to familiarize them with the problems and possible solutions.

Place women on school boards. If your state receives grants from the Vocational Education Act, it is obliged to operate a State Vocational Education Board and a State Advisory Committee. The governor appoints members to the committee or, if the board is an elected one, it does the appointing. Are women represented in these groups?

How many women serve on your regular state board, or on the local boards? If the members are appointed, see the man who chooses them. If they are elected, encourage some women to run. But don't forget the male candidates. Find out how concerned they are about school sex discrimination by mailing them questionnaires; then publish the results. Or sponsor a "candidates' night," with questions from the audience. Or visit each candidate to get his views.

Lobby. Some sex discrimination in schools can be changed by state laws. For example, Massachusetts recently passed a bill that requires each city and town with a population over 20,000 to provide a course in practical arts, including manual training and household arts, for all students—girls and boys. It's a good model for other states.

Another example: California now has a bill that requires all mandatory social studies courses in grades 1 through 12 to carry information about the contributions of women and minority groups to the state and national history. (That's Senate bill 1285, should you care to send a request to Sacramento.)

Resort to legal action. If, after all this, you're getting nowhere, file a complaint with one of the government agencies listed in the Legal Adviser section of this book.

You don't need a lawyer for this; sometimes a simple letter to the secretary of HEW or the secretary of labor is enough. Other times you may be required to provide specific instances of discrimination in your complaint. Should you have problems or questions about writing Washington, contact the education or the legal committee at WEAL's national office.

men, she and her followers are frequently seen participating in various "indecencies" on the chilly mountaintops of west Scotland. She will be hounded by outraged burghers from town to town till her death, and will die still maintaining that "it is impossible for one to commit a moral sin."

Two Girls' Experiences with Sexism

The Education Committee of NOW, New York

Excerpts from the testimony of Gigi Gordon, JHS 217, Ninth Grade.

Q: Can you tell me what shops are available at your school?

A: They have sewing and cooking available to the ninth grades. That is only for girls. And for the boys, they have metal and printing, and I think they also have ceramics.

Q: What shop are you taking now?

A: We just changed shops and I was assigned to sewing.

Q: Which shop did you want to take?

A: I wanted to take printing.

Q: Did you make any attempt to take printing?

A: Yes, I did. I went to several people, one of them was Mr. Wydlock, and he told me he would check into the matter and he would try to get me into the boys' shop. Then I saw him again and he said he thought they were all filled up. And then I saw him a third time and he said there was no room in the boys' shop for any more girls.

Q: Do you know whether there are any more girls in there now?

A: No, there aren't any girls.

Q: Did he say it was a boys' shop specifically?

A: Yes.

Q: How many shops are there for boys?

A: Two or three; it depends upon what periods. There are two in one period and three in another.

Q: How many for girls?

A: Two.

Q: Do you know what the percentage of boys and what the percentage of girls was?

A: I don't know the percentages, but it is about evenly distributed.

Q: Are there any other classes or subjects for credit that only have boys?

A: Yes. There is an AVI Squad, which is a squad with audio-visual aids, and it is for boys. And the boys are supposed to set up equipment to show films and projectors and things like that. I tried to get into that and the teacher said it would be okay to get into it. We had to fight for that, but we got into it. And the teacher said that he would show us how to work the things. And he showed us how to work them. And then we never got called to be on the squad. We never got called to set up any such equipment.

Q: Did you ask to—

A: Yes. We went to the teacher. We asked him why we weren't called. He said, "Well, there are plenty of other boys who can do the job and they have been on the squad longer than you."

Q: You mentioned Mr. Wydlock before. Can you tell me who he is?

A: He is the dean of boys. He is also in charge of the shop for girls and boys, but mostly the boys.

Q: And what did he tell you yesterday?

A: He said that the shops were all filled up with boys and that he didn't think I could get in because of the boys, because there was no room for any more girls in the shop.

Q: Now you are scheduled to take sewing, right?

A: Yes.

Q: When is that course given?

A: Mondays and Wednesdays, the third and fourth periods.

Q: And when is the printing course given?

A: The same time.

Adapted from *Report on Sex Bias in the Public Schools.* Copyright © 1973 (3rd ed.) NOW, New York, and The Education Committee of NOW, New York. Reprinted with permission.

1776. Colonial New Jersey extends the right to vote to anyone meeting standard residency and money prerequisites. However, by 1807, the privilege will be withdrawn from women, and only free white males will be permitted to cast ballots.

Q: Do you know of any other girl who tried to get into the print course?

A: Yes. Helen Kartis.

Q: Did you speak to the principal about your discussion with Mr. Wydlock?

A: No, because the principal is not available to discuss matters with students.

Q: Did you try?

A: I have tried before on different issues than this and the principal doesn't speak to the students unless it is a matter of extreme urgency; and even then he is usually at suspension hearings.

Q: Did you try this time?

A: No. But I did speak to the assistant principal, Mr. Niler.

Q: What did he say?

A: He said that I should ask the shop teachers if they wanted girls in their classes.

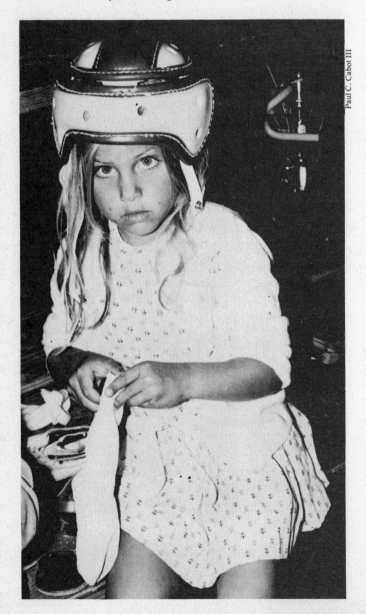

Paul C. Cabot III

Excerpts from the testimony of Julie Nives, JHS 217, Ninth Grade

Q: Could you tell me how the gym classes are set up in your school?

A: Yes, there is a boys' gym and a girls' gym. We have it once a week for two periods.

Q: What do you learn in the girls' gym?

A: At the beginning, the first marking period, we did volley ball, and after that, after the marking period was over, we continued doing that. So me and some friends complained because we were supposed to have a new curriculum each marking period. And they said, "O.K., we will try to do something," and they did. Finally they got us records which had exercises on them, but the exercises were not working out very well because they were only to slim your waistline and help you walk down the street, well, things like that. So after a while it wasn't really working out well. So then we complained again, you know, we should have something a little more, you know, better, because nobody was getting prepared—you have to wear gym suits—and so they had not done anything about it and we refused to get dressed. That day we went down, we were looking around for some guy—our assistant principal—to complain to, and he wasn't there. And the dean sent us back into gym, and since then we have not been doing anything.

Q: Can you tell me what the boys do in gym?

A: The boys do exercises. They play basketball. They can go out when it is warm, which the girls are not allowed to do. They play handball. Baseball. They have certain teams after school for just baseball, basketball, track teams, which the girls do not have.

Q: Have you asked to do any of the sports which the boys do?

A: We asked for basketball. They said there wasn't enough equipment. The boys prefer to have it first. Then we will have what is left over. We haven't really gotten anywhere.

Q: Gigi mentioned the AVI program before. Did you also try to get into that?

A: Yes, I was with her. And my teacher, who is also our science teacher, he tried. We complained to him a few times that he has not been calling us down to use the projectors. And he said that he would try to, but there were too many boys that were taken care of first. And one day he did call me down and then he said, "Oh, forget it. I have somebody else to do the job."

1776. Margaret Corbin becomes known as the "first woman to take a man's part" in the American Revolution. While she is accompanying her husband into battle, he is killed, and she takes up his position on the line. Shot three times, she defends her embankment until overrun by Hessians. The battle leaves her with a useless arm and the first pension to a woman in the United States.

The Progress of Women's Education

Matina Horner

The history of the development of higher education for women is a fascinating story. It is a story of achievement in the face of protest, active resistance, and subtle dissuasion that came in many forms, from many different sources, for many different reasons. Obstacles it encountered were rooted in an image of women that had prevailed in scholarly, literary, and popular circles for centuries—an image reminiscent of Aristotle's notion that the rational faculties of women were of innately inferior quality (which he proved with his point that women never suffered from baldness because they never used the contents of their heads) and echoed in the works of many, including so distinguished a man as Milton, who argued that "to know no more is woman's happiest knowledge and her praise."

It was not until the late eighteenth century that a few courageous women began to fight back against this image. When some went so far as to suggest the possibility of creating a university or college for women, reaction was swift—and not always as indirectly and poetically summarized as in the poem, published in 1792, titled "To a Lady Who Expressed a Desire of Seeing an University Established for Women," which includes the following lines:

> Deluded maid! thy claim forego,
> Nor fondly court thy greatest foe;
> Science has, doubtless, pow'rful charms,
> But shun ah! shun her tempting arms:
> For should'st thou feel her strict embrace,
> Farewell to ev'ry winning grace;
> Farewell to ev'ry pleasing art,
> That binds in chains the yielding heart. . . .
> There keep the station heav'n design'd,
> And reign triumphant o'er mankind;
> [a recurring theme]
> Nor ever wish, perverse, to see
> A FEMALE UNIVERSITY!

In the nineteenth century, and on into the twentieth as well, the most damaging influences against education for women came from the clergy and the medical profession, which foresaw extensive physical and moral disintegration and social ostracism for women who dared enter a life of learning. Such forebodings were explicitly portrayed in several scientific works as exemplified by the very influential *Sex and Education,* by Dr. Edward Clarke of Harvard, published in 1873.

By the second half of the nineteenth century, the Industrial Revolution had had a profound negative impact on the life-styles and status of women. With the expansion of the railroad, the development of machinery, and the resulting migration out of rural settings and into urban factories and bureaucracies, the

value placed upon the economic role of women was greatly diminished. Many of women's previous functions were eliminated by garment and food-processing factories; and men, now working off the farms and away from their homes, became increasingly independent of the economic contributions of the family as a unit. Hence, women and children became economic liabilities to be supported, rather than the "sturdy partners and helpmates," contributing to their mutual support, that they had been in rural life.

Man could afford, therefore, to be more selective and romantic in choosing a wife, since her major function was now considered to be providing him with emotional support and sustenance. In return, he provided her, if he could, with what some regarded as a life of "leisure and consumerism." In reality, of course, the life of leisure

"Out of the World"

Fred Walker, from the *Cornhill Magazine,* 1863

*Martha Carey Thomas (1857-1935), the second president of Bryn Mawr College, wrote in her diary at age fourteen: "My **one** aim . . . shall be . . . to show that women can learn, can reason, can compete, with man in the grand fields of literature and science and conjecture . . . ." She insisted that Bryn Mawr College maintain standards equal or superior to those of the best men's institutions.*

was reserved for the affluent few. In addition to housekeeping and child rearing, many poorer married women, like their single sisters, had to work for low salaries under deplorable conditions in unskilled or semiskilled jobs in factories.

Whatever the real value of women's work, however, men came to be considered the sole participators in the economic life of the community. The status of women was diminished to total dependency, and new restrictions and leisure in women's lives were justified as more appropriate and in tune with their "fragile" natures.

It was early in the industrialization process that such remarkable and dedicated women as Mary Lyon at Mount Holyoke, M. Carey Thomas at Bryn Mawr, Elizabeth Agassiz at Radcliffe, and Sophia Smith in Northampton recognized the dangers and frustrations ahead and responded to the need industrialism had created for a college education.

Not many leading educators in New England or elsewhere were ready or willing to help establish women's colleges of the kind that would, as Reverend Thomas Greene said, "give to young women educational advantages EQUAL to what our young men receive in their colleges." (Reverend Greene was instrumental in convincing Sophia Smith to leave her money for the founding of Smith College.) There was no serious objection raised to women's preparing themselves for teaching, homemaking, or "governessing." Resistance came only when they sought a "masculine" education.

Nevertheless, each of these women in her own special way worked vigorously to fulfill that dream, seeking standards in education for women comparable with the best available for men. These standards were to be a visible signal that schools for women were neither sanitariums nor sanctuaries and that women could meet the standards without any obvious negative impact on their health, reproductive organs, winsomeness, marriage, or morals (to name but a few objects of concern).

Sophia Smith insisted that men as well as women have a part in the government and instruction at the institution she founded, for "it is a misfortune for young women or young men to be educated wholly by their own kind." This point is, I think, an important one, an interesting twist on our present preoccupation and emphasis on the absence of "role models" for women, and reinforces my own feelings about the significance of the availability of "cross-sex" as well as same-sex "role models." I have argued in the past that the absence of women on the faculty, especially in tenured ranks, at primarily male institutions may be more damaging to men than to women students because it fails to prepare men for a society in which efforts to equalize access, opportunity, and ultimately the appointment of women to the professions and to executive suites are a priority of national policy and legislation. Should these efforts succeed, they may well bring young men upon graduation to jobs and careers where they will have to

physician the following day in a sort of quality-control check-up. Madame Protassov, one of the Empress's ladies, then tests him on his intelligence, character, and his abilities on "some other particulars." If he passes, he is installed in a chamber adjoining the queen's and forbidden to leave without her consent. When she tires of him, usually a short time later, he is invariably given papers to "travel" and a large estate.

work with women as colleagues and equals, and perhaps for women as bosses or superiors.

Because the pattern of socialization followed since the Industrial Revolution has stressed competitive striving and achievement for men as a major source of masculine self-confirmation, it has not prepared men to work cooperatively with or for women without challenging their self-esteem. The college years are therefore critically important for overcoming rather than reinforcing their current expectations, which are at best outdated. Primarily male institutions, without reasonable numbers of women on their faculties, are not fully addressing the educational needs of their male students for today's society.

Once women's colleges had opened their doors and women had gained access to higher education, educators began to worry not only about the personal consequences of that education but about how on earth women were to use it and what its functional significance was meant to be.

All arguments in behalf of better education for women at that time were couched in terms of what would benefit society rather than in terms of what would benefit the individual woman. Education had to be justified on the basis that it would help make women better homemakers, better mothers, and more intelligent companions for their husbands, and possibly moral crusaders as well. A common argument presented was, "If you would have the country wisely and honestly governed, give the children the right kind of mothers."

Work for female college graduates was at the turn of the century restricted primarily to the service professions (teaching, nursing, and social work), where wages were low and the work was considered appropriately feminine and complementing men's work, not conflicting or competing with it. These jobs were filled either with spinsters or with graduates who intended to marry but who were using the five- to ten- year average interim between graduation and marriage to put their education to use.

Only approximately fifty percent of female college graduates chose or were chosen for marriage in that era (a figure that, as we shall see, rapidly rose to ninety percent in the late fifties and early sixties). The rest resolved their marriage-career conflicts by repressing or sublimating their emotional and personal drives for the sake of public service. Those, like Jane Addams, who dedicated themselves to this kind of work exemplified new roles that offered "dignified and valued alternatives" to marriage in the early part of the twentieth century.

Such women were welcomed in great numbers into the service professions, but their efforts later on to gain entrance into the established professions like law and medicine, on the same terms as men, were strongly challenged, by family and friends as well as by male professional "colleagues."

Mount Holyoke College

Mary Lyon (1797-1849), founder of Mount Holyoke College (originally South Hadley Female Seminary), decided that the lack of support for women's higher education came from "good men's fear of greatness in women". She would not be turned from her purpose, responding to scorn or skepticism with the Biblical answer: "I am doing a great Work, I cannot come down."

1776. Ann Lee, a Shaker, this year heads a group of them who refuse to join the military, thereby earning the distinction of becoming America's first conscientious objectors. All are jailed without trial, not to be released until 1780.

Sophia Smith (1796-1870), founder of Smith College, foresaw the changes which an industrialized society would bring to the lives of women. In her will she suggested that with a quality college education women would be able to "have their wrongs redressed, their wages adjusted and the weight of (their) influence in reforming the evils of society greatly increased." Smith College officially opened in the fall of 1875.

By the turn of the century, there was a preponderance of women over men in sheer numbers, which attracted considerable attention on the east coast, especially in Massachusetts, where garment mills, factories, and female unmarried employees were plentiful. The problem of "superfluous women" was the subject of a group of lectures published by Mary Livermore in Boston in 1883 under the title "What Shall We Do with Our Daughters?" In it she cites the tragic fate of spinsters, widows, and those married women separated from wandering or otherwise irresponsible husbands who were left totally unprepared to support themselves. She makes a forceful case for including industrial and professional training for women in addition to education aimed at enhancing their attractiveness as potential homemakers and mothers, roles that, given the realities of the times, might or might not materialize for them. She indicated her frustration with arguments against women working, saying that no one seemed to "trumpet an alarm concerning the terrible dangers this work (would) inflict on her prospective maternity UNTIL educated women began to invade all the higher forms of labor and seek professional University education as well."

With the professionalization of many occupations in the early 1900s came an increasing concentration of efforts directed at some resolution of the marriage/career/child-producing/child-rearing dilemmas faced by women, men, and society, but most directly by women. From existing statistics it soon became clear that educational and occupational achievement exposed women to risks of nonmarriage and childlessness. Worse, the occupations available to them were "not so fulfilling, so remunerative, or so prestigious" as to make taking the risk of impairing already limited marital opportunities worthwhile. A serious setback for higher education for women came with the evidence in the early twentieth century of a serious decline in the birthrate, particularly amongst intelligent, college-educated women (most of whom were of Anglo-Saxon origin). At a time when the heredity component of intelligence was considered to be of paramount importance, there was great concern in many circles that educating women could well be the quickest path to "racial suicide"—a very serious issue. How different the issues were then compared with today's overriding concern with overpopulation, and the search for alternatives to motherhood as a lifelong career.

With the threat of potential racial suicide, "former arguments that too much brainwork was the greatest danger to women and that it was unwise, therefore, to encourage girls to endanger their true avocation of motherhood by attending college" were revived and had the sophisticated support of such eminent scholars as psychologist G. Stanley Hall (also president of Clark University). Quotas for admission of women to coed schools like the University of Michigan were introduced, separate classes for men and women were provided,

---

1776. Betsy Flanagan, barmaid at Halls Corners in Elmsford, New York, reputedly concocts the first cocktail by garnishing a mixed drink with a feather used to decorate the premises.

deans of women were appointed, and a new crusade for Moral Purity got underway.

By 1930 women had progressed enough to make up forty-five percent of professional and semiprofessional workers, but during the Great Depression the economy contracted, and women, married women in particular, were discouraged from "taking jobs away from men." Their participation in graduate study was severely slowed down, and the annual level of doctoral degrees granted to them has yet to reach that of 1930.

In 1950, with the postwar surge of education for men that was associated with the tremendous expansion of scientific and technical fields at the universities, the percentage of all degrees awarded to women graduates and undergraduates dropped precipitously. To quote Caroline Bird (*Born Female,* 1969).

The 1950s saw an unprecedented return to family life. Never had husbands, home and children been more sentimentalized. Never had so many girls married so young. Not for 50 years had American women been so fertile nor defined themselves so exclusively as mother.

There was a tremendous influx of "how-to" books relating to child care and to other aspects of family life.

Instead of preparing themselves for professional careers after World War II, girls were marrying young and working at any job that would bring in money and support husbands through graduate school. In 1950 a record 11 percent of the students graduated from medical school were women, but by 1960 this figure dropped 7 percent. The same thing happened in other professions, with the result that women lost ground or barely held their own in law, pharmacy, science, engineering, and journalism.

Another major change was reflected in the number of married women now in the work force. Employers hired more and more married women because there simply weren't enough single ones left to hire. By 1960 just about ninety percent of college women graduates were getting married (but at the same time the divorce rate was climbing)—and feminism was all but dead. To quote Caroline Bird again:

Generally speaking, frontier conditions—war, revolutions, and feverish boom times which provide urgent work for all hands—have motivated men and women to similar or androgynous goals. By contrast, periods of slow or orderly economic growth such as the first and fifth decades of this century have cultivated masculinity or femininity as goals in themselves. . .
Androgynous periods are often marked by feminist movements which assert the right of women to independent action. Male dominated or masculinist periods, on the other hand, encourage women to define themselves in terms of their relationships to men. The two philosophies have altered just frequently enough to keep every generation of American women from using their mothers as models. . .

and to intermittently reinforce the notion that achievement and femininity are not always consistent—it depends.

Elizabeth C. Agassiz (1822-1907), believed in women's education "purely for its own sake." As the first president of Radcliffe College, she was determined that women should have the benefit of the teaching of the Harvard University faculty. Although she thought that natural laws prevented women from entering certain careers, she would permit no "ladies degree" to be specially created for Radcliffe.

1777. Betje Wolff, an Amsterdam widow, persuades the poor governess Agatha Deken to quit her post and come live with her. For the next thirty years the two women are to shape Dutch literature, their romantic book *Sara Burgerhart* being the first major novel published in Holland over the past century. By their retirement they will be considered among their country's foremost writers.

The first graduating class of Radcliffe College, 1884.

With the publication of Betty Friedan's book *The Feminine Mystique* in the mid-1960s came a new wave of feminism with which we are all familiar and on which, therefore, I need not dwell.

Clearly the specific issues focused upon by the "women's movement" at the end of the nineteenth century were quite different than those focused on by today's movement. Yet both were consciousness-raising efforts highlighting new possibilities to which women might aspire. The woman question today is a human question involving the quality of life of both sexes, one which challenges the roles we have accepted for both sexes and calls into question the way we have organized society, with men immersed for longer than they would wish in remunerative work with too little time for their families—and women striving for an equal chance to become immersed in their ambitions outside the home.

There are immense adjustments in living and in outlook that the developments of our time and new levels of social consciousness will require of us, men and women alike, if those things within each of us that crave assertion and activity are to reach fullest expression (the major issue in the current movement) without enormous cost either to our physical or psychological well-being or to the society as a whole. There is an increasing awareness that the genuine experience of equality between men and women depends not only on the opportunities and barriers society has to offer but also, and perhaps most importantly, on the reactions and beliefs that those men and women involved have about themselves and about each other.

Most of us entered head first into a world of symbols, signs, and signals of manhood and womanhood—expectations about the roles we were to play were transmitted to us in a thousand different ways and are thus deeply rooted in us. Learning to substitute new roles and to accept new modes of accommodation to each other, even in the best of times, is difficult enough, but in the face of a troubled economy and scarce resources, it becomes a Herculean task. Yet it is precisely at such times that attitudes must be improved—and that we need a shared vision of the way things could be and of better ways to know and understand each other in a true spirit of mutuality. Historically, as we have seen, when resources become scarce, social consciousness diminishes, and it is considerably harder to bring valued objectives to fruition.

None of the current research with which I am familiar makes me sanguine about the possibility of revolutionary changes in the socialization of young girls and boys. But as the implicits of society become explicit, they are at least available for scrutiny, for challenge, and for affirmative action. I take great pleasure in such simple signs of progress in socialization, in education, and in action as the following.

In a report given before the Joint Economic Committee in Washington, Herbert Stein and Marina Whitman documented progressive changes in successive editions of a passage of Professor Paul Samuelson's well-known economic textbook. Lamenting the popular reaction to the results of rationing, Professor Samuelson wrote in his first edition (1948): "Of course, there are always a few women and soapbox orators, who are longer on intuition than brains and who blame their troubles on the mechanism of rationing itself rather than on the shortage."

In the seventh edition (1967), we find soapbox orators dropped and the sentence is changed to: "Of course, there are always a few women and cranks, longer on intuition than brains, who blame their troubles on the mechanism of rationing itself rather than on the shortage."

By the liberated eighth edition (1970) he writes: "Of course, there are always some cranky customers, longer on intuition than brains, who blame their troubles on the mechanism of rationing itself rather than on the shortage."

My second source of encouragement is this. We are all familiar with acknowledgements in the preface of many books recognizing a wife, who may or may not be beloved, "without whose help this book would never have been possible," whose research assistance has been crucial, and whose typing has been a godsend. On the whole this kind of assistance has not been available to women scholars, but perhaps this situation too is changing, as suggested recently by the following testimony of a woman author: "My husband has contributed to many discussions of these ideas. But perhaps a sign of greater progress—for ideas are not difficult for him—he merits thanks for doing some of the typing." (Jean Baker Miller, *Psychology and Women,* 1973.)

1777. Lydia Darragh, a Philadelphia Quaker, finds her house the unwilling headquarters of the British command. She overhears a plot to make a surprise attack on the poorly armed Americans stationed a short distance away, and, unable to confide in her husband whose Quaker beliefs forbid him from participation in military matters, she decides to

Working

Clockwise from top left, atomic scientist at Los Alamos Scientific Laboratory, Rev. Carter Heyward breaking bread at mass, Martha Johnson ready to drive a truck, Dr. Mary Helen Johnston checking the interior of a prototype of a Spacelab Crew Transfer Tunnel at the NASA - Marshall Space Flight Center. Far right: above, gathering the staves; below, women on the automobile assembly line in Detroit.

warn the patriots. She steals out into the deep snow under the pretense of fetching flour from the only mill, located between the American and British lines. Despite a raging blizzard she succeeds in alerting the Americans and returns home safe and unsuspected. The British assault is defeated.

The Working Woman: Myth and Reality

The Myth. *A woman's place is in the home.*

The Reality. Homemaking in itself is no longer a full-time job for most people. Goods and services formerly produced in the home are now commercially available; labor-saving devices have lightened or eliminated much work around the home.

Today more than half of all women between 18 and 64 years of age are in the labor force, where they are making a substantial contribution to the nation's economy. Studies show that 9 out of 10 girls will work outside the home at some time in their lives.

The Myth. *Women aren't seriously attached to the labor force; they work only for extra pocket money.*

The Reality. Of the nearly 35 million women in the labor force in March 1973, nearly half were working because of pressing economic need. They were either single, widowed, divorced, or separated or had husbands whose incomes were less than $3,000 a year. Another 4.7 million had husbands with income between $3,000 and $7,000.

The Myth. *Women are out ill more than male workers; they cost the company more.*

Reality. A recent Public Health Service study shows little difference in the absentee rate due to illness or injury: 5.6 days a year for women compared with 5.2 for men.

The Myth. *Women don't work as long or as regularly as their male coworkers; their training is costly—and largely wasted.*

The Reality. A declining number of women leave work for marriage and children. But even among those who do leave, a majority return when their children are in school. Even with a break in em-

From *The Myth and Reality*, 1974, Women's Bureau, Department of Labor.

Sophia Smith Collection, Smith College

General Motors

1778. Deborah Samson, at the outbreak of the American Revolution, runs away from home, saves her pennies, and buys herself man's clothing. In this disguise she enlists and serves three years in the patriot army under the name "Robert Chirtliffe." Wounded three times, she is recovering from yet another wound when her sex is discovered. General George Washington discharges her honorably.

Sophia Smith Collection, Smith College

Archives serendipity, clockwise from top left: a pair of "suffrage farmettes," lumberjacks during World War I, a group of carpenters, a railroad crew, and a wartime laborer at rest. Facing page, above, making pennies at the U.S. Mint, 1901; below, surgery class at Harvard University, 1930's.

1778. Mary Ludwig Hays, otherwise known as "Molly Pitcher," becomes famous this year as an American Revolutionary War heroine. At the battle of Monmouth she first carries water through the oppressive heat to exhausted and wounded troops, then, when her husband drops at the cannon he has been firing, she takes over loading and continues blasting away at the British throughout the battle.

ployment, the average woman worker has a worklife expectancy of 25 years as compared with 43 years for the average male worker. The single woman averages 45 years in the labor force.

Studies on labor turnover indicate that net differences for men and women are generally small. In manufacturing industries the 1968 rates of accessions per 100 employees were 4.4 for men and 5.3 for women; the respective separation rates were 4.4 and 5.2.

The Myth. Married women take jobs away from men; in fact, they ought to quit those jobs they now hold.

The Reality. There were 19.8 million married women (husbands present) in the labor force in March 1973; the number of unemployed men was 2.5 million. If all the married women stayed home and unemployed men were placed in their jobs, there would be 17.3 million unfilled jobs.

Moreover, most unemployed men do not have the education or the skill to qualify for many of the jobs held by women, such as secretaries, teachers, and nurses.

The Myth. Women should stick to "women's jobs" and shouldn't compete for "men's jobs."

The Reality. Job requirements, with extremely rare exceptions, are unrelated to sex. Tradition rather than job content has led to labeling certain jobs as women's and others as men's. In measuring 22 inherent aptitudes and knowledge areas, a research laboratory found that there is no sex difference in 14, women excel in 6, and men excel in 2.

The Myth. Women don't want responsibility on the job; they don't want promotions or job changes that add to their load.

The Reality. Relatively few women have been offered positions of responsibility. But when given these opportunities, women, like men, do cope with job responsibilities in addition to personal or family responsibilities. In 1973,

4.7 million women held professional and technical jobs, another 1.6 million worked as nonfarm managers and administrators. Many others held supervisory jobs at all levels in offices and factories.

The Myth. The employment of mothers leads to juvenile delinquency.

The Reality. Studies show that many factors must be considered when seeking the causes of juvenile delinquency. Whether or not a mother is employed does not appear to be a determining factor.

These studies indicate that it is the quality of a mother's care rather than the time consumed in such care that is of major significance.

The Myth. Men don't like to work for women supervisors.

The Reality. Most men who complain about women supervisors have never worked for a woman.

In one study where at least three-fourths of both the male and female respondents (all executives) had worked with women managers, their evaluation of women in management was favorable. On the other hand, the study showed a traditional cultural bias among those who reacted unfavorably to women as managers.

United States Mint

In another survey in which 41 percent of the reporting firms indicated that they hired women executives, none rated their performance as unsatisfactory; 50 percent rated them adequate; 42 percent rated them the same as their predecessors; and 8 percent rated them better than their predecessors.

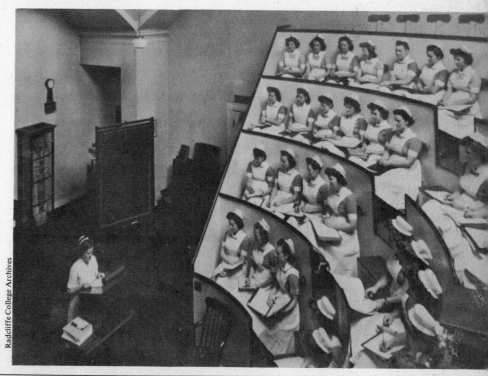

Radcliffe College Archives

1779. Margaret Shippe Arnold, pampered Philadelphia heiress of a Loyalist family, works on the allegiances of her suitor, the brilliant General Benedict Arnold. Convincing him of the unjust recognition he has received at the hands of the Continental Congress, she conspires to turn him against the patriots' cause. They are apprehended but escape to England.

What White Men Earn and Black Women Don't

THE EARNINGS OF MINORITY WOMEN, like those of white women, are substantially less than the earnings of men, either minority or white. In addition, fully employed minority women continue to earn less than white women, although the earnings gap has narrowed appreciably. In 1972 women of minority races who worked the year round at full-time jobs had a median wage or salary income of $5,320—only 87 percent of that of white women, 70 percent of that of minority men, and 49 percent of that of white men. In 1960 the corresponding proportions were 70, 63, and 42 percent.

High unemployment rates and low wages are sharp reminders that minority women, as a group, are still very vulnerable to economic changes, despite improvement during recent years in their educational attainment and occupational status. Teen-agers entering the labor force are particularly susceptible to changes in labor-market conditions. In addition, the incomes of minority women and the economic plight of those women who are heads of families show the need for increased stress on providing equal employment and training opportunities for minority women and assistance to the working poor.

	All workers		Year-round full-time workers	
Race	Women	Men	Women	Men
Total	$4,181	$8,850	$6,018	$10,384
Minority	3,944	6,261	5,320	7,548
White	4,218	9,190	6,131	10,786

Adapted from *Facts on Women Workers of Minority Races,* 1974, Women's Bureau, Department of Labor.

What Men Earn in Full-time Jobs and Women Don't

(1973 Statistics)

Major occupation group (14 years of age and over)	Median wage or salary income		Women's median wage or salary income as percent of men's
	Women	Men	
Professional, technical workers	$9,095	$13,945	65.2
Managers, administrators (except farm)	7,998	14,737	54.3
Sales workers	4,674	12,031	38.8
Clerical workers	6,458	10,619	60.8
Craft and kindred workers	6,315	11,308	55.8
Operatives (including transport)	5,420	9,481	57.2
Service workers (except private household)	4,745	8,112	58.5
Private household workers	2,243	(1/)	—
Nonfarm laborers	5,286	8,037	65.8

1/ Fewer than 75,000 men.

From *The Earnings Gap*, 1975, Women's Bureau, Department of Labor.

ca. **1780.** Marched into "marriages of convenience," many Spanish wives of the nobility find themselves with unsatisfactory mates. To remedy this need, the women acquire *cavaliere serventes,* or sophisticated gigolos, more nearly their own age and temperament. In this *menage a trois* it is considered bad form for a husband to express his jealousy.

Women in Men's Jobs

Caroline Bird

MOTHER GOOSE.

How can a woman earn more money?

She has to go where the men are—in the professions, in management, in white-collar jobs. If it's a man's job, the women who do it earn more than they would in a woman's job. If the industry or occupation employs more men than women, the women who do manage to get in earn more than in an industry where women predominate. In the clothing and related industries, where 70 percent of the workers are women, 1969 wages averaged $78 weekly. In chemicals and certain leather products, where women are only 22 percent and 11 percent of the workers respectively, weekly wages were $139 and $133.

Publishing is the field in New York City that has the highest proportion of women managers and professionals. The salaries they earn are lower than those of managers and professionals in a similar field, like advertising, where there are fewer women at the top.

How does a woman get into a male-dominated organization or profession or trade?

She finds a "woman's angle" or "feminizes" the job. Women who work at "men's jobs" have always found reasons—valid or not—to explain why they would be good at some particular job, whether they are doctors or plumbers.

Policewomen point out that in a tense situation, the presence of a woman frequently defuses violence.

Women journalists exaggerate the "woman's angle" in politics in order to get to interview Presidential candidates.

In the past, women lawyers have been funneled into trusts and estates on the theory that a woman understands the needs of widows and minors better than a man does. But now that women are demanding entry into such masculine strongholds as criminal law—with its connotations of toughness and violence—Mary B. Tarcher, assistant attorney-in-chief at the New York Legal Aid Society, points out that "women lawyers have often been known to keep their cool better than do some of the male attorneys. The expertise of women shows up in their objectivity."

Women are beginning to break into horse racing with the argument that they have always liked horses better than men do, and tender loving care counts in grooming. Donna Hincher, a pioneer woman groom, says that a famous thoroughbred trainer prefers girl grooms because they are conscientious and neater.

Small numbers of women have always gone into medicine, but they are just beginning to enter dentistry in any numbers, and one woman in a dental college says women make good dentists because they have a tender touch—and because they are good at matching colors for dentures and crowns!

Bertha Chan, who owns and operates Century Plumbers in Los Angeles, makes the most of her ability to advise on styles when installing bathroom or kitchen fixtures.

The ultimate in "feminizing" is probably the contention of a pioneer bail bondswoman that the occupation needed a woman because people accused of crime deserve special sympathy.

Isn't it contradictory to "feminize" a job when you don't really believe that women are all that different?

Possibly, but it is the first step in breaking down sex roles. When change is necessary, practical reformers know better than to attack ingrained beliefs directly. They work with them. That's the way missionaries introduced Christianity to primitives, and in our own country the way county agents got old-fashioned farmers to adopt new methods. Practically speaking, people may need reasons for anything—particularly for a change in custom—so finding reasons why a woman is better may be a better strategy than the truth, which is that sex does not make the difference. A woman who is going to be a social pioneer should do what the successful feminists in the past have done: start where the male chauvinists are, and broaden their experience.

1780. One morning this year a Spanish noble remarks to a friend, "Before I retire tonight, the whole city will be thrown into confusion." He accomplishes this by returning home one hour earlier than usual, surprising his wife's lover who is similarly forced to repair home early, and so on throughout the polite society around town.

Women in Journalism

The women's liberation movement has had a tremendous impact on the field of journalism—so much so that the term **newsmen** has now become passe and the style books require the sexless synonym **reporters** for those who ply the trade. More important, women are now accepted in newsrooms throughout the country and in every broadcast studio.

It was not always so, however, and newspapers that did have women on their staffs in past decades traditionally relegated them to the "softer" news areas such as society, fashion, and food, not to mention "sob sister" features and columns, some of which still have a wide audience today.

Ruby Black, a former reporter for United Press International (when it was known as UP),said in 1931 that "the toughest part of a woman's work in Washington journalism is to get a job. For two hundred weary days in 1925 I was told by newspapermen all the things women cannot do. I had done most of them. I knew other women who were doing the rest."

Many women who aspired to be reporters in that period told the same story. It was almost impossible for a female to get a job in the newsroom unless she came aboard for lower pay than a man who had similar training and talent.

Nevertheless, there have always been a few outstanding women in the newspaper world. One of the first of them to cover hard news was Cora Rigby, who headed the Christian Science Monitor Bureau in 1918 and was a special favorite of Mrs. Coolidge. Miss Rigby also helped to found the Women's National Press Club. A few years ago the club charter was changed to take in male members, and it became known as the Washington Press Club.

Another was Ruth Finney, of the Scripps-Howard Newspapers, who reported on the Teapot Dome oil scandal with such clarity and truth that attorneys for the principals involved barred anyone who read news stories on the subject from serving on juries that were to determine the fate of the accused.

Eleanor Roosevelt, the woman I consider to have

copyright © 1976 Helen Thomas

been the greatest libber of them all, was an important ally to women in their daily struggle to break hard news in Washington. Mrs. Roosevelt held regular news conferences in the Monroe Room—for women only. She felt that she could raise the status of women reporters and their salaries by holding such press conferences, and this had the effect of compelling those newspapers that did not want to miss out to hire women. Some of the feminist journalists at the time—and that characterization could apply to all—argued that the ban on male reporters was the kind of discrimination they were protesting against themselves. But the rule stood.

Mrs. Roosevelt talked freely and made bosom buddies of the reporters covering her. She would discourse on all the issues of the day, and if she got out on the limb on a touchy matter, one of the reporters would rise to protect her, saying, "That **is** off the record, isn't it?"

Since then, other first ladies have met from time to time with the press, but never on a regular basis. Of course, no first lady since has taken on so much political responsibility and initiative as Mrs. Roosevelt, who virtually served as eyes, ears, and legs for her crippled husband.

The drafting of young men from the staffs of newspapers during World War II forced reluctant editors to hire women. I was one of this crop. After graduating from Wayne State University in 1942, I headed for Washington. I became a copy girl and then a reporter on the **Washington Daily News**, and later got a job with United Press writing radio news at 5:30 A.M. Several other women were hired at the time, but many were lopped off after the war on grounds that the men would be coming back. As it turned out, many of the men did not return to claim their jobs, and the jobs were given to other men. I survived, presumably because nobody was begging for a job that demanded you be bright-eyed and rarin' to go at dawn.

The Washington scene during the war days and im-

1782. Elizabeth Zane, an American frontierswoman and one of several defenders of a West Virginian fort under Indian attack, realizes that the gunpowder is about to give out. Despite others' effort to restrain her, she charges out of the stockade to an isolated cabin where she remembers a keg of powder is stored. On the return trip both she and the keg

Helen Thomas

mediately after was where it was at in terms of news. The indomitable May Craig and highly respected Doris Fleeson were the celebrities in female journalism. Fleeson wrote a political column that no senator or congressman, and not even the President, ever failed to read.

Tenacious May Craig, who wrote for the **Portland (Me.) Herald**, became indignant when she was barred from traveling on a battleship with male reporters. The excuse was that there were "no powder rooms" on the ship. She put on a war of her own, gathering nationwide support, and soon there were ladies' rooms on combat ships.

She waged much the same battle on Capitol Hill and got a ladies' room built in the House press gallery.

But May, immediately recognizable in her perpetual blue suits and pastel hats, was better known for putting the fear of God into Presidents with her pointing finger and her twang. Once FDR replied to one of her questions: "I'll bet you stayed up all night thinking of that."

Another time, when Roosevelt, in an angry mood, called columnists "excrescences," May chidingly said: "But Mr. President, your wife is one." (Mrs. Roosevelt wrote a daily column entitled "My Day.")

May's appearances on "Meet the Press" were something to behold. Just before Adlai Stevenson appeared on one of the televised programs in which May was a panelist, he wrote to her: "Dear May, I shudder at the prospect of facing you again. Please be merciful."

Another woman reporter known for her formidable questioning of Presidents is Sarah McClendon, who is chief of her own Washington bureau, which serves several newspapers. Reporters used to observe the veins stand out on Dwight D. Eisenhower's forehead after Sarah asked a question. However, other Presidents found her demanding "Mr. President, sir" irresistible and would call on her. One of Sarah's questions to Eisenhower had, according to many political observers, a devastating effect on Richard M.

Nixon's bid for the Presidency against John F. Kennedy in 1960. She asked what decisions Nixon had participated in while he was Vice-President. "If you give me a week, I'll think of one," Eisenhower replied.

Sarah's questions often were news makers and resulted in banner headlines. Both she and May kept before the public the issue of discrimination against women.

"Mr. President, what have you done for women lately?" May asked Kennedy.

"Obviously not enough," he replied.

One of the greatest investigative reporters ever to hit the Washington scene—man or woman—was Miriam Ottenberg, now retired from the **Washington Star**. She won a Pulitzer Prize for her investigation of the used-car rackets, and her crime stories lined her apartment walls with awards. Among other great stories of hers were exposes of abortion rings, marriage counselors, and health-insurance regulations.

Her colleague on the **Star** and syndicated columnist Mary McGrory got her big start during the early fifties by vividly describing what it was really like in the McCarthy hearings. She had a tremendous influence on the development of a new kind of colorful interpretative journalism and won a Pulitzer Prize in 1974. Many consider her the best writer in Washington. Some say she wears her heart on her sleeve; I say, why not?

Washington would not be what it is without the reportage on society and the party circles. Both the **Washington Star** and the **Washington Post** have top-notch reporters on the staffs of their former women's sections who are the best in the business at picking up news. Tops is Betty Beale, a pro who has had innumerable scoops throughout the years. She has broken many a story the participants would have preferred not be revealed, including the dunkings of fully clothed guests at Ethel Kennedy's parties and the report that Caroline Kennedy nearly drowned in a friend's pool when she was a youngster, during her father's White House years.

become the target of countless Indian bullets and arrows, but she manages to reach the fort unharmed. With the new supply, the defenders are able to hold off defeat until help arrives a day or so later.

For several years, Beale has had a running dispute with other newswomen, mainly myself, on the propriety of carrying a notebook and pen to an elegant Washington party, and particularly at the White House. I have always maintained that we should not fly under false colors and that all guests should know that we are reporters, lest they say something they may regret. And I always introduce myself as a reporter.

Maxine Cheshire is another spectacular columnist. She has had a raft of scoops to her credit, including the story about Pat Nixon's gifts. She specializes in juicy news about Jacqueline Kennedy Onassis. Cheshire is a digger for details that other reporters despair of getting, and nothing stops her in pursuit of a story.

Women reporters are now covering all of the top beats, though still not in the numbers they should be. UPI's Charlotte Moulton has covered the Supreme Court for more than a decade, and her stories on those momentous decisions are blockbusters of accuracy and depth. **The New York Times** also has women reporters where it counts. Eileen Shanahan writes about the economy and taxes in a way that everyone can understand. Marjorie Hunter covers the House like a blanket.

Martha Rountree was a pioneer in radio and television who deserves to be more widely known as the originator of talk shows. She founded "Meet the Press" in 1945 and "Leave It to the Girls" (the former is still broadcast every Sunday), although she long ago sold her interests to her partner, Lawrence Spivak. But she was a pro who could draw some of Washington's top personalities to be interviewed on the program, including Sen. Joseph McCarthy when he was riding high and Presidents Truman and Kennedy.

Other women in the broadcast field have also racked up impressive news stories. Nancy Dickerson won a plum from Lyndon B. Johnson when he told her in an interview that he had selected Hubert H. Humphrey as his running mate in 1964.

CBS's Marya McLaughlin got the first big interview from Martha Mitchell, who called the Vietnam War protesters "liberal Communists." After that Martha was in demand for interviews by nearly every reporter—man and woman.

Out of the dozens of reporters who cover the White House on a regular basis only about ten are women, although many more women show up for presidential news conferences. I went to the White House as the first full-time woman to be assigned there by a wire service—UPI—in 1961 at the start of the Kennedy era. My friend and competitor Fran Lewine, of Associated Press, joined the White House staff in the mid-sixties. In March 1974 I was named bureau chief at the White House and had the privilege of being the first woman to close a news conference with the traditional "Thank you, Mr. President."

Women reporters have struggled for years for equal access to the news, and to some extent are still struggling, collectively as well as individually. The various press clubs have been firmly resistant to the admittance of women. In the 1950s women reporters were permitted to join the White House Correspondents Association but, believe it or not, were barred from attending its one dinner of the year. Not until the women persuaded JFK not to attend if they were barred did the wall against female members crumble. I was the first woman to become an officer of the association, of which I am now president.

For years the State Department had scheduled all visiting heads of state to make their only addresses to the press at the National Press Club, an all-male bastion from which women were barred. In the mid-fifties a concession was made, humiliating as it was, to permit newswomen to cover these appearances from a balcony, while their male colleagues sat on the floor of the ballroom enjoying the lunch. This seems incredible now. But at the time we had to kick up a storm and badger the White House, the State Department, and anyone who would listen in order to make our point and gain admittance to the luncheons for heads of state.

When I was president of the Women's National Press Club, Nikita S. Khrushchev was invited to Washington. I fired off a cable inviting him to speak at our luncheon. Confronted with several such invitations, Moscow then told the State Department that Khrush-

---

1783. Anna Goeldlin, "last of the German witches," is burnt at the stake in the marketplace of Glarus, Switzerland.

chev wanted to address a representative forum of the press. As a result, a number of women reporters were permitted to cover Khrushchev—and even to eat lunch with our male colleagues at the National Press Club. Years later, in the mid-sixties, the club finally admitted women to membership.

The last stronghold in Washington was the Gridiron Club. With the growing advent of women's lib and the breakdown of the barriers at the other press clubs, the Gridiron came under more and more pressure, from its own members as well as from outsiders, to admit women. Last March I was the first woman in its ninety-year history to be admitted to the Gridiron, and when this occurred, one of the long-time members of the club said, "Well, the roof didn't fall in, and the walls didn't cave in. I guess it will be all right."

To this day women reporters are still asked whether they use their "feminine charm" to get stories. Few do, I would say—sex appeal is not a durable commodity. But, of course, we don't ignore the woman's angle when it's useful.

When Lyndon B. Johnson was president, he made it a practice to dance with all newswomen at parties. After such an evening who could resist starting a story: "I danced with the president last night"? I couldn't—and I didn't.

Some of my male colleagues claim that all presidents in recent years have paid more attention to a woman reporter in the Oval Office than they do to men. That doesn't mean that they give us the scoops, though Lyndon Johnson sought out newspaper women at the White House because he felt that we would be more sympathetic.

But as few women reporters as there are in Washington, when we all get together to cover an event that's considered women's interest, we can be quite formidable.

Pat Nixon's social secretary called us "the leeches." Jacqueline Kennedy, who—no doubt under the illusion that JFK could influence press assignments—kept after him to get me a foreign assignment, called us "the harpies."

The British Press nominated us "the witches of Washington." They had seen nothing like the way we zeroed in on Princess Anne and Prince Charles in pack-journalism style. One night during their visit to Washington, Julie and Patricia Nixon escorted them on a tour of the monuments. At Lincoln's statue I saw Princess Anne sort of sniff and walk away, and I asked her what she thought of the Lincoln Memorial. When she just said, "I don't give interviews," I couldn't believe my ears. I couldn't believe that she wouldn't have at least some polite historical comment to make, so in case she hadn't heard me, I asked again. But the only answer I got was from a big, burly Scotland Yard man who came up to me and said, "Young lady, you have been **told**."

Surprisingly, many of the children of first families who have hated having their privacy invaded by the press have ended up working for it. Margaret Truman, Lynda Bird Johnson, Julie Nixon—all have become women journalists, writing stories, covering news, interviewing people.

Though more and more women are getting the chance to cover hard news, they're still usually the ones to cover social events and women. But even that's changing. Ever since the American public became so insatiably curious about Jacqueline Kennedy and her children, male reporters have also covered the traditionally female terrain of the first family. After all, Betty Ford's sensational statement about how she would react if she heard her daughter were having an affair was Mike Wallace's scoop.

At the same time, women journalists in many cities, though not yet in Washington, are covering sports—a sign that the line between men's and women's beats is weakening.

Many newspapers are now using the term **Ms.** instead of **Miss** or **Mrs.** because of pressure women reporters have put upon their editors and publishers.

These days, too, people in high places in Washington are responding more and more to the feminist approach of many women journalists. Recently Henry Kissinger spotted a group of newspaper women at a White House party and said, "Good night, Ladies."

Then he caught himself and said, "Good night... Women!"

1784. Hannah Adams, the first professional American woman writer, publishes her best-known work, the ponderous *An Alphabetical Compendium of the Various Sects.*

Consider an Apprenticeship

Karin Abarbanel and Gonnie McClung Siegel

Apprenticeships are programs through which workers learn a recognized trade by combining formal instruction with on-the-job training. The Bureau of Apprenticeship of the U.S. Department of Labor has set the following criteria for the registration of new apprenticeship programs:

- A clearly identified trade that can be learned in a practical way through work and on-the-job training
- A job involving manual, mechanical, or technical skills and knowledge requiring a minimum of two thousand hours of work and training
- A job requiring on-the-job training with related instruction that can be given in a classroom, through correspondence courses, self-study, or other approved means of instruction
- A job that does not fall into selling, managerial, clerical, or professional categories

Apprenticeships have long been the route by which young unskilled men have entered skilled, well-paying jobs. The length of training varies generally from one to four years, with about 144 hours of classroom instruction.

Except in a handful of female-typed trades, women, when not blatantly excluded, have been discouraged from entering apprenticeship programs. Women themselves have played their part: they have shied away from interesting, well-paying jobs in the trades to accept low-paying office work. But the attitudes of employers, unions, and the educational system have been the most formidable barriers. Schools have traditionally channeled non-college-bound boys into vocational training and girls into home economics or business courses.

Job Corps Happenings

Jobs Which Require Apprenticeships

The 79 jobs listed below have training periods of at least 2 years and some as many as 6 years. Some of the occupations are broken down into more specialized jobs, so that the total number of apprenticeable occupations is close to 350. Numbers in parentheses indicate the number of years of training required.

Aircraft fabricator (3-4)	Machinist (4)
Airplane mechanic (3-4)	Mailer (4-5)
Arborist (3)	Maintenance mechanic
Asbestos worker (4)	repairers (3-6)
Automotive body	Metal polisher and
repairman (3-4)	buffer (3-4)
Automotive mechanic (3-4)	Millwright (4)
Baker (3)	Model maker (4)
Barber (2)	Musical instrument
Blacksmith (4)	mechanic (3-4)
Boilermaker (4)	Operating engineer (3-4)
Bookbinder (2-4)	Optical technician (4)
Brewer (2-3)	Orthopedic prosthetic
Bricklayer (3)	technician (3-4)
Butcher-meat cutter (3)	Painter-decorator (2-3)
Cabinetmaker-millman (2-4)	Patternmaker (5)
Candy maker (3-4)	Photoengraver (5-6)
Canvas worker (3)	Photographer (3)
Carman (4)	Plasterer (2)
Carpenter (4)	Plate printer (4)
Cement mason (2)	Plumber-pipefitter (4-5)
Cook (3)	Printer (4)
Cosmetician (2)	Printing press operator (4)
Dairy products maker (2-3)	Rigger (2-4)
Draftsman-designer (3-5)	Roofer (2-3)
Electrical worker (4-5)	Rotogravure engraver (5-6)
Electroplater (3-4)	Sheetmetal worker (3-4)
Electrotyper (5-6)	Sign, scene, and pictorial
Engraver (4-5)	artist (3-4)
Fabric cutter (3-4)	Silversmith (3-4)
Farm-equipment	Stationary engineer (3-4)
mechanic (3-4)	Stereotyper (5-6)
Floor coverer (3-4)	Stoneworker (2-4)
Foundryman (2-4)	Stonemason (3)
Furrier (3-4)	Tailor (4)
Glazier-glass worker (2-4)	Telephone worker (4)
Heat treater (4)	Terrazzo worker (4)
Ironworker (2-4)	Textile technician (2-4)
Jeweler (2-4)	Tile setter (3)
Lather (2-3)	Tool and die maker (4-5)
Lead burner (5)	Upholsterer (3-4)
Leatherworker (3-4)	Wallpaper craftsman (4-5)
Lithographer (4-5)	Wire weaver (3-4)

Adapted from *Apprenticeship Training*, 1974, Manpower Administration, Department of Labor.

1785. The execution of women for witchcraft or treason by burning at the stake is abolished in England.

HOW IT OPERATES

Apprenticeship programs are conducted by the voluntary cooperation of labor, management, schools, and government throughout the country.

In many local areas the principal crafts have joint apprenticeship committees of six members, three from management and three from labor. These committee members are responsible for conducting and supervising their craft's local apprenticeship program.

They test, select, and sign up (indenture) the apprentice and register him with the U.S. Department of Labor's Bureau of Apprenticeship and Training, or with the State Apprenticeship Agency, if there is one.

They supervise and evaluate the variety and the quality of the apprentice's work experience.

They certify the apprentice as a journeyman.

WHO QUALIFIES

The requirements for apprenticeship vary somewhat from place to place. Generally, you should be between the ages of 17 and 26.

You must be able to work with head and hands, and be good at both. You've got to be in good physical shape, capable of performing the work of the trade.

Some trades require a high school diploma or its equivalent. Other trades prefer this, but do not insist on it.

Assistance to help pass entrance tests is being offered to those who may not have all the requirements to enter an apprenticeship program.

This help is being offered in most of the big cities through such organizations as the local AFL-CIO building and construction trades council, the Urban League, Workers' Defense League, or other community action agencies.

If you want to be an electrician, for instance, and you figure your high school studies are not enough to let you pass the mathematics and physics questions, check with the building trades council or the Urban League or the Apprenticeship Information Center at the local employment service office.

They will have information about attending one of the special 4-week courses which are conducted to prepare applicants for apprenticeship tests as openings for electrician apprentices become available.

MONEY TALK

One of the nice things about apprenticeship is that you are paid while learning. Starting pay is usually 40 to 55 percent of the journeyman's going rate. In most areas, it will vary from $2.50 to $5.00 an hour.

More than that, the apprentice making satisfactory progress gets a raise in pay every 6 months, until he is earning about 90 percent of the journeyman's current rate during the last 6-month apprenticeship period.

And then, of course, there are fringe benefits like paid vacations, paid holidays, insurance, hospitalization, and retirement pension plans.

MORE MONEY TALK

How would you like to earn $40,000 over a period of 4 years while learning a skilled trade through apprenticeship?

Let's just suppose you are a construction trades apprentice in the Washington, D.C., area. The average starting wage rate for apprentices in these trades is $3.50 an hour.

Let's say you have selected a trade which pays $7 an hour to the finished craftsman. The apprenticeship requires 4 years. The following table shows what you could be earning during each 6-month period as you move ahead:

Training period	Weekly pay	6-month total
First 6 months	$140	$ 3,640
Second 6 months	155	4,030
Third 6 months	170	4,420
Fourth 6 months	185	4,810
Fifth 6 months	200	5,200
Sixth 6 months	215	5,590
Seventh 6 months	230	5,980
Eighth 6 months	250	6,500
		$40,170

After completing a 4-year construction trades apprenticeship, you could be making an average of $280 a week as a journeyman at present rates of pay, **not including overtime** and not counting other fringe benefits.

The national average journeyman rate in all building and construction trades comes to $15,454 a year, while an apprentice starts at about $8,500 a year.

Also, an apprentice starting out now with one of the Nation's largest automobile manufacturers in any one of eight major occupational categories (mostly metal trades) would earn an average of $12,480 as a journeyman.

WHERE TO BEGIN

If you're interested in an apprenticeship get in touch with:

* The Bureau of Apprenticeship and Training regional offices. For local offices near you, consult your telephone book.

* The Apprenticeship Information Center near you

* The nearest State employment service office (consult your telephone book).

* The Urban League in your city.

* A firm that has workers in the trade in which you are interested.

* The local union that represents the trade in which you are interested.

1788. The first white settlers of Australia are 192 female and 504 male convicts, who arrive on those shores in iron and—in the case of the women—without adequate clothing. Over the next thirty years women will seldom represent more than 30 percent of the total population.

Preparing Your Resume

Catalyst

The purpose of a resume is to get an interview. Your resume actually is a sales document which should present information about your qualifications that will show how you can benefit the prospective employer. Like an advertisement, your resume should do four things: attract attention, create interest, describe accomplishments and provoke action.

Focus and Content

Follow several guidelines in preparing your resume. You will want primarily to state your qualifications, emphasizing pertinent aspects of your background and accomplishments. Detail your qualifications in a concise, accurate, readable and informative way.

The focus of your resume is important. Give a clear picture—through your past accomplishments—of how you can benefit the companies to which you will be applying.

Don't give too much information as irrelevant minutiae will dilute the strong points. Don't list anything negative. Don't use qualifying phrases—e.g. non-credit courses, unpaid work, part-time job. There's no need to separate and designate part-time and full-time or paid and unpaid work experience. Do stress positive, meaningful facts, leaving more details for the interview you hope to have. Do limit your resume to one or two pages, attaching a bibliography of additional facts if absolutely necessary (e.g. a long list of articles you may have published). Do cite on your resume your accomplishments rather than your duties. Instead of merely listing "sales manager of XYZ company," say "as sales manager of XYZ company, created promotional tools for salespersons that led to doubling of sales within six-month period." Or, instead of stating "PTA president," say "as president of the Parent/Teacher Association, coordinated annual book fair, served on search committee for new school principal, compared and evaluated science curriculae." Whether you are describing paid or unpaid work, use action words—"designed," "sold," "proposed." In fact, use jargon that pertains to that career field whenever possible.

Know what to omit from your resume. Omit extraneous personal data such as unrelated hobbies, your children's names, 10-year-old accomplishments or honors. Also omit part-time jobs of short duration that do not relate to the rest of your working experience. Omit unimportant dates. Edit out anything that could be irrelevant or superfluous. Emphasize your accomplishments and focus on your potential benefits to the prospective employers.

Form

The resume can follow either of two widely acceptable forms—the chronological and the functional. A chronological resume lists work experience and education in the reverse order of their occurrence, beginning with the most recent. On a functional resume, you organize your job experience by category, such as editorial, administrative or sales.

The functional resume allows you to cover over a spotty employment record such as two years' work experience within a 10-year period. It also provides a greater opportunity to stress skills than a chronological resume does. The chief advantage to the chronological resume is that, traditionally, it is more widely acceptable.

Samples of chronological and functional resumes appear at the end of this section. Read each line carefully because you will also want to prepare each line in your own resume carefully.

Adapted from *Your Job Campaign*. Copyright © 1974 Catalyst, Inc. Reprinted with permission.

Particularly note the paragraphs that translate volunteer service into meaningful work experience. Returning women often are uncertain as to the relevance or importance of unpaid work they have performed over the years. Assess each volunteer project in which you have participated to determine whether your unpaid work reflects capabilities and skills which can be helpful in your job campaign for a paid position. Whether you are referring to work as editor of your college newspaper or publicity coordinator of a church group, emphasize your accomplishments, particularly if your paid work experience is minimal or non-existent. In preparing either form—or both, if you'd like—keep in mind that you want to be brief but thorough in presenting the significant highlights of your background.

You may rough out the first draft of your resume with a pencil and scratch pad. Regardless of how many hours or how much paper you spend on these rough drafts, be encouraged by the progress you will make as the resume takes shape—as you edit out irrelevant material, as you strengthen pertinent material. The final typed copy of your resume should be absolutely error-free, with wide margins and limited to one or two pages. You've invested your time and energies and now you may have to invest several dollars but it is essential that you have the resume printed. Make enough copies to mail to prospective employers and to take along on interviews, allowing for copies lost in the mail or misplaced at a company and allowing for the times when several people at a company may want to review your resume simultaneously.

A clean, concise resume is important because the initial visual effect should be impressive even before the reader gets to the actual content. Both appearance and content count because your prospective employer may look at your resume as a work sample; he/she may look at the facts of your life are presented as current evidence of the way you perform insofar as organization, neatness and appropriateness are concerned. Before it leaves your hands, make sure you feel good about the way it looks and reads.

There is no rule that your resume must include personal information. Most is irrelevant. You don't have to state your age, your marital status, the number and ages of your children—or even your sex. You may prefer to use initials rather than your first name if it is one that easily indicates whether you are male or female and you'd rather not indicate this before the interview. You may feel, however, that your resume should include some dates so that an employer gets a feeling of whether you are 26 or 46.

You may or may not decide to include in your resume a brief description of your job objective. Remember that, as you proceed along a career path, your objectives may change so be careful not to state objectives too narrowly at the outset. A job objective is usually better placed in a covering letter that accompanies a resume for an interview request than in the resume itself.

Should you list your references or not? Your best approach is to include a phrase indicating that references will be furnished upon request. But make sure that you have three or four recent references ready, checking in advance that each is willing to recommend you. You will want to use references who will be respected by prospective employers such as a former employer, a former college professor, your attorney or your bank president.

Covering Letter

The covering letter that accompanies your resume should be addressed to a specific person unless you are answering a classified ad that only gives a box number. In that case, the salutation is up to you. You may be comfortable with the traditional salutations, "Dear Sir or Madam." Someone else may be more comfortable

---

1791. The French Revolution abolishes most laws and replaces them with a single code, which does not make reference to prostitution. As a result, it is interpreted as a woman's right to sell her body if she so desires. Shortly thereafter Paris is teeming with aggressive streetwalkers amid public outcry.

with "Box 1234." If the classified ad of a specific company directs all job applications and resumes to the personnel director, call the company and get the name of its personnel director so that you can address your letter and resume to that individual by name.

When you are addressing a covering letter to someone specific, be sure you have the name spelled correctly. Ms. is today's preferred title for a female employer. Also be sure that you have his/her correct job title; someone may have given you the name of "the head of the company." That person's actual title could be anything from president to executive director to chairperson of the board of directors.

Carefully consider the purpose and content of the covering letter before you write it. Be brief but remember that your goal is an interview. Your enclosed resume will give the basic information about your accomplishments and there is no need to repeat it all in your letter. You can, however, using an active and aggressive approach, cite one accomplishment which is particularly relevant to what that company is seeking so that you will immediately convey how you could be productive for that company. Your covering letter, perhaps more than your resume, is an opportunity to set yourself apart from all other applicants.

In your letter, ask for an appointment at the employer's convenience and indicate that you will call within a few days to learn if such an appointment can be arranged.

Regardless of whether you sent a resume and covering letter in response to a newspaper ad for a specific opening or as part of a campaign in which you are writing cold to a number of companies within your career field, don't forget the follow-up. If there is no pressing need to fill a job, your letter and resume may be filed for future reference and then forgotten by today's busy executive. Take the initiative and follow up each letter and resume you send with a telephone call. Ask for the interview you requested in the letter. If you are put off, call again. Remember that your persistence could pay off with the interview you're after.

Specific Steps

When you sit down with that blank sheet of paper and begin to write your first resume or even to revise an old one, remember that it is going to serve as your sales document for each job interview. Take this effort step-by-step. And here are the logical steps to follow so that your finished product will move you along in your job campaign.

- Understand your targets. Consider the job you're seeking in your career field and list what the employer would be seeking to fill that job.
- Analyze your past history and discover accomplishments. Review everything from your education and work history to your personality, awards and honors, even skills you use to run a household or committee meeting or community fair. Consider this a biographical inventory of all your accomplishments. Use action words to describe them.
- Decide on format. Determine whether your work experience is best described in the chronological or the functional format.
- Select key words and phrases appropriate to your career field. You'll then be speaking the employer's language, indicating familiarity with the jargon of that field and even taking a short cut to get your accomplishments and points across. (e.g. "reduced turnover" or "prepared mechanicals.")
- Prepare a draft. Get it all down on paper even if you feel the final draft is a long way off. Once you see progress on paper, the final step will seem, and may really be, much closer.
- Seek critique and edit. Have others look at one of your initial drafts—someone in the field, someone you know who hires staff, someone who edits—and, based on that critique and your own new ideas, revise your resume.
- Plan layout. Consider underlining key points, allow adequate "white space" between copy blocks. Your resume should be attractive and easy to read.
- Prepare the final typed copy and arrange for printing.
- Prepare a cover letter for a specific prospective employer. You should be able to proceed from a rough draft in two or three steps to the final letter.

CHRONOLOGICAL RESUME

Mary Jane Miller
105 Autenreith Lane
White Plains, New York 10504
(914) 267-2385

EXPERIENCE:
1971-74
Research Associate, Congressional Campaigns, New York City. Designed voter preference surveys, supervised teams of interviewers, assisted in analysis of data.

1966-71
Class Notes Editor, *Mount Holyoke Alumnae Quarterly*. Generated ideas for assignments and layout, wrote copy, did follow-up editing.

1964-66
Research Assistant, Institute of Government, Chapel Hill, North Carolina. Worked on study of urban development and regional planning needs for the 100 counties of North Carolina. The report, published in 1966, has served as a model in developing uniform planning standards in other states.

1961-64
Editorial Assistant, *Law Today*, monthly journal on trends in legal decisions. Read unsolicited manuscripts, verified legal citations, proofread final copy. Also served as office manager, supervised one filing clerk and two typists purchased necessary equipment, maintained financial records for a four-month period.

EDUCATION:
Mount Holyoke College, BA, 1961. Major: political science; minor: sociology. Reporter, college newspaper. Co-editor, yearbook.

Publishing Guild, New York City, 1963-64. Course in editing and publishing techniques.

New School for Social Research, 1972-73. Course in municipal government.

REFERENCES ON REQUEST.

FUNCTIONAL RESUME

Mary Jane Miller
105 Autenreith Lane
White Plains, New York 10504
(914) 267-2385

OBJECTIVE:
Legal or political research for nonprofit organization, preferably with opportunity for legal work.

WORK EXPERIENCE:
Research Assistant, Institute of Government, Chapel Hill, N.C., 1964-66

Editorial Assistant, *Law Today*, New York, N.Y., 1961-63

Research Associate, Congressional Campaigns, New York City, 1971-74

Class Notes Editor, *Mount Holyoke Alumnae Quarterly*, 1967-71

ANALYSIS OF EXPERIENCE:
Research:
In congressional campaigns, designed voter preference surveys, supervised teams of interviewers, analyzed survey data.

In university research organization, analyzed migratory patterns, vocational opportunities, natural resources and economic projections.

Verified legal citations and researched background material on landmark legal decisions for law journal.

Writing and Editing:
Drafted summary of findings on urban development and regional planning needs in North Carolina for inclusion in 400-page state report.

As class notes editor for college alumnae quarterly, generated ideas for assignments and layout, wrote copy, did follow-up editing.

Read unsolicited manuscripts for law journal, approved final copy for content and accuracy.

Administration:
Served as office manager for *Law Today*, in addition to editorial duties. Supervised one file clerk and two typists, purchased necessary equipment, maintained financial records.

EDUCATION:
Mount Holyoke College, BA, 1961. Major, political science; minor, sociology. Concentrated on courses relating to law and social institutions, including statistics.

Publishing Guild, New York, N.Y., 1963-64. Course in editing and publishing techniques.

New School for Social Research, 1972-73. Course in municipal government.

REFERENCES ON REQUEST.

1792. Mary Wollstonecraft publishes her *Vindication of the Rights of Women, with Strictures on Political and Moral Subjects,* a powerful and still oft-quoted book arguing for women's equal rights.

Getting the Perfect Job

Richard Nelson Bolles

There are a few heroes in this country, who belong to what might be called "the creative minority" in this whole field. They are a very diverse group. Some of them live in the big city; some out in the country. Some teach and do research at universities; others are professional career counselors. But, despite these outward differences, these unsung heroes have at least two denominators in common, maybe three:

First of all, they have refused to accept the idea that the job-hunting system has to be as bad as it is, or as much of an out and out gamble as it is.

Secondly, instead of just criticizing the system, they have sat down and figured out how it could be done better. And, not too surprisingly, they have all come up with methods which are strikingly similar to one another.

Third, in spite of widely teaching their methods over a number of years and in a number of places, they have been rewarded by *being studiously ignored* by the "manpower / human resources development / personnel / experts" in this country, from the Federal government on down (or up, depending on your point of view).

For *any* job-hunter, this creative minority and their insights are important.

And, when it comes time for you to seek another career, you will discover this creative minority and their insights are crucial.

THE CREATIVE MINORITY'S DIAGNOSIS

What, then, is it that makes the present job-hunting system in this country so disastrous? That was the question which the creative minority, wherever they were, first asked themselves. What are the fatal *assumptions* that are so casually made, taught, propagated, and reproduced, by some of our best business schools and job counselors, without ever being critically questioned? To the creative minority, the fatal assumptions seemed to be these:

Fatal Assumption No. 1: The job-hunter should remain somewhat loose (i.e., vague) about what he wants to do, so that he is free to take advantage of whatever vacancies may be available. Good grief, said the creative minority, this is why we have so great a percentage (80 or whatever) of Under-employment in this country. If you don't state just exactly what you want to do, first of all to yourself, and then to others, you are (in effect) handing over that decision to others. And others, vested with such awesome responsibility, are either going to dodge the decision or else make a very safe one, which is to define you as capable of doing only such and such a level of work (safe, no risk diagnosis).

Fatal Assumption No. 2: The job-hunter should spend a good deal of time identifying the organizations that might be interested in him (no matter in what part of the country they may be), since employers have the initiative and upper hand

in this whole process. Nonsense, said the creative minority. This isn't a high school prom, where the job-hunters are sitting around the edge of the dance-floor, like some shy wall-flower, while the employers are whirling around out in the center of the floor, and enjoying all the initiative. In many cases, those employers are stuck with partners (if we may pursue the metaphor) who are stepping on their toes, constantly. As a result, although the employer in theory has all the initiative as to whom he chooses to dance with, in actuality he is often praying *someone will pay no attention to this silly rule, and come to his rescue by cutting in.* And indeed, when someone takes the initiative with the employer, rather than just sitting on the sidelines with *I'll-be-very-lucky-if-you-choose-me* written all over their demeanor, the employer cannot help thinking *I-am-very-lucky-that-this-one-has-chosen-me.* People who cut in are usually pretty good dancers.

Fatal Assumption No. 3: Employers see only people who can write well. Pretty ridiculous, when it's put that way. But, say the creative minority, isn't that just exactly what our present job-hunting system is based on? To get hired, you must get an interview. To get an interview, you must let the personnel department see your resume first. Your resume will be screened out (and the interview never granted), if it doesn't make you sound good. But the resume is only as good as your writing ability (or someone else's) makes it. If you write poorly, your resume is (in effect) a Fun House mirror, which distorts you out of all proportion, so that it is impossible to tell what you really look like. *But no allowance is made for this possibility, by personnel departments, except maybe one out of a thousand.* Your resume is assumed to be an accurate mirror of you. You could be Einstein, but if you don't write well (i.e., if you write a terrible resume) you will not get an interview. Employers only see people who can write well. Ridiculous? You bet it is. And, say the creative minority, this is an assumption which is long overdue for a rest. It just doesn't have to be this way.

THE CREATIVE MINORITY'S PRESCRIPTION

Once the fatal assumptions of the present system were delineated, it wasn't all that difficult to create a new system. Once you have said that the fatal assumptions are: that the job-hunter should stay vague, that employers have all the initiative as to where a job-hunter works, and that employers only see people who write well, the prescription almost writes itself, as to *the new assumptions that are the key to success:*

Key No. 1: You must decide just exactly what you want to do.

Key No. 2: You must decide just exactly where you want to do it, through your own research and personal survey.

Key No. 3: You must research the organizations that inter-

est you at great length, and then approach the one individual in each organization who has the power to hire you for the job that you have decided you want to do.

For any job-hunter who wants more than "just-a-job," but a job which employs his abilities and interests at the highest level possible, the above prescription of the creative minority is crucial.

But, for the job-hunter who is trying to strike out in some new directions, or who must of necessity do some different things than he has done heretofore, the prescription of the creative minority is (careerwise) *a matter of life and death.* It will be a rare new careerist, indeed, who seeks employment without paying attention to these steps in the job-hunting process, and does not wind up Unemployed or, what is in some ways just as much a crime, Under-employed.

AN EXERCISE WORTH HALF A MILLION DOLLARS

As you review the three keys on the previous page, you will doubtless say to yourself something like, "My goodness, that looks like *an awful lot of work.*"

My friend, you are very very right!

Some people say *the hardest work you will ever have to do is the job of getting a job.* After all, it involves divining who you are, what you want, and where you are going with your life. So, think of it as a job in and of itself. Designate yourself Marketing Manager for the whole period of job-hunting. Marketing what?

You.

Impatience, the desire to get it over with, fast, can cost you and your loved one (or ones) many thousands of dollars over the next decade or two, as well as condemn you to a fruitless occupation in which you continually feel under-valued, misused, and miserable. So, how much time to do it right?

Well, the job-of-getting-a-job at your highest level is going to cost you something like three months (at least) on up to nine, full-time, if the average experience of others who successfully sought a job *at their highest level,* is any guide.

The higher the level of job you aim at, the more certain this time period is, since you will find decisions about hiring at higher levels—as a general rule—take longer to be made.

But, you are aiming at a package which includes job satisfaction, full use of your talents, and the stewardship of perhaps half a million dollars over the next twenty-five years.

And the irony of all this is: considering the present chaotic mess that the national "job market" is, *it can take you just as long to get a poor job which pays much less and ignores the talents God gave you, as it can take you to get a good job.*

In charting your own job-search campaign, you are going to have ample opportunity to teach yourself the importance of Commitment—commitment, whole-heartedly, to this task that is in front of you. Time, thought and action. All are going to be required of you. And, lest such categories as these remain sounding terribly hazy, let us emphasize that they are spelled: h-a-r-d w-o-r-k.

On the other hand, if you are saddled with any of the handicaps that are alleged to bog down a successful job-hunt: viz., being female, or member of a minority, or over-qualified, or under-qualified, or over forty, or under twenty-two,

or a felon, ex-mental patient, or whatever, you will find the creative minority's process so much more effective than the "numbers game," that you will thank God for every hour you spent on it.

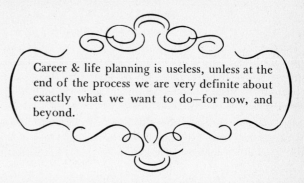

Career & life planning is useless, unless at the end of the process we are very definite about exactly what we want to do—for now, and beyond.

But let's be even more specific than this. Any career and life planning that is worth its salt should help the person who is engaged in doing it (namely, You) to do the following things:

1. You need to become more aware of your goals in life. What do you want to accomplish before you die? What is your life's "mission," as you perceive it?

You may revise this list ten more times, as life goes on (*Career and life planning is, ideally, an on-going process—not a single event, done once and for all*) but as you perceive it now what are you trying to accomplish, what are you trying to become? What's unique about *you*?

2. You need to inventory what skills you presently have—things you do well and enjoy. This inventory needs to be taken in terms of basic units—*building blocks, if you will*—so that as time goes on, these basic units can be arranged in different constellations. The creative minority insists this is the very heart of planning for first, second, etc., careers.

3. After identifying your long- and short-range goals, and inventorying your skills in terms of basic units, you need to consider and identify what Peter Drucker calls the *futurity of present decisions.*

Considering where you would like to go, and what you would like to do, what time spans are built in to present decisions (e.g., if school is demanded, how many years before you get out?), and what risks are built into present decisions? The purpose of your planning is not to eliminate risks (there can be no movement forward without them) but to be sure that the risks you take are the right ones, based on careful thought.

4. You need to basically decide who (or what) is controlling your career planning: accident, circumstance, the stars, the system, Providence, God (how?), your family, other people or—forgive us for mentioning this possibility —You. You see, ultimately, this comes down to a question of how passive you want to be about it all. (Life, career, where you

---

1794. The first American "best seller" is a novel, written this year by Susanna Haswell, entitled *Charlotte, a Tale of Truth.* By 1976 over 200 editions will have gone to press.

work, the whole bag.) We have, admittedly, an axe to grind here: we believe you will improve your effectiveness and your sense of yourself as a person 300% if you can learn to think (or already think) of yourself as *an active agent* who helps to mould his present environment and his future; rather than as a passive agent, who waits for his environment to mould him. (Or her environment to mould her.)

But, to say that your purpose is to find your goals, skills, time lines, and who's in control, is not enough. Your real purpose is to identify the core of your life, the constant thread, the constancy in you that persists through all the changing world around you.

The planning outlined above helps you to deal with change by identifying what in your life is unchanging: your sense of life "mission," your basic skills etc.—the things that continue relatively unchanging at the core of your *inner nature*. A base of constancy is necessary in order to deal with the bombardment of change that has become the hallmark of this world in which we presently live.

The secret of dealing with the future is to nail down what you have in this present—and see the different ways in which the basic units of that can be rearranged into different constellations, consistent with the goals and values that direct the inner nature which the Creator has given you, as you perceive them.

You are aiming at being able to fill in this chart:

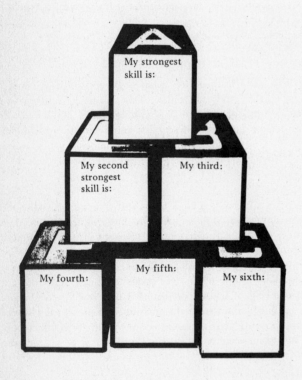

THAT BOGEY-WORD – Skills

Now many people just "freeze" when they hear the word "skills." It begins with high-school job-hunters: "I haven't really got any skills," they say. It continues with college students: "I've spent four years in college. I haven't had time to pick up any skills." And it lasts through the middle years,

especially when a person is thinking of changing his career: "I'll have to go back to college, and get re-trained, because otherwise I won't have any skills in my new field." Or: "Well, if I claim any skills, I'll start at a very nominal kind of level." All of this fright about the word "skills" is very common, and stems from a total misunderstanding of what the word means.

By understanding the word, you will automatically put yourself way ahead of most job-hunters. And, especially if you are weighing a change of career, you can save yourself much waste of time on the (currently popular) folly called "going back to school for retraining."

So, here we go:

According to the *Bible* of vocational counseling,—the third edition of the *Dictionary of Occupational Titles,* Vol. II (Washington, D.C.: U.S. Government Printing Office, 1965)—Skills break down, first of all, into three groups, according to whether or not they are being used with Things or Data or People.

Thus broken down, and arranged in a hierarchy of less skill (at the bottom) to higher skills (at the top), they come out looking like this:

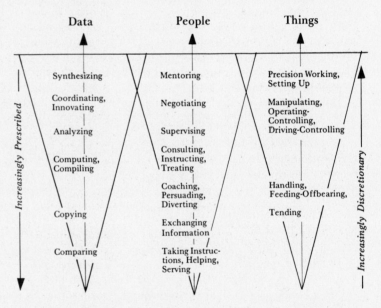

Before we explain these skills in more detail, let us look at the *most startling fact about all these skills.* It is, simply, this:

> If you graded all these skills in terms of how many of their duties are prescribed in detail vs. now many are discretionary, i.e., left to the discretion of the employee, you would discover that the lower the skill, the more its duties are prescribed, with comparatively little discretion left to the employee; but, the higher the skill, the less its duties are prescribed, and the more that is left to the discretion of the employee.

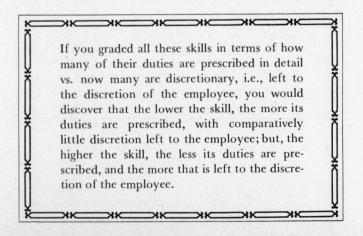

1794. Elizabeth Hog Bennett is the patient in America's first successful cesarean. Assisted by two blacks who hold her down, her husband operates—after dosing her with laudanum—on a table of two planks laid across some barrels.

This almost paradoxical meaning of the word "skill" can be easily illustrated from any, or all, of the three hierarchies on the previous page. For the sake of comparative brevity, we will take just one, namely, those which deal with people.

Each higher skill level usually or typically involves all those which preceded it.

The point of all this for you, the career changer/job-hunter, is:

1. The lower the level of your skills that you claim, the more the skills can be prescribed and measured and demanded of you. You'll have to fit in. Conversely, the higher the level of skills that you can legitimately claim, the less the skills can be prescribed and measured, and the more you will be free to carve out a job in the shape of *you*—making the fullest use of the special constellation of abilities that are you.

2. The higher level of skills that you can legitimately claim, either with people, or data or things (or, in varying degree, with all three)—depending on what *you* want to do,—the less these kinds of jobs are advertised or known through normal channels; the more you'll have to find ways of unearthing them.

3. Just because the opportunities for the higher level jobs (or careers) are harder to uncover, the higher you aim, the less people you will have to compete with—for that job. In fact, if you uncover, as you are very likely to, a need in the organization (or organizations) that you like, which you can help resolve, they are very likely to create a brand new job—for you, which means—in effect—you will be competing with practically no once, since you are virtually the sole applicant, as it were.

INCREASING LEVELS OF SKILL

Level	Definition	Level	Definition
1A	**TAKING INSTRUCTIONS—HELPING** Attends to the work assignment, instructions, or orders of supervisor. No immediate response or verbal exchange is required unless clarification of instruction is needed.	4C	**TREATING** Acts on or interacts with individuals or small groups of people or animals who need help (as in sickness) to carry out specialized therapeutic or adjustment procedures. Systematically observes results of treatment within the framework of total personal behavior because unique individual reactions to prescriptions (chemical, physician's, behavioral) may not fall within the range of prediction. Motivates, supports, and instructs individuals to accept or cooperate with therapeutic adjustment procedures, when necessary.
1B	**SERVING** Attends to the needs or requests of people or animals, or to the expressed or implicit wishes of people. Immediate response is involved.		
2	**EXCHANGING INFORMATION** Talks to, converses with, and/or signals people to convey or obtain information, or to clarify and work out details of an assignment, within the framework of well-established procedures.	5	**SUPERVISING** Determines and/or interprets work procedure for a group of workers, assigns specific duties to them (particularly those which are prescribed), maintains harmonious relations among them, evaluates performance (both prescribed and discretionary), and promotes efficiency and other organizational values. Makes decisions on procedural and technical levels.
3A	**COACHING** Befriends and encourages individuals on a personal, caring basis by approximating a peer or family-type relationship either in a one-to-one or small group situation, and gives instruction, advice, and personal assistance concerning activities of daily living, the use of various institutional services, and participation in groups.	6	**NEGOTIATING** Exchanges ideas, information, and opinions with others on a formal basis to formulate policies and programs on an initiating basis (e.g., contracts) and/or arrives at resolutions of problems growing out of administration of existing policies and programs, usually after a bargaining process.
3B	**PERSUADING** Influences others in favor of a product, service, or point of view by talks or demonstrations.		
3C	**DIVERTING** Amuses others.		
4A	**CONSULTING** Serves as a source of technical information and gives such information or provides ideas to define, clarify, enlarge upon, or sharpen procedures, capabilities, or product specifications.	7	**MENTORING** Deals with individuals in terms of their overall life adjustment behavior in order to advise, counsel, and/or guide them with regard to problems that may be resolved by legal, scientific, clinical, spiritual and/or other professional principles. Advises clients on implications of diagnostic or similar categories, courses of action open to deal with a problem, and merits of one strategy over another.
4B	**INSTRUCTING** Teaches subject matter to others, or trains others, including animals, through explanation, demonstration, practice, and test.		

1795. Sarah Waldrake and Rachael Summers are the first women employed by the fledgling United States government, weighing gold coins in the Philadelphia Mint.

The higher a skill level you can legitimately claim, the more likely you are to find a job. Just the opposite of what the typical job-hunter or second careerist starts out believing.

So, now that you know what you are looking for, on with the job:

● TOOLS & INSTRUMENTS:
MEMORIES, FEELINGS, AND VISIONS

What is needed, at this point, are some practical—some *very* practical—tools or instruments. We are going to list a lot of them. Some of you may want to try every one. Most of you will want to approach them as a kind of smorgasbord, picking and choosing from among all those that are offered. How to know which ones to choose?

If you have a reflective-type mind, it will have struck you that long range planning must include past, present and future.

Exercises 1, 2, 3, and 4— involving
YOUR MEMORIES OF THE PAST

Career and life planning involves the past, as well as the present and future, because:

1. You are being encouraged to develop a holistic (rather than atomistic) approach to life, that builds upon previous experiences rather than rejecting them.

2. You are being encouraged to see that the drives which will dictate your future course have not been inactive up until now, but have been continually manifesting themselves in what you have done best, and enjoyed most.

3. You are being encouraged to see that your life is a continuum, with a steady continuing core, no matter how the basic units or building blocks may need to be rearranged. The change lies in *the varying constellation* that these basic units are constructed in, (see page 287), but everything you enjoy most and do best will use the same building blocks that your past activities have.

Therefore, we need to look back, and see when we were (and are) enjoying life—and precisely what activities we were doing at that moment, what skills or talents we were employing, what kinds of tasks we were dealing with, what kinds of accomplishments were being done, and precisely what it was that was "turning us on."

Here, then, are some exercises and instruments designed to assist you in doing this:

Practical Exercise No. 1

A. Write your diary of your entire life. An informal essay of where you've been, what you've done. Where you were working, what you did there (not in terms of job titles—forget them—but in terms of what you achieved).

B. Boast a little. Boast a lot. Who's going to see this document, besides you, God, and any twenty people that you choose to show it to? Back up your elation and sense of pride with concrete examples, and figures.

C. Describe your spare time, in each place that you were. What did you do? What did you enjoy doing?

D. Concentrate both on the things you have done, and also the characteristics of your particular surroundings at each point in your career that were important to you, and that you really enjoyed: green grass, the theater, golfing, warm climate, skiing, or whatever?

E. Keep your eye on that "divine radar": enjoyable. It's by no means *always* a guide to what you should be doing, but it sure is more reliable than any other key that people have come up with. Sift later. For now, put down anything that helped you to enjoy a particular moment or period of your life.

F. Don't try to make the diary very structured. You can bounce back and forth (free associate) if that's more helpful; then go back later, and use the questions above (and others later) to check yourself out.

G. When your diary is all done, you may have a small book—it can run 30-200 pages. (My, you've done a lot of living, haven't you?) Now to go back over it, take a separate sheet of paper, and put two columns on it:

Things Which, On The Basis of Past Experience, I Want To Have Or Use In My Future Career(s)	Things Which, On The Basis of Past Experience, I Want To Avoid In My Future Career(s)

As you go back over the diary, each time you come to something you feel fits in the first column, put it down there. Each time you come to something that you feel fits in the second column, put that there.

H. Note particularly that when you come to a skill that you a) *enjoyed* and b) *did well* (in *your* opinion), put it down

---

1796. During the French Revolution, Marie Harel, a farm woman, makes the first Camembert cheese with the aid of an escaped priest.

in the first column and underline it twice.

I. When this is all done, choose your most important skills (*to you*—again, only your opinion counts)—choose 10, 9, 8, 7, 6, 5, but not less than five. Underline these three times.

J. Now rank them in order of decreasing importance to you.

K. What this exercise has left you with (hopefully) are: a) six or more building blocks that (when woven together) will form one coherent job description for you; b) a couple of lists which list (for your own private thinking, at the moment) some other things you want to have, or avoid, in your future employment.

So much for this exercise. If it helps, great. But maybe you want more help. Or, if you are a high-school or college student or housewife, who feels you haven't done enough yet (vocation-wise) for the exercise to be very profitable, try this one:

Practical Exercise No. 2

Analyze your hobbies (after listing all the ones you have done over the years, and then organizing them in terms of greatest enjoyment, on down) to see what you were doing, what skills you were using, and what results you were accomplishing. Here is a clue to what skills you enjoy using the most.

You can do this same exercise, of course, with your courses in school, etc. All of which is to say, what you are doing when you are *not* working (allegedly) may be even more revealing of your skills and interests, than what you do "on the job." Try it!

The above exercises, to be sure, leave you a lot of freedom to go about them however you want. But perhaps you want a little more direction and help; maybe a more systematic printed-type thing.

There are, surprisingly, quite a few such instruments floating around. They have various names (and copyrights): *Success Factor Analysis, Career Success Inventory, SIMS (System to Identify Motivated Skills), Vocational Interest Profile, Experience and Capability Inventory, Functional Self-Analysis, Inventory of Meaningful Abilities,* and a number of others.

One systematic printed-type thing you may like, is:

Practical Exercise No. 3

Bernard Haldane advertises a *Management Excellence Kit* for $3.25 . A similar instrument is described in somewhat less detail. The technique, which he was a pioneer in, consists in choosing two achievements which pleased *you* immensely from each five-year period of your life, then ordering the ten most important (to *you*) in decreasing priority, proceeding to say (about each of the ten) *why* it gave you satisfaction, *what*

you did, *and results* therefrom, finally yielding a chart in which the ten most satisfying achievements are going across the top, and then a list of *functions* or *skills* (running down the side) being checked off, to see which occur most often among the ten achievements.

Practical Exercise No. 4

When you are through with all of the above exercises, you may have a lot of data about your past life at your fingertips, but be puzzled with how you now go about making decisions concerning it. Indeed, one of the skills some of us never got any help with when we were going through our country's vaunted school-system, is that of how you go about making decisions. To meet this need, the College Entrance Examination Board has published a most useful study on how to make decisions, which you can get for $2.50. It is entitled *Deciding,* and may be ordered from Publications Order Office, College Entrance Examination Board, Box 592, Princeton, New Jersey 08540.

Exercises 5, 6, 7, and 8— involving
YOUR FEELINGS ABOUT THE PRESENT

Maybe your memory isn't so hot, lately. If so, of course the previous exercises aren't going to be very useful to you, whatever help they may be to others. Sooooo, we press on to the present. No need for memory, here; just feelings.

But what use, you may ask, are feelings, in trying to determine what kind of work one should do? Aren't we interested only in skills, talents, and all that? Well, not exactly. You see, studies have revealed that:

1. Your interests, wishes and happiness determine what you actually do well more than your intelligence, aptitudes, or skills do.

Maybe the word "feelings" or "wishes" sounds just too erratic, in your ears. OK, then borrowing a word from biology, let's speak instead of "tropisms"; things which living creatures instinctively go toward, or away from. Man is no exception, and in addition each one of us has his own personal, unique tropisms. You must know: what do you feel drawn toward, what do you instinctively go away from? Your own personal tropisms are determinative for your first, second (third, or fourth) career.

2. If you do work you really enjoy, and at the highest level that you can legitimately claim, you are bound to do an outstanding job, and be of genuine help to others.

3. No tests or other instruments have been devised yet, that measure what you want so effectively as just *asking you* or having you *ask yourself.*

Practical Exercise No. 5

This exercise consists of a very simple question indeed; write out your answer to the question: If you could have any kind of job, what would it be? (Invent your own, if need be.) Never mind what you *can* do; what do you *want* to do?

1798, *Alonin, a Dialogue,* **is written by Charles Brown. It is possibly the earliest American work arguing the rights of women and Brown is the first American writer to subsist exclusively on the earnings of his writing.**

Sometimes the question is put in other forms, or with time sequences: a year from now, ten years from now, twenty years from now? Try them all.

Exercise No. 5 presumes you know what makes you happy. Maybe, however, you have a much clearer idea of what makes you unhappy (a list, as it were, of "negative tropisms"—things you instinctively want to avoid). Okay, this exercise thrives on that:

Practical Exercise No. 6

Write a detailed answer to the question: What are the things which make me unhappy?

Analyze what you have written (afterwards) in terms of two columns, with the first one sub-divided:

THINGS THAT LIE WITHIN THE CONTROL OF MYSELF		THINGS THAT LIE WITHIN THE CONTROL OF OTHERS, OR FATE, OR CIRCUMSTANCE
Things which I could change thru a change of environment (my job, or place where I live)	Things which I could change thru working on my interior life (what's going on inside me)	

Check it over, when you are done, by reviewing the second list to be sure these things are *really* beyond your control or power to alter. Then go over the first list and decide whether the priority for you is to work on your *external* furniture (environment, work, etc.) or your *internal* furniture (personal growth, emotions or spiritual factors), or *both*. List concrete resolutions, with time goals beside them.

If you want to take a good look at the external environments that are most compatible with your internal furniture, there is an exercise you may like (and a book you *must* read):

Practical Exercise No. 7

Holland's *"The Self-directed Search"* in his *Making Vocational Choices: a theory of careers* (Prentice-Hall, 1973) helps to identify particular occupations you might be interested in, defined in terms of your preferred people-environments. Tremendously useful.

If, on the other hand (or in addition) you want to do some hard thinking about the internal "You" that—hopefully—your work environment has got to be compatible with, in order for you to be happy, then we suggest you try the following exercise:

Practical Exercise No. 8

1. Take ten sheets of paper. Write on the top of each one the words: Who am I?

2. Then write, on each sheet, *one* answer to that question. At the end of the ten sheets, you'll have the same question written, but ten different answers.
3. Now go back over the ten again, and looking at each answer, write below it on each sheet *what turns you on* about that particular answer.
4. Now go back over the ten sheets, and arrange them in order of priority. Your most important identity goes on top. Then in order, on down to the identity that is *to you* of least importance, among the ten.
5. Finally, go back over the ten sheets, looking particularly at the answers you wrote (on each page) to *What turns you on?* and see if there are some common denominators.
6. If so, you have begun to put your finger on some things that your career (calling, vocation, job or whatever) *must use* if you are to be truly happy, fulfilled, used and effective—to the height of your powers.

Since this can be an eye-opening exercise, if you possess some degree of self-knowledge, but difficult if you don't, let us show how one person filled it out. This is not in any way to suggest the kind of answers you should give, but only to flesh out the instructions above—with an example from one completed exercise:

Part 1: Who am I?

1. A man or woman
2. An urban dweller (and lover)
3. A loving person
4. A creator
5. A writer
6. An enjoyer of good movies and music
7. A skilled counselor and teacher
8. An independent
9. An executive
10. An enabler

Part 2: What Turns Me On About These?

1. Taking initiative, having inner strength; being open, growing, playful
2. Excitement, variety of choices available, crowds, faces
3. Feelings, empathizing, playfulness, sex, adoration given, happiness
4. Transforming things, making old things new, familiar wondrous
5. Beauty of words, variety of images, new perspectives, new relationships of ideas, words, understandings
6. Watching people up close, merging of color, photography, music
7. Using intuition, helping, seeing totalities of people, problem solving, long-term close helpful relationships.
8. Making own decisions, carrying out own plans
9. Taking responsibility, wise risks, using mind, seeing totalities of problems overall.
10. Helping people to become freed-up, to be what they want to be.

Part 3: Any Common Denominators? Variety, totalities, rearranging of constellations, dealing with a number of different

1800. Lady Hester Lucy Stanhope becomes one of England's most brilliant, eccentric, and adventurous women. Her wit and stately bearing place her at the head of English society, while her business sense is evident in her financial management of Sir William Pitt's affairs. She both smokes and rides horses daringly astride, horrifying her straitlaced

things and showing relationships between them all in a new way, helping others.

Part 4: What Must My Career Use (and Include) For Me To Be Truly Happy, Used and Effective? A variety of different things that have to be dealt with, with people, where seeing totalities, rearranging their relations, and interpreting them to people in a new way is at the heart of the career.

This is but one illustration. There are many other ways, and many other levels that the exercise can be done at. Be as wild, imaginative, creative as you want to be with it.

And when it is done, here are some check-back questions, to be sure you have gotten all that you can out of the exercise:

Checkback: Practical Exercise No. 8 concluded

7. What is it (or what are they/them) that, if I lost it, life would have no meaning? Is it included in the exercise above? If not, why not? (Think hard, and revise your answers, in the light of this new insight; or old.)
8. Out of the ten identifications of myself, and the ten lists of things which turn me on, which of these must be included in any job I have? *Remember the world is already filled with people who are trying to use their time after 5 p.m. to do all the things they really enjoy.*

Exercises 9 and 10 — involving
YOUR VISIONS OF THE FUTURE

If your memory groans at the idea of trying to remember the past, and if your feelings about yourself at the present are difficult for you to put into words, there is still another family of exercises available to you—which may help you pinpoint just exactly what it is that you want to do with your life. And that is, of course, those exercises which deal with the future.

The future. It sounds far away, mystical, and mysterious. But, as someone has said,

> "We ought to be interested in the future, for that is where we are going to spend the rest of our lives."

Most of us have our visions and dream our dreams. It's only when we come to our job, and what we want to do with the rest of our lives, that we think our visions and dreams must be shelved. In career planning there is a certain group of professionals, here and there, who love to play the game of getting you to say just what you want to do, and then "bringing you down to earth" by saying, "All right; now, let's get realistic." What they should ask is, "Are you *sure* this is what you really want?" because if it is, chances are you will find some way to do it.

Never mind "being realistic." For every person who "over-dreams"—of doing more than his merits would justify,—there are four people who "under-dream," and sell themselves short.

You are not going to do this task well if you keep one eye fixed on what you *think* you know about the job market, when you try to draw up what you would like to do at your job, e.g., "I'd like to be able to do this and that at my job, but I know there is no job in the world like that."

Granted, you may not be able to find a job that has all of that. But why not aim for it, and then settle for less if and when you find out that you simply have to? But don't fore-close the matter prematurely. You'd be surprised what you may be able to turn up.

Dreams may have to be taken in stages. If you want to be president of a particular enterprise, for example, you may have to work your way toward it through two or three steps. But it is quite possible you will eventually succeed—*if your whole heart is in your dream.*

Here, then, are some exercises to dust off some of those visions and dreams you may have shelved awhile back.

Practical Exercise No. **9**

Spend as much time as necessary writing an article entitled "Before I die, I want to . . . ." (Things you would like to do, before you die.) Confess them now, and maybe they'll happen.

Or you may prefer to write the article on a similar topic: "On the last day of my life, what must I have done or been so that my life will have been satisfying to me?" When it is finished, go back over it and make two lists: Things Already Accomplished, Things Yet To Be Accomplished. Then make a third column, beside the one called Things Yet To Be Accomplished, listing the particular *steps* that you will have to take, in order to accomplish these things that you have listed.

1	2	3
Things already accomplished.	Things yet to be accomplished. *(Then number them in the order in which you would like to accomplish them.)*	Steps needed in order to accomplish the things in column 2

As you get involved with these exercises you may notice that it is impossible to keep your focus only on your vocation, occupation, career or whatever you call it. You will find some dreams of places you want to visit creeping in, some experiences you want to have, that are not on-the-job, etc. *Don't omit these.* Be just as specific as possible.

Incidentally, you don't have to do the above exercise just once and for all. Some experts in career and life planning suggest making the previous exercise into a continuous one, with a list posted on your office or kitchen wall—crossing out items as you accomplish them, or do them, and adding new ones as they occur to you from month to month.

Turning from dreams (albeit, concrete, solid dreams) to visions, let us talk of goals and purposes—for these are the visions of the future which cause men and women to set their hands to present tasks.

world. Later, after the death of her uncle Pitt, she is no longer privy to political secrets; and, becoming bored, she travels first to primitive Wales and then on to the Far East. Becoming a sort of female Lawrence of Arabia, she establishes tremendous influence over Arab desert sheiks, wielding power from her home in an abandoned convent on Mount Lebanon.

Practical Exercise No. 10

Think of some practical concrete task or project in your life (hopefully in the present) that you are a) doing successfully and b) enjoying immensely. (Well, besides that!) It could be at work, at school, or in your spare time. But it must be one which really "turns you on." Put down this task in the center of a blank piece of 8½x11 paper turned on its side, then take the following steps:

1. Begin at the lower left hand side of the page, and write the word "why?" (do/did you want to do this), and on the line above it, indented, write that reason, goal, or purpose.
2. Then write "why?" after this answer, too; and on the line above *it*, indented even more, see if you can write an even more basic reason, goal or purpose.
3. Then write "why?" after it, and on the line above . . . etc. Continue this exercise up the paper, until you think you have reached a basic purpose or goal, that is rather ultimate. (You cannot think of any "why?" behind it.)
4. Now, take that most basic goal (the topmost one on the paper), and draw an arrow from it, down to the part of the paper that is beside the "task" with which you began. There write the words "how else?", and think of what other tasks or projects would accomplish the same ultimate goal (the topmost one on your paper). In the end, your exercise will look something like this:

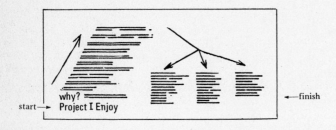

start → why? Project I Enjoy   ←finish

5. Repeat it with other projects or tasks that have really "turned you on," a new piece of paper for each one. See if you begin to see what turns you on about life, and some alternate strategies (or jobs) that could accomplish the same goals. If you "run out of gas" by step four, consult with some wise friend or vocational counselor.

JOB MARKET DIAGRAMS NEVER INCLUDE JOBS FOR WHICH NO VACANCY EXISTS

The average job-hunter—left to his own devices—is almost sure that his job-hunting task consists—in one way or another—of unearthing *jobs which someone held before, and which are now vacant. So he searches classified ads, employment agencies, etc.*

It rarely occurs to him or her that if, instead, he selects the organizations or companies that interest him, and does enough research to unearth their problems (and how he can help solve them) that they will be perfectly willing to create a new job, for which no vacancy exists just because they will ultimately save money by doing so. (Problems always cost a lot more.) Heaven knows, there are enough insiders who have

said—in print—that this hidden job market is what the job-hunter ought to be aiming at. Creation of new positions is the key to the professional job market, the creative minority have said again and again and again. This is particularly true when the economy is going through a paroxysm, like "the energy crisis" of 1974. New positions *must* be created.

Certainly, a little reflection will tell you why all of this is so. Pretend, for a moment, that you are an executive of some company or organization. Your organization exists in order to get a certain job done, or product produced. And it's doing a pretty good job. But *naturally* you've also got problems; who doesn't? Some of them are just minor, of long-standing, and probably just something you live with. Others are major, maybe even with a sense of a *time bomb*—if you don't solve these, they're going to break your back. All of them are costing you money.

Now, naturally your employees are aware of these problems—and some at least are trying to solve them. But, for one reason or another, they haven't succeeded. Then, into your office one morning comes someone who knows an amazing amount about your company or organization, including some of the major problems that you are facing. He has analyzed them, and has skills which he or she believes can help solve them. Very soon, you believe he or she can too, but *there is no vacancy in your company. Will you go and create a new job, in order to get your hands on this guy or gal? Regardless of age, background, or whatever?* Provided you have the authority (and our man or woman won't be talking to you if you don't) *you bet you will.* In fact, you may have been thinking you needed a new position, anyway.

KNOWLEDGE IS POWER

These facts about the nature of the "job market," the meaning of "skills," and the availability of "high level positions" are very strange.

They are also contrary to what many people, posing as experts, will tell you.

They are also (nonetheless) true.

And (consequently) they work.

Time after time, again and again, men and women who have comprehended the true nature of what they were facing in the matter of "the job market"—so called—have successfully found their first job, or made the transition from one career to another (without re-training or further post-graduate courses), in the area of the country that *they* chose.

And this, in spite of the fact that often the area they wanted to live and work in was designated as virtually a disaster area, unemployment-wise and job-wise.

They realized, as we said earlier, that all the unemployment figures tell you is how many people are competing with you for whatever vacancies there are, or for whatever new positions there could be.

1804. Sacajawea, her infant son strapped to her back, sets off at the head of the Lewis-Clark expedition. The Indian acts as interpreter and guide for the explorers on their lengthy and arduous trek from North Dakota across the Rockies and back. But perhaps

But, the vacancies (or potential new positions) *are there no matter how bad the economy is.* People get promoted; people move; people die; executives get tired of dealing with the same old unsolved problems and resolve to hire *anyone* capable of solving them. Young or old; male or female.

Since the vacancies or potential new jobs are there—wherever in the country one turns—you must choose where it is you want to focus.

You should not ask another man or woman to make that decision for you, nor should you ask external events (fate, coincidence, or where the "job market" is alleged to be favorable) to decide for you.

It's your move. *Your* move.

JOB MARKET FOCUSSING
(THE LASER BEAM APPROACH)

Job-hunters begin by thinking there are too few job markets (and therefore, too few jobs) "out there." Thus far, in this chapter, we have argued just the opposite. There are too many. If you try to hit them all (shot-gun style) you will only diffuse your energies and your effectiveness. Better, far better, to try concentrating your energies and effectiveness. Rifle style.

70,800,000 JOB MARKETS IN THE UNITED STATES (THAT'S THE TOTAL NUMBER OF NON-FARM PAYROLLS), including 19,400,000 Manufacturers' Job Markets. • You narrow this down by deciding just what area, city or county you want to work in. This leaves you with however many thousands or millions of job markets there are in that area or city. • You narrow this down by identifying your Strongest Skills, on their highest level that you can legitimately claim, and then thru research deciding what field you *want* to work in, above all. This leaves you with all the hundreds of businesses/ community organizations/agencies/schools/hospitals/ projects/associations/foundations/institutions/firms or government agencies there are in that area and in the field you have chosen. • You narrow this down by getting acquainted with the economy in the area thru personal interviews with various contacts; and supplementing this with study of journals in your field, in order that you can pinpoint the places that interest you the most. This leaves you with a manageable number of markets for you to do some study on. • You now narrow this down by asking yourself: *can I be happy in this place, and, do they have the kind of problems which my strongest skills can help solve for them?* This leaves you with the companies or organizations which you will now, carefully plan how to approach . . .

THE CRUCIAL MATTER: WHAT WILL GET YOU A JOB?

Suppose the time has come when you will need an alternative career. As you think about the job-hunt, very well-meaning people will tell you that the only route is to go back to college: go learn some skill or profession other than the one you had, *they say.* Go back to school. Get re-trained. Get your doctorate. *They say.*

There is, of course, a reason for this:
People think there are only two things that you can get a job with: experience, or credentials. They figure you've got to have one or the other.

With most careers, however, this is not true. No matter what others may tell you. (It is amazing how much bad advice is dispensed in our society with the sound of certainty by people who have depended either on outdated data, or on scanty sampling, or on rumor and hearsay—rather than going and doing their own research before they solemnly tell you what you must do.) Maybe you do need credentials—if you are going to set yourself up in private practice as a marriage counselor, or consultant or such; maybe. But you ought to reach this conclusion as a result of your own intensive research first, if you reach it at all. You will discover that people have gotten jobs as full professors at Universities when they did not possess a doctorate or any working credential that everyone told them they *had* to have. Likewise with other fields. And all of this because these men and women carving out a second career for themselves just didn't believe there were only two things with which to get a job. There has got to be a third thing, they reasoned, that doesn't depend on the past at all; and that is, to give a demonstration of your skills right in front of the prospective employer. Impossible, you say? Not at all. You can show him/her right in his/her own office that you have the skill he/she wants more than anything: the skill of

3. Problem-solving. No matter how much different kinds of work may vary upon the surface, underneath they have this common base: they deal with one kind of problem-solving or another. Universities, community organizations, businesses—all require people good at problem-solving *no matter what title may be tacked on the man or woman they hire in order to justify his/her salary.* Problem-solvers get hired, whether they are fresh out of college, or in later life.

Now, how do you prove you are a problem-solver right before the very eyes of a prospective employer? Forget about producing convincing Experience from the past, or producing credentials from the past. Just do the most thorough-going research imaginable of the particular company(ies), university(ies), organization(s) or other "job markets" *that you have chosen as most interesting to you,* before you ever go into the office to seek the job.

Now we said this third pathway is the key to getting a job when changing careers. But it is just as important when you are setting out to find your first job, or staying in your chosen field for your job-hunt. Therefore, we urge this path upon *all* job-hunters through your own most thorough-going research; we don't mean just an hour or two in the library. This is not what we are talking about, here.

her greatest contribution is her ability to mollify hostile Indians along the way, ensuring the safe passage of the group. During the adventure, Clark takes a liking to her boy and arranges for him to be educated first in America, then in an English public school.

DON'T PAY SOMEONE TO DO THIS RESEARCH FOR YOU, WHATEVER YOU DO.

There are a number of reasons why *no one else* can do your research for you, in this whole process.

1. Only *you* know what things you are looking for, what things you want to avoid if possible; in a word, what your *tropisms* are.

2. You need the self-confidence that comes as you practice this skill of researching *before* you go after the organizations that you have chosen.

3. You will need to use this skill after you get your job, so the time spent practicing it before you get the job will pay off directly.

Can you do it? Of course you can.

If you went to college or even post-graduate school, which over half of the high school graduates today are doing, you know exactly how to go about Researching—since you did lots of it there.

It consists, in essence, of a skillful blend of

WRITTEN STUFF, AND PEOPLE

In researching any part of this whole process: a) your skills; b) your field; c) your geographical area; or d) your chosen places to approach for a position, you will probably be dealing *alternately* with written material (books, journals, magazines, and other material librarians and such can direct you to) and with people, who are experts in one aspect or another of the subjects you are researching. You read until you need to talk to someone because you can't find more in books; then you talk to people until you know you need to get back and do some more reading. And much depends, in the end, on which you are more comfortable with.

Essential to your research (in either form) is that you know:

WHAT IT IS THAT YOU ARE LOOKING FOR

When You Are Reading or Interviewing About	Among the Things You May Be Looking for Are:
your skills	what kind of work uses *most* of these skills *together*
fields of possible work	which ones you will be happiest (and therefore most effective) in, because they fit in with your total Life Mission as you perceive it
geographical area that you have chosen	the kind of places that might need your skills, in the field you have chosen
places where you might want to work	to find out if there is any reason why you might *not* want to work there; to find out what problems they have *and* which problems are most urgent ("time-bombs") and which ones your skills can help solve.

AND JUST HOW DO YOU GO ABOUT YOUR PERSONAL SURVEY?

In visiting the geographical area where you most want to work, and conducting your own personal and organizational survey of the area, you are trying to go from one person to another, building a chain of links in which each person you see refers you to another (and hopefully sets up the appointment for you, or at least allows you to use his name).

Let's listen to an actual job-hunter describe the process:

"Suppose I arrived cold in some city, the one place in all the world I want to live—but with no idea of what that city might hold as a match and challenge for my personal talent bank. I have an economic survey to make, yes; but I also have an equally or more important personal survey to accomplish. Can this city meet my peculiarly personal needs? To find out, I meet Pastors, bankers, school principals, physicians, dentists, real estate operators, et al. I would be astonished if opportunities were not brought to my attention together with numerous offers of personal introduction to key principals. All I would be doing is forging links (references) in a chain leading to my eventual targets. *The reference is the key.*"

People who haven't tried this are understandably afraid: afraid important men won't have time to see them, afraid they won't be able to get past the secretary, etc. But, as was said above, referral is the key.

Well, suppose you just can't find a reference to a particular man you want to see?

Let's listen to John Crystal, a master in this field, describe the process:

"If you really are interested in highway carrier operations and really do know quite a bit about it, for instance, and you get to Charlotte, N.C., where you learn that one small, new company is doing something really innovative and intelligent in *your* field I would guess that the chances are that its President is just as fascinated by that subject as you are. And if you called him up—Oh, yes, the secretary, well this goes for her too—and told him the simple truth about that shared interest—if he asks if you are job hunting tell him the truth, *No*—but that you are *in truth* impressed by what you have heard about his bright ideas, and that you want to hear more about them, and that you just might possibly have a suggestion or two based on your own experience which he might find useful—Well, he just might invite you to lunch. And if he wants to offer you a job after a while, and many do, it's strictly *his* idea. And you do not accept it although you are always polite enough to say that you will be glad to consider it and perhaps talk it over with him again later on, after you have decided precisely what you want to do, where, with whom, etc. The key to the whole thing is this: treat the other guy just as you would like to be treated yourself."

If this process has been followed religiously (so to speak) you will have at the end of your initial survey:

1. A *list* of places in your chosen geographical area *that interest you, and that look as though they have problems your skills can help solve.*

What you then want to do further research about is:

2. *Identifying in detail what those problems are,* for the manageable number of organizations you have now identified in list No.1 above.

1809. Jane Todd Crawford, upon whom the first American abdominal operation is performed by Dr. Ephraim McDowell, has an ovarian tumor removed without the benefit of anesthetic.

There are resources to help you at this point, but resources are useless, unless you keep firmly in mind what kinds of questions you want the resources to help you with. So, let's list a few *samples* of the kinds of questions:

WAYS OF FINDING OUT WHAT AN ORGANIZATION'S PROBLEMS ARE

All organizations have money—to one degree or another. What I am looking for are *problems*—specifically, *problems that my skills can help solve; what problems are bugging this organization? Ask; look. (If you are talking to men within a company or organization that looks as though it might be interesting to you, ask them:* What is the biggest problem you are encountering here?)

The problem does not have to be one that is bothering only that organization. You may want to ask what problem is common to the whole industry or field—low profit, obsolescence, inadequate planning etc.? Or if there is a problem that is common to the geographic region: labor problems, minority employment, etc. All you really need is one major problem that you would delight to help solve.

How does this organization rank within its field or industry? Is this organization family owned? What effect (if so) on promotions? Where are its plants, offices or branches? What are all its projects or services? In what ways have they grown in recent years? New lines, new products, new processes, new facilities, etc? Existing political situations: imminent proxy fights, upcoming mergers, etc.? What is the general image of the organization in peoples' minds? If they have stock, what has been happening to it (see an investment broker and ask).

What kind of *turnover of staff* have they had? What is the attitude of employees toward the organization? Are their faces happy, strained, or what? Is promotion generally from within, or from outside? How long have chief executives been with the organization?

Do they encourage their employees to further their educational training? Do they help them pay for it?

How do *communications* work within the organization? How is information collected, by what paths does it flow? What methods are used to see that information gets results—to what authority do people respond there? Who reports to whom?

Is there a "time-bomb"—a problem that will kill the organization, or drastically reduce its effectiveness and efficiency if they don't solve it fast?

Some of these questions will be relevant, for you; others will not be.

Some of these questions are general in nature, and you will try to answer them about *any* organization you approach. Other questions are very specific, requiring detailed research, and you will have to keep at it, searching, digging, interviewing, until you find out. But the skills you are sharpening up will more than repay you the time spent, a thousandfold.

So much for the kinds of questions. Now, where do you turn for answers? O.K., here goes:

THE THIRD KEY TO CAREER-PLANNING AND JOB-HUNTING

As you have gone through all this intensive research concerning the particular places that you have selected as the places you would like to work, you have achieved two deliberate results:

1. *Your list is probably smaller yet,* as you discovered some of the places that interested you (even after visiting them) *did not have the kind of problems or difficulties that your strongest skills could* a) solve; and b) let you enjoy, during the process.

2. You know *a great deal* about the remaining organizations, including—most specifically—*their problems, and what you can do to help solve them.*

You are going to be a very rare bird when you walk in that front door. Organizations love to be loved (so do hospitals, colleges, and everything else). *You know far more than you are ever going to have to use*—in the hiring process anyway. But the depth of your knowledge will show, anyway, in your quiet sense of competence. You know they have problems, and you know you can help solve them.

This fact will be of great interest—most of the time—to the man you go to see, provided you have taken the trouble to identify, learn about, and ask to see *the top executive whose responsibility it is to solve the particular problems that you have zeroed in on.*

That is the man you are going to approach, by name, by appointment: the one man who has the interest, the responsibility and the motivation for hiring *this problem solver:* y·o·u·

You are going to ask to see *him,* and you are going to stay *far away* from

THAT ORGANIZATION'S PERSONNEL DEPARTMENT

This advice is given by just about every book or counselor that you can turn to: Albee, Crystal, Haldane, Harper, Kent, Miller, Miner, Shapero, Snelling, Townsend, and Uris—to name just a few.

The advice is stated strongly by many experts:

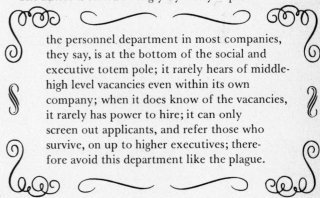

the personnel department in most companies, they say, is at the bottom of the social and executive totem pole; it rarely hears of middle-high level vacancies even within its own company; when it does know of the vacancies, it rarely has power to hire; it can only screen out applicants, and refer those who survive, on up to higher executives; therefore avoid this department like the plague.

Professors in some graduate business schools are predicting that personnel departments are either on the way out or on the way to drastic restructuring.

In the meantime, men and women aspiring to jobs above entry-level are advised to go nowhere near these departments. Even executive secretaries would be well-advised to steer clear of the personnel department, and follow these techniques.

Instead, you are going to have to do enough research—using *Poor's Register, Who's Who in Commerce and Industry,*

Who's Who In America, Who's Who in the East, and any other resources—such as periodicals—that your friendly neighborhood librarian can suggest, so that in each organization you know who is the *top man responsible for solving the problem that you can help solve*, at that organization. *If in doubt, go higher, rather than lower.*

And it will help greatly if you know something about that man too, so you don't step on his *known prejudices,* if you can help it. (After all, he's as entitled to his *tropisms—the things we instinctively go toward, or away from*—as you and I are.) If you were referred to him by someone, earlier, that someone may be able to give you some helpful background at this point.

WELL, YOU WANT TO SEE HIM, BUT DOES HE WANT TO SEE YOU?

This is the question that bothers almost everyone new to the job-hunt. We sort of just assume the answer is no. But, on the contrary,

Ten to one the answer is yes. Young or older; male or female.

First of all, you may have already met, during the process of your own personal survey of your chosen geographical area and field.

He may have liked you.

He may even have offered you a job (this happens many times) during the personal survey process. And, as we said earlier, you told him at that time the Absolute Truth: which was that you were flattered, that you would certainly keep it in mind, but that at this point you weren't ready to say yet just exactly where it was that you wanted to work. But now you are ready, and you call to tell him so.

On the other hand, maybe the two of you didn't meet before.

Even so, he's interested. The odds are 10-1 you've figured out someone who'll refer you, and act as your link to him; but, even lacking that referral you still can tell him (or his secretary) that *you want to talk to him about some of the problems of the organization, and what you've discovered that might be helpful to him.*

That's a switch!

Most of the time, when he does interviewing (for hiring, or otherwise) people are there to tell him what *he* can do for them.

Now, you offer to come in and tell him what *you* can do for *him.*

Is he interested?

Odds are ten to one he is.

(If he's not, maybe you'd better re-evaluate whether you really want to work for this kind of guy. And if you decide you still do, maybe you're going to have to convince him that he should hire you—even if he has to establish a new function or position, at a senior level, just for you.)

THIS GUY YOU ARE GOING TO SEE IS JUST LIKE YOU, BUT UNDER REAL STRESS

The creative minority in this field have correctly pointed out that one of the reasons the hiring process in America today (at the above-$10,000 level) is so difficult, is because of the great stress involved.

Let's look at some of those sources of stress:

1. The odds are very great that the executive who does the interviewing was hired because of what he could contribute to the company, and not because he was such a great interviewer. In fact, his gifts in this field may be rather miserable.

2. He can't entrust the process to someone else, because he's got to live with him/her afterward. So, hiring-interviews

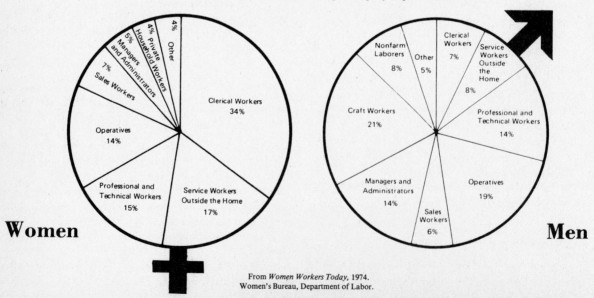

Occupational Distribution by Sex

The occupational distribution of women is very different from that of men. This is shown in the following charts for employed persons in 1973.

Women

- Clerical Workers 34%
- Service Workers Outside the Home 17%
- Professional and Technical Workers 15%
- Operatives 14%
- Sales Workers 7%
- Managers and Administrators 5%
- Private Household Workers 4%
- Other 4%

Men

- Craft Workers 21%
- Operatives 19%
- Professional and Technical Workers 14%
- Managers and Administrators 14%
- Nonfarm Laborers 8%
- Service Workers Outside the Home 8%
- Clerical Workers 7%
- Sales Workers 6%
- Other 5%

From *Women Workers Today,* 1974.
Women's Bureau, Department of Labor.

1811. Sara Payson Barton dies. She was the originator of the aphorism "The way to a man's heart is through his stomach."

for above entry-level positions have a heavy accent of "I wish I could get someone else to do this for me, but I just can't."

3. If the man with the power to hire makes a mistake, he's going to rub shoulders with that mistake, chances are. He doesn't usually hire someone, and then never see him or her ever again. An executive who has the responsibility of hiring for this position is given (or takes) that responsibility away from the personnel department *because this position is directly under his own and he is going to have to live with whomever he hires, day by day.*

4. If he hires a mistake, it's going to make him look very bad with his superiors, his board of directors, stockholders, or whoever it is that he reports to.

5. If he hires a mistake, and he isn't the chief executive yet himself, this could cost him a promotion personally—since he's proved he has bad judgment; and maybe his department is getting botched up—to boot.

6. If he hires a mistake, it's going to cost money. $30,000 for a top manager, $10-15,000 for a middle manager, $3,500 for a lower middle manager (according to a study done by R. G. Barry Corporation, of Columbus, Ohio). That's what it costs in "orientation time" for the new exec and those around him. And all wasted, if the new employee doesn't pan out; and, having to be spent all over again on whoever is hired after him or her.

Not bad. In one twenty-minute interview (or even several of same), the man with the power to hire can botch up part of the organization, cost the organization a great deal of money, lose his own promotion, be called to account, and acquire a whole new set of ulcers. No wonder hiring is such a stressful situation.

A man could be forgiven for wanting never to do it. But hiring is unavoidable. Experts estimate a good president spends 25% of his time (of necessity) in looking for new talent within his own ranks, and outside.

Failing to get rid of the responsibility entirely, a president (or whoever) could be forgiven for praying at least for a new way to do it—*one with much less stress built in.*

YOU OFFER HIM A PLEASANT LOW STRESS INTERVIEW

This is where you come in.

You are following the suggestions of the creative minority, who are all united in this: *create a situation where you and the man with the power to hire you for a position you want, can get a look at each other—without having to make a big decision.*

If the man-with-the-power-to-hire met you during your personal survey of the economic picture in the area, or while you were developing "remembrance and referral" contacts, or now—in your role of problem-solver—he had a chance to see you in what is—for him—a low stress situation. It is a form of talent *window shopping.*

You come into his office on one mission—Mr. or Ms. Researcher, or Surveyor or whatever; but the man with the power to hire you has a chance to look at you surreptitiously as Mr. or Ms. Possible-Human-Resource-for-My-Organization.

All the creative minority who have studied the career transition process and the job-hunt are agreed in this: any way you can let an executive windowshop you, without your putting him on the spot, will create a very favorable situation for you.

With this clue firmly in your hand, you may be able to think up an even more inventive approach to the man with the power to hire, in each organization. If so, more power to you.

INTERVIEW CHECK LIST

In preparing yourself for an interview (when it comes), you would do well to recall the three basic *categories* into which interview questions tend to fall—as the most expert job counselor in the country points out (John Crystal):

1. WHY ARE YOU HERE? Why have you chosen this particular place to come to? If you've done all the research recommended earlier in this book, and followed the steps in funneling (p. 295) you'll *know* the answer. If you haven't, you won't.

2. PRECISELY WHAT CAN YOU DO FOR ME? You will talk about his or her problems to the degree that you have been able to guess at them, and also listen very carefully to what he or she has to say. If new factors are revealed, field them as best you can; all the while showing how your skills can help with those problems. Within this category of questions, be prepared also for the particular form of: after you got this job, if you did, how would you start out?

3. HOW MUCH IS IT GOING TO COST ME? He or she probably has a range in mind (with a two to three thousand dollar variation), if you're seeking a job above the very lowest level. If you have done your research thoroughly, you probably have some idea at least of what that range is. Therefore, you will need to quote it at this point, adding that money isn't everything and you are interested in the opportunity and challenge as well.

Do remember to look professional. Have a good-looking dress (or suit) on, a decent haircut (or coiffure), clean fingernails, dentally cleaned teeth, deodorant, shined shoes, no smoking or pre-drinking—clean breath. It may seem like a silly game to you, but it's a game with very high stakes, in which you want to be the winner.

Whatever the interviewer may ask about your past, (like, why did you leave your last job?) remember the only thing he (or she) can possibly be really interested in is the future (under what circumstances might you leave me?).

And now for some final thoughts about this whole matter.

Never accept a job on the spot, or reject one.

Don't forget to negotiate for the future, and not just for the present. This means negotiating for promotion *now*, while you are in your best bargaining position. He has said he wants you. "Assuming I do the kind of job I want to do for this organization, when could I expect to be promoted and to what position?"

1814. Johanna Southcott, convinced that she is to be the mother of the second Christ through miraculous conception, also convinces over 100,000 others. Imagine the disappointment of her many followers when her pregnancy is discovered by British government physicians to be advanced dropsy. She dies shortly thereafter.

Getting the Job
WORKING **299**

After the Interview
Catalyst

As you leave the interview, you may feel relief or satisfaction or a combination of both. It's also possible that you'll feel discouraged and frustrated, thinking of points you forgot to mention or ways you could have better handled some questions. If you feel it's really important, correct or elaborate on these points in a letter or telephone call. In any event, use the experience of each interview to improve the next one.

It's not likely, however, that you will be confronted with the job offer or rejection during an initial interview so the follow-up, to a great extent, is up to you. Many jobs are lost because of a lack of this essential step. You must plan and carry out an appropriate follow-up strategy.

Over a cup of coffee, or whatever relaxes you, debrief yourself as soon after the interview as possible. Take out your job search work book and write down everything you feel you handled wrong. Also write down any information or job leads that came across during the interview. Write down names and titles you may need in the future. Debriefing is the first step in your follow-up strategy. Formally thanking the interviewer is the second step. In your letter, find a way to let him/her know who you are so that, again, you set yourself apart from other applicants. It's also an opportunity to strengthen or add a point about your qualifications in relation to the opening. "You may recall that when we discussed consumer relations, I described the venture I pursued in Europe and how that technique might be applicable to your company." Or "I particularly enjoyed learning that fact you mentioned about . . . ." Or "I'm taking the liberty of enclosing a copy of . . . which relates to some of the situations you described at your company."

If you are turned down for the job later, it may still be appropriate to go after some secondary benefits to that interview through a well-planned telephone call. Your end of the conversation could sound like this: "I realize this is a little unusual and I am aware that you found someone more qualified for the position at your company, but could you take just a few moments to give me some ideas as I continue with my job campaign?" You could end up with valuable advice, information, job leads—or nothing. It's worth a try.

After each interview—before an acceptance or rejection—is the time for you to decide whether you really want that job. Consider everything you've seen, heard and felt relating to such matters as atmosphere, personal relationships, job functions, commitment required and advancement prospects.

Let's say you decide you really want a particular job or, at least, want to pursue the possibility further. You have sent a prompt "thank you" letter and have not heard from the employer. A week or two have passed. Call and ask whether a decision has been made. If the job is still unfilled, you can ask whether you should call again, but tread lightly on this matter. Few people who are evaluating prospective employees want to be pushed.

Keep going to interviews even while you're waiting to hear the results of ones you've already had. It's often effective to let employers know, even if you're approaching the salary-negotiating stage, that you are considering other opportunities beside that one.

Don't be discouraged when you're turned down after one or even a number of interviews. This can and should be accepted as a way of learning more about yourself, about the job market and about what will be a good place for you in it. It's a point at which you can begin to reexamine and reassess your qualifications, your strengths and weaknesses, and your needs.

Adapted from *Your Job Campaign.* Copyright © 1974 Catalyst, Inc. Reprinted with permission.

1818. Maria Mitchell, eminent American astronomer, discoverer of a new comet and compiler of the *American Nautical Almanac,* is born. She is to become in 1848 the first woman admitted to membership in the prestigious American Academy of Arts and Sciences. She is quoted as having said, "Every formula which expresses a law of nature is a hymn of praise to God."

Talking Over Terms

Karin Abarbanel and Gonnie McClung Siegel

New York Public Library

If you fail to settle all the terms of a job before accepting the job, you can end up squarely behind the eight ball. Prospective employers are not above the "fuzz it up" approach. Many know exactly what they are doing. When they fuzz it up, you'd better clear things up or be prepared to live with costly consequences.

You cease to be a free agent the moment you accept a job. To accept a job first and *then* discuss salary, duties, and benefits puts the cart before the horse. What can you do if you don't like something? Threaten to quit and demand severance pay?

When a prospective employer wants you for a particular job, you are in a bargaining position. How strong a position depends upon how much you are wanted. It is a precarious balance; don't push your luck. Talk specifics, not generalities. Be persistent and, if possible, imply that you are weighing more than one offer. While you shouldn't lie, comparison shopping does set up an advantageous situation for you if prospective employers become bidders. But do it carefully or it will backfire.

Bargaining and bidding apply to women and men alike, but women should be extra careful to be specific about salary, duties, and chain of command. Women generally have been paid less than men for the same work. Although this practice is now against the law, it still continues in many places—it has merely gone underground. Where employers once openly paid women less for the same job, many now use deceptive titles and job descriptions to accomplish the same thing. They get away with it as long as nobody complains.

You need to know the following before you accept a job:

Salary. Is there an organizational chart with starting salary specified for each job? Was the salary for your job arrived at with you specifically in mind? If so, exactly how? Who held the job before you? What was his or her salary? (If your predecessor was a man, be sure your beginning salary is at least the same as his was.)

Advancement. Are you boxed in before you begin, or do you have room to move up? Ask the employer to chart your possible moves up the organizational pyramid, assuming you do a first-rate job.

Line of command. To whom will you report, and to whom does that person report? You can tell how far down you are in the pecking order by seeing how far your boss is from the top of the chart. Don't let anybody tell you it doesn't matter to whom you report. Buck passing begins at this point, unless the chain of responsibility is clearly established.

Job duties. Have these made as explicit as possible. It could later save you from being dumped on with duties other employees are trying to avoid. Be suspicious of any employer who reassures you, "We'll find plenty for you to do—don't worry your pretty head." Worry your pretty head.

Salary raises. Are they based on evaluation? On whatever the employer decides? Given regularly? Minimum or maximum percentage? What difference will performance make?

Where you work. Unfortunately it matters. Your office says something about how you rank in the corporation: size of office, number of windows, thickness of carpeting, the furniture, embossed stationery, and how close to the chairman of the board or the president of the company your office is located. You won't be able to change these things, but you will get an idea of how important you are.

Title. This also matters. Sometimes tiny prepositions count. "Director of marketing" often is more important than "marketing director." Discuss the structure set up by the company and where you fit into it.

1818. Hannah Crocker, living in Boston, writes her *Observations on the Rights of Women,* in which she says, "The wise Author of nature has endowed the female mind with equal powers and faculties, and given them the same right of judging and acting for themselves, as He gave to the male sex." Mrs. Crocker consulted with Mary Wollstonecraft on research for her book.

Strategies for Upward Mobility

Kathi Wakefield

Know your manager

The most important person for your career advancement (next to yourself) is your manager. This is the person who controls your raises, promotions, and day-to-day job satisfaction. When you are changing jobs, select your manager carefully. Never accept a job without meeting your boss-to-be. The only reason an organization would not want you to meet your new manager is because there is a good reason for hiding that person until you are committed to accepting the position. When you are already on the job, it does become more difficult to choose your manager because of your own promotions and changes in managerial personnel.

A good basic assumption to operate with is that you are unable to change a supervisor's behavior, so it is your task to learn to adapt to and function with the kind of boss you have. One theory (best explained by Douglas McGregor in his book, *The Human Side of Enterprise*) divides management styles into two basic types, X and Y. Type-X bosses assume that people are lazy, have to be forced to work, and lack the ability to make decisions and contribute to the organization. They also believe people have to be watched constantly to be sure that they are not making mistakes and are not goofing off. Type-Y bosses assume that work is as natural to people as play and that intelligence and the ability to make decisions are widely spread in the work force. They also believe that people will be committed to jobs that interest them and that people do not have to be closely supervised.

Some bosses fall into one of these two categories, while most bosses fall somewhere between the two extremes. Lucky you if you have chosen or have been given a manager who operates under type-Y principles; you have maximized your chance to learn and advance. Surviving under a type-X boss requires the greatest luck and ingenuity.

Managers who operate under type-Y assumptions are using a managerial style called participative management. When this management style is properly used, the manager gives an employee as much freedom, autonomy, and decision-making power as the employee is capable of handling. It is an extremely difficult style to use, because the manager is giving away a great deal of her or his authority while still maintaining responsibility for the output. It is a way of managing that permits people to develop their talents, but it requires a great deal of expertise and confidence on the part of the manager. Some managers misuse this type of management by placing too much responsibility on the employee

without giving the employee the information, guidance, and support she or he needs.

Managers who operate under the extreme type-X approach are the kind of bosses who insist on making all the decisions themselves, allow very little autonomy, and are much more concerned with production than with people. They frequently double-check all work and allow a minimum of opportunity for growth. Fortunately, the extreme type-X (often called authoritarian) managers are in the minority. It is very difficult to manage competent, responsible, intelligent people using a strictly authoritarian style. If the employees have any other options they will usually leave.

The problems in working with a participative-type manager are few unless you are very new in the field or the manager is unskilled in using this approach. If you feel that you are being given too much responsibility or not being given enough support and help in performing your job, discuss it with your manager. She or he may not realize that you are having difficulties until either you speak of them or else they are allowed to become severe enough to produce visibly inadequate results in your job performance. Most participative managers are very approachable, and, in general, they present you with an excellent opportunity to learn and to advance in your responsibilities and career.

If you are unfortunate enough to be working for a type-X manager, my advice is to start looking for ways to find a new manager. While you are working with this type of boss, keep in mind that she or he is not likely to give you many opportunities to expand your job responsibilities unless you are extremely clever in your tactics.

Since the majority of managers in this country fall somewhere between type-X and type-Y, you need to find ways to help them feel confident enough in your abilities and intelligence so that you get the opportunities needed to expand your career. What you are basically looking for is the chance to take on the kinds of responsibilities that increase your chances to make decisions, improve and broaden your skills, and be seen by the organization as a person to be promoted.

One way to help increase your responsibilities is through a version of management by objectives (MBO), a system used by many organizations. This is a process whereby a manager and her or his employee set objectives for the employee to reach during the coming year. It is a two-way process in which the employee helps to determine her or his own specific goals as well as involves the supervisor in determining what kinds of assistance the employee needs in order to reach these goals. At the end of the year the employee and manager sit

1820. Susan B. Anthony, tireless standard bearer of the suffrage movement, is born. Raised in the Quaker belief that the sexes are equal before God, Susan learns of the first women's rights convention in Seneca Falls, New York, and—in 1850— is introduced to Elizabeth Cady Stanton by Amelia Bloomer. She does not become a confirmed suffragist, however, until she is refused permission to address a New York temperance

*"I want you to know, gentlemen, that at this moment I feel
I have realized my full potential as a woman."*

• • •

down and discuss how well the employee did in reaching the goals. The results are frequently used as the basis of determining raises and promotions.

If your organization does not use such a system, it may be to your advantage to try to introduce a version of it to your own manager. Most managers are certainly willing to discuss using such a plan—particularly when they are made to realize that it can be a way to help make their jobs easier and themselves more effective.

The advantages for you are several: (1) In the process of mutually setting goals you will clarify just what it is that you are expected to do. It is amazing how many people are not clear about exactly what they are being held accountable for. (2) In discussing your goals with your manager you may find out which job elements she or he views as being important. It is not unusual to find out that a particular job function requiring only a small percentage of your time is viewed by your manager as being the most important part of your job. (3) Having successfully completed your goals and having a written record of what you have accomplished places you in a better position to negotiate for raises and promotions. (4) In the process of negotiating your goals you can frequently "win" for yourself tasks and functions that might not ordinarily be included in your job but would help you gain additional skills. (5) The process of joint goal setting should help provide a better dialogue between you and your manager. (6) The process provides you with an excellent opportunity to ask for the kinds of training, experiences, and education you feel you need to grow in your job. (You do try to take advantage of all the educational opportunities offered by your company, don't you? These are chances not only to increase your skills and knowledge but to gain visibility and increase your contacts.)

The process can begin by having your boss separately write down her or his version of your goals while you prepare your own version. The next step is to sit down together to agree on a combined modified version. It may require several individual writings and joint discussions until a final agreed-upon set of goals is reached. It is a time-consuming process, but it is time well spent since you are not only designing a written record of your performance objectives but are learning about how your manager thinks and operates. Regardless of the kinds of managers you work for, the more you know about their thinking processes the better able you are to adapt yourself to their particular style.

There is one further benefit to be had from adopting this approach in your working life: While you are learning to manage and be managed by objectives, you can apply the same process to your personal life. Setting goals for your own development and measuring yourself against your goals is an effective way to manage your entire life.

Finding a mentor

Many successful men (and women) have at some time in their careers had mentors to ease their way in the corporate world. Today, as more and better

meeting solely on the basis of her sex. Her ceaseless door-to-door canvassing and organization of conventions finally result in improved legal rights for women in New York State, including the right of a woman to sue in court and to hold property when married. Throughout her long and active career, Susan is associated with a variety of outstanding

potential jobs at the higher levels are beginning to open up to women, a mentor may be especially helpful to your upward mobility efforts.

The dictionary definition of mentor—"a wise advisor, a trusted teacher and counselor"—suggests only a part of what she or he can contribute. Besides giving you the benefit of another's greater experience and knowledge, ideally your mentor can help to make opportunities for you in the organization, acting to some extent as your personal public relations manager and using her or his power to influence your assignments and responsibilities. You can't always find all this value combined in one person but it's worth looking for.

"It sounds like a terrific idea," you may say, "but what's in it for the mentor? Why should anyone want to take me on as a protégé? And how do I find that person?"

The answer to the first two questions is that a person who has been successful in business is usually pleased to have the chance to help another individual grow and develop. People who are secure in their own power and position are not afraid that by helping someone else they will be hurting themselves. And many people find it very gratifying to know that they have had considerable influence on another person's successful career. Finally, in general almost everyone likes to be asked for advice. It flatters and it automatically engenders good will toward the asker. (That good will can mean a lot in turning your mentor into a PR manager for you, too.)

Finding the right person to be your mentor at various phases of your career is not an easy task, however. Your own boss, if you are fortunate enough to have the type-Y manager, is an obvious choice, assuming she or he can devote the kind of energy necessary for the furtherance of your career within the organization. If not, you may have to look elsewhere, or possibly find two persons with whom to establish your interests—one to give you advice, the other to further your progress in other ways.

Knowledge is widely available in any organization, and the main way to get this type of assistance is simply to ask for it. Seek out the persons who have the information you need, ask for some of their time, and ask intelligent questions. When you encounter someone who seems extremely knowledgeable and interested in your progress, follow up on the contact.

Developing visibility

Being curious and seeking out assistance is also part of the process of gaining visibility in your organization. It is simply not possible to become the protégé of powerful persons if you do not come into contact with any. One of the main blocks in the careers of women has been their lack of visibility. Women have tended to hold jobs in which the only people they come into contact with are the people they work with on a day-to-day basis.

There are many ways to develop visibility in your business community and among other professionals. Belonging to professional organizations in your field is a good start. Attend meetings regularly and get to know the other people in the organization. Find out what kinds of things are going on in their companies. This is a good way to determine where the excitement is in your field and where the openings are. You might also attend meetings of organizations in related fields or in fields that interest you, and consider joining them. If your field is advertising, for example, and you are interested as well in public relations and in marketing, try to attend some meetings of professional organizations in these fields. Professional groups frequently offer classes and seminars for the new practitioners in their field as well as for more established professionals, which can be useful for meeting people and gaining information.

Use professional associations as a basis for further visibility. Join committees that seem active, that you would enjoy working on, that are actually doing something significant. And, yes, do be the person to present the report to the entire membership.

Consider contributing an article about what you or your company are doing to a professional journal in your field. Like many other people, you may feel that you can't write, but that is not a good reason for not contributing articles. Many editors will be interested primarily in your ideas and are accustomed to major rewriting. It may even be worth your while to pay someone to put your ideas into the form of an article; there are many free-lance writers (or ghost-writers) around who love just this kind of assignment. Professional journals and magazines get passed around and read, interesting articles get saved, and the author does get contacted for further information by persons who may be sources for new job opportunities.

Attend any conventions and conferences you can, even when their programs sound dull. At any given conference the subject matter presented is probably the least important part. Your main task there is to meet new professionals, keep in touch with old contacts, and find out what is going on in the field. You may learn something from the presentations and panels, but even if you don't, your time won't be wasted. People do go to conferences with the primary purpose of recruiting new personnel for jobs in their organization. Executive recruiters often regularly attend conferences in the fields they specialize in.

In order to be considered for interesting job opportunities you must be seen by, known to, and respected by people who have the interesting

sister suffragists including Lucy Stone, Victoria Woodhull, Carrie Chapman Catt, Rachel Foster, and many others. Susan Anthony, more than any other, is considered responsible for the passage fourteen years after her death in 1906, of the Nineteenth Amendment. At her final women's convention, she proclaims, "Failure is impossible."

opportunities to offer. Jobs that offer contact with clients, key employees from other departments, outside suppliers, or the general public all put you into contact with others of importance and potential career opportunities. Certain kinds of jobs have built-in advantages of this sort, for example, positions in advertising, public relations, marketing, and particularly sales. Someone who sees you do something well and likes you may do things to help promote your career (including offering you a better job). People are much more likely to do things (hiring and promoting) for someone they have seen competently filling a particular job than for someone they have not seen perform.

If in a work situation you find yourself in the kinds of jobs that do not offer visibility to others in your own organization (as well as in outside organizations), there are several things you can do to develop this visibility. Try to get yourself on task forces or problem-solving groups that will be doing research and presenting recommendations to key policy-making executives in the organization. Develop your own research project that allows you to interview key people—and let them know what you have done with the information they provided you. Try coming in early some days and staying late others to have contact with executives who have more time for discussions then than they may have during regular working hours.

Take advantage of every opportunity to encounter people in the organization. It is well worth devoting time and thought to the process of being your own public relations agent—whether you have found a mentor or not.

Visibility outside your field

Many people lose out on significant career moves by relaxing and quitting the process of moving upward when they are relatively satisfied in their current positions. The competition is so tough for the most desirable jobs that you can never afford to stop improving yourself and looking around. No matter how satisfied you are in your present situation, you should always have in mind some possibilities for your next move and be working on ways to land the next job.

You should convey that you are satisfied for now in your current position but are always willing to consider new offers. Though most people do a better job of looking around in their own organization than they do in looking outside it, it's often possible to advance faster by zigzagging from company to company than by moving vertically within one company. But in order to be offered positions with other organizations, you have to be seen and known outside your company.

Your company may pay expenses for you to attend the pertinent conferences in your field. If they won't (and why won't they?), negotiate for the time off, with pay of course, and pay your own expenses if a conference seems worthwhile.

The next step is to try to get on the conference program itself. Leading a session obviously gives you a chance to come in contact with many people in a situation in which you can really shine. If you have never been asked to be on a program, contact members of the planning committee for the conference with an idea for a presentation you would like to make.

Ever notice how people who are frequently mentioned in the paper as successful executives are often involved in many organizations? Being active in the community (and in local politics) is an excellent way to gain visibility. Men have traditionally been involved in activities such as school boards, hospital boards, and planning boards. Such community activities offer the chance to be seen as well as to contribute your skills to the welfare of the community.

Keep in touch with people you have worked with in the past. It can be to your advantage to see them from time to time. You never know when they may hear of something that might interest you, and they are certainly in a good position to recommend you to others.

If many of the activities I have suggested sound time consuming—well, they are. However, you certainly want to consider all the ways that you can establish the contacts and develop the visibility necessary to keep your career going. You may find that some of the efforts don't pay off for you, but consider all options.

All these suggestions require a great deal of assertiveness on your part. If you are not a self-starter and find that it is extremely difficult for you to do the kinds of things that you know you should be doing, it may be worth your while to get some help in learning to do them. There are now many places available to get that help. Almost every community offers programs related to these problems. It can be very helpful to meet with other women with similar problems. Do surround yourself with the kinds of friends and associates that help you continue the constant effort required for career mobility. But always remember that you are the person in charge of your career development.

1821. Emma Willard establishes her Troy Female Seminary in New York State, the world's first school for the higher education of women. The institution, for boarding girls, will later be named the Emma Willard School.

The Working Woman and Maternity

Letty Cottin Pogrebin

Remember the old joke about the woman who has just had a physical examination?

"I have good news for you, Mrs. Brown," says the doctor.

"It's *Miss* Brown," corrects the woman.

"In that case, Miss Brown, I have bad news for you," says the doctor.

Whether the pregnancy is welcome or not, if Miss, Mrs. or Ms. Brown holds a job and wants to continue working, her impending motherhood may be very bad news from the standpoint of her employment.

Childbearing still has an honored place in our culture—*except* in the labor market. Here it's a problem situation. Once the company sets its "maternity policy"—for example, what month you must leave your job —it doesn't matter if your doctor says you can leap mountains in a single bound, or if you desperately want the job and need the income.

The employer who couldn't care less about your sciatica suddenly adopts an attitude of romantic paternalism toward your pregnancy. He may take any of these "protective" steps:

• force you to leave your job weeks or months before your due date.

• cancel your benefits and seniority during your involuntary leave.

• refuse guarantees of reinstatement to the same job or one at a comparable salary.

• forbid you to return to work for a specific period after childbirth.

• refuse cash payments to compensate for the enforced loss of income.

• omit childbirth coverage from the company health plan or say you haven't worked there long enough to qualify for it.

• or fire you, period.

Obviously maternity policies are far from uniform; the variations now range from tolerable to outrageous. Most women have accepted the indignities and the economic hardship because we've believed these policies to be immutable. But no more. Recent court cases have determined that our rights have been violated both under Title VII of the Civil Rights Act and under the Fourteenth Amendment of the U.S. Constitution (which guarantees equal protection of the laws). We realize

now that employers have been arbitrary, that their policies are based on myth and misinformation, and that penalizing us for pregnancy is not economically or morally justifiable.

As old ideas change women are beginning to expect three major pregnancy benefits as their *right*.

1. Disability Leave with Provisions for Job Security. This means that a pregnant woman should be granted a leave of absence on the same terms as any other disability —when the doctor says the patient requires it. The employer should not force pregnant women to leave their jobs, or forbid them to return to work for a specific period of time —unless the same restrictions apply to male workers on disability leaves. In other words, if an ulcer patient is carried on the rolls for benefits and seniority and gets his job back after 12 weeks, then the new mother is entitled to that same job security.

2. Cash Payments to Compensate for Loss of Wages. Most companies carry Temporary Disability Insurance, which protects the employee against loss of income resulting from sickness, ailment or bodily injury. The policy is funded by the employer or by contributions from both the company and the worker. Some states have legal requirements for disability coverage.

Once again, pregnant women should enjoy the same confidence and financial security during their period of unemployment as other afflicted employees. Whether through disability insurance or through accumulated sick leave pay, a working woman who is temporarily off salary for a legitimate reason must have a stop-gap income.

3. Allowances for Medical Care and Services. The great majority of union/management health plans include pregnancy allowances of some kind, whether flat payments for maternity expenses or specific fee schedules for prenatal care, hospitalization and delivery. Most employers agree with the wisdom of including maternity expenses in health plans. The only dispute is how much coverage is enough. What women want is realistic medical allowances and eligibility.

Don't all three maternity provisions sound eminently reasonable?

Then let's see why employers are holding out on us. And whether their arguments stand up under scrutiny.

1. *A frequent objection is that special benefits for pregnancy and childbirth would give women workers privileges not afforded to men.* We recognize that exceptional treatment for pregnant women would be resented by our co-workers. Moreover, if the special benefit costs the company money, it will be just another excuse not to hire women in the first place.

But we're not asking for *special* benefits. We only ask that childbirth be treated like any other temporary disability, and that complications of pregnancy be considered an illness like any other.

Prostate problems, for example, are unique to men. Childbirth is unique to women. Yet both conditions require medical care, hospitalization, possible surgery, a recuperative period and a temporary leave from the job. Why, then, is this uniquely male affliction just cause for sympathetic treatment while the female condition is often cause for dismissal?

It isn't, says a Virginia Federal judge in a landmark decision: "Because pregnancy, though unique to women, is like other medical conditions, the failure to treat it as such amounts to discrimination."

2. *But maternity is not like other disabilities,* goes the next argument. *It's not an illness; it's a "normal physiological condition."*

First we must divide maternity into three phases: pregnancy, childbirth itself, and the post-delivery—early-motherhood phase.

We can agree that in the first phase, a healthy, uneventful pregnancy is normal—so normal that we want the right to work through as much of the nine months as we and our doctors feel we are able! But if that pregnancy period is marked by complications, such as toxemia or hemorrhaging, it is no longer normal. Only then does it become a temporary disability.

The second phase, childbirth, may be "normal" in the sense that it is universal. However, every woman knows that labor and delivery are no picnic. They require a physician's care, hospitalization and recuperation. And there is always

1821. Clara Barton, heroine nurse, "the Good Angel of the Battlefield," is born. She is later to become organizer and the first president of the American Red Cross, founded in 1881 in Washington, D.C.

the possibility of death. For these reasons, the childbirth phase of the maternity period is as much a disability as any other.

The third phase, early motherhood, is the period when women may ask no special favors and employers may make no special prohibitions. We expect a reasonable recuperative period to be included in our disability leave. Beyond that we do not expect an open-end leave of absence for child-rearing.

The Citizens' Advisory Council on the Status of Women has issued this definitive statement: *"Childbirth and complications of pregnancy are, for all job-related purposes, the only valid temporary disabilities of maternity. It should be clear that the obligations are mutual—the employer may not be punitive and the employee may not be privileged.*

Alice Webber

3. Another argument is that pregnancy is voluntary and therefore different from all other disabilities.

Rubbish! For millions of women whose religion prohibits the use of contraceptives, and in states where abortion is illegal, pregnancy can hardly be called voluntary.

Speaking of "voluntary," what about the man who volunteers for a four-year stint in the service? Why is he granted an unlimited leave of absence from his job and all the fringes when he returns to work? Think about society's values. We recognize an employer's obligation to the man who bears arms for his country, but not his obligation to the woman who bears children for the survival of the race.
4. Some employers justify firing pregnant workers or forcing them to take unpaid maternity leaves by issuing fiats about women in general. Namely:
• Women are fragile and vulnerable during pregnancy and after birth.

That's a question for a woman and her doctor to determine—and most obstetricians authorize and even encourage women to continue working during pregnancy. According to Jacqueline Gutwillig, Chairwoman of the Citizens Advisory Council on the Status of Women, no known data indicate a higher accident rate for pregnant women.

Our bodies are our business, not businessmen's. A recent court decision corroborates this and makes new law. In Susan Cohen's case against the Chesterfield County (Va.) School Board, the judge noted that the Board's policy of enforced leave in the fifth month of pregnancy not only violated the teacher's constitutional rights but made no medical sense. "Since no two pregnancies are alike, decisions of when a pregnant teacher should discontinue working are matters best left up to the woman and her doctor."
• Women can't be effective, or be taken seriously, when they're pregnant in the working world.

I negotiated some of the biggest deals of my publishing career when I was seven months' pregnant with my twins. I had gone from 103 to 150 pounds, but my weight didn't muddle my brain. If anything, much as I deplore it, my pregnancy was an advantage. I felt buoyant and men felt kindly toward me. The combination made me an immensely effective businesswoman.
• Women don't come back to work after childbirth, so why waste benefits on them?

Of all the women executives I know, only two retired to raise their children full-time. The fact is that well-paid women with good jobs go back to work and poorly paid women in dead-end jobs (the great majority) do not. It is not a matter of sex and motherhood but of income and status. The number of working mothers with children under six years has more than doubled in the last two decades.
• Women will be absent and late more often during pregnancy.

Not so, says the Public Health Service. Time lost from work because of pregnancy and childbirth is only a fraction of the time lost because of other conditions. Then, too, a man's accidents and illnesses come without warning—and who knows how often. Conversely an employer has several month's advance notice when a woman is pregnant. Temporary help can be arranged for her absence. And the average woman is not likely to have more than two pregnancies during her working lifetime.

So much for arguments and rejoinders. The dialogue has begun—in the courts, at the bargaining tables, in

state legislatures and Federal agencies. The progress is encouraging.

Pregnant teachers have led the way. Besides Ms. Cohen's case, we have Estella Chiolino in Southgate, Mich. —a first-grade teacher who was dismissed in her fifth month "to enhance the educational process." The arbitrator rejected the notion that an expectant mother is antieducational and corrupting to six-year-olds, and granted Ms. Chiolino back pay and costs arising from expired benefits.

Two New Jersey school boards now permit teachers to work throughout their pregnancies unless they cannot produce a doctor's permission letter.

Mary Ellen Schattman, a market analyst, won her case against the Texas Employment Commission. A District Court Judge found that the Commission's policy of terminating pregnant women's employment two months before delivery was invalid under Title VII and the 14th Amendment. The restrictive policy was based on the mere fact of pregnancy, not on performance, safety or willingness to work.

Even the Army has reformed. WACs are now allowed to become mothers without facing automatic discharge.

A woman who works for the U.S. Government may accumulate sick leave indefinitely and use it for childbirth absence. And she will never be taken off the rolls because she is pregnant.

Laws in New Jersey, Rhode Island and Puerto Rico require payment of benefits for a normal delivery. Six states have government-sponsored disability insurance (but special restrictions make it imperfect). A dozen state Human Rights Commissions are tackling the question as you read this.

The Office of Federal Contract Compliance insists that any firm doing business with the Government grant a maternity disability leave with job security, *even if the employer has no leave policy.*

The Equal Employment Opportunity Commission has issued a few progressive rulings directed at private employers—among them a prohibition against special waiting periods before women can qualify for maternity medical insurance.

Yes, things are changing. But look at the many countries in Europe, Asia and Africa where the national social insurance systems entitle pregnant women to free medical care at the employer's expense (Guinea); to two months' leave with full salary (Finland); or to a legal guarantee of reinstatement to the same job (France). Where the rights of the pregnant worker are concerned, it's time America caught up with the rest of humanity.

1821. Dr. Elizabeth Blackwell is born in England. She is to become the first woman to win a medical degree in America (1849), and she also becomes the first woman entered in the *U.S. Medical Register* (1859). She will be a co-founder of the New York Infirmary for Women and Children, and will help to establish London's School of Medicine for Women in 1875.

Part-time Possibilities

Catalyst

Full-time jobs have always been more plentiful than part-time positions, particularly at managerial and professional levels. The proportion of full-time to part-time opportunities may eventually decrease. There already is evidence that nontraditional employment patterns are being studied, adapted and accepted among progressive employers here and abroad. Employment patterns so far have changed very slowly. In the future, because of changing societal needs, changing personal goals and changing life styles, more part-time positions are expected to open.

In the meantime, if you have decided on part-time work, you must understand and be prepared to discuss with prospective employers the various patterns of part-time employment that exist today and, more important, their benefits to employers. Bear in mind that, as a part-timer or full-timer, your employer's chief concern will be your capacity to "produce." Your time and skills must be converted to profits for the company, regardless of what personal needs the job is filling for you.

The advantages

The advantages of employing women as permanent part-timers are quite significant for the employer, ranging from greater productivity to lower turnover. But let's look at the benefits in greater detail so that you can clearly understand them and help your prospective employers become aware of them.

First, a larger recruitment pool is available to employers seeking part-time as well as full-time staff. This enables them to be far more selective regarding applicants' qualifications than when restricted to hiring only full-time personnel.

Second, because of the shortage of part-time jobs, the turnover rate among those who work part-time is lower than among full-timers. This factor is often reinforced by the stable life situation of the vast majority of those seeking part-time employment—women settled in their communities.

Third, studies indicate that a shorter work day or work week can increase individual productivity.

Fourth, personal chores can be done in free daytime hours by the part-timer rather than during hours taken off from work.

Finally, employment can be tailored to the time needed for the job duties rather than that needed to fill the traditional five-day, 35 or 40-hour work week. Likewise, jobs can be divided by levels of skill and pay rather than by filling the traditional work schedule of a highly-skilled person with less skilled tasks at the higher pay level.

Basic part-time patterns

Once familiar with the seven basic forms of part-time employment—and there may be other variations in the future—you can consider realistically whether any of them would be suitable for your job skills, career plans and personal life style.

Part-time Position: Any job in which one or more individuals works less than a full-time, five-day week to perform functions that

would otherwise be performed by one or more full-time individuals is a part-time position.

Job Pairing: In this flexible pattern, two women divide one full-time job with equal responsibility for the total job. Each works half-time and together they provide full-time coverage. Advantages to the employer are quite varied. Obviously, the employer gets "two heads for the price of one." Each partner works at peak efficiency, completing her tasks so that the other can proceed when she takes over. One of the pair usually is able to fill in if the job partner is unavailable for the day. Job-pairing, although by no means a widespread practice yet, has been adapted across the country—by teachers in various Massachusetts cities, by an assistant curator and research assistant at a museum in New York, by an assistant vice president and an economist at a bank in Massachusetts, by two librarians at a parochial school in New Jersey, and by a husband and wife paired as executive director and program director for a health services agency in Iowa.

Job Sharing: Two individuals divide one job between them, providing full-time coverage, but each is responsible for only half of the work. This pattern is particularly successful in such areas as social work or research, where each partner in the shared position is responsible for a separate work load. In a Catalyst demonstration project conducted for the Massachusetts Department of Public Welfare in Boston, it was shown that job-sharing case-workers on half-time schedules used their time much more efficiently than full-timers. After two years of employment, the half-time caseworkers were found to be 89 per cent as productive during their 17½-hour work week as were full-time caseworkers in 35 hours. Furthermore, the half-timers' turnover rate was 14 per cent in contrast to the prevailing turnover rate of 40 per cent.

Split-Level Position: In this employment pattern, a position is divided into two distinct levels of training or ability and the employer hires two part-time employees at different pay and skill levels to provide full-time coverage. Instead of hiring a full-time highly skilled professional who will spend part of her time in duties requiring lower-level skills, an employer may split the job between a part-time professional and a part-time skilled clerical worker, lowering the total cost and insuring optimum performance at both levels. This innovative pattern can be successful when a social worker and a community paraprofessional share a job or, in business, when a publishing company executive splits a job between a writer-researcher and an editorial assistant.

Split-Location Position: One individual performs part of her work in an office and part at home. The specific schedule usually is determined by the particular work and the need for concentration and communication. This form of part-time employment is proving to be efficient and profitable for employer and employee. There are various ways to implement split-location employment and they can add up to full work weeks or less. Some women with small children work part-time at home and part-time at the office, according to

1825. Hannah Lord Montague, weary of scrubbing her husband's shirts when only the collars require it, invents the hugely fashionable detachable collar by scissoring a few of his shirts, thereby also launching the major industry of Troy, New York, where she lives.

professional and personal needs. Many eventually return to full office schedules as home demands decrease. Various kinds of work can be adapted to split-location, particularly such creative piecework as that done by editors and commercial artists. Other career fields also lend to split-location positions. A part-time senior systems analyst in New York works two full days each week in her Manhattan office and one full day each week in her suburban home. Consultations with other analysts, part of her job responsibilities, take place during scheduled office days while the independent research-oriented work that makes up the bulk of her duties can be done in the office or at home.

Consultant or Specialist: When a particular type of expertise is not needed on a full-time basis, the progressive employer hires a part-time professional as a permanent part of the company's labor force on a regular but less than full-time schedule. Such specialists or experts range from accountants to engineering consultants, from publicists to guidance counselors. Specialists may work an abbreviated weekly schedule or only when their services are needed, paid by the hour or according to a pre-determined retainer. Specialists may, in fact, work for more than one company or organization simultaneously in the capacity of consultant. Often, in this employment pattern, the consultants are able to determine their own hours which may vary from month to month or season to season, depending on the work load. They may work in a home office or a more formal setting.

Short-Term Position: This flexible pattern is suitable when a full-time or part-time employee is hired to work on a special project for a limited time only and is not considered a permanent member of the staff. The limited time, however, could be three months for one job or three years for another. The specialist handling such a job could be an architect, an interior designer, an engineer, a publicist, a management consultant or someone in yet another field. The short-term employee is likely to handle just one special project at a time but could handle several, depending upon the field and project.

Employer concerns

Now that the benefits and basic forms of part-time employment have been detailed, let's turn to specific areas that concern employers and often cause many of them to exclude part-time scheduling entirely from their employment policies.

First, many employers feel that unless all employees work the same hours, a communications gap may occur among them or between a company and its clients. As more and more companies move away from rigid work styles and toward innovations such as part-time and other flexible work patterns, they are finding—and reporting—that variations in employees' schedules are resulting not only in increased involvement in and commitment to the job but in better internal and external communications.

Second, many employers feel it is a lot more costly to hire part-timers in terms of both overall finances and employee benefits. In general, using part-time staff can add up to a savings rather than a financial drain. Employers hiring part-timers on most of the work schedules described are reporting greater productivity, heightened efficiency, reduced absenteeism, lower turnover and reduced training costs.

Moreover, employers can construct a fringe benefits package for permanent part-time personnel that is not excessively expensive for the employer and does not exploit the part-time employee. This is possible because most fringe benefits—including vacation, holidays and sick leave—are compensatory benefits and can be pro-rated. In the case of statutory benefits such as Social Security that cannot be pro-rated, the additional cost to the employer, if any, can be offset by the deletion of supplementary benefits such as medical or life insurance in their entirety or in part. There is no significant incremental cost to the employer for two part-time employees earning a combined salary of $12,000 or less, or more than $24,000. Between $12,000 and $24,000, however, the cost to the employer of Social Security benefits is twice as much for two part-time employees as it is for one full-time employee. It is in this instance that you could suggest a deletion of some of the employer's supplementary benefits to offset the increase.

Once you are aware that employers have been wrong on both points—part-time causing a communications gap and a financial drain—and you are aware of the facts of other aspects of part-time employment, you should be convinced—and convincing to prospective employers—of the great value of part-time work.

Don't be afraid to remind your prospective employer that an increasing number of executives today are being applauded for their innovative leadership in developing part-time work schedules for college-educated women like you who are earnestly seeking responsible, less than full-time job commitments.

The Two-family Commune
Letty Cottin Pogrebin

Two couples in a large city have devised a four-way cooperative that works beautifully for them. The wives are housewives-teachers; the husbands are househusbands-law students. They live across the hall from one another in an apartment house. Each couple has two young children. Through pooled efforts each of the adults is "on duty" for three consecutive hours every day (which amounts to the total twelve hours of waking time of the kids). An intercom system keeps both apartments in touch. Each adult does the weekly marketing for both families once a month. Babysitting is cooperative. Meals, laundry and housecleaning chores are pooled and shared. In this way the adults each have nine hours of free time per day—time to work, study, read or relax. It sounds like heaven.

If the temperament of your neighbors and all of your work schedules allow it, such an experiment might be worth a try. But remember to divide the tasks four ways evenly—and not by sex-typed jobs. No cop-outs ("that's women's work") permitted.

Whether in a communal situation or in the privacy of a nuclear household, the challenge is the same: to share domestic roles, to enrich women's lives and to give dignity and value to Home Work. Admittedly, the "man-of-the-house" is being asked to give up age-old power and privilege. We know that privilege is habit-forming and power is not easily relinquished. As wives, we sympathize with our husbands' period of adjustment. But as women we must agitate and insist that working housewives get their share of justice, fairness and tangible rewards out of life.

1825. The United Tailoresses Society of New York, the first women's labor organization, is founded. In 1831, six hundred of its members will strike for over four weeks in a demand for higher wages.

She's a physician, he's a professor of chemistry. They have a two-year-old child. When the babysitter doesn't show up one morning, which parent stays home?

He's a New York lawyer, she's a book editor. He gets a fabulous job offer in Minneapolis. She can't find comparable work because there's no book publishing industry in Minneapolis. Do they move anyway?

He's a musician, she's an executive. Her company offers her a promotion with a hefty raise. Taking it means she would earn more money than her husband. Does she accept?

She has to prepare for her speech tomorrow. He's working against a deadline on his article. The kids are hungry. Who makes dinner?

These are just a few of the daily decisions faced by couples in an admittedly elite group known as the two-career families. What makes them different from other working couples is the professional nature of the wife's work. It is assumed that her career commitment is as great as her husband's, that the demands of her work are as important, and that she is motivated by intellectual rather than economic need.

Unfortunately, real life isn't that easy. Two-career families also function within our culture and are therefore subject to the same sex-role pressures and the same standards of marital "normality" as everyone else. Because of this, the difficulties experienced by two-career families are simply *intensified* examples of all couples' work-family adjustments.

In this time of radical change in women's roles, the dual-career family can be a mirror on *your future* whether or not you're a professional.

Mobility

In conventional families the wife is supposed to say, "whither thou goest I will go." If her husband is transferred to a better job, she packs and picks up stakes no matter how hard it may be to leave her job or her friends. However, for two-career couples, this rule can't be applied with biblical rigidity. Each professional person needs the freedom to move wherever opportunity beckons. He or she also needs the right to stay put in order to develop a career, rather than be uprooted by the spouse. These two provisos can easily clash. I've found that most two-career couples approach the problem from a practical standpoint, not according to "the man wears the pants" theory.

David Dretzin, an attorney, is married to Joanna Merlin, casting director and sometime actress. He speculates: "If she was unhappy here, I would think seriously about moving. We certainly would move for her physical health so why not for her mental and emotional well-being. Joanna isn't hooked on a specific job but she has to be working in some productive,

creative capacity related to the theatre. Because I understand this, I can't say I have a calling and my wife just has a job. But any specific move would have to depend on whether I could find a good position in the new location, or else whether we could all live on her income."

Many couples justify short-term separations for long term gains. Ray McGuire, a professor who teaches in Maine, cares for his two children all week while his wife, Judy, goes to graduate school in Massachusetts. The family reunites every weekend.

In contrast, Jan and Richard McLain of LaCross, Wisconsin, openly resolved that neither of them will entertain thoughts of moving just for career advancement. "He's a sales manager. I'm a newspaper reporter. We could do our kind of jobs anywhere but we love it here and it's a perfect place to raise our son, so why rock the boat," says Jan McLain.

Sometimes when one spouse is offered a good position, it's possible to negotiate with the company or university to get them to provide a good job for the other spouse too. Stanford, MIT, Oberlin and Hampshire College are among those institutions who hire married couples to share a single job. For example, Pat and Steve Brenner split one teaching job at Iowa's Grinnell College; other couples split jobs as university administrators. Such ideal situations are impossible to arrange if colleges have a nepotism rule that precludes hiring relatives onto the same staff. In most cases one job opportunity is offered to one member of the couple, and the other spouse is expected to come along and take the jobhunting risks. Usually, it's the woman who takes pot luck finding a suitable job in the wake of her husband's move. Her problems are compounded by widespread and generalized discrimination against women. Ironically, if the opposite happens and the man follows his wife's career moves, the family unit profits because he stands a better chance of finding a well-paid new job in our pro-male job market.

Money and status

If we weren't programmed from birth to believe that men must be superior to women in salary and status (as well as height, size, age and education) this subject would not arouse guilt and ego trauma. But we are, and it does—except for some.

Over three million American wives earn more than their husbands but many professional women honestly confess that they can't allow that to happen to them. "I'm balancing my career and marriage on a tightrope as it is," says one advertising woman. "If I threatened his male ego in the financial area, the whole act might tumble down."

Competition—whether in money, honors or public recognition—is a major hazard. Ursula and Warren Farrell, both feminists, moved to Washington, D.C., when she won a White

1828. The first labor strike by American women occurs this year in Dover, New Hampshire, over a wage cut and a refusal to consider their demand for the reduction of the workday from ten hours. The women are needleworkers.

310 Dual Career Family
WORKING

Letty Cottin Pogrebin

House Fellowship. Warren, a political scientist, gave up a teaching job at Rutger's University. In Washington, he was surprised at how hard it was to be introduced constantly as "the husband of." He felt the bite of being secondary—going to sherry parties while Ursula lunched with politicians and statesmen. He began to understand women's resentment about standing "behind" their men. "It can get to you after a while," he says.

To avoid the bitterness of competition, wives seem to do most of the accommodating—by consciously promoting their husband's brilliance, affecting a submissive role in their private life and curbing their own careers.

Integrating work/home/marriage/children

For professional couples, hired help seems a virtual necessity, especially when there are young children. Still, the happy, well-functioning two-career families find that balancing work schedules with the demands of the home requires the kind of sharing that ignores standard sex-role divisions of labor.

"Everybody does everything," says Gail Parker, president of Bennington College. Her husband, Thomas, vice president of the College shares the cooking and the care of their young child.

Architect Richard Newman makes breakfast and prepares his son's boxed lunch. Jay Harnick supervises bedtimes, reads stories, plays with the children in the park. Richard McLain irons and alternates cooking. David Dretzin says, "I do the grunt work and other jobs where lesser skills are required, like setting the table or doing dishes."

These men and several of those surveyed in Lynda Lytle Holmstrom's study "The Two-Career Family," commented not on the indignity of men doing housework but on the drudgery and tedium inherent in the work itself. While many women feel guilty "imposing" on their husband's time, the men take their wives' work seriously enough to assume house-

hold responsibilities so that both partners have more time to work and to enjoy each other. "I suppose I could demand my male right to relax at the end of a long, hard day," says an engineer whose wife works in government. "But then I'd never get to spend time with her. Housework gets done in half the time when two people do it—then there are hours left over for both of us to enjoy together."

Professional marriages seem to thrive on an intellectual respect that spills over into other aspects of the couple's life. Several commented that their sexual relationships were best when each partner felt a strong personal identity and particularly when the wife felt valued for herself. A few couples also made the point that busy, tired professionals feel freer to skip sex without having it interpreted as a rejection of the partner.

When babysitting problems arise or a child is sick, these couples respond to each crisis according to who can most easily accommodate that day's work schedule to the needs of the children. This might mean missing a class, postponing a meeting or working at home that day. In most cases, the professional's high status or autonomous work set-up permits maximum flexibility. People on regular eight-hour jobs alternate absences from work during those rare emergencies. But in everyday situations, babysitters or other surrogates make more than adequate stand-ins. "I've learned I'm not so indispensable," says Joanna Merlin. "Someone else can take my kids to the dentist as well as I can. I'll count the fillings when I get home."

There was overwhelming agreement among the families I questioned, that it was good for children of both sexes to perceive each of their parents in worldly roles. The kids seem to get an extra measure of excitement out of life, too.

Social lives of two-career families are generally less active than average because of the excessive career demands. But these families appear to gain great satisfaction from spending free hours with one another, their children and their professional colleagues. When they do entertain, the wives still do most of the cooking and planning. But the husbands recognize the toll on women's energies and they compensate by doing the shopping or clean-up or by planning restaurant celebrations instead of at-home parties. At social gatherings or during after-dinner discussions, these couples and their friends rarely split up according to sex. Men and women together seem as comfortable talking about their children as about their jobs, national politics or the economy.

Separate vacations may well be the last frontier for the dual-career couple. But most of their other adjustments are neither radical, nor out of reach for every working couple. They are accommodations based on an equal evaluation of the time and career commitment of both husband and wife. Ideally, none of us should have to be high-powered professionals to achieve this kind of harmony, consideration and respect.

Olschewski

1828. Sarah Josepha Hale takes charge of *The Ladies' Magazine* editorial department. In 1837 the magazine is merged into *Godey's Ladies' Book* of Philadelphia. She is America's first female magazine editor, and the author of numerous books and articles on women's interests. In addition, she devises the jingle "Mary Had a Little Lamb."

1829. Anne Royall, fearless gossipmonger and pioneer American newspaper woman, forces President John Quincy Adams to grant her an interview by sitting on his clothes while he bathes in the Potomac.

The Politics of Housework   Pat Mainardi

Liberated women—very different from women's liberation! The first signals all kinds of goodies, to warm the hearts (not to mention other parts) of the most radical men. The other signals—*housework*. The first brings sex without marriage, sex before marriage, cozy housekeeping arrangements ("You see, I'm living with this chick") and the self-content of knowing that you're not the kind of man who wants a doormat instead of a woman. That will come later. After all, who wants that old commodity anymore, the Standard American Housewife, all husband, home and kids. The New Commodity, the Liberated Woman, has sex a lot and has a Career, preferably something that can be fitted in with the household chores—like dancing, pottery, or painting.

On the other hand is women's liberation—and housework. What? You say this is all trivial? Wonderful! That's what I thought. It seemed perfectly reasonable. We both had careers, both had to work a couple of days a week to earn enough to live on, so why shouldn't we share the housework? So I suggested it to my mate and he agreed—most men are too hip to turn you down flat. "You're right," he said, "It's only fair."

Then an interesting thing happened. I can only explain it by stating that we women have been brainwashed more than even we can imagine. Probably too many years of seeing television women in ecstasy over their shiny waxed floors or breaking down over their dirty shirt collars. Men have no such conditioning. They recognize the essential fact of housework right from the very beginning. Which is that it stinks. Here's my list of dirty chores: buying groceries, carting them home and putting them away; cooking meals and washing dishes and pots; doing the laundry, digging out the place when things get out of control; washing floors. The list could go on but the sheer necessities are bad enough. All of us have to do these things, or get some one else to do them for us. The longer my husband contemplated these chores the more repulsed he became, and so proceeded the change from the normally sweet considerate Dr. Jekyll into the crafty Mr. Hyde who would stop at nothing to avoid the horrors of—*housework*. As he felt himself backed into a corner laden with dirty dishes, brooms, mops, and reeking garbage, his front teeth grew longer and pointier, his fingernails haggled and his eyes grew wild. Housework trivial? Not on your life! Just try to share the burden.

So ensued a dialogue that's been going on for several years. Here are some of the high points:

"I don't mind sharing the housework, but I don't do it very well. We should each do the things we're best at."

Meaning: Unfortunately I'm no good at things like

washing dishes or cooking. What I do best is a little light carpentry, changing light bulbs, moving furniture (*how often do you move furniture?*).

Also Meaning: Historically the lower classes (black men and us) have had hundreds of years experience doing menial jobs. It would be a waste of manpower to train someone else to do them now.

Also Meaning: I don't like the dull stupid boring jobs, so you should do them.

"I don't mind sharing the work, but you'll have to show me how to do it."

Meaning: I ask a lot of questions and you'll have to show me everything everytime I do it because I don't remember so good. Also don't try to sit down and read while I'm doing my jobs because I'm going to annoy hell out of you until it's easier to do them yourself.

"We used to be so happy!" (Said whenever it was his turn to do something.)

Meaning: I used to be so happy.

Meaning: Life without housework is bliss. (*No quarrel here. Perfect agreement.*)

"We have different standards, and why should I have to work to your standards. That's unfair."

Meaning: If I begin to get bugged by the dirt and crap I will say "This place sure is a sty" or "How can anyone live like this?" and wait for your reaction. I know that all women have a sore called "Guilt over a messy house" or "Household work is ultimately my responsibility." I know that men have caused that sore—if anyone visits and the place *is* a sty, they're not going to leave and say, "He sure is a lousy housekeeper." You'll take the rap in any case. I can outwait you.

Also Meaning: I can provoke innumerable scenes over the housework issue. Eventually doing all the housework yourself will be less painful to you than trying to get me to do half. Or I'll suggest we get a maid. She will do my share of the work. You will do yours. It's women's work.

"I've got nothing against sharing the housework, but you can't make me do it on your schedule."

Meaning: Passive resistance. I'll do it when I damned well please, if at all. If my job is doing dishes, it's easier to do them once a week. If taking out laundry, once a month. If washing the floors, once a year. If you don't like it, do it yourself oftener, and then I won't do it at all.

"I *hate* it more than you. You don't mind it so much."

Meaning: Housework is garbage work. It's the worst crap I've ever done. It's degrading and humiliating for someone of *my* intelligence to do it. But for someone of *your* intelligence . . .

"Housework is too trivial to even talk about."

Meaning: It's even more trivial to do. Housework is be-

1830. Belva Ann Lockwood, well-known American lawyer, is born. Twice nominated to the presidency of the United States, in 1879 she becomes the first woman to practice law before the American Supreme Court.

Politics of Housework
WORKING   313

neath my status. My purpose in life is to deal with matters of significance. Yours is to deal with matters of insignificance. You should do the housework.

"This problem of housework is not a man-woman problem! In any relationship between two people one is going to have a stronger personality and dominate."
Meaning: That stronger personality had better be *me*.

"In animal societies, wolves, for example, the top animal is usually a male even where he is not chosen for brute strength but on the basis of cunning and intelligence. Isn't that interesting?"
Meaning: I have historical, psychological, anthropological, and biological justification for keeping you down. How can you ask the top wolf to be equal?

"Women's liberation isn't really a political movement."
Meaning: The Revolution is coming too close to home.
Also Meaning: I am only interested in how *I* am oppressed, not how I oppress others. Therefore the war, the draft, and the university are political. Women's liberation is not.

"Man's accomplishments have always depended on getting help from other people, mostly women. What great man would have accomplished what he did if he had to do his own housework?"
Meaning: Oppression is built into the System and I, as the white American male receive the benefits of this System. I don't want to give them up.

New York Public Library

Postscript

Participatory democracy begins at home. If you are planning to implement your politics, there are certain things to remember.

1. He *is* feeling it more than you. He's losing some leisure and you're gaining it. The measure of your oppression is his resistance.

2. A great many American men are not accustomed to doing monotonous repetitive work which never ushers in any lasting let alone important achievement. This is why they would rather repair a cabinet than wash dishes. If human endeavors are like a pyramid with man's highest achievements at the top, then keeping oneself alive is at the bottom. Men have always had servants (us) to take care of this bottom strata of life while they have confined their efforts to the rarefied upper regions. It is thus ironic when they ask of women—where are your great painters, statesmen, etc? Mme. Matisse ran a millinery shop so he could paint. Mrs. Martin Luther King kept his house and raised his babies.

3. It is a traumatizing experience for someone who has always thought of himself as being against any oppression or exploitation of one human being by another to realize that in his daily life he has been accepting and implementing (and benefiting from) this exploitation; that his rationalization is little different from that of the racist who says "Black people don't feel pain" (women don't mind doing the shitwork); and that the oldest form of oppression in history has been the oppression of 50 percent of the population by the other 50 percent.

4. Arm yourself with some knowledge of the psychology of oppressed peoples everywhere, and a few facts about the animal kingdom. I admit playing top wolf or who runs the gorillas is silly but as a last resort men bring it up all the time. Talk about bees. If you feel really hostile bring up the sex life of spiders. They have sex. She bites off his head.

    The psychology of oppressed people is not silly. Jews, immigrants, black men, and all women have employed the same psychological mechanisms to survive: admiring the oppressor, glorifying the oppressor, wanting to be like the oppressor, wanting the oppressor to like them, mostly because the oppressor held all the power.

5. In a sense, all men everywhere are slightly schizoid —divorced from the reality of maintaining life. This makes it easier for them to play games with it. It is almost a cliché that women feel greater grief at sending a son off to war or losing him to that war because they bore him, suckled him, and raised him. The men who foment those wars did none of those things and have a more superficial estimate of the worth of human life. One hour a day is a low estimate of the amount of time one has to spend "keeping" oneself. By foisting this off on others, man gains seven hours

1830. Anna Slazak, a farm servant living near Prague, Bohemia, reputedly invents the Polka.

a week—one working day more to play with his mind and not his human needs. Over the course of generations it is easy to see whence evolved the horrifying abstractions of modern life.

6. With the death of each form of oppression, life changes and new forms evolve. English aristocrats at the turn of the century were horrified at the idea of enfranchising working men—were sure that it signaled the death of civilization and a return to barbarism. Some working men were even deceived by this line. Similarly with the minimum wage, abolition of slavery, and female suffrage. Life changes but it goes on. Don't fall for any line about the death of everything if men take a turn at the dishes. They will imply that you are holding back the Revolution (their Revolution). But you are advancing it (your Revolution).

7. Keep checking up. Periodically consider who's actually *doing* the jobs. These things have a way of backsliding so that a year later once again the woman is doing everything. After a year make a list of jobs the man has rarely if ever done. You will find cleaning pots, toilets, refrigerators and ovens high on the list. Use time sheets if necessary. He will accuse you of being petty. He is above that sort of thing—(housework). Bear in mind what the worst jobs are, namely the ones that have to be done every day or several times a day. Also the ones that are dirty—it's more pleasant to pick up books, newspapers, etc. than to wash dishes. Alternate the bad jobs. It's the daily grind that gets you down. Also make sure that you don't have the responsibility for the housework with occasional help from him. "I'll cook dinner for you tonight" implies it's really your job and isn't he a nice guy to do some of it for you.

8. Most men had a rich and rewarding bachelor life during which they did not starve or become encrusted with crud or buried under the litter. There is a taboo that says that women mustn't strain themselves in the presence of men: we haul around 50 pounds of groceries if we have to but aren't allowed to open a jar if there is someone around to do it for us. The reverse side of the coin is that men aren't supposed to be able to take care of themselves without a woman. Both are excuses for making women do the housework.

9. Beware of the double whammy. He won't do the little things he always did because you're now a "Liberated Woman," right? Of course he won't do anything else either . . .

I was just finishing this when my husband came in and asked what I was doing. Writing a paper on housework. Housework? He said, *Housework?* Oh my god how trivial can you get. A paper on housework.

1831. Mary Louise Booth, American author and translator, is born. Her ability during the Civil War to translate French works favoring the Union into stirring prose is to win her special praise from President Lincoln. In 1867, she will become the original editor of *Harper's Bazaar* magazine and continue there until her death in 1889.

A Model Contract for Household

Why There Should Be a Code of Standards

Household workers, who are commonly referred to as domestics, number 1.5 to 3 million. They have existed on a median annual income of about $2,365 with virtually no benefits. They were excluded from federal minimum-wage legislation until the 1974 Minimum Wage and Overtime Amendments went into effect on May 1, 1974.

Almost 98 percent of all household workers are women, most of whom are partly self-supporting or heads of families. Black women comprise over half of this segment of the labor force.

This Code of Standards was devised by the National Committee on Household Employment (NCHE) to assist in developing a responsible and responsive business relationship between the household worker and the employer.

It is the NCHE's belief that the image and dignity of household employment will be improved only through the adoption of standards which raise wages, hours and working conditions to levels which reflect the value of the services performed.

Wages

Wages should be paid according to the cost of living of a particular area. They should be at least the minimum provided by the Federal Fair Labor Standards Act: $2.00 on Jan. 1, 1975; $2.20 on Jan. 1, 1976 and $2.30 on Jan. 1, 1977. Higher wages should be paid for jobs requiring special training or skills. Pay periods should be

From *The NCHE Code of Standards for Household Employment* by the National Committee on Household Employment.

agreed upon in advance. Clothing and/or food should not be considered part of payment.

Hours

Live-in Workers. For any hours in excess of 40 hours a week, the pay should be at one and one-half the regular hourly rate. Hours in excess of 48 hours a week should be paid for at double the regular rate.

Workers employed on a **full-time** weekly basis by a single employer should be paid one and one-half the hourly rate for hours worked in excess of 48 hours a week.

Benefits

Social Security. Earnings should be reported and payments made in accordance with the 1951 law for Social Security credit toward old age, survivors, and disability insurance. Quarterly reports from the employers should be made to the Internal Revenue Service on IRS form #942. Further information about social security can be obtained from your local social security office, which can also check your record to make sure your earnings have been filed. There is no charge for this service by the Social Security Administration.

Sick Leave. Employees should receive at least one day of paid sick leave a year for each day per week worked.

Vacations. **Full-time** workers should receive two weeks of paid vacation for one year of service. **Part-time** employees should receive at least two days of paid vacation a year for each day per week worked. For longer service there should be an increase in paid vacation time.

Holidays. Live-in workers should receive a minimum of eight legal holidays with pay a year. **Full-time live-out** employees should receive the equivalent of six legal holidays with pay a year. A **day worker** should receive at least one legal holiday a year.

Facts about Private Household Workers

- Of the more than one million women who work in this occupation, 180,000 are the heads of families.

- Of the 455,000 individuals employed on a full-time basis, one out of every three works more than 40 hours a week.

- The median age of women who are employed as private household workers is over 50.

- One of every seven household workers currently employed is 65 years of age or older.

From *Women Workers Today*, 1974, Women's Bureau, Department of Labor.

1831. The British government, failing to interest its young women citizens in emigrating to Australia, presses several cargoes of girls from the workhouses and orphanages aboard ship. By 1836, 14,000 such women will have been compelled to settle in the colonies of New South Wales, till then composed almost completely of male criminals from England.

Employment

Working Relationships

A written agreement between employer and employee should clearly define the duties of the position, including specific tasks, how often they must be performed, and the desired standards. Schedules with provisions for rest periods, meal times, telephone privileges, and time out for private activities (such as church attendance for live-in employees) should be agreed upon in advance of employment.

Promptness, integrity, and courtesy should be observed by both parties.

Efficient, safe, and workable appliances and cleaning aids should be provided and used carefully.

Adequate provisions for maximum safety and health should be maintained at all times.

Pleasant and private quarters should be provided for live-in employees.

If an employer does not require the services of a day worker for the agreed upon time, the employee should be notified at least a week in advance or be compensated in full by the employer. The employee has the responsibility of notifying the employer as soon as possible if unable to report to work.

A professional working relationship should be maintained by both parties. This includes proper forms of address for both employee and employer and their respective families.

Work and work relationships should be periodically evaluated with the intent of improving efficiency and understanding.

**Model Contract Form
for Household Employment**

NAME OF EMPLOYEE _____

This contract binds each party to the terms agreed upon below. The terms shall be developed to coincide with the NCHE Code of Standards.

1. WAGES (at least the federal minimum)
2. LUNCH AND BREAK TIME
3. RAISE INCREASE PER YEAR
4. SOCIAL SECURITY
5. VACATIONS
6. PAID HOLIDAYS
7. SICK LEAVE (days per year)
8. EMPLOYEE DUTIES
9. PROBATIONARY PERIOD

_____
Employer's Signature
_____
Employee's Signature
_____
Date

1834. Sarah Flower Adams composes the immortal hymn "Nearer, My God, to Thee."

How to Organize a Union

Jean Maddox and Pamela Allen

A union is a legally recognized group of employees who negotiate their terms of employment with their employer through collective bargaining. Employees are able to deal with their employer from a position of mutual strength and respect, and to participate in the decision-making. Without a union, employees are subject to the whims of management and individual employees are often discriminated against in many ways. Thus one of the reasons for organizing is because with group strength, you have power and also protection.

Some of the aspects of work that employees can negotiate are salary ranges, raises, promotion procedures, job classification, child care, health and safety, grievance procedure, and job security.

No Blueprint. Under the National Labor Relations Act employees are guaranteed the right to organize, to form or join unions, or to engage in other concerted group activities for the purpose of collective bargaining or other mutual aid or protection. It must be group activity, not individual. But two people can be a caucus; from that you build. You should work slowly and you should know the laws before you surface.

There is no blueprint for when your caucus should surface. It depends on the existing situation. However, do not surface before your initial organizing committee has done adequate research on the company (profits, general policy, existing problems, etc.), has full knowledge of your rights under the NLRB (National Labor Relations Board), and has at least worked out a general program of what it intends to accomplish in terms of bettering existing working conditions. Write or call your area NLRB and request copies of "A Layman's Guide to Basic Law under the National Labor Relations Act."

If you have a strong, unified group in one department of your company which is ready to take action within their department to correct existing problems, it would probably be wise for that group to surface even though you have no strong overall group. You can then use this group's successes to start organizing the rest of the company. Of course, weaknesses and failures of this initial group effort should be analyzed and used to strengthen the next move.

How to Get an Election. To petition for an NLRB election an association or union must have a minimum of 30% of the employees within the bargaining unit (the company) authorizing it to represent them. This can be done either by secret authorization cards

or a petition or both. Some employees, because they are afraid of harrassment by the employer, will prefer the secret cards. Others will not hesitate to sign the petition as this provides greater protection under the NLRB. It must be made clear to all signing that both are secret and only the NLRB (and not the company) will examine them.

Most unions prefer that 50% of the employees sign up before filing for an election with the NLRB. Here proper timing is of the essence for the NLRB does not usually set the election date within 30 days and often, due to company pressure, will set the date far into the future. Under some circumstances if organizing is going well and employees are signing rapidly, you could file after obtaining 30% and utilize the time before the election to finish signing up people. But if sign-ups are slow, you probably should wait until you have obtained 50%. In any case, try to get the election set as soon as possible because once people have signed authorization for a union or association to represent them, they're ready to move forward with the work of collective bargaining.

It is possible to win representation without going through an NLRB hearing and election. Quite often, if a union is successful in getting a large majority of workers signed up for representation, they can then get a disinterested party—for example, a priest—to check the names on the sign-up cards (or petition) and inform the employer that the union does indeed have a majority of the employees interested in joining the union. The employer may agree to recognize the union. If he does, he will notify the NLRB accordingly and proceed with negotiations and setting up a bargaining unit.

Most employers push for an election, however, because they believe that in the length of time it takes before an election, they can intimidate people to keep them from voting for the union. Be prepared to counter all the employer's tactics.

Assess Your Strengths. Be sure you are strong enough to counter the employer's tactics before you surface and file for an election. For example, it might be necessary to put out a daily leaflet countering the employer's charges. (This is why it is essential that you have already done your research both of the company and the law). In assessing your strength, you will need to determine how many people you have to work on your organizing campaign, as well as how much support you have among the other employees. For example, if you worked in a company with 500 employees

and only 25 were in your organizing caucus, it might be premature to surface unless you'd had some large meetings attended by other workers or a large number who already signed authorization cards.

For your protection, it's important to have the names of all the people who are part of your organizing caucus on the letter which goes to your employer, informing him you have filed for an election. Then the employer doesn't dare fire any of those people because that is definitely an unfair labor practice.

Broaden Your Support. It is important to set up an organizational structure and to keep minutes of your meetings. This is proof that you have indeed been meeting as a group. Set up committees to research the company and labor law, to check out unions and associations, to contact other union women and women's groups, and to begin work on a shop newsletter. In the beginning move very slowly. You've got to know the facts: what goes on in your company and what the possibilities are for organizing. Below are some guidelines for an organizing caucus to follow in its preparations for surfacing.

Investigate the Company. It is a good idea to get a salary scale and figure out what everybody is making, which includes spelling out the fringe benefits (such as vacation, sick time and health plans). Research the employer: how much do he and the stockholders make? This is important in turning people off, once they see how much profit is being made from their work.

Research the physical layout of the company (who works where) and make a floor plan. Try to make contacts in each department and determine the best way to contact people. Also find out what bothers people, both the large issues and the small things, such as the bothersome "K" that's stuck on the typewriter.

Mailing List. Once you've petitioned for an election, then the employer is required to give you the names and addresses of the employees through the NLRB. But time is growing short. You need the list earlier if possible. One group circulated a peition for saving whales. This is a noncontroversial kind of petition where they nongot the names and address of everyone in the office. Another way to get a mailing list of the people you are trying to organize is Christmas lists; most large companies have them.

It is also important to make contact in the data processing department. These workers are among the most militant because their

1835. Ranavalona, queen of Madagascar, bars Christians from her island and clamps down hard on local unrest by putting over two hundred native lords to death. Eventually all Europeans are forbidden access to the land, and the queen's sea forces become infamous for their piracy against nations trading with Africa.

John Getsinger

work is boring and conditions miserable.

Meetings. When you hold meetings, make sure they aren't boring. Don't try to buy votes with prizes to people for coming to meetings; this can turn people off. When setting up a meeting, plan it. Start on time. Be sure that you have someone to chair who can stimulate the people and keep the discussion rolling and to the point. Have an agenda and stick to it. Limit the number of items to discuss; there will be other meetings.

At the meeting summarize where you are to date and what your plans are for the future. Ask for input. Make sure that every person who comes to your meetings has an assignment to do something—even if it is just to make one phone call. This builds a chain of participation. If people are just talked at and not invited to participate, they drop out.

In large companies putting out a regular shop newsletter is very important. It should emphasize two things: (1) company muck-raking and (2) how group unity and activity can be successful in changing or correcting the existing problems. Cartoons and a question-and-answer section are good methods to use.

Choosing a Union. You can remain independent or negotiate with a union to get the best deal possible for your group. Survey different contracts in your field to find which union gets the best contracts. Find out which unions will agree to your

organizing committee having input into the organizing campaign. If yours is a large company, will the union agree to hiring one of your members to work as an organizer or negotiator? Once the union has won, will the union agree to rank-and-file participation? How does the union treat women?

Many times workers believe rank-and-file members working under a union contract more than union organizers. Try to establish contact with rank-and-file organizing committees and invite some of these workers who are unionized and working under similar conditions to come to your meetings to discuss their contracts and answer questions. This can help you evaluate the particular union as well as demonstrate why you need to unionize.

Leaflets. An outside group such as WAGE can be helpful in passing out leaflets (without your names) to test interest. At the bottom of the leaflet have a coupon for people to clip out and send to an address, so you can begin to get an idea of who is interested and who is not. The address does not have to be of any person in the organizing caucus; it can be a women's group or other community group.

Overcoming Divisions. The biggest problem of all is uniting workers. Management will attempt to utilize racism, sexism and age to keep the workers divided. You must confront and fight all these attempts.

Your choice of issues can also divide workers, if you're not careful. For example,

a group of young women organized to fight for maternity benefits and maternity leaves. They were successful in winning these but it turned off the older women, who were past the child bearing age and were concerned about pensions because they could see the time drawing near when they would retire. In organizing you have to take into consideration all the various groups and degrees of consciousness of the people on the job. Use your shop newsletter to raise these points to develop understanding among the workers of the need for unity, including the need to support other workers' demands and needs.

Consciousness Raising. It is often necessary for those who are organizing to speak quietly and individually with workers, doing a sort of consciousness raising, combatting their fears and building their own self worth, strength and militancy.

A lot of women are afraid of what management will think of them because we are socialized to be good and do our job well in order to get male approval. Women can also fear the estimation of their peer group. Often in offices there is competition for who is best dressed, who can type the fastest, is most accurate with figures, etc. This type of competition is stimulated by the employers and women themselves become a part of it. Again use your shop newsletter.

Another problem is the attitude of husbands and friends. We have often had experiences where women who were very pro-union had husbands who would raise hell with them for wanting to organize. (This, or course, works both ways: wives can oppose their husbands' organizing activities too.) We have even had experiences where a pro-union man believed it was all right for him, but not for her, to organize.

Don't underestimate female supervisors who can be used against you. Once a woman is in a supervisorial job, she is forced to carry out management's orders or she is fired. Women are not always sisters, just as men are not always brothers.

Evaluate Your Work. If your efforts aren't growing, you need to evaluate why and try something new to correct it. Whatever you do, do something. Keep trying. As time goes on, people will become interested and active at different times, depending on their jobs, their other commitments, or what they think of your group and what it is doing.

Some people, when they find that signing the authorization card is secret, will sign, but they won't do anything else. Don't turn them off or make them feel they're not wanted. Be patient, good humored and motivated. One of the things you have to keep emphasizing, especially with women, is the right and importance of workers to unite on the job and fight for their rights. It's got to become a slogan for women: to unite together for those things which rightfully belong to them.

1837. South Hadley Female Seminary (later Mount Holyoke College) opens—the result of pioneer efforts by Mary Lyon. It is the first American college-level institution exclusively for women.

In Defense of Unpaid Labor

Ellen Sulzberger Straus

The official position of the National Organization for Women remains unchanged since the wordy manifesto of 1971, which challenged the "beneficial effects of service volunteering not only for women but for society" and went on to attempt a distinction between change-oriented volunteer activities and volunteer activities that serve to "maintain women's dependent and secondary status."

Congresswoman Bella Abzug (Dem.-N.Y.) recently "employed" volunteers to work in her district office to plan a community conference. Journalist Pat Joblin is charged with the task of finding volunteers to provide child-care services so that mothers may attend the meetings of the Manhattan Women's Political

Adapted from *Ms.* Magazine, February 1975. Copyright © 1975 Ms. Magazine Corporation. Reprinted with permission.

The Working Woman's Unemployment Checklist
Letty Cottin Pogrebin

Be prepared before unemployment strikes. Find out the answer to every question on this checklist.

1. Must you give advance notice of your resignation? How much notice is required? Must notice be given in writing?
2. Will you get your unused vacation and sick pay if you quit?
3. What are your chances of getting a good reference?
4. Can you continue group insurance coverage after you leave?
5. Does your firm have a voluntary or mandatory retirement policy? What are your pension and/or profit-sharing rights? Are pension benefits portable to your next job?
6. Do you know what job security measures protect you from dismissal? Have you read your employment contract, union contract, tenure provisions, or company policy statements on justifiable reasons for termination?
7. If you are fired, is there an appeals procedure? A grievance review? Were you given adequate notice?
8. What severance pay is given to fired employees? How is it correlated with duration of employment?
9. What happens to your accumulated vacation and sick leave if you are fired?
10. What termination reasons would disqualify you for unemployment insurance in your state?
11. Does your company have a layoff plan that details who will be let go first if cutbacks are necessary? Is this based on seniority or departmental priorities?
12. Is your employer a participant in the unemployment insurance program? Are you covered? Do you know where to file your claim?

From *Ladies' Home Journal*, June 1974. Copyright © 1974 Letty Cottin Pogrebin. Reprinted by permission.

Caucus. Volunteers undertake to do child care at conferences sponsored by the New York Radical Feminists. Educator Ann Welbourne supervises the most widely acclaimed Sex Information Service in the country with trained volunteers as counselors.

Who is to say which of our sisters is right or which is wrong?

Political action is often acceptable to NOW leaders. But how—NOW—do you evaluate the relative virtues of one sister who volunteered to work for CREEP in the Nixon campaign organization as against another who worked at one-to-one draft counseling? Is working (unpaid) as a file clerk for NOW so clearly a higher calling than (volunteer) advising a young woman on her abortion problem? Such questions are for individuals—not organizations—to decide. NOW's desire to be the final judge of what a woman can or cannot do with her life, either during or after working hours, is understandable, but unacceptable.

The first step when you're lost is to rethink carefully where you've been; and where you want to go. Women everywhere, recognizing the monumental contribution that NOW has made on the national scene, can help in the rethinking process.

If NOW is saying that the consciousness of volunteers needs raising, that their status must be upgraded, that they should receive benefits such as day care, out-of-pocket expenses, insurance, inclusion in the Social Security system, and tax credits, that's a path we can travel together to "bring women into the mainstream of American society." If NOW is saying that women must first of all be economically independent, but also free to choose how they intend to contribute (or not) to society, then again we must join together.

If NOW can recognize that

change seldom comes from inside the system and therefore that citizen participation on a broader scale is essential to our efforts to refind ourselves as a nation, let us all say Amen. For surely, we all wish to avoid the devastating spectacle of women, just as they achieve new status and power, turning and fighting with each other while ignoring outside goals. Consciousness-raising is crucial—but not at the cost of a lowered conscience.

In this postindustrial era, we are just beginning to grapple with new concepts of what constitutes work—and its interrelationship with service and leisure. With shorter workweeks, voluntary participation, by female and male, young and old, is becoming the norm—not the exception. But NOW continues "challenging women's traditional role as unpaid community servants."

A funny thing happened to NOW on its way to the high purpose of consciousness-raising. Following generations of men who have lost themselves in the desert of the work ethic, NOW comes to the rescue of society—and winds up worshiping the same almighty dollar. It is sad to see women embrace with such relish one of the arid features of the U.S. lifestyle: the identification of money as the *ultimate* status symbol, the amount of a paycheck as the *only* human measure of value. At the same time that many Americans are questioning their "mind-sets," desperately seeking for valid human motivations other than greed, the NOW position implies that the base of human dignity is monetary.

It is indeed essential that women become economically independent. But if we limit our sights to that goal alone, if we make economic independence our sole objective, when and if we do achieve it, the cost of that journey will be psychic bankruptcy.

1840. Elizabeth Cady Stanton meets Lucretia Mott at the World's Anti-Slavery Convention, where both discuss their anger and disappointment over the rejection of women delegates from the proceedings. Resolving to stage a women's rights convention later, they go their separate ways until 1848, when they meet again in New York State

The Big Giveaway

Margaret A. Sanborn and Caroline Bird

American women give away nearly $14.2 billion worth of work every year to worthy causes (in addition to the more than $499 billion worth of free labor they do for their families annually). By 1980, women's volunteer work may be worth more than $18 billion.

Despite occasional surveys and some theorizing, no one really knows precisely how many volunteer workers there actually are, and what percentage of them are women. "It's just an incredible guess to make," says one official of the National Center for Voluntary Action (NCVA), a federal agency that serves as a facilitator for volunteer programs. "And then to break it down into sex—very, very hard."

One source of documentation is a 1965 survey done by the Office of Manpower Research of the Department of Labor that found that of the approximately 36.6 million volunteers (excluding political, religious, and fraternal organizations) in the United States at that time, 60 percent, or 22 million, were women. Current estimates of the size of the volunteer force place the total number at at least 43 million; if past trends hold true, at the very least the women volunteers are nearly 26 million strong.

If each of these 26 million women contributes only five hours of her time each week to the various causes (a conservative figure), these women rack up an impressive total of nearly 7 billion hours of work annually. At the current federal minimum wage of $2.10 an hour—and since women are generally valued at no more than minimum wage anyway, we may as well use this figure —their donated time is worth nearly $14.2 billion annually.

In a 1969 Gallup poll, 69 million Americans of both sexes stated their

Adapted from *Ms.* Magazine, February 1975. Copyright © 1975 Ms. Magazine Corporation. Reprinted with permission.

willingness to donate their services to remedy problems in their own communities. The Department of Labor puts the total estimated economic value of these 69 million volunteers at as much as $30 billion annually by 1980. If three out of every five future volunteers are women, there will be by that time 41 million women voluntarily contributing more than $18 billion worth of work to help provide services which would not otherwise be available.

Other estimates say that there are already more women volunteers than the government surveys would suggest. A 1971 Russell Sage Foundation report, "Indicators of Trends in the Status of American Women," found that 52.7 million women were active participants in voluntary organizations. Of these women, nearly half were involved in religious-affiliated organizations. Another 316,200 were working in social service organizations; 632,400 in public affairs; and 2,793,100 in nonprofessional social welfare capacities.

Whatever the precise number of volunteers, women form the majority, having had, traditionally, more free time, or, rather, time unfilled by work with a dollar sign attached. Women are also thought to have the emotional equipment necessary to render charitable work more palatable to the recipient. But former NCVA President Douglas Kinsey, speaking to this point in late 1972, emphasized the need for more men in the volunteer forces, saying that compassion and free time are not solely the possessions of women. "People are needed in this service, so let's get men away from their TV sets and involved in their communities' problems."

Many of the tasks performed by volunteers are identical to positions found in the salaried work world, ranging from clerical work to fund-

raising and technical work in public health programs. The 3,177 local chapters of the American National Red Cross counted 1,594,020 adult volunteers of both sexes in the year ending June 30, 1973. These workers determine organizational policies, and plan and carry out Red Cross programs. Many are skilled in their fields, conducting blood-donor programs and safety and health campaigns. They work in hospitals, clinics, and relief centers in disaster-stricken areas. In addition to the tremendous volume of work accomplished by this organization, our economy is spared the burden of $1 billion that would otherwise have to be spent each year to *buy* these skilled services.

The utilization of volunteer labor not only saves money that would have gone toward salaries but in some cases actually cuts down on spending in other areas. In 1970, Women in Community Service, a federated group of women's church organizations, spent an average of $44 on seminars and other training programs for each woman enrolled in the Job Corps, while the U.S. Employment Service spent $101 in training each of its recruits less thoroughly.

The woman who remains in her home, working neither for a salary nor as an outside volunteer, may also be thought of as a volunteer, whose economic value to society can be calculated. In 1973 a research team at the New York State College of Human Ecology at Cornell University computed the number of hours a woman spends working in her home and affixed a dollar value, based on what it would cost to hire someone else for the jobs. They found that a housewife could be earning as much as $8,000 a year without leaving her home, if society found her work worth paying for.

Other estimates of the value of housework are even higher. Econo-

and make concrete plans. Then Mrs. Stanton drafts her "Declaration of Sentiments," styled after the Declaration of Independence, which lists eighteen legal disadvantages borne by women and presses for their right to vote. It is the first public presentation of a call for women's suffrage.

Volunteer Work
WORKING 321

mists at the Chase Manhattan Bank in 1970 demonstrated that an American housewife works a 99.6-hour-a-week job, and if her job paid according to its labor market value, she would be worth $13,391.56 a year, or $257.53 weekly. (Since wages in the private sector had gone up roughly 33 percent by the end of 1974, the value of the work would now be $342 a week.) For example, the original fictional salary includes 44.5 hours weekly as a nursemaid, at $2 an hour; 17.5 hours as housekeeper at $3.25 an hour; 13.1 hours as cook for $3.25 an hour; and dishwasher at $2 an hour for 6.2 hours weekly.

The more than 28 million women who remain in the home, according to the original estimate, work a total of at least 145 billion hours a year, at a monetary worth of $375 billion, a figure that represented nearly one-third of the $1.15 trillion gross national product for 1972. (Again, with inflation, the total monetary worth of this work would go up from $375 billion to $499 billion.) If, in addition, the women who work in the home were to receive Social Security old-age benefits upon reaching the retirement age of 65 (even though they never really retire), Social Security payments would rise by more than $6 billion a year, computed on the basis of the $8,000 salary suggested by the Cornell study group.

Rather than receiving any of this theoretical money, the volunteer worker in or out of the home is often out-of-pocket for expenses incurred in her volunteer career. This "cost of volunteering" is the factor that often prevents the middle- or low-income person from contributing time.

One of volunteerism's most vulnerable points has been, until recently, the lack of insurance coverage for the person engaged in volunteer activities. Unlike paid workers, who are covered by Workmen's Compensation, a volunteer injured on the job or sued in connection with her or his duties has been personally liable. In 1972, a non-profit organization, Volunteers Insurance Society, a pilot project of NCVA, provided volunteers with coverage for work accidents, personal liability, and auto damages incurred while using a car in the course of a work day. This insurance was available (at a cost of $1.50 a year, paid by the agency) to any volunteer working through a formal agency or nonprofit tax-exempt organization. The policy provided $2,500 accidental medical and death coverage for the volunteer, and $1 million in liability protection should the volunteer be sued in connection with volunteer services. Although the project is no longer in effect, a comparable insurance plan is now being worked on by NCVA.

The Internal Revenue Service permits few income-tax deductions for the volunteer. Transportation from home to the place of service is acceptable, as are meals and lodging away from home while donating services to a qualified organization, or attending a religious convention as a representative of a church. *(Other deductible expenses include automotive costs as well as upkeep of uniforms that have no general utility and that are required apparel for performing donated services.)*

The IRS treats as income a *per diem* allowance by an organization for the travel expenses of its volunteers, if the allowance exceeds the actual expenses. If the expenses exceed the allowance, the excess may be deducted.

In a recent decision the IRS ruled that one woman can deduct from her income tax the baby-sitting expenses incurred while doing volunteer work.

While income tax deductions for hours of volunteer work are still not recognized, there are now three bills before the House Ways and Means Committee. The newest twist in counting volunteer hours against income taxes is the concept of the tax credit, which is thought by some to be more equitable because it is not based solely on income.

On the volunteer's tax form a *deduction* is subtracted from the income before the tax rate is computed. The tax *credit*, as proposed by Representative Stewart McKinney (R.-Conn.) in HR 13586, would be subtracted from the total amount of taxes due after all income, other deductions, and tax rate are computed.

As always, financial donations made to a recognized charity are automatically deductible, up to 50 percent of the contributor's adjusted gross income. Typically, women may do the actual work, but in a money-oriented society where men control the economy, earn the wages, and pay conscience money to charity—the men get the credit.

Unemployment Rates by Sex, Race and Age

Unemployment rates are consistently higher for women than for men, for teenagers than for adults, and for minority races than for whites:

Race and age	Average percent unemployed in 1973	
	Women	Men
All races	6.0	4.1
16 to 19 years	15.2	13.9
20 years and over	4.8	3.2
Minority races	10.5	7.6
16 to 19 years	34.5	26.9
20 years and over	8.2	5.7

From *Women Workers Today*, 1974, Women's Bureau, Department of Labor.

1845. The first woman to receive ether as an anesthetic during childbirth is the wife of Dr. Crawford Williamson Long, who administers the drug.

Your Own Business

Do You Have What It Takes?

The Editors of *Small Business Reporter*

So you want to run your own business; but are you really prepared? It takes special skills—as well as motivation—to start a working business from scratch and to see it through to the profit margin.

YES   NO

_____ _____ I know that going into business for myself will involve the whole family.

_____ _____ My spouse thinks it's a good idea and is willing to help.

_____ _____ I like to make my own decisions and try my own ideas.

_____ _____ I enjoy being challenged and thrive on competition.

_____ _____ I want to improve my stature in the community.

_____ _____ I want to improve my financial position; build an estate for my family.

_____ _____ I know that my standard of living will be lowered for a while — until the business begins to show a profit. It may take several months, maybe even a year or two, to make a profit.

_____ _____ There's less than a 50-50 chance that I'll still be in business two years from now. I may spend the rest of my life barely making a go of it.

_____ _____ Only about 10% of the businesses started are really successful — 50% fail; 40% are marginal operations.

_____ _____ I might fail.

A note on the language in this chapter: Men own and run the great majority of businesses in this country and throughout the world. Business literature, then, is even more male-directed than the writings in almost any other field. Nevertheless, such information is still critical to any woman with business ambitions. We feel that the advantages of giving women access to this information far outweigh the irritations of some unfair sexist assumptions.—Ed.

MANAGEMENT

_____ _____ I realize that about 90% of business failures are caused by inexperience and poor management.

_____ _____ I have several years or more experience in this business.

_____ _____ I know the good things people do to improve a business. I know the mistakes that drive business away.

_____ _____ I know the suppliers and the assistance they provide.

_____ _____ I know the trade association people. I know what they expect of me and what to expect of them.

_____ _____ I have a head for figures.

_____ _____ I have experience in keeping inventory records, sales records and reports, withholding taxes for the Federal Government and making out State employee records and reports.

_____ _____ I know I'll always be able to meet my payroll.

_____ _____ I can shoulder the full responsibility of running a business.

_____ _____ I know how to juggle all the little details without cracking under the strain.

_____ _____ I know how to manage my business.

_____ _____ I've always protected myself, my family and my possessions with insurance and sensible safeguards.

1845. *Woman in the Nineteenth Century,* by Margaret Fuller, American transcendentalist, literary and art critic, mother, schoolteacher, author, feminist, journalist, and later, Italian revolutionary, is published. It directly influences the Seneca Falls women's rights convention and is to become a classic of American feminism.

_____ _____ I know that employees are the vital link between the business and its customers.

_____ _____ I've had experience in selecting, training and supervising employees.

_____ _____ I know how to develop an assistant "backup" person — to run the business when I'm not there.

_____ _____ I know how to forecast sales and expenses and how to use this information to help make my business more successful.

MERCHANDISING

_____ _____ I know how to find the right location for my business.

_____ _____ I've had experience in arranging attractive and convenient merchandise displays.

_____ _____ I can make my place of business attractive — and stay within the budget.

_____ _____ I've had experience organizing the help and establishing ways of doing things.

_____ _____ I know what, how much, when and where to buy.

_____ _____ I know how to price my goods and services competitively.

_____ _____ I know how to pay for merchandise, meet expenses and still make a profit.

_____ _____ I know how to control my inventory to coincide with peak and slack periods of the business.

_____ _____ I know how to advertise sensibly.

_____ _____ I know how to encourage customers to buy by making them feel welcome.

_____ _____ I take part in community activities.

_____ _____ I'm a good neighbor; I go out of my way sometimes to do little extra things that build good will.

_____ _____ I've always created a clean, attractive and pleasant atmosphere for customers and employees wherever I've worked.

_____ _____ I've had experience in handling merchandise efficiently.

_____ _____ I know the types of credit to offer that are appropriate to the business and the customer.

_____ _____ I know how to collect past due accounts without losing the customer.

FINANCES

_____ _____ I have some money saved that I've been putting away for my own business.

_____ _____ I have enough money to go into the business I want and I can get more from other sources — my friends and family and from my bank.

_____ _____ I know that the money must be paid back out of profits, after taxes and before I take any money for myself.

_____ _____ I realize that my savings will be the "risk capital" for my business.

_____ _____ I know that it's possible for me to lose my savings — as well as the money I borrow from others.

_____ _____ I know that even if my business fails I will have to pay back all I owe.

COMPETITION

_____ _____ I know my community wants, needs, and can support this business.

_____ _____ My community has enough people with enough inclination to spend money for the goods or services I plan to supply.

_____ _____ I've studied my competition, I know who my competitors are, and where they are.

_____ _____ I know what people think of my competition and how good they are.

_____ _____ I want to have the best business in town.

RELATIONSHIPS

_____ _____ I have friends to lean on.

_____ _____ My friends can help me because they are capable of impartial thinking and judgment when they know it will help me.

_____ _____ My banker will help me, give me counseling and advice.

_____ _____ My attorney will help me and is interested in my problems.

Among the author's close friends and associates are Ralph Waldo Emerson, Horace Greeley, Wordsworth, the Carlyles, DeQuincy, and Robert and Elizabeth Barrett Browning. She is to drown five years later in a shipwreck off Fire Island, New York, when she is returning from revolutionary activities in Italy with her husband and infant son.

_____ _____ My accountant will keep me informed of my affairs and business progress.

_____ _____ My insurance rep will help me select the best protection for my business.

_____ _____ My suppliers provide a whole range of services to help me in the conduct of my business.

PERSONAL INVENTORY

_____ _____ I know myself.

_____ _____ I know what's required of me.

_____ _____ I have evaluated my personality; it lends itself favorably to my business.

_____ _____ I am frank about discussing my financial condition. I have nothing to hide.

_____ _____ I am honest and ethical and have a good record with the people I have done business with.

_____ _____ I always get things done on time and plan ahead.

_____ _____ I have will power, lots of self-discipline.

_____ _____ I am stable. I've never jumped from job to job.

_____ _____ I like to work. My own business requires me to work hard — 12 to 16 hours each day. The work is never really done. There's always more.

_____ _____ I have the energy to do all the necessary lifting, hauling, standing, walking, talking and smiling that the day-to-day operation of my business will require.

_____ _____ I realize that I can't be all things to all people at all times — but that this will be expected of me in my own business. I can withstand the strain this will create for me.

_____ _____ I really like people; I'm friendly and outgoing by nature and I have a sincere, willing-to-serve attitude.

_____ _____ I understand people. I am the kind of person who can put myself in the other guy's shoes.

_____ _____ I don't know everything. There are still things to learn — new ideas I should consider.

_____ _____ I am adaptable. I am not so routine-bound or rigid in my ideas that I can't change if my business requires a change.

_____ _____ I make sound judgments. I know I will have to make decisions every day in my own business.

_____ _____ I can take advice from others.

_____ _____ Common sense is one of my strong points.

THE DECISION

_____ _____ I haven't reached my final decision.

_____ _____ I haven't signed anything yet. I haven't put up any non-returnable cash deposits, made any lease arrangements or merchandise commitments.

_____ _____ I've considered all of the alternatives to entering business for myself.

_____ _____ I know the advantages of a sole proprietorship, of a partnership, of incorporating my business.

_____ _____ I've investigated the possibility of a franchise operation. I'm aware of the advantages of franchising — buying someone else's know-how and proven operating techniques.

_____ _____ I'm aware of the advantages of working for someone else and not going into business for myself.

These questions should make you think about yourself, about what you need to know to go into your own business. Depending on the type of business, one question will have more weight than another. This makes it impossible to say: "If you score more than 75 right answers you're ready for your own business." It just isn't that easy.

1847. Sarah Bagley, labor leader, dies. Originally a worker in the famous cotton mills of Lowell, Massachusetts, Miss Bagley became restless under the plummeting wages and deteriorating working conditions and founded the Lowell Female Reform Association. An active lobbyist for the ten-hour workday, then considered radical, she attracted a large male following as well.

Planning Your Business

The Editors of *Small Business Reporter*

THE NEED TO PLAN

Every business begins with an idea — a product to be manufactured or sold, a service to be performed. Whatever the business or its degree of complexity, the businessman needs a comprehensive plan to translate his vision into a working operation.

A business plan should set forth, in writing and with figures, the nature of the proposed business, measurable objectives of profitability, expected sales volume over a period of time, and should map a strategy to obtain these goals. The plan will be used by prospective lenders and investors as a means of evaluating potential success, and by the businessman to continuously assess the strength of his operation.

The **nature of the product or service** must be defined. What distinguishes it from others already on the market? If production is involved, what engineering or design support will be needed? Should the product parts be manufactured or simply assembled?

The **market** must be mapped out and described. Is there evidence of a need for the prospective product or service? Is the primary market a certain type of business or a consumer of a certain age? income level? geographical area? County census data provide population figures and demographic information. Market research firms make detailed studies for the businessman who can afford this service.

Distribution methods must be determined. How will the product reach its market — through wholesalers? retailers?

The **competition** must be counted. Who and where are they? How does the proposed item or service measure up to those now in existence? Is it of higher quality? Lower cost? What are the marketable differences?

The **expense of setting up shop** must be included in the plan. Adequate funding must allow for many of the following expenses:

- Down payment on the purchase or deposit on the lease for business premises.

- Any necessary fixture or remodeling costs.

- Purchase or lease of needed equipment and machinery.

- Initial inventory purchase.

- Telephone and utility installation fees.

- Stationery and supply costs.

- Taxes and licenses.

- Professional services (accountant, attorney, etc.).

In order for the plan to be a working tool, all **income and expenses** should be estimated monthly for at least the first two years of operation. (Such figures often reveal a period of six months or longer without any profit.)

Without realistic projections, "rough periods" which could have been predicted become "crises" which cause a new business to fail.

The projected operating statement will show:

- Predicted sales volume and the rate at which it will expand.

- How much it will cost to produce or purchase the goods to be sold (materials, labor, freight, etc.).

- Fixed monthly operating expenses, including rent, utilities and insurance premiums.

- Controllable monthly operating expenses, such as advertising, salaries and accounting services.

- Net monthly profit — the amount of money left after subtracting cost of goods and expenses from sales, and before paying taxes.

Planning need not be a blind guessing game. In order to arrive at realistic projection figures, the businessman should consult trade associations, trade publications, suppliers and other sources of information to determine appropriate standards of efficiency for his type and size of business. Operating ratios common to various types of business are published by the National Cash Register Company (*Expenses in Retail Business*), Accounting Corporation of America (*Barometer of Small Business*) and The Robert Morris Associates (*Annual Statement Studies*). As an ongoing practice, the businessman should

1848. Lucretia Coffin Mott, another Quaker feminist with strong interests in abolishing slavery, organizes the Seneca Falls, New York, women's rights convention in cooperation with Elizabeth Cady Stanton. Oddly, even though a fiery opponent of inequality between the sexes, Mrs. Mott does not, now or later, consider suffrage to be a

Advisors

ADVISORS	WHAT THEY CAN DO	HOW TO FIND AND WORK WITH THEM
ACCOUNTANT	Can set up a pattern of bookkeeping that is easy for the owner to follow daily and for the accountant to work with at audit or tax time. Helps set up systems for the control of cash and handling of funds, and can suggest simple equipment like cash registers, multiple copy sales checks and .other forms.	Fees are often based on hourly rates and vary with the complexity and extent of the service. Fees should be negotiated in advance. Bankers and lawyers often know accountants who are willing to work with small businesses. Accountants are listed in the Yellow Pages. The businessman should confer with several accountants and check their experience and references before deciding on one.
BANKER	Has financial knowledge: loans, separate checking accounts for the business, other funding or bank services — such as billing service and credit systems. Is familiar with community; may suggest individuals and other institutions that can be helpful.	Where the businessman does his personal banking; near the business location for convenience. Often advisable to establish a continuing relationship with the banker and keep him informed of the progress of the business.
INSURANCE AGENT BROKER	Will evaluate insurance needs and set up packages to cover specific types of businesses. May be either an independent (dealing with several insurance companies) or a direct writer (employed by one company and writing policies only with them).	The businessman should talk with several agents, compare the coverage, costs and convenience of the insurance they can offer, and select the program that best suits his needs — comprehensively and economically. Agent requires complete information on business operations as they relate to insurance coverage and must be continuously apprised of changes that may affect insurance needs. Agents and brokers are listed in the Yellow Pages of the phone directory.
LAWYER	Can help in choosing a form of business; in drawing up partnership and incorporating agreements; making sure papers are properly filed with city, county and state governments; interpreting contracts and leases; arbitrating disputes within the business and for the business against others; consulting when the businessman is unsure of his rights and obligations under the law.	Lawyers may be located through friends, other businessmen, suppliers, consultants, trade associations or through listings in the Yellow Pages of the phone directory. In most counties, local bar association referral services can arrange for a businessman in need of legal counsel to meet with a practicing attorney in the area. The initial half-hour consultation fee ranges from $7.50 to $10.00. The consultation implies no further obligation.
MANAGEMENT & MARKETING CONSULTANT	A consultant who specializes in small business can help new businessmen determine and juggle the many facets of starting: product determination; advertising; inventory; security; filing; hiring; pricing—hidden details that a new entrepreneur may not think of. Has access to other sources of information and contacts with lawyers, accountants, advertising agencies.	Consultants are listed in the Yellow Pages and can be found by talking to friends, others in the business. The Small Business Administration sometimes has suggestions and has its own SCORE (Service Corps of Retired Executives) volunteers who counsel businessmen and charge only their out-of-pocket expenses. Consultants generally charge on an hourly, weekly, or daily basis—or on a monthly "retainer."

vital aspect of the women's movement. She votes against a convention resolution sponsored by Mrs. Stanton proclaiming women's right to vote, the only resolution not passed unanimously.

compare the performance of his operation against standard levels of performance in the trade. The history of small business failures reveals that many firms fail not from lack of capital or external economic forces, but from the cumulative effect of substandard performance and cost leaks that go undetected.

The businessman with a realistic plan has the best chance of success. Decisions regarding financing and legal organization should come only after every operating function of the proposed enterprise has been appraised.

LEGAL FORM OF BUSINESS

To move from the conceptual stage to actual formation of a new business, a prospective owner must ask himself some of the following questions:

- How much money do I need and where will it come from?

- What skills are needed that I can't provide?

- How much control will I have over the operation?

- How will the business be taxed?

- To what extent will I be personally responsible for debts or claims against the business?

- What will happen to the business if I am incapacitated?

The answers to these questions will be strongly influenced by the legal form of business the prospective owner selects. If he hasn't enough capital, for instance, he may seek a partner with available funds who may be able to provide complementary skills as well.

The organization of a business is also a continuous decision based on changing profits and growth of the operation. Partners, for example, may elect to incorporate after two or three years of operation. Though the word "corporation" calls up the image of bigness, small businesses are not excluded from the form.

Sole Proprietorship

The sole proprietor is his own man. He makes or breaks his business, which may sound singularly appealing to those instilled with the American entrepreneurial spirit. It is difficult to go it alone, however. The single owner has sole responsibility as well as sole control. He must provide or procure all the capital and he is personally liable for all claims against his business.

On the other hand, the sole proprietorship form is easy to initiate and relatively free from government regulation. The only legal procedure that may be necessary is the filing of a fictitious name statement. Business income is taxed as personal income. The form is appealing to the man who wants to stay small and keep things simple.

General Partnership

A general partnership is the pooling of capital and skills of two or more persons as co-owners to conduct business. An "idea" man and a "money" man often provide the formula for a partnership.

The general partnership is easy to set up, for it requires no official registration. A written agreement among partners is not required by law, but it is wise to have an attorney draw up a contract spelling out respective rights and duties of the partners. Almost any management and profit-sharing arrangements are possible.

Death or withdrawal of one partner or the addition of a new partner legally terminates a partnership. This may not necessarily mean liquidation of the business; a new contract can be made. But provisions for such dissolution in the original written contract ensure smooth transition of ownership and continuity of business operations.

A partnership is not an entity apart from its members to the same degree as is a corporation. Partnership liability extends to the personal assets of the general partners. And each partner is taxed on his share of the partnership income, at his personal income tax rate.

Limited Partnership

The limited partnership is a refinement of the principle of partnership. More closely regulated than the general partnership, it permits investors to become partners without assuming unlimited liability. There must be at least one general partner. The limited partner usually risks only as much as his investment and exercises limited control over the activities of the partnership.

Corporation

"A corporation is an artificial being; invisible, intangible, and existing only in contemplation of the law," wrote Chief Justice John Marshall. In other words, the corporation exists as a separate entity apart from its owners, the shareholders. It makes contracts; it is liable; it pays taxes. It is a legal person.

1848. Boston Female Medical School becomes the first American institution of its kind. Later as the New England Female Medical College, the school will merge with the Boston University School of Medicine, thereby creating the first coeducational medical school in the world.

A corporation can attract capital by selling stock in the company to selected investors or to the public. However, small, new concerns seldom "go public" before they open their doors. Generally, stockholders are not liable for claims against the corporation beyond the amount of their individual investment. Creditors have claim only against the assets of the corporation, though officers may become personally liable in some cases.

The separate identity of the corporation makes possible its continuous existence. Death of a stockholder or sale of stock will not affect the ability of a corporation's managers to continue conducting business.

Corporate taxation is heavy — 48% of net income over $25,000 goes to the federal government; the tax rate on net income under $25,000 is 22%. Income is subject to "double taxation": first when earned by the corporation; then when distributed as dividends to the stockholders.

To incorporate, the owners of a business must make application with the Commissioner of Corporations of the state, who grants charters according to state statutes. Sale and exchange of stock is governed by state "blue sky laws" for the protection of the investing public. This phrase originated with a legislator's remark that some companies sought to "capitalize the blue skies."

Incorporation can be costly. A corporation must file articles of incorporation with the Secretary of State and in the counties in which its principal offices are located and/or real estate is held. Filing fees are based on the value of corporate stock. It must also pay a franchise tax based on net income, attorney's fees and other expenses. The cost may run from $400 to $2,500 depending on the size of the business. This expense must be weighed against potential financial advantages in future years.

Subchapter S Corporation

The Subchapter S (or tax electing) corporation is a hybrid form which combines some advantages of the corporate form with federal taxation as a partnership. The Internal Revenue Code permits a closely held corporation (one with up to ten shareholders) to avoid corporate taxation by having each shareholder report his share of the corporate income on his individual tax return. The corporation itself files only an information return, just as a partnership. The business remains a corporation in the eyes of the state.

The beginning businessman may select a legal form on the basis of considerations other than taxation. But if incorporation is elected, Subchapter S status may be appealing, especially to low income businesses. An attorney can help clarify the many technical aspects of this legal form.

TAXATION

The tax liability of a business is affected not only by its legal form, but by numerous other management decisions as well. The business owner should have an accountant or tax attorney explain how his method of accounting, schedule of depreciation on property, and timing of business transactions affect his tax figure.

FINANCING

Capital required to start a business that cannot be provided by its owner(s) or investors, must be secured through loans. Every new venture is a risk. Thus, every prospective lender must evaluate the probability of success on the basis of the owner's business proposal, his experience and his potential.

As a general rule, most institutional lenders require that at least 50% of the starting capital be contributed by the entrepreneur and/or other investors from their own funds. This constitutes equity in the business, or ownership dollars. Less equity may not attract needed capital.

Banks are the primary source of commercial loans to small businesses, but not all banks are alike. The loan applicant should learn what different banks have to offer for his type and size of business.

An application for a bank loan must be accompanied by:

- Resume of the applicant, including his general background and business experience. Previous management experience in the type of business proposed is highly desirable. Advanced education is always a welcomed supplement.

- Personal financial statement of the applicant.

- In the case of a partnership or corporation, the bank will require a complete list of partners or officers and their respective percentages of interest in the business.

- Projected statement of income and expenses for the first 12 to 24 months of operation, or for the term of the loan. The applicant should make proper allowance in his projection of expenses for his own salary or withdrawal.

1848. Elizabeth Stanton meets Susan B. Anthony at the Seneca Falls convention, launching a fifty-year collaboration that culminates in the passage of the Nineteenth Amendment and is one of the most remarkable, productive relationships in the annals of womankind. Each fills the other's gaps. Elizabeth is a masterful speaker and writer,

Checklist for Beginners in Business

- **State license**

    Education and apprenticeship requirements for a specific occupation can run into years. If the candidate for business ownership has already fulfilled the occupational prerequisites, he should allow at least a month for filing and examination before a license is obtained.

- **Employer's identification number**

    An EI number should be requested from the Internal Revenue Service one month before its intended use.

- **City and county licenses**

    Licenses may be granted for a flat fee, or may be dependent upon fire, health or police permits previously obtained. Applicant should plan accordingly.

- **If incorporation is intended**

    An attorney must be retained to draw up the articles of incorporation for application to the Secretary of State. At least two weeks should be allowed for this process.

- **Seller's Permit**

    Permit must be in hand when the doors of a retail operation are opened. A permit may be secured in an hour if the applicant has the required security in cash, but a time allowance should be made for other forms of security such as a bond or time certificate of deposit. If an applicant must obtain his permit immediately, the Board of Equalization will accept a cash deposit which they will refund when security in another form is received.

- **Unemployment insurance**

    Application to the State Department of Human Resources Development should be made for such coverage within 15 days of hiring the first employee.

- **Workmen's Compensation insurance**

    Such insurance is mandatory as soon as a single employee is hired. Policy may be purchased from a private insurer or the State Compensation Insurance Fund.

- **Fictitious Name Statement**

    Filing should be made with the county within 30 days of beginning business.

- **Public utilities**

    Telephone service should be ordered several weeks in advance. Applicant should request business service, and expect to pay a deposit. A time allowance for gas and electric service is necessary if meters are not already installed on the premises. A deposit will probably be required before power is turned on.

- **Bank account**

    A bank account should be opened and kept strictly for business purposes. Checks imprinted with the business' name and address require approximately one month for delivery.

- **Business stationery**

    Business cards, forms and stationery should be ordered well in advance of opening day to allow time for printing and delivery.

Susan excels at political organization and countryside stumping. Elizabeth is later to write of their friendship, "Yes, our work is one, we are one in aim and sympathy and we should be together." Energized by deep wells of radicalism, Mrs. Stanton often alienates those within the movement who are working toward more modest goals.

- Purpose of the loan explained in detail.

Also, a bank will characteristically require as conditions for a loan:

- A security agreement on equipment, furniture and fixtures. (Such agreement offers some repayment protection to the lender; property could be sold in case of default of payment.)

- Property and casualty insurance on the business.

- Assignment of a life insurance policy on the applicant. (Cash value, or proceeds of the policy, would be paid to the bank in case of default due to death.)

Other sources of financing include commercial finance companies, which offer short-term loans for inventory and equipment purchase, as well as capital loans. Suppliers may extend short-term credit. But the new entrepreneur, without past ownership experience, may have difficulty proving his credit worthiness. Many new businesses must operate on a "cash only" basis with their suppliers until their financial stability is established.

Government Assistance

OFFICES	ASSISTANCE OFFERED	HOW TO FIND IT
INTERNAL REVENUE SERVICE	Publishes the "Tax Guide for Small Business" and advises on tax matters that concern small businessmen.	Listed under the Treasury Department in U.S. Government section of phone directory.
DEPARTMENT OF COMMERCE	Publishes statistics on business in general and does studies on various types of businesses and industries.	Has field offices throughout the United States. Listed in the phone directory under U. S. Government.
SMALL BUSINESS ADMINISTRATION	Publishes many aids for people going into business. Some of these are free; others are for sale. Conducts workshops regularly for people who want to start or improve their businesses.	Also has field offices in major U.S. cities. U.S. Government listings in phone directory.
STATE BOARD OF EQUALIZATION OR STATE TAX BOARD	Can give requirements for collecting and remitting retail sales taxes. Some states, including California, publish statistics on business, based on the amount of taxes they collect and number of seller's permits they issue.	Listed under State Government agencies.
SUPERINTENDENT OF DOCUMENTS	Distributes and sells all government publications.	Superintendent of Documents U. S. Government Printing Office Washington, D.C. 20402

Small Business Administration

The Small Business Administration is a source of capital for beginning and established small businesses. A federal agency, the SBA provides both equity financing and loans to able entrepreneurs who have sufficient capital to secure commercial loans. And, in some cases, the SBA will finance a venture with thinner capitalization than normal borrowing would require if convinced of the favorable prospects of a business and impressed with the owner's character and capability.

More common than direct SBA loans or participatory agreements, however, are bank loans guaranteed (up to 90%) by the SBA. If a business is without adequate credit standing to secure an appropriate place of business, the SBA may guarantee a lease agreement. Management assistance and published materials are provided to small businessmen, and are available at field offices of the SBA across the country.

Special programs of assistance are available to minority entrepreneurs. SBA and Department of Commerce field offices can normally supply information on the nature of these programs and the availability of funds.

INSURANCE

Small businesses, sensitive to the slightest losses, need to be especially well insured. Insurance trades a large, uncertain loss for a small but certain cost: the premium.

Prevention precedes insurance. The businessman should reduce the risk of loss to his business by taking steps to prevent fire, protect against burglary and provide for safe building construction. These

1849. Lydia Hasbrouck, women's fashion fighter, goes about in "Bloomers" as a matter of principle, three years before Amelia Bloomer publicizes them at Seneca Falls. Mrs. Hasbrouck's monthly periodical, *Sibyl*, criticizes current fashion with its dresses of "*vasty* depths and breadths" and its "senseless ninny faces and forms *deformed* and

measures can decrease the premium paid to a commercial insurer and avoid unnecessary coverage.

Insurance provides protection against losses that cannot be predictably and easily absorbed into general operating costs, or avoided through precautionary measures. Provisions for these losses would otherwise require setting aside huge amounts of money to cover potential damages. The financial stability which insurance provides makes it easier for the business to obtain credit.

SETTING UP THE BOOKS

Accurate accounting records are essential to proper management of a business. An accountant can help design a record-keeping system tailored to the nature and needs of a specific operation, but the owner/manager must be able to draw from these records the kind of financial information he needs for sound management decisions. Many studies attest that one of the big differences between successful small businesses and those that fail is the adequacy and use of accounting records.

Financial data from daily transactions, recorded first chronologically as they occur, then transferred to a permanent ledger as a debit or credit, should be compiled periodically (monthly, quarterly) into a financial statement — a balance sheet and a statement of income and expenses.

A financial statement serves as a photograph of a business. The income (or profit and loss) statement is a "moving picture" that shows income and expenses over a period of time. The balance sheet is a "still picture" of the assets, liabilities and owner's capital on a specific date.

ADVERTISING

Visibility is vital to a new business venture; a product or service may be pleading for purchase only because it is unknown in the community.

The retailer's store front and window display promote his products to passersby. Appearance of the store premises and treatment of customers by store personnel are also important in creating a favorable image in the community. Some advertising which reaches beyond the store doors is still necessary, however.

Small businessmen are advised to make advertising costs a permanent part of their business budget, allocating monthly amounts according to the changing needs of their operations.

Types of Business Organization
Small Business Administration

SINGLE PROPRIETORSHIP

ADVANTAGES
1. Low start-up costs
2. Greatest freedom from regulation
3. Owner in direct control
4. Minimal working capital requirements
5. Tax advantage to small owner
6. All profits to owner

DISADVANTAGES
1. Unlimited liability
2. Lack of continuity
3. Difficult to raise capital

PARTNERSHIP

ADVANTAGES
1. Ease of formation
2. Low start-up costs
3. Additional sources of venture capital
4. Broader management base
5. Possible tax advantage
6. Limited outside regulation

DISADVANTAGES
1. Unlimited liability
2. Lack of continuity
3. Divided authority
4. Difficulty in raising additional capital
5. Hard to find suitable partners

CORPORATION

ADVANTAGES
1. Limited liability
2. Specialized management
3. Ownership is transferrable
4. Continuous existence
5. Legal entity
6. Possible tax advantages
7. Easier to raise capital

DISADVANTAGES
1. Closely regulated
2. Most expensive form to organize
3. Charter restrictions
4. Extensive record keeping necessary
5. Double taxation

horrified by a redundancy of paints, puffs, bows, flounces and laces." Mrs. Hasbrouck bears the constant public ridicule of her position stoically. Bloomers represent a rebellion against the heavy, restrictive fashions of the day.

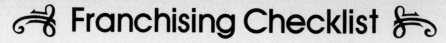

Franchising Checklist

Small Business Administration

The Franchisor

1. Has the franchisor been in business long enough (5 years or more) to have established a good reputation? ____
2. Have you checked Better Business Bureaus, Chambers of Commerce, Dun and Bradstreet, or bankers to find out about the franchisor's business reputation and credit rating? ____
3. Did the above investigations reveal that the franchisor has a good reputation and credit rating? ____
4. Does the franchising firm appear to be financed adequately so that it can carry out its stated plan of financial assistance and expansion? ____
5. Have you found out how many franchisees are now operating? ____
6. Have you found out the "mortality" or failure rate among franchisees? ____
7. Is the failure rate small? ____
8. Have you checked with some franchisees and found that the franchisor has a reputation for honesty and fair dealing among those who currently hold franchises? ____
9. Has the franchisor shown you certified figures indicating exact net profits of one or more going operations which you have personally checked yourself? ____
10. Has the franchisor given you a specimen contract to study with the advice of your legal counsel? ____
11. Will the franchisor assist you with:
    a. A management training program? ____
    b. An employee training program? ____
    c. A public relations program? ____
    d. Obtaining capital? ____
    e. Good credit terms? ____
    f. Merchandising ideas? ____
    g. Designing store layout and displays? ____
    h. Inventory control methods? ____
    i. Analyzing financial statements? ____
12. Does the franchisor provide continuing assistance for franchisees through supervisors who visit regularly? ____
13. Does the franchising firm have an experienced management trained in depth? ____
14. Will the franchisor assist you in finding a good location for your business? ____
15. Has the franchising company investigated *you* carefully enough to assure itself that you can successfully operate one of its franchises at a profit both to it and to you? ____
16. Have you determined exactly what the franchisor can do for you that you cannot do for yourself? ____

The Product Or Service

17. Has the product or service been on the market long enough to gain good consumer acceptance? ____
18. Is it priced competitively? ____
19. Is it the type of item or service which the same consumer customarily buys more than once? ____
20. Is it an all-year seller in contrast to a seasonal one? ____
21. Is it a staple item in contrast to a fad? ____
22. Does it sell well elsewhere? ____
23. Would you buy it on its merits? ____

From *Starting and Managing a Small Business of Your Own*, 1973, Small Business Administration.

24. Will it be in greater demand 5 years from now? ____
25. If it is a product rather than a service:
    a. Is it packaged attractively? ____
    b. Does it stand up well in use? ____
    c. Is it easy and safe to use? ____
    d. Is it patented? ____
    e. Does it comply with all applicable laws? ____
    f. Is it manufactured under certain quality standards? ____
    g. Do these standards compare favorably with similar products on the market? ____
    h. If the product must be purchased exclusively from the franchisor or a designated supplier, are the prices to you, as the franchisee, competitive? ____

The Franchise Contract

26. Does the franchise fee seem reasonable? ____
27. Do continuing royalties or percent of gross sales payment appear reasonable? ____
28. Is the total cash investment required and the terms for financing the balance satisfactory? ____
29. Does the cash investment include payment for fixtures and equipment? ____
30. If you will be required to participate in company sponsored promotion and publicity by contributing to an "advertising fund," will you have the right to veto any increase in contributions to the "fund?" ____
31. If the parent company's product or service is protected by patent or liability insurance, is the same protection extended to you? ____
32. Are you free to buy the amount of merchandise you believe you need rather than being required to purchase a certain amount? ____
33. Can you, as the franchisee, return merchandise for credit? ____
34. Can you engage in other business activities? ____
35. If there is an annual sales quota, can you retain your franchise if it is not met? ____
36. Does the contract give you an exclusive territory for the length of the franchise? ____
37. Is your territory protected? ____
38. Is the franchise agreement renewable? ____
39. Can you terminate your agreement if you are not happy for some reason? ____
40. Is the franchisor prohibited from selling the franchise out from under you? ____
41. May you sell the business to whomever you please? ____
42. If you sell your franchise, will you be compensated for the goodwill you have built into the business? ____
43. Does the contract obligate the franchisor to give you continuing assistance after you are operating the business? ____
44. Are you permitted a choice in determining whether you will sell any new product or service introduced by the franchisor after you have opened your business? ____

1850. Harriet Beecher Stowe writes *Uncle Tom's Cabin,* which, within three and a half years, will sell 313,000 copies in America and nearly that amount in England. More than any other written work, *Uncle Tom's Cabin* advances the cause of antislavery sentiments.

Profitability of Selected Types of Business

Line of Business	Percent Return on Investment[2] Upper quartile[3]	Median[3]	Lower quartile[3]
Manufacturing			
Coating, engraving and allied services	21.2	8.0	-18.8
Commercial Printing (except lithographic)	33.8	15.7	.0
Commercial Printing (lithographic)	33.4	17.6	2.0
Electric Components and Accessories	36.7	5.3	-21.8
Fabricated Structural Steel	25.8	8.6	3.5
Machine Shops — Jobbing and Repair	35.6	9.7	.0
Miscellaneous Plastic Products	94.4	24.3	4.7
Special dies and tools, die sets, jigs and fixtures	34.1	15.4	.0
Wholesaling			
Automotive equipment	32.8	18.8	6.4
Building materials	24.7	8.6	.0
Electrical supplies and apparatus	35.0	16.7	8.5
Fruits and vegetables	49.2	15.3	1.7
General merchandise	30.4	16.7	4.4
Heavy commercial and industrial machinery and equipment	39.6	13.3	.0
Hardware and paints	26.5	11.0	2.4
Industrial chemicals	28.9	15.7	5.3
Jewelry	33.3	16.0	8.0
Lumber and millwork	16.9	7.3	.0
Meats and meat products	58.6	24.4	10.4
Metal products (except scrap)	51.4	21.6	2.5
Mill supply houses	28.8	11.3	.9
Plumbing and heating equipment and supplies	36.9	16.0	8.8
Wine, liquor and beer	55.4	33.7	11.2
Retailing			
Automobiles, new and used	27.9	12.2	1.7
Drugs	64.0	18.4	6.1
Family clothing stores	25.9	16.2	7.5

Line of Business	Percent Return on Investment[2] Upper quartile[3]	Median[3]	Lower quartile[3]
Retailing — Continued			
Feed and Seed, farm and garden supply	23.9	9.4	.0
Floor coverings	40.8	15.1	7.9
Flowers	18.7	8.3	.0
Furniture	27.2	9.9	1.9
Groceries and meat	54.8	29.1	3.7
Hardware stores	32.1	13.3	3.7
Household appliances	32.7	12.5	1.8
House trailers	42.2	16.6	.0
Jewelry	33.9	11.3	4.2
Liquor	38.8	23.1	10.8
Lumber yards	17.0	3.4	.9
Men's and Boys' clothing	21.8	11.7	2.4
Musical instruments and supplies	19.2	8.8	.0
Office supplies and equipment	28.3	14.8	5.4
Radios, television and record players	30.8	15.0	.0
Restaurants	75.2	28.1	5.2
Shoes	25.8	14.0	2.4
Sportings goods	29.1	17.7	8.6
Women's ready-to-wear	31.3	12.3	1.2
Servicing			
Advertising agencies	101.0	35.7	11.1
Auto and truck rental and leasing			
Business and management consulting	66.5	19.9	5.4
Engineering and architectural services	100.0	51.0	9.8
Equipment rental and leasing	53.8	25.1	5.2
Laundries and dry cleaners	59.4	27.1	10.6
Local trucking — without storage	22.4	2.8	-12.0
Long distance trucking	34.6	12.2	1.4
Real estate agents and brokers	36.5	11.4	2.6

1 The ratios of only those businesses with total assets under $250,000 are quoted here.

2 The amount of net profit before taxes divided by tangible net worth. This ratio expresses the relationship between the owners' share of operations before taxes for the year and the capital already contributed by the owners.

3 These are not averages but rather are shown as the upper quartile, median and lower quartile figure. Ratios presented in this manner preclude the undue influence of extreme ratio values which would result if merely an average figure were presented. Also, and more importantly, they give you some idea of the "spread" or range of ratio value in each case.

Source.—Robert Morris Associates, the National Association of Bank Loan Officers and Credit Men. Financial Statement Studies for close to 300 lines of business are prepared each year by Robert Morris Associates, Philadelphia National Bank Building, Philadelphia, Pa. 19107.

Number of Inhabitants Per Store
[National averages]

Kind of business	Number of inhabitants per store
Food stores	
Grocery stores	1,534
Meat and Fish (sea food) markets	17,876
Candy, nut, and confectionery stores	31,409
Retail bakeries	12,563
Dairy products stores	41,587
Eating, drinking places	
Restaurants, lunchrooms, caterers	1,583
Cafeterias	19,341
Refreshment places	3,622
Drinking places (alcholic beverages)	2,414
General merchandise	
Variety stores	10,373
General merchandise stores	9,837
Apparel and accessory stores	
Women's ready-to-wear stores	7,102
Women's accessory and specialty stores	25,824
Men's and boy's clothing and furnishing stores	11,832
Family clothing stores	16,890
Shoe stores	9,350
Furniture, home furnishings and equipment stores	
Furniture stores	7,210
Floor covering stores	29,543
Drapery, curtain and upholstery stores	62,460
Household appliance stores	12,585
Radio and television stores	20,346
Record shops	112,144
Musical instrument stores	46,332

Kind of business	Number of inhabitants per store
Building material, hardware, and farm equipment dealers	
Lumber and other building materials dealers	8,124
Paint, glass, and wallpaper stores	22,454
Hardware stores	10,206
Farm equipment dealers	14,793
Automotive dealers	
Motor vehicle dealers — new and used cars	6,000
Motor vehicle dealers — used cars only	17,160
Tire, battery and accessory dealers	8,764
Boat dealers	61,526
Household trailer dealers	44,746
Gasoline service stations	1,195
Miscellaneous	
Antique and secondhand stores	17,169
Book and stationery stores	28,584
Drug stores	4,268
Florists	13,531
Fuel oil dealers	25,425
Garden supply stores	65,118
Gift, novelty and souvenir shops	26,313
Hay, grain and feed stores	16,978
Hobby, toy and game shops	61,430
Jewelry stores	13,495
Liquified petroleum gas (bottled gas) dealers	32,803
Liquor stores	6,359
Mail order houses	44,554
Merchandising machine operators	44,067
Optical goods stores	62,878
Sporting goods stores	27,063

Source: Bureau of the Census, U.S. Department of Commerce. Number of establishments with payroll from 1967 Census of Retail Trade. Number of inhabitants residing in the United States (excluding Armed Forces overseas), as of July 1, 1967.

From *Starting and Managing a Small Business of Your Own,* 1973, Small Business Administration.

1850. Great Britain declares abortion a statutory offense, the maximum penalty being life imprisonment. The law defines abortion as the attempt "to administer poison or any noxious thing to a woman with child. . .or to use any instrument. . .with intent to procure her miscarriage." The previous British law decreed the death penalty for those convicted.

45. Is there anything with respect to the franchise or its operation which would make you ineligible for special financial assistance or other benefits accorded to small business concerns by federal, state, or local governments? ____

46. Did your lawyer approve the franchise contract after he studied it paragraph by paragraph? ____

47. Is the contract free and clear of requirements which would call upon you to take any steps which are, according to your lawyer, unwise or illegal in your state, county or city? ____

48. Does the contract cover all aspects of your agreement with the franchisor? ____

49. Does it really benefit both you and the franchisor? ____

Your Market

50. Are the territorial boundaries of your market completely, accurately and understandably defined? ____

51. Have you made any study to determine whether the product or service you propose to sell has a market in your territory at the prices you will have to charge? ____

52. Does the territory provide an adequate sales potential? ____

53. Will the population in the territory given you increase over the next 5 years? ____

54. Will the average per capita income in the territory remain the same or increase over the next 5 years? ____

55. Is existing competition in your territory for the product or service not too well entrenched? ____

YOU — The Franchisee

56. Do you know where you are going to get the equity capital you will need? ____

57. Have you compared what it would take to start your own similar business with the price you must pay for the franchise? ____

58. Have you made a business plan — for example:

   a. Have you worked out what income from sales or services you can reasonably expect in the first 6 months? The first year? The second year? ____

   b. Have you made a forecast of expenses including a regular salary for yourself? ____

59. Are you prepared to give up some independence of action to secure the advantages offered by the franchise? ____

60. Are you capable of accepting supervision, even though you will presumably be your own boss? ____

61. Are you prepared to accept rules and regulations with which you may not agree? ____

62. Can you afford the period of training involved? ____

63. Are you ready to spend much or all of the remainder of your business life with this franchisor, offering his product or service to the public? ____

Conclusion

In conclusion, franchising creates distinct opportunities for the prospective small business owner. Without franchising it is doubtful that thousands of small business investors could ever have started. The American consumer might well have been denied ready access to many products and services. The system permits these goods and services to be marketed without the vast sums of money and number of managerial people possessed only by large corporations. Therefore, it opens up economic opportunities for the small business.

But not even the help of a good franchisor can guarantee success. You will still be primarily responsible for the success or failure of your venture. As in any other type of business your return will be related directly to the amount and effectiveness of your investment in time and money.

Using Other

If you are broke but want a business of your own—or at least one in which you are part owner—don't waste any more time working for someone else. Get out and start organizing one.

It may be easier to attract other investors, whether they be friends, relatives or strangers, if you can *also* put in some cash. If you can, that reduces the amount needed from outsiders and increases your ownership. Maybe you have enough to capitalize the company alone. This is ideal in terms of ownership—though it has disadvantages, too.

Whatever percentage of cash you are willing to put in, *don't* do it. Not directly in the business. Instead, develop a line of credit and borrow and put the proceeds in. As a last resort use your cash to open a savings account, then use the passbook as collateral for a loan *to the business* by a bank. Why go through all this, you may wonder, when it seems so simple to put your money right into the business?

The Small Business Administration apparently does not realize the importance of this technique. Its booklet on starting a small business, after asking where you will get the money, flatly states, "The first source is your personal savings." The booklet goes on, "Then relatives, friends, or other individuals may be found who are willing to venture their savings in your business." But there are reasons *not* to follow such advice.

First, it is psychologically unsound to manage your own funds in business. Because they are yours, it is difficult to be objective about them. This may result in an overcautious and underprofitable business.

Second, it is difficult to get your money out of your company later on. If you sell the concern, buyers will pay so much for it based on its actual value, whether you have ten dollars or a million paid into it. But if someone buys your company and it has a loan from a bank (albeit backed by your savings account), naturally they must take over such loans outstanding against the company. If you sell your company the buyer will not repay you for cash you put in. He considers that your invested capital. He usually will repay a bank loan in the company's name.

Adapted from *How to Start and Manage Your Own Business* by Gardiner G. Greene. Copyright © 1975 Gardiner G. Greene. Reprinted by arrangement with The New American Library, Inc., New York, New York.

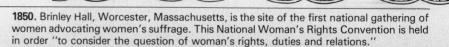

1850. Brinley Hall, Worcester, Massachusetts, is the site of the first national gathering of women advocating women's suffrage. This National Woman's Rights Convention is held in order "to consider the question of woman's rights, duties and relations."

People's Money

Gardiner G. Greene

Third, even if you do not sell the business, it is hard to get your money out without paying a double tax. You may have paid an income tax on it when you earned it originally, before you invested it in the business. Whatever method you use for getting the money out, it may again be subject to tax. You pay tax twice on the same money. How much simpler *not* to put it directly in the business and avoid the whole problem. And don't forget that the interest on your bank loan is deductible.

When you do put in cash, as above, put in somewhat *less* than the company needs. The worst thing for a small, struggling company to have is plenty of cash! Consider the story of the electric pencil sharpener.

A former employee of mine inherited some money. In keeping with my philosophy he left to start a business of his own. Soon he called me, sounding very proud, anxious to show me his new offices. He had rented a building. In it he had put the newest and best machinery and equipment. The office chairs were of fancy leather and his desk was a beauty. "Look at this," he said expansively, "we even have an electric pencil sharpener." We sat down. He put his feet up on his fine new desk and asked me, "What do you think of my business?"

"What business?" I replied.

His company had not obtained its first order! Orders and production make business, not desks and machinery. All he had was some hardware which might have the potential of a business. He did not need all that machinery. He needed no fancy office equipment. He especially did not need an electric pencil sharpener because there were no orders to dull the pencil on! Worst of all, he had spent all his cash and left none for working capital.

There is one overriding consideration for *not* putting all your own cash into your business:

If the business is successful you will need your cash later to help it grow and expand. If it is not successful you will have some cash left to start another business.

Successful businessmen seldom operate on their own money if they can possibly avoid it. That is what capitalism is: a system in which professional business operators utilize other people's money for mutual gain. Mark it down as the OPM formula. *Other people's money.*

On Being Afraid to Owe Money

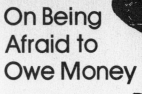

Nancy Borman

Women in business break out in hives at the thought of owing even small amounts of money. Sometimes businesses suffer under ridiculously makeshift conditions because of undercapitalization, but resist even asking for a loan.

To some women a thousand dollars is a staggering sum. Ten dollars is a burdensome debt, and the thought of owing ten or twenty thousand causes sleepless nights.

Majority Report used to save up cash for things, pay bills in time or in advance, and always in full. We got collective chills of the spine wondering if one printer would let us owe him $100 for two weeks.

Then one day we heard him discussing another publisher's bill. The publisher—a man—owed him $1300 over several months. The conversation could be described as friendly, jovial, warm, sympathetic and brief. The men were downright flippant. Neither seemed to have any hair falling out on the spot, nor to be holding his stomach in dire pain. There was some vague implication that the publisher would pay his bill when he got around to it.

We also found out that our printer got his gargantuan plant and Tom Swiftian machinery by "borrowing as much as the bank will lend me for as long as they'll let me owe." He said this with a smile. A calm, everyday kind of smile.

Businesses work on other people's money. Businessmen borrow and owe and then borrow again to pay their debts. Women are taught from childhood that they can't handle money and it's better to let Daddy buy the car, let hubby take care of the lease, let our grown son advise us on financial matters. Finance is cloaked in male mystique, especially when large sums are involved.

We must break through the male fortress if we are to succeed in business. Overcome fears of larger sums. Study banking. Share this lore with one another. Learn about bankruptcy. Find out what would really happen if you could not meet a payment on a loan. And get successful men to give away some of their "secrets."

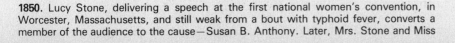

1850. Lucy Stone, delivering a speech at the first national women's convention, in Worcester, Massachusetts, and still weak from a bout with typhoid fever, converts a member of the audience to the cause—Susan B. Anthony. Later, Mrs. Stone and Miss

Dialogue Between Banker and Borrower

Deal with the highest-ranking officer you possibly can, preferably the president. At least the vice-president in charge of the commercial loan department.

If it is necessary to wait a few days for an appointment with the president, wait. This shows you are in no rush and not in trouble, or the victim of poor planning. You can usually get an appointment with a lower officer by walking in. What good can he do for you before the loan committee? Timing is one of the weapons in business dealings, as you have probably learned only too well. Banks will use it on you. So, use it on them.

When you first sit down in the luxurious leather chair, and after the phony pleasantries of the day are dispensed with, *watch out!* You are about to be trapped. The banker will say (as he quickly glances over your statement, pretending to drink it all in, but actually comprehending little), "How much money do you want?" His voice is so benign and he seems like such a nice guy that you unhesitatingly mention an amount. If you do, you have just *lost the first round.*

"Women's only" section of New Amsterdam Bank, New York, late 1880's

New York Public Library

You and your accountants have probably been wrestling with what amount is needed for weeks. It wasn't an arbitrary decision. Nor was the figure easily arrived at. Yet you tossed it off to the banker as if it were both. You have now innocently provided him with the exact location and description of his adversary. Once you reveal it, he can attack it.

"Why do you need it?" "How do you know this is enough?" "How do you know this isn't too much?" "How long do you need it for?" "Why can't you get along without it?" He may trap you still further by emphasizing his question, "Are you sure this is enough?" If you answer yes, he has really got you.

He has saved himself hours of agonizing labor in the process. Bankers are both busy and lazy (banker's hours and all that). All he has to prove now is why you either need more or shouldn't have the amount you requested. This is easy. Anyone with a smattering of business experience can rip any small business statement to shreds. Bankers sure can do this, and he is very safe in doing so because you would not be there if you didn't need money.

The I-Don't-Know Method

What you should have said, when the banker asked how much you wanted to borrow, is, "I don't know." And quickly added, "But I thought you, as my banker, could help us determine this."

This avoids all the pat questions the banker is so carefully trained to ask. He not only has to study your statements but *must* get to know something about your business. He should anyway, of course. It is amazing how little most bankers do know about their customers' businesses.

He knows he can't insult a customer by saying, "Your business isn't worthy of any loan." That is seldom the problem. The real questions are: How much? For how long? At what rate? How will it be repaid? Now *he* must discover how much your company is entitled to borrow. You won the first round by *not* answering his direct question.

You have now put your banker to work for you. Strengths or weaknesses he discovers will be pointed out to you. Policies you can improve will be questioned and suggestions made. By having him pore over your statements and material, you may learn something which only an objective outsider would catch.

More important, from now on you and your banker are negotiating *not* on whether he will make a loan, but on the

Adapted from *How to Start and Manage Your Own Business* by Gardiner G. Greene. Copyright © 1975 Gardiner G. Greene. Reprinted by arrangement with The New American Library, Inc., New York, New York.

Anthony have a falling out over several arcane political-tactical disagreements, opening a rift in the movement that was to take twenty years to heal and from which their relationship never fully recovered.

Who Needs Enemies?

Gardiner G. Greene

Alice Webber

If he had the ability to be an aggressive businessman, facing competition, taking risks, working long hours, meeting payrolls, fending off creditors and collecting from accounts, he would be your competitor, not your banker. Or, if all your competitors had his personality traits you would own the bank and be hiring him to work there for you.

The world is full of little demigods like your banker, and they must be treated so. Make him a hero. Mention a figure larger than you are after and let him act out his part by cutting it. He will probably cut down whatever figure you give, so if you mention the accurate one you will wind up with less than you need.

If you have been master of the interview, he will say, "I think I might be able to convince our loan committee that you should have twelve thousand five hundred." You look hurt and counter by saying, "You are probably right, but do you think they would consider fifteen?" Follow this up with one last sales point that you have been saving for dessert, adding quickly, "After all, our checking account balance for the past eight months has averaged twenty-eight hundred dollars."

This average—called a compensating balance—may affect the amount you can borrow. For example, if your average balance for the past year is $1,000 and the bank uses a 20% formula, you might be considered sound for a $5,000 loan. In giving your average balance, which is another exhibit you might take to the initial loan conference, pick the number of months that are the most favorable to you. If, for the past four months, the average balance was $1,500, but for the past year only $900, present the four-month figure even though it is a shorter period.

Figuring your average balance is easy. Take your bank statement and add the daily balances together. Then divide by the number of days. Include your payroll account also.

Banks use deposits to your checking account as part of their vital cash flow . . . yet they pay you nothing for it. In fact, it costs you money: no interest, service charges, etcetera. But when you use *their* money they charge interest! It is not good strategy to mention this directly. You might make a casual remark or a joke of it, just to remind your banker of the fact.

Getting the banker to visit your place is key to the I-Don't-Know method. If he turns you down without a visit, he has made an irresponsible decision. From bank management's viewpoint, the same is true in reverse. He acts irresponsibly if he approves a loan without seeing your operation.

amount. While he strives to evaluate your company scientifically, you will have the opportunity to show him things he otherwise would not know. To make the most of this, invite him to your plant or place of business. This will allow you more time to do a selling job. Now he is the stranger on *your* home ground. Fill his head and his file with all sorts of reasons why the bank should make the loan. Show him what an asset you are, or can be, to the community. Tell him, as if letting him in on a highly guarded secret, of your great plans for the future.

This technique is important even after you have a long-standing relationship with the bank and arrange loans by phone. When the banker on the other end of the line asks, "How much do you want to borrow this time?" say, "C'mon over and see what you think." Then sell, sell, sell when he gets there. Subtly, of course.

Under any circumstances, whether at your plant or his desk in the bank, do not tell him how much you want. At least not until you have done all the selling, forecasting, and convincing you can. Try to force *him* to bring the matter to a head.

If you have done all you can and he still has not mentioned any figure, you might try one or two on for size. By now you know him better and he is more familiar with your business. When you mention a figure, watch his face and especially his eyes. You might say, "Do you think we need as much as eighteen or twenty thousand?"

Actually you want $15,000, but you have got to make him a hero. He became a banker because he likes the prestige of working in the most imposing building in town.

1852. Gynecological surgery is founded as a branch of medicine through the work of Dr. Frank Marion Sims. Later, as head of the Women's Hospital in New York, Dr. Sims will perfect a technique to artificially impregnate women.

How People Lose Their Shirts

The Editors of *Small Business Reporter*

Too many entrepreneurs think extra cash will solve most every problem. But good management — not money — is the key to whether a company flourishes or dies. According to one prominent business authority, "If a company has everything except good management, it may prosper awhile, but eventually it will fold. On the other hand, if a company's strongest asset is good management, it will make the grade."

One of the best ways for a smaller businessman to learn management skills is by studying the mistakes of others. Management experts have identified those errors most often committed by managers. They include downgrading the need for experience, sloppy recordkeeping, reckless spending, failure to plan, misuse of time, ineffectual marketing programs, personnel mishandling and the failure to assume the proper role as the company grows.

These are traps of which every businessman should be wary. He must avoid such pitfalls or be prepared to see his "baby" wither and die.

1
Downgrading the Need for Experience

In larger companies, major functions of the business — such as finance, sales, personnel, research, engineering, purchasing and production — are generally departmentalized, with a key individual assuming responsibility for their accomplishment. Many smaller concerns usually rely on one man — the owner/manager — to supervise or perform most or all of these tasks. If he lacks the necessary skill and versatility, his company is doomed.

Sole proprietors, especially, must be able to wear many different hats. Superior knowledge of a few, though essential, facets of a business is not sufficient. A classic example of lop-sided experience is the star furniture salesman who started his own firm, believing his abilities were the primary reason for his employer's success. Certain that he could "pick up" whatever bookkeeping or other minor skills were necessary, he was "off and running" without proper preparation. Granted, he knew furniture — but not the furniture business. The ultimate failure of his business could be directly attributed to his lack of experience in accounting, purchasing, pricing, advertising, budgeting and other aspects of management.

Problems arising from inexperience are not limited to new enterprises. Founders often discover, after several or many years have elapsed, that they have been pushed out of their depth by the increasing complexity of the expanding venture. To stay in business, they need to learn new skills.

The obvious solution for lack of experience is to obtain ample training *prior* to launching a new enterprise. Just how much training is enough will depend on the type of business conducted. Many management authorities recommend a minimum of three years' experience in a given line of business, with some time spent in a managerial or decision-making capacity.

For the operator already in business, the only remedy is to acquire some experience — and fast. First, the top man should review his own background and current problems to discover his weak points, the missing parts of his experience. Then, concentrating on closing those gaps, he may acquire knowledgeable employees or partners, hire outside business counselors or undertake an emergency self-development program.

2
Sloppy Recordkeeping

Misleading financial records cause more havoc than any other management mistake: a poor accounting system leads to serious problems in every aspect of business, from sales to insurance, from taxes to inventory control.

Yet the need for an effective bookkeeping system is frequently overlooked. One detailed study of ten small, unsuccessful manufacturing enterprises revealed that all maintained fairly imprecise books, and more than half had systems so inadequate that the state of their businesses remained unknown even to the owners. In contrast, a similar study of ten prosperous organizations showed that each had a complete accounting system and well-informed managers who made full use of financial information in guiding the company.

Adapted and reprinted with permission from "Avoiding Management Pitfalls," *Small Business Reporter*, Vol. 11, No. 5. Copyright © 1973 Bank of America, San Francisco.

1852. Susan B. Anthony organizes the first women's state temperance society in New York.

3

Reckless Money Management

Losing sight of the importance in maintaining a healthy financial position is a grave management error. When a shortage of funds afflicts a company, the owner has little time for anything but the struggle to appease creditors.

Many independents allow capital to dip to dangerously low levels. They forget that cash and cash alone — not inventory, shiny equipment or accounts receivable — pays the bills and provides funds in an emergency.

Cash crises due to undercapitalization are common in new enterprises. But they can also arise in long-established firms if too much capital is tied up in fixed assets, if credit is not controlled, or if growth is not properly paced.

Examples of reckless money management abound. A novice beauty salon operator spent her cash reserves on store improvements without leaving enough to cover expenses or her own salary until the business started to turn a profit. A gadget-happy president of a sign-painting company faced ruin because he continued to purchase costly machinery despite a poor sales record, overdue loan payments and idle plant equipment.

In grappling with a money quandary, the entrepreneur's first move should be to consult his accountant, his banker — or both. After studying the firm's records and financial statements, these counselors can quickly point out ways to conserve cash and control costs. Indeed, a chronic shortage of funds is usually symptomatic of other operational defects. Recommendations by these experts might include (1) inventory house-cleaning, (2) elimination of borderline products and services, (3) rental of fixed assets, (4) reduction of the proprietor's salary, (5) exploitation of purchase discounts, and (6) collection of all overdue accounts.

Clearing Out Inventory

Many companies are burdened by slow-moving, out-dated or excessive inventory. Bargain-hunting managers sometimes make quantity purchases of stock that cannot be sold quickly. Warehousing slow-moving items not only adds to costs but ties up funds which could be used more effectively elsewhere. Deadweight inventory should be sold off and stock control methods revised to maximize high-return stock and minimize cash investment.

4

Failure to Plan

Ask any business advisor what he considers the most predominant failing among struggling entrepreneurs, and he will undoubtedly mention lack of planning. In fact, most business trouble-shooters cite this drawback with unending repetition. All agree with a prominent management consultant who says, "No businessman can hope to succeed unless he masters the art of formulating meaningful plans for his operation."

Planning is critically important to the small firm because it lacks the staff and finances to compete on all fronts simultaneously. Too, a rapidly changing marketplace demands forward-looking strategies. In years past, a concern could wait until a competitor's new product or process was proven before it "jumped on the bandwagon." Today, trends must be detected early in their development and followed by aggressive action.

Planned action is always more accurate than a wild shot in the dark. And while no one can control the future, well-laid plans allow the businessman to take better advantage of opportunities that arise and prevent possible difficulties.

Many businessmen believe they plan because they acknowledge the future. They often vaguely aspire to "do better next year," or contemplate activities they might perform "when business improves." However, thinking ahead is not planning. Instead, planning is a process that involves the fixation of objectives and the determination of methods for reaching them. Without these elements, the businessman is merely indulging in wishful thinking; he is not planning.

Finding the time to plan raises problems for busy executives, who, more often than not, are swamped with "yesterday's" crises. One approach is the scheduling of blocks of time for just this purpose, usually on week ends or in the evening hours. During these periods, the businessman can avoid distractions and interruptions and concentrate on thinking about the firm and its problems.

The most difficult part of plan preparation is in getting started. To trigger ideas, many businessmen undertake a step-by-step analysis of their present situation and their goals for the firm's operation.

- What business am I in?
- What is my place in the industry?
- What is my competitive niche or advantage?
- Who are my customers?
- Are these customers the type I want?
- What is my company image to potential customers?
- What is my biggest problem?
- What is my competition's biggest handicap and how can I exploit it?
- What are my specific goals for improvement?
- What percentage of the market do I want?
- What will my industry be like in five or ten years?
- How can I finance growth?

Basically, this type of session helps identify current problems and long-range goals. From this point, the planning process progresses through six steps: (1) specific goals and problems are targeted, (2) pertinent data researched, (3) possible alternatives for action determined, (4) alternatives and facts (facilities, personnel, equipment, marketing, financing) realistically analyzed, (5) course of action and logical timetable selected, (6) plans periodically reviewed and revised.

Once a company's strategy has been mapped out, it has to be implemented. Plans have no life force of their own; human attention is required if desired results are to be accomplished.

5

Misuse of Time

Typically, the small enterprise has too much to do and too little time in which to do it. Most entrepreneurs work 50- or even 60-hour weeks, with some tallying up over 70 hours a week.

Much of this activity may well be wasted. A recent study by a management consulting firm showed that executives spend more than half of their time on trivial matters. Valuable minutes and hours are often frittered away on insignificant chores while vital jobs are left undone.

Frequently a manager's work week could be reduced — and better results achieved — by sensible time management. The small businessman must learn to control the job rather than letting it control him. His objective is to work "smarter," not harder.

Efficient budgeting of work periods is a matter of self-discipline. A person must make fundamental changes in outlook and habits in order to realize progress in making better use of time. Effective managers put urgent jobs before less pressing ones — or "first things first." They rank duties according to importance, deciding, for instance, which is more urgent: planning a new advertising campaign or hiring a new assistant.

The best approach for tackling both routine duties and on-going projects is the preparation of daily, weekly and monthly schedules. Deadlines can be adjusted as interruptions or emergencies occur. Such systematic arrangement of tasks allows sufficient lead time for preparation of due-date material and eliminates disagreeable last-minute rushes, which find the manager trying to simultaneously help customers and cope with "yesterday's" paperwork.

Delegation

A critical aspect of time management is delegation — the process of assigning appropriate chores to subordinates so that managers are freed from routine, operational duties. "Failure to delegate is the chief reason a manager becomes too involved with everyday activities to perform those important jobs — like planning — that he alone can do," asserts one business authority.

Symptoms of faulty delegation are obvious: the top man is too harried to be effective and makes costly mistakes in customer, personnel and supplier relations. Or, no one is capable of taking over in emergencies and when the boss is ill or absent.

Autocratic or perfectionist executives rationalize their reluctance to delegate by insisting their employees are incompetent (otherwise known as the "I can do it better and faster myself" syndrome).

1853. Rebecca Pennell, appointed this year as a professor of physical geography, among other disciplines, at Antioch College, becomes the first female college professor granted the same professional prerogatives as her male colleagues.

6

Inattention to Marketing

The first concern of every business is to get — and keep — customers. The best products, equipment, facilities and personnel avail nothing unless they stimulate sales.

Some misguided "technicians" dislike selling and resent the time marketing takes away from production or research. Other independent businessmen are lackadaisical or overly optimistic about sales — expecting their merchandise or skills to sell themselves.

Few products are that electrifying, however, and rarely is the old myth true about a better mousetrap bringing the world to one's door. Unless revolutionary inventions or services are brought to the attention of the public, they have little chance of being sold. To build customer awareness and demand, an organized and vigorous marketing campaign is essential. A complete marketing strategy includes not only personal salesmanship, but also a saleable line of products or services, appropriate pricing, adroit advertising and promotion and a good business location.

Many independents see poor sales as an isolated problem rather than a symptom of a poorly developed and coordinated marketing effort. For example, when sales are poor, a panicky businessman may endeavor to reverse the trend through price-cutting, aggressive sales tactics or splashy advertising. However, stopgap gimmicks won't work unless the solution fits the specific marketing problem. Price-cutting rarely compensates for a poor location; increased sales calls or advertising cannot sell an obsolete product.

To combat sales difficulties, the businessman must make an objective analysis of the venture's products and services, its marketing effort, its competitive situation and its efforts to determine the real needs and wants of buyers.

7

Ignoring the Human Factor

Small firms enjoy a favorable reputation for good employer/employee relationships. In reality, a great many independents face serious personnel problems.

Even proprietors with only one employee complain about misunderstood directions, half-hearted work, frequent absences and long lunches or coffee breaks.

Salaries paid to poor producers are precious dollars lost. Studies reveal that malcontented workers not only waste time and materials, they often chase customers away. Nearly 70% of all customer losses can be attributed to indifferent employee service.

At the root of most employee difficulties is inept personnel administration. Typically, the entrepreneur worries about production, sales and finance and neglects the matter of personnel problems until a crisis develops. But to build a loyal and efficient staff, the manager of any business must devote considerable time and effort to hiring, training and managing employees.

The Art of Hiring

The common dislike for being a "small cog in a large wheel" can be turned to advantage by the small company that emphasizes close employer-employee relations and provides opportunities for rapid advancement.

Some firms, though, undercut their hiring efforts by offering less than competitive wages. To attract top-notch help, the independent must offer reasonable salaries, adequate benefits and a decent work environment.

Selecting satisfactory employees is a time-consuming job, which can force a busy executive into hasty and ill-judged choices. The following steps help to minimize the difficulties of finding well-qualified individuals:

1. Determine the specific requirements for the job and form a clear picture of the type of person needed to fill it. Write the essential points in checklist form for reference during interviews.

2. If possible, use a commercial or state employment agency to locate and screen prospects. Furnish agencies with the checklist so they can eliminate the plainly unqualified. Placement offices of secondary schools, trade schools, colleges and universities provide a good source of candidates.

3. Interview all promising applicants. Be sure to ask specific questions and refer to the checklist. Take notes on the impression each individual makes. For some jobs, the

---

1856. Elizabeth Marbury, prominent American theatrical agent and author, is born. In her book *Careers for Women* she states — making reference to her bitter disappointments — "A caress is better than a career."

employer may want to improvise practical tests of the person's skills. When filling a key position, it is often wise to have someone else in the company interview the prospect.

4. Check the applications of all candidates carefully, verifying all references and former employers by telephone. For certain jobs, a physical examination, paid for by the employer, may be desirable.

5. Before hiring, be certain the person understands fully the terms of employment, salary, company policies, work standards and the scope of the job. This avoids later complaints of "I wasn't told about that when I was hired" or "That's not part of my job."

It is pointless to hold out for the perfect employee, passing up a reasonably competent and intelligent person. Enthusiasm and cooperativeness are often more important than experience. In fact, many concerns find it advantageous to employ inexperienced youngsters, handicapped individuals or older workers who compensate for any drawbacks with a willingness to learn and above-average performance.

Placing unqualified friends or members of the family on the payroll — especially in management slots — can be disastrous. While it is admirable to want to give Cousin Bill or Uncle John a "good" job, they should only be employed if they can capably handle the responsibilities involved.

Skillful Human Relations

A manager's expectations of his subordinates and his treatment of them largely determines their job performance and career progress . . . and ultimately the success of the company.

Listed below are some guidelines for successful personnel management offered by the experts.

- Praise good work in public. Discuss grievances or offer constructive criticism in private.

- Actively solicit ideas, suggestions and opinions from employees and use the good ones, giving credit where it is due. Carefully explain why the others are unworkable.

- Respect valid differences of opinion. Not everyone views the same situation the same way.

- Make reasonable efforts to keep jobs interesting; employees are human beings, not robots or machines.

- Admit your own mistakes — it encourages subordinates to do the same.

- Keep employees up to date on all business matters affecting them and quell rumors with correct information. Members of the organization team shouldn't have to read the newspaper to know what's going on in the company.

- Always explain why things are being done as they are. It is difficult for an employee to be intelligent or enthusiastic if he doesn't know the "why" of things.

- Promote from within whenever possible (good training makes it possible). Never promote anyone, particularly a friend or relative, before a better qualified individual.

- Set up personnel policies, but avoid being rigid. Individual solutions can be found for individual problems.

- Be truthful, be consistent and — above all — be fair.

8
Failure to Assume the Proper Role

The precise skills required to be a good manager vary and change as the company grows. The managerial knowledge needed to successfully direct a company in its infancy — when primarily a one-man operation — is different from what a growing concern needs five, ten or twenty years later.

As a company reaches new stages in its development, its chief helmsman must adapt his role in concert. In effect, he must gracefully make the transition from operator, to manager and then on to executive, assuming the responsibilities that each role demands. If the businessman clings to comfortable and familiar jobs, he stymies his organization's growth as well as his own personal development.

1857. "Gentle Annie" is known as the fattest madame in Chicago. Concluding that it was high time for her lover to marry her, she invades his gambling den, drags him off his sofa, and kicks him downstairs; then she chases him through the streets with a rawhide whip. They marry in several weeks.

Woman as Inventor

Matilda Joslyn Gage

NO ASSERTION in reference to woman is more common than that she possesses no inventive or mechanical genius, even the United States census failing to enumerate her among the inventors of the country. But, while such statements are carelessly or ignorantly made, tradition, history, and experience alike prove her possession of these faculties in the highest degree. Although woman's scientific education has been grossly neglected, yet some of the most important inventions of the world are due to her.

Ancient tradition accords to woman the invention of those arts most necessary to comfort, most conducive to wealth, most promotive of civilization. Man's first needs are food, clothing, and shelter, and to woman tradition assigns their present practical forms. Isis in Egypt, Minerva in Greece, Surawatí in India, the mother of the Incas in Peru, and several empresses of China, have alike been worshiped because of their inventive genius.

But, leaving the realm of tradition and half-mythical history, we still find woman accredited with some of the earliest and most useful inventions. That she was the primitive artist is quite universally conceded. To her, as the one to prepare the food, the invention and ornamentation of pottery is ascribed. Among savage races it is still easy to trace the inception and growth of this art in woman's hands. The most ancient Chinese writers accord the invention of spinning to Yao, wife of the fourth emperor, and the discovery of silk to Si-ling-chi, wife of the Emperor Hoang-ti, four thousand years before Christ. This country was long known as Ser, or Serica—the land of silk. Its later name of China originated from Sien Tshan, under which appellation, as goddess of silk-worms, Si-ling-chi is still worshiped. When the word China is spoken, it is in perpetual honor and remembrance of this woman inventor. The unparalleled duration of Chinese civilization and the prosperity of that country are largely due to silk, the secret of which was for ages kept from other nations; and which formed an export of extraordinary value, its weight in gold being paid by Roman emperors for a garment.

As a source of wealth, lace, like silk, has largely influenced state policy. The value of the finest thread lace when wrought in points is enormous, far exceeding that of precious stones. No other art, it is said, is capable of bringing about such an extraordinary increase in value from a material worth as little as flax in the unwrought state. The early records of this art are lost in the mists of antiquity, but there is no doubt that woman was its originator. At the exposition of woman's work in Florence, a few years since, visitors were greatly interested in a specimen of the magnificent lace known as " Puleto di Venezia" (Venetian Point). Its stitch, lost since the thirteenth century, has recently been rediscovered by Madame Bessani, a humble workwoman, to whom the Italian Minister of Commerce accorded letters patent, with exclusive control of her discovery for fifteen years. The importance of Madame Bessani's invention to Italy is incalculable, opening to that country an immense source of revenue and political power.

The straw industry of the United States owes its origin to Miss Betsy Metcalf, who, in 1798, made the first straw bonnet ever manufactured in this country. Within twelve years thereafter the State of Massachusetts alone produced half a million dollars' worth of straw goods.

From *North American Review*, May 1883.

The most remarkable invention of the age, in its industrial, social, and political influence, — the cotton-gin,— owes its origin to a woman, Catharine Littlefield Greene, widow of General Greene, of Revolutionary memory, with whom the idea originated. The cotton-gin heads the list of sixteen remarkable American inventions that have been adopted by the world.

After the close of the war General Greene settled in Georgia, where he soon died. The great difficulty of separating the seed from the cotton was at that time the staple subject of conversation among planters. To separate a pound of the black seed from the lint was a day's task for a negro. The white variety, much more valuable, from its greater tenacity, was scarcely at all cultivated. It was the regular custom of the planter's family to unite in this work every evening, and a fortune was prophesied for the person who should construct a machine capable of doing the work. After a conversation of this character between some guests at her house, Mrs. Greene conceived the idea of such a machine, and intrusted its construction to the hands of Eli Whitney, then boarding with her, who possessed the usual New England facility in the use of tools. The wooden teeth at first tried not doing their work well, Mr. Whitney wished to abandon the machine altogether; but Mrs. Greene, whose faith in ultimate success never wavered, would not consent; she suggested the substitution of wire. Within ten days from the first conception of Mrs. Greene's ideas, a small model was completed, so perfect in its construction that all succeeding gins have been based upon it.

A very slight investigation proves that patents taken out in some man's name are, in many instances, due to women. A recent noted instance of this kind is Miss Louise McLaughlin's invention of underglaze painting on pottery. Miss McLaughlin, desiring that all artists should share in its benefits, explained her process to every person who asked her, and even wrote a book giving this information. But a certain man, seeing its value, took out a patent upon it, thus prohibiting even its inventor from using the fruit of her own brains. The Burden horse-shoe machine, turning out a complete shoe every three seconds, was a woman's invention. At a renewal of the patent, in 1871, it was claimed that thirty-two million dollars had been saved to the public during the fourteen years of its use.

A third great American invention, the mower and reaper, owes its early perfection to Mrs. Ann Harned Manning, of Plainfield, New Jersey, who, in 1817–18, perfected a system for the combined action of teeth and cutters, patented by her husband, William Henry Manning, as " a device for the combined action of teeth and cutters, whether in a transverse or revolving direction." Mrs. Manning also made other improvements, of which, not having been patented, she was robbed after her husband's death by a neighbor whose name appears in the list of patentees upon this machine. Mrs. Manning also invented a clover cleaner, which proved very lucrative to her husband, who took out the patent. Nor was she the only woman whose thought has been turned toward agricultural machines. The name of Elizabeth Smith, also of New Jersey, appears in 1861 among the list of patentees upon an improvement to the mower and reaper, whereby the knives could be adjusted while the machine was in motion.

The smallest inventions sometimes prove the most lucrative. A San Francisco lady, inventor of a baby carriage, received

---

1860. A huge street demonstration is staged by the girl shoe workers of Lynn, Massachusetts. Women factory workers of this time are paid between eight and fifty cents per day, and 65 percent of all jobs in Atlantic Coast factories are held by children under twelve years old and women.

"It's never occurred to you, I suppose, that they might have been done by a cave-<u>woman</u>."

fourteen thousand dollars for her patent. The paper pail, the invention of a Chicago lady, yields a large income. The gimlet-pointed screw, the idea of a little girl, has realized millions of dollars to its patentee.

Among recent inventions of importance by women, are a spinning machine, capable of running from twelve to forty threads; a rotary loom, doing three times the work of an ordinary loom; a volcanic furnace for smelting ore; an improved wood-sawing machine; a space-saving clothes-mangle; a chain elevator; screw-crank for steamships; a fire-escape; a device for correct pen-holding, invaluable in schools; a wool feeder and weigher, one of the most delicate machines ever invented, and of incalculable benefit to every woolen manufacturer; a self-fastening button; a portable reservoir for use in case of fires; a process for burning petroleum in place of wood and coal for steam generating purposes; an improvement in spark-arresters, to be applied to locomotives; a danger-signal for street-crossings on railways; a plan for heating cars without fire; a lubricating felt for subduing friction (the last five all bearing upon railroad travel); a rapid change box, a marvel of simplicity and convenience, invaluable at railway stations and ferries, the invention of a girl of sixteen; syllable type with adjustable cases and apparatus; machine for trimming pamphlets; writing-machine; signal rocket, used in the navy; deep-sea telescope; method of deadening sound on elevated railways; smoke-burner; satchel-bottom bags; bag-folding machine, etc., etc. Many improvements in sewing machines have been made by women; as a device for sewing sails and heavy cloth; quilting attachments: the magic ruffler; threading a machine when upon a full run (an idea scouted by male machinists); an adaptation of machines for sewing leather, etc. This last was the invention of a practical woman machinist, who for many years carried on a large harness manufactory in New York City.

The deep-sea telescope, invented by Mrs. Mather, and improved by her daughter, is a unique and important invention, bringing the bottom of the largest ships to view without the expense of raising them into a dry-dock. By its means wrecks can be inspected, obstructions to navigation removed, torpedoes successfully sought for, and immense sums annually saved to the marine service.

The remarkable invention of Mrs. Mary E. Walton, for deadening the noise of elevated railroads, has occasioned much comment. Edison and other inventors had for six months unsuccessfully striven to accomplish this end, when Mrs. Walton brought forward a device which was at once adopted by the Metropolitan and other elevated railways. The benefit to human health and life likely to accrue from this invention can scarcely be realized.

While passing by woman's discovery in science, where the names of Hypatia, Maria Agnesi, and Caroline Herschel shine, mention must still be made of the aquarium, the invention of Madam Jeanette Power, one of the most eminent naturalists of the century. It was used by her in making curious scientific discoveries. The value of the aquarium to marine zoölogy is incalculable.

Medicine, even in modern times, owes much to woman. It was to her knowledge of this art that woman's persecution for witchcraft in the middle ages was largely due. Through Madame de Coudray's invention of the manikin, a knowledge of physiology has been much more widely diffused than would otherwise have been possible. Many delicate and important surgical instruments owe their origin to woman, as also the adaptation of wax for recording medical observations

While, as has been shown, many of the world's most important inventions are due to woman, the proportion of feminine inventors is much less than of masculine, which arises from the fact that woman does not possess the same amount of freedom as man. Restricted in education, industrial opportunities, and political power, this is one of many instances where her degradation reacts injuriously upon the race. The majority of inventions are the result of much consideration and self-reliant thought. Inventors must not only possess full freedom

1863. Excerpt from a U.S. Civil War army-nurse recruiting poster: "No woman under thirty years need apply to serve in government hospitals. All nurses are required to be very plain-looking women. Their dresses must be brown or black, with no bows, no curls or jewelry, and no hoopskirts."

to exercise their powers, but there must also be a certain welcome and protection to their ideas. Deprived, as woman is, of political power, she has to face contempt of her sex, open and covert scorn of womanhood, depreciatory allusions to her intellectual powers, —all tending to hamper the expression of her inventive genius.

Nor is woman by law recognized as possessing full right to the use and control of her own powers. In not a single State of the Union is a married woman held to possess a right to her earnings within the family; and in not one-half of them has she a right to their control in business entered upon outside of the household. Should such a woman be successful in obtaining a patent, what then? Would she be free to do as she pleased with it? Not at all. She would hold no right, title, or power over this work of her own brain. She would possess no legal right to contract, or to license any one to use her invention. Neither, should her right be infringed, could she sue the offender. Her husband could take out the patent in his own name, sell her invention for his own sole benefit, give it away if he so chose, or refrain from using it, and for all this she would have no remedy.

It is scarcely thirty years since the first State protected a married woman in the use of her own brain property. Under these conditions, legally incapable of holding property, and trained, as she has been, to seclusion, dependence, and abeyance of thought, that woman has not been an inventor to an equal extent with man is not so much a subject of surprise as that she should have invented at all.

Matilda Joslyn Gage (1826-1898), woman's rights advocate, was known within the movement of the time for her superior writing and organizing talents. Named as president to both the National Woman Suffrage Association and the New York State Woman Suffrage Association in 1875, she was also co-author of Mrs. Stanton's famous "Declaration of Rights," and in combination with Mrs. Stanton and Susan B. Anthony she wrote the massive History of Woman Suffrage. *On her gravestone is carved her motto: "There is a word sweeter than Mother, Home, or Heaven; that word is Liberty."—Ed.*

The Measure of Success:
Return on Investment

The Editors of *Small Business Reporter*

The ultimate gauge of a business owner's success is the profit he makes from his operation. To measure return on investment, Net Profit After Taxes, derived from the Income Statement, is compared to Owner's Equity (or Capital) on the Balance Sheet.

In a corporation, a return on investment ratio usually yields a percentage ranging from 5% to 15%. However, the corporate net profit figure used in the ratio shows an amount from which all salaries have been deducted and federal income taxes have been paid.

Net Profit for the single proprietor represents not only his return on investment but also the source from which he draws his "salary" — compensation for his labor throughout the year.

To compare his return on investment with that of a similar but incorporated business, the single proprietor should deduct from his profit the amount he could earn working for someone else, as well as a hypothetical corporate tax.

Adapted and reprinted with permission from "Retail Financial Records," *Small Business Reporter*, Vol. 19, No. 5. Copyright © 1971 Bank of America, San Francisco.

Using the net profit shown on our hypothetical financial statement, the formula works out as follows:

Net Profit	$17,930
Salary could earn elsewhere	-10,000
	$ 7,930
Corporate tax (22%)	- 1,586
Comparable Net Profit Figure	$ 6,344

$$\frac{\text{Net Profit}\quad \$ 6{,}344}{\text{Owner's Equity}\quad \$45{,}820} = 14\%$$

There is no minimum percentage that indicates a "good" return on investment. Rather, financial success is relative to the return available from other sources. Perhaps the same money invested in a business would bring the owner a higher return if invested in a mutual fund or placed in a savings account.

The intangible return on investment factors should also be weighed. Long hours, hard work and occasional headaches are inevitable for the single proprietor. Nevertheless, pride, independence, and a sense of accomplishment are extremely rewarding returns for running one's own business with financial success.

1863. Lady Cough writes her famous book, *Etiquette*, a classic in its day. On page 80 the following admonition appears: "The perfect hostess will see to it that the works of male and female authors be properly separated on her bookshelves. Their proximity, unless the authors happen to be married, should not be tolerated."

Pricing Your Products
William E. Garrison

It is not easy to find someone with the right background to give advice on selling handcrafts, yet it is absolutely essential that your products are priced correctly. It is very easy to aim too low or too high. An established price structure is difficult to change. That does not mean that the changes necessary for cost increases in materials cannot be made; rather it means that it is extremely difficult to double or treble prices because they were too low initially. Real thought must be given to price structure before going into the marketplace. Pricing is not simple, and you will never make a more important decision.

It is well worth the time and effort to understand fully just what is involved in pricing before you begin selling. A brief look at the system by which most products are marketed in the United States is enlightening. The average product goes through a whole chain of marketing organizations before getting to the retail customer. Obviously, each link in the chain adds cost to the final price.

The producer (handcrafter or manufacturer) can choose to sell his product himself—by one of several methods—or to use a distribution system. While there are various levels of distributors, for our purposes we are discussing a marketing organization able to sell the products to wholesalers or retailers, or directly to retail customers—or any combination of these methods.

While it is fairly obvious that the various steps in the marketing each add to the cost of the item, people often make the mistake of thinking that direct sales do not add to the price of the item.

A typical situation can be illustrated by the plight of a craftsman who produces candles. His cost is $1 each. He feels that a markup of 35 percent will pay for his labor profitably. Thus his candles are priced at $1.35 each. He honestly thinks that he has done a good job of pricing. In fact, the whole arrangement seems great. He produces and sells a lot of candles from his home workshop. As business volume increases, however, he realizes that he is spending so much time ringing up sales that he is not producing many candles. If he hires someone to handle sales, his costs will certainly increase. If he continues to cope with it himself then his production will go down. At about that

time, he realizes that he has not based his prices correctly.

Of course, if our candle craftsman discovered that he did not have customers coming to his home workshop, he might consider that the local art festival would be the place to sell his production. Upon reading the entry requirements, however, he learns to his dismay that the festival charges a nominal fee for registration, as well as taking a commission of 30 percent on all items sold at the fair. In addition, the craftsman has to consider the setting up and dismantling of the booth, transport to and from the show, and breakage as well as his time attending the festival—time that he might have spent producing candles.

Any price increase that this craftsman considers will not be nominal. Will the radical change in prices mean that his candles are so expensive that no one will buy them? At this point, the craftsman wonders how he went so far astray in his pricing. Unfortunately, he started at the wrong point, and many of his assumptions were incorrect. His original retail price (cost + labor) was completely unreal. If the purpose of selling your handcraft is to enable you to become self-supporting, it is vital that you clarify the hidden costs.

The following list was compiled with the help of information from the Small Business and Loans Administration. Branches of this government agency are located throughout the country. Basic cost considerations are detailed as:

1. Costs of materials, labor, and overhead of premises;
2. Selling expenses, including delivery;
3. General administrative expenses, including office help;
4. Profit.

When businessmen are asked about their profit percentage, they invariably have the following reply: "If I place my money in a savings bank, it will earn a fixed percentage of interest. I will have no worries and no work. Each quarter the savings bank adds interest to my money." In the seventies, the average rate of interest paid by savings banks on money in savings accounts has been 5 percent. Thus, a business's profit margin should certainly be higher than that to justify the work and risk.

1865. Mary Surratt is among those hanged for conspiring with John Wilkes Booth to assassinate President Lincoln at Ford's Theater in Washington, D.C. The original plan was to do away with the vice-president and certain members of Congress as well.

If you use the above list, you are able to estimate 1, 3, and 4 from your own figures. You know what your materials cost you. You can run a time check on yourself (more on that later) and, when you have decided on a rate of pay, your salary is established. The tax laws specify what tax deductions can be made for businesses operating from private residences—what portion of the rent or mortgage and what portion of telephone and utilities can be deducted. An accountant can swiftly itemize these costs if you do not handle your own taxes.

Item 2 contains the pitfalls for the unwary. However you choose to sell your product, you must clarify the costs involved. Your product can go from you through all five links of the marketing chain:

> Craftsman to distributor to wholesaler to retailer to retail customer.

If you choose to follow the above, then the following percentage markups are average:

The craftsman (combining 1, 2, 3, and 4) arrives at	$1.00
The distributor adds 35 percent	$1.35
The wholesaler adds 45 percent	$1.96
The retailer adds 100 percent	$3.92

Frequently, the retail percentage is called 50 percent. It might be less confusing if we put it another way: the retail markup is never less than double the wholesale price.

While the retailer is often accused of charging high prices, he often has more marketing cost than either the distributor or wholesaler.

Often, the first reaction to the above pricing structure is outrage at the way the cost is escalated. Then, the craftsman thinks, "If I sidestep one of the links in the marketing chain I can save money." That person has fallen into one of the pitfalls that trap many. If you sell to a distributor, you have to learn his business methods. If you go directly to a wholesaler, you are taking on the salesman's job; besides, the distributor's methods will differ from those of the wholesaler. Who will pay you for your time spent in learning new conditions and selling to different links in the marketing chain?

Perhaps you are able to go directly to retail outlets. Again, the selling conditions are different.

Whatever method or system of distribution you prefer, each has its own costs. Your cost in contacting the distributor—whether he is at step 1

League of New Hampshire Craftsmen

or 3 in the marketing organization—must always be included in your analysis of expenses.

Now that we have defined the structure of pricing, we should clarify several basic points. First, and of major importance, the craftsman must determine what dollar per hour rate he is willing to work for. If he is willing to work for 25¢ an hour, that's his business. However, he must establish an hourly rate for himself. Once he has done this, he must refuse to work at a lower wage. For the sake of comparison, let's look at the nationally established minimum wage. Of course, while it keeps creeping higher, it does represent the lowest pay rate for the least skilled worker. The unskilled beginner gets the minimum wage regardless of his capability, production rate, or the number of mistakes he may make in the course of an average day. The craftsman who accepts a rate below the established minimum wage seems to be indicating that he places little value on his own work and skill. Does this indicate a positive attitude? It seems reasonable that the skilled craftsman would be paid a rate at least double that of the minimum wage.

Now to arrive at a formula by which the craftsman can price his creations. Let the letter L stand for labor cost. The time required to produce any item on a unit basis is expressed by the letter T; it may be a fraction of an hour or many hours. The formula $L \times T$ equals the labor cost for any item produced.

Example: One establishes a minimum wage of $3.50 an hour. It takes 15 minutes (0.25 hour) to

Paul C. Cabot III

make a hand-dipped candle. The labor cost of the candle is:

$$\$3.50 \times 0.25 = \$.875$$

Please do not leave off that final 5—the figure above is not $.87, it is $.875.

The letter M represents cost of materials. This varies from one craft to another. In some cases, M is so low it seems of little importance. When costly materials are used, however, M can be more important than L. M is often directly related to how the producing craftsman obtains what he needs.

This part of the cost is absolutely essential in the analysis required in pricing products. A craftsman may use items which cost nothing directly; perhaps they are found on the beach, for example. In that case, cost of materials M is not zero but is determined by how many units he finds per hour, at his regular hourly rate of pay.

Example: The candle craftsman collects beach stones to embed in his candles. On the average, he picks up thirty such stones each hour. It takes an hour each way to and from the beach. What is M, the unit cost of his beach stones?

Three hours on the beach @ $3.50 per hour	$10.50
Two hours driving time @ $3.50 per hour	7.00
Gasoline, mileage, both ways	10.00
Total	$27.50

M, the unit cost for the beach stones, is thus established for this trip at $27.50 divided by 90 (the number collected). The beach stones which supposedly cost nothing have really cost the craftsman $.305 each.

However, the candle craftsman has forgotten yet a further part of the pricing formula: Overhead. This is a somewhat mysterious term to most craftsmen. It is full of uncertainties. Overhead is the total of all costs other than direct labor and materials. Overhead covers tools, bulk supplies, paper, pencils, electricity, heat, water, telephone, and the work area in which the craftsman produces the things he sells. Everything not directly part of the production process is properly called overhead. Training, the time spent in ordering supplies, time spent on designing, time spent in talking to customers or potential buyers—all of this is hidden cost and in total is O for overhead.

Now our formula is:

$$L + M + O = \text{Wholesale Price}$$

If you come up with any other answer then you are wrong. And, as we have mentioned earlier, R—the retail price—for handcrafts is generally not less than double the wholesale price.

$$R = W \times 2 \text{ (minimum)}$$

Now let's put some numbers into the formula and make some use of it. If the candle craftsman produces 4 pieces per hour, at his self-established hourly rate of $3.50, his labor ($L$) is $.875 per unit. If we use M (cost of materials) of $.305 from our arithmetic on the unit cost of the beach stones, we have two of the three costs required to compute the wholesale price. Overhead, O, the hidden costs are not quite so easy to compute.

In the beginning, there is simply no way it can be done accurately and in the detail needed to compute O for a candle. The only way to obtain fairly meaningful data is to take an arbitrary definition of O and use that for the time being.

So long as there are no people on the payroll and all the work is handled by the craftsman himself, the rule of thumb for overhead is that O is a third of either L or M, whichever is higher. (If there is even one person on the payroll, the rule of thumb is that O is equal to a third of L plus M.)

For our purposes, we will say that the craftsman is producing the candles himself. This means that O is established (as in the above formula) as a third of either L or M, whichever is higher. In this case, L is higher at $.875 per unit. O for this illustration becomes a third of L (.333 × .875) or .291 per unit.

Thus the pricing of the hand dipped candles becomes:

$$L + M + O = W \text{ (wholesale)}$$
$$\$.875 + \$.305 + \$.291 = \$1.47 \text{ per unit}$$

If the retail price is wholesale times two, $1.47 × 2 = $2.94 per unit—or candle. That figure is a

When a *New York Herald* correspondent, charmed by her attentions, released military secrets, she instantly communicated the information to General "Stonewall" Jackson. For these and other exploits she was finally captured and sentenced to death, but at the last minute she was pardoned and went to England where she began a career on the stage.

long way from where the craftsman first established his selling price at $1.35.

At this point, the bewildered craftsman explodes, "Nobody in his right mind is going to pay $2.94 for my candles. What can I do?"

Well, Mr. Craftsman, you do have a problem and you will have to make a decision. You can establish your price at $2.94 per candle and hold it there, or you can discontinue the item. Perhaps, however, you can find a way to reduce the costs. Those are the only alternatives, and we will look at the possibilities in depth before making that final decision.

In the first place, the craftsman does not know whether anyone will pay $2.94 for one of his candles until they are put out for sale at that price. We craftsmen are frequently guilty of so seriously underpricing our work that the buying public gets the impression that it isn't worth much. It is just as easy to lose sales from underpricing as from overpricing. It is impossible to know what people will pay for a product until it is exposed to public view with a clear price tag.

Perhaps the candle craftsman considers the time when he was selling his wares from his home studio with little time and effort involved in the process. He wonders if by selling at the established retail price of $2.94 he is making an extra profit. However, he should realize that the additional money was earned because he took over the function of the retail salesman. During that selling period, he was unable to function as a craftsman.

Occasionally, you may choose to copy the retail shops' selling method of putting merchandise out at bargain prices, for a limited period. Certainly that is your right but do keep in mind that this is not changing the established retail price, it is offering a special bargain.

If you ignore the realities of this pricing formula, you will never learn to price your products and—perhaps more importantly—it will be virtually impossible for you to become self-supporting as a craftsman. You may choose to produce without having made such an analysis. Or you may choose to work for $.25 an hour. That is your business. Can you, however, live on the income you earn in this way?

To sum up, it is essential that you analyze your costs and establish a minimum wage rate. If you find that you are not earning this amount, find out what is wrong and do something about it. Either discontinue the item or find some way to make it pay off for you.

Selling Your Ideas to a Manufacturer
The Editors of *Small Business Reporter*

Despite the fact that almost all manufacturing companies are constantly on the lookout for new products to complement their existing lines, and are dependent on them for future profits, the independent inventor is not always welcomed with open arms. Getting to see the person with the necessary knowledge and authority to appraise and accept the proposed product often takes tact and time.

Many companies receive new product ideas with decided coolness. The reasons are numerous. Often, companies are besieged by unsolicited ideas from the public, very few of which are even worth serious consideration. Larger producers frequently have research and development departments into which substantial sums of money have been invested: management, naturally, favors in-house developments. Manufacturers, too, are wary of inventors who claim that their ideas have been stolen, when in fact the company may have been working on the same idea at the same time.

Larger corporations often publish their policies and procedures regarding new product ideas from outside sources. Some have "submitted ideas departments." Most companies would prefer that the inventor merely send them a copy of the patent on a new idea. In a few rare cases, the inventor might wish to submit a copy of the patent application as soon as it has been filed.

An often recommended safeguard for inventors is to submit undated descriptions and drawings of their inventions to companies, retaining dated and witnessed copies in their files. This avoids any misunderstanding later as to who thought of the idea first — the inventor or the company. Many companies, before considering a proposed idea, require the inventor's signature on a form releasing the company from obligation and responsibility.

When submitting an idea that is not patentable, the inventor should be aware of the company's policy regarding unsolicited ideas before sending it. Some companies reserve the right to make arbitrary payment for ideas as they see fit. If a patented idea is accepted, the inventor may be able to choose whether to sell the patent outright for a lump sum or to enter into a licensing agreement with the company.

Adapted and reprinted with permission from "Marketing a New Product," *Small Business Reporter*, Vol. 10, No. 5. Copyright © 1971 Bank of America, San Francisco.

1866. Boston is the site of the first American Young Women's Christian Association, whose president is a Mrs. Henry F. Durant. Later, in 1906, two national arms of the organization will join to become the YWCA of the United States, headed by Grace H. Dodge from New York.

Sources of Help in Selling Product Ideas

The Official Gazette

The Official Gazette of the U.S. Patent Office is published weekly and lists all the patents issued during that week together with an abstract and one drawing of each. It also includes a section called "Patents Available for Licensing and Sale" where, for a fee of $3.00, patents can be listed by title and number with the name and address of the inventor. Interested manufacturers can then get in touch with patent owners direct. Some 30 public and college libraries in California subscribe to the Gazette.

Other Listings

Other privately published journals periodically list patents of interest to certain trade and industry groups. These also are often subscribed to by major libraries.

National Bureau of Standards: Office of Invention and Innovation

If the inventor has a product he hopes to sell to the U.S. Government, he can submit it directly to the agency he thinks can use it, or he can send it to the Department of Commerce's Office of Invention and Innovation. This office, which is part of the National Bureau of Standards, will refer ideas to the relevant agencies without evaluating them. The inventor should make it clear that his idea is for sale, not a gift, and is submitted in confidence.

Inventors' Expositions

The Office of Invention and Innovation also works with individual states through their economic development agencies or departments, as well as with chambers of commerce, in sponsoring inventors' expositions. Patent owners (or those whose patents are pending) can rent a booth for a nominal sum and exhibit their products or ideas to interested visitors, including, hopefully, manufacturers.
These expositions may be called "congresses" or "fairs" and are sometimes part of a larger overall industry or trade show. Occasionally seminars or lectures presented by officials, manufacturers and others interested in new products and inventions, are featured during the show. Some states have never held an inventors' exposition; others, such as California, hold them almost annually. A list of upcoming inventors' expositions and more information about them can be obtained from the Office of Invention and Innovation in Washington, or field offices of the U.S. Department of Commerce.

Universities

Some state university systems, including California's, have clearing houses for patented and patentable ideas and inventions. Primarily handling the inventions of faculty and students, these clearing houses are usually only interested in off-campus ideas that will bring substantial financial return to the university. If an agreement to follow up on an idea results, they generally expend a great deal of time and effort on behalf of the inventor and, in return, expect a large slice of resulting royalties. The University of California, for example, keeps half of all resulting profits.

Private Sources

Private sources of assistance for the product inventor range from the multimillion dollar "think tanks" and institutes to the tiny, often one-man, promotion and marketing consultant offices. Called everything from "product technology consultants" to "invention brokers," consultants differ widely in the way they operate, the amount of help they can provide and the fees they charge. Some represent the inventor on a retainer basis and try to put him in touch with interested manufacturers; others will agree to work for a cut of future royalties. Many have workshops where they can produce models and drawings for the inventor. The product inventor should take time and care in selecting the right individual or firm to help him since not all are capable of rendering services commensurate with their promises and fees.

1866. Victoria Claflin Woodhull and her sister, Tennessee Celest Claflin, arrive in New York after having been inspired by a "vision" and open shop as the first woman-owned brokerage office. Their company earns, within the first six weeks of operation, a tidy net profit of $750,000. However, the volatile and highly controversial sisters, associated with

Unethical Practices

The independent inventor is extremely vulnerable. He frequently has limited business experience plus an unshakable faith in his invention which make him susceptible to flattery. His major fear is that his idea will be stolen from him by an unscrupulous company. This is probably less of a hazard, however, than the dishonest or incapable sources that try to sell him advice and services. For example:

Bargain Searches

Offers to make a patent search for $10 or even free are suspect. It is a simple matter to claim that a search has been made without doing a thorough job or without making one at all. Some of the individuals and companies offering cut-rate searches attempt to look authentic by using a name that may include the term "patent office" while having nothing to do with the U.S. Patent Office. To obtain a reliable search, a licensed patent lawyer, attorney or agent should be consulted.

Advertised "Legal" Advice

Patent attorneys and agents recognized by the U.S. Patent Office are forbidden by the Office to advertise. Anyone advertising legal patent advice is therefore suspect.

Promoters and Marketers

There are many hard-working, experienced product developers who put forth substantial effort on behalf of their inventor clients, for a reasonable fee and with a good record of success. There are also some who are less than ethical.

Most inventors whose patents are published find they receive many letters offering promotional help. These should be carefully scrutinized to ascertain exactly what the individual or company proposes to do and for what compensation.

Another aspect to be considered is the length of time any agreement reached will be in effect. Occasionally an inventor's profits have been wiped out altogether because he went to one broker with no success, and then to another later on, without setting time limits for each in which to sell the product idea. When the product is finally sold, all the brokers descend to collect their cut.

Before entering into any agreement, the inventor should make a careful and thorough check on the reputation, charges and services of the agent. The local office of the Better Business Bureau might be a good place to start. Legal implications of proposed contracts should be discussed with a lawyer.

An investigation of a business library's resources is a good beginning for any inventor.

Paul C. Cabot III

myriad shady deals and countless romances (one, in particular, with Commodore Vanderbilt), shortly go out of business. They manage, nevertheless, to retire from their Wall Street adventure with excellent returns on their efforts.

Tips on Mail-order Profit Mirages

The Better Business Bureau of Metropolitan New York

> These tested, proven mail order money makers can put you in the rich, fabulous mail order business overnight—on a shoestring.

This advertisement is typical of those that promise to make you rich by setting up a profitable mail order business in your own home. They are becoming more and more common.

A Demanding Task

Building a solid, profitable mail order business is a demanding, full-time task. Few inexperienced individuals can learn enough about the business before their capital or patience runs out. But the promoter who promises huge returns with virtually no expense or labor on your part can make it all sound quite plausible. In fact, what the promoter generally offers are shoddy products, directly or through unnamed suppliers called "drop-shippers." He also offers instructions, catalogs, mailing lists, "inside secrets," and advice, often of dubious value. He may cite unauthenticated "case histories." Here is a typical ad:

> Now you can build a profitable mail order business on your own the proven way. Use professional mail order ads. Your own catalogs. Pocket cash profits daily. Don't invest a cent in inventory. Large firms supply advertisements, catalogs and do all shipping for you. Amazing new plan for beginners requires little capital and previous experience. The ideal home business.

Possibilities of Failure

Like other new business ventures, the mail order business is fraught with possibilities of failure. No one can assure even an experienced businessman a return on his investment, let alone exceptional profits. Professional mail order men are constantly in search of new and interesting products which are not ordinarily available through regular retail or mail order channels. They depend upon list brokers who provide lists of customers likely to purchase particular products. They are adept at devising mailing material which will sell these items. Even so, they know that they may lose on their investment, despite their best efforts. For every successful sales campaign they may sustain one or more losses. When they've hit upon a successful direct mail selling campaign they strive to keep potential competitors from learning sources of supply and the like. They do not share such information with others.

Adapted from *Tips on Mail Order Profit Mirages.* Copyright © 1972 Council of Better Business Bureaus, Inc.

Why, then, would a promoter offer to share his market know-how and potential market with a beginner, a perfect stranger? Obviously, his know-how is of little value and his market potential is sheer fiction. *You* are his market potential!

Misleading Advertising

In virtually every case, this type of mail order promoter is not himself successful in mail order. His sole purpose is to sell you something—cheap catalogs listing products with stale or dubious sales appeal and near-worthless oral and printed advice. Few beginners who respond to misleading advertising making such offers can long survive and the unscrupulous promoter does not expect them to.

Responsibility in Complaints

The beginner advertising dubious products is strictly on his own when complaints start coming in. The promoter is merely a supplier. There are a few beginners who have overcome repeated failures and arrived at a point where they begin to show a modest profit. However, for most people, the fabulous returns promised by promoters are a fantasy.

Before You Invest—Investigate

There is no easy solution to the problem of questionable mail order promotions but there are some practical safeguards. People seeking "employment" and "business opportunities" on a part-time basis should:

1. Study the business and learn all they can about its pitfalls, as well as its opportunities.

2. Evaluate the risks of establishing any business successfully in the absence of prior experience.

3. Investigate the reliability of anyone offering a sales proposition with the local Better Business Bureau or Chamber of Commerce.

4. Check the performance claims made for the products involved and make sure they are supported by competent evidence.

5. Demand proof of earnings claims and verify whatever information is secured by direct contact with those whose earnings are reported.

6. Read and understand the terms of any contract or agreement before signing it.

When you become a sales agent you act as an independent businessman. Your reputation is at stake. It can be protected only if you are prepared to stand behind the product you sell and the claims made for it.

1870. Shortly after their fling in high finance, Victoria and Tennessee found *Woodhull & Claflin's Weekly,* a scandal and sensation sheet, which offers up a curious combination of feminist consciousness, mysticism, and yellow journalism. Espousing free love, the legalization of prostitution, women's rights, and various other radical causes, the sisters

The Money Manager

How the Banking System Works

Roslyn L. Kramer

The flow of money, like electric current, is fascinating not only for what it produces, but for its own exotic dynamism.

The banking system has many components, but in terms of consumer and business needs, money is ultimately exchanged and created by *commercial banks.* Commercial banks, in turn, are dependent on the *Federal Reserve* system, which has two functions. It serves as a bank for banks, lending money to member banks and holding most of their reserves—their money assets. (Reserves on deposit with the Fed are, in effect, checking accounts of member banks.) The Fed also controls the amount of money in the entire economy, thereby affecting business activity and employment.

The unique characteristic of commercial banks is their function as a depository for checking accounts, the essential mechanism for transferring money quickly and safely. The entire monetary exchange process relies on the universal and voluntary use of checking accounts to transfer money from debtor to creditor, and from buyer to seller. Because checking account balances can be used immediately, they are called *demand deposits;* they are highly liquid. Many other institutions deal with forms of money—saving banks, saving and loan associations, life insurance companies, securities brokers and dealers. But all, finally, must have checking accounts in commercial banks in order to realistically receive and pay money in our modern society, in which checkbook money is used to transact most business.

Money is created through loans. If a depositor simply takes money from Bank A to pay a creditor with an account in Bank B, no money is created; money is simply redistributed within the system. Nothing is lost, either. But if Bank A grants a loan to a customer, it has created money the customer can spend immediately. The actual increase in money materializes as soon as the bank credits the borrower's checking account with the amount of the loan.

Meanwhile, the loan churns through the banking system, as the original customer takes her or his new money from Bank A to pay a creditor, who puts the money into an account in Bank B, and who in turn pays a debt to yet another creditor who has an account in Bank C. Each bank must put aside as reserves some of the money it receives in deposits. Part of these reserves are added to the bank's account at the Fed; part remain in the bank's vault in the form of cash. The rest of the money becomes the base on which banks can create new loans. As banks lend money that becomes dispersed in many banks across the country, the total amount of money in the entire system enlarges.

The Federal Reserve System is the veins and arteries of the commercial banking system. Checks pass through the Fed on their way from one bank to another, pausing briefly while the Fed increases or decreases the member bank's account by the amount of each check.

The immediate decision to grant a specific loan is made by a commercial bank on the recommendation of an individual bank officer, or for large loans, a committee of bankers specializing in a particular industry or geographical area. But it is the Federal Reserve system that really decides whether many loans are made or not by setting conditions sympathetic or hostile to the expansion of money.

The Fed tries to maintain a healthy balance by removing money from or putting money into circulation. When it does the former, it is said to be pursuing a *tight monetary policy;* the latter, an *easy monetary policy.*

By buying securities, the Fed increases the money supply, thus creating money that was not in circulation before. The seller, whether a bank, a business, or an individual, can now use the liquid funds for all kinds of purposes: starting or expanding a business, paying employees, renting a computer, throwing a party.

When there's too much money floating around and more loans would create a dangerously inflationary situation, the Fed sells securities to sop up the extra cash that is more than the rate of the economy's productivity can absorb.

Making loans, or *discounting,* to member banks creates money. The way the Fed makes such a loan is by increasing the commercial bank's reserve assets by the amount loaned. The Fed raises and lowers the interest, or *discount rate,* at which it lends to member banks, in order to control bank lendings and thus the money supply. The lower the discount rate, the less a commercial bank has to pay for a loan and thus the more likely it is to seek one. The Fed creates the money it lends out of thin air, by writing a check drawn on itself. The member bank, however, must put up collateral, usually an I.O.U. backed by securities the bank owns, to produce this sleight of hand.

The discount rate determines the availability of money, by influencing the interest rates that the commercial bank charges its customers. Lower rates encourage borrowing, and thus monetary expansion.

The third mechanism with which the Fed can regulate the money supply—raising and lowering the reserves of member banks—is seldom used. Because it affects every bank, big and small, it is the least flexible regulating device and creates undue hardship for some banks. A slight change has a great deal of impact.

Instead of dollars, think of the Federal Reserve in another way: A tight monetary policy theoretically increases unemployment lines; an easy monetary policy decreases them. Again, a tight policy reduces grocery prices, and an easy policy raises them. The awesome interplay of private and public banking systems to produce a delicate balance in the movement of billions of dollars affects each of us.

build circulation to a healthy twenty thousand. However, the paper experiences a reversal when its publishers begin to demand $500 from New York society matrons in return for withholding details of their private lives from the public. This attempt at blackmail ultimately results in the *Weekly's* demise, but it does not stop the sisters.

Know Your Checking Account

The Editors of *Consumer Reports*

Checks are the basic mechanism by which most financial transactions are handled today. Americans wrote more than 25 billion checks in 1974 to pay for $9 out of every $10 worth of purchases. The Federal Reserve cost analysis places the average size of a personal checking account at about $900 and says the typical person writes about 20 checks a month. Generally speaking, the smaller the account the less profitable it is for the bank. A bank makes money by "selling" customers' idle funds to people or corporations seeking loans or to other banks in need of cash. It can make from 10 to 18 per cent per year just by lumping these funds together into large sums and lending them out.

Back in the early part of the century, banks acknowledged the income-producing character of checking accounts by paying interest on these deposits. But the practice was stopped by the Banking Act of 1933, passed during the Great Depression. (According to the conventional economic wisdom of the period, stiff competition for these funds forced banks to bid interest rates up so high that the increased cost contributed to the wave of bank failures in the late 1920's and early 1930's.) Now, instead of attracting depositors by paying interest for the use of funds in checking accounts, bank pay an "implicit" rate of interest (estimated to be about 3 per cent) through such "interest substitutes" as promotional gifts, "free" checking, longer hours, extra branches, and investment advice.

THE TYPES OF CHECKING ACCOUNTS

There are six basic types of checking accounts, plus combinations of those. Before examining the choices available, however, you should analyze your own checking needs.

First, figure out how many checks you write a month. You're considered a light check writer if you write 15 checks or fewer a month, average if you write 15 to 25 checks, and heavy if you average more than 25 a month.

Next, determine how much money you keep in your checking account over and above the amount of your actual transactions. Some people try to play it close, depositing in a checking account only enough to cover the checks they write. Others prefer (and are able) to maintain a cushion of a few hundred dollars against unforeseen expenses.

People who write five or six checks a month probably don't need a checking account at all. They'd be better off putting their funds in savings institutions that place no limits on withdrawals and charge a nominal fee for money orders—10c. or 15c. each. In that way they can use their savings accounts as checking accounts. Many savings institutions provide money orders free to customers who maintain savings account balances of $1000 or more. Others will write checks to third parties at no additional charge when so directed by depositors. Still others allow depositors to preauthorize payments for regularly recurring bills, such as mortgage payments and insurance premiums; payments for these bills are automatically deducted from depositors' accounts each month and sent to the apropriate creditors. Sometimes savings institutions will even allow depositors to write free checks through accounts the institutions maintain at cooperating commercial banks.

People who write more than just a handful of checks each month have a number of other choices open to them:

Analysis plan. This is a fairly complicated plan in which you're charged for every transaction you make, including deposits. These charges are reduced at the end of every month by a credit based on your balance during that month. The higher the balance you maintain, the lower the final service charge. A plan that charges 12c. for each check and 6c. for each deposit, and provides a 20c. credit for each $100 balance maintained, could cost a typical consumer $28.20 a year (this assumes the person averages 20 checks and 2½ deposits a month and maintains an average balance of $100).

Activity or "per check" plan. Another type of account is based on the amount of a depositor's activity. Frequently called "special" checking, activity accounts generally include two separate charges: a flat monthly maintenance fee and a charge for every check written. The monthly maintenance fees uncovered by our survey ranged from 25c. to 75c., and the per-check fee varied from 10c. to 15c. Assuming a maintenance fee of 75c. and a per-check fee of 10c., the annual bill for someone who averaged 20 checks a month would come to $33.

Minimum-balance plan. Under this system customers get unlimited checking at no charge per check in return for maintaining a specified balance. Often, the larger the bank, the larger the balance required. In New York City, for instance, three of the five biggest banks require balances of $500 while Barclays Bank requires only $200. (Barclays, though big internationally, is a small bank in the U.S.)

Generally, a service fee is charged if the account falls below the specified balance. The service fee is related to the size of the balance during the previous month. At the big New York banks, the charge is $1 or $2 for balances between $300 and $499, and $3 or $4 for balances under $300. These fees can mount up for those who have trouble meeting the balance requirements because of strained budgets; at some banks almost one-half of the customers fall below the limit every month. A person who doesn't maintain more than a $300 balance at a large New York City bank would pay between $36 and $48 a year under this plan.

Banks use one of two methods to determine whether or not you maintained the required balance. Under the "minimum" method, you would get charged a fee based on your *lowest* balance on any day during the month. Say you maintained a $1000 balance for every day but the final one of the month, when you dropped down to $100. You would get charged a fee based on that $100. Under the "average" method, balances are determined every day, totaled at the end of the month, and divided by the number of business days in that month. This permits your checking account balance to fluctuate widely with minimal penalty.

The "average" method is better from a consumer's viewpoint because it usually results in a smaller fee when the amount on deposit fluctuates widely. It's especially attractive to people who get paid once a month, make one relatively large deposit, and then draw down their balances until the next payday.

Minimum-balance plans are frequently advertised as "free," but they're not free at all—not even if you always keep the required balance in the account. At best, the cost of minimum-balance checking is the interest you would have earned on the maintained balance (minus a cushion of about $50 you'd keep in your account anyway) had you put that money into a savings account. The cost of a $500 minimum is thus at least $23 a year in foregone interest. (That's what $500—minus the $50 cushion—would earn in a savings account at a commercial bank paying 5 per cent compounded, meaning the earning of interest on interest.)

Free checking. One of the most desirable deals for consumers is unlimited checking at no charge, with no strings attached—no required minimum balance, no charge per check, no monthly maintenance fee. Unfortunately, this plan is not available everywhere.

Package accounts. The most recent arrival on the bank marketing scene is the package account, which individual banks peddle under such exotic names as "Gold Account," "Chextra," and "Everything Account." Under these plans you pay a flat fee of anywhere from $2 to $4 a month in exchange for a variety of services ranging from unlimited checking to lower loan rates.

Advertisements for these plans often tell consumers they can get "free" unlimited checking accounts, "free" travelers checks, and "free" safety deposit boxes. But a $4-a-month package account costs $48 a year, which is hardly "free." It can be, in fact, one of the most expensive and unnecessary accounts a consumer can choose.

Bankers concede that such package accounts benefit only the minority of customers who make very heavy use of every type of bank service. But many of the services offered in package accounts are used by a small fraction of those paying for such accounts; safe deposit boxes and personal loan discounts are used by far less than 50 per cent of package customers. Moreover, a number of the services advertised as part of the package—for example, bank credit cards and overdraft privileges (prearranged lines of credit that allow you to write checks for more than you actually have on deposit in your checking account)—are commonly available without charge to *all* depositors.

Sometimes the entire assortment of services offered in a package plan can be bought separately for less at small banks that haven't assembled them into a promotional package. Unlimited checking, as we've seen, costs nothing at some institutions. Some savings banks and S&Ls provide travelers checks free to customers, and a few banks (such as Barclays' network in New York City, Boston, and Chicago) even provide travelers

1869. In this year, Wyoming is organized as a United States territory and offers women the vote. When the territory becomes a state in 1890, it will be the first to extend the right to women.

checks free to noncustomers. Safe-deposit boxes in sizes to fit most individuals' needs can be rented for as little as $5 a year; sometimes they cost nothing at all if you maintain a large deposit at a savings institution. And by shopping for a loan the same way you shop for a checking account, you can sometimes shave your interest charges by 30 per cent—compared with the 10 per cent reduction common in package deals.

NOWs and WOWs. Probably the best banking development for consumers in this decade has been the emergence of checkable savings accounts that pay depositors interest on their balances. Called "NOWs" (short for "Negotiable Orders of Withdrawal"), they're offered by both thrifts and commercial banks in just two states: Massachusetts and New Hampshire. Congress has banned institutions in the other 48 states from offering NOWs and has directed banks in Massachusetts and New Hampshire to limit NOW advertising to persons working or living within their borders. But an out-of-state resident interested in opening such an account can do so by writing the Coolidge Bank and Trust Co., 65 Main St., Watertown, Mass. 02172.

The average interest paid on NOW accounts is almost 5 per cent (some institutions pay only 3 or 4 per cent) and the average NOW balance is a little over $1000, according to Government figures available in mid-1974. Since most institutions process NOW withdrawals at no charge per "check," many consumers in Massachusetts and New Hampshire have the best of all possible worlds: free "checking" *plus* 5 per cent interest on their "checking-account" funds. An average $1000 account would earn extra income of nearly $55 a year (assuming compounding).

NOWs were introduced by Massachusetts savings banks in 1972 as a way to circumvent the traditional prohibition against their offering checking accounts. (All savings banks in Maryland, Indiana, and New Jersey, one in Delaware, and one in Oregon have that privilege now; Connecticut banks get it this year. But none of the banks in those states can pay interest on the accounts.) Technically, NOWs are considered savings because they are subject to a legal provision that requires 30 to 60 days advance notice before withdrawal. But this provision has rarely been invoked, so, for all practical purposes, NOWs look and act like checking accounts.

THE HIDDEN COSTS OF CHECKING

In addition to the standard fees for account maintenance and activity, there are a number of potential charges that frequently are not disclosed to consumers at the time they open their accounts. Such charges can add significantly to the annual costs of a checking account.

One is a charge for a stop-payment order—when you want to invalidate a check you have already written. Our research indicates the cost can vary from nothing to $3, depending on where you live and where you bank.

Another common charge is for overdrafts, checks written by you that are returned, or bounced, for insufficient or uncollected funds. This fee generally ranges from $2 to $5. Since bounced checks probably generate more complaints than anything else, banks have moved to eliminate this source of friction by promoting automatic overdraft privileges. An overdraft is actually a loan from the bank. The finance charge can go from 12 to 18 per cent.

FACTS ABOUT THE FINE PRINT

Most banks don't provide prospective customers a list of these charges in easily understandable language. One place to look for the charges is on the signature card you sign when you open an account. This innocuous looking card, which bank personnel frequently say is just for identification purposes, is actually a legal binding document that holds you to a bank's rules and regulations. Sometimes these regulations, along with checking-account service fees, are spelled out on the face of the card. But often the signature card tells you only that you're subject to the "rules and bylaws" of the bank or to its regulations governing checking accounts.

Several of the provisions that may be spelled out on signature cards or in a bank's brochures are of particular concern to consumers. One states the bank's policy regarding deposits and withdrawals. Frequently banks do not allow customers to draw on cash deposits until the following business day and prohibit withdrawals on deposited checks until the checks have actually cleared (this latter provision is intended to prevent fraud). If a check is drawn on a bank in the same town, the clearing process may take only two or three business days. But if you live in San Francisco and the check is from New York, the process could take two weeks or more. Bankers say a major reason for bounced checks is that depositors are unaware of this provision and make withdrawals prematurely. (Sometimes exceptions are made for long-standing customers; if you need to draw right away on checks you are depositing, ask the branch manager of your bank to approve "immediate credit" on the checks.)

Another legality sometimes encountered on signature cards or brochures is the "right of offset" or "bankers' lien." Under this doctrine, embodied in common law, a bank may seize money from a borrower's checking or savings account without prior notice or court hearing in order to obtain payment for any kind of loan—installment or bank credit card—it has issued. Generally, a bank exercises this right only when a loan is long overdue and after repeated efforts to collect payments have failed. But the possibility of free entry into your checking account should make you think carefully about borrowing money at the bank where you maintain a checking account—even though having such an account at a bank often makes it easier for you to obtain credit there.

RECOMMENDATIONS

So far in this report, we've concentrated on the cost of checking accounts. But there are a number of reasons you might choose to ignore the cost of banking services. You might decide, for instance, to select a big bank that's close to work or home. Convenience is a major factor in choosing a banking institution and often small banks *are* inconvenient; there's no denying that the time you might spend traveling to and from a distant bank is worth money, too. Other valid reasons for deciding not to choose the cheapest bank in town might be the long hours offered by some institutions or the large branch network provided by others (prices may vary from branch to branch, by the way). Should you decide to choose a bank for its convenience or hours, bear in mind that you may be paying a price for your decision.

If you have resolved that it's worth your time to do some comparative shopping, begin by determining which type of account is best for you. If you write only five or six checks a month, you probably would be better off without a checking account. Keep your money in an interest-bearing savings account at a thrift institution where you can either purchase inexpensive money orders, pre-authorize payment of regular monthly bills, or get some form of free checking.

If you live or work in Massachusetts or New Hampshire, seek out the free NOWs offered by many institutions in those two states; they are the best consumer "checking" deal around. You not only earn up to 5 per cent on the funds you deposit, but you're not charged when you withdraw your money in order to pay bills—regardless of how many "checks" you write.

In the 48 states where NOWs are prohibited, unconditional free checking is the best bet. Depending on how many checks you average a month, it can save you $20 to $40 a year over the cost of other plans. If banks in your area don't offer unconditional free checking, consider going outside your area to a bank that does. You can make deposits by mail. What happens when you must write a check for cash? Neighborhood merchants who know you and value your trade are often perfectly willing to cash checks for modest amounts. And if you have a savings account at a savings bank or an S&L, it will generally cash checks up to the full amount of your balance.

If you choice is limited to the analysis plan, the activity plan, or the minimum-balance plan (and if you don't like the idea of banking by mail in another city), you must do some arithmetic to figure out which plan is cheapest for your own financial needs. Generally, the analysis plan is good for infrequent check writers or those who maintain high balances; the activity plan suits infrequent check writers who maintain low balances; and the minimum-balance plan is best for heavy check writers with high balances.

Once you've decided on the type or types of accounts that seem to suit your needs best, draw up a list of banking institutions in your city that are convenient to you. Make a special effort to include small institutions on the list, since there's a good chance they'll offer the better checking deals. Start with the Yellow Pages. Look under "banks" for commercial and savings banks, under "savings" for S&Ls. Generally, the biggest institutions have the most prominent listings, with the greatest number of branches; the smaller institutions have the more modest listings.

After your shopping list is drawn up, telephone the banks for the information on the plan—or plans—you're interested in. Ask for the operations officer or the officer in charge of checking accounts, and be sure to get the officer's name so you can get back to the person later if there are misunderstandings. Also request any brochures the bank has prepared on checking accounts.

But be ready for trouble. CU, along with every other consumer group that has tried to get information from banks, frequently encountered ill-informed or downright unpleasant bank clerks and officers. "We don't volunteer anything," bragged one banker, "but we'll tell you if you ask."

1869. Clara Colby completes all required studies for a degree at the University of Wisconsin, but President Chadbourne—opposed to coeducation—informs her that he will withhold her degree since she did not adhere to the school's "Female College" curriculum and took, instead, regular men's courses. He ultimately relents, however, and she graduates as class valedictorian.

New York Public Library

Hidden Dangers of a Joint Account

Gustave Simons

Many people, particularly married couples, hold property jointly. Their home, their stock-brokerage account, their bank account are in the names of both. This is frequently a convenience, but it does not mean that in the event of death the survivor takes over automatically. In many instances, this idea is completely false.

Let us suppose that you and your husband both work and maintain a joint savings-bank account. He dies, you automatically succeed. You will discover, to your horror, that the entire joint bank account is presumed to have belonged exclusively to your husband for the purpose of computing the amount of estate tax which has to be paid. It is up to you to come forward with proof as to what portion of the joint account came from your earnings. If the account has been maintained for many years with sums going in and coming out all the time, this will mean that you will have to know exactly what you deposited and what your husband deposited and whether the funds drawn out were to meet his obligations or merely to purchase something that you wanted for which he was not responsible. These problems of proof are almost impossible to meet adequately. Even if they can be met, they cost a small fortune in legal and accounting fees. You are more than likely to end up paying an estate tax on your own property. This is equally true of jointly held stock, real estate, or other property.

Moreover, when the survivor comes to sell jointly held property she is apt to run into a maze of complicated rules for figuring out her capital-gains tax which frequently work out very unfairly and she may end up by paying a tax on something which is not really a gain at all.

The estate tax on jointly held property has other disadvantages. If you do not have a joint estate and your husband is the sole wealth creator in your family, he can, through a properly drawn will, arrange matters so that half of his estate is taxable when he dies and half when you die. This sharply reduces the estate tax. With astute planning, the tax can be reduced even below this. But

when property is held jointly, half of it is taxed when your husband dies (because of the marital deduction) and *all* of it is taxed a second time when you die. Because of increasing tax brackets this means that the tax is increased by more than 50 per cent. Suppose your husband leaves $200,000 in a joint estate which you inherit as the survivor. When he dies there will be a tax of close to $5000 on the $100,000, payable immediately, plus a tax of close to $32,000 when you die, an over-all tax of $37,000. If there was no joint account and he had drawn up the proper will, there would be a tax of a little under $5000 when he dies and a similar amount when you die, or less than $10,000 in all. Here the use of a joint account can almost quadruple estate taxes.

If you insist on a joint account or other jointly owned property, it is particularly important that both you and your husband have a carefully drawn will. This occurs all too rarely in the case of the husband, and even less frequently in the case of the wife. Yet if both of you die in some common disaster but the wife survives the husband (as she is presumed to do in most states), the entire family estate may pass without the protection of a proper will. Under the laws of most states, property held jointly is subject in whole or in part to the claims of creditors of either party.

Money going into a joint bank account is not subject to gift tax because the gift is not complete. The person who put the money in may take the money out. But in other forms of jointly held property such as stock, a taxable gift may result where none was intended and yet the parties may not obtain the tax advantages that real gifts can achieve.

Joint bank accounts can also be dangerous in the case of a family quarrel. All too often the husband or wife, for protection or out of spite, will clean out the entire bank account.

Wealth should be shared because of the emotional and financial benefits derived, but it should be worked out through trusts, foundations, family partnerships, corporations, outright gifts, or well-drawn wills. Joint accounts, except in very extraordinary circumstances, are not the way to do it.

1869. The Daughters of Crispin, the first American national women's labor union, is organized by women shoe-factory workers. The first convention takes place this year in Lynn, Massachusetts, ending with the election of Carrie Wilson as president.

Where to Put Your Savings

The Editors of *Consumer Reports*

HOW TO PICK THE BEST SAVINGS ACCOUNT

As an investment, regular savings accounts (also called passbook accounts) provide maximum liquidity—meaning that the money is readily available and can be withdrawn at any time. (A statutory provision allows institutions to require up to 60 days' notice before withdrawal, but this provision has rarely been invoked.) Because of their greater liquidity, however, regular savings accounts pay the lowest rate of interest among the different types of savings deposits.

Time deposits (also known as certificates of deposit, savings certificates, and investment certificates, or high-interest passbooks) must be left in an institution for a specified period. They reward savers for the more limited availability of their funds by paying higher interest rates. Generally, the longer the time period, the higher the rate. Persons who withdraw their funds before the end of the specified period are subject to a stiff penalty imposed by Federal law: They forfeit one quarter's interest, and the interest rate is reduced to that paid on regular savings accounts. (The actual rate of interest earned on time deposits that are cashed in before maturity can dip as low as 2.5 per cent.)

Both regular savings accounts and time deposits are among the safest investments you can make, because most banking institutions purchase Federal insurance that covers individual accounts up to $40,000. Savings institutions in four states—Massachusetts, Ohio, Maryland, and North Carolina—may also purchase state-sponsored insurance, which is sometimes more comprehensive than the Federal plan. (This is why some Maryland thrifts can pay higher rates than their Federally insured counterparts). A small minority of institutions purchase no insurance at all.

Maximum rates for consumer savings deposits are set by the U.S. Government and have been changed about a dozen times since Federal authorities established ceilings back in the Depression (see box at right). Except for a new rate on the six-year time deposit set in December 1974, the last time these ceilings were changed was in July 1973. The table below shows the maximum rates that different banking institutions are now allowed to pay on the various types of savings deposits:

TYPE OF ACCOUNT	COMMERCIAL BANKS	THRIFT INSTITUTIONS
Regular savings	5 per cent	5¼ per cent
90-day	5½ per cent	5¾ per cent
1-to-2½ years	6 per cent	6½ per cent
2½-to-4 years	6½ per cent	6¾ per cent
4-to-6 years (minimum deposit, $1000)	7¼ per cent	7½ per cent
6 years or more (minimum deposit, $1000)	7½ per cent	7¾ per cent

WHERE TO OPEN AN ACCOUNT

How do you decide where to open a savings account? The table above shows that for equivalent types of savings deposits, the law always permits higher interest at a savings bank or S&L than at a commercial bank. The Government allows thrift institutions to pay at least one-quarter of a percentage point more on all types of accounts. The difference is intended to encourage consumers to save at those institutions and thus to provide the institutions with the funds they need to make residential mortgage loans. As a result of the law, thrift institutions do in fact usually pay higher rates on savings.

Commercial banks often disparage this rate differential. They argue that the convenience of "one-stop" banking—using the same bank for checking, savings, and credit services—more than compensates for their lower rate. CU doesn't agree. While one-quarter of a percentage point difference isn't much, it still is more. And the real difference in earnings at a thrift institution may come to more than one-quarter of a percentage point, since thrifts tend to *compute* interest in more liberal ways than commercial banks.

There are other arguments in favor of thrift institutions for savings. Should you ever need a mortgage, you're more likely to get one from a

PUNISHING THE THRIFTY: HOW REGULATION Q AFFECTS YOU

"A penny saved is a penny earned," goes the old maxim. But these days, Federal law and double-digit inflation have combined to punish the small saver. A penny deposited in an ordinary savings account last year earned less than half the value it lost through inflation. That's because the Government—at the behest of the banking institutions—has placed a ceiling on the maximum interest rates banking institutions can pay consumers with modest savings accounts. But the Government has not found any way to place a ceiling on inflation.

Why are small savers penalized this way? Much of the blame rests with a banking directive known as Regulation Q. This rule, which dates back to the Depression, was designed to curb the fierce rate competition that preceded the bank failures of the 1930's by regulating interest rates on savings accounts.

Regulation Q worked well enough as long as interest rates permitted under it kept rough pace with the gentle upward trend of interest rates in other parts of the economy. But in 1966, a business boom spurred competition for loans among borrowers big and small and sent interest rates soaring. The Government *lowered* the interest ceilings on small savings deposits. It left the rates on deposits over $100,000 virtually untouched, however, and ultimately removed ceilings on these large deposits altogether.

The Government thus created a rate structure that discriminates against the small saver. There is a regulated and artificially low savings rate for the individual of modest means and a higher free-market rate for big business and the wealthy.

The two-tier rate structure in the United States exists mainly to protect thrift institutions from competition that some might not survive. But low savings rates are also meant as an indirect subsidy to home buyers. Thrift institutions finance the bulk of home mortgages through money deposited in regular savings accounts. The lower the interest rate they need pay the six or seven savers who provide the funds for a typical mortgage, the lower the interest rate they need charge the mortgage borrower. (The real problem is that the savings institutions are full of mortgages written at low interest rates. If they had to pay the going interest rates to keep savings deposits, they would lose money.) Some economists think the system deprives consumers of as much as 3½ percentage points interest — equivalent to more than $14-billion a year — rightfully due on their savings. And during recent times, it has not helped consumers seeking mortgage loans at all.

1869. Lillie Devereux Blake, author and suffragist, writes of her experience in addressing the public on women's rights: "In all my varied life, there has never come to me a keener delight than the intoxication of thrilling a crowd with my words. . . . I am only fully satisfied when the whole throng bends and sways at my will, as a field of wheat yields to the touch of the summer wind."

These four banks all pay the same interest rate— yet interest payments range from $44.93 to $75.30.

There are many ways of computing interest, as the text of our report indicates. Here are four passbooks showing the identical deposits and withdrawals (made on the same days), with explanations of how the interest has been computed under four common methods. All four assume a 6 per cent interest rate and quarterly crediting and compounding.

IN ACCOUNT WITH

	DATE	WITHDRAWAL	DEPOSIT	INTEREST	BALANCE	TELLER
1					**1,000.00	
2	JAN 10		**2,000.00		**3,000.00	
3	FEB-6		**1,000.00		**4,000.00	
4	MAR-3	*1,000.00			**3,000.00	
5	MAR 20	**500.00			**2,500.00	
6	MAR 30	**500.00			**2,000.00	
7	APR-1			*14.79	**2,014.79	
8	JUL-1			*30.14	**2,044.93	
9						
10						

LOW BALANCE

Under this method, interest is paid only on the smallest amount of money that was in the account during the interest period. Despite a balance that reached $4000 during the first quarter, this account earned interest only on $1000—the lowest balance during that period. (There are no withdrawals during the second quarter, so the low-balance formula is not important there.) This method, which tends to discourage deposits, is the most punitive to savers. Yet 30 per cent of commercial banks still use it, according to a 1974 study by the American Bankers Association.

Interest: $44.93

IN ACCOUNT WITH

	DATE	WITHDRAWAL	DEPOSIT	INTEREST	BALANCE	TELLER
1						
2					**1,000.00	
3	JAN 10		**2,000.00		**3,000.00	
4	FEB-6		**1,000.00		**4,000.00	
5						
6	MAR-5	*1,000.00			**3,000.00	
7	MAR 20	**500.00			**2,500.00	
8	MAR 30	**500.00			**2,000.00	
9	APR-1			*22.19	**2,022.19	
10	JUL-1			*30.25	**2,052.44	
11						

FIRST-IN, FIRST-OUT (FIFO)

With this method, withdrawals are deducted first from the starting balance of the interest period and then, if the balance isn't sufficient, from later deposits. This erodes the base on which your interest is figured and means you automatically lose interest on withdrawals from the start of the interest period rather than from the dates on which the withdrawals were actually made. Another variation of this method is to apply the first withdrawal to the first deposit, rather than to the beginning balance; this would earn $53.93. About 16 per cent of commercial banks use the FIFO methods, according to the ABA.

Interest: $52.44

IN ACCOUNT WITH

	DATE	WITHDRAWAL	DEPOSIT	INTEREST	BALANCE	TELLER
1						
2					**1,000.00	
3	JAN 10		**2,000.00		**3,000.00	
4	FEB-6		**1,000.00		**4,000.00	
5						
6	MAR-5	*1,000.00			**3,000.00	
7	MAR 20	**500.00			**2,500.00	
8	MAR 30	**500.00			**2,000.00	
9	APR-1			*28.10	**2,028.10	
10	JUL-1			*30.34	**2,058.44	
11						
12						

LAST-IN, FIRST-OUT (LIFO)

Under this plan, withdrawals are deducted from the most recent deposits in the quarter and then from the next most recent ones. This method, which does not penalize savers as much as the two FIFO methods, is used by about 5 per cent of commercial banks.

Interest: $58.44

IN ACCOUNT WITH

	DATE	WITHDRAWAL	DEPOSIT	INTEREST	BALANCE	TELLER
1						
2					**1,000.00	
3	JAN 10		**2,000.00		**3,000.00	
4	FEB-6		**1,000.00		**4,000.00	
5						
6	MAR-5	*1,000.00			**3,000.00	
7	MAR 20	**500.00			**2,500.00	
8	MAR 30	**500.00			**2,000.00	
9	APR-1			*44.71	**2,044.71	
10	JUL-1			*30.59	**2,075.30	
11						
12						

DAY-OF-DEPOSIT TO DAY-OF-WITHDRAWAL

Under this arrangement, the bank pays you interest for the actual number of days the money remains in the account. This method, which is sometimes called daily interest, instant interest, or day-in day-out, is the fairest to consumers. It is used by almost 50 per cent of commercial banks and 60 per cent of insured S&Ls (there are no industry figures for savings banks). It yields the greatest return.

Interest: $75.30

1870. Ellen Richards, a chemistry graduate of Vassar, is admitted to the doctorate program at the fledgling five-year-old Massachusetts Institute of Technology, which makes her the first American woman to attend "so far as I know, *any scientific* school." She is granted a full scholarship, not so much because she needs it, but because —

lender who has enjoyed the use of your money than from who hasn't. (And remember, thrifts were specifically established to provide mortgage financing for individuals.) "I shouldn't say this," confided an officer of one of Boston's major commercial banks, "but *I* put *my* money in a savings bank that's willing to write me a mortgage. Why shouldn't I?"

BIG BANKS CAN BE STINGY

Obtaining the maximum legal rate of interest should be a major factor in selecting the institution that gets your savings funds. But not all banks actually pay the highest rate the Government allows. Often the biggest banks are the stingiest. A 1974 Federal Reserve Board study of rates paid by commercial banks noted that 23 per cent of all savings deposits were in accounts "paying a below-ceiling rate of 4½ per cent—and some were at even lower rates." In fact, a few of the banks were paying as little as 2 per cent.

The stinginess of these large banks is striking, considering that many are among the most profitable in the country and could easily afford to pay top rates. James Farley, head of consumer banking for First National City Bank, the largest bank in New York City and the second largest in the nation, says his bank's decision to pay only 4½ per cent on passbook book accounts "has to do with share of market."

"We haven't gotten hurt," Farley explains, "because people don't shop for rate."

Careful consumers *should* shop for rate. On the average account at a savings institution ($3500) First National City Bank would pay $157.50 annually while a thrift offering the maximum rate of 5¼ per cent would pay $183.75. (For illustration purposes, both calculations are done without allowances for compounding.)

If you live in a small town served by just a few banks, you may find that these institutions also pay very low rates.

Trade figures indicate you stand a better chance of obtaining the top legal interest rate at a savings bank or an S&L than at a commercial bank. A study conducted by the National Association of Mutual Savings Banks in 1974 found that more than 90 per cent of savings banks were paying the ceiling on passbook accounts and on one- and 2½ -year time deposits; and about three-quarters offered the maximum on 90-day and four-year time deposits. A survey conducted at the same time by the Federal Home Loan Bank Board, which regulates S&Ls, showed that about 90 per cent of the associations were paying the limit on regular savings accounts; about three-quarters were paying the top rate on one- and 2½-year time deposits; and two-thirds were paying the ceiling on four-year deposits. (But only one-third were paying the limit on 90-day deposits.)

FINDING THE TOP OF THE TOP

Getting the top rate allowed by law is only one part of shopping for a savings institution. Equally important is finding the most favorable method of computing interest. This is critical, because the way interest is figured on accounts containing the same amount of money and earning the same stated rate can result in an actual monetary difference of as much as 171 per cent. The variables that determine whether the amount of interest you receive is on the high end of the spectrum or the low end include such things as the formula used in calculating interest, "grace periods" for deposits and withdrawals, and the frequency of compounding and crediting.

These important policies are not regulated by the Government, and they are frequently not disclosed to consumers at the time savers open accounts. Even if the rules are stated on signature cards, brochures, or passbooks, the legalistic wording is often hard for the ordinary saver to comprehend.

The American Bankers Association says there are 50 or so widely used methods of computing interest in existence. Here are some of the important variables you should consider in selecting an institution.

Formulas for computing interest. On page 361 are explanations of four common methods used to compute interest. To demonstrate how they can affect the amount of interest paid, we followed a study by a graduate student under the supervision of Professor Richard L. D. Morse, head of the Department of Family Economics at Kansas State University and a consumer advocate who has directed significant research on savings account practices. Using the hypothetical account shown on p. 361, and assuming it earned an annual rate of 6 per cent with quarterly compounding and crediting of interest, the study found that the interest paid under the four different methods ranged from $44.93 to $75.30—a difference of nearly 68 per cent between the stingiest and most liberal methods.

Crediting and compounding. Another factor that determines how much

money your account will earn is the frequency of crediting and compounding interest. Years ago banks used to credit, or pay accrued interest to your account, just once or twice a year. Now, because of competition and the mathematical ease provided by computers, some institutions credit your account monthly, or even daily.

A similar change has taken place with the frequency of compounding— the process of earning interest on interest. Daily compounding means that the interest an account earns each day is credited that day, thus increasing the base on which interest is figured the following day (this assumes that you will leave *both* the principal and the interest to accumulate in the account).

Frequent compounding can boost a saver's yield above the stated interest rate. Banks thus like to stress frequent compounding, and the resulting high "effective yield," in their advertising. But it really doesn't amount to much in dollars and cents unless your account runs to five figures or more. The frequency of crediting and compounding should be identical to be meaningful. Beware of institutions that advertise daily compounding but credit only quarterly; such an arrangement means you don't receive the full effect of the compounding if you withdraw your money before the end of the quarter.

Grace days are also important in determining how much interest an account will earn, especially if the account is an active one with many deposits and withdrawals. A grace period for deposits commonly allows consumers to place funds in their accounts as late as the tenth of the month and earn interest on those funds from the first day of the period. Grace periods for withdrawals, sometimes called "dead days," allow consumers to withdraw funds as much as three days before the end of a quarter and still earn interest on those funds as though they were on deposit for the entire quarter. Both types of grace days can boost the "effective yield" of accounts above the stated interest rate.

Other variables. Other savings account variables include charge for "excess" withdrawals, penalties for "premature" closing of accounts, and minimum balances required in order to earn interest. Our research indicated that commercial banks levied such charges more frequently than did savings institutions.

Many commercial banks, for instance, limit withdrawals to two or three per quarter and charge fees ranging from 50 cents to $1 for each additional withdrawal. Some charge depositors fees ranging from $1 to $5 if they close accounts within the first month or quarter after the accounts are opened. Most important are provisions that stipulate a bank will not pay interest on an account unless a certain balance, which can range from $1 to $100, is left in the account until the end of a quarter. Under such a rule, you would receive no quarterly interest at all on a $5000 day-of-deposit to day-of-withdrawal account if you closed the account only one day before the quarter ended.

The Kansas State study applied 40 of these variables to the hypothetical account and found that the interest payments varied by 171 per cent. The best combination, yielding $79.13 for savers, was made on a day-of-deposit to day-of-withdrawal account that compounded and credited quarterly and offered 10 deposit grace days. The worst combination, yielding $29.25, was a low-balance formula that compounded and credited semi-annually, had no grace days, and charged a penalty for more than two withdrawals in a quarter. The study demonstrates how an accumulation of seemingly inconsequential provisions can add up and thus reduce the actual earnings of savings accounts with identical interest rates.

Even if you do open an account that pays the top rate and has the most liberal methods of calculating interest, there's a good chance you won't get your rightful due. Another study done under Professor Morse of Kansas State found that only 15 percent of 156 regular savings accounts surveyed in Kansas were credited with the correct amount of interest they should have been paid when interest was figured according to the methods the savings institutions reportedly were using. The study also found that commercial banks had a worse verification record than S&Ls (there are no savings banks in Kansas) and that both commercial banks and savings institutions tended to underpay, rather than overpay, their depositors.

SOME OTHER CONTROVERSIAL PRACTICES

A major area of controversy concerns the fees many institutions levy on accounts in which no money has been deposited or withdrawn for some time. The "maintenance" fees for handling these dormant accounts range from 50 cents to $4 per month. Some institutions also stop paying interest on accounts under a certain size. Even though an account is not considered "abandoned" until after seven years of inactivity under model regulations proposed by the National Conference of Commissioners on Uniform State Laws, a number of institutions assess maintenance fees

should controversy arise -- the administration can claim she is not a *bona fide* student. Several years later, with only her M.S. in hand, Miss Richards will quit MIT, saying the various department heads have stymied her progress toward the Ph.D. in chemistry because they did not wish the Institute's first award of the degree to go to a woman.

The Power of Compound Interest

A regular investment of $100 per year invested at:	5 years	10 years	15 years	20 years	25 years	30 years	35 years	40 years	45 years	50 years
2%	$530	$1,117	$1,764	$2,478	$ 3,267	$ 4,138	$ 5,099	$ 6,161	$ 7,333	$ 8,627
3	546	1,181	1,916	2,767	3,755	4,900	6,227	7,766	9,550	11,613
4	563	1,248	2,082	3,096	4,331	5,833	7,660	9,882	12,587	15,877
5	580	1,321	2,266	3,472	5,011	6,976	9,484	12,684	16,768	21,981
6	598	1,397	2,467	3,899	5,816	8,380	11,812	16,404	22,551	30,776
7	615	1,478	2,689	4,387	6,767	10,107	14,791	21,361	30,575	43,498
8	634	1,565	2,932	4,942	7,895	12,234	18,610	27,978	41,743	61,967
9	652	1,656	3,200	5,576	9,232	14,857	23,512	35,820	57,318	88,844
10	671	1,753	3,495	6,300	10,818	18,094	29,812	48,685	79,079	128,030

Will, compounded annually, grow to the sum shown after

To get the corresponding total for any other annually invested amount (A), multiply the dollar total given above for the interest rate and number of years assumed by $\dfrac{A}{100}$

FOR EXAMPLE: You plan to invest $75 per month or $900 per year. What capital sum will that provide after 35 years, at 7% compounded annually? Check where the lines cross for 7% and 35 years. The answer is $14,791 \times \dfrac{900}{100} = \$133,119$.

Adapted from the *Dun & Bradstreet Guide to Your Investments 1975-1976* by C. Colburn Hardy, RIA. Copyright © 1975. Reprinted by permission of Thomas Y. Crowell Company, Inc.

---

after only five years of inactivity.

The rationale for these charges is hard to understand, since dormant accounts logically should require less attention than those with frequent deposits and withdrawals. What makes these charges especially onerous is the fact that they're rarely disclosed at the time a consumer opens an account.

The problems of interest computation and disclosure that plague savings accounts are less serious for time deposits. The contract form for these types of deposits spells out almost all of the provisions exactly, according to Federal law.

There are, however, two trouble areas. One concerns the present system of penalizing persons who withdraw their funds before the specified time period has expired. Currently, a person who contracts for a four-year time deposit, then withdraws the funds after 3½ years, pays the same penalty as a person who contracts for a one-year time deposit, then withdraws the funds six months before the end of the period. The penalty: forfeiture of 90 days' interest as well as reversion to the lower passbook rate of interest on the amount withdrawn. This does not recognize that an institution has had the use of the first person's funds for a far longer time than the second person's and should therefore extract a less stringent penalty.

Freyda Koplow, former Massachusetts commissioner of banking, has proposed a "variable rate" time deposit as an alternative, which CU thinks is more reasonable. Under her plan, the rate would range from 6½ to 8 per cent, depending on how long a saver's funds actually remained on deposit; each year, the saver would have an opportunity to decide—without penalty—whether or not to "lock in" the funds for another year; the longer the funds remain on deposit, the higher the rate.

The second problem with time deposits occurs after the deposits have matured. Some institutions automatically renew time deposits unless otherwise notified by savers; other institutions automatically transfer the funds in the expiring time deposits to lower-paying passbook accounts or to noninterest-bearing checking accounts. In the case of automatic renewal, savers who had planned to withdraw their funds after the time deposit expired but failed to notify the bank would find their money tied up for another period of time and could withdraw it only with an interest penalty. (Some institutions, such as the Dime Savings Bank, in New York City, also require savers to obtain the bank's consent for early withdrawal and are balking at giving consent except in emergencies.) In the case of transfer of the funds to passbook or checking accounts, savers might mistakenly think their money was earning a higher rate of interest than it was in reality.

Some institutions remind depositors of an expiring time deposit 10 days before it is due to mature; others do it as long as 35 to 40 days before; still others send no notices at all. The best way to ensure that *you* decide what to do with these funds is to keep a list of maturity dates handy and put your decision in writing to the bank, keeping a copy of your letter for

yourself. And be sure to keep your deposit receipt in a safe place. Some banks require customers who lose these records to put up collateral or to purchase security bonds equal to *twice* the face value of the deposit until the lost receipts are produced. They say this is to prevent fraud, but consumers who lose these documents through innocent mistakes may ultimately be forced into court to retrieve their money from the banks.

OTHER PLACES TO INVEST SAVINGS

So far in this report, we've talked about how to get the best deal for your money at a commercial bank or a thrift institution. There are, however, a number of other places to invest your savings. And some pay higher interest rates than the commercial banks or thrifts and offer more safety than corporate bonds or stocks.

Credit unions. These are nonprofit saving-and-borrowing organizations, owned and run by their depositors, who generally have a common tie, such as the same employer. There are some 23,000 credit unions around the country, and about two-thirds are Federally insured for up to $40,000 per account (state insurance protects some of the other credit unions). Dividends on shares or interest on deposits are paid regularly, and the law permits the rate to go as high as 7 per cent. Trade figures gathered in mid-1974 indicate that more than half the credit unions are paying between 6 and 7 per cent on shares. But the latest Government figures (compiled at the end of 1973) show that nearly 7 per cent of Federal credit unions were paying nothing at all. Until recently, Federal law placed fairly stringent restrictions on the methods credit unions could use to compute interest, and they tended to be less liberal in this respect than commercial banks and thrifts.

Money-market funds. These are mutual funds that pool the money of individuals and invest it in the money market. Actually, the money market isn't a "market" at all, but a term that covers an array of short-term money "instruments" that the Government, corporations, and banks issue to raise funds; these instruments, which mature in just a couple of months, include such things as Government obligations (Treasury bills), commercial paper (a sort of corporate IOU), and bank paper (such as large certificates of deposit, bankers acceptances, and letters of credit). The yields on these securities are volatile but can be quite high (they soared to 12 per cent in mid-1974, then dipped to 9 per cent in the fall*) compared with the maximums on regular savings accounts. But the small saver is normally shut out of the money market because the minimum investment is at least $100,000. The advent of the money-market funds (there are now more than 20 on the scene) has changed all that. Now a minimum investment of $1000 to $5000 will get you into the money market, where your funds can earn rates comparable to those enjoyed by big corporations and wealthy investors.

*They have fallen even lower since.

1872. Victoria Claflin Woodhull is nominated as the first woman candidate for president of the United States. Her party, the "Equal Rights" party -- which she organized -- also names Frederick Douglass as her vice-president, though he declines the invitation.

There are, however, two important considerations to keep in mind when judging this alternative. First, deposits in many money-market funds are not fully insured the way deposits in commercial banks or thrifts are. Second, their rate of return is not guaranteed, as is the rate on a time deposit; the rate can vary from day to day depending on economic conditions.

An investment in a money-market fund is far more liquid than a time deposit. Many declare dividends daily, and some will wire money to you or your bank within 24 hours if you decide to sell. A few funds even allow you to withdraw money by writing checks.

Some funds, such as Anchor Reserve in Elizabeth, N.J., are known as "load" funds because they charge people sales fees of up to 8¾ per cent on the initial investment. Others are known as "no-load" funds; they charge no sales fee. (Most funds also assess a fee of up to 1 per cent of total assets for management and expenses.)

Since many of the no-loads have performed just as well as the load funds, wise investors should confine their search to the no-load funds. Some of the larger no-load funds are Capital Preservation, 459 Hamilton Ave., Palo Alto, Calif. 94301; Dreyfus Liquid Assets, 600 Madison Ave., New York, N.Y. 10022; Fidelity Daily Income Trust, 35 Congress St., Boston, Mass. 02109; Money Market Management, 421 7th Ave., Pittsburgh, Pa. 15219; Reserve Fund, 1301 Avenue of the Americas, New York, N.Y. 10019.

Government securities. In mid-1974 thousands of people bypassed the money-market funds and purchased Government securities on their own. They queued up outside Federal Reserve banks across the country to buy Treasury notes yielding 9 per cent—the highest rate since the Civil War (by winter, rates had dropped about two percentage points). These notes were part of an arsenal of securities regularly sold by the Government to raise cash; by purchasing them you help to finance the national debt. (You don't have to stand in line to buy them, though. You can purchase Treasury issues by submitting a "noncompetitive tender" in writing—along with a certified check—to the Federal Reserve bank in your area. This means you agree to purchase the issue for the average price prevailing at the sale. Or you can pay a bank or broker a fee—generally $20 or $25—to do the legwork for you.)

The great appeal of Treasury securities is their safety (they're backed by the "full faith and credit" of the U.S. Government), their relatively high rate of return, and their exemption from state and local income taxes (especially attractive if you live in a state such as New York, with a big tax bite).

Government securities issued by the Treasury come in three forms: bills, notes, and bonds. Treasury bills are the most liquid and have maturities of three, six, nine and 12 months. They are issued on a discount basis, which means they are sold at less than face value and redeemed at face value on their maturity dates. The difference between the lower issue price and the higher maturity price represents your interest.

The minimum purchase requirement for Treasury bills is currently $10,000. (In the past, the Treasury sometimes allowed the small saver to purchase bills in denominations of as little as $1000. But in the face of opposition from the thrift industry, which claimed that the practice lured savers away from their institutions, the Treasury gave it up.)

Treasury notes are securities with maturities of one to seven years; bonds mature in seven years or more. Both types of issues pay interest semi-annually. The minimum purchase denomination ranges from $1000 to $10,000.

There are three factors to keep in mind when considering the safety of Treasury issues as investments. First, if you have to sell before the securities mature, you may lose money. If interest rates have risen since you purchased the issue you may have to sell it at a discount. Second, if you purchase a bill, which matures in a very short period of time, you must be sure to reinvest your money as soon as the bill matures; you'll lose interest by allowing your money to remain idle for as little as a week or so. Third, most Treasury securities are often issued in "bearer form"; this means that they are not registered and do not bear the owner's name. They are thus as negotiable as cash, and if they are lost they can be cashed in by the finder without the necessity of identification. (Moral: be sure to keep them in a secure place, such as a safe-deposit box.)

Other types of Government securities are issued by more than a score of agencies, such as the new Federal Financing Bank, the Farmers Home Administration and the General Services Administration. These pay up to three-quarters of a percentage point more than the going Treasury rate, because the securities are backed by the agencies' own revenues or appropriations, not by the revenues of the U.S. Government (but none of these agencies has ever defaulted). The minimum investment commonly ranges from $1000 to $10,000. They are issued in bearer form, and most mature in two to five years. You can purchase these securities through a bank or broker.

Savings bonds. These familiar bonds should not be confused with other Treasury bonds, which pay higher rates. Series E and Series H bonds both yield 6 per cent. The interest on E bonds accrues in the form of semiannual increases in the redemption value over five years (this means you can sell back the bond at successively higher prices but realize full value only if you hold the bond to maturity). Interest earned on H bonds is paid each six months over a 10-year period. The rates are extremely low, considering the time period required to obtain your full interest income; CU considers these bonds unattractive forms of savings.

RECOMMENDATIONS

It seems obvious that the small saver does best these days by putting his or her funds just about any place but in a regular savings account. Yet everyone needs some surplus funds on hand in case of sudden emergency, and for this purpose savings accounts are probably the best solution. Because the Government has limited the maximum interest on these accounts to a rate that is less than half that of the current inflation, it's probably best to limit your deposit to an amount equal to two- or three-months' living expenses. (If you can accumulate more than that, it's time to think of ways to get a better return than a savings account offers.)

For such needs, open a savings account at a thrift institution; by law it can pay a higher rate than a commercial bank. Shop for an institution that offers the highest legal interest rate and the most liberal method of computing interest. This means:

1. Day-of-deposit to day-of-withdrawal formula.
2. Daily compounding *and* crediting of interest.
3. No withdrawal penalties.
4. Grace days for deposit and withdrawal.
5. No minimum balance required to earn interest.

Unfortunately, the ideal account—containing every one of these provisions—may not be available in your area because of state laws or local conditions. In such event, the way you use your account will determine how important some of these provisions are to you.

If, for instance, you make frequent deposits and withdrawals, a day-of-deposit to day-of-withdrawal feature is more important than continuous compounding and crediting. But if you make few deposits and allow the money to sit in the account for long periods of time, the frequency of compounding interest would become relatively more important.

If you routinely take funds out of your account, look for an institution that assesses no penalties for withdrawals. If you make deposits each month, but rarely before the 9th or 10th, look for an account offering the most deposit grace days. Similarly, if recurring obligations mean you must regularly withdraw funds just before the end of each quarter, seek an account with most withdrawal grace days.

Everyone should beware of provisions that require a minimum balance before any interest is paid. Such provisions mean that no matter what method of interest computation is used or how much money was on deposit during a quarter, should the end-of-quarter balance fall below the minimum, or should the account be closed out before the end of the period, no interest will be paid at all.

If you think you might need a mortgage one day, one consideration aside from computation method should figure in your shopping: an institution's mortgage policy for depositors. Ask the mortgage department if depositors at the institution get special consideration when they apply for mortgages; if they don't, we suggest you keep on shopping.

It's much harder to give advice about how to choose among the options covered in this report if you want to invest surplus funds for income growth. A lot depends on how adventurous you are and how much risk you're willing to take. Some advisers suggest that for safety and maximum return, you diversify your holdings and stagger the maturities of whatever you choose to invest in.

If you're cautious and want to be assured of a certain rate of return over a particular time period, time deposits are probably your best bet—despite the fact that their rates are not now keeping pace with the rate of inflation. At least your rate of return is guaranteed by the Government.

When money-market rates are above those on consumer time deposits, the no-load money-market funds are a much more attractive alternative for those willing to take a few chances. A big plus is that they're much more liquid than time deposits and can be easily converted into other types of securities if their rates become unattractive.

Finally, for those who have the necessary financial resources *and* an interest in keeping abreast of money-market rates, Government securities are a good bet in the present inflationary climate. They're safe, and they pay a rate of return that reflects what's happening in the marketplace.

1873. Willa Cather, American novelist, is born. Raised on the prairie, Willa refines the study of American character, stressing the values of humanity over technology. Among her best-known works are *One of Ours* and *Death Comes to the Archbishop*.

Should You Join a Credit Union?

Marylin Bender

There has been much talk in recent years about the advantages of credit unions, and what with everybody worrying about money it seemed a good time to clear up some of the confusion about just what credit unions are and what they can do for you. The name itself has the ring of labor organization about it, and many people think you have to belong to a union or work for a large corporation in order to join one. This isn't so. Credit unions have become the fastest growing species of financial institution, and the chances are you can join one if you want to. There may be some real advantages.

At this time some 30 million persons —one out of seven Americans—deposit their savings in or obtain loans from one of the 23,000 credit unions scattered about the country.

Furthermore, the federal and state regulations covering the granting of charters to credit unions have been liberalized. There are now community credit unions in which qualification for membership is simply residence in the area. The Marquette Credit Union in Rhode Island, for instance, is open to any resident of that state. The SEAL Federal Credit Union in Albany, New York, accepts anyone for membership who lives or works in the central core of that city.

There are credit unions for former drug addicts, for Arabian-horse owners, for professional golfers and nine new credit unions organized by women who identify themselves as feminists.

The definition of a credit union, flexibly interpreted of late, is a financial cooperative serving members who have a common bond—the same employer, for instance, or labor union, church, housing development. The members own and operate the credit union and make their collective savings available to each other for loans. Because the loan policies are set by directors elected by the members, the likelihood is that you can borrow money more easily from your credit union than you can from the loan officer of a commercial bank who doesn't know you.

Sometimes, but not always, the wait-

ing period for the loan is less than at a bank. That depends on the rules set by the credit-union directors. Some will grant an auto loan within half an hour after the member pays his share deposit. (Savings are called shares in credit unions and the minimum amount required is usually $10 or less.)

Also, loans will probably be less expensive; credit unions normally charge a lower interest rate for auto loans or personal loans than do many commercial banks. And it will undoubtedly be less than what you would have to pay to a finance company or for a credit-card purchase.

The federal law that regulates credit unions (and many state laws as well) holds them to a maximum rate of 1 percent monthly interest on a declining balance, which works out to 12 percent annually.

Loan limits are also set by federal or state law (depending on where the credit union obtains its charter) and by credit-union directors. Sometimes you can get as much as $2,500 on an unsecured loan, but the amount can be much less. With collateral or a co-signer, however, you may be able to borrow larger amounts.

Instead of interest on savings, credit unions pay dividends on their members' shares. In 1973 the federal ceiling on the dividend rate was raised to 7 percent to permit credit unions to compete with the higher interest rates being offered by savings banks and savings-and-loan institutions.

Most credit unions also provide free loan-protection insurance so that if the

borrower dies or is disabled, the loan is paid off instead of passing on the debt to the family. Some banks offer this service, but many charge extra for it.

In addition, many credit unions offer life-savings insurance, a form of group coverage, to match members' savings. For instance, you might get $1 worth of life coverage for every dollar you have on deposit before age 55, up to a ceiling of $1,000 or $2,000. In effect, this doubles your savings for your beneficiary.

Credit unions are reaching out to extend as many financial services as banks and more. For members, the list of consumer services—from financial counseling to group-travel and auto-purchasing discounts—keeps growing. Some of the larger credit unions even grant home-mortgage and real-estate loans, and a credit union in Ohio has established a form of credit-card system with merchants in its area.

The Credit Union National Association is pilot testing a checking-account type of service in Michigan, Georgia, California and Montana. Members can write drafts against their share (savings) accounts as payment to retailers and others. If this plan is successful, this service may be extended to other federally chartered unions, or to half of the credit unions in the country.

Credit unions and, for that matter, all financial institutions are shaping up for what some call "the battle for the deposit of the whole check."

Those who believe that the cashless society is at hand think it won't be long before all funds will be transferred electronically. Your payroll check will be credited to your account in one financial institution, and all your other transactions, from buying groceries at the supermarket to paying your electricity bill, will be handled by someone who presses a button at the point of purchase or in the utility company's office. Funds will be switched from your financial institution into their accounts.

The institution that gets your deposit will also handle your entire financial life, and credit unions want to be sure they will be filling that role. Until now credit unions have ⟶

1874. Laura Clay, suffragist, notes in her diary this year that her antislavery rearing (both parents were involved in pre-Civil War debates) has made her "hate oppression and injustice, and our own unhappy domestic life has left my eyes unblinded to the unjust relations between men and women, and the unworthy position of women."

been exempt from paying federal taxes on their income (though members pay income taxes on the dividends they receive). Bankers argue that if credit unions want to provide all financial services to practically everyone, then they should be regulated and taxed like banks and other financial institutions. The credit unions argue back that their cooperative nature gives them the right to tax exemption.

A U.S. central credit union was chartered and set up this year. This puts credit unions on the same footing as commercial banks by giving them access to large borrowings from the United States Treasury for stability in times of financial crunch.

The growing inflation has put credit unions in a squeeze because they have to pay out higher dividends to compete with the rising interest rates of savings banks, while being held to the 12 percent interest rate on the money they lend out.

Credit unions are by no means the only financial and business institutions that have had their mettle tested during the last two years. Some of the leading bankers, economists and corporation executives have become chastened by the confusing economic turns of the times. But the question of how good is

the management of the credit union you belong to or might want to join is more apt now than ever.

Unlike the corner bank, most credit unions start small and are run by volunteers who may be rank amateurs. The First Pennsylvania Feminist Credit Union was organized last year in Harrisburg by the local chapter of the National Organization for Women and two other feminist groups. Among the members are bookkeepers, accountants, lawyers and the director of public relations for the Pennsylvania Credit League, but no one with any real banking know-how. But every state has a state credit league, whose field staffs train volunteers to run credit unions.

While credit unions may start small, they tend to grow quickly. Once they reach a level of assets of $500,000 they usually hire a full-time professional staff to run them. The world's largest credit union, the Navy Federal Credit Union in Washington, D.C., has assets of over $400 million, with over 317,000 members stationed around the world.

Federal credit unions are now required by law to insure their deposits up to $40,000 each through the National Credit Union Administration, the government supervisory agency. The law extends to members the same pro-

tection that depositors in banks and savings-and-loan institutions have had since the 1930s. Federal share insurance is available to state-chartered credit unions that meet certain reserve requirements, and many states have been developing their own compulsory-insurance programs. Today most credit unions insure their members' savings.

Even though your savings are insured, they might be tied up for a while if the credit union were forced to liquidate because of bad management or a local economic disaster, such as a lengthy strike. The number of insolvencies for credit unions has been rather low, however, and even in cases of voluntary liquidation some members have received more than they originally invested. According to figures from the National Credit Union Administration, of 598 federally chartered credit unions that were liquidated in 1972, 518 paid 100 percent or more to their members. Even in the case of the 80 that paid less, the average loss per member was under $15.

To find out more about joining or starting a credit union, write to the Credit Union National Association, Inc., Box 431, Madison, Wisconsin 53701. About 90 percent of the federal and state credit unions belong to the C.U.N.A.

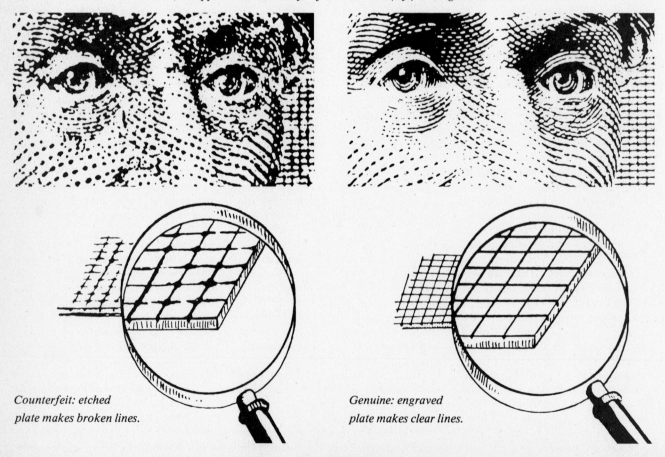

Lincoln as he appears on a counterfeit five-dollar bill (left) and a genuine note.

Counterfeit: etched plate makes broken lines.

Genuine: engraved plate makes clear lines.

1874. Mary Outerbridge plays the first lawn-tennis match in America on a Staten Island court.

Getting Credit and Loans

Roslyn L. Kramer

Note: The information in this piece was drawn from women bankers in major New York City banks and from feminist organizations.

Generally speaking, men don't know much about banking, but women know even less. Most of us lack the educational background, however casual, that men receive as they grow into their role as primary income earner. All women should make long range plans for financial self-sufficiency. In order to do so we should know more than we do about getting credit and loans.

If you do nothing more than pay taxes, you're giving banks business through federal-government deposits. If you have a savings account and a checking account, banks lend out your money for their profit. They owe you service.

Establishing and Protecting Your Credit Rating

The first step toward getting that service is establishing and maintaining an independent credit identity.

Your credit identity begins with your first application for a charge account, which triggers your existence in credit-bureau records. Your names goes into a computer, where forever after your credit history will accumulate.

Unless your income is over $15,000, establish credit on the local level by opening charge accounts with major stores before applying for national credit. Then apply for such major national credit cards as Master Charge and Bank Americard (available through banks) and American Express (highly regarded by banks because of the thorough credit check run on applicants).

Credit-card companies can wipe out the painstaking accretion of your credit

identity by trying to put you on your husband's card when you marry. The credit bureau will follow the card company's lead and fuse your account with your husband's. Which surname you use is not as important as retaining the same account number and line of credit (granted by a bank or other creditor and reflected in your credit-bureau file) without the inclusion of information on another person.

When you marry, write the credit-card company to inform it that you will retain the same account number, and that information on your husband should not be included in your file. Then write the credit bureau, notifying it that you want to keep your credit history before and after marriage segregated from your husband's (the physical file might be the same, but all your information will be on a separate sheet) and to maintain the same number and the same credit line. (After a few months of marriage, call to make sure your instructions are being carried out, advises Linda Cohen, official spokesperson for national NOW on the Equal Credit Opportunity Act.)

In an unresolved dispute over billing, write your version and send it to the credit bureau for your file. The credit bureau should send it to any organization that checks your credit standing. If credit is refused, ask to see your file immediately. You're entitled to see your credit information at no charge within thirty days of a rejection for credit.

Keep separate checking and savings accounts and a safe deposit box in addition to those shared with your husband. In case of divorce, you'll need immediate access to your own resources. If this course seems unduly pessimistic, consider that it also enhances your credit individuality and privacy. Even having a telephone listing in your own name may make a difference in

1875. From her kitchen in Lynn, Massachusetts, and with the help of her sons, Lydia Pinkham produces the first bottle of her "female remedy" which, by the time of her death, will have earned her over $3 million. For the following seventy-five years, the patent medicine will continue to be the most popular elixer in the world. It consists mainly of plant roots.

whether or not you can get a bank loan.

Nothing improves your credit rating so much as prompt payment of debts. If you're horrified at the idea of debt and never incur any—and if you always insist on paying for purchases with cash—you're a rotten credit risk. Someday you might regret your meticulousness when you want a mortgage or a large loan.

Loans

Once you've established a record of paying credit-card debts, you're ready to try for a bank loan.

Personal loans from banks (also called *installment* loans because they are repaid in predetermined installments) can be either *secured* or *unsecured* by *collateral*. In unsecured loans, which are not uncommon, your salary and employment record will be all the assurance a bank requires of your ability to repay.

One kind of *secured* loan is a passbook loan, the collateral for which is a savings account in the same bank. The cost of interest for such a loan is negligible, being the difference between the interest earned on your savings account and the interest you pay on the loan. Interest payments are tax deductible. Meanwhile, savings are removed from the reach of improvident spending habits, and you're proving yourself creditworthy. Banks are more likely to grant a passbook loan to borrowers with less than flawless credit ratings, because they have nothing to lose. The high value of the collateral also lowers the interest rate on your loan.

Signature loans is a term sometimes applied to installment loans requiring no collateral. Signature loans are not usually used for business, but they can be—and sometimes have to be since banks give small businesses a very hard time.

In order to be sure you can borrow a large sum on your signature when you really need it, begin by borrowing a small sum, say $200, when you don't need it and are sure you can repay it. Put the money in a savings account, pay the bank a few installments, and then repay the entire loan. Go back and borrow a larger amount. Based on the accretion of repaid debt, you'll eventually be able to get substantial amounts quickly when you need them.

Develop a good relationship with a banker, although your attempts might con-

Federal Credit

The Federal Equal Credit Opportunity Act states, "a creditor shall not discriminate against any applicant on the basis of sex or marital status with respect to any aspect of a credit transaction."

The act promises more in principle than is delivered in practice, which is determined by the rules implementing it (Regulation B, if you call government agencies for information or for a copy of the act).

The provisions do significantly extend protection of the law to all credit applicants, particularly where applicants are seeking small-business loans or credit for the purchase of securities. But the provisions allow creditors great leeway in gathering information from sources other than the credit applicant and permit as much as a year and a half to elapse before banks and other creditors must fully comply with some of the regulations. The act itself went into effect October 28, 1975.

Also, there is some concern among representatives of women's interests that weak state equal-credit laws can be used as loopholes.

Following are a few highlights of the regulations, along with NOW's position on them:

Creditors cannot ask if the applicant is divorced or widowed.

Sex-neutral terms must be used on applications: "spouse," rather than "husband" or "wife."

Designation of the form of address—Ms., Mrs., Miss, or Mr.—is optional and must be clearly stated as such on the loan application.

Loan applicants must be told the reason for rejection, but the explanation need not be in writing, nor is the creditor required to inform the applicant that she or he is entitled to know the reason for rejection. (The reason should be required in writing, according to Linda Cohen, official spokesperson for national NOW on the Equal Credit Opportunity Act. Ask for the reason in writing anyway, and you'll probably get it.)

Inquiries about child-rearing intentions are permitted. Inquiries about child-bearing or birth-control intentions or capability are not. However, the creditor can use this information if obtained from another source, as long as the source is not simply a generalization from statistics. (NOW supports the prohibition against basing judgments of an applicant's creditworthiness on generalizations, but is against permitting a creditor to ask about child-rearing intentions and using materials pertaining to childbearing obtained from a source other than the applicant.)

Questions on the degree to which the applicant pays alimony, or child support or maintenance or to what extent she or he relies on these payments are permitted. However, the applicant must be told that this information does not have to be disclosed if the applicant believes her or his income is sufficient for a loan. (NOW believes this is good theory but difficult in practice, since creditors don't reveal what income is necessary to support a credit extension in a given amount.)

When alimony, or child support or maintenance is a substantial part of the applicant's income, such payments must be considered as income to the extent that the

1876. Maria Spelterini walks across Niagara Falls, a length of 1,100 feet at a height of 165 feet, on a tightrope. She is one of a handful of professional acrobats ever to perform the feat.

Regulations   Roslyn L. Kramer

payments are likely to be made consistently.

An applicant has the choice of using her or his birth-given surname, married surname, or a hyphenated surname after her or his birth-given first name. (NOW feels that an applicant should be explicitly permitted to use any legal name in applying for credit.)

Income from part-time work cannot be discounted as income and should be examined for probable continuity. (NOW believes part-time work should be considered on the same basis as full-time work.)

Consumer-loan applications and all related materials must be kept by creditors for fifteen months, an extension from the previous limit of a year. This applies to loan requests of $100,000 or less where the applicant requests in writing that the creditor retain such records. Records are automatically kept for consumer loans, and the applicant need not request this be done.

A creditor may not require the signature of a spouse or other person on a credit instrument unless such a requirement is imposed without regard to sex or marital status on all similarly qualified applicants who apply for a similar type and amount of credit. This provision also applies to business and securities loans. It means that if a woman is creditworthy to the extent of bearing the credit obligation she's applying for, then the creditor cannot ask for her husband's signature unless it is required by state law in order to waive some right he might have in her property.

Accounts beginning on or after November 1, 1976, must be reported to credit-reporting agencies in the individual names of both spouses who have access to and are responsible for the account. This will enable both spouses to develop independent credit histories through use of the same account. (NOW believes this provision should have gone into effect October 28, 1975.)

For accounts established prior to November 1976, the creditor has until February 1, 1977, to inform all applicants, or all married applicants in whose name the account is carried on the creditor's records, that if they desire to have the credit information on the account furnished in the names of both spouses, they should so inform the creditor. A form will be provided for this purpose. (NOW has reservations on the length of time given creditors.)

A creditor may not use any information prohibited in evaluating an application, but the creditor can retain such information in his or her files where this information was obtained from any source prior to June 30, 1976; at any time from credit-reporting agencies; or at any time from the applicant or other, without the specific request of the creditor. (NOW doesn't think the creditor should be allowed to gather any prohibited information after the effective date of the act. The Federal Reserve explains that it would be much too expensive to sort out information in credit files that have accumulated for years.)

A word of advice: Since these regulations still don't fully protect you from discrimination, don't volunteer personal information when applying for a loan. Consider all information you do give from the perspective of whether it is advantageous to you.   copyright © 1976 Roslyn L. Kramer

clude in a brutal comedown from that mature charmer welcoming you in ads. "By all means get to know a banker—and hope he stays there a couple of weeks," one businesswoman advises glumly. You might also find that branch-bank personnel are too harried and limited in outlook to understand your goals, or are humanoid computers instead of counselors—a frequent failing, judging from the number of women I interviewed who were ready to switch banks because of a sharp decline in service at banks they had patronized for years.

Using the same bank is good for your credit history, but if you feel compelled to change, remember that your good record as a credit risk will still remain on your credit-bureau report.

But assume you've found a bank with a good reputation and a bright, understanding person longing to guide you through the spectrum of bank services for present and future needs. Be honest about your assets and liabilities when seeking a loan (you can get away with unrecorded debts to your mother, however). Prepare yourself for an intelligent discussion of your financial situation. Aside from getting advice, you're building up goodwill for a time when you might be very much in need of it. Should you hit a financial crisis after proving yourself a dependable customer, call the credit manager or your bank officer. Explain your problem and tell him or her when and how much you can pay. The loan can then be delayed, or if necessary, be renegotiated.

The foregoing suggestions are all the more important to you as a businessperson. Choose a bank that understands the peculiarities of your business. If business is off, maybe it's merely a seasonal fluctuation or a prevalent condition in the industry that only a specialized bank will recognize as a condition not unique to you.

The difficulties you may encounter in establishing a good relationship with a competent banker can be ameliorated by having your accountant or attorney introduce you to his or her banker when you're ready to open an account. Whether or not you're ready to ask for a loan, be prepared to explain every detail of your business: how it works, the direction it will take, and any data you can show to back

---

1877. Helen Magill becomes the first woman to win a Ph.D. Boston University awards her the degree on the basis of her dissertation, "The Greek Drama."

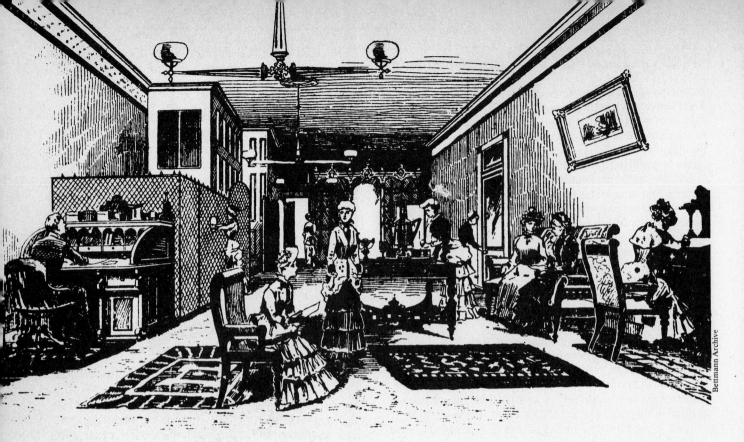

Ladies' banking room, early 19th century

your claims. Awaken the banker to the advantages your business will have for his bank.

Keep in touch by sending year-end or more frequent financial statements. Call monthly or every two weeks; frequency should depend on keeping your banker informed without being intrusive. Use other personnel at the bank, such as the adjuster, who can give your bank balance. Learn the full spectrum of business services available from a bank: payroll management, immediate payment to distant suppliers, employee benefit plans, international expansion, credit checks on prospective clients or suppliers.

Small businesses have a high rate of failure. Banks can be so supercautious, it amounts to discrimination against marginal but sound businesses—and not only banks. Banks can help obtain Small Business Administration loans, but SBA "discriminates like hell against women," one banker said. Proof of a going concern is demanded for an SBA loan before you're in business.

Loan applications can be rejected through error or discrimination, as well as a realistic appraisal of your financial position. If your application is rejected, ask for the reasons in writing. This alone sometimes produces an immediate reversal.

If the answer cites your credit report, go to the bureau or request your file. Credit bureaus have a very high rate of error. Your ex-husband might be in default, or the bureau might have pulled the wrong Jane Smith. Have your credit file cleared. Not only do banks and other creditors use it, so do employers.

You can write to the bank's consumer affairs department if you feel that your loan officer might have applied personal standards contrary to the policy of the bank. Better yet, make a personal visit to the vice president in charge of the type of loan you're seeking (vice presidents are not all that rare in banking, so don't be too humble).

Bank policy is always announced as nondiscriminatory. It has to be, by federal law. (New regulations implementing the Equal Credit Opportunity Act do give latitude for indirect discrimination, however. (See "Federal Credit Regulations.") But internal credit standards, which you're as likely to see as a General Motors bank

1879. The state of Illinois enacts the first American labor law prohibiting or limiting the employment of women. It is "an Act providing for the health and safety of persons employed in coal mines." Henceforth, women are barred from going down into Illinois mines.

statement, can very effectively subvert announced policy.

New York, for example, has an extremely liberal law, yet a woman there who takes over her husband's business after his death may find it difficult to obtain credit. Although you'll no longer be asked in any state for a certificate of sterility when you apply for a mortgage, as some women were not long ago, you may still encounter prejudice in favor of a male cosigner.

Banks everywhere take a dim view of divorce. People who engage in the practice are seen as unstable, and alimony and child support are considered undependable sources of income. If these happen to be a major source of your income but your ex-husband has made regular payments, bring the bank statements to prove it when you apply for a loan, suggests the Center for Women's Policy Studies in Washington, D.C.

If you suspect that the bank you're dealing with is discriminating against you, visit a state or local consumer protection agency or human rights commission.

You should know whether or not your state has a strong credit antidiscrimination law. Local agencies can tell you this, or go to the state attorney general's office, human rights commission, or banking agency, any of which should provide a copy of the law and regulations. And call your local chapter of NOW.

File charges of discrimination on the state or federal level, depending on whichever is most favorable to you, and lose no time in doing it. If you own a business, depending on its legal organization you might not be able to file charges through the usual channels. Call your regional Federal Reserve Board if the agencies mentioned here can't help.

The wise, friendly, trim, gray-haired financial counselor we see in television commercials insistently suggests that banking is a manly art. Perhaps he and his peers are at last beginning to realize that it's a womanly art as well. Whatever roles the recently opened women-run banks, such as the First Women's Bank in New York City, come to play in the financial community, their existence is surely a sign that change, long overdue, is on its way.

Estimating Expenses for Making a Budget

If you have records of family spending, they can serve as a basis for your budget. List items of expense that your family had, with the amount you spent for each item. Include fixed payments, contributions, and other predictable expenditures.

If you do not have records you may be able to recall some of your previous expenses. Checkbook stubs, receipts, and old bills can serve as reminders. This may be all the guide you need in estimating your expenses.

Use your records to help you decide whether to continue your present pattern of spending or to make changes.

If you are satisfied with what your dollars have given your family in the past, allow similar amounts in your estimates for the spending plan.

If you are not satisfied with what you got for your money last year or last month, look at your spending critically. Until you study your records, you may be unaware of overspending and poor buying habits.

Be realistic in revising your allowances for expenses. Resolve to cut out shopping sprees, bargains you don't need, and overuse of credit.

Of course, you will need to plan for new situations and changing conditions. For example, a child entering a new school may have increased expenses, or your property tax rate may go up.

Plan your large expenses so that they are spaced at intervals over several years. If your son gets a suit this year, your daughter may have to wait until next year for a winter coat. New curtains may take turns with baby needs, weekend trips, or a TV set.

Keep your estimate of expenses where you can refer to them as necessary.

Plan for Family Spending	
Income, set-asides, and expenses	Amount per month
Total income	_____
Set-asides:	
Emergencies and future goals _____	_____
Seasonal expenses _____	_____
Debt payments _____	_____
Regular monthly expenses:	
Rent or mortgage payment _____	_____
Utilities _____	_____
Installment payments _____	_____
Other _____	_____
Total _____	
Day-to-day expenses:	
Food and beverages _____	_____
Household operation and maintenance _____	_____
Furnishings and equipment _____	_____
Clothing _____	_____
Personal _____	_____
Transportation _____	_____
Medical care _____	_____
Recreation and education _____	_____
Gifts and contributions _____	_____
Total _____	
Total set-asides and expenses _____	

Adapted from *Steps in Making a Budget*, Consumer and Food Economics Research Division, Agricultural Research Service, 1972.

1879. Mary Baker Eddy founds the Christian Science church in Boston, based on teachings of her book, *Science and Health, with Key to the Scriptures,* published in 1875. This book is the only publication to be granted—by special congressional dispensation—an apparently perpetual copyright protection.

Financial Etiquette – For Business or Pleasure

Roslyn L. Kramer

Your hand reaches out, to be met by his enveloping, urgent grasp.

"I *never* let a woman pay," he murmurs, sweeping away the check with his free hand. Should you be pliant or insistent? Does his tone convey generosity, condescending chauvinism, or do you hear a too-intimate note of desperate masculinity better left unchallenged? Meanwhile the check disappears, covered by his twenty dollar bill.

Thank him. Mean it. He could have spent the evening anticipating your every move—lighting cigarettes, helping you on with your coat, opening doors, and grabbing the check—only to announce your share is twelve dollars, including tip.

Few rules exist to guide a woman in deciding when and how to pay for herself—and possibly for the man she's with.

"Men are all mixed up. They don't know whether to open doors or not, whether to let us call *them*," a college instructor observed after her latest adventure, a weekend to which she was invited by a college administrator who earned four times her salary but expected her to pay her way. "Southerners and European men are more confident. They have fixed values that can be altered, or at least confronted. But men who are unsure of themselves can't be confronted easily."

You're unlikely to run into a flaky Galahad who drops the bill in your lap. Men have a deep emotional stake in financing the mating ritual, even when they're with a woman who is the sole and successful supporter of three children. Women, in turn, respond with a need for the protectiveness implied by a man's willingness to pay, which in its finest flower is generosity.

Romantic dependency may have lost a lot of status lately, but don't underrate it. Ignored, it can lead you to feel obligation when there is none and, conversely, to fail to put up honest resistance to being paid for when the financial responsibility is yours. Many of the most capable, professionally secure women are ambivalent about paying their way.

Almost every decision women make about how much they will spend in the company of men flows from an acute awareness that men in general earn more. This is certainly true, but you should guard against unconsciously using it as a justification for behavior that is really dependent.

Etiquette books have always told women how to avoid direct confrontation with money and sex, and they're in no unseemly rush to change. Reluctantly they concede women might have to pay for business entertainment, but only occasionally and always unobtrusively. Protecting the male ego takes precedence over helping women skillfully execute nontraditional roles.

Business publications aren't much help either. The problem is too new, their editors too confident the readers "just *know*". But fairly well-defined rules do exist for those equipped with credit cards and expense accounts.

In general, whoever extends the invitation picks up the check. (This can be applicable in your personal life as well if your income can support it.) More important, the business relationship determines who extends the invitation to begin with. The basic rule is that the seller of a product or service takes out his or her buyer or client. But the rule isn't immutable. If a client has an irrepressible urge to entertain a supplier as a gesture of appreciation, that's no breach of etiquette.

Once you've decided to play host, stick to it. Your swift, discreet dispatch of the bill will be taken as a concrete display of your business ability.

Clearly state your intention to pay in the invitation: "I'd like to take you to lunch," rather than "Let's have lunch." If you feel that paying the check in normal fashion will cause so much awkwardness that it will interfere with business, you can prepare in advance for check payment. (But don't go to the trouble unless you think it clearly necessary.)

Arrive early to forewarn the maitre d' the meal is on you. "Lay a couple of dollars on them if they get giggly," a publicist advises. At a restaurant where you are well known ask the maitre d' to hold your bill until the next day, or quietly leave the table to sign for it. On the day before meeting at a restaurant where you're not known, ask the manager if he will take a cash deposit or otherwise arrange for the check to be taken care of.

There's no need to do more if the check won't arrive at the table. But if you intend to use a credit card, tell the waiter you are the host when drinks are ordered. Ask your guest what he'd like to order, or simply reinforce your point by saying to the waiter, "I'm not having an appetizer, but

1880. The phrase "The hand that rocks the cradle rules the world" is popularized by a current ballad and will be commonly quoted in America and England for the next fifty years.

perhaps my guest will."

If the check is placed at the opposite end of the table in spite of the buildup, place your credit card in full view. Meet objections from your guest with something like, "No, it's my treat—a thank-you lunch and a pleasure."

Anticipate the check by taking out your credit card when coffee arrives. Better yet, ask that the check be brought with the coffee. Swiftly compute the tip. "If it's done smoothly enough, the man is usually wiped out, which in a tight business situation is an advantage," a literary agent found.

Joining a professional organization or a private club with dining and drinking facilities can eliminate almost all your problems. Your guest can't pay there even if he wants to. But *you* may not even be able to join. Clubs are more than classy status symbols; they might be the only game in town when it comes to your maintaining a competitive business position. Work at breaking the barriers to admittance, and make sure you get the same expense account privileges as men.

Never fight over a check. Be gracious, the golden rule of business entertainment. Relating to a woman as a business peer might be completely new for your guest. On the other hand, in situations that could be ethically compromising (a reporter, for instance, should not relinquish a check to a new source who might be trying to buy good will), season graciousness with determination.

When you're not treating but are planning to pay for yourself, head off any dispute by arranging with the maitre d' or the waiter for a separate check and receipt. Carry single bills as well as larger denominations to cover your share of any check you weren't able to plan for in advance.

Sooner or later you'll get a vague invitation—such as "let's have lunch"—from a person with whom you don't have a well-defined business relationship. Don't assume he or she will put you on the expense account or consider your financial position in choosing a restaurant. Before agreeing to the restaurant suggested, make sure you can afford it. If you can't, suggest another place or frankly say, "That's a little more than I can spend."

Always pay your own way with office colleagues if you like getting frequent invitations and having yours accepted.

In local bars, or bars where people with similar work interests congregate, you get an interesting view of men's attitudes toward money. Male custom dictates knowing the bartender's name, leaving big tips, buying rounds, and depositing a large sum on the bar from which the bartender subtracts as the customer orders (unless a running tab is kept).

Women need to know the bartender's name and leave large tips. If you can't occasionally buy a round for the men you drink with, buy separate drinks for the really reckless spenders. The unaccustomed gesture from a woman awes men in this hothouse world.

Bartenders control their domain. Big tips generate free drinks and in time will break down a bartender's resistance to having unescorted women in his sanctuary. Tips aren't necessary each time if you don't drink much, but they

should be in bills the bartender knows came from you. Anonymous quarters don't earn good will.

If you are with a group of men in a bar, you'll probably be included in rounds and not expected to pay for your drinks. If you came alone and want to leave without the guy who's been threading passes through the conversation for the past hour, buy your own final drink.

In a large, uncoupled, mixed group it's difficult to tell what is meant when a man giving an order turns to you and asks, "What will you have?" Assume you're paying for yourself.

Poverty is a relentless condition that puts you almost beyond the pale socially or in business. Again, never assume you're being paid for. When he asks you out, don't get carried away and say yes, on the one hand or "Is this on you?" on the other. Instead of asking his intentions state yours: "I can't afford——" if you're not interested in the offer unless he pays; "I can only invest——" if you want to go. There's the rest of the evening to recover from your bluntness, which is far better than mutual bitterness at the end of the evening.

When not a cent of yours is on the line but you're asked to suggest activities, give the cost of what you'd like to do if you don't know what his resources are.

Women traditionally return male largesse with theater tickets or at-home entertainment—by-passing any direct handling of money. It can be easier to go to bed with a man than to discuss money with him. Some men adjust rapidly to women paying, but are incapable of voicing their expectations.

"Women are getting to pay a lot more, but they're not

Tips on What to Tip
The Editors of *Redbook*

When traveling in places new to them, vacationers sometimes are puzzled about how much to tip. While there are different customs and standards in many places—particularly in foreign countries—the truth is that you should tip not so much by an arbitrary standard but according to the quality of service you receive. Wherever you go, tipping should be a mark of appreciation for services well rendered, not an obligation.

On a trip abroad you will be perfectly correct in tipping the equivalent of what you would give for the same service at home. You could use your American money for tipping, but it is wiser to tip in the currency of the country. You can buy prepackaged foreign currency envelopes from foreign exchange companies and some U.S. banks before your trip. This way you can get from $10 to $50 in currencies for all the countries you plan to visit and have tipping money conveniently at hand.

Here are some guidelines for tipping, but again, remember that much depends on the quality of the service you receive.

Cab Driver:
20 cents on a 55-cent fare; 25 cents on a 75-cent or $1 fare

Doorman:
25 cents for calling a cab; more if he helps with your bags
Porter:
50 cents per bag
Chambermaid:
50 cents per night's stay, about $3 a week
Bartender:
15 percent of bar drinks
Waiter, Waitress:
15 percent to 25 percent of total food and beverage check
Wine Steward:
50 cents per person
Captain:
$1 for two persons, if special service given
Airline Personnel:
No tipping in air travel, except to porters

If you are staying at a hotel and signing for meals, you can write "Plus 15 percent" (or 20 percent or whatever percentage you choose) at the bottom of the bill to cover your tip.

A tip should always be figured on your food and beverage total, *less* tax. Some resorts and restaurants add a 15-percent service charge to meal checks automatically, making it unnecessary to leave a tip on the table. Watch for this.

Reprinted from *Redbook* Magazine, September 1972. Copyright © 1972 The Redbook Publishing Company.

1880. King Mtessa of Uganda, Africa, is permitted seven thousand wives, the high-water mark of polygamy anywhere in recorded world history.

getting much more say over where to go and how often," a sociologist feels. The basic reason for taking on a fair share of financial responsibility, no matter how minute the amount you can afford, is nothing less than keeping control over your own life. Don't make a habit of foregoing your choice in favor of his.

The compulsive chivalry that made men force dimes on you for phone calls is dead. These days you pay for your personal needs. A man riveted to the check will yield the tip to you. He won't stop you from buying popcorn at the movies. Pick up small dinner tabs with a man you see regularly, leaving larger ones to him. Buy drinks before dinner. If you are a single mother, your babysitting fees are a contribution men sometimes overlook.

Who actually gives your money to the waiter can be another problem. If you're out with a conventionally inclined man who might be humiliated by your openly handling money, you could ask if he would like you to give him the money beforehand. You might find less resistance if you use a credit card. On the other hand, *you* might resist this as an outrageous artifice to assuage his ego. You shouldn't have to hide your feelings about assuming financial responsibility.

Giving him money in advance makes sense, however, when you're bringing your children along (telling him earlier and making it clear you will pay for them) and he pays for you.

Any vacation or steady relationship deserves a frank discussion of finances. You might agree to splitting costs, keeping a record of expenses, and repaying him after your return from a trip or at the end of a week or month. You can fix a ratio reflecting your relative incomes—your one-third to his two thirds, for instance.

Offer and expect to pay your own way with men who are exclusively friends unless the rule that whoever extends the invitation pays is mutually acceptable or it's understood that he or she who can best afford it pays. Paying your own way can be a means of conveying a purely friendly—and not sexual—interest to a man, whether he's a new friend or an old lover.

A pattern few women enunciate but many have adopted as a compromise between traditional expectations and their increasing sense of financial responsibility is assuming a man will pick up the entire check when he invites her out. When the invitation is hers, she assumes he pays her share and possibly his.

You might have noticed what few rules there are conflict and must be adapted to variables—age, income, lifestyle, degrees of intimacy—that fluctuate radically with each relationship. Balance your demands with consideration of his. Take the initiative when he seems irritable over money but doesn't express it. Devise rules from your own experience. Authority over your life more than compensates for the awkward moments, to say nothing of the intellectual and financial rewards.

"I always let him pay," an ardent feminist concluded. "He has more money than I do, and besides, he's a Marxist."

Liberating

Until 1973 the Harvard Club in New York City offered limited membership to women related by academic degree or by marriage to Harvard University. This entitled them to a side entrance, a dab of red-flowered wallpaper, and a narrow staircase leading to a pleasant suite of lounges and carpeted dining room. You couldn't ask for a nicer ghetto.

With rare exception, only men could use the canopied main entrance or wide staircase, the army of black-leather armchairs, the squash courts, the library, the sleeping quarters, the vast dining hall, the telephone facing a stuffed reindeer's head, or any wood-paneled area.

This segregated club was an extension of a coeducational university. (Harvard graduate and professional schools have long been coeducational, and even Radcliffe students now get their degrees from Harvard.) In 1971, a group of alumnae women, most of them recent graduates of Harvard professional schools and all high-caliber jobholders, petitioned for all-or-nothing membership. When a peaceful victory seemed imminent a year and a half later, a publicity-bent latecomer to their group forced charges to be brought before the New York State Division of Human Rights. The women won, though with more friction than they had hoped.

Many women of the old regime preferred the status quo. Using the club for respite

Patricia Pennington

1881. Louise Bethune, opening her office in Buffalo, New York, this year, becomes the first American woman architiect.

the All-male Club
Roslyn L. Kramer with Lynn Salvage

from shopping, and paying minimal dues, they were not eager that club policy change in favor of working women who could afford full membership.

Lynn Salvage, who went from Harvard's Graduate School of Business into international banking, organized the movement for equal admittance. Here are her suggestions for taking on a local bastion of sexist aristocracy, followed by high points of the debate:

1. Gird yourself for a long stretch of exemplary behavior—diplomacy, patience, politeness, tolerance. The ultimate objective is integration in a friendly environment and your own economic survival. Demand respect as a woman; don't worry about being liked.

2. Gather support. Six Harvard women formed the active nucleus of the movement for admittance, but half the women in the graduate business school signed a protest letter to the management of the Club. Copies were generously provided to the president, deans, and members of the administration of the university.

3. Maintain a high momentum. Meet once a week or more, if only to keep up group morale. Coordinated, sustained group effort will impress the opposition. All women should meet club membership qualifications.

4. Cultivate male members who may provide a source of information about the club and sympathetic publicity among the members. Young men are not necessarily allies, nor older men opponents.

5. Spokespersons should always be women. Their work status should be high enough so that the club's establishment will perceive them as equals.

6. While wearing down the official management, also meet with individual directors. No more than three women should be present at any such meeting. Do not bring a lawyer, whose presence would indicate an adversary position. Visit segregated quarters only to show your open-mindedness when the management invites you to see how nice the quarters are.

7. Do research and get a lawyer. Tax, equal-opportunity, and liquor-licensing laws; club by-laws; and the relationship of the club to the larger community it serves will suggest strategy. (If it had been strongly pressured to do so, Harvard University would have had to acknowledge a moral obligation to back

integration of the club.) If the club management denies that substantial business activity takes place there, get the names of companies that pick up expense-account tabs for any proof of economic discrimination against women.

8. Reserve the threat of negative publicity and legal action—ultimate remedies, which you hope will never be necessary—as leverage during negotiations. A well-timed, tactful reminder that you have more than moral persuasion on your side will keep the establishment negotiating with you.

9. Be constructive. No one will have asked you, but offer to serve on committees. If physical changes are required, such as dressing rooms or bathrooms, suggest how they can be made. (The toughest objections to answer will be the ones with price tags for the club.)

10. Economic pressure is indirect and lengthy but is virtually the only way to wring concessions from private social clubs unaffected by equal-rights legislation. Convince business firms that rent private rooms at a men-only club and whose executives regularly stay there to stop patronizing it. To be effective, this strategy should be initiated internally within influential companies whose business is crucial to the club.

Clubs that allow women limited access do so for economic reasons. The Harvard

WOMEN'S LIBERATION

Prop Art

1882. The British Parliament passes the Married Women's Property Act, a legal watershed that allows married women to dispose of their possessions through a will without the intervention of any trustee. The act also permits a married woman who is a will executrix to act independently.

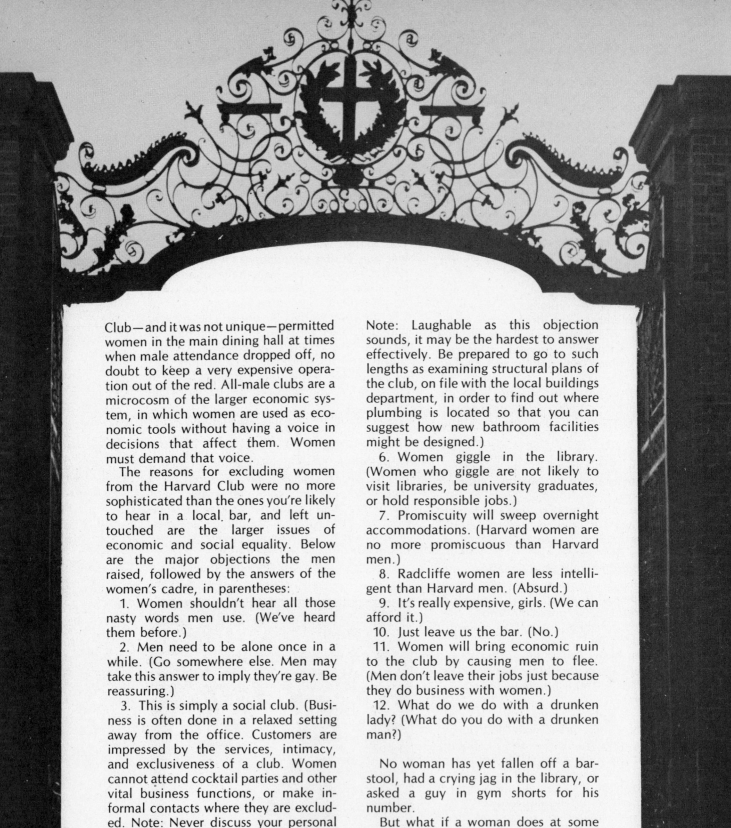

Club—and it was not unique—permitted women in the main dining hall at times when male attendance dropped off, no doubt to keep a very expensive operation out of the red. All-male clubs are a microcosm of the larger economic system, in which women are used as economic tools without having a voice in decisions that affect them. Women must demand that voice.

The reasons for excluding women from the Harvard Club were no more sophisticated than the ones you're likely to hear in a local bar, and left untouched are the larger issues of economic and social equality. Below are the major objections the men raised, followed by the answers of the women's cadre, in parentheses:

1. Women shouldn't hear all those nasty words men use. (We've heard them before.)

2. Men need to be alone once in a while. (Go somewhere else. Men may take this answer to imply they're gay. Be reassuring.)

3. This is simply a social club. (Business is often done in a relaxed setting away from the office. Customers are impressed by the services, intimacy, and exclusiveness of a club. Women cannot attend cocktail parties and other vital business functions, or make informal contacts where they are excluded. Note: Never discuss your personal social life except to say it is happily lived elsewhere.)

4. Men will be embarrassed by women seeing them half-clothed. (How do they cope with beaches?)

5. Inadequate bathrooms. (Income from female members will more than make up for the cost of new bathrooms.

Note: Laughable as this objection sounds, it may be the hardest to answer effectively. Be prepared to go to such lengths as examining structural plans of the club, on file with the local buildings department, in order to find out where plumbing is located so that you can suggest how new bathroom facilities might be designed.)

6. Women giggle in the library. (Women who giggle are not likely to visit libraries, be university graduates, or hold responsible jobs.)

7. Promiscuity will sweep overnight accommodations. (Harvard women are no more promiscuous than Harvard men.)

8. Radcliffe women are less intelligent than Harvard men. (Absurd.)

9. It's really expensive, girls. (We can afford it.)

10. Just leave us the bar. (No.)

11. Women will bring economic ruin to the club by causing men to flee. (Men don't leave their jobs just because they do business with women.)

12. What do we do with a drunken lady? (What do you do with a drunken man?)

No woman has yet fallen off a barstool, had a crying jag in the library, or asked a guy in gym shorts for his number.

But what if a woman does at some point commit such a gaucherie? It will be nothing more or less than if a male member did the equivalent.

An unrelenting chauvinist member of the Harvard Club said, "Before you know it, they'll take over the swimming pool." There is no swimming pool at the Harvard Club.

1883. Caroline Earle White founds the American Anti-Vivisection Society in Philadelphia. Its object, according to its charter, is "the prevention of suffering upon animals under the pretense of medical and scientific research."

Sex and Taxes

Marylin Bender

A reluctance to look before signing income-tax returns is one of those unfortunate female hang-ups about money. Too many women have abdicated the overwhelmingly important tax side of their lives to men—to husbands, to accountants (in whom their husbands may have put equally blind faith) and to the Internal Revenue Service.

Before I was married, I used to prepare my own tax returns. Granted my affairs were relatively simple then. But I was once challenged in an audit. I thrashed it out with an IRS man. He relented a little, I gave a little and emerged with a comforting refund.

After I was married, I lowered my eyes to the signature line of the joint returns my husband and his accountant prepared. I never peeked above because it would have seemed as though I were doubting their authority.

Besides, I might have found out how much my husband was making. He wouldn't have minded, but in those preconsciousness days I subscribed to the double standard. In taxes as in sexual morality, the double standard is arrant nonsense. Though I handled my own money and so believed I was keeping my little secrets, at tax time my husband found out everything I had done, whereas his financial affairs were a mystery to me.

In those days, though, we both indulged in fun and games about my income. There was the badinage about how it threw him into a higher tax bracket. He was doing me a favor by letting me work, an expensive gift as it were, which naturally dampened my enthusiasm for getting a better job or asking for a raise or learning more about investments so that with my own

initiative I might make a capital gain.

We don't play that silly game any more. We're both aware of how much such frilly illusions have helped to short-change women (and their families).

Since federal tax law was redrawn in 1969, many women and men have discovered that they are paying a marriage tax, a penalty for living together in legal wedlock.

While it corrected an earlier discrimination against the single taxpayer, the law now exacts a heavier tax from the two-income marriage, particularly where both partners bring in fairly equal amounts of earnings, than it does from the one-earner marriage. And the tax is considerably more than the husband and wife would pay if they divorced and lived together but filed as single taxpayers. It's tempting to try this arrangement, but it's more valorous to clamor for reform of the tax law, as a number of groups and informed individuals are now doing.

Take these examples given in a hearing before the House Ways and Means Committee by Florence B. Donohue, chairperson of the Committee on Taxation and the Working Woman of the New York Women's Bar Association. Mrs. Donohue is an executive editor with Prentice-Hall, Inc., the tax-information publisher.

Bill and Mary are married and have two children. They each make $4,000 a year. If they file a joint return, they will pay a tax of $573. If they lived in what used to be called sin but now looks like tax wisdom, each would pay a tax of $181, for a total of $362. And if one qualified as an unmarried head of household, there would be an additional $5 saving.

Bert, a young salesman, makes $12,000 a year. He and Susan, a teacher who earns $10,000 a year and with whom he shares an apartment, have talked about getting married. They almost did last Christmas, but Bert figured out the wedding license would cost them over $600. How can that be? Filing separate returns as single taxpayers, their total taxes will come to $3,312.50. Had they married and filed a joint return, the taxes would have

been $3,960. Or if they had married and filed separate returns, $3,970.

There doesn't seem to be much dollars-and-sense incentive to interrupt their unwedded bliss.

The immediate reason for this uneven treatment of taxpayers is twofold: Lower rates are given to unmarried singles and heads of households, and married couples can only use one standard deduction, currently at a maximum of $2,000.

But behind all of that is the value that our government (which reflects the opinion of society at large) places on the housewife's work. Zero.

The reason that a husband and wife each earning $8,000 will pay a combined income tax the same as one husband earning $16,000 is that no money sum is calculated for the stay-at-home wife's cooking, cleaning, chauffeuring and child-care services. If it were, the second family's income would be greater than $16,000 and so would its income tax. Furthermore, if the second wife were to take a job outside the home, she would probably have to pay someone to perform those very valuable services that the tax collector doesn't recognize when *she* does them.

The injustice here is not only to the two-income household but to the wife who is discouraged from working outside the home. The burden falls on families of all income levels. In effect, the government is subsidizing the family with one earner and is making a judgment about marital status that it has no business making.

No one has really figured out how to value the domestic services of a wife, though the subject ⎯⎯⎯⎯⎯→

1884. Frances E. Willard, reflecting an impulse common among women at the time, founds the World Women's Christian Temperance Union "to protect the home, outlaw the liquor traffic, seek and procure enfranchisement of women, work to establish courts of international arbitration, demand an equal standard of purity for men and women and labor unceasingly that justice may be opposed to greed and gain, and that Christ's

Sex and Taxes
THE MONEY MANAGER 377

keeps cropping up. But there have been several tax reforms proposed.

One would be to adopt a single tax-rate schedule instead of the four separate ones that now prevail (for single taxpayers, unmarried heads of households, married taxpayers filing joint returns and those filing separate returns). Some European countries have already done this. Into this could be cranked an earned-income credit or allowance for a percentage of the second earner's contribution. Dr. Joseph A. Pechman, a tax scholar with the Brookings Institution, would put a ceiling on the allowance so that it could just help cover the expenses the second earner incurs by leaving home to work.

A year ago, Anita and Christopher Murray, two computer specialists, organized a half dozen other married couples to fight the marriage tax. Married Americans for Tax Equality (MATE), 76 Laight Street, Seventh Floor, New York, N.Y. 10013, has had a bill introduced in Congress that would allow married persons the same tax rates as single persons.

Another major concern for many women who work or would like to is the child-care deduction. This provision of the tax law permits anyone employed to deduct up to $400 a month expenses for household services for a child under 15 or a spouse or dependent of the taxpayer who is physically or mentally incapable of caring for himself or herself. This applies, then, to an aged parent as well as a child. But the expense must be "employment related," which means you would be unable to work unless you arranged for these services, and except for the child they must be incurred for services inside the household.

Child services can include day-care-center, nursery-school or private kindergarten fees (up to $200 a month for one child, $300 for two and $400 for three or more) or payment to a babysitter (with the sitter's lunches and carfare also deductible). The difference between the amount spent for outside care and the $400 monthly limit can be given to household expenses.

The deduction is permitted to married couples only when a joint return is filed and when both husband and wife are employed full time. If the husband is a student under the G. I. Bill of Rights, he is not considered to be gainfully employed.

Once the adjusted gross income of the couple exceeds $35,000, the deduction is reduced 50 cents for each dollar of added income. This in effect means that you can't deduct for child care if your joint income is more than $44,600.

The deduction was liberalized to its present limit in 1975, but it still discriminates against women achievers. "We feel," says Dorothy Amdur, head of the committee on taxation of the National Organization for Women (NOW), that such household service is just as much of an ordinary and reasonable business expense as is the businessman's lunch where he boozes it up and takes the whole cost of the lunch as a deduction.

"The whole philosophy that woman's place is in the home runs through our tax law, and yet it's in conflict with civil-rights law," she said. (Title Seven of the Civil Rights Act of 1964 outlawed sex discrimination in employment, and the government has been enforcing the edict with lawsuits against some of our largest corporations.) "On the one hand women are encouraged to aim for management jobs," she points out, "and on the other hand, if they happen to be mothers, they are limited in the child care they can have in order to do these jobs."

Sexism rears its addled head again in the offices of the Internal Revenue Service when taxpayers are called to have their returns audited. The experience is about as agreeable as a visit to a gynecologist's office, but it may cost more if you don't have your rights about you.

You may be summoned for audit at random or because the refund you claimed seems unreasonable to the computer. Or, in the case of divorced women, because your former spouse and you may be claiming the same dependency exemption for your children.

The first step is at the desk-audit level. There's a good chance your examiner will be a woman because, according to Dorothy Amdur, who is a certified public accountant, this is a low-paying job and 95 percent of the slots are filled by women. The problem stems from the fact that they are not trained accountants, they are on a production-line quota and they tend to believe ex-husbands in these exemption disputes.

Whatever the nature of the dispute, you should not accept a desk-audit ruling contrary to your interest. "I tell my friends to go all the way to Round Two, the conference procedure," Dorothy Amdur says, "because there you meet trained accountants and lawyers." They are eager to settle disputes to cut down on the clutter in the courts, and therefore it is possible to bargain.

If your disputed tax deficiency does not involve more than $1,500, you should consider taking it to the Small Tax Case Section of the United States Tax Court. There's one in each state and as many as half a dozen in large urban areas. You do not need a lawyer, though you may bring one if you prefer. He must, however, be admitted to practice before the Tax Court.

The rules of procedure are informal. The rules of evidence are relaxed so that almost any information that would support a taxpayer's claim is allowed. You may argue your case orally and then submit a written statement afterward.

This section was created by the Tax Reform Act of 1969 to be independent of the U.S. Tax Court. Its decisions apply only to the case at hand and do not set precedent. The amount in dispute must be less than or equal to $1,500 for each taxable year. If you have been assessed a tax deficiency of $2,500 but decided the IRS may be right about $1,000 of that amount, you can fight the $1,500 in the Small Tax Case Section.

The requirements are few and simple. You must wait to receive your notice of tax deficiency from the IRS before applying to the section. Then you must file a petition to bring your case before it within 90 days of the mailing date of the deficiency notice. The filing fee is $10.

A petition form and instruction booklet can be obtained by writing to: Clerk, United States Tax Court, Box 70, Washington, D.C. 20044. Telephone: 202-964-3041.

You state your case on the petition form, request a location for a trial and within a short time you will receive a 60-day notice of the date of your trial. The case will be heard by a commissioner and his decision will be sent to you—usually with a brief summary of the reasons—within six to nine months after the trial. It will have been reviewed by the chief judge of the Tax Court and the judge sitting in charge of the Small Tax Case Section.

The decision cannot be appealed by either side, but if you are dissatisfied you can start over again in the Tax Court.

Marjorie O'Connell Amey, a Washington lawyer and NOW tax-committee member, offers this caution and encouragement about self-representation in the Small Tax Case Section. "Don't try it without appropriate research," she counsels. "You must check the points of law. However, tax cases are available at public and law libraries. On the other hand, you must realize that if the IRS is dead set against an issue's going to trial, they can say it's too important for the small tax section and that it should be handled by the Tax Court. This is not usually done, however."

Mrs. Amey asserts that, particularly in matters in which IRS agents tend to be sympathetic to alienated husbands, "the odds are eighty-five percent that the case will be settled more to the woman's advantage in the small tax section because in the relaxed manner of this forum she may be able to show, for example, that she pays more than half of the child's support."

You should recognize, though, that not all of the sexism can be blamed on the staff of the IRS. "Part of the trouble is in the law," Marjorie Amey says. "An honest and extensive use of the Small Tax Case Section by women with tax problems may eventually say something to legislators."

But don't get the impression that you have to be squabbling with a former husband to benefit from taking your case to the small tax section. Single women, widowed women and happily married couples should stand up and fight for tax equality, too.

Golden Rule may triumph in custom and law." The suffragist cause is to gain many of its strongest fighters from the ranks of frustrated temperance leaders who—when they realize that larger goals will never be met until women can command political power through the vote—stump for the Nineteenth Amendment.

What Every Working Mother Should Know
about Tax Deductions

Marion Child

If you are a mother who works or one who has thought seriously of working, you probably know that the cost of child care is now tax-deductible.

Put that way, the new provision in the tax law (enacted in 1971) sounds quite simple. But when you actually begin to grapple with it, the child-care deduction turns out to be as complicated as a Chinese puzzle. Did you know, for example, that you can deduct for nursery-school tuition? That you cannot deduct for your mother-in-law's services even if she is a trained baby nurse and you pay her a regular salary for caring for your child? That a woman who does volunteer work just may be able to count the cost of child care as a charitable contribution?

Then there are the ins and outs of actually using the deduction. There are records to keep and forms to fill out; and there is the whole moral problem, since women are finally asking the question that should have been asked years ago: Shouldn't a regularly employed baby sitter get sick leave, a paid vacation?

As a working mother I have had to come up with answers to these questions, and I recently have gone to the Internal Revenue Service for answers to others. What follows, then, is a brief guide to the use of the child-care deduction.

The first thing you need to know about the deduction is whether you are eligible. The law says you are if you maintain a household for a child or children under 15 or a disabled dependent, if you are gainfully employed, if spending money on child care is necessary to your being able to work and if the person you employ is not a relative or a dependent member of your household. You also must earn no more than $35,000 a year or lose some of the deduction; married couples must file a joint return.

What does all this mean when it comes down to cases?

Case 1: She works full time; he is a graduate student. Can they deduct their daughter's day-care expenses?

The answer is no because he is a student. Both parents must be gainfully employed.

Case 2: He works, and so did she until a month ago, when she was fired. Can they continue to deduct for babysitting expenses while she looks for a new job?

They can as long as she is actively searching for work.

Case 3: He has a salaried job and she puts in many hours as a volunteer for a local charity. To do so she must pay a baby sitter to stay with her children. Can they deduct?

They can try. One of the problems with the child-care deduction is that the Internal Revenue Service has not yet issued the regulations that eventually will spell out exactly what is allowed. The law says volunteer workers cannot claim the child-care deduction; however, a Washington, D.C., woman who applied to the I.R.S. for a private-letter ruling was told she could deduct as a charitable contribution the money she paid a sitter while she did charity work. An I.R.S. private ruling applies to just one case, but presumably it can be considered a

straw in the wind.

Under the circumstances, then, a woman who does volunteer work first of all should write to the I.R.S. to see if the regulations are finally available. If they're not, she has two choices. She can file her 1976 tax return without claiming the deduction and in the meantime write to the Assistant Commissioner, Technical, Internal Revenue Service, 1111 Constitution Avenue N.W., Washington, D.C. 20224, asking for a private ruling. It can take as long as a year to get a ruling, but if it is a favorable one, the taxpayer simply files an amended 1976 return and claims her refund.

The alternative is to make what the I.R.S. calls a "good faith" interpretation of the law and go ahead and claim the deduction—and be prepared to defend it if your return is audited. If the auditor disallows the deduction, you simply pay what you owe—the sum you withheld, plus 6 percent interest. When you choose this second course, your chances of being audited are slightly higher.

Case 4: He is an accountant; she teaches in a nursery school for four hours a day. Can they deduct child-care expenses for their two-year-old son?

The law says that both husband and wife must be employed "substantially full time" or for "at least ¾ the normal or customary work week." But it does not say whether "normal" means a given number of hours, such as 35 hours a week, or whether it means "normal" for a particular occupation, though an I.R.S. spokesman felt the second interpretation was more likely. Once again, you can claim the deduction in good faith on the assumption that a 20-hour week is normal for nursery-school teachers. Or you can file without claiming it, wait for the regulations—which will probably settle the question—and then if you qualify, file an amended return.

Case 5: Four days a week a baby sitter stays with their eight-year-old after school. On the fifth day a different woman comes in all day to clean and to keep an eye on the child. Can they deduct fully for both these employees?

Yes. The law covers "household services," which include those of a housekeeper, maid or cook.

Case 6: They have two sons in nursery school and a nine-year-old daughter in private school. Can they deduct for the three children's tuition?

Nursery-school tuition is deductible, as is tuition for camps and day camps as long as they are providing child care while both parents work. However, tuition paid for first grade and above is not deductible. So in this case school fees for the boys would qualify but not for the girl.

Case 7: Their child is bused to and from a distant day-care center. Can they deduct the bus fares as well as the center's fees?

Yes. The law states that necessary transportation costs can be included in figuring child-care expenses.

Let us move on now to the nitty-gritty—the record keeping and forms you must fill out. The first thing to know is that on your tax return you must say for each month of the year how much you spent for child care, and whether it was for care

1884. The Equal Rights Party is formed in San Francisco at a convention of the Women's Rights Party of Female Suffragettes. Belva Bennett Lockwood is nominated for president; Amarietta Stow is her vice-presidential running mate.

inside or outside your home. You will need to keep records—to save all canceled checks and write down the date and the amount whenever you pay cash.

In addition, if you hire a baby sitter and pay her more than $50 in any quarter (for tax purposes the calendar year is divided into quarters: January through March, April through June, and so on), you must pay a social security tax for that quarter—your own share of the tax as employer and the sitter's share as your employee. This is simpler than it sounds.

You start by asking your local I.R.S. office for Form 942 and for Circular E, the Employer's Tax Guide. Each time you pay your sitter, you calculate 5.85 per cent of what you owe her and hold it back from her wages; bank it, or at least keep a record of how much you deducted. At the end of the quarter you fill in Form 942; then you take the tax money you witheld, add a matching amount for your share of the tax and mail a check and the form to the I.R.S. (In New York, Hawaii and in Washington, D.C., you must pay in addition a small quarterly unemployment insurance tax for a domestic worker in a private home; you can get details from the State Department of Labor or in Washington from the D.C. Unemployment Compensation Board.)

Choosing a Stockbroker

Victoria Y. Pellegrino

1. Open up an account with a brokerage firm that is a member of the New York or the American Stock Exchange. If you have no recommendations from friends or business acquaintances, you can look in the *Yellow Pages.* Under the firm's listing, it will usually state whether they are members or not. Or you can call the firm and ask them.

2. Look for a firm that has been in business for at least ten years. Dealing with an old, reliable firm is much better than dealing with a young, inexperienced one.

3. Visit the premises of the firm to get a gut feeling about the types of people that work there. See if they are intelligent, well dressed, polite. Ask for a copy of the financial statement so that you will be able to get some idea of how well the firm is doing.

4. When and if you are directed to a particular salesman, look for signs that he is interested in forwarding your financial objectives. Beware of salesmen who are overly optimistic or who make promises of performance. Beware of salesmen who make statements such as, "You'd better get in on this now; it's a once-in-a-lifetime opportunity."

5. Get a salesman who is conservative and cautious and who recommends good stocks that are traded on the major exchanges.

6. Beware of a broker who tries to sell you low-priced securities traded over the counter.

7. Do not invest more than $1,000 in the beginning. Make a few small investments to be sure you and your broker have the same objectives and that he has your best interests in mind.

8. Never ever open a discretionary account. (That means the broker can make all decisions without consulting you. He could then buy and sell just to generate commissions for himself.) Never open a margin account in the beginning either. Open a cash account only.

9. Beware of a stockbroker—male or female—who treats you, because you're a woman, like a child or like someone not to be taken seriously.

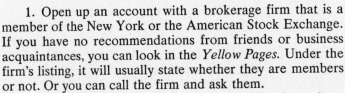

1885. Martha Canary, a.k.a. Calamity Jane, is enjoying the zenith of her fame. Supposedly skilled in such cowboy pursuits as roughriding, stagecoach driving, bullwhacking, hard drinking, and "colorful language," she is portrayed in the enormously popular dime novels of the time as a beautiful but tough woman capable of doing nearly

Investment Know-how

Marlene R. Krauss

A victory in the battle for higher wages, equal rights to own property, and the access to bank loans will be a hollow one if women continue to consider themselves incapable of intelligent money management. An artificial division in which the man—whether husband or financial adviser—makes the investment decisions while the woman spends the allowance, is crippling for women and an unfair burden for men. In reality, neither men nor women bring sex-linked inadequacies or talents to money management. Some individuals are simply more gifted at it than others.

Money management is more than just structuring a budget or saving at the nearest bank. It involves understanding and analyzing all the financial alternatives possible in our individual situations. For most people, these are saving, or investing in stocks, bonds, or mutual funds.

Because of the roles women have traditionally played, we have experience and skills we can draw on to help us become competent investors of our money. As prime consumers, women have a potential awareness of possible investments. We are usually dealing with products and services, measuring price against value. From here, it is a matter of vision and imagination. One must not be limited to viewing Tampax, for example, as merely Tampax. If three years ago you bought stock in Tampax, you would have more than doubled your money by now. If your vision of Sony television went beyond the late-night movies, the stock you bought in Sony Corporation two years ago would by now have more than tripled in price. But product knowledge is only a beginning. In itself, it is far from sufficient for making investment decisions.

The proverbial financial inexperience of women can also be turned to advantage. As novice investors, we are often willing to admit a lack of knowledge in a way that many men are not, and we are, therefore, free to question. Our uncertainty becomes a research tool.

Our traditional day-to-day handling of financial matters in the family, and sometimes in business as well, should enable us to go further to more sophisticated planning and investing. Yet in our minds, as in reality, we are always the book-keepers, never the comptrollers.

We have the ability to manage and invest our money, but we must consider whether we *want* to do so. Investments have risks not unlike gambling. However, in the stock market more than in most gambling, there are ways to reduce the element of chance, and tools that may help improve performance. You can also consider the bond market as perhaps affording more safety.

On balance, it is hard to say whether the average person makes or loses money in the stock market. In recent years, large institutional investors with superior research capabilities and huge financial resources have dominated the investment world, making it increasingly difficult for the small investor to make money. Indeed, some professional portfolio managers diligently follow the indicator of small investor decisions (the odd-lot buying and selling of less than a hundred shares) and do the opposite, using the small investor as a negative indicator.

You must carefully consider the risks as well as the possibility of financial gains, and should you decide to invest in the stock market, you should not commit any more money than you are financially and emotionally ready to lose.

Your decision about investing must also take into account any moral

objections you may have to business in general. If your moral alternative to investing has been to put your money in the bank, however, it's worth remembering that savings banks are among the largest businesses in our country and as such invest heavily in stocks. In fact, one could argue that if you buy certain municipal bonds (bonds issued by state or local governments or authorities, which may be floated to finance education, mass transit, or pollution control), you are less involved with big business than if you put your money in the bank.

You may also object to investing in certain kinds of businesses—for example, those that make war materials, pollute the environment, or discriminate against groups according to sex or race. If you strictly adhere to the last objection, you are probably limited to putting your money in your mattress—and even at that, you cannot be sure about the mattress manufacturer.

Reports that rate companies on the social issues are available from organizations like the Council on Economic Priorities at 456 Greenwich Street, New York, N.Y. 10013. And

Small Business Administration

anything as well as any man. Her inflated publicity, fueled by her occassional appearances dressed in a tailored buckskin costume as the attraction of a traveling sideshow, bears little relation to the real Calamity Jane. In fact, she spends most of her time following railroad crews and army camps about, periodically getting jailed for

Investment Clubs

How do you start an investment club?

Find 10 to 20 other women (or include men if you want) whom you like and who have similar investment objectives. They do not have to be wealthy or have experience with investing.

At your first few meetings, decide how frequently to meet and how much each person will contribute to the pool. Clubs usually meet once or twice a month and many are set up on a basis of $10 to $30 a month.

Also get some legal advice about structuring your organization and drawing up an agreement among the members.

The National Association of Investment Clubs (NAIC) at P.O. Box 220, Royal Oak, Michigan 48068, publishes "Investment Club Manual" ($3), which provides useful information on the formation and operation of investment clubs. Your club can join the NAIC for $12 a year. This entitles you to useful literature and $25,000 of insurance in case one of your members runs off with the club's money (or some such catastrophe).

How should the club function?

Initially the members should read some basic investment literature. There are a number of books and pamphlets containing valuable information for investors.

After a few meetings and a familiarity with investment concepts, choose a good broker. Make sure she or he is with a reputable firm, that you know someone who has successfully dealt with the broker and that your investment objectives are understood. Find out how the account will be opened and handled and what information on securities the broker is prepared to provide. Appoint one person to deal with the broker for the club—but don't invest until you are ready.

A way to choose the initial companies to evaluate is to have each member consider those companies in a business or industry they know because of their work, interests, or personal activities. For example, if you work with computers and are aware of the technology or market for them, you might want to look at the computer industry first for possible investments. Or a teacher might have special knowledge of the many companies dealing in textbooks and other teaching aids. Then members can be assigned to do further research.

Often the officers of companies you are researching, investment analysts, or various brokers will agree to speak to your club. Your broker should help you arrange for these guest speakers, but choose them carefully.

One main advantage of investment clubs is the ability to share knowledge, as well as risks. Discuss each investment carefully before you decide to buy—or sell.

Before your club actually takes the plunge, have a paper portfolio. Pretend you are starting with an amount of money and, on the basis of some research, buy stocks, follow them, sell them, and pick new ones—but just do so on paper. If you make money on paper, do not think you are a genius and hock everything to invest in the market. Just consider it a rehearsal for the real thing and remember that many a great rehearsal ends in a flop on opening night.

When you actually invest, don't forget the investments you hold. Assign members to follow these stocks. The entire portfolio should be reviewed two or three times a year.

How well do investment clubs perform?

The safest answer is that some make money and others lose money.

But the National Association of Investment Clubs has recent studies showing that for the year ending April 30, 1972, member clubs' investments appreciated 15.9 percent while the Dow Jones Industrial Average (an average comprised of a select group of stocks whose movement indicates the general trend of the market) rose 1.3 percent. One study also shows that over the life of the member club, female investment clubs did better than male investment clubs (16.3 percent versus 12.9 percent compound annual growth rate). But in the last year alone, women's clubs trailed men's clubs by 1.5 percent. A word of caution: only about 700 of the 12,000 members of the NAIC responded to the questionnaire for this study, and it is possible that these were the better clubs. Also, many of these clubs have been in existence a long time, and have more experience than a new club.

You must have patience, and the club should be organized for more than a year. New clubs should not expect to show immediate profits during the first year or two. In the beginning, you not only have little experience, but also your expenses (brokerage commissions, publications, and so on) are high in relation to the money you are investing. On a percentage basis, you usually pay more commission on a small investment than a large one. If you buy 20 shares of a $5 stock, the commission is usually 6.4 percent of the $100 investment. If you buy 100 shares of a $5 stock, the commission is usually 3.28 percent.

Remember, it is far from likely that you will strike it rich, and there are risks. Hopefully, over a few years your club will generate a good average return of 10 to 12 percent a year on your investment.

there are some mutual funds which consider these issues in evaluating the companies in which they invest. However, if your ethical standards limit your investment choice, it may be more difficult, although not impossible, to uncover investments that are likely to perform well.

Once you have decided to invest your money, the first question should be: what do you want out of your investments? Are you interested in seeing the money that you invest grow rapidly so that you can sell at a profit (capital appreciation)? Or is it important that your investment not decline so that you can avoid losses (safety)? Or do you want the steady income of interest or a dividend that is paid to you regularly while your money is invested (income)?

Your investment objectives should depend on such factors as your likely income and financial resources now and in the future, your age, your family situation, and your spending habits. Generally, a widowed housewife with some savings should look for income and safety. A young single woman with a good salary can afford to take a little more risk and seek capital appreciation.

Obviously you would like everything: an investment that triples in price, has no risk of going down, and pays a hefty dividend. The chart on page 52 describing *some* possible investments among stocks and bonds and the goals they best satisfy, shows that no investment optimally satisfies all three objectives; as in most things in life, there are trade-offs. An investment that pays a good dividend usually has little chance of appreciating. An investment with a good chance of appreciating often has little safety.

Since there are few hard and fast rules about investments, it should be noted that the chart is based on broad generalizations that may not always be true, and the details of a particular investment should be looked at more closely before making a choice.

After understanding your investment objectives and the alternatives, you should decide on the method of investing you prefer.

immoral conduct and disturbances of the peace. There is, however, little question that she can drink and swear enough to titillate any of the more restrained women back East. And she is known, underneath the puffed-up facade, as an exceptionally kind and loyal woman.

One way to invest is to put your money in a mutual fund: a company formed to invest in the stocks and bonds of other companies, and which hires professional money managers (usually for a management fee that runs a half percent of the assets) to make the investment decisions. Mutual funds frequently charge a sales fee of between 7 percent and 9 percent of the amount of your trade when you buy or sell shares of the fund. Some types of mutual funds are: aggressive growth funds that invest in smaller growth companies with the hope of great capital appreciation; balanced funds that invest in bonds as well as stock and usually seek both income and appreciation; and income funds that look for high dividend or interest payments. Mutual funds often accomplish diversification which helps reduce the risk of investing in just one or two stocks, but you should analyze the literature describing the structure, performance record, investment objectives, and portfolio of individual mutual funds before choosing one.

Another way to invest is to learn enough about the securities market yourself to make your own investment decisions. Forming an investment club with other women offers a way to both learn and invest as little as $10 a month. An investment club is a group of people who get together to discuss securities, and invest relatively small sums in stocks or bonds that they choose together. These clubs may be particularly appropriate for women since they enable you to share with other women, your thoughts, insights, and fears about investing, and to see that "feminine" skills and interests, contrary to popular belief, may be an asset in making investment decisions. Although this sounds a bit like a consciousness-raising group (indeed, your group could be the basis for an investment club), it is quite valid for investing since so much of investing is psychological. Understanding why you and other people decide to buy particular stocks is a key variable in predicting the price movement of those stocks.

To help you or your club follow current financial news and opinions on market trends and economic conditions, you should read the *Wall Street Journal* and the financial section of your local newspaper every day, plus, if you have time, the periodicals, *Barron's* and *Forbes.* The newspapers publish daily stock listings like this which are essential for following stock movements:

New York Stock Exchange Transactions

—1972-73— High	Low	Stocks Div.	Sales 100s	P-E Ratio	High	Low	Close	Net Chg.
45	33⅝	RalstonP .70	257	23	43⅞	43½	43½	− ¼
23¾	16¾	Rmada In .12	372	37	22	21⅝	21¾	− ¼
30⅞	19½	Ranco Inc .92	47	11	21⅜	21	21¼	
21¼	15¾	RapAm .12a	266	5	18¾	18¼	18⅝	+ ⅛
101	71¼	RapAm pf 3	6		99⅜	99¼	99⅜	+ ¼
33	25½	RaybstosM 1	27	11	32	30¾	31¾	+1⅛
13	7¾	RaymInt .20a	16	19	11¼	10⅞	11⅛	+ ¼
47½	27⅛	Raytheon .60	127	13	33⅞	33⅛	33½	+ ⅛
45	32⅛	RCA 1	3669	18	37⅛	35⅛	35⅞	− ⅞
102	80¼	RCA cv pf 4	35		87½	86	86	−2¾
33¼	19	Rdg Bate .25	250	26	28¾	27⅛	27¼	− ¼

The list may look ominous at first, but it is quite easy once you focus in. The first stock is Ralston Purina (you get accustomed to the name abbreviations). Reading from left to right, the high for 1972 and 1973 was $45, the low 33⅝ or $33.62 (each point is $1). The figures immediately following the stock's abbreviated name tell you that it pays a $.70 annual dividend, based on the last dividend paid. The next two columns record that the stock traded 25,700 shares on the previous day (the morning papers report the previous day's trading) and that its price-to-earnings ratio is 23 (a description of P/E ratio follows). On that day, the stock traded at a high of 43⅞ ($43.87), a low of 43½ ($43.50), and it closed at 43½—down ¼ (25¢).

The factual conclusions that can be made from this are that the stock is trading near its yearly high, its current yield is approximately 1.6

$$\frac{\text{(dividend—\$.70)}}{\text{(current price—\$43.50)}}$$

percent and it closed at its low for the day.

If you or your club decide to invest in stocks, you will of course want to understand the key factors responsible for stock performance. Some of these are: the potential growth of the company, the industries in vogue with investors now and possibly in the future, and the trends in the movement of the overall market. Since stocks perform primarily on the basis of expectation, stock evaluations are difficult because of the need to predict the future. But there are tools to help you in your forecasts.

To evaluate the potential growth of a company, you should first get information on the past record of earnings per share

$$\frac{\text{(yearly earnings)}}{\text{(average number of shares)}}$$

and sales (revenues). This information can be found in the company's income statement in its annual report, which can be obtained directly from the company or your broker.

The income statement for two consecutive years might look like the chart above, with the net sales and earnings highlighted.

If the company has demonstrated good growth in sales and earnings over a few years, it may be likely to continue this growth, but you should also consider other factors: if there appears to be competent management and a large enough management team to generate good sustained growth; if there is good product desirability and acceptance (here your own market research may be valuable); and how the company compares to its competition in size, product, marketing, and management (your broker should be able to get you the names of the competitors).

The performance of the company is also related to the growth of the industry it is in. The industries thought to have the most potential

1885. Annie Oakley joins Buffalo Bill's Wild West road show and is featured as the chief attraction. Her repertory includes a famous crowd pleaser in which she stands on a galloping pony and shoots out lit candles arranged in a spinning wheel.

CONSOLIDATED STATEMENT OF INCOME AND RETAINED EARNINGS FOR THE FIFTY-TWO WEEKS ENDED DECEMBER 25, 1974 AND DECEMBER 26, 1975

	1974	1975
NET SALES	$11,518,958	$8,341,105
COST AND EXPENSES		
Cost of Goods Sold	7,504,897	5,671,540
Selling, Shipping and Administrative Expenses	2,164,869	1,656,617
Interest Expense	232,738	186,023
State and Local Income Taxes	84,483	38,860
	9,986,987	7,553,040
Income Before Federal Income Taxes	1,531,971	788,065
Provision for Federal Income Taxes + Note A	720,307	384,319
Net Income	811,664	403,746
Retained Earnings, Beginning of Period	1,498,747	1,095,001
Retained Earnings, End of Period	2,310,411	1,498,747
EARNINGS PER SHARE:	$ 1.89	$ .94
Shares Outstanding	430,000	430,000

become the stock market favorites, but they can come in and out of vogue quite rapidly. Although it is hard to anticipate a new favorite, or the jilting of an old one, you should have some idea of the present feeling toward an industry before you invest in it. In the span of four years, for instance, computer time-sharing companies were in vogue, then out of vogue, and now they seem to be getting popular again. A few years ago companies owning nursing homes were popular, but now most investors will not touch them.

Stock market fluctuations, perhaps even more than industry trends, are extremely difficult for anyone, especially the small investor, to predict. However, since the stock market often moves in anticipation of future economic conditions, it is useful to read what the analysts are saying about the economy as well as the market. The Government's Composite Index of Leading Economic Indicators, published at the end of every month in many newspapers (in the *Wall Street Journal,* for example, available in most libraries), can be helpful in summarizing economic conditions. This index measures such things as corporate profits and durable goods orders, and is thought to presage broad business movements which often coincide with the movement of the market.

There is one key ratio that must be understood for stock market analysis since it is determined by many of the factors discussed above. This is the price to earnings ratio (P/E ratio), or multiple of earnings. It is derived by dividing the price of the stock by the year's earnings per share. Generally, if the expectations of a company are good, whether because of the past record or an exciting product, and if it is a popular industry, the P/E will be higher than if the opposite is true. A P/E below 10 is on the low side; above 20 is high with some very favored companies selling at as much as 80 times earnings. However, multiples are also dependent on the movement of the overall market. If the stock market is depressed, most multiples decline and a P/E of 12 may be considered high.

The multiple of a stock has meaning only when compared to that of other stocks. If a company with good growth, in a popular industry, only has a multiple of 10, it usually makes more sense to consider buying this stock rather than the stock of a company with a poor record, in an unpopular industry, that is also selling with a multiple of 10.

After you have chosen and bought your stocks, the next thing to learn is when to sell. There are no hard and fast rules but generally you should set guidelines for yourself. If a stock goes down a certain percentage (20 percent may be reasonable), it is usually wise to take your loss and sell, because it is just as likely that a further price decline will follow as that the price will return to its former level. If it reaches the price you hoped for when you made your investment, take your profit and run. Always compare your investment to other possible ones in the marketplace. If you feel you can do better than the investment you have, sell it to buy the more promising security.

Also keep in mind that you have to pay taxes on your profits when you sell your winning stocks, and on commissions when you buy and sell stocks. You should consult an expert about your particular tax situation, but generally if you hold a stock for more than six months and then sell it at a profit, you pay a capital gains tax which, for the first $50,000, is one-half of the tax rate on your ordinary income. Profits made on stock held less than six months are usually taxed at the same rate as your ordinary income. But investment factors should come ahead of tax factors: do not hold on to a stock that you think has reached its peak just because you do not want to pay taxes on the profit.

If you invest, do it seriously and give it time and thought. Your caution and good judgment should not be discarded the minute someone gives you a "hot tip." Investing is not a way to get-rich-quick; be wary of people who say it is.

Investing is not for everyone but that does not mean it is for men and not women. Whether or not we invest or make money at it, it is important that the choice is ours and a knowledgeable one, and that the responsibility for success or failure is also ours. The feeling of being in control of our financial life is necessary—especially for women.

1885. Emily Dickinson, generally recognized as one of the greatest American poets, dies. Avant-garde in her day, almost all the verse of the somewhat eccentric recluse is published posthumously. However, so sure was she of her masterful but unrevealed

Type of Investment	Income	Safety	Appreciation
stocks are shares of ownership in a corporation	*amount of dividends paid*	*likelihood of stock remaining at price paid and not going down*	*chance of price of stock going up*
DEFENSIVE STOCKS stocks of established companies relatively unaffected by business cycles (utilities, food, etc.)	high (presently 5% to 7%) depending on company	considered the safest in the stock category	usually not much appreciation
"BLUE-CHIP" STOCKS stocks of very large, well-established companies that have demonstrated reliability of earnings and dividends	usually moderate and steady (3% to 4%)	good	may be some appreciation over long term
ESTABLISHED GROWTH STOCKS "glamour stocks" which have shown consistent high growth in earnings and are now sizable companies	low (1% to 2%)	good to fair—can be quite volatile	usually continuous and often large appreciation
SPECULATIVE STOCKS stocks thought to have the potential for growth in earnings —usually smaller companies	often nil to low	risky—depends on success of company and swings in market	substantial appreciation if your choice is right

Type of Investment	Income	Safety	Appreciation
bonds are issued by a corporation or governmental unit to borrow money	*amount of interest paid; bonds usually sell on a yield to maturity basis which is the income divided by the investment cost, allowing for the proceeds realized when the bond is redeemed*	*the safety is the ability of the issuer to pay the interest, and the principal (face value) when it comes due (maturity); Standard and Poor's and Moody's rate bonds on safety—the two highest qualities are AAA and AA*	*the money made when bonds are sold or redeemed higher than the purchase price*
CORPORATE BONDS high quality	high (the average yield is presently about 7%)	excellent as to interest and principal	not much—chance for large appreciation only if there are big swings in the level of interest rates
lower quality	very high (about 9%)	good to poor	can be substantial if company issuing bond does well
U.S. GOVERNMENT BONDS	moderate (about 5½%)	considered the safest investment	not much—chance for big appreciation only when leverage with borrowed funds (strictly for professionals)
MUNICIPAL BONDS high quality	moderate—slightly less than U.S. Government bonds (about 5%) but the interest is exempt from federal income tax	excellent as to interest and principal	not much—chance for large appreciation only if there are big swings in the level of interest rates
lower quality	high (about 6%), also exempt from federal income tax	good to poor	can be substantial if finances of issuer improve

work that she wrote, "I have a horror of death; the dead are so soon forgotten. But when I die, they'll have to remember me." Our remembrance of her is due, mostly, to a massive packet of her poems found in a bureau next to her deathbed.

The Language of Investing

The New York Stock Exchange

Introduction

The language spoken in America's investment world may sound like a strange tongue to the newcomer. It is often vivid, colorful, flavored with the idioms of many eras. Some expressions have filtered down from the day when brokers traded securities under a buttonwood tree in the open air. Others are so new that they have seldom been indexed before.

Any glossary of this special language involves certain problems. Some words and phrases cannot be defined completely without going into related background material—others have nuances of meaning which even the experts may dispute.

We have tried to define terms simply and easily, trimming subtle shades of meaning in the interest of brevity and readability.

New investors, and many seasoned ones, are often puzzled by words and phrases relating to investment—we hope they find this booklet helpful. Investment, after all, is not the province of a few people but the right of men and women everywhere.

Additional information relating to any particular expressions may be obtained without obligation from a member firm of the New York Stock Exchange, or from the Exchange itself.

Accrued Interest

Interest accrued on a bond since the last interest payment was made. The buyer of the bond pays the market price plus accrued interest. Exceptions include bonds that are in default and income bonds.

Amortization

Accounting for expenses or charges as applicable rather than as paid. Includes such practices as depreciation, depletion, write-off of intangibles, prepaid expenses and deferred charges.

Annual Report

The formal financial statement issued yearly by a corporation. The annual report shows assets, liabilities, earnings—how the company stood at the close of the business year, how it fared profit-wise during the year and other information of interest to shareowners.

Arbitrage

A technique employed to take advantage of differences in price. If, for example, ABC stock can be bought in New York for $10 a share and sold in London at $10.50, an arbitrageur may simultaneously purchase ABC stock here and sell the same amount in London, making a profit of 50 cents a share, less expenses. Arbitrage may also involve the purchase of rights to subscribe to a security, or the purchase of a convertible security—and the sale at or about the same time of the security obtainable through exercise of the rights or of the security obtainable through conversion. (See: *Convertible, Rights*)

Assets

Everything a corporation owns or due to it: Cash, investments, money due it, materials and inventories, which are called current assets; buildings and machinery, which are known as fixed assets; and patents and goodwill, called intangible assets. (See: *Liabilities*)

Averages

Various ways of measuring the trend of securities prices, one of the most popular of which is the Dow-Jones average of 30 industrial stocks listed on the New York Stock Exchange.

Formulas—some very elaborate—have been devised to compensate for stock splits and stock dividends and thus give continuity to the average.

In the case of the Dow-Jones industrial average, the prices of the 30 stocks are totaled and then divided by a divisor which is intended to compensate for past stock splits and stock dividends and which is changed from time to time. As a result point changes in the average have only the vaguest relationship to dollar price changes in stocks included in the average. Currently, the divisor is 1.598, so that a one-point change in the industrial

average is actually the equivalent of 5.3 cents. (See: *NYSE Common Stock Index, Point, Split*)

Averaging

(See: *Dollar Cost Averaging*)

Balance Sheet

A condensed financial statement showing the nature and amount of a company's assets, liabilities and capital on a given date. In dollar amounts the balance sheet shows what the company owned, what it owed, and the ownership interest in the company of its stockholders. (See: *Assets, Earnings Report*)

Bear Market

A declining market. (See: *Bull Market*)

Bearer Bond

A bond which does not have the owner's name registered on the books of the issuing company and which is payable to the holder. (See: *Registered Bond*)

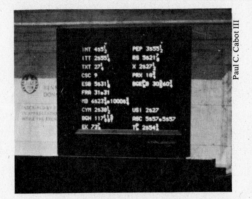

Paul C. Cabot III

Bid and Asked

Often referred to as a quotation or quote. The bid is the highest price anyone has declared that he wants to pay for a security at a given time, the asked is the lowest price anyone will take at the same time. (See: *Quotation*)

Big Board

A popular term for the New York Stock Exchange.

Block

A large holding or transaction of stock—popularly considered to be 10,000 shares or more.

Blue Chip

A company known nationally for the quality and wide acceptance of its products or services, and for its ability to make money and pay dividends.

Bond

Basically an IOU or promissory note of a corporation, usually issued in multiples of $1,000 or $5,000, although $100 and $500 denominations are not unknown. A bond is evidence of a debt on which the issuing company usually promises to pay the bondholders a specified amount of interest for a specified length of time, and to repay the loan on the expiration date. In every case a bond represents debt—its holder is a creditor of the corporation and not a part owner as is the shareholder. In most cases, bonds are secured by a mortgage. (See: *Convertible, Debenture, Income Bond*)

Book Value

An accounting term. Book value of a stock is determined from a company's records, by adding all assets (generally excluding such intangibles as good will), then deducting all debts and other liabilities, plus the liquidation price of any preferred issues. The sum arrived at is divided by the number of common shares outstanding and the result is book value per common share. Book value of the assets of a company or a security may have little or no significant relationship to market value.

Broker

An agent, who handles the public's orders to buy and sell securities, commodities or other property. For this service a commission is charged. (See: *Commission Broker, Dealer*)

Bull Market

An advancing market. (See: *Bear Market*)

Call

(See: *Option*)

Callable

A bond issue, all or part of which may be redeemed by the issuing corporation under definite conditions before maturity. The term also applies to preferred shares which may be redeemed by the issuing corporation.

Capital Gain or Capital Loss

Profit or loss from the sale of a capital asset. A capital gain, under current Federal income tax laws, may be either short-term (6 months or less) or long-term (more than 6 months). A short-term capital gain is taxed at the reporting individual's full income tax rate. A long-term capital gain is subject to a lower tax. The capital gains provisions of the tax law are complicated. You should consult your tax advisor for specific information.

Capitalization

Total amount of the various securities issued by a corporation. Capitalization may include bonds, debentures, preferred and common stock and surplus. Bonds and debentures are usually carried on the books of the issuing company in terms of their par or face value. Preferred and common shares may be carried in terms of par or stated value. Stated value may be an arbitrary figure decided upon by the directors or may represent the amount received by the company from the sale of the securities at the time of issuance. (See: *Par*)

Cash Flow

Reported net income of a corporation *plus* amounts charged off for depreciation, depletion, amortization, extraordinary charges to reserves, which are bookkeeping deductions and not paid out in actual dollars and cents. (See: *Amortization, Depletion, Depreciation*)

Cash Sale

A transaction on the floor of the Stock Exchange which calls for delivery of the securities the same day. In "regular way" trades, the seller is to deliver on the fifth business day.

Certificate

The actual piece of paper which is evidence of ownership of stock in a corporation. Watermarked paper is finely engraved with delicate etchings to discourage forgery. Loss of a certificate may at the least cause a great deal of inconvenience—at the worst, financial loss.

Collateral

Securities or other property pledged by a borrower to secure repayment of a loan.

Commission

The broker's basic fee for purchasing or selling securities or property as an agent.

Common Stock

Securities which represent an ownership interest in a corporation. If the company has also issued preferred stock, both common and preferred have ownership rights. The preferred normally is limited to a fixed dividend but has prior claim on dividends and, in the event of liquidation, assets. Claims of both common and preferred stockholders are junior to claims of bondholders or other creditors of the company. Common stockholders assume the greater risk, but generally exercise the greater control and may gain the greater reward in the form of dividends and capital appreciation. The terms common stock and capital stock are often used interchangeably when the company has no preferred stock.

1887. The Empress Taitu of Ethopia, the "Black Cleopatra," persuades her 321st husband, Emperor Menelik, to begin the settlement of Addis Ababa. She began life as a water carrier for a regiment of Negus spearmen, then periodically wed a man of increasingly higher rank until she could wed no higher.

Conglomerate

A corporation that has diversified its operations usually by acquiring enterprises in widely varied industries.

Convertible

A bond, debenture or preferred share which may be exchanged by the owner for common stock or another security, usually of the same company, in accordance with the terms of the issue.

Coupon Bond

Bond with interest coupons attached. The coupons are clipped as they come due and are presented by the holder for payment of interest. (See: *Bearer Bond, Registered Bond*)

Covering

Buying a security previously sold short. (See: *Short Sale, Short Covering*)

Cumulative Preferred

A stock having a provision that if one or more dividends are omitted, the omitted dividends must be paid before dividends may be paid on the company's common stock.

Current Assets

Those assets of a company which are reasonably expected to be realized in cash, or sold, or consumed during the normal operating cycle of the business. These include cash, U.S. Government bonds, receivables and money due usually within one year, and inventories.

Current Liabilities

Money owed and payable by a company, usually within one year.

Day Order

An order to buy or sell which, if not executed expires at the end of the trading day on which it was entered.

Dealer

An individual or firm in the securities business acting as a principal rather than as an agent. Typically, a dealer buys for his own account and sells to a customer from his own inventory. The dealer's profit or loss is the difference between the price he pays and the price he receives for the same security. The dealer's confirmation must disclose to his customer that he has acted as principal. The same individual or firm may function, at different times, either as broker or dealer. (See: *NASD, Specialist*)

Debenture

A promissory note backed by the general credit of a company and usually not secured by a mortgage or lien on any specific property. (See: *Bond*)

Debit Balance

Portion of purchase price of stock, bonds or commodities covered by credit extended by a broker to margin customers.

Depletion

Natural resources, such as metals, oils and gas, timber, which conceivably can be reduced to zero over the years, present a special problem in capital management. Depletion is an accounting practice consisting of charges against earnings based upon the amount of the asset taken out of the total reserves in the period for which accounting is made. A bookkeeping entry, it does not represent any cash outlay nor are any funds earmarked for the purpose.

Depreciation

Normally, charges against earnings to write off the cost, less salvage value, of an asset over its estimated useful life. It is a bookkeeping entry and does not represent any cash outlay or are any funds earmarked for the purpose.

Director

Person elected by shareholders to establish company policies. The directors appoint the president, vice presidents, and all other operating officers. Directors decide, among other matters, if and when dividends shall be paid. (See: *Management, Proxy*)

Discount

The amount by which a preferred stock or bond may sell below its par value. Also used as a verb to mean "takes into account" as the price of the stock has discounted the expected dividend cut. (See: *Premium*)

Discretionary Account

An account in which the customer gives the broker or someone else discretion, which may be complete or within specific limits, as to the purchase and sales of securities or commodities including selection, timing, amount, and price to be paid or received.

Diversification

Spreading investments among different companies in different fields. Another type of diversification is also offered by the securities of many individual companies because of the wide range of their activities. (See: *Investment*)

Dividend

The payment designated by the Board of Directors to be distributed pro rata among the shares outstanding. On preferred shares, it is generally a fixed amount. On common shares, the dividend varies with the fortunes of the company and the amount of cash on hand, and may be omitted if business is poor or the directors determine to withhold earnings to invest in plant and equipment. Sometimes a company will pay a dividend out of past earnings even if it is not currently operating at a profit.

Dollar Cost Averaging

A system of buying securities at regular intervals with a fixed dollar amount. Under this system the investor buys by the dollars' worth rather than by the number of shares. If each investment is of the same number of dollars, payments buy more when the price is low and fewer when it rises. Thus temporary downswings in price benefit the investor if he continues periodic purchases in both good times and bad and the price at which the shares are sold is more than their average cost. (See: *Formula Investing*)

Double Taxation

Short for Double Taxation of Dividends. The federal government taxes corporate profits once as corporate income; any part of the remaining profits distributed as dividends to stockholders may be taxed again as income to the recipient stockholder.

Dow Theory

A theory of market analysis based upon the performance of the Dow-Jones industrial and transportation stock price averages. The Theory says that the market is in a basic upward trend if one of these averages advances above a previous important high, accompanied or followed by a similar advance in the other. When the averages both dip below previous important lows, this is regarded as confirmation of a basic downward trend. The Theory does not attempt to predict how long either trend will continue, although it is widely misinterpreted as a method of forecasting future action.

Down Tick

(See: *Up Tick*)

Earnings Report

A statement—also called an income statement—issued by a company showing its earnings or losses over a given period. The earnings report lists the income earned, expenses and the net result. (See: *Balance Sheet*)

Equity

The ownership interest of common and preferred stockholders in a company. Also refers to excess of value of securities over the debit balance in a margin account.

Exchange Distribution

A method of disposing of large blocks of stock on the floor of the Exchange. Under certain circumstances, a member-broker can facilitate the sale of a block of stock by soliciting and getting other member-brokers to solicit orders to buy. Individual buy orders are lumped together and crossed with the sell order in the regular auction market. A special commission is usually paid by the seller; ordinarily the buyer pays no commission.

Ex-Dividend

A synonym for "without dividend." The buyer of a stock selling ex-dividend does not receive the recently declared dividend. Every dividend is payable on a fixed date to all shareholders recorded on the books of the company as of a previous date of record. For example, a dividend may be declared as payable to holders of record on the books of the company on a given Friday. Since five business days are allowed for delivery of stock in a "regular way" transaction on the New York Stock Exchange, the Exchange would declare the stock "ex-dividend" as of the opening of the market on the preceding Monday. That means anyone who bought it on and after Monday would not be entitled to that dividend. When stocks go ex-dividend, the stock tables include the symbol "x" following the name. (See: *Cash Sale, Net Change, Transfer*)

Ex-Rights

Without the rights. Corporations raising additional money may do so by offering their stockholders the right to subscribe to new or additional stock, usually at a discount from the prevailing market price. The buyer of a stock selling ex-rights is not entitled to the rights. (See: *Ex-Dividend, Rights*)

Face Value

The value of a bond that appears on the face of the bond, unless the value is otherwise specified by the issuing company. Face value is ordinarily the amount the issuing company promises to pay at maturity. Face value is not an indication of market value. Sometimes referred to as par value. (See: *Par*)

Fiscal Year

A corporation's accounting year. Due to the nature of their particular business, some companies do not use the calendar year for their bookkeeping. A typical example is the department store which finds December 31 too early a date to close its books after the Christmas rush. For that reason many stores wind up their accounting year January 31. Their fiscal year, therefore, runs from February 1 of one year through January 31 of the next. The fiscal year of other companies may run from July 1 through the following June 30. Most companies, though, operate on a calendar year basis.

Floor

The huge trading area—about two-thirds the size of a football field—where stocks and bonds are bought and sold on the New York Stock Exchange.

Floor Broker

A member of the Stock Exchange who executes orders on the floor of the Exchange to buy or sell any listed securities. (See: *Two-Dollar Broker*)

Formula Investing

An investment technique. One formula calls for the shifting of funds from common shares to preferred shares or bonds as the market, on average, rises above a certain predetermined point—and the return of funds to common share investments as the market average declines. (See: *Dollar Cost Averaging*)

Free and Open Market

A market in which supply and demand are freely expressed in terms of price. Contrasts with a controlled market in which supply, demand and price may all be regulated.

Good Delivery

Certain basic qualifications must be met before a security sold on the Exchange may be delivered. The security must be in proper form to comply with the contract of sale and to transfer title to the purchaser.

Good 'Til Cancelled Order (GTC) or Open Order

An order to buy or sell which remains in effect until it is either executed or cancelled.

Government Bonds

Obligations of the U. S. Government, regarded as the highest grade issues in existence.

Growth Stock

Stock of a company with a record of growth in earnings at a relatively rapid rate.

Guaranteed Bond

A bond which has interest or principal, or both, guaranteed by a company other than the issuer. Usually found in the railroad industry when large roads, leasing sections of trackage owned by small railroads, may guarantee the bonds of the smaller road.

Guaranteed Stock

Usually preferred stock on which dividends are guaranteed by another company; under much the same circumstances as a bond is guaranteed.

1887. Abigail Foster, abolitionist and feminist, dies. Of her, Lucy Stone writes: "Mrs. Foster, for more than thirty years, stood in the thick of the fight for slaves, and, at the same time, she hewed out the path over which women are now walking toward their equal political rights."

Hedge

(See: *Arbitrage, Puts & Calls, Short Sale*)

Holding Company

A corporation which owns the securities of another, in most cases with voting control.

Hypothecation

The pledging of securities as collateral—for example, to secure the debit balance in a margin account.

Inactive Stock

An issue traded on an exchange or in the over-the-counter market in which there is a relatively low volume of transactions. Volume may be no more than a few hundred shares a week or even less. On the New York Stock Exchange many inactive stocks are traded in 10-share units rather than the customary 100. (See: *Round Lot*)

In-and-Out

Purchase and sale of the same security within a short period—a day, week, even a month. An in-and-out trader is generally more interested in day-to-day price fluctuations than dividends or long-term growth.

Income Bond

Generally income bonds promise to repay principal but to pay interest only when earned. In some cases unpaid interest on an income bond may accumulate as a claim against the corporation when the bond becomes due. An income bond may also be issued in lieu of preferred stock.

Index

A statistical yardstick expressed in terms of percentages of a base year or years. For instance, the Federal Reserve Board's index of industrial production is based on 1967 as 100. In February, 1975 the index stood at 110.3, which meant that industrial production that month was about 10 per cent higher than in the base period. An Index is not an average. (See: *Averages, NYSE Common Stock Index*)

Institutional Investor

An organization whose primary purpose is to invest its own assets or those held in trust by it for others. Includes pension funds, investment companies, insurance companies, universities and banks.

Interest

Payments a borrower pays a lender for the use of his money. A corporation pays interest on its bonds to its bondholders. (See: *Bond, Dividend*)

Investment

The use of money for the purpose of making more money, to gain income or increase capital, or both. Safety of principal is an important consideration. (See: *Speculation*)

Investment Banker

Also known as an underwriter. He is the middleman between the corporation issuing new securities and the public. The usual practice is for one or more investment bankers to buy outright from a corporation a new issue of stocks or bonds. The group forms a syndicate to sell the securities to individuals and institutions. Investment bankers also distribute very large blocks of stocks or bonds—perhaps held by an estate. Thereafter the market in the security may be over-the-counter, on a regional stock exchange, the American Exchange or the New York Stock Exchange. (See: *Over-the-Counter, Primary Distribution, Syndicate*)

Investment Company

A company or trust which uses its capital to invest in other companies. There are two principal types; the closed-end and the open-end, or mutual fund. Shares in closed-end investment companies, some of which are listed on the New York Stock Exchange, are readily transferable in the open market and are bought and sold like other shares. Capitalization of these companies remains the same unless action is taken to change, which is seldom. Open-end funds sell their own new shares to investors, stand ready to buy back their old shares, and are not listed. Open-end funds are so called because their capitalization is not fixed; they issue more shares as people want them.

Specimen

Investment Counsel

One whose principal business consists of acting as investment adviser and a substantial part of his business consists of rendering investment supervisory services.

Investor

An individual whose principal concerns in the purchase of a security are regular dividend income, safety of the original investment, and, if possible, capital appreciation. (See: *Speculator*)

Issue

Any of a company's securities, or the act of distributing such securities.

Legal List

A list of investments selected by various states in which certain institutions and fiduciaries, such as insurance companies and banks, may invest. Legal lists are often restricted to high quality securities meeting certain specifications. (See: *Prudent Man Rule*)

Leverage

The effect on the per-share earnings of the common stock of a company when large sums must be paid for bond interest or preferred stock dividends, or both, before the common stock is entitled to share in earnings. Leverage may be advantageous for the common when earnings are good but may work against the common stock when earnings decline. Example: Company A has 1,000,000 shares of common stock outstanding, no other securities. Earnings drop from $1,000,000 to $800,000 or from $1 to 80 cents a share, a decline of 20 per cent. Company B also has 1,000,000 shares of common but must pay $500,000 annually in bond interest. If earnings amount to $1,000,000, there is $500,000 available for the common or 50 cents a share. But earnings drop to $800,000 so there is only $300,000 available for the common, or 30 cents a share—a drop of 40 per cent. Or suppose earnings of the company with only common stock increased from $1,000,000 to $1,500,000—earnings per share would go from $1 to $1.50, or an increase of 50 per cent. But if earnings of the company which had to pay $500,000 in bond interest increased that much—earnings per common share would jump from 50 cents to $1 a share, or 100 per cent. When a company has common stock only, no leverage exists because all earnings are available for the common, although relatively large fixed charges payable for lease of substantial plant assets may have an effect similar to that of a bond issue.

Liabilities

All the claims against a corporation. Liabilities include accounts and wages and salaries payable, dividends declared payable, accrued taxes payable, fixed or long-term liabilities such as mortgage bonds, debentures and bank loans. (See: *Assets, Balance Sheet*)

Lien

A claim against property which has been pledged or mortgaged to secure the performance of an obligation. A bond is usually secured by a lien against specified property of a company. (See: *Bond*)

Limit, Limited Order or Limited Price Order

An order to buy or sell a stated amount of a security at a specified price, or at a better price, if obtainable after the order is represented in the Trading Crowd.

Liquidation

The process of converting securities or other property into cash. The dissolution of a company, with cash remaining after sale of its assets and payment of all indebtedness being distributed to the shareholders.

Liquidity

The ability of the market in a particular security to absorb a reasonable amount of buying or selling at reasonable price changes. Liquidity is one of the most important characteristics of a good market.

Listed Stock

The stock of a company which is traded on a securities exchange, and for which a listing application and a registration statement, giving detailed information about the company and its operations, have been filed with the Securities & Exchange Commission, unless otherwise exempted, and the exchange itself. The various stock exchanges have different standards for listing. Some of the guides used by the New York Stock Exchange for an original listing are national interest in the company, a minimum of 1-million shares publicly held among not less than 2,000 round-lot stockholders. The publicly held common shares should have a minimum aggregate market value of $16 million. The company should have net income in the latest year of over $2.5-million before federal income tax and $2-million in each of the preceding two years.

Load

The portion of the offering price of shares of open-end investment companies which covers sales commissions and all other costs of distribution. The load is usually incurred only on purchase, there being, in most cases, no charge when the shares are sold (redeemed).

Locked In

An investor is said to be locked in when he has a profit on a security he owns but does not sell because his profit would immediately become subject to the capital gains tax. (See: *Capital Gain*)

Long

Signifies ownership of securities: "I am long 100 U. S.

Steel" means the speaker owns 100 shares. (See: *Short Position, Short Sale*)

Management

The Board of Directors, elected by the stockholders, and the officers of the corporation, appointed by the Board of Directors.

Manipulation

An illegal operation. Buying or selling a security for the purpose of creating false or misleading appearance of active trading or for the purpose of raising or depressing the price to induce purchase or sale by others.

Margin

The amount paid by the customer when he uses his broker's credit to buy a security. Under Federal Reserve regulations, the initial margin required in the past 20 years has ranged from 50 per cent of the purchase price all the way to 100 per cent. (See: *Equity, Margin Call*)

Margin Call

A demand upon a customer to put up money or securities with the broker. The call is made when a purchase is made; also if a customer's equity in a margin account declines below a minimum standard set by the Exchange or by the firm. (See: *Margin*)

Market Order

An order to buy or sell a stated amount of a security at the most advantageous price obtainable after the order is represented in the Trading Crowd. (See: *Good 'til Cancelled Order, Limit Order, Stop Order*)

Market Price

In the case of a security, market price is usually considered the last reported price at which the stock or bond sold.

Maturity

The date on which a loan or a bond or debenture comes due and is to be paid off.

Member Corporation

A securities brokerage firm, organized as a corporation, with at least one member of the New York Stock Exchange, Inc. who is a director and a holder of voting stock in the corporation. (See: *Member Firm*)

Member Firm

A securities brokerage firm organized as a partnership and having at least one general partner who is a member of the New York Stock Exchange, Inc. (See: *Member Corporation*)

Member Organization

This term includes New York Stock Exchange Member Firm *and* Member Corporation. The term "participant" when used with reference to a Member Organization includes general and limited partners of a Member Firm and holders of voting and non-voting stock in a Member corporation. (See: *Member Corporation, Member Firm*)

MIP

Monthly Investment Plan. A pay-as-you-go method of buying odd lots of New York Stock Exchange listed shares on a regular payment plan for as little as $40 a month or every three months and up to $1,000 per payment. Under MIP the investor buys stock by the dollars' worth—if the price advances, he gets fewer shares and if it declines, he gets more shares. He may discontinue purchases at any time without penalty. (See: *Dollar Cost Averaging, Odd Lot*)

Mortgage Bond

A bond secured by a mortgage on a property. The value of the property may or may not equal the value of the so-called mortgage bonds issued against it. (See: *Bond, Debenture*)

Municipal Bond

A bond issued by a state or a political subdivision, such as county, city, town or village. The term also designates bonds issued by state agencies and authorities. In general, interest paid on municipal bonds is exempt from federal income taxes and state and local income taxes within the state of issue.

Mutual Fund

(See: *Investment Company*)

NASD

The National Association of Securities Dealers, Inc. An association of brokers and dealers in the over-the-counter securities business. The Association has the power to expel members who have been declared guilty of unethical practices. NASD is dedicated to—among other objectives—"adopt, administer and enforce rules of fair practice and rules to prevent fraudulent and manipulative acts and practices, and in general to promote just and equitable principles of trade for the protection of investors."

NASDAQ

An automated information network which provides brokers and dealers with price quotations on securities traded over the counter. NASDAQ is an acronym for National Association of Securities Dealers Automated Quotations.

Negotiable

Refers to a security, title to which is transferable by delivery. (See: *Good Delivery*)

Net Asset Value

A term usually used in connection with investment companies, meaning net asset value per share. It is common practice for an investment company to compute its assets daily, or even twice daily, by totaling the market value of all securities owned. All liabilities are deducted, and the balance divided by the number of shares outstanding. The resulting figure is the net asset value per share. (See: *Assets, Investment Company*)

Net Change

The change in the price of a security from the closing price on one day and the closing price on the following day on which the stock is traded. The net change is ordinarily the last figure on the stock price list. The mark +1⅛ means up $1.125 a share from the last sale on the previous day the stock traded.

New Issue

A stock or bond sold by a corporation for the first time. Proceeds may be issued to retire outstanding securities of the company, for new plant or equipment or for additional working capital.

Noncumulative

A preferred stock on which unpaid dividends do not accrue. Omitted dividends are, as a rule, gone forever. (See: *Cumulative Preferred*)

NYSE Common Stock Index

A composite index covering price movements of all common stocks listed on the "Big Board." It is based on the close of the market December 31, 1965 as 50.00 and is weighted according to the number of shares listed for each issue. The index is computed continuously and printed on the ticker tape each half hour. Point changes in the index are converted to dollars and cents so as to provide a meaningful measure of changes in the average price of listed stocks. The composite index is supplemented by separate indexes for four industry groups: industrials, transportation, utilities and finances. (See: *Averages*)

Odd Lot

An amount of stock less than the established 100-share unit or 10-share unit of trading: from 1 to 99 shares for the great majority of issues, 1 to 9 for so-called inactive stocks. Odd-lot prices are geared to the auction market. On an odd-lot market order, the odd-lot dealer's price is based on the first round-lot transaction which occurs on the floor following receipt at the trading post of the odd-lot order. The differential between the odd-lot price and the "effective" round-lot price is 12½ cents a share. For example: You decide to buy 20 shares of ABC common at the market. Your order is transmitted by your commission broker to the representative of an odd lot dealer at the post where ABC is traded. A few minutes later there is a 100-share transaction in ABC at $50 a share. The odd-lot price at which your order is immediately filled by the odd-lot dealer is $50.125 a share. If you had sold 20 shares of ABC, you would have received $49.875 a share. (See: *Round Lot, Inactive Stock*)

Odd Lot Dealer

A member firm of the Exchange which buys and sells odd lots of stocks—1 to 9 shares in the case of stocks traded in 10-share units and 1 to 99 shares for 100-share units. The odd-lot dealer's customers are commission brokers acting on behalf of their customers.

Offer

The price at which a person is ready to sell. Opposed to bid, the price at which one is ready to buy. (See: *Bid and Asked*)

Option

A right to buy (call) or sell (put) a fixed amount of a given stock at a specified price within a limited period of time. The purchaser hopes that the stock's price will go up (if he bought a call) or down (if he bought a put) by an amount sufficient to provide a profit greater than the cost of the contract and the commission and other fees required to exercise the contract. If the stock price holds steady or moves in the opposite direction, the price paid for the option is lost entirely. There are several other types of options available to the public but these are basically combinations of puts and calls. Individuals may write (sell) as well as purchase options and are thereby obliged to deliver or buy the stock at the specified price.

When a put or call contract is purchased in the over the counter option market, the price at which it can be exercised is usually close to the market value at that time and is fixed for the length of the contract which is stated in days or months and is rarely longer than a year. Six months and ten days is the most common term.

There is also a listed call option market which was established recently by the Chicago Board of Trade. This differs from the over-the-counter market in that trading is limited to 32 popular stocks, expiration of contracts is standardized at 4 dates during the year, exercise prices are set at multiples of 5, and option prices are determined through a continuous competitive auction market system.

Overbought

An opinion as to price levels. May refer to a security which has had a sharp rise or to the market as a whole after a period of vigorous buying, which it may be argued, has left prices "too high."

Oversold

An opinion—the reverse of overbought. A single security or a market which, it is believed, has declined to an unreasonable level.

Over-The-Counter

A market for securities made up of securities dealers who may or may not be members of a securities exchange. Over-the-counter is mainly a market made over the telephone. Thousands of companies have insufficient shares outstanding, stockholders, or earnings to warrant application for listing on the N.Y. Stock Exchange, Inc. Securities of these companies are traded in the over-the-counter market between dealers who act either as principals or as brokers for customers. The over-the-counter market is the principal market for U.S. Government and municipal bonds. (See: *NASD, NASDAQ*)

Paper Profit

An unrealized profit on a security still held. Paper profits become realized profits only when the security is sold.

Par

In the case of a common share, par means a dollar amount assigned to the share by the company's charter. Par value may also be used to compute the dollar amount of common shares on the balance sheet. Par value has little significance so far as market value of common stock is concerned. Many companies today issue no-par stock but give a stated per share value on the balance sheet. In the case of preferred shares and bonds, however, par is important. It often signifies the dollar value upon which dividends on preferred stocks, and interest on bonds, are figured. The issuer of a 6 per cent bond promises to pay that percentage of the bond's par value annually. (See: *Capitalization, Transfer Tax*)

Participating Preferred

A preferred stock which is entitled to its stated dividend and, also, to additional dividends on a specified basis upon payment of dividends on the common stock.

Passed Dividend

Omission of a regular or scheduled dividend.

Penny Stocks

Low-priced issues often highly speculative, selling at less than $1 a share. Frequently used as a term of disparagement, although a few penny stocks have developed into investment-caliber issues.

Percentage Order

A market or limited price order to buy (or sell) a stated

---

of political organization, all recommend her to Miss Anthony who, in stepping down, passes over her closest friend and chooses Mrs. Catt as her successor. Between the years 1913 and 1920, Carrie will dedicate herself single-mindedly to the enactment of the Nineteenth Amendment, taking her campaign not only to Congress but also—in an

amount of a specified stock after a fixed number of shares of such stock have traded.

Point

In the case of shares of stock, a point means $1. If ABC shares rise 3 points, each share has risen $3. In the case of bonds a point means $10, since a bond is quoted as a percentage of $1,000. A bond which rises 3 points gains 3 per cent of $1,000, or $30 in value. An advance from 87 to 90 would mean an advance in dollar value from $870 to $900 for each $1,000 bond. In the case of market averages, the word point means merely that and no more. If, for example, the Dow-Jones Industrial average rises from 870.25 to 871.25, it has risen a point. A point in this average, however, is not equivalent to $1. (See: *Averages*)

Portfolio

Holdings of securities by an individual or institution. A portfolio may contain bonds, preferred stocks and common stocks of various types of enterprises.

Preferred Stock

A class of stock with a claim on the company's earnings before payment may be made on the common stock and usually entitled to priority over common stock if company liquidates. Usually entitled to dividends at a specified rate—when declared by the Board of Directors and before payment of a dividend on the common stock—depending upon the terms of the issue. (See: *Cumulative Preferred, Participating Preferred*)

Premium

The amount by which a preferred stock or bond may sell above its par value. In the case of a new issue of bonds or stocks, premium is the amount the market price rises over the original selling price. Also refers to a charge sometimes made when a stock is borrowed to make delivery on a short sale. May refer, also, to redemption price of a bond or preferred stock if it is higher than face value. (See: *Discount, Short Sale*)

Price-Earnings Ratio

The price of a share of stock divided by earnings per share for a twelve-month period. For example, a stock selling for $50 a share and earning $5 a share is said to be selling at a price-earnings ratio of 10 to 1.

Primary Distribution

Also called primary offering. The original sale of a company's securities. (See: *Investment Banker, Secondary Distribution*)

Principal

The person for whom a broker executes an order, or a dealer buying or selling for his own account. The term "principal" may also refer to a person's capital or to the face amount of a bond.

Profit-Taking

Selling stock which has appreciated in value since purchase, in order to realize the profit which has been made possible. The term is often used to explain a downturn in the market following a period of rising prices. (See: *Paper Profit*)

Proxy

Written authorization given by a shareholder to someone else to represent him and vote his shares at a shareholders' meeting.

Proxy Statement

Information required by SEC to be given stockholders as a prerequisite to solicitation of proxies for a security subject to the requirements of Securities Exchange Act.

Prudent Man Rule

An investment standard. In some states, the law requires that a fiduciary, such as a trustee, may invest the fund's money only in a list of securities designated by the state—the so-called legal list. In other states, the trustee may invest in a security if it is one which a prudent man of discretion and intelligence, who is seeking a reasonable income and preservation of capital, would buy.

Puts and Calls

(See: *Option*)

Quotation

Often shortened to "quote." The highest bid to buy and the lowest offer to sell a security in a given market at a given time. If you ask your broker for a "quote" on a stock, he may come back with something like "45¼ to 45½." This means that $45.25 is the highest price any buyer wanted to pay at the time the quote was given on the floor of the Exchange and that $45.50 was the lowest price which any seller would take at the same time. (See: *Bid and Asked*)

Rally

A brisk rise following a decline in the general price level of the market, or in an individual stock.

Record Date

The date on which you must be registered as a shareholder on the stock book of a company in order to receive a declared dividend or, among other things, to vote on company affairs. (See: *Ex-Dividend, Transfer*)

Redemption Price

The price at which a bond may be redeemed before maturity, at the option of the issuing company. Redemption value also applies to the price the company must pay to call in certain types of preferred stock. (See: *Callable*)

REIT

Real Estate Investment Trust, an organization similar to an investment company in some respects but concentrating its holdings in real estate investments. The yield is generally liberal since REIT's are required to distribute as much as 90% of their income. (See: *Investment Company*)

Refinancing

Same as refunding. New securities are sold by a company and the money is used to retire existing securities. Object may be to save interest costs, extend the maturity of the loan, or both.

Registered Bond

A bond which is registered on the books of the issuing company in the name of the owner. It can be transferred only when endorsed by the registered owner. (See: *Bearer Bond, Coupon Bond*)

Registered Representative

Present name for the older term "customers' man." In a New York Stock Exchange Member Organization, a Registered Representative is a full time employee who has met the requirements of the Exchange as to background and knowledge of the securities business. Also known as an Account Executive or Customer's Broker.

Registered Trader

A member of the Exchange who trades in stocks on the Floor for an account in which he has an interest.

Registrar

Usually a trust company or bank charged with the responsibility of preventing the issuance of more stock than authorized by a company. (See: *Transfer*)

Registration

Before a public offering may be made of new securities by a company, or of outstanding securities by controlling stockholders—through the mails or in interstate commerce—the securities must be registered under the Securities Act of 1933. Registration statement is filed with the SEC by the issuer. It must disclose pertinent information relating to the company's operations, securities, management and purpose of the public offering. Securities of railroads under jurisdiction of the Interstate Commerce Commission, and certain other types of securities, are exempted. On security offerings involving less than $300,000, less information is required.

Before a security may be admitted to dealings on a national securities exchange, it must be registered under the Securities Exchange Act of 1934. The application for registration must be filed with the exchange and the SEC by the company issuing the securities. It must disclose pertinent information relating to the company's operations, securities and management.

Regulation T

The federal regulation governing the amount of credit which may be advanced by brokers and dealers to customers for the purchase of securities. (See: *Margin*)

Regulation U

The federal regulation governing the amount of credit which may be advanced by a bank to its customers for the purchase of listed stocks. (See: *Margin*)

Rights

When a company wants to raise more funds by issuing additional securities, it may give its stockholders the opportunity, ahead of others, to buy the new securities in proportion to the number of shares each owns. The piece of paper evidencing this privilege is called a right. Because the additional stock is usually offered to stockholders below the current market price, rights ordinarily have a market value of their own and are actively traded. In most cases they must be exercised within a relatively short period. Failure to exercise or sell rights may result in actual loss to the holder. (See: *Warrant*)

Round Lot

A unit of trading or a multiple thereof. On the NYSE the unit of trading is generally 100 shares in stocks and $1,000 par value in the case of bonds. In some inactive stocks, the unit of trading is 10 shares.

Seat

A traditional figure-of-speech for a membership on an exchange. Price and admission requirements vary.

SEC

The Securities and Exchange Commission, established by Congress to help protect investors. The SEC administers the Securities Act of 1933, the Securities Exchange Act of 1934, the Trust Indenture Act, the Investment Company Act, the Investment Advisers Act, and the Public Utility Holding Company Act.

Secondary Distribution

Also known as a secondary offering. The redistribution of a block of stock some time after it has been sold by the issuing company. The sale is handled off the NYSE by a securities firm or group of firms and the shares are usually offered at a fixed price which is related to the current market price of the stock. Usually the block is a large one, such as might be involved in the settlement of an estate. The security may be listed or unlisted. (See: *Exchange Distribution, Investment Banker, Primary Distribution, Special Offering, Syndicate*)

Seller's Option

A special transaction on NYSE which gives the seller the right to deliver the stock or bond at any time within a specified period, ranging from not less than six business days to not more than 60 days.

Serial Bond

An issue which matures in relatively small amounts at periodic stated intervals.

Short Covering

Buying stock to return stock previously borrowed to make delivery on a short sale.

Short Position

Stocks sold short and not covered as of a particular date. On the NYSE, a tabulation is issued once a month listing all issues on the Exchange in which there was a short position of 5,000 or more shares and issues in which the short position had changed by 2,000 or more shares in the preceding month. Short position also means the total amount of stock an individual has sold short and has not covered, as of a particular date.

Short Sale

A person who believes a stock will decline and sells it though he does not own any has made a short sale. For instance: You instruct your broker to sell short 100 shares of ABC. Your broker borrows the stock so he can deliver the 100 shares to the buyer. The money value of the shares borrowed is deposited by your broker with the lender. Sooner or later you must cover your short sale by buying the same amount of stock you borrowed for return to the lender. If you are able to buy ABC at a lower price than you sold it for, your profit is the difference between the two prices—not counting commissions and taxes. But if you have to pay more for the stock than the price you received, that is the amount of your loss. Stock exchange and federal regulations govern and limit the conditions under which a short sale may be made on a national securities exchange. Sometimes a person will sell short a stock he already owns in order to protect a paper profit. This is known as selling against the box. (See: *Up Tick*)

Sinking Fund

Money regularly set aside by a company to redeem its bonds, debentures or preferred stock from time to time as specified in the indenture or charter.

Special Offering

Opposite of special bid. A notice is printed on the

---

exhausting round of cross-country travel—to the states, whose support is necessary for ratification. Next to Miss Anthony, Carrie Chapman Catt shares responsibility for the amendment's eventual passage. But not stopping with that, she is the first to propose a League of Women Voters.

ticker tape announcing the stock sale at a fixed price usually based on the last transaction in the regular auction market. If there are more buyers than stock, allotments are made. Only the seller pays the commission. (See: *Secondary Distribution*)

Specialist

A member of the New York Stock Exchange, Inc. who has two functions: First, to maintain an orderly market, insofar as reasonably practicable, in the stocks in which he is registered as a specialist. In order to maintain an orderly market, the Exchange expects the specialist to buy or sell for his own account, to a reasonable degree, when there is a temporary disparity between supply and demand. Second, the specialist acts as a broker's broker. When a commission broker on the Exchange floor receives a limit order, say, to buy at $50 a stock then selling at $60—he cannot wait at the post where the stock is traded to see if the price reaches the specified level. So he leaves the order with the specialist, who will try to execute it in the market if and when the stock declines to the specified price. At all times the specialist must put his customers' interests above his own. There are about 350 specialists on the NYSE. (See: *Limited Order*)

Speculation

The employment of funds by a speculator. Safety of principal is a secondary factor. (See: *Investment*)

Speculator

One who is willing to assume a relatively large risk in the hope of gain. His principal concern is to increase his capital rather than his dividend income. The speculator may buy and sell the same day or speculate in an enterprise which he does not expect to be profitable for years.

Split

The division of the outstanding shares of a corporation into a larger number of shares. A 3-for-1 split by a company with 1 million shares outstanding results in 3 million shares outstanding. Each holder of 100 shares before the 3-for-1 split would have 300 shares, although his proportionate equity in the company would remain the same; 100 parts of 1 million are the equivalent of 300 parts of 3 million. Ordinarily splits must be voted by directors and approved by shareholders. (See: *Stock Dividend*)

Stock Ahead

Sometimes an investor who has entered an order to buy or sell a stock at a certain price will see transactions at that price reported on the ticker tape while his own order has not been executed. The reason is that other buy and sell orders at the same price came in to the specialist ahead of his and had priority. (See: *Specialist*)

Stock Dividend

A dividend paid in securities rather than cash. The dividend may be additional shares of the issuing company, or in shares of another company (usually a subsidiary) held by the company. (See: *Ex-Dividend, Split*)

Stockholder of Record

A stockholder whose name is registered on the books of the issuing corporation. (See: *Registrar*)

Stop Limit Order

A stop order which becomes a limit order after the specified stop price has been reached. (See: *Limit Order, Stop Order*)

Stop Order

An order to buy at a price above or sell at a price below the current market. Stop buy orders are generally used to limit loss or protect unrealized profits on a short sale. Stop sell orders are generally used to protect unrealized profits or limit loss on a holding. A stop order becomes a market order when the stock sells at or beyond the specified price and, thus, may not necessarily be executed at that price.

Stopped Stock

A service performed—in most cases by the specialist—for an order given him by a commission broker. Let's say XYZ just sold at $50 a share. Broker A comes along with an order to buy 100 shares at the market. The lowest offer is $50.50. Broker A believes he can do better for his client than $50.50, perhaps might get the stock at $50.25. But he doesn't want to take a chance that he'll miss the market—that is, the next sale might be $50.50 and the following one even higher. So he asks the specialist if he will stop 100 at ½ ($50.50). The specialist agrees. The specialist guarantees Broker A he will get 100 shares at 50½ if the stock sells at that price. In the

meantime, if the specialist or Broker A succeeds in executing the order at $50.25, the stop is called off. (See: *Specialist*)

Street

The New York financial community in the Wall Street area.

Street Name

Securities held in the name of a broker instead of his customer's name are said to be carried in a "street name." This occurs when the securities have been bought on margin or when the customer wishes the security to be held by the broker.

Switching

Selling one security and buying another.

Syndicate

A group of investment bankers who together underwrite and distribute a new issue of securities or a large block of an outstanding issue. (See: *Investment Banker*)

Thin Market

A market in which there are comparatively few bids to buy or offers to sell or both. The phrase may apply to a single security or to the entire stock market. In a thin market, price fluctuations between transactions are usually larger than when the market is liquid. A thin market in a particular stock may reflect lack of interest in that issue or a limited supply of or demand for stock in the market. (See: *Bid and Asked, Liquidity, Offer*)

Ticker

The instrument which prints prices and volume of security transactions in cities and towns throughout the U.S. and Canada within minutes after each trade on the floor.

Tips

Supposedly "inside" information on corporation affairs.

Trader

One who buys and sells for his own account for short-term profit. (See: *Speculator*)

Trading Floor (See: *Floor*)

Trading Post

One of 23 trading locations on the floor of the New York Stock Exchange at which stocks assigned to that location are bought and sold. About 75 stocks are traded at each post.

Transfer

This term may refer to two different operations. For one, the delivery of a stock certificate from the seller's broker to the buyer's broker and legal change of ownership, normally accomplished within a few days. For another, to record the change of ownership on the books of the corporation by the transfer agent. When the purchaser's name is recorded on the books of the company, dividends, notices of meetings, proxies, financial reports and all pertinent literature sent by the issuer to its securities holders are mailed direct to the new owner. (See: *Registrar, Street Name*)

Transfer Agent

A transfer agent keeps a record of the name of each registered shareowner, his or her address, the number of shares owned, and sees that certificates presented to his office for transfer are properly cancelled and new certificates issued in the name of the transferee. (See: *Registrar, Transfer*)

Transfer Tax

A tax imposed by New York State when a security is sold or transferred from one person to another. The tax is paid by the seller. On sales by New York State residents, it ranges from 1.25 cents a share to 5 cents a share sold for $20 or more. Sales by out-of-state residents not employed in New York are taxed at reduced rates. There is no tax on transfers of bonds.

Treasury Stock

Stock issued by a company but later reacquired. It may be held in the company's treasury indefinitely, reissued to the public, or retired. Treasury stock receives no dividends and has no vote while held by the company.

Turnover Rate

The volume of shares traded in a year as a percentage of total shares listed on an Exchange, outstanding for

an individual issue or held in an institutional portfolio. In 1974, the turnover rate on the New York Stock Exchange was 16%.

Two-Dollar Broker

Members on the floor of the NYSE who execute orders for other brokers having more business at that time than they can handle themselves, or for firms who do not have their Exchange member on the floor. The term derives from the time when these independent brokers received $2 per hundred shares for executing such orders. The fee is paid by the broker and today it varies with the price of the stock.

Underwriter (See: *Investment Banker*)

Unlisted

A security not listed on a stock exchange. (See: *Over-the-Counter*)

Unlisted Trading Privileges

On some exchanges a stock may be traded at the request of a member without any prior application by the company itself. The company has no agreement to conform with standards of the exchange. Today admission of a stock to unlisted trading privileges requires SEC approval of an application filed by the exchange. The information in the application must be made available by the exchange to the public. No unlisted stocks are traded on the New York Stock Exchange. (See: *Listed Stock*)

Up Tick

A term used to designate a transaction made at a price higher than the preceding transaction. Also called a "plus-tick." A stock may be sold short only on an up tick, or on a "zero-plus" tick. A "zero-plus" tick is a term used for a transaction at the same price as the preceding trade but higher than the preceding different price.

Conversely, a down tick, or "minus" tick, is a term used to designate a transaction made at a price lower than the preceding trade. A "zero-minus" tick is a transaction made at the same price as the preceding sale but lower than the preceding different price.

A plus sign, or a minus sign, is displayed throughout the day next to the last price of each company's stock traded at each trading post on the floor of the New York Stock Exchange. (See: *Short Sale*)

Volume

The number of shares traded in a security or an entire market during a given period. Volume is usually considered on a daily basis and a daily average is computed for longer periods.

Voting Right

The stockholder's right to vote his stock in the affairs of his company. Most common shares have one vote each. Preferred stock usually has the right to vote when preferred dividends are in default for a specified period. The right to vote may be delegated by the stockholder to another person. (See: *Proxy*)

Warrant

A certificate giving the holder the right to purchase securities at a stipulated price within a specified time limit or perpetually. Sometimes a warrant is offered with securities as an inducement to buy. (See: *Rights*)

When Issued

A short form of "when, as and if issued." The term indicates a conditional transaction in a security authorized for issuance but not as yet actually issued. All "when issued" transactions are on an "if" basis, to be settled if and when the actual security is issued and the Exchange or National Association of Securities Dealers rules the transactions are to be settled.

Working Control

Theoretically ownership of 51 per cent of a company's voting stock is necessary to exercise control. In practice—and this is particularly true in the case of a large corporation—effective control sometimes can be exerted through ownership, individually or by a group acting in concert, of less than 50 per cent.

Yield

Also known as return. The dividends or interest paid by a company expressed as a percentage of the current price. A stock with a current market value of $40 a share which has paid $2 in dividends in the preceding 12 months is said to return 5 per cent ($2.00 ÷ $40.00). The current return on a bond is figured the same way. A 3 per cent $1,000 bond selling at $600 offers a return of 5 per cent ($30 ÷ $600). Figuring the yield of a bond to maturity calls for a bond yield table. (See: *Dividend, Interest*)

1887. Susanna Salter becomes the first woman elected mayor when her name appears—without her knowledge or permission—on the ballot, and she attracts two thirds of the Argonia, Kansas, vote. Later it is discovered that the Women's Christian Temperance Union put her up for the election.

The Benefits of Being Flimflammed

Laura Spencer Porter

Laws have been enacted to prevent the swindler from using the mails with impunity, as he did formerly; but there are ways of evading the law, and he can usually find some way of getting his proposal before the gullible. If the mails are not safe for him, the telephone is, and so are personal representatives. Lists of likely and gullible investors are kept and sold. One fake concern plays into the hands of another. The swindler can in most cases count on his prey keeping quiet about the whole transaction, because it is not pleasant to admit that one has been duped.

But what, if anything, can be done about the whole matter? Most of us who make uncertain investments in "get-rich-quick" schemes are playing a game without knowing the slightest thing about it; whereas our opponent, the fake stock-broker, knows it in and out from *a* to *z*. Now, if I am any judge, the only really sure cure for the flimflam evil is for the gullible to learn the game, and, so to speak, to beat the flimflammer at it.

Just here it is primarily important to know that the real game that the flimflammers play is not, as you might suppose, the game of stocks and bonds at all, fake or otherwise. No, indeed; the game they play, and in which they are such adepts, is the game of *human nature*, the game of human psychology.

It is not statistics, then, that we need to know—not how many people were fooled, but why they were fooled. Suppose we begin with the study of the types of people oftenest swindled. It is undoubtedly true that many persons who buy bogus stocks are of an innocent and ignorant type, unsuspecting lambs who have no knowledge of that race of wolves, the professional swindlers. Yet I feel certain that they are a rather small minority.

To judge by my own experience, rash investments are made not so often because you have never heard of flimflamming as because you would so especially like to have more money your own supply being inadequate.

Adapted from *Delineator*, February 1922.

By far the larger number are those who are so eager to mend their fortunes that they are ready to believe a miracle will be performed.

Let us say, then, that the people of the first type are duped because of their ignorance; the second, because of their desires and ambitions.

Let us take as a third type the people of gentle rather sentimental, friendly disposition, who would rather believe the world to be as they would like to have it than to know it as it really is. It is these, I believe, who offer the stock shark his largest opportunity.

But ignorance, ambition, and sentimentalism, all together do not characterize the victim of fake investments so much as does vanity. In most articles on swindling, it is pointed out that it is by no means the ignorant and constitutionally gullible who are fooled by swindler methods. The best and most frequent names on the list are, we are told, professors, lawyers, doctors, merchants, business men, business women, widows, and even bankers. The seller of fake stock approaches the ignorant and trusting as a benefactor, a kind of older brother; but when he goes to the banker, the professor, the doctor, the woman with some business experience: "A man as shrewd as you are knows a good thing when he sees it." And this, according to those who know, is the really fruitful method.

So, then, fake-stock swindling continues to thrive because of our ignorance, our am-bition, our sentimentality, and most of all because of our vanity—yes, and because of one thing more—our lack of honesty.

I DO not mean to preach morals and a sermon; but I do think, in the average article about fake stocks, there is a disproportionate blame put on the swindler and too little on the swindled.

I once overheard a clever mother berating her son, not because he had bought fake stocks, but because in so doing he had encouraged a swindler to swindle, and had been a temptation to a dishonest man to be dishonest. It may seem a novel way of looking at the matter, but it has its value.

The truth is that to have been flimflammed brings you face to face with yourself. If you are an honest person, with a love of mental integrity, you look at yourself; if you do not cherish mental integrity, you turn away from yourself as you are, and visualize yourself only as you *would like to be*. This means that you have thrown away truth and judgment, and nothing will expose you more quickly to being flimflammed repeatedly.

It is a good rule, when bonanza stocks and get-rich-quick schemes are offered you, to ask yourself promptly just which particular kind of fool you are—whether ignorant, over-ambitious, sentimental, vain, or dishonest; and then try not to be it, and keep this up until the temptation is past.

1889. "Nellie Bly" (Elizabeth Cochrane), put up to the stunt by the *New York World*, travels around the world in record-breaking time: seventy-two days, six hours, eleven minutes, and fourteen seconds. She also makes news as the first woman to take such a tour unattended.

392   Investment
THE MONEY MANAGER

Insurance, Pensions, and Social Security

Bernice J. Malamud and Nancy Eales, Women's Life Services

According to a survey by the Institute of Life Insurance, most women feel that insurance ranks right below food, clothing, and shelter as a vital necessity. Yet many women haven't given much thought to insurance, other than believing that they are protected by their husband's policies, that they have some coverage through work, or that insurance seems so confusing.

Insurance salesmen (over 95 percent of whom are male) haven't helped much. Viewing women as homemakers whose husbands buy the insurance, they rarely solicit women independently or explain insurance to them. As a result, women on the whole are underinsured.

To become adequately insured—and otherwise protected by pensions and social security—women themselves must take the initiative. A good beginning is to learn the few terms that unlock most of the mysteries in insurance policies, to find out what kinds of protection are available, and to discover what forms of discrimination women may still encounter in seeking adequate protection.

Life Insurance

People secure protection from an insurance company by signing a contract (the *policy*), which states that the company will pay (*indemnify*) you or someone you name (your *beneficiary*) a sum of money if a certain event occurs. Your part of the bargain is secured by paying the company (the *carrier* or *underwriter*) a small sum of money (the *premium*) on a regular basis. The carrier can estimate the chances of that event happening to you by consulting statistics (*actuarial tables*), which have been collected for years, and from the tables determine what your premium will be.

Most of us do not have the luxury of knowing we will never have to worry about money; so we seek to provide for a continuous source of income in various ways. Savings out of current income is one method, but it is a slow and often inadequate means of accumulating capital. Investing in securities or real estate is another, but the recent economic down cycle has shown how unreliable many investments can be. Insurance, however,

has proved itself to be a dependable means for providing continuing income should our regular source of income be cut off by untimely death or illness, or by reaching retirement age.

Most people's first question about insurance is, "How much do I need?" There is no one answer to this because everyone has different desires, obligations, and personal situations. For instance, a young, independent single woman probably doesn't need life insurance, other than for final expenses (funeral, hospital, and personal debts). If, however, she has to support dependent parents, she may want to have life insurance to protect them. Once the hypothetical single woman marries and has children, her needs change. She must then consider how her children would be affected by her death. If she provides their sole support, she should have coverage that would provide monthly income for them until they are out of school. Or, if she is a full-time mother and homemaker, she needs coverage to provide enough money to pay for housekeepers in the event of her death. Many people buy life insurance to guarantee funds for college or to pay off a mortgage.

To figure out how much insurance you need you should first estimate what your dependents' financial needs will be. Then estimate all sources of income, including savings, benefits from employer's group insurance, Social Security, and any others. Once you have figured expenses and income, you can determine how much insurance protection you should have to achieve a certain level of income per month for your dependents.

Term or Whole Life?

How much insurance you buy is, of course, also based on how much you can afford. *Term insurance* is the cheapest form of life insurance. It covers you for a certain period (the term), usually five, ten, or fifteen years; then the coverage ceases. If you choose to continue it and are still healthy, you can renew it, but at a higher premium since you are now older and more likely to die. Many people buy renewable term, which the company guarantees to renew regardless of your health. You can also buy term insurance that can be changed (*converted*) into permanent insurance without a physical examination.

Whole life, as permanent insurance is usually called, is more expensive than term, but it has values that term does not. Whole life protects you for life and its premiums, though higher at younger ages than those of term, do not go up with the years. The extra funds in the early years build up a surrender value, or *cash value,* which you will receive if you cancel the policy.

There are two types of whole-life: *straight life* and *limited-payment life.* The first requires you to make premium payments for your entire life. Many people feel premiums will be a burden after retirement so they buy limited-payment life, which is paid up after a certain number of payments or years. Protection, however, continues for life. The premiums for limited-life are higher than for straight life, but the cash values also build more quickly.

A great deal has been written on the relative advantages of term versus whole-life insurance. Term is "pure" insurance, in that it does not have the savings aspect of whole life, in the form of cash values. For young people, term provides the most insurance for the least money. Though term premiums rise steeply in later years, by then the insured's income has often increased substantially and her or his insurance needs have lessened.

Many financial advisors suggest that their clients "buy term and invest the difference," rather than buy whole-life insurance. For those who will, in fact, "invest the difference," this may be good strategy. However, those who have a great deal of trouble saving money may find it worthwhile to accumulate forced savings in the cash value of a whole-life policy.

Insurance Strategy

We believe the best strategy is to get adequate protection first—which, unless your income is substantial, likely means buying term—and consider the possible advantages of whole-life only when that criterion is met. Some people find it advantageous to buy a large term policy and a small whole-life policy or to start out with term and eventually convert it to whole life.

Because commissions are greater for whole life than term, you might possibly encounter an agent who would urge you to buy a whole life policy you're not convinced you need or can afford. Be sure you have an agent you can rely on, and buy only a policy that is within your means.

If you feel that you will eventually want to buy more insurance than you can afford right now, you should consider paying extra for a *guaranteed insurability* rider to your policy, which guarantees your right to buy additional insurance at specific periods in the future regardless of your health.

Double indemnity is an option that for a very low price will double the benefit in case of accidental death. The reason the cost is so low is that such accidents are extremely rare. In general you should buy only the insurance you need, and avoid such inessential trimmings. If you actually need the amount of insurance that a double indemnity policy would pay in event of accidental death, you should get that coverage for *all* circumstances, not just one that's extremely unlikely.

Policy Points

Your beneficiary is the one who gets the proceeds of the policy. You can name anyone or thing you desire and you can have more than one beneficiary. It is advisable to have a contingent beneficiary in case your primary beneficiary dies before you do. You may change beneficiaries as often as you desire, unless you have named an irrevocable beneficiary. In that case, you need written consent from that party. You should make sure your beneficiary is aware of the coverage and knows where your policy is.

The proceeds of the policy can be paid in a number of ways, known as settlement options. Among these are: paying the benefit in one sum; letting it remain with the insurance company for a period, during which only the interest earned on it is paid out; paying part of it in one sum and the rest in installments; paying it out in equal installments, either for a certain period or for a certain amount. The options are many; so for the best protection of your beneficiaries it is wise to consider their needs in detail and discuss the possibilities with them.

Premiums for life insurance are based on your age, sex, and health at the time the policy is purchased—all used to determine the chances of your dying (according to mortality tables). If you should accidentally give your age incorrectly, the benefit will be increased or reduced to an amount the premiums at your correct age would have purchased.

If you can't make a premium on a whole-life policy in which you have cash values,

Jane Addams and her similarly educated and moneyed volunteers at the house, "It is more for the benefit of the people who do it than the other class. . . . Jane feels that it is not the Christian spirit to go among these people as if you were bringing them a great boon: that one gets as much as one gives."

you can borrow those funds to pay the premium, in what is called an *automatic premium loan.* In fact, as the name implies, such a loan is made automatically to continue any policy in danger of lapsing. Thus, you cannot simply allow your policy to lapse and expect to receive your cash value; if you do this your cash value may be used up in paying premiums of a policy you no longer want. You must instead formally cancel the policy. However, the automatic premium loan also protects you from losing a policy because of absentmindedly forgetting to pay premiums.

Another alternative, if you're having trouble making whole-life premiums, is to use the cash values to purchase a smaller amount of paid-up whole-life insurance or to purchase term insurance for an extended period. Under an optional provision in most policies, the company will waive the premium if the insured person becomes totally disabled.

Cash values can be used for other loans, as well as premium loans, on which you pay interest, usually 5 or 6 percent. Since the policy itself is collateral, you secure the loan simply by notifying the company that you wish one. Should you fail to repay the loan, the amount of the loan and any outstanding interest is deducted from the face amount paid to your beneficiary.

Some policies pay to the holder a periodic dividend that is, in effect, a refund of part of the premium. Though the premiums of such policies are usually higher than those of comparable policies that do not give dividends, the cost of the dividend-paying policy, when the expected dividend is subtracted from the premium, may be no higher than that of the dividendless policy. To compare the actual costs of similar policies, ask for their Interest Adjusted Costs—figures that take into account dividends and cash values as well as premiums. Your agent should be able to provide you with these figures.

Women and Life Insurance

Life insurance is one type of insurance that gives women a break: Because of their greater longevity, they pay lower rates. Women are usually given a three-year advantage (called a *setback*); thus a thirty-eight year old woman pays the same as a thirty-five year old man. However, this difference should reflect the reality that women live about *seven* years longer than men. The insurance industry is not giving women the full benefit of one of the few insurance advantages they have.

Health Insurance

Health insurance can be divided into two basic types of protection: against medical expenses and against loss of income when the insured can't work because of illness or accident. The latter is called disability or loss-of-income insurance. Most people have group coverage, which has the benefits of lower rates and, if taken through one's place of work, employer contribution. Individual health insurance has the advantages of being tailored to individual needs and providing continuous protection. It can be guaranteed renewable, meaning that the premiums will stay the same as long as the premiums are paid, unless the state allows that class of insureds' rates to rise. Some disability plans are noncancelable, which means that the policy cannot be canceled or the premium raised under any circumstances. Medical-insurance plans differ, so before taking out a policy, you should determine exactly what expenses are covered, how much is paid, and for how long.

Major medical insurance is designed to protect individuals against catastrophic medical expenses. It usually covers all types of medical expenses up to stated amounts—for example, $10,000 per illness, or a lifetime total. Major medical has a *deductible* (an amount the insured must pay before benefits start), which helps lower costs to the company; the larger it is, the lower the premium. Major medical policies also have coinsurance clauses, which means that the insured pays a certain percentage, usually 20-25 per cent, and the company pays the rest. Frequently the company will assume 100 per cent of expenses after the insured has paid a certain amount, $1000 for example, in a certain year. Major medical policies can be combined with basic protection to form a comprehensive health insurance policy.

Following are some important provisions to examine in your health insurance:

1. Per-day limits on hospital costs. Many policies pay for less than the daily cost of hospital care. It may be advisable to augment such a policy with separate hospital-indemnity coverage, which pays the insured a given sum of money for each day she is hospitalized.

2. Deductible period. This is the time in which your unreimbursed health expenses must total the deductible amount before your additional expenses are covered. Less than four months is substandard. Better policies allow you to include

---

1889. Emma Ford and Flossie Moore gain notoriety as the most violent and dangerous black woman criminals in Chicago. Armed with revolvers, razors, brass knuckles, knives, and sawed-off baseball bats, the woman work as a pair by night. Emma stands over six feet and weighs 200 pounds, the terror of the town's police. (One prison guard she nearly drowned by holding his head in a water trough, another she held on the floor by his hair

expenses incurred in the last three months of the previous year in your deductible for the current year.

3. Benefit limit. A major medical policy with a $10,000 or $20,000 limit on total benefits is simply not adequate to cover a serious illness or injury. The better group coverages provide $1 million or are unlimited. If your major medical has a low benefit limit, you can gain additional protection by acquiring an excess major medical policy. These policies have a deductible of $10,000, $15,000, $20,000 or more and are specifically designed for individuals with inadequate major medical coverage.

4. Benefit period. Some policies place a limit on the duration benefits will be paid for a single illness or injury. Avoid these policies.

5. Exclusions. The better health coverages restrict exclusions to war, self-inflicted injuries, dental care, eye glasses, and normal pregnancies. Policies with other exclusions should be avoided.

6. Preexisting conditions. Examine this provision carefully. The standard is to exclude any condition for which you have received treatment prior to the effective date of the policy until you have had the policy for two years.

7. The treatment of mental disorders. Most policies severely restrict coverage for mental illnesses outside of a hospital, and coverage of treatment in hospitals varies greatly among companies. Shop around! Some companies treat hospital costs for mental illness like those for any other illness.

8. Convalescent care. There is also a great variety in coverage of prolonged convalescent treatment. Many individual policies do not provide any coverage. Better ones cover as many as 100 days.

9. Pregnancy. Better policies cover complications of pregnancy and offer coverage of normal pregnancy for an additional premium. (Note: A single woman is covered by any provision in her policy pertaining to pregnancy that a married woman would be.)

Disability income may be as important as medical coverage, since it helps replace lost earnings. Disability coverage is purchased to replace a percentage of earned income, usually limited to between 40 and 60 percent of earnings. Benefits begin after a predetermined period (called the elimination or waiting period) following the onset of the disability, for example, thirty or sixty days. The longer the waiting period, the lower the premiums will be. If you can get by on savings, or your employer will continue your income, it pays to have a long elimination period. Depending on how large a premium you are willing to pay, you can usually purchase disability insurance that provides income for as long a period as you feel you might need it. Premiums also depend on the occupation, age, and sex of the insured.

Self-inflicted injuries, mental illnesses, pregnancy, and preexisting conditions may be excluded from your policy permanently or for a stated period of time. The status of pregnancy and related disability in group coverage is currently being decided in the courts.

Women and Health Insurance

Women are at a disadvantage compared with men in medical insurance and disability income insurance. The actuarial tables that determine accident and illness (morbidity tables) indicate that women are poorer risks than men, but women are finally challenging the conclusions reached on the basis of these statistics. Women often pay twice the rate men do for the same coverage, and frequently cannot buy similar coverage at any rate.

Discrimination is very prevalent in the sale of disability income for women, except in states banning sex discrimination (Pennsylvania, New York, and New Jersey). Even then, there may still be legal rate differentials.

Examples of common discriminatory practices against women are:

- Reducing disability payments by as much as 50 percent if they are not employed outside the home at the time of the disability
- Refusing to sell disability income to housewives for fear they will fake ailments
- Giving women lower occupational ratings than men (for the same job)— low ratings mean higher premiums
- Refusing to sell noncancelable disability income policies
- Refusing pregnancy coverage to female employees, while wives of male employees are covered
- Refusing guaranteed insurability
- Requiring lengthy elimination periods for diseases of female organs (but not male), if covered at all
- Allowing men to purchase greater coverage and for longer periods
- Refusing to cover elective abortion

while plucking out his whiskers.) Flossie is known as "the most terrible female bandit that ever operated in Chicago." Her holdups will net her, in 1893, over $125,000. Arrested and released on bail as often as ten times a day, Flossie once says to a $100 fine: "Make it two hundred, I got money to burn."

Social Security

Social Security is basically a method devised by the government to provide a continuing source of income for individuals and their families whose earnings are interrupted by retirement, death, or disability. Most wage earners, whether employed or self-employed, are covered. Social Security also covers people in special categories, the blind, for example, and provides medical care for the aged via Medicare. Currently, one person in seven is receiving benefits from Social Security.

The provisions in the program, which are detailed, have changed over the years; so the best source of answers for specific questions is your local Social Security office. You can secure printed information and details of your account (ask for a "Request for Statement of Earnings") at no charge.

Wage earners build up credits by paying Social Security tax over the years on earnings up to a maximum amount that in 1975 was $14,000. Benefits, which are not subject to income tax, are determined by a person's average earnings and the time (figured in quarters) a person has worked. Benefits are now also figured with an automatic cost-of-living increase. To be fully insured, a worker needs roughly ten years under Social Security. If a worker stops work before receiving enough credits, as many women do, that worker is not entitled to benefits; but if she starts to work again, she retains previous credits.

Benefit amounts under Social Security can be affected if the retired worker elects to supplement her income. The worker is allowed only $2,520 in income, other than from pensions, savings, and investments, before benefits are reduced. Full monthly benefits are allowed for any month the worker's earnings are less than $210. Dependents' benefits can be affected by the worker's income, but after age 72 benefits remain the same for the worker or dependents regardless of earnings.

Social Security theoretically protects most workers and their families; but unfortunately for women, it contains many clauses that exclude or discriminate against them. Housewives, of course, receive no credits, because they earn no income. If they have the misfortune of being divorced prior to the 20-year marriage requirement, they have no rights to their ex-husband's retirement and survivors' benefits and may end up with literally nothing to show for those years. Married working women often cannot receive disability-income payments due to their broken work patterns. Women in general suffer from the credits/income formula because they have low-paying jobs and their work records are interrupted by family moves, child rearing, and part-time work. Each of those years out of the work force counts as zero, which pulls low pay averages down farther.

Pensions

The term pension refers to two types of retirement income: that we provide for ourselves with savings and insurance and that provided by employers.

Two of the most common forms of personally designed pension plans provide significant tax advantages to individuals eligible to set them up. One is the Individual Retirement Account (IRA) which is for employees whose employers have no pension plans. Under it, an employee can set aside 15 per cent of her salary, up to $1,500 per year, which is tax deductible. The other is the Keogh Plan, which is for self-employed persons or members of business partnerships, who can contribute 15 percent of earnings up to $7,500 per year, again tax deductible. These pensions are both subject to preretirement withdrawal penalties and are taxable upon retirement, which must be no sooner than age fifty-nine and a half nor later than age seventy. IRA and Keogh Plans are offered by insurance companies, banks, and mutual-fund sales organizations.

Another form of self-designed pension, which does not, however, have the tax advantages of the IRA and Keogh Plans, is the *insurance annuity*, which pays the holder a lifetime income, starting either immediately or in the future.

Like IRAs and Keogh Plans, pensions provided by employers can be considered deferred income and are thus tax-favored. They vary widely in the amounts they will pay at retirement and how contributions are made; so it behooves an employee to assume nothing about benefits if she is relying on pension income as retirement security.

Pensions can be separated into roughly three major categories. One is the *deferred-benefit pension,* under which the employee is assured a certain income after retirement, based on a percentage of annual salary, number of years of employment, or a combination of these two factors. Another is the *defined-contribution pension,* to which a certain amount of money is contributed each year, though the actual pension is determined by the amount in the fund at the time of retirement. Defined contribution plans can

1891. Street clothing worn by the average American and English woman at this time weighs between twenty-five and thirty pounds.

be designed so that a certain minimum benefit is ensured. In a third type, the *profit-sharing pension,* employers contribute a percentage of corporate profits each year—which may be none if there is no profit. If you work for a small corporation that offers only a profit-sharing plan, it would not be wise for you to depend on that alone for retirement income.

One of the most important things you should know about your pension is what your *vesting* rights are. Vesting means the waiting period until you are entitled to your employer's contribution to your plan. The 1974 pension act now guarantees employees minimum vesting rights that are an improvement on past practice, but many women who have had broken career patterns still fail to qualify for pensions in spite of the new regulations.

In the past, many funds paid nothing to survivors of pension holders. Now the new law ensures a minimum of 50 percent benefit to a surviving spouse. You should know what survivors' benefits your pension provides, as well as the following: the income/years-of-service formula used in determining your pension, policy on job layoffs, whether there is a cost-of-living increase, and who controls the pension fund and how it is managed.

Women and Pensions

While pension requirements are better than before the 1974 law, they still show a bias against women. Women are denied the seven-year setback, based on mortality rates, in life insurance, where it would be as advantage; in pensions, where it is a liability, they get it. What this means is that since the pension funds are paid out longer, the monthly stipend women get is reduced. Women generally earn less than men and have breaks in employment so frequently they are only entitled to small employee pensions. When the setback is added to their poorer employment records, women often end up with pitifully meager pensions.

Inadequate Protection for Women

Insurance, pensions, and Social Security are designed to protect all people, but they usually protect men better than women. Consequently, a wise woman shopping for protection will keep in mind that there are many types of discrimination but that some employers and insurance companies treat women more equitably than others.

In purchasing life and health insurance a woman may encounter the following discriminatory practices, in addition to those mentioned before:

- Refusing to sell certain types of insurance to women
- Offering fewer benefits to women
- Requiring women to take medical exams when men do not have to
- Refusing to cover women who work part time or for their husbands
- Refusing special options to women, such as the option to increase insurance at certain option dates and the option to buy lifetime accident insurance

Women should realize that they are armed with the best weapon to change such policies—consumer or purchasing power. Companies and their policies vary; so if you can't find what you want, shop around. Find an agent who is sympathetic to your desires and use his or her expertise to secure the best coverage. Employers' plans are more rigid, but if you find offensive clauses, bring them to the attention of your employer. Since Social Security must be influenced through Congress, change will necessarily be slow; but you can make your opinion known through your elected representatives and consumer groups.

If you do discover discriminatory sections in your current insurance coverage, show your displeasure by dropping the policy; but before you do so, it is very important to remember several things. The first is that after two years of being in force, a policy is incontestable by the insurance company. You will lose that benefit in any new policy. The second is that a new policy will be more expensive, since you are older. The third is that you should never drop old insurance until you are sure that you are currently insurable.

Finally, continue to educate yourself and others on insurance and pensions. Don't assume anything, because today's woman leads a very different life than the one many insurance policies and pensions were designed for. Find out whether your husband's group insurance covers you, and what happens if he dies or you get divorced. Study your own group insurance and pension plans to see if you need to secure additional protection for dependents or retirement. Review your insurance needs annually, since people's needs for protection continually change. And, to conclude, make a fuss; the best way for women to achieve a better deal in the areas of insurance, pensions, and Social Security is to let it be known that we want the same protection that is available to men.

1892. Lizzie Borden appears before court on the charge of brutally murdering her mother and father. Despite circumstantial evidence strongly implicating her guilt, the case becomes a cause of national division. Feminists—Lucy Stone and Mary A. Livermore among them—take her arrest as a clarion call to a heated defense. Amid the commotion the jury returns a not guilty verdict.

New York Public Library

Widowhood

Lynn Caine

"What you are telling me," my therapist said, "is that you are suffering from financial insecurity. So are most other people." This really brought me up short. She was not criticizing me. Simply stating a fact. But I was shocked. How self-involved, self-pitying I had become!

"You have no choice about one thing," she told me. "Your husband is dead. That's a fact and you can't alter it.

"But you do have the choice of looking on the debit side or on the credit side of your life. I suggest you count your blessings. You have two healthy children. You have a good job. You're attractive. And you are healthy. You have a lot of friends.

"Now, you can choose to look at your life any way you

want, but it seems to me that you have an awful lot going for you."

This matter-of-fact summing up pulled me out of my self-pity. At least for a time. It was another giant step into life on the other side of grief, just as my realization that I did not want to be a lonely goose, to sink into the underground of widowhood had been a step toward reestablishing myself.

Suddenly, I was no longer Lynn Caine, widow and loser. I was Lynn Caine, competent and vital mother of two. It would have been nice to have a financial buffer against the world. But I had something better. I had friends, health, children. And a good job.

I can't stress enough how important my job was to me. It was not simply that it was interesting and paid a salary that enabled me to get along. More than that, it gave structure to

1893. Marie Owen, widow of a patrolman, becomes the first American policewoman, walking the beat in Detroit.

my life. I had to get up in the morning, get dressed and get to work. Even at my lowest times, when I was torn apart by anxieties and fears, the very fact of having a job gave me emotional security. I belonged somewhere. No matter how alone I was in the world, I had a place where I belonged. Work to do.

The best single bit of advice I can give to other widows may be—keep your job if you have one, and find one if you don't. Even if you have children that need you, get a job. A part-time job, a volunteer job, anything that will provide you with a routine and stability. A paid job, of course, is preferable, both in terms of the money and of one's attitude toward it. I realize that this may be out of the question for some women, but it is the *regularity* of the job that I want to stress. I am convinced that having to go to work every day and act as if I were fine and on an even emotional keel helped me back to normality. When I was working, I had a respite from my fears, whether real or fantasy.

Slowly I began to develop confidence in myself and get my financial affairs in somewhat better order. I had done so many stupid things—partly because I hadn't known any better, but mostly because of the craziness of widowhood— that it was a slow process.

My first problem was that Martin and I had never discussed money. Just one of those unliberated things, I suppose, going back to the idea that little girls aren't good at math, a self-fulfilling prophecy that encourages financial incompetence. But the fact was that I had never shared any of the real responsibilities of the household. My job? That was just running off to play. I "ran" the household just about the way a little girl plays house. I never even knew how much money Martin earned—or how much it took to run the household.

During my crazy period, I had made terrible financial mistakes. And that's why I keep repeating my advice to widows: Sit. Be quiet. Don't move. You have to understand that your mind is not working properly. Even though you think it is. Protect yourself from yourself.

I am still very worried about money. The children and I live on my salary and Social Security and that pittance from the Veterans Administration. But I have learned to cope. I have given up most of the luxuries I used to take for granted. I don't have the paper delivered each morning. I've stopped going to the hairdresser once a week. No more steaks and chops, but lots of spaghetti and tuna fish and casseroles, casseroles, casseroles! No more French wines, but once in a while a jug of California wine. No more expensive vacations. No more summer houses.

I know I am better off than most widows. But why should any woman face deprivation and anxiety and financial terror because her husband dies? Women must learn to protect themselves and their children. We must stop playing child wife. That role hasn't been valid for a long time.

Setting Aside a Contingency Day

Lynn Caine

There is a lot to be said for those old-fashioned marriage contracts that spell out financial arrangements. The current Women's Lib marriage contracts disappoint me because they devote so much fretful concern to the question of who is going to change the sheets and take the car to be greased and have so little regard for the truly liberating matter of money.

I can't count the times I have said, "If only I had it to do over again. . ." (And, dear God, please spare me that.) But if I did, I would handle myself and my money much differently. Starting from the day we were married.

Death and widowhood are among the most shattering realities. Yet we must face them, and it would be easier to do so if we were prepared beforehand. When I wistfully think back about what I "should have" done, I realize that I *could have* done it. Martin and I *could have* provided for that final contingency of death.

Today I know how I would go about it. I would declare a Contingency Day—an annual review of the financial state of the family. And I would like to recommend such a review to

1896. Mary Grew, feminist and anti-slavery crusader, dies. Of her spirit for human rights the poet John Greenleaf Whittier wrote:
The way to make the world anew
Is just to grow—as Mary Grew!

every husband and wife. They could discuss steps to be taken if either husband or wife should die in the next twelve months. How much money the surviving spouse and children would have to live on. What changes in life-style would be necessary. Such a discussion, in the natural context of family life, would minimize some of the later trauma of widowhood (keep in mind that statistics show women usually outlive their husbands).

If Martin and I had done this I would have made fewer crazy decisions, because I would have had a guide, a plan to follow, so that grief-addled as I was, there would have been a lifeline of sanity for me to cling to.

To me, Contingency Day is an eminently reasonable concept, but so strong is the death taboo that some people with whom I've discussed the idea find it shocking.

I can understand that some women might hesitate to say, "Let's sit down tonight and talk about what's going to happen to me and the kids if you die." If this is true for you, it may be easier to start off with something like, "You know, I've never made a will." Or, "I just read that every couple should review their wills at five-year intervals." I know it is hard to talk about death. So approach it in whatever manner is easiest for you. But approach it.

There is always the possibility that your husband will refuse to join in Contingency Day.* It may make him too uncomfortable. What then? Go ahead and do it on your own. I'm serious. You owe it to yourself, to your children. I wish someone had pushed me into taking this kind of responsibility.

It should be an annual event with its own set date to be most effective—like Christmas, Thanksgiving, birthdays, anniversaries. My preference is a couple's wedding anniversary, simply because husbands and wives who have instituted this annual review report that their discussions heightened the quality of their relationship. They were brought face to face with the fact that their love was finite. They would not have each other forever. Only until death did them part. There was an increased tenderness, a kind of sweet electricity that reinforced those vows to love and to cherish.

It is important to prepare an agenda. Each family has its own special concerns, problems, hopes, but the essence of the discussions should be the future—and the direct contingency, death. What should you do if your husband dies? How will you and the children get along?

This cannot be covered in a brief half hour of general

discussion. Your first session requires advance planning and organization. In fact, I recommend that you consult your lawyer and possibly an accountant. I want to make it clear that although I am much smarter about handling money these days, I am not an expert. Do not take my suggestions as instructions that must be followed. Think about them in the context of your own needs. And remember that times change. Very rapidly. You need professional advice to plan ahead. This scares some people, because of the expense. Good advice does cost, but it may be tax deductible and it will eventually pay for itself. Ethical lawyers and accountants will charge ethical fees. Discuss the fee ahead of time. Ask if you can pay it in installments if necessary.

One important area to clarify on Contingency Day is your husband's pension plan—and yours, too, if you work. It's probably not as good as you assume it is. Find out what happens to your husband's pension if he dies. Will you get anything? What if he dies before he retires? Would you get anything then? You should, of course you should. But very few widows do. Very few private-industry plans pay off to widows. Only about 2 to 3 percent of this country's widows get any money at all from their husbands' private-industry pension plans. Half the widows who are sixty-five and over live on less than two thousand dollars a year.**

But pensions are only one item that should be part of Contingency Day discussions. Probably the top priority should go to your wills, and to the executors of those wills. It might be a good idea for you to be the executrix of your husband's will and he the executor of yours. If you can read and write and do simple arithmetic, if you are well briefed on the family finances, there is no reason you can't act as executrix. And you can save a lot of money, because you won't have to pay executors' fees.

*For husbands: If you can't bring yourself to participate in Contingency Day and discuss the very realistic issues of how your wife and child will manage in the event of your death, then at least write a letter to and for your wife that will tell her what she needs to know about such things as insurance, pensions, investments, and debts. It should contain everything your wife and lawyer need to know that is not contained in your will. Once you have written the letter, make copies. Attach one to your will. Stash one away in your safe-deposit box. Give one to your wife and encourage her to ask questions about anything that puzzles her.

**As background reading, I recommend a paperback book by Ralph Nader and Kate Blackwell, *You and Your Pension*. It's a quick survey of a subject most women don't know enough about.

1896. For the first time, Japan's new civil code places men and women on a more equal legal footing in divorce proceedings. However, while adultery on the part of the wife continues to constitute grounds for divorce, the husband's unfaithfulness does not.

I'm not going to discuss the subject matter of your wills. That is up to you and your lawyer. Just one word of advice: Don't be in awe of your lawyer. You are paying him for his advice. If you have questions, ask them. There is no such thing as a silly question. If you don't know the answer, it's not silly.

Another area that's a must for Contingency Day is insurance. To what extent are you and the children protected right now? Do you have life insurance? Major medical? Mortgage insurance? Do you need more?

If you have children, it might make a lot of sense to take out life insurance on yourself right now. If you were to be widowed, you would want to take out life insurance on yourself to protect your children. Why wait? It's cheaper now. And the premiums for women are lower than for men because of women's longer life expectancy. That's about the only break insurance companies give women.

These suggestions are just intended to start you thinking. They are not comprehensive. You lawyer and your accountant will undoubtedly indicate other areas that should be clarified. For instance, what do you know about the family's bank accounts? Stocks? Real estate? Does anyone owe you money? Do you owe anyone money?

One couple told me that they had started a Contingency Day file. It was just a big brown envelope. Every time they saw a magazine article or a newspaper story that seemed to bear on something that should be discussed, they ripped it out and filed it away to discuss on their next Contingency Day.

In her financial primer, *How to Manage Your Money: A Woman's Guide to Investing* (Little, Brown), Elizabeth M. Fowler, *New York Times* financial columnist, wrote, "I don't intend to be lugubrious, but all married women should prepare themselves to be widows, no matter what their age or status in life."

I couldn't agree more. And I'd like to carry her thought just one step further. One of the most loving acts a man can perform is to teach his wife how to be a widow. It might be that Contingency Day would give your husband the opportunity to show how much he loves you.

How to Deal

There may be a time when it seems impossible to meet a scheduled payment on a credit account. With income temporarily cut off or facing sudden unforeseen expenses it may be impossible to meet several bills when they come due.

There are times when good credit standing will serve especially well. A temporary loan of money from a reputable lending institution may be a solution; to consolidate into one the several payments we find difficult to meet. Just as possible, a temporary postponement of payment or reduction in the size of payment may tide us over.

In real emergency there are intelligent courses open to us and, on the other hand, there are very unwise things we can do, too.

If it is necessary to postpone or reduce scheduled payments, the rules of *good buymanship* (one of the newer terms in the trades) are very clear, if we will follow them.

● *Call on the credit manager, or the merchant or lender.*

Tell him the exact facts—sickness, medical expenses, loss of work, family emergency—why it is impossible to keep the payments up to date.

● *Discuss future prospects with him so he can figure out what can be done to tide the situation over and avoid loss, inconvenience, and undue hardship to both*

● *Make every effort to carry out whatever temporary or permanent revision of terms may result from the conference.*

Never do these things:

The unwise course? Pull down the shades. Answer no phone calls or letters. Refuse to answer the door bell. Stay as far away from your creditor as you can. If he should find you tell him, "Suit yourself—there is nothing I can do about it." Are not these foolish actions for an intelligent consumer to take? Surprisingly, some customers do these very things. They fail to protect their own good credit by frankness and leave their creditor no other course than to proceed to protect his own interests.

Adapted from *Using Our Credit Intelligently.* Copyright © 1970 the National Foundation for Consumer Credit, Inc. Reprinted with permission.

1896. Evylyn Thomas, bicycling down a New York City street, becomes the first victim of an auto accident when Henry Wells, piloting a Duryea Motor Wagon, knocks her to the ground and fractures her leg.

The merchant's or lender's rights if his customer defaults

The contract or note will provide, as one would expect, that if payments are not made as agreed upon, the merchant or lender may repossess or take back the purchases or security involved, if he thinks it necessary. No reputable merchant or lender wants to do this because the expense of repossessing is an added loss to him. In most states it requires legal formalities. Ordinarily, if the reasons for failure to pay are justifiable and both sides think payments can be resumed shortly, or that the customer can meet a series of smaller payments satisfactorily, an agreement that allows the goods to remain in his hands can be reached. Contract terms often are rewritten or set aside temporarily if the customer is cooperative and shows earnest interest in seeing that the obligation is paid out.

Suppose repossession seems the only course

It doesn't happen often, but family emergencies are sometimes so great that a complete reversal of plan is the only solution. Here we talk of a circumstance so difficult to manage that it will not help to rewrite the note or contract or re-arrange the instalment payments; so great that the merchant or lender and the customer, too, feel it is best to arrange for repossession.

To *arrange* for the return of the goods is a business-like procedure in an emergency. To hide out and force the creditor to repossess without working with him, is costly to our hopes for good credit standing later when the emergency is past.

In each lifetime unusual circumstances do beset us. Some of these we cannot surmount, some are too big for us at the moment. It hurts to lose a product when we have paid money on it, but we must remember also that we have had some use of it. Nor can a merchant or lender of any substance make a profit on repossessing goods from us. So repossession is a bad deal for both. Nevertheless, sometimes it is the only way out. The intelligent thing to do in such situations is to arrange a voluntary return of goods and not force the creditor to "repossess." This leaves our credit in better condition for the future when our emergency situation has passed.

What are our rights?

What are our rights in the repossession process?[1] Basically, and in most states, according to law, when the merchant or lender takes back property we are buying, he is obligated to put it up for sale and with due diligence seek a fair price for it. If he sells the product for more than enough to pay the balance of our account, usually he is obligated to repay us the difference.[2] Everyone knows, however, that secondhand prices cannot always be counted on, and nine times out of ten, the forced sale may not bring enough to pay off the balance.

Legally in most states and under most contracts, our creditor could ask us for the difference. Some state laws prevent this except when we deliberately have avoided our payments or refuse to return the goods. Ordinarily, businessmen and lenders chalk off this difference as their own loss, will not press for it. Almost all would rather see their customers back on their feet financially, able to do business with them again. But the possible problem shows how important it is to choose carefully those with whom to do business, just as the stores and lenders must be careful to know their customers.

Here again remember the rules of *good buy-manship*. Whenever it is necessary to give up merchandise because one cannot meet the payments in family emergency, *keep in touch—show good faith.* Go back and see the merchant, banker or loan company once in a while. Talk over your problem and if you are making progress explain the reason you expect soon to be in shape to do business again.

This is the secret of handling the very difficult emergency so that before long the unfortunate situation has righted itself and credit standing again is reestablished. The merchant, if treated this way, realizes you are substantial and, under reasonable circumstances, entirely credit worthy. Indeed, if you really want the articles you have returned, often the merchant will hold them for you a number of months, if you handle the situation with care.

[1] We discuss here procedures involving instalment sales and secured loan contracts and notes. While simple repossession is not the solution when "signature" or unsecured loans are the problem—the intelligent action of the debtor in emergency is exactly the same.

[2] The "Uniform Commercial Code" contains this provision. The "Code" also provides that this right can be waived—if the waiver agreement is signed *after default.* Waivers in the original contract would be void. Naturally one would waive this right only in return for the creditor's agreement not to claim any balance still unrecovered after the repossessed security has been sold and the proceeds credited to the account.

1899. Daring younger women begin to affect bloomers for bicycling wear, a vogue condemned by many clergymen as an "immoral influence."

Bankruptcy Can Be a Lifesaver

Herbert S. Denenberg

There should be no stigma attached to bankruptcy and you should not hesitate to resort to it if you need it.

Some observers have said that bankruptcy is as American as apple pie. This may be somewhat of an overstatement, but most legal experts would certainly agree that bankruptcy is part of our system and a perfectly respectable legal procedure.

The Supreme Court of the United States, itself, has explained the basic purpose of the Bankruptcy Laws: "One of the primary purposes of the Bankruptcy Act is to 'relieve the honest debtor from the weight of oppressive indebtedness, and to permit him to start afresh free from the obligations and responsibilities consequent upon business misfortunes.' "

The Court explained further: "The new opportunity in life and the clear field for the future effort, which is the purpose of the bankruptcy act to afford the emancipated debtor, would be of little value to the wage earner if he were obliged to face the necessity of devoting the whole or a considerable portion of his earnings for an indefinite time in the future to the payment of indebtedness incurred prior to bankruptcy."

This fresh start concept can be traced back as far as the Bible, which suggests the forgiveness of debtors every seven years.

Bankrupt ex-millionaires recognize the importance of the fresh start concept and so should you. After William Zeckendorf's real estate empire, Webb and Knapp, Inc., went into bankruptcy, he is reported to have said: "I did not put my brain into bankruptcy." He was already thinking of new businesses.

Even your creditors expect bankruptcies. A loan officer who never makes loans to people who go bankrupt would be accused by his superiors of being too strict in granting credit. Just as insurance companies expect fires and accidents, lending institutions and other creditors expect bankruptcies. And over 10.5 million of those bankruptcies have come to pass in the United States.

Businesses and lending institutions do not hesitate to resort to bankruptcy when it serves their purposes, and neither should you. The suggestion of stigma has probably been generated by these same businesses and lending institutions who want to collect their debts, but who wouldn't hesitate 15 seconds to go into bankruptcy themselves if it was to their advantage.

So don't be embarrassed into not going broke if that will be an answer to your problems. Bankruptcy is not leprosy. Bankruptcy is not a "Scarlet Letter." Not clearing up your debts may be a lot more hazardous than bankruptcy. According to one study, nearly one-half of debtors in default felt their health had been adversely affected by their debt problems. Thirty-six percent experienced marital strain and 9 percent were divorced because of debt problems. There are many things worse than bankruptcy, so don't hesitate to use the law if it will help. It may save your health and marriage.

Bankruptcy is designed to wipe out your debts and give you a fresh start; but there are some debts that will not be wiped out, and limits

Adapted from *A Consumer's Guide to Bankruptcy*, 1975, Pennsylvania Insurance Commission.

to how much property will be free from the claims of your creditors. So figure out where you'll stand after bankruptcy.

The fresh start of bankruptcy is subject to some heavy qualifications.

(A) *Obligations Not Wiped Out By Bankruptcy.* The first important qualification is that all debts are not wiped out by bankruptcy. The main classes of debts that you'll still be responsible for even after bankruptcy are:
—state and federal taxes (due within the last three years)
—fines and penalties arising out of criminal violations and traffic offenses
—child support
—alimony
—debts arising from willful and malicious acts
—debts incurred by fraud or false pretenses

There is one other special category of obligations—secured debts. Examples are a mortgage on your home or an encumbrance on your car.

The creditor, even if there is a bankruptcy, can still go after secured property. If you have property subject to a mortgage or other security device, you may have to give the property back to get rid of the debt. However, once the property is returned or foreclosed, you are no longer obligated on the debt.

(B) *What You Can Keep Even If You Go Bankrupt.* In addition to debts which are not wiped out, the bankruptcy court can use all of your assets to pay debts, except for the property specified in the exemption statute of your state of residence and in special federal laws. Although federal law controls bankruptcy, it also recognizes the exemption laws of the individual states.

Property exempted under Pennsylvania law from claims of creditors is as follows: wearing apparel, sewing machines, all Bibles and school books in use by the family and, in addition, $300 in real or personal property. Insurance policies and annuities are also exempt provided the beneficiary is a child, spouse or dependent relative. In addition, $100 per month on the proceeds of life insurance and annuities are exempt, as well as certain pension benefits. These exemptions vary in the different states.

In Pennsylvania if the husband and wife own real estate or personal property in what is called an estate by the entirety, such property cannot be reached by creditors unless the debt is owed by both the husband and wife.

You may also keep any wages and commissions earned after the date of filing for bankruptcy.

There are also certain exemptions created by federal law. These include Social Security payments, veterans benefits, pensions or annuities under the Railroad Retirement Act and federal government retirement plans, among others.

The federal exemptions apply in every state, but state exemptions vary widely.

1899. Generva Mudge, first female auto driver, has made regular excursions through the streets of New York during the past year. Now she participates as the first woman racer in a New York contest, in which her Locomobile skids on snow and knocks five spectators about.

Statistics on the American Family in Poverty

About 1 out of every 3 families headed by a woman lived in poverty in 1970 as compared with 1 out of 14 families headed by a man. The poverty rate was highest among Negro families headed by a woman—54 percent, more than double the 25 percent for white families headed by a woman. The proportions for Negro and white families headed by a man were 18 and 6 percent, respectively.

| | Poor Families, 1970 | | | | | |
| | Number (in millions) | | | As percent of all families | | |
Type of family	All races	White	Negro	All races	White	Negro
	5.2	*3.7*	*1.4*	*10.0*	*8.0*	*29.3*
Male head	3.3	2.6	.6	7.1	6.2	18.3
Female head	1.9	1.2	.8	32.5	25.0	54.5

The employment of women family heads takes many such families out of poverty. Among white families headed by a woman in 1969 (latest data available), 15 percent were poor where she was in the labor force; 37 percent where she was not. The comparable proportions for Negro families headed by a woman were 38 and 69 percent, respectively.

| | Percent of families below poverty level, 1970 | | |
Family characteristics	All races	White	Negro
3 children or more	16.9	12.0	44.9
Head:			
Under 25 years of age	15.5	13.1	36.1
65 years of age or over	16.3	14.1	40.8
With less than 8 years of schooling	25.3	21.0	40.3
Unemployed	16.7	13.4	38.7
Not in labor force	28.3	23.1	60.6
Worked longest in 1970 as:			
Service worker (including private household)	15.8	10.4	32.5
Nonfarm laborer	12.7	10.3	21.5
Farmer or farm laborer	27.3	23.6	67.1

Children in poverty

There were 10.5 million children under 18 years of age living in poverty in 1970—6.2 million white and 4.1 million Negro. (The total was 672,000 less than in 1969 and 6.7 million less than in 1959.) About 11 percent of all white children were members of poor families as compared with about 42 percent of all Negro children. The incidence of poverty among children was highest (68 percent) in Negro families headed by a woman.

| | Children under 18 years living in poverty, 1970 | | | | | |
| | Number (in millions) | | | As percent of all children under 18 | | |
Type of family	All races	White	Negro	All races	White	Negro
Total	*10.5*	*6.2*	*4.1*	*15.0*	*10.5*	*41.5*
Male head	5.7	3.9	1.6	9.3	7.3	26.0
Female head	4.8	2.3	2.5	53.4	43.2	67.9

Note— The figures in this fact sheet are from the U.S. Department of Commerce, Bureau of the Census: Current Population Reports, P-60, Nos. 76 and 77.

Adapted from *Fact Sheet on the American Family in Poverty,* Women's Bureau, Department of Labor.

1899. "Frankie" Baker shoots her lover, Albert Britt, in a hotel room for his infidelities to her. The following day, Britt attempts to shield her from criminal prosecution, denying that it was she who shot him; then he dies. The affair is to be commemorated in more than two hundred versions of the song *Frankie and Johnnie.* "He was her man and he done her wrong."

How Welfare Works   Timothy J. Sampson

Dealing with the welfare bureaucracy can be bewildering and frustrating even to those familiar with the ways of governments. Should you ever apply for welfare you will find it very helpful to know how a typical case might proceed.

If you are applying for AFDC[1] you are probably a mother (or soon to become one). Your child(ren) must be deprived of parental support by reason of death, physical or mental incapacitation, continued absence from the home, or (since 1961 and in **some states only**) unemployment (of the **father**).

You go to the local welfare office—your county welfare department or closest branch of the state welfare department. You will likely be seen by the eligibility worker assigned to do intake. You will be asked where you reside, when and where your children were born, who their father is and how long and why he is absent from the home (or unemployed). You will be required to cooperate with the Welfare Department in notifying local law enforcement officials of the probable whereabouts of your children's father and you will be asked to assist in his prosecution for nonsupport (if this be the case).

In determining your eligibility (and the size of your welfare grant) the Welfare Department will need to know of **any** income you (or the child) have from any source and also know the value of any real or personal property you may have. Presuming you have little or no income and that your real and personal property is below limits established by your state you will be found eligible and get "on" welfare.

All statements that you give are subject to investigation and verification. Your own parents may be held liable for your support or at least the Welfare Department may ask them if they are able to support you. The Welfare Department may (but does not have to) choose to have you "declare" all this information to be true on a "simplified" form or declaration and then routinely investigate a small sample of such declarations.

They may also **presume** you to be eligible and aid you immediately (but this also is not required). They must, under federal regulation, allow you to apply and act promptly (within thirty days) on your application.

If you are denied aid, not allowed to apply, given less than you think you are entitled to, or treated differently from others in similar circumstances in your state you are entitled to appeal and receive a fair hearing, before an "impartial" person from the state welfare agency.

Once you are on AFDC your case will usually be assigned to an "approved" file and you will ordinarily have a service worker who will talk with you about a "plan" for helping you become self-sufficient again and/or attempt to deal with problems you have (or the worker thinks you have).

The service worker will be responsible for deciding if you are employable and should be referred to the local Employment Service for training or job placement services.

You may or may not find out what medical care you and/or your children are entitled to and likewise you may or may not be given information about food stamps or surplus commodities available to welfare recipients in your county.

If you should go to work or receive any income from any source you will generally be allowed to keep only part of this money. Your budget will be figured by first looking at a table of what a family of your size, composition, and situation (rent, etc.) needs, then from this total there will be subtracted any available income, and you will be entitled to the difference un-

less (and this is **usually** the case) the state has a fixed maximum or percentage it pays instead of what is recognized as your real need!

As noted above, typically 75 percent of your service worker's salary is paid by the federal government (and 50 percent of all administrative costs). Your workers have been hired under civil service or a state merit system. Service workers have a usual case load of sixty to a hundred families and eligibility workers may have several hundred families.

About six workers (or as many as eight) make up a "unit" which has a supervisor and a clerk. Groups of units make up a district office or welfare center which usually has a director. "Downtown" there is the county administration which includes "middle-management," special investigation and fraud units (these may be directly attached to the district attorney's office), property units (to check on real and personal property), child welfare and foster home placement units, etc. The county welfare director is either responsible to the county board of supervisors or to a county welfare board appointed by elected county or state officials.

Any unusual facet of your case will go up the line for approval—from your worker to the supervisor to the district director, AFDC chief, etc.

In some counties special items of need (a refrigerator, furniture for a family who has lost theirs in a fire, for example) may be provided out of local funds with the proper approvals. Some states provide money for some of these special needs items. In many states recipients get only the "flat" monthly grant—no exceptions or adjustments for special needs.

Through routine state-case sampling (this is called "quality control") the state attempts to **supervise** the county to insure the uniform statewide administration of aid required under federal regulation. Your individual case might thus come to the attention of the state welfare department. Usually, however, you will just be a case number and a grant statistic to the state. In any event all you are likely to be to the federal government is a tiny part of the average grant payment made to all the families receiving AFDC the previous quarter, which is the basis for the quarterly federal advance payments to the state.

If there is some controversy attached to a particular state practice and question is raised about whether the state is obeying federal laws and regulations, then the federal government may hold a hearing to decide if the state is "out of conformity." The SRS[2] administrator decides this and, if he so finds, must then cut off federal assistance to the state for that program.

This has been rarely even raised. Very few such hearings have been held and no state has ever been cut off.

So, ordinarily the SRS just sends out new regulations and information about changes Congress makes in the law and then approves the changes states make in the state plan describing how welfare is supposed to work in that state. The SRS also collects statistics about how many people are getting on and off and how much money they get, etc.

However, SRS does maintain staff in all HEW[3] regional offices which can provide useful information and help in efforts to get states to comply with federal regulations.

---

[1] Aid for Families with Dependent Children. This is the largest single source of welfare monies. It is funded by both the federal government and the state, and the state determines how the funds are to be managed.

[2] Social Rehabilitation Service, which establishes the Federal rules and regulations that govern welfare policies.

[3] U.S. Department of Health, Education and Welfare.

Adapted and reprinted with permission from *Welfare: A Handbook for Friend and Foe* by Timothy J. Sampson. Copyright © 1972 United Church Press.

1901. The middle-aged Anna Taylor, harnassed and cushioned in a four-and-one-half-foot barrel, becomes the first woman to shoot Niagara Falls. She emerges scratched, shaken, but otherwise uninjured.

Bargain Calendar

Joan Bel Geddes

appliances (small)
books
china and glassware
coats (men's), hats (men's)
furniture, housewares, and lamps
furs, jewelry
gift items, toys
infants' wear, lingerie
linens and blankets, rugs
radios and stereos
refrigerators
shoes, sportswear
washing machines and dryers

appliances (small)
automobiles (used)
bedding, rugs
china and glassware
curtains and slip covers
furniture, housewares, and lamps
furs, winter clothes
hats (men's)
radios and stereos
refrigerators
silverware
sportware, toys
washing machines and dryers

hats (women's)
infants' wear

coats (women's)
infants' wear
men's clothing
spring clothes
stoves
suits (men's and boys')
washing machines and dryers

handbags
linens and blankets
lingerie
television sets
tires

building materials and lumber
piece goods
screens and storm windows
television sets

children's clothing
curtains and slip covers
furniture, housewares, and lamps
fuel oil
garden furniture
hats (women's)
radios and stereos
refrigerators
rugs
shoes
sportswear
summer clothes

air conditioners
bedding
camping supplies and sports
  equipment
coats (men's)
furniture, housewares, and lamps
furs
gardening supplies
hardware
rugs
school supplies and clothes
tires

automobiles (new)
china and glassware
furniture, housewares, and lamps
gardening supplies
hardware
piece goods

furs
school supplies and clothes

automobiles (used)
coats (women)
piece goods
stoves

automobiles (used)
children's clothing, toys
coats (women's)
suits (men's and boys')
winter clothes

1901. The "Gibson Girl," creation of artist Charles Dana Gibson, becomes the model and nationally emulated stereotype of feminine beauty in the United States.

Buying a House

Umi Hayes

The most surprising thing about buying a house, or even vacant land, is that it's romantic. Something emotional happens as you walk around the property, walk into the house, smell it, feel it, wonder what life would be like in it as the owner. But when this emotional something happens (a sudden rapture over a quaint turret), it can also obscure some less rapturous aspect of being the owner (that the turret is rotting from the base up and will cost $2,000 to repair). The trick is to balance your madness with a modicum of method. In this case that means checking details and asking questions. Do not give in to the desire to appear knowledgeable, easygoing, and a swinger about money. None of these help to make a good buy. Nor, unfortunately, does an affable broker, although she or he can be very helpful in putting you and a likely house face-to-face. You'll find brokers to be genial people. But sometimes they laugh when no one else does, probably because buyers do funny things like plunking down years of savings without asking too many questions. Hoping for the best, many people shake the broker's hand at every opportunity as though to pump out guidance and privileged information. You, too, will be tempted to enlist the broker as a friend and put the burden of making a good buy on her or him. Don't do it. Remember, the broker is the seller's agent, not yours. Just keep asking questions. The broker is there to answer you and show you property, that's all. You must take the responsibility for the buy. Here are some pointers to help you make a responsible choice.

The real estate terms that follow are explained in the glossary. Refer to that section as you read.

Now, how do you tell a broker what you want? Begin with generalities such as the size of the house (usually identified by the number of bedrooms); style (but don't box yourself into a period such as colonial or contemporary until you've seen several of each—house buyers are notoriously fickle about such things); and the location that appeals to you. What purchase price do you have in mind? Unless you're very unusual, you won't know. You should, however, know how much immediate cash you are willing to invest, and how much a month you want to pay on a mortgage, but this doesn't determine the purchase price. What you are looking for is the most house you can get for the price you can afford. I suggest you tell the broker right off where you're at on money, and let her or him work out the variables.

Start a notebook. Under the name and location of each house enter the facts: number of rooms, price, size of the property, name of the broker, zoning, taxes and how recently they were assessed, things particular to that house, and your own comments and questions. This notebook will prove to be a valuable comparison of prices against the advantages and drawbacks of each property. Also, it tends to make both you and the broker specific. If you go back to a house for another look, be sure you go with the broker who showed it to you the first time. Going with another to the same house may cost you a commission to the second broker should you buy that house. But by all means, deal with more than one broker, and go to many properties.

Caveat emptor means final sale. If the house collapses after you buy it, you don't get a penny back. Caution is the rule. Sizing up property is a profession, and unless it's yours, don't try to do it alone. Professional house inspectors are available—and expensive. But if you are nervous about your prospective home, it may be worth hiring one. What you should know are the categories of potential trouble, and who to go to for information. Incidentally, when the broker, or anyone, tells you something you don't understand because of the terms used, ask her or him to explain it on the spot.

While you are familiarizing yourself with the property and checking for secret swamps, look for a well-worn path trailing off to the next property. This may sound simpleminded, but most people never do it. Look, because such a path may indicate an easement. In other words, neighbors have used that path and have acquired the right to do it, not by agreement of the parties but by law as a result of constant use. It may not even appear in the abstract of title for the property, but nonetheless a genuine right. Your lawyer is the one to handle this.

Most other external factors are as meet the eye: the condition of paint or wood siding, the presence of aluminum siding, the solidity of the chimney, window frames, terraces, and so on. The roof is a little harder to see, but if a few of the shingles look loose or cracked, put that on your question list.

Another question for your list is the cost of any additions or subtractions you have in mind for outside or inside the house. Some, like installing electrical heat in a spare room, will be less than you expect; others, like taking down what turns out to be a supporting wall, will be very expensive or downright impossible.

Inside the house, look carefully for stained ceilings and walls. They could mean a leaky roof on the top floor, or leaking pipes elsewhere. If a roofing job has been done since the leak, ask for the name of the roofing service; if a plumbing job, ask who did it. You are free to consult with these service people to know what problems, if any, still exist. But keep in mind that it is not wise to irritate the seller. If your direct questioning is doing this, then

1902. Gertrude Stein, author and critic, Radcliffe educated, moves to Paris where she occupies the center of the American expatriate movement—the "lost generation" as she puts it. Ford Madox Ford, Hemingway, Ezra Pound, Clive Bell, all visit her salon. Her artist friends—Picasso, Matisse, Gris, Braque, and so forth—are later, of course, to

switch to listing your questions on a pad and ask the broker to get the information for you later. More questions. Ask how much electrical power the wiring can handle; how many outlets there are; if an electrician has worked on the house lately, in which case you know what to do.

Ask what other services the house has had lately, such as termite control, weather painting, perhaps additional landscaping. How's the foundation? This brings you to the basement to look at the walls. In a new house, cracks can mean just settling. In an old house, they mean trouble. Ask your lawyer for the name of a consultant. Again in the basement, look for water marks on the floor and walls. This means flooding in wet weather.

Water supply and sewage are provided in most housing developments. If the house is not part of a development, ask if there is a well on the property. If it is on a neighbor's property for shared use, your lawyer has to verify the seller's right to that use. If there is a septic tank for sewage, ask its condition, last date of cleaning, and so on.

Check the water pressure in the faucets upstairs. (Just turn them on.) If there's an attic, ask if the attic floor has been insulated. If not, the chances are the exterior walls of the house are not insulated either. In cold weather country this means a high heating bill. Look for storm windows (the extra sheeting of glass or plastic outside the regular windows). They can cut heating costs considerably. Ask what kind of heating system the house has, what it costs to operate through a winter, and the size of the water heater. Go to any local plumber and ask which is the preferred heating system and how many baths you can get from a (whatever gallon) tank the house has. These service people will help you as long as you don't put them on the spot of downgrading the seller's property. Remember, they are neighbors and very likely friends of the seller. The only time you should even identify the house in question is when they've worked on it, and then only to ask how much more work needs to be done there. After all, you are a future customer.

You will get more cooperation if you are tactful in getting your information. There's no law that says the seller must sell to you. If angered, she or he won't. Never outsmart the seller publicly. On the other hand, don't be afraid to bargain over the price. As long as you proceed diplomatically, offers and counter offers are all in the game.

If you've fallen in love with a house that has a roof about to fall in and a rowboat in the basement for rainy days, a place that has an orphan look, have it if you must—but if you think it's overpriced, list the repairs and come up with a rough estimate, all with the help of local services, and knock most of the estimate off the asking price. You may have a buy.

Above all, you need a lawyer. Of all the people you consult, this one is the most important to you. Choose one who practices real property law in the area where you will buy. Make a point of having a few preliminary talks, perhaps about the benefits of a conventional mortgage versus a Federal Housing Administration mortgage, or how the mortgage money market is these days. While you want this information, you are looking for a helpful attitude from the lawyer. If you don't find it, go to another. You must have a lawyer you can depend on for advice. She or he should direct you, when asked, to an appraiser, a consultant, or any other expert you need. It's not unusual for seller and buyer to use the same lawyer, believe it or not. In that case, particularly, be sure to get title insurance (which is often a requirement of the mortgagor anyway). From the start, don't sign anything without your lawyer's advice. Essentially, the lawyer's job is to see that you get a marketable title free from any outstanding liens, troublesome easements, missing signatures from former deeds, or any other condition that might jeopardize your investment.

The closing is momentous because a portion of the earth is literally changing ownership. Both buyer and seller are elated, which is strange when you think of it. Later, like most people, you'll probably discover surprising things on the place that need repair. No one makes a perfect buy. But if you've shopped well, you have done better than most. Give yourself credit for the good work.

  # A Glossary of Home-buying Terms

Abstract   A summary of the history of the legal title to a piece of property.

Amortization   Provision for gradually paying off the principal amount of a loan, such as a mortgage loan, at the time of each payment of interest. For example, as each payment toward principal is made, the mortgage amount is reduced or amortized by that amount.

Appraisal   An evaluation of the property to determine its value. An appraisal is concerned chiefly with market value—what the house would sell for in the market place.

Adapted from *Wise Home Buying*, 1972, Department of Housing, and Urban Development.

Binder or "Offer to Purchase"   A receipt for money paid to secure the right to purchase real estate upon agreed terms.

Certificate of Title   Like a car title, this is the paper that signifies ownership of a house. It usually contains a legal description of the house and its land.

Closing Costs   Sometimes called settlement costs. Costs in addition to price of house, including mortgage service charges, title search and insurance, and transfer of ownership charges. Be sure your sales contract clearly states who will pay each of these costs—buyer or seller.

---

become famous; but beforehand, Gertrude amasses their work in a fabulous personal collection. Her writing, often nearly unintelligible, is supposedly a reflection of the cubist style of art—and thus such phrases as "Rose is a rose is a rose." Alice B. Toklas is her constant companion and amanuensis up to Gertrude's death in 1946.

Closing Day The date on which the title for property passes from the seller to the buyer and/or the date on which the borrower signs the mortgage.

Condominium Individual ownership of a dwelling unit and an undivided interest in the common areas and facilities which serve the multi-unit project.

Cooperative Housing An apartment building or a group of dwellings owned by residents and operated for their benefit by their elected board of directors. The resident occupies but does not own his unit. Rather, he owns a share of stock in the total enterprise.

Depreciation A decline in the value of a house as the result of wear and tear, adverse changes in the neighborhood and its patterns or for any other reason.

Earnest Money The deposit money given to the seller by the potential buyer to show that he is serious about buying the house. If the deal goes through, the earnest money is applied against the downpayment. If the deal does not go through it may be forfeited.

Easement Rights A right of way granted to a person or company authorizing access to or over the owner's land. Electric companies often have easement rights across your property.

Equity A buyer's initial and increasing ownership rights in a house as he pays off the mortgage. When the mortgage is fully paid off the buyer has 100% equity in the house.

Escrow Funds Money, or papers representing financial transactions, which are given to a third party to hold until all conditions in a contract are fulfilled.

FHA Approval There is no such thing as an FHA approved house. If a builder advertises "FHA Approval" he is misleading you at worst and, at best, badly stating his belief that his house will meet standards for an FHA insured mortgage.

Hazard Insurance Insurance to protect against damages caused to property by fire, windstorm and other common hazards.

Home Mortgage Loan A special kind of long-term loan for buying a house. There are three main kinds of mortgage financing for single family homes in the United States—the conventional mortgage; the VA (Veterans Administration), sometimes called the GI mortgage; and the FHA (Federal Housing Administration) insured loan.

Mortgage Commitment The written notice from the bank or other lender saying that it will advance you the mortgage funds in a specified amount to enable you to buy the house.

Mortgage Discount "Points" Discounts (points) are a one-time charge assessed by a lending institution to increase the yield from the mortgage loan to a competitive position with the yield from other types of investments.

Mortgage Insurance Premium The payment made by a borrower to the lender for transmittal to HUD-FHA to help defray the cost of the FHA mortgage insurance program and provide a reserve fund to protect lenders against loss in insured mortgage transactions. In the case of an FHA insured mortgage this represents an annual rate of one half of one percent paid by the mortgagor on a monthly basis to FHA.

Mortgagor The homeowner who is obligated to repay a mortgage loan on a property he has purchased.

Mortgagee The bank or lender who loans the money to the mortgagor.

Prepaid Expenses The initial deposit at time of closing, for taxes and hazard insurance and the subsequent monthly deposits made to the lender for that purpose.

Repair and Maintenance The costs incurred in replacing damaged items or maintaining household systems to prevent damage.

Special Assessment A tax for a specific purpose such as providing paved streets or new sewers. People whose properties abut the improved streets or tie into the new sewer system must pay the tax.

Title The evidence of a person's legal right to possession of property, normally in the form of a deed.

Title Company A company that specializes in insuring title to property.

Title Insurance Special insurance which usually protects lenders against loss of their interest in property due to unforeseen occurrences that might be traced to legal flaws in previous ownerships. An owner can protect his interest by purchasing separate coverage.

Title Search or Examination A check of the title records, generally at the local courthouse, to make sure you are buying the house from the legal owner and that there are no liens, overdue special assessments, or other claims or outstanding restrictive covenants filed in the record.

1903. The Everleigh sisters open their famed Everleigh Club in Chicago, which shortly becomes the most consistently and highly profitable and famous house of ill repute *in the world*. Its sumptuousness is such that even the spittoons are of solid gold. Nightly receipts occasionally gross over five thousand dollars with the well-bred and stunning harlots selling at up to fifty dollars apiece. No man is admitted unless he is personally

Working with Auto Service People

Albert Lee

Would you give a carpenter, a plumber or a TV repairman a blank check when he arrived at your doorstep and tell him to fill in the correct amount when he finished the work? Of course not. Yet you are doing essentially the same thing when you sign a work order and turn your car over to a mechanic and tell him to "fix it." You're giving him an open invitation to charge whatever he wants to, along with your car as collateral.

The scales of justice are heavily tipped in favor of the mechanic in any dispute over repair charges. When you signed the work order, you gave him a lien against your car. If you don't pay the bill he presents you, whether it is a fair bill or not, he has the legal right to sell your car to collect his charges. Also, you can't even specify how much he can ask for the car, and if he wants to sell your 1973 Lincoln Continental for $200 to his brother-in-law, you've just lost a car. This legal right to sell your property without a court hearing is what the people in the service industry affectionately call the mechanic's lien. It was established when the auto industry was in its infancy as a protection for auto service people from the wily customer who would have work done and then demand to have the car back without paying. Since it was more trouble to "unfix" the car than to turn it over to the owner, the mechanic was simply cheated of his time and parts. While there is still some justification for protecting the mechanic from the public, there is even more reason for protecting the public from the mechanic, but the archaic mechanic's lien remains on the books.

The mechanic's lien can be avoided, but not without some effort on your part. Two sure ways to side-step it is to move to Texas, where such liens have been outlawed, or to never pay off your car, since the first lien from the Friendly Finance Company takes legal precedence over the mechanic's lien. A third and an infinitely more practical way to avoid it is to make sure that the work order spells out exactly what your repairs are to be so the situation never arises when you'll have to fight to get your car back. If you treat the process of working with a service shop as a business transaction, you are less likely to be given the business.

To begin with, always get a written estimate of precisely what work the mechanic will perform and how much it will cost for parts and labor. He should be able to give you the estimate right down to the last dollar. Remember you don't want a spoken estimate. It will do you no good in a small claims court later to tell the judge: "Well, the mechanic said . . ." If the estimate is in writing and in your pocket, the mechanic knows he'll have to live up to it.

Betty Medsger

The work order normally doubles as your bill when the work is completed, so it should look like an itemized bill before you sign. The mechanic should automatically itemize each part cost and labor cost; make sure that he does. Initial each item, signifying that you've approved it. Then cross out all blank lines below where more parts and labor could be listed after you leave the car. Leave no blank spaces on the work order. Then write in before the blank for your name: "ANY ADDITIONAL PARTS OR LABOR NOT AUTHORIZED WITHOUT WRITTEN CONSENT," or something to that effect. Finally, sign the work order and take a copy with you.

This may seem like a great deal of rigmarole, but actually it only takes a couple of minutes, and it avoids

known to one of the sisters or comes highly recommended both as to character and financial standing by a regular patron. Police finally close the house down after the sisters circulate a richly illustrated advertising brochure that enrages the mayor "for the audacity."

one of the most common problems arising from any repairs—misestimation. A mechanic often will estimate a repair job at half of what it will cost or less, just to get your car into his shop and torn down, before revealing the true charges. If a mechanic objects to these mild precautions, he may have a reason. Go elsewhere. This procedure also rules out another common dodge, where the mechanic takes your car in, then calls you later at home to tell you that he found some more problems, and while the car is in, shouldn't he go ahead and fix them? To say yes is to give him an open invitation to hike up your bill. Never approve additional work over the phone unless you're dealing with a mechanic who has served you faithfully for years. It may be an inconvenience to come down to the garage a second time just to approve some extra work, but it is much safer in the long run.

Also, before you leave the repair shop, ask the mechanic to check that he has the parts he'll need to do your repairs or that he can get them right away. There is nothing more annoying than to come to pick up your car at the time it was promised only to find that the job wasn't done because parts weren't available. Unless the repair job is crucial to safety or would harm the car if left undone for a few days (and few jobs fall into these categories), don't leave your car at the shop until all the parts are in. If necessary, pay a deposit to assure that parts are ordered. If there is going to be an unusually long delay for parts, telephone the local district sales manager of the manufacturer for assistance. He can usually speed up the delivery process for you. The district sales manager's number is normally listed in your car owner's manual, a valuable little document that ought to be in your glove compartment at all times.

While on the subject of parts, don't be put off if the mechanic suggests used or rebuilt parts. Used parts are employed either because new parts would take longer to get, or because they would cost a great deal more. Used parts can be just as good as new. Many reputable manufacturers rebuild carburetors, starter drives, alternators, transmissions and a number of other drive train components, and you can feel secure that such rebuilts will be comparable to new parts.

Sometimes all the repairs have not been completed by the time you return. Don't pay for the work on the mechanic's promise that he'll do it next time you come in. Even an honest repairman has a fallible memory, and arguments over verbal agreements will get nothing settled. When an insurance claim is involved, don't sign a release until the job is complete. Have everything that remains to be done and the date of completion written on your copy of the work order. Once the repairman signs your copy of the work order, he has committed himself to doing the work and can be legally coerced to do so.

When you come back to pick up the car, look it over carefully to see if the prescribed job was done. Take the car out for a test drive before paying the bill. Even the flat-rate tables make allowance for this trial run as part of the cost of repairs, and not to do it is not to get what you paid for.

Finally, always pay for auto repair work with a check. If you discover after you get the car home that the work was not done properly, or at all, you can stop payment. The garage owner will be outraged by the check stoppage and may even threaten to sue you because of it. But chances are he would rather make good the repair job than go through the expense of taking you to court.

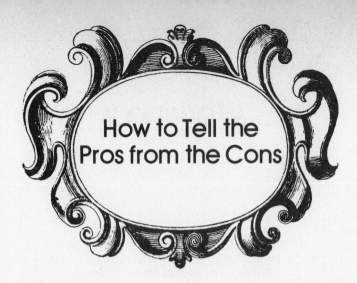

How to Tell the Pros from the Cons

Here are some of the more common tricks of the repair gouging trade and how to avoid them:

Checking under the Hood

If you innocently sit behind the wheel in a strange service station and nod complacently when the attendant asks, "Check under the hood?," you may be in for some "discovered" needs. A common trick is to cut your drive belt or puncture a radiator hose, then show you that a new one is needed. Or a mechanic may squirt oil around a seal or on your brake master cylinder to convince you that you have a dangerous leak. Another trick is to pour a little liquid laundry detergent in your battery. This makes the battery bubble and boil over and is guaranteed to scare any driver into buying a new one. Or without the use of any props, the attendant may simply announce that your engine sounds "rough" and needs a tune-up. If you're lucky, you may only get taken by the oil dodge. The service attendant pulls out the oil dip stick, then pushes it back only part way so that it appears you are a quart or two low. Then when you approve of adding oil, he takes an empty oil can, turns it upside down and punches a fresh hole in the can, then pours air into your already-well-oiled engine.

You can prevent most of these tricks by merely getting out of your car and standing by the hood when the attendant services your engine. Only the most brazen of thieves would attempt any shenanagans while you're standing an arm's reach away. Be leery of any discovered need on some part of the engine he normally would not check for routine servicing. And remember that a mechanic can't tell if you need a tune-up by just listening—an inconsistent firing can mean almost anything from the wrong grade of gas to a clogged positive crankcase ventilation valve.

Airing Your Tires

The attendant who voluntarily checks the air in your tires is either overly eager to please or out to sell some new rubber. If it's the latter case, he will let a few pounds of air out of a tire while he is checking it. Then he will either tell you that it is losing air nearly as fast as he can fill it, or he'll go about his business of servicing other parts of your car, then come back and re-check the tires a

1903. Maggie Lena Walker, a black, becomes the first American woman bank president when she founds the Saint Luke's Penny Savings Bank of Richmond, Virginia. The bank is later to become the Consolidated Bank & Trust Company.

few minutes later, discovering it is already low again and will never make it to the next station.

Next he offers to patch the tire, but alas, when he takes the tire off he discovers the cord structure inside the tire has had it. By pushing the tire inside out he spreads the cords apart, which convinces most victims that the "seams have split." If he thinks you aren't dumb enough to fall for "split seams," he may just slash the tire when you're not looking. Either way you'll pay a premium price for an unneeded replacement, and the mechanic will get your old tire, which he can resell later

The best way to avoid the tire gouge is again to stand over the service man when he is doing his initial checking. Have the attendant just put on the spare tire and drive it home where you can get a fair-priced replacement if it's necessary. Better yet, get your own gauge (available from the Tire Industry Safety Council, for $1.00), and always check your own tires. This is a good practice, not only to avoid trickery, but also to avoid sloppy checks. It makes a great deal of difference if your tires are ten pounds over or under the manufacturer's specified pressure. In fact, the tire makers have proven that the average tire loses 20 percent of its life because of typically improper inflation.

Won't Hold a Charge

Perhaps the mechanic's most common trick of all is to check your battery and announce that you will need a quick charge. This normally only takes a half hour and will cost just a couple of dollars. Obviously, you can't stand by the car for a half hour without a break, so the shyster will have an opportunity to find some other problems. You won't actually get the charge either. He'll connect the charger, not to the battery post, but to the insulated part of the battery cable. Then when the half hour is up, he'll tell you that the battery won't hold a charge and must be replaced.

Unless your battery is two or three years old or you've been having trouble starting it, don't let a strange attendant give you a quick charge. Chances are your car will be better off without it. Also, more often than not, a car won't start because corrosion has built up between the battery cable and the posts, thus blocking the flow of current. Before you start tampering with charging, clean and scrape the cables and try to start it again. This takes about three minutes and can save you the price of a new battery.

It Doesn't Feel Right

Your steering wheel shakes a little at highway speeds so you pull in to have it checked. Generally, this should indicate that you need a wheel alignment, but not if you stop at the wrong place. The mechanic will place your car on the rack, then shake a suspended wheel. It wobbles, which he says means the ball joints need replacing. Actually, a car is designed to give a good amount of movement for clearance when the weight is not on the wheels. This type of ruse has become so popular that General Motors has installed self-regulating ball joints on all of their cars since 1973. These vehicles have no play when suspended, so the trick just won't work.

Shock absorbers might also be included near the top of the list of "bad ride" repairs. Don't take anyone's word that you need new shocks, especially if the ones that are on the car have seen less than 30,000 miles of wear. It's easy to check the shock absorbers yourself. Just push down on the fender and release it. If the car returns to level immediately, the shocks are acceptable, and if the car continues to bounce, you need new ones.

Looking into the Transmission

Never let a mechanic tear down your transmission to search for a problem unless every external transmission check has been made first. Once the transmission has been torn down, it will cost you at least $75 to have it put back together again. Automotive engineers say that 80 percent of all transmission repairs can be made without taking the transmission apart. Always get at least two, and maybe three or four, estimates of what is needed before authorizing any transmission work. The transmission is by far the most complicated device in your car and repair bills of $300 to $500 are not uncommon.

One frequent trick is for a mechanic to show you metal filings from the bottom of your automatic transmission case. He says the shreds of metal mean the gears are worn out beyond repair. In truth, the meshing of gears in most transmissions causes some metal shredding in the regular course of wear. Unless there is a great deal of shredding, there is no real problem.

Impressive Credit Cards

Each impression of your credit card on a bill is as good as a blank check, and a greedy attendant can easily make a dozen such impressions while he's ringing up your bill. When stopping at a strange station, never let your card out of your sight. And do by all means go down the list of charges when your monthly bill comes in, and check the amounts against the receipts you received when you got gas or service. Major oil companies are receptive to complaints and can come down heavily on one of their outlet dealers whom they can prove has been doctoring bills.

Stranded on the Highway

If your car quits on the road or you get into an accident, beware the tow truck that just happens to come along when you need one. Some tow truckers listen to the police radio around the clock and still others maintain patrols of highly-trafficked expressways The tow truck driver will ask you to sign a contract before towing you in. The contract has clauses giving the tow truck owner the exclusive right to repair your car. Never sign such a document. The salvage value of the car plus the mechanic's lien is more than enough to cover any costs, making a towing contract unnecessary.

It's a wise move to ask the tow truck driver if he works for a repair garage. If he says yes, tell him to tow your car to another garage. He may refuse, which will tell you that he's after the repair job and not just the honest profit from towing. You're better off stranded on the highway than to accept the rescue from such an operator.

1905. Christabel Pankhurst, British suffragist, incites her followers through the barred window of her cell, where she has been imprisoned for fomenting a public disturbance. Suffragists chain themselves to trees and lampposts before the Parliament, haranguing the crowd.

New Rules for the Used Car Buyer

Wade A. Hoyt

Given the current state of the nation's economy, and the widely felt need to save pennies, many people who would otherwise be visiting showrooms in search of a new car are experiencing a resurgence of affection for the old bus—along with a determination to make it last a few more years. Others are turning to "previously owned" models—only to discover that today's used-car market is even more confusing than the new-car market. Why? Because many of the traditional ground rules for used-car buying are no longer operative. Here are a few of them:

Don't buy a used car, period; it is always "somebody else's headache."
This old saw is based on the assumption that a new car must be better than an old one—an assumption that is no longer always true. New cars cost more and may run worse than identical older models. They weigh more, have less power, and often use more gas and cost more to keep in tune. This situation is the direct result of changes mandated by the Clean Air Act and the National Traffic and Motor Vehicle Safety Act—federal legislation with the best of intentions but with grievous results in execution.

Avoid high-mileage cars. This former good advice falls apart on the definition of "high" mileage. You certainly don't want something with 120,000 miles on it. But well-kept American cars can—and do—run over 100,000 miles today without major engine repairs. In fact, the engine and drive-train will usually outlast the body chassis. Conversely, the three-year-old cream puff driven only 6000 miles on Sundays by a little old lady may not be the bargain most people think. The engine on a short-trip car never really warms up, the oil doesn't circulate properly, and undesirable acids, varnish and sludge build up in the lubrication system. And people who don't drive a lot generally feel that they needn't service their cars as often as people who do. Actually, they should service them *more* often.

Never trust the odometer. The practice of turning back the odometer to make a used car look newer was once so widespread that the best advice was to assume that it had been done, and to ignore the

mileage reading on any secondhand car. The recent federal odometer law imposes stiff penalties for such tampering. More important, car makers have, since 1972, been building "tell-tale" odometers that show white lines between the numerals of an odometer that's been spun in reverse.

Don't believe what a dealer tells you about the car's previous owner. You don't have to believe him anymore—you can ask the previous owner himself. One of the little-known provisions of the odometer law requires the dealer to obtain a mileage statement from the car's previous owner. Ask to see it and write down the name and address of the former owner. Then you can call him and ask if he had any unusual problems with the car, what repairs were made on it, even how much he sold it for.

If the owner was not an individual but a taxi company, police force, rental agency or corporate fleet, reject the car. Taxis traditionally have too much mileage (that 60,000 miles on the odometer may actually be 160,000—most odometers "start over" at 99,999). The other cars in this category usually get too little maintenance and are driven by people who treat them as though they weren't theirs (they're not).

Of course, some of the old rules still apply:

If possible, buy from the used-car lot of a new-car dealership. When a new-car dealer takes a car in poor or questionable shape as a trade-in, he normally gets rid of it at a used-car auction. Most of these wind up on used-cars-only lots. Most new-car dealers also have formal used-car programs that include a thorough inspection and refurbishing, plus a written guarantee that covers *all* parts and labor for up to 90 days.

Shop in the suburbs. If you shop for your used car in the affluent suburbs, you will pay a bit more, but you will generally find cars that have received better-than-average maintenance—simply because their owners could afford it.

Always ask for a written guarantee that the car will pass your state's safety and/or pollution inspections. And always ask the seller in advance to guarantee that he will make any necessary repairs or adjustments.

Avoid complicated equipment. Power windows, power door locks, automatic speed control and similar gizmos are just trouble waiting to happen. Look for a car without them. Likewise, air conditioning

on a car more than three years old will probably need some expensive maintenance or repairs soon. If you really need air conditioning, consider a new add-on unit for $200 to $350. You will pay that much extra for a late-model used car with air conditioning already installed, and the add-on unit will have a guarantee.

Always road-test the car. Take the car for a 15- to 20-minute drive that includes a bumpy road, some high-speed highway driving and a steep hill. Accelerate quickly, make a few sudden stops. The car should be free of excessive rattles and noises. It should hold a straight course on the highway and when braking. The steering wheel of the moving car should not turn more than two inches without starting to turn the wheels. The automatic transmission should provide smart acceleration and should shift without slipping or hesitation. As you stop, watch for prolonged flickering of the oil-pressure warning light, which could signal extensive engine wear.

Before or during your road test, check to be sure that the following work properly: interior and exterior lights, turn signals, windshield wipers and washers, heater, defroster, air conditioning, locks, windows and doors. (A door that sticks can indicate accident damage and possibly a bent frame.)

Take the car to your mechanic. Ask him to check the frame, steering, suspension and exhaust system for damage, and the brakes for wear. Have him check the engine with a vacuum gauge and a compression gauge. These instruments may reveal potential engine trouble. Have him remove a valve cover and look for sludge. If it's there, it may be throughout the engine.

If the mechanic finds some serious trouble—but you still like the car—ask for a written estimate on the necessary repairs and deduct at least that much from the sale price. The checkup is $20 to $30 well spent.

Winter is the best time to buy. Used cars, like everything else, are subject to the law of supply and demand. In late autumn the supply is generally high because of the trade-ins on new models. During the winter, demand for both new and used cars is low. Thus November through February is the time when used-car prices tend to be lowest. They skyrocket with the first robin of spring.

1905. Mistinguette, French musical comedienne and dancer, whose legs are considered the shapliest in Europe (although her face is considered the ugliest), has them insured for one million francs.

The Legal Adviser

What to Look for in a Lawyer

Women in Transition, Inc.

If you have questions about separation, divorce, child custody, or name changes.

1. What is the lawyer's *reputation*? Were you referred to her or him by someone you trust, by someone who has had experience with this lawyer's legal work?

2. Has the lawyer had *experience* with the judges and courts of your city or county? What kind of legal problems does your lawyer handle?

3. What kind of *attitudes* does your lawyer have? Does she or he make stated or unstated assumptions which would prevent her or him from working in your best interest? Does she or he assume that mothers should always have the responsibility for their children; that a woman who put her husband through school or a job-training program may be entitled to money from her husband to put her through school or a job-training program after there's a divorce (or even if there isn't a divorce); that women in general (or you in particular) are simpleminded and inferior? Does the lawyer respect you as a person? Can the lawyer imagine herself or himself in your situation?

4. What is the lawyer's *fee*? The prices private lawyers charge for their work vary from person to person and firm to firm. A standard charge for an uncontested divorce in most of the no-fault states is approximately $750 (including court costs). Anything less is a bargain (in the eyes of lawyers) and anything more is outrageous. Standard fee for a separation agreement is about $350, although you may be able to get one for less as part of a "package deal"—agreement and divorce. The charge for a support hearing is usually about $250 for the plaintiff (the person who brings the suit) and $150 for the defendant (the person who answers the charge—your husband in a support action). However, some lawyers will perform all of these services for less. If you are getting a divorce and you want

to retake your prior name, be sure to state that at the outset. Other than a nominal filing fee, there should be no additional charge in many states.

Over the telephone or at your first appointment with the lawyer, get a financial estimate for the work. Do you expect your divorce to be contested by your husband? It is important to know this from the outset. Contested divorces are much more expensive than uncontested ones. If you want a separation agreement, do you expect much resistance from your husband on the terms of the agreement (on support money, child custody, property division)? Is there much or any property to divide? Do you want the lawyer to represent you at the family court in obtaining a support order, or in determining child custody and visitation rights? Lawyers will have different fees for each of these tasks, depending on how much work is involved, how much money you or your husband have, and how much the lawyer is used to being paid.

We suggest that you and your lawyer draw up and sign a written agreement of what services the lawyer will perform, how much time the work should take, and what the lawyer's approximate or maximum fee will be. You and your lawyer can negotiate a new agreement if the conditions under which the first agreement was made

change significantly: for example, if your own financial situation changes or if more work is involved in the divorce because your husband decides to contest the divorce, or your husband disappears and must be located. The important thing is that you will know what is happening and for what and how much you are being charged.

5. Does you lawyer have good *communication* with you? Does she or he let you know what's happening with your case? Does your lawyer talk in language that you can understand? Many professionals (including lawyers) use all the technical terms they can so their clients think they are doing terribly complicated and expensive work. Others talk that way because it's a habit. If there is ever anything you don't understand, ask for an explanation. Your lawyer must have a good reason for doing something, and she or he may not. *Ask. And keep asking until you get a satisfactory answer.*

In most situations, you will probably have several options. Your lawyer should let you know what the choices are and discuss possible consequences. However, you should determine what your own goals and priorities are. Your lawyer is there to advise you, but it is your choice and you have to live with the consequences of the decision. It may be helpful to bring a friend when you see your lawyer. Remember that most decisions don't have to be made there in the lawyer's office. If you need time to think something over, take it.

Few lawyers have all the above qualities—good reputation, valuable experience, empathetic attitudes, reasonable fees, willingness to communicate. Depending on your situation and your goals, some qualities will be more important to you than others. We hope that as we become better consumers of legal services, the law will seem less mysterious, lawyers will become people just like the rest of us, and fees will drop.

1906. Elsie Parsons, noted American anthropologist and sociologist, publishes *The Family* which, despite its scholarly tone, provokes the angry cries of clergymen and politicians for its advocacy of trial marriage. In 1913 Mrs. Parsons will write *The Old-Fashioned Woman,* a popular book which holds that society begins the artificial subordination of women even in the nursery.

How to Write Your Own Marriage Contract

Susan Edmiston

First we thought marriage was when Prince Charming came and took you away with him. Then we thought that marriage was orange blossoms and Alencon lace and silver patterns. Then we thought that marriage—at least—was when you couldn't face signing the lease on the new apartment in two different names.

But most of us never even suspected the truth. Nobody ever so much as mentioned that what marriage is, at its very heart and essence, is a contract. When you say "I do," what you are doing is not, as you thought, vowing your eternal love, but rather subscribing to a whole system of rights, obligations and responsibilities that may very well be anathema to your most cherished beliefs.

Worst of all, you never even get to read the contract—to say nothing of the fine print. If you did, you probably wouldn't agree to it. Marriage, as it exists today, is a perculiarly vague, and yet inflexible, arrangement of institutionalized inequality which goes only one step beyond the English common-law concept of husband and wife as one, and, as the saying goes, "that 'one' is the husband." We have progressed from the notion of wife as legal nonentity to the notion of wife as dependent and inferior.

In recent years, many people have taken to writing their own marriage ceremonies in a desperate attempt to make the institution more relevant to their own lives. But ceremonies, they are finding, do not reach the heart of the matter. So some couples are now taking the logical next step of drawing up their own contracts. These agreements may delineate any of the financial or personal aspects of the marriage relationship— from who pays which bills to who uses what birth control. Though many of their provisions may not be legally binding, at the very least they can help us to examine the often inchoate assumptions underlying our relationships, help us come to honest and equitable terms with one another, and provide guidelines for making our marriages what we truly want them to be.

Before their first child was born, Alix Kates Shulman and her husband had an egalitarian, partnership marriage. Alix worked full time as

1906. Goldie Mabovitz (to be known later as Golda Meir) is head of her class at Milwaukee's Fourth Street elementary school. The family emigrated to Wisconsin from Russia.

an editor in New York, and both shared the chores involved in maintaining their small household. After two children, however, the couple found that they had automatically fallen into the traditional sex roles: he went out and worked all day to support his family; she stayed home and worked from 6 a.m. to 9 p.m. taking care of children and housework. Unthinkingly, they had agreed not only to the legalities of marriage but to the social contract as well.

After six years at home—six years of chronic dissatisfaction—Alix became involved in the Women's Liberation movement and realized that it might be possible to change the contract under which she and her husband lived. The arrangement they worked out (see below), basically a division of household duties and child care, rejected "the notion that the work which brings in more money is more valuable. The ability to earn . . . money is a privilege which must not be compounded by enabling the larger earner to buy out of his/her duties."

Sitting down and writing out a contract may seem a cold and formal way of working out an intimate relationship, but often it is the only way of coping with the ghosts of 2,000 years of tradition lurking in our definitions of marriage. Now, after three years, Alix has written six books, and both Shulmans find that their agreement is a new way of life rather than a document to be followed legalistically.

Agreements to disagree with the common marriage mores are nothing new. They have their roots in a fine old tradition that probably began with Mary Wollstonecraft, that first feminist of us all, who in 1792 wrote *A Vindication of the Rights of Women*. Though Mary and her husband, English essayist and political theorist William Godwin, submitted to marriage, it was on their own terms. Godwin took an apartment about twenty doors from the couple's house to which he "repaired" every morning. A letter of the time describes this arrangement: "In order to give the connection as little as possible the appearance of such a vulgar and debasing tie as matrimony, the parties have established separate establishments, and the husband only visits his mistress like a lover when each is dressed, rooms in order, etc." The couple agreed that it was wrong for husband and wife to have to be together whenever they went out into "mixed society" and therefore, as Godwin writes, "rather sought occasions of deviating from, than of complying with, this rule."

The ultimate feminist contract, however, was the one Lucy Stone and Henry Blackwell wrote when they married in 1855. Their agreement is a concise catalogue of the legal inequities of marriage in America at that time *(box, right)*.

While it is obvious that we have made some progress since Lucy Stone's day, in many ways we are still living under the heritage of the kind of laws she deplored. The American institution of marriage derives from English common law, which developed a peculiar concept, unknown on the Continent, called the "unity of spouses." As Blackstone put it, "By marriage, the husband and wife are one person in law; that is, the very being or legal existence of the woman is suspended during marriage, or at least is incorporated or consolidated into that of the husband."

Beginning in 1839, one version or another of what was called the Married Women's Property Act was passed in each state of the Union, correcting some of the gross injustices of marriage. Most of these laws granted married women the right to contract, to sue and be sued without joining their husbands, to manage and control the property they brought with them to marriage, to engage in gainful employment and retain the earnings derived from it. Like a case of bad genes, however, the fiction of the unity of the spouses has never quite gone away. Hus-

---

THE SHULMANS' MARRIAGE AGREEMENT

I. Principles.

We reject the notion that the work which brings in more money is more valuable. The ability to earn more money is a privilege which must not be compounded by enabling the larger earner to buy out of his/her duties and put the burden on the partner who earns less or on another person hired from outside.

We believe that each partner has an equal right to his/her own time, work, values, choices. As long as all duties are performed, each of us may use his/her extra time any way he/she chooses. If he/she wants to use it making money, fine. If he/she wants to spend it with spouse, fine.

As parents we believe we must share all responsibility for taking care of our children and home—and not only the work but also the responsibility. At least during the first year of this agreement, *sharing responsibility* shall mean dividing the *jobs* and dividing the *time*.

II. Job Breakdown and Schedule

(A) Children

1. Mornings: Waking children; getting their clothes out; making their lunches; seeing that they have notes, homework, money, bus passes, books; brushing their hair; giving them breakfast (making coffee for us). Every other week each parent does all.

2. Transportation: Getting children to and from lessons, doctors, dentists (including making appointments), friends' houses, etc. Parts occurring between 3 and 6 p.m. fall to wife. She must be compensated by extra work from husband (see 10 below). Husband does all weekend transportation and pick-ups after 6.

3. Help: Helping with homework, personal questions; explaining things. Parts occurring between 3 and 6 p.m. fall to wife. After 6 p.m. husband does Tuesday, Thursday and Sunday; wife does Monday, Wednesday and Saturday. Friday is free for whoever has done extra work during the week.

4. Nighttime (after 6 p.m.): Getting children to take baths, brush their teeth, put away their toys and clothes, go to bed; reading with them;

tucking them in and having nighttime talks; handling if they wake in the night. Husband does Tuesday, Thursday and Sunday. Wife does Monday, Wednesday and Saturday. Friday is split according to who has done extra work.

5. Baby sitters: Baby sitters must be called by the parent the sitter is to replace. If no sitter turns up, that parent must stay home.

6. Sick care: Calling doctors; checking symptoms; getting prescriptions filled; remembering to give medicine; taking days off to stay home with sick child, providing special activities. This must still be worked out equally, since now wife seems to do it all. In any case, wife must be compensated (see 10 below).

7. Weekends: All usual child care, plus special activities (beach, park, zoo). Split equally. Husband is free all Saturday, wife is free all Sunday.

(B) Housework

8. Cooking: Breakfasts during the week are divided equally; husband does all weekend breakfasts (including shopping for them and dishes). Wife does all dinners except Sunday nights. Husband does Sunday dinner and any other dinners on his nights of responsibility if wife isn't home. Whoever invites guests does shopping, cooking and dishes; if both invite them, split work.

9. Shopping: Food for all meals, housewares, clothing and supplies for children. Divide by convenience. Generally, wife does daily food shopping; husband does special shopping.

10. Cleaning: Husband does dishes Tuesday, Thursday and Sunday. Wife does Monday, Wednesday and Saturday. Friday is split according to who has done extra work during week. Husband does all the housecleaning in exchange for wife's extra child care (3 to 6 daily) and sick care.

11. Laundry: Home laundry, making beds, dry cleaning (take and pick up). Wife does home laundry. Husband does dry-cleaning delivery and pick-up. Wife strips beds, husband remakes them.

Copyright © 1970, 1971 Alix Kates Shulman. Reprinted by permission of Alix Kates Shulman.

1908. Julia Ward Howe becomes the first woman admitted to the select society of the American Academy of Arts and Letters for—among other accomplishments—her "Battle Hymn of the Republic."

418   Marriage Contract
THE LEGAL ADVISER

band and wife today are like Siamese twins: although largely separate persons under the law, they are still joined together in one spot or another. In one state, the wife's ability to contract may still be impaired; in another, she may not have full freedom to use her maiden name; in a third, she may not be considered capable of conspiracy with her husband.

These vestiges of the unity of spouses, however, are not the only ways in which marriage treats man and woman unequally, for we have evolved a different—but still unequal—concept of marriage. Today we regard husband as head of household and wife as housewife; husband as supporter and wife as dependent; husband as authority and wife as faithful helpmeet. This concept of marriage has not been *created* by the law but is an expression of culturally shared values which are *reflected* in the law. It is the conventional notion of marriage consciously embraced or unthinkingly accepted by many, if not most, Americans today.

What's wrong with it? The responsibility of support is commonly thought to favor women at the expense of men; I leave it for men to document how this notion injures them and will only deal here with the disabilities from a woman's point of view. Like all commonly held notions, the idea of marriage as a relationship between supporter and dependent is so much a part of our very atmosphere that it is hard to see it objectively. (To counter this difficulty, many women's groups are suggesting that people wishing to get a marriage license should have to take a test on the laws, as they do to get a driver's license.) Basically, the bargain in today's unwritten marriage contract is that the husband gets the right to the wife's services in return for supporting her. Whereas under common law the husband had "the absolute right to the product of the wife's industry," today the husband has only the absolute right to the product of the wife's industry *within the home.* "The wife's services and society are so essential a part of what the law considers the husband entitled to as part of the marriage," says Harriet Pilpel in *Your Marriage and the Law,* "that it will not recognize any agreement between the spouses which provides that the husband is to pay for such services or society."

The concept of the husband as supporter and wife as dependent underlies all the current legal inequalities of married women. To cite some specific examples:

Property. In common-law property states— like New York—husband and wife each exercise full control of what they own before, or acquire during, the marriage. But the woman who works only inside the home never has a chance to acquire property of her own, and therefore may never have any legitimate interest in, or control of, the family assets. (The only way she

Lucy Stone's Marriage Contract

While acknowledging our mutual affection by publicly assuming the relationship of husband and wife, yet in justice to ourselves and a great principle, we deem it a duty to declare that this act on our part implies no sanction of, nor promise of voluntary obedience to such of the present laws of marriage, as refuse to recognize the wife as an independent, rational being, while they confer upon the husband an injurious and unnatural superiority, investing him with legal powers which no honorable man would exercize, and which no man should possess. We protest especially against the laws which give to the husband:

1. The custody of the wife's person.

2. The exclusive control and guardianship of their children.

3. The sole ownership of her personal, and use of her real estate, unless previously settled upon her, or placed in the hands of trustees, as in the case of minors, lunatics, and idiots.

4. The absolute right to the product of her industry.

5. Also against laws which give to the widower so much larger and more permanent an interest in the property of his deceased wife, than they give to the widow in that of the deceased husband.

6. Finally, against the whole system by which "the legal existence of the wife is suspended during marriage," so that in most States, she neither has a legal part in the choice of her residence, nor can she make a will, nor sue or be sued in her own name, nor inherit property.

We believe that personal independence and equal human rights can never be forfeited, except for crime; that marriage should be an equal and permanent partnership, and so recognized by law; that until it is so recognized, married partners should provide against the radical injustice of present laws, by every means in their power.

We believe that where domestic difficulties arise, no appeal should be made to legal tribunals under existing laws, but that all difficulties should be submitted to the equitable adjustment of arbitrators mutually chosen.

Thus reverencing law, we enter our protest against rules and customs which are unworthy of the name, since they violate justice, the essence of law.

(Signed), Henry B. Blackwell, Lucy Stone.

1909. Cigarette smoking gains tentative favor among women of the upper classes and in eastern colleges, despite vocal opposition by women's clubs, reform organizations, churchmen, and masculinity in general.

can acquire property is by gift, which makes her subject to her husband's patronage.) As John Gay said in *The Beggar's Opera*, "The comfortable estate of widowhood is the only hope that keeps up a wife's spirits." Her situation is improved by her husband's death; in every common-law property state, each spouse has a non-barrable interest in the estate of the other. However, this sometimes adds up to very little. For instance, in New Jersey, a wife only has "dower rights"; if her husband dies, she is entitled to one-third of the income from his real property. If the couple lived in an apartment and didn't own any real estate, the law guarantees her nothing.

Even in six of the eight community-property states where the spouses share equally in the property acquired during the marriage, the husband is given management control. Thus a woman may earn as much as her husband and have no say in how her money is spent. In the two exceptions, Washington and Texas, husband and wife have separate control of the property each acquires. Even this arrangement leaves the non-earning spouse without any control of the purse strings.

Name. In many states the law deprives the wife of full freedom to use her own name: in Illinois in 1965 when a woman sought the right to vote although she had not registered under her married name, the Appellate Court said she couldn't. In a recent case, a three-judge Federal court upheld the Alabama law requiring a woman to assume her husband's surname upon marriage by ruling that a married woman does not have a right to have her driver's license issued in her maiden name. In Michigan, if a man changes his last name his wife must also change hers; she may not contest the change, although the couple's minor children over the age of sixteen may do so.

Domicile. Domicile is a technical term sometimes defined as a "place where a person has a settled connection for certain legal purposes." (You can live in one place and be domiciled in another.) Domicile affects various legal rights and obligations, including where a person may vote, hold public office, serve on juries, receive welfare, qualify for tuition advantages at state educational institutions, be liable for taxes, have his or her estate administered, and file for divorce. In general, a wife's domicile automatically follows that of her husband and she has no choice in the matter. (NOW members are currently challenging this law in North Carolina.)

The husband, generally, also has had the right to decide where he and his wife live, although recently he has been required to make a reasonable decision taking her wishes into account. The burden of proving she is reasonable, however, still rests with the wife.

To some women the loss of these rights may seem a small price to pay for support. In fact, the arrangement works out differently depending on economic class. The higher up the ladder her husband is, the better a woman is supported and the fewer services she gives in return. For the many millions of women who work outside the home, on the other hand, the bargain is not a terribly good one: in reality all they earn for the services they give their husbands is the responsibility of working outside the home as well as in it to help their families survive. These women learn another price they pay for the illusion of support—the low salaries they receive compared with men's are ironically justified by the argument that the "men have families to feed." This is not the fault of husbands but of a society that has structured its economy on the unpaid services of women.

But the heaviest price those women who accept the role of dependent pay is a psychological one. Economic dependency is in itself corrupting, as can be seen in rawest form in country-and-Western songs of the "I-know-he's-being-untrue-but-I-never-confront-him-with-it-because-if-he-left-me-who-would-support-the-children" variety. And economic dependency breeds other kinds of dependency. The woman who has no established legal right in the family income fares better or worse depending on how well she pleases the head of the household. In the attempt to please she may surrender her own tastes, her own opinions, her own thoughts. If she habitually defers to or depends on her husband's decisions she will eventually find herself incapable of making her own.

The solution is not that wives should never work in the home or that husbands should not share their incomes with them. The solution is that we must begin to recognize that the work wives do belongs to them, not their husbands, and should be accorded a legitimate value. If wives make the contribution of full partners in their marriages, they should receive the rights of partners—not only, like slaves, the right to be housed, clothed and fed, or in other words, supported. This is hardly a new idea: in 1963 the Report of the President's Commission on the Status of Women recommended that "during marriage each spouse should have a legally defined right in the earnings of the other, in the real and personal property acquired through these earnings, and in their management."

There is, however, hope of progress. Although the Uniform Marriage and Divorce Act drafted by the National Conference of Commissioners on Uniform State Laws has not yet been adopted anywhere (Colorado has adopted the divorce portion of the law), it embraces some of the principles of marriage as partnership. It would make irremediable breakdown of the marriage the only ground for divorce, institute

1910. Eleanora Sears, sportswoman and pedestrian, walks the 110 miles between Burlingame, California, and Del Monte in twenty-eight hours, fifteen minutes. Later, in a race between Boston, Massachusetts, and Providence, Rhode Island, she easily outdistances her two male competitors, finishing in under ten hours.

a division of property based on the assumption that husband and wife have contributed equally to the marriage, and determine custody according to the best interests of the child without the traditional bias in favor of the mother.

Should the Equal Rights Amendment be passed, it may require that most of the inequalities in the marriage relationship be abolished. According to an analysis published recently in *The Yale Law Journal*, the amendment should give women the freedom to use any name they wish, give them the same independent choice of domicile that married men have now, invalidate laws vesting management of community property in the husband alone, and prohibit enforcement of sex-based definitions of conjugal function. "Courts would not be able to assume for any purpose that women had a legal obligation to do housework, or provide affection and companionship, or to be available for sexual relations, unless men owed their wives exactly the same duties. Similarly, men could not be assigned the duty to provide financial support simply because of their sex." Even should the amendment pass, however, it will take years of action in the courts to implement it. Meanwhile, perhaps the best we can do is to say with Lucy Stone and Henry Blackwell that while we wish to acknowledge our mutual affection by publicly assuming the relationship of husband and wife, we do not promise obedience to those laws that discriminate against us. And, perhaps, by writing our own contracts we can modify the effect of the laws upon us.

The problem with a husband and wife sitting down together and drafting a legal contract incorporating their beliefs concerning marriage is that the state immediately horns its way into the act. Marriage, contrary to popular belief, is more *ménage à trois* than *folie à deux*. It is a contract to which the state is a third party, and though you and your spouse may be in perfect accord, there are certain things the state will not tolerate. Most of these things are against what is known as public policy. Under public policy, according to Harriet Pilpel, "the courts, in many states, will not enforce any agreement which attempts to free the husband from the duty of support to the wife. . . . Nor will the courts uphold any agreement which attempts to limit or eliminate the personal or conjugal rights of marriage as distinguished from property rights. An agreement that the parties will not live together after marriage is void. So is an agreement not to engage in sexual intercourse or not to have children. One court has even held that it is against public policy for an engaged couple to agree that they will live in whatever place the wife chooses. Under the law, said the court, that is the "husband's prerogative and he cannot relinquish it." Public

policy also forbids contracts which anticipate divorce in any way. Agreements defining what will happen if a couple divorces or the conditions under which they will divorce are seen as facilitating the dissolution of marriages.

There are certain contracts, called antenuptial agreements, that the state clearly permits us to make. These contracts, according to Judith Boies, a matrimonial and estates lawyer with the New York law firm Paul, Weiss, Rifkind, Wharton & Garrison, may concern property owned before marriage, property acquired after marriage by gift or inheritance, and property rights in each other's estates. A wife cannot waive support, but she can waive interest in her husband's estate.

Some lawyers believe that people should be able to make whatever marriage contracts they like with one another. "Why should marriage be any different from any other contract?" asks constitutional lawyer Kristin Booth Glen, who teaches a course in women's rights at New York University Law School. She believes that the state's intervention in people's marriages may be in violation of Article I, Section 10, of the United States Constitution, which says that the states are forbidden to pass laws "impairing the obligation of contracts." Other lawyers feel that we don't really know which of the contracts we might wish to make concerning marriage would be enforceable. "There will have to be some litigation first,' says Kathleen Carlsson, a lawyer for the Lucy Stone League. "In the light of the new feminist atmosphere, the decisions rendered today might not be the same as those rendered twenty years ago."

Judith Boies concurs with this view and feels that couples should begin right now to make whatever contracts suit their needs. If both spouses are wage-earners, they should contract how money and expenses will be divided. If they decide to have any joint bank accounts, they should sign a written agreement defining in what proportions the money in the account belongs to them. Then if one party cleans out the account—a frequent if unfortunate prelude to divorce—the contract would establish how they had intended to share the property.

Wives often assume—erroneously—that everything their husbands own belongs to them. In the common-law property states, property belongs to the person whose name it is in. When property is jointly owned, half presumably belongs to each spouse. However, this presumption is rebuttable. The husband can claim, for instance, that he and his wife only have a joint account so she can buy groceries.

The second kind of agreement couples might make is one in which the husband agrees to pay the wife a certain amount for domestic services. If there is no money to pay her, the debt accrues from year to year. When money be-

1910. Mabelle Gilman, fabulously wealthy divorcee and celebrated stage star, has a French surgeon transform her generous lips into a cupid's bow known as the "sewn smile." Thousands of other wealthy women follow suit.

Marriage Contract
THE LEGAL ADVISER   421

THE UTOPIAN MARRIAGE CONTRACT

1. The wife's right to use her maiden name or any other name she chooses.

2. What surname the children will have: husband's, wife's, a hyphenated combination, a neutral name or the name the children choose when they reach a certain age.

3. Birth control: Whether or not, what kind and who uses it. (One couple—the wife can't use the Pill—splits the responsibility 50-50. Half the time she uses a diaphragm, the other half he uses a condom.)

4. Whether or not to have children, or to adopt them, and if so how many.

5. How the children will be brought up.

6. Where the couple will live: Will the husband be willing to move if the wife gets a job offer she wants to take? Separate bedrooms? Separate apartments?

7. How child care and housework will be divided: The spouse who earns less should not be penalized for the inequities of the economic world by having to do a larger share.

8. What financial arrangement will the couple embrace? If husband and wife are both wage-earners, there are three basic possibilities:

    a) Husband and wife pool their income, pay expenses and divide any surplus. (This was Leonard and Virginia Woolf's arrangement. At the end of the year, after payment of expenses, they divided the surplus between them equally so each had what they called a personal "hoard.")

    b) Husband and wife pay shares of expenses proportional to their incomes. Each keeps whatever he or she has left.

    c) Husband and wife each pay 50 per cent of expenses. Each keeps what he or she has left.

If husband earns significantly more than wife, the couple might consider a) that the disparity is a result of sexist discrimination in employment and there should perhaps be some kind of "home reparations program" to offset this inequity, and b) whether the couple really has an equal partnership if one has greater economic strength, and therefore possibly greater power psychologically, in the relationship.

9. Sexual rights and freedoms. Although any arrangement other than monogamy would clearly be against public policy, in practice some people make arrangements such as having Tuesdays off from one another.

10. The husband might give his consent to abortion in advance. —S. E.

comes available, the wife would be a creditor and have first claim on it.

A third kind of financial contract could be made between husband and wife when one spouse puts the other through medical school or any other kind of education or training. The wife could agree to provide the husband with so much money per year to be paid back at a certain rate in subsequent years. This contract has a good chance of being enforceable, since even the tax laws recognize that husbands and wives make loans to one another.

"All these financial contracts have a reasonably good chance of standing up in court," says Judith Boies. The one with the least chance is the one providing payment for household services, although passage of the Equal Rights Amendment might strengthen its position. Since the financial contracts are more likely to be valid than those affecting personal aspects of the marriage, they should be made separately.

Judith Boies believes that, ideally, the personal contracts should also be valid. "The state shouldn't even marry people; it should just favor every contract that makes adequate provision for wife and children." The areas that might be covered in a comprehensive, total, utopian contract might include the wife's right to use the name she chooses, the children's names, division of housework and child care, finances, birth control, whether or not to have children and how many, the upbringing of the children, living arrangements, sexual rights and freedoms, and anything else of importance to the individual couple. (See box at left.)

Since the marriage relationship is not a static one, any contract should permit the couple to solve their problems on a continuing basis. It should be amendable, revisable or renewable.

At this point, many readers are probably thinking, "Why get married at all, why not just draw up a contract that covers all contingencies?" Again, the state got there first. Such an agreement would be considered a contract for the purpose of "meretricious relations," or in other words an illicit sexual relationship, and therefore would be invalid.

Other readers are probably thinking, "But we love each other, so why should we have a contract?" As Barbara Koltuv says, "Part of the reason for thinking out a contract is to find out what your problems are; it forces you to take charge of your life. Once you have the contract, you don't have to refer back to it. The process is what's important."

Whether these contracts are legally enforceable or not, just drawing them up may be of great service to many couples. What we are really doing in thrashing out a contract is finding out where we stand on issues, clearing up all the murky, unexamined areas of conflict, and unflinchingly facing up to our differences.

1911. Madame Marie Curie receives her second Nobel Prize for her work on the chemical isolation of radium. She shared the first award with her husband and another associate.

How to Change or Keep Your Name

Center for a Woman's Own Name

COMMON LAW PROCEDURE FOR NAME CHANGE

If you change your name at marriage to your husband's, no state or federal agency will give you difficulty in changing official records to your new name. Changing your name at marriage to your husband's is an example of a *common law* change of name. Your new name will be quickly recognized.

If you assume your husband's surname at marriage, you can still revert to your own name, take another name or hyphenate your name with your husband's *without formal court proceedings*. This is also a *common law* change of name. Because most women use their husbands' names, you may have more difficulty getting a name differing from that of your husband's recognized.

A woman who changes her name from that of her husband by the common law method of name change should systematically amass as much identification in the new name as possible to evidence to government officials that she is now identified by such name. In many states this is difficult once a woman has taken her husband's surname.

Deborah Taylor

Changing Identification

The following recommended procedure for women who have changed their names out of court after first using their husbands' names and who wish to procure new records is based on the laws and practices of Wisconsin, Illinois, Pennsylvania, and California agencies and institutions (states will differ).

1. Change your Social Security card.
2. Change your state university registration.
3. Change your driver's license and car registration.

After receiving the above identification,
4. Change your employment records and accompanying insurance, retirement policies, etc. (The Social Security Administration requests that one's card be in the name in which one works. Thus, sometimes employment records are most easily changed immediately after the changing of one's Social Security card.)
5. Change bank accounts, credit cards, leases, etc. (It is sometimes easiest to change these records first.)
   State and federal departments of revenue, all other creditors and interested parties should be notified of the change of name.

Although you can call yourself whatever you wish in any state, if you do so with no intent to defraud, some state and federal agencies have been known to give women difficulty in changing official records from their husbands' surnames (without a court order). If you have such difficulties, you may wish to consider taking the following legal action:

1. Go to court for a change or retention of name by court decree.
2. Appeal the decision of the administrative agent *within* the agency. Your state may require that you do this within a short period of time. You may also *have* to appeal the decision—exhaust administrative remedies— before you *can* go to court.

1912. Virginia Brooks, militant antivice crusader, after threatening fifty saloonkeepers in her Hammond, Indiana, neighborhood with hatchet brigades of aroused women, travels to Chicago where she leads a parade of over five thousand hymn-singing women and children through a torrential downpour.

3. If the agency rules against you, have the decision reviewed by a court (here again, time limits may be important), or

4. Go directly to court to compel the agent to perform his/her legal duty by what is commonly referred to as actions for declaratory judgment, writ of mandamus, and/or injunction (if all the legal prerequisites are present).

When dealing with government agencies, remember that government computers may not be programed to accept hyphenated names. If you prefer to use a hyphenated name, insist that agencies hand-type your records (as is done by the Wisconsin Division of Motor Vehicles).

State Agency's Change of Name Instructions

Office of the Secretary of State
Memorandum

TO: All Field Personnel   January 24, 1974
FROM: George D. Sibons
SUBJECT: Name Changes

The purpose of this memo is to clarify procedures relative to a request for a name change. Illinois revised statutes *do not* preclude a person from changing his or her name if the name change is not for the purpose of defrauding any person or entity or for any illegal purpose. The procedure for making application for a duplicate Illinois drivers license reflecting a name change is as follows:

1. The duplicate application is to be completed reflecting the requested name change.
2. The duplicate application must reflect the person's present Illinois drivers license number and/or the person's complete name and date of birth as shown on the person's previous application.
3. The duplicate application must be accompanied by the required statutory fee of $3.00 and the previous drivers license must be surrendered.
4. If for some reason the applicant is unable to surrender the original license, a full explanation is required.
5. Temporary drivers licenses are to be issued reflecting the requested name change.

The following procedures are to be adhered to when completing the preprinted renewal notice when a name change is requested.

1. A renewal notice is to be completed reflecting the requested name change in the space provided for in "Corrections."
2. Note in remarks, "Note Name Change."

The following procedures are to be adhered to when completing the field renewal exam form when a name change is requested.

1. The application must reflect the answer to the following question: Has the driver previously held a drivers license and if so from this state or any other state? If answered in the affirmative, list the state, country, approximate date of expiration, name and birthdate on that application.
2. In order to maintain the integrity of the files maintained by the Drivers License Division, a supplementary identification will be required on the field application. (Two supplementary documents of identification.)
3. The space provided for identification on field applications must be completed.

1912. Margaret Sanger abandons her nursing career – during which she had witnessed the tragedies wrought by unwanted pregnancy and childbirth among the poor of New York City – to pursue the cause of birth control. Though distributing contraceptive data through the mails is forbidden at the time by the Comstock Act (which classifies such information as obscene), in 1914 she will publish her magazine, *Women Rebel*, provoking

COURT PROCEDURE

If you wish to have your name changed in court, the procedure is often easy and should not require a lawyer. A judge may, however, treat your request as a trivial one and refuse to act on it until you prove your "seriousness" by hiring an attorney. In other cases, a judge may be particularly prejudiced and hostile to the idea of a woman having a name different from that of her husband, even when the husband agrees. Judges have denied petitions. Some are being appealed. One denial in Indiana has been upheld by a higher court while other petitions in that state have been and are being granted.

If your name change is denied, you can appeal. Find out from the clerk of court if other name-change petitions have been granted in the county where you are filing and by the judge hearing your case. If similar petitions have not been granted or have been denied by your judge or others in your county, you should contact a knowledgeable and sympathetic attorney to help you construct a good record on the first petition in case an appeal is necessary.

We are trying to avoid attorney fees and exercise our right to represent ourselves without critical comment, humiliation, or discouragement from clerks, lawyers and judges.

The procedure in Massachusetts is as follows (procedures vary in different states):

1. Locate the probate court in your district and pick up the necessary papers—petition and filing card—at the clerk's office. The clerks may be rude to you, but you do not have to account to them. They must give you the papers you request.
2. Some counties require you to publish your intent to change your name in a local paper.
3. Fill out the papers and explain your reasons for wanting to change your name. (Some state statutes do not require a reason.) When listing your reasons, do not stress political reasons because the court is not supposed to be a forum for political views. Emphasize individual reasons such as personal preference.
4. File your papers with your birth certificate at the clerk's office.
5. Find out your court date. On that day you may need to sign your name to the day's cases.
6. Your case will be called by the clerk of probate court. You then go before the judge. He may ask you some questions—if you have any children, if your husband consents, etc.—and upon the basis of your answers to his questions and your petition he will either grant or reject your petition.
7. To ensure that your name change is granted, have your husband sign his name below yours on your petition. This is not legally necessary but is preferred by most judges.[*] If your husband accompanies you to court, your name change will be almost certain to be granted. Often judges are prejudiced against women who appear alone in court. To make the court experience less threatening, bring someone with you even if your husband cannot be the one.

[*]"I have just handled a change of name petition for a married woman who wanted to have a court order changing her name to her maiden surname (she also wanted a change of given name).

"While the Montana statute gives the judge discretion (and no guidelines) about granting a change of name petition, the district judge involved took the position that apparently one can use any name one wishes. The husband was in the court room and would have supported the petition, if necessary, but I did not want to call him unless the judge insisted. The statute does not require consent (except in the case of a minor) and I felt it would make things difficult for other women if we volunteered his consent. The judge made no inquiry about his position at all—although he did inquire about children so he was aware there is an on-going marriage." (Attorney Emilie Loring, Montana, 1974.)

the first of several run-ins with the law. Over the next twenty-five years, Mrs. Sanger is to found a number of birth control organizations, among them the Planned Parenthood Federation. In 1953 she will carry her cause to the Far East as president of the International Planned Parenthood Federation.

● If your husband mistreats you physically or threatens to harm you, can you do anything?

Definitely. Your lawyer can go to court immediately and get a court order forbidding your husband to do these things. If your husband persists, he can be thrown into jail for disobeying the court order. If you have the feeling that your husband is all-powerful, just remember that he is not. In this situation, the law will be on your side.

● Does the husband have the right to kick his wife out of the house?

No. Courts will almost always allow the wife to remain in the house, and you can legally enforce this right the same way you enforce your right to physical safety.

● Is it all right to sleep with your husband once you have decided to get a divorce?

Never. First, in many states sleeping with your husband may prevent you from getting the divorce at all. If you have established your husband's adultery as grounds for divorce, sleeping with him after the adultery occurred is legally construed as forgiving him for his actions. Thus you lose your right to divorce him.

Second, even if the divorce is uncontested (so that you don't need to prove adultery, or any other grounds for divorce, in court), the fact that you do have strong legal grounds for divorce can put you in a strong bargaining position in negotiations over the details of the divorce. You may, for example, get a better settlement on issues like child custody and alimony simply because your husband's lawyer knows you would win in court on the question of the divorce itself. Thus your husband may have even been advised to sleep with you for just this reason: to destroy your legal grounds for divorce and thereby weaken your position in the negotiations.

● Should the woman ever pay alimony?

Yes, if she has the greater wage-earning capacity, and if the husband has taken and will continue to take the primary burden for rearing the children. If the partners are equal in both respects, presumably neither should pay alimony and each should pay an equal proportion of the child-support costs.

New York Public Library

● What kinds of expenses does alimony cover?

Alimony covers household and personal expenses, work-related costs, training and educational expenses, and recreation for the spouse.

● Is a woman entitled to child-support payments?

Of course, if she has custody of the children. Again, women should not hesitate to ask that the husband contribute his fair share. Recent studies have shown that women usually contribute a greater share of child-support costs than do their husbands.

● What should be included in child support?

The standard items are fairly obvious: food, clothing, shelter, education, medicine, medical insurance (it is usually cheaper for the kids to stay on the husband's Blue Cross program). If it is financially feasible, one should also negotiate for the costs of a college education and even the cost of graduate school (although the latter is hard to get).

● Should you negotiate with your husband about alimony, child support, property, or other matters before seeing your own lawyer?

Emphatically not. You should know your rights before making any agreement—financial or otherwise. You might be entitled to much more than you realize, or you might not have seriously analyzed your future situation—and it is always best to have the facts before making a decision.

1912. Juliette Gordon Low founds the Girl Guides, later to become the Girl Scouts. Also in this year, Mrs. Luther Halsey Gulick and her husband found the Camp Fire Girls at Lake Sebago, Maine.

about Divorce
Susan Ross

● **Should you leave your money or securities in a joint account if you are thinking about a divorce or you suspect your husband wants a divorce?**

No. Take out the money you think is your own. Men are often advised to take all the money out of a joint account as a way of preventing their wives from getting any of it. If you have even the slightest suspicion that your husband would do such a thing, out of bitterness or anger, and if you need the money, it is best to take precautionary measures.

● **If your husband has cleaned out the joint savings or checking account, or sold joint property, is there anything you can do?**

Yes. Your lawyer can get a court order forcing your husband to reimburse you in a property settlement. If he has not taken property or funds, but you suspect he plans to do so, your lawyer can also get an order forbidding any such action. This would prevent your husband from removing or selling any assets until the divorce.

Statistics on Alimony and Child Support

The following table is based on data gathered by Kenneth Eckhardt from a sample of fathers who were ordered to pay some child support in a divorce decree in a metropolitan county in the State of Wisconsin in 1955.

One man's-eye view of alimony

New York Public Library

Row 1 shows that within one year after the divorce decree, only 38 percent of the fathers were in full compliance with the support order. Twenty percent had only partially complied, and in some cases partial compliance only constituted a single payment. Forty-two percent of the fathers made no payment at all. By the tenth year, the number of open cases had dropped from 163 to 149 as a result of the death of the father, the termination of his parental rights, or the maturity of the children. By that year, only 13 percent of the fathers were fully complying, and 79 percent of the fathers were in total non-compliance. Row 5 shows the percentage of non-paying fathers against whom legal action was taken, including those taken or instigated by welfare authorities:

Years since court order	No. of cases	Compliance Full	Partial	No	Non-paying fathers-legal action taken
One	163	38%	20%	42%	19%
Two	163	28	20	52	32
Three	161	26	14	60	21
Four	161	22	11	67	18
Five	160	19	14	67	9
Six	158	17	12	71	6
Seven	157	17	12	71	4
Eight	155	17	8	75	2
Nine	155	17	8	75	0
Ten	149	13	8	79	1

From *Women in 1971*, Citizen's Advisory Council on the Status of Women, Washington, D.C.

1912. Sixty-one-year-old mountain climber Annie Peck becomes the first person to ascend Peru's Mount Coropuna (elevation: 21,250 feet). At the head of her poorly equipped and exhausted party, she plants a "Votes for Women" pennant on the summit.

Family Law

Sylvia D. Garland and Margaret S. Bearn

THE LAW AND LIVING TOGETHER

Are you and he just living together?

Don't let him tell you that sharing bed and board can bloom into a common-law marriage with the added security that would mean for you. Most states require specific civil procedures for you to be legally married. However, most of these states *do* recognize a common-law marriage if it was consummated in a state where this kind of marriage is valid.

Breaking up?

As a rule, you keep the furniture and other things you bought and he takes what he bought. If he refuses to give back your couch and you cannot shame him into compliance, you might try the Small Claims Court.

New York Public Library

Can you marry simply by mutual consent?

Absolutely not! The marriage relationship is regulated by the state. Each state has its own laws prescribing how and by whom a marriage may be solemnized—as well as how it may be dissolved.

Are you divorced and thinking of living with a man—or remarrying?

Check the terms of your decree and any agreement relating to custody, child support and, especially, ali-

mony. Alimony stops when you remarry unless there is a specific provision to the contrary in a written separation agreement. Sometimes child support also ends if you marry again. To keep the alimony coming, some divorced women just live with a man instead of marrying him. That is why more and more husbands getting divorces now insist on a provision stating that alimony will stop in such cases.

THE LAW AND ENDING A MARRIAGE

● SEPARATION

What is the purpose of a separation agreement?

The main one is to fix the property rights of wife and husband: alimony, child support, division of assets and obligations, mutual promises not to make claims against the other's estate. It may provide for custody of children and visitation rights, and for use or disposition of the marital home. Its terms may be incorporated in a divorce decree if it comes to that. These are matters far too serious to handle without a lawyer no matter how eager you are to cooperate with your husband in going your separate ways.

In New York, you can get a divorce on the basis of one year of living "separate and apart" from the time a separation agreement has been filed with the County Clerk. In those cases, adultery will not be considered unless the separation agreement forbids it. As a matter of fact, agreements are now being filed which specify that neither party will start divorce proceedings against the other on the basis of unchastity. It is also not uncommon for couples to agree on separation for a limited period with the same social privileges as if unmarried. But there may be trouble enforcing such agreements on the ground that they are against public policy—the concept of the fundamental public good underlying law.

● DIVORCE

What do you have to prove to get a divorce?

That depends on where you live. Many states used to require proof of adultery, but in recent times more lenient divorce laws have been widely adopted. Also, only a small percentage of divorces—10 or 15 per cent—are contested. Husband and wife usually agree through their at-

torneys on the tamest grounds allowed by law, for instance, incompatibility or a prescribed period of separation. More lurid grounds in various states include—besides adultery—sodomy, cruel and inhuman treatment, physical violence, abandonment, conviction of a felony, imprisonment, drunkenness, nonsupport, impotence, incurable insanity and communication of a venereal disease.

If your divorce is contested, and your husband can prove, say, that you committed adultery as well as he, the court may deny the divorce. The same goes if your husband can prove that you had sexual relations with him of your own free will *after* you found out that he had committed adultery.

What if you refuse to have sex with your husband?

That in itself is not grounds for divorce, but it can be used to prove abandonment of the marriage, or cruel and inhuman treatment if the enforced abstinence had such a traumatic effect on your husband that he needed professional care. A total sexual boycott—without a reasonable excuse like illness or childbirth—has been considered justification for the jilted spouse to walk out.

How fast can you get a divorce?

That usually depends on where the action is brought and whether you and your husband can agree in advance on the financial settlement. (A contested action may take years.) Some states require only 60 or 90 days residence before the divorce papers can be filed. It is only six weeks in Nevada, Idaho and the Virgin Islands; most states require a year.

Are foreign quickie divorces still available?

Mexico scratched its permissive one-day residency requirement for divorce a few years ago, but you can still get instant service in Haiti and the Dominican Republic. Usually only one spouse appears; the other is represented by local counsel. You could sign a separation agreement, get your husband to sign a form authorizing his representation by a Haitian attorney, and, armed with both documents, proof of citizenship, and a plane ticket, spend a night in Haiti, meet your Haitian lawyer in court the next day, fly home, and have your decree in the mail within the week.

1912. International marriages between impoverished English noblemen and title-crazed American heiresses have become so common that by this year the British peerage lists three duchesses, one marchioness, six countesses, and three baronesses as born in America.

Are foreign divorces valid in the United States?

That depends on who attacks them. If your husband consented to the divorce, he is usually in no position to complain. But anyone affected by the decree who did not consent to the court's jurisdiction may attack the divorce on the ground that you went abroad for the sole purpose of obtaining it. The safer course is to consult an attorney where you live and follow the divorce laws of your state.

● *ANNULMENT*

Can a marriage be annulled even after children?

Yes. And the children are legitimate. You can get child support and alimony just as in a divorce.

When can a marriage be annulled?

Like any other contract, a marriage can be annulled if either party was under age, or if force, duress, or deliberate misrepresentation was used to bring it about. For instance, you could have your marriage annulled if your husband refused to adopt your religious faith after having promised before the marriage to do so; or if he refused to have children and had not told you of this before you were married; or if he did not tell you in advance about a drug addiction, a chronic venereal disease, or a criminal record. A bride today, need we say, does not have to be a virgin, so that concealment of premarital frolics or even an illegitimate child are not grounds for annulment. But if you were pregnant by another man at the time of your wedding and did not tell your husband-to-be, that would be enough for him to have the marriage annulled. If he knew about your pregnancy, there would be no deception and no grounds for annulment.

● *RECONCILIATION*

Want to get back together again?

If you are separated, no remarriage is needed. If you are divorced, you just get married all over again and have a second honeymoon.

● *MONEY MATTERS*

How is alimony decided?

It depends on what he has, what you need, and what you are both used to. A caution: if you are at fault, you will not get any alimony in most states. In fact, you might have to pay it to him —there is no law against this and some courts have gone ahead and asked the women to get out her checkbook if she is very wealthy.

Lump sums?

One thing a lawyer will tell your husband is not to promise you a lump-sum settlement except if and when you get married again. The reason is this: if you get a lump sum, run through it, and are about to go on relief, he will have to help support you—divorce or no divorce. Incidentally, if you have money, you will have to help an ex-husband who has gone broke.

What if he fails or refuses to pay alimony or child support?

If he does not comply with a court order directing payment, he may be punished for contempt of court by a fine and, in some cases, a short jail sentence. You can, of course, sue him for arrears, and the sheriff may attach and sell his property to satisfy the judgment. If he is working or has any investments, you would be entitled to have the sheriff attach at least 10 per cent of his total income.

Does alimony or child support continue after your ex-husband dies?

No, unless you have a written agreement which compels his estate to make such payments.

Do you have to pay income taxes on alimony and child support?

You do have to pay taxes on alimony. Quite a few divorced women are not aware of this, and get into a lot of trouble with the IRS. Add the alimony to your own taxable income when filing your return. You should check with your lawyer or accountant to see if you must pay taxes on child support—it depends on the terms of the arrangement.

● *LIFE INSURANCE*

Can you lose out on your husband's life insurance after divorce?

Absolutely. If he owns the policy, he can change the beneficiary without your consent or knowledge. If you own it, he cannot. Quite aside from divorce, there is a big advantage to your owning the policy: you get the proceeds free of estate taxes if your husband dies. Otherwise it is part of his taxable estate.

Can the court make your husband keep you as beneficiary?

Not usually. But you could ask to be made the irrevocable beneficiary as part of the separation agreement.

● *INHERITANCE*

Can you inherit from your ex-husband's estate?

Generally not, unless he has written a new will after the divorce and named you as a legatee. Otherwise, you have no claim against his estate.

Can you inherit from your husband's estate after separation?

Yes, unless you were declared the guilty party in a separation action or you waived your right to inherit in a separation agreement.

THE LAW AND BEING A SINGLE PARENT

● *CUSTODY*

Do you usually get custody of the children in a divorce?

Usually, but not always. If the children are young and their father cannot prove that living with you would harm them, the court will award you custody. If the children are older, they are usually consulted, and the court often abides by their wishes.

Who determines visitation rights?

If the parents cannot agree, the court decides. Liberal visitation is encouraged unless it can be proved that it would have an adverse effect on the child or children.

ca. **1913.** The Settlement House (or Hull House) group is gradually drawn into the arenas of local, national, and even international social and political action programs on the behalf of the poor and disenfranchised, such as immigrants and women. In her drive toward the equality of all peoples, Jane Addams speaks and lobbies extensively for

• CHILD SUPPORT

How long is a father required to support his children?

As a rule, until they are 21. But his obligation may end earlier if the child marries or is working and self-supporting. If the child is over 21 but still at college and in need of support, the father will be liable to the extent that he is able to provide it.

When are you liable for child support?

You may become liable if the father is dead, missing or incapable of providing support. If a child is unable to support himself even past the age of 21, or is about to become a public charge, both parents are held liable for his support.

Is it worth making a will if your estate is small?

Definitely, especially if you have young children. Naming a guardian may be the most important thing: it is your only chance to decide who would raise your children and take care of their property if you should die. It is wise to review your will every few years just for that.

If you leave everything to your children, how do you know they won't spend it foolishly while they are young?

You don't know. That is why it may be advisable to leave your property in the hands of a trustee you appoint in your will. Guardianship ends when the child is 21, but the trust may continue for as long as you wish. Depending on its terms, the income or principal may go to your children in stages. •

• ILLEGITIMATE CHILDREN

Are you worried about a child born out of wedlock?

Illegitimate children have the same legal rights as those born to married couples. The child's natural father can be compelled to pay for the child's support, and the illegitimate child can inherit from his father's estate —as well as from yours. However, it must first be determined by the court, in a paternity action, that this man is actually the father.

Who may start a paternity action?

The child's natural mother or guardian; or any other person having custody of the child or a parental interest (even the father himself); or a social or welfare agency. If you consent to the adoption of an illegitimate child, you cannot later bring a paternity action against the natural father, either for child support prior to the adoption or for reimbursement of pregnancy and delivery expenses.

• ADOPTION

What are your rights if you give your child up for adoption?

Generally, you will be permitted to determine the religion of the adopting parents. But once you have executed the adoption agreement, it cannot be revoked except under the most extreme and extenuating circumstances. In most cases, the records of the adoption are sealed and neither the natural mother nor the child are ever again able to determine the location of the other. After the adoption, you are relieved of all parental duties and obligations for child support, even if the adopting parents become destitute and the child seems likely to become a public charge. The child loses all right to inherit from you or your family and you lose all right to visit the child or inherit from him or her. The child is regarded as the natural offspring of the adopting parents and is entitled to share in the inheritance of the adopting family.

Can you adopt a child if you are not married?

In most states, an adult— whether married or unmarried —can adopt another person.

Whose consent is required?

The consent of the child is required if he or she is over 14. The consent of both natural parents is needed if the child is legitimate, and only that of the natural mother if the child was born out of wedlock.

THE LAW AND BECOMING A WIDOW

• INHERITANCE

How much of your husband's estate do you normally get?

He can leave you everything he owns by will, and in most states he cannot leave you less than one third. (In community property states, you get at least one half of the property acquired during the marriage.) If there is no will, the amount depends on state law and what other close relatives there are.

Can you be disinherited by your husband?

Only if you have been guilty of misconduct such as abandonment or cruelty during the marriage.

Should your husband make a will?

By all means. (You should make one, too, for that matter.) Statistics show you will probably outlive him. If his estate is small, it may be wise to have it left entirely to you in order that you may use it to carry you through a period of adjustment or, if there are young children, for your support and theirs, without having to account for any part of the estate that would otherwise be held for the children. If the estate is large, your husband should provide that you receive at least 50 per cent of his estate since you can inherit that amount tax free. Your lawyer may recommend that the other half go in trust for your children, with the income to you during your lifetime. If there is no will and you have more than one child, under the laws of most states you will receive only one-third of your husband's estate.

If your husband was killed in an accident, how much can you expect to recover for his death?

That depends on his income and life expectancy. First, however, you must prove that his death was caused by the wrongful act of the party being sued. If successful, you can recover an amount equal to what you would have received from his earnings had he lived a normal life span. Depending on his age, health, training, ability, and position, this can range from very little up to a million dollars or more.

THE LAW AND HOUSING

Are you looking for a house, an apartment or a studio to rent or buy?

A woman living alone, or with a friend or children but without a husband, is often looked at askance by a prospective landlord. Poor risk, he may say. However, many states now have legislation similar to New York's Human Rights Law, which forbids discrimination against women in the sale or leasing of any kind of real estate or housing. The law also prohibits banks and lending institutions from denying, merely because of her sex, a women's application for a loan or mortgage to buy, build or repair a house, apartment or commercial space.

women's suffrage and the cause of world peace. In pursuit of her wide-ranging projects, she works with Carrie Chapman Catt, Grace Abbott, Florence Kelley, and many other outstanding women activists of the early twentieth century.

A Quick Course in Contracts

Carol H. Arber

Many people consider "law" to be a distant and mysterious process involving courts, judges, and lawyers, but having little relationship to themselves in their everyday lives. In fact the opposite is true. We engage in legal transactions daily—and they are not mysterious; they do not require lawyers; they need not bamboozle the ordinary individual if she or he applies some common sense and thought to them.

Most of us rent houses or apartments and sign leases. These are legal transactions. The lease is a contract between a landlord and the tenant. Its length, the amount of rent and conditions of occupancy (no dogs, no noise, etc.) will be set out in the lease, depending on what the landlord and tenant agree upon in advance.

The purchase of merchandise—a television, an electric can opener, an air conditioner—is a legal transaction. In exchange for the purchase price the consumer receives the merchandise and the seller's or manufacturer's agreement about what will be done if the merchandise is defective or breaks down before the warranty has expired.

At one time or another most of us make an agreement of some kind to have services performed. For example, you need your home or apartment painted and you hire someone to do it for an agreed-upon price. That, too, is a legal transaction—a contract.

A contract is defined simply as an agreement between parties by which each party does something or promises to do something in exchange for the other party's doing something or giving a promise to do it. Sometimes we hear a contract called an "agreement." They are the same thing; they must have the same legal elements, or they are not enforceable.

The first requirement to make a binding contract, that is, one that a court would enforce, is that the parties reach an agreement. The contract need not be in writing as long as an agreement has been reached. It sometimes occurs that the parties intend to agree, but some misunderstanding arises as to a basic element of the agreement. After Ms. Jones responds to a store's ad for a sale on color televisions and purchases one television, the store delivers the set and Ms. Jones plugs it in to find

that it is a black-and-white set. She calls the store to tell them that they have not lived up to their part of the agreement. They advertised a color set, and she paid the price for one. The store must live up to its part of the contract by delivering a color set.

Thus, an essential element of any agreement is that both parties knew and agreed about the subject of it. So if Ms. Jones telephones the store to tell them about the misunderstanding, and the store responds by saying that they thought she ordered a black-and-white set, then there is a basic lack of agreement, thus no contract. Ms. Jones gets her money back but loses the bargain television. However, if she's been careful, Ms. Jones will have retained the sales ticket, which will state that she purchased a color set. That sales ticket is strong evidence of the fact that both she and the store "agreed" on the sale to her of a color set.

The other basic element of a contract is that there be "consideration" given by both sides to an agreement. Consideration is something considered by the parties to be of value, even if it is not objectively valuable. If Jim says to Tom, "I promise to give you the first kitten born of my pregnant cat", that is not a contract. It is a promise by one person to another, and it is not enforceable. If, on the other hand, Jim said, "I promise to give you the first-born kitten *if* you promise to give me the first-born puppy of your pregnant dog," and Tom agrees, they have made a contract. Just as money for goods is "consideration," a promise for a promise is "consideration." Consideration is difficult to define because it is not the equivalent of fair value. Courts will not generally consider the adequacy of the value of any consideration given in a contract unless the disparity between what the parties are giving is so great as to render the contract "unconscionable." The courts will not simply step in and say that the used-car dealer charged too much for that heap you bought.

Contracts need not necessarily be in writing to be enforceable. There are some specific types, however, that must be written. For example, a contract involving the sale of land must be in writing. If Susan says to Sally, "I promise to sell you my house in Green Gulch for fifteen thousand dollars," and Sally says she

1913. Georgia ("Tiny") Broadwick is, at nineteen, the first woman to parachute from an airplane.

agrees, this must be committed to in writing in order to be enforceable.

As a practical matter, it is often wise to put agreements in writing so that there can be no question at a later time about what the parties intended and agreed upon. This is probably most important when the contract involves services to be rendered by one party for the other. Then the service, or the labor and materials, should be set forth with care, and the amount of the costs should be clearly stated. The parties may wish to include other provisions with regard to the time in which the contract is to be performed. For example, Mr. and Mrs. Wolfe order slipcovers from the Save-A-Penny slipcover store. Before agreeing to proceed with the work, Mr. and Mrs. Wolfe tell Save-A-Penny that they need the slipcovers by July 3 because they are having a party on July 4. If the timing of the contract is essential to it, then the time should be specified in the written contract that is entered into by the parties. In that way, if Save-A-Penny fails to produce the slipcovers on time, the Wolfes need not accept them.

In some situations the law itself reads into contracts certain obligations of the parties, even though they have not expressly assumed them. This occurs most frequently in the sale of goods. For example, when the law imposes a warranty on the seller and manufacturer, it requires that they be responsible for insuring that the product is safe and adequate for the use for which it is intended. By law, a hair dryer is guaranteed (warranted) to perform its job without burning the hair of the user. The law that codifies these obligations is called the Uniform Commercial Code and is in effect in most states. It also provides minimum time periods for the validity of warranties.

So, consumer be aware: When you buy a new toaster, you will find a card inside the box stating that it provides a "warranty" for six months or one year. The card requests that you sign and return it to the manufacturer so that the warranty will be "effective." Not so! The law has already imposed a warranty—and it is longer than the period stated on the little card. Its duration is set forth in the Uniform Commercial Code. By sending the card in you risk agreeing to shortening the length of the warranty. It is better to disregard the card and rely on the existing legal remedies.

Another type of contract that you may frequently have entered without recognizing as such, is the adhesion contract. Adhesion contracts are found on the back of claim checks, baggage tickets, and parking tickets.

They are called adhesion contracts because they adhere to these transactions; they are not explicitly agreed to but are accepted as part of accepting the service.

For example, Grace is flying to Chicago to spend a year working there and is taking along lots of baggage. At the airport she is given baggage tickets as receipts for her suitcases. When she arrives in Chicago and goes to pick up her luggage, she finds that it is missing. After extensive unsuccessful searching, the airline advises Grace that her luggage cannot be located. When she files a claim for her loss, the airline points out that the amount of her claim is limited by the maximum stated on the back of the baggage ticket. Such limitations have been upheld by the courts.

It is possible to avoid the effect of the form contract that is written on the back of the tickets by pointing out that the value of what is checked exceeds the limitation. If, for example, Grace had notified the airline before accepting the baggage checks, the airline might have agreed to insuring the full value for an additional charge.

Before accepting a ticket or receipt containing a contract, you should be aware of the limitations it may contain. To illustrate: Lenore decides to take her fur coat for cleaning and storage. At the storage company the clerk asks her how much the coat is worth and tells her that the value of the coat determines the cost of storage. Lenore decides to say that the coat is worth less than it really is so that she can save money on the cost of storage. What she does not realize is that if something happens to the coat she will be able to receive only the value of the coat as she declared it and no more. If she states the real value of the coat, she will be able to collect the full amount.

Public places often attempt to limit their responsibility for property of visitors and guests. Signs over coat racks in restaurants that disclaim responsibility for the value of lost or stolen property have been found to be valid. However, if the restaurant or public place has a check room with an attendant who takes the belongings and gives a coat check in return, the disclaimer will not be valid because there is an assumption of responsibility for the belongings.

Hotels, motels, and inns often limit liability to their guests by placing signs in the rooms disclaiming responsibility for valuables unless checked with the management. This type of limitation will be considered valid if the hotel or inn makes available vault or safe-deposit facilities so that a guest may check items of value. Even if the guest places such items in the

1913. Crystal Eastman, along with Alice Paul, Lucy Burns and others, founds the Congressional Union for Woman Suffrage, later the National Women's Party. A beautiful woman with "magnificent presence," Miss Eastman later remarks after divorcing her first husband, "No self-respecting feminist would accept alimony. It would be her own confession that she could not take care of herself." Upon her death in 1928, *Nation*

vault or safe-deposit boxes, most states place a limitation on the liability of the hotel. The only way to avoid this statutory limitation is to inform the hotel what the valuables are worth and request space to store them. If the hotel agrees to accept the valuables when it is aware of the value (whether it imposes an additional charge or not), then the hotel is liable for the full amount in the event of loss.

When you enter a contract, be sure that it reflects the entire understanding that you intend it to have. For example, Linda discusses the lease agreement with her landlord, George. George sends Linda a new lease agreement, and when Linda reads it, she finds that the rent is correct, the term of the lease is correct, but George has failed to put in a clause saying that Linda may sublet, although they have orally agreed upon that clause as well. Linda calls George and brings it to his attention. George admits that he has left it out, but he suggests that they leave it out, with their oral agreement that he will allow Linda to sublet still standing. If that clause is left out, Linda loses her legal right to sublet; she must rely upon George's good will. If the clause does not appear in the lease, it will not help Linda if George sells the building or later denies that he ever agreed to it. If the issue is taken to court, the judge will undoubtedly rely only on the words of the lease, since any modification or change of any type of contract must be in writing. It is therefore important to be sure that any contract you enter into includes all the provisions you intend to include and that are important to you.

Leases present different issues than many other kinds of contracts. For one thing, they are agreements that are generally on printed forms, and the forms are generally prepared by the real estate boards of the locality. What this generally means is that the tenant has little bargaining power against a number of the provisions in the lease, many of which clearly favor the landlord. The most hopeful thing that can be said about leases is that most courts are aware that the bargaining power is one-sided, and they approach legal problems arising out of them from that point of view. This may not be of much comfort to anyone who reads the lease

form closely, but it should put it in perspective.

When you are about to enter into an agreement, there are certain steps you should take to insure that you are protecting yourself. The first and most basic is to read the contract carefully and critically more than once. It is amazing how complicated something may appear at first glance and how much clearer it appears when you take the time to analyze it. If it happens that something is not clear after reading it over several times, it should be questioned and discussed with a view to clarifying the language in the agreement. You should remember that if you cannot understand it, there is a good chance that a judge might not understand it, and in order to prevent problems the language should be clarified in advance.

If after reading and discussing the contract it is still unclear, it may be advisable to consult an attorney to ensure that you understand what you are signing. There are many times when consulting an attorney is advisable. For example, if you contemplate signing a long lease to conduct a business, it is wise to consult with a lawyer. If you are about to buy a house, the contract should be seen by a lawyer. There are some situations where the training and experience of a lawyer will be helpful. But you should not assume in advance that anything relating to law is foreign and cannot be understood. In many day-to-day situations, legal transactions can be comprehended and entered into with confidence if you approach them in the ways suggested.

If for any reason a party to a contract does not live up to the contract, some legal action may be necessary. Not only is it possible to enter the contract on your own, it is also possible to enforce it. Many states have either a small-claims court or another court where suits may be brought without the aid of lawyers. The court personnel instruct and assist you in instituting such an action, and when the case is scheduled in court, you may tell your story without the necessity of hiring a lawyer. The important thing to remember is that the more that individuals demand access to the legal process for themselves, the more pressure there will be to make the system simpler and more accessible.

magazine will comment, "She was for thousands a symbol of what the free woman might be." Crystal Eastman will be best remembered not for her contributions to suffrage, the cause of peace, or improved working conditions for laborers — which were substantial— but for her stirring enthusiasm and *joie de vivre*.

The People's Courts: Small Claims

Ethel Lederer

A TV repair shop that does unsatisfactory work, a store selling defective merchandise, or (in states without no-fault insurance) the owner of a car that damages your car or property in a minor accident are the typical offenders that can be brought to justice through small-claims court litigations. Small-claims court is "a court of justice, often with relatively simple procedures, no requirement for a lawyer, and an upper limit to the amount of judgments which can be rendered."*

Because many of us hardly know these "people's courts" (also called conciliation courts, magistrate's courts, and justice-of-the-peace courts) exist, let alone how to use them, they are too often used primarily as collection agencies by department stores, banks, hospitals, landlords, businesses, or utility companies. They could be a potent consumer weapon. For instance, a suit can be brought against a dry cleaner for ruining or losing clothes, against an auto-repair shop (one of the most common types of suit), or against an employer who owes back wages.

Procedures for filing a small claim differ from state to state. Your local district court probably encompasses the small-claims court, but, in some areas, small claims may come under the jurisdiction of justices of the peace. (If the defendant lives or does business in another jurisdiction, you must sue in that court.) The clerk of courts can tell you how and where to file. A complaint form must be filled out. If anything about the form is unclear, the clerk can help clarify it. There is a charge of a few dollars for filing, but that will be returned to you if you win.

When suing a business, be sure you have the name of the person or persons who own the business, as well as the business address. You don't sue "Pat's Friendly Garage," for instance, but Patrick Jones d/b/a (doing business as) Pat's Friendly Garage. If you can't find out the owner's name,

the court clerk should be able to refer you to a Fictitious Firm Name Index or to another agency that can help you.

The top amount of money involved—"the jurisdictional limit"—ranges from $100 in Iowa to $3,000 in Alaska, with the average limit about $400. You must sue for a sum of money equal to or less than the jurisdictional limit. Thus, if someone sells you a faulty $500 stereo system, but your state's limit is $400, that is the most you will be able to collect. (You cannot, of course, file one claim for $400 and another for $100 in the same matter.) The court also will not award any additional money spent in ways incidental to the claim itself; for instance, traveling expenses, long-distance phone calls, or legal fees (should you choose to have a lawyer).

The fact that you don't need an attorney to represent you is a major advantage of the small-claims court: it obviates legal fees that can often be more than the actual value of a small claim. Large companies, often represented by attorneys, are usually willing to make a settlement out of court to avoid inconvenience and adverse publicity.

The first court session (and usually the only one) should take place within four or five weeks of recording the initial claim. If you are unable to attend this hearing, notify the clerk's office at least a day before and a new date can be arranged. If the defendant fails to appear on the agreed-upon date, the judge will award you the money by default. The defendant will be notified and requested to pay. If both parties are present, each tells the judge what happened and a decision is reached.

When your case does come to court, it's important to bring documentation that will support your case: canceled checks, receipts, contracts, leases, sales slips, or the damaged merchandise itself. Witnesses can be helpful and information such as hearsay is allowed as testimony. Your best assets during the trial are a calm, reasonable attitude (regardless of how angry or indignant you might feel) and accurate information.

Should you win your case but not receive your money, or should the defendant pay you with a rubber check, you can send a *capias*—an order of execution—through the clerk of courts to be delivered by a constable or another county officer. Sheriffs, marshals, and process-servers can also deliver this order. (Process servers can only serve papers and are not empowered to make an arrest, if this should be necessary.) However, there is still no feasible way to track down a fly-by-night agency or business that simply disappears.

Such was the case of a Boston couple who purchased round-trip charter plane tickets to London from a travel agency. When they went to pick up their tickets, they were given one-way tickets and told to pick up the return tickets at the firm's London office. The "London office" turned out to be nonexistent, and they were stuck for the cost of the fare home. Upon their return, they filed a small-claims suit against the travel agency. The defendant didn't show up and the couple won—on paper, at least. After sending notice to the agency, the court had its registered letter returned in the mail days later, stamped "Addressee moved—left no fowarding address."

A large portion of small-claims plaintiffs are the hapless players of the "rent deposit rip-off" game. (A Consumers Union survey in *Consumer Reports,* October, 1971, found that such landlord/tenant suits accounted for 30 percent of the small-claims cases brought by consumers.) The percentage is particularly high in areas like Boston, where there are large numbers of students and young families who move frequently. The "game" is played this way: the landlord demands a deposit against future damage or rent default, when the tenants move in; when they are about to move out, the landlord either accuses them of having damaged the apartment or simply gives them the runaround concerning the return of the rent deposit. If the tenants are moving to another city (as often happens with students and young families), the time

---

New York Public Library

panies that seem to be the object of an unusual number of complaints.

Similar efforts should be made in every community to bring about better use of the small-claims court. To do this in your own area, you can (1) get together with others interested in studying and researching how small-claims court works; (2) write up reports that include research on cases that have come to court, observe current court cases, and report on who uses small-claims court and how frequently; (3) establish liaisons with other public-interest groups who can give you both new information and feedback about what you have done; and (4) interview everyone from ex-litigants to the judges themselves for their views.

If you discover new legislation or legislative reforms that might be helpful, you may find yourself drafting a model bill to try to bring about these changes.

Besides the need for publicizing the courts so that more consumers can use them, some other needed small-claims reforms are: ensuring effective collection procedures; training paralegal persons to help the litigants; demonstrating the need for volunteer attorney-arbitrators to supplement judges, and for evening and Saturday court sessions; and preparing concise and clear manuals to be distributed free at the local court (bilingual manuals should be available wherever a large portion of the community speaks another language).

Now, with concern and awareness beginning to grow on the part of consumer groups (and with individual consumers who are becoming more and more impatient as they are shuffled from one complaint agency to another), the small-claims court is a good place to begin both action and reform. This "people's court" can bring about a new concept of justice for the little person, for poor people who are tired of being cheated, and for the average citizen who feels alienated from the impersonal system. Just as health care should begin with better services in neighborhood clinics and hospitals, judicial reforms ought to start with the local small-claims courts—with the people the legal system was supposedly designed to aid.

and bother involved in trying to get back the rent deposit doesn't seem worthwhile. When the tenant does take the trouble to make a claim, the landlord may still have the last laugh by delaying the refund or writing rubber checks until the tenant gives up. But there are many tenacious tenants who have collected.

Your chances of success in small-claims court can be improved with the help of trained paralegal community advocates. The Harlem Small-Claims Court in New York City has such a service. Narcissus Copeland is the senior member of a team of four community advocates trained by the Department of Consumer Affairs to make extensive inquiry into each case. The advocate serves as a liaison between plaintiff and defendant, helps to achieve settlements, and, when necessary, aids in bringing suits to small-claims court.

Ms. Copeland's team has made great efforts to make their existence and the existence of small-claims court itself known. TV announcements have helped in increasing the community's awareness. Community advocates speak at schools and churches and in community meetings. They also help to organize class action suits in higher courts against com-

---

1914. Rosika Schwimmer presents President Wilson with a petition signed by one million European suffragists urging an end to the war through mediation. It is through, in large part, her efforts and the organizational talents of Carrie Chapman Catt and Jane Addams that the Woman's Peace Party will be founded in 1915. Her powerful and compassionate

Making Your Will

Dorothy Tymon

Not long ago the six-room house of the late Martha Conroy was offered at public auction. All possessions of the deceased, including furniture and jewelry, were on the block as well, having been turned over to a court-appointed administrator for sale and disposal.

Among the bidders at the auction sat Helen Morton, Martha Conroy's niece by marriage. Her aunt had often told her, "Helen, I want you to have this gold necklace," and Helen finally got it, but only because she had been the highest bidder. Contrary to what her aunt believed, Helen—her nearest living relative—did not automatically inherit the property.

Because of this misconception, Martha Conroy left no will. Because she left no will, all her property was put up for public sale. Of the $51,000 the sale grossed, some $10,000 went to pay for the costs of the auction and the settling of the estate. After payment of outstanding bills and taxes, the balance was deposited in a special account with the state comptroller to await the claim of a blood relative, able to prove the relationship to the complete satisfaction of the court. (If no valid claim was made, the money belonged to the government, in this case, the government of New York State.)

Of the 10 estates included in the same auction as Martha Conroy's, nine belonged to women.

Had Martha Conroy taken the necessary steps to learn her rights and seek advice on the regulations regarding inherited property and had she left a properly drawn will, the legal disinheritance of her niece as well as the expense of the public administration of the estate, could have been avoided. But Martha Conroy had never been included in the family's financial planning. Her husband wrote his own will and took care of all financial matters without consulting or including her. Since she did not understand the mechanics of

estate planning, she neglected her own.

At least the Conroy family had one will: Martha was taken care of in her lifetime. But Florence Jones was not so lucky. Her husband, Jerry, hadn't thought that he needed to make a will, despite the fact that his business was worth $25,000, that he carried $5,000 in insurance, and had a $1,500 savings account. When he died, the insurance was paid directly to Florence, but the remainder was equally divided by the courts among his wife and their two daughters, aged 7 and 13. The court appointed Florence guardian of the children. But if for some reason she had not been appointed guardian, she would have had to obtain funds for the children's care from a court-appointed guardian.

Had Florence died along with her husband without leaving a will of her own, the situation could have been worse. Children orphaned under such circumstances have been placed in public institutions by court-appointed guardians when whatever property their parents did leave has been consumed by the court expenses of settling the estate.

Another example of what can happen to children is illustrated by the disposition of the estate of Laura Hillman, a divorcée with a nine-year-old daughter. When she remarried, she and her new husband John bought a house under joint ownership with right of survivorship (providing that if one owner dies, the other automatically inherits the property). But they did not write a will. Then they were both killed in a plane crash. John, however, survived Laura by one day. During that one day, the estate, including the house, went to him; upon his death, it all went to his two sisters. Since Laura's daughter was not related to John, she was left with nothing.

Laura should have made a will stating which assets and what percentage of them were to go to the care of her daughter, and naming a guardian for her child, as well as an executrix (female) or executor (male) to administer the money while her daughter was a minor.

Single women seem particularly indifferent to making a will. A case in point is that of Janet Cohen, 31, who had recently been promoted to vice-president of the bank in which she had been working for eight years. Janet had left home at an early age to escape her dominating father but was close to her married sister and adored her six-year-old nephew. When she died in a skiing accident, the net proceeds (after court costs) of her $6,000 bank account and $1,200 from her employee savings plan were awarded to her closest living relative, her well-off and estranged father.

To avoid such unfortunate situations, we should each have a will, regardless of our marital status or wealth. It should be drawn up with the aid of a lawyer, preferably one who specializes in trusts and estates and who knows how to minimize inheritance taxes and/or court costs. (To find an experienced estate lawyer, seek the recommendations of the trust officer of your bank, friends, your local Bar Association, or the Legal Aid Society.) If it is a simple will, not requiring extensive estate planning or complex arrangements, an estate specialist may not be needed.

When a lawyer prepares your will, the signing will take place under her or his surveillance. At least two competent witnesses (they should not be anyone who will benefit from or inherit your assets) must sign not only in your presence, but in the presence of each other. (It is not necessary for the witnesses to read the will.) Only the original of the will should be signed, and then kept in a safe place. Your executrix or executor, who can be your lawyer, should know where it is. A safe-deposit box is not the best place, because it will require a

public speeches will also be an inspiration in the founding of what is now the Women's International League for Peace and Freedom. Rosika Schwimmer typifies the fusion of feminist and pacifist beliefs common among many outspoken American and European women of the time.

court order to be opened. An unsigned copy should be kept accessible.

It is not necessary to list your exact assets, because these may change. A separate inventory should be available to make them easy to find. The list should give the name of your bank and your account number, certificate numbers of stock, and a list of jewels and other valuables.

If there are minor children, your spouse or someone in whom you have confidence should be named as a guardian.

An executrix or executor should be named to administer the will. This person receives a fee from the estate, so you don't have to feel you ought to appoint someone who will benefit from the will. In fact some lawyers advise against appointing a beneficiary and others advise strongly against appointing more than one person (even the most loving siblings have been known to lose their cool in such a situation, and hassles cause delays, as well as bad feelings, and delays can cost money).

The executrix or executor offers the will for probate (validation by the court), pays debts and taxes, and manages the assets in accordance with the terms. She or he is entitled and expected to retain a lawyer to help carry out these responsibilities, and the fee for legal services is paid by the estate.

Carefully read your will for clear, precise language. One man at age 43 is still registering for courses at a university, because the will said, "Frank is to receive income until he completes his education." No cut-off date or other specification was made.

It is advisable to review your will periodically. Since assets change and family members change, it is important that the will is current and workable. A change added to the existing will is a "codicil." If the amendments are extensive, a new will should be drawn. Since wills must be in accordance with the laws of the state of your residence, you must review your will should you move from one state to another. For example, in a so-called community-property state—Arizona, California, Idaho, Louisiana, New Mexico, Nevada, Texas, Washington—50 percent of all valuables accumulated by the couple dur-

ing the marriage automatically goes to the surviving spouse. The other portion may be disposed of by will. Many banks publish easy-to-read pamphlets on estate laws.

We must overcome the attitude of "who cares about what happens after I'm gone," or the feeling that making a will is a bad omen, or the belief that a husband's will is sufficient. A will allows us to name guardians for minor children and arrange future care according to our wishes. A will prevents the consumption of proceeds from property by court-appointed administrators. And even if there is only a small amount to be disposed of, it does seem preferable that a special friend or worthy organization be the recipient rather than an unloved relative or the government. The writing of a will is an expression of control—and love.

1916. The Russian Imperial Army equips numerous regiments of volunteer women soldiers for the front in World War I. Because of their effectiveness under fire, they become known as "Battalions of Death."

Rape and the Law

Susan Ross

Does the law protect women against rape?

Theoretically, yes; in reality, very little. The reasons stem from a complex of mutually contradictory male ideologies about women, which have been enshrined in the law of rape. Ideology number one is that women are vindictive and/or psychopathic creatures who frequently turn in an innocent sex partner to the police as a rapist out of spite or revenge. A prominent legal authority on rules of evidence asserts, for instance:

> Modern psychiatrists have amply studied the behavior of errant young girls and women coming before the courts in all sorts of cases. Their psychic complexes are multifarious, distorted partly by inherent defects, partly by diseased derangements or abnormal instincts, partly by bad social environment, partly by temporary physiological or emotional conditions. One form taken by these complexes is that of contriving false charges of sexual offenses by men.

Ideology number two is that most women want to be raped, and ask for it by wearing sexually suggestive clothing and by walking around in strange places instead of staying home. This helps account for the popularity of the suggestion, frequently advanced when a rash of rapes occurs, that a curfew ought to be imposed—but on the female victims rather than the male aggressors!

Ideology number three is that only a "pure" woman can be raped; if she has ever indulged in sex before, particularly with the accused rapist, she could not possibly have been raped. If she doesn't drink or smoke, this will strongly support her story.

Ideology number four is that women are chaste, delicate creatures, belonging to particular men, and that rape is thus a particularly heinous crime since it involves a violation of both the woman's unique purity and the man's property rights. In Bangladesh, for instance, husbands refused en masse, out of a sense of outraged male ownership, to remain with wives who had been raped by the invading Pakistanis.

These ideologies form the basis for several legal doctrines that have the net effect of making it extraordinarily difficult to convict a man of rape, but that subject the woman victim to humiliating treatment by the police and the courts. All kinds of special evidence rules, unique to the crime of rape, are set up in order to protect the accused male against women's vindictive spirit. These rules reflect two basic assumptions about women and rape: that "the woman will usually lie" and that "the woman really consented, so it wasn't rape."

"The woman will usually lie."

The most important manifestation of this assumption comes with the requirement that various aspects of the crime—unlike any other crime—be corroborated by evidence other than the victim's testimony, since it is presumed that the woman victim will lie. The word of the victim is not enough, as it is in other crimes. Thus in many states, to convict a man the prosecutor must prove through evidence independent of the woman's testimony that she was penetrated, that force was used, and/or that the man accused was the actual person who did it. In some cases, these things are difficult, if not impossible, to prove. Many women's first step after being raped will be to douche themselves, thus destroying the sperm which is the proof of penetration. In addition, many rapists are ejaculatory impotents and do not deposit sperm in the woman's vagina even when there is penetration. Proof of penetration, in these cases, is never possible. Proving force is even more difficult. A woman victim can point to her bruises to show that force was used, but many men, including judges, believe that women enjoy a little violence as part of normal sex—and thus refuse to consider bruises as evidence of sex without consent. Finally, corroborating the identity of the assailant is a third difficult problem. This rule practically requires that a third-party eyewitness be present at the rape—and that, of course, is quite rare. Such strict standards of corroboration make a conviction for the crime of rape almost impossible. The statistics for New York City show the depth of the problem: in 1971, out of 1085 arrests for rape, the state secured only eighteen convictions.

The belief that the woman will lie leads to other legal doctrines besides corroboration. A woman's failure to go to the police promptly can be used to attack her credibility on the witness stand. So deep is this distrust of women that in some states the court can allow the defendant's lawyer to have the *victim* subjected to psychiatric examination and present the results to the jury. Victims of other crimes are not normally subjected to such treatment.

"She really consented so it wasn't rape."

The second element of protection for the accused male lies in inferences the law permits in determining

1917. Mata Hari, the darling intimate of diplomats, ministers, and even kings, is executed in Paris as a German spy. Her allure to men caused the French espionage bureau to overlook her various intrigues if she would induce a certain Berlin official to reveal war secrets. Mata Hari agreed to the assignment but was stopped by the British before

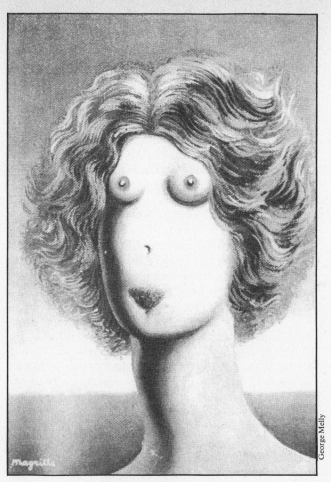

The Rape, by Magritte

ever slept with the accused, what kind of clothes she was wearing, what she was doing in that part of town anyway, and on and on. If the woman decides to go to court to testify against the rapist, much of this questioning will take place on the witness stand, often with much publicity. The best tactic the accused man's lawyer can use is to throw doubt on the woman's every word. He will do everything he can to make her appear promiscuous or vindictive or hostile toward men, or perhaps even sexually disturbed. What would a nice girl be doing at that time of day, in that part of town, with that clothing on? This will be the implication behind every question. And while it is theoretically the duty of the prosecuting lawyer to object to those questions, most of the prosecuting lawyers are men, who may secretly believe in the implications behind the questions and therefore not object to improper questioning. The net result will be that the rapist goes goes free, the woman suffers unnecessary humiliation, and other women learn the lesson: don't bother to report a rape or attempted assault to the police, because neither the police nor the courts will help you.

What can be done to make the laws more effective in protecting women against rape?

All special rules applied solely in rape trials must be done away with. This means doing away with the assumption that women will lie: there should be no special corroboration requirements, no inferences drawn from the fact that a woman didn't go to the police right away, and no suggestion that the victim be psychoanalyzed. Reform also requires a realistic notion of consent: there should be no requirement that a woman resist, and no inference drawn because she has slept with other men or even, in the past, with the rapist himself.

The requirement that a woman be penetrated should also be abolished. Whether or not a man merely touches his genitals to an unwilliing woman or penetrates her makes no diference in terms of the intended humiliation and invasion of her privacy that lie at the core of the crime of rape. And the requirement of penetration leads to degrading and meaningless searches for sperm—meaningless if the man is an ejaculatory impotent or if the victim douches before she goes to the police.

By itself, abolishing these rules will do much to eliminate the unjust treatment a woman now recieves when she is raped. Today, the woman victim is subjected to intense humiliation from the salacious inquiries the police sometimes indulge in to the outrageous cross-examination the woman is often subjected to when she testifies about the crime in court. If the special evidence rules were abolished, these humiliating questions would no longer be relevant and therefore should no longer be asked.

whether the woman was a willing partner. A woman's prior lack of virginity or her reputation for unchastity can be used by the accused rapist's lawyer as evidence to cast doubt on her claim that she did not consent. Her prior consent to intercourse with the accused male also can be used in the same way to disprove a rape. In practical effect, this can amount to licensing any man who has once slept with a woman to rape her in the future with impunity. And finally, some states require that the woman must have resisted before the state will say she did not consent to the act. This is absurd in a day when most women are told by the police themselves—and have ample reason to believe—that it is best not to resist in order to save one's life.

In conclusion, it must be said that some of these defenses have probably been created because the penalties for rape are often unreasonably high. Rape has been equated with murder in terms of the sentences imposed; understandably, this harshness contributes to an extreme reluctance to find a man guilty.

What is the practical effect of these evidence rules for the rape victim?

The rules discussed above are not mere abstract injustices. Because these rules exist, both the police and lawyers will ask the woman probing and humiliating questions about her past sex life, whether she

How do women go about changing these rules?

The first effort should take place in actual trials, where lawyers can ask the court to change judge-made rules. Feminist groups should contact prosecutors to try to convince them to raise these issues. Women victims should ⟶

reaching Germany and redirected to Spain. There she became familiar with a known German agent. Returning to Paris a few months later plentifully supplied with money by the Germans, she is suspected of a double-cross, and even though the evidence against her is inconclusive, she is shot. She dies smiling.

try to retain their own lawyers to represent them while they are testifying, and these lawyers should also challenge special rules applied solely to rape. If change cannot be achieved through the courts, a drive should be launched in the state legislatures to abolish special rules for rape.

Women should also seek new laws setting lower penalties for rape, penalties parallel to those imposed for aggravated assault, for instance. Although it sounds anomalous to urge lower sentences, actually this should help to assure more convictions. Experts are convinced that one reason the special evidence rules have been created, and so few convictions obtained, is the legitimate reluctance to give a man a life sentence or the death penalty for the act of rape. If the penalties are lowered to a more realistic level, the emotional climate in favor of the accused will be reduced.

Can any practical measures be adopted to help the rape victim?

There are several practical steps women can take to avoid some of the humiliating treatment they now receive from the time they first report the crime to the police to the time they testify in court. Until these measures are undertaken, women will remain victims—victims of the police, the lawyers, and the judges.

First, when you report the crime, take a strong friend along—possibly one who is a lawyer or law student. You want someone who is cool, calm, sure of herself, and will stand up for your rights at a time when you may be least able to do so. The role of the friend will be to help you assert your rights and to protect you against salacious questioning (such as forcing you to repeat all the details of the rape over and over to inordinately curious male police officers).

Second, refuse to answer questions about your past sex life. This is no one's business, and it is irrelevant to whether or not you have been raped. Even if the police insist that your sexual experience is relevant because of the special evidence rules, reply that you will be challenging those rules and will not answer. Go to the inquiring officers' superiors, if necessary.

Third, take a friend with you when the police send you to a doctor or hospital. The friend will help you object to improper treatment. One of the most frequent complaints rape victims make concerns the rude, abrupt, and hostile medical examinations they are given by police doctors. Such doctors often refuse to treat the victim but merely examine her to make sure that she has been raped. You should also go to your own doctor for treatment afterward, including getting an antipregnancy pill.

An important service that women's groups could perform in this area would be to meet with the police medical authorities to explain the problems with present procedures and attitudes in order to get considerate treatment for rape victims. Another service would be to set up a panel of doctors (and especially women doctors) who would be willing to give post-rape treatment in cases where police medical treatment is inadequate and women do not have family doctors they can go to immediately.

The women's groups could publicize a phone number for rape victims; women who called would be given the name of a doctor who would see them. A number of trained women could also be on hand to accompany any victim when she made her report to the police; their services could be offered at the same time the woman calls in for a doctor's name. Women's groups would thus develop relationships with sympathetic doctors and gain firsthand knowledge of the kinds of abuse most prevalent at police stations. Experience in developing a service of the kind suggested could provide ammunition for later organizational efforts to make the police change their practices.

Fourth, discuss with the prosecutor the evidence he will be using at the trial and the kinds of questions you will be asked, both by him and by the lawyer for the accused rapist. If the questions are humiliating or unnecessary, explain to him why and request that the questions not be asked or that he object to such questions by the defendant's lawyer. Go over his head, if necessary.

Fifth, try to get your own lawyer for the actual trial. You want someone who will object if improper questions, based on the special evidence rules, are asked of you by the defendant's lawyer. Of course, you will have to answer if the court orders you to do so—that is, if your lawyer has been unsuccessful in getting the court to rule that the particular questions are unnecessary.

Theoretically the prosecutor should raise objections, but he often will not, and the result can be humiliating if you don't have a lawyer whose special role is to protect your interests. Your lawyer, in fact, should explain to the judge that he or she is there to protect your reputation. Your lawyer should also discuss with you in advance the kinds of evidence that will be used at the trial so that you understand what will happen once you are in the courtroom.

Sixth, women's groups should meet with the police and prosecuting attorneys to explain what women find objectionable about present procedures, and they should seek institutional change in these procedures. The Washington, D.C., NOW group is doing just that. Contact: Carol Burris, 1345 G Street, S.E., Washington, D.C. 20003 ([202] 547-0082) for suggestions.

Seventh, use the employment-discrimination laws to get more women into the police forces, the district attorney's office, and on the bench. A major part of the problem is that the rape victim faces an essentially all-male system from the moment she reports the crime to the day of the trial. Men in our society frequently believe that all women have secret fantasies of being raped; there is seldom a discussion of male fantasies of raping women. Men with such beliefs or fantasies cannot help but be biased against the woman rape victim.

Change in this area will not be accomplished easily. Women will be dealing with very conservative forces. Policemen, lawyers, and judges are accustomed to handling rape cases in one way. They will not welcome reports from women that they themselves are mistreating rape victims, and that reforms are necessary to correct that mistreatment. Nevertheless, if women organize, they should be able to effect change in this area as in others.

1917. Jeanette Rankin, a Montana Republican, becomes the first elected congresswoman and the only member of the House to vote against America's entry into both World Wars.

440   Rape and the Law
      THE LEGAL ADVISER

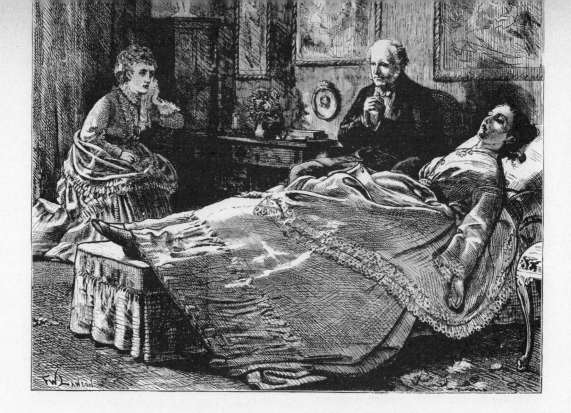

Women Patients' Rights

George J. Annas

Is the husband's consent legally necessary for any type of treatment of a married woman?

The consent of a husband is never legally necessary for the treatment of a conscious, competent, and consenting married woman. This has been consistently affirmed by the courts. Specific cases considered in the context of a husband suing the doctor for treating his wife without his consent have included both sterilization and pregnancy care. The husband's consent was determined not to be necessary. This finding, of course, works both ways, that is, the wife's consent is not required for any type of medical treatment of her husband.

Does a patient being examined by a doctor of the opposite sex have a right to have another person of the patient's sex present in the examining room during the examination?

Approximately 95 percent of all specialists in obstetrics and gynecology are men. Most routinely have a female nurse with them during all physical examinations. The reason generally given is to protect themselves from a possible charge by the woman patient of improper advances. If the doctor's practice is not to have another female present, however, a woman does have the right to demand that another female be present during the examination if she so desires. If the doctor refuses this request in the hospital context, his method of practice is open to serious ethical question, and his conduct should be reported immediately to the chief of his service. The name and phone number of his chief can be obtained from one of the nurses or

through the hospital administration. In the context of a private office, the woman's remedy is probably limited to walking out, informing the local medical society, and going to another doctor.

Increasingly, feminists are advising women to "bring a friend" with them on visits to the doctor for psychological support. Such a person can also act as a witness to what goes on and remind the patient to ask certain questions that are bothering her. No ethical doctor should object to this request.

Does a woman have a right to refuse to be examined by medical students, interns, or residents in a hospital setting?

All patients have a right to refuse to be examined by *anyone* in the hospital setting. When a woman is asked, "Do you mind if these other doctors look at you also?" she has every right to say, "*Yes*, I do mind," and refuse to permit them to examine her. One should be especially wary when the phrase "young doctor" is used since this almost always means medical student—usually a first or second-year one. In some hospitals, medical students are also referred to simply as "doctors," even though the patient has a right to know both what the extent of their training is and the purpose of their proposed examination.

In one court case from the 1930's a woman objected to being examined by a medical student just before she was due to give birth. Thereupon an older doctor came in, performed a rectal and vaginal examination, and then had the same examination performed two or three times each by "ten or twelve young men who she took to be students." She protested repeatedly and testified, "Whenever I screamed and protested they just laughed, told me to shut

1917. Frau Mathilde Kovacs, an aged widow in Vienna, Austria, revenges herself upon her relatives for their discourtesy to her pet cats by converting her large fortune into paper money (500 million kronen), then publicly burning it on the day before her death.

up." She experienced both emotional and physical damages from the delivery. The court had no difficulty in finding this conduct "revolting" and an assault on the patient. In the court's words, "A physician or a medical student has no more right to needlessly and rudely lay hands upon a patient against her will than has a layman." The court also found, over 30 years before the *Darling* case, that the hospital in which this event took place could be held liable for permitting "unlicensed students to experiment on the patient and treat her without her consent."

The lesson is not only that the medical students themselves but also the attending physician *and* the hospital are liable to the patient for any unauthorized examination or treatment. It goes almost without saying that consent by a patient based on a belief that the person examining her is a doctor is consent achieved by fraud or misrepresentation and as such is not legally valid if the examiner is not a doctor.

Can a hospital require the husband's consent as a prerequisite for a married woman's abortion?

Because of the state's asserted interest in the family, a number of state statutes require the husband's consent for an abortion. The U.S. Supreme Court specifically declined to determine whether or not this practice was constitutionally prohibited in their 1973 abortion decisions, but in early 1975 the court refused to enforce a Pennsylvania statute restricting the use of public funds to abortions consented to by spouses or parents during the time the statute's constitutionality was being challenged in lower courts. Only a few other cases on this issue have reached the courts. A Florida court refused to permit the father of an illegitimate fetus to intervene to prevent an abortion, and the Massachusetts Supreme Judicial Court refused to allow a husband separated from his wife to prohibit her from obtaining an abortion. If a hospital refuses to perform an abortion on you without your husband's permission, you should see a lawyer immediately. Legal challenges to this practice will probably be successful.

What are a woman's rights concerning childbirth in a hospital?

While more than 98 percent of all births in the United States take place in a hospital, a woman might want to have her child at home. While most obstetricians will concede that 85 to 95 percent of all births are normal and uncomplicated enough not to require any obstetrical intervention, the medical profession strongly discourages people from having their children at home. Few doctors will deliver children at home, and the competency, training, and legal status of midwives in this country is spotty. Some women have also reported having trouble getting prenatal care if they tell their doctor that they intend to have their child at home.

Inside the hospital, the woman in labor has all the rights of any other hospital patient. As such she cannot be given any specific types of treatment without her consent and has the right to refuse specifically recommended procedures. She has, for example, the right to refuse any and all drugs before and during delivery or to fully participate in deciding which drugs will be used on her, at what time, and in what doses.

No one not directly concerned with the medical care and treatment of the mother may be present in the delivery room without the consent of the mother. The harder question concerns her ability to have someone not on the hospital staff with her during the delivery. This problem is discussed in the following section.

In general, in dealing with hospitals on issues concerning birth, political pressure in the form of community organization aimed directly at the hospital administration on specific issues is likely to be most effective in producing long-term changes. Dr. Kenneth Ryan of the Boston Hospital for Women, the site of more than 6,000 deliveries annually, has asserted that his hospital is "receptive to any change that makes sense. I think that all of us subscribe to the idea of patients' rights and any responsible physician will only be delighted by a well-informed patient." Consumer-patients who desire changes in the way hospitals handle certain conditions must take people like Dr. Ryan up on this and similar assertions by presenting cogent cases for change. In this way what are currently political rights can be transformed into legal rights by being written into hospital policy. The importance of this type of pressure is well illustrated by Dr. Ryan's hospital. Historically, it has usually been the last hospital in the Boston area to change its methods and the most ardent proponent of the use of specialists during childbirth. If consumers are not able to make the community aware of what actually happens in this and other large, specialty-oriented teaching hospitals, the possibility of consumer-influenced change is minimal. Consumers should also have positions on all hospital policy-making boards and committees.

Does a woman have a right to have the father of the child present during the delivery if she so desires?

Thirteen years ago a young man in California handcuffed himself to his wife in order to witness the birth of their child. Since then much has changed, and many, perhaps most, hospitals now admit husbands into the labor and delivery rooms. Once a hospital adopts a policy of permitting this practice, it may not arbitrarily deny access to a particular husband or father on an unconstitutional basis such as race, religion, or national origin. In terms of the woman's psychological needs, it is probably even more important for her to have someone with her during labor and delivery if she is unmarried (e.g., child's father, her brother or sister, her mother, etc.). The choice of who this person is should, of course, be the woman's.

Only one case has reached a state supreme court on this subject, and that was in Montana. In that case the court decided that a Catholic hospital could reasonably deny fathers access to labor and delivery rooms on the grounds that this practice might increase the possibility of infection, increase the number of malpractice suits, disturb doctors in the doctors' locker room, increase costs, make nurses in the delivery room nervous, invade the privacy of other women in the delivery rooms, and create harmony problems among a staff of physicians who did not all ascribe to the natural childbirth method. In my view the court in this case took a far too narrow view of its role, gave the hospital far too much discretion, and did not adequately deal with the rights of the physician, the woman, or her husband. The case can be attacked on these and other grounds and should not be taken as the final word on this subject. At present, however, having the father in the delivery room is a "political" right that will most probably become a legal right only through community pressure on individual institutions to adopt desired practices.

1917. Mary Lathrop becomes the first woman member of the American Bar Association. Despite her successful legal career, she is quoted as saying, "If I had a daughter, I would bring her up as a clinging vine."

Getting Busted: Your Rights on Arrest

Oliver Rosengart

What is the general procedure that immediately follows an arrest?

After a person is arrested, he or she is brought to a police station, booked (i.e., forms are filled out about the arrest, the arrestee's background, occupation, etc.), fingerprinted, and sometimes, depending on the state and the charges, photographed. Many police departments have regulations giving arrestees the right to make a certain number of phone calls to a lawyer and a family member or friend, and providing for the care of personal property in the possession of the arrestee. In most instances these regulations are obeyed, but in many cases, where the police are hostile to the arrestee, they do not allow a phone call or feed the person or allow him to keep the personal property he is entitled to.

Do the police have to inform arrestees of the charges against them at the time of the arrest?

Yes, although in fact, some people do not even know that they have been arrested until some time after they arrive at the police station; the police, to avoid trouble, often simply tell people that they want to talk to them in the police station, and the people go along and are told later that they have been arrested. Virtually no one is informed of the charges until some time after they arrive at the precinct, and sometimes not until they get to court. The few regulations on this subject provide that people must be informed of the charges in the precinct. There is no way to enforce such rules without a lawyer in the precinct, and of course the matter is moot by the time the case gets to court and a complaint is drawn up. Also, the initial statement of charges by the police officer is not binding, since in most places it is the district attorney who decides exactly what the charges will be.

Can the police legally question arrestees in order to try to obtain a confession to use at trial?

Yes. However, a confession, or any statement, in order to be admissible in a trial, must be voluntarily given and the police must first have given certain warnings, called *Miranda* warnings, to the defendant before questioning him or her. The *Miranda* warnings, so called because they are derived from the case of *Miranda v. Arizona*, 384 U.S. 436 (1966) are: (1) you have a right to remain silent; (2) anything you say can be used as evidence against you in a trial; (3) you have a right to a lawyer; and (4) if you want a lawyer and cannot afford one, a lawyer will be appointed without cost to you. It is also required that the police give these warnings in such a manner that the person arrested understands them. If the defendant asks for a

Some Local Post-arrest Regulations

City	Regulations
Baltimore	2 phone calls; only unlawful or dangerous property, evidence and valuables removed
Chicago	reasonable number of phone calls; no property rules
Cincinnati	phone calls can be made before being assigned to a cell; 3 calls every 24 hours allowed. Only have regulations concerning confiscation of unlawfully held property
Dallas	No particular limit on calls; only valuables and items which could aid escape are taken
Detroit	arrestee can phone attorney and friend or relative; all personal property taken
Honolulu	phone calls permitted, all personal property except glasses and handkerchief removed
Indianapolis	one phone call; all personal property removed
Nashville	right to one completed call before being booked but after 1 hour arrestee can be booked without having completed call
Philadelphia	one completed phone call and jail sergeant can allow more; all personal property including belts and shoelaces and sometimes shoes are taken
Phoenix	phone calls to communicate with attorney, family, or friends; all personal property taken

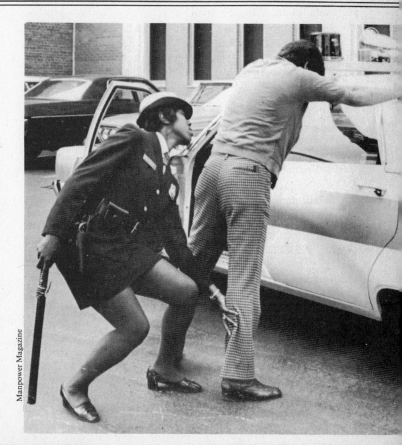

Manpower Magazine

1917. Mademoiselle Marie Rosel, a young French peasant during World War I, is surprised to have her lover appear at her home, drunk and a deserter from the front. She hides him in the barn, then fills his place on the picket line. Next morning the Germans attack and would have overrun the French had it not been for a fighting-mad soldier by the name of Nicholas.

lawyer or does not want to answer questions, the questioning must stop.

Do the police have to give the Miranda warnings to all persons who have been arrested?

No. They must give the warnings only to those persons whom they want to question.

Unlike the situation with many other post-arrest, precourt rights, there is a sanction against the police if they fail to give the warnings: any confession taken in violation of them will not be admissible in evidence. However, it is the experience of many legal workers that the police often do not give the *Miranda* warnings prior to questioning. Interrogation usually takes place in an empty room in a police station shortly after arrest before there is a lawyer on the scene; if the police are able to obtain a confession, they simply testify at the hearing on the motion to suppress the confession that they gave the required warnings. Such a hearing boils down to a swearing contest between the police and the defendant—there are almost never any nonpolice witnesses to the interrogation—and most judges, in deciding whether the confession was lawfully obtained, assume it was.

If the Miranda warnings have been properly given, are all confessions made after the warnings admissible in evidence?

No. For a confession to be admissible, it must also be voluntary under another body of case law that preceded *Miranda*. Brutality, or threats of brutality, make a confession involuntary, but the misconduct need not go that far. Frightening, undressing, denying food or medicine, promising leniency, using a friend or relative, or using a psychological trick (such as telling the defendant that his partner confessed and implicated him), can also, depending partly on the court, invalidate a confession. Physical or mental infirmities that reduce the will to resist may become factors in determining voluntariness. The length of the questioning may also be important.

What should a citizen do when being questioned by the police?

Virtually every lawyer will agree that the best advice to someone being questioned by the police is to say absolutely nothing other than your name and address. It is not easy for the average citizen to resist giving some kind of statement. The police are sometimes skilled interrogators; many have learned techniques for "opening people up." Sometimes they play the good guy–bad guy game, in which one policeman acts threatening and violent and the other acts as though he is trying to protect the defendant from his rough partner; one threatens punishment and the other promises rewards and in that way the defendant becomes frightened and also starts to trust the "good guy." As a general rule, one should never believe a promise made by a policeman, nor should one believe a threat. Another common police technique is to pursue any minor statement the defendant makes, ask him to explain it and then try to use it as a wedge to get him to say more. They may also insist that a defendant's partner confessed or relate

some misinformation they have so that you will contradict it. In spite of how difficult it is for the defendant to resist making some kind of statement the most seemingly harmless of which may be damaging at trial, the best thing to do is to say absolutely nothing. This means that to every question that is asked, you should answer that you have nothing to say. Remember that once you are being interrogated, and the police have some evidence against you, you will not be able to talk yourself out of an arrest no matter what you say. Even if you are innocent, and perhaps have an ironclad alibi, you are better off disclosing the information at a later time, after you or your lawyer have been able to check it out and make sure your witness remembers. Remember, too, that your refusal to answer any questions cannot be held against you in any way later on, but a slightly mistaken or inaccurate statement can be used against you at trial.

What if you are approached by the police and told that they want to talk to you at the police station?

In conducting an investigation, the police often pick people up, bring them to the police station and question them. They do not have enough evidence for an arrest, but they ask the person to come along to the police station, and if the person refuses they may force her. Questioning at this stage has been called "custodial interrogation"; the citizen is in a state of custody that is less than arrest.

At the point of asking you to go with them, the police will usually act very friendly and say that they just want to discuss some matters with you; don't be misled into assuming that they want to talk to you as a friend. Even in states which have the Uniform Arrest Act, covering another type of circumstance, it seems probable that, unless there is an actual arrest, the citizen has the right to refuse. You can ask if you are under arrest, and if they say no, you can tell them politely that you refuse to accompany them and that, if they order or force you to go with them, this means that they have arrested you and according to the Fourth Amendment to the United States Constitution, they cannot arrest you unless they have probable cause. If they then insist you must, of course, obey unless you want to risk being forced and/or beaten. At the police station, you can again ask if you are under arrest and if you are not, you should say that you are leaving and begin to walk out the door. If the police do not let you leave, you should insist on having a lawyer and if you cannot afford one, you can tell them that they have the responsibility to get you a lawyer free of charge. You should refuse to answer any questions; this may result in your release since, if they did not arrest you in the first place, it means that they might not have sufficient evidence to hold you.

The Supreme Court has held that the police do not have the right to round up people against whom they have no evidence and take the fingerprints of those people.

So it comes to pass that one Georges Nicholas is promoted and decorated. The war ends with Marie's lover an undeserving hero. The truth would never have been known, except that he mistreats her so badly that she sues for divorce and reveals her story of "his" courage. An army investigation confirms Marie's tale.

LINEUPS

How are identifications of suspects made by complaining witnesses?

There are two different kinds of identification procedures: "showups," in which the victim simply views the suspect by himself, either in the police precinct or wherever he happens to be, and "lineups," in which the suspect is placed among a group of persons who have somewhat similar physical characteristics, and the victim is asked to identify him. Often showups and lineups are conducted before the suspect has been formally arrested.

Table 1

States in Which Arrestees Can be Released From Police Station*

	With Bail	Without Bail
Alabama	X (M)†	
California		X (M)
Connecticut	X	X
Delaware		X (M)
Georgia	X (M)	
Indiana	X (if amount indicated on warrant)	
Hawaii	X (for crimes punishable by less than 2 years)	
Louisiana	X (violation of municipal ordinances)	
Missouri	X (M)	
Montana	X (M) (if justice of peace or police judge has posted schedule of cash bail)	
Nevada	X (M)	
New Hampshire		X (M)
New Jersey	X (M)	
New Mexico	where a warrant is issued for arrest, judge *must* indicate on it the amount of bail and authorize officer to accept it	
New York	X (M)	X (M)
Ohio	X (M, when judge not available and in accord with posted schedule)	
Oklahoma		X (only for violation of fish, game and water safety laws)
Pennsylvania	X (M)	
Texas	X (M) (F, when court is not in session in the county where defendant is in custody)	
Virginia	X (M)	
Wyoming	X (M)	

*Note: For the states not listed, the arrestee cannot be released from the police station.
†M=Misdemeanors only.

Can the police force someone whom they have not yet arrested to participate in a lineup?

Although it is not yet decided, it appears that, following the reasoning of the Supreme Court in *Davis v. Mississippi*, the police do not have the right to detain persons against whom they have no evidence for the purpose of having those persons participate in a lineup. Should you be asked to participate in a lineup, without having been formally arrested, you have the right to refuse and you may be able to physically resist participating in the lineup by turning around or covering your face.

Does a person have the right to have a lawyer present at a lineup or showup that takes place before a formal arrest has been made?

No. The Supreme Court held in the case of *Kirby v. Illinois*, 406 U.S. 682 (1972), that there was no right to a lawyer at a lineup where the defendants were not yet formally charged. The court noted, however, that the defendants did not ask for legal assistance, although even if they had requested counsel the decision by the present Supreme Court would probably have been the same. This does not mean that a person who is asked to be in a lineup should not ask for a lawyer—he should. It is possible that the police will grant the request and furnish a lawyer, or that they will give the arrestee's own lawyer a chance to get there before the lineup. A lawyer can be helpful at a lineup by making sure that the lineup or showup is not conducted in a way that leads the complaining witness or in any other way influences identification.

Does a person have the right to have a lawyer present at a lineup conducted after he has been indicted?

Yes. The Supreme Court so held in the case of *U.S. v. Wade*, 388 U.S. 218 (1967), and the present Supreme Court, in deciding *Kirby*, did not specifically overrule *Wade;* its decision in *Kirby* simply limited the right to counsel to lineups taking place after charges have been brought. If a lineup takes place after indictment, and no lawyer is present and the defendant has not waived his right to counsel, then the witness will not be able to testify at trial that he or she identified the defendant at that lineup.

THE RIGHT TO BE RELEASED FROM THE POLICE STATION

What are the conditions for release following arrest?

The rules regarding release from the police station vary from state to state and are covered in general in Table 1. For example, in New York the police-department regulations prescribe that in certain crimes (non felonies) the arresting officer is to conduct an interview pursuant to a form, on subjects indicating roots in the community, such as the number of years the person has lived at his particular address, the number of years the person has lived in the community, family ties, employment, schooling and prior criminal record. Verification by a friend or relative, either by telephone or in person, is also required. If the

1918. Margaret Sage, philanthropist, dies. The wife of New York businessman Russell B. Sage, she contributed and bequeathed a total between $70 to $80 million to public use in projects as diverse as the Russell Sage Foundation and Harvard's Cavendish Hall. The massive size of her contributions makes her one of the nation's greatest benefactors,

Judith DeLuca

Table 2 — Age at Which Persons are No Longer Treated as Juveniles

State	Age	State	Age
Alabama	16–18	Nebraska	16–18
Alaska	18	Nevada	18
Arizona	18	New Hampshire	17
Arkansas	18	New Jersey	varies from 16–18
California	18–21	New Mexico	18
Colorado	16, if punishable by death or life imprisonment, otherwise 18	New York	16–18 for girls "in need of supervision; 18 for boys"
Connecticut	16–18	North Carolina	16
Delaware	18	North Dakota	14–18
District of Columbia	18	Ohio	18
Florida	17	Oklahoma	18–girls, 16–boys, except Tulsa where it is 18 for both
Georgia	17		
Hawaii	18	Oregon	18
Idaho	18	Pennsylvania	16–18
Illinois	17–boys, 18–girls	Rhode Island	16–18
Indiana	18	South Carolina	16–18, varies by county
Iowa	18	South Dakota	18
Kansas	18	Tennessee	varies from 16 to 18, generally 17
Kentucky	18	Texas	10–17, boys; 18, girls
Louisiana	17–21	Utah	18
Maine	17	Vermont	16
Maryland	16–18	Virginia	varies from 18 to 21
Massachusetts	14–17	Washington	18
Michigan	17	West Virginia	16–18
Minnesota	18	Wisconsin	16–18
Mississippi	18	Wyoming	18–19, boys; 18–21, girls
Missouri	17		
Montana	18		

interviewee achieves a certain number of points as set forth by a formula, she is released from the police station on a summons, without bail. However, the law also prescribes that the arresting officer can refuse to issue a summons if, in his discretion, he feels that it may lead to further disorders in the community, which means in practice that the police officer can refuse to issue a summons when he is angry. The law also provides that the arrestee can be required to post bail, in the discretion of the arresting officer, of up to five hundred dollars for misdemeanors. This is called stationhouse bail.

Some special rules exist if the person arrested is a juvenile. The age at which one stops being treated as a juvenile varies from state to state and is set forth in Table 2. In most states the police must release juveniles to the custody of a parent or guardian, pending arraign-

comparable to John D. Rockefeller and Andrew Carnegie. She believed that women are men's intellectual equals and moral superiors, and as such they have a duty to improve society.

ment at a later date, except for the most serious cases such as homicide, when the juvenile can be held.

What the Lawyer Should Do

Criminal law is a very specialized field. The case law, the procedures both in and out of court, the jargon—all are peculiar to criminal law. Perhaps most important, there is an atmosphere of hostility which is much more pervasive in criminal than civil cases. In big cities, there is usually a small group of lawyers who practice only criminal law, while all others may do little or none. In small towns, what few lawyers there are do only a small amount of criminal law work as a sideline to civil law practice. In any event, none but the specialists know the finer tricks of the trade, and therefore, if you should ever be arrested, you should know what you have the right to expect from the lawyer you call to the local precinct.

What should a lawyer do at the police station?

First of all, every lawyer should tell an arrestee to make no statements other than name, address, and personal data such as employment or occupation, family, etc. Where an arrestee is being interviewed for release on a summons, the detailed questions on background are usually not damaging admissions and should be answered. The police will always ask for the particulars of any previous arrests on your part. If an arrestee refuses to be fingerprinted or photographed after an arrest, the result will almost certainly be a very high bail or no bail at all since the judge will assume that the arrestee is trying to conceal her identity.

The lawyer's basic function in the police station is to begin preparation for representing his or her client in court. The first court proceeding after arrest is the arraignment, which is a very brief proceeding in which the defendant is informed of the charges against him (unless he waives the reading of the charges, which all lawyers will do since they can simply read the written complaint), and in which the judge sets a bail or releases the defendant without bail, after the defense lawyer makes a statement to the court about the defendant's background. The lawyer must therefore get from his client what are generally referred to as "bail facts." These are all the facts that show the arrestee's roots in the community and reliability, which, together with the seriousness of the alleged crime and the defendant's prior criminal record, are the only factors that the court can consider in setting bail. (*Stack v. Boyle*, 342 U.S. 1 [1951].) In a few states (notably New York) and in federal cases the law has sanctioned preventive detention in which bail can be denied if an arrestee has a long prior record and if there is a substantial amount of proof against him on the new charge. However, in all other states there is a right to bail and it is illegal for judges to set bail at an absurdly high amount, that they know the defendant cannot post, in order to make sure that the defendant stays in jail. The fact that it is illegal does not mean that it is uncommon; in fact it is the general practice in most states. The specific bail facts include such information as the number of years the person has resided in the community, the number of years he has resided at a particular address, his employment record, his educational background, his family ties and family responsibilities (i.e., how many dependents he has), whether the defendant lives with his parents, and any civic organizations he is a member of or participates in, including regular attendance at a community center or a Y.M.C.A. or Y.W.C.A.

It is also helpful to have as many people as possible appear in court on the defendant's behalf, such as parents, social workers, ministers, employers, friends, etc., and it is appropriate in most courts for them to stand up, either at the railing separating the judge's area from the spectators' area or at their seats, when the arguments are being heard in order to show their support for the defendant. This tactic may be helpful since the judge, on occasion, may respond to the fact that many people are concerned about this individual, and their concern indicates roots in the community and reliability.

The lawyer should also be preparing to defend the case in its later stages. Information gotten at the police station can be very important at trial. For example, if the lawyer has a casual conversation with the arresting police officer, and the officer says that he gained possession of the evidence in a certain way, and if the police officer changes that story in court, the lawyer will be able to introduce into evidence the earlier statement in order to discredit the officer's testimony. Thus the defense lawyer should have a chat with the arresting officer in as friendly and casual a way as possible. If your lawyer does not talk to the police officer, you should tell him to. Although many police officers know that they have no obligation to talk to a defense lawyer, most will respond if the defense lawyer is skillful enough. If the police officer refuses to talk when first approached, it may prove successful to make several attempts, each time with a new question or statement, until he finally opens up. Or he may respond if the lawyer tells him what his client's version of the facts are, since he may want to defend himself against what he considers an unjust accusation.

Another important piece of information that the lawyer should get is the charge that the police officer initially lodges against the defendant. In case the charges are increased by the district attorney, the defense lawyer can sometimes impeach the police officer's version of the facts by pointing out that the police officer charged a lesser crime at the police station. Where there is contraband that has been seized, the lawyer should carefully examine it.

The lawyer can also be helpful in the pre-arraignment phase of the proceedings by calling people to help post bail, finding references where they are required for release on a summons, convincing police officers to issue a summons where they otherwise might not or making complaints to superiors in the police department where a police officer improperly refuses to write a summons. Such miscellaneous duties as getting food and cigarettes for the defendant if the police refuse to do so should not be considered beneath a lawyer's function.

1919. In a jolting "Westernization" program, Turkish women are no longer required to wear veils, marry for business reasons, or be confined to harems. For the next ten years, suicide rates among them are to jump drastically, and doctors will claim that fifty percent of the nation's women have been driven "either insane or neurasthenic" by their new freedoms and responsibilities.

FRONTIERO V. RICHARDSON
Cite as 93 S.Ct. 1764 (1973)

There can be no doubt that our Nation has had a long and unfortunate history of sex discrimination. Traditionally, such discrimination was rationalized by an attitude of "romantic paternalism" which, in practical effect, put women not on a pedestal, but in a cage. Indeed, this paternalistic attitude became so firmly rooted in our national consciousness that, exactly 100 years ago, a distinguished member of this Court was able to proclaim: "Man is, or should be, woman's protector and defender. The natural and proper timidity and delicacy which belongs to the female sex evidently unfits it for many of the occupations of civil life. The constitution of the family organization, which is founded in the divine ordinance, as well as in the nature of things, indicates the domestic sphere as that which properly belongs to the domain and functions of womanhood. The harmony, not to say identity, of interests and views which belong, or should belong, to the family institution is repugnant to the ideas of a woman adopting a distinct and independent career from that of her husband. . . .

". . .The paramount destiny and mission of woman are to fulfill the noble and benign offices of wife and mother. This is the law of the Creator." Bradwell v. Illinois, 83 U.S. [16 Wall.] 130, 141, 21 L.Ed. 442 (1873) (Bradley, J., concurring).

As a result of notions such as these, our statute books gradually became laden with gross, stereotypical distinctions between sexes and, indeed, throughout much of the 19th century the position of women in our society was, in many respects, comparable to that of blacks under the pre-Civil War slave codes. Neither slaves nor women could hold office, serve on juries, or bring suit in their own names, and married women traditionally were denied the legal capacity to hold or convey property or to serve as legal guardians of their own children.

SAIL'ER INN, INC. V. KIRBY
Cite as 485 P. 2d 529

Laws which disable women from full participation in the political, business and economic arenas are often characterized as "protective" and beneficial. Those same laws applied to racial or ethnic minorities would readily be recognized as invidious and impermissible. The pedestal upon which women have been placed has all too often, upon closer inspection, been revealed as a cage. We conclude that the sexual classifications are properly treated as suspect, particularly when those classifications are made with respect to a fundamental interest such as employment.

1919. Lady Astor, formerly Nancy Langhorne of Virginia and now wife of a British peer, becomes the first American woman member of Britain's House of Commons.

The Trial of Susan B. Anthony

Judge Hunt. (Ordering the defendant to stand up). Has the prisoner anything to say why sentence shall not be pronounced?

Miss Anthony. Yes, your honor, I have many things to say; for in your ordered verdict of guilty you have trampled under foot every vital principle of our government. My natural rights, my civil rights, my political rights, my judicial rights, are all alike ignored. Robbed of the fundamental privilege of citizenship, I am degraded from the status of a citizen to that of a subject; and not only myself individually but all of my sex are, by your honor's verdict, doomed to political subjection under this so-called republican form of government.

Judge Hunt. The Court can not listen to rehearsal of argument which the prisoner's counsel has already consumed three hours in presenting.

Miss Anthony. May it please your honor, I am not arguing the question, but simply stating the reasons why sentence can not, in justice, be pronounced against me. Your denial of my citizen's right to vote, is the denial of my right of consent as one of the governed, the denial of my right of representation as one of the taxed, the denial of my right to a trial by a jury of my peers as an offender against law; therefore, the denial of my sacred right to life, liberty, property and—

Judge Hunt. The Court can not allow the prisoner to go on.

Miss Anthony. But your honor will not deny me this one and only poor privilege of protest against this high-handed outrage upon my citizen's rights. May it please the Court to remember that, since the day of my arrest last November, this is the first time that either myself or any person of my disfranchised class has been allowed a word of defense before judge or jury—

Judge Hunt. The prisoner must sit down—the Court can not allow it.

Miss Anthony. Of all my prosecutors, from the corner grocery politician who entered the complaint, to the United States marshal, commissioner, district-attorney, district-judge, your honor on the bench—not one is my peer, but each and all are my political sovereigns; and had your honor submitted my case to the jury, as was clearly your duty, even then I should have had just cause of protest, for not one of those men was my peer; but, native or foreign born, white or black, rich or poor, educated or ignorant, sober or drunk, each and every man of them was my political superior; hence, in no sense, my peer. Under such circumstances, a commoner of England, tried before a jury of lords, would have far less cause to complain than have I, a woman, tried before a jury of men. Even my counsel, Hon. Henry R. Selden, who has argued my cause so ably, so earnestly, so unanswerably before your honor, is my political sovereign. Precisely as no disfranchised person is entitled to sit upon a jury, and no woman is entitled to the franchise, so none but a regularly admitted lawyer is allowed to practice in the courts, and no woman can gain admission to the bar—hence, jury, judge, counsel, all must be of the superior class.

Judge Hunt. The Court must insist—the prisoner has been tried according to the established forms of law.

The trial of Susan B. Anthony for registering to vote and voting in 1872 in Rochester began on June 17, 1873, at Canandaigua, NY.

Sophia Smith Collection, Smith College

Affectionately Yours
Susan B. Anthony

Miss Anthony. Yes, your honor, but by forms of law all made by men, interpreted by men, administered by men, in favor of men and against women; and hence your honor's ordered verdict of guilty, against a United States citizen for the exercise of the "citizen's right to vote," simply because that citizen was a woman and not a man. But yesterday, the same man-made forms of law declared it a crime punishable with $1,000 fine and six months' imprisonment to give a cup of cold water, a crust of bread or a night's shelter to a panting fugitive tracking his way to Canada; and every man or woman in whose veins coursed a drop of human sympathy violated that wicked law, reckless of consequences, and was justified in so doing. As then the slaves who got their freedom had to take it over or under or through the unjust forms of law, precisely so now must women take it to get their right to a voice in this government; and I have taken mine, and mean to take it at every opportunity.

Judge Hunt. The Court orders the prisoner to sit down. It will not allow another word.

Miss Anthony. When I was brought before your honor for trial, I hoped for a broad and liberal interpretation of the Constitution and its recent amendments, which should declare all United States citizens under its protecting aegis—which should declare equality of rights the national guarantee to all persons born or naturalized in the United States. But failing to get this justice—failing, even, to get a trial by a jury *not* of my peers—I ask not leniency at your hands but rather the full rigor of the law.

Judge Hunt. The Court must insist—(Here the prisoner sat down.) The prisoner will stand up. (Here Miss Anthony rose again.) The sentence of the Court is that you pay a fine of $100 and the costs of the prosecution.

Miss Anthony. May it please your honor, I will never pay a dollar of your unjust penalty. All the stock in trade I possess is a debt of $10,000 incurred by publishing my paper—The Revolution—the sole object of which was to educate all women to do precisely as I have done, rebel against your man-made, unjust, unconstitutional forms of law, which tax, fine, imprison and hang women, while denying them the right of representation in the government; and I will work on with might and main to pay every dollar of that honest debt, but not a penny shall go to this unjust claim. And I shall earnestly and persistently continue to urge all women to the practical recognition of the old Revolutionary maxim. "Resistance to tyranny is obedience to God."

Judge Hunt. Madam, the Court will not order you to stand committed until the fine is paid.

1919. Nonnie May Stewart, hired secretary to William B. Leeds, becomes his wife and shortly thereafter surviving heir to his tinplate fortune of $25 million. After a tour of European nobility, she marries the impoverished Prince Christopher of Greece, changes her name to Princess Anastasia, and becomes widely known to the Romans as "The Dollar Princess."

Getting Arrested
THE LEGAL ADVISER **449**

	Executive Order 11246 as amended by 11375	Title VII of the Civil Rights Act of 1964 as amended by the Equal Employment Opportunity Act of 1972	Equal Pay Act of 1963 as amended by the Education Amendments of 1972 (Higher Education Act)
Effective date	Oct. 13, 1968	March 24, 1972 (July 1965 for nonprofessional workers.) (Employers with 15-24 employees were not covered until March 24, 1973.)	July 1, 1972 (June 1964 for nonprofessional workers.)
Which employers are covered?	All employers with federal contracts of over $10,000.[5]	All employers with 15 or more employees.	Most employers.[8]
What is prohibited?[1]	Discrimination in employment (including hiring, upgrading, salaries, fringe benefits, training, and other conditions of employment) on the basis of race, color, religion, national origin, or sex. Covers all employees.	Discrimination in employment (including hiring, upgrading, salaries, fringe benefits, training, and other conditions of employment) on the basis of race, color, religion, national origin, or sex. Covers all employees.	Discrimination in salaries (including almost all fringe benefits) on the basis of sex. Covers all employees.
Exemptions from coverage	None.	Religious institutions are exempt with respect to the employment of individuals of a particular religion or religious order (including those limited to one sex) to perform work for that institution. (Such institutions are not exempt from the prohibition of discrimination based on sex, color, and national origin.)	Some retail and service establishments, certain seasonal establishments, some farm workers, all household employees.[8]
Who enforces the provisions?	Office of Federal Contract Compliance (OFCC) of the Department of Labor has policy responsibility and oversees federal agency enforcement programs. OFCC has designated agencies that control grants and contracts as Compliance Agencies to enforce the Executive Order and to conduct reviews in various industries.	Equal Employment Opportunity Commission (EEOC).[6]	Wage and Hour Division of the Employment Standards Administration of the Department of Labor.
How is a complaint made?	By letter to OFCC.	By a sworn complaint form, obtainable from EEOC.	By letter, phone call, or in person to the nearest Wage and Hour Division office.
Can complaints of a pattern of discrimination be made as well as individual complaints?	Yes. However, individual complaints are referred to EEOC.	Yes.	Yes.
Who can make a complaint?[2]	Individuals and/or organizations on own behalf or on behalf of aggrieved employee(s) or applicant(s).	Individuals and/or organizations on own behalf or on behalf of aggrieved employee(s) or applicant(s). Members of the commission may also file charges.	Individuals and/or organizations on own behalf or on behalf of aggrieved employee(s).
Time limit for filing complaints[3]	180 days.	180 days.	No official limit, but recovery of back wages is limited by statute of limitations to two years for a nonwillful violation and three years for a willful violation.
Can investigations be made without complaints?	Yes. Government can conduct periodic reviews without a reported violation, as well as in response to complaints. Pre-award reviews are mandatory for contracts over $1,000,000.	No. Government can conduct investigations only if charges have been filed.	Yes. Government can conduct periodic reviews without a reported violation as well as in response to complaints.
Can the entire establishment be reviewed?	Yes. The Compliance Agency may investigate part or all of an establishment.	Yes. EEOC may investigate part or all of an establishment.	Yes. Usually the Wage-Hour Division reviews the entire establishment.
Record keeping requirements and government access to records	Employer must keep and preserve specified records relevant to the determination of whether violations have occurred. Government is empowered to review all rele-	Employer must keep and preserve specified records relevant to the determination of whether violations have occurred. Government is empowered to review all rele-	Employer must keep and preserve specified records relevant to the determination of whether violations have occurred. Government is empowered to review all rele-

1922. A year of firsts. Rebecca Latimer Felton (Georgia) becomes the first woman to officially occupy a seat in the U.S. Senate; Florence Allen is the first American female judge to sentence a man to death; Grace Kaercher becomes the first woman clerk of a state supreme court, in Minnesota.

	Executive Order 11246	Title VII	Equal Pay Act
Enforcement power and sanctions	Government may delay new contracts, revoke current contracts, and debar employers from eligibility for future contracts.	If attempts at conciliation fail, EEOC or the U.S. Attorney General may file suit.[7] Aggrieved individuals may also initiate suits. Court may enjoin respondent from engaging in unlawful behavior, order appropriate affirmative action, order reinstatement of employees, award back pay.	If voluntary compliance fails,[9] Secretary of Labor may file suit. Aggrieved individuals may initiate suits when Department of Labor has not done so. Court may enjoin respondent from engaging in unlawful behavior, order salary raises and back pay, and assess interest.
Can back pay be awarded?[4]	Yes. OFCC will seek back pay only for employees who were not previously protected by other laws allowing back pay.	Yes. For up to two years prior to filing charges with EEOC.	Yes. For up to two years for a nonwillful violation and three years for a willful violation.
Affirmative action requirements *(There are no restrictions against affirmative action which is nonpreferential)*	Affirmative action plans (including numerical goals and timetables) are required of all contractors with contracts of $50,000 or more and 50 or more employees.	Affirmative action is not required unless charges have been filed, in which case it may be included in conciliation agreement or be ordered by the court.	Affirmative action, other than salary increases and back pay, is not required.
Coverage of labor organizations	Any agreement the contractor may have with a labor organization cannot be in conflict with the contractor's affirmative action commitment.	Labor organizations are subject to the same requirements and sanctions as employers.	Labor organizations are prohibited from causing or attempting to cause an employer to discriminate on the basis of sex. Complaints may be made and suits brought against these organizations.
Is harassment prohibited?	Employers are prohibited from discharging or discriminating against any employee or applicant for employment because he/she has made a complaint, assisted with an investigation or instituted proceedings.	Employers are prohibited from discharging or discriminating against any employee because he/she has made a complaint, assisted with an investigation or instituted proceedings.	Employers are prohibited from discharging or discriminating against any employee because he/she has made a complaint, assisted with an investigation or instituted proceedings.
Notification of complaints	Notification of complaints has been erratic in the past.	EEOC notifies employers of complaints within 10 days.	Complaint procedure is very informal. Employer under review may or may not know that a violation has been reported.
Confidentiality of names	Individual complainant's name is usually given to the employer. Investigation findings are kept confidential by government, but can be revealed by the employer. Policy concerning government disclosure concerning investigations and complaints has not yet been issued. The aggrieved party and respondent are not bound by the confidentiality requirement.	Individual complainant's name is divulged when an investigation is made. Charges are not made public by EEOC, nor can any of its efforts during the conciliation process be made public by the commission or its employees. If court action becomes necessary, the identity of the parties involved becomes a matter of public record. The aggrieved party and respondent are not bound by the confidentiality requirement.	The identity of a complainant, as well as the employer (and union, if involved), is kept in strict confidence.[10] If court action becomes necessary, the identity of the parties involved becomes a matter of public record. The aggrieved party and respondent are not bound by the confidentiality requirement.
For further information, contact	Office of Federal Compliance Employment Standards Administration Department of Labor Washington, D.C. 20210 or Regional DOL Office	Equal Employment Opportunity Commission 1800 G Street, N.W. Washington, D.C. 20506 or Regional EEOC Office	Wage and Hour Division Employment Standards Administration Department of Labor Washington, D.C. 20210, or Field, Area, or Regional Wage and Hour office

(A similar chart, "Federal Laws and Regulations Concerning Sex Discrimination in Educational Institutions," is available from the Office for Civil Rights, HEW, Washington, D.C. 20201.)

1. A bona fide seniority or merit system is permitted under all legislation, provided the system is not discriminatory on the basis of sex or any other prohibited ground.
2. There are no restrictions against making a complaint under more than one antidiscrimination law at the same time.
3. This time limit refers to the time between an alleged discriminatory act and when a complaint is made. In general, however, the time limit is interpreted liberally when a continuing practice of discrimination is being challenged, rather than a single, isolated discriminatory act.
4. Back pay cannot be awarded prior to the effective date of the legislation.

Executive Order 11246 as amended by 11375:
5. The definition of "contract" is very broad and is interpreted to cover all government contracts (even if nominally "grants") which involve a benefit to the federal government.

Title VII of the Civil Rights Act of 1964 as amended by the Equal Employment Opportunity Act
6. In certain states that have fair employment laws with prohibitions similar to those of Title VII, EEOC automatically defers investigation of charges to the state agency for 60 days. (At the end of this period, EEOC will handle the charges unless the state is actively pursuing the case. About 85 percent of deferred cases return to EEOC for processing after deferral.)
7. Due to an ambiguity in the law as it relates to public institutions, it is not yet clear whether EEOC or the Attorney General will file suit in all situations which involve public institutions.

Equal Pay Act of 1963 as amended by the Education Amendments of 1972 (Higher Education Act)
8. The following are exempted from coverage of the Equal Pay Act: (a) employees of a retail or service establishment which makes most of its sales within an individual state and the volume of whose annual sales is less than $250,000 (covered hospitals, nursing homes, laundries, dry cleaners, and educational institutions are not subject, however, to this exemption); (b) employees of certain seasonal amusement or recreational establishments, motion picture theaters and certain small newspapers, and switchboard operators of telephone companies which have fewer than 750 telephones; (c) farm workers employed on small farms; (d) household employees.
9. Over 95 percent of all Equal Pay investigations are resolved through voluntary compliance.
10. Unless court action is necessary, the name of the parties need not be revealed. The identity of a complainant or a person furnishing information is never revealed without that person's consent.

From *Federal Laws and Regulations Concerning Sex Discrimination in Educational Institutions.* Copyright © 1972 Association of American Colleges. Reprinted by permission.

1923. Aimee Semple McPherson, called by her thousands of followers "Sister Aimee" and known to her detractors as "the Barnum of Religion," sets out on her peculiar brand of barnstorm preaching, addressing tentfuls of people each night and thrice on Sunday. The service includes orchestra music, spiritual telephone "hot lines," revivalist atmosphere, and a touch of vaudeville.

Suggestions for Filing
Sex Discrimination Complaints
NOW Legal Defense and Education Fund

It is imperative to *file quickly* and *file everywhere* (with as many agencies as applicable). Your complaint may always be withdrawn.

The only exception to the "file everywhere" rule is that in many states filing with the city and state are mutually exclusive. You must therefore make a choice between the two, whichever would be most helpful. File with either the city or the state, then file immediately with the federal agencies—this will speed the complaint along.

Theoretically, the burden of proof is not on you. However, you should gather as much information as possible about your company: facts, statistics, memos, directives, employee directories. Before you file, write a short summary of your charge; this will help you organize your thoughts and helps the agency to help you. Be as concise and factual as possible.

Legislation in the area of sex discrimination is far from perfect, but the law is still far ahead of the practice. The law will not work for us unless we use it.

In some cases, you may need to file with agencies not included on the attached chart. Other federal and local agencies handling discrimination problems are:

Schlesinger Library, Radcliffe College

Benevolent Old Gentleman: "Plums are not good for little girls." (From the cover of Equal Rights, *the "Official Weekly Organ of the National Woman's party," March 24, 1923; five cents.)*

Hellmich Brothers

- **U.S. Civil Service Commission** (local branch or Washington, D.C.): Contact in cases of sex discrimination within a federal agency. This commission sponsors a "Federal Women's Program" to promote equal employment opportunity for women. Also contact FEW (Federally Employed Women), an unofficial organization for the advancement of women in the federal government.

- **U.S. Department of Justice, Civil Rights Division** (Washington, D.C.): They are interested in receiving copies of *all* charges.

- **U.S. Federal Communications Commission** (Washington, D.C.): Contact if your employer is a common carrier, such as AT&T, ITT Corp., a television station, or a radio station.

- **U.S. Labor-Management Relations Board** (local branch or Washington, D.C.): Contact when a labor union is involved.

- **National Labor Relations Board** (local branch or Washington, DC): Contact when a labor union is involved.

- **State Labor Relations Board**: Contact when a labor union is involved.

- **State Department of Law, Civil Rights Division and/or State Attorney General's Office**

- **State or City Human Rights Commission/Division**: This is the local equivalent of the U.S. EEOC.

- **State or City Department of Consumer Affairs**: Contact when the discriminating business is licensed by this department; for example, an employment agency or a home-improvement contractor.

From *Suggestions for Filing Sex Discrimination Complaints.* NOW Legal Defense and Education Fund. Reprinted with permission.

1923. Alice Paul introduces the first equal rights amendment to Congress and, when it fails to pass, undertakes to involve the League of Nations in an international drive for sex equality. She argues now, and will argue into the seventies, that much of the trouble in the world stems from the fact that women have not been able to exercise their rightful political powers.

How to Organize an
Employment Discrimination Action

Blank Goodman Rone & Stanley

The key to organizing a successful on-the-job campaign against employment discrimination can be summed up in one sentence: Involve as many women as possible. Whatever action you plan to take—negotiations, filing a lawsuit, using internal company grievance machinery—the more women who join in the effort, the better.

There are many advantages to working in a group. First, protesting is much easier psychologically. No one woman has to stand alone in criticizing management, and no one woman has to run the very real risks of being harassed, intimidated or even fired by the company.

Second, protesting as a group presents a much stronger case than if you were to complain as an individual. If there are ten or twenty women, all of them crying discrimination, a company can't explain away its practices by arguing that a particular woman employee is incompetent or just doesn't measure up to company standards.

Third, sex-discrimination cases require a lot of work. Complainants who do a thorough job of collecting statistics and documenting the company's discriminatory practices are most likely to be successful, whether they take the case to court or simply use their data as an in-house bargaining tool. Such data can be collected more easily if there are a number of women involved, not only because there are more hands to do the work but also because different women may have insights and knowledge about different parts of the company.

And, finally, employment-discrimination cases are expensive—particularly if the group decides to go to court. Even though the law provides for the recovery of fees and expenses if the plaintiffs are successful, victory is usually years away. Most lawyers require a client to pay some fees in advance, and court costs must be paid as they accrue. These expenses are a lot more manageable if

they are divided among ten women than if they are borne by one woman alone. Many a meritorious case has never reached the courts simply because an individual woman going it alone couldn't afford to subsidize the action.

Given all these advantages, it is no wonder that a company's first tactic when confronted with a group of female employees, armed with a well-documented case of sex discrimination, is to try to divide and conquer. Employers go to great lengths to discredit group leaders, to intimidate group members or—most insidiously of all—to make the kinds of cosmetic changes that, while they don't really accomplish anything very lasting for

SET HER FREE

Sophia Smith Collection, Smith College

She will be responsible for the inclusion of a statement on equal rights in the preamble of the United Nations charter and she is to become—along with her National Woman's Party—perhaps the single most important force in ERA's closing drive toward ratification over fifty years later.

WOMEN'S LIBERATION

THE WOMEN'S LIBERATION MOVEMENT

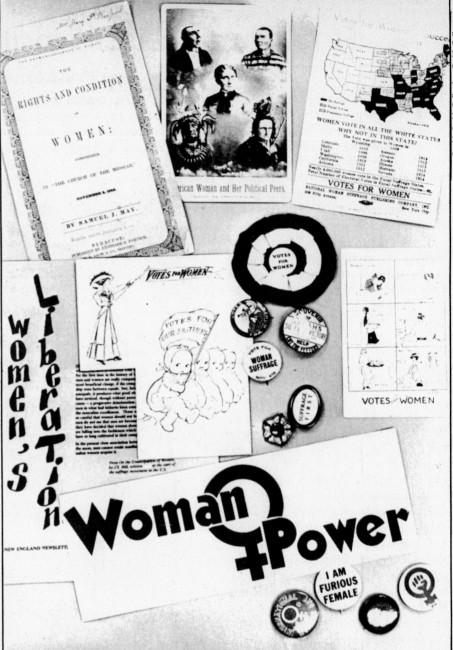

women, convince at least some members of the group that organized action isn't really necessary—"the company is doing all it can."

Faced with these kinds of tactics, many women's groups simply fold under the pressure. The groups that have been most successful, however, recognize management's tactics for what they are and refuse to be deflected from their original purpose.

Employment-discrimination actions are most successful if they draw on the concerted efforts of large groups of women employees at the company itself. They require great dedication, persistence, and, above everything else, a sense of real sisterhood and commonality of purpose among the women themselves. The women must display monumental amounts of energy, patience, and stamina; and they must be committed to working for long-range improvements at the company as a whole rather than individual promotions or monetary settlements for specific persons. It is not easy to fight an employment-discrimination battle, but without this kind of effort equal job rights will never be a reality.

1923. The clergy, reform groups, "Leagues for Decency," and local authorities violently protest the advent of shirtless, form-fitting bathing suits for women.

*Here are some of the dos and don'ts of organizing
around employment discrimination issues:*

DO organize women in every department and job category. Bring secretaries and clerical staff into your action, along with the very few women who may hold technical jobs or semimanagerial positions.

DON'T make the mistake of thinking that you have nothing in common with women from other departments. From a legal perspective, you have everything in common: You are all injured by the company's basic attitude, conscious or unconscious, that, whoever you are and whatever you do, your work is not worth as much as the work of a man.

DO develop the strongest possible case you can. Base it on statistics. Look at the overall difference between male and female salaries, the number of women versus the number of men who are in key high-paying jobs, the average number of years it takes a female employee to reach the top versus what it takes the average man.

Look at the company policies that affect women generally: Does the company exclude pregnancy coverage from its health care, sick leave, and disability plan, even though it covers virtually everything else? Does it force men and women to retire at different ages and does it give women lower retirement benefits? What about company training programs? Are women excluded from certain programs, such as those for management positions or craft jobs?

How about personnel practices? When the company hires for entry-level jobs, does it give women the clerical jobs while assigning men the technical or craft positions? Does the company rely on word-of-mouth recruitment, which results in a disproportionate number of male applicants? Are women paid less than men for what seems to be equivalent work?

If the answers to these questions are yes, then you've made out what the law calls a *prima facie* case of discrimination—enough to get you a court hearing and enough to require the company to explain away the statistics.

DON'T allow yourself to be sidetracked away from these kinds of statistics into arguing about individual cases *unless* you have cases that are extremely strong and particularly useful in highlighting the company's discriminatory practices. Focus instead on the company's general policies and practices—the conditions that affect all women.

DO present your case to management in the strongest possible way. Ask for a meeting with top company officials to discuss your findings and grievances. Attend such a meeting in a group, or else send two or three women as spokespersons.

DON'T waste too much time talking to the company's equal-employment officer or to other management personnel who may not have the authority to make major changes.

DON'T allow management to single out individual members of the group for private discussions about the sex-discrimination data or the merits of your grievances. Make sure that any discussions take place with the group as a whole or with the group spokesperson.

DO hold group meetings privately, off company premises or after hours under conditions in which management personnel cannot overhear what is being said or take notes on who is attending.

DON'T be intimidated by the company's efforts to harass the group

---

1924. Alice Astor, the only daughter of John Jacob Astor and the heir to $10 million, marries Prince Serge Platonovitch Obolensky Neledinsky Meletsky, a Russian nobleman whose pedigree allegedly is traced to Rurik, the ninth-century Viking founder of the czarist dynasty.

or to prevent it from meeting or organizing. Standard tactics are, for example, trying to keep the women from using the employee bulletin board to post notices of group meetings, or spying on the women's meetings to see who attends. A company that resorts to such tactics is clearly on the run.

DO use your lawyers effectively if you have retained lawyers. Make sure they attend or are aware of any discussions you may be having with management.

DON'T respond to any company proposals independently without discussing them with your lawyer in advance.

DO consider filing charges with the U.S. Equal Employment Opportunity Commission and your local state or city equal rights agency. It won't cost you anything, since the agencies do the work for you and since—theoretically at least—you don't need a lawyer. Some agencies, depending on where they are located and how much power they have, are fairly successful in resolving complaints and securing settlements.

Sophia Smith Collection, Smith College

DO make sure any settlement that you secure—sometimes known as an affirmative-action plan—is a good one. You're looking for meaningful goals and timetables designed to move more women into higher-paying jobs within a definite time period. You're looking for meaningful training programs and equalization of salaries. The acid test is money. If a company's affirmative-action plan requires it to spend substantial amounts of money over a period of years on women and women's programs, it's probably a decent plan.

But however good the plan may look on paper, **DON'T** be deluded into thinking it is self-enforcing. Make sure that the plan really goes into effect. Insist that your group, or some other organization, such as the state agency with which you filed your charges, has the right to police the agreement, to make sure goals and timetables are met, and to impose sanctions if they are not.

1924. Nellie Tayloe Ross becomes the first woman elected governor (Wyoming) when she fills the slot left vacant by the death of her husband.

The Equal Rights Amendment
Citizens' Advisory Council on the Status of Women

The Equal Rights Amendment. The proposed Equal Rights Amendment to the Constitution reads as follows:

> Equality of rights <u>under the law</u> shall not be denied or abridged by the United States or by any State on account of sex. (emphasis supplied)

General effect on federal and state laws and official practices. The Equal Rights Amendment would not nullify all laws distinguishing on the basis of sex, but would require that the law treat men and women equally. Equal treatment can be accomplished either by extending the law that applies only to one sex to the other sex, or by rendering the law unconstitutional as denying equality of rights to one sex. The consideration of the ratification of the Equal Rights Amendment by the individual states will give ample opportunity and time for states to decide on modifications to adjust their laws to the amendment where needed. Any modifications could be made so long as no distinctions are based on sex.

In interpreting the Equal Rights Amendment, the courts will consider the intent of Congress, particularly the views expressed by the proponents of the Amendment. The following is a summary of effects the proposed amendment would have, as reflected in the House debate on the amendment and in Senate reports in previous years.

Alimony, child support, and custody laws. Present laws will not be invalidated. In those states where alimony is limited to women, men will become eligible under the same circumstances as women. The welfare of the child will be the criterion for child custody as it is in most states now. Provisions of law giving mothers (or fathers) preference will be inoperative.

The National Commissioners on Uniform State Laws recently adopted a Uniform Marriage and Divorce Act, the terms of which are in accord with the Equal Rights Amendment. It provides for alimony for either spouse (called "maintenance"), child-support obligations for both spouses in accordance with their means, and custody of children based on the welfare of the child.

It should be kept in mind that the great majority of divorce arrangements covering these areas are agreed to by the parties without litigation.

From *The Equal Rights Amendment—What It Will and Won't Do*, Citizens' Advisory Council on the Status of Women, Washington, D.C.

Dower Rights. Dower laws will not be nullified. Dower rights will be extended to men in those few states where men do not have a right in their wives' estates.

Cary Herz, Nancy Palmer Photo Agency

Property Rights of Married Women. Special restrictions on property rights of married women would be invalidated; married women could engage in business as freely as men and manage their separate property such as inheritances and earnings.

Status of Homemaker. Congresswoman Dwyer of New Jersey said on August 10 in the debate in the House of Representatives on the Equal Rights Amendment: "It would not take women out of the home. It would not downgrade the roles of mother and housewife. Indeed, it would give new dignity to these important roles. By confirming women's equality under the law, by upholding women's right to choose her place in society, the equal rights amendment can only enhance the status of traditional women's occupa-

---

1925. Rose Knox, president of the giant Knox Company—makers of gelatin both for food and industrial use—begins to oversee the development of her business from an initial value of $300,000 to well over $1 million. She is, she says, "determined to run [the business] in. . .a woman's way." She institutes one of the first five-day workweeks,

tions. For these would become positions accepted by women as equals, not roles imposed on them as inferiors." (116 Cong. Record, H.7952)

State "Protective" Labor Laws Now Applying Only to Women. Minimum wage laws and rest period and lunch period laws will be extended to men. Laws prohibiting hours of work beyond a specified number, night work, employment in particular occupations, and weightlifting laws will be invalidated. There will probably not be any of the prohibitory laws in effect by the time the Equal Rights Amendment is ratified, as a result of Title VII of the Civil Rights Act of 1964. Leading court decisions, changes by state legislatures, rulings by state attorneys general, and guidelines of the Equal Employment Opportunity Commission all clearly point in this direction.

The Equal Rights Amendment would not prohibit special maternity benefits. Furthermore, only Puerto Rico gives any special benefit and its terms may discourage employers from hiring women. In fact, laws in several states **prohibit** employment of women during specified periods before and after childbirth but do not require reemployment or even require employers to give any of the benefits given for other forms of temporary disability. Two states have temporary disability insurance plans that include benefits for loss of employment due to childbirth along with other types of temporary disability, but this is not a special benefit.

Employment. The Equal Rights Amendment would restrict only governmental action and would not apply to purely private action. **It would not affect private employment**; it would prohibit discrimination by government as an employer—federal, state, county, and city, including school boards. One of the largest group of employees affected are teachers, professors, and other employees of public schools and state institutions of higher education. It would require equal pay for equal work only for employees of government. The coverage of private employees under present equal pay laws would not be extended or otherwise modified.

Education. The Equal Rights Amendment would prohibit restriction of public schools to one sex and it would prohibit public institutions from requiring higher admission standards for women (or men in case any exist).

Federal Social Security. The Equal Rights Amendment would extend to widowers of covered women workers the benefits now provided only to widows of covered men workers. For example, widowers with minor children would receive a benefit based on their deceased wife's employment under the same circumstances a widow with minor children would receive.

A man retiring at age sixty-two would have his benefit computed under the same formula as a woman retiring at sixty-two. (This particular inequity would be corrected by the Social Security Act Amendments that passed the House of Representatives this session and are now pending in the Senate.)

Other Governmental Pension and Retirement Plans. Any preference in treatment given to one sex or to survivors of one sex would be extended to the other sex. The Equal Rights Amendment would have no bearing on private pension and retirement plans. Many are now covered by Title VII of the Civil Rights Act of 1964.

Military Service and Jury Service. Women would be subject to jury service and military service under the same conditions as men. Women with children in their personal care could be excused from either obligation just as men could be under the same circumstances. Being subject to military service would not necessarily mean they would have to serve in all assignments any more than all men serve in all assignments. Women volunteers would have to be admitted under the same standards as men; they now have to meet higher standards. During World War II many thousands of women served, many of them in dangerous assignments. This administration is making every effort to move to a volunteer service; the issue of the draft may, therefore, be moot by the time the amendment is ratified.

Criminal Law. The Equal Rights Amendment would invalidate laws prescribing longer prison sentences for women than for men for the same offense (or vice versa, if such exists), different ages for treatment as adults for purposes of criminal law, and laws permitting imprisonment of women who have not committed any offense. It would require equal opportunity for rehabilitation, including access to treatment for drug addiction and alcoholism. It would not affect laws relating to rape.

Psychological and Social. The Equal Rights Amendment will directly affect only women's legal rights. It will not affect the social relationships between the sexes.

There are, however, intangible psychological benefits already accruing to women. The fight for the Equal Rights Amendment is forging a new solidarity among women that fosters self-confidence and the courage to use rights already theirs but not claimed because of fears.

Women of all ages and political persuasion, all occupations, black and white, union women and business women, housewives and working women, have worked together with men to secure passage of the Equal Rights Amendment in the House of Representatives.

keeps her plants spotless and pleasant, and wins exceptionally enduring loyalty from her employees. Not until she reaches her mid-eighties will she relinquish control of the operation to a son.

Politics
and the
Community

Keeping the Heat On

Election-night victories are no guarantee of legislative successes, and legislative successes are no guarantee of programs that work and laws that are enforced—in short, effective political action is more than getting out the vote. Since almost all government policy is affected by lobbies for or against an issue, to lobby for your point of view is not only a constitutional right but also a necessity.

Lobbying can be almost anything—from sending a letter to your representative to professionally organized pressure from, say, the dairy industry. A friendly visit to a lawmaker's office is traditional. Other techniques are more improvisational. (Maryland feminists recently cornered state legislators to talk about the Equal Rights Amendment by occupying all the tables in the legislators' favorite dining room at the Annapolis Hilton.) Lobbying is such an accepted and respected ingredient of the decision-making process that legislators sometimes credit lobbyists with supernatural powers. On the Monday after the special Watergate prosecutor, Archibald Cox, was fired, when Congress was flooded with letters and telegrams, one incredulous member of Congress asked Evelyn Dubrow, lobbyist for the International Ladies' Garment Workers' Union: "Evvy, did you do that?"

Shirley Downs, legislative assistant to Representative Shirley Chisholm (D.-N.Y.), reports that Senator Jacob Javits (R.-N.Y.) changed his mind on one issue of concern to women when his New York apartment building was picketed; then he told a woman lobbyist in Washington, "You can call them off now." Such is the impact—real or imagined—of a lobby. But according to Dubrow, "Lobbying is only as good as the kind of help you get back home from constituents."

It doesn't seem to be enough that a piece of legislation will work to the obvious advantage of almost everyone, as is true of many con-

sumer bills; it took Congress seven years to pass truth-in-lending legislation, mainly because business pressure against was stronger than consumer pressure for. As Jane O'Grady, lobbyist for the Amalgamated Clothing Workers, states, "The person in Washington can do a great deal in terms of legislative strategy, coalition-building, information-gathering, but there is no substitute for mass action at the grassroots level." Thus, the child-care legislation—which was passed by Congress as a result of pressure from a broad, Washington-based coalition and was then vetoed by Nixon—died because the child-care coalition did not generate enough grass-roots support for Congress to override the veto.

Carol Burris, who came to Washington to work on the ERA, formed the Women's Lobby, Inc., because "there are dairy lobbies, drug, cattle, sugar, labor, and farm lobbies. Now

it's time that 53 percent of the population lobbied for its rights." The ERA provided a training ground for women's lobbies in the states. The Women's Lobby already has coordinators in 40 states, and the staff runs lobbying training workshops in states where women are interested.

The most effective organized lobbying is done by individuals who are professional, full-time, and salaried. The legislative process, in Washington, D.C., and in the states, is not predictable—votes are not always taken when expected, unanticipated problems can arise in committee, friends can turn into enemies overnight. A lobbyist must work on a schedule created and continually revised by others, must follow the progress of a bill from inception to final vote in a process that is often erratic, must develop and maintain working relationships with other organizations, committee and legislative staff, and representatives. It's not a simple

A HARD JOB FOR JUSTICE.

"Oh, help me, Hercules! even if you have to change the course of the Potomac through the whole of Washington, and cleanse out all the departments."

1925. Marie Diers, who—during the depression following Germany's World War I defeat—writes romantic novels about young women rescuing their family fortunes from father's mismanagement, sparks a new German woman's movement for political change.

Virginia Kerr

matter of flying to the Capitol for a week. As Burris says, "It is a lot of hard work and worn-out shoes."

Most professional lobbyists think of themselves as educators. The lobbyist provides information and constituents' attitudes about an issue to legislators and also provides information and legislators' attitudes about an issue to constituents. Coalitions were fundamental to passage of the civil rights legislation of the sixties and the child-care bill. A lobbyist may spend as much time identifying and strategizing with organizational allies as in meetings with legislators. And when their constituency doesn't have the necessary clout, lobbyists lobby other lobbyists. Coalition lobbying is particularly helpful to newcomers. According to Jane O'Grady, "When you come in sort of fresh and want results right away, you make some of your worst mistakes . . . you can learn a lot from the people with experience."

Lobbying techniques depend on the issues, on the organizations, and on the individuals. Evvy Dubrow cites several rules: *Don't beg* (for votes); *Don't threaten* (confrontation is one thing, lobbying another); *Don't assume* (that someone is unalterably either for or against); *Don't pretend* (to know more than you know). She adds, "I see who I need to see, speak my piece, and get the hell out, unless they want to talk further."

Lobbying in the states can be more difficult than in Washington, D.C. State legislators may work only part-time. Some have no permanent office or staff, forcing the lobbyist to take time to find places to approach them. In addition, while lobbyists in the nation's capital can take advantage of extensive newspaper coverage of issues and of the research efforts of Congressional staffs and a variety of national organizations, state and local lobbyists often have to do all their own homework. (The greatest mistake is to begin lobbying before knowing the issue thoroughly or before knowing something about the legislators and their constituencies.)

THE WATCH ON SPOILERS.
DEMOCRATIC TIGERS AND REPUBLICAN VULTURES MUST BE KEPT AT BAY.

Mainly because of success with the ERA, women have gained a reputation in Washington as a significant political force. (Says Jane O'Grady on the subject of women and unions: "There are very few male labor leaders in Washington now who don't know that they got troubles.") But reputations die easily in politics. Women's rights organizations need support. Lobbyists' salaries cannot come from foundation grants, and even the best lobbyists can only keep representatives and organizational members informed. They need the backup letter, telegram, or phone call. Letters do not have to be elegant; they do not have to be long; they do not even have to be grammatical. All they need to do is make a point. Consider the following telegram sent to a U.S. Senator regarding the impeachment of Richard Nixon: "HIM OR YOU."

1925. Texas governor Pat Morris Neff appoints the first state supreme court composed solely of women.

The Committee
System of Congress

Nancy Cornblath

In 1789, the Standing Committee on Enrolled Bills was established in the Senate and with it came the beginning of the committee system. Today there are 18 standing (permanent) committees in the Senate and 22 in the House of Representatives. These groups of Representatives concerned with specific areas of legislative jurisdiction have become essential to the functioning of the Congress.

It is in committee that legislation is researched, formulated and written. Oversight hearings are held by these bodies and their subcommittees to gain information and to monitor the workings of other branches of the government. There are select committees appointed by the Speaker of the House or the President of the Senate, which exist for a finite amount of time to examine a particular problem area (i.e., the Watergate committee). And special committees are set up to deal with a narrowly defined sphere of jurisdiction such as aging or small business. Select and special committees do not write legislation, but use the information gathered through their investigations to make specific reports to the Congress, while standing committees work on the actual lawmaking.

Once a bill is introduced on the floor of the House or Senate, it is referred to the committee that has jurisdiction over the area with which it is concerned. The bill will usually then be assigned to a subcommittee where the process of researching and writing will begin. Currently there are 125 subs in the House and 131 in the Senate. Their major responsibility is holding hearings on bills and drafting legislation, which is then considered by the entire committee.

While a bill is usually amended after it reaches the floor, the version that emerges from committee is the point of departure, and the most effective way to influence a piece of legislation is generally as a member of the committee in which it is written. The rules state that committee assignments are made by the entire Senate and House, although they are actually determined by each party in caucus. Members can make their preferences known and geographic distribution is also a factor in the decision-making.

Power on committees has traditionally been governed by the seniority system, with the chairperson, a senior member from the majority party, having the most power—scheduling meetings, setting agendas that state the order in which bills are discussed and deciding which pieces of legislation receive hearings. She or he often hires most of the committee staff, and having access to a knowledgeable, competent staff is vital to the effective functioning of committees. Each committee also has a ranking member who is a senior representative from the minority party.

Although the privileges of the chairperson have remained intact, the basis for becoming head of a committee came under attack during the beginning of the 94th Congress. The most senior member of the majority no longer automatically assumes leadership, but must be affirmed by the party caucus and can be challenged. This change was initiated in the House when W. R. Poage of Texas lost his chairpersonship of the Agriculture Committee to Thomas S. Foley of Washington, Wright Patman of Texas was unseated as chairperson of the Banking and Currency Committee, and Melvin Price of Illinois replaced F. Edward Hebert of Louisiana as head of Armed Services. Several subcommittee chairpeople were successfully challenged as well.

Additional moves for committee reform have been brought up on the floor of both the House and the Senate. In 1973, the House established a select committee, chaired by Richard Bolling of Missouri, to study the committee system, and in the fall of 1974, House Resolution 988, Committee Reform Amendments of 1974, was passed. Resulting changes in the committee set up include:

• each committee with more than 15 members, except the Budget Committee, is required to have at least four subcommittees.

• the Speaker of the House may refer a bill to more than one committee, overriding what had been the precedent of sending a bill to only one committee. This move is aimed at eliminating jurisdictional disputes that arose in the past when two subcommittees claimed jurisdiction over the same bill.

• the number of professional staff was increased from 6 to 18 and the clerical staff was increased from 6 to 12. The minority is entitled to receive one-third in each case, but all or part of the staff may be classed as nonpartisan by agreement of both parties. Staff appointments are often patronage positions, and a recent *Washington Post* article revealed the staffers have been known to participate in campaign work.

• committee reports must now include an inflationary impact statement.

• the House Internal Security Committee (formerly the Un-American Activities Committee) was abolished.

Committees and subcommittees provide the best focus for lobbying efforts. Because their size is limited and they do most of the basic work in formulating legislation, it is in dealing with these groups that lobbyists can have the most input.

Making our views known to subcommittee staffs before a bill is written, testifying at hearings to insure our position is on the public record, preparing other language and amendments for mark up, and providing resource information to subcommittee members are all ways in which we can influence the decision-making process.

And with the challenges of new members and reevaluation by incumbents, there is little doubt that this process is changing. The committee system is evolving and slowly becoming less tradition bound.

1925. Explorers discover the "duck-billed" women of the Saras-Djinges central African tribes. Starting at the age of four, these women stretch their lips with wooden discs until they are able to accommodate fourteen-inch soup plates. They must subsist on a liquid diet, and they find speech nearly impossible.

Standing Committees of Congress

The following is a list of standing committees of Congress, their areas of jurisdiction and members.
The Senate listing contains paragraphs discussing feminist issues covered by each committee.
This information can be applied to the corresponding group in the House unless indicated.

The Senate

AERONAUTICAL AND SPACE SCIENCES: *budget for space research, NASA, aerospace activities, and science.*

This committee is difficult for women lobbyists to work with, but efforts could be made to encourage the increased employment of women by the space program. Currently few women are hired by NASA, and there are no females in executive positions in the space program.

AGRICULTURE AND FORESTRY: *general agricultural policies, forestry, timber leasing, meat inspection, nutrition and anti-hunger programs and rural electrification.*

The program handled by this committee that affects women most is food stamps. There are two areas in which we can work on this. The first centers around the problem of single parent families who receive significantly less of a subsidy than two parent families, a policy that totally ignores the possibility of teenage children who can easily eat as much or more than an adult. The second area of input concerns revision of eligibility standards and the payment schedule for the program. Nutrition programs for the aged also come through this committee and these are of importance to women, who makeup the majority of older Americans.

APPROPRIATIONS: *appropriates all federal monies.*

Once a bill has passed authorizing federal funds for a department, program, or agency, it is referred to the appropriate subcommittee of this committee. Because of the power of the purse, these subcommittees are often as important in determining policy of these agencies and departments as the standing committees with jurisdiction over the same area.

Subcommittees of special importance to women include Agriculture, Environment and Consumer Protection, which handles money for food stamps and consumer protection programs and Labor and Health, Education and Welfare, which faces pressure from anti-abortion factions when appropriating funds. The most practical approach for women to take in relation to this committee is to question its membership, which is old guard, conservative, and favors meeting in closed session. By exerting pressure, women could get more liberals on the committee who would be willing to do a lot of the detailed work involved in figuring out budgets. Although there have been some changes in the 94th Congress, this has always been a problem because, traditionally, people concerned with instituting broad social change have little interest in budgetary matters. Since all appropriations are initiated in the House, we can have more input in the committee of that body.

ARMED SERVICES: *all military programs and naval petroleum reserves.*

The most important military program of concern to women dealt with by this committee is the one denying women admission to the service academies. This discriminatory policy is a continuing focus of lobbying efforts.

There are, also, many other areas this committee could become involved in. These include the illegality of attaching an active serviceperson's pay for alimony and child support payments, and

The House

SCIENCE AND TECHNOLOGY: *weather; scientific, energy, and environmental research and development; science; technology; and space exploration, control, and programs.*

AGRICULTURE: *agriculture, commodities exchanges, farm credit, food stamps, forestry, nutrition, rural development, and sugar.*

APPROPRIATIONS: *appropriations of revenue for support of the Federal Government.*

This committee tends to meet in closed session more than others. However, women should have more input than on the Senate side now that Yvonne Brathwaite Burke of California is a member.

ARMED SERVICES: *defense, foreign military aid, and naval petroleum reserves.*

1926. Violette N. Anderson of Chicago passes the bar this year. She is later to become the first black woman lawyer to be admitted to practice before the United States Supreme Court.

keeping women out of more active roles in the service (women are not allowed in the infantry, armory, or artillery and those who are pilots and members of the corps of engineers have been coming under attack). Dependent allowances, health care, housing, and the lack of service related care within the military are additional areas that could be worked on within this committee.

The treatment of women by Armed Services has improved, however, because its chairman, John C. Stennis of Mississippi, is unhappy with the committee's behavior. He was against an all-volunteer army, and, once that passed, he decided that the status of women within the services might as well be expanded since one offends his prejudices as much as the other.

STANDARDS OF OFFICIAL CONDUCT: *campaign expenditures (House only), Code of Official Conduct, financial disclosure, and lobbying.*

BANKING, HOUSING, AND URBAN AFFAIRS: *banking and currency, all credit areas, public and private housing, controls or prices of rents, services and commodities, and financial aid to industry not covered by other committees.*

One issue to be worked on with this committee is the discrimination against women seeking to live in rental properties. Regulatory legislation for the banking industry also comes through this committee; however, the legislation is carried out by the Federal Reserve Board, which is not equipped to do any enforcement when discrimination is reported.

BANKING, CURRENCY, AND HOUSING: *banking, currency, government lending, housing, urban development, money and credit.*

Leonor Sullivan of Missouri is a high ranking member of this committee. She is a consumer rights advocate with a special interest in cosmetic safety, and this would be a good bill to work on with this committee.

BUDGET: *concurrent resolutions on the budget.*

BUDGET: *concurrent resolutions on the budget, study the effect of legislation on budget outlays, evaluate continuing studies of tax expenditures, Congressional Budget Office.*

COMMERCE: *interstate and foreign commerce, including communications, transportation, fisheries and wildlife, Coast Guard, merchant marine and navigation, and civil aeronautics.*

This committee handles legislation that concerns the Federal Communications Commission, Federal Aviation Administration, Federal Trade Commission, Office of Consumer Affairs, Environmental Protection Agency, and the Interstate Commerce Commission. The ways in which these agencies' regulatory activities affect the status of women could be worked on through Commerce and its subcommittees.

INTERSTATE AND FOREIGN COMMERCE: *communications, consumer protection, energy regulation, health care, railroads, inland waterways, and securities and exchanges.*

This committee is of interest to women because it has broad jurisdiction as well as the health subcommittee.

MERCHANT MARINE AND FISHERIES: *maritime matters, fishing and fisheries, oceanography, wildlife and wildlife refuges, merchant marine and Coast Guard, and deepwater ports.*

DISTRICT OF COLUMBIA: *District of Columbia affairs except for appropriations.*

Now that the district has homerule, it is difficult to do much within the framework of this committee.

DISTRICT OF COLUMBIA: *lawmaking for the District of Columbia except appropriations.*

1926. Percy Pearl Washington, the heaviest woman ever weighed, is born. She will eventually grow to a bulk of 880 pounds, dying at the age of forty-six.

FINANCE: *all taxation, social security, pensions, tariffs, import quotas, trade agreements, and health.*

This is a very conservative committee, and one of our highest priorities could be to work on getting good people as members. It is especially important to find individuals who are not too dependent on staff backup, because the only staff permitted to attend meetings are Chairman Russell Long's Finance Committee people. Staff aid in committee work is important for busy Congresspeople who are stretched thin or who don't understand all of the issues, and it is just not available in this committee.

Worker's compensation, unemployment compensation for women who are pregnant, tax reform, and social security reform can be worked on through Finance. It overlaps with the Labor and Public Welfare Committee in the area of health.

WAYS AND MEANS: *social security, unemployment compensation, public assistance, taxes, trade, and health.*

FOREIGN RELATIONS: *foreign affairs including all treaties.*

This committee covers little of importance to women. Occasionally bills reported out have amendments prohibiting the use of appropriated funds for abortions in other countries, and this demands our attention. Eventually we might be able to focus on the needs of women in other nations, but this would require developing expertise in an entirely new area.

INTERNATIONAL RELATIONS: *foreign affairs.*

This committee, formerly called Foreign Affairs, is generally considered less powerful than its counterpart in the Senate because the Senate Foreign Relations Committee passes on all treaties, ambassadorships, and other foreign policy posts.

GOVERNMENT OPERATIONS: *the Federal Government.*

The main function of this committee is oversight. It is an investigatory body whose purpose is to look into the workings of federal agencies. The Permanent Subcommittee on Investigations, chaired by Henry Jackson of Washington, is specifically designated to investigate abuses, although all of the subs can do this if they think it necessary—it is done rarely.

GOVERNMENT OPERATIONS: *structure of the Federal Government, executive reorganizations, intergovernmental relationships, budgeting, National Archives, and general revenue sharing.*

INTERIOR AND INSULAR AFFAIRS: *mining, oil conservation, public lands and minerals, national parks, Indians, island possessions of the United States, and irrigation and reclamation.*

This committee does a large amount of work on environmental issues such as strip mining and most areas of its jurisdiction have little effect on women in particular. However, we could work on discrimination in employment (the National Parks Service will not hire women as forest rangers).

Special concerns, such as urging the Indian Health service to offer more in the way of contraceptive services, can be worked on as well. Eventually we could start lobbying the Parks and Recreation Subcommittee to start using public funds and land to sponsor play groups and camps.

INTERIOR AND INSULAR AFFAIRS: *environment, Indians, mining, national parks and recreational areas, public lands, territories, water and power resources, and irrigation and reclamation.*

JUDICIARY: *Constitutional amendments and revision of statutes, federal judiciary, prison system, immigration and naturalization, bankruptcy, espionage, copyright, patent, and trademark law.*

This prestigious committee of lawyers handles all Constitutional amendments, including those seeking to outlaw abortion. The subcommittee on Constitutional Rights could be expanded to become an exciting sub for women now that Sam Ervin of North Carolina, its former chairman, has retired. The Juvenile Delinquency and Penitentiary subs are also places to work on wom-

JUDICIARY: *civil rights, Constitutional law, revision and codification of federal statutes, crime and criminal justice, bankruptcy, monopoly and improper trade practices, patents, trademarks and copyrights, immigration and naturalization.*

Representative Don Edwards from California heads the Constitutional Rights Subcommittee of Judiciary. He is a strong proponent of women's rights and has reported out the Educational Equity Act from that sub. All Constitutional amendments outlawing abortion must come through him. The other subcommittees are also chaired by liberals.

1927. Senora Salmonea Wolf of Jerez, Spain, has the portrait of her late husband tatooed on her tongue to atone for, according to her own testimony, having nagged him to death.

en's rights (when women commit an "unladylike" crime they often spend twice as much time in prison as men who have committed a similar act—however, women convicted for a shooting or shoplifting usually serve much less time than men in comparable situations).

LABOR AND PUBLIC WELFARE: *education, health, labor, anti-poverty programs, and vocational rehabilitation.*

This committee covers several important areas of concern to women. The Children and Youth sub handles child care legislation—the repeal of Title IX would come through the Education sub—any attempts to repeal minimum wage legislation would start in the Labor sub—national health insurance is written in the Health sub—and the Aging sub would be an effective place to hold hearings. When pension reform is expanded to cover county, state and municipal employees, it will be considered by this committee. All of these subcommittees also provide good potential for holding hearings on the problems of women because they report out a large amount of good social service legislation.

EDUCATION AND LABOR: *labor, education, and welfare.*

Tip credit, day care, and minimum wage legislation are all worked on through this committee.

POST OFFICE AND CIVIL SERVICE: *civil service, postal operations, Census Bureau, and National Archives.*

This committee does flexible hours legislation, which is of special importance to women who often can only accept parttime employment because of demands at home.

POST OFFICE AND CIVIL SERVICE: *civil service, census and collection of statistics, postal service, holidays, and celebrations.*

PUBLIC WORKS: *water pollution, rivers, harbors, bridges and dams, water power, federal buildings, and highways.*

This is a pork barrel committee and offers little opportunity for working on feminist issues.

PUBLIC WORKS AND TRANSPORTATION: *urban mass transit, surface transportation except railraods, regional development, rivers and harbors, flood control, disaster relief, and water power and quality.*

RULES AND ADMINISTRATION: *rules of the Senate, corrupt practices, and internal housekeeping matters.*

RULES: *order of business in the House, rules and joint rules of the House, and reorganization of Congress.*

Before a bill can reach the floor of the House for debate and vote, it must not only be passed on by the committee that has jurisdiction over its area of concern, but it must pass through the Rules Committee. Rules sets time limits on debate for each bill as well as establishing regulations concerning amendments. This committee has control over every bill that reaches the floor and is, thus, extremely powerful.

HOUSE ADMINISTRATION: *campaign financing and internal housekeeping.*

SMALL BUSINESS: *small business assistance and small business in federal procurement and government contracts.*

VETERANS' AFFAIRS: *the concerns of an individual after she or he becomes a veteran.*

All legislation concerned with the treatment of women veterans goes through this committee. Carol Burris has termed it "a very exciting committee in its way," and there is much that can be done in this area. Women are not able to use Veterans' Administration loans and are discriminated against under VA insurance. They don't get equal pensions because one way to supplement a VA pension is to go into the Reserves, and women who have children are not allowed to join. Expanding benefits for divorced women and working on the problems of women's hospitals can be done through this committee.

VETERANS' AFFAIRS: *the concerns of an individual after she or he becomes a veteran.*

1928. Radclyffe Hall, English novelist and poet, causes an international uproar with her novel *The Well of Loneliness.* The book is promptly banned in England and in the United States becomes the subject of a legal action brought by the American Society for the Suppression of Vice. *The Well of Loneliness* concerns a lesbian relationship.

How a Campaign Works

The Manhattan Women's Political Caucus

CAMPAIGN PERSONNEL AND STRUCTURE

We are all familiar with the various campaign titles: campaign manager, press secretary, field coordinator, office manager, research director, scheduler. But what do these people do? What are their responsibilities? In this section we will explore these titles and the functions that are associated with them.

Campaign Manager

The campaign manager is the person entrusted with the responsibility of running the campaign, and of organizing, hiring, and directing the staff into those areas deemed necessary. He or she must be able to make decisions in the candidate's absence that will be in accordance with the candidate's statements and policies; but he or she must also make decisions regarding staff that he or she feels necessary to attain the goal everyone is working toward. Most derogatory remarks made in campaign headquarters are directed at the campaign manager, and that is how it should be, for the candidate must remain above dissension , and retain the loyalties of all the workers.

Deputy Director

The deputy director actually runs the day-to-day operation of the campaign. You can usually tell who that is by the fact that his or her office is adjacent to the campaign manager's (and by the fact that he or she rarely goes to cocktail parties; there's just not enough time).

Advance Team

Have you ever noticed that in the vicinity of the candidate there are posters hung, bullhorns ask if you want to "meet the candidate," people pass out literature, and there are crowds? If you didn't, the advance team hasn't done its job properly. Once the scheduling committee, the campaign manager, deputy director, and candidate have decided to go somewhere public, it is the job of the advance people to make it look as if the whole world descended on that location. In cooperation with local clubs and elected officials, they must let everyone in the area know that the candidate has, as promised, arrived. They also ensure that the candidate meets with locally prominent rabbis, priests, or elected officials. And finally the advance team is

responsible for having the candidate's car waiting to depart at precisely the right time to get on to the next engagement and more of the same.

Schedulers

To see that the advance team knows what time the candidate will be arriving and departing and whom the candidate must acknowledge is the task of the schedulers.

The scheduling committee determines just which of the functions the candidate can or must attend, how long the candidate can remain at the function, who the candidate must see and be seen with, what issues the candidate will discuss, and lastly, what is the alternative should the function be canceled.

Citizens Committees

Some of the most important groups within the campaign structure that relate to scheduling are the various citizens' committees. Besides keeping schedulers aware of upcoming events within various communities and segments of the electorate, the function of a citizens' committee is to reach their peers and obtain their support for the candidate. Lists and friends make up the bulk of the committee's resources, and the better the lists, the better the professional contact and reputation, the better the results. For this reason the committees are usually chaired by a prominent individual in the respective field.

Field Director

The field director maintains contact with the various political organizations. He or she meets with the organizations and sees that they are adequately staffed and working, makes sure that they have and are distributing literature, and coordinates the club efforts and the efforts of various volunteers. The field director usually assigns "coordinators" who will handle a specific section of the candidate's area and who will, in turn, assign people to the various boroughs as well as various counties within his or her sphere. Because the field director and the coordinators are in daily touch with the various local clubs, and because they are the first to receive the results of various "canvassers," they are also the first to notice changes in existing patterns and shifts in attitudes among the electorate. If this information is deemed significant, immediate action must be taken and, for the most part, the advertising agency is called in.

1928. Young women are flattered at having themselves described as possessing "S.A.," or sex appeal, an attribute that would have deeply offended young American women of only a decade or so earlier.

Deborah Taylor

Political Clubs, Pressure Groups, Community Groups

Besides the campaign workers themselves, there are many other groups—political clubs, pressure groups, community groups—that may help elect the candidate.

Political Clubs

The political club is a center for party members. Although it has no official role in the party structure, the club often serves as the local campaign headquarters and a meeting and organizing center for party leaders, officials, and grass-roots members. Clubs are usually formed on a neighborhood basis and are often deeply involved in the community with a variety of social as well as economic and political undertakings. Clubs will usually circulate petitions for candidates they have endorsed, set up street corner tables, and work in conjunction with the headquarters staffs of those candidates they are supporting. However, every political club has the option not to support any candidate even if he or she has been given the official designation of the political party.

Pressure Groups

Pressure groups are groups organized around issues, ethnic affiliations, professions, or other strong interests whose members try to further the aims of their groups by lobbying and similar activities. Such voters' blocs attempt to have meaningful input and influence in campaigns. In some instances, if no candidate reflects the point of view of a pressure group, they may field their own candidate or slate.

Community Groups

In every community there are organized groups reflecting the concerns of the area ethnic and church groups, social welfare organizations, civic betterment groups, and block associations. These groups can also exert an influence on the campaign and can be helpful as a channel through which to reach a community.

1929. Ann Ronnell is paid $25,000 outright for writing the song "Who's Afraid of the Big Bad Wolf?"

Advertising

Posters, flyers, handbills, and walking tours cannot reach all the prospective voters as meaningfully and in the numbers that a sixty-second television spot can. The advertising agency must inform prospective voters of the attributes of the candidate in a positive manner. Issues must be presented clearly and honestly and shown at a time when the greatest number of prospective voters will be watching—e.g., you wouldn't run a political spot on Saturday morning since that audience is comprised largely of children who are unable to vote. You may notice that most political TV commercials will probably appear immediately before, immediately after, and during news broadcasts. The experts on whom you want to advertise to and in what tone are the agency account executive and media buyer, and the campaign's research director.

Research Director

Aside from producing a thorough demographic breakdown of the area, its income, ethnic, and religious mix, the research director must also be the most knowledgeable person on past voting records of each district, the issues—both expressed and insinuated—and the percentage of people who will likely vote in either a primary or general election, and whether they will vote as a bloc or individually.

Aside from this information, the research director must also maintain an on-going study of the opposition, what is known as negative research. If candidate X takes a position that is contrary to a position previously taken, negative research should know. When confronted with this, candidate X will probably be placed on the defensive. Candidates who are constantly defending an issue usually don't have time to present new issues, they look bad to the electorate, and they usually lose. To keep the candidate looking good is of prime importance, and the responsibility of the press secretary.

Press

The press secretary must try to obtain coverage in all forms of media from local to national newspapers, radio, and television. This is also known as free advertising, and all candidates want it. A good press secretary can get it. The press secretary is also responsible for the writing and distribution of press releases and statements, the organization of press conferences, and at times she or he is the "informed source" that reporters refer to—especially if the item has something to do with the candidate's opposition.

Since it is important for the press secretary to release items that will receive newspaper, radio, and television play, the press secretary is usually informed of all activities in all departments. What may seem trivial to the field director, deputy director, or researcher may turn out to be a "good story," and good stories are, again, free advertising.

Finance Committee

The finance committee, as its name implies, runs the monetary operation of the campaign. They not only draft budgets and supplementary budgets but also see to it that the various offices keep to their budgets.

Aside from preparing and monitoring budgets the finance committee is responsible for maintaining a positive cash flow through the campaign, for courting prospective contributors, and for successfully obtaining donations.

Volunteer Coordinator

The volunteer coordinator must ensure (because everyone else will forget) that every time the candidate makes a public appearance someone is also there with volunteer cards to take down the names and phone numbers of people who are interested in the campaign. Never overlook the volunteer-recruiting aspect of any campaign event or function. Every mailing should include a volunteer-card and tables set up on street corners should be well stocked with them.

In order to manage a smoothly running volunteer operation, the coordinator must give volunteers assignments as they arrive based upon priorities and the willingness of the individual. It is the responsibility of the volunteer coordinator to insure that those voluteers who meet the public are briefed on the issues and instructed on how to respond to questions so that they will present themselves and the candidate well.

Betty Medsger

Governor Ella Grasso campaigns in West Hartford, Connecticut

1929. Mrs. Harrison Eustis is elected the founding president of the Seeing Eye Organization, trainers of the first dog to guide the blind.

Canvassing for Suffrage

Susan B. Anthony

Women Vote in 12 States

Give the Vote to the Women of Massachusetts in November 1915

Mothers need the Vote to Protect their Homes and Children.

Working Women need the Vote to regulate conditions under which they work.

Tax paying Women need the Vote to Protect their Property.

THINK IT OVER!

By the courtesy of the Woman's Journal, Boston.

Sophia Smith Collection, Smith College

WHITE STATES   FULL SUFFRAGE
SHADED STATES   PARTIAL SUFFRAGE
ILLINOIS   PRESIDENTIAL SUFFRAGE
DARK STATES   MAN SUFFRAGE

Above, women's suffrage poster from the Women's Journal, *Boston, 1915. Facing page, clockwise from top left: a suffrage parade in New York City, 1913; suffrage activist Lucretia Mott; Carrie Chapman Catt; political cartoon — "one marcher in line is worth ten petitions in the waste basket;" Republican suffragette with suffrage plank; commemorative postage stamp; center, playing cards with a political message.*

Quotations might be made indefinitely from the master minds of the past and the present on the value of the franchise. Altho these magnificent declarations all have been made in behalf of man, they apply with equal force to woman. This knowledge took possession of me, it became the very fiber of my being, and my whole soul was absorbed in the question, "How can women be aroused to demand this right of suffrage for themselves; how can men be persuaded to the justice of granting it to them?" But where was I to make a beginning? My life had been spent in the school room. I had almost no acquaintance among prominent persons, and I did not know a dozen men and women in the whole State of New York who shared my views on this subject. This much, however, I realized, that somehow this gospel must be carried to the people.

So, with my Quaker father to map out the route, and with $50 which Wendell Phillips lent me and never allowed me to repay, I started out alone on Christmas Day, 1854, to canvass the State of New York, county by county. I carried with me two petitions, one for the franchise, and one asking for women the right to their wages and equal guardianship of their children. I took also a little pamphlet containing speeches of Phillips, Higginson, Theodore Parker, Clarinda Howard Nichols and Mrs. John Stuart Mill, on Woman's Rights, which sold for a "York shilling," twelve and half cents. With the sale of these and collections I hoped to pay my expenses. I opened in the court house at Mayville, N.Y., purchasing fifty-six cents' worth of candles to light it. I finished the canvass at Riverhead, Long Island, May 1, having spoken in fifty-four of the sixty counties, stopping only long enough to carry the petitions to the Legislature. It was one of the coldest and snowiest of winters and much of the journey was in a sleigh. My first effort in each place was to get the court house. If this was refused I tried for a church. When this was not possible I took a school house, and if all were denied I spoke in the dining room of the hotel. My placards were put up in the post office, and people came out of curiosity, as they never had heard a woman speak. The audiences were respectful, altho very cold, with a half-suppressed sneer, and an air of expecting something to call out their ridicule or disapproval, but, at the close, a few would come up, sign the petitions and speak a friendly word of sympathy. I sometimes formed a little society and always secured the names of a few people who stood firm through all the stress and storm which followed.

Adapted from *The Independent*, February 1900.

1930: Ellen Church, on a flight conducted by United Air Lines, between San Francisco and Cheyenne, Wyoming, tucks pillows behind passengers' heads as the first air stewardess.

Sophia Smith Collection, Smith College

1931. Virne Mitchell becomes, at nineteen, the first woman to pitch baseball for an organized male team, the Chattanooga Baseball Club, a member of the Southern Association.

An Insider's Guide for the Politically Innocent

Mary Anne Guitar was the first woman elected to the Redding, CT, Board of Selectmen.—Ed.

When I ran for office for the first time some years ago I knew next to nothing about politics. For example, I couldn't have named more than a few members of my party's Town Committee even though this powerful group picked candidates, made policy and got out the vote. I had been to a party caucus or two but only as a voter, not a candidate. I was absolutely astounded to find myself at the microphone spelling out my platform (just like a real politician) the night a caucus nominated me for Selectman over a Town-Committee endorsed candidate.

Astounded, because the Selectman's nomination had always gone to a man. It was the top political job in town and the Town Committee had already picked their man. He was young, personable, a born-and-raised native. He even had a war record and an attractive family. There was just one thing wrong with him. He was a builder.

The environment issue was on everybody's mind at the time and many of us were worried that the town would soon be overrun by development and lose its country atmosphere. There was some feeling that the town fathers were unduly influenced by business and commercial interests and that it might be time for a change.

I was working in private conservation/preservation groups and had served as president of our local land trust for three years but it never occurred to me that a volunteer job could be a stepping stone to elective office.

One day I was approached by a fellow conservationist who wanted to know if I would consider running for Selectman. At the time I viewed myself as an improbable candidate and I remember saying to her, "Wouldn't *that* be a George Plimpton thing to do?" At which she said, "If you're going to talk like that I'm not going to be your manager."

It was a tantalizing idea. What if I won? The notion of getting in on what is politely called "the decision-making process" (put more realistically, getting a crack at the power) had an enormous appeal. What if the outsiders became insiders? Wouldn't *we* have a chance to change things?

I told her I thought it was hopeless but if she could get somebody on the Town Committee to nominate me I was game. When I lost on their ballot (4 to 7) I wasn't a

bit surprised and figured this was the beginning and end of my political career.

However, I learned an important political truth at the caucus. Nothing political is ever sewed up. It is always possible to win if circumstances conspire in your favor. That night they did.

The chairman was unsure of his election rules. The retiring Selectman observed that the nomination meant very little any way since "it was a nothing job" and the proposed candidate seemed equally resigned to powerlessness. This display of inefficiency, indifference and defeatism so outraged my random constituency that they nominated me from the floor in a burst of defiance. To everybody's astonishment I won, 57 to 44.

All of which proves that it is entirely possible to jump into the political water and make waves the first time out if you have a strong issue to ride. In my case it was The Environment. In other towns Schools, Spending, Corruption have launched new and unlikely politicians upon the established order. Needless to say, you can't expect those who have been accustomed to running the political show to accept such an upset with good grace. The regulars are apt to call it a "power grab" and if they are seriously threatened "a naked power grab." In my case the losers promptly charged that the caucus had been rigged. Then, the party boss called on me and suggested that I withdraw from the race because "they are going to challenge you in a primary, and of course, you'll lose." At that moment, almost instinctively, I learned the political uses of righteous indignation. "What, Withdraw? When I have been chosen by MY PARTY to be its candidate." (He looked bad for even suggesting it.) At the time I must admit I had to agree with him that my chances of winning a primary against the organized efforts of party regulars were pretty chancy. Even the opposition-party boss was calling his pals on our side to tell them to get out and vote against me.

To hedge my bets, I drove to the State Capitol, with only hours to spare, to file as an Independent so that even if I lost the primary I would be assured of a spot on the ballot. (If I won the primary, I would appear twice on the ballot and that wouldn't hurt.) This was accomplished over a feverishly hot Labor Day weekend and if I had not been fighting mad I never could have done it.

You forget that politics is hustling, hard work when you are caught up in the process. The only thing that counts is winning. And, having won, you would do it all over again. Make those phone calls (I contacted every

Party member I knew personally, from my garbage man to the school superintendent), get out position papers until even my friends on the local papers complained, "What more could you possibly have to say?" Whatever it costs it's worth the effort. Nothing beats winning for pure, personal, ego-satisfying reward. Proving you can carry off an election is a singularly sweet triumph for women, the young and anyone else who has ever felt excluded from politics.

I think the best time I've just about ever had was the night the voting machines were opened and I overheard our party boss calling the other district to convey the bad news. When he reached his opposite number (we'll call him "Sidney") his tone reflected complete shock and disbelief. "Sidney," long pause, "she won." Later, in the general election, I would go on to outpoll him, 606 to 430.

Winning was only the beginning of my political education. I had to fight to get on the Town Committee (to the victor the spoils are not automatically given, not if it means sharing the power). I had to discover what was expected of the party faithful and serve my time in rain-soaked tents on election and primary days, address my share of postcards and flyers, make my quota of telephone calls to get out the vote.

The first thing you have to know if you are thinking about running is that politics-as-usual is still being waged in neighborhood clubs, small-town firehouses and private living rooms. It is wholly mysterious to those who have not been exposed to its tribal rites and even disturbing to anyone who believes, innocently, that politics should be open and high-minded.

One newcomer to my town attended her first party caucus and was appalled by the trivia being discussed. Should we have a standing committee for fund-raising? Who will see that the postcards get out? "You almost feel as though you are in a smoke-filled room with a bunch of ward-heelers," she complained. "Not that the people there aren't good types and a cross-section of the party but you look at this group and you expect issues to be discussed. In an era when ticket splitting up and down the country is the thing, when issues are vital, you sit there and feel almost tainted by what the Committee is projecting." She sighed, "I guess I'm not cut out to be a politician."

I guess she isn't. Politics *is* secretive, manipulative, often enough dirty-pool and anyone who can't take it, indeed doesn't relish the wheeling and dealing, shouldn't try to play the game. The issues change but

1931. Polygamy, though sanctioned by the Chinese Confucian religion for twenty-three hundred years as a means of ensuring male descendants should the number-one wife prove sterile, is now legally prohibited.

Mary Anne Guitar

party politics does not and those who are serious about political life should understand the system, if only to work within it for their own advantage.

First, some definitions so we'll know how the game is set up. Those who squirmed through Civics 12 can read on.

Political Party. Webster's Second gives the best definition I know. "An organized group of the electorate who attempt to control the action of the government through the election of its candidates to office."

Although "independent," more properly called "unaffiliated," voters are an increasingly important swing-bloc in elections, the two major parties—Republican and Democratic—still dominate the scene. If you don't belong to one or the other in locales where they wield power, you are going to be deprived of considerable political leverage.

Town Committee. Party business is handled through an elected (by party members) board of managers called the Town Committee. Some variation of this hardcore group of party officials will be found wherever politics is played. If you join a party the first thing you ought to do is ask for copies of the local and state party rules. Then you can find out how party officials are elected and discover what power they hold according to the rule book. This is important. Whenever you challenge any action by your party be sure you have the rules in hand. The parliamentary ploy is a powerful weapon.

The Boss. He's the one who cares passionately about playing politics. He (or she) may be the official chairman or the "titular head," i.e., top vote-getter or fundraiser. The Boss doesn't have to be a stereotype Curley, Daley, Mitchell. He may, in fact, be the local judge of probate, your uncle's law partner or even Uncle Harry himself. If so, you're in luck. A Boss likes to stick with his own kind.

If you have no "in" with the Boss, if he regards you as a troublemaker you will spend a long, long time sitting out in the cold. The strong Boss gives no quarter. He won't yield even a token spot on committees or candidacies to "the dissidents." He avoids all confrontations, competition within the party, using tactics which fall far short of sportsmanship. He will "forget" to notify you that a meeting is on, manage not to recognize you at caucus or convention, and otherwise neutralize your opposition to him, by simply not acknowledging that it (or you) exists.

He says he wants to preserve unity for the true battle with the other party. Yet, you might suspect (and rightly) that he has more

"American Woman and her Political Peers," 1893. Shows Frances Willard, 1839–1898, surrounded by an idiot, a convict, an Indian and an insane man.

in common with their leaders than with challengers in his own party.

Caucus. "A meeting of leaders of a party or faction to decide on the politics or candidates for office to be supported by their followers." (Webster's Second.)

The party chairman will call a caucus of all enrolled members to take action on such business as the election of town committee members, candidates for local elections, delegates to state conventions which pick presidential, senatorial, gubernatorial candidates.

The caucus is the heart of the party system but you must never forget that any number, of any persuasion, can caucus. A caucus occurs whenever any two or more political animals get together. They could be independents trying to figure out how to beat the party bosses. Or, they could be splinter groups within a party plotting strategy to take over a coming formal caucus. Or, a national assortment of

policy-makers, i.e., The National Women's Political Caucus.

Never go to a caucus, except as a bystander, without canvassing for votes ahead of time. If you want to win you must go with the votes in hand and that means bodies. And that means telephone calls, pressures, subtle or heavy-handed ("We need you tonight. Just think of what could happen if X gets in").

Anyone who imagines that policies and candidates emerge from a caucus without any stage-managing is naive. Somebody is always pulling strings. And beginners can be just as adept as oldtimers. At one Iowa precinct caucus to choose delegates to the Democratic National Convention a Drake University student beat out a college professor for caucus chairman simply because he bothered to gather up all the boys along fraternity row and bring them along. Never, never assume that you'll have

---

1932. Twenty-nine members incorporate the Montgomery Farm Women's Cooperative Market in Bethesda, Maryland, the first such experiment managed entirely by women. By 1945 the group will own outright property in excess of $50,000.

the votes when you get there. Make sure they are promised and that the bodies who will cast them are going to show up.

Primary. An election which is usually held for party members only. A challenge primary, for example, can be called by a group of dissidents who object to a slate endorsed by a caucus. They may feel that attendance at the caucus was unrepresentative of party membership or rigged in favor of the candidates. Or, they may decide that the candidates have not had enough public exposure and if they can publicize their supposed deficiencies they can challenge the choice and win with one of their own. Primaries are also held to pick convention delegates.

Party regulars constantly stress the importance of joining a party so you will have a chance to nominate candidates. If you are unaffiliated, they argue, you will be faced with two unappealing candidates in the election. Party members will tell you that they, too, are often forced to choose between the lesser of two evils but, certainly, you do have more of a chance to influence the choice of candidates if you are a registered party member and if you do attend the caucuses and vote in the primaries.

All politics are organization politics, whether it is the traditional *organization* made up of regulars or a group of insurgents. Somebody has to get voters together, persuade, implore or dog them to vote and "vote right." You can't do it alone. You need the troops. What you need is your own machine, a dirty word to some. Call it Movement or Machine, what it represents is a bloc of the committed who will get to the polls and see that others get there on time. This is why parties remain in power. They have access to voter lists (You, too, can get them but it calls for effort) and they have indexed and cross-indexed them so they know who comes out to vote and pretty much how they will cast their ballot. They have done their homework, thanks to the "pluggers" who carry on the real business of the party in and out of election time, keeping those lists up to date. One of the highest recommendations that can be given to a nominee for office is that he has "served The Party well." That means he has done the donkey work.

The uninitiated may wonder why such stress is put on service which has no relevance to a candidate's qualifications for, say, a job on the Board of Education or Zoning Commission. It means that he is trustworthy, will be willing to carry out the party's wishes, will not go his own way, has done his time and is therefore in line for a reward. You have to remember that parties represent uneasy coalitions. The loyalty test is really a work test. Will you come through? Can they count on you? Your ideas, your convictions, mean less than your enthusiasm for The Party.

Is party politics the only route to a political career? Not at all. Many successful campaigners take a shortcut to political power by establishing themselves as doers in civic affairs. They may call for change as concerned citizens and then find themselves sought after by their party to run for office on the issue they have so nicely dramatized.

One of my fellow politicians in Connecticut, Patsy Brescia, President of the Common Council in Norwalk, came in through the back door much as I did. She joined the PTA when she moved to Norwalk less than a decade ago and was elected "Safety Chairman" when she and other young mothers pressured the town fathers for a stop sign at a busy corner. Their next crusade was a plan to build and improve sidewalks so that children could get to school safely. Patsy and her PTA cohorts took a town map, plotted all the bus routes, measured the areas that needed sidewalks and calculated the cost, using figures supplied (at their request) by the Department of Public Works. When Patsy went to the mayor with their proposal he said soothingly, "I've put $25,000 in the budget for that this year." Having done her homework she could say with conviction, "It needs a five-year program and. . .like a million dollars." "When I look back on it," she says, recalling the work that went into the presentation, "it was something you would hire a consultant to do."

Demonstrating interest and persistence with her carefully researched programs, Patsy inevitably caught the politicians' eyes. Clearly, she was a worker. The party asked her to run for the Council even before she registered as a Democrat. She has scored impressive victories since, running well ahead of her ticket.

Suppose you don't want to work within the existing party framework. You can hope (and press) for an upset that will change the balance of power and provide access for new people and new ideas. Anything can happen to topple the leaders and create opportunities for insurgents. Local issues divide a party and someone capitalizes on the split by establishing a strong centrist position, attracting followers from both camps. More infrequently, a national issue can have a profound effect on local parties. The Vietnam War caused a cataclysmic change in the Democratic party on every level. In one small town the election of anti-Johnson delegates to the state nominating convention led to a challenge primary from the old guard. The anti-Johnson delegation won and this victory signaled a break in the ranks of regular Democrats. From that moment on there was no predicting what a caucus would do. Or, a town committee. The hold that earlier chairmen and committees held over their membership was decisively loosened. And, all because of disenchantment with national leadership.

You can start a competing party ("Taxpayers," "Good Government," "Human Rights") if you can develop an issue to compete with traditional party concerns.

You don't even have to have a party endorsement if you can rally enough supporters to your personal cause. In fact, you may decide after looking over the rituals, the creaking machinery of group politics, that you would rather go it alone, form your own campaign around a hard core of workers and petition to get on the ballot as a true independent. In some communities, particularly small towns, national political parties have no local organization, and there is total freedom to run on your own ticket.

When Jane C. Edmonds decided to try for a seat on the Sharon (Mass.) School Committee all she had to do was file the necessary papers announcing her intention to run. The mother of four small children (ages 5 to 9), Jane her husband Steven had moved to Sharon seven years earlier because the school system was considered exceptional. However, as they came to know more about it through their teenage babysitters and other parents, Jane began to wonder if the schools were really meeting the needs of the children. "Something told me they weren't, and that's what really made me want to run."

A standout candidate on many counts, Jane dropped out of Boston U., where she was a music major, to get married, and now at 30 is well launched on a career in which she hopes to specialize in legal aid to juveniles.

She is also black in a community dominated by whites and a relative newcomer at that. Her opposition in the race, four other candidates, had all lived in Sharon for at least 20 years. Yet, when the count was in, Jane had won by the biggest plurality ever tallied in Sharon for the School Committee.

How did she do it?

By concentrating on a single issue: were the schools, with all their fine facilities and devoted faculty, really doing right by the kids? As one supporter told her, after a League of Women Voters candidates' meeting, "The others were talking about taxes and curriculum but what kept coming across was that you cared about the kids."

She does, too. And the kids were her best campaigners. "They walked the streets with me. We covered all of Sharon on foot, talking to people and handing out flyers."

The flyers spelled out her campaign promises, the most important of which was a strong bid to open up communication between parents and teachers and students. Jane had opened doors for herself by persisting in an effort to find out what was happening in the schools. She was confident that she could do the same for other parents.

The first ad she ran in the local paper described her credentials and platform. The second ad was pure political inspiration. It read: "I've told you what my concerns are.

Please tell me yours." Overnight she was mobbed with calls and, naturally enough, offers of support.

What she put into the campaign was her own time and considerable energies. Fundraising was left to her volunteer workers. She says she spent about $250 for ads and buttons. On election night the kids started sporting buttons ("Jane is a Dark Horse Candidate") she had been reluctant to use until that moment.

My own campaign cost $178.10, spread over 14 donors, and if a friend from Chicago who had worked at her brother's political headquarters hadn't sent me $25 "for buttons," it wouldn't have occurred to me that I would need any cash at all to run. Then, after some of my more inspired constituents began dreaming up such slogans as "String Along with Guitar. . . She's in Tune with the Times," I began to see the possibilities in advertising. You can run, of course, without raising a dime because the press will cover your campaign if you succeed in making news. However, it is not all that difficult to raise money, in donations up to $25. You should give the donors some idea of how the money is going to be spent—buttons, advertising, mailings. Kennedys to the contrary, most candidates do not put their own money into their campaigns.

Money isn't the essential ingredient in a successful campaign. What counts is whether you can get people to work for you. How do you persuade them? That's like asking, how do you make friends. You just assume that they will want to if you project the kind of campaign that appeals. (It won't be long before you'll know whether or not you have the appeal. If nobody volunteers to help, you would be well advised to get out of politics.)

You have to speak up for yourself and your ideas. Ideally, you demonstrate what you could accomplish given the powers of office. I had been a strong advocate of land preservation, been vocally opposed to "mindless growth" and left little doubt that, if elected, I would be happy to throw sand in the wheels of "progress."

Naturally, you can't just protest the system. You have to come up with bright ideas to change it, alternative proposals. You have to lay out a platform. The more you develop your ideas, the easier it is for people to believe you are a real, live candidate, one worth working for.

Voters also seem to have an affinity for the underdog. They like to help one win if, that is, the cause isn't completely hopeless.

What politics amounts to, finally, is asserting yourself, putting yourself forward and, yes, demanding attention. It's one thing to ring doorbells for Gene or George. That's surrogate politics. Real politics is getting out there yourself. Risking it. Winning. Everybody should try it at least once.

You Can Do It
Patricia Schroeder

You can *do* the job—but first, you have to *get* the job. For those of you, and I hope there are many, who may be contemplating a run for office—whether it be party, city, state, judicial, or federal—let me offer a few suggestions from my own experience.

First: Assess critically your own qualifications. It is probably fair to say—although certainly unfair in practice—that a woman running for public office should be "overqualified." Having been chairwoman of your church's women's club may not carry the same clout as being program chairman of the local Rotary Club.

It is interesting to note that all five of this year's new Congresswomen are lawyers. Perhaps this is because, as lawyers, we have necessarily been thrust into an adverse, and often competitive, role with members of the male establishment. Furthermore, we have come into constant contact with many of the problems that face our communities, and worked on possible legislative solutions.

Second: Examine carefully the real base of your support. The support of one's family, close friends, and associates is indispensable. But what contacts or qualifications do you have that will enable you to gain the confidence and backing of other groups and allies? In my own case an extensive labor-law background was valuable in helping eventually obtain both organizational and financial support from many labor unions. Teaching contacts with three major colleges in Denver were also important. Finally, it is essential to take the pulse, and constantly stroke the brows of many of the key party leaders and workers in your area. Many of these veterans of the political wars often will make astute judgments about prospective candidates.

Third: Build credibility. Because you are a woman, you will constantly confront the attitude that you are not "a serious candidate." At our county nominating convention it is customary for candidates to have booths, give away courtesy coffee, distribute literature, placard the walls with posters, etc. I had a basic feeling of aversion to that sort of thing; but we decided it was probably more important that I do some of the traditional things, simply because I was the untraditional candidate.

Because you are a woman you may have the ability to gain more than your fair share of press and media coverage, because you are the different candidate. But the other side of the coin is that you will often be more severely cross-examined on your views and statements by newspeople than is the average male candidate.

Fourth: Develop a strong "grass-roots" organization. You will find that there are great reservoirs of dedicated, talented women who will really work for another woman. This is especially true of many older, retired women and many younger gals, such as students and working girls.

You will probably have a very hard time raising money. My husband often said that the money "is controlled by male-chauvinist pigs." Organization and union money is controlled by men, and they will usually have little confidence in the chances of a woman candidate. Hence, the bigger and better volunteer group you can muster, the better chance you will have of putting your scarce dollars into essential items like printed materials and media time.

Fifth: Use innovative and hard-hitting media. Because a woman candidate is "different," don't be afraid to run a different kind of campaign, utilizing original and different media techniques and content. Let me give you one example: the standard political brochure. You know what I am talking about—the picture of the candidate with family, with coat over the shoulder, in front of the Capitol, etc., with the standard one-liners: "X is honest; X is against pollution; X is for fiscal responsibility." We were able to achieve real impact—and also ruffle some feathers—with colorful mini-posters.

And finally, *Sixth: Be issue-oriented.* Running for public office is too time-consuming and too expensive to embark on such a venture merely for the experience or for the ego satisfaction. If you run, take a stand. Get out front on the issues that concern you, your family, your community, and the nation. The risk, of course, is great; but so are the rewards.

From *You Can Do It*, remarks of Congresswoman Patricia Schroeder at the National Women's Political Caucus, Houston, TX, February, 1973.

1933. Ruth Bryan Owen becomes the first woman diplomatic minister when President Franklin Delano Roosevelt appoints her envoy extraordinary and minister plenipotentiary to Denmark and Iceland. She is the eldest daughter of William Jennings Bryan.

This "how to" is designed to give you a few hints on how to succeed in politics by really trying hard. Although the emphasis is on running for state legislature, with certain changes it can be applied to any public office.

Stage One—Preliminaries

1. *Requirements:* In order to comply with state election laws, find out what they are. Obtain a copy of the state requirements. Study the law and be sure you meet the qualifications for the office you want.
2. *Filing:* A candidate must file her intentions with the city or town clerk and, where applicable, pay a filing fee. This must be done before a specific date and time. Check with the local election committee for rules applying to you.
3. *Contact:* If you have not done so already, notify the State Committee of your candidacy and when you would be available to appear with the major candidates when they are in your area. You may or may not seek the endorsement of your state committee, but in any case you should notify them that you are a candidate.
4. *Goal:* To win the election. That's easier said than done. Example: If you have 15,000 people in your district (varying from state to state, district to district) and half of them are registered voters, you will need about 4,000 votes to win.
5. *Approach:* The direct approach to the voter is the best system for gaining the needed majority. Meet as many of the voters as possible, tell each of them of your candidacy and convince them that you can do the best job for them as their representative.

Note: The pre-campaign work is mostly preparation. You should have the letters written, cards and posters printed and the state committee notified as soon as possible. Choose the techniques that are most suited to your personality, district and position. The following are suggested materials to be used during the next stage.

Photographs:
Have new photographs taken for use in publiciity, on posters and literature.
Printed Cards:
Have a postcard-size card printed with your name, address, telephone number and biographical sketch on it, also a slogan about your campaign and the party. You may want to have your picture on the card.
Posters:
These could be about 15" x 24", suitable for placing in store windows, etc., and should have your name, address, telephone number and slogan—if you have one. This is a good place to use the new photo.
Mailings:
If you use this method, you can state your position on key issues in the state. You should try to mail one to each voter in the district. You may want to have a new letterhead printed with your name, address and campaign slogan.

From *Tips on Running for Office,* by The Office of Women's Activities, Democratic National Committee, Washington, D.C.

Stage Two—The Campaign

1. *House to House:* Visit every home in your district, preferably on evenings or weekends when you're sure most people are home. Tell the residents you're seeking election, that you need their votes and that you will be responsible to them to do whatever is possible to be their voice in government. Be pleasant, but avoid becoming involved in prolonged discussions. You have many other houses to visit. Here may be a time to use volunteers who enjoy house-to-house canvassing. Remind them to be pleasant, informative and leave a good impression of you, the candidate.
2. *Get out the Vote:* During these house calls, ask if there is anyone in the house or neighborhood who needs an absentee ballot or ride to the polls on election day. Also, there may be some members of the household who are not registered voters. Now would be a good time to explain the voting requirements for your community and to offer help in any way to get their names on the voting lists. Don't forget to keep a record of this information for later use.
3. *Circulation:* Attend or initiate political rallies or social events in your town and attend statewide events when possible. Go to meetings of clubs and civic organizations to promote your candidacy.
4. *Innovations:* In one small town a successful candidate spent Saturday morning at the supermarket giving away coffee and literature on her campaign. She found scores of voters there only too happy to drink coffee, chat and vote for her on election day.

   In your town or district there may be a popular meeting place where you could appear regularly to campaign. Station yourself at employees' entrances to large stores or factories as people are going to work or at quitting time. Don't neglect the shut-in vote; visit convalescent and nursing homes, homes for the aged and other institutions where you can win friends and offer voting assistance.
5. *News Coverage:* Prepare a press release announcing your candidacy and send it to the papers as soon as you file. When sending the release to a newspaper, be sure you enclose a recent picture of yourself—a glossy print, head-and-shoulders type, any size.
6. *Advertising:* Weekly newspapers and local radio stations are the best and least expensive media for candidates to use. Local papers and radio-TV stations search for newsworthy items and appreciate your letting them know of future events. Remember that to the press future news is the best kind. Let the press know in plenty of time of your future activities and get free coverage.

   Your mailings, hand cards, posters and house calls are, in effect, advertising techniques, but now and then it's necessary to place an ad in a newspaper, particularly if your opponent is doing it.

   The important thing to remember about ads is that state law requires every ad to be signed either by the candidate or by her so-called fiscal agent. The agent can be a friend who has agreed to let her name be used in your campaign.

   With radio ads, part of the message has to include

1933. Frances Perkins is appointed the first woman cabinet member when President Franklin Delano Roosevelt assigns her the position of Secretary of Labor.

the fiscal agent's name, too. Thus, an ad or commercial would say something like this:

> Vote for Mary Jones, the woman who will do her best to represent you. Remember, a vote for Mary Jones is a vote for continued progress in your state. Sponsored by the Mary Jones for Legislature Committee, Sally Smith, Chairwoman.

One successful candidate used ten-second radio spots recorded by each of her three children and her husband. This showed family support and at the same time repeated the name seven times in ten seconds:

> This is Betty Doe, asking you to vote for my mother, Jane Doe, for the state House of Representatives. This is a political announcement paid for by me, Betty Doe, and by my brothers, Jack Doe and Jim Doe, my father, John Doe, and my mother, Jane Doe.

If you plan to buy radio ads, contract for them a month or so in advance. This will assure you of a good time slot. An economical technique in advertising is to associate with others on the ballot and buy some ads that mention the entire slate. Also, why not try to collect a list of supporters in your town who will let their names be used in an ad? The ad could say that the following citizens of your voting district will support you. This has the bandwagon effect on voters who haven't made up their minds. This type of advertising is most effective in the last few days of the campaign.

7. *Financing:* No matter how large or small your campaign, it will take some funds. Costs will vary according to the size of your district, or the office you're seeking, but don't let financial worries keep you from running.

Stage Three—The Election

1. *Get Voters to the Polls:* This requires the use of the telephone, newspaper, radio-TV ads and house calls even though you have been doing all of this during the campaign. Election day is the payoff! It will be the busiest day and night of the year for you. By the end of the afternoon you may find, by checking the voting list, that some of your supporters haven't shown up at the polls. Your staff can now begin calling these people, offering rides to the polls and, in some cases, going to their homes ready to escort them.

2. *Poll Watching:* If there is more than one polling place in your district, have someone at each place watching the checklist. Provide each watcher with a checklist. These can be obtained before election day from the clerk's office. Use the list to check off known supporters as they vote. (Try to do this inconspicuously. Voters don't like to be watched by obvious poll watchers.)

You Could Be a State Legislator

How many people know who their U.S. Congressman is? Surprisingly few.

Then consider how many know who their representative in the *state* legislature is. Even fewer. (Just do a quick canvass in your area and you'll be amazed.)

Now consider this proposition: A Representative whose

name isn't familiar to the voters could be easily displaced . . . by someone who *is* known to the voters.

1. Analyze your legislative districts carefully. Look for these vulnerability symptoms:
   a) An incumbent who feels "safe" and never bothers to campaign
   b) An incumbent who is colorless or relatively unknown in the district
   c) An incumbent who has taken an unpopular stand on local issues
   d) An incumbent who has remained unchallenged although the political makeup of the population has changed
   e) A district where the voter turnout has been very low.

2. A strong candidate could challenge these incumbents. The best candidate may be a woman who is well known for her political or community activities and who is respected and trusted. Women candidates are often more successful in winning bipartisan support than men.

3. That candidate could be *YOU*.

It Can Be Done!

It takes hard work and a plan—but it can be done. Here are some tips:

Have a plan. Have a carefully thought-through campaign plan and stick to it—unless, of course, it becomes obvious in the middle of its execution that you've made a mistake and it is the wrong plan for you. Understand what it is you are trying to do so that you can put the right priorities on your time and not be distracted by extraneous things. For instance, consider the size of the district; if it's small, plan to visit each house. Weigh your friends' offers to have coffees for you against reaching more people in the same amount of time by house-to-house canvassing. If it's a large district, it might call for different strategy, but don't lose sight of the importance of personal contact.

Organize. You don't have time to do everything yourself. Decide early to run so that you will have time to build a personal organization of people who will take responsibility for many of the details. Start with your friends, neighbors, and acquaintances. You'll be surprised at how many people think it's fun to be part of a political campaign.

Prepare. The secret to getting and keeping workers is to have specific jobs ready for them to do at all times. This means preparation. Have a carefully prepared instruction sheet which explains the purpose of the chore, suggested techniques, and where appropriate, provide the necessary details.

Follow-up. Somebody must keep a record of who is responsible for what, and make periodic checks to see that each job is completed on schedule.

1934. Frau Gertrud Scholtz-Klink, national Deputy Leader of Nazi Women of the Third Reich, is destined to become one of Hitler's five major executives. Largely through her influence over the 40 million women of greater Germany, the Weimar Republic is voted out and Hitler gains power.

Fundamentals of Fund Raising

The Finance Chairperson and Committee

Before any attempt is made to raise money, you must have a base of organization. Your community will probably select a finance chairperson around whom your campaign will revolve. This person is your pivotal point and has been chosen because he or she (1) has the time and desire to participate actively, (2) is a strong and articulate supporter and is able to speak in an informed way, (3) is a respected and affluent member of the community (e.g., it is very hard to turn someone like this down when they ask for money), and (4) has the leadership and organizational abilities to do the job.

Your finance chairperson cannot be effective, however, unless his or her committee is comprised of strong supporters of the campaign and who, like the chairperson, are willing to make their own contributions, either in time or money. It is the function of the chairperson and committee to actively participate in the planning and execution of all fund-raising projects. The chairperson will oversee, and each member of the committee will be responsible for, specific areas that could involve the organization of volunteers, ticket sales, publicity, or the creation and execution of an entire fund-raising event. Needless to say, all of these are key positions in your committee's fund-raising campaign.

RULE 1

Outline your fund-raising budget and goals.

Set down on paper what you want to spend and how much you want to raise—and stick to it! This is easier said than done. One often hears of a very glamorous and exciting fund-raising event only to discover it lost money! Avoid such a mistake by clearly and realistically outlining your resources and goals in advance. A good rule of thumb is: FOR EVERY DOLLAR YOU SPEND YOU MUST GET FOUR BACK. Keep this in mind when your event involves the hiring of buses or, in those last few days when excitement is high, you are thinking or ordering that extra floral centerpiece. When in doubt, do the simpler kind of event.

RULE 2

Take advantage of the resources of your community members.

You will discover many people in your community who are supporters but for some reason or another cannot give of their time. They might have access to reduced rates for printing, food, halls, prizes, etc. The law forbids an incorporated business to give contributions, but an unincorporated owner may do so. But even the owner of an incorporated business can sell you his or her product at the lowest price he sells goods or services to other bona fide customers. So try and save money by seeking out these people; the more you can get for less, the smaller your expenditures.

RULE 3

Allow yourself ample planning time.

Don't get into a position where you have to throw an event together because you did not allow enough time to work out all the details properly; there is nothing sadder than a potentially good event that comes off badly because of lack of preparation. Allow yourself at least four weeks to organize and publicize a bake sale, longer for events involving things

Reprinted with permission of the Finance Office, The Samuels Team, Inc.

1935. Amelia Earhart becomes the first women to pilot a plane solo across the Pacific, from Honolulu to Oakland, California, in eighteen hours at an average speed of 133 miles per hour. Earlier, in 1932, she became the first woman to span the country on a non-stop flight from Los Angeles to Newark, New Jersey. And, in 1928, she was the first woman to fly the Atlantic.

Finance Office, The Samuels Team, Inc.

like halls and entertainment where the number of people involved is greater and invitees must have time to plan ahead. It is also true that when you are in a hurry you tend to spend more money.

Be aware of other events planned in your community so you won't conflict. Two car-wash events on the same Saturday will surely diminish the proceeds for both groups. If you are relatively sure there are no conflicts, then all the more reason to let your plans be known as early as possible to avoid such conflicts.

You and your finance chairperson and committee must sit down—way in advance—to decide: (1) what you want to do, (2) how much you want to raise, (3) how much you can spend, and (4) when you want the event to take place.

RULE 4

Set a standard of giving prior to the event.

It is important that you know your audience and just how much they are capable of giving; don't fall into the trap of allowing someone to give you a dollar when they are capable of giving you ten or even a hundred dollars! As you plan an event, think over the list of invitees with an eye toward their ability to give; an audience of professional people should produce more revenue for you than a group of elderly, retired people living on a set income. This is not to imply one group should be approached and the other ignored. Just be aware so you can gear your requests to the audience.

RULE 5

Stress the importance of giving now— not later.

If none of us received our paychecks until December, we would probably be in a financial bind sometime during the year. The same is true of your campaign. It needs a cash flow to run smoothly from now to its completion. Stress this urgency by pointing out that "later" may be "too late."

Establish deadlines and let them be known in your community. For example:

* You must raise $1,000 at this picnic to meet your fund-raising quo-

ta for the month.
* You need $200 to pay for a newspaper ad that is to run on Saturday.
* You must raise $75 at this bake sale because a member of the community has pledged to make a matching contribution if you do so.

This kind of appeal gives you not only a deadline but a specific and limited need which the potential contributor can feel a part of. When you reach your goals, let it be known to the community with thanks and, if possible, to each person who has made a contribution. This creates immeasurable good will and makes it a lot easier to ask for another contribution in the future.

THE MISER'S GOLD.

RULE 6

Follow up on all pledges.

There are some acceptable occasions when, instead of giving you a contribution, people will pledge to give you a certain amount. The fund-raising chairperson must be informed of these instances and then remind these people of their commitments. Sometimes this is an easy job, but not often. Diplomacy, tact, and much patience are often needed. When you receive the money, even if it is late, *always* be courteous and thank them.

RULE 7

Do not assume everyone knows as much about your candidate as you do.

Many people would like to be more informed about your campaign than they are but won't admit. Emphasize

its importance and your reasons for supporting this race whenever you can. This will not only help in your fund-raising but will help build up enthusiasm for your candidate and might well be a means of getting more volunteers actively involved in campaigning. Use campaign literature.

RULE 8

In fund-raising, every member of the family can do something.

Do not underestimate the usefulness of children, teen-agers, college students, and the elderly as volunteer helpers. What they lack in some respects will be paid back tenfold in commitment and enthusiasm. You may finally be able to reap some of the benefits from all those guitar lessons you have been paying for by asking your talented son to participate in a local talent-night benefit. You may well find that an elderly member of the community who has a lifetime of experience to share with you will be your most reliable helper. Besides, making the youngsters and the oldsters feel involved almost counts as much as the money they will be able to help raise.

RULE 9

One person should be responsible for the collection of all funds.

It will not be possible for one person to attend every fund-raising event to oversee the handling of cash, checks, and pledges received, but one person should be *in charge* of this. Human errors increase as the number of persons involved increases; unless one person is held responsible for the control of the money, there may be problems. The person in charge should receive the money as soon after an event as possible with a full accounting of outstanding pledges. This information is to be passed on to the chairperson for follow-ups.

RULE 10

Seek out volunteers with special abilities to help and make sure each is motivated to keep producing.

1937. Jean Harlow, while working on the film *Saratoga,* dies at the age of twenty-six after a long history of illness. The actress was only eighteen when, after appearing in *Hell's Angels,* she became nationally known as the "Blonde Bombshell."

How to Make the Media Work for You

YOU NEED SOME TECHNICAL information in order to make the system work for you. You need to know how to write press releases, when to mail them, and to whom they should be sent; you need to know how to talk to reporters, how to organize a press conference, and how to set up radio and television interviews.

However, in order to be successful in using the media as an instrument for your concerns, you need a different kind of information as well. You need to understand what "news" is to each individual media form—to radio, to television, to daily newspapers, to weeklies, and to magazines. And then, what type of newspaper story is each of the dailies especially interested in? You need to be sensitive to the competition between media forms (especially between TV and dailies), to the relationships between competing TV networks (CBS vs. NBC), and between competing newspapers (*New York Times* and *New York Post*), and finally to the politics

within each paper, magazine, radio, or TV station. You need to understand what a reporter is looking for—a front-page story, the job of chief political reporter, or a chance to beat out the competitor on another paper for the story.

Once you have this understanding, you need to know how to use it. When do you leak information to an individual reporter? When do you give a reporter an "exclusive"—that is, give him/her the story before anyone else has it? When do you avoid the press completely? Only with experience, and a willingness to learn from each and every stituation, will you develop these skills.

Your Publicity Person

Generally, one person should coordinate publicity efforts and be the primary contact with the press. With experience, she or he will gain self-confidence and the confidence of reporters. If they have trusted her once

1937. This June, Amelia Earhart takes off on "just one more long flight," a world journey in a Lockheed Electra. On July 2, while flying to an obscure and minute island on the mid-Pacific leg of her trip, radio contact weakens and then disappears. Last messages tell

and she came through, they will likely trust her again. Also, it's important that the press know whom to contact for what. If the situation becomes too complicated, or if your person is inaccessible, you will lose the story, interview, or the chance to comment on an event.

On the other hand, many women's groups have formed PR committees that function effectively where areas of responsibility are well defined. In one group, for example, two people are responsible for oganizing press conferences and other press events, calling the press, and writing releases, though one person serves as coordinator of the event and as the press contact. At the press conferences, other members of the committee volunteer to run errands and deal with last-minute crises. Another member of the PR committee concentrates on placing group representatives on TV and radio interview programs. Two other women write brochures and other promotional material for the organization, and some new members organize a speaker's bureau. They all help with follow-up telephoning, collating, stuffing envelopes, and delivering releases by hand to certain media people. In this case, it is clear that several hands can accomplish more than just two. In addition, a group effort provides a way to develop skills in a number of women.

There are qualities that make a publicity person more effective in dealing with the press: she or he should be confident, patient, and good with details and follow-through. She or he should also be friendly and somewhat gregarious. She or he will have to call strangers cold on the telephone. She or he will have to sell them something. Reporters know that some public-relations people will sell anything without a qualm—from a leaky canoe to a device that turns tin into gold. Your group has an advantage because you are selling something you believe in. However, it is important to remember that reporters are hard-nosed, hard-working people primarily interested in a good story. Your cause is not their most pressing business unless there is something in it for them.

PUBLICITY TOOLS

Press Release

The purpose of a press release is to attract the attention of the media to your event, cause, or group. Releases take three major forms: (1) a short invitation to cover an upcoming event, (2) a long statement (released at that event or on its own) containing the information you want to have publicized (i.e. your demands or your position on an issue), (3) a backgrounder which will further educate the media on your activities and issues.

Press Release Form
by Sandy Hill

A press release should be a typewritten, double-spaced statement using standard type, and good quality 8½ by 11-inch paper. Script or italic typewriting can be difficult to read. Onionskin or tissue paper can tear, and carbon copies tend to smear easily.

Neatness counts! The press release should not contain any typos, misspellings, or crossouts.

A press release always includes the release date in the upper right-hand corner in capital letters. Generally this information, which is underlined, says FOR IMMEDIATE RELEASE. Occasionally you may want to prepare a release and have it in the editor's hands for use immediately after a newsworthy event—which you know about in advance—takes place. In that case, use a hold release, and be specific: FOR RELEASE 4 P.M. WEDNESDAY, JUNE 2, 1974.

Reference data goes on the upper left-hand side of the page and includes the name of the organization as well as the name, address, and phone number of a person to contact for further information. And make sure the contact is a person with additional information.

The text of a press release is organized with the most important and basic information first—something like an inverted pyramid—so that it's easy for the pressroom to cut it by starting with elimination of paragraphs at the bottom and working up the page. Accordingly, the first sentence or two should answer the key questions of: WHO, WHAT, WHEN, WHERE, and WHY—and, if possible, HOW.

You should use short, two-sentence paragraphs. No heading is necessary in the release, although a good title can catch a reporter's eye. Be sure to leave room for any title or directions which the news editor may want to insert.

Important details of the press release should be included next—the name of the main speaker and her topic, for example. Use the "tip" of the inverted pyramid for miscellaneous.

In closing, you should have a standard paragraph giving background information on the purpose of your group and your major activities or projects.

If you must go on to a second page, end the first page with a complete paragraph and type -MORE- at the bottom center of the page. Second sheets should contain all the reference data that the first page did. To indicate that you have reached the end of the press release, type - 30- or # # # under the last paragraph in the center of the next line.

A few words of caution:
• Never mention door prizes, raffles, or lotteries in a

---

of diminishing fuel and no land in sight. According to well-wishers who saw her off on that last flight, Miss Earhart was aware that anything less than perfect weather conditions would make her safe landing on the island impossible.

press release. Newspapers go through the United States mail, and federal law forbids their use of such information.

- Never include information about where to buy tickets for an event. After all, you are requesting free news space—not free advertising.

- You may want to include provocative quotes, but when giving straight information, avoid all unnecessary adjectives and words. Never editorialize in a news release!

- Always double-check all your data for accuracy.

The Backgrounder

Backgrounders are long releases that have all the information anyone could possibly want on your particular group and/or issue. Their purpose is to also provide all the information that a reporter would need in order to write an intelligent and factual story or feature.

Background information should be provided in your press packets whenever you are dealing with a complex issue, such as rape, sex discrimination in employment, or education. You might include relevant fact sheets and historical perspectives.

Background information on your group (its history, activities, membership) is always useful when you're announcing a specific action, project, or conference, or releasing a report.

Getting the Release to the Media

Mailing Lists

The key to good media coverage is a good mailing list. It should be extensive, covering all media and relevant reporters in the area.

Address press releases to the person most interested, or to a person with whom you have had personal contact.

Read the newspapers and follow radio and TV news to decide who would be the most logical person to contact. Call the various media offices, say who you are, and ask who should be receiving your releases.

It is important to develop personal contacts with sympathetic reporters. They will appreciate your keeping them posted and may be responsible for getting you coverage even when they cannot cover an event themselves.

Besides specific reporters, your basic mailing list should include the various assignment desks for each media:

City desk—for newspapers (dailies)
News assignment desk—for radio and TV
Local news desk—for wire services and periodicals
Political desk—for newspapers and TV
Women's labor, finance, etc. editors—where relevant
Photo desk—for newspapers, wire services, periodicals
Editors—for weeklies

In addition, college, PTA, club, church, feminist, and community group newspapers and newsletters provide another useful source for publicity. Many unions also publish newspapers and newsletters.

Lists should be broken down into groupings—dailies, TV and radio, weeklies, labor press, etc. Very often releases are earmarked for a particular audience.

Lists should be typed on carbon copy labels or Xerox labels, duplicating as many sets as possible at one time. It can be a real crisis when you have an emergency release to send and you're out of labels.

The Daybook

All press and publicity owe a debt to the Associated Press and United Press International wire services. In many major cities AP and UPI put out a complete teletype listing of upcoming events which all TV, radio, and print media receive and use. If you have a solid story, you can telephone it in to the Daybook without mailing a release, although it is preferable to send a written notice. If you are phoning in a story, do it at least twelve hours before the event.

If you telephone no one else on release follow-up (see below), *call the daybook:* "Hello, I want to make sure you have (the event) scheduled for noon tomorrow."

In many cities, there are private wire services, like the PR New York News Service, that offer the same service for about twenty-five dollars, or free to members. When you pay, you can be sure that the story will be on the wire (but not that it will be picked up by the media). The press office of your congressperson would know if such services are available in your area.

Timing

Mailing a press release too early is worse than mailing it too late. If it arrives too much in advance, it will be shunted aside and forgotten. On the other hand, if you have a hot last minute story, you can always dispense with a release and phone it in.

Releases should arrive three to five days before an event. This will provide enough time for assignment editors to put someone on your story. Weekly newspapers have earlier deadlines—so check with them on proper timing.

Telephone Follow-up

Call news desks and city desks, the Daybook, and call special reporters and those you have sent the release to by name.

Call personal contacts in advance and close to the time they have received the release. Be especially sure to follow up with people who have been assigned to you in the past. A good contact, or someone interested in your activities, may need a few days in order to free him/herself from other assignments.

When you call reporters, it is your job to let them know what is going on, and *their* job to decide whether

1937. The *Ladies' Home Journal* circulates a research questionnaire that determines that 64 percent of those women polled feel there are occasions when war is justified, 94 percent want uniform divorce laws throughout the country, 90 percent believe there is a God and life after death, and 54 percent approve of installment buying.

it is important or relevant.

There's a wrong and a right way to talk to a reporter:

WRONG:

I just wanted to call and tell you that Ms. X is having a news conference today, and since she has such a terrific position on child care, and it's so relevant, etc. . .

RIGHT:

(Who)	*This is_____ from _____.*
(Where)	*I'm calling to tell you that we're holding a*
(When)	*press conference 10 A.M. Tuesday, March*
(What/Why)	*6th at St. Gregory's Church, in order to comment on the current day-care crisis and announce a future action. The following speakers will attend _____ _____. The press conference is sponsored by a coalition of diverse community and feminist groups including _____.*
(Special Fact)	*This will be the first major response by prominent women's groups to the cut-off of funds for new child-care centers.*
(Easy Access to You)	*If you need to reach me, my name is _____. The number here is _____, and at home, it's _____. Do you have any questions? I look forward to seeing you.*

You should try to be as concise as possible. They may interrupt to say they have the story or to ask you to slow down so they can take the information down. The longer they listen, the better.

Add any last-minute facts that might not be in the release, such as the "special fact" above, or "(Celebrity) will be joining us." Try to give them a hook—why it's a hot story, personalities, photo possibilities, etc.

Don't browbeat the reporter or editor you talk to. Just make her/him feel that it's a good story, that the press event will be handled professionally, and that it will come off on time. Generally this is when you should call:

- For an event scheduled from 10:00 A.M. to noon, call between noon and 4:30 P.M. the previous day.
- For an event scheduled from noon to 2:00 P.M., call between 8:00 and 9:00 A.M. that day, or between 3:30 and 5:30 P.M. the previous day.
- For an event scheduled from 3:00 to 5:00 P.M., call between 8:00 and 10:00 A.M. the same day.

Other Ways to Reach Media in Writing
Feature Stories

Feature stories are stories that will help project a favorable image of your activities to the public and increase awareness; they are not hard news. In doing a feature, forget about self-interest. Think about what will be of interest to the public—the self-interest will be a by-product.

There are two possible approaches to feature stories: you can work with a particular reporter to place a story, or write an article and try to place that.

Interesting a newspaper in a feature is difficult. It requires a basically good idea and a persuasive approach.

Ray Pinkson

Women's Strike for Peace

Picture Story

When a picture is worth a thousand words, *use it*. Set up events that lend themselves to a picture story. Notify picture editors as well as news editors ahead of time. Put a note on the press release, "Photos available."

Generally, do not send unsolicited photos to publications. They will be thrown away 99 percent of the time.

If you have a picture story, it's a good idea to send your own photographer and let editors look at your contact sheets. This is particularly useful for local press and weeklies, and where you have established a personal working relationship with the editor.

Supply prints (glossy 5 x 7 inches or, preferably, 8 by 10 inches) on a selective basis to local editors who have already requested prints as well as to special-interest editors and publications that have demonstrated a strong interest in the topic or personality pictured.

Here is a suggested form for a photo story release:

To: Photo editors, TV or news assignment editor
From: Name, organization, telephone number

1938. Shirley Temple earns $10,000 per week in salary alone as the child star of post-Depression America.

What: Type of event
Who: People involved and participants
Where: Location
When: Day, date, time

Photo possibilities: List things that will lend themselves to a good photograph (e.g. Ms. Steinem will lead a torchlight rally; Ally Smith and Joan Weeks, of Freeport, will re-enact a scene from . . .)

Use action shots, not group portraits. Attach a caption to the photograph; do not write on the picture. Study captions in the publication in question to decide on the best form. Within the caption, identify all the people in the photo (from left to right). Include a press information name and number on the caption release. Use a headline.

Double-check photo deadlines. They usually vary from copy deadlines.

Letters to the Editor

Send well-written, concise letters to the attention of the editor. Do not deal with personalities or be petty. Do not use a hysterical or parochial approach.

You can send as many letters to the editor as you have individual allies to sign them and time to write them.

The letters are useful because they enlarge the number of voices in a campaign. Some of the most effective letters are those written by identifiable community leaders. However, all well-written letters are helpful.

Talking to Media People

Reporters

Reporters will often call with a question, to clear a fact, to clarify a position, to get an opinion. The first thing is to be sure that your phone number, or that of someone reliable, is readily available to the press, not only printed on every press release, but repeated in each conversation with the reporter.

Know the facts of your subject and be prepared to respond specifically. Also, be sure of the position your group wants to take—know the "party line."

When you are called, give an accurate answer even if it puts you temporarily in a not-so-favorable light. *Always be completely factual.*

If you don't know the answer, *don't fudge!* Just say, "I don't know, but I'll find out for you. How soon do you need an answer?" This is vital since different media have different deadlines, ranging from five minutes to a day or two from the time you've received the call. *Always call back.* You will add immeasurably to your credibility as a news source if you return calls quickly and provide complete answers.

If the reporter asks you something you don't want to answer, you can handle it honestly—"We haven't come to a conclusion about that yet." Or simply, "I can't answer that right now." Don't say you'll get an answer if you won't or can't; don't put the onus on the group to reply at a later date if you know they have no intention of doing so.

Be wary of using "off the record." The more openly you treat reporters, the more they will like and listen to you. Off-the-record stories shackle the reporter and should only be used by the most skilled press aides in the most touchy situations.

In dealing with reporters, always remember: (1) what the reporter needs—logistically and editorially; (2) what the reporter wants to know—the facts, as briefly and eloquently as possible (if you are being recorded for radio or TV, speak in twenty- or thirty-second cuts that can be used on the air).

Most important, remember how reporters see themselves—professionals with wry senses of humor and much cynicism (usually only skin-deep—they are the real idealists of the profession). Always treat them as professionals and not simply as a friend or enemy. This doesn't mean you can't have a drink with a reporter—just don't tell any reporter something you don't want known by the world, no matter how friendly the reporter may seem.

The Weekly Newspaper

Often overlooked, but certainly important to local women's groups, are the nation's weekly newspapers. These papers, which are often family owned, are major sources of information to people outside of the major metropolitan areas. Often the owner is also the editor and sometimes the reporter and advertising manager as well.

Make a point of visiting every weekly and local paper in your community. Find out about deadlines, circulation, advertising rates, and picture policies. For many, almost any picture you submit will be an added incentive to run a story about your activities. If your reception is not good, ask about advertising rates so that you can add it to your advertising budgets.

Don't forget to get a number of back issues so that you can assess editorial policy. Know how they handle issues similar to yours.

Weekly newspapers have one hectic day each week when they go to press. Find out which day it is *and stay away.*

Weekly newspapers, like major dailies, may belong to press associations. Check to see if all or any of the weeklies in your area are in this kind of organization and, if so, discuss the sharing of news.

Staging an Event

This section applies to all events you organize where you want good press coverage (demonstrations, conferences, or press conferences). Before the event, you will

1939. Eleanor Patterson, heiress and, at times, ruthless executive, combines two former Hearst Washington, D.C., papers into the *Times-Herald.* By 1943 she will have built the paper into the city's largest, though nine years later it will be merged into the *Washington Post.* On her death in 1954 she is to be called "the most hated woman in America" by *Time* magazine, and "the most powerful" by *Collier's.*

Sissy Farenthold addressing the NWPC National Convention, Boston, 1975

have sent out press releases and/or called wire services, reporters, and assignment desks. Remember, don't give them the full story by phone—just interest them in coming!

Schedule

A 10:00 A.M. event will get coverage in the afternoon newspapers, the 6:00 P.M. and 11:00 P.M. evening news, and the next day's morning papers. Eleven to 1:00 P.M. is cutting it close, but on a juicy story, it can deliver all the above, except perhaps the afternoon papers.

A 2:00 P.M. event can get you on the 6:00 P.M. evening news, although most often without film; it can also deliver the 11:00 P.M. evening news and the next day's papers.

A 6:00 P.M. story may get you the evening 11:00 P.M. news, but unless it's more of a feature than an event, it may cost you coverage for anything else the next day. By then, it will be old news.

Monday, 5:00 P.M. is the most common deadline for local weeklies. The weekly deadline for *Time* and *Newsweek* in New York is Wednesday afternoon.

Avoid Friday press events, since Saturday papers are read least. Monday morning is the time many people choose, so you may want to compete for less sought-after time by holding your conference on a mid-week morning.

On Location

Have *one* person designated in charge of press at the event, preferably the person whose name appears on the press release. The coordinator should not be the spokes-

person at the event. All the following points are duties of the coordinator and assistants.

- Arrive early.
- Have plenty of press kits.
- If the event is indoors, know where the electrical outlets and fuses are.

Greet the press. Either take the name and affiliation of each reporter and crew member, and know the difference, or have them sign in at a special table.

Know the difference between being firm about controlling *your* event and bossing the press around.

Have a list of participants and grass-roots supporters who will be available later to the press for reactions and comments or for in-depth interviews.

Make sure the media representatives know who the coordinator is, and that she or he is available if they need more information or technical help.

Have at least one person on stand-by to be a "gofer"—to get tape, get a repairman, make a phone call, pass coffee, etc.

Coordinators should help crews and photographers identify whoever is on camera. They will have your participants list, but they will need help putting faces with names.

Make sure the spokesperson of the event knows where to go and what to do. She must be prepared to change plans at any moment if the coordinator indicates there is a problem.

The Press Kit

The Press Kit is packaged in one large manila envelope or folder with pockets. It contains the following inserts

---

1940. It is reported that midwives attend only 5 percent of white infant births, and 56 percent of black infant births.

in the order they appear. Each should repeat your group's name and telephone number:

- Agenda for the day.
- List of participants, with titles, identification, and detailed biographies where needed. Make sure all names are spelled correctly—check, don't guess.
- Original press release (coverage invitiation, etc.).
- Copies of formal statements and speeches by participants.
- Background information: a brochure, one or two clippings, the organization's standard mailing piece. Be selective in materials and know why each piece is included.

A Press Conference

Press conferences can serve a variety of purposes, among them the following:

- To make announcements and statements
- To introduce personalities or specialists with a story
- To call new facts and figures to the attention of the public
- To launch campaigns and drives
- To protest or react; to praise or damn

Speakers

Unless your organization is well established or your issue especially controversial, you will have trouble attracting the press without a well-known personality.

Women Strike for Peace

Dorothy Marder

- If you have the "name," you don't need more than one or two speakers.
- If you don't have the "name," you need a package: a grass-roots cross-section, specialists you have identified, a variety of points of view. Any or all of these can make a package. However, don't have too many speakers (generally, no more than five).
- A spokesperson should clearly be in control of the conference, introducing the speakers, moving the agenda along, and should open the conference to questions from the press.
- Lead into the name speaker with one or two other speakers. The agenda should make the program clear.
- Speakers should try to keep their statements from two to five minutes, and should have copies of their statements available to the press.
- Speakers who follow the headliner or main speaker can add a one-two punch to the message but they risk getting lost in the coverage, or simply not being covered at all. It's a great spot to "waste" a potentially unfriendly friend, or to steal the show, if you know how.
- Prima donnas can turn off the press. If you are dealing with a supporter who is a prima donna, don't be afraid to put her in her place.

Timing

Start on time, if possible, and make sure you are never running more than fifteen minutes late. If most of the media is there, start it rolling, assuming anyone else who is interested will show by the time you get to your headliner. Your portion of the press conference (before questions) should be no longer than thirty to forty-five minutes, and fifteen minutes is even better.

Either the time is right for the news story, or don't bother having a press conference. You can't fake it. If you can't conveniently time a conference, maybe you can create a real, honest-to-goodness news event.

Location

Choose a symbolic place for the issue, if possible. Choose a geographically practical place, easily accessible to the press.

Beg or borrow good rooms from other organizations or corporations. Hotels are in the business of renting rooms, not lending them.

Pick a room to go with the size of your crowd. Better too small than too big. Make sure the room can accommodate lighting and sound equipment.

Radio and Television Interviews

How do you place someone on a TV or radio show?

1940. Emma Goldman—a native Russian Jew, anarchist, and birth-control advocate—dies. In 1915 she took up the banner after Margaret Sanger was arrested for speaking out on voluntary motherhood. Mrs. Goldman's example, in turn, inspired Mrs. Sanger and both, working together, brought the then radical idea of contraception before the modern public for the first time. (In 1899 Mrs. Goldman joined the anarchist

It's easy to explain and rather more difficult to accomplish.

Research your local and national TV shows, looking at their format, style, interests, and audience. There are directories of national network shows that can be helpful.

Your biggest asset is news credibility. If you've been getting good coverage, chances are that the editors on the show will know about your activities.

The best lead-in is a succinct letter of introduction that contains background information plus a clipping or two and suggests a good news angle for the show in question.

Telephone ahead to find out who screens guests and mark the envelope to that person's attention.

Ms/Mr. Host
Name of Show
Station
Address
ATT: Name of contact/assistant

Follow with a telephone call to the assistant. In most cases, the assistant does the screening and you should immediately try to establish a good rapport with that person.

Probe during this conversation and listen for a focus that will satisfy both your group and the host. Also, listen for what further material you can submit to bolster your image of newsworthiness.

Be patient. Let the show have time to call you. If this begins to seem like never, make a straightforward inquiry to see if a new angle should be developed. Present your case strongly, but don't urge—you'll lose even if you win.

On the Air

If and when a representative from your group is set to appear on a TV or radio show, make sure she understands the angle you have agreed on with the producers.

Interviewers love to create a little excitement by getting you into what they think are explosive subjects like the future of marriage or sexual freedom. It's their job to create a little controversy. It's your job to work the conversation back to your main purpose for being there.

Before you accept an appearance, always know who else is appearing on the program. Be wary of debate situations. If the station is planning a boxing match rather than a serious airing of issues, decline to appear.

Another approach is to speak to the other participants on the show and see if you can set up your own ground rules. Interviewer's intentions have often been circumvented by guests who, although they disagree on a specific issue, will refuse to attack each other.

If your purpose is to publicize an event, don't forget to give time and place and where they can get further information. Generally, *keep your goals in mind.*

Women Strike for Peace

Ray Pinkson

PROMOTION

When we talk about promotion, we mean advertising (both paid and free) and outreach efforts that don't involve dealing with the "news" media. Promotion includes brochures, posters, fliers, radio and TV spots, and speakers bureaus. It's a more expensive form of PR, but when properly planned, the money spent can be well worth it. Also there are many ways to cut costs.

Radio

Obtaining publicity on radio stations can be extremely useful to your group, especially if the station's target audience is one you're trying to reach. You can place announcements of conferences, demonstrations, or services offered by your group. You should thoroughly research each station's audience, and find out the best timing for reaching that audience before you undertake a radio campaign.

Radio time on local stations is inexpensive enough—especially in small towns or counties—for you to consider buying a few quick spots. The cost can be as little as twenty-five dollars for a sixty-second announcement. But better yet, if you listen carefully for a few days, you can find a way to work yourself into the existing program format—such as public-affairs programs, community editorials, community calendars, or public-service announcements.

Your local radio stations have agreed with the Federal Communications Commission to give free air time for

movement in New York and while there conspired with Alexander Berkman, a Russian revolutionary, in an unsuccessful effort to kill Henry Clay Frick during the Homestead clashes.) As a feminist, Mrs. Goldman spoke against the use of women as "sex commodities," but disagreed with those who would exclude men from their lives, considering them to have a "narrow, Puritanical vision."

statements of interest to the community. Generally, you are eligible for free public-service air time if your organization is a non-profit group, social or civic, and your message is directly related to the activities of your group. However, the station need *not* give this time to controversial announcements that may lead them down the path of donating endless free time for answers by your opponents, according to the Fairness Doctrine. You should call the station's manager or public relations person who will tell you how your station has interpreted the FCC's rather vague guidelines. For instance, some stations do not allow direct appeals for money. Take time to listen carefully to spots to figure out the sort of language the station requires. Some stations even have forms that you can fill out and others have handbooks that will give you sample formats for your messages as well as other media information. When you speak to the station's public-service director, ask if such a handbook has been prepared for community groups in your area.

When preparing a message for the media, plan ahead. Allow three to four weeks for preparation of the message, distribution to the media, and broadcasting. Submitting your copy early to the station will help insure its being scheduled. All stations accept written announcements, and some accept prerecorded messages.

Television

Most of the suggestions for radio promotion also apply to television, especially as they relate to acquiring public-service time. You should call the public-service director for each station and ask for their specific instructions. Some stations prefer to have public-service announcements submitted in visual form, and will give you guidelines for the preparation of your materials. Another entree to TV exposure is the requirement that all television (and radio) stations offer equal time to those who disagree with the station's editorial positions. You should monitor television editorials and learn to take advantage of these free opportunities to present your viewpoint. For information on an individual station's policies, call the editorial director.

Speaker's Bureaus

An effective tool for educating your local community and expanding your membership as well, is to organize a speaker's bureau. You should thoroughly brief your members on the issues and go through some role playing—each person taking turns asking and answering questions. You should prepare quips and serious answers to the usual questions. If feminism is your issue, get ready for questions like: "Do you think the issue of lesbianism has hurt the Movement?" or "I've talked to a lot of black women and they're against the Movement." Some groups have prepared speaker's-bureau packets containing fact sheets and sample questions with suggested responses.

Once you have a number of well-prepared speakers, you should call or write the groups you want to reach. Tell them you would like the opportunity to discuss your issue with their membership. Be sensitive to your audiences and send the speaker who could best relate to them. And when speakers go out to other organizations, they should take brochures on your group, fact sheets, and membership information. Always give people an easy way to find you again. Also, it's a good idea to debrief your speakers soon after they have addressed an audience: Was the response positive? Were there questions you couldn't answer? What follow-up do you suggest? Was it worth our time?

Brochures

Soon after your group is formed, you should develop materials describing your goals, activities, publications, services, and membership requirements. A basic brochure can be extremely useful and effective in promoting your group. Mail it to prospective members or target groups who need your services; distribute it at meetings you attend as well as through community outlets such as drugstores, supermarkets, child-care centers, women's centers, YWCA's, and social-service agencies. Also, brochures can serve as background information for all other publicity efforts.

Brochures should be straightforward, simple yet informative. They should include information on:
• *Background:* Why did you organize? What led up to your actions? Who are you—a group of community activists? a group of black feminists? a group of office workers?
• *Your Statement of Purpose:* What are your long-term goals? What do you hope to accomplish? or change? Why is what you're doing important?
• *How You Plan to Accomplish Your Goals:* Specifically, what projects, activities, publications, or services do you have? What is the goal of each project? the content of each publication? the exact cost of your services?
• *How You Function:* What is your decision-making structure? Who are the people responsible for your activities (staff, officers, boards of directors, advisory committees, or project coordinators)? Where does your funding come from?
• *How People Can Join or Get Further Information:* Who can they call or write to for information? When are you open? How much are your membership dues? Do you need contributions and are they tax-deductible? It's wise to include a tear-off form which they can fill out in order to join, to order publications, to volunteer their time, or make contributions.

If your group hasn't the money to expend on a fancy brochure, there are ways to cut costs. You can bypass typesetting, a major cost, by making your own mock-up. Press-type is do-it-yourself typesetting which is best for titles and headings. Your stationery store sells various brands of press-type.

Called by one authority "the most accomplished, magnetic woman speaker in American history," Emma Goldman—in her heyday—harangued the country from one coast to the other on topics as diverse as her disillusion with the Russian system and modern drama.

Writing and Delivering Your Speech

Dorothy Uris

To Speak or Not to Speak

Even with the nameless fears and fancies exposed and under control, women still have to deal with the actual fears of the stand-up speech. The spotlighted solo situation appears threatening; they shrink from expressing their opinions in public and from audience criticism, especially with men present; they tend to resist becoming involved and assuming responsibilities. These anxieties seesaw with universal wants—women want to be accepted, believed, admired, they want to triumph over timidity—and to move the minds and hearts of other women and of men.

If at first you do succeed, try, try again. One day you're asked to chair a small meeting of a local committee on public housing and you function with scarcely a hitch; the next week comes the suggestion that you make a plug for the new community day-care center at the membership meeting of Planned Parenthood. You swallow the "Who, me?" and fill the assignment. Before you know it, you're on your feet, explaining and persuading. Now you've got your feet wet and the water, while cold, is bracing.

Your topic and you. What *should* you, rather what do you *want* to speak about? No matter how well intentioned, no talk can mean much unless its subject moves you to express your thoughts and feelings. Problem-laden topics like the energy crisis, inflation, human rights, the divorce tangle, pollution, political corruption, concern us all. Of course, you will not be expected to deal with the totality of such subjects, any one of which could provide the basis for a full day's conference, complete with panels.

Begin with a Story

You were probably read to as a child, your grandmother may have regaled you with many a never-to-be-forgotten tale, and you may have started with your own children on picture books (an excellent speech practice for them and for you). The narration form, regardless of content, has remained with you and now that you are tackling a talk, turn to storytelling as preparation.

Write out the first draft of your maiden speech as a story by answering the questions *who, where, when, what,* and *why,* and construct a plot line in logical sequence and suspenseful telling.

Let us suppose:

You are a consumer researcher. Your topic: "Up, Up and Away—The Soaring Prices." The story: This morning at the supermarket you ran into your friend Helen, and together you investigated several items and . . .

You are a volunteer social worker. Your topic: "Even If You Win, You Lose: A Case of Rape." The story: Alice Summers, who lives down the street (fictitious name and address) was assaulted by a rapist, and she went to court to press charges without corroboration and . . .

You are a single parent. Your topic: "Single Blessedness(?)." The story: This morning the children's schoolbus was late because of the weather and you missed the commuter train to your job and . . .

You are a lawyer. Your topic: "Mum's the Word or You're Fired?" The story: Rachel Smith, your client, has an employer who refuses

illegally to hire married women, especially those with children and . . .

You were class president (Swarthmore, 1960). You are to speak at the class reunion on "Education for What?" The story: Your *cum laude* landed you a secretarial job at a large publishing house and . . .

Narration as a speech tool has many advantages: you can convert the whole of a story (if it fits) into your topic, or merely extract the nub of it to open your talk. Also, the tendency to cover nervousness with a stilted style of delivery is offset by the naturalness of recounting, rather than expounding. And with the telling on paper, you have warmed and humanized the approach to your topic, even if you eventually forgo the story itself.

The Speech as a Body

While we can dispense with some of the more complex methods of speech preparation that may hinder more than help, there are those enduring precepts, the eternal verities of speechcraft, that we cannot do without. From Plato in the fifth century B.C.: "Every speech ought to be put together like a living creature, with a body of its own, so as to be neither without head, nor without feet, but to have both a middle and extremities, described proportionately to each other and to the whole."

To develop a stable structure to lean on, *plan two-minute-by-the-clock talks on a single point;* these prepare you for the ten- to twenty-minute subjects with several points. The one-point workout gives you the bare bones of your topic, to which you later add the flesh. Following the classical image: the head is your introduction; the torso, your reasons, proofs, examples; the legs, your conclusion.

Choose a subject based on first-hand experience with the problem. You may decide on the forever-with-us fuel crisis. Your single-point topic: "A Program for Coping." To avoid bogging down on the introduction as many do by fussing with language, polishing a joke, and so on, *start with the body, not the head.*

1941. Margaret Hamma of New York City sets a new world professional record by typing 149 words per minute in a Chicago contest.

Bella Abzug

what you're gonna tell 'em—you tell 'em—you tell 'em what you told 'em.''

Keeping the head-torso-legs plan in mind, try other two-minute one-pointers:

"Shortage or Rip-off?"—another aspect of the energy crisis (statistics are required).

"Who Will Take Grandma?"—is old age a fulfillment or disaster?

"How to Needle Your Senator"—the ratification of the Equal Rights Amendment is still on the agenda.

Whether you aim to inform or persuade or both, the same abbreviated "body form" will fortify your technique and see you through to the delivery of more ambitious talks on any subject.

Delivery

The term "delivery," with its many-layered meaning, is especially expressive for women. A composite definition says why: giving birth, a "blessed event," a creative act, a handing over, any giving forth, a rescue, liberation, release, and—*the manner of style of uttering a speech!*

Nervous?

Nervousness, of varied origin, is real enough. It is often created by the gap between reality and fantasy—a sort of "colosseum complex." The antidote: instead of imagining the situation in grandiose terms, see the scene *as it is.* As you look out front, and the faces come into focus, note their humanness and friendliness. Although you refuse to believe it, also be assured that while your heart may hammer and your knees feel odd, signs of the jitters seldom show.

The best pacifier, now and always, is your rehearsed script on the

First, *state the problem:* "We lived in an immobilized community—how did we get it rolling again?" Then list your proposals to ease the energy crunch: organize car pools; pay car-sitters to wait on gasoline lines for parents at work; charter the local bus service for evenings out and Saturday outings for children; press station wagons into service as an emergency volunteer taxi service; and so on. Your conclusion: *New energy* came with sharing responsibilities—proving that the good-neighbor policy is not just a slogan for yesterday.

Now *go back to your introduction* and fashion it to match *the conclusion* so that the whole body is in alignment. As an opener, variously known as the *grabber, awakener,* or (you should pardon the expression) *hooker,* you might select a historical reference or something in a light vein. As that old chestnut reminds us, "You tell 'em

---

Ain't I a Woman? Sojourner Truth

Well, children, where there is so much racket there must be something out of kilter. I think that 'twixt the negroes of the South and the women at the North, all talking about rights, the white men will be in a fix pretty soon. But what's all this here talking about?

That man over there says that women need to be helped into carriages, and lifted over ditches, and to have the best place everywhere. Nobody ever helps me into carriages, or over mud-puddles, or gives me any best place! And ain't I a woman? Look at me! Look at my arm! I have ploughed and planted, and gathered into barns, and no man could head me! And ain't I a woman? I could work as much and eat as much as a man—when I could get it—and bear the lash as well! And ain't I a woman? I have borne thirteen children, and seen them most all sold off to slavery, and when I cried out with my mother's grief, none but Jesus heard me! And ain't I a woman?

Then they talk about this thing in the head; what's this they call it? [Intellect, someone whispers.] That's it, honey. What's that got to do with women's rights or negro's rights? If my cup won't hold but a pint, and yours holds a quart, wouldn't you be mean not to let me have my little half-measure full?

Then that little man in black there, he says women can't have as much rights as men, 'cause Christ wasn't a woman! Where did your Christ come from? Where did your Christ come from? From God and a woman! Man had nothing to do with Him.

If the first woman God ever made was strong enough to turn the world upside down all alone, these women together ought to be able to turn it back, and get it right side up again! And now they is asking to do it, the men better let them.

Obliged to you for hearing me, and now old Sojourner ain't got nothing more to say.

Sophia Smith Collection, Smith College

Sojourner Truth (ca. 1797—1883), a former slave who had seen her children sold away from her, became an enthusiastic abolitionist and reformer around 1845. In 1851, at a woman's rights convention in Akron, Ohio, she gave this electrifying speech of which Frances Dana Gage, who presided over the meeting, wrote: "I have never in my life seen anything like the magical influence that subdued the snobbish spirit of the day and turned the sneers and jeers of an excited crowd into notes of respect and admiration."

1941. Regularly enlisted regiments of women fight on the front lines of the Russian army against the invading Germans.

lectern before you and the opening and closing lines in your head. Standing feet apart, one foot slightly ahead of the other (feet *feeling the floor*), with shoulders released, your stance reassures you and the audience. Your body doesn't have that unyielding, squared-away look that some women affect. First you thank the chairperson *by name* for the pleasant introduction. *Now you're talking!*

Platform Pointers

Make a selection from this collection—yours to *work toward*.

1. *At ease.* Do you manage to appear poised at a social gathering or public function? Then consider this "speaking in public" no exception. How do you begin?

2. *Establish rapport.* Strike an informal note early with such questions as: "Anybody need to put a dime in the meter before we begin?" "Is it too hot? Shall we turn the heat down?" "Since one of our guests is late, shall we wait a few more minutes?" "Can you hear me back there?" "I see some empty rows at the front. Why don't you all move up closer?"

Always think of the audience ahead of yourself; turn the spotlight outward toward them.

3. *Smile the while.* Banish the notion that you must have a serious mien to be taken seriously. But don't overreact and grin your way through the talk; relax facial expression, smile with eyes letting your warmth come through.

4. *Shifting gears.* Stay loose by shifting your position periodically—not with a large movement when a slight one will do; begin with the feet to permit your body to follow suit.

You Amplified

5. *The mike.* Stand back about eight inches, closer if your voice doesn't carry well; but don't move in so cozily close that you feel tempted to croon. Speak *toward* the mike, *not into it.* You should dominate the instrument, not vice versa; don't keep staring at it, look beyond at the audience.

Amplification exaggerates all sound: curtail noisy breathing and watch popping consonants like /p/, /t/, and /k/. Move within the possible limits of lectern and mike. Did you remember to test the amplification before you started?

Without a mike, you'll have to amplify your own voice, turning up the volume without straining.

Our Physical Dialogue

6. *What does your body say?* Important moments in body language: your entrance and exit. So don't march on like a martinette, nor slink in like the Invisible Woman. Walk with easy, released posture—both coming and going—well rehearsed in advance.

Rest your fingers on the lectern or table. *Do* gesture by all means. Make a point of using hand and arm naturally, moving smoothly from your center. Bring your fist down to be emphatic, if you like, but don't bang.

Also, don't fidget—pulling your ear, twirling your hair, playing with jewelry, and an endless variety of attention-losers. Your voice, expression, gesture, and body are not separable.

7. *What to wear.* Choose an attractive and comfortable pantsuit or long dress with sleeves, and quiet jewelry. Be on guard with a short dress when crossing legs or bending down. Never chance a new outfit without a prior "dress rehearsal" before the meeting. Always take a jacket or sweater along just in case.

8. *If you use glasses.* Try extra-large type, or widely spaced capital letters. If they're no help, don't fret; you may choose contact lenses, half-glasses (to look over them at the audience), bifocals (these require eye coordination), or those chic glasses in large and interesting frames to complement the shape of your face. Of course, control the impulse to keep taking them off and putting them on.

Tensions, Away!

9. *A case of nerves.* Detect incipient nervousness in the act of slowing yourself down to a crawl; for the same reason, watch signs of accelerating the speed.

Don't panic if you lose your place; consult your script and *there it is;* never fear the moment of silence (the audience will catch up with you).

Breathe out frequently to counteract tension build-up (softly, during a pause).

For a dry mouth: drop your chin, opening your mouth slightly to release saliva; or hold a handkerchief to your mouth and run your tongue along the upper and lower teeth's gum line.

Final Touches

10. *Variety is the spice.* Help the audience to stay awake by changes in SPV (speed, pitch, volume). Eliminate another soporific, that dying inflection at the end of phrases.

11. *Go down, not up.* Learn to emphasize by favoring your lower, not throaty, range; as excitement mounts, your pitch may rise to shrillness. Pull your pitch down, but retain the volume for emphatic statements.

12. *Never hesitate to repeat* during a talk, an excellent form of emphasis. Let your sense of the dramatic prompt you when to reiterate.

13. *Common static.* Refrain from clearing your throat repeatedly: people out front tend to echo the contagious sound. Get it over with: turn your face away from the audience and, covering mouth with your hand, cough.

The *er's* and *um's*: Cut down these common, irritating, habit-forming fillers between words. Pause instead, and proceed with what comes next (you probably ought to pause more, anyway).

14. *Sight plus sound.* Employ visual aids (charts, blackboards, slides) *if* they add to your talk. Make sure they stay out of sight until needed; rehearse the timing or your exhibit may become a handicap rather than an aid; steer clear of overwhelming the audience with too much detail.

15. *No cocktails, please.* Celebrate *after* the event. Skip a heavy repast beforehand (sidestep that luncheon invitation). Stay away from milk products (including ice cream). Singers always do.

16. *Watch the time.* Be guided by the minute hand of a *stopwatch* or a *timer* set to buzz just before your conclusion.

17. *An "up" ending.* Build to the finish. Don't drop off to telegraph that the curtain's about to go down. Like a runner, summon your reserve energy to cross the finish with a spurt (a sustained one).

It's Over

Your sensations are a jumble of relief, damp palms, exhilaration, and the sound of clapping. You come to in time to smile your thanks. Friends gather around: "You sounded so natural—as if you were talking to each one of us individually." If they only knew how much preparation went into that talk!

It takes work to be "natural," to communicate with clear words linked together in a line of clear tone. Practice reduces anxiety to give you an *appearance* of ease, second best to *being* at ease. Naturalness also flows from letting down barriers by leveling with people, trusting them, and especially preparing for them.

1942. Current government studies reveal that less than 2 million of the 40 million women in the United States can boast "perfect figures."

The State of Womanhood
U.N. Development Programme

	MORE DEVELOPED AREAS		LESS DEVELOPED AREAS	
Female adult illiteracy	Europe North America	4.7% 1.9%	Africa Asia Latin America	83.7% 56.7% 27.3%
Percentage of females studying at: Primary level	Europe North America	87.8% 88.2%	Africa Asia Latin America	32.9% 45.2% 66.3%
Secondary level	Europe North America	32.4% 61.5%	Africa Asia Latin America	19.0% 27.9% 25 6%
University level	Europe North America	5.0% 8.0%	Africa Asia Latin America	2.0% 3.8% 4.5%
Percentage of women economically active	Europe North America	29.4% 25.0%	Africa Asia Latin America	26.3% 21.5% 17.1%
Percentage of economically active women employed in agriculture	Europe North America	23.0% 2.5%	Africa Asia Latin America	49.0% 52.0% 12.0%
Percentage of women between the ages of 15 and 19 who are married, divorced or widowed	Europe North America	6.7% 9.9%	Africa Asia Latin America	40.7% 27.9% 15.2%
Average of number of children	Europe North America	Between 2 and 4	Africa Asia Latin America	Between 5 and 7
Life expectancy		74 years		55 years
Women in national parliaments—some examples:	Denmark Finland USSR	17% 21.5% 38%	Egypt Trinidad & Tobago India	2% 7% 2.3%

From *IWY—As a Matter of Fact.* Reprinted with permission.

1943. Major Marina Raskova, a commander of a regiment of Russian dive bombers in World War II, dies in her cockpit upon returning from combat. Her ashes are buried with full military honors in a wall of the Kremlin.

Handywoman

Using Basic Tools

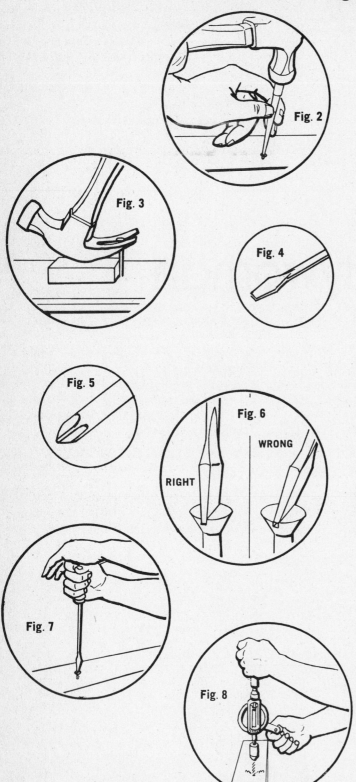

Fig. 2

Fig. 3

Fig. 4

Fig. 5

Fig. 6

RIGHT   WRONG

Fig. 7

Fig. 8

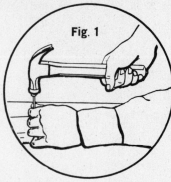

Fig. 1

HAMMER

A medium weight (12-13 ounce) claw hammer is good for general purposes.

- Hold a hammer near the end of the handle for more hitting power. To start a nail, hold it in place and tap it gently a few times until it is firmly set. Hit it straight in. (Fig. 1)

- To avoid hammer marks on the wood, use a nail set (Fig. 2) or another nail to drive a nail the last one-eighth inch into the wood.

- To remove a nail use claw end of hammer. Place a small block of wood under the head of the hammer to avoid marking the wood. (Fig. 3)

SCREWDRIVER

You need two types of screwdrivers for household repairs:

Straight blade (Fig. 4), and **Phillips** (Fig. 5). Both come in various sizes. The blade of the screwdriver should fit the slot in the screw. (Fig. 6)

- When using the screwdriver, push against the head of the screw as you turn it. (Fig. 7)

- It's easier to put a screw into wood if you make a hole first with a nail or drill. (Fig. 8) Rub wax or soap on the screw threads to make it go in easier.

PLIERS

A **slip joint pliers** can be used for many jobs around the house. (Fig. 9)

Fig. 9

Adapted from *Simple Home Repairs*, 1973 , Department of Agriculture.

1943. Nikki Giovanni, black poet, born. Of her childhood she is to write:
And I really hope that no white person ever has cause
To write about me
Because they never understand

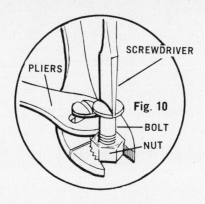

Use pliers to hold a nut while you turn a bolt with a screwdriver. (Fig. 10)

Use it to remove nails or brads. Pull the nail out at the same angle it was driven in. Use small blocks under the pliers if you need leverage. (Fig. 11)

Use it to bend or cut wire or to straighten a bent nail. (Fig. 12)

Use it to turn nuts. Wrap tape or cloth around the nut to avoid scratching it. (Fig. 13)

An **adjustable wrench** (Fig. 14) is adjustable to fit different sizes of nuts. If a nut is hard to loosen, apply a few drops of penetrating oil or kerosene. (Fig. 15) Let it soak a couple of hours or overnight. If the wrench has a tendency to slip off, try turning it over.

HANDSAW

A handsaw (Fig. 16) with about 10 teeth to the inch is good for most household work. (Fig. 17)

Mark where you want to cut. Pull the saw back and forth several times to start a groove. Let the weight of the saw do the cutting at first. If you are sawing a board, it will be easier if you support it and hold it firmly near where you're cutting. (Fig. 18)

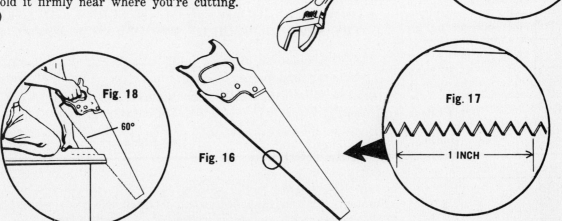

Below: Reprinted by permission of William Morrow & Company from *Black Feeling, Black Talk, Black Judgement,* by Nikki Giovanni. Copyright © 1968, 1970 by Nikki Giovanni.

Black love is Black wealth and they'll
Probably talk about my hard childhood
And never understand that
All the while I was quite happy

Tips on Using Tools and Materials
Florence Adams

Before you start any projects, there are some tips—as many as I can think of—that I will tell you about, so that you may have the edge on the me of five or so years ago, when I was bumbling around trying to do all things without foreknowledge about how things behaved under certain conditions. For example, I always thought that you simply hammered a nail into a piece of wood, through it and into another, to connect the two pieces. Did I know that often the nail displaced so much wood that the wood cracked? (And that, of course, means buying more wood.) Or, did I know that if I drilled a hole a little too big for a screw, which would then just slip in and out, I could make the hole smaller? Yes, smaller! Lots of goodies like that I know now, and many more I don't know yet, but I'm sure of picking up some more as I keep bumbling along.

ABOUT CRACKED WOOD

Think about the grain of wood as almost-openings between sections of wood, and perhaps you will avoid catastrophes. Better still, think of the grain as almost-cracks. With only a little help sometimes, the "almost" disappears and the crack is a real (and only) thing!

Cracks occur when too much wood is displaced, pushed aside, when a nail or screw enters the wood. It is often difficult to tell how much, but certainly if some were displaced (removed) before the nail entered, it would be safer—right? Thus it is often wise to predrill a hole tinier than the nail and get rid of some wood. The wood being removed by the drill kind of blows back out through the grooves of the drill bit as it's being cut away, eliminating the possibility of cracking during drilling.

Cracks are almost an inevitability when you are nailing (without predrilling) near the edge of the wood, and here is where predrilling should be used when you are unsure. Try nailing and screwing in some old wood and get the feel of the problem.

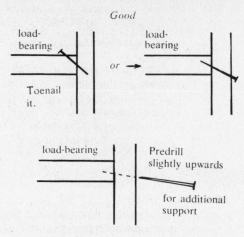

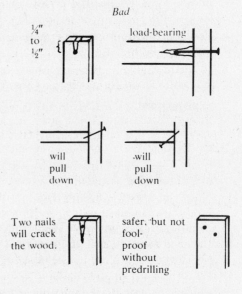

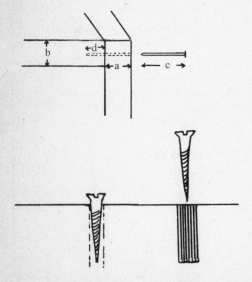

HOW FAR SHOULD A NAIL OR SCREW GO THROUGH THE SECOND PIECE OF WOOD?

Nails and screws must go in at least two-thirds as much again as through the first piece. If a, the thickness of the first piece, is ¾'', then the nail must be 2/3 longer than ¾'', or 1¼'' (c). (2/3 of ¾ = 2/4 pr ½)...(¾(a) + ½(d) = 1¼)...d = 2/3a

HOLE TOO BIG

If the hole is too big, and the screw slips out or doesn't feel tight enough, stuff into the hole some wooden matches, broken off to fit and dabbed with glue, and try again.

1944. Lauren Bacall is catapulted into instant stardom after the release of *To Have and Have Not.* The following year she marries Humphrey Bogart and at twenty-two is in voracious demand by producers eager to market her as the next sex symbol. She manages, however, to sidestep such typecasting and eventually earns a place among actresses known for their professional discipline.

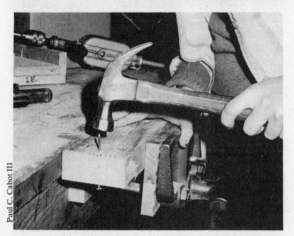

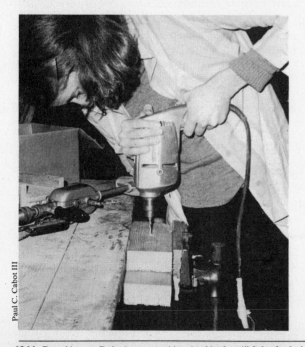

DETACHING TWO PIECES OF WOOD

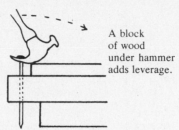

A block of wood under hammer adds leverage.

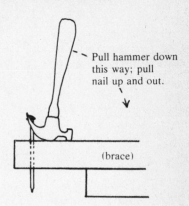

Pull hammer down this way; pull nail up and out.

(brace)

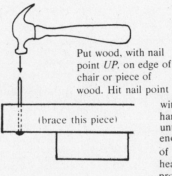

Put wood, with nail point *UP*, on edge of chair or piece of wood. Hit nail point

(brace this piece)

with hammer until enough of nail head protrudes to grab with hammer claws.

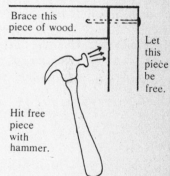

Brace this piece of wood.

Let this piece be free.

Hit free piece with hammer.

DRILLING HOLES

When drilling hole, place an old block of wood under the hole area and drill through to that piece. This will prevent splintering of the underside of the hole. The neatest hole edge will be where the drill enters the wood.

" MY HUSBAND'S THE ORIGINAL DO-IT-YOURSELF MAN.... ASK HIM TO FIX SOMETHING AND HE SAYS, 'DO-IT-YOURSELF' "

1944. Frau Hanna Reisch, termed by the Nazis a "biological phenomenon insensible to air pressure, who attained more than five hundred miles per hour while diving in gliders," is awarded the Iron Cross for secreting herself in an experimental robot flying bomb in order to determine why its wings kept falling off.

Learning Nail Language

Arthur Symons

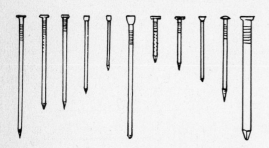

Various nails, left to right: common, box barbed, box smooth, finishing, brad, flooring (casing), roofing, slating, sinker, clinch, and spike.

Size	*Length (inches)*	*Approximate Number per Pound*
2d	1	900
3d	1¼	615
4d	1½	320
5d	1¾	250
6d	2	200
7d	2¼	150
8d	2½	100
9d	2¾	85
10d	3	75

Table of nail sizes

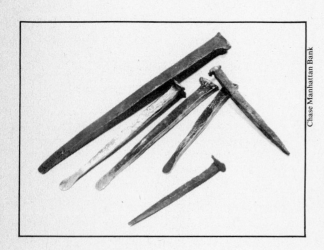

Nails were used as money in Colonial America.

There are more types and sizes of nails than there are ways of flunking algebra. The illustration will show you *some* of them:

Most of the time you will be using common nails, brads, and finishing nails. Finishing nails have small heads, which make them fairly inconspicuous and easy to cover for fine work. A brad, for all practical purposes, is a small finishing nail. Common nails are a bit thicker for their length than finishing nails and brads and are therefore easier to drive without bending.

The language used to describe the size of nails has been due for a change for many years, but nobody makes the move. Those who know what the size language means probably don't want to let anyone else in on the secret. They're like a gang with secret passwords, but the passwords aren't too hard to fathom. The "d" means penny, as in English money.

Nails run in size up to 60d spikes, but 10d is the largest you need for ordinary household do-it-yourselfing.

The trick is to choose the right nail for the job. You don't want one so big that it will go all the way through both boards, or so small that it won't hold. Oversize nails often split the wood. To nail two boards side to side, choose a nail that will go through the top board and about three quarters of the way through the bottom board. To nail two boards together, side grain to end grain, choose a nail that will go through the top board and about 1¼ to 1½ times the thickness of the top board into the edge of the other. If this means using a nail that is so thick you are afraid it will split the wood, you can get around the problem in one of two ways. You can drill a hole where the nail will go, being sure, though, that the hole is less than half the diameter of the nail; or you can cut the point of the nail off, leaving a blunt end. This will cut the wood instead of separating and splitting it.

THE RIGHT WAY TO DRIVE A NAIL

The right way to drive a nail is easy to learn, but very few people know how to do it. By learning one little trick you can drive your nail straight almost every time.

When you start the nail, place the point where it should go, but *incline the head away from you about 10 degrees.*

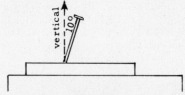

Start hammering with little taps until you are sure the friction of the board is holding the nail firmly. Then begin to whack it with long strokes, being sure that when the hammer head hits the nail head, it does so squarely and surely. The arc of the hammer swing will straighten that 10-degree "lean," and drive the nail straight down.

When you get the nail head close to the wood, be careful. If it is a very small nail, use a nail set to finish the job. A nail set is a tool for driving the head of the nail below the surface. If it is a large nail, a nail set won't help, but be sure you are hitting the nail head and not the wood.

From *The Fix-It Book* by Arthur Symons. Copyright © 1967 Sterling Publishing Co., Inc., New York 10016.

1945. Doctor Lise Meitner, eminent Austrian mathematician, is one of the several scientists responsible for splitting the uranium atom, which will directly lead to the development of the atom bomb.

Paul C. Cabot III

Building Your First Bookcase

Joyce Hartwell

Any woman who can drive a car can build a bookcase—or a table or a bed or a house. A car is a power tool much more complex than the tools used in carpentry. Actually, using power carpentry tools is even easier than driving a car—it's as simple as running a vacuum cleaner or an electric mixer. As soon as you start using them, you'll realize how silly your original fear or hesitation was.

Of course, it is possible to do carpentry with hand tools as well, but it's far more difficult and time consuming. Indeed, women benefit even more than men from using power tools, since the difference between their own muscular strength and the power of the tools is proportionately greater.

Building the simple bookcase described below will show you just how easy carpentry with power tools can be and will give you experience and confidence to undertake more ambitious projects. Today the shelf, tomorrow, the roof!

copyright © 1976 Joyce Hartwell

Tools

The two tools that are used for most projects in the home are the electric drill and the electric saw. For your bookcase a saw will be adequate. You can rent one (check the yellow pages), borrow one from a friend, or buy one for as little as thirty dollars. Wherever you rent or buy the saw, always ask for the operating instructions, and buy some extra wood to practice on. You should have the knack in fifteen minutes. Basically, the weight of the saw is rested flat on the wood. Hold the tool firmly and, using the saw's guide, move the saw as you would an iron along the straight line you will have drawn for cutting. But do follow carefully the safety rules accompanying this article.

Design

Before starting your bookcase sit down and draw up a work sheet covering the six basic steps for building: One, make a sketch and description of the project. Two, make a list of materials needed. Three, make a list of tools and materials needed for measuring and marking. Four, likewise for cutting and shaping. Five, likewise for fastening. Six, likewise for finishing.

Decide upon the space in which you want to put your bookcase and measure it. It is a good idea to make each shelf no longer than 30 inches, because, otherwise, the weight of the books will eventually cause a warp. If you wish to fit a bookcase along a whole wall, make several units each measuring 30 inches long, or if you have one long shelf, place a support under the shelf every 30 inches. Determine the height, width, and depth of your bookcase. Make it deep enough so that your largest books will not protrude over the shelf. This is usually 10 to 12 inches.

Now draw a diagram of the bookcase. Determine the space between the

1947. Florence Blanchfield is the first woman commissioned as a Regular Army officer. The colonel was previously superintendent of army nurses.

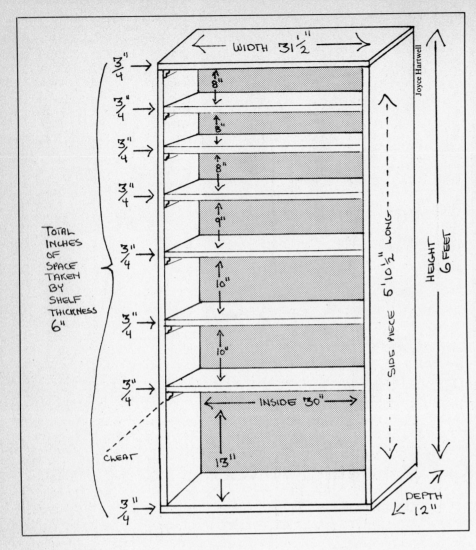

WIDTH 31½"

¾" ¾" ¾" ¾" ¾" ¾" ¾" ¾"

8"
8"
8"
9"
10"
10"
13"

TOTAL INCHES OF SPACE TAKEN BY SHELF THICKNESS 6"

CHEAT

INSIDE 30"

SIDE PIECE 5'10½" LONG

HEIGHT 6 FEET

DEPTH 12"

Joyce Hartwell

---

shelves that you need to accommodate your particular book sizes, and decide how many shelves you will need. The usual procedure is to have your shortest books on the top shelves and the larger ones below. Remember to calculate the thickness of each shelf in figuring the space for each board and the overall height.

Paul C. Cabot III

Wood

If you look at the crosscut of a log, you will see a series of circles starting at the center. Each circle represents a year's growth and is called an annual ring. When the tree is cut, the lines in the wood that we refer to as the grain are these annual rings on a crosscut. A knot marks the spot where a branch grew out of the tree. A board with knots is called common lumber and is the least expensive cut. A board without knots is called select and is the most expensive, because there's a limit to the number of cuts without knots that you can get. There are two types of lumber—the softwood family (all needle-bearing trees, like pines and firs), which is most prevalent in this country and therefore the cheapest; and the hardwood family (all leaf-bearing trees), which is the most expensive and somewhat harder to work with. For your bookcase choose a softwood to

learn on. If you are using a board with knots, check that the knots are solid, not falling out.

Softwoods are milled in specific sizes. When describing the size of a board, the thickness comes first, then the width, and finally the length. Hence a 2 x 4 x 16 is a board that is 2 inches thick, 4 inches wide, and 16 *feet* long. The thickness and width are always in inches, the length in feet. Various thicknesses are available, starting with a thickness of 1 inch, followed by 2- and 3-inch thicknesses—all of which are appropriate for shelving and bookcases. The 1-inch is most commonly used; the 2- and 3-inch thicknesses are used for a particular style, for example, a heavy Early American or Spanish appearance. Widths start at 2 inches and increase in increments of 2 up to the diameter of the largest tree the lumberyard has cut down recently. It becomes more difficult and more expensive to get boards over 18 inches wide. Lengths start at 8 feet. Everytime you want less than 8 feet you will have to pay the lumberyard to cut the board down. So when ordering your lumber, figure on lengths of at least 8 feet. Then cut them down yourself. Lengths go from 8 feet in increments of 2 up to the tallest tree they've cut down recently.

Remember that because lumber shrinks after it is milled, very often a board will be smaller than the size it is said to be. The 1-inch thickness usually measures from 3/4 to 7/8 inches; a 10-inch width will often measure 9 1/2 inches. So if you really want 10 inches, order a 12-inch board. Always ask the lumberyard for the actual specifications of their boards.

Order lumber of the same width as the depth you want for your bookcase. That is, if you have decided that it should be 10 inches deep, then order a 1 x 10 by whatever length you need to cut enough pieces. This way you only have to make one cut—the length of the shelf. The depth of the shelf is determined by the width of the lumber you have ordered.

When ordering materials, refer to the work sheet and diagram, and add together how many feet of lumber you need for your bookcase. The height of your bookcase determines what length the two sides will be: If your bookcase is 6 feet high, you need two 6-feet long pieces for the sides, that is, 12 feet of lumber. The width of your bookcase

---

1947. Carrie Chapman Catt, indefatigable American suffragist, dies. After a career first as a lawyer, then as a high school principal, and, later, as the superintendent of Iowa schools, she began her lecture tours throughout the United States and Europe advocating women's right to vote. From 1900 to 1904—around the time when she came

determines the length of the shelves. Whatever the width of your bookcase (say 31 1/2 inches) multiply that figure by the number of shelves plus top and bottom to determine how many feet of lumber you require. Always order a little over to allow for imperfections (and a learning mistake). A good board may have a few nicks, chips, or a couple of knots that are falling out—so it's a good idea to order an extra two feet. For the sides where you need two 6-foot cuts, instead of ordering a 12-foot board, order a 14-foot board, or two 8-foot boards if 14 feet is too long to get into the house.

Construction

Measuring and Marking. For measuring lengths of less than 8 feet, use an 8-foot folding rule with extension. This tool folds out to 8 feet long, each inch very clearly marked. It is used to measure the length of the sections you are cutting. The second tool you will need, in this case, is a 1-foot square. This is used to make the cutting line where you have marked the length. Very carefully line up one side of the square with the straight edge of your board, hold it in place, and mark your line. This procedure ensures that you always have a perfect 90-degree angle line or a "square cut."

Make each cut immediately after measuring and marking, and before you measure and mark for another cut. Do not do all the measuring and marking at once and then all the cutting at once, because the saw blade displaces about 1/8 inch of wood, and your boards will be too short. Measure, mark, and cut; measure, mark, and cut; until you have all your pieces for the bookcase. Cut to the outside of the line that you have measured, for if you cut right on the line, the board will again be shorter than your measurement. Careful measuring and marking is vital for a successful project.

Cutting and Shaping. Now cut each shelf 30 inches long. Then cut two 5-foot-10 1/2 inch pieces for the sides. (When top and bottom are added, the unit will measure 6 feet.) If your shelves are 30 inches long, the total width of the bookcase, including the two sides, will be 30 inches plus two times 3/4 inch (the combined thicknesses of the two sides), which equals 31 1/2 inches. Therefore, cut the top and bottom to 31

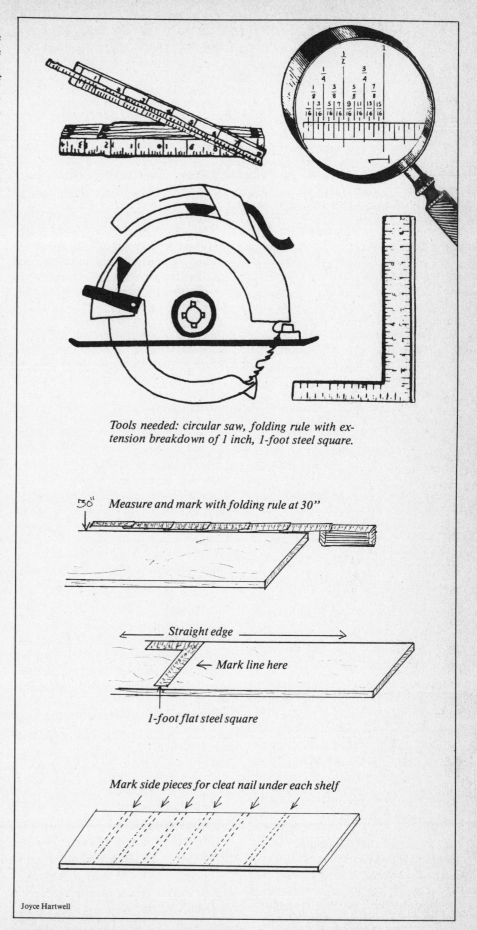

Tools needed: circular saw, folding rule with extension breakdown of 1 inch, 1-foot steel square.

30" Measure and mark with folding rule at 30"

Straight edge ← Mark line here

1-foot flat steel square

Mark side pieces for cleat nail under each shelf

Joyce Hartwell

into the public eye—she held the presidency of the National American Woman Suffrage Association and was elected to that position again in 1915. She was still in office when, five years later, the constitutional amendment granting women the right to vote was finally passed. In addition, from 1902 to 1923, she organized and led the International

Side piece with cleats in place
(before bookcase assembly)

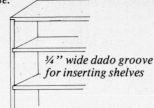

The rabbet joint, with the same groove as the dado, is on the end of the board creating the top of the bookcase.

¾" wide dado groove
for inserting shelves

Example of dado used for bookcase

1/2 inches each so that they will stretch across the total width and can be nailed down to hold the unit together. The shelves inside will measure 30 inches each.

Fastening. On your first project, for the sake of learning, I suggest you use "butt-end construction." One piece of wood is butted against the other and nailed. At the end of each shelf, against the side and under the shelf, nail an extra little strip, called a "cleat," to help support the shelf. You can use a decorative piece of molding for this to add style to your bookcase.

Another common method for fastening is the dado joint. This requires one more power tool, a router, which creates a groove that the shelf fits snugly into. (Whenever you buy or rent a router ask for instructions.) You could also build a bookcase with adjustable shelves, for which you use a metal strip and clips.

To fasten your bookcase together, measure on the sides exactly where you want the bottom of the shelf. Mark a line lightly with pencil, using your square. Under each line, nail your cleat before you attach the pieces. For fastening, use finishing nails, which have a very small head and will not be easily seen in the wood, rather than the large flat-headed nails. Nail the cleats to the side in the appropriate spot for the shelf to rest on. For added strength use a little Elmer's glue as well as finishing nails for attaching cleats and shelves. Nail the top and bottom to the sides, place the shelves on top of the cleats, and then nail into the shelves from the outside of both sides. The length of the finishing nails for this should be the thickness of the sides plus 3/4 inch, that is a 1 1/2-inch to 2-inch nail. For the last bit of hammering of the finishing nails, you will use a special tool, the nail set (see p. 494, Fig. 2).

Finishing. First sand the wood. Softwood is not usually very rough, so medium/fine sandpaper will do a good job. The fastest way to do this is to use an inexpensive electric hand sander. Always sand with the grain. Sanding against the grain will leave scratches, which will show up when you stain. It is more convenient to sand each board before you fasten them all together.

You can either paint your bookcase or stain it with any of the many products available. A natural stain will pick up the natural hue of the wood and deepen the appearance of the grain. Or you can choose a colored wood stain—mahogany, walnut, etc. A pine stain that represents the natural color of aged pine is nice if you are using a pine wood. Then put on a polyurethane finish, which is available in high gloss, satin, or eggshell, giving a highly polished, semisatin, or dull, natural appearance. If you paint the bookcase, the most durable surface is a gloss or satin finish that will not collect fingerprints or dust. An acrylic paint will dry in half an hour to an hour.

The same principles that have been applied here can be used for putting shelves into closets. Remember, one cut in a board makes a shelf. It's just that simple.

Clip

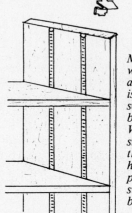

Metal wall strip which accepts adjustable clips is fastened with screws to side of bookcase. Note: When adjustable shelves are used the bookcase must have a back (¼" ply) nailed on to support top, bottom, and sides.

The router, using ¾" straight cutter, is firmly pressed down flat on board and against block of wood used as straight-edge guide then, moved slowly forward.

A postscript: Before you start any projects, be sure to have on hand the following things:

Two sturdy chairs or wooden milk boxes, to use when sawing.
One of those good mushy brooms, not the straw kind, for sweeping up the sawdust.
A medium-sized cardboard carton for saving wood scraps.
A sacred place to keep *your* tools and supplies.
A Sears, Roebuck catalog—it will be your dictionary and encyclopedia for tools and materials.
. . . And get a tetanus shot.

Reprinted by permission of William Morrow & Co., Inc., from *I Took a Hammer in My Hand* by Florence Adams. Copyright © 1973 Florence Adams.

Women Suffrage Alliance and, after the vote was won, turned her considerable energies to the search for world peace. Mrs. Catt's marriage to her second husband in 1890 was defined in a legal contract giving her two months each spring and fall for suffrage work.

Safety Rules for Power Tools

1. **WEAR APPROPRIATE CLOTHES.** Avoid loose clothing, such as big cuffs, and hanging jewelry that could possibly get caught in moving parts. Arrange hair so that it will not fall in your eyes and interfere with eyesight. **Very important—** long hair should be tied back and braids or ponytails must be positioned so that they don't fall forward when you lean over.

2. **PLAN WORK TIME** so that adult visitors and children can be kept out of the work area. You can arrange a work area especially for young children with appropriate tools and projects. (Example: handsaws, hammer and nails, files, etc.)

3. **TOOLS.** Read all literature and booklets that come with the tool. Make note of its applications and limitations, particularly the precautions necessary to avoid shock. (Example: the need to **ground** the tool if it is not an insulated model.) If you have any questions about what you read, ask at the source of purchase, or contact the manufacturer.

4. **CHOOSE THE RIGHT TOOL FOR THE JOB AT HAND.** Always ask questions when purchasing a tool. Don't force a light-duty tool to do a heavy-duty job. That will harm the motor. Always guide the tool firmly, rather than force it. **Let the tool do the job it was designed for.**

5. **MAKE SURE BLADES, BITS, AND ACCESSORIES ARE SHARP.** Dull cutting edges cause accidents and tool abuse by encouraging one to force the tool to do the job.

6. **WHEN CHANGING BLADES, BITS, OR CUTTERS, ALWAYS DISCONNECT TOOL.** Form a habit of pulling the plug out of the wall socket before making any adjustment on the tool. Make sure all adjusting keys or wrenches are removed from the tool before plugging in.

7. **BEFORE PLUGGING IN, GROUND ALL TOOLS,** unless they are especially made with double insulation. Such tools will be clearly marked that they are shockproof and will have a two-pronged plug. Make sure you understand what grounding a tool means. Ask questions when you purchase the tool. A tool with a three-pronged plug has to be grounded, for it is not shockproof. This means it should be plugged into a three-hole receptacle. If you only have two-hole receptacles, an adapter can be used.
   CAUTION: The adapter wire must be attached to the receptacle **after checking to make sure the receptacle itself is grounded.** (In many old buildings they are not. Check with the superintendent or call in an electrician, or make sure the tool you purchase is double-insulated an shockproof and does not have to be grounded.)

8. **DON'T LOSE ANY ADJUSTING KEY OR WRENCH.** Keep track of where you put it, for you will use it often. Try to attach it to the end of the tool cord, near the plug, with tape or string. This will remind you to pull the plug when changing accessories.

9. **AVOID ACCIDENTAL STARTING.** Make sure the tool switch is in the off position before plugging tool into socket. **Do not carry tool with finger on the switch.**

10. **KEEP WORK AREA CLEAR OF OBSTACLES AND CLUTTER.** An organized, clean work area encourages safety, a cluttered area invites accidents.

11. **KEEP WORK AREA WELL LIGHTED** for accurate, comfortable, and safe working conditions. Eye strain causes fatigue and invites accidents.

12. **AVOID DAMP OR WET LOCATIONS.** Do not use a power tool or any other electrical appliance **while standing on a wet floor or damp earth.** While using your power tool or other home appliance, **avoid touching pipes or fixtures attached to pipes,** such as gas stoves, sinks, bathtubs, or radiators, for these are all conductors of electrical current and could lead to a potentially hazardous situation.

13. **SECURE THE OBJECT YOU ARE WORKING ON WITH CLAMPS OR VISE WHEN POSSIBLE TO DO SO.** It is safer and easier to work when both hands are free to operate tool and help balance yourself.

14. **WEAR SAFETY GLASSES OR GOGGLES WHEN NECESSARY.** If the use of a tool causes flying particles or material, protect your eyes. If the project at hand is dusty, use a dust mask.

15. **MAKE SURE YOU DON'T HAVE TO OVERREACH TO DO A JOB.** Keep your footing and maintain a good balance.

16. **PROTECT THE TOOL CORD.** Make sure it is out of the way of the use of the tool. Do not allow it to be stepped on or abused with sharp or rough objects. Keep it away from chemicals or heat. Do not carry tool by the cord, or yank it to disconnect from receptacle.

17. **KEEP BLADE GUARDS IN PLACE.** Make sure tool is kept clean and free of excess sawdust so that blade guards move freely in working order.

18. **STORE TOOLS IN PROPER PLACE WHEN NOT IN USE.** Keep in dry, locked storage cabinet to which children do not have access.

**FOLLOW THESE RULES UNTIL THEY BECOME HABIT AND A PART OF YOU:
THEN YOU WILL BE ABLE TO CONCENTRATE ON CREATIVITY AND ENJOYMENT.**

1947. The French Institute of Public Opinion conducts a poll that shows that 71 percent of the French people believe "woman's place is in the home."

The Hang Up Hang-up

Florence Adams

So you want to hang a picture. Easy, right? Just a hammer and nail, and, besides, someone recently told you to put some Scotch tape (two pieces, crossing in an X) over the spot where you want to nail so that the plaster doesn't crack. And it works. The nail sticks, and no crumbled plaster . . . if you're lucky. But how many times has the nail gone in— and then out, sliding back and forth and ending up dangling down at a 45-degree angle? Or the nail goes exactly nowhere; you're still holding it, all bent and twisted, and the plaster is in powder at your feet? Or you *know* that a couple of nails certainly won't hold a 5-foot mirror, but what will? And how in the world do you hang flowerpots from the ceiling?

For too many years either I didn't ask the right questions or I didn't understand the answers, mainly because I couldn't visualize the inside of a wall. Then, a house bought, walls ripped out,

and many questions later, I learned about walls and all the fantastic hardware that has been invented for hanging up anything. (You could hang a bookcase.) It's really not difficult. But first, you have to understand what kind of wall you're dealing with, and what its innards are like. Every mystery solved is a plus point, so here's the scoop both on the walls and on the proper hardware for hanging things.

INTERIOR WALLS

(Separating rooms
from each other, not
from the great out-of-doors)

The interior wall is most frequently a "sandwich." From ceiling to floor, "studs" are nailed in. Studs are thick, strong beams or posts, 2-inches-by-4-inches or 4-inches-by-4-inches thick, and they are (or should be) 16 inches apart, "center to center" (measuring from the center of one stud to the center of the

next). At least, it can be expected that they are 16 inches apart in construction which has been done in the past 50 years. (For the importance of knowing where the studs are, keep reading.) There are two major types of interior walls: plaster and Sheetrock.

PLASTER WALLS: If the walls are plastered, something called lath is attached to the studs next. Lath comes in several varieties, and only poking big holes through your walls will tell you which kind you have.

Wood Lath is made up of thin, rough, wood strips nailed to the studs horizontally and fairly close together. The roughness of the wood is necessary as a surface for the plaster to adhere to. Wood lath is usually in older houses.

Wire Lath is a sheet of flat, closely meshed wire. This comes in 26-inch-by-96-inch sheets, and it is nailed onto the studs horizontally.

Rock Lath, also called board lath, is made of a mined powder called gypsum which is pressed ⟶

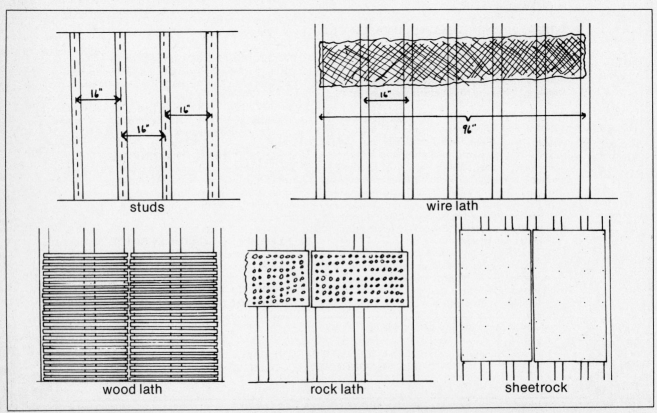

studs

wire lath

wood lath

rock lath

sheetrock

1948. Vietta M. Bates is the first woman member of the Regular Army, Women's Army Corps. She is sworn into service by General Omar Bradley during a televised ceremony.

into panels covered with strong paper, and the panels have holes. It comes in sizes from 16 inches by 32 inches to 24 inches by 64 inches. The popularity of gypsum is due to its fire-retarding quality.

Plaster comes after the lath. What is plaster? It is a powder (gypsum) which, when mixed with water and sand, will get hard, adhere to certain surfaces, and become, itself, a smooth surface. (Hit it with a hammer and it turns back to powder; thus, our hanging problems.)

Lath has to have spaces and holes so that the plaster can squish through and grab and catch itself in the back to hold better. Usually three progressively finer coats of plaster are applied; the first is the "scratch" coat, then the "brown" coat, and, finally, the "finish" coat.

Last in the sandwich (a real Dagwood at this point) is the paint or paneling—the cover for those rough walls.

SHEETROCK (wallboard, plasterboard . . . all the same): An alternate to the lath method, and popular today, is the use of Sheetrock. It comes in 4-foot-by-8-foot panels and is nailed directly to the studs. It is also made of pressed gypsum powder covered with paper, like rock lath, but without holes. The fact to remember about Sheetrock and rock lath is that they are pressed *powder*, which means they are potentially powder again. Perforated tape and a thin layer of plaster are applied at the seams of the boards to give the wall a smooth, continuous surface, but if you don't have too many layers of paint over it and you look very carefully along the wall, you can find the seams, thus the studs (see below).

SANDWICH WALL HARDWARE: Nails, hammered in at a slightly down angle (don't forget the Scotch-tape X), will hold lightweight stuff—pictures, small clocks, even stereo sound boxes—if the plaster or wallboard doesn't crumble (remember the dangling nails?). But, for hanging the heavy things, special hardware has been invented which utilizes the space behind the walls. I'll illustrate the methods in order of my preference; the strongest first.

Screw into the Studs: You can try to avoid the problem of the space behind walls by using the studs. If your walls aren't too thick, you can find the studs

by tapping on walls, listening for hollow vs. solid. Or use a long, strong nail to investigate. There is usually a stud at the corner, so measure off from there (remember, they are often 16 inches apart), and then tap, or poke around with a nail. Screwing directly into the studs in the walls is perhaps the strongest hold. However, this isn't always necessary, or esthetically desirable.

Toggle Bolt: This looks like a bolt with wings. The wings, or "butterfly," can be held closed against the bolt, or allowed to spring open. There is a tiny spring within the wings. The principle of the way it operates may be obvious from the diagram. Drill a hole, or knock one out with a big nail through everything, to get to the space behind the wall. The hole must be big enough for the widest part of the toggle (A) to fit through. As you can see from the diagram, if you unscrew the bolt from the wings after it's in the wall, the wings will drop off and fall down inside the wall. It is therefore necessary to detach the pieces, put the bolt through whatever you are attaching to the wall, and then screw the wings back on. The space that the thing you're hanging will occupy on the bolt is indicated in the diagram by (B). The toggle (with its wings closed) must then be able to pass through the hole until the wings spring open behind the wall; thus, the distance (X) must be equal to the amount of space for (B), plus the thickness of the wall (C), plus a bit more for good luck. In order to determine how thick the wall is, bend back the end of a piece of wire and push it through the hole, then pull back until it grabs the inside edge of the wall. If you mis-measure and the wings get stuck in the hole, unscrew the bolt some more and hammer it in until the wings

spring open. There will be leeway once the wings open: hold whatever you have attached outside away from the wall so that the wings grab the inside of the wall, and start screwing the bolt in. This will eventually cause the bolt to bring the wings tightly against the wall. One last word of caution: measure the space behind the wall with a long piece of wire so that you don't use a very long bolt which may hit the other wall. Toggle bolts will hold heavy items like standard and bracket bookshelves, and mirrors.

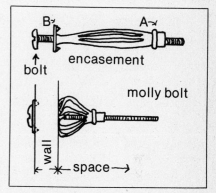

Molly Bolt: This functions similarly to the toggle. Drill a hole in the wall, only big enough for the widest part of the encasement (A) in the diagram, to fit snugly. Ask in the hardware store for a drill bit that is the right size for your molly. Or you can estimate size by rolling the encasement and then the bit between your fingers, then choosing a slightly smaller bit. The washerlike outer portion of the encasement (B) has prongs which will grab the outer wall. After the hole is made, tap the molly in. Then use a screwdriver to tighten the bolt. As the bolt is screwed in, the encasement scrunches up against the back of the wall, thus providing the support. The difference between the molly and the toggle is that once the encasement of the

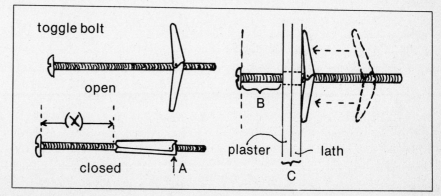

1949. Simone de Beauvoir writes *The Second Sex,* a comprehensive and learned review of woman's place in Western culture. The book will be translated into nineteen languages, spark heated and enduring controversies around the world, and become the bible of the women's movement in the United States.

molly is tight and functional, you may remove the bolt and put it back. Mollys are fine for lamps or medicine chests, but I wouldn't use them for a bookcase.

Expansion Plug: This device consists of a plastic plug and a screw. A hole is made in the wall, just big enough to tap in the plug (without screw). A hole too big is useless; a hole too small will ruin the plug. (Sometimes a package

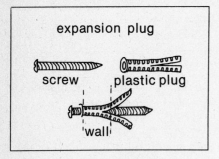

of plugs and screws includes the proper-size drill bit. Packaged hardware is more expensive than loose hardware, but, in this case, the package may be worth it.) Next, screw the screw into the plug. Because the plug is really too small for the screw, it expands as the screw comes in. It is not a good idea to ask this type of fastener to bear great weight. It will hold lamps, framed pictures, big clocks.

EXTERIOR WALLS

(The walls on the outside
outlines of the house)

These are usually the "horror walls"—brick, cement, and concrete. Here's how to proceed.

BRICK WALLS: No hollow sound in the walls when you knock, only sore knuckles. When holding strength is required, it is necessary to use Lead Plugs in the brick, not in the mortar holding bricks together. The big problem is that you need to see the bricks to know where you're at. (I think that's why I exposed my walls.) Otherwise, you'll just have to experiment. Lead plugs are the only kind of plugs that work, when they work; 3 out of 5 times on the average. (Don't tell me what I'm doing wrong, mister, I've heard it from all your brothers, and it's still 3 out of 5!) Why lead? Think of brick as sand (potentially). Therefore, the fric-

tion of something against it, pulling weight, can loosen the sand at the surface. Lead is a soft metal; it has squishability and therefore grips.

Let's look at the procedure. Drill a hole in the brick, using a carbide drill bit (recognizable by the shape of the tip). Use the proper-size bit, so that the plug may be tapped lightly into the hole. (Again, you may find the plugs and drill bit packaged together.) The depth of the hole should not be longer than the length of the plug. (Lay the bit beside the plug for measurement, and put a piece of tape on the bit as a marker to indicate when you've drilled far enough.) One more tip: before you put the plug in, vacuum the hole. This will remove all the loose sand within the hole . . . loose sand, loose plug. Okay, tap the plug in place. Now, screw in the plug. As the screw goes into the too-small plug, it expands. But this plug is solid, not sliced like the plastic one,

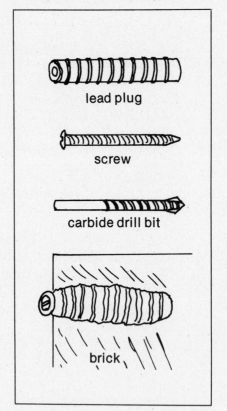

and as it expands, it squishes into all the nooks and crannies of the brick hole's uneven surface. This is why it holds.

I have recently learned of another product, called Lead Wool (looks like yarn, but is thin strands of lead), bought by the pound. Jam it into a predrilled

hole long enough for the screw, then put in the screw. (The woman who told me about it says this method was used to hang very heavy flowerpots from her concrete ceilings.)

The other way to attack brick walls is with Masonry Nails. There are two types: cut nails and ridged masonry nails. My preference is cut nails, which have a rough surface. The ridged nails feel too

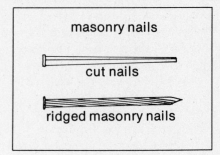

smooth to give me confidence. Cut nails look like old-fashioned, hand-hammered nails. Both of these types should be used in the mortar. (If you can't see the bricks, you'll hear a clanking sound if you're hammering into brick; besides, you won't get anywhere.) Remember, when choosing the type of hardware to use, nails are nails—in easy, out easy.

CONCRETE AND CEMENT WALLS (hah!): Well, there are those gummed, glue-on fasteners that hold some amount of weight. Otherwise, you have two choices if you can't or don't want to move, and if those of you who are tenants are allowed to tamper with walls in the first place. First, you can try drilling a hole with a carbide drill bit and use lead plugs or lead wool, as explained in the brick section. Second, there is a gadget called a stud gun, which works on the same principle as those heavy-duty staple machines: it shoots a plug into the concrete, cement, whatever. (If one of these machines is prohibitive in price, you could probably rent one.)

CEILINGS

Essentially the same as walls. If there's plaster, there's lath or there's plasterboard. And there are beams (studs). To find them, look for the light fixture; it's surely secured to a beam.

1952. The United Nations estimates that over the past ten years there has been a 93 percent increase in the number of American women employed as proprietors, directors, and managers in the work force.

Painting: The Inside and Outside Story

For an attractive, long-lasting paint job, you need to—

1. Use good-quality paint,
2. Properly prepare the surface for painting, and
3. Apply the paint correctly.

Preparation of the surface—cleaning and patching—may take the most time in painting, but it is the most important part of the job. Even the best paint will not adhere well to an excessively dirty or greasy surface or hide large cracks or other mars.

Many different kinds and formulations of paints and other finishes are available for interior use. And new ones frequently appear on the market.

Use the chart (box, right) as a general guide in making your selection. For a more specific selection consult your paint dealer. Reputable paint dealers keep abreast of the newest developments in the paint industry and stock the newest formulations.

"Dripless" paint is an example of a fairly recent development. It has a jelled consistency in the can, but it loses that form when picked up on a brush or roller and spreads evenly and smoothly. It is particularly convenient when painting a ceiling.

The usual interior paint job consists of painting wallboard or plaster walls and ceilings, woodwork, and wood windows and doors. For these surfaces you need to choose first between solvent-thinned paint (commonly called oil-based paint) and water-thinned paint (commonly called latex paint, but not necessarily latex), and then between a gloss, semigloss, or flat finish.

[Enamels, which are made with a varnish, or resin, base instead of the usual linseed-oil vehicle, are included under the broad oil-paint grouping.]

Oil-based paints are very durable, are highly resistant to staining and damage, can withstand frequent scrubbings, and give good one-coat coverage. Many latex paints are advertised as having similar properties.

The main advantages of latex paint are easier application, faster drying, and simpler tool cleanup. The brushes, rollers, and other equipment can be easily cleaned with water.

Both oil-based paint and latex paint are now available in gloss, semigloss, and flat finishes.

Guide for Selecting Paints

	Aluminum paint	Casein	Cement base paint	Emulsion paint (including latex)	Enamel	Flat paint	Floor paint or enamel	Floor varnish	Interior varnish	Metal primer	Rubber base paint (not latex)	Sealer or undercoater	Semigloss paint	Shellac	Stain	Wax (emulsion)	Wax (liquid or paste)	Wood sealer
Floors:																		
Asphalt tile																X•		
Concrete																X•	X•	
Linoleum							X							X		X	X	X
Vinyl and rubber							X	X								X	X	
Wood							X•	X•										X
Masonry:																		
Old	X	X	X	X	X•	X•					X	X	X•					
New			X	X	X•	X•					X	X	X•					
Metal:																		
Heating ducts	X				X•	X•				X	X		X•					
Radiators	X				X•	X•				X	X		X•					
Stairs:																		
Treads							X	X						X	X			
Risers					X•	X•			X			X	X•	X	X			
Walls and ceilings:																		
Kitchen and bathroom				X	X•						X	X	X•					
Plaster		X		X		X•					X	X	X•					
Wallboard		X		X		X•					X	X	X•					
Wood paneling				X•		X•			X									
Wood trim				X•	X•	X•			X		X	X	X•	X	X		X	X
Windows:																		
Aluminum	X				X•	X•				X	X		X•					
Steel	X				X•	X•				X	X		X•					
Wood sill					X•				X					X				

Black dot (X•) indicates that a primer or sealer may be necessary before the finishing coat (unless the surface has been previously finished).

Adapted from *Interior Painting*, 1971, Department of Agriculture.

1953. Frances Willis is the first woman career diplomat to receive an ambassadorship. She takes up her new post in Switzerland immediately.

SURFACE PREPARATION

In general, walls, ceilings, woodwork, and other surfaces to be painted should be clean, dry, and smooth. But read the label on the paint can before you start painting; it may contain additional or special instructions for preparing the surface.

Plaster and Wallboard

New Surfaces

New plaster walls should not be painted with oil-based paint until they have thoroughly cured—usually after about 2 months. And then a primer coat should be applied first.

If necessary to paint uncured plaster, apply *one coat only* of a latex paint or primer. Latex, or water-base, paint will not be affected by the alkali in new plaster and will allow water to escape while the plaster dries. Subsequent coats of paint—either oil based or latex—can be added when the plaster is dry.

Unpainted plaster readily picks up and absorbs dirt and is difficult to clean. The one coat of latex paint or primer will protect it.

For new drywall, a latex primer or paint is recommended for the first coat. Solvent-thinned paints tend to cause a rough surface. After the first coat of latex paint, subsequent coats can be of either type.

Clean or dust new surfaces before you apply the first coat of primer or paint.

Old Surfaces

The first step is to inspect the surface for cracks and mars. Fill small hairline cracks with spackling compound and larger cracks with special patching plaster. Follow the directions on the container label when using the patching material. When the patch is completely dry, sand it smooth and flush with the surrounding surface.

Nailheads tend to "pop out" in wallboard walls and ceilings. Countersink the projecting heads slightly and fill the hole with spackling compound. Sand the patch smooth when it is dry. It is desirable to prime newly spackled spots, particularly if you are applying only one coat.

Next, clean the surface of dirt and grease. A dry rag or mop will remove dust and some dirt. You may have to wash the surface with a household cleanser to remove stubborn dirt or grease.

Kitchen walls and ceilings are usually covered with a film of grease from cooking (which may extend to the walls and ceilings just outside the entrances to the kitchen), and bathroom walls and ceilings may have steamed-on dirt. The grease or dirt must be removed—the new paint will not adhere to it. To remove the grease or dirt, wash the surface with a strong household cleanser, turpentine, or mineral spirits.

The finish on kitchen and bathroom walls and ceiling is usually a gloss or semigloss. It must be "cut" so that the new paint can get a firm hold. Washing the surface with the household cleanser or turpentine will dull the gloss, but, for best results, rub the surface with fine sandpaper or steel wool. After using sandpaper or steel wool, wipe the surface to remove the dust.

Woodwork

Woodwork (windows, doors, and baseboards) usually has a glossy finish. First, wash the surface to remove dirt and grease, and then sand it lightly to "cut" the finish so that the new paint can get a good hold. After sanding, wipe the surface to remove the dust.

You can buy liquid preparations that will soften hard, glossy finishes to provide good adhesion for the new paint.

If there are any bare spots in the wood, touch up with an undercoater or with pigmented shellac before you paint.

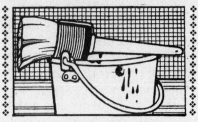

Safety Tips

For a safer paint job—

● Never paint in a completely closed room, and use caution when painting in a room where there is an open flame or fire. Some paints give off fumes that are flammable or dangerous to breathe or both.

Avoid prolonged exposure to paint fumes for a day or two after painting. Such fumes can be especially harmful to canaries or other pet birds.

● Use a sturdy stepladder or other support when painting high places. Be sure that the ladder is positioned firmly, with the legs fully opened and locked in position.

● Face the ladder when climbing up or down it, holding on with at least one hand. Lean toward the ladder when painting.

● Do not overreach when painting. Move the ladder frequently rather than risk a fall. And, to avoid spilling the paint, take the few seconds required to remove the paint can from the ladder before you move it.

● When you finish painting, dispose of the used rags by putting them in a covered metal can. If left lying around, the oily rags could catch fire by spontaneous combustion.

● Store paint in a safe, but well-ventilated, place where children and pets cannot get to it. A locked cabinet is ideal if well ventilated. Unless needed for retouching, small quantities of paint may not be worth saving.

1953. Dr. Alfred Kinsey releases his *Sexual Behavior in the Human Female,* inspiring an uproar among social commentators, especially the clergy, and the general public. Kinsey's data seem to indicate that almost all American women violate one commonly accepted sexual taboo or another. For instance, half of those subjects interviewed had

Painting Tips

For an easier and better paint job—

● Do the painting when the room temperature is comfortable for work—between 60° and 70°F. And provide good cross ventilation both to shorten the drying time and to remove fumes and odors.

Note: Check the label on the paint can for any special application and drying instructions.

● Preferably, remove all furnishings from the room. Otherwise, cover the furniture, fixtures, and floor with drop cloths or newspapers. No matter how careful you may be, you will spill, drip, or splatter some paint.

● Remove all light-switch and wall-plug plates. Paint the plates before you replace them after painting the room.

● Dip your brush into the paint no more than one-third the length of the bristles. This will minimize splattering and dripping.

● When using latex paint, wash your brush or roller occasionally with water. A buildup of the quick-drying paint in the nap of the roller or at the base of the bristles of the brush could cause excessive dripping.

● Wipe up spilled, splattered, or dripped paint as you go along. Paint is easier to clean up when wet.

● Do not let the paint dry out in the can or in brushes or rollers between jobs or during long interruptions in a job. After each job, replace the can lid, making sure that it is on tightly, and clean brushes or rollers. During long interruptions in a job, also replace the can lid, and either clean brushes or rollers or suspend them in water.

If You Have the Painting Done

You may prefer to have all or part of your painting done by a professional painter. Painting contractors usually offer three grades of paint jobs—*premium*, *standard*, and *minimum*. The difference is in the quality and cost of the work.

When you hire a contractor, it is a good idea to get a signed agreement specifying—

● The specific price for the job.

● Exactly what areas or surfaces are to be painted.

● The types, brands, and quality of paints to be used and the number of coats, including primer coats, to be applied.

● The measures to be taken to protect the floors, furnishings, and other parts of the house.

● A complete cleanup guarantee.

● A completion date (allowing for possible delays—because of bad weather for example).

Check the contractor's work with friends or neighbors who may have hired him in the past. Be sure that he is fully insured (Workmen's Compensation and Employer's Liability Insurance, Public Liability, and Property Damage Insurance). Otherwise, you could be held liable for accidents that occurred on your property.

•Check the Weather•

You can easily ruin your paint job if you forget to consider the weather. Excessive humidity, or extremely cold weather can cause you trouble. Good ventilation, regardless of the weather, is essential.

Specifically:

● unless you are using latex paint, you should not paint on damp days. Moisture on the painting surface may prevent a good bond.

● if humidity is high, check the surface before painting. If you can feel a film of moisture on the surface, it would be better to wait for a better day. If you are painting inside and the area is air-conditioned, however, neither rain nor humidity will affect the job.

● exterior painting is not recommended if the temperature is below 50 degrees or above 95 degrees Fahrenheit, since you may not be able to get a good bond. This is especially critical if you are using latex paint.

● if conditions are borderline, good ventilation will help paint to dry. Allow more drying time in damp or humid weather. The label on the can will tell you the normal drying time, but test each coat by touch before you add another. When paint is thoroughly dry, it is firm to the touch and is not sticky.

Adapted from *Paint and Painting*, 1971, General Services Administration.

•Color Do's and Dont's•

DO - Use light colors in a small room to make it seem larger.

DO - Aim for a continuing color flow through your home — from room to room — using harmonious colors in adjoining areas.

DO - Paint the ceiling of a room in a deeper color than walls, if you want it to appear lower; paint it in a ligher shade for the opposite effect.

DO - Study color swatches in both daylight and nightlight. Colors often change under artificial lighting.

DON'T - Paint woodwork and trim of a small room in a color which is different from the background color, or the room will appear cluttered and smaller.

DON'T - Paint radiators, pipes and similar projections in a color which contrasts with walls or they will be emphasized.

DON'T - Choose neutral or negative colors just because they are safe, or the result will be dull and uninteresting.

DON'T - Use glossy paints on walls or ceilings of living areas since the shiny surface creates glare.

engaged in premarital intercourse; 26 percent of those married admitted having practiced adultery; 62 percent, masturbation; and 20 percent, some homosexual activity. The figures are roundly attacked by some as patently false, praised by others as a refreshing glimpse of the reality normally obscured by sexual and social hypocrisy.

Simple Plumbing Repairs

You can save money and avoid delays by making minor plumbing repairs yourself.

Jobs that a farmer or home-owner can do with a few basic tools include:

- Repairing water faucets and valves.
- Repairing leaks in pipes and tanks.
- Thawing frozen pipes.
- Repairing water closets.
- Cleaning clogged drains.

Extensive plumbing repairs or alterations in the plumbing system usually require authorization from local authorities and possibly inspection of the completed work. Therefore such work should be done by a qualified or licensed plumber.

REPAIRING WATER FAUCETS AND VALVES

Faucets and globe valves, the type of shutoff valves commonly used in home water systems, are very similar in construction (fig. 1) and repair instructions given below apply to both. Your faucets or valves may differ somewhat in general design from the one shown in figure 1, because both faucets and valves come in a wide variety of styles.

Mixing faucets, which are found on sinks, laundry trays, and bathtubs, are actually two separate units with a common spout. Each unit is independently repaired.

Dripping faucets are the most common plumbing problem. Nor-mally a new washer is all that is required. If water leaks around the stem, either the packing is loose or needs replacing. To repair the faucet, first shut off the water at the shutoff valve nearest the particular faucet.

Disassemble the faucet by removing the handle, packing nut, packing, and stem in that order. You may have to set the handle back on the stem and use it to un-screw and remove the stem.

Remove the screw and worn washer from the stem. Clean the washer cup and install a new washer of the proper size and type.

Reassemble the faucet. Handles of mixing faucets should be in matched positions.

If a washer requires frequent replacement, it may be the wrong type or the seat may be rough and scoring the washer. Flat washers are used on seats having a crown or round ridge for the washer seat. Tapered or rounded washers are used with tapered seats. These seats may be replaced if worn or damaged.

Replaceable seats have either a square or hex shaped water passage for the seat removal tool. Seat dressing tools are available for non-replaceable seats.

Occasionally a faucet will be noisy when water is flowing. This may be due to a loose washer or worn threads on the stem and receiver, permitting the stem to vibrate or chatter. Pressing down on the handle will stop stem vibration but will not affect a loose washer.

Replacement stems are available; however, if the receiving threads are worn excessively a new stem would not eliminate the problem completely. In some faucets it is possible to replace the stem receiver, the stem, and the

Adapted from *Simple Plumbing Repairs*, 1972, Department of Agriculture.

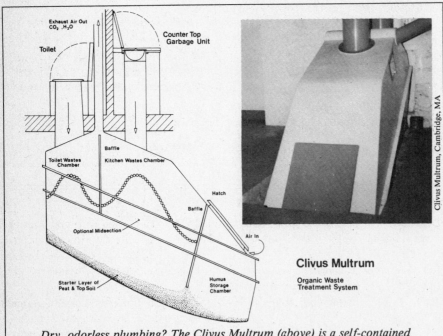

Clivus Multrum

Organic Waste Treatment System

Dry, odorless plumbing? The Clivus Multrum (above) is a self-contained system for the treatment of organic wastes. Clivus Multrum means literally "inclining compost room" and it is just that: a compost heap inside a container sitting at an angle, so that organic wastes slide in glacier-like fashion down the sloping bottom at a rate slow enough to ensure that they will be thoroughly decomposed by the time they reach the storage chamber. The end product is safe for use in gardens because of the long retention time in the container (2 to 4 years) during which the disease-producing organisms are destroyed by the normal soil bacteria. The Multrum requires virtually no maintenance, other than the removal of a few pails of humus a year.

1953. Oveta Culp Hobby becomes the first Secretary of Health, Education, Welfare—the most massive of federal bureaucracies—and the tenth member of the president's cabinet.

seat, thus restoring all normal wearing parts within the faucet.

Several new faucet designs aimed at easier operation, eliminating drip, and promoting long service life, are on the market. Instructions for repair may be obtained from dealers.

If a shower head drips, the supply valve has not been fully closed, or the valve needs repair.

After extended use and several repairs, some valves will no longer give tight shutoff and must be replaced. When this becomes necessary, it may be advisable to upgrade the quality with equipment having better flow characteristics and longer-life design and materials. In some cases, ball valves will deliver more water than globe valves. Some globe valves deliver more flow than others for identical pipe sizes. Y-pattern globe valves, in straight runs of pipe, have better flow characteristics than straight stop valves. Figure 2 shows the features of different types of valves.

WATER HAMMER

Water hammer sometimes occurs when a faucet is suddenly closed. When the flow of water is suddenly stopped, its kinetic energy is expended against the walls of the piping. This causes the piping to vibrate, and leaks or other damage may result.

Water hammer may be prevented or its severity reduced by installing an air chamber just ahead of the faucet. The air chamber may be a piece of air-filled pipe or tubing, about 2 feet long, extending vertically from the pipe. It must be airtight. Commercial devices designed to prevent water hammer are also available.

An air chamber requires occasional replenishing of the air to prevent it from becoming water-logged—that is, full of water instead of air.

A properly operating hydro-pneumatic tank, such as the type used in individual water systems, serves as an air chamber, preventing or reducing water hammer.

FROZEN WATER PIPES

In cold weather, water may freeze in underground pipes laid above the frostline or in pipes in unheated buildings, in open crawl spaces under buildings, or in outside walls.

When water freezes it expands. Unless a pipe can also expand, it may rupture when the water freezes. Iron pipe and steel pipe do not expand appreciably. Copper pipe will stretch some, but does not resume its original dimensions when thawed out; repeated freezings will cause it to fail eventually. Flexible plastic tubing can stand repeated freezes, but it is good practice to prevent it from freezing.

Preventing Freezing

Pipes may be insulated to prevent freezing, but this is not a completely dependable method. Insulation does not stop the loss of heat from the pipe—merely slows it down—and the water may freeze if it stands in the pipe long enough at below-freezing temperature. Also, if the insulation becomes wet, it may lose its effectiveness.

Electric heating cable can be used to prevent pipes from freezing. The cable should be wrapped around the pipe and covered with insulation.

Thawing

Use of electric heating cable is a good method of thawing frozen pipe, because the entire heated length of the pipe is thawed at one time.

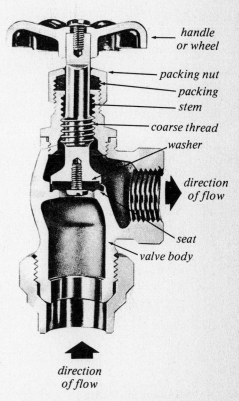

handle or wheel
packing nut
packing
stem
coarse thread
washer
direction of flow
seat
valve body

direction of flow

Figure 1. Globe type angle valve. Faucets are similar in construction.

Note drain plug; this type is often called a stop-and-waste valve

Thawing pipe with a blowtorch can be dangerous. The water may get hot enough at the point where the torch is applied to generate sufficient steam under pressure to rupture the pipe. Steam from the break could severely scald you.

Thawing pipe with hot water is safer than thawing with a blowtorch. One method is to cover the pipe with rags and then pour the hot water over the rags.

When thawing pipe with a blowtorch, hot water, or similar methods, open a faucet and start thawing at that point. The open faucet will permit steam to escape, thus reducing the chance of the buildup of dangerous pressure. Do not allow the steam to condense and refreeze before it reaches the faucet.

REPAIRING WATER CLOSETS

Water closets (commonly called toilets) vary in general design and in the design of the flushing mechanism. But they are enough alike that general repair instructions can suffice for all designs.

Flushing Mechanism

Figure 2 shows a common type of flushing mechanism. Parts that usually require repair are the flush valve, the intake (float) valve, and the float ball.

In areas of corrosive water, the usual copper flushing mechanism may deteriorate in a comparatively short time. In such cases, it may be advisable to replace the corroded parts with plastic parts. You can even buy plastic float balls.

Flush Valve

The rubber ball of the flush valve may get soft or out of shape and fail to seat properly. This causes the valve to leak. Unscrew the ball from the lift wire and install a new one.

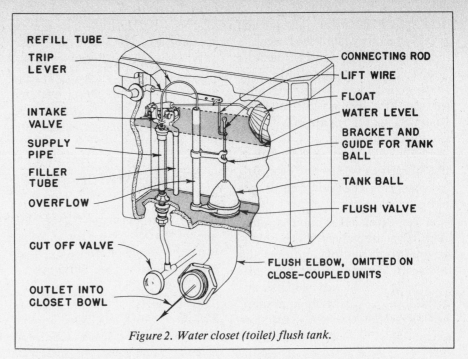

Figure 2. Water closet (toilet) flush tank.

REFILL TUBE
TRIP LEVER
INTAKE VALVE
SUPPLY PIPE
FILLER TUBE
OVERFLOW
CUT OFF VALVE
OUTLET INTO CLOSET BOWL

CONNECTING ROD
LIFT WIRE
FLOAT
WATER LEVEL
BRACKET AND GUIDE FOR TANK BALL
TANK BALL
FLUSH VALVE
FLUSH ELBOW, OMITTED ON CLOSE-COUPLED UNITS

The trip lever or lift wire may corrode and fail to work smoothly, or the lift wire may bind in the guides. Disassemble and clean off corrosion or replace parts as necessary.

Most plumbing codes require a cutoff valve in the supply line to the flush tank, which makes it unnecessary to close down the whole system (Fig. 2). If this valve was not installed, you can stop the flow of water by propping up the float with a piece of wood. Be careful not to bend the float rod out of alignment.

Intake (Float) Valve

A worn plunger washer in the supply valve will cause the valve to leak. To replace the washer—

• Shut off the water and drain the tank.

• Unscrew the two thumbscrews that hold the levers and push out the levers.

• Lift out the plunger, unscrew the cup on the bottom, and insert a new washer. The washer is made of material such as rubber or leather.

• Examine the washer seat. If nicked or rough, it may need refacing.

If the float-valve assembly is badly corroded, replace it.

Float Ball

The float ball may develop a leak and fail to rise to the proper position. (Correct water level is about 1 inch below the top of the overflow tube or enough to give a good flush.) If the ball fails to rise, the intake valve will remain open and water will continue to flow. Brass float balls can sometimes be drained and the leak soldered. Other types must be replaced. When working on the float ball, be careful to keep the rod alined so that the ball will float freely and close the valve properly.

Bowl Removal

An obstruction in the water closet trap or leakage around the bottom of the water-closet bowl may require removal of the bowl. Follow this procedure:

• Shut off the water.

• Empty the tank and bowl by siphoning or sponging out the water.

• Disconnect the water pipes to the tank (see Fig. 2).

• Disconnect the tank from the bowl if the water closet is

a two-piece unit. Set the tank where it cannot be damaged. Handle tank and bowl carefully; they are made of vitreous china or porcelain and are easily chipped or broken.

• Remove the seat and cover from the bowl.

• Carefully pry loose the bolt covers and remove the bolts holding the bowl to the floor flange (Fig. 3). Jar the bowl enough to break the seal at the bottom. Set the bowl upside down on something that will not chip or break it.

• Remove the obstruction from the discharge opening.

• Place a new wax seal around the bowl horn and press it into place. A wax seal (or gasket) may be obtained from hardware or plumbing-supply stores.

• Set the bowl in place and press it down firmly. Install the bolts that hold it to the floor flange. Draw the bolts up snugly, but not too tight because the bowl may break. The bowl must be level. Keep a carpenter's level on it while drawing up the bolts. If the house has settled, leaving the floor sloping, it may be necessary to use shims to make the bowl set level. Replace the bolt covers.

• Install the tank and connect the water pipes to it. It is advisable to replace all gaskets, after first cleaning the surfaces thoroughly.

• Test for leaks by flushing a few times.

• Install the seat and cover.

Tank "Sweating"

When cold water enters a water closet tank, it may chill the tank enough to cause "sweating" (condensation of atmospheric moisture on the outer surface of the tank). This can be prevented by insulating the tank to keep the temperature of the outer surface above the dew point temperature of surrounding air. Insulating jackets or liners that fit inside water-closet tanks and serve to keep the outer surface warm are available from plumbing-supply dealers.

CLEARING CLOGGED DRAINS

Drains may become clogged by objects dropped into them or by accumulations of grease, dirt, or other matter.

Fixture and Floor Drains

If the obstruction is in a fixture trap, usually the trap can be removed and cleared. If the obstruction is elsewhere in the pipe other means must be used.

Cleanout augers—long, flexible, steel cables commonly called "snakes"—may be run down drainpipes to break up obstructions or to hook onto and pull out objects. Augers are made in various lengths and diameters and are available at hardware and plumbing-supply stores. (In some cases, you may have to call a plumber, who will probably have a power-driven auger.)

Small obstructions can sometimes be forced down or drawn up by use of an ordinary rubber force cup (plunger or "plumber's friend").

Grease and soap clinging to a pipe can sometimes be removed by flushing with hot water. Lye or lye mixed with a small amount of aluminum shavings may also be used. When water is added to the mixture, the violent gas-forming reaction and production of heat that takes place loosens the grease and soap so that they can be flushed away. *Use cold water only.* Chemical cleaners should not be used in pipes that are completely stopped up, because they must be brought into direct contact with the stoppage to be effective. Handle the material with extreme care and follow directions on the container. If lye spills on the hands or clothing, wash with cold water immediate-

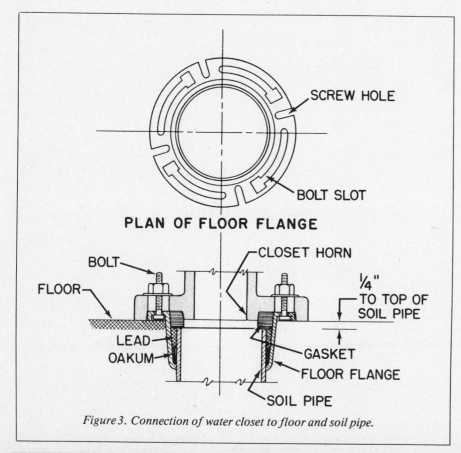

PLAN OF FLOOR FLANGE

SCREW HOLE

BOLT SLOT

BOLT

FLOOR

CLOSET HORN

¼"
TO TOP OF
SOIL PIPE

LEAD
OAKUM

GASKET
FLOOR FLANGE

SOIL PIPE

Figure 3. Connection of water closet to floor and soil pipe.

1961. Mrs. Saadet Cor of Turkey bears the heaviest child on record, a boy who weighs twenty-four pounds, four ounces.

ly. If any gets into the eyes, flush with cold water and call a doctor.

Sand, dirt, or clothing lint sometimes clogs floor drains. Remove the strainer and ladle out as much of the sediment as possible. You may have to carefully chip away the concrete around the strainer to free it. Flush the drain with clean water.

When drains have become partially clogged due to lack of water to transport all solids through them, large buckets or other containers should be used to flush them. Water should be poured fast enough to nearly fill the drain.

Occasional flushing of floor drains may prevent clogging.

CAUTION: Augers, rubber force cups, and other tools used in direct contact with sewage are subject to contamination. Do not later use them for work on your potable water supply system unless they have been properly sterilized.

Outside Drains

Roots growing through cracks or defective joints sometimes clog outside drains or sewers. You can clear the stoppage temporarily by using a root-cutting tool. However, to prevent future trouble, you should re-lay the defective portion of the line, using sound pipe and making sure that all joints are watertight.

If possible, sewer lines should be laid out of the reach of roots. But if this is impossible or impracticable, consider using impregnated fiber pipe which tends to repel roots.

EMERGENCIES

Grouped below are emergencies that may occur and the action to take. The name, address, and phone number of a plumber who offers 24-hour service should be posted in a conspicuous place.

Burst pipe or tank.—Immedi-ately cut off the flow of water by closing the shutoff valve nearest to the break. Then arrange for repair.

Water closet overflow.—Do not use water closet until back in working order. Check for and remove stoppage in closet bowl outlet, drain line from closet to sewer, or sewer or septic tank. If stoppage is due to root entry into pipe, repair of pipe at that point is recommended.

Rumbling noise in hot water tank.—This is likely a sign of overheating which could lead to the development of explosive pressure. (Another indication of overheating is hot water backing up in the cold-water supply pipe.) Cut off the burner immediately. Be sure that the pressure-relief valve is operative. Then check (with a thermometer) the temperature of the water at the near-est outlet. If above that for which the gage is set, check the thermostat that controls burner cut-off. If you cannot correct the trouble, call a plumber.

Cold house.—If the heating system fails (or if you close the house and turn off the heat) when there is a chance of sub-freezing weather, completely drain the plumbing system. A drain valve is usually provided at the low point of the water supply piping for this purpose. A pump, storage tank, hot-water tank, water closet tank, water-treatment apparatus, and other water-system appliances or accessories should also be drained. Put antifreeze in all fixture and drain traps.

Hot-water and steam heating systems should also be drained when the house temperature may drop below freezing.

TOOLS AND SPARE PARTS

Basic tools that you should have on hand to make simple plumbing repairs include:

Wrenches, including pipe wrenches, in a range of sizes to fit the pipe, fittings, fixtures, equipment, and appliances in the system.

Screwdrivers in a range of sizes to fit the faucets, valves, and other parts of the system.

Ball peen hammer or a 12- or 16-ounce clawhammer.

Rubber force cup (plunger or "plumber's friend").

Cold chisel and center punch.

Cleanout auger ("snake").

Friction tape.

Adjustable pliers.

Additional tools required for more extensive plumbing repairs include:

Pipe vise.

Set of pipe threading dies and stocks.

Hacksaw and blades (blades should have 32 teeth per inch).

Pipe cutter, roller type.

Tapered reamer or half-round file.

Carpenter's brace.

Set of wood bits.

Gasoline blowtorch.

Lead pot and ladle.

Calking tools.

Copper tube cutter with reamer (if you have copper tubing).

Always use the proper size wrench or screwdriver. Do not use pipe wrenches on nuts with flat surfaces; use an adjustable or open-end wrench. Do not use pipe wrenches on polished-surface tubings or fittings, such as found on plumbing fixtures; use a strap wrench. Tight nuts or fittings can sometimes be loosened by tapping lightly with a hammer or mallet.

It should not be necessary to stock a large number of spare parts. Past plumbing troubles may give some indication as to the kind of parts most likely to be needed. Spare parts should include:

Faucet washers and packing.

One or two lengths of the most common type and size of piping in the plumbing system.

Several unions and gaskets or unions with ground surfaces.

Several couplings and elbows.

A few feet of pipe strap.

An extra hose connection.

1963. Congress passes the Equal Pay Act, which requires most companies to pay equal wages regardless of sex to all those performing equal tasks.

Electricity without Fear

Lady Borton

I used to be scared of electricity, afraid that tampering with anything more complex than replacing a light bulb would bring disaster. But then our family moved to an old farmhouse without electricity. Since the cost of paying an electrician to wire the house was prohibitive, we decided to do it ourselves. We spent several hours with our noses in a guide to household wiring, planned our own electrical system, bought supplies, and started. It was easier than I had thought possible.

Much of the work in electrical wiring involves simple carpentry skills which you may already have. As for the electrical skills, some reading and a little practice can provide them easily. This article won't give you enough knowledge to undertake ambitious wiring projects, but it will provide those of you who know nothing about electricity with a basic understanding of how the wiring in your home works. If you understand the how and why of wiring, you can not only figure out what's wrong when it doesn't work, but you can fix it.

We'll start with basics. Electric current is generated by harnessing waterpower, burning fuel, or using certain chemical reactions. That current can be stored in batteries. Electricity is conducted on wires made of metal to outlets (lights or receptacles, i.e., wall plugs).

The "flow" of electric current is measured in amps. Newer homes have 100 amps of current coming in at the service entrance; older ones may have 60 amps. This current is divided into several branches or circuits of 15 or 20 amps. (In examples, we'll assume you have 100 amps divided into 20-amp branch circuits.)

Electricity under pressure is measured in volts. The dry-cell battery used in a standard flashlight stores one and a half volts. Most buildings are wired for 115 volts (sometimes 110, 220, or 230 volts). The power transmission lines along highways may carry as much as 345,000 volts.

The difference between low and high voltage is the difference between dump-

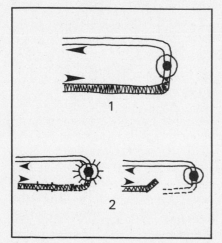

ing a bucket of water over your head and aiming a fire hose at your face—it's the amount of pressure. A low-voltage electric fence won't harm you, but touching an uninsulated section of a high-voltage transmission line could kill you. Under some conditions, such as standing in water, a shock of 115 volts (the voltage found in most houses) can be fatal. All of which is to say that the electric current you use deserves your knowledgeable caution.

Suppose we take a simple light as an example of how electric current is used. The current comes from a source (such as a battery or the service entrance of a building), and follows a wire (usually covered with black insulation, thus called the black wire) to the light. It returns to the source on another wire (usually covered with white insulation, thus called the white wire). (See Figure 1.) We call the path of electric current from source to outlet (light or receptacle) and back to the source a circuit. A heavy line in diagrams indicates a black wire; a thin line indicates a white wire. For simplicity, diagrams show the black and white wires separated. In actual practice, though, a single cable carries the two wires together in another sheath of insulation.

The black wire is the current-carrying wire. In any circuit there is a circuit breaker or fuse in the black or "hot" wire. Circuit breakers and fuses are safety features which we'll talk about later. The white wire is the grounded or

neutral wire. It connects the electrical system to the earth via the electrical ground, usually one of the buried pipes in the household water system. This protects against electrical shock by providing a path for current to flow out of the system.

Follow the current through the circuit in Figure 1, which shows how a simple light works. In Figure 2, when the switch is "on," electric current passes through the switch to the light on a switched black wire. When the switch is "off," no current passes along the switched black wire to the light and the light is off. A heavy dotted line in diagrams indicates a switched black wire.

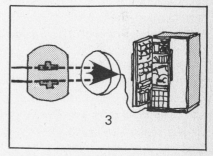

A receptacle (wall plug) works on the same principle, as seen in Figure 3. Current comes from the source to the receptacle on a black wire and returns to the source on a white wire. When you plug into a receptacle, the prongs in the plug of your appliance cord connect with the wires of the circuit inside the receptacle as in Figure 3. In effect, then, your appliance becomes part of the circuit. Thus, a flow of 20 amps at 115 volts passes through the appliance.

The same thing happens when a toddler pokes a fork into the slits of a receptacle. The metal can act just like the prongs of an appliance plug and conduct the flow of current through the child's body and possibly electrocute her or him. If you live with a child who is inclined to experiment, cover receptacles not in use with the plastic plugs available at any hardware store.

Figure 4 illustrates a flashlight lighting circuit, which works on the same principle as the electricity in your home but

---

1963. Betty Friedan, author of *The Feminine Mystique*, remarks to an interviewer about her book, "Some people thought I said, 'Women of the world unite—you have nothing to lose but your men.' It's not true. You have nothing to lose but your vacuum cleaner."

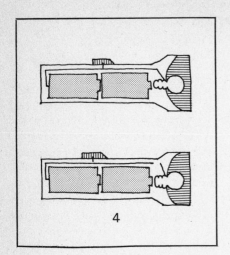

4

is easier to experiment with. Take it apart and see what its source of electric current is. What conducts the current from the source to the light bulb? Bear in mind that the metal conductor does not have to be a wire. Flick the switch on and off. What happens *mechanically* inside the flashlight when you switch it on and off? How does the current get from the light bulb back to the source?

In the home, each light and receptacle is not on a separate circuit. To save wire, several lights and/or receptables are connected to form one circuit. In Example A of Figure 5 the current comes from the source on a black wire, passes through the switch, and then runs on a switched black wire to the first light. From that light it runs to the second light, to the third light and back to the source on a white wire.

Suppose you remove the second light bulb in Example C of Figure 5—you will break the circuit at that point. Since the circuit is broken, current no longer flows from the source to the lights. The first and third lights will shut off. This type of wiring, in which you *cannot* trace the current directly back to the source from each fixture, is called series wiring. Old fashioned Christmas tree lights were on series wiring. If one bulb burned out, then none of the bulbs would light until you had replaced the culprit.

For this and other reasons, lights and receptacles in your house are wired in parallel. In parallel wiring you can trace the current from *each* fixture directly back to the source. Figure 6 shows lights connected in parallel. Current comes from the source to Point A where it di-

vides, going to Switch 1 and Point B. At Point B it divides again, going to Switch 2 and also to Switch 3, and on to Lights 2 and 3. From each light you can trace the current directly back to the source without going through another outlet. If you remove one of the bulbs in this group, current still runs to the other two lights.

It would be possible to route the 100-amp flow of current coming in at the service entrance through a house in only one circuit, but there are two disadvantages to this. First, should that one circuit break, the house would be completely without electricity. Second, a 100-amp current requires thick, cumbersome cable. Thus, it's easier to divide the 100 amps into several lower amperage

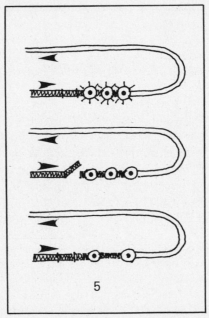

5

branch circuits—usually 15 or 20 amps each. For simplicity, we'll talk about 20-amp circuits, as I mentioned before.

Any one room may have several branch circuits in it, and one branch circuit may run through several rooms. Figure 7 shows

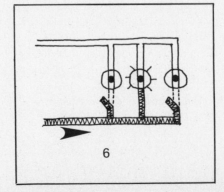

6

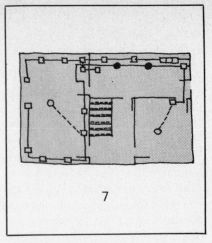

7

a possible living-room wiring plan. There are two branch circuits in the room, and each circuit comes from another room. This diagram shows two junction boxes. As the name implies, the circuits branch at points A and B with connections made inside the junction boxes. You'll probably find several junction boxes in your attic, basement, or utility room.

We'll do some experimenting now so you can figure out where the branch circuits run in your house or apartment. In apartments the circuit breaker—used in newer buildings—or fuse box is apt to be in a closet or the kitchen. Some apartments may not have a circuit breaker (or fuse box) for each living unit, in which case you're out of luck. Those who live in houses will probably find it in the basement, utility room, or kitchen.

What you find will be some variation of Figure 8. One circuit breaker (or main switch in a fuse box) controls the 100-amp flow of current at the service entrance, and another circuit breaker (or fuse) controls each 20-amp branch circuit. All are important safety features that warn you when something is wrong in your electrical system, and protect you from fire and electrical shock.

Figure 7 shows a circuit breaker at the beginning of each circuit. Circuit breakers and fuses should be labeled according to the circuits they control. (If yours aren't, then do that little chore now.)

Switch a 20-amp circuit breaker off or unscrew a 20-amp fuse. If some of your lights should go out or appliances shut off, don't worry. *Don't stick curious fingers or anything else in the fuse socket.* If you do, you'll complete a circuit carry-

1963. Valentina Tereshkova, at twenty-six one of Russia's youngest Communist Party members, is launched into orbit to become the first woman in space. Her call name while aloft is "Seagull."

516 Electricity
HANDYWOMAN

ing 20 amps of current at 115 volts with your body and receive a nasty and possibly fatal shock.

The wires in any one branch circuit of your house or apartment are designed to carry a certain flow or amperage. If a higher amperage flows over the circuit, that extra current may melt the insulation covering the wires, thereby letting the black and white wires, once protected from each other by insulation, touch and cause a short circuit. Instead of flowing through the entire circuit, the current takes the shorter, uninsulated route with less resistance to its flow. This can result in sparks and fire. Circuit breakers and fuses are designed to break the path of electrical current if there is a short circuit.

Circuit breakers or fuses are marked with an amperage, say 20 amps. If more than 20 amps of current pass over the circuit, the circuit breaker or fuse breaks the circuit near the source, and everything on that circuit shuts off. When you switched the breaker (or unscrewed the fuse) a few minutes ago, you broke the circuit near its source.

After you have turned off one branch circuit, use a switched-on desk lamp or some other appliance to figure out which receptacles are no longer current-carrying or "hot," and try the light switches. Using this system you can map the wiring plan of your house, as in Figure 7. Ignore any lights controlled by two switches The outlet nearest the source is probably "first" in the circuit. Then where would the current go? It is likely that the circuit divides at a junction box into several directions (see Figure 7). You may come up with several possible wiring circuits. The one requiring the least electrical cable is probably the one used.

Now that you know how to break the circuit, you can cut off the current and safely explore the way a receptacle, switch, and light are wired.

Choose a receptacle on the circuit, and just to be sure, use some easily portable appliance (switched on) to check that the circuit is off. Take off the plastic receptacle cover and unscrew the two screws that attach the receptacle to its box. Gently pull the receptacle out so you can peer in behind it.

8

What you see should look something like Figure 9. There are probably two cables coming into the box, one coming from the source to the receptacle and the other going to the next outlet. (If there is one cable only, then it comes from the source and the receptacle is the "last" one in the circuit.)

The cable insulation has been stripped to free the black and white wires. Though you may not be able to see it, about a half inch of wire insulation has also been stripped from each wire. The wires connect to the receptacle either around screw terminals on the receptacles (black wires on copper screws, white wires on

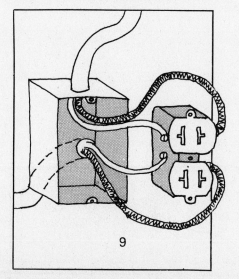

9

white screws) or inside special slits in the back of the receptacle.

Newer wiring systems have grounding receptacles with a third hole below the familiar two. These accommodate the three-pronged plugs found on such appliances as stoves, washers, dryers, air-conditioners, drills, and saws. Both the appliance cords and the electrical cables running to grounding receptacles have a third wire in addition to the black and white ones. This wire is called a grounding wire, and it connects the frame of an appliance or motor to the ground (a pipe buried in the earth). Thus it prevents electrical shock from the appliance frame, should there be a short circuit. The National Electrical Code, which establishes regulations for safe electrical wiring, requires that all new building construction use grounding receptacles.

The terms "ground," "grounded wire," and "grounding wire" refer to different parts of an electrical system. The ground, as I mentioned earlier, is a device such as a buried water pipe connecting the system to the earth. Grounded wires are the white neutral wires which connect all outlets of a circuit to the ground. Grounding wires are uninsulated wires connecting the frames of appliances or motors to the ground. All three—ground, grounded wires, and grounding wires—provide protection from electrical shock by providing a path to carry current in case of short circuit.

Now choose a light which is controlled by only one wall switch. This is a single pole switch. Flick the switch to check that the current is off. Unscrew the switch cover and the switch. Gently pull the switch a peeking distance from its box. Unscrew the light fixture controlled by that switch so that it hangs down enough for you to see inside. There are several ways to wire a light and its switch, depending on the type of fixture and its location in the circuit. Figures 10 and 11 show two basic possibilities: a light that is the last outlet on the circuit and one that is somewhere in the middle of the circuit.

In Figure 10 there are two cables coming in to the single-pole switch indicating that the current comes to the switch first and then goes to the light.

1964. Margaret Chase Smith, senator from Maine, attracts twenty-seven votes at the Republican National Convention, thereby becoming the first woman ever nominated for president by an established political party.

The black wire running between the switch and the light is a switched wire. It carries current only when the switch is on. Current returns to the source on the white neutral or grounded wire.

In Figure 11, the current goes from the light to another outlet. In this case, the current comes first to the light-fixture out-

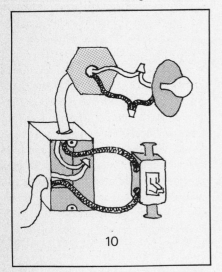

10

let box where it sidetracks to the switch before it actually connects to the light. The current comes in from the source to wire nut 1 in the outlet box. A wire nut is a small piece of plastic which, when screwed on two or more wires, connects them together. (Wrapping the ends of wires together with electrical tape accomplishes the same thing.)

At wire nut 1, the current goes on to the next outlet, and also runs to the switch on the white wire. This is a special exception in which a white wire is a current-carrying wire. You can follow the current with a pencil on the switched black wire through wire nut 2 to the light.

When the switch is on, current passes through the switched black wire to the light. The other white wires, which are the grounded or neutral wires, join in wire nut 3 and connect the fixture to the electrical ground.

Screw the light and switch back into their boxes, put the covers on, and turn the circuit back on. To turn on a circuit you need only reset the circuit breaker or screw the fuse back into its socket.

Now you're ready to try a little practice at troubleshooting. Suppose you plug in your electric coffeepot—and *zap!* sparks fly out of the receptacle and several lights and/or appliances, possibly in different rooms, go out. This means that a circuit breaker switched off or a fuse blew on one of your branch circuits.

Since the circuit broke when you plugged in the coffeepot, that appliance is a likely first suspect. Since the circuit is off, you can feel comfortable about snooping around for the cause. A frayed cord could cause a short circuit. If the cord is in good condition, then the short circuit may be inside the appliance itself. If you think there is something wrong with the appliance, unplug it and don't use it until it's fixed.

Another common cause of a thrown circuit breaker or blown fuse is an over-loaded circuit caused by too many appliances drawing too much current. Sometimes this happens when a motor (such as a washing machine or an air conditioner) starts, since a motor uses more current during the first few starting seconds than after it is running. If it seems the circuit was overloaded, change some of that load to another circuit.

Another, but less likely, suspect is the outlet itself. If you think this is the problem, take it apart and examine it while the circuit is off. The outlet may be faulty, or, more likely, there is a loose connection or a loose wire. Check to be sure that all wires connect tightly and properly at the terminals.

Once you have isolated the problem and either solved or removed it, you're ready to reset the circuit breaker (just the flick of a switch), or replace a blown fuse, which deserves some thought. It is important to replace a fuse only with one of the same amperage. Replacing a 20-amp fuse in a 20-amp circuit with a 35-amp fuse will not be a protection against overload. It will actually be a hazard since it may allow more current to flow through the circuit than the wires are designed to carry.

Now you probably know more than most people about electrical wiring. You can see that twisting wires around screw terminals isn't difficult but that the theory involved is more challenging. If you'd like to do some wiring yourself (say, extending a circuit), pick up a wiring handbook at your local hardware store. One clear, concise guide (about 140 pages) is *Wiring Simplified* by H. P. Richter (Park Publishing, Inc., P.O. Box 5527, Lake St. Station, Minneapolis, Minn. 55408). You do not need a license to do your own wiring, though in some localities you may need a permit which covers the cost of inspection. Always be sure that any electrical materials you purchase are stamped with the Underwriters' Laboratories seal which guarantees their safety.

The carpentry involved in concealing wires in the finished walls of our old farmhouse was the most frustrating and time-consuming part of our wiring job. Braces, studs, and joists appeared where we had figured there were none. The thick, hard beams were thicker and harder to drill through than we had anticipated. And the narrow crawl space under the house provided a challenge to our tall frames and long drill bits. But planning circuits to suit our own electrical needs was an exciting challenge and the actual electrical work was remarkably simple. In fact, we've just moved to another old farmhouse without electricity.

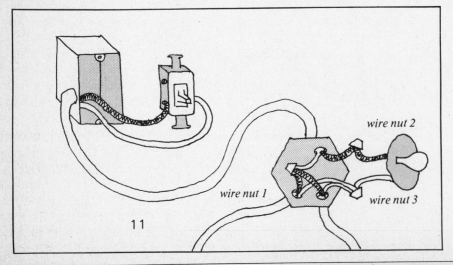

wire nut 2

wire nut 1

wire nut 3

11

1966. The National Organization for Women (NOW) is founded, the first organized group associated with the modern resurgence of feminism. Betty Friedan is its president.

Simple Electrical Repairs

Kay B. Ward

Rewiring a plug. If an appliance or lamp doesn't work and the trouble isn't something obvious like a burned-out light bulb, check the prongs on the plug.

1. Perhaps you are not getting proper contact in the wall outlet. Bend the two prongs in the plug slightly apart (not together) to obtain a firmer fit and better contact.

2. If this is unsuccessful, face the plug toward you (after unplugging it of course) and make sure that the wires inside have not worked loose from the terminal screws. If this has happened, look at another plug, loosen the screws and reset the wires, copying the second plug. Tighten the screws.

3. If the prongs of the plug are loose, if the small wires in the plug are split or broken, if the plug casing is broken or cracked or if the cord is broken or exposed near the plug, replace the plug.

A. With the cord unplugged, cut off the plug and at least an inch of cord, removing all the broken or cracked portion of the cord.

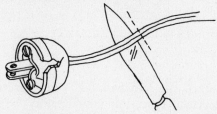

B. Strip off the insulation for about two inches from the end of the cord. Do this carefully so that when the two individual wires are exposed, their insulation is not damaged. (You may want to purchase a tool which easily strips the insulation.)

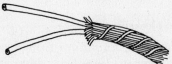

If the cord looks like two wires with rubber molded over them, split the two sections apart for about two inches.

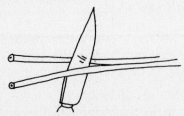

C. Strip off about ½ to ¾ inch of insulation from each wire with a sharp knife or a wire stripper. This will expose many little wires. Try to keep these little wires bunched together and do not cut into the little wires with that sharp knife.

D. Push both wires through the top of the new plug. With the pulled-through wires, tie a special knot called an underwriters' knot in the wire just above the exposed little wires.

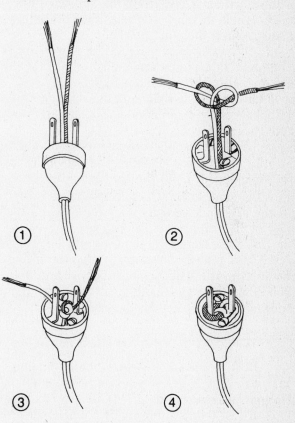

Pull this knot back into the plug, nesting it in between the two prongs. Then loop one wire around one prong and wrap the exposed little wires *clockwise* around the closest terminal screw. Tighten the screw. Wrap the other wire around the other prong and wrap the little wires *clockwise* around the other screw in the same manner. Be sure that neither bunch of little wires touches the other bunch of little wires. Also be certain

Adapted and reprinted from *The Feminine Fix – It Handbook* by Kay B. Ward. Copyright © 1972 Kay B. Ward. Used by permission of Grosset & Dunlap, Inc.

1967. About thirty women civil-rights and "New Left" workers, dissatisfied with the treatment they have been receiving at the hands of their groups, break away and form the first true women's-liberation organization.

that each bunch of little wires is gathered under its screw and that no loose strands stick out.

The above steps A–D show the best method of replacing most plugs. However, for lamps and light extension cords you can use the newer clamp-on plugs. Just cut off the old plug, insert the end of the cord in the clamp-on plug and clamp it in place according to the directions that come with the plug.

Female appliance plug (named by a male chauvinist). Many cords have a big, flat plug at one end which fastens directly into a particular appliance (electric coffee maker, frying pan, grill). These plugs take a lot of hard use and as their casings are often made of a brittle material they are easily chipped or broken. Very often the wires inside become worn from pulling the plug in and out.

So don't despair if you think the appliance has gone kerflooey. It may be only this plug. Before running to a serviceman, check the plug yourself.

Be sure the wall outlet you're using is working properly. To prove this, plug a working lamp into the outlet. If the lamp lights, the outlet is working.

If you have a cord like the questionable one from another appliance, try it out on the problem appliance. If the appliance now works, great!

If you have no second cord and plug to test with, unplug the one from the outlet and see if its case is cracked or chipped. Does the cord going into the case seem insecure and loose? Does it look frayed or burned? Check the case and see if its two halves seem loose and wobbly.

If any of these things are so, it's worth investing in a new cord and plug because if it isn't now giving you trouble it soon will. They're not expensive and both five and ten cent stores and hardware stores carry them. If your new plug doesn't remedy the situation, see a serviceman.

A damaged electric cord.   Do not try to repair a heater cord (for toaster, iron, coffee pot or other heating appliances). Have a serviceman replace the cord with a new one.

You can repair a damaged lamp cord or extension cord as follows:

1. If only the outer insulation is frayed or broken, wrap the damaged area well with electrical tape.

2. If the inner wires are damaged too and the cut or break goes deep, cut off the offending area.

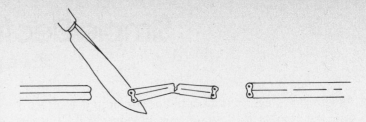

3. With a wire stripper or sharp paring knife, strip off about two inches of insulation on each side of the cut.

4. Twist the opposite wires together.

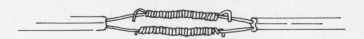

5. Wrap each wire with electrical tape making sure that the tape covers *all* exposed metal wire. In fact, it's a good idea to wrap two layers of tape to be absolutely sure all exposed wire is covered.

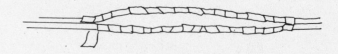

6. Last wrap the two wrapped wires together with more electrical tape. For added safety, wrap a second coat of tape around the item.

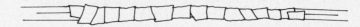

WALL SWITCHES

It is actually a simple job to replace a defective wall switch. The most important thing is to shut off the power to that switch. If you don't do this it could kill you!

If after that dire warning you're still game to continue, here's what to do.

1. Shut off the power either by pulling the main switch or by unscrewing the correct fuse. Be sure you *know* it's the correct fuse.

2. As a double safety against a shock, you may want to work with a rubber-handled screwdriver. If you have them, wear sneakers. Never work in bare feet.

Unscrew the two screws from the switch-plate cover and remove the cover. Do *not* do this before the power is shut off.

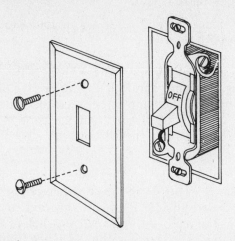

3. Unscrew the two screws at the top and bottom which hold the switch in position against the wall and the switch box.

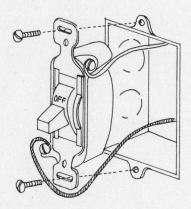

4. After pulling the switch carefully out of the box, you will see that it is tethered by two wires. Unhook these wires by loosening the terminal screws mounted on the switch.

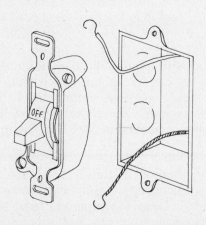

5. Hook these two wires to the new switch. Be sure to hook the black wire to the brass-colored terminal and the white or red wire to the silver-colored terminal.

6. Bend the wires back into the switch box and replace the screws which hold the switch on the wall.

7. Replace the switch plate.

In many newer houses, after you have removed the switch you will see a third wire called a ground wire in the switch box. This wire is frequently green and is usually attached to the back of the switch. If this is true of your switch box check with your hardware store on installation or check the instructions on the packaging.

LAMPS

Rewiring a lamp.　Your lamp needs fixing if the light is fluttering or buzzing or if you have to switch it on and off a couple of times before it makes contact.

1. Check the lamp plug as described earlier in the section Rewiring a Plug. If it needs replacing, use one of the new, easy snap-on varieties. More than likely, however, your problem is in the lamp's socket.

2. Unplug the lamp! Remove the lampshade and bulb. The socket into which the bulb screws has a springy metal tab in it. With a screwdriver, bend this tab slightly upward to make a tighter contact between the tab and the end of the bulb.

1968. Dr. Elizabeth Boyer and other disaffected former members of NOW (who have disagreed with NOW's stand on the repeal of criminal abortion laws, among other things) found the Women's Equity Action League (WEAL) in Washington, D.C.

Screw in the light bulb, plug in the lamp and try it. It works? Good! But if it doesn't, check the socket.

3. Unplug the lamp! Remove the bulb again. Pull the shell apart from the cap, leaving the cap in position. Be sure the terminal screws around which the wires are wrapped are tight and examine all of the cord to make sure it isn't worn or broken anywhere (if the cord needs replacing, see the section Replacing the Lamp Cord). Put the lamp together again and try it. If there is still no light, the switch may be faulty and you need to replace the socket.

Replacing the socket

1. Unplug the lamp! Pull the socket shell from the cap, leaving the cap in position. If the old cord is not broken you may proceed, using the existing cord. Loosen the two terminal screws inside the socket and remove each wire. Throw the old socket away.

2. Pull apart the new socket to reveal the terminal screws. Discard the new cap part as it is interchangeable with the old cap already in position. Trying to remove the old cap can loosen the whole lamp mechanism. If at all possible, leave the old cap.

3. Twist each wire clockwise around each terminal screw, taking care to match the dark wire to the bronze-colored screw and the light (or red) wire to the aluminum-colored screw.

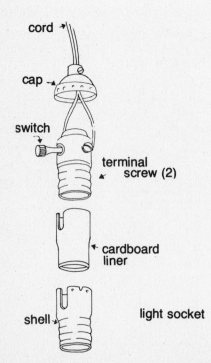

cord

cap

switch

terminal screw (2)

cardboard liner

shell

light socket

Put the socket shell back on the cap. Do not forget the cardboard liner as it is protection against short circuits. Pull the cord gently at the bottom of the lamp to make it taut.

4. Replace the bulb and plug in your lamp as good as new.

Replacing the lamp cord.

Is the cord damaged inside the body of the lamp or between the lamp and the plug? Does the light flicker when the cord is wriggled? Play it safe and replace the full cord as well as the socket.

1. Unplug the lamp! Unscrew the bulb and remove the harp. (This is the curved wire section that holds on the lampshade. It usually squeezes in and pulls upward to remove.) Pull apart the shell of the socket from the cap. Unscrew the old wires from the two terminals. A smart move at this point would be to tie a long string onto the top of the old lamp cord.

You'll understand as you read on. Discard all the old parts: the old switch, plug, socket.

Pull the cord out through the bottom of the lamp. The string will remain inside the lamp, sticking out from the top. Untie the string from the old cord. Tie on the new cord and from the top of the lamp, pull the string, drawing the new cord through the lamp.

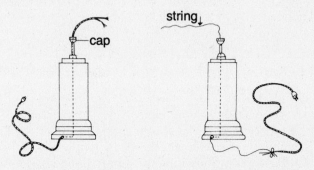

cap   string

2. Using wire strippers, strip off about three quarters of an inch of insulation at the top end of the lamp cord, revealing the two bunches of small wires. Twist each bunch of wires tightly together, making two tight bunches. Wrap the bunch from the black wire clockwise around the dark terminal screw of the new socket. Wrap the bunch from the white (or red) wire clockwise around the light terminal screw. Reassemble the socket and shell onto the lamp cap as described in Step 3 in the previous section.

All the information in this section should give you hints on how to convert an antique gas lamp or a handsome vase into a lamp. Go to an electrical supply store or a good hardware store and look around at the kits, supplies and instruction booklets which are available.

1968. In an interview with *Playboy* magazine, Timothy Leary maintains that LSD has an unusually aphrodisiacal effect on women:
Playboy: We've heard that some women who ordinarily have difficulty achieving orgasm find themselves capable of multiple orgasms under LSD. Is this true?

You flick the switch on your dependable appliance . . . nothing happens. "It's broken!" you exclaim. But, before you jump to conclusions, or to the telephone, ask yourself — IS IT PLUGGED IN? A simple point, this, but one so largely ignored that it accounts for numerous unnecessary service calls that cost money as well as embarrassment. National statistics tell us that about 40 percent of all service calls are unwarranted, wasting about $80 million yearly.

HANDY CHECKLIST FOR INDIVIDUAL APPLIANCES

RANGE AND OVEN

Problem: Single surface unit does not heat
1. **Cause:** Loose connection or broken wire to unit.
   Remedy: Cut all power to range by removing fuse or switching circuit breaker to OFF position. Lift up heating element and reflector to see if one of the wires is broken at terminal screws on surface unit. If it is, clean ends of wire with fine sandpaper — not moist steel wool (this dampens wire, which can then cause a short circuit when switched on). Connect securely to terminal screw. If the wire is broken anyplace except at the terminal screw, call a serviceman.

Problem: Convenience outlet does not supply power
1. **Cause:** Range fuse or circuit breaker has blown or plug-type fuse has worked loose.
   Remedy: Replace range fuse, reset circuit breaker or check plug-type fuse to be sure it is secure. Check manufacturer's instructions for exact location of range fuse or circuit breaker.

Problem: Oven unit won't heat
1. **Cause:** Timer set on OFF or AUTOMATIC position and/or selector switch set in wrong position.
   Remedy: Reset timer to MANUAL position and/or set selector to BAKE.
2. **Cause:** Terminals of removable heating unit are not pushed firmly into receptacle and/or they are dirty.
   Remedy: Cut all power to range by removing fuse or switching circuit breaker to OFF position. Make sure terminals are clean and fit securely into receptacle at back of oven.

Problem: Food overcooks in oven
1. **Cause:** Oven temperature too high.
   Remedy: Follow manufacturer's directions for proper temperature setting.
2. **Cause:** Oven thermostat out of adjustment.
   Remedy: Call serviceman to make an adjustment or replace with new thermostat if necessary.
3. **Cause:** Oven door not tightly closed.
   Remedy: Call serviceman to make adjustment.
4. **Cause:** Incorrect type or size pans, incorrect pan placement in oven, overcrowded oven.
   Remedy: Follow manufacturer's directions for proper type, size, placement and number of pans to use.

Adapted from *How to Avoid Unnecessary Service Calls on Your Electrical Appliances*. Reprinted with permission of Electric Energy Association.

Problem: Food undercooks in oven
1. **Cause:** Oven door opened too often while cooking.
   Remedy: Do not open door until cooking time is up.
2. **Cause:** Oven thermostat out of adjustment.
   Remedy: Call serviceman to make an adjustment or replace with new thermostat if necessary.
3. **Cause:** Improper pan for recipe needs.
   Remedy: Follow reliable recipe. Use size and type pan specified in recipe.

Problem: Food browns or bakes unevenly
1. **Cause:** Range not level.
   Remedy: Check position of range with a level. If not perfectly level, adjust leveling screws on base of range. If there are no leveling screws, insert thin strips of wood under base to bring unit level.
2. **Cause:** Incorrect placement of pans in oven.
   Remedy: Allow at least 1" between cake pans and 1" between pans and sides of oven.

REFRIGERATOR OR FREEZER

Problem: Failure to operate
1. **Cause:** Temperature control set at OFF or DEFROST.
   Remedy: If model defrosts manually, adjust temperature control to correct setting. Check manufacturer's instructions on timing of automatic defrost cycle.
2. **Cause:** Use of long extension cord, smaller than No. 14 wire.
   Remedy: Extension cords of any kind should not be used. If there is no alternative, the cord should be 3-wire, No. 14 or heavier.
3. **Cause:** Fuse blown or circuit breaker open.
   Remedy: Test outlet with lamp. Check fuse box for blown fuse or close circuit breaker.

Problem: Motor seems to run too often or too long
1. **Cause:** Door opened frequently or allowed to remain open too long.
   Remedy: Plan meal preparation to avoid constant opening of refrigerator door; close promptly after use.
2. **Cause:** Dust on condenser.
   Remedy: Turn off or disconnect appliance. Clean condenser according to manufacturer's instructions.
3. **Cause:** Door leaking air.
   Remedy: Clean door gasket with mild soap and water. If gasket is torn or worn, call serviceman. He will replace it and, if necessary, adjust so it closes tightly.
4. **Cause:** Unit too near heat source — range, radiator warm-air register — or too close to wall or cabinets.
   Remedy: Move unit to a location in the kitchen away from trouble spots.

Problem: Inside light fails to operate
1. **Cause:** Bulb burned out.
   Remedy: Replace bulb with one of same type and size.
2. **Cause:** Bulb loose in socket.
   Remedy: Tighten bulb.
3. **Cause:** Door-switch button sticking.
   Remedy: Press button in and out several times. If this measure fails, call serviceman.

Problem: Unit noisy when motor is running
1. **Cause:** Unit not level on floor.
   Remedy: Check with a level and adjust leveling screws at base. If there are no leveling screws,

---

Leary: In a carefully prepared, loving LSD session, a woman can have several hundred orgasms.
Playboy: Several *hundred*?
Leary: Yes. Several hundred.

insert thin strips of wood under base
to bring unit level.

2. **Cause:** Objects placed on top of unit rattling
from slight vibration when motor is running.
Remedy: Remove or cushion objects.

3. **Cause:** Items inside the refrigerator vibrate.
Remedy: Reposition contents of refrigerator
so items are solidly placed.

Problem: Food slow to freeze

1. **Cause:** Freezing too much food at one time.
Remedy: Freeze no more than 2 to 3 pounds of food per
cubic foot of freezer space in a 24-hour period.

2. **Cause:** Excessive frost built up inside cabinet
or on cooling coils.
Remedy: Defrost before ice becomes ¼″ thick.

Problem: Freezer collects too much frost

1. **Cause:** Door leaking air.
Remedy: Clean door gasket with mild soap and
water. If gasket is torn or worn, call serviceman.

2. **Cause:** Temperature too low.
Remedy: Follow manufacturer's instructions for
proper temperature setting.

3. **Cause:** Incomplete defrosting.
Remedy: Defrost completely and wipe inside of
freezer unit dry with soft cloth or sponge.

4. **Cause:** Door opened too frequently or allowed
to remain open too long.
Remedy: Plan meal preparation to avoid constant
opening of freezer door; close promptly after use.

5. **Cause:** Uncovered foods.
Remedy: Cover or seal all foods.

Problem: Excessive condensation in fresh foods section

1. **Cause:** Opening door too often, leaving it open too long.
Remedy: Avoid frequent and prolonged opening
of door, particularly in hot, humid weather.
Remember that some condensation is normal.

DISHWASHER

Problem: Does not operate

1. **Cause:** No power to unit.
Remedy: Check fuse in dishwasher circuit.
Make sure plug is in securely when using a
portable unit.

2. **Cause:** Door latch not completely closed.
Remedy: Reclose door and latch securely.

3. **Cause:** Cycle control not on proper setting.
Remedy: Adjust control to proper setting
per manufacturer's instructions.

Problem: Does not fill with water and light is on, indicating there is power to the dishwasher

1. **Cause:** Faucet not open (portable models) or
shut-off valves on water lines are closed.
Remedy: Check faucets or shut-off valves to
be sure they are open.

2. **Cause:** Low water pressure in plumbing system.
Remedy: Check for adequate water pressure by
opening a faucet in another area of the house.
If pressure is low, call the water company or
a plumber. Do not use water for other purposes
requiring large quantities — showers, clothes
washing — while dishwasher is operating.

Problem: Motor hums but dishwasher does not operate

1. **Cause:** Object jamming the impeller or
spray arm.
Remedy: Turn off dishwasher — remove object.
If this is not possible, call serviceman.

Problem: Detergent remains in cup dispenser after washing cycle has been completed

1. **Cause:** Old detergent caked in cup, or detergent
allowed to stand in cup too long before

dishwasher is turned on.
Remedy: Follow manufacturer's instructions on
amount and correct type of detergent to use.
To prevent detergent from caking in cup, always make
sure cup is dry before filling with detergent.
Also check to see if water is hot enough, or
whether dishes or pots and pans could be blocking flow of water to dispenser.

2. **Cause:** Control malfunction.
Remedy: If malfunction continues,
call serviceman.

Problem: Water won't empty out

1. **Cause:** Restriction or kink in drain hose or
obstruction in house drainage system.
Remedy: Remove obstruction or straighten drain hose.
If house drainage system is clogged, call plumber.

2. **Cause:** Dishwasher drain outlet clogged.
Remedy: Turn off dishwasher, clean strainer
and drain according to manufacturer's instructions.

Problem: Dishes not clean

1. **Cause:** Water not hot enough.
Remedy: For proper dishwashing, water should be
150° at faucet. Have water-heater thermostat adjusted per
manufacturer's instructions. On portable dish-
washers, allow water to run hot from faucet
before starting dishwasher.

2. **Cause:** Dishes and/or cutlery not properly prepared or loaded.
Remedy: Scrape dishes. Follow manufacturer's
instructions for proper loading.

3. **Cause:** Dishwasher drain clogged.
Remedy: Clean drain and strainer in accordance
with manufacturer's instructions.

Problem: Dishwasher leaks when in operation

1. **Cause:** Wrong type of detergent.
Remedy: Follow manufacturer's instructions on
type and amount of detergent to use. Use dishwasher detergent only.

2. **Cause:** Dishwasher not level.
Remedy: Check position of dishwasher with level.
If not perfectly level, adjust leveling screws
on base. If there are no leveling screws, insert
thin strips of wood under base to bring unit level.

3. **Cause:** Faulty gasket on door.
Remedy: Have gasket replaced.

Problem: Loud noises inside dishwasher when in operation

1. **Cause:** Improper loading or loosely loaded utensils.
Remedy: Follow manufacturer's instructions for loading.

AUTOMATIC CLOTHES WASHER

Problem: Water does not run into washer

1. **Cause:** Faucets not open.
Remedy: Check faucets to be sure they are open.

2. **Cause:** Kink in hose.
Remedy: Straighten hose.

3. **Cause:** Screens stopped up.
Remedy: Remove hose at faucets and/or washer
and clean screens.

Problem: Water to washer is cold

1. **Cause:** Inadequate hot water supply.
Remedy: Do not use hot water for other major purposes while washer is in operation. Or, install an
electric water heater with a larger capacity or an
additional heater to furnish adequate hot water
for all purposes.

2. **Cause:** Water heater thermostat set too low.
Remedy: Have thermostat adjusted per manufacturer's
instructions to obtain 150° temperature at faucet.

3. **Cause:** Hoses reversed.
Remedy: Check hoses; if reversed, switch
to proper position.

1969. Cornell University becomes the site of the first women's studies course. By the
following spring, student demand has swelled course enrollment to lecture-hall
dimensions.

Problem: Water does not drain from washer
1. **Cause:** Kink in discharge hose.
   Remedy: Straighten hose. If this does not eliminate the problem, call serviceman.

Problem: Water leaks on floor
1. **Cause:** Faucet or hose connections loose.
   Remedy: Turn off water faucets and tighten connections. See if mixing valve is cracked.
2. **Cause:** Wrong kind of detergent.
   Remedy: Follow manufacturer's instructions.

Problem: Water pipes vibrate excessively when washing
1. **Cause:** Water hammer in pipes.
   Remedy: Have risers installed in supply lines to absorb shock.

Problem: Washer vibrates when in operation, especially in spin cycle
1. **Cause:** Washer not level.
   Remedy: Check position of washer with level. If not perfectly level, adjust leveling screws or insert thin strips of wood under base to bring unit level.
2. **Cause:** Improper loading.
   Remedy: Follow manufacturer's instructions on proper loading of washer.

Problems: Clothes do not get clean
1. **Cause:** Water not hot enough.
   Remedy: Check temperature of water with a thermometer. It should be 150°. Turn up water-heater thermostat if necessary, per manufacturer's instructions. Avoid laundering right after heavy use of hot water for other purposes.
2. **Cause:** Insufficient detergent.
   Remedy: Follow detergent manufacturer's instructions for recommended amount to use.

Problem: Clothes come out of washer too wet
1. **Cause:** Controls not properly set.
   Remedy: Follow manufacturer's instructions on proper control setting.
2. **Cause:** Washer shut off automatically because of vibration during spin cycle.
   Remedy: Rearrange load to prevent vibration.
3. **Cause:** Not spinning properly at high speed.
   Remedy: Call serviceman.

CLOTHES DRYER
Problem: Dryer does not operate
1. **Cause:** Door not firmly closed.
   Remedy: Reclose door firmly.
2. **Cause:** Controls not properly set.
   Remedy: Check position of controls and adjust to proper setting. Make sure START control has been set.

Problem: Clothes do not dry in proper time
1. **Cause:** Dryer overloaded.
   Remedy: Follow manufacturer's instructions for loading.
2. **Cause:** Lint tray full.
   Remedy: Clean lint tray; empty after each use.
3. **Cause:** Clothes too wet when put in dryer.
   Remedy: Check washer to be sure that spin cycle is operating properly.

Problem: Clothes shrink
1. **Cause:** Controls not set at proper temperature for type of fabric.
   Remedy: Follow manufacturer's instructions on suggested temperatures for various fabrics and do not over-dry.

Problem: Fabrics yellow during drying process
1. **Cause:** Improper washing that has failed to remove oily substance from fabrics or the use of too much detergent — problem not caused by dryer.
   Remedy: Follow manufacturer's instructions on recommended amount of detergent.

WATER HEATER
Problem: Water not hot enough
1. **Cause:** Thermostat on heater set too low.
   Remedy: Have thermostat adjusted per manufacturer's instructions. Avoid using too much hot water at one time.
2. **Cause:** Inoperative element.
   Remedy: Call serviceman.

Problem: Insufficient hot water
1. **Cause:** Thermostat set too low.
   Remedy: Have thermostat adjusted per manufacturer's instructions for water temperature of 140° to 160°.
2. **Cause:** Water heater undersized for present needs.
   Remedy: Replace with larger-capacity water heater or add a second one.
3. **Cause:** Unit too far from faucets, causing water to cool in pipes.
   Remedy: Insulate pipes or relocate heater.

Problem: Hot water costs appear high
1. **Cause:** Thermostat set too high.
   Remedy: Never have thermostat set higher than 160°.
2. **Cause:** Dripping faucets (can waste 300 gallons per month).
   Remedy: Always turn off faucets completely. If they still leak, replace gasket, packing or washer.
3. **Cause:** Unit too far from point of use.
   Remedy: Check manufacturer's directions. Call a plumber if necessary to relocate water heater.

ROOM AIR CONDITIONER
Problem: Fuse or breaker on air-conditioner circuit frequently blows
1. **Cause:** Circuit overloaded.
   Remedy: Remove other electric equipment from air-conditioning circuit. Better yet, have special circuit installed for unit.

Problem: Unit operates but room not cool enough
1. **Cause:** Dirty filter in unit.
   Remedy: Clean or replace filter.
2. **Cause:** Insufficient circuit capacity.
   Remedy: Have separate circuit installed for air conditioner.
3. **Cause:** Bushes or other obstruction interfering with air flow through outdoor portion of unit.
   Remedy: Clear shrubbery or ANY other obstruction at least a foot away from unit.
4. **Cause:** Too much heat buildup before unit is started.
   Remedy: Turn unit on earlier. Keep shades drawn, windows and doors closed to reduce heat load wherever possible. Avoid unnecessary cooking, ironing and other heat-producing activities.
5. **Cause:** Heat or hot-water vapor from kitchen or bathroom coming into room.
   Remedy: Release heat or vapor through windows in kitchen or bathroom, preferably with an exhaust fan. Keep kitchen or bathroom door closed as much as possible.
6. **Cause:** Drapes or furniture blocking front of unit.
   Remedy: Tie back drapes; relocate furniture.
7. **Cause:** Round-the-clock use can cause ice to build on coils and block air flow.
   Remedy: Turn unit off until ice melts.

Problem: Room feels clammy
1. **Cause:** Chores using water (mopping, window-washing, ironing) release moisture faster than unit can remove it.
   Remedy: Whenever possible, schedule such chores for cooler part of the day.
2. **Cause:** Bathroom or kitchen moisture coming into room.
   Remedy: Release moisture through window in bathroom and kitchen, preferably with exhaust fans.

1969. Among those countries reporting such statistics, the United States leads the world in divorce rates, followed by Russia and Hungary.

Homeowner Emergencies

The Editors of *American Home*

No homeowner is a stranger to emergencies. Most of these problems merely disrupt your household operations for a while; a few can bring everything to a halt.

1 **Your roof springs a leak.** If you can get to the underside of your roof, try to trace the drip to its source. Usually this will be a distance away from the drip. Use a flashlight to spot it—or simply look for the daylight shining through. When you find the hole, poke a long, thin wire through it for easy spotting when you're up on the roof. (If you can't get to the underside of your roof, you must go topside to check; you may not find the leak even then, unless it's sizable. To stop leak, use fiber-reinforced asphalt roofing cement on the outside: Dry the area around the hole and smear a thick dab of cement over it. If the hole is large, flatten a piece of sheet metal and shove way up under leaky shingle or tile. Winter leaks are caused by water freezing in gutters, creating ice dams that force water to back up under roofing. Stop this by chopping channels through the dams with an ax.

2 **Water pours into your basement during a storm.** If it's coming through an areaway window, bail and clean out the areaway, then dig a ditch sloping away from it so no more wa-

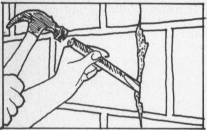

ter will run in. If the water comes through a sloping cellar door over stairs, throw a tarpaulin over the door and repair it later. If the water is coming through a hole in cellar walls or floor, open up the hole with a cold chisel and hammer, making it wider in back than in front. Mix a little quick-setting hydraulic cement with water, mold until it begins to stiffen, then cram it in the hole and hold for 5 minutes.

3 **A winter storm knocks out your electricity.** To protect your home from costly consequences, keep the

*The Day Technology
Fell Down*

heat up as best you can. With a gas-fired warm-air heating system, remove the furnace filters and adjust burner valve to cut flame in half. Check hourly to prevent overheating. If you leave, turn it off. With a gas-fired hot-water or steam system, call the gas company to get precise instructions for adjusting your system; if you can't get the company, turn it off. If heat goes off, hopefully you'll have a fireplace to depend on. Burn wood only; charcoal or briquets give off carbon monoxide. Open curtains to let in the sun; cover windows at night. Plug up all air leaks around windows, doors. Keep faucets slightly open; if the inside temperature dips very far below freezing, shut off the water at the house main; open all faucets and main valve and drain the system. Drain water heater and toilets; pour denatured alcohol into toilet tanks and bowls.

4 **Voltage drops sharply.** Drops that cause lights to dim sharply and appliances to labor can damage your large electrical appliances—refrigerator, freezer, washer, dryer, furnace and boiler, water pump, swimming pool pump. Turn off or unplug all large motors and motor-driven equipment.

By doing this, you protect the motors against a sudden surge of power when the outage ends; if this surge were to hit them when they were on, it would knock them out completely.

5 **Your freezer stops. Don't panic:** Most freezers will keep food frozen for a bare minimum of 24 hours after the power goes off. Try not to open the freezer. To be super safe, get some dry ice and put it in—you need about 3 pounds of ice for each cubic foot of storage space.

6 **A door is locked and you don't have the key.** If the lock is a modern one operated by a key in the knob, you might disengage the latch tongue by inserting a short, thin knife blade into the crack and pushing back the latch tongue. (If you can't get at the crack because you're on the wrong side of the door, pry off the stop—the thin molding strip against which the door bears when closed.) If you can't open the door with a knife, your only quick solution (but one damaging to the trim) is to wedge the thin end of a wrecking bar or heavy chisel in the crack. Push to force the door away from the lock jamb and toward the hinge jamb.

1970. Thousands of women take to the streets in scattered cities throughout America to demonstrate "Women's Strike for Equality" and to observe the fiftieth anniversary of women's suffrage. Three central demands are: equal opportunity in jobs and education,

Why Not Fix Your Car Yourself?

The Editors of *Changing Times*

Tʜᴀᴛ ᴍᴇᴄʜᴀɴɪᴄᴀʟ mélange of wires, hoses and gadgets under the hood of your car looks intimidating, but it needn't be—and therein lies the key to saving money, time and trouble in having your car repaired.

Here is a basic list of chores you can do, starting with the simplest. Even advanced jobs aren't beyond the reach of the average person once he—or she—has learned to raise the hood with confidence.

Air filter. This rests inside that round container that looks like a covered cake pan on top of the engine. The cover is generally held on with wing nuts or clamps that come off easily. Lift out the filter and take a look at it. Most these days are the paper throwaway type. If it is clearly dirty, buy a replacement at prices ranging from about $1.50 to $3. Look also for a small piece of filter material tucked away at the side of the container. This filters fumes being fed back into your engine. It sometimes can be cleaned with kerosene, left to dry and reinstalled. Or you can buy a new one for about 50 cents.

Fuses. When one or more of the electrical appliances on your car refuses to work, the cause may be a burned-out fuse. Manufacturers often hide fuse boxes under the dash, so if your owner's manual doesn't tell you where it is, check with the man at the gas station. Knowing the location and having a spare set of fuses and a fuse puller—total cost about $1.25—can be very handy in an emergency.

Tail and backup lights. On some models you must unscrew the lens covering to replace a burned-out bulb, but on many you just reach inside the trunk, grasp the rubber fitting and twist it either right or left, so that the bulb and socket pull free. Twist the old bulb out and put the new one in the same way. Bulbs cost less than $1 a pair.

Minor lubrication. You can get rid of many of your car's annoying squeaks and rattles and even make some parts work better by doing a little lubrication. A can of silicone spray for about a dollar will work wonders on hinges and catches. Powdered graphite will make door locks work smoothly. Automatic-choke cleaner will help your carburetor work smoothly if you follow the directions on the spray can.

Fluid checks. Periodic checks of the fluid levels in the power steering, automatic transmission and brake master cylinder can save a lot of grief. Your owner's manual may tell you where these are, or you may have to search a bit.

The power steering pump is at the front of the engine. Unscrew the top, and if the level is low and the steering has been making growling noises, you should add fluid.

The automatic transmission dipstick—at the rear of the engine—looks like the engine oil dipstick and has the same "add" and "full" marks on it. Check the transmission fluid level with the engine running at an idle, car in "park" on level ground. You need an inexpensive tool to add this fluid—a funnel with a tube on the end to get the fluid into the tube where the dipstick rests.

The master cylinder is located near the rear of the engine compartment. Wipe all dirt away from the edges of the cover and take it off; many covers are held with a wire clamp, some have a screw top. Fluid should be within a quarter to a half inch of the top. The owner's manual will tell you which types of fluid to use. Do not overfill any of the components.

Headlights. Replacing a burned-out lamp merely in-

Framingham Resources for Equal Education

free twenty-four-hour day-care service, and free abortion on demand. It is the first large-scale protest for women's rights since agitation over the vote fifty years ago, and many mark the birth of modern feminism from this date.

volves buying the right size and taking out a few screws from the trim ring covering the light. You then will see the headlight held in place by a metal retainer ring that usually is secured by three screws. Loosen these and rotate the ring counterclockwise so that you can lift it off. Don't touch the aiming screws or you will have to get the aim readjusted. As you lift out the lamp, you will see that it is plugged into a socket. Unplug the old, plug in the new and reverse your work procedure to put everything back in place. On some cars, those made by General Motors, for instance, the rings are held by springs, which usually can be disengaged with a hook made of coat hanger wire or with a pair of needle nose pliers.

Gas filter. A dirty filter can stop your car from running and mean an expensive trouble call. A new one costs only a dollar or so. Many are in plain sight— a little container clamped into the fuel line running to the carburetor. Some require a brief but worthwhile search. Loosen the clamps and pull out the old filter. This may take some tugging and a little gas may spill, but you can wipe it up later. Install the new filter in the same direction as the old one and make sure the clamps are tight.

PCV valve. A dirty positive crankcase ventilation valve can cause plenty of engine problems. A new one costs about a dollar or two, and once you find its location in your engine it's quickly installed. On four- or six-cylinder engines the PCV valve is usually stuck at the end of a rubber tube that emerges from a rubber fitting atop the valve cover. On V-8's it is often at the end of a tube emerging from the intake manifold, the casting on which the carburetor sits. Some are held by a clip or clamp, others will come out with just a sharp tug. If the tubing appears gummy inside, you should remove it and clean it by running a piece of heavy wire and kerosene through it. Let it dry and replace everything.

Checking and replacing coolant. For a couple of dollars you can buy a four-ball hydrometer, a gadget that measures the strength of your radiator's coolant. Follow the directions on the box, and take the worry out of winter freeze-ups. You can buy antifreeze at sales and add it as your checks show it's needed. And it is far cheaper and often more prudent than waiting until you can get to a gas station.

Replacing hoses. A radiator hose that appears cracked or brittle is existing on borrowed time. You may need a flashlight to see those at the bottom of the engine. To replace a top radiator hose, put a drain pan under the radiator, open the petcock at the bottom with pliers and run off enough coolant to lower the level below the hose. To replace the bottom hose, you must drain all the coolant. If it is still fresh, you can pour it back when you finish.

Take the clamps off the hose and pry the hose off the connecting necks with a screwdriver. Make sure the necks are clean and then slide the new hose on. You can use a thin coat of sealing compound on the necks, but a good clamp usually will hold the hose tightly enough. Buy the metal-band type that tightens with a screw at about 50 cents a pair. Hoses average $1.50 to $2. If the system is dirty and needs flushing, buy a can of radiator flush.

Battery care. Take off the caps on your battery and look inside. Water should just reach the filler rings. with clean water without getting any inside the battery. You can also pull the cable clamps from the terminal posts and scour the inside of the clamps and the terminal posts with a piece of emery paper. Put them back so tightly that you can't move them, and coat the terminals and cable clamps with a nonmetallic grease. Vaseline works well. If the cables are corroded, you can replace them for $1 apiece. A terminal You may need a flashlight to see properly. Never use a match. Unless the local water has a lot of iron in it, you can safely use tap water, although many people prefer to stick with distilled. A plastic squeeze bottle allows neat, quick filling.

The terminal posts should be kept clean. You can remove some of the white deposits with a wire brush, then cover them with a paste of baking soda and water. While this is eating away the deposits, stick toothpicks temporarily in the vent holes on the cell caps, if there are any, so you can wash the mess away

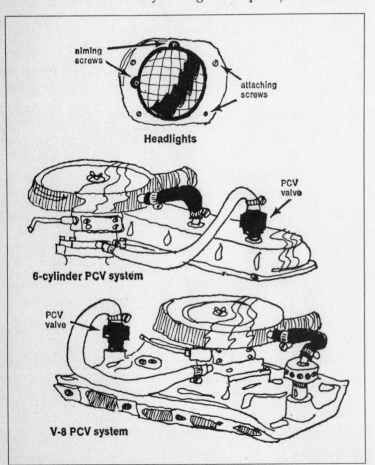

Headlights — aiming screws, attaching screws

6-cylinder PCV system — PCV valve

V-8 PCV system — PCV valve

1970. Diane Crump, competing in the 96th Kentucky Derby, becomes the first woman ever to do so, finishing second to last among eighteen jockeys.

with clean water without getting any inside the battery. You can also pull the cable clamps from the terminal posts and scour the inside of the clamps and the terminal posts with a piece of emery paper. Put them back so tightly that you can't move them, and coat the terminals and the cable clamps with a nonmetallic grease. Vaseline works well. If the cables are corroded, you can replace them for $1 apiece. A terminal lifter tool, for about $3.50, simplifies the job.

Fan and other belts. Every 5,000 to 6,000 miles you should check the belts that run the fan, power steering and air-conditioning. *The engine must be off when you do this.* A loose fan belt can cause overheating; a loose power steering belt can cause an annoying squeal when you turn the wheel. You can test the tension by pressing hard on the belt with your thumb midway between pulleys. The belt should deflect about half an inch if the center-to-center distance between pulleys is 13 to 16 inches. It should deflect a quarter of an inch if the distance is 7 to 10 inches. A more precise method is to use a belt tension gauge, but these are relatively expensive.

Adjusting the tension is not too difficult in many cases. Loosen the holding bolts of the component involved—alternator, power steering pump or the idler pulley for the air-conditioner. Using a pry bar, press the component back to firm up the tension. Tighten the bolts and check the tension. When adjusting the fan belt, press only against the center of the alternator. Pressing on the back portion of the casing may cause damage. Frayed or cracked belts should be replaced—about $1.50 apiece. New belts will stretch a bit almost immediately, so recheck the tension after idling the engine for several minutes. Do not overtighten the belts; this could strain and damage components.

Oil and filter change. This is seldom a neat job, but it is not difficult. Buying at sales, you can often find a good-quality Pennsylvania base oil at prices as low as 50 cents a quart. Filters may be less than $2. You'll also need a wrench to take out the drain bolt on the oil pan and a pan to catch the old oil. For the common screw-on type of oil filter you'll need a filter wrench, which costs less than $2.

Park on a level spot, run the engine briefly to warm the oil, then turn it off and make sure the car is securely braced and braked. Crawl underneath to loosen the drain plug. Have the pan ready to catch the oil and make the final turns with your fingers. Try to keep your arm up and out of the way. When the oil has drained, use your filter wrench to loosen the filter. Drain the old oil from it and throw the filter away. Put the old oil into plastic milk jugs and take it to a gas station for disposal.

Put the drain plug back tightly and, with a clean cloth, wipe the area where the filter fits. With your finger, spread some new engine oil around the gasket of the new filter and screw it on hand tight. Do not use the filter wrench. You can use a cheap funnel to pour the oil into the filler neck—your owner's manual will tell you how much. Run the engine for about five minutes, turn off the engine and check underneath for leaks. Then pull out the dipstick to check the oil level. Remember that a new filter soaks up about a quart of oil.

A Home Mechanic's Toolbox

If you get serious about "shade tree" car repairs, assembling a basic set of tools can be expensive. Sales can save some money but stick to name brands, such as Craftsman, S-K, Mac, Snap-On and Crescent. Good wrenches carry a lifetime guarantee against defects. The tool set below, compiled by a group of working mechanics who teach a repairs course for beginners at Northern Virginia Community College, would total $125 to $150 at a minimum. If you work on foreign cars, as well as domestics, you'll probably also need metric wrenches and sockets.
• Socket and rachet sets in ½", 3/8" and ¼" drive. (Beginners could acquire the heavy ½" drive set later.)
• Combination box/open-end wrenches from 5/16" through 7/8".
• Spark plug sockets in 5/8" and 13/16" to fit a 3/8" drive rachet.
• Screwdrivers: Various sizes from large to stubby in both regular and Phillips head, and a tension-screw holding type.
• Pliers: Regular, water pump and side cutter.
• Hacksaw, ignition wrenches and feeler gauges in wire and blade type.
• Tachometer—dwell meter, timing light, compression gauge and test light.

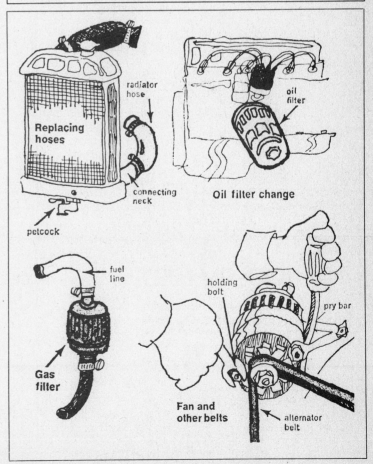

Replacing hoses

radiator hose

connecting neck

petcock

Oil filter change

oil filter

Gas filter

fuel line

Fan and other belts

holding bolt

pry bar

alternator belt

How to Prepare Your Car for Winter

Mort Schultz

Don't wait until the middle of winter to prepare your car for cold weather. The American Automobile Assn. claims that more than 50 million U.S. motorists "Mayday" the association for AAA service trucks to help them get their cars started when temperatures drop below freezing. This represents more than 45 percent of all AAA service calls, and is more than double the rate of calls resulting from flat tires and almost triple the rate of motorists calling to get their stuck cars out of snow and mud.

Prewinter preparation will help you keep your car moving. It will also assure you that your car is safe to meet the foul-weather driving ahead. By doing the work yourself you will save $30 to $50 and can make sure that the job is done right.

TOOLS NEEDED

Cooling-system hydrometer (inexpensive ball-type is adequate)	Battery terminal and post-cleaning tool	Distributor breaker-point feeler gauge
Cooling-system thermometer rated to at least 212°F.	Dwell/tachometer	Ignition wrench set
	Stroboscopic timing light	Ignition point file
Battery hydrometer	Ratchet wrench set with sparkplug socket	Assorted wrenches and pliers
Battery cable puller		Phillips and straight-slotted screwdrivers
Battery carrier strap	Sparkplug-gapping tool	

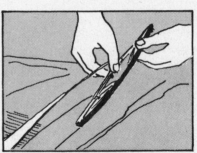

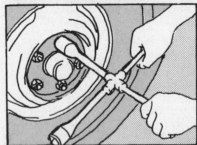

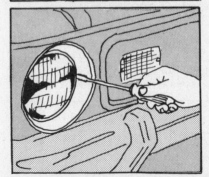

Safety first

■ Check that headlights, parking lights, taillights, stoplights, side-marker lights, backup lights, direction signals and hazard warning flashers are working. Replace burned out bulbs.

■ Replace windshield wiper blades (illustration, left) if rubber isn't firm and resilient or if blades streak glass.

■ Check windshield-washer system. Fill reservoir with 1:1 solution of windshield washer fluid and water. Bend nozzles carefully so they squirt solution at top of the areas swept by blades.

■ Prepare snow tires. Check for cuts, safe tread and correct inflation. Check state laws concerning use of studs and dates. Mount snow tires following correct lug-tightening pattern (illustration left).

■ Road test brakes. They must stop car evenly with no trace of pulling. Uneven braking can cause skidding on slippery roads.

■ Check exhaust system for leaks.

■ Adjust headlights to specification. Use adjusting screws or controls to aim beams horizontally and vertically. Adjustment screws are accessible either through bezel (illustration left) behind lights through engine compartment or when bezel is removed.

■ Prepare a list of, and purchase aids you feel necessary for, your winter driving habits. For example: windshield ice scraper, aerosol deicers and defrosters, compact or fold-up shovel and emergency blanket.

Adapted from *Popular Mechanics*, October 1974. Copyright © 1974 the Hearst Corporation.

1970. The rate of U.S. illegitimate births is 398.7 per thousand, a fourfold increase over the 89.5-per-thousand rate of 1940.

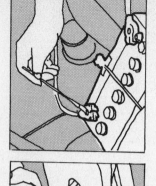

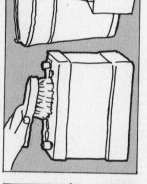

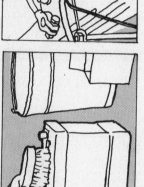

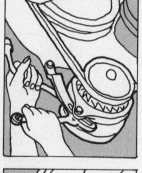

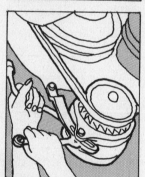

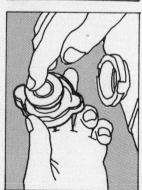

Checking the cooling system

Test coolant with a cooling-system hydrometer. Its strength must be sufficient to protect your engine against the lowest anticipated temperature in your area. If coolant meets requirements but is more than two years old, replace it.

Check the rubber gasket on the radiator cap (above). If it is cracked or has lost pliability, or if the spring is not firm, replace the gasket and/or cap. Squeeze top and bottom radiator hoses, water-pump bypass hose (if there is one) and heater hoses. Replace hoses that show cracks or feel mushy.

Check water pump. Press the drive belt midway between the pulleys. It should give no more than ¼ to ½ inch. To tighten the belt, loosen the alternator adjusting-arm bracket bolt and place a tire iron against the middle of the alternator housing (above). Exert pressure until the belt is taut. Tighten the bolt and recheck tension. Replace a cracked or glazed belt.

With the engine cold, insert a cooling-system thermometer into the radiator filler neck. Let the engine idle. The thermometer should reach 190°-210°F. and stabilize. Squeeze the top radiator hose. You should feel coolant surging. If the thermometer never reaches this temperature range, replace the thermostat by draining the radiator to below the level of the top radiator hose and unbolting the thermostat housing. Replace the gasket if it is damaged.

If there has been a loss of coolant from the radiator during the last few months, inspect the cooling system for leaks with a cooling-system pressure tester. Fit tester to radiator filler neck and

pump its arm to place cooling system under pressure. Leaks will reveal themselves.

If ethylene glycol coolant is two years old, replace it. Remove the radiator cap and open the pet cock at the bottom of the radiator (below). Turn on heater controls and remove engine-block drain plug(s) (below). In-line engines have one drain plug; V8s have two, one on each side of the block. When coolant has drained off completely, tighten the pet cock and reinstall drain plug(s).

Fill radiator with plain water, add a can of fast-flush cleaning solvent and let engine idle 15 to 30 minutes (see instructions on the container). Turn off engine and again drain the system.

With the pet cock open and drain plug(s) removed, insert a garden hose into the radiator filler neck and turn it on to flush the cooling system. Reverse flushing is also desirable. As water is being injected into the radiator, start the engine and let idle for about five minutes. Then remove the hose, tighten the radiator pet cock and reinstall engine drain plug(s).

Pour a solution of high-quality ethylene glycol and water into the radiator. Adequate protection will be afforded to engines in most parts of the country by mixing a 50:50 solution, but if you live in a subzero climate consult your car owner's manual or instruction on the ethylene glycol container for correct mixture. Test coolant with hydrometer after it's in radiator (below).

Replace radiator-pressure cap, start engine and let it idle. Check for leaks at pet cock and drain plug(s). Continue to check system for leaks for a few days to ensure that all is well.

Cleaning the battery

It doesn't take much corrosion and dirt to prevent delivery of maximum current needed to start an engine in cold weather when maximum cranking power is required. Turn off the ignition switch and all accessories, and disconnect battery cables (ground cable first). Use a battery cable puller. Don't use screwdriver, hammer or pliers—you may damage the battery.

Take the battery from the car with a battery carrier strap and place it on a wooden plank. Tighten all vent caps and cover them with small strips of masking tape to keep cleaning solution from leaking through the vent holes into the battery and neutralizing the acid.

Mix a solution of baking soda and water, and wash the top, sides and bottom of the battery

(above). Then flush thoroughly with water. Repeat this cleaning procedure until a fresh application of solution no longer fizzes when applied. Clean the battery holder in the car in the same way.

Wipe battery cables with a dry rag. Replace the cables if internal wiring shows or if insulation is brittle and cracked. Clean terminals with a battery terminal cleaning tool until bright (above).

Place the battery back into the car and reconnect cables (positive cable first). Connections must be tight. Apply a thin coat of petroleum jelly to terminals and battery posts (above). Finally, bring battery water up to the rings in the bottom of the filler wells. Use drinking water or, better yet, distilled water or rainwater that you have caught in a plastic container.

Testing the battery

A fully charged battery in winter is a must. That's because its capacity lowers as the temperature goes down. When the temperature drops to 32°F., your battery produces only 60 percent of its rated capacity. At 0°F., only 46 percent of capacity is available. Test the battery (but never immediately after adding water) one cell at a time by drawing electrolyte into a battery hydrometer (left). Note readings and return acid to the cell from which it was drawn.

It's generally not necessary, but for a very accurate reading, compensate for the temperature of electrolyte since specific gravity varies with temperature. Some hydrometers have built-in temperature correction scales. With others, you have to insert a thermometer into the battery's center cell, read the temperature and correct the reading.

A battery with a corrected average specific gravity reading of 1.250 or less should be charged. A fully charged battery has an average specific gravity reading of 1.260 or more.

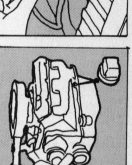

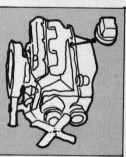

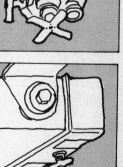

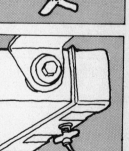

1971. Pat Palinkas, a young schoolteacher, becomes the first woman to play professional football. On her first play she is hit by a 235-pound linebacker, who claims he was trying to "break her neck" for her "making folly with a man's game."

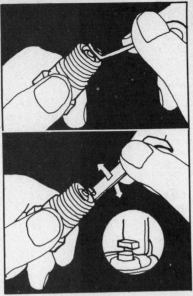
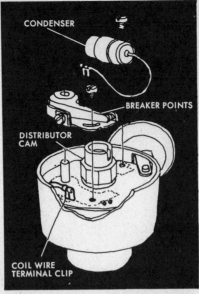

CONDENSER

BREAKER POINTS

DISTRIBUTOR CAM

COIL WIRE TERMINAL CLIP

Tuning the engine *

An engine in a poor state of tune may start now, but won't when the temperature drops. A tune-up, which consists of the following, will assure that your engine always starts—even on coldest days.

Replace worn or damaged sparkplugs. Good sparkplugs can be cleaned by removing deposits from between electrodes with a wire brush and lightly filling electrodes with an ignition point file until square and bright. All sparkplugs, new or old, must be adjusted to specification, which can be obtained from the owner's manual or the tune-up decal mounted in the engine compartment. Bend the side electrode to gap plugs (left). They are adjusted properly when the specified gauge passes smoothly between electrodes with minimum resistance (left, top).

Examine distributor components (left). If breaker points are badly pitted or eroded, replace them. If points are still usable, clean them by passing the ignition point file between them once or twice; then wipe them with a cloth dampened in mineral spirits. Gap points to specification by inserting the proper-size feeler gauge between them. Slide gauge back and forth. You should feel slight friction. To adjust points, insert a screwdriver in notch or slot near the mounting screw, loosen screw and twist. Or insert an Allen wrench in the hole in adjustment screw and turn. It depends on the type of distributor.

Inspect distributor cap and rotor. Replace a cracked distributor cap or rotor and ignition wires that are damaged.

Be sure you have the right oil in your crankcase to meet the lowest anticipated temperature in your area. Above 0°F., you can use SAE 10W-30 or SAE 10W-40. Below 0°F., use SAE 5W-20 or SAE 5W-30; while using this oil you should avoid sustained high-speed driving.

A complete tune-up involves more than the above. For more details, consult your car manufacturer's manual.

Troubleshooting Common Engine Problems

The Editors of *Popular Science*

Symptom	Compression or manifold system	Carburetor or fuel system	Ignition or electrical system
1. Hard starting	Manifold leak Burned or sticky valves	Inoperative choke Flooding	Worn points Defective condenser Burned or cracked cap or rotor Weak coil Burned coil tower Bad ignition cables Worn plugs Faulty starter Weak battery Faulty generator or regulator Improper timing
2. Rough idle	Manifold leak Burned or sticky valves Stuck heat-riser valve	Inoperative choke Flooding Improper idle adjustment Leaking gaskets Worn fuel pump	Worn points Burned or cracked cap or rotor Leaking vacuum advance Burned coil tower Bad ignition cables Worn plugs Improper timing
3. Poor gas mileage	Restricted air cleaner Burned or sticky valves Stuck heat-riser valve	Inoperative choke Flooding Leaking gaskets High pump pressure	Worn points Leaking vacuum advance Inoperative mechanical advance Weak coil Wrong polarity Worn plugs Improper timing
4. Engine misses	Manifold leak Exhaust system restricted Burned or sticky valves	Flooding Worn fuel pump	Worn points Defective condenser Burned or cracked cap or rotor Leaking vacuum advance Weak coil Burned coil tower Wrong polarity Bad ignition cables Worn plugs
5. Engine lacks top speed	Exhaust system restricted Air cleaner restricted Burned or sticky valves Stuck heat-riser valve	Improperly adjusted throttle linkage Low pressure	Worn points Burned or cracked cap and/or rotor Leaking vacuum advance Inoperative mechanical advance Weak coil Wrong polarity Worn plugs Improper timing
6. Engine sluggish	Stuck heat-riser valve	Inoperative choke	Worn points Leaking vacuum advance Inoperative mechanical advance Wrong polarity Worn plugs Improper timing
7. Engine ping		Improper fuel grade	Improper timing
8. Engine dies	Manifold leak	Inoperative choke Flooding Improper idle adjustment Leaking gaskets	Worn points Improper timing
9. Hesitation	Stuck heat-riser valve	Inoperative choke Leaking gaskets Worn accelerator pump	Worn points Leaking vacuum advance Inoperative mechanical advance

1971. The U.S. House of Representatives approves an Equal Rights Amendment to the Constitution that is meant to guarantee equal rights for women under law. The measure now goes to the Senate.

Quick Solutions to Six Car Dilemmas

The Editors of *Reader's Digest*

Starting difficulties

If your car refuses to start, but the battery has enough power to crank the engine, you may not be using the correct starting procedure. For most cars, starting the engine when it is cold requires that you depress the accelerator to the floor and then release it. Turn on the ignition and attempt to start the car; the engine should come to life. If it doesn't, pump the accelerator two or three times, then try

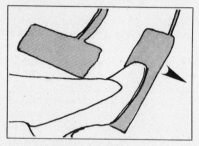

For sure starts, depress accelerator fully to floor and release before engaging starter.

starting. If the car is properly tuned, and the weather is not extremely cold or damp, this procedure will ensure smooth starts. If for some reason you have tried pumping the accelerator several times and there is a faint odor of gasoline, you may have flooded the engine. This simply means that too much gasoline has gone into the engine as a result of your pumping. The best solution for this is to wait two or three minutes, then depress the accelerator all the way to the floor and hold it there while you turn on the ignition and engage the starter. If this fails to start the engine, there is probably some mechanical difficulty.

Damp-weather starts. A well-tuned engine should not present starting problems in damp weather. If the car has been sitting out in the rain for several days, however, you may have difficulty getting it going. If the engine has not come to life after several attempts, do not persist in trying until the battery is too weak to

crank the engine. The wiring under the hood is probably laden with condensation, causing the spark to short circuit. You can usually remedy this by wiping the spark plug wires with a dry rag. If possible, direct the rays of a heat lamp at the distributor cap. This cap is a round, usually black, plastic cylinder from which numerous wires lead out to the spark plugs. It is usually located in plain view at the rear, front, or side of the engine.

After about 15 or 20 minutes the heat from the lamp should have dried the moisture inside the cap sufficiently for the car to start.

Cold-weather starts. If the temperature has been close to freezing for several hours, your car may be difficult to start. Be sure to depress the accelerator to the floor and release it at least twice under such conditions, then switch on the ignition and engage the starter. At first the engine will turn over sluggishly and slowly pick up momentum. Wait for a minute or two between starting attempts. This will give the battery a chance to rebuild its power. Try four or five times,

Distributor cap is a plastic cylinder with wires leading to the spark plugs. If cap is moisture laden in damp weather, it could be the cause of engine-starting problems.

but no more unless the engine is showing some signs of life. To try more would only run the battery down. Call for a service truck. If none is available, you might try removing the battery from the car and taking it indoors if the outside

temperature is extremely low. At temperatures below zero batteries lose up to 75 percent of their power. An hour or two of warmth will allow battery power to build up, often sufficiently to get the car started.

Battery removal is not very difficult. Use an adjustable wrench to remove the two nuts that hold the metal battery frame. Then remove the positive (+) cable and the negative (−) cable. Do not place the battery in an oven or atop a stove. It could explode.

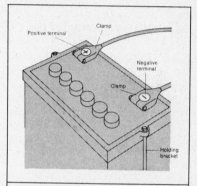

To remove the battery from the car, first unscrew the two nuts on the hold-down arms. Then remove the clamps on the battery terminals. You will need a wrench for this on some cars; others have spring-type clamps requiring only a pair of pliers. When replacing the battery, be certain that the cables are placed on the same terminals they were removed from.

When replacing a battery, be sure that positive and negative cables are attached to the correct terminals. This is easy to tell since all battery terminals are marked with a plus or a minus symbol.

There are other tricks for cold-weather starts. Chemical preparations in aerosol cans, for example, can be sprayed into the air intake unit that sits on top of the engine. Be sure to follow the spray manufacturer's instructions to the letter since these sprays are highly flammable.

Having your car pushed by another is one way of getting it started, but this is not recommended if your car has an automatic transmission. Also, it is not recommended unless the roads are free of snow and ice.

1971. More than two hundred women gather in Washington, D.C., this July to organize the National Women's Political Caucus (NWPC) in an effort to equip the women's rights movement with independent political power. NWPC issues a declaration of its opposition to "sexism, racism, violence and poverty."

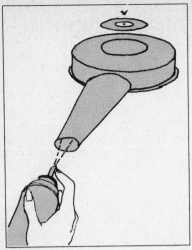

Chemical preparations in aerosol cans are designed to be sprayed into the car's air cleaner. Spray two or three short bursts into the mouth of the cleaner's air intake. The air cleaner is located atop the engine.

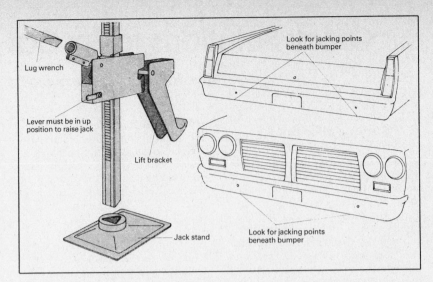

Lug wrench

Lever must be in up position to raise jack

Lift bracket

Jack stand

Look for jacking points beneath bumper

Look for jacking points beneath bumper

The jack is stored disassembled in the trunk of your car. To jack up the car, fit the pieces together as shown. Place the jack under the car bumper only at designated jacking points. These are usually indicated by slots or holes in the underside of the bumper.

What to do for a flat tire

Make certain that the car you are driving is equipped with a proper jack and a lug wrench to remove the nuts that hold the wheel onto the axle. A good safety idea is to carry in the trunk two large blocks of wood about the size of a brick to keep the car from rolling when it is jacked up. It is wise to carry an 8-inch-square piece of ¾-inch plywood as well; this can be placed under the jack if you have to raise the car while it is resting in mud or on sand.

Since you might have a flat tire anytime, anywhere, make sure that the spare tire is kept inflated to the proper pressure.

It is a good idea to keep work gloves and coveralls (paper ones are available) in the trunk. And a drop cloth or large sheet of plastic or even some old newspapers may come in handy.

Most cars are equipped with jacks that must be assembled a specific way to jack up the car. Often the jack assembly for raising the car at the front bumper is different from that required for raising the rear of the car. Familiarize yourself with the jack assembly and jacking procedure for the car you drive. The owner's manual is not always clear enough to help; and although some cars have jacking instruction labels in the trunk, they often get torn off.

Every car has its specific jacking points located on the chassis or somewhere along the bumper. If the instructions that come with your car aren't clear, have someone who knows explain and demonstrate the jacking procedure. It is a good idea to practice a tire change once or twice until you get the hang of it.

ACTION:
If a tire goes flat while you are on the highway, pull well off the road. Have anyone in the car stand away from the car and off the road. Small children are safer remaining still in the rear seat of the car. Switch on the emergency flashers. Turn off the ignition. Apply the parking brake. Leave the car in gear if it has a standard transmission (stick shift). Put the transmission selector in "park" if the vehicle has an automatic transmission. If you have a safety flare or similar warning device, set it up on the road at least 100 feet behind you.

Remove the jack and the spare tire from the trunk. Wedge a large

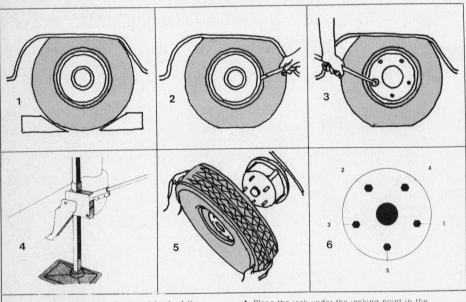

1. First, place chocks in front and back of the wheels on the opposite end of the car from the flat tire. Rocks will do.

2. Remove the jack and spare tire from the trunk of car. Use the lug wrench to pry the wheel cover off the wheel.

3. Loosen the lug nuts with the lug wrench. On most cars, the nuts must be turned counterclockwise. Loosen the nuts, but do not remove.

4. Place the jack under the jacking point in the bumper. Make sure the jack base is on firm, even ground. Jack car until wheel lifts.

5. Make sure the car is stable on the jack. Remove lug nuts and place them in wheel cover. Lift the wheel off. Replace with spare.

6. Follow the above sequence of numbers to tighten the wheel nuts. This will ensure that the wheel seats properly.

1971. Chi Cheng, a Taiwanese runner training in Los Angeles, breaks five female world dash and hurdle records within a six-month period.

block of wood or a stone under the wheels of the car at the end opposite the one that will be raised. Use the flat end of the lug wrench to pry the wheel cover or hubcap off the wheel with the flat tire.

Fit the lug wrench firmly over one of the wheel nuts. These nuts are usually very tight. On most cars they must be turned counterclockwise to be removed. If you can't budge them using all your strength, try standing on extension arm of the wrench. Loosen all the nuts two or three turns only. Do not remove them.

Assemble the jack and fit it under the jacking point of the car. Raise the car until the flat tire is off the ground, leaving several inches' clearance. Try shaking the car gently to make sure that it is firmly on the jack. If the jack begins to sway or angle off to one side, lower the car, reposition the jack, and raise the car again.

Remove the nuts. Drop them into the wheel cover for safe keeping. Pull the wheel off and roll it behind the car. Line up the spare wheel so that the holes are in approximately the same position as the studs on the wheel hub of the car. Lift the wheel onto the studs. Replace the nuts so that they are all finger-tight. Lower the car until the fresh tire is just resting on the ground but not carrying the full weight of the car. Tighten the nuts with the lug wrench. Lower the car completely and tighten the nuts with as much force as possible.

Do not waste time on the roadside. Place the flat tire and jack assembly in the trunk. To avoid wasting time at the roadside, it is safer to put the wheel cover in the trunk and put it on the wheel later. Remove the blocks from the wheels before driving away. Stop at the nearest service station and have the wheel nuts checked to be sure they are fully tightened. Also, have the condition of the newly mounted tire checked. Make sure that the air pressure in it is equal to that of the tire on the opposite side of the car. If you are on a trip, it would be safer to have the flat tire repaired immediately.

Running out of gas

It is not good under any circumstances to allow the gasoline level to get too low in the tank. Rust and sediment in the tank bottom can be drawn into the fuel line where it can cause blockage. In addition, condensation that forms on the inside of an empty tank mixes with the gasoline and can cause the engine to falter or run erratically. In below-freezing temperatures the condensation forms more rapidly and can result in a frozen fuel line. Symptoms of running out of gas, whether caused by an empty tank or a frozen fuel line, are similar: The car will be running smoothly, then suddenly it will begin to hesitate, come to life again, and cough erratically. If this starts to happen while you are driving on a major highway, pull well off the road at the first sign of trouble.

ACTION:
Turn on the emergency flashers. Check the fuel gauge to see if it registers "empty." Flick it with your finger to be sure that the needle is not stuck. In many cars the gauge does not register unless the ignition is on. If the gauge does not read "empty," remove the gas tank cap and rock the car; you should be able to hear gas sloshing around.

If the tank is empty, lock the car but leave the emergency flashers on. If you are on a limited-access highway, stay safely off the road and wait for help from the highway patrol. On other roads walk to or telephone the nearest service station. A gallon of gas is generally enough to get you to the nearest gas pump. It is a good idea to carry an empty gallon container and a suitable funnel in your trunk for such emergencies. Gas stations do not always have containers available. If the filler neck of your fuel tank is hard to get at—if, for example, it is behind the license plate —a funnel with a flexible spout is a must for your trunk's safety equipment.

When you return to the car, pour all but a cupful of the gasoline into the tank. Try starting the engine. Let it crank over several times; stop for a moment, then try again. If the battery seems to be weakening, stop cranking the engine. You will have to prime the carburetor. Do this by lifting the hood and removing the air cleaner top (above). This is accomplished by unscrewing the wing nut and lifting off the cleaner's disk-like lid. On some cars you can easily lift out the entire filter unit. Pour about a quarter of the remaining gasoline into the car-

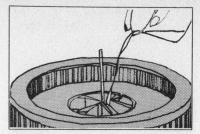

To prime a carburetor after you have run out of gas, pour about ¼ cup of gasoline directly into the throat of the carburetor. To do this, first remove the air cleaner unit.

buretor opening. Replace the air cleaner and try starting the engine. It will probably take several seconds of cranking before the engine comes to life. Once it does, it will probably die again almost immediately. This is because the fuel pump, which works only when the engine is running, has not had time to pump fuel from the tank into the carburetor. (This is not a problem for many foreign cars that are equipped with electrical fuel pumps.) At this point, remove the air cleaner top again and prime the carburetor once more with the remaining gas. Replace the air cleaner top and start the engine once more. It should keep running this time. Let it run for a minute or so before pulling back onto the highway.

Frozen fuel line. If the temperature is below freezing, and you have ascertained that there is gasoline in the tank, try starting the car again. It may catch and falter again, or it may not start at all. Under these conditions the problem is most likely an accumulation of water that has frozen in the fuel line. In extremely cold weather the solution is to get the car into a heated garage until it thaws out. Buy some gas line anti-freeze ("dry gas") and pour it into the tank. If this product is not available, two tablespoons of alcohol in the tank will absorb moisture and avert future freeze-ups.

Some gasolines contain moisture-absorbent additives. If your fuel line tends to freeze up easily, try filling your tank with a gasoline that promises to prevent fuel-line freeze.

Radiator boils over

Driving in heavy traffic during warm weather may cause the engine of your car to overheat. This is especially true in city driving where there is a lot of stop-and-go

1971. Teresa Levitin, a researcher at the University of Michigan, releases a study that shows that the average American woman worker would require a raise of 71 percent to match the pay of a similarly qualified and employed man.

traffic. Whenever you are in such a situation, watch the water temperature gauge, if your car is so equipped. Otherwise, be alert for the red light on the dashboard that warns of overheating.

You can avoid an overheated engine by taking the following steps. Turn off the car's air conditioner. Every time you stop, slip the transmission into neutral and race the engine; this will make the fan turn faster, drawing more cooling air through the radiator. Pull off the road and race the engine for a few minutes, or turn the engine off and leave the car hood raised; give it at least half an hour to cool.

If an engine overheats under normal driving conditions, there is probably a mechanical problem. The coolant level may be low; perhaps there is a leak in one of the radiator hoses, or the fan belt may have broken. Usually, a broken fan belt will be evident long before the engine overheats. The fan belt also drives the car's alternator or generator; if the belt breaks, the ignition warning light will flash on. If this happens, it is still safe to drive at least a mile or so to the nearest service station for repairs.

If the engine does overheat, the coolant will boil in the radiator. Pressure builds up, and the boiling coolant escapes in the form of steam that billows from under the hood. If this happens, pull off the road and turn off the engine. Lift the hood but do not touch the radiator cap.

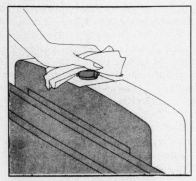

Protect your hand with a rag when releasing the cap of a boiled-over radiator. Turn the cap part way and let the steam escape before removing it completely.

ACTION:
Wait until the bubbling and steam have subsided, then wrap a rag around your hand and carefully turn the radiator cap counterclockwise. Twist it half a turn only. If

more steam shoots out, let go of the cap and back away until the steam subsides. Then remove the cap completely.

Before driving again, you will have to fill the radiator with water. Before adding water, allow the engine to cool for 40 to 60 minutes. Adding cold water to a hot engine could result in serious mechanical damage. Check the various hoses and connections under the hood for signs of obvious leaks that might have caused the trouble. If a hose is damaged, it will have to be replaced; but even with a hose leak, you can probably make it to the nearest service station with a fresh supply of water. Refill the radiator slowly. Once it is approximately half full, start the engine. Continue to add water until it is about 1 inch below the neck of the filler tube. Replace the cap.

Frozen door locks

An immediate freeze following rain or wet snow can cause trapped water to freeze in car door locks. Similarly, locks will freeze if you have the car washed during below-freezing weather. After going through the car wash, avoid locking the doors for several hours. Also, wipe around the rubber door seals with a dry towel. This will keep doors from freezing shut.

Many people who have to leave their cars outdoors in winter, keep a small container of lock deicer taped underneath the hood. Be sure to store aerosol deicers away from areas subject to engine heat. If your door locks are frozen and no deicer is available, try one of the following suggestions.

ACTION:
First, be sure to try all the doors. One of them may not be frozen. If the car has been sitting in the wind, start working on the door that is away from the wind.

Heat the key with a flame from a match or a lighter, then insert it into the lock.

Often body warmth will ease the ice enough to free the lock. Lean against the car or blow warm breath onto the lock.

The ultimate solution is to pour boiling water down the side of the car door. Once you get into the vehicle, avoid opening other frozen doors until the car has had a

chance to warm up. Otherwise, you may not be able to close them properly.

Keys locked in car

Some cars can be locked while the keys are inside. If your car is one of these, consider taping a key in a hidden location under the hood.

ACTION:
If you do not have a spare key conveniently nearby, a wire coat hanger can be a great help. First, make sure that all doors are indeed locked. Next, check for any windows that may be open just a fraction. If the windows are tightly closed, and the car is locked, you will have to use the hanger. Straighten it out but leave a rounded hook at one end. Force the hanger between the car window and the rubber molding. Work the hanger down to the door lock and try to engage the hooked end of the hanger over the lock button. It will take patience, but eventually you will be able to pull the lock button up.

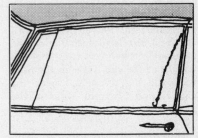

A hooked length of wire (straightened coat hanger) can be wedged between the rubber seal and the window to unlock the car in the event that the key gets locked inside. This method is effective only on cars that have no center posts.

If your car has no space between window glass and the rubber molding, the alternatives are to call a lock specialist or break a window.

The easiest window to force in most cars is the side vent window. Try putting pressure on the forward part. This will generally break the lock mechanism, and you can reach in to unlock the door.

If you must break a large area of glass to get into the car, choose a window that will not cause inconvenience while you are driving. Usually, a sharp blow with a hammer or a rock will open a large enough hole for you to get a hand in and reach the lock.

If Your Battery Goes Dead

Before the development of automatic transmissions for automobiles, failure of a battery meant asking a friendly neighbor or a passing motorist for a push. But with many of today's cars, if the battery is dead the car cannot be started by towing or pushing with the engine in gear. Consequently, the "jumper cable" is now a common emergency accessory. With it, you can borrow power from the battery of the friendly neighbor or passing motorist and start your car. Unfortunately, many people do not understand how to use jumper cables or how damaging they can be if improperly used.*

Adapted from *Automobile Batteries,* 1971, General Services Administration.

How to Use Jumper Cables

Before you attempt to connect jumper cables, there are several precautions which should be taken:

● In very cold weather, check the battery to see if the electrolyte is frozen. Do not use jumper cables if the electrolyte is frozen—you may damage the battery beyond repair!

● Check to see that both the booster battery and the rundown battery have the same voltage — six-volt or 12-volt.

● Turn all accessory switches and the ignition key to the OFF position.

● Place the gearshift or gear selector in the NEUTRAL or PARK position.

● Remove vent caps from both the booster battery and your rundown battery. This will release any accumulated gases.

Now follow the procedure outlined in the pictures, left, in the exact sequence shown.

A. On rundown battery, find terminal connected to starter switch or solenoid. Note if positive or negative. Then (step 1) clip one end of jumper cable to like marked terminal of booster battery.

B. Clip the other end of the same jumper cable (step 2) to the terminal of the rundown battery having the same marking; that is, *positive* to *positive* or *negative* to *negative.*

C. Connect one end of the second jumper cable (step 3) to the other terminal of the booster battery. The other end of this cable (step 4) should be fastened securely to the bumper or engine block of the car with the rundown battery

D. Engage the starter of your car. If it does not start immediately, it is well to start the engine of the other car to avoid excessive drain on the booster battery.

E. Restore the cell caps to both batteries after your car starts and is running normally.

F. Remove the ground connection from the bumper or engine block of your car.

G. Remove the other end of the cable from the booster battery.

H. Remove the other cable first from your car; then the other end from the booster battery.

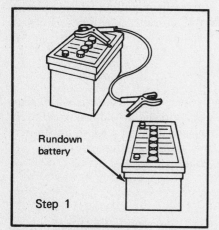

Rundown battery

Step 1

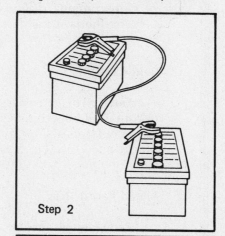

Step 2

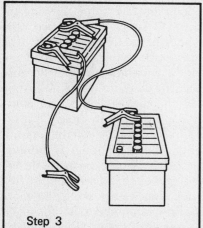

Step 3

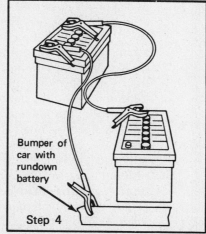

Bumper of car with rundown battery

Step 4

Be sure that the positive terminal marked (POS), (P), or (+) of one battery is connected to the positve terminal of the other; and that the negative terminal marked (NEG), (N), or (-) is connected to the negative terminal of the other. Connection of a positive terminal to a negative terminal may result in alternator damage or a possible explosion! Sparks given off by the short circuit of an incorrect jumper cable connection may ignite the inflammable gases normally found near battery vents. The explosion, which can occur in either the charger battery or the rundown battery, may rupture the battery case and splatter electrolyte acid.

There's no danger of getting a shock, even if you deliberately touch both battery terminals with your fingers.

1972. Congress passes the Equal Opportunity Employment Act, which outlines sex-discrimination guidelines for the employer in detail. For instance, under the act fringe benefits available from employers and unions must be identical for both men and women, and women with disabilities related to their pregnancies must be treated like any employee with a temporary disability.

BEFORE you buy a replacement battery.

1. Be sure you need one. Have the old battery checked by your service station or battery dealer to ensure that the run-down condition is not due to a loose connection, corrosion, or other correctible cause.

2. Be sure that the new battery has an electrical rating at least equal to your old battery, and fits the hold-down brackets and battery tray.

3. Compare prices, ratings and warranties. You will find substantial differences in batteries of the same size. Be sure the warranty is in writing and dated.

4. Be wary of bargain batteries—they may be low in both capacity and quality. As in most everything else, you get about what you pay for.

5. If your car came equipped with a six-cell, 12-volt battery, replace it with a six-cell, 12-volt battery. Similarly, replace a three-cell, 6-volt battery with another three-cell, 6-volt battery. They are NOT interchangeable.

AFTER you buy a replacement battery.

1. Keep the engine tuned to avoid excessive drain on the battery.

2. Keep lights and accessories off when starting the car.

3. Keep the battery clean and free of corrosion, including the case, terminals, vent caps, cable clamps and hold-downs.

4. Check cable clamps periodically to ensure that they are tight and free from corrosion. If slow starting or non-starting is encountered, remove cable clamps from battery posts; scrape or brush the battery posts and the inside of cable clamps until bright and shiny; then reinstall clamps to the battery posts. This should solve well over half of the starting problems encountered in early battery life.

5. Check the water (electrolyte) at regular intervals, especially in hot weather. If you need water too often, have the alternator and voltage regulator checked—they may be overcharging.

6. Use the proper weight motor oil to avoid excessive battery discharge while starting.

7. Have the battery checked periodically when it is getting old, whenever the engine appears balky in starting, and especially before arrival of cold weather.

Tires:
Materials, Types, and Maintenance
Dorothy Jackson

The three tire types we will discuss are: bias ply, belted bias ply and belted radial tires. The plies make up the structure of a tire and they are layers of rayon, nylon, polyester or steel cords beneath the tread and inside the rubber sidewalls. When you hear of a two or four ply tire, it only means the number of these plies (no matter what the material) beneath the tread.

Bias Ply

If you look at this type of tire head-on and could see beneath the tread, you would see a layer of cords running diagonally down from left to right and on top of that layer would be another layer of cords running diagonally down from right to left. By crisscrossing the layers and cords, the strength of the tire is greatly increased.

Belted Bias Ply

This type of tire construction uses the same crisscrossing layers of cords, but between these layers and the actual tire tread there are more layers of finer cords running around the circumference, or "belting" the tire. Doing this minimizes tire squirming and keeps the tread flatter on the road.

Belted Radial Tires

Radial design tires also use layers or plies of cords but instead of diagonally crisscrossing each other, the layers run from side-to-side or across the tire. Then, beneath these layers at least two more layers run around the circumference of the tire, or "belt" it. The advantage here is that the tread is much firmer on the road and squirms less even though the sidewalls are more flexible. Because the tread is firm and the sidewalls flexible, the radial tire often looks soft or slightly flat even with the correct air pressure. Don't be alarmed, this is the way they are supposed to look.

Most professionals and consumers will agree that the superior tire is steel belted and radial design. The radial design is stronger, safer and lasts longer and the steel belts make it extremely safe and resistant to early wear. Although steel belted radials are quite a bit more expensive than other types, they can prove to be more economical in the long run. Most are guaranteed to last for 40,000 miles or about twice as long as polyester belted tires; they are almost impervious to blowouts and punctures and because of their tread design they eliminate the need for snow tires in all but severe winter areas.

Now that you know the differences among tires, don't make the mistake of mixing different designs and sizes on the same car. All four tires on any car should be the same size and radials should *never* be mixed with other tire types.

1972. Though the Census Bureau reports that the number of American poor families has decreased 4 percent in the past decade, the amount of poor families headed by a woman has increased 4.6 percent.

Pressure

Do not exceed the maximum pressure rating on the sidewall of your tires.

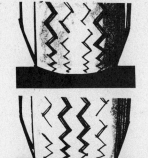

If you habitually drive with air pressures far from normal, your tires will give you warning, as follows:

- Excessive wear on the center of the tread and a "hard" ride indicate too much pressure; and
- Excessive wear on the outside of the tread, a "mushy" ride, and a tendency for tires to "squeal" on corners indicate too little pressure.

Mixing Tire Types

For better handling mount the bias tires on the front, and the belted bias on the rear.

Do not mix radials with other tires unless the tire manufacturer specifically recommends it. For optimum handling, use tires of the same type all around.

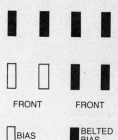

FRONT   FRONT

☐ BIAS TIRE   ■ BELTED BIAS TIRE

Out of Balance

If tires are not balanced properly the wheels vibrate, and tire wear is increased. Balance all four tires, particularly if your car has an independently sprung suspension. If in doubt, seek expert advice.

Worn wheel bearings, worn shock absorbers, loose tie rods or wobbly wheels cause vibration and various types of uneven and excessive wear. **When you notice uneven or excessive wear on one or more tires, take the car in for inspection. The chances are it is in need of service.**

Rotation

In normal city driving, cornering tends to wear the front tires more than the back; in turnpike driving, the rear tires tend to wear more. Frontwheel drive cars, of course, show more wear on the front tires in turnpike driving. Rotation distributes the wear more evenly.

Five tire rotation, including the spare, at 5,000 mile intervals is good economics, as well as good safety practice.

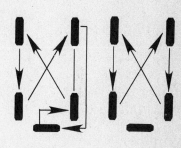

Alignment

This is the angle of the wheel in relation to the direction of travel—just like your feet in relation to the direction you are walking.

TOE-IN - TOE-OUT Too much toe-in produces a feathered edge on the **inside** of the tread design; too much toe-out produces a feathered edge on the **outside** of the tread design.

Camber

This is the angle the wheel makes with the surface of the road. The wrong camber angle causes excessive **even** wear on one or the other side of the tread, depending on the way the wheel leans.

The backward tilt of the axle structure can also cause trouble. Too little tilt can result in poor handling and spotty wear. Unequal tilt can cause one tire to pull, resulting in uneven wear on one tire.

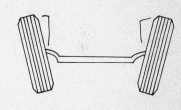

Tread Depth

Modern tires have built-in wear indicators which appear as smooth narrow bands across the face of the tire when the tread depth gets down to 1/16th inch. Beyond this point the tire may be extremely dangerous, particularly on wet roads.

If a tire wears unevenly so that **any considerable portion** of the tread is below the 1/16th inch minimum, the tire should be replaced, and the cause of the uneven wear corrected.

Adapted from *Tires: Their Selection and Care,* 1970, Department of Commerce.

Grabby Brakes

Poorly adjusted brakes cause tires to wear unevenly; out-of-round brake drums can be the cause of excessive wear in a single spot.

Pocket Gauge

To be sure that you are maintaining the correct, safe pressure in your tires, buy a good pocket gage at an auto supply store and see that it is used to check your tires at least once a month.

HAND GAGE ACCURACY

35% DIFFERED BY LESS THAN 0.5psi*

75% DIFFERED BY LESS THAN 1.5psi*

90% DIFFERED BY LESS THAN 2.5psi*

97% DIFFERED BY LESS THAN 3.5psi*

*Pounds per square inch

1972. Twenty percent of this year's entering American medical school students are women, up from 1971's 13.5 percent. Twelve percent of the nation's first-year law students are also women, compared to 4.6 percent in 1967.

Corrosion—at first just a tiny speck, then a tiny hole, then. . .if it isn't checked it just continues spreading. When it reaches the advanced stages shown here, where holes are eaten through sheet metal and edges have fallen away, the only solution is to replace the missing metal either with more metal or with fiberglass. Rocker panels, which until about 10 years ago were a serious problem, are much less prone to corrode now because they are made of galvanized steel, like many other parts.

Paul C. Cabot III

If Your Car Rusts Out, It's Your Fault

The Editors of *Popular Science*

What can you do to keep your car corrosion-free?

● Wash your car frequently. And wash the underbody, too. If you use an automatic car wash, make sure it sprays the underbody, not just the top and sides.

● If you use a car wash, make sure that recycled water isn't used. It contains salt, acids, oil, or whatever else that people before you have washed from their cars.

● Don't wash or steam clean your car when the temperature is below freezing. Ice remains in cracks and crevices.

● Give immediate first-aid to scratches. Scratches left unpainted can eventually become corroded holes in the sheet metal.

Adapted from *Popular Science*, May 1975. Copyright © 1975 Popular Science. Reprinted by permission of the Edward Haggerty Publishing Co.

● Make sure all drain holes are open. Find out where these holes are (by checking a body manual for your car, or by consulting the service manager at your local dealer), and periodically unclog them with a stiff wire.

● If front and rear fenders wrap under to the extent that the wheels splatter them, an abrasive effect is created that can chip off paint. Periodically inspect and repair any paint chipping.

Should you have your new car undercoated? That depends. Asphalt-based undercoating, the kind used by most car dealers, acts more as a sound deadener than a rust preventer. If this type of undercoating is applied poorly, it can promote corrosion instead of hindering it.

If the undercoater is careless, drain holes can become clogged with the undercoating material, trapping moisture in boxed-in areas

Corrosion experts from the car makers say that if you keep the underbody clean (spray it regularly at a car wash or with your garden hose), undercoating is unnecessary. If you decide to have your car undercoated anyway, watch while it's done. Make sure the underbody metal is absolutely clean so the undercoating can adhere properly. Have the undercoater clean out the drain holes in the body, and be sure he doesn't clog them.

Then, periodically check the underbody for chipped undercoating. Remove chipped or cracked undercoating, along with whatever rust that may have accumulated, and spray the exposed metal with an underbody anti-corrosion spray.

1972. The 76th Boston Marathon carries women on its roster of starters for the first time. Of the nine entrants, Nina Kuscsik finishes first with a time of 3:08.58, placing ahead of 800 male competitors in the field of 1,081 participants.

Surviving a Car Crash

Anthony Greenbank

Any speed is fast enough to kill when the unexpected happens. Mesmerized as you approach collision-point—whether at 10 or 100 mph—what you should do to survive and actually *do* do are very different things.

Speeding across the median on a freeway or tumbling in an avalanche, only chaos prevails: Those without an earthly hope sometimes escape, while someone else with every chance dies. And vice versa.

There is no set law—save anticipating things going too fast with you on board by (1) preparing ahead as in fitting seat belts to car, and (2) knowing the best you can do when totally unprotected (given presence of mind to act in time).

CAR CRASH

FITTING SEAT BELTS—AND WEARING THEM —IS THE PRIORITY RULE IN SURVIVING CAR TRAVEL. Yet however strongly you agree, and fit them to *your* car, you might have to travel in a beltless car. Or some similar vehicle. Anywhere. Any time. Possibly at speed.

Given time to think, fast reactions can do *something* to help you as crash approaches a second or two away. Car driver braced so savagely on steering wheel in 80 mph crash (in expensive car) that his grip twisted steering wheel—and he escaped; girl driver leaped into back of sports car as crash loomed ahead—and lived. Such instances are very much exceptions to the general rule that a car crash means virtually inevitable injury or death.

It is impossible to be dogmatic about beltless crash survival. But following points MAY help you survive as they have others (and are backed up by motoring authorities as scientifically realistic).

PRECOLLISION ACTION WHEN NOT STRAPPED IN

1. DO OPPOSITE OF NATURAL INSTINCT TO PUSH AWAY FROM CRASH.
2. FLING YOURSELF TOWARD POINT OF IMPACT.
3. WRAPPING ARMS ROUND HEAD . . .
4. TWISTING SIDEWAYS AND LYING WITH FLANK ACROSS FRONT.

If driving, hold steering wheel tightly. Aim to get car out of as much trouble as possible.

Back-seat passengers lie (as above) against back of front seats.

This is very much a last-stand tactic. Usually there is no time to think. But with two or three seconds' warning, quick reaction and knowing right thing to do, you can take advantage this way of energy-absorbing capability of car as hood crumples in head-on crash.

Never sit back and try to brace against oncoming crunch. No matter how well braced you are, first the car will stop (say from 30 mph to zero in 2 feet). And then you, still traveling at pre-accident speed, will have second collision with car's windshield/door frame/dashboard/steering column/seats in front.

Going with car from very beginning heightens your chance of survival. Technically—the method of surviving crash once it is determined to happen, is to get passengers

to lose their speed over greatest possible distance and hence reduce to absolute minimum the deceleration to which they are subjected.

Nontechnically: *Go with it* (most serious impact accidents happen at combined speeds of less than 40 mph).

WHEN DRIVER IS DRUNK/SUICIDAL/OUT OF CONTROL

If very good chance car is soon going to crash, and driver is acting fantastically irresponsible, protect yourself.

1. Feign sickness and vomiting all over car interior to make him stop. Then whip out ignition key.
2. Lie on floor, in back of car if possible.
3. Or lie braced against front of car.

(Note. Climbing into back from front seat so you can get down on floor might distract and make drunk or suicidal driver lose control.)

Switching off and pulling out ignition key while car is traveling has worked—obviously last resort. Dangerous.

Make sure you have clear/straight/wide stretch of road. Take a firm grip of wheel (after noting where handbrake is) as you reach across to turn and pull out key. Easier to do this—by virtue of key position—in some cars than in others.

Important. Realize that steering car with hand on steering wheel while seated in passenger seat is very tricky. A last resort.

SNEEZING

A-TISHOO! at 70 mph makes car driver cover length of big cemetery half-blind and dazed. Three sneezes in 16-mph rush-hour crawl carries him the length of 220 big wreaths in a row—snorting/grimacing/head jerking/eye wiping/blinking.

Stop sneezing in good time by . . .

1. PRESSING FINGER HARD ON UPPER LIP, or
2. SLAPPING THIGH HARD.

WHEN BRAKES GO

Shift down. Pull on handbrake. If no use, drive off road. If you bounce back out, keep repeating until stopped. Use headlights/horn.

If not possible to drive straight off road, brush against side of road (walls/banks/buildings) to give slowing effect. Don't think about ruining vehicle—think about surviving.

Brace as best you can if crash comes.

ACTION WHEN SKIDDING

Driver should try to reduce the steering angle of car.

If front wheels have lost their grip, a smaller steering angle can help regain control by completing a wider turn than was intended. Trying to sharpen the turn will aggravate the skid more. So will braking.

If back wheels slide, say to left, and car starts spinning to the right, turn steering wheel to left very briefly. This is natural way, but it must be instant and not violent.

Overcorrection of skids is common—due to steering wheel being yanked too far over and for too long. Only way to cope with skiddy surfaces is to slow down and drive steadily.

When taxed to your limit on a bend, watch outside shoulder for only true indication of its sharpness.

1972. Joanne Pierce and Susan Roley are sworn in as the FBI's first women agents.

PREVENTING SKIDDING

Basically when roads are not dry:

1. BRAKE ON STRAITAWAY, NOT ON BENDS.
2. DRIVE MUCH SLOWER THAN ON DRY ROADS.
3. LEAVE EXTRA ROOM BETWEEN YOU AND VEHICLE AHEAD.
4. BRAKE GENTLY. DON'T STEER FORCEFULLY.

Special hazards are: fog, strong winds, rain; darkness as well as conditions on the road surface. For example, overtaking truck in clear patch on misty road could run you head-on into wall of fog again during passing time, with real skid risk on damp surface.

Cutting speed on wet road—especially with worn tires—necessary. At 50 mph in rain your car surfs along with tires off the road on a wedge of water. Even with reasonable tire tread, car is partly out of contact with road for same reason at 60 mph.

Slow down well ahead of hazard points:

Traffic circles
Bends
Steep hills
Junctions
Obstacles/diversions/emergency signs.

Read road surfaces between the lines—certain skiddy surfaces are not always obvious. Rough/gravelly/knobby surface could prove skiddiest of any. Summer roads after rain shower often more skiddy than same road after rain in winter.

Lightness in steering is good warning sign generally.

Have your steering and brakes garage-tested all around frequently. Inspect tires often. Check with a penny. Insert coin upside down in tread of most worn part of tire. If the top of Abraham Lincoln's head is still in view it is time to change the tire.

(Note: Fast motoring is made safer by increasing tire pressure as makers recommend, usually between 2 to 6 lbs. per square inch above normal.)

OVERTAKING SAFELY

Overtaking means speed. And risk of escalating chaos. Think hard before you judge whether to pull out and increase speed, or stay put.

1. DON'T CLOSE UP ON CAR IN FRONT.
2. DON'T WORRY ABOUT ANYONE JUMPING INTO THAT GAP.
3. ASSESS ANY HAZARDS AHEAD FROM YOUR SUPERIOR ROAD POSITION.

Keeping your distance behind vehicle to be overtaken means you don't blind/mask/shade your vital view ahead. Keep two car lengths behind at 25 mph and eight lengths at 60 mph. This gives adequate sight of road ahead, bends, junctions, corners, obstructions forcing vehicle in front to pull out suddenly, oncoming traffic.

Check in rear mirror for line jumper coming up behind, but don't let this force you to close that gap between you and vehicle in front. When ready to overtake you will be the one to go first.

When it is time to pass . . . in quick succession:

4. CHECK REAR MIRROR.
5. PULL OUT AND ACCELERATE IN GEAR WHICH WILL LET YOU PASS FAST WITHOUT HAVING TO CHANGE GEAR.
6. TOUCH HORN OR FLASH HEADLIGHTS.
7. IF OTHER CAR ACCELERATES, DROP BACK.

A car in front doing 60 mph needs your doing 70 mph to pass—and you must ensure you don't have to cut in immediately afterwards. Drop back if this looks probable.

SEAT BELTS FOR SURVIVAL

Seat belts definitely reduce risk of death or maiming by as much as 70 percent. Examples of ways seat belts save:

(a) Stop your being thrown from car, almost certain cause of death or injury (locking doors often fails as crash distorts bodywork and door flies open).
(b) Stop head being done in on windshield or frame.
(c) Stop face being cut on bits of broken glass.
(d) Stop chest and intestines being smashed on dashboard or steering column for driver.

Buy best belt you can afford. Don't be put off and buy none if full harness is too expensive. Buy diagonal and lap straps. Check with garage for more recent developments on belt safety since time of writing.

(Note: Lap straps on their own should only be fitted to back seats as they allow head to be thrown forward to hit front of car interior if used for front seats.)

It is better to have some protection all the time than the best protection only some of the time.

1. ALWAYS WEAR BELTS.
2. ALWAYS ADJUST TIGHT.

Imagine ignition key won't start car until belts are all fitted to car passengers and driver—and adjust (some cars actually have this safeguard). Make it a rigid rule—even when in a tearing hurry.

Three more points:

(a) Make sure belt you buy is tested to comply with standard specifications.
(b) Have it garage-fitted.
(c) Check that anchorage for diagonal strap crossing body is as far behind you as possible. It should NOT cross shoulder, descend over back of seat and be anchored below on floor behind, as then it is depending partly on seat for support and this could buckle immediately in a crash.

You may not agree with seat belts, but you should still have them . . . and give passengers the choice.

SAVING CHILDREN

Buy seat and harness for child under 80 lbs. Fit to back seat. If over 80 lbs. child can use adult harness on back seat.

Children should always sit in the back (whether strapped in or not). Doors should have childproof locks. Ways to get them to wear the harness: Tell them car won't start until they do/they're astronauts going to moon/they'd better hurry up, or else.

Never allow:

Children to sit on front passenger's seat.
Child to sit on mother's knee in front.
Child to be tucked between mother and her seat belt.

AFTER THE CRASH

Control other road-users by signaling (get help from other motorists and onlookers). In fog, darkness, rain and twisty road especially, light flare (oily rags burning inside levered-off hub caps), placed some way from wreck to warn others.

Only move someone badly hurt if danger of fire from spilled gasoline (no one should smoke), or if danger from traffic cannot be avoided. Treat for injuries (see p.64). But where casualty must be moved handle *very* carefully, especially if broken bones suspected or complaint of pain in back (spinal-injury risk).

1972. The U.S. Supreme Court rules that unwed fathers have the same rights as unwed mothers in demonstrating their fitness to parent and to take custody of any child born of the relationship.

Simple
Pleasures

Jim Corrieri and Ralph Baxter, with Salah of the Round Table

The Compleat Belly Dancer

Julie Russo Mishkin and Marta Schill

In the land of its origin, it was just dance. The Arabs called it Beledi, which means, simply, native dance or native rhythm. It is an alliterative coincidence that the Arabic word also sounds like belly. Oriental dance, Middle Eastern dance, or Arabic dance are some nice ethnic euphemisms for it. Just don't call it hootchie-kootch.

Oriental dancing derives from much more than Arabia proper. It encompasses Morocco, West Africa, Algiers, the African borderland of the Mediterranean through Syria, Iraq, Turkey, Persia, and even Greece and Northern India. The Arabs mingled with all the nations of the Near East, and their musical life had an international, inter-oriental character we call Arabian. When Islam unified the Middle East in the seventh century, the culture became homogenous.

In these lands, the passions of birth and life and love are woven into every facet of the culture with a special earthy quality that transcends morality in the Western sense. Because of this, the Westerner has often misunderstood the dance, giving it his notoriety and striptease condescension. The music is highly emotional and very free rhythmically. Naturally, the dance, as a physical expression of that sensual, mystical music, is of the same stuff. There is magic in these parts of the world, and the music reflects thousands of regional customs, practices, and celebrations.

And now there is you. Whatever your reasons for pursuing the High Priestess and her secret lore, there is something herein to enrich your awareness. If you don't have a particular motive in mind, let us suggest a few reliable ones. They may all apply.

You may decide to learn belly dancing because you want to tone your muscles, improve your posture, develop more grace and balance in all your movements, increase your stamina, and perhaps decrease your girth. Belly dancing is one of the best all-around body improvers you'll ever find.

Or it may appeal to you because you feel your body and soul are dangerously out of reach.

Whatever your reason for calling on the Ancient Lady, whether you call her Belly or Arabic or Beledi or Oriental, she responds only to the desire to dance. She will like you all the more if you're a bit on the plump side; give you extra grace and dimension if you are over thirty (even a professional well within her forties can mesmerize her audiences).

She'll set your body moving in an entirely new way—every part of you will move on its own, rotating or wiggling as though detached from the rest. The hands, legs, breasts, and, of course, the belly will say things you never even heard before. The Lady will mostly make herself felt in your hips,

THE BASIC BELLY-DANCE POSITION

Belly dancing is a matter of engineering. If you think it is just the tummy that sways around, you won't be moving much at all. The way you stand,

1972. The Senate approves the ERA (Equal Rights Amendment) by an 84-8 margin and passes it on to the states for ratification by 1979. The development culminates forty-nine years of feminist lobbying.

your use of weight change, your understanding of your own center of gravity . . . and USING those joints and bendable places to give you more freedom of movement all go into play.

Just to prove to yourself how much engineering adds to your movability . . . try this. Remember the old twist? Stand straight (well, slump your shoulders if that's what you've been doing anyway) and twist that derriere. Now, bend your knees as though you were about to start sitting down. Now twist a few sweeps with your derriere. Get the difference? You have engineered your body into a posture that allows for much more freedom of movement in the hips—and the belly.

The look of belly dancing is one which is set-up to provide the most freedom of movement. You can't disengage the hips from the torso, but you can master a few basic engineering techniques that will start you moving and undulating right away.

So, the first and most important thing a belly dancer must learn is how to stand, how to hold herself, how to distribute her weight, how to make gravity work for her.

This "Basic Position" is the foundation of all your movements.

1. Knees slightly bent. (Tiring at first, until you have strengthened leg muscles.)

2. Weight on heels. (Gives you backward emphasis and frees hips.)

3. Rib cage up. (A puppeteer's string is pulling it up from above.)

4. Shoulders down and relaxed (not hunched up or pulled back *a la militaire*).

5. Abdominal muscles relaxed. (Let it all hang out.)

Visual images help: A puppeteer's string is attached to your sternum (right between the breasts on the rib cage), pulling from above to give you a good lift.

A slender pole runs plumb from the top of the head to the ground. At times this pole coincides with the spinal column. Usually, it becomes an imaginary center of gravity around which all movements revolve, undulate, and bend.

An invisible chair is always right behind you (perhaps one of those stump stools used on the farm by maidens milking the cows). You are often in a position to just about sit back on it.

Your feet are always ready to sift sand or work a little hole in the earth. A belly dancer's toes are her earthy contact.

THE SHIMMY SHAKEDOWN

What makes the belly dancer jingle so? Her belt of coins or beaded fringe quiver so? It's the Shimmy, of course . . . most exciting and colorful quiver ever to come from a dancing body. It looks fantastic and sexy —and it is. It also looks very difficult—which it isn't. Actually, the Shimmy is a movement requiring less muscle ability than most. It's main prerequisite is in learning to relax—to let it all hang out and flap around like a bowlful of jelly being gently jiggled. Many dancers shift into a Shimmy just to give themselves a rest from the more taxing movements. You can use the

1972. District Court Judge Richard McLaren rules that a state's Board of Education stipulation requiring pregnant teachers to take a six-month unpaid leave after the fifth month of pregnancy is unconstitutional. Instead, he says, teachers can remain on the job as long as their doctors permit.

Shimmy in discothèque rock dancing too—it can be added to any kind of step to inject an electrical quality.

When practicing this, it is very helpful to wear coins around your hips . . . if you haven't gotten around to making your own, tie on a big scarf and attach the noisiest jangles and baubles you have. The jingle will let you know when your Shimmy is at least a reasonable one.

BREAKING IT DOWN

1. Assume the Basic Position. Knees bent. Relax torso; let that belly and derriere hang out. Relax internal (*sphincter*) muscles.

2. Shift weight to right foot, keeping upper body in central position. Do not stiffen shoulders.

3. Let right hip fall to right side as weight is being shifted to right foot. This is the same hip thrust you may have used to tote schoolbooks or a toddler. Left foot rests in place.

4. SMOOTHLY NOW—shift weight to left foot, letting left hip fall to left side to "hold books."

5. THE BASIC SHIMMY IS EXECUTED BY SIMPLY REPEATING THIS WEIGHT CHANGE SMOOTHLY AND WITH INCREASING RAPIDITY.

CLUE: You should feel a pleasant loose vibration—a flopping kind of quiver—in the buttocks and upper inner thighs as you make your Shimmy.

KEEP YOUR KNEES BENT . . . SHOULDERS DOWN . . . ARMS RELAXED TRY TO HOLD RIB CAGE AND UPPER TORSO IN PLACE . . . RELAX.

WALKING WITH THE SHIMMY

This one is a bitch! Keep it for your more advanced practice . . . it is WELL worth the effort.

1. Assume Basic Position.

2. Begin Basic Shimmy.

3. Listening to the music, SHIFT WEIGHT slightly to right foot on downbeat.

4. SHIFT WEIGHT slightly to left foot on next downbeat. DON'T STOP THE SHIMMY! Your rhythm count is:

RIGHT-two-three-four
    shift
LEFT-two-three-four
    shift
RIGHT-two-three-four, etc.

This is similar to how you learned the Basic Shimmy. Now you are shifting weight within the Shimmy. You will find that when you are able to put some speed into this movement, it becomes much easier. The impetus of your movement carries you along as much as your muscular efforts.

5. NOW FOR THE WALK. Relax! You're not really going far. To begin, just move a couple of inches with each step . . . even one inch.

6. Continuing the weight-shift Shimmy, your first forward step will come when the weight is on the right foot—at that moment, the left foot will

The Compleat Belly Dancer

1972. President Nixon declares August 26 Woman's Rights Day, and states, "Today, more women than ever before serve in policy-making positions in the executive branch of our government."

inch forward. On the next downbeat, the weight will shift to the left foot, and the right foot will inch forward. Between steps, the weight will be on both feet as usual.

YOU MIGHT FEEL LIKE A WADDLING DUCK AT FIRST . . . GO RIGHT AHEAD AND WADDLE. ONCE YOU'VE GOTTEN THE KNACK, THEN YOU CAN WORK ON MAKING THE SHIMMY WALK PRETTY.

THE HIP LIFTS

One of the belly dancer's most rhythmically provocative movements. The angular leaning comes from proper use of bent knees. Use it for sultry emphasis of your lower-torso roundnesses, or bounce it around for lively abandon.

BREAKING IT DOWN

1. Assume Basic Position, with knees DEEPLY bent. Extend left foot slightly forward. Incline weight on right leg.

2. Rise up to ball of left foot, keeping heel high off floor. Keep both knees bent . . . but weight on right.

3. Now—for the Hip Lift—straighten left leg, pushing hip and thigh forward (not to side). Keep heel of left foot off ground. Right knee will straighten only slightly.

4. Let hip fall back into Basic Position, allowing left knee to bend again.

5. Repeat lift.

MAKING IT GREAT

LEANING BACK WITH THE HIP LIFT

1. Lean back to accentuate the angle of your body. BUT DON'T BEND YOUR BACK . . . as your muscles get conditioned, you will be able to bend that RIGHT KNEE even more.

2. Lean your torso backward, TUCK THE PELVIS so that you keep your center of gravity over the right foot . . . and proceed with the Hip Lift.

KEEPING TIME WITH THE HIP LIFT

1. To develop rhythmic use of the Hip Lift, add doubles and triples:

A. In Basic Position for Hip Lift.

B. Execute a Hip Lift forward.

C. Let hip fall back only SLIGHTLY, and push it forward again. Push into floor with ball of left foot to increase control.

D. Practice to music—accentuate the rhythm by combining single, double, and triple Hip Lifts.

MOVING WITH THE HIP LIFT

You can use the Hip Lift to propel yourself in a circle or to the side.

HIP-LIFT CIRCLE

1. Assume Basic Hip-Lift Position.

2. Execute a Hip Lift, let hip fall back again.

3. NOW, AS YOU BEGIN TO EXECUTE A SECOND HIP LIFT, PLACE BALL OF LEFT FOOT SLIGHTLY MORE TOWARD RIGHT. DO YOUR HIP LIFT, LETTING LEFT FOOT PULL YOU TOWARD RIGHT. RIGHT FOOT WILL PIVOT SLIGHTLY.

The Compleat Belly Dancer

The Compleat Belly Dancer

1972. A number of studies indicate that women inseminated early in their menstrual cycle (or, that is, women who have intercourse frequently) are more likely to give birth to boys. This, it is thought, may explain why women under twenty-five tend to conceive a higher proportion of boys while for women over thirty-five the opposite is true.

The Compleat Belly Dancer

4. Continue in a circle until you have returned to original position. (A circle in place.)

5. The more you allow hip to fall back with each step, the more you allow left knee to bend on its return to Basic Position, the more of a movement will be executed in the rise and fall of the hip.

MOVING SIDEWAYS WITH HIP LIFT

1. Assume Basic Hip-Lift Position.
2. Execute Hip Lift, to side, not forward.
3. Hold all weight on LEFT FOOT . . . so that right foot is free. Straighten left leg.
4. As Hip Lift is at peak, lift right foot slightly and bring it back down toward left foot.
5. With each Hip Lift, left leg moves slightly to left.
6. KEEP LIFTS AND MOVEMENT OF RIGHT FOOT SMALL. MOVE A FEW STEPS TO LEFT, THEN TRY USING RIGHT HIP AND REVERSE HIP-LIFT PROCEDURE TO RIGHT.

THE ROLLING HIP LIFT

1. Place index finger on hip.
2. Move hip in circle, using finger to describe the roundness. Work that knee!
3. Remove finger and dance it.

"FIGURE 8" SWAYS

A very usable movement that involves a side-to-side and back-and-fro twist and sway. Produces fascinating side effects in the belly muscles. May be done with large, sweeping motions or very subtly, in standing or kneeling position.

BREAKING IT DOWN

1. Assume Basic Position. The more you bend your knees, the more movement you will get.
2. Bring your right hip back as far as it can go.
3. Swing the right hip as far forward as it can go, as if it were a swinging door.
4. You will notice that as your right hip swings forward the left hip will have swung backward.
5. Slide your weight, now on your right hip, back through your body until weight is resting on left hip in back. Now swing your left hip forward. Repeat weight shift.

CLUE: Imagine you are tracing a figure 8 with your hips. The right hip traces one half of the 8, the left traces the other.

Using your legs to engineer the weight transfer, concentrate on the diagonal line that connects the two sides. This is the crucial part of the movement, for the diagonal crossover line is where smoothness is achieved.

NOTE: Another step—the Half Moon—is similar to a reverse Figure 8, in which hips move from front to back.

The Compleat Belly Dancer

1972. The U.S. Supreme Court rules this year that a state has the authority to require a wife to assume her husband's surname at time of marriage. The case in question concerns an Alabama woman's right to possess a driver's license in her own name, and "to demonstrate the equality of contract and commitment. . .felt in her marriage."

MAKING IT GREAT

1. Minimize the movement from the rib cage up. Try to achieve a twist in the hips and legs only.

2. Vary the movement—make it small and subtle. Get down on your knees and do it. Bend your knees more and swing those doors around with a smooth fervor.

3. To make it a more controlled movement, practice it like this:

Bend knees, but tuck in derriere. As you now enact the Figure 8, it will pull on your belly muscles even more.

Now, get down on your knees and, with derriere still tucked under, repeat.

When standing, *do not* attempt this step in a fixed position—it will be jerky and "cut off" at every turn. Learn to pivot gracefully on the toe that brings the hip around. If it looks strange and "pigeon-toed," you're doing it right! Your long skirt (when dancing) will cover those hard-working feet —and your torso will appear to be almost magically floating in a graceful Figure 8.

THE BASIC LIFT STEP

When a village woman heard the insistent rhythms of the drummer, her first inclination was to mark time with her feet. Since she was looser and freer moving than her civilized sisters, her body swayed as her feet softly kept time in the dusty earth.

When a belly dancer executes this rhythmic, Basic Lift-Sway Step, she is merely exaggerating the native principle . . . by means of a constant swaying in belly.

This is a step that becomes a good basic for improvisation . . . it can be walked, twisted, and varied.

BREAKING IT DOWN

Assume Basic Position—arms out at shoulder height.

1. Right leg extends forward.

2. Touch floor with right heel and roll up onto ball of foot (just like walking).

3. As foot rolls, lift leg slightly and bring it back to standing position. Belly sways forward with foot.

4. Pelvis sways forward again when right foot is in place.

5. Now, left leg extends forward. Touch floor with left heel and roll up onto ball. As you roll forward and lift to return leg, belly sways.

6. Belly sways again as left foot is in standing position.

UNDERSTANDING IT

If we concentrate on this movement's footwork and leg engineering only, we have this:

1. Right step-roll forward. Lift back.

2. Feet both in place.

3. Left step-roll forward. Lift back.

4. Feet both in place.

The Compleat Belly Dancer

The Compleat Belly Dancer

1973. After some unrest and confusion among the local organizations, the seventy-man national board of the Jaycees (the Junior Chamber of Commerce) votes decisively to exclude women from membership.

The Compleat Belly Dancer

Assume basic position—arms out at shoulder height. Touch floor with right heel and roll up onto ball of foot (just like walking). As foot rolls, lift leg slightly and bring it back to standing position. Belly sways forward with foot.

Lean back to accentuate the angle of your body. BUT DON'T BEND YOUR BACK. . .as your muscles get conditioned, you will be able to bend that right knee even more.

The Compleat Belly Dancer

If we concentrate on the pendulum sway of the belly, achieved by allowing the belly to move back and forth from the rib cage like a loose swing, we have this:

1. Belly sways as if sliding out to cover front foot.

2. Belly sways just as far forward AND BACKWARD with both feet in place.

MOVING WITH IT

To walk with the Lift-Sway Step, make this simple change:

1. Foot extends forward. Roll from heel up to ball of foot and lift hip.

2. NOW, INSTEAD OF BRINGING FOOT BACK TO STANDING POSITION, make lift but step down on foot to walk forward.

3. Bring left foot in front and repeat. Then continue walking, swaying belly (1) as foot touches forward and (2) as foot steps down.

MAKING IT GREAT

1. Once you have gotten the swing of the basic step, use your arms to accentuate the movements. (Arm movements should originate in the torso and work outward so that they are full, smooth gestures and not flappy, stiff flailings.)

2. Add countermovement with the rib cage or shoulders. PRETEND YOU ARE MOVING UNDER WATER—push and pull against an imaginary weight. RESIST the air around you.

3. Add a twist of the hip . . . as the foot rolls in front of you, bring the round part of the hip around to the front with each leg lift.

4. Practice this step with finger cymbals. A good basic rhythm for this step involves three clacks of the cymbals (left-right-left . . . right-left-right . . . left-right-left, etc.) with each of the step's four main movements.

1973. After investigating charges of employment discrimination, the federal government orders AT&T to award 15,000 employees with $15 million in back pay. Eventually, under the combined pressure of the Equal Opportunity Employment Act and NOW suits, AT&T pays out a total of $60 million.

A Woman's Guide to Yoga

Joy F. Herrick

When people learn that I practice Yoga, one of the first questions they ask is, "Do you stand on your head?" I do, and I enjoy it very much. Before Yoga, it never occurred to me that I would be *able* to do a headstand, much less want to. In school, I had been aptly known as the Crisco Kid, and later, as an overweight adult, the idea of getting my bottom half raised above the top half seemed wildly improbable. However, after building up to it for half a year, I could finally do it, and I am now on my way to perfecting the position.

Confidence is half the battle, so before I stand on my head I always pile a lot of pillows behind me. This takes away the fear of being hurt, and when I do go too far and roll over it doesn't bother me. The headstand has helped me beat hunger, fatigue, and tension. By concentrating on the position I have no room in my mind for negative thoughts. When I let go of these —and the headstand forces me to—I relax and have more energy.

The first time I was able to achieve this position it took every bit of concentration I had, but one day I was balanced well enough to look around from my upside-down perspective. Under the record player, I discovered quantities of rolling dust and cobwebs. The whole picture tickled my sense of humor and I immediately lost my concentration and somersaulted over in a heap of giggles.

Until I saw the Yoga postures performed by a master, I had an absolutely crazy conception of them. In the beginning it was difficult for me to relate to the photographs and illustrations of Yogis in what appeared to be grotesque, unnecessary positions. They seemed senseless and ugly until the magic day I saw them done by an expert. It was like watching ballet. One posture flowed into the next with total grace and harmony. Mind, body, spirit, and space became one. What surprised me most was the feeling that I was watching a form of meditation. It was an uplifting, opening experience, and everyone else who was watching felt its magnetism.

APPROACHING THE POSTURES

The postures are for total health and development. As with the other Yoga disciplines, you are working on two levels: the material (finite) and the spiritual (infinite).

Physically, each posture is designed to benefit specific organs or bodily systems, as well as to improve general body tone, circulation, and limberness. For example, if kidney benefits are indicated, the posture is intended to promote the optimum health and functioning of that organ.

Mentally, as you practice and advance in your prowess, the postures calm the mind and thus increase your sense of harmony and oneness. You become able to use your body as a channel to perfect, peaceful consciousness, and to let that consciousness work through you with all its creative energy and healing power.

When I first started doing the postures, I made the mistake of falling into a set routine, a kind of inflexible ritual, and this took away the spontaneity and joy. Instead of being sensitive to what

Adapted from *Something's Got to Help and Yoga Can* by Joy F. Herrick. Copyright © 1974 Joy F. Herrick and Nancy Schraffenberger. Reprinted by permission of the publisher, M. Evans and Co., Inc., 216 East 49th Street, New York, New York.

my body felt, I was doing what I thought would be good for me; by my dogmatic effort, I shut out the energy and meditativeness I was looking for. Filled with false pride, I pushed myself past my own limit. I was going to do a certain posture come what may—I felt it was just a case of mind over matter. Naturally, with an attitude like that, I overexerted myself, which didn't help my back or my morale.

Another possible hang-up: if you attend a class in Yoga postures you may feel self-conscious or competitive and try to do the exercises too vigorously and too fast. I was guilty of this, and it took a while to let the tranquillity and proper attitudes sink in. It was only when I began to concentrate on the harmony and stillness that I finally began to enjoy myself.

Don't be discouraged if you, too, are tense, tired, or in a foul mood when you start doing the postures. You'll find that concentrating on doing them correctly takes your mind off your troubles. As you strive to hold the postures motionless, and to do them *slowly,* smoothly, and with right attitudes, your energy increases and your fatigue and tension slip away. The better you become at them, the calmer you feel for longer periods of time.

Bodily discipline is a step toward mental discipline. If our bodies control us, either by sickness or emotion, we are thrown out of harmony. The Yoga postures teach us control and concentration and help us to be masters of our bodies under all conditions.

If you want to do the postures, you have more than three thousand to choose from to build your own routine. I do the ones described in this chapter because they are basic and are included by most teachers. Remember that all the postures are not meant to be done by everyone, and you must proceed *at your own rate* of speed. Don't push past your limit or compete with anyone else, and if you have any medical problems—with your blood pressure, for example—check with your doctor before beginning.

Often the postures are misunderstood in our culture. They are right for the Hatha Yogi, but not for everyone. Spending a lot of time doing the postures isn't necessary, although some practice is recommended and is extremely beneficial. My purpose is to expose you to all eight steps of basic Yoga, and to demonstrate the great flexibility of this ancient system.

GENERAL RULES

1. The following postures are given in the order in which I do them. However, feel free to start with any position that seems easy to you—perhaps the alternate Leg Pull or Head to Knee postures—and move on to the others when you feel ready.

2. After you master a posture, in most cases you will do it *once,* stretching to *your own* limit, and holding completely still as long as possible. (*Asana* means to hold motionless and relaxed for a period of time.) When you are holding a posture perfectly still and comfortably, relax; *visualize* yourself doing it correctly. Concentrate on what you are doing. Think positive thoughts— you can even meditate. *Make* yourself forget the office, boy scout supper, finances, etcetera.

1973. Eight women begin pilot training for the U.S. Navy. Those who pass the eighteen-month course will become the first women to do so.

3. Rhythmical breathing is germane to the postures. As a general rule, inhale when raising up and exhale when going down. Visualize yourself as an empty glass and pour in the air as if it were a liquid. Fill your lungs from the bottom (way down, almost to the base of your spine) to the top. You should feel the air pushing itself up, expanding your lungs toward your shoulder blades and sideways under your arms. Continue pouring air in until you're full to the tip of your nose.

Exhale as if you were pouring the air out, from the top to the bottom. *Make sure you get all the old stale air out before starting a new breath.*

4. Alternate forward-bending postures with backward-bending ones. On leg pulls and other postures involving alternate limbs, be sure you do them on both left and right sides.

5. Rest after doing two or three *asanas*—assume the Corpse or Folded Leaf position and relax completely.

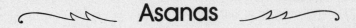

Asanas

TWIST

Benefits: adrenal glands, kidney, liver, spleen; helpful in connection with obesity, indigestion, constipation, asthma; improves stooping shoulders, bent back, poor posture.

a. Sit with legs outstretched.

b. Bend right leg back so right foot is next to left buttock.

c. Put left foot on floor over right knee.

d. Raise and straighten right arm, then place right palm on left knee and slide it down left side of knee until you can reach your ankle.

e. Put left arm behind back, palm out.

f. Take a deep breath; exhale while twisting to the left. Keep back straight, chin up and look back over your left shoulder.

g. *Hold ten seconds at first;* inhale as you slowly untwist and face forward. Exhale.

h. Reverse the positions of your arms and legs and twist in the other direction. This is a very difficult position, so go slowly—it takes most people a long time to master it.

PLOUGH

Benefits: thyroid gland, liver, spleen, sex glands, improves spinal arthritis.

a. Lie on back, arms at sides, palms down.

b. Inhale while going into Shoulder Stand.

c. Exhale while lowering legs (keep them straight) to the floor behind your head. Breathe deeply; *hold three to five minutes.*

d. Inhale while raising legs toward ceiling (going back into Shoulder Stand), still keeping legs straight, your weight supported on your shoulders.

e. Exhale while gradually lowering legs to floor, uncurling spine vertebra by vertebra.

SHOULDER STAND (Can be part of a series with Plough and Fish— see following two postures. However, don't try to link the postures until you are fairly proficient in each one.)

a. Lie on back, arms at sides.

b. Inhale while raising legs over head; use arms to support back. Get up as high on shoulders and neck as possible.

Benefits: thyroid gland (governs metabolism, obesity, water retention), sex glands; purifies blood; strengthens lower organs.

c. Keep body straight, chin pressed into neck. Breathe deeply; *hold three to five minutes.*

d. Exhale while lowering legs and back slowly to floor. Keep legs straight if possible and uncurl vertebra by vertebra.

1973. The Gallup pollsters discover that only 20 percent of all American women consider four or more children in a family to be an ideal number, a significant drop from the 40 percent of a 1967 poll.

FISH

Benefits: thyroid gland, pelvic organs, reproductive organs; tones back and nerves.

a. Sit with crossed legs or in Lotus or Half-Lotus. Inhale.

b. Exhale, leaning slowly backward until the top of your head is on the floor behind you. Arch your back. Breathe deeply; *hold thirty seconds to one minute.*

c. Inhale and return slowly to a sitting position.

ALTERNATE LEG PULL

Benefits: digestion, spleen, abdomen, spine, leg and back muscles.

a. Sit with legs straight out, place left foot against inside of right thigh.

b. Inhale while rising arms over head and lifting trunk up slightly.

c. Lower arms forward; slowly exhale while sliding hands down right leg (bend from base of spine) until you reach your toes and touch your head to your knee. Breathe deeply; *hold thirty seconds to one minute.*

d. Inhale while slowly returning to starting position.

e. Repeat with other leg.

Anne Fiske

HEAD TO KNEE

Benefits: kidneys, spine, digestion, heart; reduces abdominal fat; strengthens sciatic nerve.

a. Sit straight with legs outstretched and together; palms on floor.

b. Inhale while stretching trunk up slightly.

c. Exhale slowly while working hands down legs until you reach your feet. Touch head to knees, trying to get elbows to floor. Breathe deeply; *hold one to three minutes.*

d. Inhale while straightening up slowly. Uncurl; don't straighten your back abruptly.

HALF-LOCUST and LOCUST (Can be part of a backward-bending series with Bow and Cobra—see following two postures)

Benefits: lower spine, backs of legs and knees, pelvic area, abdominal organs and muscles, bladder, prostate gland.

Half-Locust:

a. Lie on stomach, hands in fists at sides, chin just off the floor.

b. Inhale while rising one leg, keeping it straight. Push floor with fists. Hold breath; *hold position as long as you can.*

c. Exhale while lowering leg slowly to floor.

d. Repeat with opposite leg.

Locust:

a. Lie on stomach, hands in fists at sides, chin just off the floor.

b. Inhale, thrust *both* legs up quickly, chin off floor, fists pressed to floor for support. This is one of the most difficult positions. Hold breath if possible; *hold position as long as you can.*

c. Exhale as you lower legs slowly to floor.

1973. Three women (''the Three Marias'') are arraigned this year in Lisbon, Portugal, on charges of flouting public morals by publishing their *New Portuguese Letters,* a book of essays, letters, and poems. The authorities maintain that the book carries obscene passages.

BOW

Benefits: helpful in connection with constipation, rheumatism; reduces fat in abdomen, hips, and thighs; develops chest and bust; improves posture.

a. Lie on your stomach, hands at sides, cheek on floor. Relax.

b. Turn head so chin is just touching the floor. Bend knees and bring legs back over thighs. Reach back and grasp your ankles with your hands. Exhale.

position a few seconds to begin with, later as long as you can increase to.

c. Inhale as you arch your body upward. Pull with your arms, arching your back as much as possible, raising knees and trunk from floor. Bend head back so you feel the stretch. Try to keep knees together as much as possible. Hold breath if you can; *hold*

d. Exhale as you slowly come down, lowering trunk and knees to floor. Don't jerk, don't let go of ankles until there is no strain left on your arms.

e. Release ankles, let your legs down slowly. Return to starting position and relax.

COBRA

Benefits: adrenal glands, spine, disks, nerves, ovaries, uterus, back and chest muscles.

a. Lie on stomach, arms at sides.

b. Inhale while raising head and chest off the floor. When up as far as possible, place hands under shoulders, elbows bent. Continue to curl back, vertebra by vertebra, putting head back first, then shoulders . . . chest . . . back. Keep abdomen on floor. Hold breath if possible; *hold thirty seconds to two minutes.*

c. Exhale slowly, uncurling back to floor; keep head back until you've uncurled to the starting point.

CORPSE (or SPONGE)

Benefits: renewal of life force; rest and relaxation between and after a series of postures—or any time you feel you need it.

a. Lie flat on back, arms out comfortably at sides, palms up.

b. Concentrate on tensing and relaxing your entire body, part by part, starting from the toes and working up. Let the tiredness flow out and away from you, and visualize it being replaced by energy and vitality.

c. Stay in the position for at least three to five minutes—longer if you like.

While I was washing windows last year, I had a thrilling experience—and I know it was directly attributable to my practicing Yoga, and especially Yogic breathing. It happened on one of those sunny, alive, spring days. As I worked, I noticed a wood thrush on the grass outside. He was so still I thought perhaps he had hit the window and been stunned, and I kept glancing at him. When the windows were finished, he was in the same place on the grass, so I decided to make sure he wasn't injured.

I went outside, and when I was about twenty feet away I consciously slowed my breathing and started to project thoughts of calm and love. I felt totally calm myself, and as I drew nearer the thrush he continued to stay still and watch me. By then, I was less than five feet away and he didn't seem hurt, nor was he frightened. Usually injured birds will panic when you come close. Their hearts pump faster and they struggle to get away. No such thing happened this time.

While we were both watching each other, I slowly lay down on the grass next to him, all the time trying to wrap him in calm and love. By now we were eye to eye. Carefully I extended my first finger and gently stroked his breast. He tolerated me for several seconds—still watchful, but trusting—before he hopped a few inches away. Again we watched each other and then, without hurry or fear, he flew off.

I couldn't believe it! Even if he *had* been stunned, I've picked up enough half-conscious birds to know how panicky they act. This was different. I had consciously slowed my breathing to calm myself, and then transmitted love to the wood thrush. It was communication of the most beautiful kind.

This experience is an example of how breathing can be controlled deliberately to exert a beneficial influence. Have you ever thought about how your own breathing behaves in different situations?

When you're fiercely angry, or filled with fear, what happens to your breath? Your heart pounds and your breathing is rapid and erratic.

When you're trying to thread a needle, or do a delicate job, or making a concentrated physical effort such as a dive from a high board, you're apt to hold your breath at the critical point.

When you're sunbathing on the beach, relaxed and happy, think what happens to your breathing then. It's slow and rhythmical, and you are calm in mind and body.

Clearly, the state of our breathing reflects the state of our minds and bodies. When the mind is calm, and we are free of desires and fears, our breathing is calm. When we are anxious or tense, our breathing is agitated and unrhythmic.

You can learn to control your breathing through practice, just as you can learn to ride a bicycle or knit. When you get into a jam or get excited, you can make a conscious effort to quiet your breathing. This will help you keep in control of your emotions, and *it works.* The next time your boss gets to you, or the children are impossible, don't just count to ten. Count as you do deep breathing. Even as a beginner, you'll be astonished at how effective it is in helping your control your temper.

Breathing should be thought of as a constant prayer. Yoga associates three steps with each complete breath. (1) With inhalation, think and *know* you are taking in inspiration, cosmic perfection, energy, and life force. (2) With breath retention,

---

realize you are filled with this cosmic perfection. You are one with the universal life force. (3) With exhalation, tell yourself that you are expelling all the impurity and toxic matter from your body. You are emptying your mind of all negatives and illusion.

These three steps will help you realize the *significance* of your breathing. They are guideposts or symbols of the goals of Yogic breath control. Breath is our most important connection with *pranic* energy. When we breathe air, we are taking in two things: air and *prana*. *Prana* is absolute energy, the life substance existing in and around all things. Just as we are immersed in air, we are also immersed in *prana*. As we learn to control breathing, we learn to control *prana* at the same time.

Controlled breathing can be done at any time; it is traditional to practice it with and after the postures and before meditation. Here are the general rules for Yogic breathing, followed by two exercises: (1) The Complete Breath, which is basic and commonly used with the postures as well as separately, and (2) The Alternate Breath, which is used as a cleansing and calming exercise.

GENERAL RULES

1. Always sit with your spine straight. If you can't sit in the Lotus, Half-Lotus, or cross-legged, sit on the edge of a hard chair.

2. As described on page 552, visualize yourself as an empty pitcher with air pouring in. During inhalation, fill the lower lungs first, then the middle and upper parts. During exhalation, empty the upper lungs first, then the middle and bottom.

3. Never strain or lose control of your breath. Strive for a continuous, subtle, unbroken flow.

4. Try to maintain an easy rhythm. *Don't push past your own limit.* Start slowly and build up to your desired goal. Perfecting this may take a year or longer.

5. The ratios of inhalation-retention-exhalation should be 1:4:2. In other words, retention should be four times longer than inhalation. For example, the most basic intermediate-level ratio is to inhale 4 counts, retain 16 counts, exhale 8 counts. Beginners should start with a 1:1:1 ratio, then 1:2:2, 1:3:2, and so on, working up gradually.

6. Make sure all the old stale air is out before you take a new breath. *This is most important,* and it is the reason for exhaling to a longer count than you inhale.

THE COMPLETE BREATH

a. Sit with your spine straight. Exhale completely.

b. Inhale 4 counts. Use your nostrils, but draw the breath in from the area at the back wall of your throat. Let your stomach expand a little, but keep chest and shoulders practically motionless. Let your ribs do the expanding and contracting.

c. Retain 16 counts. Stay relaxed; nothing should be strained or forced.

d. Exhale 8 counts through nose. You should feel the air at the back of your throat and only gently at your nostrils. Empty the air from top to bottom.

THE ALTERNATE BREATH

While doing the alternate breath, which calls for breathing through alternate nostrils, you can use one of several Yogic hand positions. Here are the two most used positions—do whichever is comfortable and natural for you.

1. Place the first and second fingers of your right hand against the palm; your thumb and third finger will be used to open and close your nostrils. Your arm and elbow should be down. Traditionally, this position is preferred because of energy patterns. Or . . .

2. Rest the first and second fingers of your right hand between your eyebrows—the seat of the "third eye," according to Yoga—for support. This leaves your thumb and third finger free to open and close your nostrils.

Now, to do the alternate breath, sit with your spine straight and take one of the hand positions just described.

a. Exhale. Close right nostril with your thumb. Inhale 4 counts through the left nostril.

b. Close left nostril with your finger. With both nostrils closed, retain the breath 16 counts.

c. Release right nostril and exhale 8 counts, keeping the left nostril closed.

d. With left nostril still closed and right one open, inhale 4 counts through the right nostril.

e. Close right nostril. With both nostrils closed, retain the breath 16 counts.

f. Release left nostril and exhale 8 counts, keeping right nostril closed.

The above a–f sequence is known as one round: inhale-retain-exhale; inhale-retain-exhale. Do from three to five rounds.

RECOMMENDED IN-HOLD-OUT RATIOS

	Inhale	Retain	Exhale
Beginners	4	4	4
	4	8	8
	4	12	8
Intermediate	4	16	8*
	5	20	10
Advanced	6	24	12
Maximum	8	32	16

* I don't go past this level; it seems to be the most commonly used ratio.

When doing controlled breathing, it's essential to keep a steady, unstrained rhythm. *Do not go past your own capacity.* Increase the ratio only if it's comfortable for you to do so. You'll do much more harm than good if you try to advance too quickly.

1973. Carol Downer and Lorraine Rothman publicize a device called the Del-'Em, which consists of a cannula, normally used for vacuum-aspiration abortions, connected to a syringe and two bottles. Self-help clinics are to use the apparatus for menstrual extraction. Margaret Mead is quoted as saying that the "Del-'Em is the greatest thing since the development of the wheel."

Massage: The Basic Strokes

Constance Young

There are several basic movements at the root of all systems of massage; the names may vary from system to system, but the principles remain the same. Some movements are applicable to all parts of the body, others only to specific areas. Where a particular stroke is contraindicated in an area, I am careful to mention it. Usually, however, if the wrong stroke is used, the person doing the massage soon becomes well aware of it by the displeased response from the subject. For the most part, there is room for trial and error once certain important massage rules are followed. These basic rules are given at the end of this article.

As mentioned earlier, experimentation is an important aspect of recent developments in massage, and this is obvious by the names of some of the new strokes: "rocking horse," "swimming," "raking," where once only such names as "kneading" and "petrissage" were used. One physical therapist I interviewed mentioned that he wasn't sure of the names of the strokes he used; his technique, as that of all people doing massage, developed largely out of trial and error, as in any other "art form." The human potential movement may use the new "rocking horse" or "swimming," but it still uses age-old techniques—Chinese "cupping," for one, which dates back at least 2,500 years. I include some of the old and much of the new, in order to present the best of all methods.

All massage movements fall basically into three categories: stroking, (also called effleurage), compression, and percussion (also called tapotement). Every person doing massage has his or her own method of using these movements. They can be varied by pressure, direction, or the part of the hand being used. One masseur may use one hand for a stroke; one may use both hands. But the massage should always be performed at a uniform rate of speed and in a slow and even rhythm. At almost all times throughout the massage, one hand is always kept in contact with the subject's body.

Stroking

In the Bible and in Homer's *Odyssey* when they speak of "anointing thyself with oil," they were very likely referring to the stroking movement. To my knowledge it is used in all systems of massage.

Generally, stroking, or effleurage, is of two types—superficial or deep. The term effleurage is usually used in Western massage when referring to a light pressure, and this includes strokes with the fingertips alone as well as return strokes with the whole hand.

The usual procedure for stroking is to hold hands palms down, fingers close together and cupped to fit

the contours of the subject's body. The thumbs may be spread or closed. One or both hands are used, depending on the area of the body or on the practitioner's preference.

The direction of the stroke—particularly in deep stroking—should be centripetal, or toward the center. This means that most deep stroking is done in the direction of the heart or in the direction of the veins that bring blood to the heart. Stroking is also done following the contours of a muscle. It is sometimes helpful to study a chart of the main muscle groups of the body before doing a massage for the first time. But even without such a chart, if the person doing the massage is really attuned to the other person's body as well as to his own, and if the massage is conducted gently at first, with pressure built up as needed, the muscles can be felt under the fingers. It is a little more difficult to do this during superficial stroking, as there is rarely enough pressure applied to define the muscles with the fingers.

It is important to maintain a uniform and unvarying pressure during each stroke, and when moving from stroke to stroke and area to area, and always to keep one hand lightly in contact with the subject's body. There may be times when contact must be lost briefly, but this will seldom happen during a movement. If, at the end of a stroke, hands must briefly lose contact, a rhythmic and gentle motion should be maintained so that the moment of noncontact acts something like a pause in music. Any abruptness of movement might jolt the person being massaged out of his or her relaxed mood.

Superficial stroking requires the use of extremely light pressure, much as Lucas-Championnière described—"little more than a caress." Usually the entire hand is used, with fingers held together and the thumb spread or opened to suit the needs of the part of the body being massaged. In superficial stroking, movements may be centrifugal, or away from the heart. This is true for legs and arms, because the hair falls that way and the usual centripetal strokes might be uncomfortable.

The Oriental method of stroking is similar to the Western method. The rubbing and stroking are usually done with the hand flat on the body or with the balls of the fingers alone. In Japan there is also a complete system of fingertip massage, called *Shiatsu*, in which specific points on the body (acupuncture points) are pressed.

Deep stroking is done with sufficient pressure to produce mechanical effects as well as reflex effects; the

---

1973. In the United States, arrests of women under the age of eighteen increase 62 percent over the rates of 1967. During the same period of time, arrests for males under eighteen increase 21 percent.

blood is actually squeezed and pushed through the veins so that it flows more rapidly to the heart. In deep stroking, movements are *always* performed in the direction of the veins, or toward the heart. The purpose of this deep-stroking massage is generally to assist the venous and lymphatic circulation. Such stroking relieves fatigue and improves the tone of the skin and muscles. To perform deep massage, any part of one hand or both hands could be used. Usually it's done with the entire hand. The hand is kept in contact with the body during the entire stroke to avoid stimulating the nervous system by breaking contact with the skin. During return strokes, pressure is kept light, as in superficial stroking, so that it does not interfere with the mechanical effect of the deep stroke. Deep stroking should not induce pain under ordinary circumstances. Pressure should be uniform and vary only according to the bulk of the massage being massaged or the body type being manipulated. (A frail girl will usually require less pressure than a bulky, muscular male.)

Usually, superficial stroking is done prior to deep stroking to help the muscles relax.

Compression

Kneading. Some people use the term "kneading," interchangeably with the French word "petrissage." I call it kneading because it's easier and more descriptive. Generally, kneading is very relaxing.

To do it, the masseur grasps loose flesh . . . or a muscle . . . or a part of a muscle . . . between the thumbs and fingers, taking as much as can comfortably be held onto. The muscle is then allowed to slip slowly from between the fingers. It is repeated for adjacent areas. Kneading may also be done with the palms or with the thumbs and the second and third fingers of one or both hands—whatever works best for the masseur or subject. Usually both hands are used for the bulkier muscles.

Movements are kept slow, gentle, and rhythmic, and care must be taken to avoid pinching. The part of the

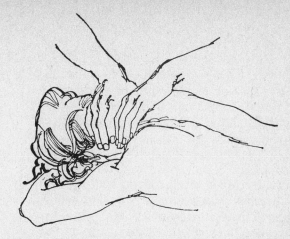

hand being used conforms to the contour of the area. As a rule, heavy pressure is directed toward the veins and heart. The muscles for which kneading works best are the larger, thicker ones of the torso and extremities, or those which are usually extremely tight or tense (trapezius, pectorals, latissimus dorsi, triceps, biceps gluteus maximus, gracilis, rectus femorus, and gastrocnemius). These are generally the muscles of the neck, upper arms, back, hips and buttocks.

Oriental kneading massage. The ancient Chinese system contains many shaking or vibrating movements that are at first gentle and then gradually build up in intensity. They are used to tone up the muscles and joints. There are a number of variations of the grasping movement: (1) "rolling of the muscles": individual muscle cords are grasped between the fingertips or between the palms of the hands and rolled backward or forward in a linear or circular motion; (2) "shrinking": the skin and muscles of the neck and shoulders are compressed into folds; (3) "shaking": individual muscle cords are grasped between the fingertips and shaken vigorously backward and forward. This is done for the arms, legs, neck, and back.

In modern Japanese systems, which are based on the ancient Chinese, kneading is done either with the thumb and index finger or with all four fingers, or the middle finger alone. The tendons which cross the joints are massaged in this manner. This motion is supposed to break up any pathological deposits that may collect in these areas, and relieve symptoms that occur after an acute attack of rheumatism of the joints has subsided. It is thought to correct the enlargement and hardening that make the joints difficult to bend, as well as bring relief to some cases of partial paralysis.

Friction. Physical therapists consider these movements good for loosening scars and helping to absorb fluids around joints. The whole palm can be used, or part of the palm, or the thumb or fingers alone. These strokes are done by moving the superficial tissues over the underlying structures by keeping the hand in firm contact and making circular movements over a small area at a time. Pressure should be firm but not heavy. The part of the hand being used is always in contact with the subject's skin.

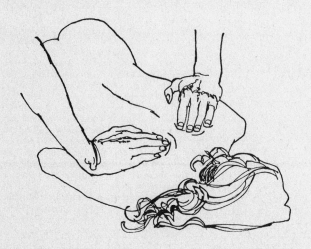

1973. The U.S. Supreme Court makes two landmark decisions in *Roe v. Wade* and *Doe v. Bolton,* rendering the abortion laws of Texas and Georgia unconstitutional, and, in effect, declaring all laws prohibiting abortion to be unconstitutional.

Percussion

There are any number of percussion movements that date back to ancient Rome, when masseurs used a wooden palette to restore tone to the body. The movements are usually brief, brisk, and rapidly applied contacts with one hand or both hands alternately. There is "hacking"—done with the outer border of the hand, or the relaxed fingers, bouncing the hands alternately off the part being treated as in the drawing above. It may also be done with a kind of whipping motion, using fingers as the flexible portion of the whip. There is also "clapping," in which the fingers and palms form a concave surface. If the hands are cupped, there is a deeper sound. "Beating" is done with the fists half-closed or closed. Then, also, there is "tapping," which is done with the tips of the fingers. None of the movements are intended to produce pain, but to stimulate the body.

Vibration and shaking movements are sometimes included among the percussive movements. Vibration is produced by placing the fingertips in contact with the skin, and shaking the entire arm, thereby transmitting a trembling movement to the subject.

Professional masseurs like to do percussive movements at the end of the session. But Beard's textbook expresses the need for caution and urges physical therapists not to do these movements on any person with a serious disorder. They feel that the benefits of these percussive motions, which is increased circulation of the capillaries, may be achieved by other methods, such as the use of heat.

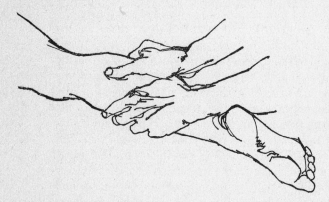

Other, less commonly used Western massage techniques are "swimming," which is a stroke that is good for the broad muscles of the thorax. To do the swimming stroke on the abdomen, hands are placed flat on either side, with fingers pointing toward each other to the center. Hands should glide, pressing gently to the opposite side. This should be a gradual movement up and down the abdomen and chest. Then there are such strokes as "throwing," "shaking," "pulling," and "sawing," which are essentially what their names imply. To "throw" the subjects arm, do just that; "shaking" a limb or "pulling," also need no explanation.

The ABC's of Ice Cream
Mrs. S. T. Rorer

Two different kinds of ice cream are known to the confectioner: the Philadelphia, which might correctly be called the American cream, and its foreign rival, the Neapolitan. The first, when prepared properly, is made from good cream, scalded, flavored and sweetened. Neapolitan ice cream differs in that it contains the yolks of eggs.

Prepare carefully the mixture and allow it to cool while you chip the ice and pack the can. Before beginning, read carefully the receipt and the method employed for packing.

Where cream alone is used one-half or one-third of the quantity used should be scalded, the sugar dissolved in the scalded portion, and when cool added to the remaining quantity of cream. Where cream is not obtainable, milk may be used enriched by the yolks of eggs, allowing four to each quart of milk. Scald the milk in a double boiler; beat the eggs and sugar together; add to the hot milk, cook for a moment, then strain into the ice cream mould and freeze.

Care Must be Used in Every Part of the Work

Always use earthen or porcelain dishes, wooden spoons and granite colanders for the mashing and straining of fruits. Never use in the preparation of ice cream any utensils that have been used for cooking vegetables.

Thoroughly scald the ice-cream can each time before using, no matter how carefully it was cleaned before being put away. Never allow the ice cream to remain in the can over night. This cannot be done with safety.

Where part milk and part cream are to be used for ice cream the milk should be heated, the sugar added, the mixture cooled and frozen, and the cream whipped to a stiff froth and stirred into the frozen mixture. Avoid gelatine and arrowroot if you can afford cream. One quart of raw cream will make two quarts of vanilla ice cream, and two quarts and a pint of fruit cream.

Where such flavorings as orange, lemon or vanilla extracts, chocolate or coffee are used add them to the cream before freezing. For fruit ice creams add the fruit after the mixture is frozen. This will prevent curdling and give a better flavor. This rule also applies to brown bread or bisque ice creams. If such articles are added first they become soft and pasty in the stirring.

How the Freezing is Accomplished

The time and manner of freezing do not depend so much upon the construction of the machine or the rapidity of the turning as upon the fineness of the ice and the coarseness of the salt. It is a well-known fact that when snow or fine ice and salt are mixed together a degree of cold is produced by the rapid melting of the ice that will draw the heat from any mixture placed within their grasp, bringing it down to freezing point. Place the freezer on a bench or chair of convenient height to the person who is to do the freezing, securing it firmly to the bench.

Have ready the finely chopped ice and salt. These may be mixed in a pan, allowing one part of salt to four of ice. Fill the space around the can in the tub to the very top, packing the mixture down until quite firm; give the handle a turn to settle the ice below the lid. Remove the cross-bar and lid and put in the mixture to be frozen. Readjust and begin to turn slowly and carefully for at least five minutes. As the ice melts refill the tub, turning more rapidly as the mixture freezes until it becomes difficult to turn which should be in at least fifteen minutes. Ice cream frozen in

From *Ladies' Home Journal*, Vol. 16, No. 7, 1889.

1973. The president's Council of Economic Advisors estimates that American women are paid as much as 20 percent less than men; that nearly half of all U.S. women over the age of sixteen are working; that women make up almost 40 percent of the total work force; and that of the 15 percent of working women comprising the professional or technical class, over 5 percent are teachers.

Making

from five to seven minutes is apt to be buttery.

Caring for the Cream After it is Frozen

After the mixture is frozen take off the crank with its cross-bar, carefully remove the lid, take out the dasher, and with a wooden spoon smooth down the cream. Do not let a grain of salt or a drop of brine fall into the cream. Replace the lid, closing the hole in it with an ordinary cork. Draw off the water by removing the lower plug. Repack with salt and ice, covering the entire top of the can. Put over this a piece of brown paper tucked carefully around the edge, and over the whole a piece of blanket or carpet dipped in the brine you have just drawn off. Stand in a cold place for an hour or an hour and a half to ripen. If the ice melts repack with more ice and salt.

When Small Forms are to be Used

Where the cream is to be served in forms have ready an ordinary bucket or tub the bottom of which is filled with coarse salt and ice; the pieces may be as large as hens' eggs. Dip the mould in cold water, press it down into the mixture, leaving it open, of course, at the top. When you have removed the dasher from your freezer and beaten the cream for a moment with a wooden spoon, fill the mould solidly and quickly and smooth the top. Lay over a piece of wax paper large enough to project beyond the edges when the lid is firmly pressed on. Cement the joint with a strip of muslin dipped in melted suet. As soon as the suet touches the cold cream it hardens, forming a protection from the brine. Bury this thoroughly in the ice and salt, cover with a piece of carpet and stand aside for one or two hours. When ready to serve take the mould from the ice, wipe it carefully, plunge it into a pan of warm water and wipe off the mould; lift off the lid, turn the cream out carefully on a napkin placed on a pretty dish. All ices or creams should be served on a napkin. If the cream should happen to stick to the mould wait a moment; the heat of the room will soon loosen it. A second plunge into the warm water may remove the gloss or melt the cream, spoiling the impressions. The brick and melon moulds are the cheapest, best and most easily handled by the average person.

Sherbets, Sorbets and Vanilla Ice Cream

Sherbets, sorbets and punches are really one and the same, differing only from the ordinary water ice in that they are lighter in texture, made so by constant stirring during the freezing process, while a water ice is frozen with but little motion.

A frappe is almost a water ice, save that it is a little heavier, and should resemble, if properly made, moist or wet snow. Frappe is usually served with the meat course at a dinner, or as a drink for evening affairs or at afternoon teas, and not as a dessert.

A parfait is made from cream whipped to a froth and then frozen slowly in a mould.

A mousse is much the same as a parfait.

To make vanilla ice cream, scald one pint of fresh cream in a double boiler; add half a pound of granulated sugar and stir constantly until the sugar is dissolved; take from the fire; add another pint of cream, and. when cold, add a tablespoonful of ordinary vanilla extract. Of some of the better grades of vanilla a teaspoonful, or at most two, will be quite sufficient. Turn the mixture into the freezer and freeze as directed. Where the vanilla bean can be obtained it makes a far better flavoring. Put the cream then into a double boiler, split the bean into halves, scrape out and add the seeds to the sugar. If the bean is good and oily one-half of it will be quite sufficient. Add the seeds and sugar to the hot cream, then throw in the pod; stir it around carefully. When hot take from the fire, remove the pod. When cold add the remaining pint of cream, turn into the freezer and freeze. Vanilla ice cream is frequently served with a hot chocolate sauce.

Neapolitan and Caramel Ice Creams

All Neapolitan creams contain eggs; the same flavorings in the same way are used for both caramel and Neapolitan cream. Put a pint of cream into a double boiler over the fire; beat the yolks of three eggs and half a pound of sugar together until light; add to the cream; cook just a moment. Whisk the whites to a stiff froth, pour the hot mixture into them, and pour it backward and forward from one vessel to another until the whole is light. When cold add another pint of cream, three tablespoonfuls of caramel and one teaspoonful of vanilla; strain and freeze. The yolks only must be used.

When using chocolate or cocoa dissolve it in the pint of hot cream; the vanilla may be added, and you may then proceed as when making plain vanilla cream.

Strawberry and Other Fruit Creams

Stem and mash a quart and a pint of strawberries; add to them half a pound of sugar; stir until the sugar is dissolved; cover and stand aside while you prepare the cream. Put a pint of cream in a double boiler; add another half pound of sugar and stir until the sugar is dissolved. Take the mixture from the fire and when cold add another pint of cream. Freeze until the consistency of a thick batter. Remove the lid carefully and stir in the strawberries; readjust the lid and crank and turn slowly until the mixture becomes hard and dry. Remove the dasher and repack.

All fruit creams may be made after this recipe. Raspberries are often better for the addition of the juice of a lemon with the sugar. Peach, pineapple and apricot should have the fruit mashed, grated and sweetened.

Brown Bread, Bisque and Coffee Ice Cream

Toast dry in the oven three slices of Boston brown bread, then pound and rub through a sieve. Put one pint of cream in a double boiler; add to it half a pound of sugar; stir until the sugar is dissolved; take from the fire, and when cold add another pint of cream, a teaspoonful of caramel and a teaspoonful of vanilla. Freeze until the consistency of batter; remove the dasher; add the brown bread crumbs and turn slowly until thoroughly mixed; repack for ripening.

Bisque ice cream is made much after the same manner, using instead of the brown bread a quarter of a pound of stale macaroons grated, two stale lady fingers and four kisses rolled and put through a sieve.

To make coffee ice cream, put four ounces of the best Mocha or three ounces of the best Java coffee, freshly browned and coarsely ground, into a double boiler with one pint of cream. Cover the boiler and put it on the back part of the stove so that the mixture may steep for ten minutes; then strain through two thicknesses of cheesecloth, pressing very hard to get out all the strength of the coffee. Add half a pound of sugar and stir until the sugar is dissolved; take from the fire, and when cold add another pint of cream, pour into mould or can, and freeze as you would any other kind of ice cream.

Several Other Kinds of Ice Cream

To make ice cream from condensed milk, add sufficient boiling water to one can to make it the proper consistency. Moisten two tablespoonfuls of arrowroot with a little cold milk; add to the hot milk and cook in a double boiler for five minutes; take from the fire; add two teaspoonfuls of good vanilla, and when cold freeze as directed.

Hokey-pokey is made much after this rule. If hot milk instead of hot water is added to the condensed milk better and much more satisfactory results will be obtained.

To make frozen strawberries, mash one quart of the berries and add to them the juice of two lemons and one pound of sugar; stir until the sugar is dissolved; cover and stand aside for an hour; then add one quart of water; turn into the freezer and freeze slowly much the same as you would freeze water ice, except at the end of the time turn the dasher rapidly for about one minute. Repack for ripening. All fruits may be prepared and frozen in the same way, and all will be found most satisfactory if the directions are carefully followed.

Making and Serving Sherbet and Water Ice

To make water ice into a sherbet or sorbet, or an orange punch, turn the dasher rapidly from the beginning until the mixture is frozen. Beat the white of an egg until stiff; add a tablespoonful of powdered sugar and beat again. Remove the dasher from the can, stir in this meringue mixture, re-cover the can and stand aside until wanted.

Water ice may be served in the same way and in the same dishes as ice cream. Sherbet, sorbet and frappe are, as a rule, served in lemonade glasses or small tumblers. The best selections to serve with meat would be ginger, grape, lemon, mint or cherry.

To make orange water ice, select twelve medium-sized juicy oranges. Put one pound of granulated sugar and one quart of water over the fire; add the chipped yellow rind of three oranges and boil the mixture for five minutes; strain at once. When cold add the strained juice of the twelve oranges and strain again through two thicknesses of cheesecloth; turn the mixture into a freezer; give the crank a few slow turns and let it rest; then turn slowly as before and rest again; and so continue until the water ice is sufficiently frozen. It must not be light nor frothy. A much longer time is required for freezing water ice than for making ice cream. When the mass is frozen it may be repacked.

Where an ordinary patent freezer cannot be afforded a tin kettle packed in a common water bucket with a paddle to be used for the stirring will make exceedingly good ice cream. Where time, however, is counted as money the patent freezers are the best.

Some General Rules to Follow

Allow a half pound of granulated sugar to each quart of cream unless acid fruits are used; then add an extra quarter of a pound. A little gelatine dissolved in "milk creams" gives them body.

Where the freezing tub has two holes, one near the top and the other near the bottom, keep the bottom one always closed, and the upper one open, or the salt water may overflow the freezing can.

If the salt water is allowed to dry on the cross-bar or in the cogs the wheels will refuse to turn. Do not hammer nor force them into place; dip the whole into hot water, soak a moment, then put on a few drops of machine oil and wipe and adjust the cross-bar. To prevent a recurrence, wash the cross-bar thoroughly each time before putting it away. Wash and dry the tub thoroughly, scald the can, and put it away in a perfectly dry place.

The finer the ice is chipped the closer it packs, the less waste there is, and the more quickly the mixture freezes.

1973. The Senate unanimously passes bill S.2102, which proscribes credit merchants from discriminating on the basis of sex or marital status.

Brown & Bigelow

Poker to Win

Clement McQuaid

Poker is, in the final analysis, a kind of rummy game, a game in which you try to acquire certain combinations of cards. The two main types of poker are Draw and Stud, but there are as many variations as there are cards in a deck. Even a long-experienced poker player in a "Dealer's Choice" game occasionally comes up against a variation he's never seen before.

The variations are usually a combination of wild cards and wild rule changes. The expert player may not like some of these off-beat games, but he isn't bothered by them because he knows that the most skillful player has the advantage in "wild" games.

The object of all poker games except "Low" games is to wind up with the best hand in the game.

Draw Poker

In draw poker, each player is dealt five face-down cards. The players are, in turn starting at the dealer's left, given an opportunity to "open," or make a bet. A common variation is the requirement of a pair of Jacks or better to open.

Those who want to "stay" in the game either match the opener's bet or raise it, in accordance with rules for betting which have been established before the cards are dealt. The three general classifications of betting start with table stakes, and any player may bet all his chips at any time. The second is pot-limit table stakes, in which a raise may be made up to the current amount of the pot until the table stake is reached, and the third and commonest is the fixed limit game. This is often linked with a fixed number of raises.

Each player who "stays" has the privilege of discarding part of his hand and drawing new cards, with the dealer dealing around the table, starting at his left. A player may discard up to three cards, and in some rule variations may discard four cards or draw an entire new hand. With the hands completed, betting resumes.

The original opener either bets or "checks." Each player in rotation has the opportunity to "stay" by meeting whatever bet has been made or "raise" by meeting the previous bet and betting an additional amount. If he elects not to meet the bet or raise, he drops out. When all players meet a bet without raising, a bettor is said to be "called," and exposes his hand, along with the hands of the "callers." The best hand wins the pot.

From a deck of 52 cards, it is possible to deal 2,598,960 different five-card hands—poker hands. Of those hands, 1,098,240 will contain a pair. Other

HOLDING HANDS—CHEATER'S STYLE

"If you're in a poker game with strangers, perish the thought," the old gambler said, "watch how every player holds the deck when he deals the cards.

"When a dealer holds the cards with a wide space between his first and second fingers, he may not be cheating, but he's holding the deck in such a way that he can, whenever he has a mind to. He always holds the deck that way, so that nobody will notice anything different about his deal if he decides to cheat.

"It's known as a 'Mechanic's Grip,' and a good card mechanic can deal cards off the bottom of the deck without anybody in the game knowin' what's happening. He can't do it if he's holding that left-hand first and second finger close together.

"Whenever I spot a mechanic's grip in a card game, I get out. The guy may not be cheating me, but I know he can do it and get away with it if he wants to. Somehow, I can't play my usual game under such conditions."

Aside from moral scruples, few "friendly game" participants are willing to risk getting caught. Not many social stigmas equal that faced by the known gambling cheat, and the ostracism carries over into other parts of his life.

A player who "welches" on his gambling losses faces social ostracism, too. Gambling debts are uncollectable in a court of law, and so a strict Code of Honor has been built up to assure payment of them. A man may be excused for non-payment of his grocery bill or the interest on his mortgage, but let him ignore a gambling loss and he is in deep trouble with his area of society.

For the most part, the player has a right to assume that most friendly games are honest and that those involved will pay their losses. He knows there is no built-in house "edge." He is matching his luck and ability against those of other players and if he is properly informed has an "even money" chance of winning.

1973. Billie Jean King beats Bobby Riggs in a much ballyhooed tennis match billed as a battle of the sexes.

possibilities out of 2,598,960 possible hands will result in:

4 Royal Flushes
36 Straight Flushes
624 Four-of-a-Kind Hands
3,744 Full Houses
5,108 Flushes
10,200 Straights
54,912 Three-of-a-Kind Hands
123,552 Two Pair Hands

This means you have one chance out of 21 of being dealt two pairs, 1 chance in 47 of getting three of a kind, 1 in 255 of getting a straight, 1 in 509 of getting a flush, 1 in 694 of a full house, and 1 in 4,165 of getting four of a kind in a pat hand.

From the multi-million possibilities, any player quickly realizes that the odds in draw poker are fairly complex. In drawing three cards to a pair, the odds against making any improvement are roughly 2½ to 1. Other percentages are:

Arriving at:	Odds Against:
Two Pairs	5.25 to 1
Three of a Kind	7.74 to 1
Full House	97.3 to 1
Four of a Kind	359 to 1

Knowing the rules of the game is elementary in poker. Knowing the mathematical possibilities of filling out a hand is tremendously important. There's much more to the game, however, than knowing the data. You can get the necessary information from books, but it won't make you a superior poker player.

For one thing, you have to know the Poker Attitude of the other players in the game. Knowing them away from the poker table isn't enough; you must know how they bet and how they play. You need to be a good psychologist.

While poker is one of the greatest of all gambling games, never forget that it is also a game of skill. In *Oswald Jacoby on Gambling,* the card expert says, "If you play poker and lose more often than you win, don't place the blame upon your luck—you are being outplayed."

Remember that the best hand doesn't always win in poker; the best hand still in at the finish of the game is the winner, and many winning hands are frozen out or bluffed out before the showdown.

A good poker player needs something you can't buy —daring. Call it "guts," courage or what you will, every superior poker player has it. When he thinks he holds the winning hand, he backs his judgment to the limit.

People who make money at poker are generally agreed that the best hand going *into* a draw poker game is usually the best hand at the finish. In a six or seven-handed game, a pair of Kings will stand up more often than it will lose.

Tom James says, "I've spent a lifetime learning to play winning poker, and the big thing I've learned is how to figure what the other players have in their hands. I don't often miss, but when I do, I get hurt bad, because I back my judgment to the limit. Teaching anybody else how to read draw poker hands is out

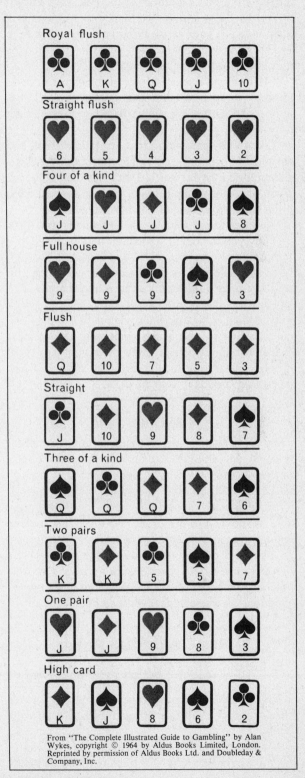

From "The Complete Illustrated Guide to Gambling" by Alan Wykes, copyright © 1964 by Aldus Books Limited, London. Reprinted by permission of Aldus Books Ltd. and Doubleday & Company, Inc.

of the question. It's something you've gotta learn for yourself.

"One important thing I've learned is to run for the woods when I think I'm beat. There's players who think it's a sign of weakness to drop out of a round. They're real proud of saying that they can't be bluffed. Man, I'd like to play against those dudes seven days a week.

"A poor player sticks in the game because he's already got a big investment in the pot. That's absolutely crazy. The minute you think you're gonna lose a hand, toss in your cards. What you already have in the pot has nothin' to do with it. Throwin' good money after bad is no way to get ahead.

"Bluffing's an important part of the game, but you gotta know when to bluff. One thing I can tell you, don't try to bluff a big winner or a big loser and get away with it.

"Like in any gambling game, try to lose small and win big. If you think you've got the winning tickets, bet 'em for all they're worth. Don't lose the old moxie. If you're afraid with what you think is the best hand in the game, you shouldn't be playing poker.

"Another thing, gamble when the odds are right. Let's say you're holding a medium high pair and you think the guy who just raised has a pair of Aces. If the pot's small, toss in your hand. But count the pot. Let's say there's fifteen bucks in it and the guy with the Aces has just raised a buck. Call.

"The chances against improving your hand to two pair are five to one against you, and the chances against winding up with three of a kind are eight to one against you. But the payoff is 15 to 1. Don't pass up good odds in your favor."

MR. ODDS-MAKER'S BEST BET

Mr. Odds-Maker says, "The game doesn't call for as much skill as Stud. Mix up your play; don't set a pattern. If you stay with a weak hand that doesn't get better with the draw, toss it in. There's no point in throwing good money after bad. One of the great old-time poker players once told me, 'The hardest poker player in the world to bluff is a lousy player.' He also said, 'Know what's saved me more money than anything else in poker? Knowing when I'm over-matched and having the sense to get out of the game.' Of course, he was seldom over-matched."

Five-Card Stud Poker

In five-card Stud Poker, a first card is dealt face down to each player in rotation, and a second card face up. High card showing opens the betting. Three more cards are dealt face up, with betting after each round.

A rule of thumb in a conservative game is not to stay unless you can beat what's showing. If one player

has an Ace up and you have nothing as good, get out. Only if you have another Ace up or a pair do you stay. A pair of deuces on the first two cards, incidentally, will win more pots than it will lose, depending in some measure, of course, on how many people are in the game. On the first two cards, however, any pair is considered worth staying on. A high pair is always a betting hand.

As the hands progress, you must observe all the up-cards. If one player has an Ace up, and so do two others, the chance of any one of them having an Ace in the hole is lessened.

When an up-pair shows in an opponent's hand and has you beaten, you are playing a losing game to stay for another card or cards in the hope of beating his hand.

How to bet your hands in five-card Stud depends in large part on the characteristics of the game. If all the players are playing cautiously, it behooves you to play the same way. If everybody is staying, let 'em, but you get out if you don't have the cards.

Tom James says, "There's times in Stud when you know for sure that you've got the best hand. There's no guesswork. You've got a high pair, with one of 'em face down—let's say, a pair of Aces. Nobody else has anything higher than a King up, and there's no possible flushes or straights.

"You've got a sure winner, but your object oughta be to win as much as you can. If you start bettin' big, you'll scare everybody out. Wait 'til the last round to raise, and then kick the pot as high as it'll go.

"Here's another tip that's made me a bundle over the years. Once in a blue moon, you'll find a really smart poker player who'll fool you on this, but not often. When a player keeps lookin' at his hole card, the chances are 99 to 1 that it's a big, fat nothing. If it's any good, he'll remember it after one glance.

"Another thing, you gotta bet a face-up pair to the limit. If the other players know what they're doin', they'll drop out unless they got you beaten, but you gotta do it to win the maximum when your hole card makes what's showin' three of a kind.

"Only a lame-brain draws to two or three-card flushes or straights in five-card stud. Another thing,

1974. The U.S. Department of Labor announces that 142,597 women employees are owed over $65 million in back pay for alleged sex discrimination directed against them by their employers while on the job.

562   Poker
SIMPLE PLEASURES

don't bet into a hand that must either raise or drop, like a possible flush or straight. If he has it, he'll raise you right back, and if he doesn't, he won't even call."

Seven-Card Stud

While the object of the game is the same, seven-card Stud is as different from the five-card variety as day is from night. The big difference is that each player makes a five-card hand from seven cards. Given this extra choice, the hands are invariably better than in draw or five-card stud.

The game is much more deceptive than five-card stud in another respect. With three cards face down and four face-up, a powerful winning hand can be well concealed.

Many good players won't stay in a seven-card stud game unless they get a concealed pair, a 7-spot or better split pair (one up and one in the hole) or three cards of the same suit on the first three cards.

Other good players contend that it takes a second up-card to let you know whether your hand is going anywhere or not. They stay for a second up-card, but drop fast if it doesn't improve the original holding.

Betting is much the same in seven-card as in five-card, but the player must bear in mind that the winning hand will almost invariably be better.

There is usually more money in the pot than in the five-card game, not only because there's an extra round of betting, but because the potentialities for good betting hands are better.

Tom James says, "I love the game. To me, it combines the best features of both Stud and Draw. And it's the game where the experts come off best.

"There's a tendency in seven-card to stick around, even when you have a rotten hand. Most players do it. Actually, you don't have to stay as often to make a lot of money as you do in five-card, because the pots are bigger. It costs money to stay, and there's no point unless you think you're gonna win.

"Whenever anybody in the game has two cards face up that have me beaten, I get out. I'll take the second face-up card to see what happens, but when it's on the table and I'm beaten, I won't stick around to make anybody prove it to me.

'Studying the face-up cards is even more important in Seven-Card than in Five-Card. Like in Draw, you gotta try to figure what everybody has, and the face-up cards can tell you a lot."

Lowball

This is a weird variation of draw poker in which the low hand wins. The official rules say that straights and flushes don't count and Ace is low, so the perfect hand is Ace,2,3,4 and 5. A pair of Aces, incidently, is considered lower than a pair of deuces. In some variations, straights count, in which case Ace,2,3,4 and 6 is a perfect hand.

Most hands that stay draw one card or are pat. The lowest hand after the draw is usually an eight-high bust.

High-Low Draw

This is draw poker in which high hand and low hand split the pot. The Ace is not customarily ranked as low card, and straights and flushes count as in regular draw poker.

For some reason, more players go for "low" in this game than for "high," although it is usually sounder to draw to a good high hand than to a good low one, because a low hand may be "improved" right out of contention.

High-Low Seven-Card Stud

This variation is popular because it is often possible for one hand to win both "high" and "low." The player is entitled to use his seven cards in any way he likes to put together both a high and low hand.

Tom James advises the player to try for low. Sometimes, he points out, low cards can be put together so that they will not only win "low" but will make a flush or straight that will win "high."

One variation of this game stipulates that you must win both high and low or you lose, if you try for both high and low.

Wild Card Poker

All forms of poker are sometimes played with "wild" cards, the commonest being deuces, one-eyed Jacks and Joker. With any wild cards, the hands are naturally better. Two pairs will often induce an optimistic player to bet, although anything less than three Aces seldom wins. Since the wild cards increase every player's chance for a good hand, heavier betting results.

1974. The Ninety-Fourth Congress carries a record high enrollment of women members. Of the eighteen originally seated, a nineteenth is added later in 1975 as the result of a special election.

Wild-card varieties of poker such as Baseball, Spit in the Ocean, Whiskey Poker, Wild Widow and others enjoy regional popularity. In most wild-card games, five-of-a-kind beats a straight flush. Any player in a wild-card game should get comparative values of various holdings stipulated before play starts.

WINNING HANDS

The best hand still in the game at the show-down is the winner, and it may vary from a Royal Flush to a face-card high "bust."

To say that any hand other than a Royal Flush or four-of-a-kind is a "sure-winner" has to be imprecise —and in the case of four-of-a-kind, four Aces beat four Kings.

Any flat statement as to what hand will win an "average" game is open to argument. What constitutes an "average" game? How many hands contain an "average" run of cards?

Tom James approaches the problem from a slightly different angle. He says, "You've gotta have certain minimums to stand any *chance* of winning in an average game. For example, any player who expects to win a hand of draw poker with less than Jacks Up is too optimistic for me. I've lost more three-of-a-kind hands to Full Houses than I like to remember, but I'd bet 'em again.

"I'd say you've got a fair chance of winning a hand of Draw with Queens Up. In five-card stud, I'd be happy with Aces or Kings. In seven-card stud, I'd want three-of-a-kind, preferably tens or face cards. In Deuces Wild Draw, it takes three Aces to make me feel I've got a chance.

"Even though these hands will win an 'average' round, I wouldn't bet a dime on 'em without knowing the circumstances. How many cards the other players draw and how they bet may make me think I've got a lead-pipe cinch or may convince me that my hand is borderline, a 'maybe' winner.

"Don't ever forget that your chances of winning depend on who you're playing with, almost as much as on the cards you draw. A Big-League poker player wins more often than he loses, but he doesn't always win on the best hand in the game. He may win with a 'bust,' and he may win with what's really the second or third-high hand. But one thing for sure, he *never, never* loses on the best hand in the game. He plays it right down to his bottom dollar."

Poker Etiquette

John Moss

Contrary to the assumption, echoed below, that poker is a man's game, of nearly 50 million poker players in the United States, nearly half are women.

1. Before you deal, always offer the cards to the man on your right to cut. This is an important part of the etiquette of poker. Also it is clear indication of your honesty. Even if you are playing in an informal game in which the cards are dealt without being cut, offer them for the cut when you deal. It is well to get in the habit of doing things right, and it will help you to play more naturally in another game in which the rules are closely followed.

2. Deal the cards down, holding the deck close to the table, with the front of the deck turned down slightly. This reduces the chances of your flashing a card. In addition, players watching for their own cards in draw or their down cards in stud do not like to see what they are going to get. They want to squeeze them out, and this is their privilege.

3. Shuffle the cards with care, making particularly sure that, after a hand in which three of a kind showed, the cards are well mixed. It is always annoying to the others to have the three kings of a previous hand come one after the other in a hand of stud.

4. Call the cards as you deal them. When dealing the first round,

call: "queen," "seven," "jack," etc., as you deal the up-cards. On the second round, announce the hands: "queen–six," "jack–nine—two spades," "pair of sevens," etc. Always call every pair and call all possible straights or flushes (three cards showing is enough to make the holding possible). After dealing the round of up-cards, designate the first bettor with the statement: "pair of sevens bet" or "ace bets," etc. This speeds up the game. While every player normally watches the fall of the cards, the dealer should call each holding as he deals.

Don't peek

5. Never, never peek at cards coming up in later rounds, even though you are out of the hand. This is a bad breach of poker etiquette and causes distrust and ill-will. Nor should you permit anybody else to peep at cards still in the deck that will be dealt in the next round. The suspense of a critical hand may be intense, but that does not excuse riffling through the deck to see if that flush is going to come in.

6. Even though you are out of the hand, do not attempt to look at any other player's hole cards or watch him squeeze out his draw,

1974. Maria de los Angelos becomes Spain's first female bullfighter in a controversial ruling by the Supreme Labor Court of Spain. Previously, the Spanish Bullfighter's Union had denied her a license to practice her art.

unless he states that it is all right for you to do so. If he has anything, you'll see it soon enough anyway, and by waiting you will not antagonize anyone. Needless to say, after having been given the courtesy of seeing another man's holding, you must not give any indication of the nature of his hand. Nor should you then look at anybody else's hand.

7. Under no circumstances should you attempt to see the hand of a player who has bet and won the pot when no one called. This is inexcusable. The whole idea of poker is to get others to pay to see your cards, and whether you are in the pot or not you have no right to look at an uncalled hand. If, for example, a man opens and has several callers, draws three cards and bets and no one calls, he must show his openers, but you are not entitled to see his other cards. Remember, though, that when a hand is checked* or called, all players in the game (whether in this particular hand all the way or not) are equally entitled to see every hand—both the winning hand and the others. Thus, if somebody asks to see your cards after the hand is over, you are bound to show them, regardless of whether or not you won the pot, provided the hand was either checked on the last round, or there was a bet and you were a caller.

If you drop out before the last round, you are not required to show your cards to anybody, and doing so is a courtesy only. You may, of course, refuse. But it is important to remember that everybody has an equal right to see every hand on a checked last round or to see all of the caller's hands on a bet-and-called last round. If there is a bettor and no one calls, no one in the game is entitled to see the winning hand, and to try to see it either openly or as you pick up and arrange the cards is in very bad taste and upsets the game.

Stay alert

8. Do not delay the game. Bet promptly when it is your turn. If you raise, say it so that the others hear. If you fold, turn your cards at once. No one is entitled to ask what up-cards you folded, and you should not answer, as it is unfair to the other players. Some will have noted your up-cards before you folded, and if a player who failed to do this can ask you what you had and get an answer, there is no longer any premium on alertness. But bet, raise, fold, and check in turn. Do the thing right! Doing any of these out of turn disrupts the game. It is unfair to the other players. If you fold out of turn it has a psychological effect on the other players who are still making up their minds what to do.

Betting out of turn is careless and unfair to the others. If you raise out of turn you are likely to hurt yourself, because it often means those who might have stayed for the original bet and then felt forced to see the raise will fold up, glad to have saved some money. All of these admonitions may seem elementary, but the fact is they are violated repeatedly by hundreds of thousands of poker players. Learn to play right! For all its seemingly informal nature, poker is an exacting game, with an etiquette comparable to that of golf. Do it right—and insist that the others do so. No game can survive sloppy play. No one enjoys a careless game as much as he does a correct one. Discipline yourself to play properly; it will help your game.

Remember each draw

9. Do not ask how many cards anybody drew in draw poker. The dealer should announce each draw—including his own, if he stays—and it is up to the other players to be alert and notice what each man takes. Very often one finds instances such as this: opener draws three cards; B draws one; C two. Opener bets, B raises. C folds. Opener turns to B and says: "How many cards did you take?" B, of course, is not required to answer this question and should, in fact, remain silent. It is the opener's hard luck, and he is not entitled to an

*"Check" and other expressions used in different localities all mean the same thing: I'm staying but not betting (no one else has bet).

answer. Nevertheless, B often answers out of courtesy. In my opinion, this is unfair to the other players (when there are others in the hand), and, in any case, the opener is taking advantage of B's sense of fair play. It is quite true that in most cases, if the situation were reversed, the opener would answer the question as to his draw. But it is not good poker, and it makes for a sloppy game. If you refuse to answer when asked, others may do likewise, and soon you will have strengthened the game generally by making the players conform to this rule. One way to stop such questions is to give a wrong answer. Tell the man that you took two, when you took only one. It may not be exactly ethical, but neither is his question—and it will eventually discourage such questions.

10. Don't beef about your bad luck. Nothing is more annoying in a poker game than to have some guy grousing about his bad luck all the time. No one cares to hear about your bad luck—or that you haven't won a hand for an hour. No one is sympathetic—any more than you are when somebody else is grumbling. Learn to take the bad luck with the good, and don't throw the cards around, or complain unduly, or make a nuisance of yourself. It's never easy to sit and lose money, but everyone has to from time to time, and if you learn to lose gracefully it will not only make you more welcome in a poker game, but will put you in a better frame of mind.

11. Never criticize the play of others, either to them personally or to a third player. If a man makes a poor play, note it for your own future reference, but don't embarrass him by calling his attention to it. A man should be entitled to lose his own money any way he wants to. You should rejoice in bad plays you see around you. But don't talk about them.

Don't be unreasonable

Nor should you complain to the man on your right that he should have stayed (when he folded and your card dropped on the immediate left) or folded (when he catches the card you want). This is silly, of course, but many players do it constantly. Even when he stays on nothing in a hand when he should have folded, and catches your card, you should keep quiet. Good players don't complain about such things, but many not-so-good ones do. It is always a man's privilege to stay or fold as he wishes, and you cannot expect him to do anything except in the interests of his own cards and himself. His rights are equal to yours, and no matter how correct your raise was, for example, and how little he was justified in staying in, the fact is that if the raise fails to fold him and he then catches a card you wanted, you should still keep quiet about it.

12. Ante in turn, and get the others to do so. The pot will be found to be light sometimes, and everybody will insist he is in. Perhaps each player thinks he really is in. But somebody is light. Anteing in turn will prevent such needless situations and misunderstandings.

13. In draw poker, when you take one card to a straight or flush and fail to catch, don't throw in your hand until the betting has reached you. (I shall dwell on this repeatedly in this book, because it is most important and yet is violated repeatedly by far too many players.) It is unfair to the others for you to fold out of turn. Whereas the opener might check to your one-card draw, if he sees that you didn't catch he may go ahead and bet. Then the other players who hoped to have the round checked will have to pay to see the bettor. They resent your folding out of turn, because it makes the hand more expensive for them. If the betting is checked to you, you must check, too, even though you failed to catch. You cannot fold until somebody has bet and it is your turn to act. The same applies to stud poker.

Similarly, with any holding you must fold in turn. Suppose somebody bets and a second man raises (whether draw or stud makes no difference). If a man folds out of turn it is bad psychologically for the others. Beyond any question, anybody who cannot learn to play by the rules should not sit in any poker game. Though it is an individual game, all have equal rights.

1975. Jill Ruckelshaus is appointed by President Ford presiding officer of the National Commission on the Observance of International Women's Year (IWY).

Bee-keeping by Women

Hester M. Poole

We—the members of a small household in the pretty little Jersey village of M_____, were startled one pleasant morning in the early summer of 188__ by discovering a swarm of honey bees hovering over one corner of the rose-embowered cottage.

How we watched the interesting creatures while warm weather lasted, as they sped on their thrifty errands and stored sweets during the long procession of honey-bearing flowers with which the vicinage of New York is so richly supplied, it is not the province of these pages to describe. From them we learned about many laws which apply to larger lives, and gained other sweets than those so deftly gathered.

In every hive are found three kinds of honey-bees, the queen, workers, and drones. And it must be observed that however positive the masculine principle may be elsewhere, it is the feminine principle which here rules. The drone, or male, exists solely for prolification. He has nothing to do with the management of the hive; he cannot even gather the honey on which he feeds. The queen is the mother of the entire colony, and the workers are undeveloped females whose maternal instincts are directed to the care of the young, in addition to their incessant toil. The offices and functions of these three kinds of bees, the manner in which they are developed, and the agencies employed in producing them, are among the most wonderful facts which the naturalist has observed and tabulated.

In shape the queen-bee is long, slender, and about twice the size of the worker. Her color varies from a rich gold to a dark velvety brown, and she is destitute of that silky down or hair seen upon the others. Sometimes her body is crossed from side to side with a band of yellow. Always shy and retiring, a close search of the comb frames is often necessary in order to find her elusive form hidden under her subjects. But once seen, the inexperienced bee-keeper will afterward have no difficulty in recognizing her majesty.

As the prosperity of the swarm depends upon the queen, apiarians closely watch the habits of the mother, first being sure that she is of the best or the Italian stock. The common black bee indigenous to this country has been found far interior to its transatlantic cousin. It is more irritable and pugnacious and less thrifty, docile, and industrious. Hence the best breed is that in which two distinct strains of Italian stock unite in the queen-mother. There are men who make a business of rearing them for

From *Home-maker* Magazine, Vol. 4, Nos. 3 and 4, 1890.

sale. Imprisoned in wire-cloth cages, with an opening in the stopper filled with pure candy for food, the queen may be sent a long distance through the mails.

Sixteen days suffice from the laying of the egg to the maturation of the young queen. A few days after hatching out she emerges from the hive on a nuptial flight, the only occasion on which she ever leaves her quarters, unless it be at the head of a young colony to settle in a new home. From this time, for about three years,—the period of her natural life,—the queen-bee attends as strictly to her maternal duties as the most exacting advocate of domesticity would require. During the honey harvest, when workers are in great demand, the queen-mother lays no less than two thousand eggs every twenty-four hours. Her efforts relax as flowers decline, and still further decrease during the winter, but never entirely cease.

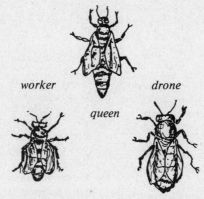

worker   *drone*
queen

The relationship between the queen-mother and the workers is close and reciprocal. The more eggs she lays the greater is their activity, and, on the other hand, she is stimulated to prodigious efforts when the workers are overwhelmed with excess of sweets. Should she become infertile they lose energy and spirit, as if conscious of the approaching extinction of the swarm. An old queen deposits but few eggs and these produce only drones, a state of things remedied by the apiarian, who then supplants her ladyship by a young successor,—a process to be described hereafter. Sometimes the workers take the matter in hand themselves, and, forgetful of past services, gently put the queen to death. In this case, by one of the most remarkable processes known in insect economy, they have already prepared the way for the rearing of a young mother in her place. The queen is dead. Long live the queen! For the bee is a true Positivist. It lives for future generations. As if conscious, from birth of the brief span of life allotted it, the first care is for the continuance of the species. To this

all else is secondary. The wisdom with which this purpose is carried out deserves close study.

The worker-bees, numbering from twenty to thirty thousand in each hive, are smaller than either the queen or the drones. An examination of the illustrations will show that while the queen is long and slender, and the drone large and clumsy like a bluebottle fly, the worker is small, compact, and trimly formed for speed and work. Its peculiarities consist of a sac below the throat in which honey is conveyed from flowers to hive, and small basket cavities on the posterior legs in which pollen is stored. Its duties are to forage for provisions, make combs and fill them, prepare food for the young, bring water and propolis (that gum or resinous coating found in such trees as the Balsam Poplar), to seal up cracks and crevices, and also to stand as sentinels in order to keep out moths and other intrusive enemies.

The workers' length of life varies from one month to eight. When flowers overflow with honey, these little creatures fairly tumble over each other in their mad flights to and from the hive, so that in a few weeks their wings are literally worn out.

With a proper degree of caution, bee stings need not be dreaded. In approaching a hive the attendant ought to be gentle and slow of gait. Quick and abrupt movements excite fear and invite attack. The ruling spirit of our apiary often handled swarms fearlessly and without protection, a practice hardly to be commended. Occasionally bees object to the personal exhalations of a visitor, who would then do well to remember the poet's aphorism and seek the enchantment of distance. They also dislike the human breath. They seldom sting at a distance from the hive or when laden with honey. An injured bee makes a peculiar noise which alarms his fellow-workers and renders them liable to attack

sting of a worker, and dart

Annals of Womankind is based mostly on the research of De Lysle Ferree Cass (1887–1973) who for thirty years compiled 30,000 file cards in his study of "facts about women in their every aspect and activity, public and private," from the farthest reaches of recorded history to 1952.

the apiarian. Other motives, in addition to those of humanity, therefore, make the attendant cautious about crushing them.

The sting of the worker-bee is composed of a sheath and two enclosed darts through which a drop of poison is thrust into the flesh. If these are not withdrawn, the bee loses its life. The sting should be scraped off and the poison squeezed out: then apply ammonia or a mixture of soda and salt. Apiarians soon grow indifferent to stings, which generally lose their virulence after the system has received repeated inoculations. Some aver that their effect is decidedly beneficient. The master of our apiary frequently went about with sting-swollen hands from which he suffered no discomfort.

While the fear of stings should prove no hindrance to bee-culture, it is well to guard the face with a veil of mosquito-netting or coarse lace. It should be three fourths of a yard wide by twice that length. Sew the ends together, and run an elastic along one edge, which must be fitted closely around the crown of a man's hat of felt or straw.

In front of the veil insert a piece of fine wire cloth having coarse meshes. It must be large enough to enable the wearer to see in all directions, say five or six inches by nine. At the bottom attach a tape to tie about the neck, and the head is safe from stings. For the hands there are long rubber gloves, and for the arms short cotton oversleeves, reaching from wrist to elbow and kept in place at either extremity with elastic bands.

Add to these precautions, the use of a "smoker," a most necessary adjunct to subdue the irascibility of these "skittish cattle," and woman is master of the situation.

bee veil

The third and last variety of the honey-bee, the loud-buzzing, stingless drones, vary in number according to the season and the quantity of prospective food. When the honey crop is small, but few are allowed to live; in a season of scarcity and in autumn all are destroyed. Then the sight of a drone escorted to the edge of the "alighting-board" in front of the hive, by a worker on either side, is a common spectacle. He is bitten by their strong mandibles, and dropped on the ground to perish. They who work not, die.

Meantime spring has come and our tenants under the flooring are growing restless.

From the winter's sleep our guests awoke in spring and proceeded so faithfully to multiply and replenish beedom, that we found it needful to establish over them that kind of parental government which men usually exercise over inferiors, that is, to provide a local habitation and then despoil them of the fruits of their labor, save only so much as is necessary to sustain life. Early in June, therefore, they were reduced to subjection by the following method:

Closing doors, windows, and blinds,—with the exception of one of the latter,—the Master sawed through the flooring directly over the bee-colony, and exposed to view a remarkable scene. Extending back from the small aperture through which the insects had gained access to the space between the floor and ceiling, the area between two sills to the length of four feet was literally packed with brood and honeycomb. Winding galleries penetrated every portion, and gave entrance to innumerable cells crowded with life in all stages of development. Here were tiny eggs, larvae, unfolding chrysalis and young bees. Swarms of bewildered workers flew up in our faces, expostulating against such vandalism in that pointed way peculiar to bees; but protected by our smokers and veils, and assisted by two friends, we conquered.

It was hard work, demanding caution, strength, and swiftness. By sunset that room looked like a miniature battlefield in which countless Lilliputians had been vanquished. The comb had been sawed from sills and flooring, broken bits dripping with amber sweetness were thrown into pails while the larger pieces and broodcomb were fitted and fastened into frames enough to make the nuclei of four colonies; that is, eight frames to each hive, or thirty-two in all.

It was estimated that in all we had taken out at least two hundred pounds of the products of the bee, including brood. The dripping mass of sweets was taken to a close room from which it could not be rifled by its little makers; the old opening to their improvised hive was closed; the bees brushed from the sole windows which admitted light, and dusk fell like a curtain upon the scene. Then three of the new colonies were carefully carried out and placed on low stands ready to receive them on the lawn, fronting south, and only a short distance from the cottage.

The fourth colony we proposed to keep in the house subject to daily inspection. One might suppose bees to be peppery inmates, but they were given no opportunity to express disapprobation. Quarters were provided in such manner that it became an "observatory hive," and during four successive years it furnished our friends and ourselves with unlimited delight and instruction. By this means we were able to

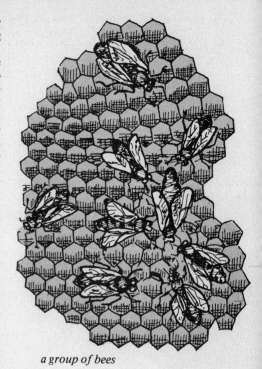
a group of bees

watch all departments of bee-housekeeping, and to admire every day something new about those instincts which act more swiftly and surely than the hard-won lore of men.

One thing more, the most important of all, was needed in each colony—a fertilized queen. As we hoped, the old hybrid queen was lost in the melee and four pure Italian majesties, which had been ordered, duly arrived. They were accompanied, as usual, by a few attendant workers. Lifting the covers, the queens, still caged, were placed upon pieces of unsealed comb where they could partake of their native ambrosia. While the bees are making their acquaintance through the bars, we will proceed to examine their little communal dwellings.

observatory hive

"In ye olden time" bees were kept in box-hives, having neither divisions nor compartments. From them honey could only

Mr. Cass—magazine contributor, illustrator, publisher, and novelist—held a lifelong interest in the accomplishments of women. One of his magazines, *Babyhood*, was the only infant and maternity periodical available in this country at its publication in 1923. In his admiration for woman's capabilities he was a man ahead of his time.

be procured by that cruel and wasteful process, the destruction of the entire swarm by sulphur. Afterward, boxes were inserted for the deposit of comb-honey and finally the present improved "movable frame" hive was evolved.

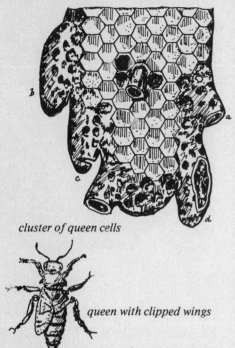

cluster of queen cells

queen with clipped wings

The one most in use is the "Simplicity Hive." In size, roughly measured, it is about two feet deep, one high, and fifteen inches wide. During prosperous seasons, a second and similar story is placed over the first to contain "section boxes," those small, square, glass-covered cubes in which comb-honey presents such an attractive appearance. After the workers have filled the lower story, they are provided with the upper hive, which they proceed to fill in like manner.

Evidently the first work of the bee is the making of a foundation upon which to build cells through all this space. Here science steps in to help by the manufacture of artificial "comb-foundations."

In this way are saved much valuable time and work, for it is estimated that no less than twenty-five pounds of honey must be gathered in order to furnish material enough for one pound of that peculiar natural exudation of the bee. Sometimes during a prosperous season a swarm will draw out into cells a sheet of foundation in a single night.

Two kinds of comb are found in every hive. The bulk of it, the worker comb measures five cells to the inch, the drone comb being one fourth wider. There is a difference in colonies, some making coarse and clumsy cells, others those as thin as tissue paper. Whenever queen cells are needed, the workers tear down the partitions between three of their own

brooding apartments to give room for the future royal highness. These cells in appearance greatly resemble small dark-colored peanuts. They are generally found on the bottom edges of the comb, but only in small numbers. When the hive is crowded with bees and in the height of the flowering season it desires to send out new colonies, there are from five to fifteen of these cells in various stages of development.

And now let us return to the four hives into which, the previous day, as many queens had been introduced. The cage containing each had been placed over an old piece of comb and the bees were left to their own devices. Readily adapting themselves to their new homes, they went in and out bringing honey as usual; opening the hives cautiously and removing the enamelled cloth covering, one could hear that low "hum of content" which is real music to the lover of bees. None of them were clinging like balls to the queen-cages, nor could we detect that peculiar hissing sound which indicates bad temper.

Where a home-reared queen is desired, a frame containing worker brood may be inserted in the queenless swarm. Move along the division board which separates the frames from the vacant chamber and in the middle of the hive place a frame of brood containing larvae two days old. This should be taken from a strong adjacent hive which can well spare some of its incipient population. Replace the cover and let the bees work out their own form of perpetuity.

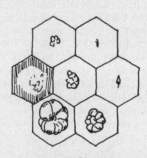

eggs and larvae

By one of the most marvellous processes known, they will at once begin to develop from several larvae a new and higher order,—the Queen. After enlarging the cells the inmates are fed on "royal jelly," which is much richer than the food usually doled out in the nursery. It has the effect of changing the worker into the fully developed female. This food is a creamy mixture of pollen and honey, and, like the other food, is first partially digested in the stomachs of the nurses.

When the larvae are six days old, or nine days after the laying of the eggs, these queen-cells are sealed up under a convex lid. In one week more the first fully grown insect bites off the end of her roomy prison and emerges, a slim dainty creature ready to examine her environments.

Her first work is to look about for other unhatched queen-cells, since her majesty allows no rival within the hive. With her strong mandibles she bites apart their prison-doors, not to give them freedom but to sting them to death. Unless it is preparing to send out a new colony the swarm will not interfere.

The newly hatched queen, now monarch of all she surveys, crawls about on the comb, and usually a week afterward,—it may be either a few days sooner or later—takes her virgin flight into space. Returning in matronly guise she settles down to serious work. Before she is three weeks old she begins to deposit eggs. During the next three years, unless overtaken by misfortune, the queen will become the mother of thirty thousand insects, each perfect in instinct and volition.

The first eggs are laid in or near the centre of one of the middle frames, the quietest, warmest and most secluded portion of the hive. Take out such a frame and you will see, attached to the base of the cells, small white objects no larger than pin-heads. These are eggs.

Then follows another wonderful transformation. In twelve days more, or three weeks from the laying of the egg, the larvae gnaws open its tissue-like cap and steps out a beautiful little creature with gentle bee-baby wings and graceful mien.

In power of vision the bee is no doubt telescopic. He is also attracted by color. In consequence, it is a good plan to have the several hives in an apiary painted with different tints. The bright colors of flowers attract them, so that nature had somewhat in addition to gratifying the love of beauty when she clothed the lily and the rose in ineffable loveliness. While "beauty has its own excuse for being," it has an added one in securing the fertilization of the plant through the office of the bee who unwittingly carries pollen from one flower to its neighbor. And it is a curious fact, as Darwin has pointed out, that flowers with deep cups, spurs or bells, which cannot readily shed their pollen, are those which secrete a precious drop of condensed sweetness within petals glowing with richest coloring. In like manner do all the processes of nature play and interplay. And in no other form of life is there found greater evidence of intelligence and design than in the honey-bee.

In the preface to the *Annals* he used a poem by Kate Fields that reads, in part:
There's not life, or death, or birth
That has a feather's weight of worth
Without a woman in it.

Suggested Reading

In addition to the books excerpted in the *Almanac,* the editors recommend the following.
We have listed paperback editions, when available.

AGING

Curtin, Sharon R., *Nobody Ever Died of Old Age*. Boston: Little, Brown, 1974. (paper)

De Beauvoir, Simone. *Coming of Age*. New York: Warner Books, 1973. (paper)

Olsen, Tillie. *Tell Me a Riddle*. New York: Dell, 1971. (paper)

ANTHROPOLOGY

Boserup, Ester. *Woman's Role in Economic Development*. New York: St. Martin's Press, 1970.

Briffault, Robert. *The Mothers: The Matriarchal Theory of Social Origins*. 1927. Reprint. Atlantic Highlands, N.J.: Humanities Press, 1959.

Davis, Elizabeth Gould. *The First Sex*. Baltimore, Md.: Penguin Books, 1972. (paper)

Mead, Margaret. *Male and Female*. 1949. Reprint. New York: Dell, 1968. (paper)
———. *Sex and Temperament in Three Primitive Societies*. 1935. Reprint. New York: Morrow, 1963.

Morgan, Elaine. *The Descent of Woman*. New York: Stein and Day, 1972. (paper)

BIOGRAPHY AND AUTOBIOGRAPHY

Angelou, Maya. *I Know Why the Caged Bird Sings*. New York: Bantam Books, 1970. (paper)

Davis, Rebecca Harding. *Life in the Iron Mills*. 1861. Reprint. With a biographical interpretation by Tillie Olsen. Old Westbury, N.Y.: The Feminist Press, 1972. (paper)

Devlin, Bernadette. *The Price of My Soul*. New York: Random House/Vintage Books, 1970. (paper)

Dunway, Abigail Scott. *Path Breaking: An Autobiographical History of the Equal Suffrage Movement in the Pacific Coast States*. New York: Schocken Books, 1971. (paper)

Gilman, Charlotte Perkins. *The Living of Charlotte Perkins Gilman*. 1935. Reprint. New York: Harper Colophon Books, 1975. (paper)

Goldman, Emma. *Living My Life*. 2 vols. New York: Dover Publications, 1930. (paper)

Hellman, Lillian. *An Unfinished Woman*. New York: Bantam Books, 1974. (paper)

Holt, Rackham. *Mary McLeod Bethune: A Biography*. New York: Doubleday, 1964.

Johnston, Jill. *Lesbian Nation: The Feminist Solution*. New York: Simon and Schuster, 1974. (paper)

Krueger, Starry. *The Whole Works: The Autobiography of a Young American Couple*. New York: Random House/Vintage Books, 1973. (paper)

Lerner, Gerda. *The Grimke Sisters from South Carolina*. Boston: Houghton Mifflin, 1969.

Reitman, Dr. Ben L. *Sister of the Road: The Autobiography of Box-Car Bertha*. 1937. Reprint. New York: Harper Colophon Books, 1975. (paper)

Stanton, Elizabeth Cady. *Eighty Years and More: Reminiscences 1815-1897*. 1898. Reprint. New York: Schocken Books, 1971.

EDUCATION

Ahlum, Carol and Fralley, Jacqueline M. *Feminist Resources for Schools and Colleges*. Old Westbury, N.Y.: The Feminist Press, 1974. (paper)

Dennison, George. *The Lives of Children*. New York: Random House/Vintage Books, 1970. (paper)

Harrison, Barbara. *Unlearning the Lie: Sexism in School*. New York: Morrow, 1974. (paper)

Holt, John. *How Children Fail*. New York: Dell, 1964. (paper)

Neill, A.S. *Summerhill*. New York: Hart Publishing Co., 1960. (paper)

Rasberry, Salli, and Greenway, Robert. *Rasberry Exercises: How to Start a School and Make a Book*. Freestone, Calif.: Freestone Publishing Co., 1970. (440 Bohemian Highway, Freestone, Calif. 95472)

Woolf, Virginia. *Three Guineas*. New York: Harcourt, Brace, Janovitch, 1963. (paper)

FEMINISM

Allen, Pamela. *Free Space: A Perspective on the Small Group in Women's Liberation*. New York: Times Change Press, 1970. (1023 Sixth Avenue, New York, N.Y. 10028)

Cade, Toni, ed. *The Black Woman*. New York: NAL/Signet Books, 1970. (paper)

Daly, Mary. *The Church and the Second Sex*. Rev. ed. New York: Harper and Row, 1975.

De Beauvoir, Simone. *The Second Sex*. 1952. Reprint. New York: Bantam Books, 1961. (paper)

Dreifus, Claudia. *Woman's Fate*. New York: Bantam Books, 1973. (paper)

Engels, Friedrich. *The Origin of the Family, Private Property and the State*. New York: International Publishers, 1972. (paper)

Ephron, Nora. *Crazy Salad: Some Things about Women*. New York: Knopf, 1975.

Friedan, Betty. *The Feminine Mystique*. New York: Dell, 1970. (paper)

Goldman, Emma. *Anarchism and Other Essays*. 1910. Reprint. New York: Dover Publications, 1969. (paper)
———. *Red Emma Speaks: Selected Writings and Speeches by Emma Goldman*. Edited by Alix Kates Shulman. New York: Random House/Vintage Books, 1972. (paper)

Gornick, Vivian, and Moran, Barbara K., eds. *Women in Sexist Society: Studies in Power and Powerlessness*. New York: NAL/Signet Books, 1971. (paper)

Grimstad, Kirsten, and Rennie, Susan. *New Woman's Survival Sourcebook*. New York: Knopf, 1975. (paper)

Hole, Judith, and Levine, Ellen. *Rebirth of Feminism*. New York: Quadrangle Books, 1971. (paper)

Janeway, Elizabeth. *Man's World, Woman's Place*. New York: Dell, 1972. (paper)

Koedt, Anne; Levine, Ellen; and Rapone, Anita; eds. *Radical Feminism*. New York: Quadrangle Books, 1972. (paper)

Marx, et al. *The Woman Question: Selections from the Writings of Karl Marx, Frederick Engels, V.I. Lenin, Joseph Stalin*. New York: International Publishers, 1970. (paper)

Mill, John Stuart. *The Subjection of Women*. 1869. Reprint. Cambridge, Mass.: MIT Press, 1970. (paper)

Mill, John Stuart, and Mill, Harriet Taylor. *Essays on Sex Equality*. Edited by Alice Rossi. Chicago: Univ. of Chicago Press, 1970. (paper)

Millet, Kate. *Sexual Politics*. New York: Avon, 1971. (paper)

Mitchell, Juliet. *Woman's Estate*. Baltimore, Md.: Penguin Books, 1971. (paper)

Morgan, Robin, ed. *Sisterhood Is Powerful*. New York: Random House/Vintage Books, 1971. (paper)

New York Radical Feminists. *Notes from the Third Year*. New York: New York Radical Feminists, 1971. (Box AA, Old Chelsea Station, New York City 10011)

Rossi, Alice S., ed. *The Feminist Papers: From Adams to De Beauvoir*. New York: Bantam Books, 1974. (paper)

Roszak, Betty, and Roszak, Theodore. *Masculine/Feminine*. New York: Harper Colophon Books, 1969. (paper)

Schneir, Miriam, ed. *Feminism: The Essential Historical Writings*. New York: Random House/Vintage Books, 1972. (paper)

Tanner, Leslie., ed. *Voices for Women's Liberation*. New York: NAL/Mentor, 1970. (paper)

Ware, Cellestine. *Women Power*. New York: Tower Publications, 1970. (paper)

Wollstonecraft, Mary. *A Vindication of the Rights of Women*. 1792. Reprint. New York: Norton, 1967. (paper)

HANDYWOMAN

Brightman, Robert. *The Home Owner Handbook of Carpentry and Woodworking*. New York: Crown, 1974. (paper)

Chilton's Repair and Tune-up Guides. New York: Chilton Publishing Co. (paper)

Consumer Guide. *How It Works and How to Fix It*. New York: NAL/Signet Books, 1975. (paper)

Curry, Barbara. *Okay, I'll Do It Myself: A Handy Woman's Primer*. New York: Random House, 1971.

Daniels, George. *The Unhandy Handyman's Book*. New York: Harper/Perennial Library, 1974. (paper)

Day, Richard. *The Home Owner Handbook of Concrete and Masonry*. New York: Crown, 1974. (paper)
———. *The Home Owner Handbook of Plumbing and Heating*. New York: Crown, 1974. (paper)

Hentzberg, Robert. *The Home Owner Handbook of Electrical Repairs*. New York: Crown, 1974. (paper)

Herchy, Harry. *Fix It Yourself: The Modern Woman's Handbook of Home Repair*. New York: Western Publishing Co./Golden Press, 1975.

Philbin, Tom. *Home Repairs Any Woman Can Do*. Englewood Cliffs, N.J.: Prentice-Hall, 1973.

Poriss, Martin. *How to Live Cheap But Good*. New York: American Heritage Press, 1971. (paper)

Schremp, William E. *Designer Furniture Anyone Can Make*. New York: Simon and Schuster, 1972. (paper)

Singerie, Ann. *How to Fix It*. New York: Doubleday, 1975. (paper)

Squeglia, Michael. *All About Repairing Small Appliances*. New York: Hawthorne, 1975. (paper)

HEALTH

Boston Women's Health Book Collective. *Our Bodies, Ourselves*. Rev. 2nd ed. New York: Simon and Schuster, 1976. (paper)

Burack, Richard. *New Handbook of Prescription Drugs*. New York: Pantheon, 1970. (paper)

Cooper, Kenneth, M.D. *The New Aerobics*. New York: Bantam Books, 1970. (paper)

Ehrenreich, Barbara, and English, Deirdre. *Witches, Midwives and Nurses: A History of Women Healers*. Old Westbury, N.Y.: The Feminist Press, 1973. (paper)

Frank, Arthur, M.D., and Frank, Stuart, M.D. *People's Handbook of Medical Care*. New York: Random House/Vintage Books, 1972. (paper)

Frankfort, Ellen. *Vaginal Politics*. New York: Bantam Books, 1973. (paper)

Kushner, Rose. *Breast Cancer: A Personal History and an Investigative Report*. New York: Harcourt, Brace, Jovanovitch, 1975.

Lappe, Frances, M. *Diet for a Small Planet*. New York: Ballantine Books, 1971. (paper)

Phelan, Nancy, and Volin, Michael. *Yoga for Women*. New York: Harper and Row, 1973. (paper)

Pomeranz, Virginia, M.D., and Schultz, Dodi. *The Mother's Medical Encyclopedia*. New York: NAL/Signet Books, 1972. (paper)

Samuels, Mike, M.D., and Bennett, Hal. *The Well Body Book*. New York: Random House, 1973. (paper)

Source Collective. *Organizing for Health Care: A Tool for Change*. Boston: Beacon Press, 1974. (paper)

HISTORY

Aries, Philippe. *Centuries of Childhood*. New York: Random House/Vintage Books, 1965. (paper)

Flexner, Eleanor. *A Century of Struggle*. 1959. Reprint. New York: Atheneum, 1968. (paper)

Fuller, Margaret. *Woman in the Nineteenth Century*. 1855. Reprint. New York: Norton, 1971. (paper)

Kraditor, Aileen. *Ideas of the Woman Suffrage Movement, 1890-1920*. Garden City, New York: Doubleday, 1971. (paper)

O'Neill, William L. *Everyone Was Brave: The Rise and Fall of Feminism in America*. New York: Quadrangle Books, 1969. (paper)

Scott, Anne Firor, ed. *The American Woman: Who Was She?* Englewood Cliffs, N.J.: Prentice-Hall, 1971. (paper)

. *The Southern Lady: From Pedestal to Politics 1830-1930*. Chicago: Univ. of Chicago Press, 1972. (paper)

Stein, Leon. *The Triangle Fire*. New York: Lippincott, 1962.

LAW

Fraenkel, Osmond K. *The Rights You Have*. New York: Warner Paperback Library, 1972. (paper)

Goodman, Emily Jane. *The Tenant Survival Book*. New York:NAL/Signet Books, 1974. (paper)

Hirsch, Barbara. *Divorce: What a Woman Needs to Know*. New York: Bantam Books, 1975. (paper)

Kanowitz, Leo. *Women and the Law: The Unfinished Revolution*. Albuquerque, N.M.: Univ. of New Mexico Press, 1969. (paper)

Matthews, Douglas. *Sue the Bastards*. New York: Dell, 1975. (paper)

Samuels, Catherine. *The Forgotten Five Million: Women in Public Employment*. New York: Women's Action Alliance, 1975. (370 Lexington Ave., New York, N.Y. 10017)

Strouse, Jean. *Up Against the Law: The Legal Rights of People Under 21*. New York: NAL/Signet Books, 1971. (paper)

ACLU Handbook Series:

Boggan, E. Carrington. *The Rights of Gay People*. New York: Avon, 1975. (paper)

Ennis, Bruce, and Siegel, Loren. *The Rights of Mental Patients*. New York: Avon, 1973. (paper)

Law, Sylvia. *The Rights of the Poor*. New York: Avon, 1974. (paper)

MONEY AND BUSINESS

Bernstein, Peter L. *A Primer on Money, Banking and Gold*. New York: Random House, 1969. (paper)

Dacey, Norman F. *What's Wrong with Your Life Insurance?* New York: Macmillan, 1966. (paper)

Graham, Benjamin. *The Intelligent Investor*. Rev. 4th ed., New York: Harper and Row, 1973.

Mayer, Martin. *The Bankers*. New York: Weybright, and Talley, 1975.

Ney, Richard. *The Wall Street Jungle*. New York: Ballantine Books, 1973. (paper)

Porter, Sylvia. *Sylvia Porter's Money Book*. New York: Doubleday, 1975.

MOTHERHOOD

Bettelheim, Bruno. *The Children of the Dream*. New York: Avon, 1971. (paper)

Bing, Elisabeth. *Six Practical Lessons for an Easier Childbirth*. New York: Bantam Books, 1973. (paper)

Boguslawski, Dorothy Beers. *Guide for Establishing and Operating Day Care Centers for Young Children*. New York: Child Welfare League of America, 1970. (paper)

Bradley, Robert A., M.D. *Husband-Coached Childbirth*. New York: Harper and Row, 1974.

Brazelton, T. Berry, M.D. *Infants and Mothers: Differences in Development*. New York: Dell, 1969. (paper)

Brutten, Milton; Richardson, Sylvia O.; and Mange, Charles. *Something's Wrong with My Child: A Parents' Book about Children with Learning Disabilities*. New York: Harcourt, Brace, Jovanovitch, 1975.

Caplan, Frank, ed. *The First Twelve Months of Life*. New York: Grosset and Dunlap, 1973. (paper)

Chess, Stella, M.D.; Thomas, Alexander, M.D.; and Birch, Herbert G., M.D., Ph.D. *Your Child Is a Person*. New York: Simon and Schuster, 1965. (paper)

Dodson, Dr. Fitzhugh. *How to Parent*. New York: NAL/Signet Books, 1971. (paper)

Ewy, Donna and Roger. *Preparation for Childbirth*. New York: NAL, 1974. (paper)

Feingold, Dr. Ben F. *Why Your Child Is Hyperactive*. New York: Random House, 1975.

Gardner, Richard. *The Boys' and Girls' Book about Divorce*. New York: Bantam Books, 1971. (paper)

Gil, David G. *Violence against Children: Physical Child Abuse in the United States*. Cambridge, Mass.: Harvard Univ. Press, 1973.

Ginott, Dr. Haim G. *Between Parent and Child*. New York: Avon, 1965. (paper)

Gordon, Thomas. *Parent Effectiveness Training*. New York: Peter H. Wyden, 1970.

Hartman, Rhonda Evans. *Exercises for True Natural Childbirth*. New York: Harper and Row, 1975.

Kitzinger, Sheila. *The Experience of Childbirth*. Baltimore, Md.: Penguin Books, 1972. (paper)

McBride, Angela Barron. *The Growth and Development of Mothers*. New York: Harper and Row, 1973.

Olds, Sally Wendkos, and Eiger, Marvin S., M.D. *The Complete Book of Breast-feeding*. New York: Bantam Books, 1973. (paper)

Pomeranz, Virginia E., M.D., with Dodi Schultz. *The First Five Years*. New York: Doubleday, 1973.

Pryor, Karen. *Nursing Your Baby*. New York: Pocket Books, 1973. (paper)

Scharlatt, Elizabeth, and Shushan, Ronnie. *Kids' Catalogue*. New York: Simon and Schuster, 1975.

Spock, Dr. Benjamin. *Baby and Child Care*. New York: Pocket Books, 1972. (paper)

Spotnitz, Hyman, M.D., and Freeman, Lucy. *How to Be Happy Though Pregnant*. New York: Berkley, 1974.

PSYCHOLOGY

Bardwick, Judith M. *Psychology of Women: A Study of Bio-Cultural Conflicts*. New York: Harper and Row, 1971. (paper)

. *Readings on the Psychology of Women*. New York: Harper and Row, 1972. (paper)

Berne, Eric. *Games Alcoholics Play*. New York: Ballantine Books, 1974. (paper)

Chesler, Phyllis. *Women and Madness*. New York: Doubleday, 1972.

Flach, Frederic F. *The Secret Strength of Depression*. New York: Lippincott, 1974.

Freud, Sigmund. *The Interpretation of Dreams*. New York: Avon, 1967. (paper)

Three Essays on the Theory of Sexuality. Translated by James Strachey. New York: Avon, 1965. (paper)

Hammer, Signe. *Women: Body and Culture: Essays on the Sexuality of Women*. New York: Harper/Perennial Library, 1975. (paper)

Horney, Karen. *Feminine Psychology*. New York: Norton, 1967. (paper)

. *Self Analysis*. New York: Norton, 1942. (paper)

. *The Neurotic Personality of Our Time*. New York: Norton, 1937. (paper)

. *Our Inner Conflicts*. New York: Norton, 1945. (paper)

. *Neurosis and Human Growth*. New York: Norton, 1950. (paper)

Kubler-Ross, Elisabeth. *On Death and Dying*. New York: Macmillan, 1969. (paper)

. *Questions and Answers on Death and Dying*. New York: Macmillan/Collier Books, 1974. (paper)

Miller, Jean Baker, ed. *Psychoanalysis and Women*. Baltimore, Md.: Penguin Books, 1973. (paper)

Naranja, Claudio, and Ornstein, Robert. *On the Psychology of Meditation*. New York: Viking Compass, 1971. (paper)

O'Brien, Patricia. *The Woman Alone*. New York: Quadrangle Books, 1973.

Ornstein, Robert E. *The Psychology of Consciousness*. New York: Viking Press, 1973.

Perls, Fritz. *Gestalt Therapy Verbatim*. New York: Bantam Books, 1971. (paper)

Radical Therapist Collective. *The Radical Therapist*. Edited by Jerome Agel. New York: Ballantine Books, 1971. (paper)

Rough Times. Edited by Jerome Agel. New York: Ballantine Books, 1973. (paper)

Rogers, Carl. *On Becoming a Person*. Boston: Houghton Mifflin, 1970. (paper)

Strouse, Jean, ed. *Women and Analysis*. New York: Dell, 1975. (paper)

Szasz, Dr. Thomas. *The Myth of Mental Illness: Foundations of a Theory of Personal Conduct*. Rev. ed. New York: Harper and Row, 1974. (paper)

Tennov, Dorothy. *Psychotherapy: The Hazardous Cure*. New York: Abelard-Schuman, 1975.

Thompson, Clara. *Interpersonal Psychoanalysis: The Selected Papers of Clara Thompson*. New York: Basic Books, 1964.

RAPE

Brownmiller, Susan. *Against Our Will*. New York: Simon and Schuster, 1975.

SEX

Belliveau, Fred, and Richter, Lin. *Understanding Human Sexual Inadequacy*. New York: Bantam Books, 1970. (paper)

Breasted, Mary. *Oh! Sex Education*. New York: Praeger, 1970.

Brecher, Ruth and Edward, eds. *An Analysis of Human Sexual Response*. New York: NAL/Signet Books, 1966. (paper)

Friday, Nancy. *My Secret Garden*. New York: Pocket Books, 1974. (paper)

Greer, Germaine. *The Female Eunich*. New York: Bantam Books, 1972. (paper)

Heilbrun, Carolyn G. *Toward a Recognition of Androgyny*. New York: Harper Collophon Books, 1974. (paper)

Herschberger, Ruth. *Adam's Rib*. 1948. Reprint. New York: Harper and Row, 1970. (paper)

Masters, William H., M.D., and Johnson, Virginia. *Human Sexual Inadequacy*. Boston: Little, Brown, 1970.

. *Human Sexual Response*. Boston: Little, Brown, 1966. (paper)

Pomeroy, Wardell, B. *Boys and Sex*. New York: Dell, 1968. (paper)

. *Girls and Sex*. New York: Dell, 1969. (paper)

Sherfey, Mary Jane. *The Nature and Evolution of Female Sexuality*. New York: Random House/Vintage Books, 1973. (paper)

WORK

Benet, Mary Kathleen. *The Secretarial Ghetto*. New York: McGraw-Hill, 1973.

Bird, Caroline. *Born Female*. New York: Pocket Books, 1974. (paper)

Epstein, Cynthia. *Woman's Place: Options and Limits in Professional Careers*. Berkeley, Calif.: Univ. of California Press, 1970. (paper)

Friedman, Sande, and Schwartz, Lois C. *No Experience Necessary*. New York: Dell, 1971. (paper)

Gilman, Charlotte Perkins. *Women and Economics*. 1898. Reprint. New York: Harper and Row, 1970. (paper)

Holland, John L. *Making Vocational Choices: A Theory of Careers*. Englewood Cliffs, N.J.: Prentice-Hall, 1973. (paper)

Lopata, Helena Z. *Occupation: Housewife*. New York: Oxford Univ. Press, 1971. (paper)

Oakley, Ann. *Woman's Work: The Housewife, Past and Present*. New York: Random House, 1974.

Smuts, Robert W. *Women and Work in America*. New York: Schocken Books, 1971. (paper)

Index of Articles

Index of Authors

of "Annals of Womankind"

About the Authors of
Specially Commissioned Articles

Carol H. Arber (*A Quick Course in Contracts*) is a partner of Lefcourt, Kraft and Arber, an all-woman law firm in New York City.

Blank Goodman Rone & Stanley *(How to Organize an Employment Discrimination Action)* is an all-woman law firm in New York City.

Joyce Hartwell (*Building Your First Bookcase*) is founder and director of the Lady Carpenter ® All-Craft Institute in New York City. She has taught and practiced carpentry since 1963.

Matina Horner (*The Progress of Women's Education*) is president of Radcliffe College and founder of the Office of Women's Education at Harvard. She has published original research on women's fear of success.

Roslyn Kramer (*Financial Etiquette, Getting Credit and Loans, How the Banking System Works, Liberating the All-male Club*) is a freelance writer in New York City who has written for the Family/Style section of *The New York Times* and on a variety of subjects for the *Soho Weekly News.*

Bernice J. Malamud and Nancy Eales (*Insurance, Pensions, and Social Security*) are associated with Women's Life Services in New York City and Philadelphia, a firm which specializes in women's insurance.

Kristine Paulsen (*Help in Rearing the Handicapped Child*) teaches retarded and special children in Michigan.

Marcia L. Storch, M.D. (*Menstrual Extraction, Self-Help Groups, Your Medical Data Bank*) is an obstetrician and gynecologist practicing in New York City. She is co-author of *Woman's Body, Man's World. . .The Female Patient,* to be published by Holt, Rinehart and Winston.

Helen Thomas (*Women in Journalism*) is White House Correspondent for United Press International.

Barbara Trecker (*Problems of the Single Mother*) is a reporter for the *New York Post,* who specializes in women's interests.

Kathi Wakefield (*Strategies for Upward Mobility*) is a founder of MORE for Women, a career counseling service.

Dr. Eleanor Yachnes (*Self Analysis*) is a psychoanalyst associated with the Karen Horney Clinic in New York City and is also in private practice in Brooklyn, New York.

Woman's Directory

Abortion

see also—Family Planning, Health Care Services, Pregnancy & Childbirth

American Civil Liberties Union, Women's Rights Project
22 E 40th St, New York, NY 10017
The ACLU has launched a drive to force all hospitals receiving federal funds either to conform to the Supreme Court ruling allowing abortions, or to give up those funds. (212-725-1222)

Association for the Study of Abortion
120 W 57th St, New York, NY 10019
Formed 10 years ago to study the constitutionality of women's right to abortion, ASA disseminates information through films, brochures, articles, and its own newsletter (free). Those in search of legal or medical facts about abortion, in any state, will probably find answers here. (212-245-2360)

Catholic Women for the Right to Choose
36 Ashley St, Hartford, CT 06105
This group is evidence that the Catholic church is not united on the question of women's rights to control reproduction.

Catholics for a Free Choice
515 Madison Ave, New York, NY 10022
Same as above. (212-541-7939)

Clergy Consultation Service
The CCS is a nonprofit volunteer organization that evaluates the medical/professional qualifications of abortion clinics before making referrals, and will help to secure special financial arrangements for individuals. See phone book for local number and address.

National Abortion Rights Action League
250 W 57th St, New York, NY 10019
Created to preserve the US Supreme Court abortion decision, NARAL "recognizes the basic human right of a woman to limit her own reproduction, and is dedicated to guaranteeing the constitutional right to a safe and legal abortion." Write for information on local action groups. (212-265-5125)

Preterm
Preterm is a nonprofit, tax-exempt agency "founded by women for women" for the termination of pregnancy. Staff physicians perform abortions using the vacuum-aspiration method under local anesthesia. There is no charge for pregnancy tests. Counseling, abortion, laboratory tests, birth-control information, and supplies are included in the fee. See your phone directory for the nearest office.

Women's National Abortion Action Coalition
150 Fifth Ave, New York, NY 10011
WONAAC focuses on the Supreme Court ruling and other related abortion issues, as well as publishing a newsletter. (212-691-3495)

In most instances, the local office of NOW, Planned Parenthood (*see* Family Planning for regional office), or the Dept of Health will assist with information and/or referrals.

Denver, CO
Boulder Valley Clinic
2346 Broadway 80205
BVC, a private, nonprofit community clinic, is staffed by medical doctors who perform safe, low-cost abortions. Counseling is available before and after the abortion. Eligibility is limited to women over 18, and women under 18 who have parental consent or are married. (303-442-5160)

Denver, CO
Ministerial Council Abortion Referral and Counseling Service
1400 Lafayette 80218 (303-832-2293)

New Haven, CT
The New Haven Women's Abortion Referral Service
215 Park St 06520
Helps arrange pregnancy tests, and will find a clinic that meets one's needs. The service is free. (203-776-3182)

New Haven, CT
Women Versus Connecticut
2505B Sterling Law Bldg 06520
This organization works to liberalize the state abortion laws. (203-436-0364)

Washington, DC
Abortion Assistance Association
AAA acts as a hotline for abortion and contraception information; it furnishes names of certified doctors for abortions, clinics for pregnancy or pelvic exams, and new facilities in the DC area for contraception instruction and materials. (202-523-5101)

Washington, DC
Abortion and Family Planning Organization
919 18th St NW 20002
The AFPO gives information about the how, when, and where of abortion and contraception methods. Members have referral lists for doctors, clinics, and hospitals. There is no charge. (202-785-1077)

Preterm Institute

Washington, DC
Abortion Information Services of Washington, Inc
1010 Vermont Ave NW 20005
These services offer assistance to women seeking safe and legal therapeutic abortions; provide information on vasectomies and the detection and control of venereal disease; provide nonprescription contraceptives, and birth-control and sex-education materials through the mails. (202-628-5098)

Washington, DC
New Women's Clinic
1990 M St NW 20036
The New Women's Clinic offers vacuum-aspiration abortions with preabortion counseling. Free pregnancy tests, VD screening, and birth-control information. (202-452-8400)

Chicago, IL
Concord Medical Center
17 W Grand 60610
This clinic, directed and staffed by women, offers supportive individual and group birth-control information and pre- and postabortion counseling. The CMC is approved by the Health Evaluation and Referral Service and by the Planned Parenthood Association. (312-467-6555)

Chicago, IL
Illinois Citizens for the Medical Control of Abortion
100 E Ohio St 60611
This group supports the 1973 Supreme Court decision. (312-644-0972)

W Des Moines, IA
Iowans for Medical Control of Abortion
Box 232 50265
IMCA supports the 1973 Supreme Court decision. (515-277-0886)

Boston, MA
Massachusetts Organization to Repeal Abortion Laws
Box 238 02134
Organized to implement the 1973 Supreme Court decision. (617-426-0382)

Ann Arbor, MI
Michigan Citizens for Medical Control of Abortion
201 E Liberty St 48108
Supports the 1973 Supreme Court decision and monitors abortion safety in Michigan.

Detroit, MI
Keemer Clinic
1105 David Whitney Bldg, 1553 Woodward Ave 48226
Use of relaxing taped hypnotic suggestions in addition to local anesthesia makes this abortion clinic unique in the country. (313-961-9779)

Detroit, MI
Legal Abortions for Women
This north-suburban nonprofit abortion referral service also offers free handbooks on control and VD. (313-548-8300)

Detroit, MI
Women's Health Services
16401 Grand River 48227
WHS is one of the 3 abortion cinics in Detroit approved by the Clergy Council for Problem Pregnancy, NOW, and Planned Parenthood. (313-272-2100)

Minneapolis, MN
Minnesota Organization for Repeal of Abortion Laws
5205 Duneraig Rd 55436
MORAL promotes education to prevent unwanted pregnancies and supports the 1973 Supreme Court decision on abortion. (612-929-0941)

Buffalo, NY
Erie Medical Center
50 High St 14203
Confidential medical service includes information on outpatient abortion facilities. (716-883-2213)

"No woman can call herself free until she can choose consciously whether she will or will not be a mother."
—*Margaret Sanger*

New York, NY
Abortion Rights Association of New York
250 W 57th St   10019
ARANY provides lists of selected clinics and general information on abortion. (212-541-8887)

Winston-Salem, NC
Forsyth Pregnancy Termination Clinic, Inc
3000 Maplewood Ave   27103
Abortions are performed only on Saturdays and every other Wednesday night. A full-time counselor is on duty during the week. (919-768-2980)

Cincinnati, OH
Choice
1107 St. Gregory   45202
Choice operates an abortion clinic and provides birth-control information. (513-241-9335)

Cleveland, OH
Cleveland Center for Reproductive Health
11955 Shaker Blvd   44120
CCRH offers medical care for women seeking 1st-trimester abortion. (216-421-8600)

Cleveland, OH
Concerned Women's Clinic
10605 Chester Ave   44106
Women in their 1st trimester of pregnancy may receive an abortion by D&C-suction procedure. (216-231-2622)

Cleveland, OH
National Health Care Services
10605 Chester Ave   44106
Gynecologists, nurses, and experienced counselors provide counseling and medical services for the termination of pregnancy up to the 12th week. (216-795-1900)

Bethlehem, PA
Lehigh Valley Abortion Rights Association
Box 252   18015
Information on abortions and birth control in the area is provided by a 24-hour answering service. (215-435-2502)

Havertown, PA
Abortion Assistance Agency
149 Lewis Rd   19083
Pregnancy tests cost $4; the agency also does counseling and abortion referrals. (215-449-2006)

Pittsburgh, PA
Women's Health Services, Inc
1209 Allegheny Tower, 625 Stanwix St   15222
Women's Health Services performs 1st-trimester abortions by vacuum aspiration. (412-562-1910)

Providence, RI
Rhode Island Coalition to Repeal Abortion Laws
21 Oriole Ave   02906
Organized to persuade hospitals and clinics to expand their services and to support the 1973 Supreme Court decision on abortion. (401-751-7648)

Providence, RI
Special Procedures Clinic
Women and Infants Hospital, 50 Maude St   02908
Located in the old Lying-in Hospital, the Special Procedures Clinic is the only Rhode Island clinic performing abortions. (401-274-1100 ext. 270)

Memphis, TN
Center for Reproductive Health
202 Union Ave   38103
The Center performs abortions by vacuum aspiration up to the 12th week of pregnancy. The service includes counseling. (615-527-3505)

Austin, TX
Problem Pregnancy Counseling Agency
2434 Guadalupe   78705
The agency provides birth-control and abortion information. (512-474-5321)

Seattle, WA
Birth Control-Abortion Referral Service
BC-ARS provides birth-control education and abortion referrals; drivers are provided for abortion patients when necessary. (206-634-3460)

Madison, WI
Midwest Medical Center
1020 Regent St   53715
MMC performs abortions only up to 12 weeks. (608-251-8500)

Madison, WI
Women's Medical Fund
This organization lends money to women seeking abortions. (608-233-3388)

Adoption

Adoption Resource Exchange of North America
67 Irving Pl, New York, NY   10003
ARENA is affiliated with the Child Welfare League of America, one of the major standard–setters in adoption. Children and families are listed with ARENA by agencies from all over the US and Canada. Monthly newsletters sent to adoption agencies and parent groups contain pictures and descriptions of children, along with current information on the availability of adoptable children and adoptive homes. Most children registered with ARENA are considered by their local adoption agencies to be difficult to place in their own locale. (212-254-7410)

American-Korean Foundation
345 E 46th St, New York, NY   10017
AKF is involved with social welfare in Korea. One of its programs is Operation Outreach, aiding Korean lepers and their families. Although AKF itself is not an adoption agency, one part of the Operation Outreach program is arranging adoption of some children, mostly of school age, by American families. (212-697-1960)

Holt Adoption Program
The Holt Adoption Program started in the early 1950s and is now the largest adoption agency in the world, placing almost 3,000 children from 5 countries with families in every state, with Americans abroad, and in 8 foreign countries. Check your local phone book for the nearest Holt office.

International Social Service American Branch, Inc
345 E 46th St, New York, NY   10017
This agency works with other organizations and counsels when adoption problems involve different countries. It finds homes for children from abroad. (212-687-2747)

International Union for Child Welfare
Centre Internationale, Rue de Varembe 1, 1211 Geneva 20, Switzerland
IUCW is an international nongovernmental organization for service of children and adolescents. It has consultative status with the United Nations and is affiliated with public and voluntary agencies around the world.

Welcome House
Box 836, Doylestown, PA   18901
Welcome House was originally established to place Oriental and part-Oriental American children in adoptive homes, but now places only foreign-born children, primarily from Korea. It is licensed as an adoption agency in several states. (215-345-0430)

The Open Door Society, Inc
5 Weredale Park, Montreal, Quebec Canada

This is Canada's national headquarters for ODS, primarily a group committed to transracial adoption. (514-331-3823)

Citizens Groups
Various organizations of adoptive parents and concerned professionals supply supportive aid for the hard-to-place child and encourage transracial adoption. A North

American Council on Adoptable Children is being formed as a national clearinghouse on citizens groups. At least one of the organizations listed below should exist in your area.

Adoptive Parent Association
Council on Adoptable Children
Open Door Society
Organization for a United Response
Spaulding for Children

Government Agencies

City, county, and state offices list licensed adoption agencies, resource exchanges, and foster-care services. They can also provide consultation and complaint services to parents, adoptees, and other interested parties. Telephone numbers can be found in the city, county, or state-government section under one of these department headings:

Child Services   Human Resources
Child Welfare   Public Welfare
Family Services   Social Services

Erika Stone

Huntington Beach, CA

Orange County Adoptive Parents' Association
Box 1314   92647   (213-839-0897)

Los Angeles, CA

Adoptive Parents Association of Los Angeles
13141   Lake   St   90066   (213-390-6380)

Oakland, CA

Aid to the Adoption of Special Kids
Box 11212   94611   (415-451-1748)

Ontario, CA

Adoptive Family Association, Inc
Box 1236   91762 (213-983-6801)

Yuba City, CA

League of Adoptive Parent Services
1141   Helen   Ave   95991   (916-673-0867)

Aruada, CO

North Area Mothers Club
Mrs Judy Martine, 6238 Ingalls St 80002 (303-423-0272)

Boulder, CO

Colorado Parents for All Children
Box 4132   80303   (303-449-1450)

Cedaredge, CO

Orphan Voyage
Jean Paton   81413 (303-856-3937)

Denver, CO

Colorado Adoptive Parents' Association
Mrs Sam Dalton, 1331 W Evans 80223 (303-935-3566)

Lakewood, CO

Foothills Mothers' Club
Mrs Sandra True, 120 Flower   80026 (303-237-4624)

Darien, CT

Friends of Children, Inc
14   Brookside   Rd   06820   (203-655-2218)

Washington, DC

Barker Foundation
4708   Wisconsin   Ave   NW   20016 (202-363-7751)

Washington, DC

Pierce-Warwick Adoption Service of the Washington Home for Foundlings
5229 Connecticut Ave NW 20015 (202-966-2531)

Altamont Springs, FL

We Kare
Mr William Clark, 200 Grace Blvd 32701 (305-862-2130)

Atlanta, GA

NAACP Adoption Project
70   Hunter   St 30314   (912-522-4373)

Augusta, GA

CSRA Adoptive Parents Organization
c/o Mrs Morgan Wheeler, 1652 Pendleton Rd   30904 (912-733-3964)

Chicago, IL

Adoption Information Service
1439   S   Michigan   Ave   60605 (312-793-4834)

Raritan, IL

Chosen Parents of Illinois
c/o Mrs Herman H. Harden, Box 7 61471 (309-343-6741)

Springfield, IL

Child Care Association of Illinois
2101   W   Laurence   Ave   62704 (217-787-1715)

Lawrence, KS

Families of Adopted Mixed-Race Children
c/o Mrs John Boulton, 1721 Kentucky 66044 (316-842-4429)

Topeka, KS

Adoptive Mothers' Club
c/o   Mrs Nancee Price, 1206 High 66604 (913-357-7695)

Boston, MA

Massachusetts Adoption Resource Exchange
600   Washington   St   02111   (617-727-6180)

Muskegon, MI

Muskegon Mothers' Group
c/o Henry Dejong, 1363 Amity St 49442 (616-773-4222)

Minneapolis, MN

Lutheran Social Service of Minnesota
2414 Park Ave   55404 (612-871-0221)

Illmo, MO

The Adoptive Mothers' Club
c/o Mrs Raymond Eifert, Box 382 63754 (314-264-2516)

Lincoln, NB

Nebraska Foster and Adoptive Parents Club
1911 S 20th St   68502 (402-432-9496)

Concord, NH

Frontiers in Adoption
RFD 4   03301 (603-798-5392)

Dobbs Ferry, NY

Adoptive Families of Westchester
Box 127   10522 (914-762-4727)

Kingston, NY

Parents and Children Together
28 Tietjen Ave   12401 (914-339-4872)

New York, NY

Adoptees Liberty Movement Associates
Box 154, Washington Bridge Sta 10033 (212-581-1568)

New York, NY

Adoptive Parents Committee, Inc
210 Fifth Ave   10010 (212-683-9221)

New York, NY

The New York City Adoption Exchange Book
New York City Special Services for Children, 80 Lafayette St 10013 (212-433-3573)

Ouaguaga, NY

Families for All Children Today
Box 27   13826 (607-655-1721)

Rochester, NY

Council of Adoptive Parents
Manual of Waiting Children
425 Mt Vernon Ave 14620 (716-436-5070)

Schenectady, NY

Families for the Future, Inc
Box 725   12301 (518-377-8249)

Schenectady, NY

New York Citizens Coalition for Children
2361 Algonquin Rd 12309 (518-374-7175)

''Children sweeten labours; but they make misfortunes more bitter: they increase the cares of Life; but they mitigate the remembrance of Death.''
—*Francis Bacon*

Eastlake, OH

Project Orphans Abroad
34500 Grovewood Dr 44094 (216-946-3418)

Rocky River, OH

Adopt a Child Today, Inc
19438 Laurel Ave 44116 (216-331-7636)

Tulsa, OK

David Livingston Missionary Foundation Adoption Program
Box 232 74101 (918-747-3401)

Portland, OR

Open Home Association
c/o Meskimon, 4054 N Colonial 97227 (503-288-8515)

San Antonio, TX

Texas Cradle Society Maternity Home
8222 Wurzbach 78228 (512-696-8800)

Springville, UT

The Parents of Adopted Orientals of Utah County
c/o Mrs Black (801-489-7877)

Essex Junction, VT

Room for One More
Star Rte 05452 (802-878-2657)

Bellingham, WA

Adoptive Parents Group
c/o Mrs Catherine Donner, Dept of Social and Health Services, Community Services Div, Bellingham Office L37-1, Box 639 98225

Seattle, WA

Adoptive Family Association
1004 S 208th 98148 (206-839-8236)

Seattle, WA

Interracial Family Association
3332 Hunter Blvd S 98144 (206-722-7862)

Adult Education

Adult Education Association of the US
810 18th St NW, Washington, DC 20006
The AEA supports relevant research and publishes journals, pamphlets, books, and monographs on adult and continuing education. Services are primarily for members, but individual requests for information will be answered. (202-347-9574)

American Management Association
135 W 50th St, New York, NY 10020
An in-house management training course, EXCEL, is for management employees, most of whom are women clerical workers. (212-586-8100)

Association for Women's Active Return to Education
5820 Wilshire Blvd, Los Angeles, CA 90036
This program encourages women to return to school.

College Examination Board
Publications Order Office, Box 592, Princeton, NJ 08540
Those omnipresent computers that guide our educational careers offer the "Wom-en's Higher and Continuing Education, An Annotated Bibliography."

Continuing Education for Women
Adult Education Association of the US, 810 18th St NW, Washington, DC 20036
CEW works to improve and expand the resources available to women wishing to pursue educational and/or vocational goals, and to enhance opportunities for students, paraprofessionals, and professionals. CEW does not, however, have the resources to provide information for research projects or financial aid. (202-347-9574)

Courses by Newspaper
U of California Extension—San Diego, Box 109, La Jolla, CA 92037
Daily and weekly texts are carried by 270 newspapers providing credit courses with exams. Nearly 180 colleges and universities give academic credit for these courses.

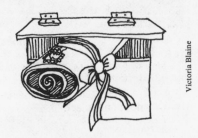

Victoria Blaine

Extension Service, US Dept of Agriculture
Washington, DC 20250
The Extension Service reaches 45 million people annually, providing personal help to farmers and ranchers, programs on nutrition, home management, clothing, and consumer information for homemakers. It also conducts 4-H and FFA programs for young people and aids community leaders in analyzing needs and developing appropriate programs. Address local inquiries to state universities, land-grant colleges, or to county extension agents. For printed material explaining the Extension Service send written requests to the Dept of Agriculture in Washington, DC. (202-447-6283)

Foundation Management Seminars, Business and Professional Women's Foundation
2012 Massachusetts Ave NW, Washington, DC 20036
These training courses are offered around the country for $25. (202-293-1200)

National Advisory Council on Extension and Continuing Education
1325 G St NW, Washington, DC 20005
NACECE is the watchdog for quality of extension courses. (202-382-7985)

National Center for Higher Education
1 Dupont Circle, Washington, DC 20036
NCHE promotes and evaluates higher education throughout the country. (202-659-4197)

National Community School Education Association
1017 Avon St, Flint, MI 48502
NCSEA believes that a public school should serve all those who live in its surrounding geographic area, and that these people should have a voice in school administration. It acts as a clearinghouse for the exchange of ideas and information on community schools. (313-234-1634)

National Home Study Council
1601 18th ST NW, Washington, DC 20036 (202-234-5100)

National University Extension Association, National Center for Higher Education
1 Dupont Circle NW, Washington, DC 20036
Because of an increased demand for continuing education, many colleges and universities have grouped extra and special classes into "extension divisions." The NUEA **Guide to Independent Study** lists correspondence courses available from member institutions, all accredited. (202-659-3130)

The New York Times Guide to Continuing Education in America
c/o Frances Thompson, Quadrangle Books, New York
The most comprehensive, well-organized guide to what is available—found in most libraries.

Project on the Status and Education of Women
Association of American Collges, 1818 R St NW, Washington, DC 10009
This clearinghouse and research center can provide bibliographies on women in education. (202-387-1300)

Women's Bureau, US Dept of Labor
Washington, DC 20402
Continuing Education Programs and Services for Women (with over 450 entries) can be obtained from the Women's Bureau. (202-523-6611)

The Women's Medical College of Pennsylvania
3300 Henry Ave, Philadelphia, PA 19129
WMC operates a training program for women physicians to enable them to return, after a long absence, to residency or active practice. (215-842-6000)

Hartford, CT

Board for State Academic Awards
340 Capitol Ave 06115
This state agency has recently instituted a program of awarding college degrees for a variety of jobs and experiences as well as traditional academic training. The agency has also compiled a helpful booklet listing counseling centers in Connecticut, many of which offer employment referrals as well. (203-566-7230)

Atlanta, GA

Office of Adult and Vocational Education
312 State Office Bldg 30334
This is an information center for those seeking adult education. Call to find out where courses are available. (404-656-2538)

Chicago, IL

Adult Education Council of Greater Chicago
332 S Michigan Ave 60604
The Council provides information on lectures, debates, forums, and conferences. It publishes a directory of educational opportunities for adults in the Greater Chicago area. (312-427-2670)

Adult Learning Skills Program   *Chicago, IL*

Chicago Urban Skills Institute, City College of Chicago, 3901 S State St 60609

The program offers residents of Chicago, 18 years old and over, both day- and night-school courses in General Educational Development, English as a Second Language, and studies leading toward high school graduation and college preparation. ALSP also offers a wide range of technical classes that include carpentry, woodshop, interior design, blueprint reading, plumbing, and electricity. Tuition fees vary with the courses, and special financial arrangements are available. Call or write for class schedules and school locations near you. (312-642-7300 ext 10)

Evanston, IL

The Learning Exchange

Box 920   60204

The Learning Exchange is a free educational referral service that matches people who want to learn with the proper school. (312-864-4133)

Indianapolis, IN

Emmerich Manual High School, Adult Evening School

2405 S Madison Ave   46227

Learn to take care of your car and know exactly what the mechanic is talking about when she or he estimates repairs. Many other courses are offered. (317-784-2405)

Boston, MA

Women's Inner-City Education Resource Service

90 Warren St   02119

A group of women put together *The Urban Women's Guide to Higher Education*, a directory of Boston's continuing-education opportunities for lower-income, inner-city women. (617-440-9150)

Cambridge, MA

Cambridge Center for Adult Education

42 Brattle St   02138

Subjects range from faucet repair to Socrates. A 10-week course costs about $30. (617-547-6789)

Cambridge, MA

The Educational Exchange of Greater Boston

17 Dunster St   02138

The Educational Exchange publishes directories of educational resources for Boston-area adults. (617-876-3080)

Cambridge, MA

Radcliffe Institute

3 James St   02138

The Institute is a place for women to research and create. Fellowships for one year are offered to scholars, artists, and professional women. (617-495-8211)

Cambridge, MA

The Women's School

595 Massachusetts Ave   02139

Courses on women's liberation, lesbianism, women in fiction, the family, and other topics are offered for a minimal fee. (617-492-4845)

Detroit, MI

Institute for Continuing Education

Archdiocese of Detroit
305 Michigan Ave   48226

The Institute offers classes, educational TV, and special lectures to anyone in the community 18 or older. (313-237-5981)

Detroit, MI

University Courses in Adult Education

60 Farnsworth   48202

Lifework Planning, Film, Art History, Studio Art, Insurance, Food and Wine, and Edible Wild Plants are some of the wide variety of noncredit adult-education classes offered in conjunction with U of Michigan, Wayne State, and the College of Lifelong Learning. (313-577-4665)

Minneapolis, MN

Loring Nicollet-Bethlehem Community Centers, Inc

1920 Pillsbury Ave   55403

Among many other programs, these centers offer tutoring for the Graduate Equivalency Diploma, and do-it-yourself programs in health, nutrition, economics, and home decoration. Free. (612-871-0230)

St Louis, MO

Adult Education Council

607 N Grand   63103

AEC acts as the coordinating and referral agency for all phases of local adult education. As a clearinghouse for adult-education teachers, the Council also sponsors new services, workshops, and seminars. Services are gratis. AEC also publishes an excellent *Directory of Adult Education*. (314-625-1335)

New York, NY

Graduate Management Program for Women

Pace University, Pace Plaza   10038

This 2-year MBA program offers two options: The Internship Program includes a 5-month business internship and is designed for women just entering business; the Friday-Saturday program is for women whose employers recognize their potential and support their efforts by letting them attend Friday classes as a regular working day.

Syracuse, NY

Board of Co-operative Educational Services

Adult Education Program, 6820 Thompson Rd   13211

Helen Keller

Sophia Smith Collection, Smith College

BOCES offers over 70 different courses during the school year (and mini-courses in the summer) in many employment skills—data processing, auto mechanics, drafting, tractor-trailer driving, to name a few. Courses are held at BOCES centers throughout Onondaga County. (315-437-1631)

Cincinnati, OH

Adult Education Booklet

Cincinnati Public Library   45202

An expansive list of classes given by various schools and programs in the Cincinnati area is available free from the Public Library. (513-241-2636 ext 67)

Cincinnati, OH

Continuing Education in the Cincinnati Public Schools

230 E Ninth St   45202

This booklet contains a complete listing of all courses offered by the public school system for adult education and vocational training. (513-369-4015)

Portland, OR

Women's Liberation School

Women's Place, 706 SE Grand   97214

The school offers nontraditional academic opportunities. The courses, taught by women, cover the women's liberation movement, poetry, history, auto mechanics, and self-defense. Child care provided. Nominal fee per course. (503-234-7044)

Portland, OR

Women's Programs, Division of Continuing Education and Volunteers in Educating Women

1633 SW Park Ave   97207

DCE holds 2 workshops throughout the year: "Search and Discovery" and "Job or Career," both of which explore alternatives for working or job hunting. (503-229-4866)

Providence, RI

Career Education Project

10 Dorrance St   02903

CEP provides career counseling for the "home-based population" and informs clients, mostly women, of the adult-education opportunities available in the state. The Project, funded by the National Institute of Education, constitutes one of the largest educational grants in the state's history. (401-272-5300)

Dallas, TX

Institute for Women in Business

School of Business Administration, Southern Methodist U, 75222

The Institute gives special attention to the recruiting, course development, and career counseling of women students. (214-692-2000)

Houston, TX

The Women's Institute

2202 Westgate Dr   77019

WI provides continuing opportunities for the Lecture Luncheon Series and the Cultural Studies, which are tailored to fit the schedules and conveniences of busy women. (713-529-7123)

"Educate a boy and you educate an individual; educate a girl and you educate a family."
—*John Crumpton Hardy*

Affirmative Action
see — Discrimination,
Employment Rights

Aging
see — Senior Citizens

Alternative Education
see — Adult Education,
Free Schools,
Handywoman

Apprenticeships

Bureau of Apprenticeship and Training
Manpower Administration, US Dept of Labor, Washington, DC 20210
Write for information on apprenticeship, including a list of apprenticeable occupations. (202-376-6585)

State Employment Office
For information on local apprenticeship opportunities consult your state employment office.

San Francisco, CA
Women in Apprenticeship
593 Market 94105
This program guides women into nontraditional technical areas of employment through apprenticeship. (415-495-6752)

Denver, CO
Better Jobs for Women
1554 Tremont Pl 80204
A program of Outreach, funded by the US Dept of Labor and sponsored by the YWCA of Metro Denver, this association places women into registered apprenticeship programs in skilled trades and crafts. Counseling is by appointment only. (303-893-3534)

Madison, WI
Women in Wisconsin Apprenticeships
Dept of Industry, Labor and Human Relations, Box 2209 53702
General information and referral are available at this progressive government agency. (608-266-3131)

Manpower Administration

"The median income of year-round, full-time working women with college degrees is lower than that of male high school drop-outs."
—*Susan Edmiston*

Art

Women's Art Registry
55 Mercer St, New York, NY 10013
Mail to: Box 539, Canal St Sta, New York, NY 10013
Open to all women artists, the Registry maintains slide files on members for museums and colleges.

Los Angeles, CA
Feminist Studio Workshop
The Center for Feminist Art Historical Studies, 743 S Grandview 90057
An ambitious and exciting women's art center, with studios and shops.

Los Angeles, CA
Womanspace
11007 Venice Blvd 90034
A feminist gallery and performance center, Womanspace provides space, lectures, films, and special programs by/for/about women. (213-838-9668)

San Francisco, CA
San Francisco Women Artists
1407 Gough St 94109
The artists, about 500 of them, put together group shows of members' work about once a month. (415-567-1850)

Chicago, IL
Women's Graphic Collective
3100 W Southport 60657
Members of the Collective display and sell their work in the store and have access to the group's equipment. Two annual workshops are conducted to teach silk screening and poster design. (312-447-6070)

Oak Park, IL
Women's Exchange
237 South Blvd 60302
The Exchange is an outlet for arts and crafts by local people. Members of the Exchange give their handiwork to the store on a consignment basis, and receive 75% of the sale price. In return, each member works for the Exchange at least 4 hours a month. (312-848-4693)

Detroit, MI
Women's Cultural Center
926 W 7 Mile Dr 48203
Women artists and others who support women's culture share their creativity at the storefront WCC. The collective sponsors communitywide art fairs, exhibitions, poetry readings, and a weekend coffee house. (313-891-9516)

Rochester, MI
Objects and Images, Inc
202 E Fourth St 48063
A council of women artists operates this shop of fine arts and crafts. Member artists, who come from all over Detroit, display their work in the store, sponsor an annual spring outdoor art show, conduct classes and workshops, and display their work in malls 3 times a year. Classes include instruction in arts ranging from oil painting and sandcasting to leaded glass and macrame. (313-652-1770)

St. Louis, MO
Women's Art Center
7587 Olive St Rd 63130
An adjunct of the Community of Women Artists, the WAC provides studio space and is a place to begin your own workshop or join one. You'll find, among others,

groups in print making, welding, and feminist readings. A $5 fee is required to participate in group shows, meetings, speaking engagements, and to receive their newsletter. To join the Center a $25 fee is charged. The building is open to women's groups involved in feminist projects. (314-721-9333)

New Paltz, NY
Women's Media Exchange
RD 2, Box 131 12561
The Exchange fosters professional attitudes, arranges exhibits, runs workshops, and provides other services for women artists. (914-658-5821)

New York, NY
Women's Interart Center
549 W 52nd St 10019
WIC rents working space to women artists; but the supply is limited and there is a long waiting list. (212-246-6570)

Philadelphia, PA
Women's Art Center of Philadelphia
c/o Joan Hubbard
The center encourages women's creative endeavors. (215-686-5129)

Wakefield, RI
Women's Cooperative Art Center and Gallery
546 Main St 02879
The women-oriented art center in South County promotes feminist art. It offers courses in weaving, painting, drawing, and other handicrafts during the fall and spring. Special exhibits of women's art, and cheese parties make for occasional pleasant evening gatherings. (401-789-1488)

Austin, TX
Women Artists' Guild
c/o Gwen Hill
The Art Guild helps women artists to meet and discuss art, promotes women's work in the city, and holds frequent art shows at various Austin locations. (512-474-5255)

Birth Control
see — Abortion, Family Planning, Health Care Services, Pregnancy and Childbirth

Bookstores

Government Printing Office
N Capital St, Washington, DC 20401
Most government documents in print can be ordered from GPO. Don't waste time when you know of something you want; they run out fast and don't reprint. There may be local branch stores of the GPO listed under US Government in your phone book. (For orders, call 202-783-3238)

Tucson, AZ
Antigone Bookstore
415 Fourth Ave S 85701
This store stocks a good selection of feminist literature. (602-792-3715)

Hayward, CA
The Oracle
1024 B St 94541
Owned and operated by women, this bookstore serves as a center for feminist literature and information, particularly about community activities in the East Bay area,

below Oakland. As Marilyn Shatzen, an owner, puts it, "It's not really a business; it's a service." (415-886-1268)

Los Angeles, CA

Sisterhood Bookstore
   743 S Grandview   90066
   1351 Westwood Blvd   90024
Books, posters, jewelry, pottery, and art are among the items available for purchase from the Sisterhood. (213-473-9090) (213-384-6516)

Oakland, CA

A Woman's Place
   5251 Broadway   94618
This Bay Area bookstore features literature of special interest to women. (415-654-9920)

San Diego, CA

Women's Store
   2965 Beech St   92102
This store carries feminist books, many of them small-press books, and also some crafts by local women. In addition, the store is sometimes open for poetry readings and meetings. Some referrals to medical, legal, and child-care services are also handled. (714-233-4164)

Somerville, MA

New Words Bookstore
   419 Washington St   02143
New Words is a feminist bookstore, a clearinghouse for books about women and the women's movement, and a center for books and journals by women writers. (617-876-5310)

Minneapolis, MN

Amazon Book Store
   26 Hennepin Ave   55401
Filling a need for the feminist movement, this bookstore sells only feminist and nonsexist children's books. A revised bibliography is furnished upon request. (612-374-5507)

Kansas City, MO

New Earth Bookstore
   24 E 39th St   64111
This nonprofit bookstore is operated by a collective of the Women's Liberation Union. Available are books and papers on all types of radical social change as well as news of what's going on locally in the women's movement. The bookstore also periodically has films and discussions. (816-931-5794)

Flushing, NY

Feminist Book Mart
   47-17 150th St   11355
This retailer and wholesaler handles feminist and nonsexist children's books. (212-767-0633)

New York, NY

Labyris
   33 Barrow St   10014
In addition to current feminist literature, this store carries used books. (212-741-3460)

New York, NY

Womanbooks
   255 W 92nd St   10025
This store carries a good selection of feminist reading. (212-873-4121)

Portland, OR

A Woman's Place Bookstore
   1533 E Burnside Ave   97214
This bookstore has a reading room, but no books can be taken out unless purchased.

It is the best place in town to find just-published works. Call before going, since hours seem to be variable. (503-234-8703)

Philadelphia, PA

Women's Cultural Trust
   3601 Locust St   19104
The Trust stocks a good selection of publications written by and about women, as well as an art gallery and many other interesting feminist projects. (215-243-5110)

Houston, TX

Prairie Fire Bookstore
   2912 Wentworth   77004
A good selection of women's literature and radical compositions for browsers is available. Jewelry, posters, and buttons are also sold. (713-529-1641)

Houston, TX

University Boulevard Bookstore
   2437 University Blvd   77005
Has the best selection of feminist books sold in the Houston area. (713-527-8522)

Seattle, WA

It's About Time
   5502 University Way NE   98105
This women's book center is run collectively by a group of feminists, who turn profits back into the center. They are establishing a bulletin board listing women's groups and activities in Seattle. (206-525-0999)

Seattle, WA

Madwoman
   317 Pine St   98101
The store carries a wide selection of feminist literature and features an exhibit area for women artists. Topical women's groups meet here regularly. (206-624-4775)

Madison, WI

A Room of One's Own
   Box 2193   53701
The bookstore markets all varieties of women's literature, including periodicals, fiction, records, posters, and nonsexist technical and professional books. It has a mail-order service, reading room, and information and referrals on housing, employment, counseling, and day care. (608-275-7888)

Breast Exam
see — Health Care Services

Breast Feeding
see — Pregnancy and Childbirth

Business Assistance

Chamber of Commerce of the US
   1420 N St NW, Washington, DC 20005
The Chamber of Commerce will supply information on business in your area and try to help business in whatever way possible. See the phone directory for local chambers. (202-659-6000)

Department of Commerce
   14th St NW, Washington, DC   20230
Your state or city Dept of Commerce advises and consults with small-business owners, giving them help in starting and running their own businesses. See your phone book under the state- or city-government listings. (202-783-9200)

"No girl was ever ruined by a book."
   —*James J. Walker*

Alice Webber

Directory of State and Federal Funds for Business Development
   Pilot Books, 347 Fifth Ave, New York, NY   10016
This publication contains a geographically arranged grouping of 60 entries giving basic data on the financial assistance programs of the 50 states and federal agencies offering funds to business. (212-685-0736)

National Association of Minority Women in Business
   Inez Kaiser & Associates, Inc, 906 Grand St, Kansas City, MO   64106
Members are minority women owners or managers of businesses who work to further the image of businesswomen, share their experiences, and encourage others to enter the field. (816-421-3335)

Office of Invention and Innovation
   Rm B-146, Technology Bldg, National Bureau of Standards, Washington, DC   20234
This new government office is ready to assist anyone who has an idea for a new gadget to improve the quality of public life. If you can sell it, perhaps the quality of your private life will improve too. (202-921-1000)

Small Business Administration
   1441 L St NW, Washington, DC   20005
The SBA was formed in 1953 to help keep small businesses alive and thriving. Any small, independent business is eligible for managerial, technical, and some financial assistance and counseling, as long as it is not a gambling or speculative enterprise, or media firm. SBA will help small businesspeople get loans, either by participating with the bank or by guaranteeing up to 90% of the loan, which may be as high as $350,000 with a maximum interest rate of 10-1/4%. Consult your phone book for the nearest branch office. (202-393-3111)

"Business? It's quite simple. It's other people's money."
   —*Alexander Dumas, the younger*

The Active Corps of Executives

ACE was established as a supplement to SCORE and is also a part of the SBA program. Businessmen counsel small businessmen on an "as needed" basis. Qualifications and areas of work are identical to SCORE. Assistance with expenses is also provided.

SCORE

A service of the SBA, the Service Corps of Retired Executives is an organization of retired businesspeople who furnish advice, based on their own experience, to owners of small businesses and people in the process of starting a venture.

San Francisco, CA

Advocates for Women

593 Market St   94105

The country's first economic-development center for women acts as an advisory and referral service in several fields. Employment Center works with employers to find job candidates and maintains an information center. Affirmative Action Center encourages employers to develop better programs for women and to increase benefits. It has begun organizing apprenticeship programs for women in major trade unions. Business Development Center assists women who want to develop businesses that would employ others. Credit Center assists and advises women on how to establish and use credit. Resource Center finds ways to tap into existing programs for training, financing child-care facilities and flexible work-hours programs. Information Service Center assists women in locating counsel and maintains a list of professional women and a business women's directory. (415-495-6750)

Atlanta, GA

Atlanta Business League

2001 Gordon Rd   30310

Anyone who owns a small business or is considering starting one in the Atlanta area may get information, referral, or assistance from the ABL. (404-758-8751)

Atlanta, GA

Interracial Council for Business Opportunity

40 Marietta St NW   30303

ICBO provides managerial, technical, and financial assistance to minority business operators. If you want to start a business or expand your present one, ICBO will assist you in filing for loans. It also has a loan guarantee fund. Market research and assistance in finding federal agencies that will buy your product are two other very valuable services rendered. (404-577-2570)

Kansas City, KS

Loans and Investments for a Future Together

1 Gateway Ctr   66101

LIFT helps minority business entrepreneurs by providing assistance in the areas of management, accounting, sales, advertising, marketing, and legal aid. It also sponsors an annual minority trade exposition in Kansas City. (913-281-0862)

Baltimore, MD

Mayor's Advisory Committee on Small Business

230 Tower Bldg   21202

The Committee plans and directs programs to aid small retail businesses and rehabilitate older shopping neighborhoods in the city of Baltimore. Aid to small businesses includes providing information to assist in understanding and solving business problems, along with financial counseling for those having difficulty obtaining financial assistance. (301-396-3954)

Boston, MA

Department of Commerce and Development, Women's Bureau

100 Cambridge St   02202

The Women's Bureau will give you free counsel as you start your business, as well as leads on other sources that provide specific information. (617-727-3210)

Detroit, MI

Urban Bankers Forum

c/o Lee Aubrey, National Bank of Detroit, Metro Division, Uptown Office, General Motors Bldg   48202

The Forum is composed of black bankers in managerial or officers' positions who assist businessmen of minority groups in matters of business, credit, loans, and banking. General information is given through panel discussions or talks to various groups. (313-225-3386)

St. Paul, MN

Minnesota Dept of Economic Development

51 Eighth St   55101

People interested in starting a business but who want to check out the market first or who need information on where to find help might try DED, which helps along anything promising economic expansion for the state. No fee. (612-296-5005)

Kansas City, MO

Black Economic Union

2502 Prospect   64127

Although BEU cannot grant loans, it counsels potential minority entrepreneurs on how to put together loan packages. Management and technical assistance, which go all the way from accounting and control systems to legal affairs, are also part of BEU's services. A minority business exposition, cosponsored every year by the Chamber of Commerce and BEU, has been a successful vehicle for establishing contacts between buyers and minority sellers and also an aid in procuring contracts for minority enterprise. (816-924-6181)

Philadelphia, PA

Self-assessed Taxes Department

City of Philadelphia, Municipal Services Bldg   19102

If you have plans for starting a business in the city, this is the first place to visit. After filling out the application, take advantage of their free tax advice: Any questions are entertained. Possible future problems, or obligations are all discussed. No other comparable official agency in Philadelphia is as well equipped to dispense this information. (215-686-1776)

"Business is really more agreeable than pleasure; it interests the whole mind, the aggregate nature of man more continuously, and more deeply. But it does not *look* as if it did."

—Bagehot

Providence, RI

Business Opportunity, Inc

40 Westminister St   02903

This agency, like the SBA, offers financial and counseling assistance to small businesses in the community. (401-751-1000)

Houston, TX

Forty Plus Club of Houston

The Forty Plus Club is a useful resource for employers who need advice on running their businesses. The club consists of successful executives over 40 years old who are currently employed and are willing to disclose the secrets of management to struggling entrepreneurs. (713-224-3314)

Career Counseling
see — Employment

Child Abuse
see — Parents

Childbirth
see — Pregnancy and Childbirth

Bank Street College of Education

Day Care Consultation Service, 610 W 112th St, New York, NY   10025

Assistance is offered on day-care-center organization and Title IV-A funding. (212-663-7200)

Child Welfare League of America, Inc

67 Irving Pl, New York, NY   10003

CWLA offers a monthly journal as well as a book list on child-care topics. They can also assist in the organization of child-care centers. (212-254-7410)

Community Coordinated Child Care

4-C, a nonprofit agency operating independently within the guidelines of the federal 4-C program, offers several services: (1) refers people seeking day care for their children, (2) works to upgrade and promote day care, (3) monitors legislation affecting children, (4) establishes parent groups, (5) publishes a newsletter, (6) has begun a resource center, and (7) continually seeks to promote projects of benefit to children. Your phone book will list a local number for you to call.

Day Care and Child Development Council of America, Inc

1012 14th St NW, Washington, DC   20005

This national, nonprofit organization is dedicated to establishing a system of child care for all families who need and want it. Through conferences, volunteer workshops, technical assistance, and publications, DCCDC advocates quality child care. (202-638-2316)

Department of Human Resources
Your city or state dept will explain local laws and regulations governing local child-care centers. Consult your local phone directory.

Movement for Economic Justice
1609 Connecticut Ave NW, Washington, DC   20009
Help in finding day-care funding is readily offered at MEJ. (202-462-4200)

National Day Care Association
Box 62, Porter Sq, Cambridge, MA 02140
NDCA provides day-care information, a newsletter, and resource files for members.

NOW National Task Force on Child Care
Mary Grace Plaskett, 934 Florida Ave, Mt Lebanon, PA 15228 (412-343-6675)

National Parents Federation for Day Care and Child Development
429 Lewis St, Somerset, NJ 08873
A membership organization that can provide information and assistance to those beginning day-care centers. (201-846-3730)

National Welfare Rights Organization
1426 16th St NW, Washington, DC 20036 (202-628-6800)
NWRO provides organizing assistance for day-care centers.

Office of Child Development
400 Sixth St SW, Washington, DC 20024
OCD provides information on federal funds and curriculum for day care and acts as a resource center for teaching materials. (202-755-7762)

Social and Rehabilitation Service
Community Services Administration, HEW, 330 C St SW, Washington, DC 20250
Information on Title IV-A funding for day-care centers is available. (202-245-8717)

Child Development/ Education

Action for Children's Television
46 Austin St, Newtonville, MA 02160
Concerned with children's programming, these parents and professionals work for better TV fare and tasteful advertising for children. (617-527-7870)

Association for Childhood Education International
3615 Wisconsin Ave NW, Washington, DC   20016 (202-363-6963)

Association for Children with Learning Disabilities
2200 Brownsville Rd, Pittsburgh, PA 15210 (412-881-1191)

Association for Education of the Visually Handicapped
1604 Spruce St, Philadelphia, PA 19103 (215-732-0100)

"The most deadly of all possible sins is the mutilation of a child's spirit."
—*Erik E. Erikson*

Black Child Development Institute
1028 Connecticut Ave NW, Washington, DC   20036 (202-659-4010)

Center for Exceptional Children
1920 Association Dr, Reston, VA 22070 (703-620-3660)

Change for Children
2588 Mission St, San Francisco, CA 94110
In an effort to help children develop interests along nonsexist, nonracist lines, this parent-teacher organization supplies teaching aids, conducts workshops, and maintains a resource center. (415-282-3142)

Child Study Association of America
50 Madison Ave, New York, NY 10010 (212-889-3450)

The Children's Foundation
1028 Connecticut Ave NW, Washington, DC   20036
Among other services, the Foundation can advise on school meal programs for your community. (202-296-4451)

Closer Look
1201 16th St NW, Washington, DC 20036
If you have an inkling that something may be wrong with your child physically or emotionally, Closer Look, a government-funded agency, will advise on identifying a disability, where to find special education and job training, and how to find financial aid and supportive parents' organizations. (202-833-4163)

Educational Resources Information Center
HEW Office of Education, Washington, DC   20202
ERIC Document Reproduction Service, The National Cash Register Company, 4936 Fairmont Ave, Bethesda, MD 20014
ERIC is a clearinghouse for information on education and schools. (202-245-8710)

Emma Willard Task Force on Education
University Sta, Box 14229, Minneapolis, MN   55414
The Task Force works to eradicate sexism in education through courses, committees, and workshops. They have also written a book, *Sexism and Education,* which is available at the office.

Human Services Institute for Children and Families
1701 18th St NW, Washington, DC 20009 (202-232-1898)

Lollipop Power, Inc.
Box 1171, Chapel Hill, NC 27514
Lollipop Power is a women's liberation collective that writes, illustrates, and publishes books for the liberation of young children from sex-stereotyped behavior and role models. Copies are often sent to nonprofit day-care centers. (919-929-4857)

National Association for Child Development and Education
500 12th St SW, Washington, DC 20024
NACDE represents private proprietary child-care centers providing information and promotional assistance. (202-484-0140)

National Association for Education of Young Children
1834 Connecticut Ave NW, Washington, DC   20009
NAEYC provides information for professional and non-professional day-care personnel through 180 affiliates nationwide. (202-232-877)

National Association for Gifted Children
8080 Spring Valley Dr, Cincinnati, OH 45236
NAGC are the publishers of *Gifted Child Quarterly.* (513-631-1777)

National Association for Retarded Children
420 Lexington Ave, New York, NY 10017 (212-689-9290)

National Association of the Deaf
814 Thayer Ave, Silver Spring, MD 20910 (301-587-1788)

National Council of Organizations for Children and Youth
1910 K St NW, Washington, DC   20036
This coalition of groups acts as an information clearinghouse. (202-785-4180)

National Easter Seal Society for Crippled Children and Adults
2023 W Ogden Ave, Chicago, IL 60612 (312-243-8400)

National Epilepsy League, Inc
6 N Michigan Ave, Chicago, IL 60602 (312-332-6888)

NOW Educational Task Force
Call your local NOW branch for information on the current education coordinator.

Erika Stone

National Rehabilitation Association
1522 K St NW, Washington, DC 20005 (202-659-2430)

Office of Child Development
400 Sixth St SW, Washington, DC 20024
Operates programs such as Head Start, develops new programs for parents and children, coordinates federal programs for children, and brings children's needs to the attention of the government. (202-655-4000)

Recreation for the Handicapped, Information Center
Outdoor Laboratory, Little Grassy, S Illinois U, Carbondale, IL 62901 (618-453-2121)

Resource Center on Sex Roles in Education
National Foundation for the Improvement of Education, 1156 15th St NW, Washington, DC 20005
The Center assists those researching and producing nonsexist educational material and provides technical services as well as a clearinghouse for school and community groups. (202-833-4402)

Women on Words and Images
38 Jefferson Rd, Princeton, NJ 08540
WWI is fighting sexism in education, especially in children's education. They have published a study of children's readers and have prepared a slide show on the same subject. (609-921-8653)

Women's Action Alliance, Inc
Nonsexist Early Childhood Education Project, 370 Lexington Ave, New York, NY 10017
Book lists, suggested readings, and resource lists of nonsexist educational materials are available from WAA. Ask for their pamphlets on child care. A small contribution toward printing and postage is appreciated. (212-685-0800)

Child Education, Sexism in
see — Child Development/Education

"The future destiny of a child is always the work of the mother."
—*Napoleon Bonaparte*

New York Public Library

Clinics, Medical
see — Health Care Services
Clubs
see — Women's Associations
College
see — Adult Education
Consciousness Raising
see — Women's Centers

Consumer Protection

American Association of Concerned Investors
27 Main St, Keene, NH 03431
A nonprofit organization that testifies on behalf of investor interests at public hearings. (603-352-2000)

American Council on Consumer Interests
283 Stanley Hall, U of Missouri, Columbia, MO 65201
ACCI publishes a monthly newsletter with an annotated bibliography. (314-882-2121)

Attorney General's Office, Consumer Protection Division
Your state attorney general's office has the duty to investigate complaints brought by the public regarding fraudulent business practices. See your local phone directory under the government listings.

Call for Action
CA is a nationwide volunteer information-referral and consumer-advocacy service operating under the auspices of local radio and TV stations. At present, CA is in 45 major US cities. See your phone book for local numbers.

Carpet and Rug Institute
Box 2048, Dalton, GA 30720
An industry complaint and information service, the institute answers questions and handles consumer problems. (404-287-3176)

Center for Auto Safety
Dupont Circle Bldg, Washington, DC 20036
The Center refers complaints, recommends appropriate consumer action, and is involved in auto-recall campaigns. (202-659-1126)

Chamber of Commerce
Composed of businessmen, the C of C is most anxious to maintain professional

ethics, and will try to assist you with consumer problems. Call your local chapter.

Common Cause
2030 M St NW, Washington, DC 20036
Common Cause, the rapidly growing national citizen's lobby, works to promote the public interest in all levels of government, favoring programs to revitalize self-government, and working both to eliminate corruption in political and governmental institutions and to reduce the influence of special interests. (202-833-1200)

Consumer Action Now
30 E 68th St, New York, NY 10021
CAN, publishers of *CAN*, is a grass-roots environmental organization. (202-628-2295)

Consumer Federation of America
1012 14th St NW, Washington, DC 20005
CFA undertakes legal and economic research and acts as a clearinghouse for local groups. (202-737-3732)

Consumer Product Information Center
Seventh & D Sts NW, Washington, DC 20407 (202-343-6171)
CPIC encourages the development of meaningful consumer-product information by appropriate federal departments and agencies and promotes public awareness of federal consumer-product information. Copies of the quarterly *Index of Consumer Product Information* and a weekly release highlighting selected new products may be obtained from: CPI, Pueblo, Colorado 81009.

Consumer Product Safety Commission
1750 K St NW, Washington, DC 20006
The Commission conducts research, providing information on consumer-product safety standards. (202-634-7700)

Consumers Research, Inc
Consumers Rd, Washington, NJ 07882
CRI publishes *Consumer Bulletin* and *Handbook of Buying*, describing the results of their product testing. (201-689-3300)

Consumers Union of US, Inc
256 Washington St, Mt Vernon, NY 10550
The well-known *Consumer Reports* is published by this group. The information comes from their own testing and research facilities. (914-664-6400)

Council of Better Business Bureaus, Inc
845 Third Ave, New York, NY 10022
BBB seeks to root out shady businesses, frauds, and hucksters. It promotes truth in advertising and reliability in selling by providing information about specific companies, monitoring advertising, and handling consumer complaints. It cannot undertake matters requiring the services of an attorney, nor can it provide credit information or endorse individual companies or products. Your phone book has the local number. (212-754-1320)

"The want of a thing is perplexing enough, but the possession of it is intolerable."
—*Sir John Vanbrugh*

Council on Economic Priorities

84 Fifth Ave, New York, NY 10011
This nonprofit organization evaluates the comparative social responsibility of corporations and publishes its findings. Studies on women in diverse professions are released as well as a bimonthly publication, *Economic Priorities Report*. (212-691-8550)

Dept of Consumer Affairs Protection

City, county, and state governments all have departments or offices for the protection of consumer interest. Mayors' and governors' offices may also have complaint offices or ombudsmen who can cut through governmental red tape. Check your phone book under the government listings.

Direct Mail Marketing Association

968 National Press Bldg, Washington, DC 20004
If you are tired of being deluged with catalogues, advertisements, and solicitations, write to DMMA for a form to fill out. They will in turn inform their 1800 member companies to take your name off mailing lists. (202-347-1222)

Direct Selling Association

1730 M St NW, Washington, DC 20036
The Association will handle complaints of harassment in door-to-door solicitation. (202-293-5760)

Environmental Protection Agency

401 M St SW, Washington, DC 20460
EPA assures the quality of water, air, and land through research, standard-setting, monitoring, and enforcement. (202-655-4000)

Federal Information Centers

These centers, located in key metropolitan areas across the country, serve as clearinghouses for all types of information about the federal government. US citizens can address questions about the federal government to the nearest FIC, and will be provided with the complete information on the spot—or directed to the closest office able to help. The staff will also try to answer questions about state- and city-government services. The centers stock federal publications advising the consumer on how to buy, use, and care for a variety of consumer products and federal programs. Look under US government listings in your phone directory.

Federal Trade Commission

Pennsylvania Ave at Sixth St NW, Washington, DC 20580
The FTC can protect the consumer from false advertising, untruthful labeling, flammable fabrics, deceptive packaging, dubious credit practices, and the circulation of inaccurate credit reports. (202-963-1110)

Food and Drug Administration, HEW

5600 Fishers Ln, Rockville, MD 20852
The watchdog of foods and drugs through research and standards. (301-443-1544)

GET

Box 355, Ansonia Sta, New York, NY 10023
GET (Gas, Electric, Telephone) can advise you of your rights in resolving disagreements with these utilities. Among other things, GET opposes phone-rate increases on the local level and organizes seminars for colleges and groups. Oddly, GET has no phone.

Movement for Economic Justice

1609 Connecticut Ave NW, Washington, DC 20009
MEJ organized to investigate possible restructuring of the economy through tax equality, revenue sharing, and other consumer-oriented programs. (202-462-4200)

National Association of Furniture Manufacturers

8401 Connecticut Ave NW, Washington, DC 20009
This industry association will handle problems and complaints. (202-657-4442)

National Consumer Congress

1346 Connecticut Ave NW, Washington, DC 20036 (202-833-9704)

National Consumer League

1785 Massachusetts Ave NW, Washington, DC 20036
Most consumer issues are promoted by the League. (202-797-7600)

National Tenants Organization, inc.

1346 Connecticut Ave NW, Washington, DC 20036
NTO links more than 400 local tenant groups from across the country in an effort to strengthen the movement for housing reform, and provides assistance and advice for tenants in public and private housing. *Tenants Outlook* gives a monthly analysis of the tenant housing situation as well as local activities. (202-785-4730)

Obscene or Harassing Phone Calls

If you are the victim of an obscene or harassing caller, hang up, call the police, and then call the telephone business office. New equipment and procedures enable the phone company to trace such calls.

Office of Consumer Affairs

New Executive Office Bldg, Washington, DC 20506 (202-245-6158)
The office coordinates existing federal programs, recommends new ones, and advises the President. Its booklet *Forming Consumer Organizations* is available for 35 cents from the Supt of Documents, US Government Printing Office, Washington, DC 20402.

Public Interest Research Group

2000 P St NW, Washington, DC 20036
Student-run PIRG's have been established throughout the country to support Ralph Nader's consumer investigations. See your phone book for local office. (202-833-9700)

Claremont, CA

Center for California Public Affairs

226 W Foothill Blvd 91711
The CCPA publishes the *California Handbook*, a comprehensive guide to sources of information and organizations in CA.

"If the present unused potential of women in our economy were realized by ending limitations and discrimination, a gain of perhaps 10 to 15 percent in living standards might be achieved."

—*Paul Samuelson*

The book contains a selected bibliography, 55 chapters, and detailed indexes. (213-624-5212)

San Francisco, CA

Consumer Action

26 Seventh St 94103
This volunteer collective offers free advice on consumer affairs and problems. Membership dues cover legal advice and a monthly newsletter. Pamphlets are also available for a small fee. (415-626-2510)

Boston, MA

Consumer Affairs Foundation, Inc

150 Tremont St 02111
The Consumer Affairs Foundation mediates disputes between customer and the retail merchant and checks false or misleading advertising. (617-482-6194)

Detroit, MI

Bureau of Information and Complaints

City-County Bldg 48226
If you have a question or complaint about city services, call the Bureau. (313-224-3000)

Kansas City, MO

Action Center of Kansas City

City Hall, 414 E 12th St 64106
This service for citizens who have problems with city government channels complaints to the proper department, follows through until problems are resolved, and notifies the citizen of the action taken. Citizens can call, write, or walk in. (816-274-2222)

Kansas City, MO

Jackson County Area Information Department

415 E 12th St 64106
AID claims it can find answers to all consumer questions and problems. This information and complaint service refers a call only when it must be handled personally by a specific individual. (816-881-3322)

St. Louis, MO

St. Louis Consumer Federation

7526 Byron Ave 63105
The Federation acts as a clearinghouse for information on improving the standard of living. It informs consumers so that they may buy wisely, know grades and standards, read labels, and learn to plan expenditures. The Federation seeks to organize consumers for increased political effectiveness. (314-721-5136)

New York, NY

New York Banking Department

Consumer Complaints, 100 Church St 10007
The Department investigates written complaints about sales-finance companies and insurance-premium-finance companies. To get the facts on buying on time, order the *Consumer Credit Guide* free from the above address. (212-488-2353)

Philadelphia, PA

Consumers Education and Protective Association

6048 Ogontz Ave 19141
The voluntary, nonprofit CEPA was formed when consumers banded together for mutual protection and education. Their newsletter, *Consumers Voice*, is an excellent publication. (215-424-1441)

Pittsburgh, PA
Alliance for Consumer Protection
Box 1354   15230
This voluntary citizen group helps the public with information for consumer-oriented laws and regulations, researches consumer concerns in the Allegheny County area, educates members and the public through monthly meetings and newsletters, sponsors a speakers service, and mediates consumer complaints. (412-241-8778)

Providence, RI
Consumer Protection Center, Inc
71 Rugby St   02903
CPC helps state residents with problems concerning fraud, misrepresentation, and defective merchandise. It educates the poor in better consumer protection and tries to make public agencies more responsive to public needs. (401-467-5807)

Milwaukee, WI
Concerned Consumers' League
524 National Ave   53204
CCL listens to consumers' complaints, plans how to take direct action, and then arbitrates a settlement. In the majority of cases it handles, CCL uses moral and fair-play arguments to make its point for the consumer. (414-645-1808)

Continuing Education
see — Adult Education, Handywoman
Contraception
see — Family Planning,
Health Care Services,
Pregnancy & Childbirth
Counseling, Women's
see — Mental Health
Crafts
see — Handywoman

Credit

Consumer Credit Commissioner
Cities and states frequently employ a Commissioner who will assist if you have any difficulty establishing consumer credit. Consult your phone directory under local government listings.

Credit Bureau
Virtually every city has a credit bureau that collects information on your credit records. Under the Fair Credit Reporting Act you have the right to check your file to make sure it is accurate. Check your local phone directory for number.

National Foundation for Consumer Credit
1819 H St NW, Washington, DC 20006
NFCC provides an intermediary between the individual consumer and the increasingly complex economy, maintaining an extensive program of education and public information, as well as research and counseling. (202-223-2040)

NOW National Task Force on Credit and Finance
3408 N St NW, Washington, DC 20007
The Task Force was organized by NOW to fight for legislation prohibiting discrimination on the basis of sex or marital status in granting consumer credit, and to educate women to the ways of credit unions. The Task Force offers a credit manual. (202-872-0133)

Credit Counseling
see — Financial Counseling

Credit Unions

American Federation of Community Credit Unions, Inc
2436½ 18th ST NW, Washington, DC 20009
The Federation promotes the continued growth of community-based credit unions and fosters resident leadership of each local facility. (202-332-7567)

Credit Union National Association, Inc
Box 431, Madison, WI 53701
Ninety percent of the federal and state credit unions belong to this association. (608-241-1211)

National Credit Union Administration
2025 M St NW, Washington, DC 20036
To apply for a federal charter for a credit union write to NCUA for information, or call your local chapter. (202-254-9800)

New Haven, CT
Women's Credit Union
170 York St   06511
The credit union is open to any member of the Connecticut Women's Political Caucus, the Women's Liberation Center, or Black Women United in Struggle. Membership costs $1. (203-777-6339)

Cambridge, MA
Feminist Credit Union
186½ Hampshire St   02139
A recently formed women's credit union, in need of your support. (617-661-0450)

Detroit, MI
Feminist Federal Credit Union
18700 Woodward Ave   48023
The first feminist credit union in the country, FFCU has been instructing feminists around the country on how to open their own credit unions. Any woman can join the union by paying the 50¢ membership fee, opening a shares account with $5 or more, and belonging to a feminist organization. FFCU is a nonprofit savings and loan cooperative, offering the same services as any other credit union. (313-892-7160)

Harrisburg, PA
First Pennsylvania Feminist Credit Union
126 Paxtang Ave   17111
Credit is available for members of Harrisburg NOW, the Harrisburg Women's Rights Movement, and the Harrisburg Women's Political Caucus. Contact Doris Ellis or Virginia Sassaman.

Pittsburgh, PA
Southwestern Pennsylvania NOW Federal Credit Union
6811 McPherson Blvd   15208
This newly formed credit union extends credit to NOW members. (412-363-2599)

Dallas, TX
Feminist Southwest Credit Union
Box 431   75221
A federally chartered women's credit union, FSCU provides low-cost loans to individuals and small businesses, credit counseling, and credit referrals. According to federal regulations, a woman must first belong to a women's group that is, in turn, a member of the Credit Union. She must then buy a $5 share to be eligible for the services. (214-521-1780)

Day Care
see — Child Care

Discrimination
see also— Employment Rights,
Women's Rights

American Civil Liberties Union
410 First St, Washington, DC   20003
The ACLU is dedicated to protecting the Constitution and, in particular, the Bill of Rights. It provides consultation and litigation at no charge to defendants or people needing aid. Members receive *Civil Liberties,* the official ACLU publication, 9 times a year, as well as reduced prices on a number of books and pamphlets dealing with civil liberties. (202-544-1681)

US Civil Rights Commission
1121 Vermont Ave NW, Washington, DC   20425
Although without enforcement powers, the Commission refers discrimination cases and complaints to the proper authority. It also publishes studies on deficiencies in federal laws and agencies. Contact your regional office:

NORTHEAST
26 Federal Plaza, New York, NY   10007
(212-264-0400)

MID-ATLANTIC
2120 L St NW, Washington, DC   20425
(202-254-6717)

SOUTH
75 Piedmont Ave NE, Atlanta, GA 30303 (404-526-4391)

MIDWEST
219 S Dearborn St, Chicago, IL   60604
(312-353-7371)

"Women need the same opportunity as men to use their brains and should then not be confined to making pudding or knit stockings."
—*Charlotte Bronte*

CENTRAL STATES
911 Walnut St, Kansas City, MO   64106
(816-374-5253)

SOUTHWEST
106 Broadway, San Antonio, TX   78205
(512-225-4764)

MOUNTAIN STATES
1726 Champa St, Denver, CO   80202
(303-837-2211)

WEST
312 N Spring St, Los Angeles, CA
90012 (213-688-3437)

Government Agencies

States, counties, cities, governors, and mayors all have various commissions or departments that handle discrimination complaints concerning housing, employment, credit, public accommodations, education, and other areas. Consult your phone directory's government listings for commissions under these key words:

Civil Rights	Equal Opportunity
Community	Human Relations
Relations	Human Rights
Discrimination	Women's Advocate

Divorce

National Organization to Improve Support Enforcement
12 W 72nd St, New York, NY   10023
NOISE is a one-woman organization founded by Ms. Diana DuBroff to fight for divorce insurance. (212-595-5299)

Women in Transition
4634 Chester Ave, Philadelphia, PA 19143
WIT provides support and discussion groups and publishes *Women in Transition* for women in the midst of divorce. (215-724-9511)

"Is not marriage an open question, when it is alleged, from the beginning of the world, that such as are in the institution wish to get out, and such as are out wish to get in?"
—*Ralph Waldo Emerson*

Doctor Referral
see — Health Care Services

Educational Financial Aid

Altrusa International Foundation, Inc
332 S Michigan Ave, Chicago, Il 60604
Altrusa awards grants to women for training or retraining to qualify for employment, with an emphasis on vocational education rather than a college degree. Stipends average $350 per year. (312-341-0818) See also Grants-in-Aid (this page).

American Association of University Women Educational Foundation
2401 Virginia Ave NW, Washington, DC 20037
The Foundation funds graduate fellowships for women and sponsors educational awards and programs, pilot projects, and basic studies and publications.   (202-785-7700)

Business and Professional Women's Foundation
2012 Massachusetts Ave NE, Washington, DC   20036
Services include a special-use library of more than 75,000 items; research grants and fellowships; management-training seminars; career-advancement scholarships open to mature women needing more training to reenter the job market, obtain a promotion, or enter a new career; grants to Latin American women for graduate study in the US in any field beneficial to their country; and special grants for outstanding projects of interest to BPW Club members. (202-293-1100)

Carnegie-Mellon Mid-Career Women's Fellowship Program
Admissions Officer, Graduate School of Public and International Affairs, Bruce Hall, U of Pittsburgh, Pittsburgh, PA 15213
Women between 30 and 50 who wish to pursue graduate studies in urban affairs or public administration can apply for fellowships for full or part-time study. (412-624-4744)

Danforth Graduate Fellowship for Women
Danforth Foundation, 222 S Central Ave, St. Louis, MO   63105
Fellowships for graduate study are available for women who want to pursue a career in secondary or college teaching or administration. (314-862-6200)

Diuguid Fellowship Program
Council of Southern Universities, Inc, 795 Peachtree St NE, Atlanta, GA 30308
Funds from $3,000 to $6,000 are for one year of retraining or formal study, leading to career advancement. Applicants must live and attend school in the South. (404-874-4891)

Educational and Cultural Exchange Opportunities
Dept of State, Bureau of Educational and Cultural Affairs, Washington, DC   20520 (202-655-4000)

Financial Aids for Higher Education
Oreon Kessler, Wm C Brown, 1974
A valuable reference book.

Financing a Graduate Education
Bulletin #OE-55036, Supt of Documents, Washington, DC 20402

Founders Fund Vocational Aid
c/o Altrusa International Foundation, 332 S Michigan Ave, Chicago, IL 60604
FFVA awards from $50 to $350 for training, retraining, or purchase of necessary equipment to women who plan to enter the job market, move to a more highly skilled occupation, or become self-employed. (312-341-0818)

General Federation of Women's Clubs
In the past two years approximately $2.5 million has been awarded to women through local and state chapters of Women's Clubs. For further information contact the president of the Women's Club in your community. If you have trouble finding a listing, contact the Chamber of Commerce to determine the name of the local club.

Lillian Moller Gilbreth Scholarship
Society of Women Engineers, United Engineering Center, 345 E 47th St, New York, NY   10017
The $500 scholarship has been awarded annually since 1958 to a woman enrolled in her 3rd, 4th, or 5th year as a full-time student in an engineering BA program at an accredited college or university. (212-752-6800)

Grant and Award Programs of the Public Health Service
US Public Health Service, HEW, Supt of Documents, Washington, DC 20402 (202-245-1638)

Grants-In-Aid
Altrusa International Foundation, 332 S Michigan Ave,   60604
Women graduate students from Africa, Asia, Latin America, and the Middle East enrolled in accredited colleges outside their own country and needing emergency funds to complete their studies qualify for grants ranging from $250 to $1,000, provided that they return home to work after receiving their degrees. (312-341-0818)

HEW Fact Sheet
HEW Educational Div, Washington, DC 20202
The pamphlet gives information about 5 federal financial programs: Basic Educational Opportunity Grants, Supplemental Educational Opportunity Grants; College Work-Study, National Direct Student Loans, and Guaranteed Student Loans. Free. (202-245-8710)

How About College Financing
American Personnel and Guidance Association, 1607 New Hampshire Ave NW, Washington, DC   20009 (202-483-4633)

Philip Morris Scholarship Fund
Ms Carole Johnson, Mgr of Urban Affairs, Philip Morris, Inc, 100 Park Ave, NY   10017
For women over 25, the fund provides grants for part-time undergraduate study at either a 4-year or community college in southwest Michigan. (212-679-1800 ext 788)

Need a Lift
American Legion, Dept S, Box 1055, Indianapolis, IN   46206
This 50¢ directory includes over 475 services of career and scholarship information. (317-635-8411)

Phi Chi Theta Foundation
2939 Van Ness St, Washington, DC 20008
The Foundation provides scholarships in business and economics to qualified and deserving women. (202-966-6049)

Helena Rubinstein Foundation
261 Madison Ave, New York, NY 10016
For women selected by the schools they attend, scholarships are based on financial need and academic ability. (212-751-9100)

A Selected List of Major Fellowship Opportunities and Aids to Advanced Education for US Citizens
National Academy of Sciences, 2101 Constitution Ave NW, Washington, DC 20418
Undergraduate, graduate, and postdoctoral-study financial assistance programs are described in this pamphlet. (202-393-8100)

Soroptimist Awards
1616 Walnut St, Philadelphia, PA 19103
Awards of up to $2,000 for training or re-training in vocational or technical study are given through local clubs. (215-732-0512)

The Student Assistance Handbook: A Guide to Financial Assistance for Education Beyond High School
Supt of Documents, Washington, DC 20402

Study Abroad
UNESCO Publications Ctr, 317 E 34th St, New York, NY 10016
Study Abroad presents an arrangement of information on about 100,000 fellowships and scholarships offered by governments, universities, foundations, and other institutions throughout the world. (212-686-4707)

Women in Leadership
United Presbyterian Church, 730 Witherspoon Bldg, Philadelphia, PA 19107
WIL is a national program that funds local groups working to improve their communities. The grants, ranging from $500 to $2,000, are awarded on the merits of the local projects, irrespective of religious, racial, or cultural backgrounds of participants. (215-893-4400)

Employment

Americans for Indian Opportunity
1820 Jefferson Pl NW, Washington, DC 20036
This is a free job-referral and placement service for native Americans. (202-466-8420)

Boyle Kirkman Associates, Inc
230 Park Ave, New York, NY 10028
This firm assists companies in utilizing women more effectively through personnel procedures, executive presentations

"Oh, if our high born girls knew only the grace, the attraction, labour, and labour alone, can add to the beauty of woman."
—*A.H. Clough*

on Equal Employment Opportunity guide-lines, training programs for women, and management-awareness seminars. (212-689-2061)

Catalyst
6 E 82nd St, New York, NY 10028
Catalyst helps women reenter the work force. It is now compiling a computerized list of women with at least one year of college and making it available to potential employers. If you want a job in administration, management, or technical or professional work, send a resume; there is no charge. Other job-finding materials are distributed at a minimal cost. (212-628-2200)

Civil Service Commission
CCS is in charge of testing and hiring for state and federal employment. Check the phone directory for nearest office.

Employment Security Division/ Commission
States fund these information centers that offer job placement, aptitude testing, job counseling, and referral for complaints. See state-government listings in your white pages.

Federal Job Information Center
US Civil Service Commission
The Job Information Center publishes listings of federal-employment opportunities available in your area and disseminates information about civil-service examining and appointment procedures and the benefits a federal employee receives. (202-737-9616)

Higher Education Resource Services
Brown U, Providence, RI 02912
HERS, a nationwide clearinghouse, finds faculty and administrative jobs for qualified women. They prefer that applicants for this service have PhD's or ABD's for faculty positions. (401-863-2197)

Jewish Vocational Service
Educational, career, and vocational-rehabilitation counseling; job placement; and psychological testing are all available to women; JVS fees vary according to individual income. Check your phone book for local branch address.

Job Corps for Women
JCW provides job referrals and personal help to young women 16 to 21 years of age who are members of low-income families and are high school dropouts. After interviewing, counseling and testing the girls, JCW arranges for their training in centers throughout the country and works toward their job placement and orientation in suitable employment areas. It also offers employment-readiness courses and training programs in adult-education centers. Check the phone book for your nearest office.

Labor Statistics
US Dept of Labor, 200 Constitution Ave NW, Washington, DC 20210
The *Occupational Outlook Handbook* is published every 2 years, with information on the future prospects of over 850 careers. This is a basic reference book for anyone seeking employment. (202-393-2420)

Manpower Administration
City, county, state, and federal Manpower offices channel Dept of Labor funds for employment and employment-training programs. Consult your phone book for the nearest office.

National Federation of Business and Professional Women
2012 Massachusetts Ave NW, Washington, DC 20036
A talent bank in operation since 1970, it collects the resumes of job applicants from the coalition of 26 women's professional organizations. Information includes the candidate's job objectives and desired salary range. Employers are given this information on request, at no fee. (202-293-1100)

Today's Woman Placement Service
21 Charles St, Westport, CT 06880
A national employment service for professional women, this agency screens women applicants for jobs in $10,000-to-$30,000 salary range. *Today's Woman in the Business World* is their management-digest newsletter, listing available job applicants, from chemists to sales managers. (203-266-4451)

The following local organizations offer a wide range of services including job placement, career counseling, vocational training, job banks, aptitude testing, and temporary employment. Call or write for specifics.

Tucson, AZ

Urban League
745 N Fourth Ave   85701 (602-623-6458)

Los Angeles, CA

Career Planning Center
1623 S La Cienega   90025 (213-273-6633)

Los Angeles, CA

Chicana Service Action Center
5340 E Olympic Blvd   90022 (213-728-0168)

Oakland, CA

Vocations for Social Change
4911 Telegraph Ave   94609 (415-653-6535)

Palo Alto, CA

New Ways to Work
475 Kingsley Ave   94301 (415-321-9675)

Sacramento, CA

Sacramento Concilio
911 F St   95814 (916-444-9665)

Sacramento, CA

Senior Citizen Job Mart
916 23rd St   95816 (916-446-6103)

San Anselmo, CA

Woman's Way
412 Red Hill Ave   94960 (415-453-4490)

San Francisco, CA
Careers Unlimited for Women Agency, Inc
Fairmont Hotel   94108 (415-397-3436)

San Francisco, CA
Chamber of Commerce Job Forum
465 California   94104 (415-392-4511)

San Francisco, CA
Women's Chamber of Commerce
922 Monadnock Bldg, 681 Market St
94105 (415-986-2807)

San Francisco, CA
Women's Vocational Institute
593 Market   94105 (415-495-8044)

Boulder, CO
Wo-Man Power
2750 Spruce St   80302 (303-447-9670)

Denver, CO
Better Jobs for Women—YWCA
1545 Tremont PL   80202 (303-244-4180)

Hartford, CT
Connecticut Institute for Health Manpower Resources, Inc
770 Asylum St   06105 (203-247-5677)

Hartford, CT
Health Job Bank
90 Washington St   06611 (203-566-5067)

New Haven, CT
Dixwell Neighborhood Employment Center
226 Dixwell Ave   06511 (203-562-2178)

Washington, DC
Job Market, Inc
1816 Jefferson Pl NW   20036 (202-785-4155)

Washington, DC
Washington Opportunities for Women
1111 20th St NW   20036 (202-293-2853)

Atlanta, GA
Black Women Employment Program
52 Fairlie St NW   30303 (404-522-8764)

Chicago, IL
Chicago Opportunities Industrialization Center
7 E 73rd St   60619 (312-651-8800)

Indianapolis, IN
IUPUI Continuing Education Courses
1201 E 38th St   46205 (317-264-4501)

Indianapolis, IN
J Everett Light Career Center
1901 E 86th St   46240 (317-259-5265)

Bedford, MA
Women's Opportunity Research Center
Div of Continuing Ed, Middlesex Community College, Springs Rd   01730
(617-275-1590)

Boston, MA
Wider Opportunities for Women
C F Hurley Bldg, Government Ctr
02114 (617-727-8978)

Boston, MA
Women's Educational and Industrial Union
264 Boylston St   02116 (617-536-5651)

Boston, MA
University Center, Inc
650 Beacon St   02215 (617-261-3313)

Marblehead, MA
Success, Inc
1 Auburndale Rd   01945

Newton, MA
Boston Project for Careers
83 Prospect St   02165 (617-969-2339)

N Cambridge, MA
New Environments for Women
Box 37   02140 (617-643-2228)

Detroit, MI
New Options Personnel, Inc
1249 Washington Blvd   48226 (313-961-8337)

Detroit, MI
Public Job Information Center
Lobby of City-County Bldg, 2 Woodward Ave   48226

Minneapolis, MN
Minnesota Planning and Counseling Center for Women
301 Walter Library, U of Minnesota
55455

Newark, NJ
EVE (Education, Volunteering, Employment)
Kean Bldg, Newark State College
07083

Union, NJ
EVE
Kean College of New Jersey, Morris Ave   07083 (201-527-2210)

Huntington, NY
Career Counseling for Women
13 W Tenth St   11743 (212-421-1948)

Mineola, NY
Nassau County Vocational Center for Women
33 Willis Ave   11501 (212-535-4646)

New York, NY
Career Workshop for Women
245 E 30th St   10016 (212-759-8080)

New York, NY
More for Women
52 Gramercy Park N   10010 (212-647-4090)

Cincinnati, OH
Job Information Center
Cincinnati Public Library, Eighth & Vine St   45202 (513-241-2636)

Cleveland, OH
Aim—Jobs
2310 Superior Ave   44113 (216-696-6171)

Philadelphia, PA
Distaffers, Inc
1130 Western Savings Fund Bldg
19107 (215-732-6666)

Philadelphia, PA
Options for Women, Inc
8419 Germantown Ave   19118 (215-242-4955)

Providence, RI
Opportunities for Women
72 Pine St   02903 (401-331-3315)

Houston, TX
Minority Women's Employment Program
2626 Calumet   77004 (713-526-3495)

Arlington, VA
Arlington Community Action Program
2410 Columbia Pike   22204 (703-979-2400)

Seattle, WA
Individual Development Center
1020 E John   98102 (206-329-0600)

Milwaukee, WI
Labor Education Advancement Program
930 W Center   53206 (414-374-0300)

Employment Rights

American Association of University Professors
1 Dupont Circle, Washington, DC 20036
A national committee of AAUP, the Committee on the Status of Women in the Academic Profession, was first established in 1918 and was reactivated in 1970. Committee W has reviewed existing AAUP policies in regard to women and equal-employment opportunity, and has examined its own past in an effort to correct discrimination against women. Local chapters work with women on campuses, support coalitions working for change, and sponsor various conferences and symposia on the topic of women in academe. (202-466-8050)

Attorney General
US Dept of Justice, Washington, DC 20036
This office has the responsibility for enforcing the equal-employment laws in governmental agencies. (202-737-8200)

Center for United Labor Action
167 W 21st St, New York, NY   10011
CULA supports strikes and advocates better living and working conditions for working women. (212-741-0633)

Equal Employment Opportunity Commission
EEOC enforces antidiscrimination laws regarding hiring, promotion, and benefits by employers, employment agencies, and labor unions. (The law applies to employers with 25 or more employees.) Individuals or groups may file charges against employers for such faults as underrepresentation of women in certain job categories. For more information, contact EEOC by checking the white pages of the phone book.

Fair Employment Practices Commission
The Commission researches, informs about, investigates, and enforces laws dealing with equality of employment opportunity. It has jurisdiction over labor unions, employment agencies, public agencies, and private employers of 25 or more people. Contact your local branch office for further information.

Federal Women's Program, HEW
330 Independence Ave SW, Washington, DC   20201
FWP develops and orchestrates programs to eradicate employment discrimination. (202-962-5311)

"Of course, women should have equal job opportunity and equal pay, but to pretend that being a mother and having a home is demeaning and not worthy, I think, is ridiculous."
—*Mrs. Arthur H. Sulzberger*

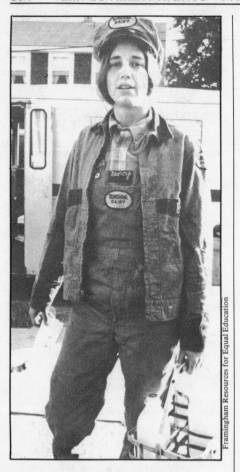

Framingham Resources for Equal Education

Federally Employed Women, Inc

487 National Press Bldg, Washington, DC 20004

FEW seeks to end sex discrimination in government service employment, to increase job opportunities for women, and to improve the merit system in government promotions. FEW also sponsors speakers and seminars, provides information to members on developments in equal employment opportunity, and publishes a newsletter. (202-638-4404)

National Committee on Household Employment

8120 Fenton St, Silver Springs, MD 20910

The average income of a household employee working full time with no vacation is about $2,000 per year. NCHE has prepared a model contract form, of use to both employer and employee. NCHE works to upgrade household employment, to extend the minimum-wage laws to include domestics, and to establish co-ops. (301-587-3335)

Office of Federal Contract Compliance

US Dept of Labor, Washington, DC 20210

Laws prohibit discrimination because of race, color, religion, sex, or national origin, and require affirmative action to ensure equality of opportunity in all aspects of employment by all federal-government contractors and subcontractors, and by contractors and subcontractors performing work under a federally assisted construction contract, regardless of the number of employees in either case. Contact OFCC if you think you have been discriminated against. (202-523-7981)

Womanpower

Betsy Hogan Associates, 222 Rawson Rd, Brookline, MA 02146

This newsletter covers women's rights in employment and monitors American industry for affirmative action. (617-232-0066)

Women's Bureau

Employment Standards Administration, US Dept of Labor, 200 Constitution Ave NW, Washington, DC 20212

The Women's Bureau promotes women's rights by serving as an information clearinghouse on working women, as well as studying the education and training of women and legislation pertaining to women workers. The Bureau provides resource people to many groups and referral information to local resources. There are publications on a wide variety of subjects including job opportunities, equal pay, economic-political-legal status, recent employment trends, and labor participation. (202-523-6611)

Beverly Hills, CA

Wells Associates

Box 3392   90212

Wells consults on the organizational and personnel changes resulting from equal-employment enforcement. (213-652-6661)

San Francisco, CA

Women's Job Rights

593 Market St   94105

WJR publishes the *Women's Job Rights Advocate Handbook,* which outlines what constitutes sex discrimination in hiring and employment practices and tells what steps to take if you feel you have been discriminated against. (415-495-0923)

Boston, MA

City Women for Action

Boston YWCA, 140 Clarendon St 02116

If you are an employee of the City of Boston with a complaint, call the City Women for Action. They share an office with Nine to Five, an association of Boston women office workers, but deal more specifically with problems of city employees. (617-536-6002)

Detroit, MI

New Options, Inc

2908 Book Bldg   48226

Michigan's only women consultants on affirmative action for women help employers comply with the law on equal rights. (313-961-8337)

New York, NY

Executive Enterprises Publications

10 Columbus Circle   10019

EEP publishes an affirmative-action-compliance guide for employers. (212-489-2670)

Philadelphia, PA

Lawyers' Committee for Civil Rights Under Law

1 N 13th St   19107

This Committee maintains an Employment Discrimination Panel consisting of a group of lawyers specializing in sex-discrimination cases in employment. Services are free, unless amount of damages won enables client to pay court costs. (215-735-7200)

Environmental Protection

see — Consumer Protection

Equal Employment Opportunity

see — Employment Rights

Extension Schools

see — Adult Education

Family Planning

see also—Abortion, Health Care Services, Pregnancy & Childbirth

American Family Planning

149 Lewis Rd, Havertown, PA 19083

AFP staffs counseling services in hospitals throughout the US for abortion, birth control, and other alternatives. (800-523-5101, toll free)

Association for Voluntary Sterilization, Inc

708 Third Ave, New York, NY 10017

AVS devotes its time to the increasingly controversial issues of voluntary sterilization. A nationwide referral service is provided for men and women seeking this permanent form of birth control. (212-986-3830)

The National Genetics Foundation

250 W 57th St, New York, NY 10019

NGF sponsors genetic-counseling centers throughout the US and is dedicated to the prevention and treatment of inherited disorders. (212-265-3166)

Victoria Blaine

Planned Parenthood Federation of America, Inc

810 Seventh Ave, New York, NY 10019 (212-541-7800)

This national headquarters for all Planned Parenthood affiliates provides only educational services. A library devoted to information on sexuality, birth control, and family planning is open to the public. For medical services, however, check with one of the clinics or regional offices:
GREAT LAKES

234 State St, Detroit, MI 48226 (313-962-4390)

"You know, of course, that the Tasmanians, who never committed adultery, are now extinct."

—*W. Somerset Maugham*

MID-ATLANTIC
Medical Towers Bldg, 255 17th St, Philadelphia, PA 19103 (215-732-4744)

MIDWEST
406 W 34th St, Kansas City, MO 64111 (816-531-2243)

NORTHEAST
810 Seventh Ave, New York, NY 10019 (212-541-7800)

SOUTHEAST
3030 Peachtree Rd NW, Atlanta, GA 30305 (404-233-7117)

SOUTHWEST
4928 Burnet Rd, Austin, TX 78756 (512-452-6417)

WESTERN
680 Beach St, San Francisco 94109 (415-673-0297)

Population Crisis Committee
1835 K St NW, Washington, DC 20006 (202-659-1833)
The Committee raises and channels funds to population-planning organizations.

The Population Institute
110 Maryland Ave NE, Washington, DC 20002
PI supplies information and educational material to promote population control. (202-544-2202)

Population Reference Bureau
1754 N St NW, Washington, DC 20036
Since 1929, the Bureau has provided any interested individual or group with information on all aspects of population. (202-638-5500)

Zero Population Growth
1346 Connecticut Ave NW, Washington, DC 20036
ZPG is a national organization formed in 1968 to stabilize US population through political, educational, and legal action. ZPG has set the year of 1990 as target date for zero growth, and now maintains full-time lobbyists in DC. It publishes the monthly *PG National Reporter;* obtains media coverage of the population problem; and distributes a wide variety of public announcements over TV and radio. (202-785-0100)

Family Services

Catholic Social Service
Under the direction of the State Archdiocese, these organizations offer many services for adoption, family counseling, foster-family care, the homemaker, resettlement, and unmarried parents. Fees are determined by ability to pay. See your phone book for local address.

Family Service Association of America
44 E 23rd St, New York, NY 10010 (212-674-6100)
FSAA is the national accrediting, standard-setting federation for more than 330 agencies throughout North America. They spearhead a battery of services to strengthen family life and alleviate family stress by professional counseling, specialized help, and advocacy to improve social conditions affecting family life. Check your phone directory for local listings under the following titles:

Community Chest
Community Council
Community Planning Council
Council for Community Services
Counseling Clinic
County Department of Health
Health and Welfare Council
Information and Referral Service
Mental Health Clinic
United Fund

Lutheran Social Services
Pastoral counseling, marriage counseling, individual therapy, family counseling, group therapy, and couples' group psychocounseling supervision are offered by these organizations. Fees are based on a sliding scale according to salary. Check your phone for a local outlet.

Financial Counseling

Consumer Credit Counseling Services
Anyone in financial difficulties may take advantage of CCCS's free, confidential services. The organization works out a plan of liquidation that suits both creditors and debtors, then distributes money to creditors from a set monthly payment from the debtor, simultaneously advising and educating the debtor in budgeting and money management. See your phone book for local listing.

Foster Parents
see — Adoption

Free Schools

American Association for Higher Education
1 Dupont Circle, Washington, DC 20036
AAHE publishes *The Free University Directory,* which lists most major schools offering nontraditional subjects. (202-293-6440)

Free Universities
As an offshoot of the late-sixties youth movement, many colleges established free schools. Check the university nearest you for further information.

Denver, CO

Denver Free University
1122 E 17th Ave 80218
"Anyone may teach anything" at DFU. Teachers do not have to have a degree: they're all volunteers interested in a subject, with some experience. The school makes general public announcements for volunteers, determines the curriculum a quarter in advance, and prepares a catalogue. (303-832-6688)

Chicago, IL

Alternative Schools Network
c/o American Friends Service Committee, 407 S Dearborn 60605
The Network's aim is to create places where the natural learning processes of dialogue, trial and error, and trusting relationships between young and old can thrive. Task forces concentrate on funding, gathering resources and information, and documenting ways in which alternative schools can function cooperatively. (312-427-2533)

Minneapolis, MN

Education Exploration Center, Inc
3104 16th Ave S 55407
The Center makes information available on alternative education resources in the Midwest. Members publish a newsletter, run a Speakers Bureau, and sponsor parent-student-teacher conferences. (612-722-6613)

Cincinnati, OH

East End Alternative School
c/o East End Area Council, 3527 Columbia Pkwy 45226
East End provides free skill and hobby classes, such as auto mechanics and woodworking, as well as vocational training and counseling. (513-281-1929)

Philadelphia, PA

Free University of U of Pennsylvania
34th & Spruce Sts 19104
Over 100 courses in a wide variety of subjects are offered each semester. (215-594-8908)

Milwaukee, WI

Independent Learning Center
1437 W Lincoln Ave 53212
Students who are having difficulty with institutional education can enroll in this alternative accredited high school program, based on the self-motivating interest of the student, emphasizing new options for the student. (414-384-4760)

Genetic Counseling
see — Family Planning

Grants
see — Educational Financial Aid

Handywoman

Van Nuys, CA

Everywoman's Village
5650 Sepulveda Blvd 91401
Offerings include car maintenance and repair, wallpapering, carpentry, tennis, Kung Fu, woodcarving, silk screen, gymnastics, tumbling, and acrobatics. Classes are limited, but late fees are prorated. (213-787-5100)

Chicago, IL

Bug Identification
U of Illinois Cooperative Extension Service, 10 N LaSalle St 60602
The Service will identify household and garden bugs, and give advice on how to exterminate them.

Chicago, IL

Kennedy-King College
6800 S Wentworth Ave 60621
Specialties include nursing, child care and human development, air conditioning and refrigeration, automotive services, photo-offset printing, theater arts, radio and television broadcasting. (312-962-3200)

Indianapolis, IN

Thomas Carr Howe High School Evening School
An 8-week comprehensive course on auto mechanics, for women only, costs $20. A 6-week photography course costs $15; an 8-week First Aid course, $2. (317-353-1326)

Indianapolis, IN

J Everett Light Career Center Adult Education
1901 E 86th St 46240

Courses include woodworking, welding, upholstery, tailoring, small-engine repair, radio-TV repair, printing, mechanics, picture framing, drafting, canoe construction, basic electronics, auto mechanics, and antiquing. Classes are 2½ hours once a week for 9 weeks. Fees range from $15 to $25. (317-259-5275)

Detroit, MI
East Detroit Adult Education Program
15501 Couzens Ave   48021
Home, general, and auto-mechanics courses as well as woodworking are offered to women. (313-776-9780)

Grosse Pointe, MI
Grosse Pointe Dept of Community Services
11 Grosse Pointe Blvd   48236
Classes in home repair, auto mechanics, upholstery, and woodworking are offered to women for about $10. (313-885-3808)

Minneapolis, MN
Project for Pride in Living
1527 E 26th St   55404
PPL helps people repair, decorate, and improve their homes. Clients must own their homes, have a low income, and be willing to do most of the work. U of Minnesota students from the Interior Design Dept draw up plans, secure materials, and provide expertise as needed. (612-721-6469)

Kansas City, MO
Communiversity's Skills Courses
5100 Rockhill Rd   64110
Course offerings usually include a session on basic auto care and repair for women, home repair, and home improvement. (816-276-1000)

Charlotte, NC
Central Piedmont Community College
1141 Elizabeth Ave   28204
Courses in auto care, furniture restoration, basic woodwork, general housewiring, and drafting cost only about $3. (704-373-6535)

New York, NY
Lady Carpenter® All-Craft Institute
20 St. Marks Pl   10003
Classes and facilities are provided for home-repair and maintenance instruction. (212-982-7166)

Cincinnati, OH
Continuing Education in the Cincinnati Public Schools
230 E Ninth St   45202
Vocational and hobby courses are offered through the Cincinnati Public School System. (513-369-4015)

Cincinnati, OH
Great Oaks Career Development Center
3254 E Kemper Rd   45241
GOCDC offers adult evening classes in auto mechanics, electricity, woodworking,

carpentry , and many other interesting disciplines. (513-771-8840)

Cleveland Hts, OH
Cleveland Heights—University Heights City School District
2155 Miramar   44118
Adult classes, open to all residents of the Cleveland area on a first-come first-served basis, usually meet in the evening for 10-week sessions. All types of handiwork are taught. (216-371-7171)

Memphis, TN
Woman's Exchange of Memphis
88 Racine   38111
If you are running a cottage industry and are having trouble selling your products, the Woman's Exchange will help you to spruce up your goods and find an outlet. (615-327-5681)

Seattle, WA
Experimental College
U of Washington, 203 HUB   98195
At this school anyone may take a course for a minimal fee or may offer to teach one. (206-543-2100)

Health Care Services

see also—Abortion, Family Planning, Pregnancy & Childbirth

County Medical Society
The Medical Society investigates legitimate complaints against members, finds qualified physicians for people who have none, and provides emergency medical help when other channels fail. Check your phone book for your local County Medical Society.

Dept of Public Health
The state, county, or city Health Dept offers a variety of services, including pregnancy testing, birth control, tuberculin testing, lead testing, diabetic screening, immunization clinics, and VD clinics, on a first-come first-served basis. Fees vary according to the patient's ability to pay. Look under local government listings in the phone directory.

Health Policy Advisory Center [Health-PAC]
17 Murray St, New York, NY   10007
Health-PAC keeps track of new developments and potential inequities in the health-care system and organizes workshops and speakers. (212-267-8890)

National Women's Coalition
222 E 35th St, New York, NY   10016
The Coalition will send a team of experts anywhere in the country, free of charge, to help set up a women's health center. Other services are abortion referrals, phone counseling, investigation of complaints about medical care, and information on health questions. (212-684-0217)

Reach to Recovery
Part of the American Cancer Society, Reach to Recovery includes women who

have undergone partial or complete mastectomies. Volunteers visit mastectomy patients still in the hospital, giving them practical advice and emotional support. See your phone book under American Cancer Society for local listing.

Well Baby Clinics
Sponsored by county health departments, these clinics offer free shots and preschool examinations for reasonably healthy children. If an illness is discovered, parents are advised where to seek medical treatment. Refer to the county-government listings in your local phone directory.

Women's Health Forum
155 Fifth Ave, New York, NY   10010
Research on women's health concerns, youth and community education projects, consumer education on the use of health facilities and personnel, and career guidance for women wishing to enter the health field are all part of this group's work. (212-674-3660)

Tucson, AZ
Tucson Health Resource Directory
Pima Health Systems, Inc.,
2302 E Speedway   85719
This comprehensive guide to over 250 health care facilities, programs, and equipment sources in Pima County is well worth the $3.50 asked, but PHS data is also available without charge on a walk-in or phone basis. PHS offers no direct health services. (602-881-4770)

Berkeley, CA
Berkeley Women's Health Collective
2908 Ellsworth   94705
Major services provided include free health care for women and children, birth control, abortion counseling and referral, sterilization referral, and psychological counseling. (415-843-6194)

Davis, CA
Davis Free Clinic
604 Fourth St   95616
Absolutely free and confidential medical care and advice is available to anyone in need. Special women's clinics offering pregnancy testing and various gynecological services are conducted. (916-758-2060)

Los Angeles, CA
Feminist Women's Health Center
1112 S Crenshaw Blvd   90019
(213-936-6293)

Los Angeles, CA
Women's Clinic
6423 Wilshire Blvd   90048
(213-655-5410)

Oakland, CA
Feminist Women's Health Center
2930 McClure St   94706
(415-444-5676)

Palo Alto, CA
Our Health Center
270 Grant   94306
Self-help groups for women run 4 or more sessions. Designed to teach women self-examination and to present information on diseases, birth control, and abortion, the groups gradually evolve into rap sessions, and take up massage, consciousness-raising, or whatever the particular group of women are into. (415-327-8717)

San Diego, CA

Womancare, Inc.
150 Garnet Ave   92109
(714-488-7591)

San Pedro, CA

Harbor Free Clinic
615 S Mesa   90731 (213-547-0202)

San Rafael, CA

Marin Women's Health Center
1618 Mission   94901 (415-456-2171)

Santa Ana, CA

Feminist Women's Health Center
429 S Sycamore   92701
Clinic services include pregnancy screening, birth control, and abortion referral. (213-836-1941)

Boulder, CO

People Clinic
2760 29th St   80301
Baby exams, birth control, and other medical services by volunteer physicians and trained paramedical persons is provided free or for a donation. (303-449-6050)

Colorado Springs, CO

Women's Clinic
801 N Cascade   80903
(303-471-3260)

Colorado Springs, CO

Women's Health Service
601 N Tejon   80902 (303-471-4127)

Washington, DC

Washington Free Clinic
1556 Wisconsin Ave NW   20007
The Free Clinic, in the basement of Georgetown Lutheran Church, offers night-time services, including general medical treatment, birth-control information, VD and pregnancy testing and counseling, and mental-health counseling, all of which begin at 6:30 p.m. There is a pediatrics clinic for children up to 12 years old. (202-965-5476)

Washington, DC

Women's Medical Center
1712 I St NW   20006
By appointment only, women can find medical care for birth control and abortion, at the hands of women doctors. (202-298-9227)

Gainesville, FL

Women's Health Center
805 Fourth Ave SW   32601
Services include pregnancy testing, pelvic examination, comprehensive gynecological checkups, low-cost Pap smears, 1st trimester abortion by vacuum aspiration, and pre- and post-procedure counseling accompanied by birth-control information. Sickle-cell screening and VD testing and treatment are free of charge. Arrangements for free day care of clients' children must be made in advance. (904-377-5055)

Tallahassee, FL

Feminist Women's Health Center
1126 Lee Ave   32303
(904-222-9600)

Atlanta, GA

Community Crisis Center Women's Clinic
40 Peachtree Pl NW   30309
The Women's Clinic provides family planning, abortion referral, VD testing, pregnancy tests, and counseling to young people. (404-892-1358)

Atlanta, GA

The Ladies Center
1211 W Peachtree St NE   30309
TLC maintains a sex- and health-education clinic offering birth-control and sex education, pregnancy tests and exams, VD tests, and other information. (404-872-7359)

Honolulu, HI

Women's Health Center
1820 University Ave   96816
(808-964-8844)

Chicago, IL

Emma Goldman Women's Health Center
1317 Loyola   60626
The EGWHC is a feminist paramedical collective. Trained and guided by a woman doctor, the staff offers the following tests and services: pregnancy testing, Pap smears, VD screening, contraceptives, pelvic exams, birth-control and abortion counseling, rape counseling, and self-help clinics. (312-262-8870)

Chicago, IL

Health Evaluation and Referral Service
2748 N Lincoln   60614
HERS screens information about women's health-care facilities in Chicago, and offers 24-hour call-back phone service with complete information concerning pregnancy testing, abortion facilities, evaluations of family-planning clinics, birth-control services, and private physicians. Chicago abortion facilities are closely monitored and evaluated. (312-528-2736)

Maywood, IL

Loyola Fertility Clinic
2160 S First Ave   60153
Married people are accepted by appointment at the Clinic, where both are thoroughly examined. Women are asked to keep temperature charts to check on ovulation, and sperm count is analyzed by a urologist. (312-531-3817)

Iowa City, IA

Emma Goldman Clinic for Women
715 N Dodge   52240 (319-337-2111)

Brighton, MA

Crittenton Hastings House Clinic
10 Pertshire Rd   02135
The Clinic offers GYN services and an abortion clinic, and maintains a residential program for unwed mothers. (617-782-7600)

Somerville, MA

Women's Health Project
326 Somerville Ave   02143
(617-666-5290)

Detroit, MI

Feminist Women's Health Center
2445 W 8 Mile Rd   48203
Women paramedics run pregnancy and vaginal-infection screenings, gonorrhea

"To insure good health: eat lightly, breathe deeply; live moderately, cultivate cheerfulness, and maintain an interest in life."
—*William Louden*

tests, abortion counseling and aftercare, birth-control counseling, and a doctor's referral system for a fee of $1 to $3. In the self-help clinic women learn to examine themselves and to detect problems in their earliest stages. (313-892-7790)

Mt Pleasant, MI

Women's Health and Information Project
Box 110 Worriner, Central Michigan U
48859 (517-774-3762)

Minneapolis, MN

Neighborhood Involvement Program Health Clinic
2617 Hennepin Ave   55408
(612-374-4089)

Minneapolis, MN

Women's Health Center
2000 S Fifth St   55404
(612-335-7669)

Minnetonka, MN

West Suburban Teen Clinic
15320 Minnetonka Blvd   55343
A drop-in center with clients from 12 to 20, the Clinic provides free medical treatment of venereal disease, pregnancy diagnosis, physical examinations, and birth-control help. (612-933-5290)

Kansas City, MO

Westport Free Health Clinic
4008 Baltimore   64111
Free diagnosis and treatment, or referral to a specialist, are available to all. The Clinic is extremely popular, and there is a long wait for service. (816-931-3236)

St. Louis, MO

Reproductive Health Services, Inc.
100 N Euclid   63108
RHS's services include crisis-oriented counseling, abortion prior to the 12th week of pregnancy, with post-procedure instructions, contraceptive counseling, VD screening, and referrals for childbirth counseling. Male and female sterilization will be offered. (314-367-0300)

St. Louis, MO

Wohl Health Centers
3200 S 13th   63118 (314-771-6776)
1501 S Grand   63104 (314-773-2666)
1528 N Kingshighway   63116 (314-367-4280)
The Dept of Health and Hospitals offers free services to women during pregnancy and after delivery at several health centers. Two of the centers have intensive-care programs for high-risk pregnancies. Family planning, social services, and nutritional services are provided for fees determined according to means.

New York, NY

Eastern Women's Center
14 E 60th St   10022
A complete range of abortion and gynecological services is offered for a fee; this state-licensed group does provide free pregnancy testing. (212-832-0033)

Rochester, NY

Rochester Health Network
360 East Ave   14604
Four gynecologists and obstetricians, along with family practitioners, assure comprehensive care for mother and child. The Childbirth Education Association also conducts natural-childbirth classes in conjunction with RHN, at a cost of $15 to $25 per 8-week session. (716-546-4200)

Rochester, NY
Women's Health Collective
713 Monroe Ave   14607
The organization has extensive files on health issues, as well as written records of local women's reactions to nearby physicians. Monthly meetings are held to discuss specific prearranged topics. (716-271-0680)

Cincinnati, OH
Vasectomy Services
3333 Vine St   45220
VS gives counseling and performs surgery. (513-961-3542)

Cleveland, OH
The Free Clinic
12201 Euclid Ave   44106
A staff of physicians, dentists, and 275 volunteers provide medical, dental, and mental-health care at no cost. The clinic is open to anyone from 5:00 to 10:30 p.m. (216-721-4010)

Cleveland, OH
Maternity and Infant Care Project
Cleveland Metropolitan General Hospital, 3395 Scranton   44109
Six clinics offer free maternity care, family-planning services, mobile dental clinic, and infant care up to one year to anyone in the Central, Central-East, Central-West, Glenville, Hough, Near Westside, or Tremont areas and to anyone enrolled in the Hough-Norwood Family Health Care Center. Appointments are not necessary. Call for information on the clinic nearest you. (216-351-7435)

Dayton, OH
Dayton Free Clinic and Counseling Center
1005 N Main St   45405
(513-228-2226)

Mentor, OH
Free Clinic of Lake County
9652 Old Johnny Cake Ridge   44060
There is no fee for any of the services rendered by the FCLC, which include treatment for VD, drug abuse, and other medical problems, as well as counseling and referrals. (216-255-6783)

Portland, OR
Women's Health Clinic
4160 SE Division   97202
The Clinic provides instruction on general health care and self-examination and offers Pap smears, pregnancy and abortion counseling, and referrals to doctors for more serious problems. (503-234-9774)

Philadelphia, PA
Breast Diagnostic Center
Thomas Jefferson U   19107
The Center offers free breast examinations to women between the ages of 45 and 64 who have had no previous history of breast malignancy. Women will be examined periodically during the 5-year program. Call for information. (215-829-6000)

Philadelphia, PA
Choice
A nonprofit consumer-advocate organization concerned with reproductive health care for women, CHOICE has collected and evaluated information on women's health-care services. The organization provides counseling, referral, and the *Resource and News Bulletin.* (215-932-0912)

Providence, RI
Maternal Infant Childcare Project
Women's and Infants' Hospital, 50 Maude   02908
MICP offers prenatal and infant care, provides dental services, and follows the health of the baby up to a year after birth. Patients are seen by appointment only. (401-274-1100)

Dallas, TX
Women's Health Forums
2917 Gladiolus Ln   75233
The Women's Health Coalition offers 3-hour health forums 3 to 4 times annually. The forums assist women in understanding their own bodies and emotions. (214-337-1895)

Houston, TX
Cullen Women's Center
7443 Cullen Blvd   77051
This specialized hospital, staffed by 8 gynecologists, offers pre- and post-abortion counseling as well as birth-control information and services. (713-733-5421)

Burlington, VT
Vermont Women's Health Center
Box 29   05401
Health education and services for women. (802-863-1386)

Rutland, VT
Southern Vermont Women's Health Center
187 N Main St   05701 (802-775-1056)

Richmond, VA
Fertility Clinic
A D Williams Clinic, 12th & Marshall Sts   23219
For a medical diagnosis and treatment of infertility, and also of hormonal problems, call the Clinic for an appointment. (703-770-4111)

Seattle, WA
Aradia Women's Clinic
4224 University Wy NE   98105
One of 4 free women's clinics in Seattle encouraging women to participate more actively in their health care, Aradia offers pregnancy detection and counseling, routine pelvic examinations, contraceptive information and supply, and information about menstruation, conception, and menopause. Appointments are necessary. (206-634-2090)

Millie and Christine, Siamese twins

Sophia Smith Collection, Smith College

Seattle, WA
Birth Control Information Family Planning Clinic
140 Public Safety Bldg   98104
All forms of birth control, birth-control classes, some sexual counseling, and referrals for sexuality problems are available at the 8 clinics throughout the city. (206-583-2530)

Seattle, WA
Country Doctor Women's Clinic
402 15th St   98112 (206-322-6698)

Seattle, WA
Fremont Women's Clinic
6817 Greenwood Ave N   98103
(206-782-5788)

Seattle, WA
Open Door Clinic
5012 Roosevelt Wy NW   98105
This is the oldest free medical clinic in the country. Its services include a crisis phone, referral system, and a women's clinic on Wednesday evenings. (206-524-7404)

Madison, WI
Near Eastside Community Health Center
1133 Williamson St   53703
The Health Center is a free clinic, giving checkups, VD screening, birth-control counseling, medical referrals, classes on health problems, and preventive health care. Appointments are usually made a week in advance. (608-255-0704)

Milwaukee, WI
People's Free Health Clinic
2621 W Center   53206
This walk-in center offers free health services to local residents, providing limited diagnostic treatment, and referrals. A free dental clinic is also available to children from ages 3 to 15. (414-264-1435)

Vancouver, BC (Canada)
Vancouver Women's Health Collective
146 E 18th St   9
This collective is dedicated to self-help clinics and health-education services. (604-873-3984)

Home Study
see — Adult Education

Insurance

Health Insurance Institute
277 Park Ave, New York, NY   10017
The Institute offers a simple husband-and-wife quiz, with a records form, which can make it easier to figure out what insurance you really need. *New ABC's of Health Insurance,* a booklet covering more detailed questions, is also available. (212-922-3000)

Insurance Information
State governments have a Dept or Div of Insurance that can handle complaints and provide information on the reputation of a company, as well as the types of policies and benefits offered. See your phone book under the government listings.

"Nature has given women so much power that the law has very wisely given them little."
—Dr. Samuel Johnson

Paul C. Cabot III

Legal Aid

American Bar Association
1705 DeSales St NW, Washington, DC 20036
The ABA sponsors citizen's-advocate centers, monitors the standards of the legal profession, and provides referrals for those in need of legal advice (see also "Lawyer Referral Service" below). (202-659-1330)

Black Women's Employment Project, NAACP Legal Defense Fund
10 Columbus Circle, New York, NY 10019
The Project investigates job discrimination against black women and initiates class-action suits in order to set the tone for more equitable job practices. (212-586-8397)

Ford Associates, Inc
701 S Federal Ave, Butler, IN 46721
These lawyers publish a *Directory of Women Attorneys in the US,* as well as a legal handbook on discrimination. (219-868-5331)

Lawyer Referral Service
The local Bar Association refers persons in need of legal advice to attorneys in appropriate fields of practice. A small fee is charged for the first half-hour of consultation in the attorney's office; fees for additional services are a matter of agreement between attorney and client. Check your local phone directory under Bar Association.

Legal Aid
For those who cannot afford a lawyer, Legal Aid handles civil litigation and some criminal cases. For the office nearest you, check the phone directory under Legal Aid or Legal Services.

National Organization for Women Legal Defense and Education Fund, Inc
47 E 19th St, New York, NY 10003
NLDEF does the research for educational and legal work for NOW; and assists in court cases involving precedents or class actions. It also sponsors public-service advertising and education projects. (212-674-8950)

Women's Equity Action League Legal Defense and Educational Fund, Inc
795 National Press Bldg, Washington, DC 20004
The Fund conducts research, contributes to costs of landmark women's cases, writes proposals for massive legal and educational work, and works for enforcement of anti-sex-discrimination laws in education. (202-638-1961)

San Francisco, CA
Women's Legal Center
558 Capp St 94110
The Center sponsors a number of projects in the Bay Area: a divorce clinic, an information and referral service, and *"Women and the Law,"* a directory of women lawyers. The staff writes a column for the National Lawyers Guild. (415-285-5066)

New Haven, CT
Connecticut Women's Education and Legal Fund, Inc
33 Whitney Ave 06510
This organization fights sex discrimination, usually on behalf of groups rather than individuals. (203-865-0188)

New Haven, CT
Women's Law Fund, Inc
35 Elm St 06510
The Fund engages in suits for the benefit of women in Connecticut. (203-562-8993)

Washington, DC
Women's Legal Defense Fund
1424 16th St NW 20036
WLDF provides legal assistance and counseling for cases involving employment and credit discrimination, abortion, domestic relations, and child-care facilities. A screening committee selects cases that will help establish precedents in the fight for equal rights. (202-232-5293)

Sophia Smith Collection, Smith College

Indianapolis, IN
Laws of Special Interest to Women
M Catherine Barton and Glenn Grampp, Rm 211, State House 46204
This leaflet is not a compilation of all Indiana laws; it's merely meant to acquaint you with some of them, by answering questions women frequently ask about matters that touch their daily lives.

Baltimore, MD
Women's Law Center
Box 1934 21203
The Center provides advice, assistance, and representation to individual women encountering sex-based discrimination, and also serves as a focal point for those interested in the legal issues involved in sexism. (301-366-2232)

Cambridge, MA
Women's Law Collective
698 Massachusetts Ave 02138
WLC provides information and referrals for women with legal hassles. (415-492-5110)

St. Paul, MN
Women's Advocates
500 Grand 55105
Women's Advocates helps women to find attorneys and operates a telephone-information service. (612-227-8284)

Cleveland, OH
Women's Law Fund, Inc
620 Keith Bldg, 1621 Euclid Ave 44114
WLF assists and represents women who have encountered sex discrimination in their jobs, in housing, or in insurance, by private or public persons. (216-621-3443)

Legal Defense Funds
see — Legal Aid

Lesbians

Daughters of Bilitis
1005 Market St, San Francisco, CA 94103
DOB aims to aid the lesbian in discovering her place in society and to educate society to understand and accept her without prejudice. (415-861-8689)

Gay Community Services Center
1614 Wilshire Blvd 90017
Various services for gay persons are provided by this nonprofit organization. (213-482-3062)

Lesbian Speakers' Bureau
3028 Greenmount Ave, Baltimore, MD 21218
Pairs of women from this Bureau visit schools and civic and religious groups for an adjustable fee of $25. Their intention is to educate the public about lesbianism and change the attitudes that lead to oppression of homosexuals. (301-235-8593)

National Gay Student Center
2115 S St NW, Washington, DC 20008
NGSC serves as an information clearinghouse and resource center for newly formed gay campus groups. (202-265-9890)

San Francisco, CA
Lesbian Mothers Union
c/o Metropolitan Community Church, 1074 Guerrero 94110
LMU aids lesbian mothers in contested custody cases, conducts research on legal precedents, and facilitates contacts among lesbian mothers. (415-285-0392)

Atlanta, GA
Atlanta Lesbian Feminist Alliance
Box 7684 30309
ALFA maintains a library, hosts social functions, provides speakers to the community, and actively supports local political action. (404-523-7786)

Chicago, IL
Lavender Women
1723 W Devon St 60660
This "journal of lesbian/feminist opinion" is published every 6 weeks by a creative women's collective.

Chicago, IL
Lesbian Feminist Center
3523 N Halsted 60657
The Center houses 2 autonomous groups —the policy branch, staffed exclusively by lesbians, and a counseling resource center, which provides information on local lesbian activities. (312-935-4270)

Ann Arbor, MI

Gay Liberation Front
530 S State 48104
GLF promotes gay liberation. (313-761-2044)

Minneapolis, MN

Lesbian Resource Center
2104 Stevens 55405
The Center offers consciousness-raising groups, a coffeehouse, counseling, sports, and courses in various subjects, as well as a newsletter and a magazine. (612-871-2601)

Buffalo, NY

Sisters of Sappho Gay Community Services Center
1350 Main St 14209
This group of lesbian women meets twice a month for a rap session, sponsors women's dances, and runs a speakers' bureau. (716-881-5335)

New York, NY

Homosexual Community Counseling Center, Inc
45 E 74th St 10021
The Center offers a staff of psychiatrists, psychologists, and psychoanalysts, as well as lay people, for counseling homosexuals and lesbians. (212-988-7632)

New York, NY

Lesbian Feminist Liberation
Box 243, Village Sta 10014
LFL supplies understanding and help to lesbians who are beginning to find their identities, publishes a newsletter, sells a lesbian record—*A Few Loving Women*—and maintains a speakers' bureau. (212-691-5460)

Cincinnati, OH

Labyris
Box 6302 45206
A lesbian group, Labyris sponsors social and political activities and has a printing press and lesbian-feminist bookstore, besides offering various courses such as auto mechanics. (513-475-3967)

Philadelphia, PA

Gay Switchboard
Call this number if you'd like counseling or information about the gay movement and related self-help groups. (215-978-5700)

Philadelphia, PA

Lesbian Hot-line
A group of trained counselors is available to talk to women about lesbian issues by phone. (215-729-2001)

Pittsburgh, PA

Gay Alternatives Pittsburgh
This group provides information and group counseling for sexual minorities and is involved in political action. (412-363-0594)

Seattle, WA

Seattle Counseling Center for Sexual Minorities
1720 16th Ave 98134 (206-329-8707)

Madison, WI

Lesbian Switchboard
306 N Brooks 53715
The Switchboard will answer questions or discuss problems about lesbianism. (608-257-7378)

Milwaukee, WI

Grapevine Women's Coalition c/o Women's Coalition
2211 E Kenwood 53211
Grapevine is a collective of activist lesbian-feminists seeking to eliminate male domination and to free women to pursue their needs and goals. (414-964-8135)

Libraries

Venice, CA

Feminist History Research Project
218 S Venice Blvd 90291
This group is assembling primary source material on twentieth-century women and plans to publish a research digest journal. (213-823-4774)

New London, CT

American Woman's Collection
Connecticut College Library 06320
Uncatalogued material is available on Alice Hamilton, Belle Moskowitz, Frances Perkins, Prudence Crandall Philleo, and Lydia Sigourney. (203-442-1630)

Washington, DC

Business and Professional Women's Foundation Library
2012 Massachusetts Ave NW 20036
The BPW Library collects materials devoted to women in contemporary American society. (202-293-2100)

Washington, DC

Library of Congress
First St NW 20540
The LC offers full or partial collections on Susan B. Anthony, Carrie Chapman Catt, and the National American Woman Suffrage Association. (202-426-5000)

Washington, DC

National Woman's Party Library
144 Constitution Ave NE 20002
Manuscripts, maps, and slides are housed in this library with about 3,000 volumes. (202-546-1210/1211)

Evanston, IL

Women's History Research Center Library
Northwestern U, 633 Clark St 60201
WHRC has a large collection of contemporary materials dealing with all aspects of the women's movement. Formerly at Berkeley, initiated by Laura X. (312-492-3741)

Boston, MA

Zion Research Library
771 Commonwealth Ave 02215
The library, dedicated to nonsectarian Protestant research for the study of the Bible and the Christian Church, has a small collection on women and the Church. (617-353-3724)

"The best method of guarding against the danger of reading what is useless is to read only what is interesting."

—*Lord Balfour*

Cambridge, MA

Schlesinger Library on the History of Women in America
3 James St 02138
The Schlesinger houses an outstanding collection of papers and writing of distinguished American women, from the earliest writers to the suffragists and the liberationists, including official NOW papers. (617-495-8647)

Northampton, MA

Sophia Smith Collection
Smith College 01060
This collection documents the retrospective and contemporary intellectual and social history of the world's women. Especially strong holdings relate to birth control, the humanities, fine and applied arts, education, suffrage, women in the professions and industry, women's rights and women's liberation. (413-584-2700)

Ann Arbor, MI

Bentley Historical Library
Michigan Historical Collections, Beal & Bonisteel Sts 48104
Women's history material relating to Michigan is available here. (313-769-1828)

New York, NY

New York Public Library
Research Libraries & Special Collections, Fifth Ave & 42nd St 10017
The full or partial records of Lillian Wald, Fania Cohn, Emma Goldman, Carrie Chapman Catt and Elizabeth Oakes Smith, as well as partial records of the National American Women Suffrage Association, are housed in the Special Collections. (212-790-6161)

Greensboro, NC

Walter Clinton Jackson Library
U of North Carolina 27412
Special collections on physical education for women and on women from 1500 to 1900. (319-379-5284)

Philadelphia, PA

Women's Medical College Library
3300 Henry Ave 19129
The American Medical Women's Association has presented the Library with a strong collection on women in medicine. (215-842-6000)

Swarthmore, PA

Friends Historical Library
Swarthmore College 19081
The Lucretia Mott Collection is contained in this library. (215-574-7900)

Madison, WI

Helen C White Women's File
Corner of Park St & Observatory Dr 53706
The File includes current information on local women's groups and their publications.

Milwaukee, WI

Research Center on Women
Alverno College, 3401 S 39th St 53215
Files contain film, reports from the Women's Bureau, seminar reports, bibliographies, and considerable material on sexism and discrimination. (514-671-5400)

Lobbies
see — Politics

Magazines/Newspapers
see — Publications

Management Training
see — Adult Education

Media

Features and News
333 N Michigan, Chicago, IL 60601
FAN is a national news service supplying women's features and news articles to 30 newspapers across the country. (312-346-7037)

Feminist Radio Network
Box 5537, Washington, DC 20016
FRN is a central clearinghouse for feminist audio tapes produced by women all over the country. Write for the catalogue of prices and descriptions.

Women's Institute for Freedom of the Press
3306 Ross Pl NW, Washington, DC 20008
In addition to publishing a newsletter, *Media Report to Women,* the Institute researches the economic and organizational structure of the communications industry and its role in maintaining male dominance in society. (202-966-7783)

Clearinghouse for Feminist Media
Box 207, Ancaster, Ontario
CFM provides information for women entering media.

Northampton, MA
Women's Film Co-op
c/o Valley Women's Center
200 Main St 01060
The Co-op lends films to groups for a small fee, trains women in the visual arts, and publishes a catalogue of films and reading lists on women in the media. (413-586-2011)

Detroit, MI
Women's Radio Collective
WDET, 5035 Woodward 48202
Members of the Collective write, announce, produce, direct and engineer *All Together Now,* a weekly radio program. The Collective also provides free public-service announcements of activities and events of general interest to women. (313-577-4147)

Minneapolis, MN
Twin City Women's Film Collective
c/o Darlene Marvy
This group produces films and video tapes that illuminate the history of women. (612-473-2373)

Mental Health

American Institute for Mental Studies Referral Service
Vineland, NJ 08360
The Service helps parents select appropriate diagnostic facilities for children who may be retarded. (609-691-0021)

Community Mental Health Centers
Mental health centers provide counseling, group and family therapy, emergency service, referrals, diagnostic testing, and treatment for adults and children. Look up the nearest center in your phone book.

The International Association of Counseling Services
1607 New Hampshire Ave NW, Washington, DC 20009
IACS issues a *Directory of Approved Counseling Agencies* listing types of service and fees for agencies throughout the country. (202-232-6729)

Mental Health Depts
States, counties, and cities have departments or committees that investigate, administrate, and monitor government mental-health programs. Besides coordinating area programs, most will handle complaints and make referrals.

National Association for Mental Health, Inc
1800 N Kent St, Arlington, VA 22209
NAMH is committed to helping the mentally ill, their families, and the community. The program emphasizes improved care and treatment for mental-hospital patients, aftercare and rehabilitation services, treatment, education and special services for mentally ill children, and community mental-health services. (703-528-6405)

National Clearinghouse for Mental Health Information
5600 Fishers Ln, Rockville, MD 20852
The Public Inquiries Section at NCMHI maintains an updated collection of publications, articles, and reference lists on the many forms of mental illness. All this material is available to those interested in learning more about mental-health theory and practice. The staff also compiles lists of psychiatric facilities and organizations offering help to troubled people. (301-443-4515)

Neurotics Anonymous
1341 G St NW, Washington, DC 20005
This program, which offers help to mentally and emotionally disturbed people, is staffed by people who have been successfully helped by the program. (202-628-4379)

Recovery, Inc
116 S Michigan Ave, Chicago, IL 60603
Chicago is the national office for this nonprofit organization that offers self-help care to chronically nervous people and former mental patients. At the weekly group encounters members help each other by giving examples of how they practiced the Recovery method in facing specific difficulties. (312-263-2292)

Tucson, AZ
Alternatives for Women
40 E 14th St 85705
Professional counselors help women gain control of their lives, discover their strengths, and learn techniques for dealing with fear. (602-884-9776)

San Francisco, CA
Women for Women, Institute and Educational Center
4220 California St 94118
W for W acts as an umbrella agency for

female therapists, as well as offering individual and group sessions for problem solving. (415-668-7111)

San Francisco, CA
Women's Center for Creative Counseling
Call for appointment. (415-648-1509)

San Francisco, CA
Women's Counseling Service
Individual, group, and family counseling is provided by trained psychologists. (415-392-0400)

New Haven, CT
Women's Counseling Center
Yale U 06520
Trained counselors discuss a wide range of personal problems and make referrals to sympathetic therapists. (203-436-0272)

Norwalk, CT
Counseling Center for Women
Norwalk Community College, 33 Wilson Ave 06854 (203-853-2040)

Carbondale, IL
Feminist Therapists
c/o Annette M Brodsky, 1600 W Freeman 62901
A directory of feminist therapists is offered for 35 cents.

Chicago, IL
Woman's Institute
4180 N Marine Dr 60613
The Woman's Institute is primarily concerned with providing feminist therapists for women. (312-334-1198)

Cambridge, MA
Focus
186½ Hampshire St 02139
Women can be treated by women at this therapy center staffed by professionals. Fees are arranged on a sliding scale, and hours are flexible. Group as well as individual therapy is available. (617-876-4488)

Cambridge, MA
Women's Counseling and Resources Center, Inc
1555 Massachusetts Ave 02192 (617-492-8568)

Minneapolis, MN
Elizabeth Blackwell Women's Health Center
2000 S Fifth St 55404
The Health Center is dedicated to helping women emotionally, politically, and medically. Individual and group counseling is available. (612-335-7669)

Minneapolis, MN
Feminists' Therapists
Women's Mental Health Center, General Hospital, 6195 Fifth St 55415
The center offers walk-in counseling for people with emotional and mental-health problems. (612-926-9297)

Minneapolis, MN
New Hope Center for Women
3125 Clinton Ave S 55408
New Hope Center offers help and spiritual rehabilitation for women. (612-822-1935)

New York, NY
New York Counseling and Guidance Service
110 W 86th St 10024
The Service provides individual and group therapy for marital and personal problems. (212-362-1086)

New York, NY

New York Feminist Therapist
Referral Service
c/o Tina Mandel, 334 W 87th St
10024 (212-724-1157)

New York, NY

Women's Counseling Project
Columbia U, 117th St & Broadway
10027 (212-280-5133)

Cincinnati, OH

Human Potential Specialists
2928 Linwood Ave   45208
HPS is a resource center and counseling service devoted to helping women of all ages achieve their utmost potential. (513-871-1844)

Cincinnati, OH

Women Helping Women
2933 Clifton   45220
WHW is a crisis counseling center and referral service for women facing any type of problem. (513-861-8616)

Cincinnati, OH

Women Into Tomorrow
5105 Ivyform Rd   45243
WIT helps women unsure of the meaning and value of their lives through programs of group interaction and training. The Ella Snook Traver Scholarship is awarded yearly. (513-821-1698)

Cleveland, OH

Cleveland Women's Counseling
Box 20279   44120
CWC refers women to consciousness-raising groups, helps to start groups, and sponsors a network of women dedicated to helping other women in need. (216-321-8585)

Portland, OR

Women's Psychological Clinic
Portland State U   97207
The Clinic offers a variety of counseling and aptitude testing. (503-229-4459)

Philadelphia, PA

Feminist Therapy Collective
2132 Lombard St   19146
Individual and group therapy is provided for women who want to explore alternative roles and life-styles. (215-546-1234)

Philadelphia, PA

Institute of Awareness
401 S Broad St   19147
Adult women can attend courses in personal growth, transactional analysis, career exploration, personal finances, female sexuality, interpersonal communication, women in literature, and mysticism. (215-545-3770)

Philadelphia, PA

Wives' Self-help
Women with marital problems can call for help from married non-professionals. (215-667-9262)

Dallas, TX

Explore
3935 Boca Bay   75234
A unique 8-week course for women, Explore has taken a thousand women through this unique program of self-evaluation and goal-setting. (214-247-6397)

"The true way of softening one's troubles is to solace those of others."
—*Mme de Maintenon*

Dallas, TX

Women for Change Center
Center for Personal Growth,
3220 Lemmon Ave   75204
At the Center, women examine their potentials with professional guidance and group support in a variety of organized settings. (214-522-3560)

Houston, TX

Changing Life Is My Beginning
Box 55683   77055
Small groups of women meet every other week to discuss the physical and psychological problems of menopause.

Richmond, VA

Women Helping Women
Women's Resource and Referral Line
6 N Fifth St   23219
Women counselors offer a sympathetic ear for women trying to work out problems in their lives; referrals are made. (703-649-2211)

Seattle, WA

Seattle Counseling Center
1720 16th St   98112 (206-329-8737)

Seattle, WA

Women's Institute of the Northwest
2102 NE 50th St   98116
WIN offers individual group and family counseling from a feminist perspective. (206-522-7039)

Madison, WI

Women's Place
St. Francis House, 1001 Ave   53715
A group of motivated women started Women's Place to provide a mental-health counseling service to women in the Madison area. (608-256-0446)

Babyhood

Parents

Guild for Infant Survival, Inc
6822 Brompton Rd, Baltimore, MD 21207
An international group of parents who have lost a child through crib death, the Guild's purpose is to support other parents who go through this traumatic experience. GIS meetings are generally held 3 times a year; one of its main functions is to raise money for research on the cause of crib death. (301-944-2502)

Momma
Box 5759, Santa Monica, CA 90405
This group is composed of mothers who are widowed, divorced, separated, or never married, and who seek a supportive atmosphere to help them face the challenge of their position. The underlying theme is that the woman must return to living her own life and not live in waiting for another man. Activities include investigation and evaluation of

child-care facilities; cooperative babysitting; recreational activities; investigation of discrimination against single mothers by employers, landlords; and the publication of a monthly newsletter.

National Foundation for Sudden Infant Death, Inc
1501 Broadway, New York, NY 10036
NFSID was the first lay organization to propose a plan of public education about the sudden-infant-death syndrome, as well as to provide authoritative information and understanding to stricken families. The goals are the prevention of SID and the eradication of needless guilt reaction. (212-563-4630)

National Organization for Non-parents
Box 10495, Baltimore, MD 21209
NON feels that in our overpopulated society, persons who choose to be child free should not be discriminated against through economic and cultural bias. Members are parents and nonparents who encourage societal acceptance of child-free life-styles. Meetings are announced in the monthly newsletter. (301-484-7433)

Parents Anonymous, Inc
Parents Anonymous is a supportive group for parents with negative feelings toward their children. It emphasizes methods of preventing child abuse by learning positive expressions of feelings. Check your phone book for local address.

Parents Without Partners International
7910 Woodmont Ave, Bethesda, MD 20014
PWP is devoted to the well-being of single parents and their children. Program activities are sponsored by local groups. (301-654-8850)

Political Parties
see — Politics

Politics

Another Mother for Peace
407 N Maple Dr, Beverly Hills, CA 90210
This organization works to promote peace and eliminate war. (213-278-3476)

Center for the American Woman in Politics
Eagleton Institute of Politics at Rutgers University, New Brunswick, NJ 08903
This nonpartisan information and research center investigates the role of American women in government and develops conferences and model education programs. (201-932-1766)

Democratic National Committee, Office of Women's Activities
1625 Massachusetts Ave NW, Washington, DC 20036

Aiming to serve all Democratic women and encourage their participation in the political process, the committee publishes information on fund raising, political clubs, elections, and other aspects of politics. (202-797-5900)

The Feminist Party
c/o Irene Davall, 311 W 24th St, New York, NY 10011

Sophia Smith Collection, Smith College

Maud Wood Park, first president of the League of Women Voters

League of Women Voters
1730 M St NW, Washington, DC 20036
The League encourages citizen participation in the political process, supplying information on candidates, platforms, and issues to local chapters (see phone book for your local chapter). The League's active publications program covers diverse topics. (202-296-1770)

National Black Feminist Organization
285 Madison Ave, New York, NY 10017
NBFO was established by black feminists to meet the needs of black women; it deals with such issues as the black woman's self-image, unemployment, welfare, and black women prisoners. (212-889-5881)

National Federation of Republican Women
310 I St SE, Washington, DC 20003
NFRW is a partisan political group that educates women on political matters and coordinates efforts toward the election of Republican candidates. (202-484-6670)

National Peace Action Coalition Women's Contingent
150 Fifth Ave, New York, NY 10011
(212-741-1960)

National Woman's Party
Alva Belmont House, 144 Constitution Ave NE, Washington, DC 20002
Founded in 1913 by Alice Paul, Crystal Eastman, and others to spearhead the woman's suffrage movement, the Party introduced the first Equal Rights Amendment bill in 1923 and has been obtaining more sponsors every year. (202-546-1210)

National Women's Political Caucus
1921 Pennsylvania Ave NW, Washington, DC 20006
With members from every political party and a great variety of women's organiza-

tions, NWPC seeks to place women in decision-making positions at every level of government. It lobbies to end discrimination based on sex and to change national priorities to meet the needs of the young, elderly, ill, and poor. Write for the address of your local chapter. (202-785-2911)

Nurses Coalition for Action in Politics
1030 15th St NW, Washington, DC 20005 (202-296-8015)

Republican National Committee, Women's Division
310 First St SE, Washington, DC 20003
The Division encourages the activity of women in the political process, specifically the Republican party. (202-484-6500)

Women Strike for Peace
145 S 13th St, Philadelphia, PA 19107
WSP was founded in 1961 to organize a one-day strike. Since then it has opened several offices in cities throughout the country. It now works to reallocate the military budget to serve humanitarian needs. (215-923-0861)

Women United
2001 Jefferson Davis Hwy, Arlington, VA 22202
This organization lobbies for legislation benefiting women, spearheading the fight for states' ratification of the ERA. (703-892-4248)

Women United for Action
58 W 25th St, New York, NY 10010
This volunteer group organizes demonstrations protesting high costs, particularly of food, and studies the economic effects of cuts in services and layoffs on women's lives. (212-989-1252)

Women's International League for Peace and Freedom
120 Maryland Ave NE, Washington, DC 20002
The League works by nonviolent means to establish the political, economic, social, and psychological conditions necessary for world peace. Its monthly newsletter, *Peace and Freedom*, reports on current legislation. (202-546-8814)

Women's Lobby, Inc
1345 G St SE, Washington, DC 20003
WL lobbies for child care, pension reform, abortion rights, women's education, and minimum wages for domestics. A $10 contribution brings both a quarterly, which concentrates on one topic per issue, and *Alert* which puts out the alarm on important legislation. (202-547-0082)

"No calling in the life of the city belongs to woman as woman or to man as man; by nature the woman has a share in all practices, and so has the man. For a woman to hold office she will not need special education. We will be dealing with the same nature in woman as in man and the same education will be required for both."

—Plato

Women's National Democratic Club
1526 New Hampshire Ave NW, Washington, DC 20036
WNDC offers Democratic women an opportunity to obtain information about problems and issues confronting the US, to discuss Democratic ideals and programs, to participate in educational and community service, and to meet the nation's lawmakers. (202-232-7363)

Oakland, CA
Women's Action Training Center
1941 High St 95601
WATC serves the Bay Area by offering classes for women who wish to improve their skills and understanding of social action. (415-533-2000)

Miami, FL
ERA Coalition
1174 NE 110th St 33161
The coalition coordinates the activities of over 50 organizations in the Greater Miami area working to obtain ratification of the ERA. (305-895-0648)

Miami, FL
Women's Committee of 100
5835 SW 50th Terr 33155
The committee works on the solution of community problems and emphasizes the need for qualified women to seek involvement in public affairs. (305-665-3027)

New Orleans, LA
Independent Women's Organization
IWO endorses candidates for office and takes stands on issues. Any woman who is a registered Democrat is eligible for membership. A newsletter keeps members informed on group activities. (504-482-2427)

Boston, MA
Women's Lobby
State House, Rm 275 02233
The Lobby traces the progress of legislation affecting women. Member organizations and individuals contribute fact sheets for hearings on bills pending. (617-868-4738)

Cleveland, OH
Women Speak Out for Peace and Justice
Box 18138 44148
WSPJ is a group of concerned women who take an active interest in political and social problems. Send for a free newsletter. (216-371-4027)

Philadelphia, PA
Philadelphians Who Care
1420 Walnut St 19102
Acting as a clearinghouse on civil and legal matters, PWC also publishes the *News Report* which describes the actions of city government and various citizen's groups. (215-546-5950)

Pregnancy & Childbirth

see also—Abortion, Family Planning, Health Care Services

American College of Obstetricians and Gynecologists
1 E Wacker Dr, Chicago, IL 60601
For booklets about myriad aspects of pregnancy, prenatal care, labor, birth control, abortion, hormones during the menstrual cycle, genetic counseling, high

Babyhood

blood pressure during pregnancy, hysterectomy, infertility, how to deliver a baby in an emergency, and many other related subjects, request *ACOG Booklets* from ACOG. A directory of other sex-education materials separated into preschool, elementary, junior and senior high school, college, and graduate levels is also available. (312-222-1600)

American Society for Psycho-Prophylaxis in Obstetrics, Inc
1523 L St NW, Washington, DC 20005
Classes in the Lamaze method of childbirth start in the last 6 to 8 weeks of pregnancy and are taught by certified instructors. ASPO is a national nonprofit educational organization. (202-783-7050)

Association of Mothers for Educated Childbirth
Box 9030, Far Rockaway, NY 11691
Home delivery and its safe practice are the concerns of this group.

Birthright
For "Right to Life" alternatives to abortion in cases of problem pregnancies, Birthright can help. Consult your phone book for the local address.

Catholic Social Service
CSS helps unwed parents to make sound decisions regarding their future and their child's. Check your phone book for your local branch.

Childbirth Education Association
Registered nurses teach the Lamaze technique of childbirth. Single women are accepted—bring a friend to help with the timing. Check your phone directory for a local branch.

Clergy Consultation Service on Problem Pregnancies
CCSPP provides referrals on abortion clinics, maternity homes, and psychiatric and prenatal care. There is no fee, and the service is nondenominational. A local branch is listed in your phone directory.

Florence Crittenton Association of America
67 Irving Pl, New York, NY 10003
Local branches provide comprehensive programs of residential, day care, and outpatient services for young women whose out-of-wedlock pregnancies create social and psychological problems. There are no age, race, or religious restrictions. Pregnancy testing is offered along with abortion planning, maternity home, adoption planning, and single-parent programs. Fees based on actual cost of care and ability to pay.

Department of Public Health
Information and referrals for pre- and postnatal care, childbirth classes, pregnancy counseling, and other services are offered. Look under the phone book's city, county and/or state government listings for numbers and addresses.

International Childbirth Education Association
Box 5852, Milwaukee, WI 53220
ICEA will direct you to the closest source of information on the modified Lamaze method of childbirth. (414-476-0130)

La Leche League International
9616 Minneapolis Ave, Franklin Park, IL 60131
Guided by a professional medical advisory board, LLL instructs mothers throughout the world in all phases of breast feeding. Call or write for further information concerning LLL instructors and classes in your area. (312-455-7730)

La Leche League

Lamaze
Many hospitals and clinics offer childbirth education classes, including exercises and instructions. Call your local hospital for information on Lamaze in your community. Classes meet once a week for 6 weeks; you should register by the 5th month of pregnancy.

Maternity Center Association
48 E 92nd St, New York, NY 10028
MCA gives classes on pregnancy, childbearing, and baby care for expectant mothers, and information on other facets of family life. An extensive bibliography of books and pamphlets is available. (212-369-7300)

Planned Parenthood
Local PP branches have pregnancy testing and counseling services. Check your phone book or see listing under Family Planning for regional offices.

Right to Life
In place of abortion, RTL supports such solutions as counseling for women distressed by their pregnancies, comprehensive medical, social, economic, educational, vocational, and recreational care for pregnant, unwed mothers, and the removal of the word *illegitimate* from birth certificates. A speakers bureau and extensive pamphlets are available. Check your phone book for a local branch.

Society for the Protection of the Unborn Through Nutrition
17 N Wabash, Chicago, IL 60602

To protect the mother and her unborn child, SPUN counsels women, provides speakers, and disseminates literature. (312-332-2334)

Tucson, AZ

Free Clinic of Tucson, Inc
256 S Scott Ave 85701
Pregnancy testing and counseling, drug-crisis help, and VD tests are given at this walk-in clinic. There is also a Women's Gyn and Self-Help clinic. (602-622-8221)

Sacramento, CA

Pregnancy Hot Line
The Hot Line gives information on alternatives to abortion. (916-482-8488)

Boulder, CO

Alternatives, Inc
1345 Spruce 80302
This organization provides pregnancy tests, pre- and postnatal medical care, psychological support, shelter for unwed mothers, food and clothing needs for the mother and baby, financial and welfare assistance, adoption services, and assistance in child rearing. The service is free. (303-449-6565)

Denver, CO

Connection
1309 Kearney 80220
Connection's staff will talk with anyone about pregnancy, childbirth, and other health matters. (303-321-5709)

Southbury, CT

Parents Association for the Lamaze Method
PALM, a consumer group, aims to improve childbirth conditions in hospitals. It sponsors films on the Lamaze method each month and maintains a speakers bureau. (203-264-7758)

Miami, FL

Women's Aid
Box 630374 33163
Women's Aid offers free pregnancy tests, abortion advice, and adoption arrangements. (305-949-4972)

Winter Park, FL

Prenatal Classes
Ms Louis Forthuber RN, Director, 200 N Lakemont Ave 32789
All aspects of pregnancy, labor and delivery, and care of the baby are covered during 6 weeks of classes. (305-646-7111)

Chicago, IL

Midwest Population Center
100 E Ohio 60611
This clinic, run by women, offers comprehensive pre- and postabortion and birth-control counseling and gynecological care; services include a 24-hour emergency phone service, pregnancy testing, and pelvic examinations. Medical eligibility cards are accepted; sliding-scale fee arrangements are made with Health Evaluation Referral Service guidance. MPC is approved by HERS. (312-644-3410)

Glenview, IL

Midwest Parentcraft Center, Inc
627 Beaver Rd 60025
MPC offers classes for mothers and partners that concentrate on relaxation, breathing patterns, and body mechanics, starting in the 4th month of pregnancy. (312-724-5488)

Palatine, IL

Society for the Preservation of Human Dignity Helpline
Box 574 60067
The Helpline is a volunteer phone counseling service which offers alternatives to abortion for women with problem pregnancies. (312-359-4919)

New Orleans, LA

New Life
211 Camp St 70130
Abortion is not considered an alternative by the New Life Staff, which will help the mother keep her baby or put it up for adoption. New Life offers pregnancy tests free of charge. (504-581-5433)

Annapolis, MD

Anne Arundel General Hospital Prepared Childbirth Classes
Franklin St 21401
Registered nurses instruct groups of about 12 couples in the Lamaze method. A woman must attend with her coach, must deliver at AA Gen, and must have her obstetrician's permission. (301-268-4444)

Baltimore, MD

Maryland Children's Aid Society, Inc
2502 St Paul St 21218
Children's Aid is a voluntary agency offering various services to unmarried or expectant mothers, temporary placement of children in foster homes, an adoption service, counseling service to parents and children, and a referral service. (301-366-1430)

Bethesda, MD

Parent and Child, Inc
5914 Greenlawn Dr 20014
The directors of P & C believe that it is as important for the father as it is for the mother to receive childbirth training. Classes meet both in Maryland and in Washington. (301-530-6263)

Boston, MA

Coping with the Overall Pregnancy Experience
2 Hanson St 02118
COPE helps the pregnant woman and her family deal with all aspects of her pregnancy through small counseling sessions. (617-357-5588)

Lexington, MA

Boston Association for Childbirth Education
14 Cottage St 02173
BACE runs a consumer forum in maternal and child health, provides an educational service for professional health workers and parents, reports on innovative approaches and services related to childbearing, and conducts a childbirth education class for expectant parents. (617-861-0569)

North Adams, MA

Birth Control Information Center
45 Eagle St 02147
Birth control and abortion counseling from the feminist viewpoint are the strong points of BCIC. (413-663-8846)

Springfield, MA

Women's Services Association
78 Chestnut St 01103
WSA specializes in the evaluation, counseling, and treatment of problem pregnancies. All examinations and procedures are performed by certified staff gyne-

cologists at Wesson Women's Hospital next door. (413-788-0886)

Worcester, MA

Worcester Pregnancy Counseling Service, Inc
104 Chandler 01609
Information on adoption, health-care services, abortion, prenatal care, and hospital resources in Massachusetts. (617-791-7201)

Detroit, MI

Childbirth Without Pain Education Association
8448 W McNichols 48221
CWPEA trains couples in the Lamaze childbirth technique in classes in Highland Park, Warren, Royal Oak, Berkley, Southfield, Westland, and Detroit. (313-345-9850)

Detroit, MI

Women's Counseling Center
13040 W 7 Mile Rd 48235
WCC is a complete gynecological clinic, staffed mostly by women. (313-861-3939)

Lincoln Park, MI

Childbirth Preparation Association
2962 Ford St 48146
CPA conducts classes in the Lamaze childbirth technique in the Garden City, Taylor, Dearborn, Redford, Trenton, Lincoln Park, Dearborn Heights, and Wyandotte areas. (313-388-2229)

St Louis, MO

Children's Home Society
9445 Litzsinger 63144
The Home Society provides assistance to women with unwanted pregnancies and arranges for adoption if the mother so desires. (314-968-2350)

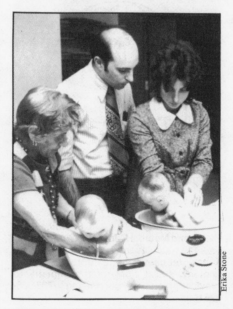

Erika Stone

Winston-Salem, NC

Birthchoice
Birthchoice is a nonjudgmental group formed to provide information on pregnancy including medical, legal, financial, or emotional problems. (919-723-8218)

New York, NY

Parents Workshop
St Luke's Hospital, 411 W 114th St 10025
Parents groups run by the workshop function as support systems for new parents—

both men and women. They help women to cope with the loss of identity they may experience upon becoming mothers. (212-362-3314)

Cincinnati, OH

Cincinnati Women's Services
1433 McMillan E 45206
Besides free pregnancy tests and birth-control information, Women's Services provides counseling and an abortion clinic. (513-961-5544)

Cincinnati, OH

Total Parent Education
Box 39382 45239
TPE presents educational programs, classes, and films on childbirth. (513-385-8793)

Cleveland, OH

Association for Parent Education
Box 727 44121
Weekly classes led by registered nurses, instruction centers in Cleveland Hts, Mayfield Hts, University Hts, Euclid, and other southeast suburbs, are offered. Cost for the 7-week course and a monthly newsletter is $20. (216-283-0904)

Columbus, OH

Columbus Association for Childbirth Education
Box 1062 43216
A general prenatal course deals specifically with the Lamaze method of special exercise to aid in labor and delivery. Instructors are RNs who have gone through an intensive 18-week training period. (614-864-0948)

Lakewood, OH

Educated Childbirth, Inc
Box 2613 44107
ECI expects to train 1,200 prospective parents in safe childbirth procedures per year. (216-734-0161)

Portland, OR

Prepared Childbirth Association
PCA runs a 7-week course to prepare couples for family-centered childbirth. The prospective father is taught to coach breathing exercises and to help during labor and delivery. (503-244-9392)

Columbus, OH

Lamaze Childbirth Association
3950 Milton Ave 43214
It is the philosophy of Lamaze to have husbands participate in the program and at baby's birth. The 6-week course costs $20; however, LCA never turns anyone away who is interested. (614-261-1112)

Portland, OR

Portland Association for Childbirth Education
PACE runs classes in childbirth preparation for prospective mothers and fathers including information on nutrition and medication. (503-284-0591)

Chester, PA

Reproductive Health and Counseling Center
Crozer Chester Medical Annex, 15th & Upland Ave 19013
(215-874-4361)

Philadelphia, PA

Concern for Health Options: Information, Care and Education
1421 Arch St 19102
Affiliated with the Clergy Consultation Service, CHOICE is a free pregnancy

counseling service. (215-547-2904)

Pittsburgh, PA

Alternatives to Abortion, Inc
Box 8297   15218
This service gives telephone counseling and referrals to women with unplanned pregnancies. Information and group lectures are also available. (412-731-2420)

Pittsburgh, PA

People Concerned for the Unborn Child
1760 Potomac Ave   15216
This group provides educational programs for interested persons and maintains a resource center. (412-531-9272)

Pittsburgh, PA

Pittsburgh Organization for Childbirth Education
Box 10480   15234
Women may enroll for classes taught by registered nurses on anatomy, physiology, labor process, relaxation, body-building exercises, Lamaze breathing exercises, and the husband's role. (412-221-3066)

Pittsburgh, PA

Women's Health Services, Inc
1209 Allegheny Tower, 625 Stanwix St 15222
WHS provides free pregnancy tests and abortion by the vacuum-aspiration method for a fee. (412-562-1910)

Austin, TX

Austin Parent-Child Association
Box 1141   78767
APCA sponsors childbirth-education classes for expectant parents based on the Lamaze technique. (512-453-2477)

Austin, TX

Problem Pregnancy Counseling Agency
2434 Guadalupe   78705
The agency suggests ways of dealing with an unwanted pregnancy and will find legal help if necessary. Its services are free. (512-474-5321)

Dallas, TX

Dallas Association for Parent Education, Inc
5531 Dyer, Rm 203   75206
Childbirth education classes start every 7 weeks. They train the husband as a labor coach. (214-692-0790)

Dallas, TX

St Paul Hospital Parenting Classes
5909 Harry Hines Blvd   75235
The classes prepare couples for labor and delivery and for care of the newborn at home. Men assist during labor and help with breathing and relaxing exercises; they may accompany their wives in the delivery room. (214-631-4040)

Houston, TX

Houston Organizing for Parent Education
3311 Richmond   77006
Cooperative childbirth (Lamaze), breast feeding, and family-centered maternity-care classes are taught by qualified instructors. (713-534-3089)

Houston, TX

Pregnancy Counseling Service
7030 Bretshire   77016
PCS disseminates free information on abortion, adoption, and maternity care. (713-633-3958)

Houston, TX

Reproductive Services, Inc
6243 Bissonnet   77036
Contraceptive and abortion information and services are offered. (713-771-4336)

San Antonio, TX

Alamo Childbirth Training Association
Box 1884   78297
ACTA teaches the Lamaze method of prepared childbirth. (512-342-3311)

San Antonio, TX

Reproductive Services
4810 San Pedro   78212
This nonprofit corporation's services include pregnancy testing, counseling, vacuum-aspiration and curettage abortions, and a follow-up examination. (512-826-6336)

Richmond, VA

Daily Planet
1422 Floyd Ave   23221
Pregnancy and abortion counseling are provided by the Daily Planet. There is no fee. (703-355-2375)

Richmond, VA

Fan Free Clinic
1721 Hanover Ave   23221
Social workers, ministers, nurses, and doctors provide birth control, pregnancy tests, and counseling. (703-358-8538)

Richmond, VA

MCV Ob/Gyn
Broad & 12th Sts   23219
Classes in childcare for fathers as well as mothers cover all the basic problems of a new baby. Pre- and postnatal training are available for a fee based on ability to pay. (703-770-5977)

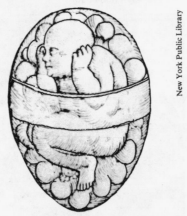

New York Public Library

Richmond, VA

Richmond Medical Center for Women
112 N Boulevard   23220
The center uses volunteers trained in psychology, social work, or the ministry to provide pregnancy counseling. (703-335-3751)

Madison, WI

Parentcraft
Parentcraft conducts classes in early pregnancy, Lamaze childbirth, and child-care; and operates consumer-advocate services. (608-271-7785)

Madison, WI

Women's Counseling Service
731 State St   53703
Women's Counseling has free information and counseling on birth control, pregnancy, abortion, VD, sterilization, and sexuality. (608-255-9149)

Milwaukee, WI

Problem Pregnancy Information Service, Inc
2266 N Prospect Ave   53211
This proabortion volunteer group directs pregnant women to outlets where safe, legal abortions can be obtained. Counseling services are also available. Since there is no fee, low-income women can find confidential help here. (414-271-2610)

Prisons

National Female Offender Resource Center
Commission on Correctional Facilities & Services, 1705 De Sales St NW, Washington, DC   20036 (202-293-1715)

Brooklyn, NY

Co-workers Development Corp
108 Lawrence St   11201
Training programs, residences, and workshops for ex-offenders are provided to help the women become economically productive and self-supporting. Write for their brochures and enclose a stamped, self-addressed envelope for the reply mail. (212-858-0880)

New York, NY

Puerto Rican Women's Prison Project
Puerto Rican Forum, 296 Fifth Ave 10001   (212-244-1110)

New York, NY

Women's Prison Association
110 Second Ave   10003
Many services such as job counseling and placement, and child care are offered by WPA. (212-674-1163)

New York, NY

Women's Prison Project: Legal, Education and Counseling Clinic
c/o Marilyn Haft, ACLU Women's Rights Project, 22 E 40th St   10017
Inmates are taught law and given legal counseling through this group. (212-725-1222)

Cleveland, OH

Library for Women Prisoners
Box 18072   44118
A library for women prisoners in the Cuyahoga County jail accepts books and pamphlets on women's lib or general reading material.

Columbus, OH

Ohio Woman-to-Woman
935 E Broad St   43205
WTW, started by Man-to-Man Associates in March, 1971, matches women volunteers with inmates in Marysville Reformatory for Women to bring the offender into contact with society and to provide assistance once she is paroled. Matches are made on the basis of applications from would-be volunteers and inmates. (614-253-0936)

Dallas, TX

Institute of Women's Wrongs
Box 19987   75219
IWW researches and studies the conditions of women in prisons and what happens to their infants and minors; and it raises funds to try to improve these conditions. There is a book club for resource material and a speakers bureau. (214-521-6507)

Richmond, VA

Sisters in Prison
Women's Center, 6 N Fifth St   23219
Women interested in working in the city
jail can contact this group through the
Women's Center. (703-649-2211)

Professional Women

The majority of these professional
organizations maintain a roster of women
in the field and will provide career
information on request.

Association of Feminist Consultants
222 Rawson Rd, Brookline, MA
02146 (617-232-0066)

**Federation of Organizations for
Professional Women**
828 Washington St, Wellesley, MA
02181 (617-235-8624)
Rm 1122, 1346 Connecticut Ave NW,
Washington, DC   20036 (202-833-
1998)

Accountancy
**American Women's Society of Certified
Public Accountants**
327 S LaSalle St, Chicago, IL   60604
(312-427-1989)

Advertising
**American Advertising Federation
Women's Division**
1225 Connecticut Ave NW, Washington, DC   20036 (202-659-1800)

Agriculture
American Farm Bureau Federation
Women's Committee, Park Ridge, IL
60068 (312-689-2020)

Anthropology
American Anthropological Association
1703 New Hampshire Ave NW,
Washington, DC   10009 (202-232-
8800)

Architecture
American Institute of Architects
Women in Architecture Task Force,
1735 New York Ave NW, Washington, DC   20000 (202-785-7300)

**American Society of Landscape
Architecture**
Committee for Women in Landscape
Architecture, 2511 Q St NW, Wash-
ington, DC   20007

Association of Women in Architecture
Ms Dorothy Gray Harrison, 2155
Pine Crest Dr, Altadena, CA   91001

**Women Architects, Landscape Archi-
tects, and Planners**
The Boston Architecture Center
320 Newbury St, Boston MA   02115
(617-536-3170)

Art
**National Association of Women
Artists, Inc**
156 Fifth Ave, New York, NY
10010 (212-675-1616)

Women's Caucus for Art
c/o College Art Association of
America, 16 E 52nd St, New York,
NY   10019 (212-755-3532)

Astronomy
American Astronomical Society
c/o Dr B T Lynds, Kitt Peak Observatory, 950 Cherry Ave, Tucson,
AZ   85717 (602-327-5511)

Banking
**National Association for Bank Women,
Inc**
1730 Pennsylvania Ave NW, Washington, DC   20006 (202-785-0500)

Biology
American Society for Cell Biology
Women in Cell Biology, Dr. Mary
Clutter, Dept of Biology, Yale U,
New Haven, CT   06520 (203-432-
4298)

American Society for Microbiology
Committee on the Status of Women
Microbiologists, 1913 I St NW,
Washington, DC   20006 (202-833-
9680)

Biophysics
Biophysical Society
Professional Opportunities for
Women, Dr. Mary Jacobs McCrea,
George Washington U, Medical
School, Washington, DC   20037
(202-331-6897)

Business
**American Business Women's
Association**
9100 Ward Pky, Kansas City, Mo
64114 (816-361-6621)

Association of Women Administrators
U of Cincinnati, Cincinnati, OH
45221 (513-475-8000)

**National Association of Female Execu-
tives, Inc**
1251 Ave of the Americas, New York
NY   10016 (212-586-1123)

**National Association of Negro Business
and Professional Women's Clubs**
2861 Urban Ave, Columbus, GA
31907 (404-561-3472)

"If the Women's Movement were to
become less visible, less influential,
it would reduce the psychological
pressure on the courts to enhance
the status of women in the long run."
—*Leo Kanowitz*

**National Federation of Business and
Professional Women's Clubs, Inc**
2012 Massachusetts Ave NW,
Washington, DC   20036 (202-293-
1100)

Chemistry
American Chemical Society
Women Chemists Committee, Dr.
Susan Collier, Research Lab, East-
man Kodak Co, Rochester, NY
14650

American Society of Biological Chemists
Subcommittee on the Status of
Women, 9650 Rockville Pike, Beth-
esda, MD   20014 (301-530-7145)

Construction
**National Association of Women in
Construction**
2800 W Lancaster, Ft Worth, TX
76107 (817-335-9711)

Cosmetics
Cosmetic Career Women, Inc
614 W 51st St, New York, NY
10019 (212-765-8406)

Dentistry
**Association of American Women
Dentists**
435 N Michigan Ave, Chicago,
IL   60611 (312-644-0828)

National Dental Association
Box 197, Charlottesville, VA
22902 (703-293-8253)

Economics
American Economic Association
Commission on the Status of
Women, Dept of Economics, SMU,
Dallas, TX   75275 (214-837-5275)

Society for International Development
Committee on Women in Development, Pushpa Schwartz, 8510 Fenway Rd, Bethesda, MD 20034

Education
Adult Education Association of the US
810 18th St, NW, Washington,
DC   20006 (202-347-9574)

**American Association for Higher
Education**
1 DuPont Circle, Washington,
DC 20036 (202-293-6440)

**American Association of University
Professors**
Committee on the Status of Women,
Ms Carolyn Polowy, 1 Dupont
Circle, Washington, DC   20036
(202-466-8050)

**American Association of University
Women**
2401 Virginia Ave NW, Washington,
DC   20037 (202-785-7700)

American College Personnel Association
Task Force on Women, 1607 New
Hampshire Ave NW, Washington
DC   20036

American Council on Education
Office of Women in Higher Education, 1 Dupont Circle NW, Washington, DC 20036 (202-833-4700)

American Educational Research Association
Committee on Women in Educational Research, Dr. Carol Kittle, CUNY, 1411 Broadway, New York NY 10018

American Federation of Teachers
Women's Rights Committee, 11 Dupont Circle, NW, Washington, DC 20036 (202-737-6141)

American Society for Training and Development
Women's Caucus, Ms Kate Kirkham, NEA, 1201 16th St, Washington, DC 20036 (202-833-4292)

Association of American Colleges
Project on the Status and Education of Women, 1818 R St NW, Washington, DC 20009 (202-387-3760)

Intercollegiate Association of Women Students
Box 3028, University Sta, Columbus, OH 43120

National Association for Women Deans, Administrators and Counselors
1028 Connecticut Ave NW, Washington, DC 20036 (202-659-9330)

National Coalition for Research on Women's Education and Development, Inc
160 Harper Hall, Tenth St & College Ave, Claremont, CA 91711 (714-626-8511)

National Council of Administrative Women in Education
1815 Ft Myer Dr, N Arlington, VA 22209 (703-528-6111)

National Council of Teachers of English
Women's Committee, Dr Janet Emig, Dept of English, Rutgers U, New Brunswick, NJ 08903 (201-329-1766)

National Education Association
Women's Caucus & Teachers Rights, 1201 16th St NW, Washington, DC 20036 (202-833-4000)

National University Extension Association
Div of Women's Education, Betty Siegal, Dean of Continuing Education U of Florida, Gainesville, FL 32601 (904-392-3265)

Philosophy of Education Society
Committee on the Status of Women, Dept of History & Philosophy of Education, Indiana U, Bloomington, IN 47401 (812-332-0211)

Women Educators
Dr. Noele Krenkel, 45 Valdez Ave, San Francisco, CA 94112

Engineering
Society of Women Engineers
United Engineering Ctr, 345 E 47th St, New York, NY 10017 (212-752-6800)

Family Relations
National Council on Family Relations
Task Force on Women's Rights and Responsibilities, 1219 University Ave, Minneapolis, MN 55414 (612-331-2774)

Geography
Association of American Geographers
Committee on the Status of Women Geographers, Dixie Ann Pemberton, UMCEES, College Park, MD 20742 (301-454-5641)

Society of Women Geographers
1619 New Hampshire Ave NW, Washington, DC 20009 (202-265-2669)

Government
American Society for Public Administration
Standing Committee on Women in Public Administration, 1225 Connecticut Ave NW, Washington, DC 20036 (202-785-3255)

Federally Employed Women
Rm 1249, National Press Bldg, Washington, DC 20004 (202-638-4404)

Health
American Public Health Association, Inc
1015 18th St NW, Washington, DC 20036 (202-467-5000)

National Institute of Health
Organization for Women, Box 105, Garrett Park Sta, Garrett Park, MD 20766

History
American Historical Association
Committee on Women Historians, 400 A St SE, Washington, DC 20003 (202-544-2422)

Coordinating Committee on Women in the Historical Profession
Richmond College, CUNY, Staten Island, NY 10301 (212-448-8433)

Home Economics
American Home Economics Association
2010 Massachusetts Ave NW, Washington, DC 20036 (202-833-3100)

National Executive Housekeepers Association, Inc
Alberta Wetherholt, Exec Sec, Business and Professional Bldg, Gallipolis, OH 45631 (614-446-4800)

Insurance
National Association of Insurance Women
1847 E 15th St, Tulsa, OK 74105 (918-932-5195)

Law
Association of American Law Schools
Section on Women in the Legal Education, Prof Mary Wenig, St. Johns U School of Law, Jamaica, NY 11439 (212-969-8000)

International Federation of Women Lawyers
150 Nassau St, New York, NY 10038 (212-227-8339)

National Association of Women Lawyers
American Bar Ctr, 1705 De Sales NW, Washington, DC 20036 (202-659-1330)

National Lawyer's Guild
Women's Caucus, 930 F St NW, Washington, DC 20006

Women's Law Forum
Seton Hall School of Law, 1095 Raymond Blvd, Newark, NJ 07102 (201-642-8500)

Library Science
American Library Association
Social Responsibilities Round Table, Task Force on the Status of Women, 50 E Huron St, Chicago, IL 60611 (312-944-6780)

Society of American Archivists
Committee on the Status of Women, Dr. Mabel Deutrich, Dir Military Archives, Div, National Archives and Records Services, Washington, DC 20408 (202-963-1110)

Linguistics
American Philological Association
Committee on the Status of Women and Minority Groups, Prof Jane McIntosh Snyder, Dept of Classics, Ohio State U, Columbus, OH 43210

Modern Language Association
Commission on the Status of Women, 62 Fifth Ave, New York, NY 10011 (212-741-5588)

Mathematics
Association for Women in Mathematics
Lenore Blum, Dept of Mathematics, Mills College, Oakland, CA 94613 (415-632-2700)

Media
Ad Hoc Committee on the Status of Women in Journalism Education
U of Nebraska School of Journalism, Lincoln, NB 68508 (402-472-3045)

American Newspaper Women's Club, Inc
1607 22nd St NW, Washington, DC 20008 (202-332-6770)

American Women in Radio and Television, Inc
1321 Connecticut Ave NW, Washington, DC 20036 (202-296-0009)

Committee on the Status of Women in Journalism
College of Journalism and Communications, U of Florida, 234 Stadium St, Gainesville, FL 32601 (904-392-6558)

Journalists for Professional Equality
Eileen Shanahan, **New York Times,** 1920 L St NW, Washington, DC 20036 (202-864-8815)

National Association of Media Women, Inc
157 W 126th St, New York, NY 10027 (212-850-1886)

National Federation of Press Women
Status of Women Committee, Marva Gay, NFPW, 1148 Kiawa Trail, Frankfurt, KY 40601

National League of American Pen Women, Inc
1300 17th St NW, Washington, DC 20036 (202-785-1997)

National Press Club
National Press Bldg, 529 14th St NW, Washington, DC 20004 (202-727-2500)

Washington Press Club for Women
505 National Press Bldg, Washington, DC 20004 (202-393-3418)

Women in Communications, Inc
8305 A Shoal Creek Blvd, Austin, TX 78758 (512-452-0119)

Medicine
American Association of Immunologists
Committee on the Status of Women, 9650 Rockville Pike, Bethesda, MD 20014 (301-530-7178)

American Medical Women's Association
1740 Broadway, New York, NY 10019 (212-586-8683)

Center for Women in Medicine
The Medical College of Pennsylvania, 3300 Henry Ave, Philadelphia, PA 19129 (215-849-0400)

Midwifery
American College of Nurse-Midwives
1000 Vermont Ave NW, Washington, DC 20005 (202-628-4642)

Music
College Music Society
Women's Caucus, Dr. Carolyn Raney, Peabody Conservatory of Music, Baltimore, MD 21202

Nursing
American Nurses' Association, Inc
2420 Pershing Rd, Kansas City, MO 64108 (816-474-5720)

National Association for Practical Nurse Education and Service
Rose G Martin RN, Exec Dir, 122 E 42nd St, New York, NY 10017 (212-682-3400)

"If there be difficult murder 'tis to kill the unfilled gaps of time, to suffocate the tedium of occupation, to live unbusy in a busy world."
—Heather Bigg

Performing Arts
Women in Performing Arts
c/o Mary Saboe, 4208 Nawadaha Blvd, Minneapolis, MN 55406

Personnel
American Personnel and Guidance Association
Women's Caucus, Dr. Helen Roehlke, Counseling Center, U of Missouri, Columbia, MO 65210 (314-822-2121)

International Association of Personnel Women
2017 Walnut St, Philadelphia, PA 19103

National Association of Student Personnel Administrators
Task Force on Women, E Susan Petering, Dean of Students, Wheaton College, Norton, MA 02766 (617-285-7722)

Philosophy
American Philosophical Association
Ingrid Stadler, Dept of Philosophy, Wellesley College, Wellesley, MA 02181 (617-235-0320)

Physical Education
American Alliance for Health, Physical Education and Recreation
Task Force on Equal Opportunity & Human Rights, 1201 16th St NW, Washington, DC 20036 (202-833-5553)

American Association for Health and Physical Education
Committee on Women, Prof Ione G Shadduck, Drake U, Des Moines, IA 50311 (515-271-2011)

Physics
American Physical Society
Committee on Women in Physics, 335 E 45th St, New York, NY 10017 (212-685-9422)

Physiology
American Physiological Society
Task Force on Women in Physiology, 9650 Rockville Pike, Bethesda, MD 20014 (301-530-7164)

Planning
American Institute of Planners
1776 Massachusetts Ave NW, Washington, DC 20036 (202-872-0611)

Political Science
American Political Science Association
1527 New Hampshire Ave NW, Washington, DC 20036 (202-483-2512)
Women's Caucus for Political Science, Mt Vernon College, 2100 Foxhall Rd NW, Washington, DC 20007

Psychiatry
American Psychiatric Association
Task Force on Women, Dr. Nancy Roeske, 1700 18th St NW, Washington, DC 20009 (202-232-7878)

Psychology
American Psychological Association
Committee on Women, 1200 17th St NW, Washington, DC 20036 (202-833-7600)

Association for Women in Psychology
Joyce Walstedt, 243 Russell Rd, Princeton, NJ 08540 (609-924-2346)

Public Relations
Public Relations Society of America
Committee on Women in Public Relations, 8150 Leesburg Pike, McLean, VA 22101 (703-790-8500)

Women Executives in Public Relations
Lever Brothers Co, 390 Park Ave, New York, NY 10022 (212-688-6000)

Publishing
Women's National Book Association
National Book Committee, Inc, 1564 Broadway, New York, NY 10016 (212-575-1070)

Union Pacific Railroad

Railroad
American Council of Railroad Women
Marguerite Holden, Accounting Systems, Burlington Northern, 176 E Fifth St, St. Paul, MN 55101 (612-298-2121)

Real Estate
Women's Council of the National Association of Real Estate Boards
155 E Superior St, Chicago, IL 60611 (312-440-8000)

Religion
Church Employed Women
475 Riverside Dr, New York, NY 10027 (212-870-2981)

United Presbyterian Church in the US
475 Riverside Dr, New York, NY 10027 (212-870-2515)

Women's Caucus for Religious Studies
Dept of Religious Studies, U of North Carolina, Greensboro, NC 27412

Science
American Association for the Advancement of Science
Office of Opportunities in Science, 1515 Massachusetts Ave NW,

Washington, DC 20036 (202-467-4400)

Association for Women in Science
1346 Connecticut Ave NW, Washington, DC 20009 (202-833-1998)

Graduate Women in Science
Sigma Delta Epsilon, Dr. Margaret Stone, 1447 Ellis Hollow Rd, Ithaca, NY 14850
Alpha Chapter, Prof Betty A Lewis, 285 Van Renssalear Hall, Cornell U, Ithaca, NY 14850
Rho Chapter, Dr. Eva Weinreb, 328 Overhill Rd, Wayne, PA 19087

Engineering

Registry of Women in Science and Engineering
Rush Medical College, 1753 W Congress Pkwy, Chicago, IL 60612 (312-942-6900)

Women in Science and Engineering
Dr. Margaret E. Law, 80 Richmond Rd, Belmont, MA 02178

Secretarial Work

National Association of Educational Secretaries
1801 N Moore St, Arlington, VA 22212 (703-526-4400)

National Secretaries Association
2440 Pershing Rd, Kansas City, MO 64108 (816-474-5755)

Social Studies

African Studies Association
Committee on Women, 218 Chestnut St, Cambridge, MA 02139 (617-323-4082)

American Studies Association
4025 Chestnut St, U of Pennsylvania, Philadelphia, PA 19174 (215-243-6252 ext 5408)

Association for Asian Studies
Committee on the Status of Women, 1 Lane Hall, U of Michigan, Ann Arbor, MI 48104 (313-665-2490)

Latin American Studies Association
Women's Committee, Dr. Evelyn P Stevens, 14609 S Woodland Rd, Shaker Heights, OH 44120 (216-283-7859)

National Council for the Social Studies
1515 Wilson Blvd, Arlington, VA 22209 (703-527-4954)

Women's Coalition of Latin-Americanists
Dr. Elas Chaney, Box 712, Fordham U, Bronx, NY 10458

Sociology

American Sociological Association
1722 N St NW, Washington, DC 20036 (202-833-3410)

Sociologists for Women in Society
Dr. Joan Huber, Dept of Sociology, U of Illinois, Urbana, Il 61801 (217-333-1000)

Speech and Hearing

Speech Communication Association
Women's Caucus, Bonnie Ritter Patton, Dir, Office of Affirmative Action, 235 Strong, U of Kansas, Lawrence, KS 66044

American Speech and Hearing Association
Caucus on the Status of Women, 9039 Old Georgetown Rd, Wash-

ington, DC 20014 (301-530-3400)

Statistics

American Statistical Association
Caucus for Women in Statistics, Ms. Regina Loewenstein, 165 West End Ave, New York, NY 10023

Vocational Guidance

National Vocational Guidance Association
Commission on the Occupational Status of Women, Ms Thelma C Lennon, Dir Public Personnel Services, Dept of Public Instruction, Raleigh, NC 27602 (919-829-4258)

Publications

Amazon
Women's Coalition, 2211 E Kenwood Blvd, Milwaukee, WI 53211
Amazon is a feminist journal that includes articles, poems, announcements, and graphics by local women. (414-964-7535)

Aphra
Box 893, Ansonia Sta, New York 10023
This feminist literary magazine welcomes articles and graphic material. Include a stamped, self-addressed envelope for returns. (212-595-0622)

Artemis
525 West End Ave, New York, NY 10024
Artemis searches for creative women's enterprises nationwide. (212-787-6780)

Daughters, Inc
Plainfield, VT 05667
This publishing company produces only books written by women. (802-454-7141)

Diana Press
12 W 25th St, Baltimore, MD 21218
Diana Press is a feminist publishing and printing company. (301-366-9262)

The Eve News
Kean College, Union, NJ 07083
This publication tells of development groups, workshops, and job openings and gives general help to today's woman. (201-527-2210)

The Executive Woman
747 Third Ave, New York, NY 10017
This newsletter tries to give women an edge in the male-oriented business world. (212-688-4601)

Feminist Art Journal
41 Montgomery Pl, Brooklyn, NY 11215
Reviews, scholarly articles, and current

activities are the substance of this periodical.

Feminist Press
Box 334, College at Old Westbury, Old Westbury, NY 11568
Feminist Press specializes in biographies of women and nonsexist children's books. (516-876-3000)

Feminist Printing Collective
Milwaukee, WI 53202
The main objective of this working collective is to meet the printing needs of the Women's Coalition and its feminist members. (414-964-8135)

Les Femmes Publishing
231 Adrian Rd, Millbrae, CA 94030
LFP serves as a publishing outlet for women, with emphasis on feminist literature. (415-692-4500)

First Things First
321 Seventh St NE, Washington, DC 20003
A "fe-mail order house" for books on, for, by, and about women. First Things First is working on a comprehensive list of nonsexist children's materials along with records, posters, and similar stock. (202-546-2335)

Gidra
Box 18649, Los Angeles, CA 90018
Gidra is not exclusively a women's paper, but certain issues concentrate on the exploitation of Asian-American women.

Goldflower
c/o Mary Hastings, 710 W 22nd St, Minneapolis, MN 55405
This monthly tabloid for women covers a wide range of issues. It is looking for volunteer staff members and writers, and nonstaff contributors in writing, art, and photography. (612-389-1848)

Joyful World Press
468 Belvedere St, San Francisco, CA 94117
Feminist posters and nonsexist children's books are the staple of this small group. (415-566-2787)

Know, Inc
Box 86031, Pittsburgh, PA 15221
They reprint feminist articles on a variety of topics, including the Female Studies Series, a collection of course designs and essays. (412-241-4844)

Libera
Eshleman Hall, U of California, Berkeley, CA 94720
Libera, a new woman's journal, features selections of prose by women writers.

Matrix
Box 4218, N Hollywood, CA 91607
Illustrations and prose by women writers are featured in this publication.

Moving Out
169 MacKenzie Hall, Wayne State U, Detroit, MI 48202
Edited by a cooperative of women from the Wayne area, *MO* is a biannual feminist magazine. It welcomes contributions of artwork, short stories, essays, poetry, or photographs. (313-577-3409)

Holly Alderman McLellan

Ms Magazine
370 Lexington Ave, New York, NY 10017
Poems, features, and events for the liberated woman in a glossy, monthly-magazine format. (212-725-2666)

New England Free Press
60 Union Sq, Somerville, MA 02143
A cooperative publishing and printing company, the Free Press is committed to distribution of radical and feminist pamphlets. (617-628-2450)

Off Our Backs
1724 20th St NW, Washington, DC 20009
A monthly paper collectively run by women, OOB is an alternative to straight news media and solicits articles for which it is as yet unable to pay. (202-234-8072)

Paid My Dues
Box 11646, Milwaukee, WI 53211
This new journal provides exposure for feminist music and prints information about women musicians. It welcomes contributions of songs, articles, or drawings by women musicians. (414-263-7792)

El Pop Femenil
Chicano Studies Dept, California State U, Northridge, CA 91324
This bilingual paper features articles discussing relationships between Chicano and Anglo women, the effect of the Women's Movement on Mexican-American women, and Chicanos in law school. (213-885-2734)

Prime Time
345 E 86th St, New York, NY 10028
An independent feminist monthly, *Prime Time* is the national forum for older women who advocate women's liberation. The publication solicits articles, editorials, poems, illustrations, cartoons, and news from women "in the prime of life." (212-876-3683)

Siren
c/o Solidarity Bookshop, 713 W Armitage Ave, Chicago, IL 60614
Created to encourage the growth of radical feminist consciousness and activism, this newsletter features articles, essays, letters, and fiction written from an anarchofeminist point of view. (312-327-9155)

The Spokeswoman
5456 S Shore Dr, Chicago, IL 60615
This national monthly newsletter features breaking feminist news not available through establishment media, the latest developments in employment, politics, legal action, reviews, and an extensive help-wanted section. (312-363-2580)

Elizabeth Cady Stanton Publishing Co
5857 Marbury Rd, Bethesda, MD 20034
The main work published to date is the *Women's Rights Almanac 1975,* which is updated annually. (301-229-7067)

The Successful Woman
Box 2068, Santa Barbara, CA 93102
This monthly newsletter is directed to ambitious women who hope to sidestep traditional barriers, and concentrates on profiles, resources, and financial advice.

Up From Under
339 Lafayette St, New York, NY 10012
Up From Under is edited for the working class woman. (212-260-1040)

Whirlwind
c/o Fredrik Baer, 3214 N California, Chicago, IL 60618
The purpose of this bimonthly literary magazine is to create a means by which anarchist women can communicate their common experiences through their art.

Wollstonecraft, Inc
6399 Wilshire Blvd, Los Angeles, CA 09948
Wollstonecraft concentrates primarily on feminist books "that will make people think."

The Woman Activist
2310 Barbour Rd, Falls Church, VA 22043
The *Activist* reprints sections of the *Congressional Record* relevant to women and reports on recent legislation before Congress. (703-573-8716)

The Woman Executive's Bulletin
Bureau of Business Practice, 24 Rope Ferry Rd, Waterford, CT 06285
A semimonthly newsletter that examines the unique problems of women executives in business. (203-442-4365)

Women in Film
2802 Arizona Ave, Santa Monica, CA 90402
This publication analyzes the image of women in film from a feminist perspective and contains the latest on current feminist filmmakers.

Women Today
621 National Press Bldg, Washington, DC 20004
This fact-filled newsletter is dedicated to the dissemination of up-to-date information about today's women. Published biweekly, it provides news on topics ranging from day care to Constitutional law. (202-628-6663)

Women's Guide to Books
MSS Information Corp, 655 Madison Ave, New York, NY 10021
The Board of Advisors (including Nora Ephron, Ellen Frankfort, Elizabeth Janeway, Florynce Kennedy, Cindy Memser, Letty Cottin Pogrebin, Barbara Seaman, Sheila Tobias, and many others) selects current and past writings on women and womanhood for an annotated catalogue.

Women's Studies: An Interdisciplinary Journal
Dept of English, Queens College, Flushing, NY 11367
A forum for criticism and scholarly presentations on women in all fields of endeavor. (212-445-7500)

Canada

Canadian Newsletter of Research on Women
Dept of Sociology, U of Waterloo, Waterloo, Ontario
This newsletter publishes research on women in Canada. (519-885-1211)

Canadian Women's Educational Press
280 Bloor St W, Toronto, Ontario
CWEP publishes new material arising from the movement in Canada. (416-962-3904)

Montreal Health Press, Inc
Box 1000, Station G, Montreal 130, Quebec, Canada
MHP publishes inexpensive health handbooks in English, French, and Spanish for mass distribution. (514-844-5838)

Los Angeles, CA

Now!
743 Grand View St 90057
Published monthly by the LA chapter of the National Organization for Women, *NOW!* is filled with a wealth of feminist information plus a calendar of events.

Sacramento, CA

Skirting the Capitol
Box 4569 95825
This biweekly publication covers local lobbying activities in the California capitol.

San Diego, CA

Goodbye to All That
Box 3092 92103
Published every 3 weeks, *Goodbye* is a guide to women's rights (political and social) and to festivals, meetings, and caucuses in San Diego and around the country.

San Francisco, CA

Mother Lode
Box 40213 94140
Mother Lode is a feminist publication.

Venice, CA

Everywoman
10438 W Washington Blvd 90291
Issues ranging from news to pornography are covered in this movement newspaper.

Denver, CO

Big Mama Rag
1724 Gaylor 80206
Colorado's only feminist newspaper features articles of special interest to women. (303-322-2010)

Waterbury, CT

On Our Way
Box 2085 06702
Published by Waterbury's Women's Center, this monthly newsletter is full of news of feminist events. (203-753-4540)

Miami, FL

Herstory
7801 SW 134th St 33156
Mindful of the contributions made by women to the development of Dade County, a coalition of local women has formed a nonprofit organization dedicated to the

telling of their story. (305-235-6364)

Tampa, FL

Us Magazine
    4213 W Bay Ave   33616
A literary feminist publication for Florida women. (813-839-2892)

Chicago, IL

Act Now
    W Jackson   60626
Act Now provides information on feminist issues as well as a meeting-place arrangement service for feminist groups. (312-922-0025)

Chicago, IL

Black Maria
    815 W Wrightwood   60614
Black Maria is a quarterly publication offering articles for minority women. The magazine welcomes contributions.

Morton Grove, IL

Chicago Women in Publishing
    Box 392   60053
The group attempts to improve the status of women in publishing in Chicago.

New Orleans, LA

Distaff
    Box 15639   70124
Distaff is a local monthly magazine published by women for women. (504-525-9194)

Boston, MA

Focus: A Journal for Gay Women
    Daughters of Bilitis, 419 Boylston St 02116
Advocating the acceptance of Lesbianism, *Focus* features events, poetry, and recent legislation pertaining to gay affairs. (617-262-1592)

Cambridge, MA

Second Wave
    74 Mt Auburn St   02138
A monthly journal of liberation and lesbianism. (617-491-1071)

Kansas City, MO

Women in Kansas City
    Dolan Communications, 8037 N Stoddard   64152
Local women's issues and activities. (816-587-9583)

Dover, NJ

New Directions for Women
    Box 27   07801
This quarterly newspaper is for women in today's world. (201-366-6036)

Trenton, NJ

In Touch
    NJ State Commission on Women, Dept of Community Affairs, Box 2768   07007
This newsletter tells of the latest happenings, symposia, and conference meetings concerning women in government.

New York, NY

Majority Report
    74 Grove St   10014
A monthly feminist publication, it will fill you in on what New York women's groups are up to. (212-691-4950)

Scarborough, NY

The Feminist Bulletin
    Box 262   10510
TFB is a monthly newsletter featuring listings of feminist meetings as well as reports of previous meetings. (914-762-3541)

Portland, OR

The Changing Woman
This monthly coordinates women's news, publishes book reviews, and provides a calendar of events. (503-232-3859)

Seattle, WA

Pandora
    Box 94   98105
Pandora covers local events and projects and attempts to improve communication between sisters on all levels. (206-525-6398)

Madison, WI

Whole Woman Newspaper
    1628 Winnebago   53704
Whole Woman is written by local women for local women. (608-244-0773)

Madison, WI

Wisconsin Women Newsletter
    428 Lowell Hall, U of Wisconsin Extension, 610 Langdon St   53706
Wisconsin Women carries stories of statewide interest, including news on the ERA, reports on women's conferences, and feminist editorials.

Madison, WI

Women's Communication Network
    c/o Kathy Vorel, 1631 Monroe St 53711
The group publishes a newsletter listing organizations and services for women in the area. (608-256-8523)

Winneconne, WI

Women in Struggle
    Box 325   54986
A newsletter for Wisconsin women.

Publishers/Presses
see — Publications

Rape Crisis

Tempe, AZ

Assault Crisis Center
    Box 26851   85282 (602-257-8095)

Tucson, AZ

Women Against Rape
    Alternatives for Women (602-884-9776)

Bay Area, CA

Women Against Rape
    (415-845-7273)

Berkeley, CA

Bay Area Women Against Rape
    2490 Channing Wy 94704 (415-841-0370)

Inglewood, CA

Rape Crisis Hot Line
    (213-677-8116)

Fresno, CA

Rape Counseling Service of Fresno
    Box 708   93612 (209-222-7273)

Kentfield, CA

Marin County Rape Crisis Center
    Box 823   94904 (415-924-2100)

Los Angeles, CA

Anti-Rape Squad
    Women's Center, 743 S Grand View 90057 (213-388-3491)

Los Angeles, CA

Women Against Sexual Abuse
    (213-868-3783)

Placentia, CA

Stop Rape Hotline
    Box 651   92670 (714-525-4357)

Sacramento, CA

Sacramento Rape Crisis Line
    1221 20th St   95814 (916-447-7273)

San Bernardino, CA

Suicide and Crisis Intervention
    Rape Crisis Service, Family Service Agency, 1669 N E St 92405 (714-886-4889)

San Diego, CA

Rape Crisis Center
    Box 16205   (714-239-7273)

San Fernando Valley, CA

Rape Information and Prevention Center
    (213-888-6515)

San Francisco, CA

San Francisco Women Against Rape
    (415-647-7273)

San Jose, CA

San Jose Women Against Rape
    Ninth & Carlos Sts   95192 (408-287-3000)

Boulder, CO

Rape Counseling Team
    Mental Health Center of Boulder County, Inc, 1333 Iris Ave   80302 (303-443-8500)

Denver, CO

Coalition of Sexual Assault
    227 Clayton   80206 (303-321-8191)

Denver, CO

Denver Anti-Crime Council
    1313 Tremont Pl   80204 (303-893-8581)

Denver, CO

Rape Prevention Program
    Dept of Psychiatry, Denver General Hospital, Eighth & Cherokee Sts 80204 (303-893-7001)

Fairfield, CT

People Against Rape
    448 Birch Rd   06430 (a.m. 203-366-0664; p.m. 255-4752)

Hartford, CT

Rape Crisis Center YWCA
    135 Broad St   (203-522-6666)

Milford, CT

Rape Crisis Hotline of Milford
    (203-878-1212)

New Haven, CT

Rape Crisis Center
    215 Park St   (202-397-2273)

Washington, DC

Feminist Alliance Against Rape
    Box 21033   20009 (202-833-1273)

Washington, DC

Rape Crisis Center
    (202-333-7273)

Ft Lauderdale, FL

Boward County Women Against Rape, Inc
    Box 41011   33304 (305-584-4357)

Gainesville, FL
Rape Information and Counseling Service
(904-377-7273)

Sarasota, FL
Rape Prevention and Crisis Center
Box 74   33578 (813-958-8222;
hotline: 955-8153)

Tallahassee, FL
Rape Crisis Service
c/o Women's Center, 212 Mabury Hts,
Florida State U   32306 (904-644-2525)

Tampa, FL
Help Stop Rape
Hillsborough Community College
(813-879-7222 ext 380)

Atlanta, GA
Metropolitan Atlanta Rape Crisis Committee
Grady Memorial Hospital   30303
(404-659-1212)

Chicago, IL
Rape Crisis Center
North (312-728-1920)
South (312-667-1929)

Chicago, IL
Women Against Rape
Loop YWCA, 37 S Wabash   60657
(312-372-6600)

Lombard, IL
Dupage Women Against Rape YWCA
1 S Park   60142 (312-629-0170)

Peoria, IL
NOW Rape Task Force
902 W Moss Ave   61606 (309-688-2253)

Bloomington, IN
Rape Crisis Center of Bloomington-Normal
(812-828-8725)

Indianapolis, IN
Center for Rape Investigation
School of Medicine, Indiana U
46205 (317-635-8431)

Indianapolis, IN
Women United Against Rape
5343 N Arlington Ave   46226
(317-633-9130)

Cedar Rapids, IA
Rape Crisis Line
3011 Sixth St SW   52404 (319-366-7351)

Iowa City, IA
Iowa City Crisis Line
c/o The Women's Center, 3 E Market
St   52240
(319-353-2121)

Iowa City, IA
Rape Crisis Line
c/o Law Office, 300 Whetstone Bldg
52240
(319-338-4800)

Baton Rouge, LA
Women's Crisis Center
(504-383-7273)

New Orleans, LA
Rape Crisis-Information Service YWCA
3433 Tulane Ave   70119 (504-486-6041)

Baltimore, MD
University Women's Crisis Hotline
U of Maryland   21201 (301-454-4616)

Amherst, MA
Rape Hotline
(413-545-2121)

Cambridge, MA
Rape Crisis Center
46 Pleasant St   02139 (617-492-7273)

Springfield, MA
Rape Crisis Hotline
(413-737-7273)

Ann Arbor, MI
Women's Crisis Center
306 N Division St   48108 (313-994-9100)

Detroit, MI
Detroit Rape Crisis Line
Box 35271, Seven Oaks Sta   48235
(313-872-7273)

Detroit, MI
Women Against Rape
18700 Woodward Ave   48023 (313-892-7160)

Detroit, MI
Women's Crisis Center
4105 Cass St   48201 (313-831-2606)

Grand Rapids, MI
Rape Crisis Team
Box 6161, Sta C   49506 (616-456-3535)

Ypsilanti, MI
Ypsilanti Rape Relief
(313-485-3222)

Minneapolis, MN
Rape Crisis Center
(612-374-4357)

St. Paul, MN
Sex Offense Services of Ramsey County
529 Jackson   55101 (612-222-4260
ext 402)

St. Louis, MO
West End Feminists
(814-726-0642)

University City, MO
Rape Crisis Center
(314-773-1313)

Missoula, MT
Rape Relief Program
Women's Place (406-543-7606)

Lincoln, NB
Rape Center
U of Nebraska, YWCA,
Nebraska Union 345, Rm 4   68508
(402-472-7211)

The Police Foundation

Reno, NV
Women's Center and Rape Crisis Line
Box 8448   89507 (702-329-7273)

Collingswood, NJ
Women Against Rape
Box 346   08108 (609-854-0050;
hotline: 667-3000)

Englewood, NJ
Women Against Rape
Box 624   07631 (201-569-7273)

New Brunswick, NJ
Women's Crisis Center
56 College Ave   08901 (201-828-7273)

Albuquerque, NM
Rape Crisis Center and Women's Center
U of New Mexico   87131 (505-277-3717)

New York, NY
Mayor's Task Force on Rape
52 Chambers St   10007 (212-566-5700)

New York, NY
New York Women Against Rape
150 Amsterdam Ave   10023 (212-877-8700)

New York, NY
Rape Prevention of New York NOW
(212-684-0367)

Rochester, NY
Rape Crisis Service
38 Windsor St   14605   (716-546-2595)

Syracuse, NY
Rape Crisis Center
113 Concord Pl   13210 (315-422-7273)

Chapel Hill, NC
Rape Crisis Center
Dept of Psychiatry, School of
Medicine, U of North Carolina   27514
(919-433-2211)

Chapel Hill, NC
Women's Assault Line
c/o Switchboard, 402 W Rosemary St
27514   (919-929-7177)

Greensboro, NC
Rape Action Prevention and Education Center
(919-273-7273)

Winston-Salem, NC
Winston Women Against Rape
c/o Unitarian Fellowship,
2873 Robin Hood Rd   27106
(919-723-7633)

Akron, OH
Akron Women Against Rape
Humanity House, 475 W Market St
44303 (216-253-7151)

Cleveland, OH
Rape Crisis Center
3201 Euclid Ave   44115
(216-391-3912)

Columbus, OH
Feminist Rape Crisis Center
Box 4442   43212 (614-221-4447)

Dayton, OH
Ombudsman Office Victimization Center
40 E First St   45402 (513-223-4613)

Kent, OH
University Rape Crisis Project
Center for Peaceful Change,
Kent State U   44242 (216-672-3143)

Oklahoma City, OK
Oklahoma County Rape Crisis Center
YWCA Women's Resource Center
73102   (405-528-5508)

Eugene, OR
Rape Crisis Center
(503-485-0234)

Portland, OR
Rape Hotline
4160 SE Division   97202 (503-235-5333)

McKeesport, PA
Rape Crisis Center
810 Walnut St   15132 (412-678-8895)

Philadelphia, PA
Center for Rape Concern
Philadelphia General Hospital
700 Civic Center Blvd   19104
(215-823-7000)

Philadelphia, PA
Women Organized Against Rape
Box 17374   19105 (215-823-7997)

Pittsburgh, PA
Action Against Rape
(412-664-0788)

Pawtucket, RI
Rape Crisis Center
34 Broad St   02860 (401-851-4040)

Providence, RI
Committee on Criminal Sex Offenses
c/o Women's Liberation Union of RI,
Box 2302, East Side Sta   02806
(401-861-2910)

Austin, TX
Austin Rape Crisis Center
24th St & San Gabriel   78714
(512-472-7273)

Dallas, TX
Rape Crisis Center
(214-341-9400)

El Paso, TX
Rape Crisis Center
(915-545-1500)

Ft Worth, TX
Task Force on Rape YWCA
512 W Fourth St   76102
(817-332-6191)

Houston, TX
Rape Crisis Center
3602 Milam   77002 (713-524-5743)

Houston, TX
Rape Crisis Hotline
(713-228-1505)

Richardson, TX
Dallas Women Against Rape
1700 Baltimore Dr   75080   (214-341-9400)

San Antonio, TX
Rape Crisis Center
Box 28061   78228 (512-433-1251)

Roanoke, VA
Rape Crisis Center
(703-366-6030)

Seattle, WA
Rape Relief
(206-632-7273)

Seattie, WA
Sexual Assault Care Center
Harborview Medical Center
325 Ninth Ave   98104 (206-223-3047)

Madison, WI
Dane County Project on Rape
120 W Mifflin St   53703 (608-251-5440)

Madison, WI
Rape Crisis Center
(608-251-7273)

Milwaukee, WI
Anti-Rape Council
Women's Coalition, 2211 E Kenwood
53211 (414-964-7535)

Shorewood, WI
Wisconsin Task Force on Rape
Box 11408   53211 (414-964-0869)

Recreation
see — Sportswomen

Religion

American Baptist Women
Valley Forge, PA   19481
Open to all Baptist women, the organization aims to unite all the women of the church. (215-768-2000)

American Jewish Congress, National Women's Division
15 E 84th St, New York, NY   10028
(212-879-4500)

B'nai B'rith Women
1640 Rhode Island Ave NW, Washington, DC   20036 (202-393-5284)
A Jewish women's service organization engaging in educational, civic, and philanthropic programs. (202-393-5284)

Catholic Daughters of America
10 W 71st St, New York, NY   10023
(212-877-3041)

Christian Women's Fellowship
222 S Downey Ave, Indianapolis, IN
46219 (317-353-1491)

Church Women United
475 Riverside Dr, New York, NY
10027
CWU works generally for "justice and liberation," sponsoring volunteer programs for adult basic education, prison reform, and health services, especially for women. (212-870-2347)

Coalition Task Force on Women and Religion
4759 15th Ave NE, Seattle, WA
98125
An interfaith women's action group concerned with the issues of women's liberation as affected by religious tradition, history, sacred writings, theology, and contemporary practices, the Task Force has published *Woman's Bible* as well as maintaining a women's religious library and endorsing legislation in the interests of women. (206-522-1955)

Hadassah
Women's Zionist Organization of America, Inc, 65 E 52nd St, New York, NY   10022
Through support of schools and medical centers, Hadassah women devote their service to the people of Israel and the US. (212-355-7900)

Joint Committee of Organizations Concerned with the Status of Women in the Church
1600 Sunset Ave, Waukegan, IL
60085
An overview group meeting to attain an equal status for women in the Catholic Church.

Lutheran Church Women
2900 Queen Ln, Philadelphia, PA
19129
These women promote the overall mission of the Lutheran Church and publish a magazine called *Lutheran Women.* (215-438-2200)

National Assembly of Women Religious
201 E Ohio St, Chicago, IL   60611
(312-751-2797)

National Coalition of American Nuns
1307 S Wabash St, Chicago, IL
60605
With concern for women in the Church and society, NCAN develops projects and speaks out for the Gospel values. (312-341-9159)

National Conference of Christians and Jews
Southern Bldg, Washington, DC
20005
NCCJ promotes good will and humanitarian service and has recently begun to focus on the special circumstances of the mature woman. (202-737-5353)

National Council of Catholic Women
1312 Massachusetts Ave NW, Washington, DC   20005
NCCW was formed to "unite Catholic organizations and individual Catholic women of the US." (202-659-6777)

National Council of Jewish Women, Inc
4908 Wisconsin Ave NW, Washington, DC   20016
NCJW educates women for constructive action in the community. Its objective is to improve the quality of life for all people through education, social action, and community service. (202-244-9450)

Reorganized Church of Jesus Christ of Latter Day Saints, General Department of Women
The Auditorium, Independence, MO
64051
Mormon women work to promote their religion and the role of women in the ministry. (816-833-1000)

Unitarian Universalist Women's Federation
25 Beacon St, Boston, MA   02108
The Federation stresses meeting the spiritual and social needs of women through work in the Church and in society. (617-742-2100)

United Church of Christ, Task Force on Women in Church and Society
297 Park Ave S, New York, NY
10010
This task force works to increase opportunities for women within the Church

and to eliminate discrimination in work and in society as a whole. (212-475-2121)

United Methodist Women

475 Riverside Dr, New York, NY 10027

UMW provides legislative contacts for individuals within the organization working on the ERA, abortion reform, and minimum wage for household workers. They publish a monthly newsletter. (212-663-8900)

United Presbyterian Church, Task Force on Women

730 Witherspoon Bldg, Philadelphia, PA 19109

Founded in 1969 to promote justice for women in Church and society, the Task Force publishes a monthly newsletter. (215-893-4400)

Senior Citizens

Administration on Aging

HEW, Washington, DC 20201

Extensive information can be obtained from HEW concerning the Older Americans Comprehensive Services Amendment of 1973; the agency is directly responsible for carrying out the provisions of the Act. (202-245-0827)

American Association of Homes for the Aging

529 14th St NW, Washington, DC 20004

The AAHA provides information on initiating senior-citizen programs. The booklet *Let's End Isolation* lists individuals and organizations that have agreed to share details of their programs with others. (203-347-2000)

American Association of Retired Persons

1909 K St NW, Washington, DC 20006

AARP provides new direction for more than 5½ million persons over the age of 55. One membership fee ($2) covers both husband and wife. Health insurance, home-delivery pharmacy service, travel programs, and life-insurance information are a few of the benefits. AARP endorses legislation that favors the senior citizen. (202-872-4700)

Gray Panthers

3700 Chestnut St, Philadelphia, PA 19104

The Panthers believe that when young and old work together on projects and issues of public concern, the young benefit from the experience and wisdom of the elderly and learn that aging itself need not be viewed as a problem. (215-382-6644)

Tax Facts for Older Americans

American Association of Retired Persons-National Retired Teachers Association, Box 199, Long Beach, CA 90801

Many older people are unaware of legitimate deductions and are paying more tax than they should be. This AARP-NRTA tax guide summarizes federal and state retirement income-tax credits.

"Housework is no longer an excuse for growing old."

—Lilly Dache

Sex Education

American Association of Sex Educators and Counselors

815 13th St NW, Washington, DC 20005

AASEC assists schools, colleges, and social agencies in developing sex and human-relations curricula. It publishes a quarterly newsletter. (202-638-2523)

ACLU National Project on Sexual Privacy

American Civil Liberties Union, 22 E 40th St, New York, NY 10017

This project is attempting to abolish laws restricting private sexual activity between consenting adults and the discrimination that follows from those laws. (212-725-1222)

International Institute of Sexual Identity

1346 Connecticut Ave NW, Washington, DC 20036

The Institute collects scientific information about human sexual identity and disseminates it through scholarly journals and seminars. (202-723-4341)

Sex Information and Education Council of the US

122 E 42nd St, New York, NY 10023 (212-661-7010)

Single Parents
see — Parents

Special Children
see — Child Development/Education

Sportswomen

International Association of Physical Education and Sports for Girls and Women

Dr Edith Betts, U of Idaho, Moscow, ID 83843 (208-885-6111)

National Association for Girls and Women in Sport

1201 16th St NW, Washington, DC 20036 (202-833-5541)

Sterilization
see — Family Planning

Technical Education
see — Handywoman, Vocational Education

Unions

Distributive Workers of America

13 Astor Pl, New York, NY 10003

DWA organizes women office workers and assists anyone in the employment struggle. (212-673-5120)

National Labor Relations Board

1717 Pennsylvania Ave NW, Washington, DC 20570

NLRB prevents discrimination within unions and protects employees who are dismissed for attempting to unionize. (202-655-4000)

Union Women's Alliance to Gain Equality

Box 462, Berkeley, CA 9470

Union WAGE agitates for equality of pay and aims to elevate the status of women who work. Order their book, *ORGANIZE: A Working Woman's Handbook.* Price

$2.50 plus postage 25 cents; bulk of ten or more, $2.00 plus postage; special discount to bookstores only for orders of ten or more, $1.75 plus postage. (415-444-8757)

Women's Rights Committee, AFT, AFL-CIO

1012 14th St NW, Washington, DC 20005

Under the umbrella of the American Federation of Teachers, the committee helps form union policy regarding parental leave, sexism in teaching materials, curricula reform (emphasizing the equality of women), continuing education, counseling, children's centers, early childhood education, etc. (202-737-6141)

Chicago, IL

Women Employed

37 S Wabash 60603

Women Employed, a group of Chicago working women, is pressuring employers to hire, pay, train, and promote women on the same basis as men. (312-372-7822)

Boston, MA

Nine to Five

140 Clarendon St 02116

These women office workers hold meetings open to all women to discuss on-the-job organizing with the goal of improving working conditions. (617-536-6002)

Detroit, MI

UAW International Staff

Solidarity House, 8000 E Jefferson Ave 48214

Its purpose is to bring women into the mainstream of organized labor. (313-926-5335)

New York, NY

Trade Unions Women's Program

New York State School of Industrial and Labor Relations 9 E 43rd St 10017

The program organizes workshops dealing with the problems of women in industry. (212-697-2247)

New York, NY

Women Office Workers

Box 439, Planetarium Sta 10024

WOW is agitating for better salaries as well as greater respect and dignity for workers in offices.

Venereal Disease

see also—Health Care Services, Pregnancy & Childbirth

American Social Health Association

1740 Broadway, New York, NY 10019

For more information on venereal disease, contact the ASHA. (212-582-3553)

National Free Clinic Council

1304 Haight St, San Francisco, CA 94117

Referral to VD clinics. (415-864-6232)

National Operation Venus Program

1620 Summer St, Philadelphia, PA 19103

This national, toll-free hotline, run by teenagers, supplies information about venereal disease and makes referrals to treatment facilities. (800-523-1885)

Vocational Education

Board of Education
Both city and state boards can provide information on local technical and vocational courses. Ask for the Blue Book of occupational and vocational schools.

National Association of Trade and Technical schools
2021 L St NW, Washington, DC 20036
This center will investigate your doubts about the ethics and business practices of member trade and technical schools. A membership directory is available free. (202-296-8892)

A Selected List of Professional Training Programs and Internships
American Association of University Women, 2401 Virginia Ave NW, Washington, DC 20037
Major training and intern programs, short workshops for administrators, and other resources are listed by annotation. (202-785-7700)

Vocational Rehabilitation
see — Employment

Volunteering

Action
806 Connecticut Ave NW, Washington, DC 20006
This federal agency administers the Peace Corps, VISTA, Retired Senior Volunteer Program, and Service Corps of Retired Executives. (202-655-4000)

American Women's Voluntary Services, Inc
125 E 65th St, New York, NY 10021
AWVS works to make volunteer opportunities available to all women. (212-535-8886)

Commission on Voluntary Service and Action
475 Riverside Dr, New York, NY 10027
Coordinating various private voluntary-service organizations, both secular and religious, the commission publishes *Invest Yourself,* a catalog of service opportunities. (212-870-2707)

National Center for Voluntary Action
1785 Massachusetts Ave NW, Washington, DC 20005
NCVA is organized to coordinate voluntary action through its 177 locally based Voluntary Action Centers (see your phone book). It publishes a monthly newsletter and acts as a clearinghouse for information on volunteer activities. (202-797-7800)

Voluntary Action News
1625 Massachusetts Ave NW, Washington, DC 20036
For those interested in nationwide volunteer opportunities, the VAN information center is the place to look. There are descriptions of volunteer programs from all over the country. (202-797-7800)

Voter Registration
see — Politics

Widowhood

Chicago, IL
Crane Fund for Widows and Children
4100 S Kedzie Ave 60632
This fund supplies financial help to children and widows in their homes. (312-523-3404)

New York, NY
Widow's Consultation Center
136 E 57th St 10022
The center arranges small group sessions with a professional leader for widows to discuss their common problems and experiences. (212-688-8850)

Rocky River, OH
Chapter 11
Box 2854 44116
This nonsectarian, interfaith organization provides help for the recently widowed person. (216-842-9916)

Salem, OR
They Help Each Other Spiritually
868 Shenandoah Dr SE 97302
THEOS lends a helping hand to recent widows, and points out ways to adjust to living alone.

Milwaukee, WI
Widowed Persons Service
U of Wisconsin Extension,
600 W Kilbourn Ave 53233
This nonsectarian program is ready to help. (414-224-4688)

Women's Associations

International Federation of University Women
17a King's Rd, Sloane Sq, London SW3
The IFUW promotes understanding and friendship among the university women of the world.

Alpha Kappa Sorority
5211 S Greenwood Ave, Chicago, IL 60615
This black sorority of college-educated women is devoted to encouraging "high scholastic and ethical standards." (312-684-1284)

Altrusa International, Inc
332 S Michigan Ave, Chicago, IL 60604
Altrusa is an international service organization for professional and executive women. (312-341-0818)

American Association of University Women
2401 Virginia Ave NW, Washington, DC 20037
AAUW provides an opportunity for college-educated women of all ages to further their education, promote the advancement of women, and open new avenues for effective community service. (202-785-7700)

American Mothers Committee, Inc
Waldorf Astoria, 301 Park Ave, New York, NY 10022
Open to mothers selected through State Committees. AMC awards an annual Mother of the Year award. (212-355-3000)

Association of the Junior Leagues of America, Inc
Waldorf-Astoria, 301 Park Ave, New York, NY 10022
The League fosters interest among its members in the social, economic, educational, cultural, and civic conditions of the community and encourages volunteer service. (212-355-3000)

Black Women's Community Development Foundation
1028 Connecticut Ave NW, Washington, DC 20036
The Foundation works to improve conditions for blacks and publishes a newsletter called *Binding Ties.* (202-296-7656)

Chinese Women's Association, Inc
5432 152nd St, Flushing, NY 11355
Open to Chinese Women in the New York, Oakland, and Los Angeles areas, the Association works to promote better understanding of the Chinese and their customs and provides assistance to the needy in Hong Kong and Taiwan.

Directory of Women's Organizations and Leaders
Today Publications, National Press Bldg, Washington, DC 20004
Myra Barrer coordinates this useful guide. (202-628-6663)

General Federation of Women's Clubs
1734 N St NW, Washington, DC 20036
The Federation works to unite women's clubs and similar organizations. Check your local phone book or chamber of commerce for a women's club near you. (202-347-3168)

National American Indian Women Association
3201 Shadybrook Dr, Midwest City, OK 73110
Open to all Indian women, the association works to improve social conditions and intertribal communication and to increase awareness of Indian culture and fellowship among all people.

National Association of Colored Women's Clubs, Inc
1601 R St NW, Washington, DC 20009
NACWC promotes, the physical, moral, intellectual, and spiritual welfare of women and girls. (202-726-2044)

National Council of Negro Women, Inc
1346 Connecticut Ave NW, Washington, DC 20036
Organized in 1935, the Council seeks the cooperation and membership of all races and works for integration. (202-223-2363)

National Council of Women in the United States
345 E 46th St, New York, NY 10017
Founded by Susan B. Anthony, Elizabeth Cady Stanton, Frances Willard, and Clara Barton, it is a clearinghouse of information on women's issues. (212-679-1278)

National Federation of Grandmothers Clubs of America
203 N Wabash Ave, Chicago, IL 60601
(312-372-5437)

National Order of Women Legislators
RFD 2, Lisbon, CT 06351
NOWL encourages the participation of women in public affairs and their appointment and election to public

office, and serves as a clearinghouse for members. NOWL Letter is its quarterly bulletin.

National Women's Christian Temperance Union
425 13th St NW, Washington, DC 20004

NWCTU seeks to unite Christian women to educate the public to a standard of total abstinence from alcoholic beverages and abolition of liquor traffic. (202-628-0822)

National Women's Education Fund
1532 16th St NW, Washington, DC 20036

NWEF is a public foundation that supports the broad goals of the women's movement through education and research programs. (202-462-8606)

Pilot Club International
244 College St, Macon, GA 31201

Open to executive and professional women, the club works to encourage high ethical standards in business and to improve the civic, social, industrial, and commercial welfare of the community.

Quota International, Inc
1828 L St NW, Washington, DC 20036

Quota is a service club of women executives. Emphasizing the worth of useful occupation, it promotes international friendship. (202-331-9694)

Soroptimist International Association
1616 Walnut St, Philadelphia, PA 19103

Open to business and professional women, Soroptimist programs seek to increase international understanding. It encourages the programs of the U.N. Commission on the Status of Men and Women. (213-347-7054)

Spanish Speaking Women's National Caucus
State Human Rights Appeal Board, 250 Broadway, New York, NY 10007 (212-488-2377)

Women in Community Service, Inc
1730 Rhode Island Ave NW, Washington, DC 20036

Members help organize the Jobs Corps to assist girls in job training and in finding steady employment. (202-293-1343)

Women's Action Alliance
370 Lexington Ave, New York, NY 10017

WAA is attempting to set up an information and referral network to aid women in organizations of all kinds. It provides literature at minimal cost on many aspects of the movement. (212-685-0800)

Young Women's Christian Association of the USA
600 Lexington Ave, New York, NY 10022

Open to any woman over 12 years, the YWCA offers a variety of continuing education, exercise and travel programs at more than 8,000 chapters around the country. Contact your local "Y" for more information. (212-755-2700)

Zeta Phi Eta
Box 1201, Evanston, IL 60201

Founded to "provide incentives and opportunities for women students to develop professional competency in communicative skills," ZPE has 45 university and 14 professional chapters.

Zonta Club
915 19th St NW, Washington, DC 20006

Zonta encourages high ethical standards in business through a world fellowship of executive women. (202-331-1081)

Davis, CA
Sisters Getting Ourselves Together
624 Adeline Pl 95616

Organized to foster a sense of unity among black women, SGOT members meet regularly for discussions. (916-758-0923)

Chicago, IL
Chicago Woman's Club
8 S Michigan Ave 60603

The Woman's Club is an organization dedicated to civilizing humanity through literary and financial efforts. (312-372-9443)

Boston, MA
Women's Service Club of Boston
464 Massachusetts Ave 02118

The club helps women become involved in community affairs, assists women who are newcomers to Boston in finding jobs and housing, and works to upgrade the position of household workers as a whole. (617-262-3935)

New York, NY
League of Black Women
841 E 63rd St 60637

This organization is studying black family life, economic conditions, and health. The League also operates a consumer action group. (212-667-4010)

Charlotte, NC
Charlotte Council of Women's Civic Organizations
50001 Kuykendall Rd 28211

This clearinghouse is composed of 2 representatives of each of the 25 member organizations. Inquiries are welcome. (704-374-6364)

Cincinnati, OH
Coalition of Campus Women
U of Cincinnati 45221

CCW's purpose is to advance the status of women on campus, to facilitate communication between women's groups, and to provide an information exchange and legal-aid counseling. (513-475-2831)

Portland, OR
Portland Feminist Coordinating Council
Composed of representatives of each of the women's groups in the area, the Council maintains communication between groups in Portland. (503-771-4082)

Pittsburgh, PA
Allegheny County Federation of Women's Clubs
Joseph Horne Co, Pennsylvania Ave & Stanwix St 15222

ACFWC tries to consolidate the forces of local women's clubs in their efforts to promote educational, moral, and social measures. (412-281-8138)

Houston, TX
Women in Action
629 W Alabama 77006

WIA has programs in criminal justice, education, welfare, and health. All services are free, and volunteers are always needed. (713-523-5339)

Milwaukee, WI
Face to Face with the 70's
1360 N Prospect 53202

About 40 diverse women's groups comprise this umbrella organization that aims to persuade women to look seriously at the problems of the 1970s and to consider the impact that women can have on the quality of life. (414-962-0882)

Milwaukee, WI
Feminist for Life
3932 N Farwell St 53211

A prowoman, prolife group, these feminists are against abortion. They support the ERA and a human-life amendment.

Women's Centers

National Board YWCA
Resource Center on Women, 135 E 52nd St, New York, NY 10022

A wide range of evaluation and information services are provided for local YWCAs, many of which have local women's centers as well as programs and residences for women. (212-753-4700)

Women's centers offer an assortment of referral services, education programs, consciousness-raising groups, feminist reading rooms, self-help health clinics, and social and cultural activities.

Birmingham, AL
Women's Center
Office of Women's Affairs, Miles College, 5500 Ave G 35208
(205-780-6490)

Mobile, AL
The Association for New Women
Box U-27, 307 Gaillard Dr 36688

Fairbanks, AK
Fairbanks Women's Coop
U of Alaska Student Activities 99701
(907-479-7211)

Junea, AK
Women's Resource Center
570 Seatter St 99801

Tempe, AZ
Associated Women Students
Arizona State U, Memorial Union 85281 (602-965-3438)

Tempe, AZ
The Women's Center
1414 S McAllister 85281 (602-968-0743)

Tucson, AZ
Alternatives for Women
40 E 14th St, 85701 (602-884-9776)

Tucson, AZ
Women's Center
912 E Sixth St 85719 (602-792-1929)

Tucson, AZ
Women's Collective
829 N Fifth Ave 85705 (602-792-1890)

Fayetteville, AR

Women's Center
U of Arkansas, 902 W Maple St
72701 (501-575-2000)

Berkeley, CA

Female Liberation
U of California at Berkeley 94720
(415-642-6000)

Berkeley, CA

Women's Center
2134 Allston 94704 (415-548-4343)

Berkeley, CA

Women's Center
Graduate Theological Union, 2378
Virginia Ave 94709 (415-848-0373)

Berkeley, CA

Women's Coffee House
Unitas House, 2700 Bancroft 94704
(415-845-2727)

Costa Mesa, CA

Women's Center
Orange Coast College, 2701 Fairview
Rd 92626 (916-556-5651)

Cupertino, CA

Women's Opportunity Center
De Anza College, 21250 Stevens
Creek Blvd 95014 (408-257-5550)

Davis, CA

Women's Center
Bldg 124, U of California (916-752-
1011)

El Camino, CA

Women's Center
El Camino College, 16007 Crenshaw
Blvd 90506 (213-532-3670)

Fremont, CA

Women's Task Force
Ohlone College, Box 909 94537
(414-657-2100)

Fresno, CA

Women's Center
Fresno City College, 1101 University
Ave 93741 (209-442-4600)

Fullerton, CA

Women's Center
California State U 92634 (714-870-
2011)

Glendale, CA

Women's Center
Glendale Community College, E
1500 N Verdugo Rd 91208 (213-
240-1000)

Goleta, CA

Isla Vista Women's Center
6504 Pardall Rd 93107 (805-968-5774)

Hayward, CA

South County Women's Center
25036 Hillary 94542 (415-886-1268)

Irvine, CA

Irvine Women's Center
Associated Students, UCI 92664
(714-883-6000)

Irvine, CA

Women's Center
24552 Dardania Ave 92675 (714-
833-5011)

Irvine, CA

Women's Opportunities Center
U of California 92664 (714-833-7128)

La Jolla, CA

The Women's Center
1121 Torrey Pines Rd 92037
(714-459-3864)

La Jolla, CA

Women's Programs—Extension
U of California, Box 109 92037
(714-452-2230)

Long Beach, CA

Women's Center
California State U, 6407 Bayard St
90815 (213-498-4111)

Los Angeles, CA

Chicana Service Center
5340 E Olympic 90022 (213-
728-0168)

Los Angeles, CA

Women's Building
743 S Grandview 90057 (213-
389-6241)

Los Angeles, CA

Women's Resource Center
90 Powell Library, 405 Hilgard Ave
90024 (213-825-3945)

Oakland, CA

Women's Action Training Center
2735 MacArthur Blvd 94602
(415-533-3200)

Pt. Richmond, CA

**Women's Information and Counseling
Center**
Contra Costa College, 405 Santa Fe
Ave 94801 (415-235-7800)

Redwood City, CA

Women's Center
Canada College, 4200 Farm Hill Blvd
94061 (415-364-1212)

Riverside, CA

Women's Center
3354 Orange Grove 92501
(714-787-0389)

Rohnert Park, CA

Women's Survival Center
California State U, Sonoma, 1801 E
Cotati Ave 94928 (707-795-2495)

Sacramento, CA

Sacramento Women's Center
2220 J St 95814 (916-446-7663)

Sacramento, CA

Sacramento Women's Center
YWCA Bldg, 1122 17th St 95819
(916-442-4741)

San Anselmo, CA

Woman's Way
412 Red Hill Ave 94960

San Diego, CA

Center for Women's Studies and Services
908 F St 92101 (714-233-8984)

San Diego, CA

Women's Liberation
Aztec Center, San Diego State College 92105 (714-286-6551)

San Francisco, CA

American Indian Women's Center
229 Valencia St 94103 (415-431-1180)

San Francisco, CA

San Francisco Women's Center
63 Brady St 94103 (415-431-1180)

San Francisco, CA

San Francisco Women's Switchboard
620 Sutter St 94102 (415-775-6500)

San Francisco, CA

Women's Need Center
558 Clayton St 94117 (415-621-1003)

San Jose, CA

San Jose Women's Center
177 S Tenth St 95114 (408-294-7265)

San Jose, CA

The Woman's Alliance
1509 E Santa Clara 95126
(408-251-5522)

San Jose, CA

Women's Center
San Jose State U, Bldg S, 177 S Tenth
St 94192 (408-277-2000)

San Luis Obispo, CA

Women's Resource Center
2293 Santa Ynez St 93401

San Mateo, CA

Women's Center
College of San Mateo, 1700 W
Hillsdale Blvd 94402 (415-574-6161)

San Raphael, CA

Women's Center and Emergency Housing
YWCA, 1618 Mission St 94901
(415-456-0782)

Santa Monica, CA

West Side Women's Center
237 Hill St 90231 (213-399-9512)

Stanford, CA

Stanford Women's Center
Stanford U 94305 (415-321-2300
ext. 3114)

Stockton, CA

Women's Union
Anderson Y Center, U of the Pacific
95211 (209-946-2011)

Venice, CA

Women's Switchboard
Box 597 90201 (213-388-3491)

Alamosa, CO

Resource Center for Women
Adams State College, San Luis Ranch
81101 (303-879-7011)

Boulder, CO

**Boulder County Women's Resource and
Counseling Center**
St. John's Episcopal Church, 1419
Pine St 80302 (303-447-9670)

Boulder, CO

U of Colorado Women's Center
U of Colorado 80302 (303-443-2211)

Colorado Springs, CO

Virginia Neal Blue Women's Center
First Methodist Church, 420 N
Nevada Ave 80902 (303-471-3170)

Denver, CO

Denver Women's Resources Center
25 E 16th St 80202 (303-222-0870)

Denver, CO

Research Center on Women
Loretto Heights College, 3001 S
Federal Blvd 80236 (303-936-8441)

Denver, CO

Women's Resource Center
U of Denver, University Park 80210
(303-753-1964)

Ft Collins, CO

Women's Crisis and Information Center
Colorado State U, 629 S Howes St
80521 (303-491-5744)

Ft Collins, CO

Women's Research Center
Office of Women's Relations,
Colorado State U 80521
(303-491-1101)

Grand Junction, CO

Center for Women
Mesa Junior College   81501 (303-748-1020)

Littleton, CO

Virginia Neal Blue Women's Center
Arapahoe Community College
80120 (303-794-1550)

Monta Vista, CO

Virginia Neal Blue Women's Resource Center
San Luis Valley Area Vocational
School, Sherman Ave   81144
(303-852-5977)

Pueblo, CO

Virginia Neal Blue Women's Center
Southern Colorado State College
81001 (303-549-2461)

Pueblo, CO

Women's Information Service of Pueblo
330 Lake Ave   81004 (303-543-0245)

Bridgeport, CT

Every Woman's Center
YWCA of Greater Bridgeport, 968
Fairfield   06606 (203-334-6154)

Enfield, CT

Women's Center
Amuntuck Community College, Box
68   06082 (203-745-1603)

Hartford, CT

Women's Liberation Center of Greater Hartford, Inc.
11 Amity St   06106 (203-523-8949)

Middletown, CT

Wesleyan Women's Center
High St   06520 (203-347-9411)

Middletown, CT

Women's Center
115 College St   06457 (203-346-4042)

New Britain, CT

Prudence Crandall Center for Women
Box 895   06050 (203-229-6939)

New Haven, CT

Women's Liberation Center
215 Park St   06511 (203-436-0272)

Storrs, CT

Women's Center
U of Connecticut   06286
(203-486-4738)

Waterbury, CT

Waterbury Area Women's Center
Box 2085   06702 (203-753-4540)

Washington, DC

Washington Area Women's Center
2452 18th NW   20009 (202-232-5145)

Washington, DC

Women's Center
Catholic U, Michigan Ave NE   20017
(202-635-5000)

Washington, DC

Women's Center
Trinity College, Michigan Ave NE
20002 (202-296-2000)

Newark, DE

Women's Center
Episcopal Student Center, U of Delaware, 57 E Park Pl   19711
(201-738-2000)

Coral Gables, FL

Women's Commission
U of Miami   33124 (305-284-2211)

Gainesville, FL

Women's Walk-in Counseling Service
U of Florida   32601 (904-392-1575)

Jacksonville, FL

Jacksonville Women's Movement
1825 Hendricks Ave   32207
(904-398-7728)

Miami, FL

Institute for Women
Florida International U, Tamiami
Trail   33144 (305-552-2000)

Tallahassee, FL

Tallahassee Women's Educational and Cultural Center
Florida State U   32306 (904-644-2525)

Tampa, FL

Women's Center
U of South Florida   33620
(813-947-2687)

Atlanta, GA

Atlanta Women on the Way
161 Peachtree St NE   30303
(404-656-5911)

Atlanta, GA

YWCA Women's Center
45 11th St NE   30309 (404-892-3476)

Macon, GA

Women's Center
Box 58, Mercer U   31207
(912-743-1511)

Honolulu, HI

Women's Center YWCA
1820 University Ave   96822
(808-947-3351)

Boise, ID

Women's Center Alliance
YWCA, 720 Washington   83704
(208-343-3688)

Moscow, ID

Women's Center
U of Idaho, 108 Administration Bldg
83843 (208-885-6111)

Pocatello, ID

Women's Center
Idaho State U   83201 (208-236-0211)

Aurora, IL

Women's Center
Aurora College   60507 (312-892-6431)

Carbondale, IL

The Women's Center, Inc.
404 W Walnut St   62901
(618-549-4215)

Chicago, IL

Chicago Women's Liberation Union
2748 Lincoln Ave N   60614
(312-953-6808)

Chicago, IL

Ecumenical Women's Center
1653 W School St   60657
(312-348-4970)

Chicago, IL

Loop Center YWCA
37 S Wabash   60603 (312-372-6600)

Chicago, IL

Sister Center
United Church of Rogers Park, Morris
at Ashland   60626 (312-761-2500)

Chicago, IL

Women's Center
6200 S Drexel St   60637
(312-955-3100)

Chicago, IL

Women's Center
3322 N Halsted St   60657
(312-935-4270)

Chicago, IL

Women's Center
436 E 39th St   60653 (312-285-1434)

Chicago, IL

Women's Center North Area
1016 N Dearborn St   60610
(312-337-4385)

Chicago, IL

Women's Center South Suburban
45 Plaza Park Forest   60466
(312-748-5660)

Chicago, IL

Women's Center Southwest Area
3134 W Marquette Rd   60629
(312-436-3500)

Chicago, IL

Women's Center
U of Chicago, 5655 S University Ave
60637 (312-648-3189)

Chicago, IL

Women's Center Uptown
4409 N Sheridan Rd   60640
(312-561-6737)

Chicago, IL

Women's Center West Side
5082 W Jackson Blvd   60644
(312-379-8332)

Chicago, IL

Women's Institute
4334 N Clarendon   60640
(312-525-1722)

Evanston, IL

Women of Northwestern
Northwestern U   60201
(312-492-3741)

Evanston, IL

Women's Center
Kendall College, 2408 Orrington
60201 (312-869-5240)

Evanston, IL

Women's Liberation Center of Evanston
2214 Ridge Ave   60201 (312-475-4480)

Lombard, IL

Women's Center West Suburban
1 S Park St   60148 (312-629-0170)

Morton Grove, IL

Women's Resource Center
Oakton Community College, 7900
Nagle   60053 (312-966-3830)

Des Moines, IA

Women's Information Center YWCA
Eighth and Grand   50309
(515-244-8961)

Iowa City, IA

Women's Center
U of Iowa, 3 E Market St   52240
(319-353-2121)

Pella, IA

Women's Committee
Central College   50219
(515-628-4151)

Lawrence, KS

Lawrence Women's Center
Kansas U   66044 (913-864-2700)

Manhattan, KS

Women's Resource Center
Kansas State U   66506 (913-532-6011)

Owensboro, KY
Women's Center
Brescia College, 120 W Seventh
42301 (502-685-3131)

New Orleans, LA
Tulane Women for Change
6823 St. Charles Ave   70118
(504-865-4735)

New Orleans, LA
Women's Center
2106 General Pershing   70130
(504-899-0175)

Augusta, ME
Women's Center
U of Maine   04330 (207-622-7131)

Baltimore, MD
Women's Growth Center
862 Park Ave   21201 (301-539-3588)

Baltimore, MD
Women's Liberation
101 E 25th St   21218 (301-366-6475)

Baltimore, MD
Women's Center
Essex Community College   21237
(301-682-6000)

Baltimore, MD
Women's Center
Johns Hopkins U   21218
(301-955-5000)

Baltimore, MD
Women's Center
St. Mary's College   21210
(301-744-3227)

Baltimore, MD
Women's Center
Towson State College   21204
(301-823-7500)

Baltimore, MD
Women Together
1530 Bolton St   20217
(301-837-5424)

Catonsville, MD
Women's Center
Catonsville Community College, 800
S Rolling Rd   21228 (301-747-3220)

College Park, MD
Women's Center
U of Maryland   20742 (301-454-0100)

Columbia, MD
Women's Resource Center
8905 Footed Ridge   21045
(301-454-5411)

Essex, MD
Women's Center
Essex Community College   21221
(301-682-6000)

Rockville, MD
Women's Center
Montgomery College   20830
(301-762-6088)

Towson, MD
Women's Center
Goucher College, Box 1434   21204
(301-825-3300)

Amherst, MA
Everywoman's Center
U of Massachusetts   01002
(413-545-0883)

Amherst, MA
Southwest Women's Center
Southwest U of Massachusetts
01002 (413-545-0626)

Amherst, MA
Third World Women's Center
U of Massachusetts   01002
(413-545-0111)

Bedford, MA
Women's Opportunity Research Center
Middlesex Community College,
Springs Rd   01730 (617-275-8910)

Boston, MA
Women's Center
Boston State College, 174 Ipswich St
02115 (617-731-3300)

Boston, MA
Women's Center
Boston U, 185 Bay State Rd   02215
(617-353-4240)

Boston, MA
Women's Center
Simmons College, 300 The Fenway
02115 (617-738-2000)

Brockton, MA
Center for Women at Massasoit
290 Thatcher St   02402
(617-588-2152)

Cambridge, MA
Cell 16
2 Brewer St   02138 (617-491-5820)

Cambridge, MA
Women's Center
46 Pleasant St   02139 (617-345-8807)

Cambridge, MA
Women's Research Center of Boston
6 Laurel St   02138 (617-876-2128)

Dorchester, MA
Alternative Center
1882 Dorchester Ave   02124
(617-436-0541)

Fall River, MA
Women's Center
Bristol Community College, 64 Durfee
St   02720 (617-674-4483)

Framingham, MA
YWCA Women's Resource Center
66 Irving St   01701 (617-873-9781)

New Bedford, MA
New Bedford Women's Center
374 County   02747 (617-996-3341)

Newton Centre, MA
Women's Resource Center
Andover-Newton Theological School,
215 Herrick Rd   02159 (617-964-1100)

North Dartmouth, MA
Women's Center
Southeastern Massachusetts U
02747 (617-997-9321)

Northampton, MA
Valley Women's Union
200 Main St   01060 (413-586-2011)

Provincetown, MA
Women's Center
Center St   02675 (617-487-3075)

Salem, MA
Florence Luscomb Women's Center
Salem State College   01970
(617-745-0556)

"I am the way I am. I look the way I
look. I am my age."
—*Abigail McCarthy*

South Hadley, MA
Women's Center
Mt Holyoke College   01075
(413-538-2000)

Springfield, MA
Jewish Women's Resources Center
Kodimoh Synagogue, 124 Sumner
Ave   01108 (413-781-0171)

Springfield, MA
Springfield Women's Center YWCA
26 Howard St   01105 (413-732-3121)

Springfield, MA
Springfield Women's Union
292 Worthington St   01103
(413-732-1852)

Worcester, MA
Women's Center
Clark U   01610 (617-793-7711)

Worcester, MA
Worcester Women's Center
905 Main St   01610 (617-753-9622)

Battle Creek, MI
Women's Resource Center
Kellogg Community College   49016
(616-965-3931)

Bay City, MI
Women's Center
Delta College   48710 (517-686-0400)

Benton Harbor, MI
The Women's Center
Lake Michigan College   49022
(616-927-3571)

Detroit, MI
Women's Center
4105 Cass   48201 (313-831-2606)

Detroit, MI
Women's United Action and Aid Center
103 W Alexandrine   48201
(313-832-4848)

Grand Rapids, MI
Women's Resource Center
226 Bostwick NE   49503
(616-456-8571)

Kalamazoo, MI
Kalamazoo Women's Center
211 S Rose   49006 (616-345-3036)

Kalamazoo, MI
Women's Center
Western Michigan U, 2210 Wilbur
49001 (616-383-1600)

Rochester, MI
Continuum Center for Women
Oakland U   48063 (313-377-2100)

Saginaw, MI
Chrysallis Center
Saginaw Valley College   48710
(517-793-9800)

Duluth, MN
North Country Women's Center
2205 E Fifth St   55802 (218-728-3705)

Duluth, MN
Women to Women Center
U of Minnesota   55812

Duluth, MN
Women's Center
U of Duluth Medical School   55812
(218-726-7571)

Mankato, MN
Women's Center
Mankato State College   56001 (507-
389-2463)

Minneapolis, MN
New Hope Center for Women
3125 Clinton Ave S 55408
(612-882-1935)

Minneapolis, MN
Twin City Women's Union
2953 Bloomington 55407 (612-729-6200)

Minneapolis, MN
Women's Center
U of Minnesota 55455 (612-373-3850)

Moorhead, MN
Women's Center
Concordia College 56560 (218-646-6157)

Northfield, MN
Women's Resource Lounge
St. Olaf College 55057 (507-663-2222)

St. Paul, MN
Women's Advocates
584 Grand Ave 55102 (612-227-8284)

Starkville, MS
Women's Action Movement
Mississippi State U, Box 1328 39762
(601-325-2131)

Kansas City, MO
Women's Liberation Union
3621 Charlotte 64109 (816-753-2634)

Kansas City, MO
Women's Resource Center
5325 Rockhill Rd 64110 (816-276-1442)

Kansas City, MO
Women's Resource Service
U of Missouri, 1020 E 63rd St 64110
(816-276-1470)

Liberty, MO
Women's Resource Center
William Jewel College 64068 (816-781-6400)

St. Louis, MO
Coalition of St. Louis Women
612 N Second St 63102 (314-241-0522)

St. Louis, MO
Women's Center
Florissant Valley Community College,
3400 Pershall Rd 63135 (314-524-2020)

St. Louis, MO
Women's Center
St. Louis U, 3801 W Pine Blvd 63108
(314-535-3300)

St. Louis, MO
Women's Center
U Missouri, 8001 Natural Bridge Rd
63121 (314-453-0111)

St. Louis, MO
Women's Resource Center
Washington U 63130 (314-863-0100)

Missoula, MT
Woman's Place
Broadway 59801 (406-543-7606)

Missoula, MT
Women's Resource Center
U of Montana 59801 (406-243-4153)

Crete, NB
Women's Study Group
Doane College 68333 (402-826-2161)

Lincoln, NB
University Women's Action Group
(402-472-7211)

Reno, NV
Women's Center
Box 8448 89507 (702-329-7273)

Reno, NV
Women's Resource Center
U of Nevada 49507 (702-784-1110)

Franconia, NH
Women's Center
Franconia College 03580 (603-823-5545)

Hanover, NH
Women's Information Service, Inc
38 S Main St 03755 (603-643-5133)

Keene, NH
Women's Center
Keene State College 03430 (603-622-9721)

Manchester, NH
The Women's Center
Unitarian Church, Myrtle and
Union Sts 03104 (603-625-6854)

Portsmouth, NH
Women's Center YWCA
40 Merrimac St 03801 (603-436-0162)

East Orange, NJ
YWCA Women's Center
Upsala College 07019 (201-266-7213)

Glassboro, NJ
Together
7 State St 08028 (215-881-4040)

Hackensack, NJ
Women's Center of Bergen County
166 Main St 07601 (201-342-8958)

Hackensack, NJ
The Women's Rights Information Center
100 Main St 07601 (201-342-4737)

Montclair, NJ
Women's Center YWCA
159 Glenridge Ave 07042 (201-742-5400)

New Brunswick, NJ
Women's Center
Douglass College 08903 (201-932-1766)

Newark, NJ
Feminist Resource Center
108 Washington St 07102 (201-622-1765)

Orange, NJ
YWCA Women's Center
395 Main St 07050 (201-672-9500)

Princeton, NJ
Princeton Seminary Women's Center
Princeton Theological Seminary
08540 (609-921-8300)

Princeton, NJ
Woman's Place
14½ Witherspoon St 08540 (609-924-8989)

Summit, NJ
Women's Center of the Unitarian Church
4 Waldron Ave 07901 (201-273-2383)

Upper Montclair, NJ
Women's Center
Montclair State College 07405
(201-893-5106)

West Paterson, NJ
Women's Center
Tombrock College 07424 (201-345-2020)

Alburquerque, NM
Women's Center
1824 Las Lomas NE 87131 (505-277-3717)

Bayside, NY
The Women's Research and Resource Center
Queensborough Community College
222-03 Garland Dr 11364 (516-423-0666)

Bronx, NY
The Women's Center
Lehman College, 2468 Jerome Ave
10468 (212-960-8881)

Bronxville, NY
Women's Center
Sarah Lawrence College 10708
(914-337-0700)

Brooklyn, NY
Union Center for Women
8101 Ridge Blvd 11209 (212-748-7708)

Brooklyn, NY
Women's Center YWCA
30 Third Ave 11217 (212-875-1190)

Clinton, NY
Women's Center
Kirkland College 13323 (315-859-4011)

Hempstead, NY
Women's Center
Hofstra U 11550 (516-560-0500)

Hempstead, NY
Women's Liberation Center of Nassau
14 W Columbia Ave 11550 (516-292-8160)

Ithaca, NY
Women's Center
101 N Geneva St 14850 (607-272-6922)

Ithaca, NY
Women's Center
Cornell U 14850 (607-256-1000)

New York, NY
Women's Center
243 W 20th St 10011 (212-255-9802)

New York, NY
Women's Center
Barnard College, 117th & Broadway
10027 (212-280-2067)

New York, NY
Women's Center
NY Theological Seminary,
235 E 49th St 10017 (212-355-4434)

Oakdale, NY

Women's Center in Islip
855 Montauk 11769 (516-567-0772)

Oswego, NY

Women's Center
286 Washington Blvd 13126 (315-342-1294)

Pearl River, NY

Rockland City Women's Liberation Women's Center
St. Stephen's Episcopal Church 10965 (914-354-7442)

Poughkeepsie, NY

Mid-Hudson Women's Center
27 Franklin St 12601 (914-472-1796)

Poughkeepsie, NY

Poughkeepsie Women's Center
96 Market St 12601 (914-454-9487)

Poughkeepsie, NY

Women's Center
Vassar College 12601 (914-452-7000)

Seldon, NY

Women's Group
Suffolk Community College 533 College Rd 11784 (516-233-5172)

Staten Island, NY

Women's Center
Richmond College, 130 Stuyvesant Pl 10301 (212-273-0287)

Staten Island, NY

Women's Center
Staten Island Community College, 715 Ocean Terr 10301 (212-390-7602)

Syracuse, NY

The Women's Center
750 Ostrom Ave 13210 (315-423-4268)

Syracuse, NY

Women's Information Center
113 Concord Pl 13210 (315-478-4636)

Yonkers, NY

Women's Center
Elizabeth Seton College 1061 N Broadway 10701 (914-969-4000)

Charlotte, NC

Charlotte Women's Center
1615 Lynhurst St 28203 (704-334-9655)

Durham, NC

Durham Women's Center YWCA
515 W Chapel Hill St 27701 (919-688-4396)

Greensboro, NC

Women's Center
Guilford College Campus 27401 (919-292-5511)

Murfreesboro, NC

Women's Center
Chowan College 27855 (919-398-4101)

Cincinnati, OH

Womanpower Unlimited
Ninth & Walnut St 45215 (513-241-7090)

Cincinnati, OH

Women's Affairs Council Women's Center
U of Cincinnati 45221 (513-475-3967)

Cincinnati, OH

Women's Center
173 E McMillan 45236 (513-621-1515)

Cincinnati, OH

Xavier Women's Center
Breen Lodge, Victory Pkwy 45207 (513-745-3322)

Cleveland, OH

Women's Center
Case Western Reserve, 11205 Euclid Ave 45387 (216-368-2647)

Columbus, OH

Women's Liberation
38 E 12th Ave 43201 (614-291-9317)

Prop Art

Dayton, OH

Dayton Women's Liberation
1309 N Main St 45405 (513-274-7084)

Dayton, OH

Women's Center
U of Dayton 45469 (513-229-3026)

Kent, OH

Women's Center
Kent State 44242 (216-672-2121)

Oberlin, OH

Women's Service Center
92 Spring St 44074 (216-774-4377)

Oxford, OH

Oxford Women's Liberation
Miami U 45056 (513-529-2161)

Springfield, OH

Women's Center
Wittenberg U, 966 Pythian Ave 45504 (513-327-6231)

Toledo, OH

Women's Programs
U of Toledo, 2801 Bancroft St 43606 (419-537-2072)

Yellow Springs, OH

Women's Center
Antioch College 45387 (513-767-7331)

Tulsa, OK

Women's Resource Center
U of Tulsa, 600 S College 74104 (918-939-6351)

Monmouth, OR

Women's Collective
Oregon College of Education 97361 (503-838-1220)

Portland, OR

Women's Institute and Resource Center
Portland State U 97207 (503-229-2000)

Portland, OR

Women's Resource Center
YWCA, 1111 SW Tenth St 97205 (503-223-6281)

Easton, PA

YWCA Women's Center
41 N Third St 18042 (215-253-2523)

Lancaster, PA

Women's Center
230 W Chestnut St 17603 (717-229-5381)

Newtown, PA

Women's Caucus
Bucks County Community College 18940 (215-968-5861)

Philadelphia, PA

Kensington Women's Resource Center YWCA
174 W Allegheny 19133 (215-739-1430)

Philadelphia, PA

Philadelphia Opportunities for Women
Eighth & Market Sts 19107 (215-886-8268)

Philadelphia, PA

Resources for Women
36th & Locust Walk 19104 (215-243-5537)

Philadelphia, PA

Women's Center
Temple U 19122 (215-787-7990)

Philadelphia, PA

Women's Cultural Center
2027 Chestnut St 19103 (215-564-3430)

Philadelphia, PA

Women's Liberation Center
4216 Chester Ave 19143 (215-387-6626)

Philadelphia, PA

YWCA Women's Center
5820 Germantown Ave 19144 (215-438-6266)

Pittsburgh, PA

Women's Center
Community College of Allegheny County 15212 (412-237-2525)

Pittsburgh, PA

Women's Center South
2929 Brownsville Rd 15227 (412-563-5043)

Kingston, RI

Women's Liberation
U of Rhode Island 02881 (401-792-1000)

Providence, RI

Women's Center
62 Jackson St 02903 (401-861-2910)

Providence, RI

Women's Liberation Union
Box 2302, East Side Sta 02806 (401-861-2910)

Rock Hill, SC

Women's Center
Winthrop College, Box 6763 29730 (803-323-2211)

Knoxville, TN

Knoxville Women's Center
507 Mulvaney St 37901 (615-546-1873)

Memphis, TN

Memphis Women's Resource Center, Inc
Wesley Foundation, 3625 Midland Ave 38111 (901-323-4790)

Sewanee, TN

Women's Center
U of the South 37375 (615-598-5274)